W9-CTW-248

Contemporary
Literary Criticism

Guide to Gale Literary Criticism Series

For criticism on	Consult these Gale series
Authors now living or who died after December 31, 1959	*CONTEMPORARY LITERARY CRITICISM (CLC)*
Authors who died between 1900 and 1959	*TWENTIETH-CENTURY LITERARY CRITICISM (TCLC)*
Authors who died between 1800 and 1899	*NINETEENTH-CENTURY LITERATURE CRITICISM (NCLC)*
Authors who died between 1400 and 1799	*LITERATURE CRITICISM FROM 1400 TO 1800 (LC)* *SHAKESPEAREAN CRITICISM (SC)*
Authors who died before 1400	*CLASSICAL AND MEDIEVAL LITERATURE CRITICISM (CMLC)*
Black writers of the past two hundred years	*BLACK LITERATURE CRITICISM (BLC) AND BLACK LITERATURE CRITICISM SUPPLEMENT (BLCS)*
Authors of books for children and young adults	*CHILDREN'S LITERATURE REVIEW (CLR)*
Dramatists	*DRAMA CRITICISM (DC)*
Hispanic writers of the late nineteenth and twentieth centuries	*HISPANIC LITERATURE CRITICISM (HLC)*
Native North American writers and orators of the eighteenth, nineteenth, and twentieth centuries	*NATIVE NORTH AMERICAN LITERATURE (NNAL)*
Poets	*POETRY CRITICISM (PC)*
Short story writers	*SHORT STORY CRITICISM (SSC)*
Major authors from the Renaissance to the present	*WORLD LITERATURE CRITICISM, 1500 TO THE PRESENT (WLC)*
Major authors and works from the Bible to the present	*WORLD LITERATURE CRITICISM SUPPLEMENT (WLCS)*

ISSN 0091-3421

R

Volume 118

Contemporary Literary Criticism

Criticism of the Works
of Today's Novelists, Poets, Playwrights,
Short Story Writers, Scriptwriters, and
Other Creative Writers

Jeffrey W. Hunter
Timothy J. White
EDITORS

Tim Akers
Angela Y. Jones
Daniel Jones
Deborah A. Schmitt
Polly A. Vedder
Kathleen Wilson
ASSOCIATE EDITORS

The Gale Group

DETROIT • SAN FRANCISCO • LONDON • BOSTON • WOODBRIDGE, CT

Library of Congress Catalog Card Number 76-46132
ISBN 0-7876-3193-0
ISSN 0091-3421

Printed in the United States of America
10 9 8 7 6 5 4 3 2 1

Contents

Preface vii

Acknowledgments xi

Preface

A Comprehensive Information Source
on Contemporary Literature

Named "one of the twenty-five most distinguished reference titles published during the past twenty-five years" by *Reference Quarterly,* the *Contemporary Literary Criticism (CLC)* series provides readers with critical commentary and general information on more than 2,000 authors now living or who died after December 31, 1959. Previous to the publication of the first volume of *CLC* in 1973, there was no ongoing digest monitoring scholarly and popular sources of critical opinion and explication of modern literature. *CLC,* therefore, has fulfilled an essential need, particularly since the complexity and variety of contemporary literature makes the function of criticism especially important to today's reader.

Scope of the Series

CLC presents significant passages from published criticism of works by creative writers. Since many of the authors covered by *CLC* inspire continual critical commentary, writers are often represented in more than one volume. There is, of course, no duplication of reprinted criticism.

Authors are selected for inclusion for a variety of reasons, among them the publication or dramatic production of a critically acclaimed new work, the reception of a major literary award, revival of interest in past writings, or the adaptation of a literary work to film or television.

Attention is also given to several other groups of writers—authors of considerable public interest—about whose work criticism is often difficult to locate. These include mystery and science fiction writers, literary and social critics, foreign writers, and authors who represent particular ethnic groups.

Format of the Book

Each *CLC* volume contains individual essays and reviews taken from hundreds of book review periodicals, general magazines, scholarly journals, monographs, and books. Entries include critical evaluations spanning from the beginning of an author's career to the most current commentary. Interviews, feature articles, and other published writings that offer insight into the author's works are also presented. Students, teachers, librarians, and researchers will find that the generous critical and biographical material in *CLC* provides them with vital information required to write a term paper, analyze a poem, or lead a book discussion group. In addition, complete bibliographical citations note the original source and all of the information necessary for a term paper footnote or bibliography.

Features

A *CLC* author entry consists of the following elements:

- The **Author Heading** cites the author's name in the form under which the author has most commonly published, followed by birth date, and death date when applicable. Uncertainty as to a birth or death date is indicated by a question mark.

- A **Portrait** of the author is included when available.

- A brief **Biographical and Critical Introduction** to the author and his or her work precedes the criticism. The first line of the introduction provides the author's full name, pseudonyms (if applicable), nationality, and a listing of genres in which the author has written. To provide users with easier access to information, the biographical and critical essay included in each author entry is divided into four categories: "Introduction," "Biographical Information," "Major Works," and "Critical Reception." The introductions to single-work entries—entries that focus on well known and frequently studied books, short stories, and poems—are similarly organized to quickly provide readers with information on the plot and major characters of the work being discussed, its major themes, and its critical reception. Previous volumes of *CLC* in which the author has been featured are also listed in the introduction.

- A list of **Principal Works** notes the most important writings by the author. When foreign-language works have been translated into English, the English-language version of the title follows in brackets.

- The **Criticism** represents various kinds of critical writing, ranging in form from the brief review to the scholarly exegesis. Essays are selected by the editors to reflect the spectrum of opinion about a specific work or about an author's literary career in general. The critical and biographical materials are presented chronologically, adding a useful perspective to the entry. All titles by the author featured in the entry are printed in boldface type, which enables the reader to easily identify the works being discussed. Publication information (such as publisher names and book prices) and parenthetical numerical references (such as footnotes or page and line references to specific editions of a work) have been deleted at the editor's discretion to provide smoother reading of the text.

- Critical essays are prefaced by **Explanatory Notes** as an additional aid to readers. These notes may provide several types of valuable information, including: the reputation of the critic, the importance of the work of criticism, the commentator's approach to the author's work, the purpose of the criticism, and changes in critical trends regarding the author.

- A complete **Bibliographical Citation** designed to help the user find the original essay or book precedes each critical piece.

- Whenever possible, a recent **Author Interview** accompanies each entry.

- A concise **Further Reading** section appears at the end of entries on authors for whom a significant amount of criticism exists in addition to the pieces reprinted in *CLC*. Each citation in this section is accompanied by a descriptive annotation describing the content of that article. Materials included in this section are grouped under various headings (e.g., Biography, Bibliography, Criticism, and Interviews) to aid users in their search for additional information. Cross-references to other useful sources published by The Gale Group in which the author has appeared are also included: *Authors in the News, Black Writers, Children's Literature Review, Contemporary Authors, Dictionary of Literary Biography, DISCovering Authors, Drama Criticism, Hispanic Literature Criticism, Hispanic Writers, Native North American Literature, Poetry Criticism, Something about the Author, Short Story Criticism, Contemporary Authors Autobiography Series,* and *Something about the Author Autobiography Series.*

Other Features

CLC also includes the following features:

- An **Acknowledgments** section lists the copyright holders who have granted permission to reprint material in this volume of *CLC*. It does not, however, list every book or periodical reprinted or consulted during the preparation of the volume.

- Each new volume of *CLC* includes a **Cumulative Topic Index,** which lists all literary topics treated in *CLC, NCLC, TCLC,* and *LC 1400-1800.*

- A **Cumulative Author Index** lists all the authors who have appeared in the various literary criticism series published by The Gale Group, with cross-references to Gale's biographical and auto-biographical series. A full listing of the series referenced there appears on the first page of the indexes of this volume. Readers will welcome this cumulated author index as a useful tool for locating an author within the various series. The index, which lists birth and death dates when available, will be particularly valuable for those authors who are identified with a certain period but whose death dates cause them to be placed in another, or for those authors whose careers span two periods. For example, Ernest Hemingway is found in *CLC,* yet F. Scott Fitzgerald, a writer often associated with him, is found in *Twentieth-Century Literary Criticism.*

- A **Cumulative Nationality Index** alphabetically lists all authors featured in *CLC* by nationality, followed by numbers corresponding to the volumes in which the authors appear.

- An alphabetical **Title Index** accompanies each volume of *CLC*. Listings are followed by the author's name and the corresponding page numbers where the titles are discussed. English translations of foreign titles and variations of titles are cross-referenced to the title under which a work was originally published. Titles of novels, novellas, dramas, films, record albums, and poetry, short story, and essay collections are printed in italics, while all individual poems, short stories, essays, and songs are printed in roman type within quotation marks; when published separately (e.g., T. S. Eliot's poem *The Waste Land),* the titles of long poems are printed in italics.

- In response to numerous suggestions from librarians, Gale has also produced a **Special Paperbound Edition** of the *CLC* title index. This annual cumulation, which alphabetically lists all titles reviewed in the series, is available to all customers. Additional copies of the index are available upon request. Librarians and patrons will welcome this separate index: it saves shelf space, is easy to use, and is recyclable upon receipt of the next edition.

Citing *Contemporary Literary Criticism*

When writing papers, students who quote directly from any volume in the Literary Criticism Series may use the following general forms to footnote reprinted criticism. The first example pertains to material drawn from periodicals, the second to material reprinted in books:

[1] Alfred Cismaru, "Making the Best of It," *The New Republic,* 207, No. 24, (December 7, 1992), 30, 32; excerpted and reprinted in *Contemporary Literary Criticism,* Vol. 85, ed. Christopher Giroux (Detroit: Gale, 1995), pp. 73-4.

[2] Yvor Winters, *The Post-Symbolist Methods* (Allen Swallow, 1967); excerpted and reprinted in *Contemporary Literary Criticism,* Vol. 85, ed. Christopher Giroux (Detroit: Gale, 1995), pp. 223-26.

Suggestions Are Welcome

The editors hope that readers will find *CLC* a useful reference tool and welcome comments about the work. Send comments and suggestions to: Editors, *Contemporary Literary Criticism,* The Gale Group, 27500 Drake Rd., Farmington Hills, MI 48333-3535.

Acknowledgments

The editors wish to thank the copyright holders of the criticism included in this volume and the permissions managers of many book and magazine publishing companies for assisting us in securing reproduction rights. We are also grateful to the staffs of the Detroit Public Library, the Library of Congress, the University of Detroit Mercy Library, Wayne State University Purdy/Kresge Library Complex, and the University of Michigan Libraries for making their resources available to us. Following is a list of the copyright holders who have granted us permission to reproduce material in this volume of. Every effort has been made to trace copyright, but if omissions have been made, please let us know.

COPYRIGHTED MATERIALS IN *CLC* VOLUME 118, WERE REPRODUCED FROM THE FOLLOWING PERIODICALS:

African American Review, v. 29, Spring, 1995 for "The African American Historian: David Bradley's **The Chaneysville Incident** by Matthew Wilson Copyright © 1995 by Matthew Wilson. Reproduced by permission the author; v. 30, Summer, 1996 for "Syndetic Redemption: Above-Underground Emergence in David Bradley's **The Chaneysville Incident** by Edward Pavlic. Copyright © 1995, 1996 by Edward Pavlic. Both reproduced by permission of the authors—**American Imago,** Summer, 1986. Copyright 1986 by The Association for Applied Psychoanalysis, Inc. Reproduced by permission of the publisher.—**The American Poetry Review**, May-June, 1977 for "Philip Levine: Naming the Lost" by Richard Hugo; v. 16, March/ April, 1987 for "Comment/ Memory Theater" by Marianne Boruch. Copyright © 1977, 1987 by World Poetry, Inc. Both reproduced by permission of the authors.—**American Theatre,** v. 13, January, 1987; v. 13, April, 1996. Both reproduced by permission.—**The Bloomsbury Review,** May/June, 1990 for a review of The Book of Evidence by James Sattler. Copyright © by Owaissa Communications Company, Inc. 1990. Reproduced by permission of the author.—**Books and Bookmen,** January, 1983 for a review of **The Newton Letter**: An Interlude by Derek Stanford. © copyright the author 1983. Reproduced by permission of the author.—**The Antioch Review,** v. 44, Spring, 1986. Copyright © 1986 by the Antioch Review Inc. Reproduced by permission of the Editors—. **Boston Review,** v. 13, June, 1988 for "A Walk with Tom Jefferson" by Frederick J. Marchant. Copyright © 1988 by the Boston Critic, Inc. Reproduced by permission of the author.—**Boulevard,** Spring, 1994 for "Why 'Nothing Is Pas't: Philip Levine's Conversation with History" by Kevin Stein. Reproduced by permissionof the author.—**Cahiers-Irlandais,** v. 4-5, 1976. Reproduced by permission.—**Calllaloo,** v. 7, Summer, 1984 for n a review of The Chaneysville Incident, by Thomas Gannon. Copyright © 1984 by Charles H. Powell. Reproduced by permission of the author.—**Canadian Literature,** n. 118, Spring, 1988 for "Narrative, Carnival, and Parody: Intertextuality in Antonine Maillet's **Pélagie-la-Charrette**" by Michéle Lacombe. Reproduced by permission of the author.—**The Canadian Modern Language Review/La Revue Canadienne d es Langues,** v. 36, March, 1980. Reproduced by permission of University of Toronto Press Incorporated.—**The Canadian Review of American Studies**, v. 23, Fall, 1992. © Canadian Review of American Studies 1992. Reproduced by permission of the publisher.—**The Chicago Tribune,** July 9, 1995 for "Irish Eyes Unsmiling: A Baroque Vision of Despair' in **Fog and Darkness** from John Banville" by Douglas Glover. © copyrighted 1995, Chicago Tribune Company. All rights reserved. Reproduced by permission of the author..—**CLA Journal,** v. 38, June, 1995; v. LX, June, 1997. Copyright, 1995, 1997 by The College Language Association. Both reproduced by permission of The College Language Association.—**Contemporary Literature,** v. 33, Summer, 1992; v. 38, Fall, 1997. © 1992, 1997 by the Board of Regents of the University of Wisconsin.Both reproduced by permission of The University of Wisconsin Press.—**The Durham University Journal**, v. 82, July, 1990 ;v. 84, July, 1992. Both reproduced by permission.—**Éire-Ireland,**v. XXIII, Fall, 1988; v. 21, Spring, 1986. Copyright © 1986, 1988 by the Irish American Cultural Institute.Both reproduced by permission of the publisher.—**Imagine,** v. I, Winter, 1984 for "Cipriano Mera and the Lion: A Reading of Philip Levine." Reproduced by permission of the author.—**The Hollins Critic,** v. XXXII, December, 1995. Copyright 1995 by Hollins College. Reproduced by permission.—**The Hudson Reveiw,**, v. XXXV, Summer, 1982; Winter, 1992. Copyright © 1982,1992 by The Hudson Review, Inc. Both reproduced by permission.—**Irish Literary Supplement,** Fall, 1995. Copyright 1995 Irish Literary Supplement. Reproduced by permission of the publisher.—**Journal of the Short Story in English,** Spring, 1987. © Université d'Angers, 1987. Reproduced by permission.—**London Review of Books,** December 4, 1986 for "Liza Jarrett's Hard Life" by Paul Drive; v. 15, April 22, 1993 for "A Whole Lot of Faking" by Valentine Cunningham; v. 19, June 5, 1997 for "Gossip" by Frank Kermode.All appear here by permission of the London Review

John Banville

1945-

Irish novelist, short story writer, critic, and editor.

The following entry presents an overview of Banville's career through 1997. For further information on his life and works, see *CLC,* Volume 46.

INTRODUCTION

One of the foremost contemporary authors to experiment with the format of the traditional Irish novel, Banville makes extensive use of metaphors, literary allusions, and elements from various genres to create complex aesthetic effects. His narratives are usually enigmatic and ambiguous, reflecting his belief that reality cannot be accurately mirrored by the conventional realistic novel.

Biographical Information

Banville was born in Wexford, Ireland, on December 8, 1945. He was educated at the Christian Brothers primary school and St. Peter's College secondary school. Instead of attending university, Banville became a clerk at Aer Lingus for a brief period of years. Banville's initial artistic interest was painting, but after moving to London with his wife, he began writing short stories. After publishing his stories in several periodicals, Banville published his first book, a collection of short stories called *Lord Lankin,* in 1970. Shortly afterward, Banville moved just outside Dublin, where he became chief sub-editor for the *Irish Press.* Banville worked at the *Irish Press* until 1983, when he left to pursue writing full time. When he found that his fiction writing did not pay the bills, he returned to the *Irish Press* as literary editor in 1986. Throughout his career Banville has won numerous awards, including the Allied Irish Banks prize for *Birchwood* (1973), an Irish Arts Council Macauley Fellowship, the Irish-American Foundation Literary Award in 1976, and the James Tait Black Memorial Prize for *Dr. Copernicus* in 1976.

Major Works

Banville's fiction studies the relationship between reality and art, and departs from a traditional focus in Irish fiction on historical and social concerns. Banville is also more concerned with the aesthetic aspects of fiction than his Irish literary predecessors. Each of his novels has a first-person narrative voice; *Long Lankin* is his only work with a third-person narrator, and it is his only collection of short stories. The stories present different stages of life in the *nouveau riche* contemporary suburbs of Dublin, including childhood,

adolescence, and adulthood. The stories present the common conflicts which arise from personal relationships and address such topics as guilt, loss, destructive love, and the pain inherent in attaining freedom. *Nightspawn* (1971) is a parody of several genres in which Banville endeavors to expose the limitations of the traditional novel through an intentionally chaotic narrative in which he merges the narrator, protagonist, and writer. Set on a Greek island, the story involves a potential military coup, a highly sought-after document, a plenitude of sex, and a murder. *Birchwood,* a modern-day Gothic novel about a decaying Irish estate and a disturbed family, centers on Gabriel Godkin, the son and heir, who gains independence and maturity through his involvement in a circus and a revolutionary coup. Next Banville produced novels toward a proposed tetralogy influenced by *The Sleepwalkers: A History of Man's Changing Vision of the Universe,* Arthur Koestler's study of notable astronomers. In the tetralogy, Banville analyzes the relationship between creation and reality by presenting the lives and scientific quests of several famous intellectuals, including Polish astronomer Nicolaus Copernicus in *Dr. Copernicus,* German astronomer Johannes Kepler in *Kepler* (1983), and Isaac Newton in *The*

Newton Letter (1987). *The Book of Evidence* (1990) is the first of a trilogy which centers on the mind of narrator Freddie Montgomery. Montgomery becomes enamored with a painting in the home of a friend and impulsively steals it. When a maid catches him in the act, he forces her to leave with him and eventually kills her with a hammer. The book is his confession of the crime to police. *Ghosts* (1993) again takes up the story of Freddie Montgomery as he re-enters life after serving a ten-year prison sentence. He finds a job on an island as an apprentice to an art historian. *Athena* (1995) completes the Montgomery trilogy. Montgomery, now called Morrow, has become an authority on art and is called upon to authenticate pictures stolen from the same house in which he stumbled into his own criminal life. Banville tackled another genre with *The Untouchable* (1997) which charts the world of espionage during the 1930s by fictionalizing the story of Russian spy Anthony Blunt. The novel is unique because it lacks the romantic excess of most spy novels and instead delineates the day-to-day minutia of its characters' lives.

Critical Reception

Critics often refer to the Nabokovian influences in Banville's fiction. Many commentators praise his lavish prose style; Erica Abeel calls him "a landscape painter with language." Others, however, are critical of the self-conscious impulses of his language and his use of obscure vocabulary. Paul Driver asserts that *Mefisto* (1986) is "massively overwritten" and states, "There is so much verbal flesh on the book that its moral backbone is difficult to discern." Reviewers point out Banville's preoccupation with the relationship between art and reality. Most note Banville's tendency to celebrate the unreality of the fictional world. Philip MacCann states, "Banville's art eschews the vulgar artificiality of life in favor of the stylish artificiality of art itself." Banville is generally respected for his well-researched and erudite books, and critics have credited him for his influence on contemporary Irish literature. Valentine Cunningham posits that Banville is "one of the most important writers now at work in English—a key thinker, in fact, in fiction."

PRINCIPAL WORKS

Long Lankin (short stories) 1970
Nightspawn (novel) 1971
Birchwood (novel) 1973
Doctor Copernicus (novel) 1976
Kepler (novel) 1983
Mefisto (novel) 1986
The Newton Letter (novel) 1987
The Book of Evidence (novel) 1990
Ghosts (novel) 1993
The Broken Jug (play) 1994

Athena (novel) 1995
The Untouchable (novel) 1997

CRITICISM

Seamus Deane (essay date 1976)

SOURCE: "'Be Assured I Am Inventing': The Fiction of John Banville," in *Cahiers-Irlandais,* Vols. 4-5, 1976, pp. 329-39.

[*In the following essay, Deane, a well-known poet, discusses Banville's awareness that the world he creates in his books is fictive.*]

John Banville has so far produced three books: **Long Lankin, Nightspawn,** and the prizewinning **Birchwood.** In each one of them he shows himself to be very conscious of the fact that he is writing fiction, and this lends to his work both a literary and an introverted humour which relieves him from the accusations of monotony, plagiarism and preciousness which could otherwise be justifiably levelled against him. He is a *litterateur* who has a horror of producing 'literature'. This horror is equalled only by his amusement at the notion that literature might (by accident or innate capacity) reproduce life. He rejects mimetic realism by practising it in the avowed consciousness of its incompetence. Various authors betray their influence on his writings— Nabokov, Henry Green, Hermann Hesse—and, in addition, he makes his relationship to the reader as quizzically autocratic as does John Barth, Borges or even Richard Brautigan. He favours his sensibility as something so electrically endowed that it can only be glimpsed in its movements with the help of modern, high-speed, novelistic lenses. Like some of those authors mentioned, he joyfully commits technical narcissism over and over again, photographing every mutation of the self in the act of mutation, reproducing in words a wordless process, recording for ever a fugitive experience:

> Only here, in these sinister pages, can time be vanquished. These little keys on which I dance transfix eternity with every tap.

The three books are all interlocked in their sets of characters and preoccupations. Each is an odyssey of a writer for whom the act of writing is itself the only Ithaca and the only Penelope his Muse or his memory. (The fact that **Nightspawn** and **Birchwood** are both told in the first person and in the past tense is a trite but important one. The pastness of that which is written about is the source of much of the writing's grief.) There is a good deal of Gothic glare, and glamour—exotic parties and exotic parts, revolutions, Greek and Irish, famine, circus, arcane relationships, codes, puns and riddles—but, basically, Mr. Banville writes about writing and the relation of the thing written to the thing written about. Like many modern novelists, he is a scholastic, one of the *cymini sectores,* splitting atom-sized distinctions, watching the flight and disappearance of neutron sensations in the quantum world of the self and yet always aware of the fact that the self and its sensations are always determined by the very act of watching. Consciousness is, for his heroes, a burden and it creates other burdens which are in direct proportion to its own mass. The plot of his fictions is Sisyphean, repetitive. Their structure, which in its inner parts is largely a matter of consequential images, is outwardly (and sometimes pretentiously), that of a myth.

It is difficult to describe Banville's stylism. Take for instance, the opening of *Nightspawn* (and admitting the heavy Dostoievskian overtones):

> I am a sick man. I am a spiteful man. I think my life is diseased. Only a flood of spleen could cauterize my wounds.

Or, the opening of *Birchwood:*

> I am, therefore I think. That seems inescapable. In this lawless house I spend the nights poring over my memories, fingering them, like an impotent casanova his old love letters, sniffing the dusty scent of violets.

Compare these openings with those of novels like Robbe-Grillet's *Dans Le Labyrinthe* or Michel Butor's *La Modification:*

> Vous avez le pied gauche sur la rainure de cuivre, et de votre épaule droite vous essayez en vain de pousser un peu plus le panneau coulissant

The comparison (which can be extended far beyond these openings) is useful because its shows, I think, how aggressively solipsistic Banville is and also how incompletely so. For the 'vous' of Butor creates a wider chasm than the 'I' of Banville. Banville's gap is between himself and his reader; Butor's gap is between himself and what he has written. The 'vous' is an 'I' that has become, not self-reflexive and therefore the centre of its own panoramic world, but merely observed as something living in a world of silent objects. 'To restore silence is the role of objects' says Beckett's Molloy and the kinds of silence we meet with in Robbe-Grillet and Butor exemplifies this submission of the subjective self to the foreignness and inexhaustibility of the phenomenal world. One major form of the Romantic imagination has always believed in possessing the world entirely, consuming everything in the flames of self; another has always believed in itself as essentially foreign to all that the world contains, Banville begins by belonging to the first opinion and gradually seems to come towards the latter. In *Long Lankin* and *Nightspawn* even the oddity of the world is, we are persuaded, really a function of the perceiver's brilliant eccentricity. The observed world becomes (especially when written about, since writing is a form of re-observation) a dream locked in the mind of the observer. Or the dream perhaps constitutes a perception about the world which it exceeds the power of mere observation to command. Symbolism outmatches realism. But then, Mr. Banville will not allow us this either, because he creates and hunts for his own symbols and leaves the critic (or a chosen version of the critic anyway) without a job or at least without self-respect:

> Sweaty pencils poised, panting hunters of the symbol?
> There is wealth in store.

Given such warnings, who would dare pant, especially when the author does it so well himself? He wishes to be as much as possible his own critic, since criticism too is a satisfactory kind of authorship, being in effect a stance whereby one can watch oneself being someone other than oneself, even though that other is one's own creation. And by pretending to be a critic one can save oneself from the grosser defects of the symbolic method by committing them and then pointing them out. The varieties of narcissism are, as I have already mentioned, irresistible to Mr. Banville, but they can also be very usefully defensive too.

So, all this is very obviously a kind of fiction that is no longer either strange or new in itself. Anyone who has read John Fowles' *The Magus* would not find *Nightspawn* unique or incomprehensible; similarly, to have read *Steppenwolf* and/or Henry Green's *Loving* is to have been prepared for *Birchwood.* The Banville novels are clearly more Nabokovian than any of these others; Nabokov seems to be as much of a genre indeed as an influence for this author. Yet, although Mr. Banville's dependence on other writers might at times appear irritating or even parasitical, his work is not, nevertheless, mere pastiche. Its experimentalism is of a curious kind. If we except the nine short stories that make up Part I of *Long Lankin,* everything this author has written strikes me as being a prolegomena to a fiction, rather than a fiction itself. Even those nine stories lose some of their stability when seen in the retrospect of *The Possessed,* the *novella* which comprises Part II of that volume, and which in one sense completes them while it in another sense opens the way for the next book, *Nightspawn.* Mr. Banville is not really a writer of novels *tout court.* He is a writer working in a medium by testing its possibilities to the point of exhaustion. His fiction is dominated by his fascination with the nature of fiction. The impedimenta we meet with there from other writers, obtrusive as they sometimes are, is part of this fascination. We could put it more clearly perhaps by saying that Mr. Banville cannot write a novel until he sees what a novel is and that he cannot see what a novel is until he writes one. The preoccupation with the act of writing itself, both in its formal and in its philosophical aspects, is scarcely exaggerated, I believe, by this kind of statement. But there are, of course, other considerations which make this interest less professionally barren than I have so far given any ground to expect.

In this respect, the epigraph to *The Possessed,* (Part II of *Long Lankin*) is worth quoting; it is taken from Gide's *L'Immoraliste:*

> Take me away from here and give me some reason for living. I have none left. I have freed myself. That may be. But what does it signify? This objectless liberty is a burden to me.

Mr. Banville often seems to conceive of the imagination as a faculty which allows the creation of such a complete and purposeless liberty. Against that kind of freedom, there is lodged the world of necessity, the world of time, in which man is constantly reminded of minor and major loss, nostalgia and death. One passage, from *Birchwood,* gives us the effect of the imagination operating on the world of fact:

> Such scenes as this I see, or imagine I see, no difference, through a glass sharply. The light is lucid, steady and does not glance in spikes or stars from bright things, but shines in cool cubes, planes and violet lines and lines within planes, as light, trapped in polished crystal will shine. Indeed, now that I think of it, I feel it is not a glass through which I see, but rather a gathering of perfect prisms. There is hardly any sound, except for now and then a faint ringing chime, or a distant twittering, strange, unsettling. Outside my memories, this silence and harmony, this brilliance I find again in that second silent world which exists, independent, ordered by unknown laws, in the depths of mirrors. This is how I remember such scenes. If I provide something otherwise than this, be assured that I am inventing.

The point is that he must invent, and therefore our assurance is justified. This independent world, typically enunciated for us in mirror and prism images, in a mode of perception that has temperature rather than content, has to be colonised, alas, by the actual world of pain and torment. When he describes this, Banville sometimes comes close to the world of Butor, the world of the phenomenal, exact object bearing to the human perceiver his own refracted pain. But it is also true that Mr. Banville does tend to make the mystique of the moment a little too evident and appealing. In *Nightspawn,* we read:

> I thought of that four-letter word of which

Heraclitus was so fond. Things fluctuate, merge, nothing remains still. A late September day, say, and you pause in a deserted corner of a strange town. There is a white sunlit wall, and a patch of dark shadow. Dandelions nod among sparse grass. All is silent, but for an intimation of music somewhere, just beyond hearing. The leaning lid of a dustbin beckons you around the corner. You step forward, and come suddenly, breathtakingly upon the river, far below, calm and blue, with a small white cloud swimming in it. You think that this has all been arranged, that some hand has set up the props, that wall, those flowers, all of them exact and perfect and inimitable, so that you may catch a strange memory of something extraordinary and beautiful. . . . You have touched the mystery of things. In time that moment in a strange town becomes itself a memory, and merges with the one which eluded you. Life goes on. Spring sunshine wrings your heart, spring rain. Love and hate eventually become one. I am talking about the past, about remembrance. You find no answers, only questions. It is enough, almost enough. That day I thought about the island, and now I think about thinking about the island, and tomorrow, tomorrow I shall think about the thinking about thinking about the island, and all will be one, however I try, and there will be no separate thoughts, but only one thought, one memory, and I shall still know nothing. What am I talking about, what are these ravings? About the past, of course, and about Mnemosyne, that lying whore. And I am talking about torment.

Thus it is as a war of attrition between imagination and time, with all its variants of Memory, Dream and Fantasy that John Banville defines the act of writing and treasures the written thing. What we meet in his work is another version of that brand of self-consciousness which has been such a distinctive feature of one tradition (and that the major one) of Irish fiction which includes Joyce, Flann O'Brien, and Beckett on one level, and accommodates a variety of people, from Jack Yeats to George Fitzmaurice to Aidan Higgins on another. All of them are at times masters of the boredom which comes from self-contemplation, solipsism carried to a degree of scientific precision, some of them are equally at times mastered by it.

This is a strange tradition to which John Banville belongs, for it is not a political literature by any means, yet it is not at all a literature without politics. Its removal from the public world is contemptuous. But the removal itself expresses a deep disillusion, not only with Irish politics as such but with the very idea basic to most politics—that the world is subject to improvement if not to change or transformation. For them all, it is a place of proverbial and archetypal corruption. One could, I believe, argue that the degree of introversion in the major Irish fictions of this century is in exact ratio to the degree of political disillusion. Both *Nightspawn* and *Birchwood,* with their complicated political backgrounds, offer us exemplary instances of this. In the first case, post-war Greece forms the backdrop to a confusing if not confused story of murder, rape, espionage and betrayal. Julian Kyd acts the part of Master of the Revels (which Ben had played in *The Possessed*) while the Irish writer and exotic Dubliner Ben White plays out a Nabokovian twin game with the German agent Erik Weiss and his hunchbacked partner Andreas. The chronology is deliberately disturbed and in case we should forget this obvious fact we are several times reminded of it. We also have an arcane relationship within the Kyd family. Ben stalks and even rapes the beautiful Helena but perhaps truly seeks the brother Yacinth (Hyacinth). Myth is constantly rattling about in this Hiberno-Anglo-Greek cupboard, although sometimes it would be, like the family skeletons, better hidden.

[*Birchwood*] . . . is a story of the fall of the Anglo-Irish Ascendancy house, but this Godkin/Lawless home wears its rue with a difference.
—*Seamus Deane*

The novel is fundamentally concerned with pursuit and immunity. A magic document which gives immunity is at the centre of all the espionage as of all the myth. Perhaps Marvell's lines would be a cooler epigraph than any:

> Apollo hunted Daphne so,
> Only that she might laurel grow;
> And Pan did after Syrinx speed,
> Not as a nymph, but for a reed.

Yet the novel does not keep its various levels of 'significance' alive, although it misses no opportunity to remind us of Significance whenever it should appear. A spy story which is also a myth, it has at its centre what Erik wrote down after Ben had said it:

> What the heart desires, the world is incapable of giving.

Maybe so, but even in that sentence there is, I think, visible a heavy sag towards cliché. The second time this is said it comes without the usual and attendant irony. If we read again the passage where it originally occurs, we have this:

> 'Isn't it strange how all these things work together',
> I mused. 'The wind lifts the waves, and the waves
> pound the shore. These strange cycles. People too,

with their cycles and reversals that cause so much anguish. It's amazing.'

> I looked at Erik. Erik looked at the sea. I went on,
> 'Imitating the seasons, I suppose. The rages and
> storms, the silences. If only the world would imi-
> tate us once in a while. That would be something,
> wouldn't it? But the world mountains a contemp-
> tuous silence, and what the heart desires, the world
> is incapable of giving.'

> A pretty speech. I would refuse to believe that I had
> made it, did I not have evidence, which I have. Erik
> hitched up his trousers, and blew his nose. I won-
> dered if he had been listening to me. He had.

The irony does not rescue the passage, it simply gives its superficial gloss a higher sheen. *Nightspawn* is characterised all through by this device—attempts at solemn truth subverted by a supposedly wicked or devastatingly deadpan humour. Instead of finding a way in which the commentary on time and freedom will arise naturally from the story and its circumstances, Mr. Banville makes the story into an exotic mode of talking about these problems. The most harmful exoticism is not of background, but that of anguish, torment, art. The idiom of an adolescent romanticism is strong here, and the rhetoric, while spending itself in cliché, is also congratulating itself on its power of insight. Take, for instance,

> The wind lifts the waves, and the waves pound the
> shore. Whatever I did, or might do, the world went
> on, with or without me, always, and I was but a
> small part of an eternal confluence which I could
> not understand, and had no need of understanding.
> I am talking about the healing of wounds. I am talk-
> ing about art.

But talking about it in this way is not at all the same as creating it. The thing itself is at some distance from commonplace ruminations upon the *ding an sich.* The best comment on this sort of thing is Mr. Banville's own. In *Birchwood* we read:

> The Exotic, once experienced, becomes common-
> place, that is a great drawback of this world.

It is also the great drawback of *Nightspawn* and of *The Possessed.* A brilliant, lyric phrasing does not redeem either from its adolescent softness, a softness which largely arises from the self-enhancement which Mr. Banville allows himself in the character of Ben. His is a Portrait of the Artist as a Cryptic or as a Corrupt Young Man, but Mr. Banville forgets Ben's youth and forgives it as Joyce never does Stephen's. The result is that much that would have been structurally ironic—i.e. belonging to a sustained view of Ben as a projection in fiction of certain possibilities in the self—becomes instead merely a matter of self-conscious embarrassment. The biggest danger about solipsistic novels is that the author may forget to disengage his solipsism from that of the hero. When that happens, even the author's occasional self-consciousness at the figure he is cutting may appear to the reader to be sadly belated and never enough.

Birchwood, the most recent of Mr. Banville's novels, is, however, a different matter. It is a story of the fall of the Anglo-Irish Ascendancy house, but this Godkin/Lawless home wears its rue with a difference. (The name games in these novels are intricate and sometimes very funny.) Gabriel Godkin has to discover that he is twin to his sinister cousin Michael, and therefore child of 'Aunt' Martha. The relationship, in its horrible intimacy and in its secrecy, is typical of the kind of plot device upon which Mr. Banville weaves a good deal of symbolic tapestry. Equally though, the eerie power with which these relationships are evoked is at times reminiscent of the atmosphere in a Julien Green novel. In fact what Green said of his own fiction in 1929 could in many ways be applied to Mr. Banville's, although *Birchwood* is the work to which it can most reasonably be referred. Since ordinary life supplied him with nothing, Green said,

> J'en suis réduit à inventer . . . c'était toujours le fait réel qui avait l'air faux et le fait inventé, la fiction, qui avait l'air vrai.

The same is true here. The grotesque deaths of Granny Godkin and of Aunt Martha, the first certainly, the second possibly filched from Dickens, the volatile chronology which moves us from the world of the Troubles in this century to the world of last century's Famine, the juxtaposition of the political against the familial and circus worlds, the occurrence of manic forms of cruelty and violence, of mutants, physical and moral cripples—all of these things make *Birchwood* one of those rare books in which phantasmagoria has all the presence of a reality. The hero's sensibility is as precious as ever, but it discovers itself through this phantasmal world, it does not merely use it as an excuse for some kinds of reaction. Anguish is real here. It has a political and a social expression. Psychosis is no longer simply the determinant of circumstances but their product. Then it appears to be their determinant. The relationship is so close that one cannot ask of Mr. Banville's world that it become more historically actual, since it has a psychiatric accuracy which is itself part of the Irish historical experience. The favourite motif of distant, almost unheard music, the favourite technique of the frozen instant of crisis in which a Beckett-like mania for precision occupies the shocked consciousness, the swirl of secret relationships and initiations, which shadow the more overt social and familial groupings, these all oc-

cur in new systematic combinations, the force of which is to bring to bear upon the reader the awareness of some wildly inexplicable yet radical grief at the heart of all personal and social existence. It evokes a metaphysical shudder in the true modern Gothic way (although besides Julien Green and Mervyn Peake, I would most strongly be reminded here of the most unGothic *Loving* by Henry Green). Prospero does not exist, yet his circus does. God does not exist, yet His world does. And so too, the novelist and his novel. Mr. Banville has provided, in *Birchwood,* a complicated metaphor of the world as book and the author as God.

Birchwood [is] one of those rare books in which phantasmagoria has all the presence of a reality. The hero's sensibility is as precious as ever, but it discovers itself through this phantasmal world, it does not merely use it as an excuse for some kinds of reaction. Anguish is real here.
—*Seamus Deane*

For his interest is obsessively of this kind, and in this area. The author who is a God within his world of book, enjoys complete liberty, especially liberty from time. Art abolishes sequence, allows invention. It makes plots into structures, stories into fables. Yet in order to exist, art must make use of the world which, unlike itself, is death-driven, disordered, meaningless. The imagination of a writer like Mr. Banville, therefore, hovers and hesitates over this paradox. Like the theology of transubstantiation, the theology of art asks the fundamental questions. Does the world exist in art as a Real or merely as a Symbolic Presence. Or, to put it in Gabriel Godkin's more electric terminology:

> I find the world always odd, but odder still, I suppose, is the fact that I find it so, for what are the eternal verities by which I measure these temporal aberrations? Intimations abound, but they are felt only, and words fail to transfix them. Anyway, some secrets are not to be disclosed under pain of who knows what retribution, and whereof I cannot speak, thereof I must be silent.

Whatever the retribution, John Banville will hardly be silent. For even *Birchwood,* for all its manifest achievement, still appears as if it were no more than a preparation for something other, something more exclusively Banvillean to come. One can be more assured that he is inventing as we see his heavily dislocated fictions move in their typical constellations of event—incest, murder, inconsequence, breakdown—around their inner subjects of time, memory, freedom, and death, converting these stiff concepts more and more surely and profoundly into the substance of our consciousness. No other Irish novelist seeks the effect of time-lessness more hungrily than this one. For he is interested in serious events, and as Borges tells us in a short story,

> Serious events are outside time, either because the immediate past is as if disconnected from the future, or because the parts which form these events do not seem to be consecutive.

Such events and the nature of such dislocation form the basis of John Banville's fiction so far. It is an achievement to greet and even more, to wait for.

Derek Stanford (review date January 1983)

SOURCE: A review of *The Newton Letter,* in *Books and Bookmen,* No. 328, January, 1983, p. 32.

[*In the following review, Stanford states, "Mr Banville's surface technique* [*in* The Newton Letter] *presents no difficulties and few idiosyncrasies whilst nevertheless leaving us with a feeling of experience steeped in all its local habitation."*]

C. P. Snow once opined that "James Joyce led novels up a blind alley" (and *Finnegan's Wake* is clearly sign-posted "No thoroughfare for most fiction readers"). Mr Banville's surface technique presents no difficulties and few idiosyncrasies whilst nevertheless leaving us with a feeling of experience steeped in all its local habitation (a lodge cottage and half ruined 'great house' in the deep country of the south of Ireland). By frequently using short chapters or sections, he guards against our ever getting satiated with the atmosphere each so differingly conveys. That was a ploy the de Goncourt brothers first introduced into the novel; and Mr Banville uses it with the greatest effect.

The under-surface structure of **The Newton Letter** can be likened to a concerto, with the solo instrument becoming fainter and fainter until, at the end, it returns more emphatically. Although there are no needless games with the chronology of the action, the story progresses by episodic development. Which means that the 'plot' also operates in a largely submerged state. What we get is 'reality', 'the feel of things', and not an invitation to reconstruct a jig-saw of events.

Basically the substance of action is as follows. A post graduate student (from a Catholic southern background) takes a lodge cottage to complete his work on Isaac Newton. He gets held up at the point of Newton's mental breakdown and becomes involved in the family who still inhabit the run-down 'big house'. They are of the Ascendancy (but Catholic) and

are also next door to bankrupt and live by running a nursery. The group also includes a drunken husband (dying of cancer), an illegitimate boy, and two sisters, one of whom the narrator beds and gets with child, while falling in love with the married elder sister.

Newton goes to the wall. The summer ends; and our author leaves for Dublin. He is offered a university post, but wonders if he will not be drawn back, next summer, to finish his book on Newton and pick up the end of his relationship with the come-down county family.

I can only suggest my enjoyment of the book by comparing it with John Fowles's novella *The Ebony Tower* which seems to me one of the finest pieces of writing of recent years.

Paul Driver (review date 4 December 1986)

SOURCE: "Liza Jarrett's Hard Life," in *London Review of Books,* December 4, 1986, pp. 24, 26.

[*In the following excerpt, Driver complains that Banville's* Mefisto *"is massively overwritten with a distinctly Irish lyrical imperative and studious lexicality."*]

. . . **Mefisto** is the most ambitious of these five works, yet in some ways the least successful. It is massively overwritten with a distinctly Irish lyrical imperative and studious lexicality. Rare words are preferred: 'auscultating', 'exsanguinated', 'incarnadined', 'labiate', 'vermiform', 'psittacine', 'rufous', 'lentor', 'strabismic', 'gibbous', 'snathed'. There are too many descriptions like 'a flash of opalescent silk' or 'the air a sheen of damp pearl', and there is too much seasonal reference of the 'It was a hot, hazy day, one of the first of summer' kind. Its ambition is roughly to be a sort of Beckettian comedy of drabness, to maintain a firm hold of childhood perceptions, but not to scruple to render death, disfigurement, indigence and despair. The book's scope is too wide, in fact, and one is never properly sure what kind of novel one is in.

Apart from the narrator when he is young—and a mathematical prodigy—and his immediate kin, the characters (Mephistophelean, spivish Felix, the deaf-mute Sophie, the mine-owner and mathematician Mr Kasperl, et al.) are only elusively real—shadows on an indeterminate geography. The humour is equally nebulous; and the narrative points of view are occasionally mixed up, deliberately but awkwardly. As in *Kramer's Goats,* there are irritating authorial intrusions: 'How do I know these things? I just do. I am omniscient, sometimes.' It is very difficult to tell whether **Mefisto** is primarily a record of actual memories (the early part, recalling *A Portrait of the Artist as a Young Man,* has a glow of poignant recollection) or a novel whose chief concern is to build an imaginative structure: if the novel is somewhat laboured, it is nonetheless vague and wavering.

Twinship is again the theme: the opening section was entitled 'Gemini' when first published in one of the *Firebird* anthologies; and the opening sentence, 'Chance was in the beginning' ('chance' is also, Joyceanly, the book's last word), refers to the narrator's luck in being born when a twin foetus had died. The lost kinship haunts him *en passant,* but the deep significance which presumably attaches to it as the opening motif is diffused and then lost. The twinship of the two main parts, 'Marionettes' and 'Angels'—almost exactly equal in length—is a more palpable notion.

The misty actions of Part One are mimed in matching circumstances in Part Two, which finds equivalents for those characters not retained from before and suggests a pattern of endless drudging repetition. The narrator is occupied throughout with numbers and calculations: he is seeking a sort of mathematical epiphany, and perhaps he finds one: it is hard to tell. There is so much verbal flesh on the book that its moral backbone is difficult to discern. At any rate, the publisher's reference to Yeatsian man forced to choose between life and work seems an undue clarification. If there has to be a high-falutin reference of this kind it might be better made to some such document of enveloping contingency as Hofmannsthal's 'Letter of Lord Chandos'.

The narrative is prone to sudden plunges: disaster strikes repeatedly at the end of Part One, sweeping off half the characters, but at least Banville is good at describing death. The sickness and passing of the narrator's grandfather, Jack Kay, are beautifully written:

> He lay against us stiffly, a big chalk statue, mute and furious. He was unexpectedly light. The years had been working away at him in secret, hollowing him out. . . . He gazed up at us fearfully, like a child, his mouth working, his fingers clamped on the folds of the blankets at his chest as if it were the rim of a parapet behind which he was slowly, helplessly falling . . . There was no way out of the huge confusion into which he had blundered . . . He turned his eyes to the window, and one fat, lugubrious tear ran down his temple, over the livid vein pulsing there.

Joe McMinn (essay date Fall 1988)

SOURCE: "Stereotypical Images of Ireland in John Banville's Fiction," in *Eire-Ireland,* Vol. XXIII, No. 3, Fall, 1988, pp. 94-102.

[*In the following essay, McMinn analyzes the way Banville portrays Ireland and its people in his fiction.*]

To examine the imaginative role which Ireland plays in the novels of John Banville might seem like missing the point of a fiction which shows little regard for historical fact and less faith in the narrative manoeuvres of realism. Like the young Gabriel Godkin in *Birchwood,* who learned geography from his Aunt Martha, "not its facts but its poetry," Banville employs images of Ireland as metaphors for emotion and perception. Some of these images—such as the Big House—are almost institutionalised literary fictions. This is precisely why Banville likes them: they are fictional counters to play with in his own self-enclosed literary design. The wealth of literary cliché and stereotype in Irish literature has a special attraction for this writer who wishes to forge a style answerable to imagination not fact. It provides ammunition for the literary parodist—indeed, an ironic token of freedom from tradition—and concentrates the task of the novelist on the refinement of language itself.

> **Like the young Gabriel Godkin in *Birchwood,* who learned geography from his Aunt Martha, "not its facts but its poetry," Banville employs images of Ireland as metaphors for emotion and perception. Some of these images—such as the Big House—are almost institutionalised literary fictions. This is precisely why Banville likes them: they are fictional counters to play with in his own self-enclosed literary design.**
> **—Joe McMinn**

The self-conscious interaction between Irish identity and the English language, an important literary fiction since Stephen Daedalus's conversation with the Dean of Studies in *Portrait of the Artist as a Young Man,* reinforces Banville's sense of caution in regard to the deeply ambiguous medium of language. In terms of metafiction, this peculiar Irish unease about the relation of language and identity has now become a literary virtue and marks a distinctively self-conscious tradition in the modern Irish novel. This modernism is closely allied to an older, Romantic stereotype of the Irish gift for words, an imaginative and poetic adaptation of rational English. Banville accepts these images and the following stereotypes for the purposes of his writing:

> For the Irish, language is not primarily a tool for expressing what we mean. Sometimes I think it is quite the opposite. We have profound misgivings about words. We love them—all too passionately, some of us—but we do not trust them. Therefore

we play with them. I am well aware of the danger there is in saying these things. Shamrocks. Leprechauns. The gift of the gab. Little old men with pipes in their gobs sitting on ditches and maundering on about how things were in their fathers' time. In a word, pronounced chaarrm. If I have conjured these images, please banish them at once from your minds. What I am talking about is something subversive, destructive even, and in a way profoundly despairing. Listen to any group of Irish people conversing, from whatever class, in whatever circumstances, and behind the humour and the rhetoric and the slyness you will detect a dark note of hopelessness before the phenomenon of a world that is always *out there.*

There is no advantage to be gained from an academic argument over the factual basis of such declarations. Banville accepts the myth and the stereotype as having a special kind of reality which suits his imaginative purpose and formalist design. Like much self-conscious fiction, stereotypes and myths have a basis in reality but are not to be confused with reality. They are attractive and meaningful because they are primitive and simple forms of dramatic expression, images of national character which satisfy an imagination discontented with facts. The loss of the Irish language, the irrational savagery of Irish political history, the rise of a peasantry hungry for land and revenge, the ambiguous and fatal position of the ascendancy class—these are the essential images of Ireland which Banville adapts to his poetic fictions where they serve as metaphors for an experience which is tragic, chaotic, but occasionally illuminated through the very medium of writing about it.

Irish literary types and genres provided Banville with a dramatic series of metaphors for *Birchwood,* a story which includes a haunting parody of the Big House novel. Asked about his interest in this particular genre, Banville makes it clear that such a convention provides a useful narrative structure—no more:

> Obviously, I was thinking about Carleton, Somerville and Ross, but no one book in particular. I took stock characters, you know, the overbearing father, long-suffering mother, sensitive son, and then also other strands, the quest, the lost child, the doppelgänger.

Once the scaffolding of the Big House genre is in place, Banville is free to embellish it with a poetical character. *Birchwood* is a form of memoir written by Gabriel Godkin, the sole survivor of his family which rose from nowhere to take over the Lawless estate, only to lose it through the violence and confusion of a country in revolt. The historical background to Godkin's tale is deliberately confused and confusing. The early part of the story is set in Ireland during the Great Famine, but the narrative very soon switches to the land war of the early twentieth century. Agents of unpredictable and terrible violence, the British Army and the Molly Maguires, drift in and out of the plot with dramatic and wholly illogical effect. The anachronisms and narrative discontinuities have a dramatic purpose, however disconcerting for the reader. They are there to emphasise Godkin's entirely subjective view of a past which can only be invented but never really understood:

> All that blood! That slaughter! And for what? For the same reason that Papa released his father into the birch wood to die, that Granny Godkin tormented poor mad Beatrice, that Beatrice made Martha believe that Michael was in the burning shed, the same reason that brought about all their absurd tragedies, the reason which does not have a name. So here then is an ending, of a kind, to my story. It may not have been like that, any of it. I invent, necessarily.

There are no absolute truths or certainties about history or personal experience and, so, language has to be satisfied with the unknowable and the mysterious. Some kind of order to experience is desperately needed, however; and only an imagined order is possible. The Big House fiction serves the "necessary" fiction of consolation. The demented, violent and irrational sketches of Godkin's memoir are a personal nightmare which recalls images and sensations rather than facts or continuities. The narrative structure is that of a dream. The Irish landscapes situated within that memory give a special emotional quality to the narrative, usually a contradictory quality of emotion, joy blended with sadness, beauty amidst disorder.

There is an extraordinary description of such sensations in *Birchwood* when Godkin recalls a visit to a West of Ireland pub with his circus companions:

> That was my first taste of porter. Frightful stuff, I must admit, for I am no hard-drinking broth of a boy, but taken there, that brew, black and bitter, harbinger of a wild mordant gaiety, seemed to me, and still seems, to carry the savour of the country itself, this old little land ... The topers were dressed in their Sunday best. It must have been a holiday, or a holy day, perhaps some feast of the Queen of May. Much raucous laughter tumbled out of gap-toothed mouths, and the voices and the strange macaronic talk clashed in the smoky air like the sounds of battle. A fat woman with a red face was copiously weeping, rocking back and forth on a stool between two sheepish, speechless men. The cadaverous piper, hunched over his reeds, swung into a gay

dance tune, but his long face registered only a deeper melancholy. There is in the happiest of that music a profound thread of grief, never broken, equivalent to but not springing from the sustained drone note, an implacable mournfulness, and so, although the jig made the glasses sing, the fat woman wept and wept, rocking her sadness to sleep, and the two old men, with their hands on their knees and their jaws munching, sat and stared, with nothing to say.

In retrospect, every detail is invested with symbolic significance, but the tone is cautiously ironic, aware of the constant presence of contradiction and deflation. The porter's taste, "black and bitter," becomes a kind of synecdoche for Ireland's "wild mordant gaiety." The "topers" in their "Sunday best" all appear grotesque. The piper's "gay dance tune" is spoilt by his face of "deeper melancholy," and, while the jig "made the glasses sing," the audience sits silent and weeps.

Irish literary types and genres provided Banville with a dramatic series of metaphors for *Birchwood*, a story which includes a haunting parody of the Big House novel.
—*Joe McMinn*

This passage contains a carefully composed image of some terrible but fascinating asylum where drink and music seem to represent with unbearable accuracy the essential strangeness of existence. Even the talk is "macaronic," intensifying the boy's sense of contradiction and ambiguity. There is no need for Banville to reproduce this strange talk—the idea and the accompanying images convey the necessary effect. The confusion of language, typified here by a *Gaeltacht* culture, depressed and isolated, comes directly from Irish historical experience, a feeling picked up later by Godkin when he writes: "I do not speak the language of this wild country," and resigns himself to solitude. The cultural experience of loss and inarticulateness provides the Modernist in Banville with an effective fiction of remoteness in order to dramatise a contemporary sense of alienation. The story remains one of personal failure and individual survival, a defiantly private vision of language and reality. The unique effect sustained in *Birchwood* results from the manner in which Banville has converted so many Irish literacy fictions, many of them from the Romantic period, into a style and a consciousness which belong to the modern sense of the Absurd. This tension between the past and the present, between faith and scepticism, is at the heart of *Birchwood.*

While all of Banville's fiction exploits the artificial nature of narrative conventions, constantly drawing attention to their limitation and deceptiveness, it also tries to expose the fictional nature of rationality. This is the major theme of Banville's tetralogy on astronomy and science: *Doctor Copernicus, Kepler, The Newton Letter,* and his latest novel, *Mefisto.* The protagonists of these novels come to realise that science develops systems which, like Banville's fiction, are quite distinct from the realities which they claim to represent. The narrators suffer from a shared sense of having been tricked by the intellect away from a real, sensuous appreciation of human existence. Science cannot reproduce reality, only dream versions of it. The same is true of literature and art. A certain kind of abstraction common to both science and language is the prime culprit in Banville's interrogation of versions of reality. Only imagination, heightened by a tragic sense of life's fragility and irrationality, can retrieve some compensatory, personal sense of order and purpose. Systems of knowledge, whether geometry or language, are either merely elaborate diversions or, worse, paths of ignorance. In this regard, Banville would certainly endorse Blake's distinction between knowledge and perception.

The Newton Letter combines an astronomical motif with the Big House setting to produce a story about the relation between scientific and cultural fictions. The nameless narrator, like Gabriel Godkin in *Birchwood,* has written an account of a personal experience whose significance remains a mystery. Trying to finish his biography of Newton, he lodges in County Wexford at a Big House owned by the Lawlesses. In the following excerpt he remembers his early, confident assumptions about the nature of both his academic work and his neighbours:

> I had them spotted for patricians from the start. The big house, Edward's tweeds, Charlotte's fine-boned slender grace that the dowdiest of clothes could not mask, even Ottilie's awkwardness, all this seemed the unmistakable stamp of their class. Protestants, of course, landed, the land gone now to gombeen men and compulsory purchase, the family fortune wasted by tax, death duties, inflation. But how bravely, how beautifully they bore their losses! Observing them, I understood that breeding such as theirs is a preparation not for squiredom itself, but for that distant day, which for the Lawlesses had arrived, when the trappings of glory had gone and only style remains. All nonsense, of course, but to me, product of a post-peasant Catholic upbringing, they appeared perfected creatures.

The narrator's fictional stereotype of the Protestant gentry is no less real because explained only in the context of his own cultural background. The reality seems uncannily like the fiction. This correspondence confirms his assumptions, and he is pleased with his observation. But from then onwards, through a series of increasingly strange and shocking episodes, like those of a domestic mystery-tale, he comes to an embarrassed awareness of his total ignorance and delusion with regard to those about him.

The Lawlesses are, needless to say, Catholic. There is a young boy in the house, Michael, who never speaks and whose mother is either Charlotte or Ottilie. Edward dies from cancer, which the narrator mistook for moodiness. An eccentric neighbour horrifies him by drinking a toast to the murder of Mountbatten and eighteen British soldiers and, then, praises the afternoon cake. Reduced to silence by confusion and fear, the narrator abandons his research on Newton. Paradoxically, however, this personal defeat opens up a new perception to him of the importance of the ordinary and the immediate in human affairs, "At once commonplace and unique, like clues at the scene of a crime." The most significant events are now eloquent images perceived afresh, not the abstractions of intellectual design. Like the subject of his own book on Newton, so much speculative knowledge only results in his feeling like a child with the real world yet to be discovered.

To some extent, Banville caricatures Science in order to achieve this effect. In a parodic footnote in *The Newton Letter,* having wondered whether the local town has a bawdy-house, he writes: I have since learned that this contention is mistaken; cf. Polkolski, F X., Interface Tribal Situations in Southeast Ireland: a structuralist study. So much for the pretensions of anthropological science to explain the innermost lives of people in the tribal culture of modern Ireland. The kind of poetical perception by which academic knowledge is judged is always a personal—never a social—experience. Banville's romantic anti-intellectualism comes from a despair with modern rationalism and a simultaneous faith in primitive, direct perception. In a curious way, the enduring fiction that the Irish are more imaginative than rational suits Banville's fiction admirably. Of course, this is only part of his complex view of the relation between intellect and emotion. Banville is no Wordsworth. The Irish fictions in Banville are always held in check by irony and self-consciousness. Moments of exquisite pastoral beauty are usually followed—promptly—by disaster.

The final novel of the tetralogy, *Mefisto,* is the darkest fiction of the series, a coda of unmitigated pain. More like the brashly self-conscious Gothic of Banville's early *Nightspawn,* it is a disappointing story. It has many familiar elements and motifs—a mathematical prodigy as narrator, an elaborately contrived mystery plot involving all kinds of bizarre and sinister characters, the anguish of trying to write about the incommunicable, and a setting which moves from rural Wexford to contemporary urban Dublin. Like *Birchwood,* it is a story about a boy's initiation into an evil world. The narrator, Gabriel Swan, comes under the malign influence of Felix, a kind of theatrical pimp, and he ends up in the Dublin underworld of drugs and violence. Like his scientific and academic predecessors, Swan's search for the absolute order which mathematics promises is brutally overwhelmed by personal tragedy when his body is burned in an accident leaving him hideously deformed. *Mefisto,* his "black book," is Swan's inadequate but necessary attempt to recreate and possibly understand the hollow meaninglessness of his youthful quest.

> *The Newton Letter* combines an astronomical motif with the Big House setting to produce a story about the relation between scientific and cultural fictions.
> —*Joe McMinn*

The contrasting Irish settings of rural Wexford and urban Dublin, apart from their obvious metaphorical association with innocence and experience, show Banville at his most stylish and, unfortunately, his most studied. In the first part of the novel, Swan recalls the countryside where he walked with his mother, always ending up at the Big House:

> Ashburn would be for her always an idyll. The life of the big house, at the far fringes of which she had hovered longingly, she remembered as a languorous mime to the music of tick-tocking tennis balls across green lawns and the far-off bleat of the huntsman's horn on frosty mornings, a scene small and distant, yet perfectly, preciously detailed, atwinkle with tiny laughter, like a picture glimpsed of eighteenth-century aristocrats at play in a dappled glade.

Here, memory becomes a kind of dreaming. Banville excels at lyrical descriptions like this which are deliberately contrived and transparent but delivered in such a tone as to commend their reality to the imagination.

According to the novel, the invented is always real, even if untrue. Swan's family works for the Big House, and their peasants' suspicion of everything outside their class makes Gabriel conceal his curiosity about the house as well as his mathematical dreams. Like his namesake in *Birchwood,* Gabriel follows his obsession in order to escape from the boredom and pain of family. But, whereas Godkin's adventures throughout an imaginative version of nineteenth-century Ireland have a very unified effect and always preserve dramatic tension in the character of a narrator caught between love and hate, Swan's nightmarish experience in Dublin seems all too cleverly rehearsed. It is also difficult to see why he needs to be cast in the role of mathematical prodigy, except that it is a blatantly abstract comfort. The grotesque and the inexplicable events of his story arrive just a bit too easily and predictably and have a deadening effect on a fiction which is trying to express a frightful sense of physical and spiritual pain:

> Grief, of course, and guilt. I shall not go into it. Pain too, but not so much as before, and every day a little less. My face is almost mended, one morning I'll wake up and not recognise myself in the mirror. A new man. I stay away from the hospital. What is there for me there, any more? I want no protectors now. I want to be, to be, what, I don't know. Naked. Flayed. A howling babe, waving furious fists. I don't know.

> Have I tied up all the ends? Even an invented world has its rules, tedious, absurd perhaps, but not to be gainsaid.

At this point the story seems tired of its preoccupation with the relentless imagery of evil and leaves no room for those redemptive moments of perception and joy which occur in Banville's best work. Occasional moments like these do occur but, unfortunately, do not convince. One of them, when Swan experiences an insight into the order behind the seeming chaos of existence, takes place in a country pub full of evil freaks and feels like a borrowed response from **Birchwood.** The final lines in the above quotation about the necessary but tiresome job of making a story coherent is a bad sign, especially so late in Banville's mature work. It sounds a bit like a defence of a story which has run out of fiction.

Mefisto has some powerful and compelling moments, especially in the section which deals with memories of childhood. But the shift into the drug-underworld of contemporary Dublin is the least satisfying of Banville's Irish metaphors. It is, perhaps, too close to the reality of contemporary public opinion to suit this novelist's more detached imagination.

As with so many Irish writers, especially novelists, Banville both denies and exploits the attractions of tradition. The familiar antagonism between the struggling artist and a philistine, provincial culture appeared early in his work. In **"Nightwind,"** one of the short stories of **Long Lankin,** a character called "Mor" who wishes to write a novel, declares passionately:

> This place produced me and will destroy me if I try to break free. All this crowd understands is the price of a heifer and the size of the new car and the holiday in Spain and those godblasted dogs howling for blood.

This updated echo of Stephen Daedalus did not become the basis of a self-dramatising fiction of spiritual martyrdom in the cause of literature. Instead, Banville's personal argument with Ireland's new middle class and its old literary conventions developed into his more impersonal art based on a series of original metaphors for the individual imagination seeking to recover a language to express lost innocence. Freedom for a writer like John Banville comes from finding a style which creates and sustains an alternative vision of reality, dramatised through metaphors which speak for themselves. Those metaphors may be independent of—but not out of sympathy with—reality. Samuel Beckett resonates as a strong presence here. Like him, Banville has found a distinctive voice for his tragic narrators, nostalgic but defiant. Both writers have often turned to Irish images of landscape and character, familiar but fictive, to suggest a recognisable and melancholic sense of loss and isolation. Banville's adventurous and iconoclastic imagination and his necessary formalism question the limitations of tradition and convention in Irish literary culture and discover, in its stead, a European character. Banville's stereotypical images of Ireland have helped secure that achievement without compromising the originality of his fiction.

Erica Abeel (review date 15 April 1990)

SOURCE: "He Killed Her Because He Could," in *New York Times Book Review,* April 15, 1990, p. 11.

[*In the following review, Abeel asserts that in* The Book of Evidence *"Mr. Banville has gambled that he could write a mesmerizing tale about a monster—and he has won."*]

Here is an astonishing, disturbing little novel [**The Book of Evidence**] that might have been coughed up from hell. A first-person narrator confesses to a murder. It's soon apparent, though, that the crime was not inspired by greed, revenge or any other discernible motive. The narrator is a sort of accidental killer—Everyman as monster.

Freddie Montgomery, a gifted scientist, presents his confession as he sits in jail awaiting trial. He imagines his ruminations as a courtroom statement and posits his readers as judge and jury. John Banville, the author of **Doctor Copernicus, Kepler** and other novels, has made his Freddie a thoroughly bad apple, who has spent the last 10 years drifting about on various southerly islands, wife and child in tow. He gets into a scrape with some island lowlifes and returns to Ireland (leaving his wife as hostage) to raise some cash. There he stages an absurdly clumsy theft, stealing a painting from a friend's estate in daylight and in view of some dozen people. During the getaway, he kills a maid. The homages to illustrious predecessors in **The Book of Evidence** are unmistakable. Albert Camus's Meursault, in *The Stranger,* also blundered into a senseless murder, maddened—as is Freddie—by blinding sunlight. Like Meursault, Freddie feels that he is a stranger on this planet and can't quite marshal the appropriate responses (Meursault is condemned for not crying at his mother's funeral), and Freddie wanders through life with "an amnesiac's numbed amazement." Mr. Banville has resurrected the world of the post-World War II existentialists, a universe bled of significance or meaning. "Nothing cared," marvels Freddie of nature's indifference to human suffering. The dark spirit of Dostoyevsky's Raskolnikov also permeates Freddie's confession: the notions of crime as a journey toward self-knowledge and the joys of self-degradation. Freddie even says, "I felt like the gloomy hero in a Russian novel."

Still, Freddie is very much his own man. In fact, he comes across with such immediacy, we almost empathize with him, even when he is most depraved. Acutely self-conscious and observant, he's a man who loves gin and sleazy dives, hates dogs and mustaches, desires his wife—along with her best friend and assorted other women. He's contrary, spiteful and fond of teasing us. "I was ashamed," he confesses at one point. "I can't explain it. That is, I could, but won't." He has flashes of sardonic humor, especially in scenes with his mother, who triggers attacks of "filial heartburn." Parodying the blame-it-all-on-mom approach, he cracks, "Is it any wonder I have ended up in jail?" And he seldom reacts predictably—even to himself. After his capture he observes, "There was something about being manacled that I found almost soothing, as if it were a more natural state than that of untrammelled freedom."

Freddie has reason to fear untrammeled freedom. By his own admission he is "bifurcate." Inside him resides his very own Mr. Hyde, a grumbling brute he dubs "Bunter," who is itching to break out of his cage and pull down the rafters.

Mr. Banville's agenda is not simply to offer a portrait of the intellectual as psychopath. He's a demolition artist, dynamiting received ideas and basic assumptions at every turn. Freddie refuses to honor the notion of crucial turning points in a life, or even causality. His explanations for behavior are tautological: "My journey, like everyone else's . . . had not been a thing of signposts and decisive marching, but drift only. . . . I was living like that because I was living like that, there is no other answer." Under Freddie's scrutiny, the very concept of evil evaporates; "badness" is just a word, "a kind of elaborate cover for the fact that nothing is there. Or perhaps the words are an attempt to make it be there? Or, again, perhaps there is something but the words invented it."

Through Freddie, Mr. Banville dismantles conventional thinking about crime—and human behavior—including the notion of motives. Not only had Freddie no reason for kill-

ing the maid, there was no moment at which he even decided to kill. The murder was just an unleashing of primal anger. The monster inside "leaped out, frothing and flailing. He had scores to settle with the world, and she, at that moment, was world enough for him." In a comic passage, the police try to extract from Freddie his murder plan, and like a good schoolboy, he tries to comply. But Freddie's flaw has never been dishonesty. There was no plan, he insists—"I killed her because I could."

Mr. Banville even subverts the reality of Freddie's confession, casting doubts on its veracity. Studded with minutely observed detail (in keeping with his scientific training), Freddie's story has the weight of lived experience. But look again. Balking at the rigors of describing minor players in his tale, he remarks, "For God's sake, how many of these grotesques am I expected to invent?" Invent? Is Freddie's "evidence" based on an actual murder, or are we privy to the fantasies of a madman? Toward the end, he concludes that his greatest sin was having never imagined the maid vividly enough: "I never made her be there sufficiently. . . . Yes, that failure of imagination is my real crime." He means that he was able to kill the maid because she never existed for him as a person. But possibly Mr. Banville also intends a gloss on the art of the storyteller, whose greatest sin is an insufficiently vivid character.

To capture the full spectrum of Freddie's lunatic moods, Mr. Banville has forged a most supple, most fluid prose. He has a kind of fiber-optic vision that sees where no one else can see ("I might have been no more than a flaw in the air," Freddie remarks about his own inconsequence). The author is a landscape painter with language ("the houses along the coast shimmered in a pale-blue haze, as if the sky had crumbled into airy geometry there"). The novel's centerpiece is the murder scene itself, conveyed with lapidary precision, a horrible jewel held up to light; at its climax there's a salute to Henri-Georges Clouzot's film *Diabolique.* And always, humor alleviates the blackness. Post-gallows humor, you might say. Just as Freddie watches the passing parade from beyond life, "behind leaf-reflecting glass," Mr. Banville's laughter emanates from an eerie fourth dimension. A current refrain in the publishing world has it that a writer must create a sympathetic hero. Mr. Banville has gambled that he could write a mesmerizing tale about a monster—and he has won.

James Sattler (review date May/June 1990)

SOURCE: A review of *The Book of Evidence,* in *Bloomsbury Review,* May/June, 1990, pp. 2-3.

[*In the following review, Sattler asserts that* The Book of

Evidence *is about the disintegration of its protagonist Freddie Montgomery.*]

"Well, Well, That's the advantage of jail, one has the time and leisure really to get to the heart of things," says Freddie Montgomery at one point during his confession of murder which comprises *The Book of Evidence.* Through this sometimes seemingly random rambling, characterized by minute expansion on a relatively simple string of events, emerges the substance of Freddie's life.

Freddie, a thirty-eight-year-old husband, father, failed son, and onetime scientist, travels aimlessly, never losing a sense of alienation. He imagines that a cosmic mistake placed humans on the earth and put the real earthlings somewhere else: "No, they would have become extinct long ago. How could they survive, these gentle earthlings, in a world that was made to contain us?" While vacationing on an island in the Mediterranean he borrows money from the "wrong people" and must return home to Ireland to try to get the money from his widowed mother. His wife and daughter are left behind under the watchful eyes of the local crime organization.

Freddie finds little comfort or hope of assistance at home, with his mother fed up with his profligacy. A row with her, sparked by the absence of paintings he thought might be of value, sends him wandering to the house of an old acquaintance. To Freddie's dismay, he finds that the paintings were sold to the friend who, in turn, sold them again. While visiting, he becomes obsessed with the woman in the seventeenth-century Dutch painting *Portrait of a Woman with Gloves.*

Freddie returns to steal the painting, only to be interrupted by a servant girl whom he abducts along with the painting. In a petulant rage he brutally murders the servant girl with a hammer. After a short time undercover, he is jailed and begins his confession.

Evoking comparisons to Dostoyevsky's *Crime and Punishment,* Camus' *The Stranger,* and even some of Beckett's early fiction, Banville's novel is an existential portrait that maps an internal landscape through the narrator's perceptions and reactions to the external, looking at seemingly unimportant details, giving every event equal weight no matter how mundane or extraordinary.

"I only wish to explain my motives, I mean the deepest ones, if such a thing is possible," Freddie says. With a stunning precision of expression Banville exposes the reality beneath Freddie's actions. What seems like merely pricking the surface often inundates the reader with what has been festering below.

Unaware of any vaginal connotations, Freddie can't explain his pronounced aversion to moustaches and disguises his latent homosexuality in homophobia. Once home, he spends time in a bar frequented by homosexuals but denies any sexual interest, and his relationship with Charlie, an old friend of the family who later hides him, seems purposefully ambiguous. After recalling childhood events—having to wait outside while his father visited his mistress—Freddie dismisses the idea of Oedipal feelings, yet there is always an undercurrent of hate for his father.

Freddie's relationships with women are less than satisfying. His intimacy with Daphne, who becomes his wife, begins only with the break-up of her relationship with her roommate Anne. His mother dies while he's in jail, leaving behind a will that disinherited him and replaced him with the stable girl long before the murder. The only sympathetic woman from whom Freddie gets unconditional affection is a total stranger he meets while in hiding. He refers to her only as Foxey, because of her red hair:

> She trusted me. She smelled the blood and the horror and did not recoil, but opened herself like a flower and let me rest in her for a moment, my heart shaking, as we exchanged our wordless secret.

Fulfillment of simple, childish wants makes the greatest impression on Freddie. In a self-indulgent trip to the hardware store he buys a hammer, the murder weapon, to gratify the deprived child he once was. After the murder he yearns to be caught and even becomes upset at having to wait for the police to find him:

> The least I had expected from the enormities of which I was guilty was that they would change my life, that they would make things happen, however awful, that there would be a constant succession of heart-stopping events, of alarms and sudden frights and hairbreadth escapes.

Finally, he revels in being brought before some authority: "From now on I would be watched over, I would be tended and fed and listened to, like a big dangerous baby." He enjoys being handcuffed, and although he gets offended when he doesn't receive the attention he thinks he deserves, Freddie finally seems satisfied under the paternal authority of the police.

"Now and then I am afforded a glimpse into what seems a new world, but which I realise has been there all along, without my noticing." Throughout the monologue, Freddie evinces a new sense of consciousness to which he seems to have been boosted through his actions and his reflections on them. But he can find little consolation because he feels he's spent a life walking past doorways never daring to enter; now he is an explorer "glimpsing a new continent from a sinking ship."

Through razor sharp observations and scintillating prose, Banville creates a voice true to its pathology. American readers might experience a slight feeling of distance from the voice because it is not always the English of America, but the difference can be appreciated as the subtle flavor of a slightly different culture. And although Freddie's obsession with the woman in the painting seems less convincing and more of a device than his other impulses, it is still effective as an indication of the extent to which Freddie is losing touch with reality.

[*The Book of Evidence*] . . . is an existential portrait that maps an internal landscape through the narrator's perceptions and reactions to the external, looking at seemingly unimportant details, giving every event equal weight no matter how mundane or extraordinary.
—*James Sattler*

In explaining what he thinks are his motives, Freddie reveals the real forces at work, conditions such that a man functioning relatively acceptably in the world can commit murder without hesitation. The reader must confront the potential damage resulting from emotional disorder and the fallacy of functioning normally as any measure of mental health.

Freddie muses about his future: "By the way, what an odd formulation that is: to get life. Words so rarely mean what they mean." So it is with Banville's story but so much the better when an artist can convey what isn't or can't be expressed. The evidence of the title is not of the murder of the servant girl but of the gradual, lifelong disintegration of the being that was Freddie.

Brian McIlroy (essay date Winter 1992)

SOURCE: "Reconstructing Artistic and Scientific Paradigms: John Banville's *The Newton Letter*," in *Mosaic*, Vol. 25, No. 1, Winter, 1992, pp. 121-33.

[*In the following essay, McIlroy examines the connection between scientific and literary pursuits in Banville's* The Newton Letter, *and asserts that it "is an ingenious exploration of how conceptual frames, both artistic and scientific, are imagined and reimagined to produce new syntheses."*]

John Banville's *The Newton Letter* is the third volume in the contemporary Irish novelist's scientific tetralogy, which includes *Doctor Copernicus, Kepler* and *Mefisto.* Attempts to coordinate the four works have thus far taken the form of noting their intertextuality or their Irish themes. As I see it, a stronger case for their coherence can be made by focusing on their collective concern with what literary and scientific pursuits have in common. My specific focus on *The Newton Letter* derives from the way that this novella seems best to illustrate Banville's artistry in dramatizing this connection.

The narrator of *The Newton Letter* is a nameless Dublin historian who is attempting to write a biography of this great scientist. Frustrated in completing his chapter on Newton's breakdown in 1693, and looking for inspiration, the narrator moves from Dublin to Fern House, a country-house estate in the south of Ireland. There he becomes fascinated with the Lawless family from whom he has rented his accommodation, in particular Charlotte, who along with her husband Edward owns the estate; Ottilie, a younger woman; and a young boy named Michael. The narrator initially finds the exact relationships among these people elusive. He begins a sexual relationship with Ottilie, while secretly harboring desires for Charlotte, who we gradually learn is under sedation and preoccupied with Edward's stomach cancer and the possible loss of her home-based business (market-gardening). In the process of socializing with this enigmatic family, the narrator finds great difficulty in returning to his biography of Newton. Following a traumatic evening when Edward has to be attended to by a doctor after a bout of heavy drinking, the narrator leaves, but keeps up a correspondence with Ottilie and learns that he is the father of her soon-to-be-born child. The novella ends with the seeming optimism of the narrator's determination to resume work on his Newton biography and to continue his relationship with Ottilie.

At first glance, *The Newton Letter* appears to constitute a radical departure from the two previous works of the tetralogy. Whereas earlier Banville had interwoven first- and third-person narratives, in *The Newton Letter* the whole discourse is channeled through a first-person narrator who is also a major participant in the action, and the entire narrative takes the form of a letter in which a key concern of the narrator is two letters written by Newton. Whereas *Doctor Copernicus* and *Kepler* are set in the times of their scientific subjects, in *The Newton Letter* the setting is not Newton's eighteenth-century England but twentieth-century Ireland. Despite these differences, however, *The Newton Letter* continues to examine, albeit indirectly, the issues that confront a great scientist.

The general tone of the novella is one of somber reflection at past mistakes, and one senses that Banville decided at this juncture to narrow his focus to a specific time and place because his concern was with the way a specific crisis in the life of Newton served to call into question the validity of totalizing systems—such as Newton's clockwork model of the universe. Banville's decision to structure the novella in the form of a letter and to use Newton's letters as a basis for exploration can perhaps be traced to the seeming absence of personal philosophy in Newton's official formulations; as M. H. Nicolson has observed, "There is little enough metaphysics in Newton's scientific writings, and students have been forced to deduce many of his philosophical opinions from his letters."

As Banville's narrator tries to come to terms with his writer's block, it becomes clear that his feelings of uncertainty and hesitation resemble those he sees in Newton and that in both cases the cause for the most part is an inability to provide a theoretical framework with which to account for new empirical and conceptual data. Some general connections between the narrator's project and the problems confronting his subject can thus easily be made. In the first place, the biographer/narrator must deal with the eighteenth-century influences on Newton and the twentieth-century influences on his own reinterpretation; equally, a scientific theorist must examine the social reasons for a previous theory to have been popular in the past and the current reasons for accepting or rejecting it. Second, the narrator must account for sudden "revolutions" or paradigm changes in Newton's life and thought, just as a scientific theorist must clarify what is original, staid or simply wrong in the work of other theorists. Third, the narrator must endeavor to explain Newton's creative and non-creative periods, just as the scientific theorist must puzzle out what creative thought actually is, if he is to make claims for his own forays in the field. It might be further argued that scientific theorists such as Newton are, in fact, historians, since they must build upon previous work. Newton always claimed he could see so far because he had giants like Kepler to help him. Crucial differences in time and location may exist between the narrator's project and Newton's, but perhaps not in abstract concepts, such as the recognition of a gulf between the knowable and the unknowable.

What Banville seems to be attempting through the structure and concerns of *The Newton Letter* is a humanistic fleshing out of the theories of Thomas Kuhn on "Scientific Revolutions."
—*Brian McIlroy*

What Banville seems to be attempting through the structure and concerns of *The Newton Letter* is a humanistic fleshing out of the theories of Thomas Kuhn on "Scientific Revo-

lutions." We know that Banville read Kuhn closely: he acknowledges his work in the foreword to *Doctor Copernicus.* In my view, this personalizing of Kuhn's theories is the cornerstone of the novella's provocativeness; in *The Newton Letter* Banville is exploring the wider applicability of Kuhn's concept of paradigm change.

Scientific paradigms can be described as conceptual frameworks which are generally agreed upon by a community of practitioners and theoreticians who can then concur on the nature of the problems still to be solved. According to Kuhn, when crises in science occur they are solved in one of three ways: (1) by an ingenious reworking of the existing paradigm; (2) by a move to label them as "insoluble" or "time-wasting"; or (3) by constructing a new paradigm, over which there is much disagreement. The narrator's Newton takes the second course of action *vis a vis* doubts concerning the absolute nature of space, time and motion, while Banville's narrator progresses through all three stages in the understanding of his own life and relationships. More specifically, what Banville's protagonist experiences is the foregrounding of a new paradigm, a process which involves "the previous awareness of anomaly, the gradual and simultaneous experience of both observational and conceptual recognition, and the consequent change of paradigm categories and procedures often accompanied by resistance." This three-step process is mirrored both by the narrator and by the narrator's understanding of Newton's activities in 1693. The narrator assumes that Newton's work subsequent to his *Principia* began to cast doubts on his previous achievements. This "breakdown" period, the narrator believes, emerged because of an undismissable anomaly which began to move from the periphery to the center of Newton's thoughts and which thus required the construction of a new model.

The narrator expresses this torturous re-thinking via the self-reflexive form of autobiographical reminiscence, in the midst of which he attempts to distance himself through recourse to traditional methods and views. These attempts, however, are short-lived and often flippantly undermined. Ultimately, the narrator has decided to work through his writer's block by writing a confessional missive to the muse of history, "Clio" or "Cliona." The novella opens with a paradoxical invocation: "Words fail me, Clio. How did you track me down, did I leave bloodstains in the snow? I won't try to apologise. Instead, I want simply to explain, so that we both might understand." In attempting to explain, however, he is caught in the typical conundrum of the scientist and artist: how does one validate subjective experiences and achieve objective truth?

The narrator's awareness of the anomaly he must address is crystallized in the "flawed" Newton he has come to see as a result of his examination of the scientist's intellectual and personal problems. Although the Newton letter "discourse" appears very briefly in the text, it is part of the new paradigm at work on the narrator, and I want first to isolate it to emphasize its ultimate importance. In the context of the novella, the narrator is stymied by two letters written by Newton to John Locke in 1693: one a factual document, the other Banville's fabrication. The first or authentic letter reveals the passionate and irrational side of Newton the scientist. Never reproduced directly, this letter is present in the form of the narrator's attempts to account for it. Initially he assumes the pose of a sympathetic inquirer:

> Remember that mad letter Newton wrote to John Locke in September of 1693, accusing the philosopher out of the blue of being immoral, and a Hobbist, and of having tried to embroil him with women? I picture old Locke pacing the great garden at Oates, eyebrows leaping higher and higher as he goggles at these wild charges. I wonder if he felt the special pang which I feel reading the subscription: *I am your most humble and unfortunate servant, Is. Newton.* It seems to me to express better than anything that has gone before it Newton's pain and anguished bafflement. I compare it to the way a few weeks later he signed, with just the stark surname, another, and altogether different, letter. What happened in the interval, what knowledge dawned on him?

Having hinted briefly at the second fictional letter, the narrator then assumes the pose of an academic historian:

> We have speculated a great deal, you [Clio] and I, on his nervous collapse late in that summer of '93. He was fifty, his greatest work was behind him, the Principia and the gravity laws, the discoveries in optics. He was giving himself up more and more to interpretative study of the Bible, and to that darker work in alchemy which so embarrasses his biographers. He was a great man now, his fame was assured, all Europe honoured him. But his life as a scientist was over. The process of lapidescence had begun: the world was turning him into a monument to himself. He was cold, arrogant, lonely. He was still obsessively jealous—his hatred of Hooke was to endure, indeed to intensify, even beyond the death of his old adversary. He was—
>
> Look at me, writing history; old habits die hard.

By not citing the Newton letter directly but rather in terms of the narrator's attempt to analyze it for clues to Newton's character and value system, Banville highlights the way that the charges in question apply to the narrator's own situation. According to one of Newton's actual biographers, Frank Manuel, the word "immorality" concerns not sexual rela-

tions, but the greedy seeking of a "place" or "position." The narrator is also clearly desirous of reputation and acclaim for *his* work: "It would be a splendid book, fresh and clean as this bright scene before me. . . . and Cambridge would offer me a big job." Equally self-reflexive is the narrator's concern with the "Hobbist" accusation. Hobbes believed that absolute government was necessary because of the selfishness of human beings which—left unchecked—leads to chaos and disorder; a totalizing concept, Hobbism involves adherence to a monolithic structure or entity, somewhat resembling the power the narrator gives to the muse of history, Clio or Cliona, to whom he is confessing. Lastly, it is not surprising that the narrator finds significance in Newton's paranoid feelings concerning "entrapment by Women," since he himself fornicates with one woman while having adulterous desires for another.

Where Newton and the narrator seem to part company is in Newton's perception of Nature and in his belief that many unanswerable questions were inappropriate or dismissable because the pure absolutes were to be found in God; the narrator, however, appears to have no faith and is subsequently at variance with the natural world, exemplified by his fear of animals, birds and insects and his bemusement at the various kinds of trees. Thus he becomes and feels detached, "an interloper," so much so that even his manuscript appears to be severed from him.

The second Newton letter is supposed to have been written a few weeks after the first. In an endnote, Banville tells us that the letter is a fiction, "the tone and some of the text of which is taken from Hugo von Hofmannsthal's *Ein Brief* ("The Letter of Lord Chandos")." The fictional letter of Hofmannsthal imagines a correspondence between Lord Chandos and Francis Bacon, in which the former laments his inability to make meaningful sense of reality and the inadequacy of language to mediate experience: "My case, in short, is this: I have lost completely the ability to think or to speak of anything coherently." In Banville's fictional letter, Newton plays Lord Chandos to Locke's Bacon.

The facts of the matter, according to Manuel's biography, are that when Newton gave up his Cambridge position as lecturer, he had a reputation for speaking to empty halls, so incomprehensible was his discourse; in fact, only two accounts of his lectures have come down to us. He then took up an administrative position at the Royal Mint, a job of immense routine dealing primarily with everyday matters. Historians of science believe that Newton's relinquishment of scientific pursuits was intentional, and that he realized that his great creative period was over. Through the fictional letter Banville suggests that possibly this change was dictated by unwillingness to address an anomaly in his previous theoretical system.

The centrality of this second letter is highlighted in the title of the novella itself, which suggests one particular piece of correspondence, and the narrator specifically encourages us to see the fictional letter as the one at issue. In doing so, he also suggests how this anomalous letter serves to integrate his biographical project and his personal experiences at Fern House: "The letter seemed to me now to lie at the centre of my work, perhaps of Newton's too, reflecting and containing all the rest, as the image of Charlotte contained, as in a convex mirror, the entire world of Ferns." The inscrutable Charlotte would appear to be at the core of the family drama at Fern House, just as the narrator sees the fictive letter to be at the core of Newton's fluctuations in thought. It is also significant that Newton is writing to John Locke, who denied the concept of innate ideas and located knowledge in experience.

In this fictive letter to Locke, Newton complains of an intellectual impasse. He shifts away from the mere pronouncements of beliefs in God and in a mechanistic universe to that which is creating doubt in his mind, his everyday meetings with tradesmen:

> *They would seem to have something to tell me; not of their trades, nor even of how they conduct their lives; nothing, I believe, in words. They are, if you will understand it, themselves the things they might tell. They are all a form of saying*—and there it breaks off, the rest of that page illegible (because of a scorch mark perhaps?). All that remains is the brief close: *My dear Doctor, expect no more philosophy from my pen. The language in which I might be able not only to write but to think is neither Latin nor English, but a language none of whose words is known to me; a language in which commonplace things speak to me; and wherein I may one day have to justify myself before an unknown judge.*

The inadequacy of human language to explain the phenomena of life is a constant theme throughout Banville's tetralogy: Copernicus and Kepler constantly revise their writings, admitting at least to themselves that errors have been made. Here Banville has Newton ascribe to these laborers a form of knowledge which is unspeakable and untransmissible, but which he also feels must be the site of future philosophy. In turn, he presents as his final judges not God but his fellow man, the tradesmen who are supposedly his intellectual inferiors but in whom he finds power.

A sense of the reductiveness of his scientific endeavors underlies this fictive letter, wherein Newton appears to be admitting before his peers (Locke) and superior (God) that his discoveries and theories are in reality minuscule. Such humility is consistent with the quotation from Newton that Banville includes in the novella's preface: "I seem to have been only as a boy playing on the seashore, and diverting myself in now and then finding a smoother pebble or a prettier shell than ordinary, whilst the great ocean of truth lay all undiscovered before me." Similarly, what interests Banville and the narrator are the limitations of one intellect to understand the world. The "secondary" nature of a history, biography or even autobiography/personal memoir—an uncertain writer dealing with an uncertain subject—promotes the debilitating feeling that empirical exactitude is illusory and that subjectivity is the only reality worth attempting to articulate.

To the narrator, the "story" of Newton's "madness" in the autumn of 1693, following a fire in his room which destroyed a number of his papers (including a manuscript on optics), is to be understood in terms of his discovery of pleasure in the minutiae of everyday life: "He notices details, early morning light through a window, his rescuer's one unshod foot and yellow toenails, the velvet blackness of burnt paper. He smiles." As in Banville's portrait of *Kepler,* the reassuring elements are apparently trivial.

The narrator's contention is that to Newton the destruction of his work mattered little because the great ocean of truth lay around him in this real, observable, though inexplicable, world. As the narrator informs Charlotte, Newton's absolutes of space, time and motion upon which he based his theories had to be revised the more he thought about his science. The grand design or system, seemingly absolute and closed, became unnervingly relative and open in tandem with the chaos and disorder of the human life around him. This "confused mix" is succinctly conveyed when the narrator *marries* his scientific speech to Charlotte with his feelings for her, during the dinner table chaos when a guest attempts to focus conversation on buying out the Lawlesses' business. For the first time, Charlotte seems to recognize the narrator and his work, and he is eager to impress, even if he has to be pedantic:

> "Because he had to have certain absolutes," I said, look at me, keep looking at me, "certain absolutes of of of [sic], of space, time, motion to found his theories on. But space, time, and motion," beats, soft beats, soft heartbeats, "can only be relative, for us, he knew that, had to admit it, had to let them go, and when they went," O my darling, "everything else went with them." Ah!

The realization of an undismissible anomaly in his work led Newton to give up science. Equally, the narrator's difficulty in writing about Newton's breakdown consists of his inability to determine at what juncture the scientist refused to continue supporting a flawed paradigm, and at what point he withdrew from constructing a new one. Commenting directly on a scientist's choices when faced with such a situation, Stephen Hawking has observed:

> What should you do when you find you have made a mistake like that? Some people never admit that they are wrong and continue to find new, and often mutually inconsistent, arguments to support their case—as Eddington did in opposing black hole theory. Others claim to have never really supported the incorrect view in the first place or, if they did, it was only to show that it was inconsistent. It seems to me much better and less confusing if you admit in print that you were wrong. A good example of this was Einstein, who called the cosmological constant, which he introduced when he was trying to make a static model of the universe, the biggest mistake of his life.

What Hawking omits are two other possibilities: silence and Newton's "solution," that of shifting to other pursuits. The appeal of Banville's novella is that we see the narrator advance (as if having read Hawking) in this area of cognition to the point of beginning to construct a new paradigm (concerning Newton), despite his own resistance. The latter is rooted in the traditional biographer's reluctance to argue that the man to whom he has devoted a great deal of time and energy had a breakdown and changed occupations primarily because his celebrated theories did not square either with experience or with further reflection. The problem he is faced with is that of a biographer whose subject renounces his philosophy. Having constructed a suitable paradigm for his subject's ideas, he is faced with doubt when the "Odd behaviour" of his subject challenges the pre-established profile—even if in the case of Banville's Newton this renunciation occurs only once, in the fictive letter to John Locke.

One of the major features of *The Newton Letter* is the humbling of the intellectual in the face of the natural, arbitrary, tragic, disorganized world. Both Copernicus and Kepler face similar embarrassments. The narrator of the novella experiences such a humbling in his relationships with Ottilie and Charlotte.

—*Brian McIlroy*

The narrator's initial entrapment in his traditionalist biographical model and the beginnings of his construction of a new humanistic paradigm are neatly coordinated when he observes: "Sitting at my table before the window and the sunlit lilacs, I thought of Canon Koppernigk at Frauenberg, of Nietzsche in the Engadine, of Newton himself, all those high cold heroes who renounced the world and human happiness

to pursue the big game of the intellect." Such an observation might seem to constitute an appropriate introduction to a great scientist's biography, and to some critics it reflects Banville's own attitude throughout the tetralogy. The narrator, however, goes on to add: "A pretty picture—but hardly a true one." This demythologizing rejoinder better describes Banville's approach and in the case of Newton suggests that he was a man who desired to interact with the observable world of everyday life in the hope of finding a different kind of knowledge there.

As the result of his research and speculation, the narrator has come to feel that the effect of Newton's personal tragedy (madness), was his desire for a life of action over thought, and moreover that Newton did lead an active life (in a narrow sense) by casting out old, worn theories, just as the narrator turns aside from his scholarly project in the interests of his more real and urgent personal experiences. He and Newton have seen the light and that the light is the real world of action and feelings. Tellingly, in the narrator's account of the burning, Newton smiles and cries (Newton is believed to have laughed only once in company!).

One of the major features of *The Newton Letter* is the humbling of the intellectual in the face of the natural, arbitrary, tragic, disorganized world. Both Copernicus and Kepler face similar embarrassments. The narrator of the novella experiences such a humbling in his relationships with Ottilie and Charlotte. Their influence, which serves as the Kuhnian introduction of new conceptual and empirical data, displaces the writing of his biography of Newton as he had initially planned—ironically enough, by providing the narrator with an unsettling experience which parallels Newton's breakdown. Whenever the narrator attempts to put names to his experiences, he inevitably fails to give a fair account. At base, there exists a definite flaw or weakness in the intellectual endeavor of any attempt to universalize one's subjective feelings, for no surety exists that these feelings and instincts are valid for others.

The narrator of *The Newton Letter* is at the outset a man of hubris, arrogance and misogyny. Initially, he sees Fern House as the kind of place where a "mad stepdaughter" would be locked up. Even from the very first meeting with the two women who are to dominate his summer break, he assumes, incorrectly, a great deal. Seeing them from a distance, he concludes that Charlotte is the younger sister of Ottilie; it is not until he is up close and after she takes off her straw hat that he sees a middle-aged woman. This initial incident is an index to the narrator's peculiar vision. What he sees is actually there; the faultiness lies in his perception: "I had got them nearly right, but the wrong way round." Such disjunctions between his subjective vision and the facts disrupt the narrator's concentration. He has brought guidebooks to trees and birds, but he cannot connect their descriptions to what he sees. He begins to feel detached from his manuscript on Newton, even entertaining the notion that it had been written "not by someone else, but by another version of myself." This awareness of anomaly is reinforced when in the forest he at first thinks he sees a rat. "To smell a rat" is a saying that suggests a crack in some existing system. The narrator, however, dismisses this awareness by reversing the notion: "I never saw sign of a rat. It was only the idea." In the same way the narrator is struggling to rescue his previous models of Newton in order to make his book a seamless whole.

In the early sections of the novella, we also sense a superimposition of the narrator's academic life onto that of Newton's. As he sees it, "time is different in the country" and Fern House becomes a kind of Woolsthorpe, a quiet place to add the final touches to a major tome or report on a discovery. Woolsthorpe Manor in Lincolnshire was Newton's mother's home. It was here in the period between 1665-67 (during the plague) that Newton is thought to have made major advances in celestial dynamics, mathematics and optics.

Seeing himself as a type of replica of Newton, the narrator adopts a superior air. He immediately concludes that Edward, Charlotte, and Ottilie are "Protestants, of course, landed," and observes that "to me, product of a post-peasant Catholic upbringing, they appeared perfected creatures." When he learns that the family are in fact Catholics, not Protestants, he admits his faulty assumptions but does not necessarily heed his conclusion: "My entire conception of them had to be revised." As readers, we are also intrigued why a Catholic (albeit lapsed) historian would devote his major work to a Protestant genius, especially one who had been involved in anti-Catholic politics in the British parliament.

The narrator is entranced by Charlotte who, unlike him, can name things very exactly. He is mystified by the presence of young Michael, who seems to constitute the human anomaly of the Fern House system: "I couldn't fit him to the Lawlesses." As the narrator reads under a tree (a proverbial apple with Newtonian echoes) he spies Michael perched among the branches. Later, Ottilie brings the "fallen" Michael to the narrator's lodge, an incident that sparks the relationship between them.

Although the narrator is confronted with many flaws in his conceptual system, he often overlooks them. For example when he is invited up to the Big House for a meal, he assumes a grandness consistent with the architecture of the place. The Big House is like a massive and impressive theoretical system inside of which anomalies and incongruities flourish. He observes but does not take in the significance of a hurley stick in the umbrella stand—how many Protestants in Ireland play hurley! During the unexpectedly meagre meal served on a plastic tablecloth he hears, though does

not understand the meaning of, Edward's outburst: "Well what's wrong with being ordinary?" The narrator's educated guesses prove to be only half-truths. Although he correctly believes that he has been invited to dinner to prevent discussion about Edward's drinking, his other assumption is extremely askew: "I saw the whole thing now, of course: he was a waster, Charlotte kept the place going, everything had been a mistake, even the child. It all fitted. . . ." His subsequent ruminations are even more farfetched; he sees Edward as a "fortune hunter" in marrying Charlotte. In turn, the embarrassing silence that follows his reference to Michael as Charlotte's child leads him to the erroneous assumption that Ottilie is the mother. Such a febrile imagination is consistent with the role of a biographical historian who seeks out extraordinary events to make his narrative compelling. Yet possibly the "insistent enigma of other people" is as much created as it is founded in fact.

The narrator of *The Newton Letter* is at the outset a man of hubris, arrogance and misogyny. Initially, he sees Fern House as the kind of place where a "mad stepdaughter" would be locked up.
—*Brian McIlroy*

Ottilie actually clues the narrator to the problem that is besetting Edward and Charlotte, when she asks him if he had ever taken drugs, such as the ones they give people dying of cancer. The narrator does not pick up on this nuance. Ironically, Edward himself tries to give him good advice: "It goes to show, you should listen to people, eh?" The narrator also seems unable to shake off his various prejudices. When Edward's sister arrives, he expects her to be the "West Brit," but quite the reverse is true: instead of uttering laments at the violent deaths of Mountbatten and eighteen paratroopers, she wants to celebrate the slaughter by naming a street after the date it occurred.

The narrator is unceasingly patronizing toward Ottilie, seeing himself as "one of those tragic gentlemen in old novels who solace themselves with a shopgirl, or a little actress, a sort of semi-animate doll with childlike ways and no name, a part for which my big blonde girl was hardly fitted." Only when she approaches him and sexual activity results does he begin to dispense with such categorizations. Another attempt at cognition involves his belief that he is in love with Charlotte. He is troubled that he can find no words which are adequate to describe her. When he articulates his difficulties, he seems to be re-enacting Newton's difficulties in the fictive letter to John Locke:

> When I search for the words to describe her I can't find them. Such words don't exist. They would need

to be no more than forms of intent, balanced on the brink of saying, another version of silence. Every mention I make of her is a failure. Even when I say just her name it sounds like an exaggeration. When I write it down it seems impossibly swollen, as if my pen had slipped eight or nine redundant letters into it. Her physical presence itself seemed overdone, a clumsy representation of the essential she. That essence was only to be glimpsed obliquely, on the outer edge of vision, an image always there and always fleeting, like the afterglow of a bright light on the retina.

Like the nature of the Newtonian universe itself, his estimation or picture of her relies on a fair degree of imagination and fabrication, a consciously false fiction; his is, in truth, a very immature unrequited love.

Constantly, he misunderstands Charlotte; her blankness (induced by drugs) creates in her conversation many *longueurs* and disconnected speeches. His inability to discern what is the matter with his would-be love is highlighted when they drive to the town together and stop suddenly. He thinks that this is the opportunity for a move (sexual perhaps) on his part, and although a sixth sense prevents him from doing so, he is oblivious to the important statement, "Edward is not well." Unable to see beyond his infatuation, he even merges the two women in his portmanteau exclamation: "Charlottilie!" By bringing two unlike concepts together, he hopes to create a Koestlerian synthesis (one not just combining "ripeness" and "chance" but also one which merges two disciplines to create a third). The more closely he examines his sense of anomaly, the more complex it appears, although he attempts to relegate it to his feeling that "this summer [was] a self-contained unit separate from the time of the ordinary world." One anomaly breeds another.

With even more hubris, he assumes a number of things about Ottilie, whom he thinks he sees more clearly than ever before: "Receding from me, she took on the high definition of a figure seen through the wrong end of a telescope, fixed, tiny, complete in every detail." Ironically, his metaphor is perceptive: he repeatedly looks through the wrong end of the telescope in judging character or coordinates in a system. For example, he assumes that Michael is Ottilie's child, born when she was around sixteen: "That she was the mother I never doubted." At Michael's birthday party, he compounds the error by assuming that Edward is the father.

Although Ottilie does lead the narrator astray when she brings him into Charlotte's bedroom to make love and maintains that it is her own, he can also be faulted for overlooking the anomalous fact that he sees: a black hair on the pillow, "like a tiny crack in the enamel." Once tricked and told of the true state of affairs, he loses his temper, forcing

Ottilie to utter a perceptive comment: "You think you're so clever, but you don't know a thing." Refusing to believe Ottilie's story that Michael is not her child but one adopted by Charlotte because she could not have any children herself, he also fails to see the depth of feeling Ottilie has for him. When it does dawn upon him, he is aghast and surprised. It is not until Edward's bout of drinking and the Doctor's suggestive comments that the narrator can find the right questions. Even then, he has to weed it out of Ottilie: "Valium, seconal. . . . Six months she's been on it. She's like a zombie—didn't you notice?" she asks, realizing that he has not understood Charlotte, Edward, or her. Later, he also lies when he states that he knew that Edward "has it in the gut," as another character puts it.

The narrator's admission of his limitations, and the burgeoning awareness of rampant anomalies, begins with his failure to deal adequately with Newton's period of breakdown. Matching his failure as a biographer is the way he has failed adequately to interpret events surrounding him. The cyclic inscription at the end of the novella—"Dublin-Iowa-Dublin Summer 1979-Spring 1981"—suggests that the narrator is on his way back to Ireland after his American sojourn, from where we assume he has written this entire novella/letter to Clio (I take this inscription to be the narrator's and not Banville's). In retrospect, his account is a humble one, anxious to show that in terms of chronology, remembered of course, he has not been very perceptive. After his query whether or not he has "lost [his] faith in the primacy of text?" (an ironic question, for why then write a letter?), he remembers his first visit to Ferns past Killiney Bay. The visual images that he conjures up appear "at once commonplace and unique." These two apparently oppositional notions are at the core of his experiences at Fern House.

In the process of writing his retrospective confession the narrator reluctantly recognizes the need for periodic scientific and humanistic revolutions. Gradual change to a new paradigm is effected by the lengthy time and thought he expends at Fern House on the Lawlesses—a surname of Beckettian proportions, which serves to parody Newton's exact laws by suggesting entropy or increasing disorder. By the end of his discourse, he is able to construct a new workable paradigm: "I shall take up the book and finish it: such a renunciation is not of this world." Nevertheless, he is wary, worried that in time he will have to construct yet another paradigm to keep in step with scientific progress and areas of human feeling.

The Newton Letter is an ingenious exploration of how conceptual frames, both artistic and scientific, are imagined and reimagined to produce new syntheses. As we have seen, the first-person narrative, structured in the form of a letter to history, contains within its frame two letters which the narrator sees as the kernel of his own surrounding text. Yet he is at first *resistant* to the message these inner texts seem to imply—that theories of the world are valid only unto themselves—for when the subjective view of the observable world is introduced, anomalies appear and theories must be recast accordingly.

> ***The Newton Letter* is an ingenious exploration of how conceptual frames, both artistic and scientific, are imagined and reimagined to produce new syntheses.**
> **—Brian McIlroy**

As a result, *The Newton Letter* also sheds an interesting light on literary trends and the formation and dismantling of the canon. Artistic paradigms may be understood as generally accepted "coordinates"—such as character types, a consistent narrative frame, and the unities of time and space—which combine to convey an apparently settled system that is agreed upon by the scholarly community but that is also repeatedly challenged. Literary movements—realism, naturalism, magic realism, modernism, and postmodernism—have their proponents and detractors, a struggle for dominance not unlike competing scientific theories. This explains why so-called outmoded paradigms can make a comeback wearing only slightly new clothes. In this way, motions of linearity and of circularity can be reconciled, in the sense of Koestlerian "ripeness."

Shaun Whiteside (review date 16 April 1993)

SOURCE: "Shadow Plays," in *New Statesman & Society,* Vol. 6, No. 248, April 16, 1993, p. 41.

[*In the following review, Whiteside praises Banville's* Ghosts, *but calls it a difficult book.*]

It's fair to say that anyone approaching this dense, elusive, richly allusive novel without prior knowledge of John Banville's work will be at something of a disadvantage. Readers of the darkly ironic *Book of Evidence* will remember Freddie Montgomery, the empty soul who stole a portrait and dashed in the brains of a hapless maidservant before racking his own in vain to find out why he had done it. Here is Freddie again, named once only, his narratorial voice unmistakable. But *Ghosts* is altogether more difficult of access than that other novel, and marks a return to the more metaphysical speculations of Banville's earlier works, particularly his reworkings of Goethe in *The Newton Letter* and *Mefisto.*

"It was like hiding inside a head," said Gabriel Swan in *Mefisto* of a room with two windows. Reading *Ghosts* is a little like hiding inside a head as well, although it's not always clear whose head. Here, on an oak-wooded island off the south coast of Ireland, a troupe of mismatched, shipwrecked *commedia dell'arte* figures make their way to the house of Professor Kreutznaer, superannuated scholar of the painter Vaublin, whose amanuensis Montgomery has become. There are three children, a woman, the aged and ungainly Croke, the obscene clown Felix and the beautiful Flora, with whom everyone falls in love and whom Felix fucks. Each seems in search of something, but pawky Felix seems in search of Freddie and Kreutznaer, perhaps to remind them of the retribution that awaits them for deeds past or of the possibility of atonement.

The novel's first half is dark and dreamy. Flora sees a painting of a pierrot, a harlequin astride a donkey and an assortment of people making their way down a hill to a ship. In a dream she takes refuge in the donkey's head, up a flight of stairs. Kreutznaer is reminded of his mother, two boys fight on a beach, Flora seems to clutch a grail or monstrance and Croke croaks, or nearly. "Oh life!" muses Montgomery; "And I in flames."

And suddenly the sleepy, purgatorial atmosphere lifts, as if in the wake of a general epiphany. At this point you might half-expect Elizabeth Welch to turn up singing *Stormy Weather,* Flora to say something about a brave new world and somebody—who?—to drown a book. But *The Tempest* is not Banville's only model. Readers of *Mefisto* may remember Prospero's masque mingling with Faust's *Walpurgisnacht* in a Dublin dive, with Felix as guide. It might be useful for potentially baffled readers to know that the sinister Felix has appeared before in Banville's work, in the guise of Mephistopheles, something hinted at here by means of the whiff of sulphur that accompanies his presence.

Now, amid scurrilous comic cross-talk, Freddie Montgomery is recalled to a kind of life by recognising that Flora is "no longer Our Lady of the Enigmas, but a girl, just a girl". Mulling over his past, his release from prison and his journey to the island, he becomes aware of the possibility of redemption through love and the embrace of the things of this world, although redemption itself must remain out of reach.

Multi-layered, and written in Banville's impeccable poetic prose, *Ghosts* is a haunting but a difficult book: ("balneation", anybody? Or "popliteal"?). Larded with veiled references to Wittgenstein and Frankenstein, to Nietzsche, Goethe and Shakespeare, to Beckett and, indeed, to Banville, it sometimes seems a little like a crossword puzzle with unnumbered lights. But if it doesn't yield up everything on a first reading, *Ghosts* has a melancholy power that will draw the reader back for further bids to plumb its mysteries.

Valentine Cunningham (review date 22 April 1993)

SOURCE: "A Whole Lot of Faking," in *London Review of Books,* Vol. 15, No. 8, April 22, 1993, pp. 10-1.

[*In the following review, Cunningham discusses the inter-rogative nature of Banville's* Ghosts *and asserts that, "It's at the centre of his power that his mood, his people's mood, the mood of his writing, is interrogative. And in best Mod-ernist fashion, these interrogations don't have straight an-swers."*]

'The philosopher asks: *Can the style of an evil man have any unity?*' It's a wonderfully sharp question, marrying mor-als to aesthetics in a challenging new-old fashion. And it's a question, as ever with John Banville, within other ques-tions. Who, for instance, you're made to wonder at this point in *Ghosts,* is actually asking? Some anonymous narrator? The author? The novel's own enigmatic 'evil man', the one who does so much of its telling and, it turns out, has a lot morally to answer for? You never know. It's hard to tell; it's always hard to tell with this author. It's at the centre of his power that his mood, his people's mood, the mood of his writing, is interrogative. And in best Modernist fashion, these interrogations don't have straight answers.

So can the style of an evil man—those fallen aestheticians Banville is drawn to, the compulsive counters and writers, the book-keepers and keepers of the books, notes, novels, those custodians of black books, Big Books, words, even of the Word—have, in fact, unity? The question drives right to the heart of the ordering, sense-making, story-telling, fiction-writing that preoccupies Banville's novels, not least this one. The rather higgledy-piggledy structure of *Ghosts*—its abrupt to-ing and fro-ing; its throwing of chronological switches between a present in which a curious troupe of pleasure-boat passengers is briefly thrown up on a small Irish island, and the past lives of the island's art-historical inhabitants, espe-cially of the novel's 'evil man', its ex-con main narrator; the plethora of ancillary voices, stories, modes (including the sudden late intrusion of an art-critical passage in which an anonymous painting gets lengthily scrutinised); the unsmooth mix of action, reflection, question—all this, which makes this the most contrivedly ragged of Banville's novels so far, cer-tainly appears to challenge any ready reply in the affirma-tive. Unity? Not really. But then, a simple negative reply is hard too. More is going on, or might be going on, in the mat-ter of order, than immediately meets the eye.

On the island so rudely invaded by the flock of castaways. Professor Krutznaer, art-historian now *manqué,* occupies his time up his panoptical tower with what he calls 'the old ques-tions'. Are chance, disorder, incongruity the 'only constants' uniting the 'disparate things' which he observes Banville-wise—'that wind, this fly, himself brooding here'? These

questions, of order, pattern, deep arrangement in things, are old not least because they're asked by a long line of Banville intellectuals: Koppernigk of *Copernicus,* Kepler of *Kepler,* Kasperl and Kosok of *Mefisto.* The air of Banville's fiction is thick with such issues. His people squirm and wriggle away from the idea that chaos, or chaos theory, are all. They're eager to ponder the counter-claims of necessity. Was the ex-jailbird's arrival on the island, Krutznaer wonders, arranged? Can he be a 'required' man? Surely his old ac-quaintance Felix, who knows a discomforting mite or two too much about his sticky ways with picture provenances, cannot be among the castaways by 'pure chance'.

As for provenance, it has this way, especially in the mouths of babes and sucklings (and there are some among the cast-aways), of sliding over into its allied vocable Providence. Indeed, if arrangements exist they presuppose arrangers, even—especially in the minds of the great Doctores Mathematici, the pioneering Scientific Christians whose nosings about the universe concern and haunt *Copernicus* and *Kepler* and *Newton's Letter*—a great Arranger. But then, if provenances can be, as Felix alleges, faked, maybe Provi-dence can be a grand faker, or fake, too. Certainly when it comes to the narrative arrangements made by the 'evil man' of *Ghosts* and his fellow conspirators, the Author, the Narrator(s), the Text, there seems ample room for a whole lot of faking.

Banville has always been a classic Modernist, committed to an exemplary Modernist programme of narrative self-doubt-ing, tricksy uncertainty-mongering, caginess, the unsettling of readers—what *Finnegans Wake* knows as HeCitEncy, hesitation about citing. And *Ghosts* keeps up the old Mod-ernist ways. 'Here they are. There are seven of them. Or bet-ter say, half a dozen or so, that gives more leeway.' Thus the opening of *Ghosts.* It could be the first paragraph of Ford Madox Ford's *The Good Soldier.* Better for whom, one won-ders? And leeway for what, exactly? Why, for more such cal-culated inexactness. 'Tell them I'm alright. Tell them I'm asleep. Tell them I . . .' From her temporary bed-clothed ref-uge the much-desired Flora could be Lord Jim tailing off into ellipsis, caesura, the cut-off. She could also, of course, be on a page of dotted Irish playfulness by Sterne or Beckett. Banville knows, hereabouts what his house and lineage are. And his readers should be up on what to expect in the way of random naming by now ('My wife. What shall I call her this time—Judy?'), that defiant unfixing of the novel's old sense, the modern world's sense, of the fixity and unique-ness of names. The painter studied on the island, is he Vaublin or Vanhoblin or Van Hobellijn? The infection of this kind of uncertainty spreads all over. The monologic murderer of *The Book of Evidence* made a point of wondering repeat-edly whether he'd mentioned this or that, and the ex-con of *Ghosts* avidly continues the device. 'Have I said this al-ready?' 'Have we met Alice?' 'Have I mentioned My Search for God?' As for the rig of the old actor Croke, one of the castaways, is he wearing a boater or a panama? It's a question Beckett would have relished.

Words, in general, tend to fail old Croke. 'My son, the comedian', his father used to say, not intending a joke. And verbal failure on his scale is certainly not funny. Croke is called the '*homo verus* of myth and legend', but he can't ever drag up from his linguistic resources the name for 'that thing they keep the host in to show at Benediction'. No monstrance of the Word made flesh for him. Even at the fifth, or even sixth, time of asking this verbal entity eludes. No wonder the jailbird reflects on the slipperiness of his pen, its tendency to go 'prattling along all by itself', making it the instrument and accomplice of a deviousness implicit in language itself. Small wonder, either, that there's a continual celebration here of behind-hand, uncovenanted linguistic resources, of communication occurring despite the opacities and trickiness of words. 'Thus they converse'—this of Krutznaer and Sophie, another of the castaways, a refugee photographer from post-war Germany, as they prowl about each other like a wary pair of lapsing communicators out of some late piece of Henry James—'haltingly, between long pauses. Behind the language that they speak other languages speak in silence, ones that they know and yet avoid, the languages of childhood and of loss. This reticence seems imperative.'

The imperative of reticence is one Banville's people very commonly knuckle under to. One way or another, all Banville's roads lead to the ample condition of silence, whether as grace or as curse. 'What a connoisseur of silences I have become over the years!' concludes the ex-con. He'd struck up a liaison with the island's widowed Mrs Vanden that was satisfactory to both precisely in its tendency to 'ruminant silence', phrases spaced out like the slow lobs of gerontic tennis players, 'not exactly a conversation, more a sort of laborious intermittent batting'. Banville's early novel *Birchwood* ended with a deference to Wittgenstein. 'Anyway, some secrets are not to be disclosed under pain of who knows what retribution, and whereof I cannot speak, thereof I must be silent.' It's a thought that keeps striking in Banville's pages.

In these texts, among these people, some secrets remain secret. Secrets are the domesticity Banville's people customarily inhabit. What's secreted away, the past, buried lives, old actions, intrigues and frightens. These people are continually anxious to grapple with the dead old thing or truth, to winkle it out into the open, to have Lazarus come forth, stinking grave-clothes and all. At the same time they'd rather some deeds got forgotten. Isn't forgetting a way, perhaps, to forgiveness? (Doesn't God, in forgiving, promise to remember your sins no more?) Wouldn't it be better for ev-

eryone if Lazarus stayed well swaddled in his grave-clothes and Banquo's accusing ghostly presence were dissipated?

It's this fraught margin where the recurrence of ghosts is in question—as solution, even salvation, but also as grievous problem—that *Ghosts* patrols with such telling alertness. It is, of course, a mighty echo-chamber of a novel, whose mode is echo upon echo, echolalic to a daunting degree. Take the island. Arrivals hear it making a lovely, musical noise. This echoes, of course, the island in *The Tempest,* the one that was full of noises. More, the inhabitants keep hearing, and reminding us of, ghostly echoes of other notorious fictional and historical islands and islanders—Devil's Island, Treasure Island, the Swiss Family Robinson, Crusoe. On such an echoing island Banville's readers will of course pick up strong echoes of Banville's earlier interest in Prospero. The carnival troupe of castaways inevitably recalls Prospero's Magic Circus in *Birchwood.* And still there's more. It gradually dawns on one that the blackmailer Felix seems to be the same person as the slouching Mephistophelean pander in Banville's *Mefisto.* What's even more, the ex-con soon manifests himself as Freddie Montgomery, the picture-thief and killer of the female domestic whose story was told in Banville's last novel, *The Book of Evidence.* *Ghosts* brings home the issue of the power and readability of the past not least by being a sort of sequel to *Mefisto* and *The Book of Evidence.* 'Everybody,' it's said of the island people, 'feels they have been here before.' They have. And so have we.

Repeating himself is by no means new in Banville's work. The same or similar names, favourite tropes (metallic tastes in the mouth, or the bed that sags as if it had just borne a corpse), trademark adjectives ('brumous', for example) travel freely across the oeuvre. Banville devotedly supplements and footnotes history and literary history; he writes supplements and footnotes to his own writing. It comes as little surprise, for instance, after the nice way in which the picture thief in *The Book of Evidence* obtained employment at an institution whose computer was worked on at night by a zany prof and a youth with a burnt face—so that he was, as it were, actually in *Mefisto*—when we find *Ghosts* recounting the story of *The Book of Evidence* and picking up the picture-taker's life at the point where he's released from his life sentence with a self-educated yen for art-history, clutching a reference from the stolen picture's owner.

What's intriguing, and commanding, is how these resurrections are by no means just simple returns of the chronologically repressed. Felix still has coppery pubic hair, but the hair on his head is black—dyed to evade the scrutiny of plodding Sergeant Toner and his kind. *Ghosts* is clearly the story of Freddie Montgomery, but he's only Montgomery now, and that only once. What's held out is the possibility—faint, but still a possibility—of the redemption that Montgomery dreams of, a rebirth into a forgetting, an innocence, an innocent place.

It is, of course, a dream. The island could, perhaps, be paradisal. But, alas for all the wonderful pastoralia that Banville's prose is so extraordinarily good at, the place of refuge is already fallen. As arcadias go, this one is blazingly unarcadian. This novel and its predecessor are mightily taken with a painting entitled *Le Monde d'or,* which turns out to have been dubiously provenanced by Krutznaer. So much for the Realms of Gold. Mephistopheles turns up in the shape of Felix. The Bad boy Hatch, aka Bunter (one name for the killer's Double in **Evidence**), chivvies Croke into a heart attack. The hands so carefully rinsed of gore in **Evidence** still have 'greasy black stuff flecked with blood and hair' stuck 'immovably under my splintered nails'. It's a besmirched condition said to be normal, the natural accumulation of humans 'as they claw their way through this filthy world'.

Ghosts brings home the issue of the power and readability of the past not least by being a sort of sequel to *Mefisto* and *The Book of Evidence.* 'Everybody,' it's said of the island people, 'feels they have been here before.' They have. And so have we.
—*Shaun Whiteside*

The rot the death of the Great Houses of Ireland that populate Banville's pages—heavily mortgaged, ghostly, gothic effigies of splendours and riches long past—become a symbol of permanent Fall in the Garden. Birchwood, that 'baroque madhouse', scene of cut-throat greeds and vile passions, sets a tone. Whitewater, where Montgomery steals and abducts the maidservant he kills, is a grim centrepiece of both *Evidence* and *Ghosts.* The glory of its great picture collection is the dubious *Monde d'or.* Whatever aesthetic glory there was is now illusory. Perhaps it always was. In one of Banville's most telling moments, the scholar-narrator of *The Newton Letter* yearns Yeatsianly after the mistress of Fern House—'Light of evening, the tall windows—Oh, a gazelle'. She's the Protestant Ascendancy still on the ascendant. But it's all a private fantasy and delusion. The House is mortgaged to the hilt; soon he hears the admired family talking of going to Mass. They're not even Protestants. The let-down is as much a blow to the Yeatsian vision as to his own. 'Farewell Happy Fields', Banville's people keep crying. Felix does so twice, once in *Mefisto,* again in *Ghosts.* It's the valedictory apostrophe of Satan, quitting heaven for hell, his paradise well and truly lost. In such a context, if there be a divine Arranger, it would perhaps be the 'supreme malignancy' of Montgomery's gloomiest musings.

But are things always so awfully dark as all this suggests?

St Paul's seeing through a glass darkly, *per speculum in aenigmate,* is clearly a mode of vision that attracts Banville. But it also provokes a kind of resistant counter-seeing. Again and again Banville returns us to some scene utterly lucid with brilliant light, takes us through the brightest days of childhood summers, sets us down under those large limpid skies and vistas of his many seasides. It's surely no accident that Krutznaer's oldest sidekick—the owner, it turns out, of his speculative tower—is named Licht; nor that Sophia is a photographer, an artist in light. 'I see,' says the narrator of **Birchwood,** 'through a glass sharply.' And if those Great Houses of Yeatsian celebration prove crumbling illusions, there are always the counter-possibilities of those manifestly delusive, but still significant and suggestive, pools of light in the Christianised garden of T. S. Eliot's ruined Great House, Burnt Norton, echoes of which keep recurring in the grounds of Banville's dilapidated mansions. For every Lisadell, in other words, there's a Burnt Norton—a potential theatre of redemption, the place where the voices of dead children echo, greatly suggestive of transcendence, where Prufrock-Lazarus might indeed have come happily forth. In the emptiness of his old home, with its reminders of church, Montgomery meets Van, his son, the boy he once thought might be the saving of him, the absolver of the sins of the father. Van, we learn with some shock, is dead. He's a real ghost.

That the world is all there is, is one of Banville's persisting Wittgensteinian cornerstones. The mere phenomena are what his Kepler and Copernicus fight to save from the doxa-men, the priests and believers, But what seems to attract Banville to these mathematically-minded clue-seekers is the way that the utter given otherness of things was for them still, possibly, a manifestation of some sort of arranging and arranged Otherness. Of course, it has to be said that in his later novels the suggestive, crypto-religiose wonders of the natural world—so magnificent a part of earlier works like **Birchwood** and **Kepler**—have been toned down, quietened, darkened. They're not what they once were. But still, in **Ghosts** Montgomery does say that he 'could rhapsodise about . . . the simple goodness of the commonplace . . . the quiet delights of drudgery'. And still, to an extent, Banville does. His prose can still work miracles, still turn on stunning rhapsodies of enchanting thinginess. 'A few big stalks of last year's cabbages, knobbed like backbones, leaned this way and that, and there were hens that high-stepped worriedly away from me in slow motion, or stood canted over on one leg with their heads inclined, shaking their wattles and uttering mournful croaks of alarm.' This prose, with its virtuosity of simultaneous acquaintance and estrangement, is not just there for purposes of display. It's part of a sequence of brilliant gestures to the possibility of a ghost in the machine, some big Arranger, if only a *deus ridens,* as Montgomery puts it, a comic one with funny ways with cabbages and funny bones. This is not the least of what makes this astonishingly attractive novelist one of the most important writers now at work in English—a key thinker, in fact, in fiction.

Richard Eder (review date 7 November 1993)

SOURCE: "Raskolnikov on the Couch," in *Los Angeles Times Book Review,* November 7, 1993, pp. 3, 12.

[*In the following review, Eder complains of the flat characterization in Banville's* Ghosts.]

Call me Ishmael.

No.

It's not that Melville needs us to say "yes" right at the start, so that he and we can get on with Moby Dick. "Maybe" or "let's see" will do; the "yes" can take its time. "I" in a first-person narrative invites us to a game and must charm, puzzle, annoy or even terrify us into wanting to play; but not immediately. What would stop things dead is a "no." The invitation extended by the narrator of *Ghosts* is all too easy for the reader to turn down.

The ghost in John Banville's novel about the aftermath of a gratuitous crime is the criminal. He is not literally dead but his sense of self is so shattered that even serving out his punishment—10 years in jail—did not restore him. Perhaps it is because he cannot really repent; repentance belonging to a pre-therapeutic era when the chief import of a transgression was what it did to others, not its disorienting effect on oneself. The nameless narrator, an art expert who impulsively removed a valuable painting from the wall of his host's country house and killed the maid who found him at it, is Raskolnikov on a couch. Even if jail might seem to be the narrator's redemptive equivalent of Siberia, it wasn't; the couch went with him.

Ghosts is written with the subtlety and cultural erudition that is characteristic of Banville, literary editor of the Irish Times and author of the intellectually demanding *Dr. Copernicus* and *The Book of Evidence.* It carries his trademark use of a few words—*nimbed, luminance* and *popliteal*—that only the Oxford Dictionary could love. This is a dandified flourish, like the tip of a silk handkerchief protruding from the breast pocket; and there is nothing wrong with a flourish. The trouble with *Ghosts* is not these few words but a fair number of the others.

The first part of the narrator's story was told in *Book of Evidence:* his intellectual's self-estrangement, his gradual loss of human contact with his past and his family, his crime and

imprisonment. In *Ghosts* these things are alluded to and in some sense relived. It is a kind of sequel but in a different mode. Where the first book was told as confessional realism, with narrative and moral suspense and a tone of cold passion, *Ghosts* moves in the fog of limbo. The narrator haunts his story instead of living it. Its setting—a derelict mansion on an island off the Irish coast—could be the land of the dead, and its characters and the sparse action they engage in skip about in sequence and logic, as if dreaming about such a land.

Released from prison, the narrator first makes an abortive effort to see his wife, who rejects him, and then visits their house in her absence. He is looking for remnants of himself before the fall; he finds none. With a letter of introduction he travels to the island, seeking a job assisting the aged Silas Kreutznaer, a world-famous but dubiously ethical art expert now in shabby seclusion. He is accepted and takes up residence.

It is a ghostly residence: Kreutznaer spends most of his time looking out of a turret window; Licht, who seems to be his servant but in fact is his landlord, lurks about sullenly. The narrator, between spells of writing a book for his employer, flits solitarily about, emerging at one point to have an enigmatic non-affair with an old woman. The cast suggests the emblematic and utterly arbitrary characters of Iris Murdoch, but without their comically perverse humanity.

A boatload of visitors wades ashore—their boat having grounded a little way out—and drifts about the premises. There is Croke, an old actor—he is dying; hence, perhaps, the pun—Sophie, a world-weary photographer; Flora, a wraith-like young woman; two obnoxious little boys, and an obnoxious little girl. There is also a cheroot-puffing, saturnine seducer named Felix, with dyed hair and a criminal record.

There are only a few events. Licht cooks and complains, Croke collapses walking on the beach, Felix has sex with Flora, who develops a sick headache. The real action takes place in the narrator's mind. In his dead state, the visitors seem to represent an eruption of human life; he hides and then fearfully joins them. In Flora, in particular, he sees the hope of becoming human once more. It is a futile hope, proffered and then mocked by the mysterious Felix. He is the narrator's nemesis and alter ego; he has followed him to the island and brought the others to taunt him with the suggestion that his isolation can be overcome. When he approaches them they turn as ghostly as he. They leave; Flora stays for a while but will soon leave as well. Felix, his dark double, will remain; and the narrator's work with Kreutznaer will go on.

Partly, but not altogether, it is a matter of art being the redeemer of humanity's darkness. The artist whom the narrator is writing about is Vaublin, a fictional contemporary of Watteau, whose reputed masterpiece is a work—reminiscent of Watteau's Journey to Cythera—called "The Golden World." Kreutznaer's crime, which has placed him in a ghostly limbo similar to the narrator's, is to have authenticated it for a commission. It is a forgery yet its magic is real. Its figures, in mythic procession from an Arcadian landscape to a waiting ship, are precisely those who have visited the narrator's retreat: an old man, a blond woman, three children, a wraithlike girl peering from a tower. Harlequin—the grinning Felix—rides on a donkey; in the foreground stands the pale Pierrot—the narrator—holding a club that Harlequin has given him.

As symbol and idea it all fits neatly, even suggestively. Yet Banville does not manage to fuse his figures with the eternal painted ones. A painting may imply an idea but we only care about this idea through the allure of the image and the brush strokes. Banville writes well enough about art to convince us of the timeless allure of the Vaublin forgery, but he doesn't do the same for his characters.

The denizens of the island and the visitors are flat and schematic. Their emotions and movements are geometric. None of them remotely approaches the sorrow or exuberance of a painted glance, let alone a human one. As for the narrator, his confession is a web of well thought-out moral complexity. But it is sterile and self-regarding. It illuminates nothing beyond itself, so what it illuminates is not much worth seeing. It is gymnastics performed in front of a mirror. It may call itself Ishmael but I won't.

John Banville with Katharine Weber (interview date 15 November 1993)

SOURCE: "John Banville," in *Publishers Weekly,* November 15, 1993, pp. 55-6.

[*In the following interview, Banville talks about his career and his approach to literature.*]

John Banville's narrators despair over the intractable chaos of life. They worry that chance and incongruity weave the patternless patterns of existence. Each of his eight novels tells a story from the point of view of a tormented, agonized soul.

In *Nightspawn, Birchwood* and *Doctor Copernicus,* all published here by Norton; in *Kepler, The Newton Letter* and *Mefisto,* all published by Godine; and in *The Book of Evidence* and *Ghosts,* the new novel just out from Knopf, Banville's characters float in a sea of grandiose shame.

The Irish author of this melancholic philosophizing, however, comes across as comparatively cheerful and unassuming, resembling none of his self-loathing narrators. A compact, graceful man, the 47-year-old Banville has the air of a somber pixie.

Over a leisurely lunch in Cork City, Banville, who is down for the day from Dublin, where he is the literary editor at the *Irish Times,* talks with *PW* about these voices and the recurring themes and images that link his books.

"We all have those darkest thoughts that come unbidden, those thoughts you would never tell anybody about," he says in a soft, Wexford buzz. When asked if he would agree that his narrators seem to be pure id in psychoanalytic terms, he replies, "I don't really believe in Freudianism, though I'm fascinated by Freud as an artist. He was a good writer, though he overwrote a bit. He was immensely creative in the way that he would put his desire for stories and plots onto the chaos of dreams."

Ghosts, a novel its author says has "almost no plot, to speak of," opens with a group of characters arriving on an island off the coast of Ireland, their boat having gone aground. Alert readers who enjoy Banville's games, which include subtle evocations of works of art, will identify the dreamlike scene as a reference to Watteau's *Embarcation from Cythera,* and Banville says he wrote the book hoping to give it the "glittery, silken surface" of a Watteau. At the dark center of the story is the unnamed narrator, a convicted murderer who has served his time and now devotes himself to art history while dreaming of redemption. Those familiar with *The Book of Evidence* will soon recognize him as another version of Freddy Montgomery, the hapless, homicidal source of that confessional monologue.

Banville admits this, saying, "There is a very strange mind at work there. I'm fascinated by that voice. I never gave him a name in *Ghosts.* It's some kind of superstitious thing; I could never refer to this character as the same man, though obviously it is the same man." The novel Banville is writing now, *Athena,* once again features the same character, though he is still metamorphosing, "fading, going out of existence." Banville says, "In the present book, if I can do it, he will have no name, no characteristics—he'll just be a voice."

The Book of Evidence, which in 1989 was shortlisted for the Booker Prize and was selected by Graham Greene for the Guinness Peat Aviation Award, finally brought the haunted and haunting literary voice of John Banville to the attention of a larger audience, especially in the U.S. Although his previous books have been praised in most of the right places and have sold reasonably well, and although Banville has received numerous European literary awards—

including the Allied Irish Banks Prize, a Macaulay Fellowship from the Irish Arts Council, the James Tait Black Memorial Prize, the American-Irish Foundation Literary Award and the Guardian Fiction Prize—Banville was long viewed as a challenging, stylistically complicated, highly literary writer: a writer's writer.

When *The Book of Evidence,* which has been translated into 11 languages, was published here in 1990, Scribners brought Banville over for his first American author tour, which he enjoyed immensely, despite his aversion to all literary scenes wherein "people look over your shoulder to see if somebody more important is coming into the room."

Though Banville is very happy to be at Knopf, he was sorry to leave the people with whom he worked at Scribners, and refers apologetically to "money, you know," as the reason for decamping. As he anticipates his upcoming eight-city U.S. author tour, he reminisces with a grin about his first introduction to publishing on this side of the Atlantic.

"I had never dealt directly with American publishers before, and I expected tough guys in suspenders. Instead, I found all these marvelous women, all of whose names ended in 'man'—Barbara Grossman, Susan Richman, Erika Goldman—so I always thought of them as the Scribners Men."

He doesn't agree with critics who find his work excessive, is amused by literal-minded reviewers who completely miss or misunderstand irony and allusion, and characterizes most of them as "people in the literature business." (In the novel-in-progress, Banville says he's enjoyed having the narrator write about a collection of paintings using the same language of criticism that has been applied to his books.)

But Banville points out that, through no particular plan, he has produced books that are alternately "easy" and "difficult," the difference being partly attributable to the presence or absence of a concrete plot that drives the narrative. Thus, he calls *The Newton Letter* easy, *Mefisto* difficult, *The Book of Evidence* easy, *Ghosts* difficult, and the book he is now writing easy.

"*Ghosts* is a very difficult one, both to write and to read," says Banville. (The *London Review of Books* calls its structure "higgledy-piggledy" and says *Ghosts* "is the most contrivedly ragged" of his novels, while at the same time calling Banville "one of the most important writers now at work in English." Significantly, it has also been shortlisted for this year's Whitbread Literary Award.) "If I look at *The Book of Evidence,* I can find stretches of pages that are essentially as I wrote them. Whereas the manuscript for *Ghosts* is in boxes and boxes. *Ghosts* has no organic coherence."

If the past is burdened by shameful secrets for Banville's characters, his own history, as he tells it, is both curiously devoid of darkness and at the same time lacking in any expectable early sources of his ferociously intellectual grasp of, and curiosity about, all aspects of history, culture and the arts. Born in Wexford in 1945, Banville, whose family name can be traced to a French cotton merchant who arrived in Ireland in the 1600s, says he had a "horribly happy" childhood growing up in a lower-middle-class family.

His father, who was an office worker in a Wexford garage, wanted him to be an architect, on the practical theory that the youngest of his three children, who intended to be a painter (writing came later, in Banville's early teens), should choose one of the few artistic professions that could earn him a proper living.

But instead of going to university, Banville went to work as a clerk at Aer Lingus. "I wanted to get away from my family, whom I loved, but disliked," he says. "So I worked for the airline for two or three years, really for the free travel."

In 1968, while visiting the U.S. courtesy of Aer Lingus, he met his wife, neé Janet Dunham, a weaver from St. Louis, "at a ghastly party in San Francisco on St. Patrick's Day." They moved to London together, after Janet had finished her degree at Berkeley, and were married. At 24, Banville finished his first book, *Long Lankin,* a novella and nine stories.

Having published some of the stories in magazines, Banville had been approached by a several literary agents. He chose Anthony Sheil (then of Anthony Sheil Associates, now of Sheil Land Associates in London), who placed the book with David Farrer at Secker & Warburg, which published it in 1970, and has since issued all his books in England. Banville only writes novels now, and can't imagine returning to the story form.

"All Irish writers have to produce one book of short stories, as Joyce did," he says, though he winces over the book now, pronouncing parts of it "really awful." (He also dislikes Joyce, calling him "the coldest writer ever," and saying of Molly Bloom's soliloquy, "It's bad, just bad. If I were a woman I'd throw it through the window.") . . .

Banville's first novel, *Nightspawn,* followed in 1971, by which time the Banvilles had moved to the coastal village of Howth, outside Dublin, where they live today in a house above the harbor with their two grown sons.

Banville was the chief sub-editor at the *Irish Press* for about 12 years. He left journalism in 1983 to write fiction full-time when *The Newton Letter* was being filmed for television. (It was shown during the 1984 Olympics, to Banville's chagrin.) But the three-year period that followed was "a disaster, because I discovered that I simply couldn't make a living." He returned to journalism as the literary editor at the *Irish Times,* a position he has held for almost a decade. "I like office life because I don't have to be part of it. But I would never leave the house were it not for my job," he says.

The work itself, which he does part-time, Banville characterizes as "chaos, really." He manages the weekly book page more or less on his own, doing everything from choosing books to assigning reviewers, copy editing, and laying out the page. He himself reviews a book perhaps once a month.

Though he writes at home for two or three hours every morning, Banville doesn't think of himself as particularly productive. "The first hour is just sitting down with yourself." He usually writes "a couple of hundred words, like a snail, you know," by hand in notebooks made for him by a bookbinder friend. ("I just cover the pages line by line. I have to have that resistance, to slow down the thought process.") From that first draft he revises on a word processor—"Stone Age meets the future." He tries to follow Hemingway's advice to leave off for the day in mid-sentence.

Banville is thoughtful and deliberate as he searches for the precisely right word to express his meaning as he talks about writing. "Every choice . . . is a wrong choice. Whatever you put down is a horribly clumsy attempt at that perfect, ideal sentence that you have in your head."

When asked what it is that makes a John Banville novel, the author closes his eyes in concentration. "What I try to do is to give to prose the kind of denseness and thickness that poetry has. Auden said you cannot half-read a poem. You can look at a picture and be thinking of something else, you can listen to a piece of music—you can be at the opera and be making love to somebody in a box—but a poem—you either read it or you don't."

He opens his eyes and continues, "I would like to think that with my novels, you either read them or you don't. To me, the late works of Samuel Beckett are possibly the greatest prose written in this century, just ravishingly beautiful texts. They take a lot of work, but it's wonderful work because it's like a rose that's furled. What makes a rose unfurl is light. What makes a Beckett text unfurl is the attention of the reader. You throw light on it and it just opens up."

Does Banville agree, then, that his writing requires concentrated effort on the part of the ideal reader he has earlier characterized as "someone with no specialized knowledge, just an open mind"? He does, and goes on to talk about creative conception:

"The artist concentrates on the object so strongly that the object begins to blush, and says, 'I'm not supposed to be looked at like this, I'm only an object,' but the artist's attention makes the thing begin to glow. That's what art is. Otherwise, it's just stories and characters."

Wendy Lesser (review date 28 November 1993)

SOURCE: "Violently Obsessed With Art," in *New York Times Book Review,* November 28, 1993, p. 1.

[*In the following review, Lesser discusses the narrator which appears in both* The Book of Evidence *and* Ghosts, *and asserts that, "Where the narrator in* The Book of Evidence *was always striving for effect, the narrator in* Ghosts *quietly achieves it."*]

The latest novel by the Irish writer John Banville, [*Ghosts,*] is a bit like a Peter Greenaway film: the visual elements are entrancing, the mystery plot is intricate and obscure, and the characters are all faintly (sometimes aggressively) threatening oddballs. Like Mr. Greenaway, Mr. Banville is particularly interested in humankind's strange mixture of passions for the beautiful and the violent, especially in combination.

> **. . . . [*Ghosts,*] is a bit like a Peter Greenaway film: the visual elements are entrancing, the mystery plot is intricate and obscure, and the characters are all faintly (sometimes aggressively) threatening oddballs.**
> **—*Wendy Lesser***

But while we have come to expect this mixture in movies (think of Alfred Hitchcock and Michael Powell, Martin Scorsese and Brian De Palma), it is less common to come across it in a novel. Mr. Banville has made it his turf. In his previous novel, *The Book of Evidence,* published in 1989, he gave us a main character who set out to steal a privately owned portrait of a young woman (it sounded, from the description, like a Vermeer) and ended up murdering her flesh-and-blood counterpart, a maid who worked for the portrait's owner. Now, in *Ghosts,* Mr. Banville offers us a houseful of eccentric, mainly criminal, sometimes violent characters who are all obsessed with the visual arts.

Ghosts is set on an unnamed island, presumably off the coast of Ireland. Like *The Tempest,* which it explicitly echoes in places, the novel begins with a shipwreck. Among those who straggle onto the beach are Sophie, a black-clad photographer; Flora, described as looking like a Modigliani; and Felix, whose shady past includes evil doings in art forgery. They and their companions make their way to a large house inhabited by one Professor Kreutznaer and his assistant, Licht, who are engaged in studying the work of a famous painter named Vaublin. For some unspecified time past, they have been helped in their research by another art expert, a nameless man recently released from prison, who also serves as the novel's narrator. "Serves" is not exactly right, for this narrator considers himself the novel's master, the Prospero-like figure who has created the entire cast. "A little world is coming into being," he tells us on the second page. "Who speaks? I do. Little god."

If you are looking for a plot in any conventional sense, you may as well give up on *Ghosts* right now. Though there are elements of suspense (Why is Kreutznaer afraid of Felix? What happened in the past with a Vaublin painting called "The Golden World"? And what is the narrator's connection to all this?), they are hardly the motivating forces in this novel. The achievement of *Ghosts* is to use words as brushstrokes, to create in language an artwork that has all the appeal of a complex painting. Our eye roves over it and back again, not in linear, chronological order but in a state of suspended time, picking up new details and drawing new conclusions with each concentrated gaze. "They have a presence that is at once fugitive and fixed," the narrator says of his characters when he finally, and explicitly, presents them as figures in a Vaublin painting. "They seem to be at ease, languorous almost, yet when we look close we see how tense they are with self-awareness. We have the feeling they are conscious of being watched." This is the language of sensitive, intelligent art criticism, heightened and transformed into the realm of fiction.

> If you are looking for a plot in any conventional sense, you may as well give up on *Ghosts* right now. Though there are elements of suspense . . . . they are hardly the motivating forces in this novel. The achievement of *Ghosts* is to use words as brushstrokes, to create in language an artwork that has all the appeal of a complex painting.
>
> —*Wendy Lesser*

One of Mr. Banville's victories in *Ghosts* is to have created a famous painter out of whole cloth. True, Vaublin's work contains elements of the Dutch and Flemish masters—Vermeer's crystalline stillness, Rembrandt's luminous darkness, Bruegel's antic figures at play. And with their Pierrots, their cherubs, their allegorical nature scenes, Vaublin's paintings also have affinities with those of French artists like Watteau, Poussin and Fragonard. But there is no single artist on whom Mr. Banville is drawing when he gives his vivid

descriptions of Vaublin's work. We cannot simply hunt up the key and insert it in the novel to unlock its mysteries of identity. Instead, we need to give our minds over to imagining Vaublin's paintings, which exist nowhere else but in our imaginations.

The descriptive felicities of *Ghosts* extend beyond the paintings themselves. There are moments of evocation here, in sentences and vignettes, that capture the physical details of reality in a startling, witty and genuinely pleasing way. Take, for example, the portrayal of an alcoholic about to take his first drink out of a new bottle of gin: "I love that little click when the metal cap gives; it is like the noise of the neck of some small, toothsome creature being snapped." Or the throwaway aside about a concert pianist: "Yes, laugh, as I want to laugh for instance in the concert hall when the orchestra trundles to a stop and the virtuoso at his piano, hunched like a demented vet before the bared teeth of this enormous black beast of sound, lifts up deliquescent hands and prepares to plunge into the cadenza." And the same narrator who perceives reality so well is also an expert at unreality, for the dreams rendered in *Ghosts* are truly, convincingly dreamlike.

Mr. Banville received a great deal of acclaim for *The Book of Evidence,* which—with its lovingly enunciated, self-distanced chronicling of the murderer's deed—was hailed as a worthy successor to Camus's *Stranger* and Dostoyevsky's *Crime and Punishment.* Such praise is bound to be overpraise, and in fact *The Book of Evidence* struck me as a coy and artificial work, with a narrator who was constantly searching for the highest-priced word on the menu. *Ghosts* is a far better novel, though it is also a more difficult one. Where the narrator in *The Book of Evidence* was always striving for effect, the narrator in *Ghosts* quietly achieves it. The irony is that they are intended to be the same person.

I do not know what people who have not read the previous novel will make of this new one. Many of the central questions in *Ghosts*—who the narrator is, what his crime was, how he has dealt with women, how he knows so much about art—are answered only in *The Book of Evidence.* The very motivation that fuels *Ghosts,* its explicitly Pygmalion-like desire to create a living woman out of a work of art, is a response to a problem raised in its predecessor. "I killed her because I could kill her, and I could kill her because for me she was not alive," the narrator said in *The Book of Evidence.* "And so my task now is to bring her back to life. . . . How am I to make it come about, this act of parturition?" *Ghosts* is that same character's answer to that question.

Hence many of the technical mysteries of *Ghosts* dissolve if you have read *The Book of Evidence.* The plot becomes straightforward rather than contorted, the narrator gains a name and a history, the motivations come clear. But one unresolvable mystery remains. How did the coldly and flagrantly self-dramatizing narrator of the earlier novel become the elusive, evocative artist of the present work? One wants to know if this is the character's moral progress or John Banville's. But, as another Irishman famously remarked, how can you tell the dancer from the dance?

Lawrence Norfolk (review date 12 December 1993)

SOURCE: "A World Elsewhere," in *Washington Post Book World,* December 12, 1993, p. 3.

[*In the following review, Norfolk calls Banville's* Ghosts *"a strange and austere book."*]

[In John Banville's **Ghosts,** a] drunken captain runs his boat aground, stranding seven passengers on an island. They are watched, wading ashore; Croke, "an old boy in a boater," Felix, "a thin lithe sallow man with bad teeth and hair dyed black," Flora, "a pretty young woman," Sophie, "in a black skirt with a black leather jacket" who totes cameras with the purpose of capturing what she terms "*tableaux morts,*" and three children: Pound, Hatch, Alice.

The unmagical Prospero of this island is Professor Silas Kreutznaer, an art historian specializing in the work of "Vaublin," who is served by two lackluster Calibans: Licht, a graceless and insecure factotum, and another, who watches, comments and dribbles out the events of the life which brought him here. The "other" is the narrator and principal subject of this new novel from John Banville, literary editor of the Irish Times and author of **The Book of Evidence** and **Doctor Copernicus,** among other books.

This unnamed observer reports, twice-weekly, to one Sgt. Toner, which suggests some former wrongdoing. Later, we learn of a 10-year stretch in prison, and later still the nature of the crime—the murder of a young girl. The protagonist is now in retreat from his past, from the world at large, but most of all from himself. His time on the island has been spent in writing, in the maintenance of a wordless, eventless liaison with the widow of a South African colonial officer, and in gardening. The seven strangers provide unwanted new grist to this decelerated mental mill. He is propelled reluctantly into watchfulness, into engagement, and ultimately back into life.

The action of **Ghosts** is pitched at so low a level that a banal conversation with Flora, the young castaway, is enough to effect his conversion. The novel is grounded in mental interiors; Banville's bravura descriptions—of weather, or the island's landscape—are glimpses of a very distant Arcadia,

tokens of forestalled longing. A much-anticipated meeting between the narrator and his estranged wife finally fails to happen, although we do meet his mentally retarded son, whose existence and condition had hitherto remained unguessed. The murder itself is handed to the reader thus, "Here the plot does not so much thicken as coagulate."

Banville evinces a certain discomfort with the habitual gestures of the form in which he has chosen to work. "Let us regress. Imagine the poor old globe grinding to a halt and then with a cosmic creak starting up again but in the opposite direction. Events whiz past in reverse, the little stick-figures hurrying backwards, the boat pulling itself off the sandbank with a bump and putting out stern-first to fasten the unzipped sea . . ." The flashback is a familiar enough workhorse in contemporary fiction and of itself does not require so fulsome a confession that artifice is at work. On the other hand, the passage itself is a beautiful piece of trickery, enjoyable in terms just as nugatory and slippery as "artifice." What exactly is it that we enjoy when we enjoy good prose?

Or art, for that matter? The painter "Jean Vaublin" is a brilliantly plausible creation, established early on in a scattering of asides, more substantially later when his masterpiece, "*Le monde d'or*" (the Golden World) is exhaustively described and Vaublin himself emerges as a cross between Claude and Fragonard, with perhaps a dash of Piero di Cosimo besides. And remains, naturally, wholly nonexistent. The entrance fee to "*Le monde d'or,*" as with any work of art, is payable in empathy and belief.

"The objects that I looked at seemed insulated, as if they had been painted with a protective coating of some invisible stuff, cool and thick and smooth as enamel," remarks the protagonist before he finds the willingness to pay up. The murder itself turns on a ghastly confusion between a painting and a living, breathing human being. The ghosts of the title are the real presences behind their images, whether painted, written, or remembered. "Artifice" and "Life" form a notoriously woolly syzygy and wedding it to the human values of the novel constantly threatens to inflate the world that Banville has created. Like John Hawkes, whose *The Blood Oranges* this novel resembles in some ways, Banville resists by resolutely sticking to the particulars. "Details, details: pile them on," urges his narrator, who happily can lean on the skills of a prose stylist in his prime.

Ghosts is a strange and austere book. It is not an anti-novel in either the happy (Queneau) or unhappy (Robbe-Grillet) sense, but the outrageous evenness of its tone, the thoroughness of its self-inquisition, and the elaborate courtesy by which it exposes its own narrative machinery all betray a deep unease with its own "novelishness." Behind the confession, agonizing and restitution of its protagonist lie

Banville's own. Is it acceptable to shape the narrative like this? asks the book's structure. Is it desirable to convince so completely? asks the characterization. Is it right to write this well? asks Banville's coruscating prose.

It is.

Philip MacCann (review date 17 February 1995)

SOURCE: "Profoundly Superficial," in *New Statesman & Society,* Vol. 8, No. 340, February 17, 1995, pp. 38-9.

[*In the following review, MacCann discusses Banville's* Athena *and concludes that "At the heart of his writing appears to be a fear of uglification by the ordinary."*]

Joyce described respectable society in Dublin as suffering from a particular unreality: perhaps colonial mimicry, perhaps also the result of a great literary tradition, disproportionately dominant for such a small culture. In Ireland there is a sense in which one's every gesture is a literary cliché; there are more scenes in books than things to do.

A major theme in Irish (and much other) literature is the threat of lifeless conformity and overfamiliar material to individual imagination. For this reason some Irish writers still exile themselves. A few have looked to the vibrant working-class culture, previously excluded from the canon and thus free from literary self-consciousness. John Banville, who along with William Trevor occupies the pinnacle of contemporary Irish writing, has his own solution. He transforms the Ireland around him into the unfamiliar world of stylised art. You won't recognise an Irish pub scene or pervy priest in Banville. At the heart of his writing appears to be a fear of uglification by the ordinary.

To some, this appears European. For others, Banville is Irish in a sense that has yet to emerge. But his aestheticist task—to improve on life by artificial representation—tackles an international dilemma. Fredric Jameson writes that: "We have become incapable of achieving aesthetic representations of our current experience." Thus Banville's art eschews the vulgar artificiality of life in favour of the stylish artificiality of art itself. He paints a painted world. Characters are caricatures, images are ice-bright hypermetaphors, narrative knows it is so.

Artificial structures and pattern-making are often Banville's material. It comes as no surprise that short spoof critiques of Dutch Baroque mythological paintings form intervals in the monologue of his new novel. For *Athena* continues an appropriate theme: writing aspires to the condition of painting.

Montgomery's story, begun in *The Book of Evidence,* is concluded by this third novel in a trilogy that continued with *Ghosts.* His *crimes passionnels* were the theft of a painting, and—less-importantly—murder. Now he is back with a new identity, drawn once again to art and shady dealings. He is distracted by the subplot of a dying aunt and his own more interesting philosophising. The total picture is complete when that original preoccupying artistic image of female perfection takes physical form in the dealer's sister, to whom the novel is addressed.

This "solipsistic", Nabokovian narrator (we get flashbacks to *Lolita*), with pretensions of villainy he can only struggle to imagine, shows greatest self-awareness by his self-description: cyclops. He is the agent of Banville's artistic vision, which sees itself ironically as two-dimensional exaggeration. There is a Banvillesque image of "windows below which the sunlight's geometry was laid out in complicated sections". This has the freshness of a child's vision. Is it limited by being disengaged from the world? Montgomery's thought in *The Book of Evidence*—"on the surface, that's where there is depth"—recalls Derek Mahon's complimentary remark about the "profoundly superficial" Louis MacNeice. It could equally have been said of Cubism, Surrealism, Abstract Expressionism . . .

"A row of shops with delivery vans, dogs, defeated-looking women pushing prams: how little I know of what they call the real world," the new narrator, Morrow admits, doubtful that writing should provide the only set of references in the novel he is creating. So he undermines his own narrative constantly. He subverts the tradition of writing from experience: one moment is like "a spring day in Clichy (I have never been in Clichy)".

He may fear that his narrative is like Klee's *Twittering Machine,* an elaborate, absurd structure that simply works. But any style is limited to itself. This novel is *total* writing which, like any exciting style, is arrogant, gorgeous and usually uncompromising. Yet unlike Banville's early novels, *Athena* relaxes into more ordinary colloquialism and Irishness, though this does not bring more emotional truth. I like best those moments when the stylisation is so powerful that, rather as in Wedekind and Genet, it can support the translation of emotion into affecting expressionism: "Three things the thought of you conjures up: the gullet of a dying fish into which I have thrust my thumb, the grainy inner lining of your most secret parts, ditto . . ." Here is a novel by a painter who writes philosophy for writers, imparting what the Dutch call *wijsbegeerte* or "lust for knowledge". He's an artist's artist.

Patricia Craig (review date 18 February 1995)

SOURCE: "This is Such Stuff as Dreams Are Made On," in *The Spectator,* Vol. 274, No. 8693, pp. 30-1.

[*In the following review, Craig discusses the dream-like quality of Banville's* Athena.]

> I've always likened writing a novel to a very powerful dream that you know is going to haunt you for days. If you sit down at the breakfast table and start to try to explain the dream to someone, they yawn and look at you and they can't understand what you're on about.

If—John Banville goes on in an *Irish Times* interview with Fintan O'Toole in 1989—if you try to imagine an author sitting down with such a dream for three years or so, refining and refining it into an elaborate work of fiction, 'then you're close to the impulse of my novels'. It's an illuminating analogy. The supercharged realism and lucidity of Banville's prose do not preclude a sense of somnambular unreality.

The events of *Athena,* in particular, are set out like the bits and pieces of a dream, a dream with a rational outline superimposed on top of it, but retaining an essential strangeness and perplexity. It proceeds—in Banville's phrase—'in a fog of ambiguity and dissimulation'. It continues the story of Freddie Montgomery of *The Book of Evidence*—Banville's ex-thief and murderer last met in *Ghosts,* and now appearing under a different name entirely (by means of the deed poll), Morrow. Morrow—like Montgomery—is a monologist. Returned to society after serving his sentence, he's co-opted at the start of this novel by a bull-like individual named Morden to cast his expert's eye over a cache of 17th-century Dutch paintings, which may or may not be the real thing. Soon a dark girl, whose provenance is no less dubious than the pictures', has Morrow in thrall. Is she Alpha, or Athena, or even Aisling (vision)? Whichever it is, she gets no more identification than the letter A and a taste for extreme sexual practices. When he's not recalling his clandestine couplings with A at a house in Rue Street (tautology or pun or a bit of both?), Morrow is coming face-to-face with a jovial/sinister policeman named Hackett, or getting himself lumbered with a geriatric aunt. Characters in this novel are few and outré, and its set-pieces come furnished with a comic-surreal quality: for example, the episode in which Morrow's Aunt Corky, on her last legs, takes tea with a master criminal known as the Da. The Da, for the occasion, has got himself up in a black velvet dress and a hat with a veil. This 'master of disguise', as he's sardonically dubbed, is no less adept than T. S. Eliot's Mr Mistoffelees at creating eccentric confusions. Nor, for that matter, is Banville himself. His aim, or one of his aims, is to embody duplicity in the most labyrinthine manner imaginable. His work puts forward the notion of fiction itself as a shady business, stressing its connection with feigning. He teases us constantly with his refusal to differentiate explicitly between the real and counterfeit. Even Dublin—the setting for *Athena*—is recast as an unreal city, with its Dickensian down-and-outs, its cobbled alleyways and the 'cavernous gloom' of its pub interiors. Even the phrase, 'a self-made man', applied to the narrator, takes on a new—a literal—connotation.

> **The events of *Athena,* in particular, are set out like the bits and pieces of a dream, a dream with a rational outline superimposed on top of it, but retaining an essential strangeness and perplexity.**
> **—Patricia Craig**

Banville's well-known rage for order, in the face of endemic chaos and uncertainty, lends a peculiar tension to his novels; at the same time, they derive their density from some accompanying system or motif which is hitched to the narrative—be it astronomical, mythological or whatever. The paintings in *Athena,* for example, function as part of the plot and also as clues to its import: each of the seven (seven, though the number specified at the beginning is eight)—each of the seven gets a critical appraisal at some point in the course of the novel, and this somehow works to stabilise its more bizarre goings-on (amongst which we might include a series of Jack-the-Ripper-type killings, if these didn't clearly suggest themselves as an additional bit of gruesome ornamentation on the body of the story).

Athena is the third part of a trilogy, but it also harks back to earlier Banville novels such as *Mefisto,* whose burnt narrator Gabriel Swan is evoked in the playful juxtaposing of Gabriel Street and Swan Alley (home territory of a derelict named Barbarossa). It's part of an intricate, unsettling fictional enterprise—strongly imagined and rigorously planned—in which all the characters are pushed to extremes, and a kind of mordant dislocation prevails.

Michael Gorra (review date 21 May 1995)

SOURCE: "Irish Baroque," in *New York Times Book Review,* May 21, 1995, p. 15.

[*In the following review, Gorra describes the mood of Banville's* Athena *and states that, "Plot counts for nothing here, or seems not to, and mood becomes all—a mood sustained by a prose of idiosyncratic and appalling charm."*]

Murder as sex, sex as murder, murder instead of sex—why do so many recent Irish novels worry away at the relation between the big death and the little one? John Banville writes with his eyes on a European past, and not a narrowly national one; writes without the customary parade of politics and priests. But murder and sex, those he does share with his contemporaries, with writers like Bernard MacLaverty, Patrick McCabe and William Trevor. Mr. Banville's peculiar genius is to bleed this promising material dry, draining it of suspense; reading him, you never taste the stomach-turning urge to know what's going to happen that so flavors Mr. Trevor's recent novel, *Felicia's Journey.* Plot counts for nothing here, or seems not to, and mood becomes all—a mood sustained by a prose of idiosyncratic and appalling charm.

Athena concludes the trilogy Mr. Banville began with the jailhouse gibbering of his first-person narrator Freddie Montgomery in *The Book of Evidence.* In that novel Freddie, overeducated, underachieving, the Irishman as Eurotrash, abandons his wife on a Mediterranean island and returns to Dublin to beg from his mother. On a visit to a friend's country house he stops dead in front of a portrait—a woman, Dutch, 1660, with a "querulous, mute insistence" in her eyes. "It is as if she were asking me to let her live." Freddie decides he has to have her. Then a housemaid gets in the way, and with a hammer he smashes her, the housemaid, and dumps the painting in a ditch. In *Ghosts* the now-unnamed narrator is out on probation, working as a dogsbody for an art historian. In *Athena* Mr. Banville's protagonist has taken a new name (Mr. Morrow) and set up as an "expert" himself. But the past seems always there, for his employers have given him a tantalizing task: writing descriptions of and authenticating a batch of pictures stolen from the same house where Freddie began what one might call his career.

Those paintings. They carry titles like "The Rape of Proserpine," "Pursuit of Daphne," "Revenge of Diana"—images of Ovidian transformation from the Dutch Golden Age. But here metamorphosis carries always the note of decay, and the paintings all seem just a little bit off, canvases that can't quite sustain the full glory of the Baroque. In one, "the loftiness of the classical theme is sacrificed for the sake of showiness and vulgar effects"; another is marred by "jumbled perspectives and heavy-handed symbolism." Heavy-handed indeed: the god of the underworld carries off a maiden; a virgin goddess takes revenge on an intrusive male. It's as if Freddie's employers had chosen such subjects as a crude joke. And Mr. Banville's description of these imaginary daubs is of course a reflection of *Athena* itself, a book that "gives more the impression of a still life" than it does of the "passionate activity" it is intended to represent.

Intended to, and maybe finally does. For in its last pages *Athena* suggests that both Freddie and we as readers have had our own perspectives jumbled, ensnared in plots—different ones—whose contours we only belatedly perceive. But the impression of a still life remains so strong that one's

opinion of the novel will depend almost entirely on how one responds to its narrator's voice. "Here, in me, in this Bermuda Triangle of the soul, the fine discriminations that are a prerequisite for moral health disappear into empty air and silence and are never heard of again." It's a voice not only mannered but Mannerist, vigorously handled, yet in a way that makes human longing a cartoon of itself; a voice at once taut and yet florid, as if there had been some mythic coupling of Beckett and Nabokov, and this were the misshapen offspring. "Do we really need all this, these touches of local color and so on?" Freddie asks at the start of the novel. But if we don't, he does, for "what would I do to divert myself if I had not language to play with?" On a bright day along the shore "the sun was resplendent on the mud flats and the verdant algae"; sex becomes "the act, as it is interestingly called."

In his description of "The Rape of Proserpine" Freddie draws our attention to the fact that "the girdle . . . has not yet fallen from her waist: in this painted world all time is eternally present, and redeemable." That's just what he would wish; he clings "to the present tense as to a sheer cliff's last handhold." Yet though he's changed his name by deed poll, there is no "poll by which past deeds might be changed," and now there's someone else who's always "asking me to let her live." But Freddie can no more make that housemaid live again than he can liberate that painted Dutchwoman. Or can he? On his first day with the paintings, a chink in the wall discloses a flash of stocking and a stiletto heel. Soon he meets their owner, a woman called "A," and begins an affair with her. Yet her character never quite becomes clear to us. The things she says seem too naive to match the chic black in which she's mostly unclothed. And gradually his life, the "intricate dance of desire and deceit at the center of which A. and I had whirled and twined," and his descriptions of those paintings begin to invade each other. *Athena* is as grotesque as a portrait by Arcimboldo, in which flowers and fruit and even fish can become the features of a human face, and every bit as beautiful.

Douglas Glover (review date 9 July 1995)

SOURCE: "Irish Eyes Unsmiling," in *Chicago Tribune,* July 9, 1995, p. 3.

[*In the following review, Glover asserts that Banville's* Athena *has a much more conventional plot than his earlier novels.*]

John Banville is an Irish author singularly unafraid of the stigma of hyperbole and baroque excess. His novels are littered with incestuous, decaying families, waifish women inviting the whip or the hammer, and drunken, ineffectual male orphans (real or figurative) who move through a fog of decadence, drift and dread worthy of the great Gothic masters.

Known best in America for his historical novels **Kepler** and **Dr. Copernicus,** Banville has lately been mining a vein of contemporary Irish grotesquerie centered on a serial character called Freddie Montgomery. In **The Book of Evidence,** Freddie, drinking too much and down on his luck, tried to steal a painting from a squire's country house and ended by murdering the maid with a hammer. In **Ghosts,** free after serving 10 years in prison (a life sentence in Ireland), Freddie turned up on a sparsely populated island where he had been hired as secretary to an aging professor whose specialty was a little known Parisian painter named Vaublin.

If there can be said to be a conventional plot in **Ghosts,** it turned on Freddie's abortive love affair with a young woman dropped ashore by a drunken ferryboat captain. This woman and her shipmates bore a striking resemblance to figures in a Vaublin painting called "The Golden World"—part of the collection Freddie pillaged in **The Book of Evidence** and probably a fake.

In Banville's new novel, **Athena,** Freddie's back, this time in Dublin under the assumed name Morrow, hired by a man called Morden (who works on a street called Rue) to authenticate a cache of 17th Century paintings on classical themes. In contrast to **Ghosts, Athena** is knee-deep in conventional plot elements. There is a cockamamie art fraud plot—something out of "The Rockford Files"—with a cop called Hackett and a sinister transvestite gangster called Da. There is a plot of sexual obsession and sadomasochistic love between Freddie/Morrow and a girl called A. And there is an astringently tender subplot involving Morrow's elderly Aunt Corky (not a blood aunt; the connection is vague), who moves into his dingy flat to die. In the background lurks a mysterious serial killer who drains his victims' blood.

For much of the novel, the cracked love story between Morrow and A., a young woman with preternaturally white skin and bruised lips, takes center stage. From the outset, the bumbling, chronically depressed Morrow (not since *The Ginger Man* have we met a character so engagingly and self-destructively melancholy) is besotted and yet knows that she will leave. His breathless, goggle-eyed account (reminiscent of Humbert Humbert's in *Lolita*) of their wanton trajectory, from innocent abandon, to voyeurism, to a *menage a trois* in a seedy brothel, to spanking and whipping and complicit infidelity, is a droll parody of Victorian pornography—melodramatic, perfervid and decidedly unsexy as the situations become more bizarre and mechanical.

Though Freddie/Morrow has taken pains to conceal his identity, everyone else in the novel seems to know exactly who Morrow is—from the criminals who hire him to authenticate

their paintings, to the investigating detective, to A. herself, who shocks Morrow one day by asking him to strike her the way he struck that unfortunate maid in **The Book of Evidence.** Even Aunt Corky hints that she may not be his aunt but his mother. At every turn, an atmosphere of mystery, unreality and downright fraud dogs his steps, so that, though Morrow is telling the story, he seems more and more like a character in someone else's book, a cog in someone else's plot.

And interspersed throughout **Athena** there are catalog descriptions of the paintings entrusted to Morrow, paintings on classical themes of violence, rape and transformation that bear, on the face of it, a strong resemblance to the events of the book (just as in **Ghosts** the characters seem to have walked out of the Vaublin painting).

So **Athena** becomes a kind of echo chamber of comic despair in which everything seems fated or written by another hand, where gods toy with humans and turn them into beasts, where a miasma of solipsism hangs in a world of dream, and mysterious lost children, doubles and putative parents hover just out of focus. When A. disappears near the end of the novel, she leaves a note: "Must go. Sorry. Write to me." But there is no signature and no address, and Morrow is left with only the presence of her loss, a pneumatic void into which he writes his words.

> *. . . Athena* **becomes a kind of echo chamber of comic despair in which everything seems fated or written by another hand, where gods toy with humans and turn them into beasts, where a miasma of solipsism hangs in a world of dream, and mysterious lost children, doubles and putative parents hover just out of focus.**
> **—Robert Tracy**

All this is peculiar stuff—heady, hilarious, hyperbolic and strange. Banville's literary ancestors are writers like Poe, Beckett and Nabokov. His novels are little wars between a repressive, fusty, petty bourgeois sensibility (Irish, Victorian and Modern, with a capital M) and the dark, bubbling, drunken, violent, godlike forces of sex and madness that lurk beneath the surface of life and language.

On the strength of his novels, Banville is not so much a postmodern writer as a pre-modernist, and his critique of modernity rests on a romantic, Arcadian vision of our pre-Renaissance past. Part-way through **Athena,** Morrow explains how the invention of perspective in painting destroyed the blissful, circular forgetfulness of the past, "spawning upon the world the chimeras of progress and the perfectibility of man and all the rest of it. Illusion followed rapidly by delusion: that, in nutshell, is the history of our culture. Oh, a bad day's work!"

From this vision, everything else follows: Morrow's confusion, the novel's atmosphere of fog and drift result from the application of narrowly rigid concepts of self and reality to a world that is ever and always mysteriously other. Stripped clean of contemporary talk show anodynes and psychobabble bromides, the world of *Athena* is finally hyperreal—one in which loneliness, loss and despair throb at the very center of being, and poetry, once again, is possible.

Robert Tracy (review date Fall 1995)

SOURCE: "The Broken Lights of Irish Myth," in *Irish Literary Supplement,* Fall, 1995, p. 18.

[*In the following review, Tracy praises Banville's adaptation of Heinrich von Kleist's* The Broken Jug *as "funnier and grimmer" than the original.*]

Der Zerbrochene Krug/The Broken Jug (1807), by Heinrich von Kleist, is a renowned classic of German drama, which means that, like Goethe's *Faust* or Schiller's *Die Räuber,* it is virtually unknown to the English-speaking playgoer. John Banville's lively adaptation employs a subtly colloquial verse line, and transfers the action from the Netherlands in 1700 to "Ballybog . . . in the West of Ireland, in August, 1846," making the play accessible at least to Irish playgoers.

As adapted by Banville and directed by Ben Barnes at the Peacock Theatre, *The Broken Jug* is in many respects a version of the German original. But Banville has also localized—Hibernicized—the play, making it at once funnier and grimmer. "If . . . all men had green glasses," Kleist once remarked, "they would have to conclude that the objects which they perceived through them were green." In a slightly different sense, Banville makes us see the play through green glasses, as an Irish tragicomedy mocking certain sacred cows—and bulls.

Kleist's plot is comic and reassuring. Judge Adam is a local magistrate, ignorant and corrupt. We watch him in action along with Walter (Upholder), an inspector from the capital, who recognizes Adam's incompetence and disregard for justice, and catches him in a particularly vile trick: Adam has persuaded young Eve that her beloved Ruprecht is to be drafted overseas. He gains admission to her chamber by promising her a medical certificate exempting Ruprecht from military service. Then he tries to rape Eve. Ruprecht arrives and thinks the worst. Adam escapes out a window, breaking the jug, a family heirloom. Ruprecht scorns Eve for having

a man in her room; she proudly asks him to trust her, and protects him from conscription, as she thinks, by refusing to explain. Eventually all is revealed. Walter dismisses Adam, and replaces him with his clerk, Licht (Light), as a promise of better days. The lovers fall into one another's arms. The system may occasion fail to perform justly, Kleist tells us, but sooner or later government, through its efficient and fair-minded agents, will unmask and punish the wrongdoer.

Banville describes his play as "after Kleist," freeing himself to make some interesting changes, signaled by ominously rechristening Licht, Adam's clerk/successor, as Lynch, and suggesting that Lynch as judge will be equally corrupt, though subtler. It is little like the shift from the flamboyant Rackrents to the cautious Jason Quirk. Adam is Protestant, Lynch Catholic, retained to spy on "them." The relationship between Eve and her lover, now Robert Temple, draws on two Irish preoccupations, history and land. Robert is suspected of rebel leanings. As played by Pat Kinevane, he posed like a waxwork of Robert Emmet. Alone among the characters, he talks at times in heroic couplets. "It is not anger that I feel towards you," he tells Eve; "But disappointment: that, and bitter rue. / When we first met, I gave you all my heart, / And swore that from your side I'd never part."

Like most things Irish, the relationship between Robert and Eve is complicated by national and local history. Robert is Catholic, Eve's "a Prod." Eve's father has acquired the lands once owned by Robert's father. By marrying Eve, he will get them back. To woo her, he "fed her with a lot of poppycock," Adam tells Sir Walter, "About the Planter and the noble Gael . . . She fell for it, of course." As for Eve, nobly played by Amelia Crowley, she is "damaged goods," with a withered leg, a crippled Kathleen ni Houlihan without the walk of a queen. "That withered leg discourages the boys," Adam opines; "Round here they want their mares fit in all fours." At the end of the play she has bleakly taken Robert's measure, and realized he is the poor best that she can get. Her clear-eyed acceptance of things as they are and must be makes her the play's heroine in every sense.

As Judge Adam, Eamon Morrissey was a marvelous combination of overextended villainy and impotent guile. His personality was beautifully reflected by Joe Vanek's setting, a rural courtroom looking as if it had been inhabited by chickens for years, slovenly, stained, broken, the "records" a heap of dusty papers thrown into a closet. Adam is as battered as his court, his wig gone as he escaped from Eve's room—breaking the jug in passing—and his face marked by Robert's attack.

Banville supplies Sir Walter (Des Braiden) with a clerk of his own, Ball (Joe Savino), who joins Lynch (Mark O'Regan) in providing a sardonic choric commentary on the action. And he supplies most of his principals with at least one solo turn. Adam has more than one, as he wriggles and schemes his way through the play, now fawning, now blustering, now explaining Ireland to Sir Walter. Robert Temple delivers a spirited account of what happened in Eve's room, and his simultaneous efforts to identify and damage the other man. Eve's testimony is moving as she blames Robert for his lack of trust. Best of all is the history of the jug, as delivered by Eve's mother (Maria McDermottroe), which displays selected clichés of Irish history and legend delivered with great speed and passion. Captured from a rebel "In Enniscorthy after '98," the jug

> . . . told old Ireland's history, all in scenes.
> See here, where there's now nothing but a hole,
> The Firbolgs and the Tuatha Dé Danaan
> Were shown in mighty battle on the plain,
> And there Cuchulain swung his hurley stick:
> Those are his legs, that's all that's left of him.
> There's Brian Boru, at prayer before Clontarf;
> You see him kneeling?—That's his backside, see?
> . . .
> The walls of Limerick, look, the siege of Derry.
> The glorious victory at the River Boyne—
> Our country's history, broken up in bits!

Katy Emck (review date 16 May 1997)

SOURCE: "An Elegy for the Lost World of Espionage," in *New Statesman*, Vol. 126, No. 4334, May 16, 1997, p. 46.

[*In the following review, Emck lauds Banville's* The Untouchable *saying, "Banville's achievement is to show the tragic consequences of Maskell's detachment while making him an appealingly human, even noble, figure."*]

Victor Maskell, anti-hero of John Banville's *The Untouchable,* is based on Anthony Blunt, the Fourth Man: he is curator of the Queen's art collection, a spy of culture and owner of a painting by Poussin. This portrait of Seneca's "fortitude and dignity" when forced to commit suicide for conspiracy is symbolic of Maskell's own fate. On the one hand, the painting suggests the traitor is a man of noble resolve. On the other, it suggests he is just an aesthete, a collector of *objets d'art* without a heart.

John Banville embellishes brilliantly on the facts of Blunt's life in this poignant meditation on loyalty, love and identity. Maskell is divided on every conceivable level. He is a closet homosexual as well as a married man; a communist but also an Irish Protestant and a personal friend of the Queen; but also a man with an emblematically seedy sex life. This, paradoxically, gives him a peculiar and moving capacity for the

truth. Maskell's "all-corroding scepticism" burns away the debris of cliché.

At the same time Maskell is an effete, social-climbing sleazeball. He is fastidious and something of a pedant. He prides himself on being "scrupulous with tenses"; he is liable to describe an ordinary blue sky as "pellucid bleu céleste"; and he is fond of comparing people and things to paintings and books. His capacity for betrayal is related to his dislike for things that offend his sense of beauty (a mentally subnormal brother, a shabbily countrified father, a spouse of the wrong sex).

Banville's achievement is to show the tragic consequences of Maskell's detachment while making him an appealingly human, even noble, figure. The novel is Maskell's confession after being outed as a spy. His narrative voice is a marvellous invention—by turns caustic, wistful, lush, self-mocking and filled with regret. It is permeated by a sense that political commitment and ideals are futile, which is what makes them beautiful. Maskell's ideals have a kind of art-for-art's-sake value as saving images of immutability where none exists—rather like the classical paintings that are his true love in life.

The Untouchable brilliantly evokes the way youth and love fomented espionage. Drunken debates about art and Marxism between Cambridge Apostles relocate to London parties with flappers and champagne: "Deep down it was all no more than a striking of attitudes to make ourselves feel more serious, more weighty, more authentic."

> *The Untouchable* **brilliantly evokes the way youth and love fomented espionage. Drunken debates about art and Marxism between Cambridge Apostles relocate to London parties with flappers and champagne: "Deep down it was all no more than a striking of attitudes to make ourselves feel more serious, more weighty, more authentic."**
> —*Katy Emck*

The tales of cold-war espionage capture the inadvertently comical, B-movie quality of the entire rickety enterprise. The Cambridge graduates go for it with camped-up *Boy's Own* derring-do, while one Russian agent dresses like a "mythical version of John Bull" for a meeting in a London pub—"something a scouting party from another world might send ahead to mingle with Earthlings and transmit back vital data".

He compares a trip to Moscow laid on for communist

sympathisers in the 1930s to the journey made on the Ship of Fools. Although Maskell is glad to get back home, realising that underneath it all he is "nothing less than an old-fashioned patriot", he nevertheless continues to spy. With yet another comical inconsistency, he ends up being sent by King George to Germany after the war to smuggle back papers that show the Duke of Windsor's Nazi sympathies.

"You really cannot beat royalty for poise in adversity," says Maskell. Like any old royal on their uppers, like Seneca on the verge of death, the hunted-down spy has an old-world dignity, a kind of *sprezzatura* that blends lightness of touch with respect for form. In some ways *The Untouchable* is an elegy for espionage as it once was. But then you can never quite pin down this marvellous novel. After his exposure, Maskell wears slippers out of doors, and carries a string bag containing a gun.

John Bayley (review date 29 May 1997)

SOURCE: "The Double Life," in *New York Review of Books,* Vol. XLIV, No. 9, May 29, 1997, pp. 17-8.

[*In the following review, Bayley delineates the major theme of Banville's* The Untouchable *and observes that Banville's books provide "a joyful and durable source of aesthetic satisfaction."*]

John Banville occupies a very definite and indeed almost unique place among contemporary novelists. He is not fashionable. Indeed he disregards fashion, even the extent to which most novelists, however independent in their natures and talents, keep an eye on what is "in" or "out," and are often insensibly influenced by this awareness. He shows no interest in discovering in his fiction who he "really is"; nor does he consciously explore the predicament of a class or a society. Social indignation, or powerful statements about the inner life, are not for him: nor is the fantasy projection of the self that goes with magic realism.

Instead he has thoroughly learned what Henry James called "the Lesson of Balzac." It was a lesson which James himself mastered, and used with the greatest skill. The novelist, like the scientist, picks his theme, and lets nothing about it be lost upon him. He explores it coolly but imaginatively, without recourse to plotting devices or adventitious effect. The subject may be the natural history of a murder, as in Banville's *The Book of Evidence.* It might be the history and implications of a scientific mind and its theory, as with the biographical novel *Kepler,* themes further taken up in *The Newton Letter* and in *Doctor Copernicus.* It might be an oblique study of the world of mythology and belief, as

in *Mefisto,* and in Banville's recent novel, *Athena.* Banville is above all a learned novelist, who bears his learning lightly.

> *The Untouchable* **takes as its theme the psychology and the natural history of treachery and the treacherous person.**
> —*John Bayley*

His new novel, *The Untouchable,* takes as its theme the psychology and the natural history of treachery and the treacherous person. In one sense such a subject may seem to belong to the past: since the collapse of the Soviet Union the role of the master spy has been greatly diminished, perhaps even abolished; and with it has gone the fascination the public once felt about such men and their activities. But this does not deter Banville, just as it would not have deterred Henry James. This challenging theme has its own interest, irrespective of its immediate or contemporary relevance. With such a subject men's motives, their personalities, obsessions, and hidden desires, have a timeless quality. The field in which the classic traitors once operated deserves to be chronicled and comprehended by the imagination, as Balzac once chronicled the corruptions of French society, or Scott the mind and heart of historic legend. The novelist can work in a medium more intuitive than that of the historian, giving his personae from the past a view of their own actions, and a voice of their own.

The past in this novel is not far away, but in our time even the immediate achieves its own kind of distance very quickly. The once-famous traitors—Burgess and Maclean, Philby and Blunt—are already historic figures. It is the last of them that Banville takes as his "hero," making him the annalist of his own downfall and compiler of the memoir he wishes in his last days, stricken with cancer, to survive him. The same technique was effectively used by Banville on another historic figure, Copernicus; and similar judicious liberties with the facts are taken here but in harmony with history.

The real Anthony Blunt—once Sir Anthony, but his treachery eventually cost him his knighthood—was born, like Kim Philby, in the bosom of the English governing upper class. He was an aesthete and an art expert, who before being demoted had become Master of the Queen's Pictures and an acknowledged authority on many important painters. Like Philby, he was a Cambridge spy, recruited as a "sleeper" while still an undergraduate, and at a time and place when loyalty to friends and to the ideology of friendship was a paramount feature of the youthful English intelligentsia. E. M. Forster, one of its heroes, had notoriously stated that if he had to choose he would betray his country rather than betray a friend. The act of betrayal required no dramatic decision, no conscious leap in the dark.

Nor of course was it done for money, although the Russian spymasters usually insisted on token payment as a matter of protocol, part of the decorum, as it were, of professional treachery. But Blunt and his fellows were very much amateurs—though Philby at the Foreign Office later acquired a chilling expertise—and it will probably never become clear just how much harm an amateur like Blunt actually did. Before the war the willingness of Blunt and his friends to be recruited was a matter of romantic protest against economic defeatism and depression in England—the graphic background of W. H. Auden's early poems—and what might be termed a *Princesse Lointaine* complex in politics. Russia was the unknown wonderful country where people were happy and the future was working. There was also sex. Blunt was homosexual from undergraduate days, and hence habituated to the undercover double life, and to secret protest justified by persecution.

Much of this Banville has altered, but in so subtly imaginative a way that a new character is created who gives his own style of intimacy and individuality to our public portrait of the man on whom he is based. Banville's Victor Maskell is a Northern Irishman whose father is a bishop in the Irish Protestant Church. He is conditioned to a repressive atmosphere, in a country where repression by an external country, and even more by the Catholic or the Protestant Church, has become habitual. Like Blunt he goes to Cambridge, becomes an art expert, makes close friends, is drawn into the atmosphere and the camaraderie of dissent. He is secretly recruited. A slow process of psychological attrition begins.

This would land many novelists in difficulty, for the drama—usually melodrama—that the reader associates with espionage is conspicuously lacking. In real life, of course, the whole process takes place in very slow motion indeed, both invisibly and ambiguously. It is only the highlights that are usually offered to the public, as newspaper stories or later on by the writers of spy thrillers. But there is no field of human activity where the simplifications and stark contrasts of drama are more misleading—and it is this that makes even great classics of the genre, like Conrad's *The Secret Agent,* seem in the end artificial, necessarily contrived. For a masterpiece like Conrad's it is worth paying that price. But lesser spy writers such as Graham Greene try to make a virtue out of necessity by stressing the falsifying artifice of their technique: Greene often referred to the product itself as an "entertainment."

Banville tightly eschews entertainment. For the reader, the compulsion of his novel is secured by much more convincing and interesting means. Naturally enough the risk is one of monotony. Spies lead day-to-day lives like other people: falling in love, getting married, worrying about friends and family, indulging in routine pleasures. They are also apt to

be relentless self-justifiers, and for the fellow at the other end of it such self-justification—whether it takes the form of guilty deprecation or of boasting—can easily become the most boring thing in the world. And yet all these formidable hazards Banville has miraculously managed to turn to his own writerly advantage, so that his reader remains gripped, not by a dramatic tale but by the gradual unfolding of a personal history, a kind of home movie or album of self-taken pictures. How is it done?

Banville has always been a fastidious writer, but the manner in which he has chosen to explore this latest theme presents the greatest challenge he has faced yet to his own virtuosity of style. In a sense his greatest display of virtuosity can show itself in a successful downplaying of things, as in his description of Maskell's encounter with a doctor, after his treachery has been revealed and his disgrace made decorously public.

> Old age, as someone whom I love once said, is not a venture to be embarked on lightly. Today I went to see my doctor, the first such visit since my disgrace. He was a little cool, I thought, but not hostile. I wonder what his politics are, or if he has any. He's a bit of a dry old article, to be honest, tall and gaunt, like me, but with a very good line in suits: I feel quite shabby beside his dark, measured, faintly weary elegance. In the midst of the usual poking and prodding he startled me by saying suddenly, but in a tone of complete detachment, "Sorry to hear about that business over your spying for the Russians; must have been an annoyance." Well, yes, an annoyance: not a word anyone else would have thought of employing in the circumstances. While I was putting on my trousers he sat down at his desk and began writing in my file.
>
> "You're in pretty good shape," he said absently, "considering."
>
> His pen made a scratching sound.
>
> "Am I going to die?" I said.
>
> He continued writing for a minute, and I thought he might not have heard, but then he paused and lifted his head and looked upward as if searching for just the right formula of words.
>
> "Well, we shall all die, you know," he said. "I realise that's not a satisfactory answer, but it's the only one I can give. It's the only one I ever give."
>
> "Considering," I said.

He glanced at me with a wintry smile. And then returning to his writing, he said the oddest thing.

"I should have thought you had died already, in a way."

I knew what he meant, of course—public humiliation on the scale that I have experienced it is indeed a version of death, a practice run at extinction, as it were—but it's not the kind of thing you expect to hear from a Harley Street consultant, is it.

Style here is all the more masterly for not being on view. The social implication of the passage suggests the whole world in which Maskell/Blunt has moved and had his precariously elegant being, but the suggestiveness is deliberately kept unobtrusive; except, perhaps, to a connoisseur of Banville's wide range of aesthetic effect. It is a stylistic tradition that goes straight back to James Joyce, who used all the resources of language to reveal the richness of the most ordinary and homely daily experience. Banville uses them here to explore the edgy boredom, with nothing thrilling about it, of having to lead a double life; and the even more desolating and solitary boredom awaiting the agent who has been "blown" but left contemptuously in place: a pariah who for a number of reasons is not even worth awarding the martyrdom of prosecution. The novel, as a case history, is anticlimactic, and yet just as Joyce is never banal as he explores the dailiness of our daily routines, so Banville is never boring as he leads us from day to day through the dreary corridors of espionage. He has no melodramatic gambit in store—he does not need one—and no contrived dénouement in the style of Ambler or Le Carré: such things do not go with the real work the spy is doing, or with any true exploration of it.

Instead he deftly imagines and reveals a patrician world and class which have lost their nerve and know it. Being Irish himself Banville may be taking a sly pleasure here in English social and political embarrassments, as he may do also in the fact that his hero's father, the upright man, is a Protestant bishop in the Church of Ireland, not the Roman Catholic Church. If so it is a private joke, for the ordinary reader will have no trouble in accepting what is in fact the highly implausible scenario of an Ulsterman at ease among the English spying coterie, who hang together by reason of class and background. If it is a private joke it is not the only one. The novelist Graham Greene makes a thinly disguised appearance as the odious Querell, another English spy who has been in the spy business longer than Maskell himself, and there is a good deal of vindictiveness in this mordant sketch by Banville of a novelist for whom he clearly feels no affection.

The real Graham Greene liked to hint, no doubt out of van-

ity, that he was not only familiar with the world of espionage but had participated in it. He had certainly known Burgess and Maclean and their friends, and worked himself briefly for MIS during the war, though only in an innocuous role. Querell, however, both cuckolds and betrays Banville's hero, perhaps because the latter despises the spy stories that he writes (". . . That thriller of his about the murderer with the club foot. What was it called? *Now and in the Hour,* something pretentiously Papist like that.") The detestable Querell remains triumphantly unsuspected (writing spy stories would be excellent cover for a real spy?) and appears like death itself at the book's ending, waving a sardonic farewell to the hero, who is himself on the edge of death. His world is in ruins. His children may not be his own, and even his precious picture by Poussin turns out to be probably a fake.

It appears too that yet another man remains unexposed, a shadowy figure of such eminence in the British Conservative establishment that he is literally "untouchable." But as with the Graham Greene ploy these nods and hints appear over-contrived—Henry James would not have approved of them in a novel with such a sober and intelligent approach—and it is no less than a compliment to Banville's book to point out that such occasional devices represent its weakest side. However many hidden higher-ups may remain unrevealed, the real imagination of the book goes into its sense of events in the past. All these doings seem very long ago, and hardly even very real anymore. Banville turns history into the kind of reality which can be possessed by the novel as a work of art.

Spain, the kulaks, the machinations of the Trotskyites . . . how antique it all seems now, almost quaint, and yet how seriously we took ourselves and our place on the world stage. I often have the idea that what drove those of us who went on to become active agents was the burden of deep—of intolerable—embarrassment that the talk-drunk thirties left us with.

That sense of futility haunts the novel, and in his unobtrusive way its author draws it forward into our present age—into any age—by indicating how perennial is the gap between those who talk and those who act—and adding the grotesquely true paradox that some are driven to the latter course merely by a sense of shame at their own impotence as chatterers and theorists. Active treachery is at least doing something, giving an active idealist the illusion of bringing society nearer to the Promised Land—the Promised Land Maskell would never reach, and never really wanted to reach. The members of any such dedicated, secular body, among the few that are left today—the ETA, the IRA, and a few others—are doing their thing for its own sake, and resolutely refusing to face the consequences for themselves of their dream's fulfillment.

Burgess and Maclean escaped to Moscow in 1951, a more sensational event at the time than the later defection of the much more damaging traitor Kim Philby, who does not appear in the book. The other couple, who had always been absurdly indiscreet, were on the verge of being picked up by the counterespionage authorities. Unlike Philby, or Maskell/Blunt, they were also picturesque figures, whose sexuality and drunkenness could be gloated over by newspapers and public. Banville is very successful in creating Victor Maskell ("code-name John") and beguiling us throughout a longish first-person novel with the way he talks, thinks, and behaves. Maskell himself is fascinated by the personality of "Boy" Bannister, a creation based on the real Burgess, just as Maskell himself is based on the real Blunt. Burgess was a legendary figure, appearing in many memoirs of the time. A Falstaffian bisexual, he was habitually drunk and reckless, but his charm protected him by ravish-' ing most people with whom he came in contact, women as well as men. The "Boy" even appeals to the pregnant wife of one of Maskell's spy colleagues.

> We climbed to Nick's rooms and found Baby, in a smock, big-bellied, sitting in a wicker armchair by the window with her knees splayed, a dozen records strewn at her feet and Nick's gramophone going full blast. I leaned down and kissed her cheek. She smelled, not unpleasantly, of milk and something like stale flower-water. She was a week overdue; I had hoped to miss the birth.
>
> "Nice trip?" she said. "So glad for you; Boy, darling: kiss-kiss."
>
> Boy lumbered to his knees before her and pressed his face against the great taut mound of her belly, mewling in mock adoration, while she gripped him by the ears and laughed. Boy was good with women. I wondered idly, as I often did, if he and Baby might have had an affair, in one of his hetero phases. She pushed his face away, and he rolled over and sat at her feet with an elbow propped on her knee.

Domestic and period aspects of the story are vividly sketched; and there is a good deal of history and action thrown in as well—Dunkirk; Bletchley Park, the code-breaking center; a panorama of the last great war—but recalled with a certain absentmindedness which brings us back to the narrating hero's present fate as an outcast and solitary, as untouchable as the mysterious grandee whose social and political status means that he never has been and never can be unmasked. The title has a triple ironic twist, referring as it

does simultaneously to this figure, to the whole caste of untouchables shunned by society, and to a special criminal status in which the guilty man is revealed but left alone. Blunt was publicly exposed but never punished or prosecuted, seemingly because of his social status, and his once close connections with the Royals as their art expert. A man of great charm himself, he had been a friend both of the Queen and of her father, King George VI, with whom the young Victor Maskell has in the novel a notable and almost Shakespearean interview. Indeed Banville's technique in exposing the progress of this unusual spy is to let him chronicle the events of his own life in a series of brilliant portraits and life studies not so unlike the multiple succession of scenes in the playwright's historical chronicles. Although sedulously avoiding any contemporary version of spy-style drama, Banville employs the traditional kind of account to great effect.

Blunt was homosexual and a bachelor. Maskell is married, although his mode of life makes him not unduly in love with domesticity. His "friends" are either the professionals who are periodically recalled into Russia, usually never to be heard of again, or his own amateur colleagues, like Boy Bannister. It is this last who turns out, after his flight to Moscow, to have left Maskell an unusual legacy in the shape of a young man called Danny, an expert but genial practitioner of the homosexual "rough trade." In his isolation and his inner exile, condemned to continue with his "normal" life as a professor and aesthete while being shunned by all, Danny constitutes for Maskell a kind of ironic lifeline back to humanity. This sexual transformation in himself, observed by Maskell with his own sort of wry and urbane intelligence, becomes in his singular circumstances both moving and convincing. So is the picture of Danny.

> Immediately, like a fond old toué, I sought to introduce Danny to what used to be called the finer things of life. I brought him—my God, I burn with shame to think of it—I brought him to the Institute and made him sit and listen while I lectured on Poussin's second period in Rome, on Claude Lorrain and the cult of landscape, on Francois Mansart and the French baroque style. While I spoke, his attention would decline in three distinct stages. For five minutes or so he would sit up very straight with his hands folded in his lap, watching me with the concentration of a retriever on point; then would come a long, central period of increasing agitation, during which he would study the other students, or lean over at the window to follow the progress of someone crossing the courtyard below, or bite his nails with tiny, darting movements, like a jeweller cutting and shaping a row of precious stones; after that, until the end of the lecture, he would sink into a trance of boredom, head sunk on

neck, his eyelids drooping at the corners and his lips slackly parted. I covered up my disappointment in him on these occasions as best I could. Yet he did so try to keep up, to seem interested and impressed. He would turn to me afterwards and say, "What you said about the Greek stuff in that picture, the one with the fellow in the skirt—you know, that one by what's-his-name—that was very good, that was; I thought that was very good." And he would frown, and nod gravely, and look at his boots.

As with his study of a murderer, *The Book of Evidence,* there is about Banville's method his own highly original style of detachment. True, there are moments in all his novels when this technique seems to be enjoying itself for its own sake: and moments when Banville seems deliberately to wear what Elizabeth Bowen memorably described as a face not infrequently to be met with in Ireland—"an unkind Celtic mask." But on the whole the author's pose is not unlike that of his own consultant physician in *The Untouchable:* dry and humorous, a little world-weary, but by no means inhumane. Above all, highly individual. In an age in which conventional pieties and a standardized "seriousness" have tended to rob the novel of the lightness and capacity for surprise which should be its great asset, Banville's books are not only an illumination to read—for they are always packed with information and learning—but a joyful and durable source of aesthetic satisfaction.

Frank Kermode (review date 5 June 1997)

SOURCE: "Gossip," in *London Review of Books,* Vol. 19, No. 11, June 5, 1997, p. 23.

[*In the following review, Kermode discusses Banville's* The Untouchable *and asserts, "As to plot and scene and dialogue all is competent, even, at times, rich or funny. But again and again one feels that the writing is more assured when the story reaches a pause. . . ."*]

[Banville's *Untouchable*] ought to be a good novel, for it is by a good writer and deals intelligently with a bit of British history that continues to interest us. And it certainly gives pleasure; so it seems a shade ungrateful to be asking what's wrong with it. Is this all? Is this the best a lively imagination can make of the plight of the virtuous spy, whether wild or sober, dedicated or not, Blunt or Burgess?

There is nothing much here to conflict with the stereotypical idea of the Thirties, the afternoon men in their Soho clubs and hideouts, their lust for working-class boys, their not wonderfully well-informed Marxism, and their easy way of arranging matters to suit themselves, whether in the choice of

wartime careers, say at Bletchley, or perhaps in some other establishment where scraps of secret could be salvaged to keep their Russian contacts happy.

As to plot and scene and dialogue all is competent, even, at times, rich or funny. But again and again one feels that the writing is more assured when the story reaches a pause, when Maskell, the hero based on Blunt, contemplates a moment or a view and records some sort of epiphany. There is one near the beginning of the book, just before Maskell is being vetted for recruitment: 'The moment stretched. Neither of us spoke. Time can stand still, I am convinced of it; something snags and stops, turning and turning, like a leaf on a stream. A thick drop of sunlight seethed in a glass paperweight on a low table.' Light seething in glasses is a recurring figure, perhaps random, perhaps a leitmotif about the significance of which one can only speculate: it could have to do with seduction, or with the sensitive eye of the art expert, or something else; or maybe it's a figuration that exists simply for itself.

Some of these epiphanies are related to paintings, most often to a small Poussin depicting the death of Seneca, bought for Maskell by Leo, later Lord Rothenstein, an identifiable fellow-traveller who has 'the matt sheen of the very rich'. The theme of the picture is obligingly explained in detail to a tedious young woman interviewer. It keeps coming up, not only for its ecstatic potential but because of its subject, the compulsory suicide of Seneca, who was given no choice by an ungrateful Nero. Maskell claims to be a Stoic, too, and similarly situated.

In another light, the painting offers the novel its whole programme: 'The problem for Poussin in the depiction of suffering is how to stylise it, as the rules of classical art demand, while yet making it immediately felt.' But this problem is not solved here, because what is stylised is not so much the hero's suffering as his unlovely detachment from ordinary human concerns (wife, children). He tries to make himself a bit more like Seneca by pointing out that the philosopher had his faults, too; but it doesn't really work.

Maskell, who is the narrator, moves from Trinity College, Cambridge to what is evidently the Courtauld Institute, where he rather improbably (but, as we know, the whole tale of the Spies is profoundly implausible) keeps a catamite in the director's top-floor flat. He begins his story when it is almost over; finally, after long delay (not expressly connected with his boasted closeness to top Royals), he is exposed and disgraced, de-knighted, ill, harried by the press, and is writing a sort of journal-autobiography.

He is the son of an Irish bishop (this genealogy is presumably borrowed from Louis MacNeice, who became a friend of Blunt's at Marlborough) and above all he is a connoisseur. 'Art was the only thing in my life that was untainted.' Art offered 'the possibility of transcendence, even for the space of a quarter of an hour'. He owns a Bonington as well as the Poussin—the authenticity of which is authoritatively but impudently questioned at about the time its owner's was demolished. He is not at all repentant about his career as a traitor, and claims never to have had his heart in the cause for which, eventually, he suffered.

What interested his foreign masters was his closeness to the Palace, where he looked after the pictures. He had chats with the King, whom he liked, knew his wife well enough to despise her, and even carried out a secret post-war royal mission to Bavaria. 'Your value for us,' said his contacts, 'is that you are at the heart of the English establishment.' Sometimes he saw himself less as a spy than as a very high-class gossip writer. He may have allowed men to go to their deaths, and even taken some risks himself, but he has trouble believing that the information he conveys is of any importance. Anyway, as he tells his interviewer, 'I did not spy for the Russians. I spied for Europe.' And indeed a pre-war visit to Russia did nothing to alleviate his dislike of Russians. They just happened, unfortunately, to live where the Revolution happened.

Elsewhere, however, he says 'we did not care a damn about the world, much as we might shout about freedom and justice and the plight of the masses. All selfishness.' He and his friends did not bother to read Marx: 'we had others to do that for us. The working-class Comrades were great readers.' They were spared contact with 'such an essentially *vulgar* ideology'. Maskell prefers Blake, whom, when drunk, he declaims, much in the manner of that other failed artist, Gully Jimson.

He was, though it would have been anachronistic to say so, gay, but he entered late, well over thirty, one guesses, and after a cold marriage, into 'queerdom'. 'The Fifties was the last great age of queerdom. All the talk now is of freedom and pride (pride!), but these young hotheads in their pink bell-bottoms, clamouring for the right to do it in the streets if they feel like it, do not seem to appreciate, or at least seem to wish to deny, the aphrodisiac properties of secrecy and fear.' He is an old-fashioned gentleman, from the days when it was necessary to consider (defy) the risks of exposure, which appeared not to trouble some at least of his more rampant friends.

His circle included a rather sinister libertine novelist who said things like 'a sense of humour is nothing but the other face of despair' and later went off to live in Antibes; and a strange, rather proletarian Cambridge mathematician who cracked the Enigma code and made the operation at Bletchley possible; but this man was found out, and, follow-

ing the example of the Stoic Seneca, killed himself by eating an apple he had laced with cyanide. Chief among his associates was Bannister, called simply 'Boy', an extremely dissolute, drunken, cottaging risk-taker from his Cambridge days on. Bannister happened to be, of the whole group, the most ideologically committed, though socially the most madly irresponsible. He was admired for his wildness, amply chronicled here, up to the moment of his escape, in which our hero had a part.

All is here done with much knowingness, not only about the lives of the Spies but also about London, still Dickensian until the Blitz; and about the life of these privileged young fellows in their time, a combination of booze, snobbery, sodomy and that hopelessly abstract tenderness for the lower classes, unknown except as subordinates and bedfellows. Some scenes, some dialogue, remind one of the early Angus Wilson. Others recall Anthony Powell's Poussin-dominated series of novels and also, at moments, that writer's earlier work. Yet Banville's own style is distinctive, especially at those epiphanic time-stopped moments (there is a cluster of them in an episode describing the hero's visit to his father's house in Northern Ireland) and the prose is usually fresh, though a 'glans-brown sky' seems a trifle forced, and there are occasional sentences that trespass on banality, as when bafflement comes over Maskell 'like a fog'.

[*The Untouchable*]. . . . will please because of its intelligence and skill. If it leaves some readers a little discontented, that will perhaps be because it occurs to them to speculate as to what Ford Madox Ford might have made of this material; or because they rather greedily expected even more from a novelist they had long since learnt to admire.
—*Frank Kermode*

Like all good novelists, Banville knows a lot, even about matters with which he cannot have had direct contact: not only the war, Bletchley and so on, but the fact that people carried cigarette-cases and tapped cigarettes briskly before lighting them. Why? he asks. Good question, one answers; but people do these things because they have seen them done, and stop when they see them done no more. However, it is a convincing accent, one of many such. On the other hand, Maskell, who is supposed to have been educated in Cambridge, has really no more idea than his Russian contact of what Syndics are and do in that university. But of course the great thing, as Kingsley Amis pointed out, is to sound as if you know some things well, and the rest will be taken on trust (except by readers who happen to have privileged information).

For the rest, this novel (sometimes possibly a shade too expansive, as in the accounts of Maskell's journeys to Ireland, France and Russia) will please because of its intelligence and skill. If it leaves some readers a little discontented, that will perhaps be because it occurs to them to speculate as to what Ford Madox Ford might have made of this material; or because they rather greedily expected even more from a novelist they had long since learnt to admire.

Patrick McGrath (review date 8 June 1997)

SOURCE: "The Fourth Man," in *New York Times Book Review,* June 8, 1997, p. 10.

[*In the following review, McGrath lauds Banville's* The Untouchable *and concludes, "Contemporary fiction gets no better than this."*]

A leitmotif in the recent fiction of John Banville has been the elusive and unstable nature of identity. It's apt, then, that in *The Untouchable,* his 11th novel, he should seize upon the historical figure of Anthony Blunt as his point of departure. Blunt, a homosexual esthete of the 1930's generation at Cambridge, was a distinguished English art historian, an expert on Poussin, curator of the Queen's art collection and director of the Courtauld Institute of Art. He was also a spy. Blunt worked for the Kremlin from the 1930's to the 1960's. In 1979, he was exposed in Parliament by Margaret Thatcher and publicly disgraced as the fourth of the "Cambridge spies" (the others, of course, being Guy Burgess, Donald Maclean and Kim Philby). He died of a heart attack in 1983. Refracted through the novelist's imagination, Blunt becomes Victor Maskell, the untouchable of the book's title.

In his recent fiction, Mr. Banville has explored various themes suggested by the study of art: the relationship of painting to the real world, the process of restoration, the distinction between the fake and the authentic, the futility of representation, its compensatory pleasures and so on. One of the finest stylists at work in the English language, he has woven these ideas into morally complex stories about violence and passion, guilt and redemption. In the novels immediately preceding this one (*The Book of Evidence, Ghosts* and *Athena*), he elaborates on these concerns through a central character called Freddie Montgomery. In the first of these books, Freddie murders a maid while stealing a painting from a country house. The repercussions of that act are worked out in the following two.

There is a Freddie in *The Untouchable* as well: the narrator's imbecile brother, who, midway through the novel, is sent away to a private nursing home where, shortly afterward, he dies. To the watchful Banvillean, the death of the idiot Freddie is charged with significance. Whether it marks the end of the Freddie Montgomery sequence we cannot yet know, but what we do know is that Freddie Maskell was not named carelessly: this is an author who is never careless with names. The plot of *Athena* involves a number of paintings, almost all of them fakes, by equally fake artists with names like Jean Vaublin, Johann Livelb, Giovanni Belli and L. E. van Ohlbijn—all anagrams, more or less, of "John Banville." The point is that we come to Mr. Banville's work with the expectation of encountering mirrored surfaces, of nothing and nobody being what they seem, with all attempts to depict the real clearly doomed to failure—ideal conditions for a spy story with an unreliable narrator at the controls.

Intellectually playful though they are, Mr. Banville's books never display the aridity of much self-reflective fiction. Infected, rather, with the antic spirit of Samuel Beckett and Flann O'Brien, they teem with life and humor, with vivid characters thrust into bewildering and sometimes absurd situations—a tendency that's only somewhat subdued here, where the dominant register is a sort of confessional realism. Victor Maskell is the son of an Anglo-Irish bishop, and his Irishness, as he moves through the higher strata of English society, adds a further layer of duality to what is already a baroquely divided character: "And then, for me, there were other forces at work, ambiguous, ecstatic, anguished: the obsession with art, for instance; the tricky question of nationality, that constant drone-note in the bagpipe music of my life; and, deeper again than any of these, the murk and slither of sex."

We meet Victor just after he has been "outed" by Mrs. Thatcher and is preparing to deal with the coming public humiliation. He is an old man now; at times, in fact, a rather precious old queen—"Did men die because of you? Yes, dearie, swooned quite away"—and what follows will be his reminiscences of a life spent largely among the sort of people one meets in the novels of Evelyn Waugh. His thoughts are directed to Serena Vandeleur, a young woman who wishes to write his biography. Serena listens while Victor dishes. The first thing she asks is, "Why did you do it?" Victor will spend the rest of the novel circling round this question; indeed, it is the very heart and core of the novel, and of the character who animates it. He will provide not one answer but several. The question then becomes: which, if any, can be believed?

Victor tells us that self-revelation is like the restoration of a painting: "I shall strip away layer after layer of grime—the toffee-colored varnish and caked soot left by a lifetime of dissembling—until I come to the very thing itself and know it for what it is. My soul. My self." Our confidence in his sincerity is not helped by the laughter this statement provokes in him. "I have lived decorously here, I must not now turn into a shrieking hysteric." Thus do the intertwined themes of art and deception announce themselves. Though there is, it seems, one work of art that does not dissemble: Victor's own Poussin, a small painting called "The Death of Seneca."

He will refer to it throughout the novel. First, the joy of finding it, early in his career, in a dusty stack at the back of a gallery: "And then there it was, in its chipped gilt frame, with a cracked coating of varnish that made it seem as if hundreds of shriveled toenails had been carefully glued to the surface." (Anthony Blunt's Poussin, "Eliezer and Rebecca at the Well," found in identical circumstances, was got for 100 in 1933; it is now valued at a million pounds.) Then later: "In the ever shifting, myriad worlds through which I moved, Poussin was the singular, unchanging, wholly authentic thing." In 1940, when Victor is in mortal peril during the evacuation of Boulogne, it is not of his wife or his child, his father or his brother, that he thinks—it's of "The Death of Seneca." "I thought, God forgive me, of what I truly loved. Things, for me, have always been of more import than people."

Things may be of more import than people, but Victor, especially in his youth, is surrounded by some very colorful characters indeed. Boy Bannister is a large, loud, boozy, slovenly fellow, obviously based on Guy Burgess, who creates glorious havoc wherever he goes, usually drinking vast quantities of Champagne and reeking of "semen and stale garlic." He too spies for the Russians and later, aided by Victor, flees England for Moscow.

Querell is a cold, sly, slightly reptilian Roman Catholic writer. After the war, "his bleak little novels had at last caught on, reflecting as they did the spiritual exhaustion of the times, and he was enjoying sudden and lavish success, which was a surprise to everyone except him." Graham Greene? Then there's the Brevoort clan. Nick Brevoort is for years Victor's best friend, a beautiful young man who in later life will turn into a fat, red-jowled Tory Cabinet minister. Victor marries Nick's sister, Baby, who reminds one strongly of a Waugh heroine: arch, flippant, sophisticated, vulnerable, eventually pathetic.

These and others like them are the constants in Victor's life, from university days through the war and on up into the 1980's. Their endless parties, their politics (or lack thereof), their brittle wit, their affairs, their casual anti-Semitism, but most of all their intimate connections to the real sources of wealth and power in Britain during the last half-century— all lend them a furious and often febrile vitality on the page.

But at heart *The Untouchable* is about the strangely compulsive appeal that Communism held for so many of these people. Victor's case is particularly tantalizing. He is no man of the people and marvels that he "could have given myself

over to such an essentially vulgar ideology." In fact, he freely admits to being a royalist. Nor has he read much Marx. Was it, then, guilty embarrassment at being so privileged? He says not. Perhaps the need to believe in something, anything? "Oh, no doubt for me Marxism was a recrudescence, in a not greatly altered form, of the faith of my fathers; any backstreet Freudian could tease that one out." But we don't really believe this, and neither does he.

Then, in a quite breathtaking metaphor, he supplies a more satisfactory psychological explanation. He is describing the way a believer's "conscious mind can separate itself into many compartments containing many, conflicting, dogmas. These are not sealed compartments; they are like the cells of a battery . . . over which the electrical charge plays, leaping from one cell to another, gathering force and direction as it goes. You put in the acid of world-historical necessity and the distilled water of pure theory and connect up your points and with a flash and a shudder the patched-together monster of commitment, sutures straining and ape brow clenched, rises in jerky slow motion from Dr. Diabolo's operating table."

Having made his commitment, then, he allows his career as a spy to go forward. It is not glamorous. He meets his Russian control in seedy London pubs. He is asked for information of such comic banality that most of it is already freely available to the public. He visits Moscow and is disillusioned. On the map, "the Soviet Union looked like nothing so much as a big old dying dog with its head hanging, peering westward, all rheum and slobber, barking its last barks." Somehow he weathers the Hitler-Stalin pact: "Surely by now it is clear where my loyalties would always lie, whatever worthless treaty this or that vile tyrant might put his name to." Still faithful to his failing god, eventually he gets some serious espionage work to do, and carries it off with dispatch.

There is also an energetic private life: an initiation into the gay world of the time, after which a love story unfolds. The predictable parallel is drawn between the life of the spy and the life of the closeted homosexual. And, as in all the best spy stories, the last chapters bring startling revelations, genuinely surprising denouements. We are made to see that nothing is as it seems (not even that ultimate index of authenticity, the Poussin) and nobody is who he or she seems to be (perhaps not even Miss Vandeleur). In addition, a quite plausible theory is put forward as to why Victor Maskell (and Anthony Blunt) was unmasked when he was.

There is much, much more to celebrate in this extraordinary book: prose of a glorious verve and originality, in the service of a richly painted portrait of a man and a period and a society and a political order—the whole governed by an exquisite thematic design. Contemporary fiction gets no better than this.

Tony E. Jackson (essay date Fall 1997)

SOURCE: "Science, Art, and the Shipwreck of Knowledge: The Novels of John Banville," in *Contemporary Literature*, Vol. 38, No. 3, Fall, 1997, pp. 510-33.

[*In the following essay, Jackson traces one of Banville's major themes: "the situation of living everyday life in the context of postmodern understandings of knowledge and truth."*]

The novels of Irish writer John Banville make for uncommonly rich reading. His fictional fabrics are always finely textured, often movingly poetic, threading together various narrative styles and genres. Because he is a very literate writer (he is the literary editor of the Irish *Times*), his pages abound with allusions to other great literature. At times his writing is straightforwardly realistic, at times surreal, at all times extremely well crafted: repeated visits to his books only increase our awareness of the subtle and complex figures woven into the mesh of his stories. There are many interpretive considerations that could be (and no doubt will be) made of Banville's work. Here I will examine one of the major concerns in his last several novels: the situation of living everyday life in the context of postmodern understandings of knowledge and truth.

The term "postmodernism" can be defined in many ways. For my purposes here it has to do with certain ideas about knowledge, truth, and desire that have become common in the twentieth century in general, but especially in the last decades. There are a number of sources for these ideas, but certainly a generally acknowledged source would be Friedrich Nietzsche. Nietzsche forced upon the world in a new and powerful way certain truths about the truth: no matter how absolute a truth appears to be, no matter how exactly words appear to be equivalent to the thinks to which they refer, the truth is always, ultimately, a set of "arbitrary metaphors" that are subject to "the legislature of language" and not to the thing in itself. As we know, the kind of thing Nietzsche says about the nature of language and its consequences gets formalized into structuralist linguistics by Ferdinand de Saussure, and then of course such thinkers as Jacques Derrida come along to show how this structuralism in its turn undoes its own attempts at grounding language.

Historically we have two primary responses to the kind of thinking that Nietzsche most fully sets into motion. The first, which we associate more with naturalism and modernism in literature, involves nihilism. As I have argued elsewhere, one ready reaction to Nietzschean claims is a leap to the conclusion that there is no truth at all, that the truth in general is simply an illusion or a batch of lies perpetrated by whoever happens to have power. And even Nietzsche himself falls into this at times. But this nihilistic conclusion is in fact the same *kind* of absolute truth claim that Nietzsche's arguments disallow. Only in relation to some absolutely true truth could you judge the truth in general to be a lie; but Nietzsche's arguments rule out such an absolutely true truth. If we do not think his claims through thoroughly, we can easily and without realizing it end up judging the new idea of truth by the standard of the old idea of truth that we have agreed has been disproved by, precisely, the new. This latter is what nihilism always unwittingly does.

"Postmodernism" is one way of describing the second primary response to Nietzsche. And despite the fact that it has been regularly attacked as nihilistic, postmodernism constitutes itself in part through the recognition of that which nihilism misses in Nietzschean claims about the nature of truth. For in fact Nietzsche only shows the unsustainability of certain *kinds* of truth, namely those that present themselves as entirely self-consistent, eternal, changeless, outside of history and desire. Postmodern understandings do not find the truth in general to be simply false, nor the world to be meaningless; rather, we have truth and meaning in a different way than had previously most commonly been thought. The postmodern project involves the investigation of how actual truths have been constituted in actual historical situations. More theoretical writers, such as Derrida, Paul de Man, Jacques Lacan, and Michel Foucault, have become famous for revealing certain large-scale linguistic or psychological or discursive structures that have operated toward the production of ostensibly universal, self-evident truths. Most of the practical interpretive activities—that is, certain feminisms, new historicism, postcolonial studies, cultural studies, and so forth—that would fall into the postmodern category have tended to show how desire or ideology of whatever kind has produced truths in specific cultural settings.

But although Nietzsche and postmodernism do not destroy the truth and meaning in general, they end up leaving us with a truth and meaning that seem for many people unsatisfying in fundamental ways. Evidently our desire is always, impossibly enough, for the absolute, and we are disappointed with anything less. What are the consequences for everyday life if Nietzschean or postmodern understandings are true? After all, it is one thing to demonstrate logically the end of absolute truths or grounds or centers or selves, but it is another thing to live life without them. Banville's work has considered just this situation, specifically in the context of scientific kinds of knowledge. If we look over a series of his most recent novels, we find that Banville gives us a kind of history. In several earlier novels he imagines what we now see as postmodern understandings of knowledge appearing individually to an array of great Renaissance scientific thinkers. It is as if the most intense thinking will naturally tend to press ever onward until it strikes the kinds of perimeters that postmodernism has taken as its center of interest. And this makes sense. Postmodern conceptuality is not in some radical way unprecedented. Of course thinkers have run up on all this before. But though postmodern conceptuality is not new in itself, it is historically significant that it has now spread into a wide array of intellectual arenas and even into everyday life. And it is this latter case that Banville considers in his more recent books, particularly **The Book of Evidence** and **Ghosts,** at which I will look in most detail.

A string of three books—**Doctor Copernicus, Kepler** (winner of the *Guardian* Prize for fiction), and **The Newton Letter**—most established Banville's international reputation. The first two of these are fictional biographies of the real historical figures. Banville portrays both men as having an almost religious conception of mathematics and geometry, as being possessed by the idea that quantification and geometrization can embrace the entire material world as it really is in its essence. Nicolaus Copernicus experiences a calling to forge a "new beginning . . . a new science, one that would be objective, open-minded, above all honest, a beam of stark cold light trained unflinchingly upon the world as it is and not as men, out of a desire for reassurance or mathematical elegance or whatever, wished it to be." Similarly, Johannes Kepler, with his religious conviction that "[t]he world works by geometry, for geometry is the earthly paradigm of divine thought," searches "after the eternal laws that govern the harmony of the world." "To enquire into nature," he says, "is to trace geometrical relationships." But though Banville vividly paints each man's intellectual drive to get at the real truth of nature, he also shows us the eventual sense of failure that haunts each of them. Despite their great successes navigating the sea of knowledge, in the end both men finally run aground on the impossibility of their desire. Copernicus, after a series of disappointments and defeats, comes to lose his basic belief that the world is "amenable to physical investigation, that the principal thing could be deduced, that the thing itself could be said." He keeps on working, continues to make discoveries, but underneath it all, as his amanuensis tells us, "All that mattered to him was the saying, not what was said; words were the empty rituals with which he held the world at bay. Copernicus did not believe in truth." Kepler never despairs to the extent of Copernicus, but still, after a series of devastating real-life events, he writes in a letter to his daughter that he had thought the great human task was "the transformation of the chaos without, into a perfect harmony & balance within us." Now he says this is "Wrong, wrong: for our lives contain us, *we* are the flaw in the crystal, the speck of grit which must be ejected from the spinning sphere." Though he continues to work, at the very last he things: "Everything is told us, but nothing explained. . . . We must take it all on trust."

With **The Newton Letter** Banville turns from the life stories of the great astronomical wizards to the twentieth-century biographer who finds them fascinating. This short novel features a first-person retelling of how a historian comes, after seven years of research, to give up not only his major project, a biography of Isaac Newton, but his calling as a historian. A key document in his research, one of Newton's letters to John Locke, turns out to "lie at the centre of [the unnamed narrator's own] work." Paradoxically though, in the letter Newton has come to the margins of his own circle of knowledge. After arguing with Locke about some of the grounding claims of the *Principia,* Newton abruptly turns away from the subject of science, formulas, and laws to speak of everyday people: "They would seem to have something to tell me; not of their trades, nor even of how they conduct their lives; nothing, I believe, in words. They are . . . themselves the things they might tell. They are all a form of saying." Therefore, he continues, "expect no more philosophy from my pen. The language in which I might be able not only to write but to think is neither Latin nor English, but a language none of whose words is known to me." No matter his immense successes, in the end the old philosopher finds that the net of his knowledge has failed to capture the essential reality. Newton's recognition of the failure of his scientific knowledge is mirrored in the academic historian's recognition of the failure of history. The narrator has "lost [his] faith in the primacy" of the historical text. "Real people keep getting in the way now, objects, landscapes even." Finally, he simply says, "I can't go on. I'm not a historian anymore."

> *Mefisto* **is again a fictional autobiography, but written in a surreal style, with a cast of strange, almost figmentary characters and a bizarre plot that slips back and forth between a macabre realism and postmodern science fiction.**
> **—Tony Jackson**

In his next novel, **Mefisto,** Banville takes a new tack both stylistically and in terms of his interest in the mathematization of the world. **Mefisto** is again a fictional autobiography, but written in a surreal style, with a cast of strange, almost figmentary characters and a bizarre plot that slips back and forth between a macabre realism and postmodern science fiction. The main character, Gabriel Swan, is born with a "gift for numbers," able to count before he can talk. In fact, Swan's gift is such that he is "at ease only with pure numbers." In contrast with his great Renaissance predecessors, the twentieth-century mathematician does not have to prove any link between mathematics and the material world: he simply assumes it. But he, too, finally sees his desire crack up on the reef of the real. Late in the novel, after the accidental deaths of his mother, father, and uncle, and after being horribly disfigured in a mysterious explosion, he ends up having to abandon the language of mathematics, but he still listens for the voice of the thing itself. "I woke up one morning," he writes, "and found I could no longer add together two and two. Something had given way, the ice had shattered. Things crowded in, the mere things themselves. One drop of water plus one drop of water will not make two drops, but one. Two oranges and two apples do not make four of some new synthesis, but remain stubbornly themselves."

As we have seen, all these novels tell in different ways stories of the same kind of desire and the same kind of failure. Each man, after much study and thought, after producing true and useful knowledge about certain aspects of the world, discovers, typically in a striking flash of realization, that some essential, most basic quality of the real world has slipped through his intellectual embrace, and more specifically has eluded a certain kind of mathematical and/or geometrical formalization. With *The Book of Evidence* and *Ghosts,* we begin where these previous stories end. In fact the thoroughly twentieth century protagonist of these two novels is in many ways the historical result of the Copernican determination to look "unflinchingly upon the world as it is and not as men, out of a desire for reassurance or mathematical elegance or whatever, wished it to be." *The Book of Evidence* and *Ghosts* both revolve around a character who lives in a world that in some senses takes for granted the disillusionment with knowledge that had come belatedly to the astronomers.

And just here we may turn to the thought of Friedrich Nietzsche to consider all this, for Banville has represented the desire of scientific knowledge much after Nietzsche's representation of Socratic knowledge in *The Birth of Tragedy.* There, Socrates is described as operating under a productive illusion: "the unshakable faith that thought, using the thread of logic, can penetrate the deepest abysses of being." And of course this faith has been immensely successful. It has "led science onto the high seas from which it has never again been driven altogether." Alluding to the Copernican revolution, Nietzsche continues that science has cast "a common net of thought over the whole globe, actually holding out the prospect of the lawfulness of an entire solar system." Insatiable, even violent in its desire, this faith, this knowledge cannot rest without roping everything into its domain. "Anyone who has ever experienced the pleasure of Socratic insight and felt how, spreading in ever-widening circles, it seeks to embrace the whole world of appearances, will never again find any stimulus toward existence more violent than the craving to complete this conquest and to weave the net impenetrably tight." Nietzsche himself has of course experienced just this craving, and his philosophical project tries to make sense out of what we know and who we are once we have realized just these truths about Socratic knowledge. Banville has given us portraits of actual men driven with uncommon force to complete the "conquest and to weave the net impenetrably tight."

But Nietzsche goes on to claim that "science, spurred by its powerful illusion, speeds irresistibly toward its limits where its optimism, concealed in the essence of logic, suffers shipwreck. For the periphery of the circle of science has an infinite number of points; and while there is no telling how this circle could ever be surveyed completely, noble and gifted men nevertheless reach, e'er half their time and inevitably, such boundary points on the periphery from which one gazes into what defies illumination." All this is to say that scientific knowledge has been driven by an at least implicit faith that the world in its entirety can be known within the same *kind* of knowledge. The "essence of logic" conceals the fact that this is simply a faith or optimism, because logic seems self-evidently to be the infallible means to the whole truth. Nietzsche, however, argues that all logic sooner or later runs into its limit, the point at which it turns back upon itself and fails to maintain itself consistently within its own bases for truth. Just this latter truth about the necessary shipwreck of logic, arrived at through logic itself, is of course the point from which deconstructive and post-structuralist arguments typically take off. For Nietzsche it is at this boundary point, the point at which "logic coils up . . . and finally bites its own tail," that a "new form of insight breaks through, *tragic insight* which, merely to be endured, needs art as a protection and remedy."

Along with the "shipwreck" of knowledge, Banville has considered the dialectical emergence of art out of the failed desire of science, especially in the very last pages of *Doctor Copernicus.* In his dying moments, Copernicus is visited by the ghost of his brother, Andreas, who has been the dark opposite of Copernicus for all their lives. A kind of deathbed realization occurs. Andreas says to the doctor, of his astronomical discoveries, "You thought to discern the thing itself, the eternal truths, the pure forms that lie behind the chaos of the world." But anything ascribed to lights in the sky beyond their simple existence is only a function of what must finally be a matter of "faith . . . belief in the possibility of apprehending reality." Such an attitude, Copernicus protests, attempts to reject knowledge altogether. But Andreas says, "It is the manner of knowing that is important," at least when we come to knowing the thing itself. Though Copernicus has established certain truths, the truth that most matters cannot be apprehended within the kind of knowledge to which Copernicus has been committed. In fact this kind of truth in some sense falls outside even the clutch of language: it "may not be spoken . . . but perhaps it may be . . . shown." And art—"disposing the commonplace, the names, in a beautiful and orderly pattern"—is the means by which this could happen. So Copernicus does recognize the significance of art as it emerges from the failure of scientific knowledge, but he does so only at the last minute.

With *The Book of Evidence* and *Ghosts,* we have a rather more in-depth look at the disillusionment with Socratic knowledge and the consequent turning to art. The books are sequels of a sort. *The Book of Evidence* is the written confession (which will be submitted as evidence) of a captured but not yet tried murderer, Freddie Montgomery. *Ghosts* is the story of Freddie (though his name is never mentioned) when he gets out of jail ten years after the events of *The Book of Evidence.* The central dramatic event of the earlier novels—the disillusionment with science, history, and so with knowledge in general—has, with Freddie, already happened in the past. And this is of course in part because Freddie lives after Nietzsche, whose thinking marks a historical boundary of Socratic thought. Early in his confession, Freddie explains that as a young man he "took up the study of science in order to. . . . make the lack of certainty more manageable. Here was a way, I thought, of erecting a solid structure on the very sands that were everywhere, always, shifting under me." This relates Freddie to, but also distinguishes him from, Copernicus, Kepler, and Newton. The earlier men simply thought of themselves as looking for objective truth. Freddie, coming after the progress of science since the seventeenth century, has a Nietzschean conception of what actually brings about scientific truth: the desire for some kind of solid ground of knowledge. But we live in the century of Albert Einstein and Werner Heisenberg, and from the perspective of the previous, which is to say Newtonian, scientific paradigm, our present knowledge consists of very watery certainties. Freddie has studied "statistics, probability theory. . . . Esoteric stuff." Further, as a twentieth-century citizen, Freddie can state freely and even cavalierly that he had a head start in his study of modern science because he was from the beginning "without convictions as to the nature of reality, truth, ethics, all those big things."

With respect to history, Freddie says, "I used to believe . . . I was determining the course of my own life, according to my own decisions, but gradually, as I accumulated more and more past to look back on, I realized that I had done the things I did because I could do no other." He now looks on his life "as a prison in which all actions are determined according to a random pattern thrown down by an unknown and insensate authority." The most striking areas of modern science—from quantum theory to contemporary Darwinism—give us a natural "order" that consists of just this contradictory mix of determinacy and randomness. But this kind of order, from a certain point of view, does not satisfy. In *Ghosts,* looking back on the past of *The Book of Evidence,* Freddie describes himself as someone who had been "trained to reason and compute" but "in the face of a manifestly chaotic world ha[d] lost his faith in the possibility of order."

So Freddie in *The Book of Evidence* lives out his adult life in the situation that came only as a revelation late in the lives of the great astronomers. In fact, Freddie's general awareness, at least in this book, remains stuck in a very particular way in the limbo realm just at the self-undoing of Socratic

knowledge. Like Nietzsche, Banville will carry us on past this boundary-condition to present us with a turning to art, and it is a turning that seeks out in its own way "protection and remedy." But the presence of a "tragic insight" is another issue. For Freddie commits murder in the act of stealing a seventeenth-century Dutch painting. He encounters the painting—of a woman standing in a doorway, entitled *Portrait of a Woman with Gloves*—by chance at the manorial home of an old lover, whose father is a famous art collector. Freddie is swept away, overwhelmed. The painted image seems to reverse the normal relationship between viewer and representation. Everything in the painting suddenly seems to be "an eye fixed on [him] unblinkingly." The painted gaze affects his sense of himself. As he stares at the painting, gradually "a kind of embarrassment" takes hold of him. He feels, he says, a "shamefaced awareness of myself, as if somehow I, this soiled sack of flesh, were the one who was being scrutinized." The portrait's gaze carries a "mute insistence . . . which [he] can neither escape nor assuage." "She requires of me," he says, "some great effort, some tremendous feat of scrutiny and attention. . . . It is as if she were asking me to let her live." He realizes that "[t]here is no she, of course . . . . only an organization of shapes and colors," but he is struck by her presence more forcibly than he has been struck by any living human. In *Ghosts,* Freddie briefly retells the story of the theft and murder, speaking of himself in the third person. He says of himself that he was "surprised by love, not for a living woman—he ha[d] never been able to care much for the living—but for the figure of a woman in . . . a painting." Though the woman in the painting is not beautiful, nonetheless, "in her portrait she has presence, she is unignorably *there,* more real than the majority of her sisters out here in what we call real life." Almost instantly Freddie decides he must have the painting. This italicized "thereness," this sense of being fully and uniquely present in space and time, Freddie has never experienced in himself or in others. All his life he has had the "sense of [himself] as something without weight, without moorings, a floating phantom." Of his own history, he says, "I was always a little way behind, trotting in the rear of my own life." But the painting brings about a spontaneous experience of fullness in the here and now. As Freddie retells his story in *Ghosts,* he says of the painting, "It is *being* that he has encountered here, the thing itself, the pure, unmediated essence, in which, he thinks, he will at last find himself and his true home, his place in the world."

This sense of presence is that aspect of "the thing itself" that has escaped the mathematical grasp of Freddie's predecessors in Banville's work. Given this, and given what Freddie apprehends in the painting, the turn to art begins to look like a means of success, a means of finally fulfilling the most fundamental desire, and so securing a remedy for what he perceives as the disease of existence. But this is not the idea of art Banville is after. In the act of stealing the painting,

Freddie is surprised by a flesh-and-blood maid who works at the house. He forces her to leave with him and murders her with a hammer when she tries to escape. In the instant before striking her, Freddie is "filled with a kind of wonder." "I had never," he says, "felt another's presence so immediately and with such raw force. I saw her now, really saw her, for the first time. . . . She was quite ordinary, and yet . . . somehow radiant." Now this, though without the sense of wonder, is the kind of "presence" that Freddie has felt in the painted image. He responds to the painting with an almost mindless desire to possess it, to have it for his own. How does this relate to his response to the maid?

Only as Freddie is about to take the maid's life does he see her life as it really is. But this vision does not stop him. It is as if he must go on to complete this ultimately negating action, in the same way that he must possess the painting. The painting makes the perfect, albeit illusory, lover, because a painted woman, unlike a real woman, cannot differ from his perception of it, cannot ultimately be anything other than what he projects upon it. Further, by possessing the painting, he will end its public existence, will close it off from the rest of the world, shut down the possibility that other eyes might see in it either what he has seen or, worse, some other meaning. In fact, Banville makes a point of this. An art historian and her tour group interrupt, without realizing it, Freddie's stealing of the portrait. They look at the paintings in the room with "respectful vacancy." "[T]he picture," he says in disgust, "*my* picture, was given two sentences, and a misattribution." The italicized "my" captures what has happened. The glimpse of some kind of pure being in the painting has given material manifestation to the emptiness, the homelessness of his own sense of self. He could not have seen the painting as he has seen it unless he himself were empty or deficient in a crucial way. Looking back from *Ghosts,* he will say that suddenly falling for the portrait reveals that a "need was there all along, awaiting its fulfillment in whatever form chance might provide." This particular painting has exactly expressed the nature of being that Freddie most wants, and so least has. In a sense the picture is *of* him. The "love" he feels for the painted image is entirely narcissistic. The living woman, then, accidentally gets in the way of Freddie having himself as he most wants to be. In a way he kills her out of self-defense.

And yet her death changes everything, for what Freddie sees in the living woman's eyes silences the appeal of the portrait: just after killing the maid, with one last look he throws the painting into a ditch and walks away. Recalling in *Ghosts* the moment of "sudden access to another's being" when he looks into the maid's eyes, he says that "he had never known another creature—not mother, wife, child, not anyone—so intimately, so invasively, to such indecent depths, as he did just then this woman whom he was about to bludgeon to death." The crucial word that distinguishes what he has seen

in the painting and what he sees in the woman is "another." With respect to the maid, he has mentioned "another's presence," "another's being," "another creature." In the painting, he sees, though he does not think of it this way, only himself. As he is about to kill the maid, he has his first experience of the essential self-presence of another person. But although Freddie suddenly apprehends the intimacy of *another* person's sense of being, he does not recognize the significance of what he has apprehended. At the end of *The Book of Evidence* Freddie himself offers an explanation of the "essential sin" in murdering the woman. The sin "for which there will be no forgiveness," he says, is "that I never imagined her vividly enough, that I never made her be there sufficiently, that I did not make her live. Yes, that failure of imagination is my real crime." "I killed her," he continues, "because I could kill her, and I could kill her because for me she was not alive." Obviously, "alive" in this sense involves more than just biology. Imagination, then, is that extra quality of understanding that can enable us to grasp the essential reality of another human being's unique aliveness. So after the fact, when he has had time to consider the horror of his failure of imagination, he begins to have an updated version of the tragic insight about which Nietzsche wrote.

What makes Banville's representation of all this in fact post-Nietzschean is that there is no mythification to be had, no invocation of dionysian or apollonian essences. Both the theft and the murder seem simply to happen. If it were left at this point, we would have another version of *The Stranger,* but Freddie, unlike Meursault, feels guilt and remorse. At the end of *The Book of Evidence,* he says that his "task now is to bring [the maid] back to life." In *Ghosts,* still recalling these past events, he says that prison, "punishment, paying his debt to society, all that was nothing, was merely how he would pass the time while he got on with the real business of atonement, which was nothing less than the restitution of a life." *Ghosts* is the story of this atonement, this restitution.

In *Ghosts,* Freddie, freed after ten years in jail, has sought refuge on an island. While in jail he had become an authority on Dutch painting, and he applies to become an assistant to a famous but reclusive art historian, Professor Kreutznaer, who lives on the island. The professor takes Freddie on, and Freddie moves into the house in which the professor and his secretary live. All this is told as a long flashback in the middle of the book. Most of the rest of the story involves the arrival on the island of a tour group whose boat has run aground. They end up spending the day at the professor's house, until the tide turns and they can refloat the boat. One member of the tour group, a woman named Flora, remains behind. The immediate present of the novel, the (impossible) point of time from which the whole tale is being told, occurs on the day in which she has revealed that she, too, is getting ready to leave.

The professor is a famous authority on the great, mysterious painter Vaublin. Vaublin's masterpiece *Le Monde d'Or* plays a much larger part here than did the painting in **The Book of Evidence,** as much a part as geometry and mathematics in the earlier novels. In fact the characters in the story may be only Freddie's imaginary projections of real people *from* the painting. Since Freddie describes the painting in great detail, often in the language of an art critic, we can readily discover what Banville never reveals outright: that the fictional painting *Le Monde d'Or* in fact blends together two of eighteenth-century French painter Antoine Watteau's later, most famous works, *Gilles* and *A Pilgrimage to Cythera.* Watteau's *Gilles* features a life-size, standing image of the commedia dell'arte clown known as Gilles, but also called Pierrot. Behind and beneath him, we see four other traditional members of the standard commedia cast as well as a donkey that they are trying to coax into movement. In the descriptions of *Le Monde d'Or,* the Pierrot figure, the donkey, and one other of the players from *Gilles* are discussed at length. But Freddie describes the figures ranged behind Pierrot setting "off down the slope towards that magically insubstantial ship wreathed round with cherubs that awaits them on the amber shore," which is plainly from Watteau's painting *A Pilgrimage to Cythera.* So Banville has created one fictional painting from the two real ones.

Aside from this, Banville also changes elements of the originals. In **Ghosts** the figure of the clown holds a club, which is not true of the original. In the original *A Pilgrimage to Cythera,* we see a number of adult couples gradually moving off down a hill toward a waiting ship. But in **Ghosts,** the group setting off down the hill consists of an old man, a blond-haired woman, two young boys, a teenage girl, and a man on a donkey. These characters do not appear in Watteau's painting, but they are a painted version of the "actual" characters, the stranded tourists, who appear in this novel. That is, this group behind Pierrot makes up not only the figures in the fictional painting but the principal cast of characters in this fictional world. Similarly, the image of the clown with a club is both in *Le Monde d'Or* and a representation of Freddie himself. So it could be that Freddie is somehow simply imagining the painting into "real" life, looking at *Le Monde d'Or* and dreaming (the book has much of dreams in it) a reality for these images. And even if he is not, the crossover between painted and real is a central quality of the "reality" of the world Banville has created. Banville pointedly does not provide us with any definite certainty about the location of the real thing, fictional, painted, or historical. In fact we cannot even know with clear certainty who the narrator is. At times he seems to be an actual character, at times a kind of ghost. All this is in stark formal contrast with **The Book of Evidence,** which reads in a very conventional way. Since both books are told in first person by the same speaker, we may take it that the difference in the kind

of telling has more than incidental importance. I shall return to this later.

Assessing his situation upon arriving at the island, Freddie can at least say that he feels in a very qualified way "at home" there. Having always felt the world to be incomprehensible on some most basic level, he now hopes he "might come to understand things," at least simple, basic things. But the problem is that the manner in which he knows things disallows such understanding. "The object," he says, that which he would come to know, "splits, flips, doubles back, becomes something else. Under the slightest pressure the seeming unit falls into a million pieces and every piece into a million more. I was myself no unitary thing." If the analytical attitude of scientific knowledge is not simply arbitrarily cut off, then it will go on, apparently without end, finding smaller and smaller "unitary things," arriving in the late twentieth century at the incomprehensibly tiny "things" of quantum theory. This realization is one of those boundaries of knowledge mentioned by Nietzsche. In modern (or postmodern) times this boundary-awareness becomes unavoidable—indeed, in some ways seems to become the norm. Freddie cannot even speak simply: "I would open my mouth and a babble would come pouring out, a hopeless glossolalia. The most elementary bit of speech was a cacophony. To choose one word was to exclude countless others." "My case," he concludes, "was what it always had been, namely, that I did one thing while thinking another and in this welter of difference I did not know what I was. How then was I to be expected to know what others are, to imagine them so vividly as to make them quicken into a sort of life?"

Freddie, after his time in jail, still sees the necessity of imagination, but given his sense of being an unanchored self, he cannot see how imagination is to work. Just here we have a key to his dilemma, and we can see the way nihilism on the one hand and postmodernism on the other arise out of the situation Nietzsche described in *The Birth of Tragedy.* Freddie is caught between two ideas of knowledge. In a way he knows this, and in a way he does not know it. He has described his own situation a number of times in both books, but without being able to grasp its significance. In **The Book of Evidence,** after becoming obsessed by the portrait, Freddie imagines a story to go with the painted woman: the story of how she came to be painted. In his imagination, when she sees the finished portrait of herself, she has a moment of disorientation: "She had expected it would be like looking in a mirror, but this is someone she does not recognize, and yet knows." This is in fact a projected image of Freddie himself. He is constantly in the situation of knowing and yet not recognizing. We can see this in the way he doubts (in the quotation above) the possibility of someone such as himself being able to imagine others into life. He does not doubt himself because he is a murderer; he has thought of himself this way for most of his adult life. Something else is going on. On the one hand, he clearly knows his own "case." He gives us an accurate description of his own sense of self and the sense of knowledge and language that accompany and are accompanied by that sense of self. So what he has described is obviously what he knows, but he cannot recognize what he actually knows *as* knowledge. In other words, when he says, "I did not know what I was," this statement can only be true in relation to some notion of knowledge and self that is so taken for granted as to be invisible, "concealed," as Nietzsche puts it, "in the essence of logic." His self-criticism assumes some right idea of what a person is, but what Freddie actually lives does not fall within that idea (again not simply because of his crime); this unseen, governing right idea will not allow him to recognize his actual state of being as a positively existing, alternative *kind* of self. He can only conclude, nihilistically and in contradiction with actuality, that he has no real self, no real language, no real knowledge. Again, on some level he "knows" this contradiction, but he cannot recognize it for what it is. The version of knowledge by which he automatically judges himself, as Nietzsche showed, underlies the achievements of Copernicus, Kepler, and Newton and is taken for granted by modernity as the right kind of knowledge.

This contradictory state of mind can help us better understand Freddie's relationship with the portrait in *The Book of Evidence.* Seeing the portrait, Freddie is struck by a knowledge that falls outside the boundary of what can typically be considered knowledge, but his instant response is to possess the painting in just the way Socratic knowledge sets out to possess whatever appears to fall outside its established limits. Of course it is not that he wants to pull the painting into a formulated system of knowledge: unlike his predecessors, he has already given up on that, and in any case Banville is now exploring all this on a more everyday level. But the almost mindless craving to hold the painting to himself operates in the same manner. Freddie grasps the potent "thereness" of the painted image, but he cannot allow this most fully present "object" to exist outside the orbit of a center in himself, a center that he does not even know exists. Thus he seems to act spontaneously, obsessively. Just before he kills the maid, he fully realizes the otherness of a living self outside his own confused center, but in going on to kill her, he disallows that otherness. In both cases he has been suddenly opened to the knowledge that all Banville's protagonists have most wanted and, at the same moment, has violently shut down that knowledge.

Perhaps the largest-scale sign of this great contradiction appears in the different manner of telling the two stories. In *The Book of Evidence* Freddie lives a life on the boundary of the kind of knowledge that the conventional realistic novel both supports and is supported by, and yet he still employs that mode of narration—realism—to tell his story. In effect, the life he actually lives calls for a different narrative mode,

a different net of art by which to catch his life's mysterious, uncatchable essence, in much the same way that Nietzsche's philosophical message required a different mode of philosophical discourse. The narrative net of *Ghosts,* like the narrative form of all thoroughly postmodern literature (as well as certain postmodern philosophical writings) attempts to capture an existence that occupies the strange boundary-area defined by Nietzsche. It will necessarily fail, but it will fail in a significantly different way from how conventional realism fails, and with failure, as with knowing, it is the manner in which it is done that is important.

As knowledge and misrecognition came in the forms of a painting and a woman, so atonement and restitution will come in the forms of a painting and a woman. At the end of *The Book of Evidence,* after being in jail only a few weeks, Freddie has already begun studying Dutch painting, from biographies to histories to techniques, even to "the methods of grinding colours" and the like. All the learning, though, all the researched information, fails to give him what he wants to know: "How could mere facts compare with the amazing knowledge that had flared out at me as I stood and stared at the painting lying on its edge in the ditch where I dropped it that last time?" But of course here again we run into an unrecognized confusion of ways of understanding. Studying, in the way Freddie approaches it, cannot begin to bring the kind of knowledge he seeks. It does, however, prepare the way for what may be had of knowledge.

Chapter 3 of *Ghosts* is an interpretation of *Le Monde d'Or.* It begins: "He stands before us like our own reflection distorted in a mirror, known yet strange." Already, this interpretation in a sense diagnoses, and so remedies, what was wrong with Freddie's response to the portrait in *The Book of Evidence.* Some version of "we" is consciously being brought into the experience. Freddie consciously recognizes the projection of his self into the work, so that he does not simply mistake the painting as an independent, freestanding thing in itself, an object to be possessed that can, conversely, possess him. The rest of the opening passage consists of strings of questions that bring forth meaning without solidifying it. In spite of what he said about historical research at the end of the previous book, he brings it readily into this interpretation. He has not, that is, closed off the material world and history as meaningless in favor of the meaningfulness of art. Also, certain puzzles are simply left standing: "It is difficult to say which effects are intentional and which accidental." In fact, the central discovery of his interpretation is that something in the very nature of the painting eludes the net of his comprehension. On the one hand the painting is "a masterpiece of pure composition, of the architectonic arrangement of light and shade." In this sense he sees the painting in the way that the scientist sees the natural world. On the other hand, being art, it thrusts forward that which science must ignore: it "carries a weight of unaccountable significance that is disproportionate to any possible programme or hidden discourse." And this—both the architectonic arrangement and the *lack* of a hidden program—is precisely its significance. The nature of the painted image is such that it is "hardly present at all and at the same time profoundly, palpably *there.*" So the restitutive response to this painting does not simply reject the previous moment of misrecognition in *The Book of Evidence.* In both experiences of art Freddie has a moment of knowing what he most wants to know. But as Andreas said in *Doctor Copernicus,* "It is the manner of knowing that is important." "Who is [the clown]?" Freddie asks. "[W]e shall not know. What we seek are those evidences of origin, will and action that make up what we think of as identity. We shall not find them." The "what we think" is of course a key phrase: since he no longer takes for granted the version of identity that he himself has never in fact experienced, he is no longer doomed to the misrecognitions that were explored in the previous book. We could say, in other words, that now he is not unconsciously judging a Nietzschean identity by the unrecognized standards of a Socratic identity.

In the end Freddie concludes that the painter has created "a world where nothing is lost, where all is accounted for while yet the mystery of things is preserved." From this, again, we can see that it is not so much that the knowledge of art is opposed to or destroys scientific knowledge. The scientific desire, too, is that nothing be lost. But the "mystery of things" must be given up or ignored in order to produce certain kinds of knowledge, some very useful, some very destructive. Nor does art simply appear as the success in relation to science's failure. As Nietzsche himself points out, there is not "*necessarily* only an antipodal relation between Socratism and art."

As Freddie's experience of the painting in *Ghosts* does not simply discredit the experience of the painting in *The Book of Evidence,* so his experience of the woman, Flora, does not somehow reverse or make up for the crime in the earlier book. Nonetheless, in the world Banville has created, it is as close to an atonement as can be expected. We know little of Flora, except that she is young, has been hired as a nanny for the two obnoxious boys who accompany her on the boat tour, and is being pursued by the sinister, Mephistophelean Felix, another member of the tour. She comes down with a fever as soon as she arrives and stays in bed alone all day. When it is time for the group to leave, she asks Freddie two things: if she can stay on at the house when the others leave, and if Felix, who has himself been talking of staying on, will in fact be going. Freddie says yes, and this modest guarantee of a shelter and safety becomes, for a man wracked with guilt and self-doubt, a monumental act. "Something had happened," he says. A "solemn warrant had been issued on me, and I felt more than ever like the hero in a tale of chivalry commanded to perform a task of

rescue and reconciliation." Flora remains for, as nearly as we can tell, a few weeks. Other than being temporary housemates, no relationship appears to develop between her and Freddie. In fact they have apparently hardly spoken until the morning of the present moment of the telling of the story, when the climactic event occurs.

The event is singularly unsingular and yet for Freddie means everything. Flora simply begins to talk with him at breakfast. Significantly, they speak of history. "What interested her was the same thing that interested me, namely. . . . [h]ow the present feeds on the past, or versions of the past. How pieces of lost time surface suddenly in the murky sea of memory." As I noted earlier in my consideration of *The Book of Evidence,* Freddie has always felt that history, being "determined according to a random pattern," is a kind of prison. But his earlier understanding of history, as with his other understandings, has been involved with the unseen contradiction he has been living. The ineluctable mix of randomness and determinacy appears as a "prison" only from the perspective of a version of history that no longer stands as the obvious story of change over time. One quality of this moment with Flora is an acceptance of this changed notion of history: he no longer unwittingly judges this *different* understanding of history as a failed or wrong or menacing history.

The unfolding of the rich moment of knowledge reveals the conceptual depth and density of these two novels. The large-scale, structural crossover between "real" and "painting" in the book becomes integrated with a thematic crossover here at the end. The experience of the "moment" with Flora happens as a mixed return to, and surpassing of, what Freddie has experienced with both the painted portrait and the flesh-and-blood maid in *The Book of Evidence.* As with the portrait of the woman, the knowledge that matters comes "out of nowhere" and as the result of a perfectly everyday event: Flora begins to talk. But then echoing almost verbatim the moment of recognition of the maid in *The Book of Evidence,* Freddie says that "as [Flora] talked I found myself looking at her and seeing her as if for the first time." And he sees her "not as a gathering of details, but all of a piece, solid and singular," as well as "amazing," the same word he had used to describe the knowledge that flared out at him from the painting in the previous book. But then he goes on, as if now seeing the difference between the experience of being in art and the experience of being human: "No, not amazing. That is the point. She was simply there, an incarnation of herself, no longer a nexus of adjectives," such as "amazing," "but pure and present noun." He says that the event of her beginning to speak "transfigured everything," but of course it is actually he who has been changed (we have no evidence that Flora perceives any of this). For now, "by being suddenly herself like this she made the things around her be there too. In her, and in what she spoke, the world . . . found its grounding and was realised." The recognition of another human *being* can never involve simply one separate individual peering into another, like a scientist looking at a particularly amazing specimen. As Freddie himself has said of his moment with the maid, it was as much an invasion, an indecency as it was a recognition. Really to recognize a single human being is to recognize the essence of the human world in general.

Carrying forth the mix of painting and real, Freddie goes on to say, "It was as if she had dropped a condensed drop of colour into the water of the world and the colour had spread and the outlines of things had sprung into bright relief." Listening and watching, he feels "everyone and everything shiver and shift, falling into vividest forms, detaching themselves from me and my conception of them and changing themselves instead into what they were, no longer figment, no longer mystery, no longer a part of my imagining." With this summary statement, it turns out that this experience of another's being not only surpasses, as had the experience in *The Book of Evidence,* the conventions of scientific knowledge, but also the kind of imaginative knowledge that Freddie has demonstrated in his understanding of *Le Monde d'Or.* The word "vividest" specifically recalls the two previous passages in which he has lamented the failure of his imagination, so it seems that this time his imagination has not failed. But on the other hand, if the rejection of "amazing" indirectly points out the inadequacy of his understanding of the portrait in *The Book of Evidence,* the rejection of "mystery" must indirectly point out an inadequacy of his concluding assessment of the Vaublin painting (in which the "mystery of things" was preserved). And more obviously, he says outright that this experience of being does not have to do with his imagining.

So what are we to make of this? The moment combines elements of the experiences of both paintings and of the maid but seems to go beyond them. What is the extra wind that blows this experience into yet another current in the sea of knowledge? The answer comes to us only very indirectly, primarily through hints and imagery. Once again, however, it has been previsioned in *Doctor Copernicus.* At the very last, the ghost of Copernicus's brother, Andreas, says that what Copernicus has most missed is "the thing itself, the vivid thing. . . . that thing, passionate and yet calm . . . fabulous and yet ordinary. . . . Call it acceptance, call it love if you wish." And we may call the extra knowledge gained through Flora love or acceptance, as we wish. The last pages of the novel confirm this. Having taken on his "task of rescue and reconciliation," Freddie escorts the rest of the tourists back to their boat, in a replay of Watteau's *A Pilgrimage to Cythera.* "We walked down the hill road in the blued evening under the vast, light dome of sky where Venus had risen." And of course Cythera in myth is the island near which the goddess of love arose from the foam. At the very

end, we are brought to the immediate present, again some weeks after the tour group's visit and departure, and the same day on which Flora has spoken and given Freddie the experience of being that he has most wanted. Significantly, having brought about this event, she "is getting ready to leave." In the end, Freddie is, like Nietzsche, "[c]oncerned but not disconsolate" at the way things have turned out. "I shall be glad to see her go," he says. "There was never any question but that I would lift her up and let her go; what else have I been doing here but trying to beget a girl?" He imagines soon watching her, in the image of the risen Venus, "skim away over the waves." Thus we can conclude that the extra knowledge that surpasses the knowledge of art, that in its turn has surpassed Socratic knowledge, is, modestly enough, love. The difference between love in this instance as opposed to the "love" in *The Book of Evidence* is apparent.

Hopefully it need not be said, but Banville is hardly suggesting that only through brutal violence can the decentered modern human come to a healthy understanding of the self and others: violence here is not redemptive, but the sign of a horrific failure of knowledge; or as Freddie calls it, of imagination; or as we have seen in the end, of love. Rather, Banville has given us a fictional exploration of what it can be like to live life in the turbulent historical wake of the Nietzschean understanding of knowledge and desire. As with any other identifiable historical epoch, the one considered here by Banville can, and perhaps must, produce new versions of ancient forms of human ugliness and cruelty. But the epoch will just as necessarily produce new forms of beauty and charity. As always, we can depend upon literature to help us see just these truths.

FURTHER READING

Criticism

Black, Campbell. "To Act or Not." *New Statesman* 81, No. 2082 (12 February 1971): 217-18.
    Compares Banville's *Nightspawn* to a nightmare.

Levin, Martin. A review of *Birchwood,* by John Banville. *New York Times Book Review* (17 June 1973): 28.
    Asserts that in *Birchwood* Banville has employed "an unusual poetic style that makes his book fairly glow in the dark."

Prescott, Peter S. "Ultimate Designs." *Newsweek* CI, No. 18 (2 May 1983): 78.
    Asserts that Banville's *Kepler* is more of a novel than a biography, although it is historically accurate.

Walters, Margaret. "Middle Distance Man." *Observer Review* (14 September 1986): 27.
> Complains that in *Mefisto* Banville "seems to be working much too hard at his melodramas and mysteries."

Additional coverage of Banville's life and career is contained in the following sources published by Gale: *Contemporary Authors*, Vols. 117 and 128; and *Dictionary of Literary Biography*, Vol. 14.

Elizabeth Bowen
1899-1973

Anglo-Irish novelist, short story writer, essayist, nonfiction writer, autobiographer, and critic.

The following entry presents an overview of Bowen's career. For further information on her life and works, see *CLC,* Volumes 1, 3, 6, 11, 15, and 22.

INTRODUCTION

Bowen was proficient in many fictional genres, from comedies of manners to mystery stories that include elements of horror and the supernatural. All of her work, however, is strongly informed by the cultural shift toward modernism that occurred after World War I. Marked by alienation, disillusionment, and a sense that twentieth-century life was essentially monstrous, this shift was highlighted to great effect by Bowen and other writers of her generation who witnessed the comparative serenity of the Edwardian period shattered by modern warfare.

Biographical Information

Bowen was born in Dublin, Ireland, in 1899, the only child of Henry Cole Bowen and Florence Colley Brown Bowen, who traced their family history to Wales but considered themselves Anglo-Irish. Despite spending much of her early childhood in Dublin, Bowen was heavily influenced by the genteel life at her family's seventeenth-century estate, Bowen's Court, in County Cork, Ireland. In 1905 Henry Bowen suffered a nervous breakdown; unprepared to support herself and her child, Florence Bowen moved with Elizabeth to southern England, where she had family. Around this time, Bowen developed a life-long problem with stammering. When she was twelve, Bowen's father was recovering from his breakdown and planning to reunite his family in Ireland. But a year later, Bowen's mother died of cancer, leaving Bowen in the care of her aunts, who sent her to Downe House boarding school in Kent. While at Downe House, Bowen met novelist Rose Macauley, who became her mentor and introduced her to influential people in the literary community; Macauley may also have been instrumental in the publication of Bowen's first book of short stories, Encounters (1923). She continued to spend her summers at Bowen's Court with her father and one of his unmarried sisters. When Bowen finished school in 1917, she returned to Dublin to work in a hospital for shell-shocked soldiers, memories of whom remained with Bowen the rest of her life. She later infused her characters with many of their most notable traits. At the end of World War I, Bowen returned to

England to attend the London County Council School of Art, but withdrew after two terms, disappointed with her abilities in painting and drawing. When her father remarried in 1918, Bowen felt she had no focus in her life; she spent the next several years taking classes and traveling abroad with her aunts. Social and political conflict in Ireland erupted into civil war in 1921. Ancestral homes—known as the "Big Houses"—such as Bowen's Court were occupied by soldiers or burned as symbols of British oppression. Bowen's Court escaped major damage, but with the demise of other Big Houses, Bowen's world changed permanently. In 1923 she married Alan Cameron, an assistant secretary for education. Two years later, when Cameron was appointed Secretary for Education in Oxford, Bowen entered the Oxford intellectual circle, befriending many of the leading thinkers in England at the time. By the time she became the first woman in the family to inherit Bowen's Court after the death of her father in 1930, Bowen was a well-known and highly respected figure in the literary world, often compared to her friend Virginia Woolf. In 1948 Bowen was made a Commander of the British Empire and was awarded an honorary Doctor of Letters by Trinity College in Dublin in 1949. Bowen and her husband moved from London to Bowen's Court in 1952; Cameron died later that year. Bowen lived at her family estate until 1959, when she sold it. She received a Doctor of Letters from Oxford University in 1957. Several more moves and many more highly lauded published works followed. Bowen died of lung cancer in 1973.

Major Works

Bowen frequently used her own life as a starting point for her fiction. Having lived through both world wars and the Irish civil war, she had experienced the horror of war and its aftermath firsthand. Hence, many of her characters reflect her own sense of disillusionment and displacement. Her protagonists, notably in *Encounters, Ann Lee's and Other Stories* (1926), and *The Hotel* (1927), are often inexperienced young women who have been separated for from their homes and families for various reasons—sometimes deliberately—and who have failed to develop meaningful emotional attachments. *The Last September* (1929) portrays life in the Irish Big Houses during the Irish civil war. Lois Farquar desperately tries to escape the suffocating life at Danielstown, her family estate, while her uncle and his neighbors ignore the war and attempt to maintain their way of life. Eventually, Danielstown is burned by Irish rebels, and Lois is released from her emotional prison. *Friends and Relations* (1931) draws attention to upper-class society life in England. Stale, unloving marriages and the resulting infidelities appear in *Friends and Relations.* Similarly, the protagonist of *The House in Paris* (1935) makes a socially advantageous match with a man to whom she feels indifferent. When he leaves on a diplomatic assignment, she begins an affair with a friend's fiancé, which results in an unwanted pregnancy. *The Death of the Heart* (1938) returns to the plight of innocent young women without family to instruc or guide them. The most critically acclaimed of Bowen's novels, *The Death of the Heart* compares favorably to James Joyce's *Ulysses* because of its technical innovation. Her short fiction explores the sense of alienation engendered by World War I and uses elements of horror and mystery, notably in *The Cat Jumps and Other Stories* (1934), *Look at All Those Roses* (1941), and *The Demon Lover and Other Stories* (1945). Explicit reference to the widespread psychological repercussions of the first World War appears in the widely anthologized "The Demon Lover," in which a woman returns to her old home and receives a vengeful message from her fiancé, who died in the war.

Critical Reception

Bowen earned a reputation with her early work as an observer of social absurdities among the upper classes. Her comedies of manners are considered witty and delicately handled satire. Gradually, her work moved into the more serious, and tragic, realm of psychological realism, where her focus shifted to the decadent but emotionally stunted post-War period of the 1920s and 1930s in Europe and Great Britain. Bowen's novels that fall into this phase of her writing—especially *The Last September, Friends and Relations, The House in Paris,* and *The Death of the Heart*—are among her most critically admired work. However, many commentators believe Bowen's technical and artistic achievement reached its peak in her short stories, particularly the supernatural stories in *The Cat Jumps and Other Stories, Look at All Those Roses,* and *The Demon Lover and Other Stories.*

PRINCIPAL WORKS

Encounters (short stories) 1923

Ann Lee's and Other Stories (short stories) 1926

The Hotel (novel) 1927

Joining Charles and Other Stories (short stories) 1929

The Last September (novel) 1929

Friends and Relations (novel) 1931

To the North (novel) 1932

The Cat Jumps and Other Stories (short stories) 1934

The House in Paris (novel) 1935

The Death of the Heart (novel) 1938

Look at All Those Roses (short stories) 1941

Bowen's Court (nonfiction) 1942

English Novelists (criticism) 1942

Seven Winters (autobiography) 1942

The Demon Lover and Other Stories (short stories) 1945; also published as *Ivy Gripped the Steps and Other Stories*

Anthony Trollope: A New Judgement (criticism) 1946

Selected Stories (short stories) 1946

The Heat of the Day (novel) 1948

Why Do I Write? An Exchange of Views between Elizabeth Bowen, Graham Greene, and V. S. Pritchett (nonfiction) 1948

Collected Impressions (nonfiction) 1950

*Early Stories (short stories) 1951

The Shelbourne Hotel (nonfiction) 1951

A World of Love (novel) 1955

Stories (short stories) 1959

A Time in Rome (nonfiction) 1959

Afterthought: Pieces about Writing (essays and lectures) 1962

The Little Girls (novel) 1963

A Day in the Dark and Other Stories (short stories) 1965

The Good Tiger (juvenile) 1965

Eva Trout; or, Changing Scenes (novel) 1968

Pictures and Conversations (memoirs) 1975

Irish Stories (short stories) 1978

The Collected Stories of Elizabeth Bowen (short stories) 1981

The Mulberry Tree: Writings of Elizabeth Bowen (collected works) 1987

*This work contains *Encounters* and *Ann Lee's and Other Stories.*

CRITICISM

Sean O'Faolain (essay date 1948)

SOURCE: In his *The Short Story,* Devin-Adair Co., 1951, 370 p.

[*In the following excerpt from his acclaimed critical study of the short story genre first published in 1948, O'Faolain gives a detailed evaluation and appreciation of Bowen's techniques of characterization, language, and construction in "Her Table Spread."*]

"The Good Girl" is a characteristic [Elizabeth Bowen] story, among her best twelve. It is witty, malicious, intelligent, satirical, amusing. Uncle Porgie, who is not really an uncle, is Rolls-Royceing in Italy with his niece Monica, who is not his niece, and the lovely Dagmar who is not Monica's aunt though Captain Montparnesi is polite enough to pretend to think so. (We are left in no doubt as to Uncle Porgie's relations with Dagmar.) The Captain proposes to Monica who, rather helplessly, for she is a bit of a goose, permits an attachment, if not an engagement. One night she stays out late in his company—to the horror of Uncle Porgie, Dagmar and the proprietors of the hotel. Ladies and gentlemen do not do *this* sort of thing. Is not the hotel fully appointed? The gallant Captain disappears, having found that Monica is not an heiress. The 'good girl' is whirled off to Rome, very exhausted with Virtue, her own especially, and sadly sensible that it is her doom.

Now, the methods Miss Bowen employs to outline her characters—no short-story writer can do more—are of the swiftest. Monica has charm as well as virtue, we gather:

> Uncle Porgie, lifting his glass to twinkle in the pink lamplight, paid Monica tribute: "She's a damn pretty girl and a good girl, too!" Yet, all the time under the table he had been pursuing Dagmar's foot.

It is almost a statement. She is a good girl whom one admires while playing footy with some other girl. That disposes of two characters. Captain Montparnesi is outlined brutally. He proposes, he kisses Monica's hands, she asks for time to think (she would), and when she has walked away:—'Captain Montparnesi brought his pocket-book from against his heart and made some calculations.' No more need be said.

The story can now proceed to display its wit and malice at its ease, and further minor elaborations of character may be picked up on the way, or not, according as the reader is alert or merely passing the time. Thus when Monica finishes reading a book on Leonardo da Vinci (poor child) she takes a walking stick and the hotel-dog (poor child) and walks down to the lake (poor child): if you do not bother to note the little stabs you will not murmur 'poor child.' At the end of her walk

> she found mud-flats, washing, stark damp reeds, no one about. The lake was intended for distant scenery. She spoke Italian to a child who ran away, then she walked up again. On the terrace she had come upon Captain Montparnesi, engaged in sadness. He patted the dog. "I love dogs," he said: "it is almost a passion with me."

Naturally, he being a solitary man . . . and so on, with poor Monica gulping it all in. Or one may appreciate her natural resentment at Dagmar's smooth progress through the bewildering narrows of passion where she alone is lost; or Uncle Porgie's kindness in giving her a pair of coral ear-rings, since a good girl must have some compensations; or we may be amused by Captain Montparnesi's solemn family-council. But, whatever one does or does not find amusing and illuminating, one cannot fail to observe that this entire comedy creates its illusion with a minimum of characterisation.

[Bowen's **"Her Table Spread"**] compresses into the usual modern length of three thousand words material for which Turgenev would have needed twice or three times the space. The scene is Ireland, a castle on the coast, a rainy summer night, the candle-lit dinner table, a friendly party which includes the unromantic Mr. Alban from London, whom the heiress Valeria Cuffe is vaguely expected to marry. In the bay there is a British destroyer whose ambience, all the more romantic by its nearness combined with its inaccessibility, emotionally disturbs them all. Valeria is especially affected. She is a very romantic young lady indeed who has, apparently, dreamed much of 'the Navy' and of marrying one Mr. Garrett who had visited them the previous Easter, when another destroyer was anchored in the estuary. Mr. Alban plays Mendelssohn, and then a Viennese waltz, while Valeria, now quite overbalanced, rushes out into the wet bushes to look at the misty portholes, and hug her dreams under the leaves in the moist night-air, and wave a mad lantern out to the rain-pocked sea. Her uncle and poor, abandoned, self-pitying, civilian Mr. Alban go in agitation to the boat-house to search for her. There is a bottle of whisky in the boat and a bat in the rafters, and the uncle talks of marriage and the parlour-maid. The Irish are, it is evident to Mr. Alban from London, just as dotty as people say. He flies from the bat and the bottle, and runs into Valeria, now beside herself, crying joyously that Mr. Garrett has landed; indeed Mr. Alban *is*

Mr. Garrett. It becomes a moment when even Mr. Alban is unmanned and manned, a fleeting mad moment of sheer abandonment to the excitement of the dark, wet summer's night, the creaking satin and the bare shoulders of the woman, a moment of rampant Celtic emotion. . . . The story concludes, or rather exhausts itself:

> Perhaps it was best for them all that early, when next day first lightened the rain, the destroyer steamed out—below the extinguished Castle where Valeria lay with her arms wide, past the boat-house where Mr. Rossiter lay insensible and the bat hung masked in its wings—down the estuary to the open sea.

The compression of this story is in such enormous degree due to the suggestive style (e.g. a word like 'extinguished' above, saves a whole phrase; or the word 'lightened,' which gives a double sense of brightness and diminution) that we should keep this most difficult part of the analysis for [a discussion of language]. When we try to separate construction from situation the subtle management of the tale likewise resists dissection. I have long wondered whether the situation, the group, the place, or the atmosphere may have been felt first by the author; and whether Valeria came first, or Mr. Alban, and felt that nobody would ever know, least of all the author; for the story has such thirst and urge that it looks as if it had sprung from Jove's forehead fully armed, complete when first conceived. When I asked Miss Bowen this question she said that she saw a castle like this and wanted at once to write 'something' about it; only a somewhat odd and rather dotty girl seemed to fit the mood of the place. The 'mood'? But whose mood? We are back at the indefinable; a writer's own personality seeing things in her own unique way.

One may appreciate the cohesion of **"Her Table Spread"** by trying to imagine the story as Turgenev might have written it: the lonely girl (*a*), the remote place (*b*), the timid suitor (*c*), the anxious aunt (*d*), the Navy arriving (*e*)—step by step, leaf laid on delicate leaf, lyric note on lyric note. Here all occurs together. The three unities of Place, Time and Character weld everything like a handgrip. For Place we keep to the castle dining-room, with a slight extension in lamplight to the garden (and for Mr. Alban and Mr. Rossiter a slightly wider but brief extension to the boathouse), all but Mr. Rossiter coming back to the dining-room for the climax. For Time, all occurs within about an hour, possibly two, except for the epilogue I have quoted, which passes to the following dawn. For character Alban is the focus. I cannot explain how much skill all this involves without a digression to what, for convenience, I call the technique of the camera-angle.

By camera-angle I mean the technique by which the writer of short-stories 'sights' his characters one by one without creating an uncomfortable feeling that we are wandering all over the caste; and without breaking the form of the story. As we read a short-story by Maupassant, or Chekov, or O. Henry, or Frank O'Connor, or Liam O'Flaherty, or A. E. Coppard—and as I mention the names a score or more of their stories pass quickly before me—we do not notice how the mental camera moves, withdraws to a distance to enclose a larger view, slips deftly from one character to another, while all the time holding one main direction of which these are only variations. This mobility as to the detail combined with the rigidity of the general direction is one of the great technical pleasures of the modern short-story. . . .

This matter of the angle is paramount. It is a way of answering the question, 'What is the story about?' without being too obvious in the answer. So, I remember reading a story somewhere about a daughter which was really a story about the father, as did not appear until the last few lines. Or, in that story of Chekov's *Gooseberries,* the story was ostensibly about one man, and was so, but when we close the book we find that the narrator, the brother of the subject of the tale, has also unconsciously been revealing himself. . . .

Having explained what I mean by camera-angle we can now come back to **"Her Table Spread,"** and observe how Elizabeth Bowen, while presenting a number of characters, has kept her Unity of Character. I have said that Alban is the focus. The story opens with him. 'Alban had few opinions on the subject of marriage . . .' When the other characters steal into the story we may still feel that it is he who is observing them; some reaction from him is indicated in each paragraph to convey this impression of his pervasiveness. The fourth paragraph breaks into conversation, and the atmosphere of excitement is gradually released. Conversation is every writer's favourite way of escaping from his centre to his circumference. Everybody may share it. All overhear. The writer vanishes. And Mr. Alban may see as well as hear. They have been speaking of the Navy's visit last Easter:

> Will they remember? Valeria's bust was almost on the table. But with a rustle Mrs. Treve pressed Valeria's toe. For the dining-room also looked out across the estuary, and the great girl had not once taken her eyes from the window. Perhaps it was unfortunate that Mr. Alban should have coincided with the destroyer. Perhaps it was unfortunate for Mr. Alban too. For he saw now he was less than half the feast. . .

That rustle of Mrs. Treve's skirt is delicate. He could have heard that. One may presume that he looked up and saw Valeria staring out of the window. The next two sentences belong to anybody. Mrs. Treve's thought? Guessed at by Mr. Alban? They are interesting sentences, technically, because they illustrate how a writer may, having slipped his camera across a scene which includes the main character, quietly pick up other characters on the way. There is, as it were, an elastic bond of thought that ties us to the main character; we may stray from him quite a distance.

There is a nice example of this gentle truancy in the paragraph which follows; the reader will observe the sentence where we slip from Alban to their thoughts of him, and, later, where the writer slips in her own comment on him. (Valeria has meanwhile skipped out into the garden.)

> In the drawing-room, empty of Valeria, the standard-lamps had been lit. Through their ballet-skirt shades, rose and lemon, they gave out a deep welcoming light. Alban, at the ladies' invitation, undraped the piano. He played, but they could see he was not pleased. It was obvious he had always been a civilian, and when he had taken his place on the piano-stool—which he twirled around three times rather fussily—his dinner-jacket wrinkled across his shoulders. It was sad they should feel indifferent, for he came from London. Mendelssohn was exasperating to them—they opened all four windows to let the music downhill. They preferred not to draw the curtains; the air, though damp, being pleasant tonight, they said.

To be sure, we do *not,* in reading for pleasure, observe anything very technical here. It would be obtrusive technique if we did. Indeed, it would not be technique at all since the function of technique is to create illusion, not to break illusion by poking its nose through it. There are hints and suggestions in that paragraph which we will quite unwittingly take; for example, they do not listen well—they get up in the middle of the music to open windows; they speak of the weather. There is more to it than that. They are troubled by Valeria's behaviour and seek to excuse it. 'The air is damp, but it's pleasant,' they said. It is natural for Valeria to have wished to stroll in it. This is true short-story writing; beautiful suggestibility all through.

The camera has stayed long enough away from Alban, so the next sentence returns full-face. 'The piano was damp but Alban played all his heart out ...' etc. 'The piano was damp.' What compression of suggestion there! This is genuine poetic realism. Damp. The wet night. Neglect all round. The untended castle. And poor Alban playing his civilian heart out on the damp keys while they chatter. More general conversation allows the camera to wander again and this time the atmosphere becomes hysterical, and floating away on it, in the middle of a waltz played by Mr. Alban (still, doubtless, brooding on himself, on her, on everything), Valeria is given the stage, racing past the window with her mad lantern. This is the most daring part of the story, and it comes off. She has robbed the stage from Alban and done

it triumphantly. After two pages in which she and her crazy romantic dreams hold all our interest we return to Alban. He and the uncle go down to the boat-house in the rain after her and there is some secret drinking and maudlin chatter about marriage. When he flies from the boat-house he and she will rush into one another in the darkness, and she will take him into her dream and he will, in his woe and excitement, respond to her wild fancy and the climax will mount and topple. That moment is an emotional *tour de force.*

> **... Elizabeth Bowen was probably unaware of her own cleverness in all this; long practice, a gift of emotional combustibility, a great gift of words, an eye of a hawk, a special sympathy for the Valeria type—in one form or another Valeria turns up in all Miss Bowen's novels—combined to cast this perfectly fashioned story as freely and as unconsciously and as perfectly and as successfully as a fisherman casts his invisible line. ...**
> **—*Sean O'Faolain***

Not until we are thinking back on the story, perhaps days after, do we realise that it all began and ended with Mr. Alban, and yet was called **"Her Table Spread."** It had been a story about a *girl's* romance all the time.

Naturally, Elizabeth Bowen was probably unaware of her own cleverness in all this; long practice, a gift of emotional combustibility, a great gift of words, an eye of a hawk, a special sympathy for the Valeria type—in one form or another Valeria turns up in all Miss Bowen's novels—combined to cast this perfectly fashioned story as freely and as unconsciously and as perfectly and as successfully as a fisherman casts his invisible line. ...

Here is the opening of ["Her Table Spread"]. ... What individual words in the opening passage strike us by their suggestiveness?:

> Alban had few opinions on the subject of marriage; his attitude to women was negative but in particular he was not attracted to Miss Cuffe. Coming down early for dinner, red satin dress cut low, she attacked the silence with loud laughter before he had spoken. He recollected having heard that she was abnormal—at twenty-five, of statuesque development, still detained in childhood ...

For me the word 'red' seems deliberately chosen. It may, lightly, suggest Miss Cuffe's dramatic taste in dress. The word 'attacked' (the silence) suggests her strident personality; the word 'recollected' implies that Alban is disturbed, thinks back, perks up, is suddenly alert. The word 'detained' in childhood has ominous undertones as applied to this slightly batty lady. It suggests the dog-house.

This language of undertones is Miss Bowen's specialty. Thus, when Miss Cuffe becomes 'preoccupied' with attempts at gravity we may see her as looking even more vacant in her efforts to look less flighty. When Mr. Alban begins to feel miserable by this 'indifferent shore' the adjective has a treble meaning—heedless, not so hopeless, quite hopeless. When Miss Cuffe proposes a row in the bay, rain or no rain, and the ladies 'produced indignation' we may feel that even these dotty Irish ladies are not wholly averse to the idea which they condemn; they have to force their indignation.

As the excitement mounts the language becomes more and more charged and less and less literal. Mr. Alban's state of mind is proposed metaphorically.

> Wandering among the apples and amphoras of an art school he had blundered into the life room; woman revolved gravely. "Hell," he said to the steps, mounting, his mind blank to the outcome.

Words now begin to extend freely, quite dilated.

> Behind, through the windows, lamps spread great skirts of light, and Mars and Mercury, unable to contain themselves, stooped from their pedestals. . . . Close by Valeria's fingers creaked on her warm wet satin. She laughed like a princess, magnificently justified. Their unseen faces were all three lovely, and, in the silence after the laughter, such a strong tenderness reached him that, standing there in full manhood, he was for a moment not exiled. For the moment, without moving or speaking, he stood, in the dark, in a flame, as though all three said, "My darling . . ."

Elsewhere in the story 'a smothered island' gives an immediate bosky effect without labouring for the picture. We see, or do not see, an 'extinguished Castle.' The striking image of 'The bat hung masked in its wings' is a sentence which gives the clue: this is the language of poetry magnificently taken over by prose. 'La poésie ne consiste pas,' says Saint Beuve, 'à tout dire mais à tout faire rêver.'

It is difficult to find a label for this modern use of English. Some of it is frankly neologistic. Some almost catachresis, or extravagant metaphor: cf. our now-common use of the word to 'jockey'; Miss Bowen's 'attacked' the silence. Most of it is what is technically known as radiation of meaning,

which is not only legitimate but the normal process of dilating language in poetry.

> By a succession of radiations the development of meaning may become almost infinitely complex. No dictionary can ever register a tithe of them, for, so long as language is alive, every speaker is constantly making new specialised amplifications of its words. . . . The limits of the definition must always be vague and even within these limits there is always scope for variety. If the speaker does not transgress these limits in a given instance we understand his meaning. . . . He has given us a conventional sign or symbol of his idea. Our interpretation of the sign will depend partly on the context, partly on what we know of the speaker, partly on the associations which we ourselves attach to the word . . . [In a footnote, the critic attributes the quote to Greenough and Kittredge, *Words and Their Ways in English* (1926).]

All these three elements are at work in the witty phrase 'detained in childhood,' with its radiated meanings: that Miss Cuffe has got stuck (in the queue), is engaged (in the nursery), has not been allowed to proceed (by Nursey), or is already in the Big House.

It may be said that such use of language does not make for clarity; it does not. Neither does it make pictures; it is impressionistic, in letters a special feminine strength or weakness. It makes stringent demands on the wit and the intelligence lest it become just too, too clever or an end in itself, or 'transgress the limits.' Yet in this language some of the wittiest things in English have been written and without it we should not have had the romantic music of such as Carlyle or Browne. Its value for the writer of short-stories is at least indisputable in one respect: so alert a language helps to make short-stories shorter. . . .

Sean O'Faolain (essay date 1956)

SOURCE: "Elizabeth Bowen; or, Romance Does Not Pay," in *The Vanishing Hero: Studies in Novelists of the Twenties,* Eyre & Spottiswoode, 1956, pp. 167-90.

[*In the following excerpt, O'Faolain asserts that Bowen's writing was influenced by her Anglo-Irish background and its accompanying sense of exile. O'Faolain also considers Bowen's relationship to the French novelist and short story writer Gustave Flaubert and discusses Bowen as a romantic in an anti-romantic age.*]

Elizabeth Bowen is detached by birth from that society she

describes. She is an Irishwoman, at least one sea apart from English traditions. She descends from that sturdy and creative sub-race we call the Anglo-Irish. At least a part of her literary loyalties are with that long and honourable pedigree that goes back through Shaw, Joyce, George Moore, Somerville and Ross, Yeats, Wilde, Goldsmith, Sheridan, Burke, Swift and Berkeley to the forced marriage of two races, two islands. . . .

The effects of this detachment seem to be mainly two. Malice would naturally be more free, and the play of sentiment more indulgent. It is a nice ambivalence. No English writer can have quite the same liberty. . . .

Miss Bowen is indebted to another influence besides her race and her exile to stiffen her own natural, shrewd intelligence, her own natural integrity as an observer. This is the early influence of Flaubert. And when we recall the romantic-realist conflict within Flaubert we may see another reason for thinking of Elizabeth Bowen as a bifrontine writer. The conflict in her work is, in fact, not dissimilar. She wavers between two methods of approach.

The essence of her way of seeing life is that, like the singer who was supposed to be able to break a champagne glass by singing at it, she exposes the brittleness of romance by soliciting it ruthlessly. Time, for her characters, is very far removed from Faulkner's continuum, or Hemingway's feeling for events enclosed-at-both-ends. It is a brittle moment, snatched from fate. Happiness in her novels is rapt away, shop-lifted, and always dearly paid for. God is the shopwalker who makes her characters pay, and we vulgar citizens, the run-of-the-mill of ordinary people, decent fathers of families, impatient of all youthful aberrations cannot deny His justice.

Happiness may even have to be snatched between the moments. She pursues these golden if elusive hours on behalf of her heroines. So, in *The Last September* Francie Montmorency found that during her honeymoon time had been "loose-textured, had had a shining undertone, happiness glittered between the moments". In *To the North* when Cecilia returns to her flat and looks about her at the unfamiliar-familiar . . . "Life here, still not quite her own, kept for those few moments unknown tranquillity." Happiness is thus interleaved in the book of life. It is a bonus, a wad of dollars smuggled through the customs of life. But to go after this happiness too hard is, one is led to feel, to wrench from life something that it can only give arbitrarily like a Fairy Godmother. One is not therefore surprised to discover that there is nothing of the Hemingwayan will in her characters. They may seem wilful; they are, in practice, the passive recipients of fate. All they receive from fate is passion, and this receipt is like a soldier's calling-to-the-colours. Her characters are conscripted by passion into action. Once in ac-

tion they fight well, but what Arnold said of the Celt may be said of them: they go into battle and they always fall. It is true that they may also and for long have desired passion, but the desire is never so powerful as the impulse of chance. Her characters are all played upon.

> There is an atmosphere of ancient fable behind all of Miss Bowen's fiction. Her persons are recognisable temperaments rather than composed characters. . . . Her characters are the modern, sophisticated, naturalistic novelist's versions of primitive urges. One feels that if she had lived three hundred and fifty years ago when passions rode freely and fiercely she would have described the dreams that drove Ophelia, Juliet and Desdemona to love and to death. . . .
>
> —*Sean O'Faolain*

There is a short story in her second book, *Ann Lee's,* written before she had published her first novel, which neatly illustrates this fateful element in all her later work. It is called **"The Parrot"**. A young girl, Eleanor Fitch, is a companion to an old lady, Mrs Willesden, in whose life nothing ever happens. One morning Eleanor accidentally lets her old lady's parrot fly away. She pursues the gaudy bird in its wayward flight from garden to garden until it pauses in the garden of a Mr Lennicott, a novelist of doubtful repute according to Mrs Willesden. Palpitating, Eleanor enters the garden of this fabulous person, enters his house, meets him in his dressing-gown, has the great adventure of capturing the multi-coloured bird with his assistance. When Lennicott kindly wishes to detain her, offering her fruit, she refuses. "Nobody had ever reached out for her like that so eagerly; she did not want to go back to that house of shut-out sunshine and great furniture where the parrot was royally carried from room to room on trays, and where she was nothing." Eleanor goes back unscathed to her dull routine, thinking: "How world overlapped with world; visible each from the other, yet never to be one."

Now, I have a profound suspicion of that technique of criticism which elucidates the interior meaning of stories, and the secret meanings of an author's mind, by his unconscious use of symbols, but whether this brilliant and far-faring bird luring a potential Proserpine from garden to garden to the haunts of Pluto is or is not—and I think it is—in the full tradition of Flaubertian symbolism (the blueness of Emma Bovary's dream-curtains suggesting the Virgin; and such-like symbols) one may fairly use this fable as a symbol of one of Miss Bowen's favoured types: the dreaming but recusant girl. Longing but vigilant, troubled by her own eagerness, she will, one fine day, follow the bright bird of her dreams into the woods of life and suffer the fate of Proserpine, or worse. There is an atmosphere of ancient fable behind all of Miss Bowen's fiction. Her persons are recognisable temperaments rather than composed characters. Flaubert merely overlays the fabulous. Her characters are the modern, sophisticated, naturalistic novelist's versions of primitive urges. One feels that if she had lived three hundred and fifty years ago when passions rode freely and fiercely she would have described the dreams that drove Ophelia, Juliet and Desdemona to love and to death. . . .

Elizabeth Bowen is a romantic up against the despotism of reality. So many other Irish writers are. The metallic brilliance, even the occasional jarring brassiness and jauntiness of her style is, in an admirable sense, a fake, a deceptive cocoon wrapped about the central precious, tender thing. One could imagine a hare settling into her form, a sticky little leveret between her paws, or perhaps a lioness growling over her young. It is the growl of *Ich grolle nicht,* the Flaubertian coldness imposed on Irish feeling, and the theme is so heartbreaking that it would be embarrassing if she were not tight-lipped about those heroines who just do not know what o'clock it is once love enters their unwary lives. She writes of romantic heroines in an age that has made the two words pejorative. The underlying assumptions here are very much of the Twenties. The conflicts are no longer clear enough to justify bold affirmations, positive statements of loyalty, straight fights or declared aims or ends. Miss Bowen's heroines are, after all, always defeated. In Mauriac's phrase their beauty is borrowed from despair. Not, as we have seen, that she is anti-heroic, but that she must state coldly that heroism, the absolute aim, does not stand a chance in modern society, even while she still insists passionately that it is always worth while to try. She has not assumed that we must therefore reject tradition, but she is plainly unenthusiastic about it. She does not assume that violence is the only possible alternative in fiction to thought. She does not assume that the intellect must be abdicated by the modern novelist. She hovers patiently over her subjects. But the prime technical characteristic of her work, as of other modern women writers, such as Virginia Woolf, is that she fills the vacuum which the general disintegration of belief has created in life by the pursuit of sensibility. It is a highly sophisticated pursuit. Sometimes it is over-conscious and overdone.

Her sensibility can be witty; it can also be catty, even brassy, too smart like an over-clever *décor* for a ballet. I do not mind that it is, to my taste, on occasion vulgar, though not quite in the sense in which her young girls are vulgar. She has defended, or at least pleaded, for sympathy with vulgarity, and are there not times when good taste is itself a little vulgar? One thinks of the ghastly good taste of Mr Charles Morgan. But what one means by finding this kind of good taste rather vulgar is that it is bloodless, and that one longs occasion-

ally for a good, warm, passionate howl like an Italian mother baying over her dead child. This sort of earthiness is outside the range of any English-trained writer. When Elizabeth Bowen is dealing with elemental things she skirts around them with too much elegance. There are certain things she will not deign to describe. The actual falling in love of her people is one. . . .

The one place where she is really earthy is when she is being humorous, and would, many times over, that she were humorous more often, for when she is being humorous she is also most human. Louie in *The Heat of the Day* is not only good fun but real; down to earth; far more so than Robert, Harrison and Stella pirouetting about each other exhaustingly. Yet, to take a fair measure of the humanity (as against the elegance) of her sensibilities, one may compare them with the sensibilities of Virginia Woolf whose antennae are as sensitive as remote radar, but who reacts not so much to human beings as to things and "states of mind". Miss Bowen is also responsive to things and states of mind, but she responds chiefly, and warmly, to her own favoured types of people. "Things," Mrs Woolf characteristically makes Terence Hewitt say in *The Voyage Out,* "things I feel come to me like lights. I want to combine them. Have you ever seen fireworks that make figures? I want to make figures." That also, to my taste, is a form of vulgarity through elegance. Miss Bowen would never be quite so refined. She wants to make people not figures, to put them into conflict with society, and her explorations of their feelings are never just an exploitation of her own.

Her outer-imposed limitations do, nevertheless, obtrude themselves. *The Death of the Heart* was, indeed, a firm and passionately felt protest against the modern desiccation of feeling, but one could not help noting that it offered no moral approach to the problem: meaning that it intimated no norm to set against the subnormal. But can one reasonably blame Miss Bowen for this? We are brought back by this longing for a norm to the death of the traditional Hero, that symbol of the norm in all traditional literature. She, too, can only present us with the martyr in place of the Hero, the representative not of the norm but of the disease. Greene's alternative is God. Miss Bowen is too deeply rooted in the great, central humanist tradition of European culture to take refuge in hereafters. What she directs our eyes towards is the malady of our times that breaks the dreaming and gallant few. It is what her master Flaubert did with Emma Bovary, more ruthlessly. She has described the dilemma of our times honestly, beautifully and at times movingly. To have done so much, and done it so well, is to have done a great deal. . . .

Jeslyn Medoff (essay date Spring 1984)

SOURCE: "'There Is No Elsewhere': Elizabeth Bowen's Perceptions of War," in *Modern Fiction Studies,* Vol. 30, No. 1, Spring, 1984, pp. 73-81.

[*In the following essay, Medoff examines Bowen's descriptions of life during wartime in her short fiction.*]

On book application forms at the British Library there occasionally appears this notation: "It is regretted that this work was destroyed by bombing in the war; we have not been able to acquire a replacement." This statement serves as a reminder of the irreparable damages of war, which destroys history even as it is created. The intricate fabric of British history, woven with a sense of cultural permanence, was burned through during the Blitz. Lives were lost, books were burned, works of art and architecture vanished, a way of life disappeared. Even amid this destruction, however, creativity continued. Elizabeth Bowen's wartime short stories speak to later generations, answering the question: "what must it have been like to live in that place at that time?"

Eudora Welty aptly expressed an appreciation of Bowen's skill: "Elizabeth Bowen's awareness of place, of *where she was,* seemed to approach the seismetic; it was equaled only by her close touch with the passage, the pulse, of time."
—*Jeslyn Medoff*

A chronicler of life during the bombing, Bowen recorded the emotional and psychological tenor of a city under siege. She was specially qualified for this task, working as an ARP warden and narrowly missing death when her Regent's Park home was bombed. But the "action" of wartime London, people scurrying to bomb shelters, corpses lying in the streets, children crying in the night, is not the stuff of Bowen's fictional documentary. Instead her war manifests itself in strained social encounters, in changing mores, in the dreams and memories of shattered psyches. Already a respected author, recognized for the "comedy of manners" of her novels and early short stories, Bowen transcends that category with these wartime works, showing in her mature and subtle style a gift for treating serious issues and a mastery of her craft.

A great deal has been written on Bowen's art as demonstrated in her novels; far less attention has been paid to her short stories. The recent publication in America of her collected stories provides a perspective for the study of Bowen's canon. In her review of the collection, Eudora Welty aptly expressed an appreciation of Bowen's skill: "Elizabeth Bowen's awareness of place, of *where she was,* seemed to approach the seismetic; it was equaled only by her close

touch with the passage, the pulse, of time." She is indeed a gifted fabricator of atmosphere and climate, both psychological and physical. An examination of three stories—one set in Ireland during the early years of war, another in the heart of London in the midst of war, and a third in the city just after V. E. day—provides at once an understanding of Bowen's wartime perceptions and an appreciation of her artistry as short-story writer.

In the neutral Ireland of **"Summer Night,"** everyday· life continues uninterrupted; beneath the calm surface, however, the reverberations of war's destructiveness and moral disintegration are palpable. Peace and beauty exist as mirages. In the opening paragraph a bright, burning reality contrasts with a golden other-worldliness:

> As the sun set its light slowly melted the landscape, till everything was made of fire and glass. Released from the glare of noon, the haycocks now seemed to float on the aftergrass: their freshness penetrated the air. In the not far distance hills with woods up their flanks lay in light like hills in another world— it would be a pleasure of heaven to stand up there, where no foot ever seemed to have trodden, on the spaces between the woods soft as powder dusted over with gold. Against those hills, the burning red rambler roses in cottage gardens along the roadside looked earthy—they were too near the eye.

Light, color, and texture create landscapes in two different worlds. The first is one of escape. The hills are those of "another world . . . a pleasure of heaven." Haycocks are "released," floating as the landscape melts. All "in the not far distance" is "soft as powder dusted over with gold." Fresh air carries the pleasing scent of hay. But closer in, by the road, burn "earthy" roses "too near the eye," part of a more tangible world. The senses—sight, smell, nearly even touch—are alive and alert. The hills also seem alive, like animals, possessing "flanks." In this beautifully constructed paragraph Bowen foreshadows the perspective afforded the characters in **"Summer Night."** A look at life close up is, at the very least, disconcerting; one looks with pleasure only into the distance of memories, dreams, and illusions.

Through this peaceful landscape speeds Emma, a married woman anxiously en route to a rendezvous with her lover. Emma envisions her encounter with her ever-practical, more experienced lover as a romantic adventure. That illusion is dispelled later when she realizes that she is "being settled down to as calmly as he might settle down to a meal." The distant dream is converted, close up, into a much colder reality. The idealistic immaturity that Emma has harbored and cherished dies: "The adventure (even, the pilgrimage) died at its root, in the childish part of her mind. . . . She thought for a minute he had broken her heart, and she knew now he had broken her fairy tale."

Emma's romantic adventure, like the strange summer night, affects others in her life. Back home in her bed, Emma's little girl, Vivie, responds to the night in her own way. "One arbitrary line only divided this child from the animal: all her senses stood up, wanting to run the night." She impishly strips off her nightclothes, chalks colorful snakes and stars on her body, and dances wildly on her mother's empty bed. Savage young Vivie responds to the night in a sensuous way that unwittingly imitates her mother's own pursuit of pleasure and release. Her flame is extinguished when great-Aunt Fran envelopes her in a proper pink eider-down, makes her say prayers, and sends her back to bed.

The disintegration of life as it once was, represented by Emma's extramarital affair, is inseparable from war. Old Aunt Fran senses that something is not quite right about Emma's trip away from home, about the world, about the night. Disturbed by the unsettling evening, she tries to pray and to sleep, but she cannot:

> The blood of the world is poisoned, feels Aunt Fran.... There are no more children: the children are born knowing.... There is not even the past: our memories share with us the infected zone; not a memory does not lead up to this. Each moment is everywhere, it holds the war in its crystal; there is no elsewhere; no other place.... What is the matter tonight—is there a battle? This is a threatened night.

Aunt Fran mourns the loss of innocence of the young, "born knowing." All is now tainted by the war; there is no purity, no past, no holiness. "Each moment ... holds the war in its crystal," and the war, in turn, holds everything in its grasp. Something infectious is in the air; it is war.

A fourth perception of the night is offered in the dreams of middle-aged Queenie, a quiet, deaf, pretty woman who has paid Emma's lover a social call just before Emma's arrival. In her silent world, solitary, chaste Queenie is the only character affected calmly by the night. Her experience balances Aunt Fran's feeling that memories are no longer·possible. She drifts off to sleep, ending the story with her peaceful dream:

> This was the night she knew she would find again. It had stayed living under a film of time. On just such a summer night, once only, she had walked with a lover in the demesne.... That had been twenty years ago, till tonight when it was now.

The best elements of Bowen's short-story writing are found here: the delicate and subtle creation of environment, a blurring of margins between the real and the unreal, the destruction of a romantic ideal, the perspectives of sensitive female characters who seem to function as emotional barometers. Bowen exercises a steady though unobtrusive control over her subject and theme. Through the many impressive images of **"Summer Night"** one never loses grasp of the story's major thread: summer night, not-so-distant war, a household without its mistress, a shattered illusion. Ireland hardly seems "neutral." There is no escape; war pervades the environment like the night. Only Queenie, living in "a world to herself," finds peace in distant dreams. Life, close up, burns like "red rambler roses," like Vivie's flushed little form.

A story comparable to **"Summer Night"** is **"Mysterious Kôr,"** the last story in the early collection *The Demon Lover*. This tale is the highwater mark in Bowen's self-defined "rising tide of hallucination." The wave of illusion and dreams in the original collection crests in this story, one of Bowen's best. As in **"Summer Night,"** the story's power is evident in the opening paragraph:

> Full moonlight drenched the city and searched it; there was not a niche left to stand in. The effect was remorseless: London looked like the moon's capital—shallow, cratered, extinct. It was late, but not yet midnight; now the buses had stopped the polished roads and streets in this region sent for minutes together a ghostly unbroken reflection up. The soaring new flats and the crouching old shops and houses looked equally brittle under the moon, which blazed in windows that looked its way. The futility of the black-out became laughable: from the sky, presumably, you could see every slate in the roofs; every whited kerb, every contour of the naked winter flowerbeds in the park; and the lake, with its shining twists and tree-darkened islands would be a landmark for miles, yes, miles, overhead.

Here Bowen distinguishes three cities: the "real" London; the London that is the "moon's capital"; and the London that strangely combines both the real and the unreal, that place the reader will come to know as **"Mysterious Kôr."** Time is also carefully presented. "Late, but not yet midnight" reveals the time of night; the reference to a blackout gives the story its place in the century; "naked winter flowerbeds" establishes the season. Like the opening passage from **"Summer Night,"** evocation of atmosphere and the juxtaposition of reality and illusion prefigure the experiences of the characters. The theme of **"Mysterious Kôr,"** survival in fantastic conditions, is presented in five succinct sentences.

Appropriately, Bowen employs the light of the moon, a traditional symbol of fantasy and magic, to create atmosphere. Like the sunset on Irish hills, the near-midnight moonlight creates another world. In a less sinister but equally powerful way, the searching, drenching moonlight pursues the city as German bombers might. The city lies stretched out beneath its full impact; the moon is "full," "remorseless," blazing. All else is "polished," "shining," "whited," "ghostly," "brittle," "naked." London is a corpse, or perhaps T. S. Eliot's "evening . . . spread out against the sky / Like a patient etherized upon a table." A similar sense of desolation, passivity, and sterility is conveyed in the prose. Human action is mocked by the moon: "The futility of the black-out became laughable." London is truly leveled by the moon's strength. Whether "soaring" or "crouching," buildings look alike; every nook, cranny, and "niche" has disappeared. Depth cannot be found on earth but in the sky above, which reaches "miles, yes, miles, overhead." The moon's-eye-view, like a camera, sweeps across the city's once-varied levels all at once; roofs, curbs, flowerbeds, the lake all meld to form one shadow reflection of their purveyor. The moon creates a futuristic city, exposing the ultimate threat of this world war, that the earth may become a barren planet, another reflector, like the moon, "shallow, cratered, extinct."

But the moon is no collaborator. It is its own power. The political enemy is absent from this picture:

> However, the sky, in whose glassiness floated no clouds but only opaque balloons, remained glassy-silent. The Germans no longer came by the full moon. Something more immaterial seemed to threaten, and to be keeping people at home. This day between days, this extra tax, was perhaps more than senses and nerves could bear. People stayed indoors with a fervour that could be felt: the buildings strained with battened-down human life, but not a beam, not a voice, not a note from a radio escaped. Now and then under streets and buildings the earth rumbled: the Underground sounded loudest at this time.

Life in London is almost unbearably tense and feverish. The "extra tax," the strain, the tangible "fervour" are all shut up within. Dwellings teem with human inhabitants, "battened-down human life," like ships' holds in a storm-tossed sea. The sky, now "glassy," is as silent as the world's surface; it is the earth beneath that rumbles. This second paragraph communicates a feeling of repression and imprisonment more than of sterility and desolation. Life, here insulated and enclosed, goes on despite threats of bombs or "something more immaterial."

Into this unnatural, surreal scene, up from the Underground, emerge a girl and a soldier with nowhere to go. Glancing around the city Pepita shares her vision with boyfriend Arthur, baptizing this new place "mysterious Kôr." When Arthur protests that there is no such place, Pepita explains:

> What it tries to say doesn't matter: I see what it makes me see. . . . This war shows we've by no means come to the end. If you can blow whole places out of existence, you can blow whole places into it. . . . By the time we've come to the end, Kôr may be the one city left: The abiding city.

The vision to which Pepita so tenaciously clings, her fantasy city, is a sort of spiritual bomb shelter, a place for the soul to seek safety when there is literally no refuge for the body.

Pepita's device for escape contrasts with that of her roommate, Callie, with whom Pepita and Arthur will have to share a small flat that night. Virginal Callie, "the guardian of that ideality which for Pepita was constantly lost to view," is "sedate, waxy and tall—an unlit candle," like that other symbol of purity for which she seems to be named, the calla lily. Callie hides within her naiveté, her innocence, her "still unsought-out state." She reacts to the moonlight with a half-formed understanding. "At once she knew that something was happening—outdoors, in the street, the whole of London, the world. An advance, an extraordinary movement was silently taking place." Callie copes with the bombed-out world not by escaping through fantasy but by seeing that world only partially—through a veil of inexperience. The ironies of a suppressed life do not strike her as strongly as they do Pepita because she has not yet begun to live fully. When Pepita and Arthur arrive at the flat, Callie's old-fashioned expectation that she will share a bed with her roommate kills any hope that the other two may have had for lovemaking. Betrayed by the radiance of the moon and by Callie's ingenuousness, and unable to find a dark corner, the young couple settle down to sleep in separate beds.

In the middle of the night, when Arthur wakes from a restless sleep, Callie joins him for a brief conversation in the dark. Arthur tries to explain how the night and Pepita's vision have affected his fatalism:

> "A game's a game, but what's a hallucination? You begin by laughing, then it gets in you and you can't laugh it off. . . . Now I see why she sleeps like that if that's where she goes. . . . when two people have got no place, why not want Kôr, as a start? There are no restrictions on wanting, at any rate."

> "But, oh, Arthur, can't wanting want what's human?"

> He yawned. "To be human's to be at a dead loss."

To have lived in that place at that time, according to Bowen, one would have been forced to seek shelter. One shelters oneself in naiveté and innocence, if possible; if not, one can try dreams, dreams so powerful they exist even in waking hours. Neither innocent nor dreaming, Arthur states the wisdom of the disenchanted, the harsh fatalism of a restricted, seemingly doomed generation. His view of life impinges on Callie's world, bringing about a loss of innocence. Marking the waning of the moon, Callie returns to her bed, thinking:

> . . . it seemed likely that there would never be such a moon again; and on the whole she felt this was for the best. . . . she tried to compose her limbs; even they quivered after Arthur's words in the dark. . . . The loss of her own mysterious expectation, her love of love, was a small thing beside the war's total of unlived lives.

Beside her, Pepita sleeps, dreaming of Kôr.

In **"Mysterious Kôr"** one finds the same elements as in **"Summer Night."** The night air that affected the Irish women becomes haunting moonlight in the later story. Queenie's memory-dream that ends **"Summer Night"** is echoed in Pepita's concluding fantasy-dream. Though Pepita is the woman in love, it is Callie who, like Emma, suffers the loss of a romantic ideal. In both stories the stolid, relatively sanguine male is the agent of this new awareness. Interestingly, Emma's lover and the young soldier, Arthur, share a similar treatment at Bowen's hands. The male characters are depicted almost exclusively through dialogue and action. Bowen rarely represents the male psyche as thoroughly as the female.

This pattern is repeated in a third story, **"I Hear You Say So,"** in which the people's reaction to armistice is expressed almost solely in terms of the female. Here one finds as well thematic and technical echoes of the previous two stories.

It is a warm night in London a week after V. E. Day. A nightingale's song travels through the air, shaking the city's inhabitants out of a postwar numbness. Everyone within hearing distance of the bird is disturbed: lovers in the grass, families in the park, old ladies on a park bench, young widows in their beds. London is already on its way to restoring itself. Victory flags wave in the breeze; lights blaze; windows are audaciously flung open. It is a markedly different city from the "battened-down" London of **"Mysterious Kôr"**:

> High up, low down, the fearlessly lit-up windows were like exclamations. Many stood wide open. Inside their tawny squares the rooms, to be seen into, were sublimated: not an object inside them appeared gimcrack or trivial, standing up with stereoscopic sharpness in this intensified element of life. The knobbed or fluted stem of a standard lamp, the bustlike curves of a settee, the couples of photo-

graphs hung level, the fidgeting of a cockatoo up and down its perch, the balance of vases on brackets and pyramids of mock fruit in bowls all seemed miraculous after all that had happened. . . . Each of these theatres was its own drama—a moment perpetuated, an integration of all these living-unliving objects in surviving and shining and being seen. Through the windows, standing lamps and hanging bowls overflowed, spilling hot light into the warm dark.

Now that the war is over, it is permissible to use words such as "miraculous" again. One may now consider "a moment perpetuated," conceive of "integration" and the possibility of something "surviving and shining and being seen." This time the scene is illuminated artificially; there is no longer a danger in "being seen." Man is in the process of reclaiming his own.

The first perceivers of the nightingale's song are Violet and Fred, lovers lying casually in the park grass. They debate whether it is a thrush or a nightingale singing on someone's wireless:

> She said: "Funny if you and me heard a nightingale."
>
> "You and me don't look for that sort of thing. It may have been all very well for them in the past."
>
> "Still, there must still *be* nightingales, or they couldn't have put one on to the wireless."
>
> "I didn't say they'd died out; I said they don't come round. Why should they? They can't sell us anything."

Later Violet says, "You begin to wonder. . . . suppose the world was made for happiness, after all?" The nightingale sings again, "drawing out longings, sending them back again frozen, piercing, not again to be borne." Fred's unwillingness to be moved by the nightingale's song dampens Violet's reaction. "'He was right,' she thought, 'we're not made for this; we can't take it.'"

Two middle-aged women sitting on a park bench wonder why the bird has stopped singing. Mary speculates that he has paused to listen. Naomi observes, "Disappointing for them to listen, perhaps. But why not? Why should a nightingale get off scot free, after everything it is able to do to us?" On their way home she comments:

> Apart from anything, it's too soon. Much too soon, after a war like this. Even Victory's nearly been too much. There ought not to have been a nightingale

in the same week. The important thing is that people should go carefully. They'd much better not feel at all till they feel normal. The first thing must be, to get everything organized.

Of course, it is impossible for people to "go carefully." Aunt Fran and Callie realize this, one with aged weariness, the other with new understanding. People had been existing during the war years in the futility of "unlived lives." They will no longer do so.

Ursula, a young widow, is awakened from her sleepwalking by the nightingale's song. It draws her attention to the no-longer enclosed park: "Every place was invaded and desecrated." She remembers her husband's grandmother saying earlier in the evening, "I shall be glad to go. Look at the shameless people rolling on the grass. Is it for this we have given Roland?" Ursula does not share this sense of indignation and regret. The nightingale symbolizes for Ursula her husband's youth. She realizes that "all they had hoped of the future had been, really, a magic recapturing of the past." Past, present, and future become one for Ursula. Somehow the bird's song fills her with a "profound happiness." Restoration to a sense of normality will be painful, "too much" perhaps, but it is already in process. Ursula is another of Bowen's women whose perceptions and reactions help explain the times.

Populating her stories with impressionable and impressive women of various ages, Bowen looks at the psychological impact of war, the emotional mending and patching that goes on when people find themselves under attack. According to Bowen, people cope by dreaming, whether awake or asleep, of other times and of other places or by assuming a kind of fatalistic numbness or naive blindness. In dialogue, description, and characterization she recreates a special period in history, at once fashioning credible, living characters, evoking the essence of a particular environment, and revealing truths about the human psyche. It is particularly fortunate that we have been left the fictional "reports" of a writer whose talent lies not only in the telling of who, when, and where, but also in the exploring of why and how.

Phyllis Lassner (essay date Spring 1986)

SOURCE: "The Past Is a Burning Pattern: Elizabeth Bowen's *The Last September*," in *Éire-Ireland,* Vol. 21, No. 1, Spring, 1986, pp. 40-54.

[*In the following essay, Lassner examines the Anglo-Irish myth of the ancestral home in* The Last September, *focusing on the narcissim, false privelege, and fatalism it fosters.*]

Although Elizabeth Bowen's Anglo-Irish background has been acknowledged as a powerful influence on her fiction, scant attention has been given to *The Last September,* the novel which deals most directly with the political and social forces that shaped her life and creative vision. Bowen sets the novel during the Troubles at Danielstown, an Anglo-Irish country estate greatly resembling Bowen's Court, her ancestral home in County Cork. Moreover, the last days of the big house clearly rely on Bowen's appraisal of the Ascendancy. The Ascendancy, in Bowen's view of her family history, "drew [its] power from a situation that shows an inherent wrong. . . . Having obtained their position through an injustice, they enjoyed that position through privilege." The terrible price of exploiting the local populace was to be Irish rebellion that brought disaster to many of the families descended from the original English settlers. Bowen did not applaud the destruction of the big houses, but she did regard it as the inevitable result of entrenched and unchanging attitudes on the part of an unassimilated and exclusive population. As *The Last September* reveals, the Anglo-Irish failed to assume direct responsibility for the well-being of that country which bore the weight of their self-proclaimed aristocracy.

The subject of the novel is the twilight of Anglo-Ireland and the fate of those younger people born to inherit the myth of the ancestral home. Tied to the ancestral home by a belief in its power to endow identity and security, "order and a reason for living," those younger people also suffer its "innate" isolation as well as its "intense centripetal life." The big house represents the moral, political, and psychological contradictions that shape the Anglo-Irish. Bowen's Court, the inspiration for all such houses, provided a compelling tie to the past as well as traditions and values that were to shape the future. Many years after writing *The Last September,* Bowen chronicled her family history which comprises the myth of the ancestral home. She writes of "the strong rule of [her] family myth . . . A Bowen, in the first place, made Bowen's Court. Since then, with a rather alarming sureness, Bowen's Court has made all the succeeding Bowens." Describing a stay at Bowen's Court, Bowen reflects how the emotional and political legacy of past inhabitants is felt to be part of its walls and atmosphere. Indeed, the big house seems to haunt and ultimately absorb "the lives that submerged here." In turn, the accumulated perceptions of those who lived at Bowen's Court assume an implicit, sentient power felt only by those who belong at the big house and tying them to one another, to the past and to the house in a mutually dependent relationship.

Bowen reconstitutes her conception of her family home in the relationship between Danielstown and its residents—a relationship immutably grounded in her characters' personal and cultural histories and, consequently, in their feelings about themselves and one another. Emotionally isolated, these people remain nevertheless bound to one another by the pull of the big house. Clearly, Bowen's design suggests that the house and the characters serve as metaphors for each other's destinies. Indeed, the presence of Danielstown structures the novel. Through a series of dialogues between the Naylors and their friends, and through the reflections of the characters about themselves and one another, the novel reveals the story of the life and death of Danielstown. Despite what happens to them outside Danielstown, the characters formulate their plans, examine their pasts, and speculate about their futures under the influence of values inherent in the life and history of the estate.

Bowen's dramatized evaluation of big house culture centers on Lois Farquar, the orphaned niece of Sir Richard Naylor. Contemplating the possibilities for her future amidst repressive social conventions and political chaos, she nevertheless sees herself as part of a world clinging to its privilege. Enacting the attitudes and experiences that constitute Anglo-Irish country life, the other characters foreshadow the meager possibilities available to those trying to escape the confines of Anglo-Ireland but unable to divorce their expectations from its traditions. For example, Hugo Montmorency's dream of a new start in Canada shrinks to plans for the next country house visit. The dreams of younger characters are also portrayed as self-deceptions. At face value, Livvy Thompson's romance with a British soldier serves as a comic counterweight to Lois's quest for love and personal expression. The narrator's mocking tone, however, suggests that Livvy is as trapped as the others. A would-be novelist, Laurence understands that his need for self-expression may very well be frustrated. Identifying with Lois's mother, Laura Naylor, Laurence also recognizes the futility of rebellion. The mirror image of her friends and relatives, Lois will also discover that her future can be defined only in terms of Danielstown's legacies. Whether she considers a career of marriage, she reflects that "the unbelievable future became as fixed as the past."

> **Staring "coldly over its mounting lawns" and dependents, the house has been anthropomorphised by the lives it has absorbed, exactly as Bowen describes Bowen's Court. In fact, Bowen's method recreates the house as a symbol of maternal omniscience and omnipotence.**
> —*Phyllis Lassner*

Danielstown embodies a fantasy of limitless nurture and control. Staring "coldly over its mounting lawns" and dependents, the house has been anthropomorphised by the lives it has absorbed, exactly as Bowen describes Bowen's Court. In fact, Bowen's method recreates the house as a symbol of maternal omniscience and omnipotence. Its coldness, remoteness, and emptiness, however, suggest a decidedly rejecting mother who commits her children to a cruel bind. Represented by Danielstown, Anglo-Ireland is an "unloving country" whose "unwilling bosom" threatens to "smother her children." Yet, its inhabitants experience the house as "a magnet to their dependence." Such visitors as Marda Norton and the Montmorencys endure the awful weather, the desolate insularity, and the inevitable rejections served up at Danielstown—along with antique plumbing and lack of electricity—because they feel compelled to return to the world that made them.

Lois wavers in the shadow of two dubious legacies: her mother's impulsive rebellion and Danielstown's "magnetism." Like her mother, she stands between the two opposing and compelling forces of a man who represents a world outside the big house and secure tradition: "And she could not try to explain . . . how after every return—awakening, even, from sleep or preoccupation—she and these home surroundings still further penetrated each other mutually in the discovery of a lack." So complete is the desire to be part of the house's structure, to fuse with the power projected onto it, that the heirs of Danielstown cannot assess with any detachment the attractions of the external world. It is as though they imagine the house as a human rival to foreign lovers and yet also as empty of fulfillment. How, indeed, can one otherwise explain a building and a human being "mutually penetrating each other with a lack?" The language indicates that Lois has confused home, lover, mother, and herself. Lois's dependence on her surroundings ultimately proves unfulfilling because whatever power the house once represented is being destroyed from inside and out—its "lack" points ironically to its inhabitants' capabilities. Lois's lack is the mark of her frustrated attempts to locate her own needs and find a mode of self-expression within an environment capable of both nurturing and letting go. She discovers, instead, only the suffocating bonds of family expectation.

Sir Richard and Lady Naylor preside over their cloistered estate and young wards as clients of the house and its traditions. They rule with an intensely social design for living which excludes, however, all human realities residing between the gates of their demesne and those of other gentry. Despite expressions of sympathy for local families, the Naylors essentially ignore the Irish, but Bowen does not. While the Irish have no plot of their own, Bowen so implants them in the Naylor's story so that they become the sole agents for change in Anglo-Ireland.

The world of Danielstown, of course, falls victim to its own designs. In all her writing about Ireland, Bowen exposes the Anglo-Irish obsession with their homes, an investment necessarily excluding the interests of the outside world and assuring self-absorption. But Bowen does not suggest that those in power, like the Naylors, would have it any other way. Indeed, in order to insure against rivals for that singular, if precarious place in the "unwilling bosom," they perform an act of self-justification. They mystify their own power to themselves and to others by creating a myth of the big house. With each new generation they duplicate themselves and the conventions defining their "intense centripetal life." Their conventions give them an encoded language by which they communicate only with themselves, about themselves, reinforcing a kind of narcissism born out of loneliness and deprivation, not nurture and love.

Bowen's Anglo-Irish create an artificial world whose only proclaimed inhabitants are themselves. In turn, their political and personal passions have only one object of desire—the estate, which becomes its own island-nation. The compulsion to keep the estate going above all signifies the crippling debt paid by the Anglo-Irish to those limestone shrines to the past. According to Bowen, the big house had no future because by "living for a myth . . . they refused to give history direction." The realities denied by the Naylors come home to haunt them in the form they most fear—they are dispossessed. What Bowen refers to as "keeping the lid on," proves to be a fatal strategy for coping with the threat of imagined or real danger. Ignoring the capture of their Irish neighbors and even the gunfire outside the house, they fall victim to their own unpreparedness. The world of the Naylors must ultimately burn because "with a kind of fatedness, a passivity, they resumed the operation of living." Only the invited penetrate Danielstown, so the Naylors think. Social obligations become ceremonial acts celebrating the Ascendancy. Sir Richard worries more about visitors coming down too early for dinner than about his role in Danielstown's destiny. Only his dreams are beset by the political violence that threatens his absolute control. Although political matters do not come to the fore of the novel's actions, all actions are, nevertheless, really subordinate to their political implications.

Bowen portrays Danielstown as an analogue to its inhabitants' emotional and political blindness, suggesting that the house's apparent omniscience reflects its owners' narcissism. Historically, it has stood only for its own maintenance, ignoring the needs and individuality of its dependents. In turn, its heirs assume others are only variations of each other. Thus, Hugo's brief infatuation with Marda repeats his misperception of Laura Naylor, the love of his youth. The characters seem imbued with the residual effects of those qualities ascribed to the house. Francie's ghost-like presence reflects "the imposingly vacant house." Lois laments the Naylors' rejection of Gerald Lesworth's unauthorized warmth: "You'd think this was the emptiest house in Ireland—we have no family life." By discouraging free expression of feeling, the social conventions ruling Danielstown reinforce "the lack" its heirs feel.

The only survivor in this impoverished world is the actual story of Danielstown. The characters become prisoners to those traditions upholding the "family myth." By living as though they are replicas of their ancestors and their aristocratic codes, they transform themselves into figures in an historical romance, important only to the imagined continuity of Danielstown. Before the young have even the chance to live as characters in a more realistic fiction, they become conventional, thus sacrificing contingency and indeterminacy to the myth of Danielstown's immortality. Bowen uses the conventions of realism to promise her heroine an open ending and self-determination while simultaneously building a case for the futility of such a promise. Such a transformation renders the characters passive and, hence, incapable of action.

Every character who lives at or visits Danielstown is fated to experience a struggle with the domination of the past; making any plans for the future seems like an exercise in futility or at best, an act of whimsey. Even Marda, whose marriage plans mean that she may escape her own transience and the doom of Anglo-Ireland, assesses herself in relation to Danielstown: "She might not be fatal, but *here* she was certainly fated." Marda also sees Lois "pray[ing] for somebody to be fatal." Although the literal meaning here indicates that Lois is looking for someone to love, the use of the word "fatal" betrays a connection between Lois's feelings and the fatalism enshrouding the big house. The foreboding ascribed to Lois indeed proves true: her would-be suitor, Gerald, is killed in an Irish Revolutionary Army ambush. Moreover, Lady Naylor's reaction to Gerald's death negates the value of his personal sacrifice by emphasizing that the incident was destined: "he could not help it . . . ." It seems that any force mediating between Anglo-Irish arrogance and ambivalence, on the one hand, and the unacknowledged violent fate or Ireland on the other, is doomed.

Like the inhabitants who live within its limits, the outsider who dares to set foot inside the ancestral demesne is also sacrificed to the history of Anglo-Ireland. An unacceptable suitor partly because he is English, middle-class, and has no money, but mostly because he is not Anglo-Irish gentry, Gerald is dismissed by Myra Naylor as "irrelevant," a rather strange usage reducing him to a nonperson. He is, in effect, treated like the Irish revolutionaries, rendered "superfluous" by her commitment to the myth of the ancestral home. Hugo and Francie Montmorency illustrate further the infection of Anglo-Irish fatedness and passivity. Francie's weak heart has left her too tired to feel, but most significantly, unable to make a permanent home in Ireland. Hugo's passivity betrays the mistake fatal to his sense of self. He sold his ancestral home, Rockriver, without which he has no occupation, no identity, no need for vitality, and no feeling.

Whatever passion and energy went into the conquest of Ireland and the construction of the big houses, the Naylors and the Montmorencys seem to be paying for the moral wrongs of the system they perpetuate by being sterile. Indeed, their generation is but an effete version of their most violent and crude ancestors. They both suffer the "lack" that haunts Lois. Unlike the Montmorencys, however, the Naylors attempt to revive their family tree by directing their energies towards raising Lois and Laurence as replicas of their forbears. Kept under wraps, the young people are virtually suffocated. Lois muses: "How is it that in this country that ought to be full of such violent realness there seems nothing for me but clothes and what people say? I might as well be in some kind of cocoon." They are not only unseen, but unheard as well, as Lady Naylor's strategy reveals: "From all the talk, you might think almost anything was going to happen, but we never listen. I have made it a rule not to talk, either.'" Later she says: "'I make it a point of not knowing.'"

The need of the younger generation neither to be absorbed nor to have its individuality destroyed and the need to insist on its identity are regarded as precisely that kind of disturbance considered anarchy by its guardians. To experience external reality, the young must first know how their guardians feel about themselves and the world beyond Danielstown. The Naylors succeed in keeping the outside world at bay at a tremendous price to the spirit of those who depend on them. Lois and Laurence do not know how to feel about themselves because no one has ever communicated to them thoughts and feelings that might free them from their closed world. For the young, even life within the big house is never spoken of directly. The walls themselves appear to reverberate with sounds of whispers and secrets—"what people feel but never openly express." What *is* said comes as a sinister revelation to those who overhear their lives being discussed. The effect of being talked about instead of being spoken to—of overhearing indirectly the determination of one's fate—is to diminish the sense of a living self. The young of Danielstown thus become someone else's fictional creation. When Lois overhears a conversation about her art school career, she reacts with anxiety: "Was she now to be clapped down under an adjective, to crawl round lifelong inside some quality like a fly in a tumbler?" Indeed, because Anglo-Irish family character is modeled on one's ancestors, the individual becomes submerged in a rigid pattern. Note that even Bowen's proliferation of names beginning with "L" mocks this inbred society: Lois, Laura, Laurence, Livvy, and even the English Lesworth and Leslie Lawes.

A direct confrontation with the old order is of course impossible, for there exist no common language and convention of behavior with which to express deep emotion. If the young could only articulate their unformed feelings, they would begin to resist having their lives trapped in an unalterable historical pattern. But, as Lois and Gerald's frustrated relationship illustrates, without a language of their own they must become what the Naylors conceive them to be. Gerald can only report to Lois what her aunt has distorted about their feelings for each other, thereby falling into the doyenne's trap. The lovers' failure is mutual because, while Gerald lacks the self-possession to help resolve her conflicting needs, Lois lacks the sense of purpose with which to influence him. She tells him: "Even what I think isn't my own.'" Laurence at least can mock Lady Naylor's strategy and express bitterness at his unsatisfactory dependence. He wishes upon Danielstown the very anarchy its owners dread in the form that haunted Bowen: "I should like . . . some crude intrusion of the actual . . . I should like to be here when this house burns. . . . And we shall all be so careful not to notice." Without independent minds, language, or perceptions, the young cannot see their problem to act on it. Dependence thus leads to bitter passivity, which undermines the urge to live. Marda links the fatalism infecting life at the big house to the Troubles with words that echo Laurence's bitterness and mock Danielstown's strategies for survival. Of Lady Naylor's "despairing optimism," Marda asks: "'Will there ever be anything we can all do except not notice?'"

In *The Last September,* adolescence, the Anglo-Irish presence, and the subjugation of the Irish appear to be interchangeable states of being suspended between imagining a self and protecting oneself from annihilation. Lois is trapped between her desire for an orderly life and her fear of the "actual" that Laurence craves. This "actual"—emphasized by its echoed use—is clearly for Laurence the political turbulence that brings on the destruction of Danielstown. For Lois, the "actual" is emotional turbulence—indeed, rage—that threatens to break through the constricted language of the Naylors. While Laurence may wish for someone else to enact his rage, Lois fears it entirely. At first glance it seems to be her own awakening sense of womanhood—her sexuality. Later, it emerges as the aggression underlying Lois's urge to live. Lois uses the word "*actual*"—Bowen's italics—in response to her suitor's spontaneous and uninvited arrival at the house. Gerald may be "ordinary," but what Lois desires and fears about him endows him with extraordinary power.

Gerald's love violates her unformed sense of self—that part requiring nurture and unprepared for sexual aggression. Gerald's sexuality makes him a real person and, hence, dangerous. If given his desires, he has the power to overcome Danielstown's rigid codes. Hence, the conflict between Lois's desperate need of his passion and her strong desire to retain what she feels is the nurturing quality of her environment. Lois experiences Gerald's kiss as "an impact, with inside blankness," recalling her feelings about her home and its "penetration" which "discovers a lack." Bowen's similar metaphors indicate a fear of being absorbed, by sex or by home, into emptiness. The sensation also reaffirms Lois's troubled feelings about approaching womanhood which, on another occasion, she refers to as a "merciless penetration." Thus, if Lois is not absorbed and suffocated by union, she suffers an assault by and on herself. As antidote against such fears, Lois imagines sexual love as a sanctuary from feelings of emptiness:

> Lois felt she was home again: safe from deserted rooms, the penetration of silences, rain, homelessness. Nothing mattered: she could have gone to sleep. But he woke her.

The associative strategies of Bowen's narrative, however, link such a relationship to the very home that promises nurture and, yet, violates the boundaries of selfhood. Thus, any other body of needs and the need to feel threaten to be both smothering and violating. It is no surprise therefore, that Lois, hardly capable of self-expression, does not know what to expect of others. She is afraid of being shattered, either by her own desire to live, by the possibility of mutual sexual need, or by her own rage—any or all of which could destroy her carefully constructed cocoon. If feeling is dangerous, action could be deadly.

Bowen's young characters feel that to rebel is to destroy that very source of nurture necessary to life itself. Therefore, Lois submerges her need in the oppressive security of her family home. In a sense, she resembles the subjugated Irish who, for generations, bore their resentment, eking out a minimal existence. While the Irish tenants have been denied autonomy and escape by real or "actual" political and economic structures that existed before they were born, Lois is governed by a self-perpetuating myth endowed with power by her own belief. What is lacking in the lives of these young characters Bowen ascribes to the big house when it becomes, in their minds, another holding environment. The real ability of the house to fulfill such needs, remains of course, highly questionable; the house only reflects traditions towards which Bowen and her characters feel ambivalent.

Bowen writes many times of the importance of place as an inspiration, an "actor," in her fiction. . . . for Bowen relationships become synonymous with places. In her fiction, family life and the family home are characterized as places that fail to communicate feeling and intimacy.
—*Phyllis Lassner*

Bowen writes many times of the importance of place as an inspiration, an "actor," in her fiction. In her autobiographical *Seven Winters,* she reveals that her sense of place de-rived from her reaction to her parents' marriage as a "private kingdom"—a place which seemed to exclude everyone but them. Thus, for Bowen relationships become synonymous with places. In her fiction, family life and the family home are characterized as places that fail to communicate feeling and intimacy. For Bowen, such isolation led to creativity. For her characters, no such transformation takes place. What, then, happens to feelings that result from experiencing the isolated but claustrophobic family home as a place which both suppresses imagination and vitality and is fast becoming an anomaly in times of revolution? Where is the rage accompanying the loss, frustration and anxiety that Bowen attributes to Lois, to Laura, to Laurence, and to Hugo, but which seems to dissipate within the characters' reveries? Bowen gives her characters no means by which to enact this rage. Even when they expressed it verbally, it seems to lose its power in the frustrated attempt to transform words into acts.

In two important scenes, however, both taking place away from Danielstown, this rage is suggested by imagery, if not directly by the characters. Hugo, Lois, and Marda confront rage and rebellion in the mill scene in a way they cannot at Danielstown, because Bowen there separates them from the action that precipitates and enacts such feeling. The event becomes central to the novel's meaning precisely because it indicates that the characters of the big house may be "superfluous" to the political realities of Ireland and to the expression of feeling within the novel. Indeed, the "dead" mill is a sinister version of the place symbolizing Anglo-Ireland's "lack": "the house of Usher . . . like corpses at their most horrible . . . another . . . of our national grievances." These references connect personal, cultural, and political deprivation. Ireland may be a country full of decayed monuments to Irish powerlessness and to the lifeless domination of the Anglo-Irish, but such quiescence proves deceptive. Entering the mill, Marda and Lois surprise a sleeping rebel into brandishing a pistol. Although Bowen does not dramatize the accidental firing of the pistol, the mill scene suggests that violence is embedded in the novel, even if no one seems capable of committing it. By witnessing the event, the two women take part in a way that suggests that only someone else's violence can express the rage the characters feel but cannot enact themselves. Moreover, no one is made responsible for its action.

Lois's confrontation with this external reality signifies her ability to grow up. By keeping the Irishman's presence a secret, Lois and Marda attempt to discover and preserve a reality that Danielstown conceals from them. They safeguard it from becoming a conventional fiction, victim of Danielstown's need to censor a story foretelling its own violent end. In this way Lois's secret remains an untold story; however, as with any well-guarded secret, its impact dies with suppression. Thus, neither Lois nor Marda can be rebels. Lois's only autonomy is to usurp Danielstown's method of suppression and reconstitute it. She turns the event into an expression of feeling that she and Marda share.

The barracks dance, like the mill scene, illustrates the radical disjunction between moral and emotional life in the Ireland of Bowen's girlhood. Lois both reflects and struggles to overcome Anglo-Irish political and personal indifference. A British officer named Daventry is the counterweight to the Irish rebel in the mill. An outsider in Anglo-Ireland, Daventry, too, is both sinister and psychically wounded, in this case, by orders to assert a power of dubious value: ransacking beds for guns in "houses where men were absent and old women or women with babies wept loudly and prayed." The scene establishes a tension between the sexual energy generated by the dance and the alienation Daventry, Lois, and Gerald feel, but neither condition has an outlet. Lois and Gerald attempt one tentative embrace, but fail to connect. Lois and Daventry also experience a brief moment of recognition, but only to reinforce their mutual sense of displacement, dehumanization, and powerlessness. As the characters retreat from each other, intense feeling finds expression only in the spontaneous explosion of objects: balloons explode, a gramaphone is upset, and a room throbs as though it would burst.

The juxtaposition of incapacitated people and energized objects, however, is not as comic as one could expect, for it suggests, instead, an absurd and horrifying relationship between the inability to feel and the eruption of violence. The echoes of the mill scene in this scene thus establish a link between the repression both of violence and of responsibility. Those whose feeling is preserved in an object—the big house—literally sit around or disappear from the novel while their country explodes around them. The separation of concealed rage from the outbreak of violence shapes the novel's violent ending while revealing Bowen's ambivalence about her ancestral home.

In **"The Big House"** Bowen expresses reverence for the comforting forms of gracious living that aestheticized an otherwise gloomy and precarious existence. In *The Last September,* however, such justification breaks down. After all, for Lois, as for her mother, "in the interest of good manners and good behavior, people learned to subdue their feelings." Twenty-five years after writing *The Last September,* Bowen admits that such a strategy might also have been "foolhardy or inhuman," for Lois's "acquiescence to strife, abnormalities and danger" deflects what she might feel toward the family and home which not only fail to nurture her, but threaten to incorporate her.

The portrait of Lois may have been a means of diffusing the powerful emotions which bound Bowen to her heroine and to Danielstown, for, as Bowen admits, "This, which of all my books is nearest my heart, has a deep, unclouded spontaneous source. . . . It is a work of instinct, rather than knowledge." Examining her work in retrospect, Bowen appears uneasy about Lois's indifference to "the national struggle around her." The response may describe her own reaction as well as that of her heroine: "In part, would not this be self-defence?" At the time Bowen wrote the novel, she apparently felt a strong need to distance herself from her heroine and to keep Danielstown discrete from Bowen's Court. As a "niece always, never child of that house," Lois cannot feel the full emotional and economic impact of the big house as did her creator. With twenty-five years of distance, Bowen wonders whether it was "sorrow to [Lois], Danielstown's burning?" One supposes that Bowen is asking about her own reaction, should Bowen's Court have been burned. Although it was spared, the destruction of Bowen's Court was a grim possibility that haunted Bowen during those difficult years. She describes the feelings that compelled her to write *The Last September* a short time later:

> I *was* the child of the house from which Danielstown derives. Bowen's Court survived— nevertheless, so often in my mind's eye did I see it burning that the terrible last event in *The Last September* is more real than anything I have lived through.

Bowen's ambivalence about the big house is divided between the pain of imagining her family home in flames and the wish to be free of its burdens and constraints.

Bowen employs another strategy to express and deflect her conflicting feelings. While the heroine and her friends safely leave the stage of war, and the Naylors suffer in appropriate silence, the writer, with the help of Irish rebels, sets fire to the big house. Again, the object bears the brunt of human feeling, but here people alien to the big house are responsible for its destruction. The language describing the conflagration testifies to the strange relationship between the house and its inhabitants. The "open and empty country" burning against a "bosom of night" suggests once again that the house represents Anglo-Ireland as a rejecting but controlling mother now suffering poetic justice. Devoid of nurture, compassion or stability, its fragile and insular interior is appropriately gutted. It is as though enraged children reciprocate her maternal favors through the "fearful scarlet [which] ate up the house that threatened to eat them." Thus, they deliver an "abortive birth" to the myth of Danielstown's continuity, committing its rejecting door to infinite "hospitality."

Rebelling against oppressive landlords, the Irish also express the rage of the big house characters, thus becoming the instruments of action and feeling that Bowen denies Lois, Laura and Laurence. As the big house embodies both the emptiness and suffocation that comes with withholding and control, so Bowen's novel implies that the relation between the Irish and the big house is also that of deprived and oppressed children and controlling and indifferent parents. Thus, the Irish fulfill Laurence's wish and burn the cocoon—freeing the children of the Ascendancy to realize their own capacity for life. Although Danielstown is destroyed, the myth of the ancestral home thrives, however, in the wishes, needs, and fantasies of Bowen's characters in future novels. Even in those works set far from Ireland, characters desperately yearn for the power, identity, and sense of purpose they feel comes with belonging to a family home. With *The Last September* Bowen became a successful novelist, exploring characters who desire the nurturing promise of home and family, but who experience their overwhelming demands instead. Regardless of the setting of her subsequent novels, Bowen is never far removed in her imagination from the world she knew so well and described so evocatively in *The Last September*.

Mary Jarrett (essay date Spring 1987)

SOURCE: "Ambiguous Ghosts: The Short Stories of Elizabeth Bowen," in *Journal of the Short Story in English*, No. 8, Spring, 1987, pp. 71-9.

[*In the following essay, Jarrett discusses the ambiguous line between reality and fiction in Bowen's short stories.*]

Elizabeth Bowen felt early what she called the 'Anglo-Irish ambivalence to all things English, a blend of impatience and evasiveness, a reluctance to be pinned down to a relationship.' This, I would argue, richly affected her fiction.

Bowen may be compared with the Anglo-Indian Kipling, with his similar ambivalence to all things English. Each was early exposed to betrayal, alienation, and compromise, and each sought refuge through 'magical' fictions. Kipling, born in Bombay, was abandoned as a small child in England. The hell of bullying into which he was delivered laid, he says, 'the foundation of literary effort.' He played imaginary games in which he literally fenced himself off from the alien world in which he had been made a prisoner, making the later comment that 'The magic, you see, lies in the ring or fence that you take refuge in.' And it was in his House of Desolation that he learnt to read: 'on a day that I remember it came to me that "reading" was not "the Cat lay on the Mat," but a means to everything that would make me happy.'

Elizabeth Bowen suffered feelings of dislocation and betrayal as a child from the lies told to her about her father's mental breakdown and her mother's cancer, and Edwin J. Kenney has pointed out that she learnt to read, at the age of

seven, precisely at the time 'when her family catastrophes began to enter her consciousness with her removal to England. As she said later, "All susceptibility belongs to the age of magic, the Eden where fact and fiction were the same; the imaginative writer was the imaginative child, who relied for life upon being lied to." So from this time on, she said, 'Nothing made full sense to me that was not in print.' She instinctively connected being a grown-up with being a writer—that is, being in control of one's own fictions. For her, as for Kipling, fiction was a way of escape, a powerful magic, a means of creating another, more tolerable, reality and identity.

Yet this identity could be a shifting one. Elizabeth Bowen, who was the first Bowen child to live and be educated in England since the family settled in Ireland in the seventeenth century, could never decide at school whether to present herself as Irish or as ultra-English, and this 'evasiveness' stayed with her all her life, this 'reluctance to be pinned down to a relationship' affected the way in which she presented her fictions. In all her best stories there is a refusal to pronounce on the validity of the worlds her characters create for themselves. Many of her characters share the fervent wish of Lydia in **'The Return'**: 'if she had only a few feet of silence of her own, to exclude the world from, to build up in something of herself.' But the nature of the silence, like the nature of the building up, in all her best stories is always left open to question. This is true too of Kipling: I would name in particular 'Mrs Bathurst' and 'The Wish House'. Kipling, however, draws attention to his ambivalence by the use of the frame of an outer narrator (in 'Mrs Bathurst' a double frame) in a way Elizabeth Bowen does not.

Nor do all Bowen's short stories have this richness of ambivalence. She wrote in 1959, of her art as a short story writer: 'More than half my life is under the steadying influence of the novel, with its calmer, stricter, more orthodox demands: into the novel goes such taste as I have for rational behaviour and social portraiture. The short story, as I see it to be, allows for what is crazy about humanity: obstinacies, inordinate heroisms, "immortal longings".' Some of this craziness and these immortal longings are made explicitly supernatural, for example in **'The Cheery Soul'**, **'The Demon Lover'**, **'Green Holly'**, and **'Hand in Glove'**. That is to say, they are stories in which the surface of ordinary life cracks. This is to use Elizabeth Bowen's own image; in a broadcast discussion of 1948 she explained that she was fascinated with the surface of life not so much for its own sake, as for the dangerous sense it gives of being a thin crust above a bottomless abyss: 'the more the surface seems to heave or threaten to crack, the more its actual pattern fascinates me.' I would argue that in her finest stories the surface only seems to heave but never finally cracks.

One consistent cause of surface-heaving in Bowen is alienation, a loss of identity, like Mrs Watson's in **'Attractive Modern Homes'**, who begins to doubt her own existence when she moves to a new housing estate, or that of the drifting Tibbie, **'The Girl with the Stoop'**, who 'had not learnt yet how to feel like a resident'. Bowen remarks of the Londoners in **'A Walk in the Woods'** that 'Not to be sure where one is induces panic'. Yet in this same story the 'city woman' exclaims to the young lover she has brought to the woods, '"Before you came, I was walled in alive."' Imprisonment, the ultimate loss of control of one's environment, is another major preoccupation of the stories.

Imprisonment takes many forms. The prison can be one of vulgarity, an intolerable aesthetic assault, as it is for Mr Rossiter in **'Breakfast'**, trapped by the lodging-house's 'thick fumes of coffee and bacon, the doggy-smelling carpet, the tight, glazed noses of the family ready to split loudly from their skins'—an image in which even the family's noses become impatient prisoners. Cicely in **'The New House'** makes her escape into marriage, with the claim—which would be merely whimsical in another writer—that she was imprisoned in her life with her brother in the old house by the way the furniture was arranged. Oliver and Davina fail to escape into marriage, and their imprisonment is inaction: 'Their May had been blighted. Now, each immobile from poverty, each frozen into their settings like leaves in the dull ice of different puddles, they seldom met.'

Very often the imprisonment is the capture of one person by another. It can be deliberate, like the social capture of the young wife in 'Mrs Windermere': 'Firmly encircling Esmée's wrist with a thumb and forefinger she led her down Regent Street.' Or it can be involuntary, like the enslavement of the hapless Mr Richardson in **'Ann Lee's'** by someone 'as indifferent as a magnet'. Ann Lee, the mysterious enslaver and hat-creator, incidentally appears to derive her power from the fact that she eludes identification: 'Letty Ames had said that she was practically a lady; a queer creature, Letty couldn't place her.'

For other characters, imprisonment can actually be the pressure of being a magnet, of feeling other people's needs. Clifford in **'A Love Story'** feels that 'the nightmare of being wanted was beginning, in this room, to close in round him again.' In **'The Dancing-Mistress'** Peelie the pianist, who wears a slave bangle on each arm, and Lulu, the male hotel secretary, are in thrall to their 'dancing mistress' Joyce James, whose name is perhaps an allusion to the 'paralysis' of James Joyce's *Dubliners,* since she is the prisoner of her own stupor of weariness. Bullying a clumsy pupil is all that affords her 'a little shudder of pleasure' and she is dismayed by Peelie's bright suggestion that the pupil might die, because 'She couldn't do without Margery Mannering: she wanted to kill her.' She wants, that is, the perpetual pleasure of hating and tormenting Margery. But, on another level,

to kill Margery would mean that she need never do without her, for the Metropole ballroom in which Joyce and Peelie work is a vision of Hell. As Joyce says to her friend: '"Oh, Peelie, I'm *dead*!"', and when her would-be lover Lulu tries to hold Joyce's sleeping body in the taxi, Peelie implicitly warns him: '"You'll be as stiff as hell in a few minutes—I am, always."' The story balances exactly between the real and the supernatural.

In many of the 'ghost' stories the ghost may be seen as the conscious or unconscious fiction of one of the characters. In **'Making Arrangements'** a deserted husband is asked to send on all his wife's dresses, and his perception of her shallowness and her social dependence on him becomes his perception that 'From the hotel by the river the disembodied ghost of Margery was crying thinly to him for her body, her innumerable lovely bodies.' In **'The Shadowy Third'** the second wife is haunted by the *idea* of the unloved first wife—although she does supply a technically correct explanation (murder) for the existence of a ghost by saying that she thinks '"that not to want a person must be a sort, a sort of murder."'

Some ghosts are seen by the characters themselves as fictions. Thomas, a ghostlike figure himself who must never enter the world of the couple's children, visits Gerard and Janet. He is treated to a sickening, civilized display of luxurious acquisitions, but the fly in the ointment is Janet's acquisition of a ghost called Clara. It gradually becomes apparent that the ghost is the embodiment of Janet's own loneliness and unhappiness, so that Thomas feels how much less humiliating it would have been for Gerard for Janet to have taken a lover, and Gerard complains petulantly, '"She's seeing too much of this ghost."'

In **'Dead Mabelle'** the ghost is the dead film star whose films go on playing. Like Vickery in Kipling's 'Mrs Bathurst', Mabelle's fan William is drawn obsessively to her phantom image. The different worlds of reality comically collide when the distraught William returns home and jerks open a drawer for the pistol for a cinematic suicide, only to find a litter of odds and ends. Another collision of realities, or fictions, occurs in **'The Back Drawing-Room'**. This story is relatively unusual for Elizabeth Bowen in having an outer framework of narrators. As one of the characters mutters disgustedly under her breath, '"Hell! . . . Bring in the Yule log, this is a Dickens Christmas. We're going to tell ghost stories."' But the guileless little man who tells of his own supernatural experience in Ireland has no notion of the proper, literary way to tell a ghost story, despite hints about the House of Usher. He is actually presented as the prisoner of his ignorance as 'the others peered curiously, as though through bars, at the little man who sat perplexed and baffled, knowing nothing of atmosphere.' Mrs Henneker, the acknowledged arbiter of atmosphere, acts as a marvellous parody of Elizabeth Bowen herself as she urges the little man to recall correctly his entry into the phantom country house.

> 'You had a sense of immanence', said Mrs Henneker authoritatively. 'Something was overtaking you, challenging you, embracing yet repelling you. Something was coming up from the earth, down from the skies, in from the mountains, that was stranger than the gathered rain. Deep from out of the depths of those dark windows, something beckoned'.

This is a brisker, more peremptory version of the atmosphere Bowen herself establishes in **'Human Habitation'**, published in the same volume (*Ann Lee's,* 1926), in which two students on a walking tour blunder out of the rain into a heavily atmosphere-laden house. The pelting rain, and the physical exhaustion of the students, serve as the bridge into what one of them perceives as 'some dead and empty hulk of a world drawn up alongside, at times dangerously accessible to the unwary'. In his zombie-like state of weariness, he had already begun to doubt his own existence: 'He was, he decided, something somebody else had thought.'

Bowen uses a similar bridge in **'Look at All Those Roses'**, the story I would select as the best example of her delicate balancing of fictions against realities. Here the bridge is the 'endless drive' of Lou and Edward through the Suffolk countryside back to London. We are reminded that 'there is a point when an afternoon oppresses one with fatigue and a feeling of unreality. Relentless, pointless, unwinding summer country made nerves ache at the back of both of their eyes.' Beyond a certain point the route becomes pointless: unmappable. In any case it has always been a 'curious route', since Edward detests the main roads, and we are therefore prepared for the fact that when they break down 'Where they were seemed to be highly improbable'. They have already 'felt bound up in the tired impotence of a dream'. Lou and Edward may have driven over the borderline into another kind of reality—or they may not.

The title of the story becomes its first sentence.

'Look at All Those Roses'

Lou exclaimed at that glimpse of a house in a sheath of startling flowers.

The word 'sheath' has a sinister connotation. But the third sentence of the story runs, 'To reach the corner, it struck her, Edward accelerated, as though he were jealous of the rosy house—a house with gables, flat-fronted, whose dark windows stared with no expression through the flowers.' The curious syntax of 'To reach the corner, it struck her, Edward accelerated' emphasizes Lou's subjectivity. It is only her 'as-

tounding fancy', later in the story, that the murdered father lies at the roses' roots.

The perhaps unsurprising lack of expression of the house's dark windows gains a resonance not only from Mrs Mather's greeting them with 'no expression at all', but from Edward's and Lou's reaction when the car breaks down: 'He and she confronted each other with that completely dramatic lack of expression they kept for occasions when the car went wrong.' The car's breakdown itself is completely realistic and simultaneously a kind of magic spell: 'A ghastly knocking had started. It seemed to come from everywhere, and at the same time to be a special attack on them.' There is a 'magic' which is suggested by the curious isolation of the house and its dislocation: Edward speaks of the rest of the country looking like something lived in by '"poor whites"', although this is, on one level, Suffolk and not the American South. But Lou and Edward are themselves isolated and dislocated. Lou is perpetually anxious that Edward, who is not her husband, will escape her, whereas Edward feels that 'life without people was absolutely impossible'—by which he means life only with Lou. Lou is presented as rather less than a person: during the course of the story she is compared with a monkey, a cat, and a bird. When she says longingly of the 'rosy house', '"I wish we lived *there* . . . It really looked like somewhere"', Edward replies tartly, '"It wouldn't if we did."' Mrs Mather is also isolated, but it is a powerful isolation, like Ann Lee's, and one disconcerting to Lou and Edward, who cannot make out whether she is a woman or a lady. She has no 'outside attachments—hopes, claims, curiosities, desires, little touches of greed—that put a label on one to help strangers.' By contrast, her crippled daughter Josephine has 'an unresigned, living face'. She asks Lou which are the parts of London with the most traffic, and her restlessness is expressed by her canary 'springing to and fro in its cage'. Josephine is described as 'burning', just as the rose garden has a 'silent, burning gaiety'.

Various interpretations of the 'rosy house' and its occupants are possible for the reader who is searching for a label. One is that Josephine's father had escaped after injuring her back. (This would have happened when Josephine was seven, the age at which Elizabeth Bowen left her father and felt abandoned by him.) As Lou, whose 'idea of love was adhesiveness', thinks bitterly: 'He had bolted off down that path, as Edward had just done.' Another is that he has been murdered by Mrs Mather, a view which obviously enjoys much local support. The murder weapon was possibly the lump of quartz, the 'bizarre object' which props open the front door, wielded by Mrs Mather's 'powerful-looking hands.' This leads to another interpretation, that the house and garden are in effect haunted, and that the murder is manifested by the over-profuse roses, 'over-charged with colour' and 'frighteningly bright'. When Lou sees the same roses that Josephine sees, 'she thought they looked like forced roses, magnetized into being. 'This would explain why the farm is '"unlucky"', and why there is only one servant for the house, '"not very clear in her mind'." This in turn leads to another interpretation, that the 'rosy house' is a place of enchantment, which it is impossible to leave. Lou says jokingly to Josephine that she put the evil eye on the car, and when Lou refuses to eat tea, Josephine says, '"She thinks if she eats she may have to stay here for ever.'" (Eleanor in **'The Parrot'** remembers Proserpine when she is offered figs by the Lennicotts.) The enchantment, however, may be either good or bad. Is Lou's 'ecstasy of indifference' to life, experienced as she lies beside Josephine's invalid carriage, an unaccustomed peep into the nature of things—one of her 'ideal moments'? Or is she succumbing to the lure of death, so that Edward rightly realizes that he had 'parked' her, like the car, in the wrong place? Lou realizes that she has always wanted 'to keep everything inside her own power', but to abandon this desire to control one's own fictions may be to abandon life.

The story is alive with ambiguities, like Josephine's '"We don't wonder where my father is.'" This reminds us of Edward's taunting Lou with '"You like to be sure where I am, don't you?'" Edward, who is a writer, comments on the episode, '"There's a story there"', which may reveal him either as a sensitive artist or a shallow journalist.

The title of the story is the first sentence, Lou's exclamation. It is also an exhortation to the reader to look at all those roses—and make what you can of them.

John Coates (essay date July 1990)

SOURCE: "Elizabeth Bowen's *The Last September:* The Loss of the Past and the Modern Consciousness," in *Durham University Journal,* Vol. 82, No. 2, July, 1990, pp. 205-16.

[*In the following essay, Coates examines the narrative tension in* The Last September *in terms of the cultural shift that occurred after World War I.*]

The existence of a seemingly obvious frame of reference for **The Last September** may mislead the critic. Given the intrinsic interest of the Irish "Troubles" and of the last phase of the Protestant Ascendancy, the historical setting of **The Last September,** it is tempting to see them as the defining factors of the book's meaning. The strongly autobiographical derivation of the novel which its author herself emphasized ("I *was* the child of the house from which Danielstown derives"), seems to enforce attention to the Anglo-Irish predicament. As a result critics have often approached the novel as if called upon to strongly disapprove of its inhabitants. The Anglo-Irish were casualties of an "inevitable" historical process which they ought, nevertheless, to have foreseen

or prevented in some way. Danielstown is burned down so, obviously, its inhabitants must have deserved their fate. For example, E. J. Kenney's condemnation of the "guilty void at the center of such a life" as that of the Anglo-Irish landowners colours his view of Lois Farquar, the novel's heroine. She has a fundamental affinity with them because both lack "any vital connection with life". Kenney sees the Anglo-Irish as a whole, as "adolescent only children". Hermione Lee's position is subtler. She sees the "satiric mode" of the comic scenes of **The Last September** as a "form of elegy" for the Ascendancy in decline. The poignance of this decline is that it involves the loss of those qualities recorded in **Bowen's Court** "the 'grand idea', the sense of family pride, the almost mystical apartness". Hermione Lee's mention of **Bowen's Court** is apt, because Elizabeth Bowen's long family history provides an essential context for **The Last September.** It records a much more complex and ambivalent attitude to her Anglo-Irish heritage, and her Bowen ancestors than some critics have allowed:

> In the main, I do not feel they require defence—you, on the other hand, may consider them indefensible. Having obtained their position through an injustice, they enjoyed that position through privilege. But while they wasted no breath in deprecating an injustice it would not have been to their interest to set right, they did not abuse their privilege—on the whole.

The situation of the Anglo-Irish, intruders in an alien land, is not in itself unnatural. Rather, as Antonia, a character in the much later novel *A World of Love,* reflects, it is a paradigm of the condition of man. The Anglo-Irish landowners may have had to maintain a "hostile watch" against a potentially rebellious population, yet, after all "everywhere is a frontier" where the "outposted few", the "living" must never be off their guard. One recalls, too, Elizabeth Bowen's comment in **The Big House** that the struggles of the owners of great Irish houses to maintain themselves were part of a struggle which goes on everywhere and that "may be said, in fact, to be life itself".

Critics' insistence that the Anglo-Irish political crisis is the subject of **The Last September** and hostile view they sometimes take of the Anglo-Irish themselves tend to drain the novel's events of significance. The people in the book are doomed and irrelevant to the process of political events. Therefore their doings must lack substance and appear only as "aimlessness and malaise". Tempting as it may be to view Danielstown simply as a historical limbo it is a mistake to do so. If the meaning of **The Last September** is that its characters and actions are nugatory then it hardly seems worthwhile to give them close attention. Critics have chosen instead to emphasize the atmosphere or mood of the novel. Jocelyn Brooke, for example, asserts that what the reader remembers best about *The Last September* was a "brooding nostalgic melancholy". Such concentration on atmosphere neglects the intellectual meaning of Elizabeth Bowen's work. (In any case the distinction between atmosphere and intellectual meaning is a dubious one with her). Discussion of *The Last September* in terms of its general mood also neglects the architecture of the novel.

One of the most obvious features of *The Last September* is its unusually symmetrical structure, the three parts of almost equal length, drawing attention to a design. These divisions and their titles, 'The Arrival of Mr and Mrs Montmorency', 'The Visit of Miss Norton', and 'The Departure of Gerald' unavoidably suggest a pattern rather than simply the ebbs and flows of an empty emotion critics have seen. Elizabeth Bowen's own subsequent comments are also suggestive. She was "most oppressed" by the technical difficulty of "assembling the novel's cast", of bringing the characters to the same place and keeping them there in order "to provide the interplay known as plot". Clearly she thought the interplay important. The encounters and conversations of the novel, above all the choice of just that particular "cast" of characters and of the particular way in which they interact, are meant to be significant. The inner dynamics of *The Last September* clearly require a much closer attention if its meaning is to be fully elicited.

Elizabeth Bowen's opposition to retrospectively seen historical inevitability and the facile and complacent moralising it involves is as obvious in *The Last September* as it is in her later treatments of the Anglo-Irish decline.
—*John Coates*

The second critical preconception about the novel, that the owners of Danielstown are living a false life, "in a vacuum", in fact rests on very little either in the text or in the way of external evidence from Elizabeth Bowen's own comments. *The Last September* does not endorse that quirk of thinking which has long fascinated social psychologists, and from which historians and political writers enjoy no exemption, of holding the victim responsible for his own ruin. Elizabeth Bowen's opposition to retrospectively seen historical inevitability and the facile and complacent moralising it involves is as obvious in *The Last September* as it is in her later treatments of the Anglo-Irish decline. The burning of Danielstown is not "death", the result of inevitable internal organic decay, but "execution rather". The book's final description emphasizes violation of the seasons and of the pattern of light and dark. At the burning of the house an "extra day" comes to "abortive birth". The roads run dark through

"unnatural dusk" in a landscape which is a crazy "design of order and panic". Those who carry out the burning do so with a cold fanatical assurance, "executioners bland from accomplished duty". A flow of life has been broken. There will be "no more autumns" after this "hard spring darkness". All the visiting and parties of the novel rise to an unnatural climax as the door of the house stands "open hospitably on a furnace". The accent throughout that crucial last passage is on an abrupt ending by superior force of what had been earlier described as the "vital pattern" of expected continuity. Elizabeth Bowen's remark that the novel "from first to last takes its pitch from the month of its name" reinforces this sense of the breaking of a seasonal rhythm as the primary fact of *The Last September.* The chief point about the Naylors and the life of places like Danielstown is not that they and it were decadent or wilfully blind. It is that they were erased.

It is worth comparing the impression of this final scene with that important earlier passage describing the response of Laurence, Lois's cousin, to the watcher on the mountain, the I.R.A. man looking down at Danielstown. Laurence is aware of *force,* a "reserve of energy and intention" which "impinges to the point of transformation" on the "pattern below." Force, it is implied, can make or unmake "reality", can change the way in which a pattern of living is perceived, even by those within it. It is the property of overwhelming hostile "energy and intention" to deny not merely the life but the meaning of what they set themselves to destroy. Whatever general historical views the reader may entertain of the Anglo-Irish landowners outside the scope of *The Last September,* it is impossible to deny that within the novel the Naylors, for all their obvious limitations, are the only example of a fairly happy relationship and a degree of stability. It is as this that they are destroyed, not as the representatives of an unjust social order, the question of whose injustice is not, in any case, the subject of the novel. (This, of course, is not to deny that the Naylors' weaknesses and the weaknesses of the Anglo-Irish position are, incidentally, shown in *The Last September. Bowen's Court* was later to sum up one of the most salient of them in the remark that the Protestant landowners had "formed a too-grand idea of themselves".)

Elizabeth Bowen accepts the process of history and the destruction it brings about with a matter of factness which critics of her work have not shown. This view of history has to be taken into account in reading *The Last September.* Although it violates a complex work to name some one theme as its "subject", the book is essentially an exploration of the individual's search for meaning and order at a time of cultural fracture. Apart from their personal significance to the author, the Troubles and the downfall of the Anglo-Irish landowners offer the setting for a peculiarly vivid instance of that displacement of sensibility which has come subsequently to be widely known as the "Modernist Crisis". The focal point of *The Last September* is not a political crisis or a social upheaval but one of those moments when it becomes obvious that, in Thomas Mann's well-known phrase, "the wisdom of the past has become non-transferable" or in D. H. Lawrence's remark in *Kangaroo:* "It was in 1915 the old world ended".

Although not experimental in form, *The Last September* has many of the most significant "modernist" hallmarks, especially an emphasis on cultural breakdown, severance from past traditions, the failure or at least inadequacy of communication, the isolation of the individual and the uncertain nature of selfhood.
—*John Coates*

One early comment is particularly illuminating. *The Times Literary Supplement* reviewer (February 7, 1929), sedulously adopting the "plain man" standpoint, saw the novel as displaying "too much cleverness" and its story as no more "than a framework for a flickering study of human convolutions", a vision of life as "fundamentally absurd". Although this early reviewer does not develop his perception, his reaction is more authentic than most of the later repeated generalizations about "mood" and "atmosphere". *The Last September* belongs, with an important part of its vision, to a 1920's preoccupation with the discontinuity of the world, with disorientation and the loss of a communal reality. "Flickering studies of human convulsions", or "visions of life as fundamentally absurd" are irritated but not inaccurate descriptions, from the contemporary conventional point of view, of the work of Proust, Joyce or Virginia Woolf. Although not experimental in form, *The Last September* has many of the most significant "modernist" hallmarks, especially an emphasis on cultural breakdown, severance from past traditions, the failure or at least inadequacy of communication, the isolation of the individual and the uncertain nature of selfhood. It is typical of such a "Modernist" climate that Marda Norton, for example, should consider that her own experience must be meaningless to Lois, because the individual's relation to life is one of "infinite variation" which

> breaks the span of comprehension between being and being and makes an attempt at sympathy the merest fumbling for an outlet along the boundaries of the self.

The Naylors' life and attitudes are presented not as a testimony to some peculiar decadence in the Anglo-Irish landlords but as an example of a 1920's avant-garde truism best known in Virginia Woolf's formulation "On or about December 1910 human character changed". Elizabeth Bowen's subsequent comment merely confirms what the novel itself shows. The Naylors are meant to seem historically dated rather than guilty:

> If it seems that Sir Richard and Lady Naylor are snobs with regard to Lois's young officers, recall that the uncle and aunt's ideas dated back to the impeccable years before 1914.

Mrs Ramsay in *To The Lighthouse* (published two years before *The Last September*) provides an excellent analogy for the Naylors and their function. Like Virginia Woolf's hostess and homemaker, Sir Richard and his wife have an assured sense of their roles both social and sexual. (Their stability is suggested by, among much else, the Victorian wholesomeness of dreams when "soundly asleep" in a night that rolls over them "thickly and uneventfully"). When her old friend Francie sees Lady Naylor again, after a lapse of years, she sees her as "happier, harder". In her face is a record not of failure but of toughness and coping. Myra Naylor is someone who "goes on with" life, who discharges "the duty of love and pleasure". Like Mrs Ramsay, Lady Naylor stresses the personal rather than the abstract and concentrates on the achieving of pleasant social occasions, and the maintaining of emotional stability. Her view of her own particular historical situation is neither foolish nor incomprehensible. Although cancelled by events, it is not wrong or escapist. Rather it reflects her reliance on the restraints, tolerances and little acts of personal kindness which soften the edges of social and economic systems. The Naylors' fuzziness and vagueness, their deliberate ignoring of provocations and alarms, their agreeable manners and solicitude for their native Irish neighbours (because "it's not a good thing to have made an enemy") prevents lines being drawn too sharply. There is, in fact, some political wisdom in such behavior. Those enjoying privileges or a position others question may help themselves by being personally pleasant. The Naylors are destroyed not by their own lack of perception but by the British parade of naked force, the countryside "altogether too full of soldiers" which shows too clearly the mechanism of society which the tact of Danielstown's owners had helped to disguise. Elizabeth Bowen's own later comment that the Anglo-Irish keeping up of their "orthodox conventional social life", as the Naylors did at Danielstown, seemed "the best thing to do" in circumstances "more tragic than they cared to show" suggests a different interpretation of Sir Richard and his wife from the one adopted by almost all critics of *The Last September:* (Read in the light of such a comment for example, the early scene in which the "crowd of portraits" reflecting an earlier ease and confidence, give the present inhabitants of Danielstown "a thin, over-bright look" in their "lower cheerfulness, dining and talking" is sympathetic rather than condemnatory. It suggests not some process of historical degeneration but the poignancy of the effort to maintain social life against a threatening background). As Mrs Ramsay's world of elaborate hospitality, of chaos kept at bay by adroit charm, represents an ideal the young cannot accept and do not wish to follow, so the Naylors' delicate scheme of pleasantness, evasion and sociability finds few imitators in a new generation. Mrs Ramsay's and the Naylors' pattern of life are alike in another respect too. Both codes and their representatives are destroyed by sheer force, the brutalities of individual death and the Great War in one case, the Troubles in the other.

Arguably the most original feature of *The Last September,* and the most suggestive for its author's future development, is the odd angle from which it views the "Modernist Crisis" and cultural deracination. Indeed, the novel's epigraph, from Proust's *Le Temps Retrouvé,* seems to announce the solution to discontinuity and deracination, to failures of communication between individuals and to the meaninglessness of experience, on which the great Modernist works were built. Proust had stated that the materials of art could come "in frivolous pleasures, in idleness . . . , in unhappiness" and that art, by creating significant harmony from these materials, can redeem them. This could be said to be the faith of Modernism, of Proust, Joyce or Virginia Woolf. It is exemplified by the great and well-known moment in *To The Lighthouse* when Lily Briscoe completes her painting.

At first sight, it might seem that this "Proustian paradox" (in Hermione Lee's phrase) of tedious, poverty-stricken experience being redeemed by an aesthetic achievement for which tedium has itself provided the materials or the preconditions is to be the ultimate meaning of *The Last September.* The "Proustian paradox" raises a problem. It clearly does have a significance in Elizabeth Bowen's own life. One might well argue that she is presenting herself as Lois and suggesting that experiences which for her seemed thin at the time will become the novel itself, that the writing of the book comes out of what appeared at a time of "impatience, frivolity or lassitude". However, if one reads *The Last September* as it stands and without this external autobiographical information the expectation of the "Proustian paradox" is raised only to be challenged. Some support is given for such a reading in Elizabeth Bowen's remark that the novel does deal with "invented happenings, imagined persons" and is "at many, many removes from reality". There is no moment of artistic transcendence for Lois within the novel. Her painting, the conversation with Marda makes clear, is weak and derivative. (She is "cleverer", the older woman apologetically remarks, than her drawings suggest.) The sardonic authorial comment on Lois's writing is even more decisive:

> She took all this merciless penetration for maturity.

Any artistic promise she may have remains not only unfulfilled, but unrevealed when the book ends and the "Proustian

paradox" has no significance for her, whatever its significance for her creator. Perhaps one should read the epigraph of *The Last September* more carefully. It comes from that passage in *Le Temps Retrouvé* where Proust is describing those with an artistic temperament or leanings but who are unwilling to undertake the concentration and labour of creation:

> They suffer but their sufferings, like the sufferings of virgins and lazy people, are of a kind that fecundity or work would cure.

The Proustian epigraph offers no possibility of a Modernist aesthetic transcendency but rather emphasizes a peculiar kind of failure, not necessarily permanent or irremediable, but not remedied within the bounds of *The Last September.*

In order to understand the failure the novel records, it is necessary to look more closely at that structural symmetry already referred to. The opening episode of *The Last September* is dominated by two factors. The reader is made aware of the difference between the generation of Francie Montmorency and the Naylors and that of Lois and her cousin Laurence. Secondly, attention is drawn to Lois's expectations about her meeting with Mr Montmorency, the object of one of her most important childhood memories. It is at once made clear that some substantial alterations in the quality and nature of personal relationships, the way in which they are conceived and valued, has occurred between one generation and another. The Naylors' and Montmorencys' acquaintance with each other "was an affair of generations". More important, out of this now fading context of stability and habitude, had grown the particular friendship of Myra, Lady Naylor and Francie Montmorency. Francie's feeling for Myra, it is established, grew out of her feeling for the old presence of Danielstown in her consciousness. She had "heard all her life" of its inhabitants before she met them. "There had been no beginning". She has a "sense of return" because of this old family connection, "of having awaited". This security is, it appears, the necessary background to the young womens' enthusiastic discovery of each other. The house "lying secretly at the back" of Francie's mind is the setting for talks "confidential if not alarmingly intimate". This whole past episode connects a certain kind of order with a certain kind of intimacy, both of which are fact vanishing in the present.

Here, the older generations' confidence and readiness to enter into relationships seems to have evaporated. To Laurence and Lois emotional commitments are awkward, embarrassing, even incredible. They are like the debris of the Imperial and Ascendancy past among the Danielstown furniture, including those photographs of reunions "a generation ago" which seems to Lois to give out "a vague depression" from the wall. Laurence sits carefully out of the way on a "not very comfortable" chair because he "dared not go down" for another book, fearing to meet the visitors and have to talk to them. Lois feels a similar unease. She prefers Laurence's cold egocentricity and indifference to "every shade of her personality" to the tender and receptive listeners with whom she feels she has exposed too much of herself. Both cousins share a wariness, a refusal of involvement or commitment. Laurence boasts of having "no emotional life". Lois notes the warm meeting of her aunt and Francie like an anthropologist noting the customs of a remote tribe. She remarks calmly that "There was a good deal of emotion". The opening juxtaposition of Lois and Laurence helps, of course, to broaden the observation of the novel to an affair of generations. Lois's characteristics cannot be seen as mere personal idiosyncrasies or products of her own raw youth.

However, a second and vital point is made in these opening pages of *The Last September.* While Lois shares Laurence's "post-War" edginess and general lack of confidence in human relations, there is another and contradictory element in her character. Mr Montmorency has been the focus of her "illusions" since she was ten and the reason for this childhood memory, which causes her to be interested in the reunion in spite of her awkwardness, is a curious and symptomatic one. She remembered Hugo, as her mother's guest, falling asleep in the garden in a "perfectly simple exposed way". He seemed without pretence and unlike other visitors who were "noisy at one" as a child. What Lois apparently values is a quality of *repose* she once thought she detected in her aunt's guest, a "melancholy and exhausted and wise" readiness to be himself, a wholeness of nature which needs no effort or attitudinisings. In fact, Lois is wrong about Hugo Montmorency. What she hoped for in a minor way from meeting him again, however, is what she pursues, much more deeply, in her relationship with Gerald, the possibility of a connection of intellect with instinct, in a life free from self-consciousness and self-division. (It is suggestive that she should recall Hugo's unembarrassed sleeping immediately after her own almost dottily self-conscious reflections on how her fingernails grow inexhaustibly "out of" her and that they are the only part of one's person "of which it is possible to be conscious socially"). Elizabeth Bowen's places Lois firmly in a post-War context in the later Preface to the novel:

> World War had shadowed her school days: *that* was enough—now she wanted order.

The order which Lois wants, involves an emotional and personal stability, even more than a social one. Yet such a desire, it is plain, must involve a placing of the self in a social context for which neither Lois nor her cousin Laurence appear to have the desire or the confidence.

Hugo Montmorency, through his relationship to the Naylors

and to Laura, Lois's dead mother, introduces another significant factor into the book's design. The dimension of past events is insisted upon for various reasons. One of the most important of these is that figures in the present, such as Lois or Laurence, and the emotional and cultural climate which they represent have, we are meant to see a context in the choices or refusals of the previous generation. The "Modernist Crisis" is the result, not of a sudden cataclysm, but of a number of complex processes, some of which are typified in the lives of Hugo and Francie and in Hugo's early decision to sell his property. At first sight, Hugo's conduct might have seemed that of a realist, one who has read a historical situation aright and salvaged something from the downfall of the Anglo-Irish landowners. Surely it was better to have sold his house Rockriver long before the Troubles, rather than to have hung on, like the Naylors, until Danielstown was burned. Yet, the novel early makes clear, what purported to be sensible, a making of his peace with circumstances, was, in fact, ignoble, an uprooting and a destruction of some part of Hugo's life from which it has never really recovered. Francie, with "a delicate woman's strong feeling for 'naturalness'" always blamed herself for not having dissuaded him from the sale. She had been pained by his lack of feeling for his home "as by an expression of irreligion". "Religion" and "nature" are strong and challenging terms. They insist uncompromisingly, and in a novel otherwise so aware of the Modernist climate, so unfashionably, on the real value of the home, the family past, the pieties of ancestry. Even if, for some reason, they are impossible to get or to keep, these are the essential preconditions of emotional health. Hugo sells Rockriver not, we are to believe, from a wise and necessary yielding to historical processes but because "he had expected little of life". This chosen homelessness and resulting debility of the Montmorencys is emphasized by their weak notion of buying a bungalow somewhere which is then as weakly abandoned. Hugo's uprooting of himself has prepared the way for the self-pitying anticlimax of his later life, a "net of small complications" without the dignity of tragedy. Especially, it explains the emotional failure of his marriage to Francie. Since "they had no house" and Francie "no vocation", they have drifted about, Hugo steering his wife into the role of a permanent invalid. The closest part of their marital bond seems to be his nightly combing out of her hair. (Hugo and Francie are, of course, one of many other instances of displacement and deracination resulting in emotional damage in Elizabeth Bowen's work. One recalls the way in which the rootlessness of Theodora Thirdman's parents in *Friends and Relations* is linked to her own disastrous emotional development or the context given to Robert's betrayal of his country in *The Heat of the Day* in the impermanence of his family home, Holme Dene, a house like a stage set, practically always for sale).

If we are meant to compare the older and younger generation in *The Last September* we are equally meant to compare the two specimens of the older generation itself. The Naylors and their real, if conventional, happiness take on another light when compared with the choices their contemporaries the Montmorencys have made. Myra, who would not have her husband "otherwise" has made a better bargain, within the limits of the established duties of family and position, than her friend Francie has with a husband who has drifted away from them. Hugo's failure is, significantly, twofold. It involved the sale of his home and the choice of a wandering life spent largely in hotels. Also, and equally important, was his failure to love Laura, Lois's mother, no doubt a difficult woman, but one whose restlessness had been an "irradiation" as he recalls years later. This earlier betrayal of love, linked to the failure to establish one's life, is echoed and amplified in the second generation, in Lois.

The background of Hugo's failure, and his vanity, posturing and self-deception throughout *The Last September* undermines the "wisdom" of his view of the Anglo-Irish dilemma, whatever its apparent plausibility. His answer to Marda's question about the Troubles, "Will there ever be anything we can all do except not notice?" is to deny any point or meaning to the Anglo-Irish. Their collective personality is merely "a sense of outrage and we'll never get outside it". Marda Norton's response to this pseudo-omniscience, this moral and emotional bankruptcy masquerading as maturity, defines the spiritual landscape of *The Last September* with peculiar accuracy:

> But the hold of the country *was* that she considered, it could be thought of in terms of oneself, so interpreted. Or seemed so—"Like Shakespeare", she added more vaguely, "or isn't it?"

She half recollects, is dimly aware, of some universe of moral discourse in which instincts are their own arguments, or rather need no arguments. Love of land, of family, home or country cannot be rationally defended against a determinedly nihilistic scepticism any more than can the moral pieties or imperatives of Shakespeare's tragedies or histories. Such pieties are simply, in life as they are in Shakespeare, the bases and the perameters of a human existence. Marda's vague half-awareness, her sliding away from her own perception, shows that she knows this but cannot hold onto her knowledge. This little exchange, itself an epitome of Elizabeth Bowen's management throughout the novel of undeveloped communications and abortive arguments, suggest the presence of needs which cannot be satisfied, because they cannot be articulated, as Marda here, somehow, lacks the will to state them.

Hugo Montmorency's languid and somewhat precious nihilism, redolent of the *fin de siécle,* is a reminder that the crisis of meaning and order, of relationships and communication, which lies behind *The Last September* has

been developing for many years. The opening of the novel presents two lines of approach, the realization of a gap between the generations in their perceptions and emotions and, by contrast, the sense of historical and psychological processes which *link* the generations in an unfolding development. The choice between the stability and "despairing optimism" of Lady Naylor and Hugo's narcissism and surrender was an earlier and simpler picture of the problems which in Lois's life have become more intractable. The suggestion is made that at least part of the climate of the 1920's was created by earlier abandonings of hope, and lack of energy and purpose, veiling themselves, as in Hugo's case by a pretence of superior sensitivity and refinement.

One of the most subtle and amusing facets of this unfolding of tendencies in *The Last September* is illustrated by Hugo's encounters with Laurence. It is clear that nihilism in the mode of Maeterlinck does not care for nihilism in the mode of Aldous Huxley. It is also clear that the two are connected. (The affinity between Laurence and the boorish intellectuals in Huxley's recent novels was noted by the *Times Literary Supplement* reviewer). Hugo is offended by Laurence's clever conversation and asks, as an attempted snub, "Are you the undergraduate of today?" The "overfine machinery" of his own mind revolts from the details of living but, in the manner of his generation, prefers "manly talk" as a refuge rather than "articulate" cynicism. Marda Norton, however, tells Laurence that he is in danger of growing up into another version of Mr Montmorency.

Laurence himself notices the affinity, detecting the fact that Hugo "hated parties and conversation" as much as he did but was less "adept" at avoiding them or less fierce in honouring "the virginity of the intelligence". When asked by Marda Norton what he thinks about Lois, Hugo is about to reply that he is "no good at people" but refrains because "he reminded himself of Laurence". Hugo's stance is an 1890's melancholy fastidiousness. He is like a less successful member of the "Souls":

> His nostrils contracted slightly as though the smell drawn up from the roots of the grass . . . were more offensive than he cared to explain.

In Laurence, the façade of sensitivity has been dispensed with and the underlying misanthropy and egocentricity he shares with Hugo has become obvious. Where Hugo and those of his generation who shared his pose affected a flaccid ennui, Laurence is briskly malicious, exaggerating his Bloomsbury-like patter "his vein of third or fourth quality", or bringing up Hugo's failure to settle in Canada in order to needle the older man.

Hugo is (mentally) unfaithful to his wife Francie, or almost worse, to the memory of Laura, Lois's mother. Once recollections of her had filled the valley through which he walks with Marda but now "he and she might never have come here; they were disowned". The rocks are "transmuted" by his new found, or fancied, love for his new companion, who, comically, finds him unsympathetic and is even exasperated "past caution" with him. All Hugo's "unordered moods" are merely sentimentalisings of his own egotism:

> He loved her; a sense of himself rushed up, filling the valley.

Laurence, and those of the younger generation he typifies, need no such romantic clothing for *their* selfishness. Where Hugo used women for private fantasies, without ever really knowing or caring about them, Laurence discards them altogether, regarding Hugo as one who "had given away his integrity, had not even a bed to himself". It is interesting too, to notice affinities between Laurence and Francie, Hugo's wife. Neither of them, we are told, wanted to know "how anyone was" at the tennis party, or what they thought or wanted, but while Francie is all tremulous sensibility on the surface and egocentric beneath, Laurence is simply egocentric.

It may seem that too much may be read into Laurence's would-be clever chatter and cynicism. Is there really more in them than in those of many tiresome or pretentious undergraduates? A partial answer to the question is to consider Laurence's place in the scheme of *The Last September.* He clearly offers a contrast with Gerald, Lois's fiancé, as the important passage which juxtaposes the two young men's view of what civilization consists makes plain. At the same time, Laurence, as has been suggested, represents a continuation to a point of graceless absurdity of the selfishness and narcissism of the previous generation. What Laurence and the other characters around Lois are intended to embody is that "shape" which Elizabeth Bowen was later to describe as "*the* important thing". The juxtapositions, oppositions and developments between persons and generations in *The Last September* fulfils her later pronouncement that "in a novel every action or word on the part of any one of the characters has meaning . . . and the whole trend of the story suggests direction". Each member of the small, carefully chosen "cast" of *The Last September* has a cultural significance, a representational quality Laurence's elevation of his own refusal to *know,* or to be interested in, others into a sign of superior intelligence ("I never can conceive of anybody else's mentality") is to be judged against Elizabeth Bowen's constant preoccupation with the individual's duty to society. The ability of people to talk to each other in pleasant and easy ways, the capacity to like one's kind and to want to find out about them are indices of psychological health in the individual and cultural health in a society. Laurence anticipates Elizabeth Bowen's fuller treatment of the intellectual who betrays the duties of human sympathy, St Quentin in *The*

Death of the Heart. In fact, Laurence and St Quentin both offer the same manifesto of aloofness, in almost the same words.

More significantly, the view civilization which Laurence is made to hold is not some trivial, purely personal affair. It is the epitome of the rationalist, hedonist "progressive" 1920's thinking of which, no doubt, Elizabeth Bowen was fully aware when she was writing *The Last September.* This was a period, she remarked, when "Civilization (a word constantly on my 1928 lips) was now around me". Laurence's view of civilization as "an unemotional kindness withering to assertion selfish or racial; silence cold with a comprehension in which the explaining clamour died away" recalls the ambience of Lytton Strachey or of Bertrand Russell's popular writings, among so many others.

> **The comparison which the reader is invited to draw between Lois and her mother is a vital part of the novel's historical dimension, a reinforcement of the sense, fundamental to *The Last September,* of changes in moral feeling and emotional response.**
>
> —*John Coates*

It is an ideal to which Elizabeth Bowen is as merciless as D. H. Lawrence had been while adopting at the same time a much calmer and more matter of fact tone. She agrees with Lawrence's perception of the sterility, even suppressed hatred, behind the "progressive" ideals of the day. Under the rationalism and civilized irony of Lois's cousin lies the desire for "a faceless and beautiful negation", an end of "art, of desire" as well as of battle, effectively for a kind of death. The novel underlines this point elsewhere in Laurence's daydreams about violent destruction, his longing to "be here when this house burns" or for the arrival of the raiders whose non-appearance "pricked his egotism". In that curious passage, informed with the new psychological preoccupations of the period, which describes his fantasizing when unable to go to sleep it becomes clear that what Laurence enjoys is a frivolous mental manipulation of his relations and acquaintances, placing them, for his amusement, in imaginary scenarios, remaking marriages. Superficially amusing, it is a somewhat chilling passage suggesting Laurence's indifference to, even dislike, of people and relationships which actually exist. In superficial contrast Hugo "sets up a stage for himself" where, "divorced from fact and probability", he can indulge in erotic day-dreams about Marda. Underneath the romantic trappings and self-deception ("and if this were not love") there is a substantial similarity with Laurence in Hugo's manipulations of "power disconnected with life".

If it is interesting to see Laurence and his type as a continuation and development of the predilections of people like Hugo Montmorency, it is *essential* to see Lois in relation to her family past. Hugo's account of Laura, the dead girl's mother, may, perhaps must, be coloured by his unsatisfactory relationship with her, but there are striking likenesses between what we learn of the dead woman and what we see of her daughter. Like Lois, in her own way, Laura had "wanted her mind made up" by a relationship with a man. This Hugo felt unable to do for her: "I had enough to do with my own mind". In any case, she was never "real" in the way that he wanted. Her endless talk was a camouflage, he felt, for a wish to avoid personal contact or being known. If she thought he had succeeded in knowing she would "start a crying fit". Her throwing of herself into a marriage with Farquar, Lois's father, was an impulsive and muddled affair, completed before she "had time to get out of it". Her subsequent unhappy life gave her something concrete to be miserable about. Hugo's waspish recollections contain a substantial truth about the externals of Laura's behaviour, although he makes no attempt to understand the inner reasons for her actions. Hugo's version of these external details is confirmed when Sir Richard applies the very phrase to Lois which Hugo had used to describe her mother:

> She was just like Laura, poor Laura's own child in fact; she would talk and talk and you never knew where you had her.

The existence in her dead mother of a kind of prototype for Lois and an earlier version of some of the problems she faces might be a way of making the simple point that Lois has inherited something of her temperament. More than this is involved however. Laura's uncertainty about *her* role had fed those "epic rages", which Laurence remembered "against Hugo, against Richard against any prospect of life at all". The bitter quarrels, the "eroding companionship" with Hugo, to whom Laura was attracted but whose unresponsive nature could not provide what she needed, bred a "confusion which clotted up the air" of Laura's life. She raged impotently, scrawling "with passion" an insulting drawing of Hugo whose failure to marry was, in Lady Naylor's view part of his general "way of avoiding things". Finally, in her frustration, she "hotly" went North to marry Mr Farquar "the rudest man in Ulster". In these fragmentary references to her enough of Laura's character has been preserved to suggest an intelligent, spirited woman, reacting against the sentimental and limited role imposed on her sex, as in her abrasive rejection of "being loved" and gushed over by Miss Part, Lois's governess. We are reminded, however, that she belonged to a different world from the one Lois inhabits and a simpler. In Laurence's recollection the "dated" quality of Laura's impulsive marriage is what is emphasized. She

> buttoned a tight sleek dress of that day's elegance

> over her heaving bosom, packed her dresses in arched trunks (that had come back since to rot in the attics)

before embarking on her despairing flight. In its late romantic melodrama, such a scene belongs to the same world as Hugo's melancholy sensitivity, or Lady Naylor's sleeping when young and a "rebel" with a copy of Shelley's poems under her pillow.

The comparison which the reader is invited to draw between Lois and her mother is a vital part of the novel's historical dimension, a reinforcement of the sense, fundamental to *The Last September,* of changes in moral feeling and emotional response. Essentially the changes are in the direction of a greater complexity where the confidence to make even the wholehearted, if disastrous, gestures Laura made in the 1890's has been sapped. Lois recognizes that she is "twice as complex" as the older generation, because of the multiplicity of elements which have gone into her making. This feeling is accompanied by a sense of the passing of time, like a ship "rushing" onwards. The fact that she will penetrate "thirty years deeper" into it than her uncle, her aunt and than Hugo who "belonged" to their world, enhances Lois's awareness of "mystery and destination".

Lois looks in three directions in order to find answers to the problems raised by her apprehensions, needs and expectations of living. The tripartite division of *The Last September* corresponds to the three fields of her quest. In the novel's first section she is shown turning her eyes at the past, at Mr Montmorency, the lover who had failed her mother. Hugo's desertion of Laura and the resulting marriage to Farquar brought about Lois's birth and the identity with which she finds it so hard to cope. It might well seem that her problems might be clarified, if not solved, by going back into the past where they originated. Hugo, the missed possibility in her mother's life, is the missed possibility in her own, since he was the father she did not have. The journey back into the past is a frequently used narrative device, with its own mythic power. However, it is Elizabeth Bowen's purpose to raise the possibility of such a narrative line, or personal quest, only to disappoint it. She suggests an obvious and pleasing way in which *The Last September* might develop and then deliberately balks expectation. Hugo possesses none of that repose with which Lois's childhood memory had endowed him and for which she herself is seeking. He is vain, restless and self-deluding. Almost at once, on meeting him, she recognizes that though he was so subtle he "would not take the trouble to understand her". When he does look at her, it is with a cold, bored intelligence, superficially perceptive, actually dismissive:

> He supposed that unformed, anxious to make an effort, she would marry early.

It is, of course, a sound enough assumption, since she almost does. Hugo, however, is judging Lois by the choices and limitations available in his own generation and exemplified in the action of her mother Laura, the woman he emotionally betrayed.

If the past, incarnated in Hugo, has nothing to offer or to teach, it is natural to assume that one must look towards the future. The second section of *The Last September,* accordingly, is built round the visit of Marda Norton to Danielstown. Marda's stay, and its effect on Lois, represent a second aborted narrative possibility, a second potent myth deliberately discarded. If one cannot explore and redeem the past, then one can discard its elaborate and outworn claims and face the world in a spirit of "existential choice" (before the name), of rational unencumbered freedom.

Marda is introduced as a disrupter of social ease through her accidents and gaucheries on previous occasions at Danielstown. Her first effect on Lois is to accelerate the girl's emancipation from romantic illusions of the past in general and Hugo, in particular, through her open derision of him as a man married to a woman old enough to be his mother. In other ways, too, Marda's "sophistication opened further horizons to Lois". The new woman of the 1920's, she has shed the "feminine" sweetness of Francie and the assiduous charm of Lady Naylor along with "feminine pear-shape". She watches and assesses others, challenging their "integrity" and the sincerity of their social postures from "the stronghold of her indifference". By these astringent standards, Hugo is quickly disposed of. She treats his infatuation with her as an irrelevant nuisance which does not concern her in the least.

In Lois's first fairly lengthy conversation with Marda, however, the younger woman quickly detects an underlying insecurity beneath the surface elegance and ease. Lois's attitude changes in this encounter. She starts from admiration of Marda's "inimitable deftness" with her make-up, those casual gestures which, like Stella's as seen by Harrison in *The Heat of the Day,* are the outward tokens of a "brilliant life". Lois yearns to purchase a place in the memory of this distinguished being even at the cost of the burning of the house in "one scarlet night". The room in which they sit seems, like Lois's own existence, hopelessly devalued, full of the "dusk of oblivion", compared with the nature promise of Marda's forthcoming marriage. However, the turning point in their talk comes quickly and decisively. Lois attempts, in a long passage, left in reported speech perhaps to suggest its breathlessness and incoherence, to explain her need "to go wherever the war hadn't", to travel "alone", to look at sights "unprepared" and "unadmonished". Her daydreams, although inchoate, involve a reaction against wartime restrictions but even more, a revolt against the limited role of women, "of being not noticed because she is a lady",

a demand for wider experience. Marda's reply reveals that her emancipation is superficial. She advises Lois not to "expect to be touched or changed—or to be in anything that you do". The comment is "unwisdom" since, in a somewhat cryptic but telling authorial phrase, it lacks "the sublimer banality". In order to live, one must have an appetite for living, a hopefulness or idealism prepared to risk sounding naive or banal. This Marda, in spite of her poise and air of independence, does not possess. When Lois tries to explain that she wants to be "in a pattern", to be "related", her companion immediately sees this in the narrow formalized terms of being "a wife and mother". Marda's praise of this "traditional" feminine role is vitiated by her own adoption of it out of a search for financial security and in a weary spirit of "we can always be women".

Lois, watching the deferential stoop of the older woman's head, as she writes to her fiancé Leslie Lawe, thinks "how anxious to marry Marda must really be" and "her distantness and her quick, rejecting air must be a false effect". This intimation about Marda's deliberate choice of the conventional role out of mere expedience, does not, at once, form a final verdict on her in Lois's mind. The delay in Lois's reaction is one of the characteristic subtleties in Elizabeth Bowen's writing. Rather (and this is surely more true to the way in which individuals do perceive each other) Lois's insight remains, beneath many pleasant and interesting exchanges, to surface again, after the failure of her relationship with Gerald, in a poignant complaint:

> Even Marda—nothing we said to each other mattered, it hasn't stayed, she goes off to get married
> in a mechanical sort of way. She thinks herself so
> damned funny—it's cheap, really.

Marda's modishly tough and disengaged manner is as deceptive as Laurence's Bloomsbury "civilization". Embracing the future with Miss Norton is no more of an answer than disentangling the past with Hugo.

One of the most curious features of *The Last September* is the significance of events which do not happen. Indeed what does not take place (but very well might have done) is as important as what actually does. The novel propounds the features of the crisis familiar in Modernist literature, the abrupt break in the pattern of history, the loss of confidence in the autonomous personality, the discontinuity of the self and the uncertainty of its contact with the outside world, the failure of social contact and communication. Where *The Last September* differs from other books which examine this crisis is partly in its diagnosis of the problem and partly in what seems a resolute refusal of the solutions most commonly offered. The most popular of these, the aesthetic transcendence of chaos, the solution of *A Portrait of the Artist as a Young Man* and *To The Lighthouse,* is emphatically rejected, by disallowing Lois artistic talent and success. More traditional solutions, the search and understanding of the past or the open-eyed facing of the future are denied with equal force.

There remains one final solution, that of synthesis, the possibility that a split culture or a splintered vision of reality may be healed by the joining through love of rival and originally incompatible visions. Perhaps the best known example of such a synthesis is E. M. Forster's enterprise in *Howards End.* Lois's relationship with Gerald clearly does have resonance far beyond that of a purely personal love affair. To the shattered Daventry, it is primarily Gerald's youth that is striking. He looks across a gulf at "our young friend", and his capacity for hope. In Lady Naylor's view, however, "no amount of experience shook these young Englishmen up". Gerald is primarily a study in the success and failure of training, in the nature of the public school product. His conditioning is thorough, an imbibing of simple healthy sentimental images, of the ideal life as

> a fixed leisured glow, and relaxation, as on coming in to tea from an afternoon's gardening with his mother in autumn.

At first sight in such passages and others, we seem to be being offered a version of E. M. Forster's critique of the "undeveloped heart" of the English professional and middle-class. However, one has only to think of Gerald Dawes in *The Longest Journey,* of Ronnie in *A Passage to India* or even of the Wilcoxes in *Howards End* to realize that a satirical intention is not predominant in the portrait of Gerald in *The Last September.* Instead, one might even view him as a recapitulation of some Forsterian material from a non-Forsterian standpoint, as a partial answer or alternative to that "unfairness" with which, a few years later, Elizabeth Bowen suggested Forster had treated "half his cast in *A Passage to India*".

Gerald is unfailingly amiable. Betty Vermont's description of him as "so absolutely nice-minded" is sustained by his behaviour throughout the novel. The key incident in his severance from Lois is caused not by an instance of insensitivity but by one of mistaken chivalry and decency. He refrains from making a physical response to her appeal, which might have saved the situation. He does this, however, not out of lack of feeling but because he earlier promised Lady Naylor not to try to kiss her. Lois feels not so much that she is the victim of emotional shallowness or refusal to feel as of a refusal to see her as she really is. She tells Gerald "I don't believe you know what I'm like a bit". Some idea he has formed of her remains "inaccessible to her" and she cannot affect it. He, for his part, is convinced that "his darling Lois . . . had no idea what she was".

Comparison is one of the most significant devices in *The Last September.* The reader is meant to infer meaning by the carefully placed moral and historical juxtapositions of Lois and Laura, the Montmorencies and the Naylors, Gerald and Laurence, and Laurence and Hugo. Among the less obvious, but nevertheless useful, of these comparisons is that of Lois and Gerald with Livvy and David. What the contrast of Lois's love relationship with that of her much simpler friend, whom she suddenly outgrows and drops, is that Lois has a much more complex organization. She reveals a need to express, to explore and to understand her own needs. Her conception of love is, like her conception of herself, one which rejects the premature closing down of the development of feeling and of mutual emotional exploration. Gerald's reserve is, on the contrary, a matter of "convenience", undeserving of the "sensitive reverence with which such a quality is apt to be treated". He avoids emotional communication because it embarrasses, not because it is too sacred to discuss. Lois was Gerald's

> integrity of which he might speak to strangers but of which to her he would never speak.

There is obviously a serious defect in the training which prevents a lack of emotional articulacy, even though such a lack is not the final truth about Gerald.

Lois's predicament is not specifically an Anglo-Irish one. Rather it is, in considerable part, the product of the need felt by some women for a less stereotyped role, for a freer and more open way of feeling, for a greater respect for the individual identity. Lois feels the need for "some incalculable shifting of perspectives that would bring him wholly into focus, mind and spirit" before she can wholeheartedly love him. For her, love must involve a communion of intelligences, a growth of understanding not simply a meeting of instincts, of "unclothed" emotion where a kiss is "an impact with inside blankness". It is, perhaps, this refusal to accept that instinct can be all in all which caused Jocelyn Brooke to note a cerebral quality in Elizabeth Bowen's description of sexual feeling.

However there is a contradiction at the heart of Lois's problem. While she desires the openness to development, the avoidance of some narrow role as Gerald's "lovely woman", she does at the same time, desire "something beyond sensation", a "quiet beyond experience", a kind of wholeness and calm which exists beyond the "little twists of conversation all knotted together". It is a misreading of her relationship with Gerald to ignore her own persistent sense of being "lonely", without a future, "ruled out", of lacking the stability such a love might bring. Besides, the reader's awareness that the inability of Lois to love Gerald is a failure is sharpened by the existence in the novel of a wider context of rootlessness and refusal to feel, deepening from Hugo's generation to Laurence's. It is also worth giving weight to Elizabeth Bowen's later remark that Lois "touches the margins of tragedy, not in Gerald's death, but in her failure to love".

However, no external evidence is needed since the text makes it clear that Lois chooses to abandon the possibilities of this love and supplies her motive for doing so. When all is allowed for Gerald's limitations and for Lady Naylor's interference (well meant according to her lights, since she wishes to spare Lois the poverty she foresees for Livvy), it is Lois who cannot bring herself to make the choice, which, like all choice, contains some sacrifice. In a crucial incident she overhears her aunt and Mrs Montmorency discussing her relationship with Gerald. Lois is aware of the disadvantages of marrying to a woman:

> Love, she had learnt to assume, was the mainspring
> of womens' grievances.

(The parenthesis is significant, of course, because it implies that some of these disadvantages may be subjective and ignores any possible gains). The overheard conversation proceeds and Lois is about to hear Mrs Montmorency make some definite statement about her. This Lois cannot bear. "She didn't want to know what she was" since she feels "such knowledge would finish one". The rejection of final self-knowledge is linked here with the rejection of the confinement, as it's seen, of a relationship.

> The "creation of atmosphere", or the evocation of minute notations of feeling for which [Bowen] is celebrated are, in fact, subordinate to a far more striking quality in *The Last September,* that of a judicious moral assessment which treats every feature of a problem with scrupulous fairness, combined with a tough-mindedness which does not attempt to suggest that there is some compromise in which every incompatible good can be combined.
>
> —*John Coates*

The Last September nowhere pretends that Gerald does not have very obvious limitations. However, in a superb passage, Elizabeth Bowen underlines the fact that, in rejecting love, even with its attendant restrictions, Lois has denied herself the chance of understanding herself and of achieving some final fruition. Lois bangs her water-jug about in her basin to draw attention to her presence and stop the two women talking. In this she succeeds.

It was victory. Later on, she noticed a crack in the basin, running between a sheaf and an cornucopia; a harvest richness to which she each day bent down her face. Every time, before the water clouded, she would see the crack: every time she would wonder: what Lois *was*—She would never know.

The image is an apt suggestion of the failure of any "harvest richness" in Lois's own life. The last sentence of the chapter is ominous with its implication of some definite and final turning away, some willed refusal. There will, indeed, be no more Septembers.

This sense of refusal is reinforced later when Gerald utters words which have a "solemn echo", "You know I'd die for you". In Lois's mind these words evoke the high arches of a church, where the young pair are to be married. What he says has too a "warmth and weight" and a "quiet" as though "for many nights he had been sleeping beside her". It is the promise of a bond, a progress to stability and peace, "beyond experience", perhaps because nothing in her experience affords evidence for what she yet nevertheless intuitively senses is possible and which she desires. Then, with a deliberate baldness, and a bleakness, unexplained here but perhaps explained by the breaking of the "Golden Bowl", the novel states the fact of her refusal:

> But she turned away from some approach in his
> look.

What Gerald had said and what Lois had felt is proof of the existence of words of power, offers, promises, or kinds of loyalty which bind individuals to each other and on which "quiet" can be built. What Gerald had offered was significantly different from the "future" envisaged by Marda or Laurence or the "past" incarnated in Hugo. In a final scene with her cousin, Lois tentatively admits the existence of a range of feeling from which she has chosen to exclude herself. Laurence comes to Lois in the garden of Danielstown after Daventry has brought the news of Gerald's death. She explains that she is "just thinking". This seems to be a mood Laurence can understand, in which by a process of reflection one can reach a kind of indifference or detachment where everything appears relative, without ultimate meaning or value and at last without power to hurt. This is the consolation he promises Lois:

> I think I should, I expect—I don't know—one probably gets past things.

Lois replies that "there are things one can't get past", meaning Gerald's love of her and of his country: "At least, I don't want to". Laurence, perhaps out of politeness, agrees, "studying, with an effort of sight and comprehension, some unfamiliar landscape". Gerald's fumbling sense that Laurence's earlier idea of civilization reflected "a wrongness that was the outcome of too much thinking" receives a posthumous confirmation.

If one gives due weight to this exchange, our last glimpse of Lois, then it signifies an affirmation of certain values. These values had been preserved in a fossilised form by the Naylors, before being engulfed by historical change. They had been denied by the modern consciousness, developing from Hugo to Laurence. They are values which, it appears, survive their association with Gerald's naivety and emotional immaturity, his young man's awareness of Lois's needs and feelings at a time when women's image and expectations were changing.

The Last September has many titles to distinction but perhaps the greatest use of them is its handling of a complex moral and emotional problem. This problem, born of long-standing cultural change, now sharpened by war and social upheaval, is, essentially the conflict between the claims of development and those of stability. Lois is a microcosm of that conflict, to which Elizabeth Bowen returns in her later novels, and which is, perhaps, their essential subject. The "creation of atmosphere", or the evocation of minute notations of feeling for which she is celebrated are, in fact, subordinate to a far more striking quality in *The Last September,* that of a judicious moral assessment which treats every feature of a problem with scrupulous fairness, combined with a tough-mindedness which does not attempt to suggest that there is some compromise in which every incompatible good can be combined. As the rootless Stella finds in *The Heat of the Day,* the stability of Mountmorris had its price. There is no easy answer. In *The Last September,* current solutions to the "Modernist" crisis of meaning, having been tried and found wanting, another choice was left. It again was not without its price, one which Lois was unwilling to pay. However, *The Last September* does not enforce a sense of futility so much as that of an unanswered question. It can claim the giving of that sense of "direction" which Elizabeth Bowen, later offered as one of the reasons she wrote:

> Even stories which end in the air, which are comments on and pointers to futility imply that men and women are too good for the futility in which they are involved.

John Coates (essay date July 1992)

SOURCE: "The Tree of Jesse and the Voyage Out: Stability and Disorder in Elizabeth Bowen's *Friends and Relations,*" in *Durham University Journal,* Vol. 84, No. 2, July, 1992, pp. 291-302.

[*In the following essay, Coates examines the essentially conservative framework of* Friends and Relations, *arguing that the narrative defends family and social institutions despite its characters' personal weaknesses.*]

Elizabeth Bowen (1899-1973) is a novelist highly praised in standard works of reference and literary histories. Yet, oddly, critical attention has not kept pace with general acclaim. There is an obvious reason for this. Academics, at least in Britain, are not, on the whole, sympathetic to Bowen's conservative social and moral position. They cannot and do not deny the distinction of her style and the skill of her design but her vision does not appeal to them.

In many ways this is unfortunate. Whatever the reader's own political or moral sympathies, there is no denying Bowen's subtlety and intelligence. Her Anglo-Irish inheritence might be bound (if one was not utterly stupid and perverse) to make for a sharpened consciousness of the problem of any order or any attempt to build stability or permanence. The achievement of the 'people of Burke and Grattan' was one of glorious distinction but the injustices and cruelties it involved were blatant. At least some of Bowen's density of texture comes from the great value she placed on order and rootedness while acknowledging that the two are insecure and precarious and may (perhaps *must*) involve some pain or loss of oneself or to others. What is inescapably the good, the natural life is, at some time, difficult, threatened, undermined. Order and rootedness can never be merely assumed or taken for granted either as facts which will continue or as values to be endorsed. The object of this paper is to examine one of the most interesting of Elizabeth Bowen's studies of the problems of rootedness and order in her novel *Friends and Relations* (1931).

Clearly enough *Friends and Relations* has its basis in the contrast between two instincts, the first locating the emotional life in institutions such as marriage, the home or the family, and the second desiring to reject those institutions in favour of the autonomy of the self without ties. It is possibly that basis itself which has irritated critics and led them to undervalue the novel. Hermione Lee, for instance, attributes what she feels is an 'affectation' of language to the novels being 'reduced to investigating compromises and repressed emotions'. Yet the basic premise of *Friends and Relations* is the direct opposite of the one which underlies Lee's criticism. The compromises and 'repressions' (or rather acts of self-control) which the work examines are the foundations of social living, ultimately of civilisation. Far from being 'pointlessness', they are also the conditions of limited but substantial victories in the emotional life, of creation over destruction, of a difficult but rewarding art of the possible in the pursuit of happiness.

The first scene of *Friends and Relations* introduces many

of its themes and many of those contrasts around which its structure is organised. One of the simplest and yet most fundamental of these is the dichotomy between stasis and mobility. Laurel Studdart's sense that the hours before her wedding to Edward Tilney are 'like a too long wait on the platform of some familiar station' whose associations have become 'irksome' is a preliminary hint of an appetite for movement, for the cutting of ties, the taking of the individual out of a family or communal context. It is an appetite which is seen as a pervasive and deeply damaging feature of the contemporary world. The image is echoed, within a few pages, when Theodora Thirdman, who epitomises this destructive current in the novel, reproaches her parents for failing to live in such a fashion that they 'mattered' in a place, for failing to be other than 'superfluous'. It is a failure which helps to launch their daughter on her course:

> Arn't we ever going to begin? Mother, you're like someone sitting for always on a suitcase in a railway station. Such a comfortable suitcase, such a magnificent station!

Friends and Relations, like its successor *To the North* (1932), is concerned to explore the true nature and effects of this questing, unsettled spirit.

One of the two most important extended passages of imagery in the earlier novel is a revaluation of movement towards an unknown future. Lewis, Edward's closest friend, is 'stung to the personal quick' by the thought that Edward has, as he imagines, deserted his wife Laurel and gone off with her sister Janet. (The somewhat fragile but worthwhile marriages of the two Studdart sisters, Janet and Laurel, are the essential subject of the novel.) The 'guilty' couple are 'now out at sea', as it were, looking back at 'the whole town'. This image of the ship, sailing away with brave voyagers, out of the bounds of the known and conventional into the untried where risks must be taken, new values discovered, new emotions experienced, draws on a stock of feeling which Modernism inherited from the Romantic Movement. It is the mood of Virginia Woolf's *The Voyage Out* as much as Tennyson's *Ulysses.* Both the image and the mood behind it are questioned and subverted by Bowen as Lewis ponders what he feels was his friends' failure and betrayal: 'Landbound, he hated their damned ship, all damned ships and hated those everlasting departures'. The travellers are not going towards a 'trackless' and exciting future but towards a knowledge 'scored bewilderingly'. Even more significantly, the perspective from which the voyage is being made is altered. In this frequently recurring image the journey was invariably seen through the eyes of those who are setting out towards freedom or selfhood. The version of *Friends and Relations* makes a number of delicate adjustments. Lewis projects himself into the minds of those who, he supposes, are sailing away on their moral and emotional adventure.

However, what they see in the town they are leaving behind are its unexplored possibilities, 'some unknown relation' between its buildings or the church 'you often went in without looking up' and the steep avenue 'never mounted'. The angle of vision then shifts in Lewis's mind to those left behind. They 'relinquish the travellers, the ship vanishes'. Even regret is lost in 'that last exchange' and the town received the observers back into its 'confusion'. The point (one rarely made) is that those who remain within have a view of things just as much as those who reject or leave the community.

The very end of the novel offers another shift of perspective on this basic contrast of movement and stasis, or journeying to the unknown or remaining in the habitual. *Friends and Relations* begins with Laurel impatient to depart from the 'familiar station' of her old home to a new destination. It ends with both of Colonel Studdart's daughters, Laurel and Janet, back at their home, accompanying their father down the Cheltenham street, 'smiling to left and right'. American tourists are startled by 'a horn in the street, some alarm of departure', but the hotel down whose steps they hurry is the one in which Edward, Laurel's husband, stayed in before his marriage. The continuities of the novel's world have contained and neutralised the forces of departure and disruption. At the same time the resolution is qualified with sorrow. Mrs Studdart worries about Laurel though not about Janet: 'What became of her? She has never been away. When this house goes—I don't know'.

The sophistication and unpredictability of the novel's patterning of order and stasis are only part of its wider complexities. Many of these relate to the nuances of an attitude to human beings in society which the first chapter begins to define. *Friends and Relations* opens in that somewhat unfashionable literary territory of 'social comedy'. It is not one which many critics currently find interesting. Why describe the postures and pretensions of the public man or woman, the snobberies of class or money, or the minute gradations of position in some artificial hierarchy, when one ought to question the whole foundations of such a society or even help to hasten its disintegration? A recent and very influential account of the English novel sums up the common current dismissal of social comedy: 'At its lower levels, which have been very popular, it is the mode of an anxious society—an anxious class preoccupied with placing, grading, defining. . . . It's the staple of familiar sometimes witty, sometimes malicious minor fiction.' The description of the Tilney-Studdart wedding at the opening of *Friends and Relations* seems to go out of its way to emphasise the strain and artificiality of the event. Edward's 'wonderfully self-possessed' manner, too studied to be entirely pleasing, is the result of his determination that his wedding should pass off, like Julien Sorel's execution, simply, suitably, 'without any affectation on his part'. His mother, Lady Elfrida, 'over-acted a little' in her attempts to charm. In order to have a 'summer wedding' the bridal pair had 'devoured' each other through their endless winter engagement. Strain and artifice are the keynotes of the wedding photograph. The young couple wait 'for the curtain to rise' in a garden 'staged in light'. Yet it is not a successful piece of theatre. The photograph, when it is developed, is a partial failure, the young bridesmaids looking 'over-posed', the married pair suggesting 'the heroic perhaps exaggerated a little'. Yet Mrs Studdart can never resist showing the photograph to her visitors. It is a hint of the ambivalence the novel explores.

These are reinforced by a number of echoes of Jane Austen throughout *Friends and Relations.* The name of the richer and somewhat intimidating family with a 'dark' secret about whom the Studdarts know little is Tilney, an allusion to *Northanger Abbey.* There are verbal echoes, too, as in Janet's letters to her mother describing Rodney's courtship which, it appears, resulted from the fact that 'weather in —shire was uncertain' or in her parent's delight that Laurel has been given an 'establishment' through her marriage. Sometimes the echo is continued into a short passage of pastiche. When Janet's marriage is endangered, 'letters on this affair of extreme delicacy shot to and fro between the distracted Studdarts in Cheltenham and the distracted young Tilneys honeymooning in Dalmatia'. The Austen echoes suggest a continuity both in English social life and in the way that life has been described in English novels. They recall a mode of perception which views society as necessarily involving both pretension and a contrast between the unaccommodated individual and his or her social role. In that perception the existence of property necessarily colours views taken of marriage. Yet this coexists with an entire acceptance of both property and marriage as necessary and inevitable. The comedy is concerned with excesses within a recognised framework, not with a questioning of the framework itself.

The embarrassments of the Studdart-Tilney wedding set the tone for a whole view of society in *Friends and Relations.* Its starting point is a recognition of the limitations and inherent comedy of social gatherings. Almost anyone who has ever been to any wedding would understand such a standing joke as the penumbra of 'friends' and relations one hardly ever sees and scarcely knows now, yet who have to be invited: 'Many old friends whose persistence has become a reproach and cousins receding in the distance almost to vanishing point'. In such situations, and they are many, social exchange involves certain conventional responses, a common acceptance of certain codes which channel feeling and avoid fuss and friction. No sensible person would dream of taking such useful devices and guidelines for the realities of the private emotional life of individuals. As Mrs Studdart remarks, having 'learned to reply by formula' to the congratulations which 'come in steadily' on Janet's engagement to Rodney Megatt, 'I suppose it's never possible to be absolutely sincere'. As if to suggest what the use of

social conventions consists in, the reader is allowed a brief glimpse in the opening wedding scene of nature untrammeled by convention. The bride's two attendants, little girls 'with pink knickers', are typical of the unidealistic view *Friends and Relations* takes of young children generally:

'Cheat!' shrieked Prue.

'Are you allowed almond-paste?' Dilly countered.

'Oo, I'm sick of old almond-paste.'

The Jane Austen references have a second and more important function, however. By their contrast with the present they remind the reader of disruption as well as continuity. The Studdarts, in their Cheltenham seclusion, may carry on the older modes of life but their daughters' marriages thrust them into a current of radical moral change. It is bad enough to discover that one daughter, Janet, is to marry the nephew of the man who had been the lover of their other son-in-law's mother, Lady Elfrida. It is much more disorientating to find that their delicacies, doubts and moral quandary seem to mean nothing whatever to others. Lady Elfrida 'didn't consider the situation awkward at all. Not nowadays when everybody was different'. The Studdarts are left confused about their own behaviour. They do not know any longer whether they are being worldly or unworldly about the matter 'high-handed or simple'. It is perhaps significant that this amiable couple's home is called 'Corunna Lodge' with its suggestion of a gallant last stand. In their case it is a defence of failing standards and attitudes.

Yet the battle of Corunna was not an entire defeat, but a kind of Napoleonic Dunkirk. What the introductory chapters of *Friends and Relations* record is just such a narrow escape against the odds. They explore a victory against forces that make for disintegration. The compromise, the adjustments, the acts of self-command, the settling for what is less than one might have dreamed of but still a substantial contentment, all make up the map of civilised and adult life. The scheme is briefly suggested in the description of Janet's marriage to Rodney Megatt: 'No one knew what she thought. She had now, of course, her happiness, but it had been difficult—Cheltenham did not know'. What Cheltenham did not know has, however, been made clear enough to the reader. It is a mistake to see the structure of *Friends and Relations* as being based on two 'scandals', the overt one of Lady Elfrida's adulterous affair with Considine Meggatt, uncle of the Rodney who marries her daughter-in-law's sister, and the far more serious one of Janet's passionate but suppressed love for her sister's husband. This design could have made a striking plot and an interesting theme for a novel, but it is not the one Elizabeth Bowen chose to write. In fact, both 'scandals' are equally obvious from the beginning of *Friends and Relations.* The schoolgirl Theodora Thirdman, who is later to be developed as the main example and source of modern disorder, detects the emotional trouble behind Janet's impassive manner. Overhearing Lady Elfrida's loaded remarks, 'Theodora, intently listening, inferred that Janet loved Edward, that his mother preferred Janet; that for Janet this was a day of chagrin, possibly of despair'. The weight of interest in *Friends and Relations* rests not on the revelation of a secret to the reader but in examining the problem of maintaining order in the personal life and the poignancy of carrying out duties undertaken within relationships. It is concerned with the quality of love viewed as an institution rather than as a form of self-fulfilment.

> **The weight of interest in *Friends and Relations* rests not on the revelation of a secret to the reader but in examining the problem of maintaining order in the personal life and the poignancy of carrying out duties undertaken within relationships.**
> **—*John Coates***

The strains of maintaining the two sisters' marriages and the limitations of each relationship are made sufficiently clear for the question of whether they are worth maintaining to become unavoidable. Neither marriage is based on deep and whole-hearted love or romantic self-abandonment. In one case, that of Laurel and Edward, it is not what is somewhat intimidatingly called a mature or adult relationship at all. Rodney, Janet's husband, is an admitted second best. A somewhat colourless man, 'fair, lean and solid', he was 'very much liked in the neighbourhood'. What Janet values is his calming sympathy and undeniable physical attractiveness as she 'wept on his shoulder': 'Though she did not love him she began to understand desire. He comforted her a little'. However, Rodney's behaviour during the meal at the Ionides Restaurant, his first, extremely difficult meeting with his future brother-in-law Edward, reveals his more substantial qualities. It also defines much more clearly the novel's moral attitudes. The meal is a test of the two sisters' husbands' ability to get on with each other and of the future family relationship to cohere. The test is passed. Potentially explosive material is rendered manageable by manners and the exercise of self-control. The scene is a paradigm of that social loving which secures the individual's peace of mind and realisable happiness and skirts around possible disasters. There is a suggestion of a code in which thought and emotion may be free but in which it is not possible or worthwhile to express everything one thinks or feels. Rodney's low-key 'impassable' manner, his equable cordiality, deflects Edward's suspicion of the nephew of the man who caused the collapse of his mother's marriage and his own miserable childhood. An even more dangerous area is avoided by Janet's self-suppression. Her brooding obsessive love for her

sister's husband is even more likely to wreck the future family alliance than scandals from the previous generation. Yet, while Janet thinks with 'cold dispassionate passion' how easy it would be to make Edward fall in love with her and make him 'run about' in the palm of her hand, she thinks this while 'deliberately not looking' at him. Janet's behaviour is best understood by comparing it with her sister's on the same occasion. Laurel 'forgot herself—an objective in manners her mother had constantly put before her—in the determination to set them all at ease'. Both Laurel and Janet are, in fact, their mother's daughters and their standards are, in important ways, those of Corunna Lodge, Cheltenham.

The predicaments of Lady Elfrida and of the would-be destroyer Theodora are not caused primarily by either woman's sexual tastes or 'failings'. Both Janet and Laurel are faced by dilemmas at least as serious, but which are surmounted. What lay at the heart of Lady Elfrida's earlier unhappiness is what lies, in a far grosser form, at the heart of Theodora's nearly disastrous activities. It is an egotism which will not admit the duties of social living. Lady Elfrida 'had few friends, for she appeared to lack reticence and talked extravagantly, exaggerating her idea of herself'. It was this self-dramatisation, this playing up of her own postures and attitudes without a regard to others, which, much more than the single fact of her adultery, destroyed her marriage. She 'exasperated' the affection of those who had loved her, especially her husband 'Edward's gentle father'. It was this 'cumulative' indignation which led him to divorce her 'punitively'.

It is worth comparing the cause of Lady Elfrida's marital breakdown and subsequent relative isolation with the causes of Theodora's disruptive career. Theodora is more complex and interesting than is suggested by critical descriptions of her as a 'ghoulish lesbian' providing the only vivid patches in the novel or as 'an awful irresponsible female adolescent'. A useful starting point is the perception that the problem Theodora poses, like that posed by Lady Elfrida, is wider and deeper than the isolated facts of a sexual transgression or a sexual unorthodoxy. At the end of the novel, Theodora has broken up the family party at Batts by her malicious letter, but her interference has, apparently, had the effect she least desires, of driving Janet, with whom she is infatuated, into the arms of Laurel's husband Edward. This is Theodora's tragic moment. She is about to launch into a great confession scene ('I tell you, idiot, I love her beyond propriety') when it is cut off by Lewis: 'And never, never think of anyone but yourself. It would be fatal, wouldn't it, Theodora?' Like Lady Elfrida, Theodora has an 'idea of herself' which overrides any notion of the obligations of corporate living or the duties of relationships. Far from being 'destined' to grow up as she does, by some impersonal fate, she is the product of a particular modern ambience, implicitly contrasted both with the Studdart family home at

Cheltenham and the more precarious and self-conscious achievements of order and stability in the marriages of Janet and Laurel which she threatens. Alex and Willa Thirdman, Theodora's parents, embody a devitalised intellectualism which possesses neither a social function nor a sense of social responsibility. (Their very name, perhaps, suggests this supernumerary quality.) They have returned to England from Switzerland but really prefer their hygienic exile with its 'arrangement of scenery; there but never too close'. That last phrase is, perhaps, the clue. The older Thirdmans seek disengagement from living. They do not want the sharp experience of places or people which, risky or painful as it might be, is the inevitable accompaniment of really knowing them. They can never be made to understand that the individual is responsible for making his or her life count and that this 'affair' is a 'desperate' one. Their only response to experience is 'a little mild fortitude'. The Thirdman's spiritlessness, lack of appetite and of the habits and idiosyncrasies which are the tokens of spirit and appetite, their refusal of the particular and the exciting are directly responsible for their daughter's attempts to grab at associations, friendships, or any kind of emotional intensity to be had on the instant and on the cheap. In reaction to Alex and Willa, Theodora 'armed herself like a bandit, to hold up anything, anyone and wreak pillage on the years'. The Thirdman parents are a serious critique of 'progressive' thought and styles of living, as well as a pair of comic minor characters. They are, it is clear, far from unique oddities. 'Hundreds of English families' live like them, 'happy in their translation' from England to Geneva, where they can enjoy modish, antiseptic and undemanding pleasures: 'boating, botany, the dear League of Nations'. The last reference to an institution whose well-intentioned futility was apparent at the time when *Friends and Relations* was published, helps to define the Thirdman ambience of advanced thought in the 1920s, already wearing thin.

The futility, and worse, of Alex and Willa's values becomes clearer in the description of the 'rigorous education' to which they have subjected their daughter from the age of six. Under their up-to-date allegiances lies an emotional rejection of Theodora. Her father would have preferred a boy. Both parents have taken no care to understand her feelings or affections and 'hardly knew' whether she formed 'strong attachments'. Instead of the bonding of family life, they fob her off with a cultural package deal in which the 'bleak excellence of her Swiss education' is succeeded by the pretentious absurdities of an innovative English schooling. Miss Byng's establishment is obviously a foretaste of Miss Paullie's in *The Death of the Heart* (1938) and touches on some similar preoccupations. Portia in the later novel is a poignant examination of that violation of childhood sensibility and that refusal of love which is handled mainly as grotesque comedy in the figure of Theodora. Both schools are establishments to which the

unwanted child, awkward and embarrassing for whatever reasons, can be packed off. Thomas and Anna in the later novel salve their consciences with the pretence that Portia is imbibing culture and lady-like ways at Miss Paullie's. In *Friends and Relations* Alex and Willa's ostensible educational aims are those fashionable in more 'liberal' circles. The headmistress of their chosen school, Mellyfield, 'sets great store by individual development'. Theodora is to be exposed to a diluted Freudianism. 'Neurosis had a high value at Mellyfield' and the girls are absorbed by their own personalities which 'they displayed, discussed and altered'. They 'read psychology to each other' on Sunday afternoons. It is in this heady atmosphere that Theodora develops her interest in alternative sexual orientation through male roles in amateur theatricals ('"You make a marvellous man," said Jane and Ludmilla') and falls under the influence of Marise, Lewis's young sister, a 'bleak fair girl' with whom she later sets up house. The relationship begins not in an atmosphere of affection but of appraisal. Marise, who, significantly, is 'too thoroughly the Statue' in a school production of *Don Giovanni,* takes the measure of Theodora and her situation: 'The one thing she oughtn't to be is taken notice of. She's probably been sent here to make nice friends'. Her future 'nice friend's' hold over Theodora is based on this cold knowingness rather than emotional closeness.

It is at Mellyfield, too, that Theodora's need for vicarious emotional satisfaction becomes dominant. Earlier this had been little more than childish mischief, a lonely and bored girl's attempt to connect herself with some life outside her parent's flat with its 'hired bric-a-brac'. All the Thirdmans can suggest to their daughter is a kind of dim parody of the modernist aesthetic solution to the problem of living, the notion that one can make life bearable by converting it into art, already rejected in *The Last September* (1929). The earlier novel's epigraph, from Proust's *Le temps retrouvé,* seemed to suggest that the meaninglessness of experience might be redeemed by art. Yet Lois's writing, in *The Last September,* is dismissed as weak and derivative. It is interesting, in this connection, that the attempt of Theodora's friend Marise to write a novel on 'women's difficulties, difficulties about women' is, like Lois's artistic velleities in *The Last September,* dismissed as without merit. The Thirdmans go about on buses, 'looking at all the types', and Willa expects that 'Art will come' for Theodora and that 'she will write'. (The first phrase may be an echo of Pater's *The Renaissance* and a hint of that connection established in *The Last September* between the deracination of the 1920s and the moral climate of the 1890s and the Edwardians.) The Thirdmans' 'calm parental faces' and tones of sweet reasonableness cannot disguise their fundamental lack of love for their daughter. She recognises the emotional void in which she has been living and knows that her progressive school is a device to dispose of her: '"I am being put out of the way," she thought of Mellyfield angrily. "I am like a dog going to the lethal chamber".'

In such a context, Theodora's earlier antics with the telephone become only too understandable. Having no place, no world, no love of her own, she takes to ringing 'several prominent people' in disguised voices and maintaining conversations with them: 'Passionately passing along the wire she became for those moments the very nerve of some unseen house'. These forays into other lives are too brief and disconnected to do other than produce 'bitterness'. At Mellyfield, however, Theodora moves from idle mischief to a more fully developed emotional parasitism, focused on the Studdart sisters and their marriages and especially on the figure of Janet, whose kindly sensible letter, extorted after constant pressure, she folds in her camisole until it 'became limper and limper'. She develops this emotional interest partly to impress her new associate Marise and partly in response to the theoretical interest in psychology and relationships manifested around her.

The account of the way in which Theodora Thirdman is shaped towards the sterile and destructive role she is later to occupy in *Friends and Relations* is important for two reasons. Firstly, it emphasises that Theodora's case grows out of a moral and intellectual context in a particular society at a particular time, a context produced by the choices of individuals like her parents. Secondly, the account forces the reader to revalue what it is that both Janet and Laurel do in their marriages and, perhaps, something of the nature of marriage itself.

The other of the two main images in *Friends and Relations,* equal in importance to the departing ship which in Lewis's reflections deflates the 'poetry of departure', is like the ship, unexpected and challenging in its implications. In the striking 'Tree of Jesse' passage, Janet reflects on the old branchings 'like the fatal apple tree in a stained-glass window', the affair of Lady Elfrida with Considine Meggatt, the uncle of her own husband Rodney:

> And in her confused thought this one painted tree
> associated itself, changed to another, the tree of
> Jesse; that springing—not, you would think, without pain somewhere—from a human side, went on
> up florescent with faces, to some bright crest or climax or final flowering to which they all looked up.

The passage is a conflation of two historical and religious metaphors familiar in earlier writings and iconography. The fatal apple tree with the man and woman on either side was often seen as part of a process which was to culminate in the Redemption of mankind. Popular medieval legend suggested that the wood of the Tree of the Knowledge of Good and Evil was actually used to make the Cross on which

Christ was crucified and that when Eve left Eden she carried away a branch which 'betokened a great happiness . . . a sign of our return hereafter'. The movement from Fall to Redemption was even seen as in some sense dynamic, a way to a better state than the first innocence, as the well-known carol 'Adam Lay Abounden' suggests.

At the same time this pivotal passage in *Friends and Relations* draws on a second medieval mythic mode for understanding history and the relationship between individual choice and action to its wider social context. The Tree of Jesse first appeared in iconography in the twelfth century, one of the first examples being in the psalter of Henry of Blois, Winchester 1140-1160. Based on Isaiah, II, 1-2, it is a genealogical linking of David's father with Christ and the Virgin Mary, a means by which the most private and domestic of Old Testament stories, that of Naomi, Ruth and Boaz, is joined to the ultimate cosmic drama.

It is worth dwelling on the full implications of this passage in *Friends and Relations* because it offers a radically alternative vision to that of the discredited 'voyage out', a way of seeing feeling as private and yet joined by a web of connection to other lives, other choices, the actions of the past, the consequences in the future. The individuals, the 'perplexed similar faces', are part of a wider process of institutional and familial growth which contains but does not suppress their identities. Lady Elfrida may regret for herself but she must not disown the act of adultery which is the ultimate origin, the 'pain somewhere', from which the Studdart marriages have emerged in their present form. That act must, in a manner, be regarded as a 'fortunate Fall' since it has produced the fabric of friends and relations, the family connections whose potentialities the novel explores and whose virtues it celebrates:

> If you felled the tree, or made even a vital incision,
> as Elfrida impatient of all this burden now seemed
> to desire (for if her heart were the root it had contracted, if hers were the side, it ached) down they
> all came from the branches and scattered, still green
> to the core like July apples, having no more part in
> each other at all: strangers.

The fear expressed here is that, by her denial of the inheritance of marriage and relationship brought about by her own action, Lady Elfrida risks destroying a complex growth of mutual dependence before its fruits have ripened.

It is here that the novel is most challenging. Superficially, it is only too easy to read the situation as Lady Elfrida reads it here, when she wishes to 'fell the tree' her actions have planted. It seems hard to deny the force of her own conclusion that, by destroying her marriage and breaking up his childhood home, she damaged her son emotionally, rendering him incapable of a fully adult relationship such as marriage with Janet would have offered. As it is, 'scared' by his mother's actions, he is 'fit for no one but little Laurel' with whom his life is 'nursery tea' or 'miniature happiness'. However, the validity of this passional view of relationships is at once checked. It is the biased response of one who by nature and circumstances is unable 'to conceive of love' except as 'a very high kind of overruling disorder'. Clearly unless one does accept the conclusion of *Friends and Relations* as a whole that love is other than solely a quest for emotional and sexual satisfaction, one will agree with Lady Elfrida here or with those critics who regret that Edward's and Janet's suppressed love 'doesn't have enough force to persist against the family' or that their 'prospect of sexual fulfilment is relinquished'.

In fact, by the time Janet has this conversation with her mother-in-law, the novel has investigated both sisters' marriages, suggesting the climate and quality of each. What emerges are not two cases of conventionality and personal frustration but two examples of growth and ripening which promise to heal the past (as much as it can be healed) and to make the future. The love of Laurel and Edward may be 'childish' or 'retrogressive'. Yet while they 'lay side by side on their two low beds as on tombs', they remain 'aware' of each other over the 'chasm' and a 'small thrill animated the tombs'. The account of Laurel and Edward is a gently amusing yet effective plea for remembering that there are many kinds of love which may be worthwhile in many kinds of ways. 'Nursery tea' is better than starvation.

The account of Laurel and Edward is a gently amusing yet effective plea for remembering that there are many kinds of love which may be worthwhile in many kinds of ways.
—John Coates

What his marriage offers Edward is, confessedly, an opportunity to regress, to have with his wife the happy childhood he should have had and to gradually erase the pain inflicted upon him. In the early period of their life together, he tells Laurel of the shattering effect of the loss of his childhood home and of his desertion by his mother: 'It really did seem as though she had thought out what she ought not to do, what to avoid, what would hurt people most, and done it all'. Without explanation the child Edward was carried off by his Tilney aunts to 'a dreadful house in Buckinghamshire' to which bits of the furniture he had known 'like wreckage came down on a flood'. This, of course, is the price paid by the innocent victims of the view of love as 'a very high kind of overruling disorder' and who are left behind when others make the voyage out.

It is particularly significant that Laurel can offer Edward sympathy which Janet, who loved him in a far more full-blooded fashion, could not. While Janet dismisses Edward's early traumas ('It's time you gave him something else to think about'), Laurel readily takes on the comforting role the situation requires of her:

> Her husband had told Laurel all about this in the dark, with his head close to hers and his arms round her. Had he spoke of this before? He said, till now he had not let himself think or feel. Once she comforted him so much that he wept. They had designed, wordlessly, that he must re-live his childhood.

Friends and Relations makes it abundantly clear that Janet's predicament is that she has fallen in love with a man who cannot respond to the kind of feeling she has to offer. It is not a question of compromise or conventionality strangling love or of passion being 'relinquished'. Such passion is never possibility. Forced to a point 'where dread and desire ran round the circle to meet' in one of those brief self-revealing encounters with Janet brought about by Theodora's interference, Edward admits this fact about his own nature: 'If you and I had fallen in love—but I didn't want that, he said clearly'. His and Laurel's alternative, of life as an 'affair of charm, not an affair of passion', is, the text makes clear, a workable choice, and, for some temperaments, a perfectly sensible one. (To Janet's suggestion that it must be a good thing for people to harden, Laurel aptly replies, 'If people can'.) Laurel's 'childishness', her very lack of emotional depth, provides her husband with exactly what he needs. She turns their inevitable quarrels into 'burlesque', throwing everything into a 'harmless light by exaggeration' and making up arrears of nonsense right back to his infancy.

Friends and Relations posits a real and credible dilemma. Whatever the pain and sterility of the view of love as an imperative of personal fulfilment (and it is clear from the affair of Lady Elfrida and Considine that it may be both painful and sterile), there must be situations in which such love is, in any case, unavailable. Janet rears the edifice of her life in recognition of that fact. Her 'conventional' marriage to Rodney is intended to secure happiness both through that marriage itself and because it is a means to have a connection, 'to be related', in some way to Edward who cannot return her love. At first sight, and bearing in mind Henry James's acknowledged influence on at least Elizabeth Bowen's early work, it is tempting to see Janet's conduct as some recondite psychological case history. It might seem to rival the moral curios in what Chesterton called James's 'treasury of unique inventions'. In fact, such a response is itself testimony to the hold of romantic and sub-romantic conceptions of love on the minds of readers and critics.

Janet's actions are understandable against a background suggested by the 'Tree of Jesse' passage, an emotional context which gives more weight to family, both as an inheritance and as an atmosphere, and less to the romantic satisfaction of any given pair of its members. Such an emotional context would have seemed comprehensible and valid in other times and cultures, as the medieval image reminds us. Begging Edward not to quarrel with her because she has married the nephew of his mother's lover, she assures him that 'we are relations for life' always meeting and 'talking over arrangements' for the next fifty years. Above all, the family connection offers its own kind of quietness and order: 'You must see what families are; it's possible to be so ordinary; it's possible not to say such a lot'.

Much of *Friends and Relations* is, in fact, a celebration of these qualities in family life, of its power to cure the past and to build the future. The 'recurrence', even 'monotony', of domestic life has its own delicate rhythm for Janet. Her and Rodney's marriage, without being a great meeting of mind and spirit, is a testimony to the force of kindly habit. 'Ten years work on a calm lover' can produce in the inarticulate husband 'a strong natural law' that his wife should be at his side. He follows her movements about the house, and looks for her shadow on the 'curved white wall'. The family, however, involves much more than the relation of husband and wife. It is shown as an increasingly complex interaction of all its members in somewhat unexpected but rewarding combinations. Edward's friend Lewis forms a pleasant companionship ('an unequivocal success') with Janet's and Laurel's father. Janet as an aunt is beneficial to her sister's children. The fact that she leaves them alone, 'is not concerned with them', is a healthy relief from the somewhat overwrought attentiveness of their own parents. Above all, it is in the cases of Elfrida and Considine that the developing family works its most profound effect. The 'guilty pair' become the indulgent grandmother and uncle to the Studdart children. The scandal and, more important, the pain of the past is assuaged and overlaid by the new relationship.

The suspicion of sentimentality is challenged by the novel's insistence that family occasions and festivities are not outmoded or irrelevant. Rather, they correspond to natural, if unfashionable, appetites. Elfrida's fear that she will not be able to 'be together for Christmas' with her grandchildren 'was the nearest she ever came to penitence' for her past escapades. Considine, we are told, 'loved gatherings', and Elfrida fears that this wish for future meetings will be rejected, like her own for family Christmases. She does not care to think of her former lover as 'sentimentally wounded'. If the peculiar moral landscape of *Friends and Relations* could be summed up in any one sentence, it is the next. Elfrida reflects: 'to be rebuffed as an uncle would be disastrous'. Much of the originality of the book lies in its unfashionable insistence on the value of the wider family

connection, of the relationships which grow up on the penumbra of the married couple. The opportunities to be an uncle, an aunt, a grandparent or a family friend correspond to real emotional needs which individuals have, even if the climate and ideologies of a rootless and atomised society do not encourage their discussion. The chief 'event' of the novel's second section is bound up with the natural dynamic of this wider familial living.

Janet gradually becomes aware that in spite of the unremitting courtesy and loyalty of her husband's uncle, 'she was not his type'. This lack of sympathy is due partly to the 'lenten' quality of the 'daily companionship' at her husband's house, but the main reason lies in the changing climate of society between Considine's Edwardian generation and that of the late 1920s and early 1930s. There may, Edward's friend Lewis admits, be an 'asexuality, a competitiveness' in talk and less enjoyment in the contemporary world. However, there is a natural and easy solution to this social difficulty. If Considine lacks his 'pair' in the 'smallish, equable and domestic' home his nephew and Janet have set up, then that 'pair' can easily be found. Elfrida is the obvious person to provide companionship and 'entertainment' for him. Whatever the burnt-out scandals of their past, the elderly couple do belong to the same generation and besides, share an interest in and connection with the family now growing up around them.

The passage which describes how, and more importantly why, the taboo about Elfrida and Considine staying at the same time as Edward's children melts away is particularly significant. It is made clear that this 'moral front of a lifetime is abandoned calmly', simply out of a desire to make existence as pleasant as possible within the family circle. As Rodney remarks, although he is sorry for Edward, 'life has really got to be lived somehow'. It is the undramatic but sensible reaction of one who 'so seldom spoke of life'.

The scene of domestic comedy in which Considine and Lady Elfrida take Edward's children to have their hair cut and eat ices, which one of the first reviewers rightly called 'delightful' is so for two reasons. Like the comedy of the hordes of unknown 'friends' and relatives at Laurel's wedding, it is an immediately recognisable human situation, the harassed grandmother or uncle dealing with the childrens' demands for sweets. Secondly, and more subtly, the comedy lies in the two worldly people with their 'wicked' past being brought into that common domestic and family situation. To their young charges, they are harmless and amusing. Elfrida is a lady with a Petunia-coloured hat, who at one time 'had been very much in the papers'. Considine is 'a daddy-long-legs rather than a spider', in spite of all Anna has heard about his 'bad character'. The bleak and dismal episode of Edward's ruined boyhood Christmas, with an unwanted teddy-bear from his mother's lover, is recalled now by

Edward's son Simon as an 'awful' hint to Considine to buy *him* a camera.

This capacity of family growth to change and mitigate past attitudes is suggested by Elfrida's reaction to Considine when she meets him again at Janet and Rodney's house: 'He took on as much, in her view, from this domestic setting as he did in Janet's from the social heightening and brightening Elfrida's presence set up'. In the 'ordinariness' and ease of this new life, the two erring members of the older generation are allowed to forget their past defeats and disasters. Elfrida 'had certainly sinned' in bygone years but she can now enjoy having an egg for breakfast with her grandchildren looking on. The new light in which she and her lover can see each other originates from their being both involved in new relationships in a new setting. Escaping from the 'sad conventionality' of their sterile and rigid roles as failed adulterers, they relax into an easy friendliness.

These are the hopeful and developing prospects which Theodora Thirdman attempts to blight by her interference. That attempt and its failure are the core of the novel's plot, the essence of its moral diagnosis. To say that Theodora embodies forces hostile to the family might have been to credit her with a certain boldness or courage, a creative adventurousness, given the notion that a defence of this family would only be mounted or believed by the stuffy or unimaginative. *Friends and Relations* launches a radical attack on this notion. Since the reasons for Theodora's behavior in her parents' failure and rejection and in her school experiences have already been given, that behavior seems a compulsive needling and undermining born out of emotional parasitism, rather than a deliberate gesture of emancipation. More important, however, it is the family, viewed in all the temporal and spiritual perspective of the 'Tree of Jesse', which brings about interesting changes, cuts across stereotyped relations and images of the self which revolt from it does not bring.

One of Elizabeth Bowen's constant preoccupations, here as elsewhere in her work, is with the connection between the minutiae of domestic life and the broader issues of social and spiritual health.
—*John Coates*

Even on the mundane level of easy daily living, Theodora's appearance as a house guest at Batts, to which she invites herself after the failure of her Austrian holiday, marks disruption. She is an irritant, glancing at the company 'casually, superciliously', grinding out 'cigarette after cigarette' against the range, the churn or the mangle. Her 'ironic patience' and 'lucid perplexity' are, it is plain, techniques intended to unsettle others, to make them self-conscious, to devalue their mode of living or their activities. She follows Janet about weighing her movements down with her 'attention'. One of Elizabeth Bowen's constant preoccupations, here as elsewhere in her work, is with the connection between the minutiae of domestic life and the broader issues of social and spiritual health. The whole passage in which Theodora refuses to sit down, keep still or to leave objects or people alone epitomises this approach, the inability to make oneself agreeable or even to be quiet is one index of a much deeper and more widespread sickness. Elizabeth Bowen shows, too that such emotional derangement, no mere matter of sexual preference, disguises itself by an air of sophistication. Theodora may emulate her friend Marise's 'cool little air of self-sufficiency that discredited marriage' and may attempt to impale others on smart prepared phrases but these are far less impressive than she intends ('"Nonsense," said Janet kindly, hoping it pleased Theodora to be so clever').

Emotionally dependent in the worst sense, Theodora battens on others, looking for drama, 'situations' or excitement. She cannot keep off the subject of Lady Elfrida's past, that 'extinct sin' in spite of the fact that the old crater is 'now so cheerfully verdant'. She loves, too, to dwell Edward's 'victimization', unlike Janet who, 'impatient for order', regards grievances as a 'delay of the faculties'.

A substantial part of the problem Theodora poses lies in the fact that others do not grasp her skill in wrecking and undermining or the need she feels to do so. Lady Elfrida, while seeing her, probably rightly, as a product of contemporary life with its 'still recent sense of catastrophe', dismisses her emotional oddity and exorbitance as 'awkward . . . like nausea at meals'. Janet is unable to quite focus her attention on Theodora, only registering in a vague, good-natured way that 'something is the matter' with her. She cannot concern herself with the younger woman's complexities: 'she supposed, Theodora is bored, Theodora is fond of me'.

If *Friends and Relations* celebrates the values and explores the potentialities of an emotional order based on the family and its wider connection, it also shows poignantly that such an order, perhaps all order, is deeply vulnerable. The making of stability, the striking of roots, depend on vigilant self-command. Since her passionate love for her brother-in-law has been smothered but not eradicated, there are moments when 'Janet's composure became something precariously but calmly held, some very delicate glass dish piled high with fruit that balanced curve on curve just not tottering'. The accent here is not on the keeping up of a facade but on the maintenance of something fragile and precious. The 'Tree of Jesse' may reach into both past and future but its growth might be broken at any point.

Theodora, then, is dangerously destructive as well as fatuous and pathetic. Even after the earlier evidence of her background and upbringing there is still something shocking in the 'potent vulgarity' of her final definition, of the stance she has taken up by the end of the novel. The letter she writes to Laurel, letting her know that Edward's and her children are staying at Batts and precipitating a predictable scene over the improper visit and, less predictably, to a surfacing of Edward's and Janet's feelings for each other, is one of the most brilliant stylistic *tours de force* in *Friends and Relations.* 'Clever' as one of the first reviewers called it, it is the epitome of clever futility. Theodora's response to her supposed friends is revealed as that of glib and malicious psychological speculation. Above all, she is guilty of presumption. Unable to make or maintain any home or relationship of her own, she yet feels able to judge or dismiss the mutual feelings of others. What has been shown of the admittedly imperfect marriage of Rodney and Janet in any case disproves her suggestion that they 'can't love reciprocally'.

A final proof that the order Theodora attempted to destroy was worthwhile is to be found in Willa Thirdman's visit to the flat her daughter shares with Marise Gibson. This place is one of Elizabeth Bowen's finest domestic nightmares, a worthy anticipation of Eddie's flat in *The Death of the Heart* or Holme Dene in *The Heat of the Day* (1949). It shares some of the features of the much more fully developed later settings. Here, as later, discomfort is not merely an awkward atmosphere or a lack of pleasant arrangements. It involves the refusal of relationships and communication, the denial of the wish to sit and talk. Marise had had the mantelpieces removed 'so there's no dust', but really, one suspects, to deprive each room of a focus. Offering Willa 'an edge of the divan', she 'groaned in the Kitchenette' while making her visitor what she almost boasts will be 'impossible' tea. Marise repudiates the most elementary gestures of friendliness or hospitality as if they were crude and pointless ('You don't eat, do you?') and refuses even to share the tea she has made for Mrs Thirdman.

When Marise suggests that Janet might like to come over ('She need not talk to us'), Willa reflects that she would be far happier in the mediocre little hotel she uses on her London visits where, if the brass bed-knobs are unpolished, the maid 'who forgot the hot water remembered Rodney's grandfather'. In the bleak flat Theodora and Marise share, Willa Thirdman for a moment glimpses the futility of her daughter's life which, at the same time, is the futility of her own motherhood: 'Twenty-six years ago she had borne Theodora—to what? For this?'

Friends and Relations has set itself a difficult subject in the avoiding of tragedy. Survival, the maintenance of what is threatened, may, as themes, disappoint some readers' expectation that only the harrowing is ultimately significant, and

they may feel that the novel's characters show a failure to rise to crisis. However, the book's choice of subject is deliberate and important, a difficult and threatened course of action pursued because it alone affords the means of growth and life, and after the alternative has been fully shown. The determining interview between Edward and Janet hinges on their recognition that in the marriage of each they have created a wider world which sustains them. They are unlike Edward's mother Lady Elfrida, who 'spent her own life' because it was all she had to spend.

This exchange between Edward and Janet means a dispelling of 'the obscurity of the years', the facing of the hidden feeling between them. They now know themselves and each other but neither is prepared to destroy the marriages they have made. What they realise is that the emotion may be powerful but can lead to nothing and that not merely because Edward does not have Janet's range of feeling. Curiously and interestingly, what overlays the possibility now overt in his mind, enabling him to bear it 'without regret or desire', is simply the existence of domestic patterns, the bonds of habit, the events of day to day in his sister-in-law's life and his own. The 'flickering little sequences' of his intimacy with his own wife, memories of her habitual acts (throwing him a cushion, patting cream on her face 'from the chin up'), are *facts* more concrete and valid than a world of notional erotic fulfilment. The weight in the novel's rejection of passion falls, after the context that has been built up, on the preference for the actual, in all its satisfying detail, over the formless and partly imaginary might have been.

To rely on the institutional view of marriage, to merge individual passion in the social framework of friends and relations, of the past and the future, is to avoid the 'bitter necessity' of the unaccommodated individual and the voyage out. For all its limited scale, Elizabeth Bowen's novel is one of her most coherent and thorough examinations of these potent, and in her view, debilitating modern myths.

Alexander G. Gonzalez (essay date Summer 1993)

SOURCE: "Elizabeth Bowen's 'Her Table Spread': A Joycean Irish Story," in *Studies in Short Fiction,* Vol. 30, No. 3, Summer, 1993, pp. 343-48.

[*In the following essay, Gonzalez explores the symbolic, thematic, and technical similarities between "Her Table Spread" and James Joyce's "The Dead."*]

One of Elizabeth Bowen's earliest published Irish short stories, **"Her Table Spread"** (1930), merits serious attention for two central reasons: not only is it an engrossing and rewarding work of art but it also reveals yet one more Irish fiction writer contemporary with James Joyce who was clearly influenced by him. Moreover, Bowen's story demonstrates surprisingly similar aesthetic and social attitudes—despite obvious differences in the authors' social classes and general cultural upbringing—which are a testament to how strong an influence Joyce was. Bowen's Court and the streets of Dublin are as strikingly diverse raw materials of experience as one may imagine in Ireland. At first **"Her Table Spread"** would appear to have nothing Joycean about it, since it involves Ireland's Protestant upper class during the twenties; Dublin's slums and middle-class neighborhoods are nowhere in sight. However, further connections do exist once we consider certain significant subtleties of symbol, theme, and technique—all of which Bowen successfully adapts to suit her own purposes.

Not much has been written on Bowen's short stories, and precious little is dedicated to the study of her *Irish* stories. Antoinette Quinn, the only recent scholar to focus specifically on Bowen's Irish stories, unfortunately restricts herself to the period 1939 to 1945. Heather Jordan, however, not only lists Joyce among those authors Bowen most admired but also reminds us that Bowen's first published book, a volume of short stories, was titled ***Encounters***—a fact of some significance for two fairly obvious reasons: it echoes the title of Joyce's second *Dubliners* story, "An Encounter," and it suggests Joyce's epiphanic method in his collection, a method utilized by Bowen in **"Her Table Spread"** to imbue the story with significant depth and poignancy. Mary Jarrett has noted Bowen's use of paralysis as spiritual metaphor in another of her stories, **"The Dancing Mistress,"** likening it to something out of *Dubliners*; the same metaphor is clearly at work in **"Her Table Spread,"** whose protagonist has much in common with Gabriel Conroy of "The Dead" both in terms of character traits and in the narrator's rhetorical stance toward the protagonist.

Bowen makes it very clear throughout her story that she is criticizing not only a handful of upper-class individuals, and one in particular, but also the remnants of Ireland's formerly powerful ascendancy as a whole. In fact, Bowen's story seems the logical ending point of a tradition in Irish fiction concerned with exposing the ascendancy's ailing spiritual condition. Beginning with George Moore's *A Drama in Muslin* (1886) and continuing through Seumas O'Kelly's *The Lady of Deerpark* (1917) and various short stories by Daniel Corkery, Brinsley MacNamara, and others, this tradition has always emphasized the ascendancy's paralysis in parallel fashion to the better-known tradition that criticizes Ireland's other classes for having the same disease—as manifested in *Dubliners,* its most salient example. Even though Valeria Cuffe may own her palatial home while Joyce's Misses Morkan merely rent their sprawling second-floor middle-class apartment, considerable similarities exist between the dinner parties in the two stories, especially since the events presented at each party occupy the bulk of each story. The party in Bowen's story is something of a reduced version of the one in Joyce's, for it involves far fewer participants. Still, when the story's protagonist, Mr. Alban, plays the piano, no one listens; Mr. Rossiter, Bowen's version of Mr. Browne, drinks to excess and has some ridiculous flirtation—or worse—going on with the parlor maid; and the general veneer of good manners hides only temporarily the underlying indelicacies of human nature.

The role of Mr. Rossiter, who conceals his bottle of whiskey in the most undetectable places, seems to be to show the debauched and seedy side of the self-consciously polite aristocracy—to expose the falseness skulking behind refined airs. Valeria's aunt, Mrs. Treye, and her younger friend and associate, Miss Carbin, are snooty, two-faced, and patronizing—and since they insist on treating the 25-year-old heiress as a child, they play a part in enabling Valeria to continue her bizarre puerility. Their only stake in Valeria's well-being seems to be that if she were to remain unwedded and childless, "the Castle would have to be sold and where would they all be?" Their fortunes are, apparently, legally tied to Valeria's. Mannerly and controlled to the utmost, these two older women seem intent upon suppressing the spontaneous actions and ejaculations of the effervescent Valeria—as when she excitedly contorts her body so that her "bust [is] almost on the table" and Mrs. Treye is forced to step on her toe from beneath the table in an effort to rein in her niece's enthusiasm.

In contrast to the general paralysis suffered by her class, Valeria maintains a vibrancy that cannot be effectively controlled. Though her passions may seem silly, they are at least genuinely felt and emanate from an independent-spirited soul. In this respect she continues the tradition in Irish fiction of such women: Moore's Alice Barton, Rose Leicester, and even Esther Waters; O'Kelly's Mary Heffernan; and, ultimately, Joyce's Gretta. There are more. Yet though none of these lives a vigorous peasant life, conversely, none suffers from upper- or even middle-class inertia. In fact, except for her age, level of maturity, and probably intelligence, Valeria shares a good deal with Gretta Conroy. Caught up in her wildly romantic imaginings, Valeria runs out into the rain and mud with no concern for her shoes or her satin dress; at times like these she seems much like Gretta, who, according to the fearful Gabriel, "would walk home in the snow if she were let." Valeria's spontaneous and heartfelt responses to life are found throughout Bowen's story and remind us of Gretta's similar reactions, as when she "clasped her hands excitedly and gave a little jump" at the thought of a trip to romantic Galway. And while Gretta has really lived through a highly romantic episode in her life—her involvement with Michael Furey—Valeria has at least a similar receptivity to romance, a state of being to which we are directly exposed via the device of narrated interior monologue. Valeria's consciousness reveals not only a strange and immature propensity for romantic reverie, but an almost incredible naïveté, a flightiness that is like a child's, and a fertile imagination that is wildly out of control—picturing, for example, a fight for her honor between two naval officers she has never even met. But why would Bowen create such an abnormally childish young woman as a major character in her story? Valeria's behavior has led at least one critic to call her "demented," but Bowen's vision of the protagonist's epiphanic moment requires just such a character.

The story's protagonist, Mr. Alban, whose name suggests his colorless, unromantic nature, is every bit as paralyzed as Gabriel Conroy, though obviously his malaise is not of exactly the same sort. For instance, while Gabriel has the consolation of being much sought-after for conversation throughout the Morkans' party, Mr. Alban is remote from Valeria and her guests, and, because he is colorless, he easily becomes socially invisible. He is described as one who "disappeared personally" from the rest of the company; later he feels that the party sits "looking through him"; and, finally, when the best he can attract is "less than half their attention," his instant thought is that "some spring had dried up at the root of the world." This is the man invited as a suitor to Valeria's symbolic table spread but who finds himself to be "less than half the feast" when he discovers that a naval destroyer, with its imagined romantic officers, has usurped his position as the gathering's main point of interest.

Like Gabriel, Alban is highly controlled and unspontaneous. While Gabriel has his prophylactic galoshes, Alban has his mackintosh buttoned tight up to the very collar. Gabriel worries if his literary references will be above the heads of his listeners, for whom he feels some obvious cultural contempt; Alban also feels culturally superior to the other guests, finding it "sad" that they should feel so "indifferent" to a man who comes from London and plays Mendelssohn on the piano for them (an exercise they find so "exasperating [that] they open all four windows to let the music downhill"). Finally, just as Gabriel fails several times in his dealings with women (with Lily, with Miss Ivors, and, most poignantly, with his own wife), Alban, actually a reluctant suitor, is twice described as having a "negative . . . attitude to[ward] women." This unromantic figure, with his fussiness and constant adjusting of his glasses and clothing, is, like Gabriel, so self-absorbed that he is described as having "failed to love" ever in his life. We cannot miss one of Gabriel's chief epiphanic revelations: that "he had never felt [as Michael Furey had] towards any woman but he knew such a feeling must be love." However, this is not the stuff of Alban's epiphany, since we are apprised of his misogynous attitude early in the story, well before the epiphanic moment itself; rather, Alban's loveless condition is more like an attendant detail that lends additional meaning to his coming revelation.

Significantly, Alban begins to shed his paralytic constraints by degrees, thus clearing the way for his epiphany to occur with full force. When Valeria runs off into the rainy night in search of her imagined naval officers, Alban feels—reluctantly—obliged to follow her and bring her back. He worries about his expensive shoes—his treasured pumps—for once they are destroyed with mud and scuffs, he has "no idea where to buy them . . . in this country" and he has "a ducal visit ahead." But let go he must, and as he uncharacteristically mutters a minor expletive he finally breaks loose and charges off gallantly into the downpour, for the first time "his mind blank to the outcome"; he has acted spontaneously even though pushed to it by circumstances. Finally locating Valeria in the dark after her lantern has gone out, he attempts to communicate with her but finds it impossible because the voluble Valeria has mistakenly assumed he is one of her much-desired naval officers come to rescue her—and she gives Alban little opportunity to make any explanations. She does not even recognize his voice—evidence of how invisible Alban has indeed become over the course of the evening. But for these few moments, Alban is unwillingly and suddenly thrust into the role of the romantic lover. Finding himself in an uncontrolled situation, "madly" out in the rain and the dark—muddy, dirty, and sopping wet—he realizes that he is standing very close to a warm, beautiful young woman, whom he can feel next to him better than he can see. It is for him an exciting moment, almost purely romantic and sensory: for once his all-controlling intellect is inoperative.

These stimuli bring on his epiphany, but one that is not as limited as it may seem. It is not the mere sexual arousal he is feeling, which would hardly constitute an epiphany, but a much broader and more significant insight that includes *all* women. This is so because just above him and Valeria, up on the balcony, are the story's two other female characters, the middle-aged Miss Carbin and the older Mrs. Treye. Among the three women all ages are represented, especially if we remember that Valeria, though in her twenties, behaves much like a young, teenaged girl, "still detained in childhood." As Bowen's narrator puts it, "their unseen faces were all three lovely, and . . . such a strong tenderness reached him that, standing there in full manhood, he was for a moment not exiled." Alban's awakening, then, has very broad implications, reaching beyond Valeria to include all women and an appreciation of womanhood itself; ultimately, through the three women's agency, he also arrives at a new and vital understanding of his own manhood. These emanating ripples of insight are, on a far smaller scale, similar to the waves of new vision that Gabriel Conroy experiences—going beyond Michael Furey's death to a far broader contemplation of death itself. Bowen's stuffy protagonist has been enabled to reach his fullest potential as a sentient human being by an epiphany of such magnitude that his former self has been momentarily obliterated.

The role of the destroyer (which is actually anchored far below in the estuary) and its crew is, strangely, comparable to that played by Michael Furey: both are catalysts. Unchanged themselves, they have been the chief agents in permanently changing the life perspectives of the protagonists. Hence, the destroyer in Bowen's story appropriately heads out to sea as the story's final detail. The significance of Bowen's title becomes fully clear now: Valeria's table has obviously been spread for a suitor. Originally that suitor is supposed to be Alban; then he is replaced by the never-seen naval officers; and, finally, it is Alban who replaces the naval officers by unwittingly impersonating one of them and thereby assumes the role of suitor in a totally new way. It can also be said that her table has been spread to enable Alban to reach his epiphany.

Mary Jarrett has argued that in all of Bowen's best stories "there is a refusal to pronounce on the validity of the worlds her characters create for themselves." This is most certainly true for Alban—and Valeria for that matter—in **"Her Table Spread."** What we have, then, is an ambiguity very similar to that at the end of "The Dead." Is Alban to change as a result of his epiphany? Is Gabriel? Is either capable of change? Are they too old, chronologically or emotionally? Or is each man terminally paralyzed and now painfully aware of it—and of what each, somnambulistically, has missed in his life? Such ambiguity is both meaningful and intended. As is the case at the end of Joyce's story, multiple perspectives emerge as possibilities. Those of us who are optimists would hope that significant change will occur in each protagonist.

Harold Bloom finds Bowen's stories to be "even . . . more remarkable than [her] novels" and he places Bowen only after Joyce and Lawrence as possibly "the most distinguished writer of short stories in our time." Once again we have Bowen and Joyce linked, this time in terms of quality. **"Her Table Spread"** is by no means on the level of "The Dead," but then not many stories are. Bowen's story is, however, qualitatively comparable to other *Dubliners* stories that demonstrate both spiritual paralysis and then the use of epiphany as the means by which a character becomes acutely aware of his of her affliction. This level of quality acts to reinforce the argument that Bowen, perhaps idealizing Joyce's work as a level of art to which to aspire, read him carefully and probably subconsciously—imitated some of the effects he had perfected, especially in "The Dead." When she applied her considerable talents to writing the story of Mr. Alban and Valeria Cuffe, what emerged was a thoroughly Joycean story—except for the merely surface differences of setting and social class. The imitation may possibly have been a

conscious effect, but it seems to me more likely that it was a subconscious phenomenon that Bowen could not have helped noticing soon after the composing process had begun. The aesthetic stance and the multiplicity of connections between Bowen's story and "The Dead"—on the level of character, theme, symbol, and technique—make the case for influence considerably strong.

Robert L. Calder (essay date Winter 1994)

SOURCE: "'A More Sinister Troth': Elizabeth Bowen's 'The Demon Lover' as Allegory," in *Studies in Short Fiction,* Vol. 31, No. 1, Winter, 1994, pp. 91-7.

[*In the following essay, Calder suggests that "The Demon Lover" is an allegory of war, drawing parallels between the story's imagery and the cultural context of its composition.*]

Of all of Elizabeth Bowen's short stories, none has been anthologized as often as **"The Demon Lover."** First published in *The Listener* in November 1941 and reprinted in *The Demon Lover and Other Stories* (1945) and *Ivy Gripped the Steps and Other Stories* (1946), it is usually introduced as a clever tale of occult possession. Early critical commentary is typified by Allen E. Austin's remark that "**'The Demon Lover'** is a ghost story that builds up and then culminates like an Alfred Hitchcock movie."

This interpretation was first challenged by Douglas A. Hughes in his 1973 note "Cracks in the Psyche: Elizabeth Bowen's 'The Demon Lover.'" "Far from being a supernatural story," he argued, "**'The Demon Lover'** is a masterful dramatization of acute psychological delusion, of the culmination of paranoia in a time of war." The ghostly threat, rather than having any external reality, is a product of the disturbed mental state of the protagonist, Mrs. Kathleen Drover. Her guilt over her fiancé's disappearance and presumed death in the First World War, buried by years of conventional marriage, has been reawakened by another war, and she hallucinates his vengeful return. The inconstant woman in the English ballad "The Demon Lover" discovers that the lover is in fact the devil; in Bowen's story, "war, not the vengeful lover, is the demon that overwhelms this rueful woman" because it strips her of her recent memories and plunges her back to her betraying past.

In 1980, in an article entitled "Elizabeth Bowen's "'The Demon Lover': Psychosis or Seduction?," Daniel V. Fraustino disputed Hughes's interpretation, arguing that it interpolates several key points in the text. There is no evidence, says Fraustino, that Mrs. Drover suffered an emotional collapse after the loss of her fiancé or was gripped by "psychotic guilt," and nothing in her thought processes indicate incipient mania. To the contrary, the fiancé was clearly a psychopath who survived the war and has now returned to kill Mrs. Drover on the twenty-fifth anniversary of their parting. Impelled by an unconscious desire to escape from an impoverished and unfulfilling marriage, she becomes the victim in a "murder mystery of high drama."

Fraustino's analysis rightly identifies some serious flaws in Hughes's reading—there is indeed little evidence that Mrs. Drover suffered an emotional collapse after the loss of her fiancé—but in making his own case he is guilty, if not of interpolation, certainly of exaggeration. To counter Hughes's argument that Mrs. Drover's disarrayed house, which Bowen describes in characteristic detail, reflects her internal collapse, Fraustino claims that she has had an unsatisfactory marriage, marked by years of "accumulated emptiness." Her London house is an objective correlative, not of Mrs. Drover's psychological state, but of her "impoverished married life."

There is nothing in **"The Demon Lover,"** however, to indicate that Mrs. Drover is dissatisfied with her marriage. After some years without being courted, she married William Drover at the age of 32, settled down in a "quiet, arboreal part of Kensington," and began to raise three children. When the bombs drove the family out of London, they settled in the country, and on the day of the story, wearing the pearls her husband had given her on their wedding, she has returned to the city to retrieve some things from their house. Empty of any human presence, it now seems to her full of "dead air" and "traces of her long former habit of life": a smoke stain up the fireplace, a watermark left by a vase on an escritoire, and scratch marks left on the floor by a piano. These may be images of emptiness, repetition, and stagnation, but they underline the absence of the family and its normal human interaction, not dissatisfaction with the marriage. She is a "prosaic" woman, whose "movements as Mrs. Drover [are] circumscribed," and her marriage is simply conventional.

Fraustino's view of Mrs. Drover as a discontented wife in an unfulfilling marriage runs into difficulty when he attempts to make her behavior relevant to the murder mystery plot. Like Hughes, he regards the title of **"The Demon Lover"** as an allusion to the English ballad about an absent lover, an intervening marriage, and a desertion from that marriage upon the lover's return. Bowen's story, however, has no indication whatsoever that Mrs. Drover intends or attempts, even fleetingly, to abandon her marriage. As a result, Fraustino can voice only the vaguest, most guarded of suppositions: "is it not possible that Bowen at least suggests Mrs. Drover's desertion?"

Finally, to build his case for murder, Fraustino interprets the character of the fiancé in a way surely not justified by the text. He rightly emphasizes that the young soldier was never tender and loving, that he was "without feeling," and that he extracted an "unnatural promise" from Kathleen. When, however, he notes that she left the encounter with a weal on her palm, which he had "pressed, without very much kindness and painfully, on to one of the breast buttons of his uniform," Fraustino concludes that "the soldier is a sadist of the most deranged kind . . . a psychopath." Cold, unfeeling, and disconcerting the fiancé certainly is, but can his behavior really be called sadistic, deranged, or psychopathic? If not, how credible is it that he would return to kill his lover of 25 years earlier?

As Fraustino admits, his reading of **"The Demon Lover"** as a realistic murder story invites several practically unanswerable questions: "how the taxi-driver knew that Mrs. Drover would be visiting her London house on that particular day, or how he managed to engineer events so cleverly that she would inevitably seek a taxi precisely on the hour of seven, can only be guessed." After suggesting that Mrs. Drover may have gone to London in an unconscious response to the twenty-fifth anniversary and arranged in advance for a taxi, he confesses that the story does not provide enough information "to reconstruct a completely rational, satisfying interpretation of events."

If, then, there is no completely "rational" interpretation—and both the Hughes and Fraustino readings are attempts at rational explanations—could the story be operating on another level? Given her other writing, Bowen is unlikely merely to have written a ghost story or a tale of murder, though she does elsewhere explore psychological breakdown. In connection with this last point, however, it is important to see **"The Demon Lover"** in the context of the period in which it was written and of the collection in which it was published. In writing of the wartime milieu in the preface to the American edition, Bowen states that the stories "may be found interesting as documents, even if they are negligible as art. This discontinuous writing, nominally 'inventive,' is the only diary I have kept." It is as a wartime "document," then, a "diary" entry of a woman's response to yet another war, that **"The Demon Lover"** perhaps can be most clearly understood.

> **It is as a wartime "document," then, a "diary" entry of a woman's response to yet another war, that "The Demon Lover" perhaps can be most clearly understood.**
> —*Robert L. Calder*

Elizabeth Bowen was not only keenly sensitive to political and social developments around her—witness her article on Ireland's neutrality in *The Spectator* in 1941—but immersed in the British literary scene. As such, she is likely to have read Vera Brittain's book about another writer, Winnifred Holtby, *Testament of Friendship,* first published in January 1940. There she would have seen the following passage:

> There are to day in England and in France and Germany and Austria and Italy, one imagines—women peacefully married to men whom they respect, for whom they feel deep affection and whose children they have borne, who will yet turn heartsick and lose colour at the sight of a khaki clad figure, a lean ghost from a lost age, a word, a memory. These are they whose youth was violently severed by war and death; a word on the telephone, a scribbled line on paper, and their future ceased. They have built up their lives again, but their safety is not absolute, their fortress not impregnable.

Brittain is here quoting Holtby's review of Pamela Hinkson's novel *The Deeply Rooted,* published in *Good Housekeeping* in 1935, and the phenomenon it describes was common enough that Frances Partridge, on reading the passage, noted in his diary:

> Vera Brittain writes of the number of women now happily married and with children who still hark back to a khaki ghost which stands for the most acute and upsetting feelings they have ever had in their lives. Which is true, I think, and the worst of it is that the ghost is almost entirely a creature of their imagination.

There is no proof that Bowen read either Holtby's review or Brittain's reiteration of it, but its similarity to the plot of **"The Demon Lover"** is so striking that it could well have provided the idea for her story. Mrs. Drover has built up her life after losing a fiancé through war, has peacefully married and raised children, and certainly has her safety shattered and her "fortress" proven not to be "impregnable" by the appearance of some "lean ghost from a lost age."

If Bowen were writing only about the women haunted by the memories of lovers lost in the First World War, however, she is hardly likely to portray Mrs. Drover's fiancé in such harsh, negative terms. After all, few women would mourn the loss of a painful presence or have their present settled lives dislocated by its return. The formula demands a loving fiancé described in such detail as to evoke a sense of poignancy when he is lost. In Bowen's story, there is nothing sensitive or kind about the soldier, and, more remarkably, he is in no way individualized. We are given the barest of details, not about his features, but about his uniform, and his face remains hidden by the darkness. This lack of identity is emphasized again later when Bowen writes: "She re-

membered—but with one white burning blank as where acid has dropped on a photograph: *Under no conditions* could she remember his face" (original italics). Though this is obviously a very significant element in the story, both Hughes and Fraustino give it little attention. Hughes briefly suggests that the facelessness is the result of Mrs. Drover's faulty memory 25 years after the event, and Fraustino makes no mention of it.

Such an unusual treatment of the soldier suggests that he is meant to represent something quite different from the conventional lost lover, something perhaps arising from the conditions and times in which **"The Demon Lover"** was written. In 1935, sparked by Holtby's review, Bowen might well have described the unsettling recollection of lost love. Several years into the Second World War, when Britons were facing the real possibility of annihilation of their culture and civilization, she is more likely to have invested the soldier with a more ominous significance. In the midst of one war, a relic from an earlier one that was to have been the war to end all wars, would be a ghastly symbol of endless, inescapable violence.

In his forward to *Writers on World War II,* Mordecai Richler calls the Second World War "no more than a second act," and it has become commonplace to refer to the inter-war period as "the Long Armistice." The realization that the years from 1919 to 1939 were merely a temporary respite from armed conflict, however, came early to many thinking Britons. The Yorkshire novelist Phyllis Bentley, for example, wrote of "the armistice period [1919-1939] in British fiction" in the *New York Times* in August of 1941. Bowen, born in 1899 and having worked in a hospital for shell-shocked soldiers in 1916, could hardly have escaped feeling that the violence of one war had been let loose again in another.

Looked at as allegory, much in **"The Demon Lover"** becomes explicable. The present action takes place in August 1941, and the earlier parting took place in August 1916, almost exactly half way through a war that began in August—just as August 1939 had seen Europe rushing into another conflagration. The faceless, featureless soldier becomes a representative figure, a threatening everyman in military uniform. The absence of kindness, his not "meaning a person well," his being "set upon" Kathleen rather than in love with her, suggest that she is gripped by a force that is seductive but not benign. That she is in the presence of something demonic is conveyed by the "spectral glitters" she imagines "in the place of his eyes." The experience of war could hardly be more vividly embodied than in the image of the young woman's hand being so forcefully pressed onto the buttons of a military uniform that they leave a weal on her palm. Tennessee Williams employs a similar metaphor in *The Glass Menagerie* when he describes the American middle class "having their fingers pressed forcibly down on the fiery Braille alphabet of a dissolving economy." In Bowen's story, "the cut on the palm of her hand was, principally, what [Kathleen] was to carry away."

Kathleen takes something else away from her encounter with the soldier, though it becomes forgotten in her subsequent inter-war life: "the unnatural promise." Inexplicable in conventional terms, Bowen's language here becomes more understandable if it suggests complicity with war. In perhaps the last major war that the public approached with zealous idealism, in which women saw men off to battle amid banners and brass bands, and in which they gave white feathers to young men not in uniform, it would seem that they "could not have plighted a more sinister troth."

Just as war subsumes normal human life and interaction, Kathleen experienced a "complete suspension of her existence during that August week" when, she is told, she was not herself. In the years immediately following her loss, she suffered a "complete dislocation from everything," just as the western world went through a decade of dislocation—whether it was the Roaring Twenties in America or the era of Evelyn Waugh's Bright Young Things in Britain—in reaction to the disillusionment and horror of the First World War. And just as the 1930s brought the world back to a sober confrontation with serious issues of economics and politics, Kathleen's thirties made her again "natural enough" (as opposed to the "unnatural promise") to return to a conventional pattern of living. She married the prosaically named William Drover, and settled complacently down, convinced that they were not "still watched."

For many people in Britain, the 1930s was a period of similar complacency, grounded on the assumption that war had been "presumed killed" by the Treaty of Versailles and the creation of the League of Nations, and that appeasement would prevent its return. As we now know, however, the seeds of the second armed conflict had been sown and not eradicated in the first. Kathleen had thought that her khaki-clad demon was "going away such a long way," but his reply, "not so far as you think" suggests that war was never remote, no matter how normal and settled her life and that of her fellow citizens. The inevitability in his "I shall be with you, sooner on later. . . . You need do nothing but wait" matches the seeming inexorable march to September 1939 when, in the words of his letter, "in view of the fact that nothing has changed" the European powers had to return to their "sinister troth" with war.

But Kathleen is not haunted by her demon lover in September 1939. Total war did not really touch those in Britain until the following summer, and then she and her family were isolated from its full horror by living in the country. It is when she returns to London's deserted streets, cracked chimneys, and her shut-up, bomb-damaged house that she receives the letter. "The hollowness of the house this evening canceled years on years of voices, habits and steps," putting her back into the more dominant awareness of war, and so her demon soldier appears—on one level perhaps an hallucination but on another a symbol of war that will not go away.

In her 1916 parting from her fiancé, Kathleen had suffered a "complete suspension of her existence" when she was "not herself"; and the final lines of the story return to this idea, but much more dramatically and terrifyingly. Several moments after the taxi moves off, she remembers that she has not "said where," in other words that she has given no instruction and that she no longer controls the direction of her life. Bowen treats the taxi, normally an island of security in London's streets, as a brutal machine in a brutally mechanized age; the jolt of the driver's braking throws Kathleen forward so violently that her head is nearly forced into the glass. This places her six inches from the driver's face, and as they stare "for an eternity eye to eye," she recognizes what she could not remember in the features of her fiancé 25 years earlier: the face of war itself.

Like most allegorical readings, this interpretation of **"The Demon Lover"** will invite questions, and some of the suggested parallels may not persuade everyone. It should be remembered, though, that other tales in *Ivy Gripped the Steps and Other Stories* are fantastic and hallucinatory but above all about people's experience of war. In **"Mysterious Kôr"** a young woman is preoccupied by a waking dream of escape to the mythical city of Kôr, arguing that "if you can blow places out of existence, you can blow places into it." In **"The Happy Autumn Fields,"** another young woman seems to lead a dual existence: one in London during the Blitz and one in the country at the turn of the century. Neither story is totally explicable in rational terms, but both dramatize what Bowen called "resistance to the annihilation that was threatening [them]—war."

"The Demon Lover" is another reaction to that threatened annihilation but also a reminder of its origins. Always conscious of the formative influence of the past, Bowen wrote a book about her family home, *Bowen's Court,* in 1942, and in an afterword stated: "War is not an accident: it is an outcome. One cannot look back too far to ask, of what?" **"The Demon Lover"** links the Second World War to the First and concludes horrifically that our "sinister troth" with war is inescapable. The final image of Kathleen trapped in a taxi "accelerating without mercy" into the "hinterland of deserted streets" perfectly captures the feelings of millions of people who in 1941 seemed to be propelled at an increasingly frenzied pace into a European wasteland of rubble and death. Like Kathleen, they could only scream.

Richard Tillinghast (essay date December 1994)

SOURCE: "Elizabeth Bowen: The House, the Hotel & and the Child," in *The New Criterion,* Vol. 13, No. 4, December, 1994, pp. 24-33.

[*In the following essay, Tillinghast traces biographical influences in Bowen's fiction as allegories of innocence and experience, noting in particular the importance of displacement and abandonment among her characters.*]

To read Elizabeth Bowen is to enter, both with pleasure and with consternation, the world of the Anglo-Irish: that spiritually hyphenated class which has all but vanished from Ireland since the Easter Rebellion of 1916 and the foundation of the Republic. As a British Protestant ruling class which owned land taken by force from the Irish Catholic population, the Anglo-Irish were always, from the sixteenth century on, to some degree rootless and insecure in the country they governed. But the Land Wars and legislation of the late nineteenth century set into motion forces that would soon deprive the Protestant land-owning classes of whatever *raison d'être* they had. By the time Bowen was born in 1899, the shadows of what Mark Bence-Jones has called, in his 1987 book of the same name, the "Twilight of the Ascendancy," had already lengthened dramatically.

Though she spent most of her adult life in England, and London is in some ways the center of her fictional world, Elizabeth Bowen was the daughter of a County Cork "big house" called Bowen's Court, which she inherited and, unable to afford its upkeep on her earnings as a writer, eventually had to sell in 1959. She was born into a Protestant Ascendancy that rose to power and distinction in the eighteenth century and went into decline by the late nineteenth. Comparisons to the planter aristocracy of the American South are roughly, but only roughly, apt. The alienation of the Anglo-Irish landowner, set above and isolated from the "native" population, is a vantage point to which Bowen refers often when writing of Ireland. "I have grown up," she writes in her essay **"The Big House"** (1940), "accustomed to seeing out of my windows nothing but grass, sky, tree, to being enclosed in a ring of almost complete silence and to making journeys for anything that I want."

The sense of the house "contemplating" its surroundings [in her essay "The Big House"] is pure Bowen—one of many instances of a house as a living entity: an Irish house or just any house.
—*Robert L. Calder*

Visiting these houses today as a guest or a tourist, one feels the uncanny accuracy with which Bowen captures the strangeness emanating from these gray limestone piles, Palladian or neo-Gothic, set starkly against the primal green of the Irish countryside:

> Each house seems to live under its own spell, and that is the spell that falls on the visitor from the moment he passes in at the gates. The ring of woods inside the demesne wall conceals, at first, the whole demesne from the eye: this looks, from the road, like a *bois dormant,* with a great glade inside. Inside the gates the avenue often describes loops, to make itself of still more extravagant length; it is sometimes arched by beeches, sometimes silent with moss. On each side lie those tree-studded grass spaces we Anglo-Irish call lawns and English people puzzle us by speaking of as "the park." On these browse cattle, or there may be horses out on the grass. A second gate—(generally white-painted, so that one may not drive into it in the dark)—keeps these away from the house in its inner circle of trees. Having shut this clanking white gate behind one, one takes the last reach of avenue and meets the faded, dark-windowed and somehow hypnotic stare of the big house. Often a line of mountains rises above it, or a river is seen through a break in woods. But the house, in its silence, seems to be contemplating the swell or fall of its own lawns.

The sense of the house "contemplating" its surroundings is pure Bowen—one of many instances of a house as a living entity: an Irish house or just any house. In her novel *The House in Paris* (1949), she writes: "The cautious steps of women when something has happened came downstairs, sending vibrations up the spine of the house." Just how remote, how starved for company, the houses must have seemed when their day had passed can be gathered from the opening sentences of *The Last September* (1929):

> About six o'clock the sound of a motor, collected out of the wide country and narrowed under the trees of the avenue, brought the household out in excitement on to the steps. Up among the beeches, a thin iron gate twanged; the car slid out of a net of shadow down the slope to the house. Behind the flashing windscreen Mr. and Mrs. Montmorency produced—arms waving and a wild escape to the wind of her mauve motor veil—an agitation of greeting. They were long-promised visitors.

Many of the Anglo-Irish found it convenient to forget how they came by their land in the first place. In *Bowen's Court* (1942, revised 1964), her classic family history, and elsewhere, Elizabeth Bowen does not shy away from admitting that her original Welsh ancestor (the name Bowen derives from the Welsh *ap Owen,* "son of Owen") was granted land taken from the defeated Irish owners as booty from Oliver Cromwell's campaign to put down the rebellion of the 1640s. At the same time she makes a positive claim for the value of the country-house culture founded by people of her class. This culture, molded in the age of Gandon and Swift and Burke, retained in its architecture and its literary style the clean lines of classicism. And Bowen saw in big-house life, too, a ritualistic element that was practically religious. How the housemaid Matchett, in *The Death of the Heart* (1938), prepares for the night in the London establishment that she serves is informed by her English country-house training:

> About now [i.e., about 10:30 P.M.], she served the idea of sleep with a series of little ceremonials— laying out night clothes, levelling fallen pillows, hospitably opening up the beds. Kneeling to turn on bedroom fires, stooping to slip bottles between sheets, she seemed to abase herself to the overcoming night. The impassive solemnity of her preparations made a sort of an altar of each bed: in big houses in which things are done properly, there is always the religious element.

As its last owner, Elizabeth Bowen describes her house, built in 1776, as "a high bare Italianate house" and elsewhere as a "great bare block," "severely classical." Like Newbridge in County Dublin, Castle Ward in County Down, the ruin of Tyrone House in County Galway, and many another Irish big house, Bowen's Court, which was pulled down in 1960, was an austere rectangle of limestone that dominated the landscape from its imposing elevation. "After an era of greed, roughness and panic, after an era of camping in charred or desolate ruins (as my Cromwellian ancestors did certainly), these new settlers who had been imposed on Ireland," she writes in **"The Big House,"** "began to wish to add something to life. The security that they had, by the eighteenth century, however ignobly gained, they did not use quite ignobly. They began to feel, and exert, the European idea— to seek what was humanistic, classic and disciplined."

For the full flavor of the Anglo-Irish in their ridin', fishin,' and shootin' prime, the reader should turn to the two cousins who published from 1889 to 1949 under the names Somerville & Ross (Edith Somerville continued to regard Martin Ross—the pseudonym of Violet Martin—as a collaborator even beyond the latter's death in 1915). Somerville & Ross picture an Anglo-Irish ruling class characterized by vigor, *sangfroid,* eccentricity, and a habit of command, at ease with their neighbors among the native Irish. This is a world where a favorite hunting dog wipes his muddy paws on a priceless Oriental rug, where the squire goes on a tear with the poacher. As portrayed in the stories brought together in collections like *Experiences of an Irish R.M.,* the Anglo-Irish played a vital role in their adopted country. The Resi-

dent Magistrate of Somerville & Ross's stories adjudicated— often with hilarious results—the disputes of the Catholic majority, while other members of this group functioned in the economy as large farmers, bankers, merchants, and administrators. The never less than outspoken Edith Somerville reprimanded her brother, who had written her that he had come to regard himself as English: "Nonsense about being 'English'! I don't mind if you say 'British' if you like. . . . My family has eaten Irish food and shared Irish life for nearly three hundred years, and if that doesn't make me Irish I might as well say I was Scotch, or Norman, or Pre-Diluvian!"

The attenuation and malaise one feels among Bowen's characters springs, historically, from the growing isolation of the Anglo-Irish in an Ireland increasingly bent on controlling its own destiny and increasingly successful in moving toward that goal. Only four years after Bowen was born, the Wyndham Act—engineered by George Wyndham, Chief Secretary of Ireland at the turn of the century—was passed, enabling landlords to sell their farms to their tenants in transactions financed by the government, with an added Bonus of 12 percent paid by the British Treasury. By 1914 three-fourths of the former tenants had bought the lands they farmed, leaving landlords with only their big houses and a few hundred acres of surrounding land. This put them in the position of being (relatively) rich men living in islands of leisure, with no useful function in the country. "The story is told," writes Mark Bence-Jones, "of how when Wyndham was walking through one of the gaming rooms at Monte Carlo a few years after the passing of his Act, he was greeted by an Irish peer of his acquaintance who pointed to the large pile of counters in front of him and said gratefully: "'George, George, the Bonus!'"

I would not want to claim that such irresponsible attitudes toward the ownership of property in a poor country were typical: in landed or monied classes the socially responsible and the scrupulous always co-exist cheek by jowl with the callous and the profligate. *The Last September,* set in 1920 during the Troubles of that period, is Bowen's most sustained look at the predicament of Anglo-Irish big-house people— caught between the nationalist agitation of the Irish, with whom, temperamentally, they feel they had so much in common, and the protection of the British military, whom they really don't like very much. Perhaps because of their hyphenated position between England and Ireland, the Anglo-Irish have produced several masters of the comedy of manners— Oscar Wilde, Richard Brinsley Sheridan, and William Trevor among them. Bowen's writings are sprinkled with delicious little moments of social comedy, and the latitude she allowed herself in using the omniscient point of view lets us see into the minds of widely incompatible characters whose thoughts are inaccessible to each other. Here, in *The Last September,* we have a British officer's wife, Mrs. Vermont, and an

Irish lady, Mrs. Carey, conversing at a tea and tennis party at a country house called Danielstown:

> "Hoity-toity!" thought Betty Vermont (she never used the expression aloud, as she was not certain how one pronounced it: it was one of her inner luxuries). Turning to Mrs Carey (the Honourable Mrs Carey), who sat on her other side, she said frankly:
>
> "Your scrumptious Irish teas make a perfect piggy-wig of me. And dining-room tea, of course, makes me a kiddy again."
>
> "Does it really?" said Mrs Carey, and helped herself placidly to another slice of chocolate cake. She thought of Mrs Vermont as "a little person" and feared she detected in her a tendency, common to most English people, to talk about her inside. She often wondered if the War had not made everybody from England a little commoner. She added pleasantly: "This chocolate cake is a specialty of Danielstown's. I believe it's a charm that they make it by, not a recipe."
>
> "Things do run in families, don't they? Now I am sure you've all got ghosts."
>
> "I can't think of any," said Mrs Carey, accepting another cup of tea . . .

Edith Somerville wrote in *Irish Memories* (1917) of "English people whose honesty and innocence would be endearing, if they were a little less overlaid by condescension." The patronizing tone adopted seemingly unconsciously by the English when speaking of or to the Irish shows no signs of abating even in our own day. The revulsion and hostility occasioned by IRA bombs going off near the Bank of England, by the mortar attacks on Heathrow Airport, are made all the more virulent by the sense that one is being betrayed by people who were considered to be loyally subservient—when, in the language of an older generation of American Southerners, the "good nigger" suddenly and inexplicably becomes the "bad nigger."

Speaking to an Anglo-Irishwoman, Mrs. Vermont will naturally presume that they are both of the same breed, unaware how complicated questions of identity were for the Anglo-Irish, who thought of themselves as Irish, while to their tenants they were "the English." This was brought home to me recently in a conversation with a friend from Connemara whose first language was Irish—a great fan of Elizabeth Bowen's writing. I was speaking to her of the ease with which Bowen used French words in her writing. "Yes of course," my friend said. "That would have been typical for an Englishwoman of her time."

To return to the conversation between Mrs. Vermont and Mrs. Carey, however. Here are the terms in which the English officer's wife commiserates with her Anglo-Irish acquaintance about the armed rebels in the hills above her house:

> "All this is terrible for you all, isn't it? I do think you're so sporting the way you just stay where you are and keep going on. Who would ever have thought the Irish would turn out so disloyal—I mean, of course, the lower classes! I remember Mother saying in 1916—you know, when that dreadful rebellion broke out—she said 'This *has* been a shock to me; I never shall feel the same about the Irish again.' You see, she had brought us all up as kiddies to be so keen on the Irish, and Irish songs. I still have a little bog-oak pig she brought me back from an exhibition. She always said they were the most humorous people in the world, and with hearts of gold. Though of course we had none of us ever been in Ireland."

If you add to the isolation common to other members of her class in the twentieth century the peculiar circumstances of Elizabeth Bowen's childhood, you find yourself face to face with an individual perilously, heroically it seems to me, cut off from nurturing influences. Her father, Henry, broke with a family tradition that expected the master of Bowen's Court to live there and manage the affairs of the estate. He studied law, eventually becoming an examiner of landlords' titles for the Irish Land Commission, and set up housekeeping in Dublin. After suffering a nervous breakdown apparently brought on by overwork, Henry Bowen succumbed to a life-long mental illness. His daughter responded with a "campaign of not noticing," which may be related to the subtlety and indirectness of her fiction: the reader must often follow barely detectable nuances in the development of character and plot. Not uncommonly in Bowen's work, something that is never mentioned—or that is alluded to ten pages later—may be the most important thing that is going on.

"I had come out of the tension and mystery of my father's illness, the apprehensive silence or chaotic shoutings," Bowen would later write, "with nothing more disastrous than a stammer." Great artists by definition turn defects into distinctions, and she would turn her speech impediment to advantage. As an internal British Council memo regarding Bowen as a lecturer put it in 1950: "She is a *most* successful lecturer with a *most* successful stammer." With Henry Bowen confined to a mental hospital near Dublin, his wife and daughter left for England, where they bounced from one relative and one rented house to another. In 1912 her mother told her sister-in-law, "I have good news, now I'm going to see what Heaven's like." She had cancer, and she died when Elizabeth was thirteen. As Victoria Glendinning writes in her biography, "One of the words at which her stammer consistently baulked her was 'mother.'"

From her first novel, *The Hotel* (1927), to her last, *Eva Trout* (1968), the isolated or orphaned girl is a recurring character in Bowen's fiction: the girl who lives much of her life in hotels, the girl who gets fobbed off on relatives.
—*Robert L. Calder*

From her first novel, *The Hotel* (1927), to her last, *Eva Trout* (1968), the isolated or orphaned girl is a recurring character in Bowen's fiction: the girl who lives much of her life in hotels, the girl who gets fobbed off on relatives. In *The Death of the Heart,* Bowen's best-known novel, Portia, the isolated, in-the-way girl, with her outsider's point of view, reminds one of the way Robert Lowell writes of himself as a child: "I wasn't a child at all— / unseen and all-seeing, I was Agrippina / in the Golden House of Nero." The conflict with which *The Death of the Heart* opens is initiated when Portia's sister-in-law, Anna, finds and reads her diary, which contains disturbing though vague comments about Anna and St. Quentin, Anna's presumed lover (I say "presumed" because Bowen is not one to make such relationships explicit). "Fancy her watching me!" St. Quentin exclaims. "What a little monster she must be. And she looks so aloof." Anna responds: "She does not seem to think you are a snake in the grass, though she sees a good deal of grass for a snake to be in. There does not seem to be a single thing that she misses."

Portia Quayne is the daughter of a love-match. Her father, an older man, had fallen in love with Louise—this is his daughter-in-law Anna telling the story—"a scrap of a widow, ever so plucky, just back from China, with damp little hands, a husky voice and defective tear-ducts that gave her eyes always rather a swimmy look." How unerringly, in these thumbnail sketches, Bowen places her characters: "[Louise] had a prostrated way of looking up at you," continues Anna,

> "and that fluffy, bird's-nesty hair that hairpins get lost in. At that time, she must have been about twenty-nine. She knew almost nobody, but, because she was so plucky, someone had got her a job in a flower shop. She lived in a flatlet in Notting Hill Gate.... I often think of those dawns in Notting Hill Gate, with Irene leaking tears and looking for hairpins, and Mr. Quayne sitting up denouncing himself.... She would not be everyone's money.

You may be sure that she let Mr. Quayne know that her little life was from now on entirely in his hands. By the end of those ten days he cannot have known, himself, whether he was a big brute or St. George."

No fool like an old fool, of course, and Mr. Quayne confesses the affair to his wife. "Mrs. Quayne was quite as splendid as ever: she stopped Mr. Quayne crying, then went straight down to the kitchen and made tea." Before he knows it, the poor man has been kicked out of his comfortable country house and finds himself living out the rest of his life on a reduced income with his new little family of three in hotels, pensions, and rented villas in the least fashionable parts of the Riviera. Portia's half-brother and his wife, Anna, take the orphan to live with them after both her parents have died. "A house *is* quiet, after a hotel," Portia tells her brother. "In a way, I am not used to it yet. In hotels you keep hearing other people, and in flats you had to be quiet for fear they should hear you."

Perhaps it is the habit of keeping quiet and listening that has sharpened Portia's attentiveness to the nuances of life in her new surroundings. "Mother and I got fond of it, in some ways. We used to make up stories about the people at dinner, and it was fun to watch people come and go." This outsider's point of view—cold-eyed, unillusioned—places Portia beyond the cozy circle of civilized mutual accommodation practiced by Anna and Thomas, and thus makes their visitor a dangerous presence.

What Portia's inner wounds might be, we are never quite sure. Of her mother, the child's constant companion, we learn little, even about the circumstances of her final illness. We only catch a glimpse—poignant for anyone who has ever lived on the cheap in Europe during the off-season—of the last little pension where they lived in Switzerland:

> They always stayed in places before the season, when the funicular was not working yet.... Their room, though it was a back room facing into the pinewoods, had a balcony; they would run away from the salon and spend the long wet afternoons there. They would lie down covered with coats, leaving the window open, smelling the wet woodwork, hearing the gutters run. Turn abouts, they would read aloud to each other the Tauchnitz novels they had bought in Lucerne. Things for tea, the little stove and a bottle of violet methylated spirits stood on the wobbly commode between their beds, and at four o'clock Portia would make tea. They ate, in alternate mouthfuls, block chocolate and *brioches*. Postcards they liked, and Irene's and Portia's sketches were pinned to the pine walls.

And finally we see them leaving:

When they left that high-up village, when they left for ever, the big hotels were just being thrown open, the funicular would begin in another day. They drove down in a fly, down the familiar zigzag, Irene moaning and clutching Portia's hand. Portia could not weep at leaving the village, because her mother was in such pain. But she used to think of it while she waited at the Lucerne clinic, where Irene had the operation and died: she died at six in the evening, which had always been their happiest hour.

In Anna's relations with Thomas Quayne, one guesses there is something of Elizabeth Bowen's own·marriage to Alan Cameron, an ex-army officer who bored the London literary crowd—perhaps deliberately, as a way of getting even for being ignored—by telling long war stories. One anecdote that Victoria Glendinning repeats has a guest at a Bowen's Court party, while searching through the old house trying to find a lavatory, opening a door and finding Alan Cameron "alone in a small room eating his supper off a tray." Thomas chafes in his study with a large whiskey while Anna has her *tête-á-têtes* with her friend St. Quentin and the *enfant terrible,* Eddie, whose relationship with Anna is even more equivocal than what the reader gathers about St. Quentin. The situation might remind someone who has read Bowen's biography of Mr. Cameron's complaints about the "Black Hats"—so-called from the rows of men's hats hanging in the hall of their house in Regent's Park when he would come home from his office at the BBC—who visited his wife. A complex and interesting marriage in which "married love" was less a factor than a mutual dependence and affection. "I never saw real strain or needling between them," May Sarton writes, "never for a second. Love affairs were a counterpoint."

Perhaps drawing parallels between marriages, fictional and real, even after husband and wife are dead, is an exercise in frivolous presumption. In *The Death of the Heart,* at any rate, Anna is rattled by her young sister-in-law's observant eye. "I cannot stand being watched. She watches us." Bowen renders the tense accommodation between this man and woman with her own keen eye:

> She posted herself at the far side of the fire, in her close-fitting black dress, with her folded arms locked, wrapped up in tense thoughts. For those minutes of silence, Thomas fixed on her his considering eyes. Then he got up, took her by one elbow and angrily kissed her. "I'm never with you," he said.
>
> "Well, look how we live."
>
> "The way we live is hopeless."

Anna said, much more kindly: "Darling, don't be neurotic. I have had such a day."

> He left her and looked round for his glass again. Meanwhile, he said to himself in a quoting voice: "We are minor in everything but our passions."
>
> "Wherever did you read that?"
>
> "Nowhere: I woke up and heard myself saying it, one night."
>
> "How pompous you were in the night. I'm so glad I was asleep."

In a house galvanized by these tensions only Matchett, the impassive family retainer, one of the best serious portraits of a servant in fiction since Proust's Françoise, has very definite ideas about what is to be done with Portia. And with Bowen's beautifully specific imagination, the details of Matchett's standards ring with authenticity:

> Matchett's ideas must date from the family house, where the young ladies, with bows on flowing horsetails of hair, supped upstairs with their governess, making toast, telling stories, telling each other's fortunes with apple peel. In the home of today there is no place for the miss: she has got to sink or swim. But Matchett, upstairs and down with her solid impassive tread, did not recognize that some tracts no longer exist. She seemed, instead, to detect some lack of life in the house, some organic failure in its propriety. Lack in the Quaynes' life of family custom seemed not only to disorientate Matchett but to rouse her contempt—family custom, partly kind, partly cruel, that has long been rationalised away. In this airy vivacious house, all mirrors and polish, there was no place where shadows lodged, no point where feeling could thicken.

Portia, like Bowen's other orphans, is in dire need of affection, unequipped by her experience with the means to ask for love. She turns to the massively self-controlled Matchett, whose very name tells us how stiff and contained a creature she is. A poignant scene in *The Death of the Heart* has Matchett sitting on Portia's bed, reluctantly drawn into the sort of confidential talk Portia had ought to be having with her sister-in-law if Anna were not so cold:

> "She had a right, of course, to be where I am this minute," Matchett went on in a cold, dispassionate voice. "I've no call to be dawdling up here, not with all that sewing." Her weight stiffened on the bed; drawing herself up straight she folded her arms sternly, as though locking love for ever from her

breast. Portia saw her outline against the window and knew this was not pique but arrogant rectitude—which sent her voice into distance two tones away. "I have my duties," she said, "and you should look for your fond-ofs where it is more proper."

Matchett is only one of the servants who appear in Bowen's pages—though a distinction should be made between Irish servants and English servants, in houses and thus in books. Irish people curiously manage to be both egalitarian and hierarchical at the same time. Hierarchical because traces of a feudal society endured perhaps as late as the 1950s on this little island with its bogs and mountains and months of rain. The Middle Ages were slow to disappear in a "land of saints and scholars" and large land holdings where even today, driving through the Irish countryside, the visitor is struck by mile after mile of demesne walls, perforated every so often by baronial gates and Gothic gate-lodges. Egalitarian, perhaps because the Irish are religious people whose church teaches that all souls are equal in the eyes of God.

And perhaps also because the man saddling the horse of his jumped-up Anglo-Irish squire or squireen may have, or fancy he has, noble blood running in his veins. The Kerry poet Egan O'Rahilly (1670-1726), of whom Brendan Kennelly has written, "O'Rahilly *is* a snob, but one of the great snobs of literature," wrote a great contemptuous putdown of the new Cromwellian adventurers who had conquered Ireland and usurped the land of the Irish nobility, using the house, as Bowen habitually does, as an emblem of a way of life:

> That royal Cashel is bare of house and guest,
> That Brian's turreted home is the otter's nest,
> That the kings of the land have neither land nor
>   crown
> Has made me a beggar before you, Valentine
>   Brown.

This is Frank O'Connor's translation from the Irish lament, where O'Rahilly characterizes himself in a haunting synecdoche as "An old grey eye, weeping for lost renown." The last line, in which the English name Valentine Brown would undoubtedly sound even more contemptible in the context of the Gaelic words of the original, recurs as the burden of every stanza in the poem. Kennelly comments: "O'Rahilly himself would have considered 'Valentine' a ridiculous name for anyone calling himself a gentleman, and as for 'Brown,' he would as soon have addressed a 'Jones' or a 'Robinson.'" I mention O'Rahilly and his great poem of hauteur and despair because he lived in the next county over from Elizabeth Bowen's County Cork, and because the people he so eloquently despised were of the same ilk as the Bowens.

Bowen never committed the modern heresy—inspired, I suppose, by what might be called a romantic Marxism—of want-ing to become a member of the working class. Servants—or Mrs. Vermont, of the bog-oak pigs and the tendency to talk about her inside—were simply not her social equals. In the eyes of many readers, Americans especially, this makes her a snob. Even as sensible a reader as Elizabeth Bishop, in a letter to Robert Lowell expressing reservations about the Boston poet Anne Sexton, criticizes Bowen for her gentility:

> Anne Sexton I think still has a bit too much romanticism and what I think of as the "our beautiful old silver" school of female writing, which is really boasting about how "nice" *we* were. V. Woolf, E. Bowen, R. West, etc.—they are all full of it. They have to make quite sure that the reader is not going to misplace them socially, first—and that nervousness interferes constantly with what they think they'd like to say.

I think Bishop mostly has it wrong. I would agree with her about Rebecca West, the precariousness of whose family origins and social status I touched on in my essay on her in these pages [in *The New Criterion*]. On the other hand, Anne Sexton in her poetry never struck me as being out to impress anyone about her social standing, which takes a back seat to her emotional problems and her drinking and drugging. In terms of social standing, Woolf and Bowen had nothing to prove; both wrote within the social context they were born into.

Bowen to a large extent took the world as she found it, and was more interested in her characters as people—with likes and dislikes, and especially with a desperate and often frustrated need for love—than as exemplars of social class. When she writes in **"A Love Story"** (1939), "Servants love love and money, but the Perry-Durhams bored the servants by now," at first one's radar of political correctness beeps; then one thinks again about the sentence and says, "How true that is!" When politics, as the modern substitute for religion that it has become among what are called in Britain "the chattering classes," arises in Bowen's novels—and it rarely arises—it is seen as a form of emotional desperation. Here is part of an exchange from ***The House in Paris*** between Karen, who has grave doubts about her impending marriage, and her upper-middle-class Aunt Violet. The time would be the early 1930s.

> "Things one can do have no value. I don't mind feeling small myself, but I dread finding the world is. With Ray I shall be so safe. I wish the Revolution would come soon; I should like to start fresh while I am still young, with everything that I had to depend on gone. I sometimes think it is people like us, Aunt Violet, people of consequence, who

are unfortunate: we have nothing ahead. I feel it's time something happened."

"Surely so much has happened," said Aunt Violet. "And mightn't a Revolution be rather unfair?"

"I shall always work against it," said Karen grandly. "But I should like it to happen in spite of me."

Except for saying she wants to work *against* the Revolution, how much Karen sounds like W. H. Auden at this same time!

The "lack of life" Matchett regretted would not, I suspect, have been found at Bowen's Court when Elizabeth Bowen was mistress there. Something of the insouciance, the gay defiance of adversity, to be found at all levels of Irish society can be seen in Bowen's remark from the essay I have quoted:

> the big house people were handicapped, shadowed and to an extent queered—by their pride, by their indignation at their decline and by their divorce from the countryside in whose heart their struggle was carried on. . . . These big house people admit only one class-distinction: they instinctively "place" a person who makes a poor mouth.

It is, I think, to the credit of big house people that they concealed their struggles with such nonchalance and for so long continued to throw about what did not really amount to much weight. It is to their credit that, with grass almost up to their doors and hardly a six-pence to turn over, they continued to be resented by the rest of Ireland as being the heartless rich.

The strengths of Bowen's big-house people—pluck, style, common sense, decency, and a sense of community—are what several of her orphans and heart-wounded girls yearn for, often without even understanding this.
—*Robert L. Calder*

The strengths of Bowen's big-house people—pluck, style, common sense, decency, and a sense of community—are what several of her orphans and heart-wounded girls yearn for, often without even understanding this. A question Bowen implicitly asks over and over is: What precisely is the emotional damage inflicted on her orphaned heroines (herself included) by the circumstances of their lives? In **"The Easter Egg Party"** (1940), Hermione, taken in for a long visit in the country by two maiden ladies who are friends of her recently divorced mother, frustrates the ladies' desire to help her. "Their object was to restore her childhood to her," the

story begins. But there is some basic human generosity, some sense of give and take, that she has simply missed out on. A spoiled child, she can appreciate things only by owning them: "'I think those lambs are pretty,' said Hermione, suddenly pointing over a wall. 'I should like a pet lamb of my own; I should call it Percy.'" After she demands to leave the sisters' home, seeing that they refuse to cater to her self-centeredness, she leaves a sadness behind her, because they realize her childhood is beyond the power of their wholesome kindness to restore: "The sisters seldom speak of her even between themselves; she has left a sort of scar, like a flattened grave, in their hearts."

As implied by the age and nature of many of her characters, Bowen's novels and stories are songs of innocence and experience. The innocence is not necessarily pure, and the experience may be benign or sinister. In **The House in Paris,** astounded by a lie that the tyrannical Leopold, the illegitimate child of a troubled and unfortunate affair, is willing to tell, Henrietta, the settled, "normal" child, finds herself thinking: "'But we're children, people's belongings: we can't—' Incredulity made her go scarlet . . ." Leopold observes cynically: "Nobody speaks the truth when there's something they must have." Emma, beginning an adulterous affair in **"Summer Night"** (1941), realizes: "Yes, here she was, being settled down to as calmly as he might settle down to a meal." Portia in **The Death of the Heart,** because she is such a sacrificial lamb, is easy prey for the heartbreaker Eddie, Anna's young protégé. The novel, as its title implies, is almost an allegory, a Unicorn Tapestry in which the "pure"—Portia, Thomas—are victimized by the worldly and corrupt—Anna, St. Quentin, Eddie.

Unstrung by Eddie's betrayal, and disoriented by Anna's rejection of her, Portia takes the extraordinary step of going to the decent, avuncular old Major Brutt, a demobbed colonial ex-army officer who is floundering around trying to find his way in the fast-changing Britain of the Thirties, living in an attic room of a cheap hotel in the Cromwell Road. After she has told the Major how unhappy she is with her brother and sister-in-law, he asks quietly what she wants to do:

> "Stay here with you," she said. "You do like me," she added. "You write to me; you send me puzzles; you say you think about me. . . . I could do things for you: we could have a home; we would not have to live in a hotel. . . . I could cook; my mother cooked when she lived in Notting Hill Gate. Why could you not marry me? I could cheer you up. I would not get in your way, and we should not be half so lonely."

Eva Trout, the rich young heiress and title character of Bowen's last, rather odd, and not very satisfactory novel, buys through the mail, in a similar effort to settle herself, a seaside house—sight unseen. When she descends on the small town to take possession, she startles the real-estate agent by her rather mad-seeming peremptoriness.

> "Now," she announced, looking round for her charioteer, "I want to go home."
>
> "*Home?*" cried he, fearing all was lost.
>
> "Where is my house?"

Ireland and England, house and hotel, innocence and experience, the child and the world—these are the boundaries between which Elizabeth Bowen's fiction runs its supple and sinuous course. With a touch of the worldly French moralist, she is fond of delivering maxims reminiscent of Madame de Sévigné. In thinking about the way she mediates between her classic polarities, one might ponder the following formulation from the last part of *The Death of the Heart:* "Happy that few of us are aware of the world until we are already in league with it."

Martin Bidney (essay date Winter 1996)

SOURCE: "Nostalgic Narcissism in Comic and Tragic Perspectives: Elizabeth Bowen's Two Fictional Reworkings of a Tennyson Lyric," in *Studies in Short Fiction,* Vol. 33, No. 1, Winter, 1996, pp. 59-68.

[*In the following essay, Bidney examines the Tennysonian context of "Tears, Idle Tears" and "The Happy Autumn Fields," deconstructing the psychological tensions of their representations of nostalgic melancholy.*]

"Tennis, anyone?" is the opening of Peter De Vries's delightful "Touch and Go (With a Low Bow to Elizabeth Bowen)," and its closing words are "Tennyson, anyone?" Surprisingly, "in conversation Miss Bowen said that she had not realized," until she read this parody, "how often she relied on Victorian poetry for her titles (e.g., **'Tears, Idle Tears,' 'The Happy Autumn Fields,'** etc.)," according to William Heath's report in 1961. Bowen was not necessarily disingenuous: the creative process arises from deep levels of preverbal awareness; memory is unreliable; influences operate deviously (creating and overcoming anxieties as they do so). What is important is the way Tennysonian allusive structures shed light on the two stories Heath has named. The fact that **"Tears, Idle Tears"** and **"The Happy Autumn Fields"** are both rewritings of the same lyric is of special interest, for it shows us Bowen's ingenuity and breadth of resource as she considers alternative ways to rethink a celebrated poem— and a provocative one.

Tennyson's "Tears, Idle Tears," a poem evoking the sense of strangeness, vivid freshness, and sudden melancholy brought on by memory, was lauded in an essay by Cleanth Brooks as rich in the ironic tensions beloved of New Criticism: "The days that are no more are *deep* and *wild,* buried but not dead—below the surface and unthought of, yet at the deepest core of being, secretly alive." Bowen's own **"Tears, Idle Tears"** has never been studied in detail, so far as I can find. **"The Happy Autumn Fields,"** with its title taken from line 4 of the same Tennyson lyric, has often been looked at, but never in a detailed Tennysonian context, and never in concert with its Tennysonian companion piece (as we may call it). Yet the two short stories belong together, and not only for their shared Victorian allusions.

The theme of both tales, I suggest, is nostalgic narcissism— presented from a comic perspective in **"Tears, Idle Tears,"** from a tragic one in **"The Happy Autumn Fields."** The ostensible theme of the Tennyson lyric is, of course, nostalgia: "So sad, so fresh, the days that are no more." But the nostalgia develops from melancholia to morbidity by the poem's conclusion: "O Death in life, the days that are no more!" Though psychoanalysis of the speaker of such a brief (if evocative) lyric might perhaps seem risky, in previous investigation of lyrical masterworks of a nostalgic kind (Goethe's "Kennst du das Land," Blake's "The Land of Dreams") I found a pattern suggesting the presence of narcissism at the heart of all nostalgia. So it is appropriate that Tennyson's concentrated distillation of extreme nostalgic melancholia should have stimulated, in the psychological imagination of Elizabeth Bowen, brilliant fictional studies of narcissism—its potential pathology and (more surprisingly, given the gloom of Tennyson's lyric dirge) its possible remediation.

Bowen, I am suggesting, radically re-imagines in these two stories a Victorian lyric of nostalgic melancholia, and she does so in order to show how this condition fosters, and is fostered by, a regressive, narcissistic mindset. In contrast to traditional Freudian theory, recent psychological scrutiny of the origins of narcissism has focused not on the oedipal struggles of father and son but on the child's first (pre-oedipal) relation to the primary caregiver, traditionally the mother. As Barbara Schapiro explains in summing up the work of Otto Kernberg, "Due to the unavoidable shortcomings of maternal care, the relationship with the mother as our first love object is primarily characterized by ambivalence," which also "results in a corresponding split in the ego" because the "child internalizes both the 'good,' loving mother and the 'bad,' frustrating one. If the relation with the mother imago is damaged" by some trauma such as "emotional rejection, the internal splitting becomes even more intense."

Splitting the mother image emphatically into Good Mother and Bad Mother leads toward unreality because the child wants to deny the existence of Bad Mother, an unloving, dis-approving, and cruel figure. The narcissistic ideal is to sup-press Bad Mother by insisting on the all-loving Good Mother whose loving gaze guarantees the preservation of the child's (equally fictitious) idealized or "grandiose self"—a defense against the child's "real feelings of deprivation and rage." This idealization of both self and Good Mother doesn't work: Bad Mother refuses to stay repressed. The child's ef-fort at shoring up the all-beloved "grandiose self" must be perpetually renewed, for it is perpetually frustrated. The only way to grow up (into reality) is by learning to form a mother image that includes both good and bad. The self image, too, can then be realistically ambivalent, not idealized or "gran-diose."

We will see that the source of seven-year-old Frederick's narcissism in Bowen's neo-Tennysonian **"Tears, Idle Tears"** is illuminated by this psychological pattern. Frederick has continually suffered emotional rejection: he is not so much cast aside as simply disregarded, and in the first part of the story we can hardly resist being deeply sympathetic—until finally it dawns on us that Frederick may be more than half responsible for ensuring his own continued misery. Tennyson writes: "Tears, idle tears, I *know not* what they mean, / Tears from the *depth* of some divine *despair* / Rise in the heart, and *gather to the eyes*" (italics added). Bowen elaborates the theme of mystery or not-knowing and also the deep de-spair that is felt as tears unexplainably rise from a similarly deep and hidden source and suddenly break out at the eyes: Frederick "*never knew* what happened . . . a red-hot bellwire jagged up through him from the *pit* of his frozen belly *to the caves of his eyes*. Then the hot gummy rush of tears"; "*Despair* howled round his inside like a wind" (italics added).

Even the artificial and "terrible *square* grin" that Frederick "felt his mouth take" and the "plate-glass *windows* of the lordly houses" that "looked at him" with "judges' eyes" are grotesque but appropriate variants of Tennyson's melan-cholic scenario where "unto dying eyes / the *casement* [win-dow] slowly grows a glimmering *square*" (italics added). Tennyson concludes:

> Dear as remembered kisses after death,
> And sweet as those by hopeless fancy feigned
> On lips that are for others; deep as love,
> Deep as first love, and wild with all regret;
> O Death in life, the days that are no more.

We may easily see this as the key to Frederick's sorrows, for Frederick's very "first love," his mother, has lips that are perhaps "for others" but certainly not for him. When Frederick's father dies in the war, his mother offers no so-lace. Instead, all her concentration goes into playing the role of noble, stoic widow. The only time she permits herself

something like "convulsions" of frustrated grief is at her baby's bedside; it is terrifying for Frederick, but she simply and selfishly ignores his presence. Frederick is indeed "wild with all regret," for the only kisses of which he may be aware are "remembered kisses after death"—kisses he may remem-ber having received before the age of two, the time when his father died. For Frederick, the nostalgically remembered or idyllically imagined "days that are no more" lie very far back indeed—in infancy, largely in fancy.

But the Frederick I have been describing in Bowen's Tennysonian terms—Frederick as we see him before the lib-erating epiphany that will happen shortly—is no mere mar-tyr, nothing so simple as that. When he starts a crying fit, "Frederick, knees trembling, butted towards his mother a crimson, convulsed face, as though he had the idea of bury-ing himself in her." His butting is aggressive, defying the Bad Mother who neglects him as she continually preens herself, continually entranced—herself a veritable female Narcis-sus—with the image of her own stately and comely deport-ment ("What a lovely mother to have," she thinks): "His mother seldom openly punished him, but often revenged her-self on him in small ways. He could feel how just this was. His own incontinence in the matter of tears was as shock-ing to him" as "it could be to her."

By insisting on the justice of Mrs. Dickinson's frequent little revenges, Frederick makes her into Good Mother: if she pun-ishes him, he deserves it. If he admits he deserves it, he will continue to be Good Son. But this attempted self-abasement is unbearably frustrating—and so tomorrow, or next minute, he will uncontrollably (with motives unconscious to him) stage another aggressive crying fit. Frederick wants to be continually "burying himself in her," merging his idealized self-image with the specular idealized image of his mother. Only the loving image of Good Mother will guarantee the stability of his own Grandiose Self, the sole focus of his daily concerns, of his despairing crying fits.

But Bowen does not simply rewrite Tennyson's lyric in a modern psychological context: she radically revises it to show how narcissistic melancholy may be cured. In a lakeside epiphany, the story shows that there is hope for Frederick, and that this hope lies in a change from seeking attention to lending attention—preferably by attending to something that will not even flatter the perceiver by look-ing back.

What turns pathos into quirky humor and enlightenment at the wonderful outing by the lake in the park is Frederick's acquisition of new ways of looking—different from the nar-cissistic ones. Frederick sees "with joy a quivering bough of willow" that "looked as pure and strong as something af-ter the Flood"—a cooling draught of aesthetic vision after Frederick's flood of hot tears. A lady he meets at the park tells him about another world-class weeper named George ("Funny to meet two of you"), and Frederick becomes genuinely interested. Best of all and most deeply memorable for Frederick is the duck in the lake: "When it rolled one eye open over a curve, something unseeing in its expression calmed him," so that "Years later, Frederick could still remember, with ease, pleasure and with a sense of lonely shame being gone, that calm, white duck swimming off round the bank." Glimpsing the willow bough Frederick learns to look at something else than his mother; the lady with her talk of George makes him think about somebody other than himself; the duck, most refreshingly of all, looks at neither son nor mother. The daily deadlock of intertwined mother-and-son glances, of intertwined narcissisms, has been broken, at least for a while.

And it is the new, momentarily liberated Frederick who has the story's last (cheerful) word—implicitly refuting the gloomy musings of the lady at the park, who indulges some exaggeratedly Tennysonian thoughts on "tears" that "rise" from a "depth" of despair and "gather to the eyes": "The eyes of George and Frederick seemed to her to be wounds, in the world's surface, through which its inner, terrible unassuageable, necessary sorrow constantly bled away and as constantly welled up." Such thoughts might well induce philosophic melancholia of the *Sunt lacrimae rerum* sort—tears rising out of a gloomy metaphysics. Bowen, however, through her story of the momentary freeing of Frederick, strongly hints that self-pitying tears may be—from another point of view or in another mood—fully as "idle" as the Tennysonian persona himself had at first suspected; that melodramatic ruminations on human grief may be largely a rationale for narcissistic fixation on a grandiose self.

One sees more clearly "after the Flood," and what one sees may be reassuringly whimsical and comic. In fact, in a final stroke of telling humor, Bowen informs us that both the lady (with her pretentious elegiac philosophizing) and even "George's trouble" (the self-absorbed, perseverating melancholy that made George a narcissistic twin to the earlier lachrymose Frederick) fall quickly through a "cleft" in Frederick's memory and are "soon forgotten." Only the wonderful, unseeing eye of the quirky duck remains.

In **"The Happy Autumn Fields"** the focus changes from the possible cure of regressive sadness to the deadly lure of nostalgia, its power to keep one's selfish will fixated on preserving an idealized mind-set held over from childhood. We will see that the narcissism here, though less evident at first glance, is darkly pervasive, even tragic. A box of letters and photos, coming to the attention of Mary in blitzed-out London, serves as a departure-point for her dreams of a Victorian past, though her lover Travis, wanting to curb her melancholy fancies, eventually takes the letters away and reads them himself. Having dreamed herself into the life of mid-Victorian Sarah, Mary protests to Travis, "I cannot forget the climate of those hours. Or life at that pitch, eventful—not happy, no, but strung like a harp."

The harp metaphor is double-valued: the story, true to its Tennysonian name, will play variations on a melody from the Victorian laureate's lyre, but the unendurable psychological tensions pervading it make the visionary episode "strung" in a far less soothing way—nervously tense and taut. Since Digby and Lucius and Robert must leave for school (Fitzgeorge is already away, serving in the army), the family is having a farewell outing. Yet, paradoxically, their leaving is not as fraught with imminent loss as is the prospective *arrival* of Eugene: he is in love with Sarah, and Henrietta is intensely, narcissistically jealous of her dear sister's love.

Appropriately, in this episode of problematic arrival and loss—a dawn of prospective arrival that is even more melancholy than a sunset of departure—Bowen focuses her allusive variations on the second stanza of Tennyson's lyric:

> Fresh as the *first beam* glittering *on a sail,*
> That brings our friends up from the underworld,
> Sad as the last which *reddens over one*
> *That sinks* with all we love below the verge:
> So sad, so fresh, the days that are no more.
>
> (italics added)

The sail, the sinking, the reddening of a sunset that offers a melancholy, darkly ironic comment on all seemingly happy dawns of arrival—these are the Tennysonian themes Bowen will elaborate in depicting Henrietta's bitter reaction to Eugene's unwished-for approach.

Thus, when Henrietta sees her sister's unwelcome suitor coming to disrupt her own comfortable ride with Sarah, "A resigned sigh, or perhaps the pretence of one, heaved up Henrietta's still narrow bosom. To delay matters for just a moment more she shaded her eyes with one hand, to search the distance *like a sailor looking for a sail*" (italics added). The "underworld" from which the Tennysonian "sail" rises may be simply the part of the ocean below the horizon, but for jealous Henrietta it is a dark place indeed. Ironically, she would like to blot out Eugene's image, like the night succeeding the last ray that "reddens" over "all we love" in Tennyson's poem, but no redness seems capable of spreading its shade over this detested rival: "The dark *red* shadows gathering in the drawing room as the trees drowned more and more of the sun would reach him last, perhaps never" (italics added). Instead, like a defiant mockery of Tennyson's image of sunset redness, "The wallpaper now flamed scarlet behind his shoulder." Henrietta would like to return to that moment in her walk with Sarah when "The mansion and the home farm had *sunk* forever below them in the expanse of woods" (italics added), but since Eugene has arrived it is clearer than ever that it is Sarah instead, the loved one, who in Henrietta's prophetic vision already "sinks . . . below the verge."

Sarah and Henrietta are in fact entrapped in an alarming *égoïsme à deux.* Tennyson writes of the vanished past, "Ah, sad and strange as in dark summer dawns / The *earliest pipe of half-awakened birds* / To dying ears" (italics added), and Bowen uses similar imagery to show us, in free indirect discourse, how intensely Sarah echoes Henrietta's inordinate love in her own narcissistic fantasizings: "She must never have to wake in the *early morning* except to the *birdlike stirrings* of Henrietta, or have her cheek brushed in the dark by the frill of another pillow in whose hollow did not repose Henrietta's check. Rather than they should cease to lie in the same bed she prayed they might lie in the same grave" (italics added). Evidently Sarah's own regressive love for Henrietta as mirror-image of a nostalgically idealized childhood (when they first began to "lie in the same bed") is much deeper than her love for Eugene. Better than a prospective marriage to Eugene would be the fulfilling return of the two sisters to good Mother Earth.

Surely this is a vividly imagined "Death in Life": Tennyson's phrase could hardly be more apposite. Moreover, when Sarah says to Henrietta, "You and I will stay as we are, . . . then nothing can touch one without touching the other," she pictures a situation that could be much more readily envisioned if the two girls were not sisters but mother and baby, two beings habitually conjoined or juxtaposed in a literal, physical way because of the unremitting necessities of child care. Both the Tennysonian allusions to nostalgia, to "days that are no more," and the odd imagery of constant bodily contact of a seemingly maternal type would suggest that the underlying motive of both Sarah and Henrietta in desperately envisioning their eternal life together is to preserve an intimacy remembered from memories or submerged fantasies of the ideal mother image, the Good Mother. The good mother in the Victorian dreamings of Mary is largely absent—she does not participate in the family's farewell walk. But at one point, when Eugene holds up his handkerchief in what oddly seems to be a "final act," Mamma instinctively murmured to Henrietta, "but you will be my child when Arthur is gone." Perhaps Arthur—and other males in the family—have had primacy so far in Mother's life, and the girls have felt left out.

One thing about this troubled family is clear and it is clarified by the pre-oedipal narcissism theory outlined above. I refer to the essential unreality of the Good Mother figure, the idealized image of mother, displaced by both Sarah and Henrietta onto a sibling substitute, as it is used to guarantee or idealize a "grandiose self" portrayal. The unreality of the idealized mother is based on its existence at the expense of the repressed Bad Mother image of the child's resentments.

Narcissistic behavior reveals a tension between the willed idealization of Good Mother and the involuntary response to the Bad Mother who will not stay repressed: thus, Frederick in **"Tears, Idle Tears"** tried to idealize Mrs. Dickinson's justice but also aggressively persevered (not consciously knowing why) in weeping incessantly so as to tarnish the noble, stately image of his mother as she liked to present it in public ("Such a lovely mother to have"). Similarly, in **"The Happy Autumn Fields,"** we should expect some powerful fantasy of aggression against the repressed Bad Maternal Figure—perhaps from the younger of the sisters.

That is what happens: Henrietta, the younger one, expresses a narcissistic resentment of Sarah that proves fatal in its effects. She begins by oddly reproaching Sarah, with very forced humor, for being older, for being born first. "But I cannot forget that you chose to be born without me; that you would not wait—." This is the blatant expression of an infantile wish for ultimate primacy. And eventually, Henrietta shockingly says to Eugene, "Whatever tries to come between me and Sarah becomes nothing." In some occult way reminiscent of Edgar Allan Poe or the ghost stories of Henry James, Henrietta evidently has her wish, for (as we and Mary learn from Travis, who has read the Victorian letters), a certain "friend of their youth" was "thrown from his horse and killed, riding back after a visit to their home." Folding up his handkerchief before departing was indeed Eugene's "final act." Sarah was at least partly in love with Eugene; therefore, by wishing his death, Henrietta knows that her love for Sarah is also unconscious jealous hate. Narcissistic love for an idealized imago reveals its cruel underside.

"The Happy Autumn Fields" is the story of Henrietta and Sarah's attempt to bring back or somehow willfully preserve the "days that are no more," a nostalgically idealized childhood-like state of "first love" for a close family member. Mary, too, in her Victorian dream has tried to bring back a happier time, for her current relationship with Travis displeases her: preferring to be the imagined Sarah, she thinks of the "grotesquerie of being saddled with Mary's body and lover"; and she notes distastefully the "possessive angry fondness" of Travis. Commenting on the wished-for death of Eugene, Phyllis Lassner suggests that "violence is a saving grace here because it forces the women to recognize the disorder hidden in their lives"—and only women "are capable of composing a new story out of disturbing old ones" as "Mary and Sarah together wrest their stories away from Travis and Papa to create an altogether-new kind of tale."

To this I would reply: insofar as the violence of **"The Happy Autumn Fields"** is in any way a "saving grace," it is salvific only for Elizabeth Bowen, for she can consciously "recognize the disorder" in the narcissistic nostalgia of Mary and Sarah and Henrietta as none of these women themselves can.

That is why, for the protagonists, the tale is a tragedy, its uncomprehended psychological problems and dangers repeating themselves in successive generations, just as in classical Greek drama. Sarah and Henrietta apparently both died young; in the story's ghostly mental dreamworld, Henrietta's ill wishes eliminate Eugene. And if the tale of these three Victorians also represents a fantasy of Mary's, what is being hinted about her covert wishes concerning Travis? The Victorian "days that are no more" become a frighteningly ironic "Death in Life," disturbingly prophetic of Mary's present morbidity and apparent hostile resentment.

In **"Tears, Idle Tears"** and **"The Happy Autumn Fields"** Elizabeth Bowen seeks to deconstruct Tennysonian nostalgia by laying bare the narcissistic tensions that give it its melancholy life, or death in life. What I find refreshing about these paired meditations on Tennyson is that the deconstruction is carried out in two alternative modes, with two contrasting kinds of irony: tragic and comic. Playfully, Bowen shows how a seven-year-old child can enjoy a fine deconstructive epiphany as the oblivious "unseeing" gaze of a duck on a pond momentarily breaks a narcissistic mental deadlock of the kind that—magnified on the screen of history—can keep generations tragically in thrall.

FURTHER READING

Criticism

Jordan, Heather Bryant. "Rifling the Past: Elizabeth Bowen's Wartime Autobiography." *Notes on Modern Irish Literature* 2 (1990): 52-57.

> Examines the ways in which Bowen came to terms with her family's past while writing her autobiography.

Watson, Barbara Bellow. "Variations on an Enigma: Elizabeth Bowen's War Novel." *Southern Humanities Review* XV, No. 2 (Spring 1981): 131-51.

> Discusses the sensibilities imparted by World War II onto Bowen's novel *The Heat of the Day.*

Additional coverage of Bowen's life and career is available in the following sources published by Gale: *Contemporary Authors,* **Vols. 2, 17-18;** *Contemporary Authors New Revision Series,* **Vol. 35;** *Concise Dictionary of British Literary Biography,* **1945-1960;** *Dictionary of Literary Biography,* **Vols. 15, 162;** *DISCovering Authors Modules: Novelists; Major Twentieth-Century Writers; Short Story Criticism,* **Vol. 3.**

The Chaneysville Incident
David (Henry) Bradley, Jr.

The following entry presents criticism on David Bradley's novel *The Chaneysville Incident* (1981).

For further information on Bradley's life and works, see *CLC,* Volume 23.

INTRODUCTION

An expansive and innovative novel, *The Chaneysville Incident* took a decade for Bradley to develop. Beginning with an incident that Bradley discovered in historical papers belonging to his mother, the author used his imagination to breathe fictional life into a story based on the facts presented in the papers. Bradley's technique of merging history and fiction challenges traditional notions of historical and narrative processes.

Plot and Major Characters

The Chaneysville Incident is based on a historical event in which a group of slaves fleeing through the underground railroad committed suicide when faced with capture. Bradley takes this historical incident and creates a fictional narrative around it. The novel focuses on John Washington, an African-American historian who is searching for his identity by connecting with his familial past. He journeys to his home in western Pennsylvania to take care of his ailing surrogate father, Old Jack Crawley. When Old Jack dies, Washington is compelled to visit his real parents' home to study his late father's collection of old journals. Washington feels incomplete due to several gaps in his personal family history, including the ambiguity surrounding his father's and his paternal grandfather's deaths. Looking through his father's papers, Washington begins a journey which merges his personal ancestry with history. He learns that his father, Moses, committed suicide and begins to understand its connection to the suicide of the slaves at Chaneysville. The tale unfolds as Washington describes his findings to his girlfriend, a white psychiatrist named Judith. Washington's trip home causes him to recall how Old Jack took him under his wing after Moses's death. Old Jack taught Washington the skills of a woodsman and recounted tales of Washington's grandfather, also named Moses. There are several threads to the narrative, including sections told from Washington's perspective and some from Old Jack's. Eventually Washington's journey ends when he merges the stories with history to conclude that his grandfather, C. K., was a member of the Chaneysville incident, and that C. K. killed the woman he loved, several other slaves, and himself in order to avoid capture. This rev-

elation leads Washington to understand that his father committed suicide after he had discovered the same information. Washington now understands the effect of his familial history on the reality of his present, and he feels complete.

Major Themes

The major themes of *The Chaneysville Incident* focus on history's influence on the present and explore historical process itself. John Washington uses history, in the form of Moses's papers, and imagination, in the form of Old Jack's stories, to develop a knowledge of the past. The novel departs from a typical view of history as an accumulation of empirical data. Other major themes focus on racism and racial stereotypes, specifically the conflict between Washington's "white" education and his organic common sense acquired from Old Jack. Washington tries to flee what he considers to be a stereotypical African-American heritage, including a reliance on intuition and imagination, by becoming a historian who relies on facts and evidence. Ironically, Washington is unable to piece together his own past without merging his skills as a historian and his imagination.

Critical Reception

Most reviewers discuss what *The Chaneysville Incident* implies about historical perspective. W. Lawrence Hogue states that *The Chaneysville Incident* "shows that history itself depends on the conventions of narrative, language, discourse, and ideology in order to present what happened." Many reviewers praise Bradley for his skill at bringing the narrative to life. Paul Gilroy lauds Bradley's accomplishment: "Employing a variety of genres and literary techniques with great skill, not as pastiche but for the substantive value of each differing register of address, Bradley brings this story to life at an extraordinary intensity." Many reviewers note the theme of withdrawal in the book, which connects it to a tradition in African-American literature, and compare Bradley to Ralph Ellison and James Baldwin. Gilroy says, "the motif of withdrawal without retreat is a sign that Bradley recognises his own literary heritage." Critics also compare Bradley to William Faulkner and Ernest Hemingway. A few critics condemn Bradley for the misogyny presented in *The Chaneysville Incident,* but others note Washington's rehabilitation at the end of the novel. Critics praise Bradley for his innovative exploration of the narrative form and consider him a prominent writer of contemporary fiction.

PRINCIPAL WORKS

South Street (novel) 1975
The Chaneysville Incident (novel) 1981

CRITICISM

David Bradley with Patricia Holt (interview date 10 April 1981)

SOURCE: An interview with David Bradley in *Publishers Weekly,* Vol. 219, No. 15, April 10, 1981, pp. 12-4.

[*In the following interview, Bradley discusses his development of* The Chaneysville Incident.]

It seems incredible to David Bradley that his new book, ***The Chaneysville Incident,*** which Harper & Row published April 8, took 11 years and almost as many drafts to write. Although his highly acclaimed first novel, ***South Street,*** had taken him less than a year, he says that ***Chaneysville,*** a much longer book, involved "quite a bit of digging."

Author of articles for publications as various as *The Village Voice, Quest, Signature, The New York Arts Journal, The American Photographer* and the *Philadelphia Bulletin,* Bradley is currently an assistant professor of creative writing at Temple University who has taken a year "away from the cold winters of Pennsylvania" to become visiting professor at San Diego State University.

The experience has served him well. At 30, Bradley is slim, lithe and athletic—a devoted runner who puts in 12 to 13 miles a day. When *PW* meets him over lunch in Los Angeles, his dark eyes penetrate the thick lenses of his frameless glasses with an intensity that is at first unsettling. Then, suddenly, the eyes crinkle up with laughter as he sees what has been placed before him: a runny omelet and two chopsticks. "Well, *this* should be interesting," he grins. Smoothing his magnificently fluffy beard out of the way, he leans forward to tell us why the research and writing of ***The Chaneysville Incident*** took him, as he says, "so damn long."

As he talks, it is apparent that Bradley is a good-humored scholar without a trace of snobbery, having earned his B.A. on a scholarship at the University of Pennsylvania and his M.S. from the University of London. He is "a lucky man," he says, who was "encouraged if not pushed" by his mother, his teachers and local librarians to get out of the racially claustrophobic environs of his hometown of Bedford, Pa.

"Writing this book," he says, speaking perhaps for many novelists, "has been a growing-up process for me because when I started 11 years ago, I knew nothing about where I grew up. It was as if I had no psyche—as if whatever I had experienced there had made no impression. All I remembered was that I was always coming down with bronchitis or pneumonia or some sort of allergy. Later on I realized that like John Washington in the novel, I was just *allergic* to the place, you know?" A smile cuts across his beard as if all that is over now, although he quips that he still comes down with a cold "just thinking about the place."

It was during his research for the book that Bradley began to remember incidents in his childhood that he had apparently suppressed before: what it was like for blacks to live on Gravel Hill (known by whites in town as "Niggers Knob," "Boogie Bend" or "Spade Hollow"); how it felt never to talk about racial fragmentation ("We were north of the Mason-Dixon line, and racism didn't happen in our town the way it did in the South"); how it felt at age six to accompany his father into the deep South, where "Whites Only" signs were still prominent, and wonder why he felt so *comfortable* there ("It was because they were so up front about blacks staying out of white districts that for once there was nothing personal about it"); and, finally, how it felt to be befriended by older black men who lived in dirt-floor shacks on what was called the "far side" of the hill. "These were men who taught me to hunt and live in the woods, who fixed hot toddies for me when I was 10 or 12 and who told me stories—legends, really, mixed with history and myth—about people before my time, about a near-lynching close to the town, about the town's Klan sheriff, that sort of thing."

Some of the stories concerned a "station" of the Underground Railroad near town that had been supported almost entirely by black people, and this Bradley confirmed as historical fact years later while plowing through local county records. But the incident to which the title refers was actually discovered by Bradley's mother during her own research into the history of the town's black community for a locally published book.

In a letter to Bradley, she wrote that during the mid-1800s, a group of runaway slaves had traveled across the Mason-Dixon line via the Railroad to Chaneysville (a town near Bedford), where they were captured. Rather than face jail, beatings or return to the South, they asked to be shot to death by their captors, and—as Bradley's mother wrote after she uncovered the graves where they had been buried for over 100 years—"someone obliged."

"I began to research this story with a scholar's interest," Bradley recalls. "I wasn't a historian, but my father [the minister of the local African Methodist Episcopal Zion Church] had been trained as one, and I know how these guys think. For them, all the stuff about people who died a long time ago actually exists, and you've got to know it, got to *see* it all, to understand what really went on."

Bradley admits to becoming "a bit exercised" about this because he believes that "too often history is translated into novels about the Old South that read like a black version of the Regency romance. You know: the sweet old darkies down by the cabin singing by the light of the moon, slavery portrayed as a condition of life that was not really so hard or bad, girls who wear crinolines and Miz Scarletts who behaved so kindly to their slaves. Well, all that is bullshit. Slavery was a dirty, nasty, disgusting business for every one of the 13-million Africans brought to the New World, and the fact is that it went on for *400 years*—almost twice as long as this country has been a nation."

The thousands of historical documents Bradley examined and his belief in using a historian's approach to the Chaneysville incident convinced him that the book couldn't be written as a conventional novel. "I tried at first to write it as nonfiction, as history," he recalls, "but that didn't work. History, after all, is pretty dry. Then I tried telling the story in a traditional way, but that didn't work either because I couldn't give the reader enough historical data to explain the larger forces at work on whites and blacks alike."

So Bradley finally combined it all—the stories of the old men on the "far side," the mountain of facts from the past, his own childhood in Bedford and the search of historian protagonist John Washington to find the truth about the 13 people who one night asked to be killed rather than recaptured.

The result is a complicated book, with long historical passages that are so readable they go down like cream, primarily because John Washington is very much like David Bradley—a historian and an incorrigible wiseacre whose meanderings are as fascinating as his central story. But this is another reason the book took so long to complete. As a former assistant editor at Lippincott, Bradley had sensed a trend in publishing that he felt was harmful to writers and, ultimately, to publishers. "It may have been naive of me," he says, "but I felt when I was an editor that if you took some extra time with an author you might be able to help make the book better.

"The only problem was that no one ever demonstrated that a better book *sells* better. And with corporate pressures taking their toll, the trend now is that if you get a book that's publishable, do it. If not, decline it. So I knew that if I was going to write a book that ultimately would be what I had hoped it would be, I couldn't rely on an editor saying, 'Well, this isn't good enough yet, but we'll help you.' It was going to be, 'Well, this isn't good enough yet so we're going to dump you.' I think that's a continuing problem that many writers have to face."

Bradley himself also had to face the musical chairs syndrome that increasingly affects editor-writer relationships. In his case, the book was acquired at Harper, first by Jonathan Dolger, who subsequently left and turned it over to Harvey Ginsberg, who subsequently left and turned it over to Jake Ross. By this time the book was big, bulky—and risky. In spite of the success of *Roots,* Bradley says, "Publishers still don't believe that black people buy books or that black novels sell."

Soon Bradley, in consultation with his agent Wendy Weil, began considering the possibility of taking the book back and returning the advance. "There's just no way a writer can ask a publishing house to carry out with full enthusiasm the plans and directions of an editor who is no longer there," he says. But during meetings with Harper management, Bradley says he was "really quite gratified by their support" and feels he is "coming out of this a lucky man indeed."

With a 25,000-copy first printing, a $25,000 advertising budget and selection by both Book-of-the-Month Club and Playboy Book Club, it does seem that *The Chaneysville Incident* finally reached the marketplace with a good launching. Meanwhile, Bradley is finding life in San Diego "bland but warm," does not know where he will be teaching next year—and has started a new book, about which he has little to say.

"I'll tell you one thing," he grins, pushing the heavy glasses up his nose, "this time it's going to take considerably less than 11 years."

David Bradley with Susan L. Blake and James A. Miller (interview date Spring-Summer 1984)

SOURCE: An interview with David Bradley, in *Callaloo*, Vol. 7, No. 2, Spring-Summer, 1984, pp. 19-39.

[*In the following interview, Bradley discusses* South Street *and* The Chaneysville Incident, *focusing on the characters John Washington and Judith from the latter work.*]

[Miller]: *We were talking earlier about what it meant to travel as a black person, back home, to the South, before the age of the super highway. How did those experiences affect you? We're talking about how relationships changed once you crossed the Mason-Dixon line. What did you gather there? How did it shape your perception of the South, of Bedford?*

[Bradley]: I always liked the South because you knew what was happening there. Nobody ever said this stuff—this is the amazing thing—nobody ever said "This is the South, now." But if you place somebody who doesn't know what they're doing in a context where everybody knows what to do, they start knowing what to do. Bedford had the same racist structures, but nobody would acknowledge it. And so, for the first time in my life, for three weeks in the year, I knew what to do. Another thing; I never saw any white folks. Except in gas stations. Dinwiddie was sort of an old plantation. You were back in there and you never saw anybody. You camped out basically. Racism: I didn't know that word. That was before Martin Luther King was on TV. Later on, I found out. My father would carefully avoid anyplace where we might get into trouble. Anywhere. We'd be low on gas, and he would look for a *big* gas station. The more pumps, the safer he felt.

[Miller]: *How did that experience shape your view of Bedford? Coming back, did you have any conscious awareness that those forays into the South were shaping your social, political perspective toward life in Bedford at all?*

Well, you see, I'm stupid. I'm slow. I didn't know what was going on until after I left. All I knew was that it was different. What happened was—and this is bizarre—I would go down South and I would meet these girls, and would write these passionate letters, all the rest of the year. Mostly I'd never see them again. I'd go back the next year and there would be different girls. But, see, there were only fifty black people in Bedford and only one black girl who was about my age who had somewhat similar interests, and she didn't do it.

[Miller]: *They never do.*

It was a logical match to everybody but her. And this was a very important thing to me, 'cause this meant that the South was associated with every kind of release that there was. So I always loved those trips. And Bedford was just hell.

[Blake]: *You've said in another context that you felt alienated at the University of Pennsylvania. What exactly did you feel alienated from?*

Not alienated in the common sense, or the sociological or whatever sense, of the term. It was simply this: I came from a rural background. It was black, rural, less black than rural. At this time the image of blacks that was acceptable to that sort of institution was urban black, and so it wasn't that I got to a place where they were not prepared to have black people, but where they were prepared to have a particular kind of black people, and where the black people were prepared to have a particular set of problems in dealing with white institutions. I didn't have any problem like that because I had been dealing with white institutions all my life. My problem was people would say, you know, we had rats at home. Well, we didn't have rats, we had field mice. We had chickens. So they couldn't deal with that. And it meant that the kinds of programs that were set up to make black people welcome—which weren't doing that anyway, but which were set up for that—didn't apply to me, and nobody really understood what I was doing. It was not so much that I was alienated, but that I didn't fit into the mold of what I was supposed to do, and how to satisfy my contract with the institution—because they gave me money. And being raised as a Protestant, I believed if people give you money, that means you have a job, and there's something you're supposed to do. And it took me a while to figure out what I was supposed to do. Eventually, I did; I was supposed to fuck up, but I didn't do that.

[Miller]: *What did you find on South Street that constituted an alternative to the style you found at Penn in the late sixties?*

First of all, it was a small town—South Street was a small town. People related to each other, people had histories, people knew each other's mothers, you know, that sort of thing. Secondly, nobody was an intellectual. People were not prepared to intellectualize their experience all the time, and that's what went on at the university. Even the black people went around mouthing rhetoric; these people on South Street were dealing with real problems. The other thing was that the rhetoric of the time was that the horrible experience of being black in America, of being poor, of being oppressed had irrevocably damaged black people to the point where they were dehumanized, incapable of love, only capable of anger, and directing it towards each other. I didn't feel that way—and these people on South Street demonstrated love for themselves, as people. They didn't know they were dehumanized. And that was incredibly comforting. The other thing was they didn't care I went to college. I remember going to a bar once where there was this beautiful barmaid named Leola. She leaned over to me one day—and I was wearing jeans and a T-shirt—she leaned over, and she said, "You go to college, doncha?" And I thought, O.K., Penn, this is going to impress the hell out of this woman; I'm going to get over. I said "Yeah," I said, "Yeah." And she said, "That's all right, I won't tell nobody." When you're a dumb kid, who is scared to death you're going to flunk out—which I was—and somebody says, "Hey, I won't tell anybody you're in college," it's an incredibly liberating kind of thing. You drink your gin, you pay your money.

[Miller]: *The character Brown in* **South Street** *is a model of a kind of aspiring artist who is also attracted to the values of this community. He's trying to come to terms with South Street. At some levels he does; at some levels he doesn't. How complete is the fusion?*

Brown was really a plot device. That book was written in a particular kind of way. The first third of it was written in a writing workshop.

[Miller]: *With whom?*

Hiram Haydn. But also three other people—three other students and myself. With only four people, every four weeks, you had to come up with stuff. And so the first three chapters of **South Street** were done almost like Charles Dickens would have done it. O.K., it's time for me to come up with forty pages for the folks. And I did. It was submitted . . . What I would do was write out a rough draft, throw away pages that I didn't want, cross out stuff with a black felt-tipped marker, so nobody could see the mistakes, and xerox it, and hand it in and get reactions. Those people were into the characters; me, I'm into plot. But there was an influence that propelled the first part of that novel—somebody'd constantly say, "Gee, I liked that; gee, I liked him; gee, I liked her." So, when I left that group, and wrote the end of the book, it was *entirely* different. It was all about Brown, Brown coming from the country, Brown . . . It shifted to the first person at one point. And when I sold it, I had to write a letter telling how I was going to revise it. And I looked at it and said the best thing to do is to continue this thing. In a way, you know, it's the outsider theme. And I realized that Brown was really a plot device; he's the one that makes all these other things hold together; he's the impetus.

[Miller]: *There's a relationship in the novel that interests me between Brown and the old wino Jake. Jake seems to embody a certain kind of wisdom, a certain kind of understanding of experience, and it occurred to me that the relationship seems to prefigure the relationship between John Washington and Jack Crawley later on in* **Chaneysville.**

O.K., but there's something else you gotta remember, and that's that I wrote the beginning of **Chaneysville**—and particularly that old Jack Crawley and John Washington existed—before **South Street.** They were both characters in this other novel that will never see the light of day—it was really a collection of short stories. The tale-telling, in fact the story of the Chaneysville incident, was part of that.

[Blake]: *Did you ever know anybody like Jack Crawley?*

Yes. Three people. My own father—see my own father was forty-five years old when I was born. By the time I was old enough to start understanding what a man was, my father was sixty, and was starting to get—a little crusty. And it was difficult to see him as a father. At the same time, while I was very young, there was a man named Dan Harris, an old guy who, when I was four or five years old, was basically my playmate. And my Uncle John, who always was crusty; he was the black sheep of the family. Did nasty stuff. But also I was always around old preachers, and, you know, a seventy-year-old preacher, having been a preacher for some time, has given up most of the vices, or is beyond most of the vices, and what he's left with is the ability to tell lies. And they sit around and they lie. And preaching is sort of lying anyway. And I would sit listening to these guys for days. And it was amazing to hear how a pious preacher, without ever using profanity or anything else, could suggest almost every funky human interaction. These were men who'd seen life. Readers respond to that, too. I don't know whether they respond to it because I respond to it or just, you know, love old men.

[Blake]: **Chaneysville** *is a historical novel—*

That's what you say!

[Blake]: *Well, it has this historical incident at the core. How much of it is researchable history?*

The further back you get, and the more objective you get, the more researchable it is. There was never a C. K. Washington. There was never a C. K. Washington's father, Zack. There was a rebellion in Louisiana at that time, and they did place heads on stakes. There was a man named Lewis Bolah, who betrayed that rebellion, who did serve with Commodore Perry, did petition the legislature of Virginia for permission to live in Virginia. There was a Cherokee nation that had slaves, and experienced difficulties because gold was discovered on their land. There were the things C. K. Washington supposedly wrote. They were usually listed as anonymous.

[Blake]: *So you picked out some anonymous things that fit the character of C. K.?*

I decided I wanted him to have written some things, and I wanted him to be able to speak in that way. I needed things that pushed him forward. I needed documents, and so I found documents that were anonymous. There was a character named Pettis, who did advertise in southern newspapers. There were rebellions in Kentucky, although there was no evidence Pettis was involved with them. Basically what I did was I found the beginnings of lines in history, and I sort of filled in the dots.

[Blake]: *You've said that the gravestones are there near Chaneysville.*

Not in that pattern.

[Blake]: *Are they associated in the legend with the escaped slaves?*

O yeah, yeah. They're right next to the family graveyard. It's very clear where the Iiames family starts and these people stop. The gravestones are of a different character.

[Blake]: *So you have John Washington in the novel making that connection imaginatively, but actually in local legend, the connection between the escaped slaves and the stones is there—something John discovers when he's kicking at the stones.*

Well, what he discovers is the pattern, which allows him to reconstruct the family structure and everything else, but the stones are there.

[Blake]: *You said last night that the material was "so wonderful." What was "so wonderful" about it? Why did it appeal to you?*

It bothered me as a person. It appealed to me as a fiction writer. Here you've got a story of thirteen people who take a dramatic act. O.K., so you tell somebody this story—my mother wrote it, and she wrote it in two sentences. The questions that sprang to my mind when I read it were, Who were these people? Where did they come from? Why did they do this? That's a novel. Characterization: who were they? Background: where did they come from? Motivation: why did they do it? It's *all* right there. All you have to do is invent the beginning; you've got the end. Everything else in that book is a means to that end. All those characters—Old Jack, John Washington, all those things—came *after* the story.

[Miller]: *You said your mother wrote it in two sentences. Was that because the legend was so pervasive in the community?*

No, it wasn't pervasive; she discovered it. Well, she didn't discover it; she was told it. But I've never seen it written anywhere else. She was told it by a guy in a store in a town called Clearville, about fifteen miles from Chaneysville. He told her to go there and look for these graves. She says that when she first went there, the guy, Iiames, who was then alive, told her that, yeah, yeah, the graves were up there. When I went there, he either had forgotten or had changed his mind and said that he hadn't known the story until my mother came and told him. He possibly just knew the graves were there and didn't know the story. But she's the one who brought those two things together.

[Miller]: *How did she respond to it? I mean what was her sense of . . .*

To the story?

[Miller]: *Yes . . . discovery?*

My mother is a lot like John Washington. Nobody knows what the hell she thinks about anything. She's the kind of person who would have stood there and cried her eyes out and not told anybody. So I really don't know. I know she never asked me why I was doing this, and I know she called me up and told me the story. She found out a lot of things about the county. She was doing research for a local history. It was the county bicentennial. They wanted a black person to write the history of the black community.

[Miller]: *This was Bicentennial?*

Well, it was the county bicentennial, which preceded the U.S. Bicentennial by three or four years or so. It was late 1969 when she did it—'71 was the bicentennial. And first, they thought of my father, who was a trained historian, but they decided that his writing style was rather dry, and they asked me, and I wanted as little to do with Bedford at that time as possible. So they asked my mother, and she just went crazy. She went to my father, she said, "what do I do?" He said, you go to the graveyards and the courthouse. And that's what she did. She looked at these records and slavery transactions. Because these little courthouses preserve everything, and this one never burned. And the graveyards, the old graveyards. I think those are the two places that people don't lie.

[Miller]: *That suggests another issue—that is the predominance of images of fire in* **Chaneysville.** *There are so many other things in* **Chaneysville** *that do burn. Records burn, and files burn. Part of the process that seems to be going on in the novel is that a lot is being burned away to get at the real stuff.*

That's too critical. The only explicit thing about fire in there is about fire and power. At that point fire is the means to an end, because the power had to be the power to destroy. Call it death if you want to. That fire image started out as an antithesis to the cold. 'Cause if you're cold, you build a fire.

That was something I stole from Jack London. I think, of all the things I ever read, that short story made the most impression on me. Just at a real visceral level, 'cause, man, I hate the cold. I really hate it.

[Miller]: *To go back to the question of history, there are some very, very complex evaluations being made about history and how we look at history and what's the appropriate thing to do within history. For example, C. K. is very involved in the Abolitionist movement, and then he drops out . . .*

You see, I hate it. I hate history on account of my father because my father refused to have any fun with the stuff. And it's, you know, it's a style of black history, *name* history; you read a bibliography or a book, it consists almost entirely of names, no faces, no events, and you don't know what's going on. I mean it's boring. It was boring to me. I like stories. So, that's when I decided that John had to be a historian; I figured, O.K., I'm gonna let the guy talk about history.

[Blake]: *You said this morning, in answer to a student's question, that the reason there were historical lectures in the novel was that Americans, black and white, didn't know history, and needed to know some things in order to understand the story that you wanted to tell. Does that imply that the history you have John say in these lectures is history you want people to understand? Your interpretation of events?*

No, it's history that's necessary to understand the incident, understand what those people did on the Hill.

[Blake]: *But, essentially what you're giving John to say there is what you would say, too.*

I hate history on account of my father because my father refused to have any fun with the stuff. And it's, you know, it's a style of black history, name history; you read a bibliography or a book, it consists almost entirely of names, no faces, no events, and you don't know what's going on.

—David Bradley

Sometimes. I mean John is a little extreme about a lot of things. John is extreme about his detachment. I mean, John's concept of an incident—that you take an event, and you put it on a card, and you can tear it away from everything else—is totally bullshit. But, yeah, he says things that are historical. For example, the dissertation about the slave trade—all his facts are true. The little philippic about minority set-

asides—that's sort of funny, or it's supposed to be sort of funny. Is that interpretation or fact? I'd say fact. There are other things I wouldn't say that of. I don't worry that much about knowing the truth about things, as he does in the book. In a word, he's a historian, I'm not.

[Blake]: *You told Mel Watkins that one of the reasons you abandoned your first approach to the* **Chaneysville** *material was that, despite the violence and tragedy, it was funny. It seems to me that this evaluation fits Jack Crawley's story of the near-lynching of Josh White and most of* **South Street** *. . .*

I said that?

[Blake]: *Well, he claims you did. And I wonder how you would characterize the relationship between humor and tragedy.*

Well, I don't know if I do. In **South Street,** I had no problem because I could always get the jokes in. **South Street** conforms to a Shakespearean comedy. Low comedy, low characters, lots of bawdy jokes, Falstaffian people, whores, the whole business. **Chaneysville** is a tragedy. The problem with **Chaneysville** is getting any jokes in there, getting any humor in there at all. And that's one of the reasons that Old Jack stayed. After the lynching story—all the jokes are over. You get a couple of them here and there, you get a couple of ironic twists, but John is not a funny guy. And I knew I had to relieve that first-person narration some way, because nobody was going to listen to that guy for nine chapters or whatever there are unless I put some funny stuff up front. So that's why I had to keep Old Jack's voice. I don't know if that answers your question, but that's the way I approach the problem. Some of John's dissertations are there for that reason, too.

[Blake]: *In a broad sense, you and John Washington have gone through similar processes; that is, you've both taken a historical situation, researched it, and told a story about it. Are there any similarities in the two experiences? Did you go through any of the processes you have John going through?*

I would like to say no, but there is one very important one.

[Blake]: *What's that?*

He doesn't think he can do this thing; he goes through the whole thing maintaining he can't imagine anything. And I would like to say that all the way through I knew I could, but in fact I could tell you almost, to the minute, the moment I knew that I was going to be able to pull this off—and it was extremely late; it was in March of 1980.

[Blake]: *A year before the book came out.*

It was a year before the book came out, but what's more it was about three months after the book was due to be delivered. I mean, I was three months late on the contract and I still did not know I could pull this off. So, there is that; there is certainly a parallel in that sense. And there's the process of going through anger—which he denies and I never denied. Other things like that. There's duplication, but he's reluctant to imagine and I just do it all the time.

[Blake]: *How would you explain Judith's role in the novel?*

I wouldn't . . . I would actually. Judith is one of the latest structures in the whole business and she's peripheral in this sense, that it's not about her . . . Let me just tell you how she came about. I knew that John had to have someone to tell this to, because I didn't want him just telling it to a reader—there was no point—and there would be no reaction to direct him in the right ways. So the questions she asks move him to talk to the topic, and so forth and so on. I also knew that I needed some reason for him to have to come to terms with all this because he's been sitting on this stuff for years. Why, all of a sudden, does he have to deal with this? Well, there's the whole thing that she's going to leave him. I started out with Judith being a black woman. Then I realized that black people don't talk about this stuff. Once every three weeks, you know, and they'd agree with each other. Who wants to hear two niggers sitting around complaining about white folks? So she had to be white. Which opened up the door to miscegenation, and all that other stuff—and it did. Then I needed a job for her . . . because I think people should have jobs; John had one and I thought she should have one, too. Because he's not the kind of guy who . . . I mean he's not going to have a white lover and *keep* her. I knew they couldn't be married because marriage implies that he has accepted her totally, and he wasn't going to do that. So what's she going to do? She had to be a professional of some sort, because if she were an academic she would be inclined to approach things in the same way he did, and she doesn't; she's more practical. O.K., so she's a professional. A lawyer? She can't be a lawyer because law is basically history. Anybody who knows the law knows history. She can't, she's got to be ignorant of that stuff. So she's got to be a doctor.

[Blake]: *There're only two alternatives?*

Or she could be a dentist, but, I mean, come on, a dentist didn't make it, you know? Although talking to John Washington is like pulling teeth. So now we're down to doctor. Well, what kind of doctor? Now, this guy's crazy. What kind of person would be willing to sit there and say, "Uh huh, and how long have you felt this way?," be capable of listening to somebody say "I raped a woman just like you" and

conceal her reaction to this? So that's how she became a shrink. But that was late. In fact, John Washington didn't exist until 1978.

[Blake]: *I was wondering when we were talking earlier, about the novel and its development and culmination as though it were the story John discovers and tells rather than the framework . . .*

I didn't know . . . John existed because of that earlier novel but I didn't know I was going to use him until real late. And then he was a kid. At one point it was in the third person and it started as sort of cinematic thing with this cabin and this one kid coming down and the old man telling him stories. And, at that point, he didn't really have an identity, and he was going to grow up and then he was going to start to talk, and I decided that that was hokey as hell and it took too damn long. And, so, he didn't become a historian until much later either, when I realized I had to get all this history in, and how was I going to do that unless this guy was a historian. So all these things came about as a result of wanting to tell the old story. Essentially, the old story existed first, then Moses Washington, as a bridge. Then I realized the generations wouldn't work out, so I needed C. K. C. K. was real late, too. C. K. came along about 1978. By the time it ran to contract, by the time it was submitted, there were two proposals, and I don't think the first proposal mentioned C. K. Washington at all; the second one did. So, somewhere in there, all these things developed.

[Miller]: *To go back to the relationship between John and Judith for a minute, one of the things that becomes clear is that John is reluctant to apply his imagination to . . .*

He doesn't have one.

[Blake]: *Well, he obviously has one, doesn't he? It develops toward the end.*

[Miller]: *And John finally learns to apply his imagination to this incident and therefore unlocks that key to the history that's been tormenting him. Although Judith is very, very practical and has these qualities of a trained professional, Judith also has to learn to be able to imagine John's situation.*

I'm not sure she doesn't all along. Like he says, he underestimated her . . .

[Miller]: *What does that imply? John has to change, right? John, as an individual, as a professional, John as a historian has to learn how to get rid of all that academic apparatus that stands between him and his ability to imagine, imaginatively re-create history.*

I wouldn't put it that way. I would put it that he has to learn to do both things at the same time. You know, in the funeral chapter, what he's talking about is not choosing one or the other but applying both of them. It's the fact that he knows all these things that allows him to imagine. And the fact of imagining does involve the use of names and places and people that he knows. I mean, he doesn't . . . he still doesn't make anything up.

[Miller]: *But he has to go through this process. You said that Judith is really an auditor, she has a certain structural role, a certain . . .*

She changes, too, though; she changes; she starts to drink. All right, you guys, I'm going to be a literary critic, too. There is a theme of drinking together in this novel.

[Miller]: *Yes . . .*

With coffee with the mother . . .

[Miller]: *As ritual?*

All right. At the beginning he says there would have been more Wild Turkey, although Judith didn't drink, implying that she doesn't. By the end of the novel, she too drinks a toddy. But before that, she's drinking coffee, they drink water together, and there's a progression. First, she makes him toddies, she's willing to become complicit to that extent, and then she wants one herself.

[Miller]: *Are you suggesting that the ritual of drinking really requires two acts of complicity: that John has to learn how to recreate his imagination and, simultaneously, Judith has to learn how to participate in those rituals that bond them together?*

Yeah, well she wouldn't let him drink; she didn't like his drinking. She didn't understand it, she thought it was weakness, and, you know, she gave him a hard time about it. And, you know, by the end of the novel, she's willing to say: "O.K., maybe the guy has reason to drink; maybe I need a drink, too." The reason I can talk about that is because I put that one in.

[Blake]: *Well, to get back to Jim's question, it seems as though her learning to drink a toddy is an indicator of another kind of change . . .*

A symbol.

[Blake]: *Yes, well I thought I would avoid that terminology.*

No, you can use it, you can use it, I just can't.

[Blake]: *O.K., a change that's expressed when Judith asks who buried the fugitives and John says it was Iiames and Judith says, "why would a white man or why would you think a white man . . ."*

She says both.

[Blake]: *Yes. And that indicates an absorption into John's point of view there. And John's analysis indicates a kind of ability to trust a white person. But, as you've suggested in the novel, the fundamental changes are John's. Judith learns to see John's point of view, but she's been willing and ready all along, it's just that John hasn't given her any opportunity. To the extent that these two individuals represent black and white—and both of their personal histories seem to represent general history and the whole problem in their relationship has been related to race—*

No, I don't think so. I think, first of all, they're very atypical. John Washington, for sure, is not the typical black.

[Blake]: *It's not typicality: it's that their personal identities, their family histories, are linked to general racial history. Judith comes from a genteel Southern family that is connected to what John has learned about the history of the area, for example. John is preoccupied with his relationship to ancestors who were slaves, fought against slavery, escaped from slavery, and so forth.*

One's black and one's white, all right? I mean, that's what it comes down to.

[Blake]: *At any rate, what does the fact that John is the one that has to change imply?*

Nothing. I'll tell you what it *doesn't* imply. His changing is not something that has to do with race; it's something that has to do with his point of view; and her changing has something to do with her point of view.

[Blake]: *And are their points of view strictly individual?*

I wouldn't say they're strictly individual, but . . . certainly everything somebody is grows out of something else. If you want to you can, but I would not generalize it to some sort of grand message about who should change and who should not change from the point of view of society.

[Miller]: *This is another question about the meaning of history and historical pattern, coming from a different angle. Does the novel suggest that John must confront his history, not as Moses has—to reduplicate or re-enact a historical pattern—but to overcome it, to change it, transform it, to get rid of it?*

I can tell you what I believe about that in the abstract. History to me is raw material, the past is raw material. We can't be governed by it. Now, I stole half, or a third, of the book from Robert Penn Warren, and he ends *All the King's Men* with "out of history, into history, and the awful responsibility of time." O.K.? That's it.

[Miller]: *One thing that's clear to me is that you tend to resist interpretations of the novel that propose it as a metaphor for the broad scale racial agonies of America in the seventies, eighties . . .*

It's not that I resist it; it's that I haven't thought about it, and didn't conceive it that way. It's not an allegory. And, I think, certainly a novelist gets in trouble when he gets himself into the process of making an allegory.

[Blake]: *Do you imagine an audience as you write?*

Me. Me. I write things that please me. See, I'm into form and plot. The details that make a character alive for a reader are fully arbitrary; you can juggle a character around a lot more easily than you can juggle the plot because there's no causality in the character. Once you're locked into a plot sequence, you make maybe three decisions having to do with the plot, and that's *it*; everything else is logical. Some student today asked something about the bus passage, and the reason that I kept the bus passage in—apart from the fact that I liked it—was that I had a character who was going to have to sit on a bus for four hours, and so had to convey to the reader the passage of time. I couldn't say, "four hours later." So I put in something that takes up a little time. The solutions to those problems are what please me. And I don't worry about whether people get it. I know for a fact that most readers aren't going to understand why that section's there, anymore than when you start your car up and you drive down the road, you think about the valves and the pistons. Maybe the mechanic does and maybe the guy who works on the assembly line does, but you don't. All you know is, your car goes. So, I'm a mechanic, I'm a guy on an assembly line.

Lynn Veach Sadler (essay date 1986)

SOURCE: "The Black Man's Burden: The Pursuit of Nonconformity in David Bradley's *The Chaneysville Incident*," in *Philological Papers*, Vol. 32, 1986, pp. 119-27.

[*In the following essay, Sadler discusses the roles of stereotypes and nonconformity in* The Chaneysville Incident, *focusing on the problems of imagination.*]

John Washington, the Black historian in David Bradley's ***The Chaneysville Incident,*** is in rebellion not only against his

family but the world in general and particularly against the preconceptions it has imposed on his race. One enforced stereotype that drives John, though unwittingly, is the imagination of Blacks and its end product, superstition. Accordingly, he will not conform to expectation; he turns himself into the man of facts, the historian who will not let emotion get in his way. Yet imagination turns out to be the core of his quest and the synthesizing element in both his family and his racial "roots." Ironically, he ends affirming the necessity for a faculty that is distinctly and generally *human.* His search in the novel curves more and more surely toward an identity that transcends both race and sex and that denies the Black man's burden of nonconformity to racial stereotypes.

The book spans a week and two days of real time (from Saturday, March 3, to Monday, March 12, 1979) but hundreds of years of human, racial, and family time through reminiscence and imagination. All of John's faculties are engaged to unravel the mystery of his father, but the key to that effort is his imagination, which he has always insisted that he, in contrast to his brother Bill, lacks. Bradley drives his protagonist rather mercilessly toward wholeness.

Always a spirit in rebellion, even against his own race, John has forced aside his natural instincts and looked for propriety and formality. He never stoops to street language, for example. Judith, the White psychiatrist with whom he lives, does, and she is a member of one of the first families of Virginia and has waged her own rebellions against sexism. To keep others at a distance, he uses knowledge as an iron grating. When the phone awakens them with his mother's news that old Jack Crawley is sick and calling for him, he puts Judith off with a disquisition on the history of the telephone, an ironic commentary on his misuse of the historian's art. She later accuses him of throwing out webs of logical discourse to keep others at bay, as when his amusing commentary on the unsanitary facilities of buses circumvents his communicating that she should not drink a lot of coffee before she boards a bus.

The imagery of the book also supports wholeness. Edenic images abound and suggest John as the new Adam, Judith as the new Eve, who, together, Black and White, seem to be ready to start the historical process over with the child she has wanted him to father. The other dominant image, the candle, relates in a standard way to knowledge but also helps to explore the true and the arcane at the heart, Bradley suggests, of the everyday and the mundane. The seal of candle wax protects Moses Washington's folio of secrets far in excess of its literal power to do so, and John is initiated into symbol, as well as the workings of power, through it. Again, his recognition that things look different and are different by candle and lamp light moves him from the literal, fact-driven world of the historian to the work of the empathic imagination.

The world of story-telling, another art based in the imagination, also figures in the education—or reeducation—and quest of John Washington. So vivid is Jack in John's recreation that Judith actually thinks he has made up "the old man with the stories": "It's just that the way you talked about him, he was sort of a legend. I would have thought he was indestructible. Or a lie." Since Moses has never communicated his thoughts to his son, John must piece together what he knows of his father from Jack's stories, a blending of the factual and the imaginative, as well as from the artifacts Moses leaves behind. Conflation and wholeness are again the end products of the quest, and John's bent is toward conflation if in a somewhat sterile, scholarly manner; for example, he moves from the "ancient adage 'Red sky at night . . .'" to Shakespeare's "Venus and Adonis" and then to the Bible. Similarly, his use of the term *story* for a man's *history* demonstrates that he is not so arid as he proclaims: "And then I began to think about what a man's dying really means: his story is lost. Bits and pieces of it remain, but they are all secondhand tales and hearsay, or cold official records that preserve the facts and spoil the truth; the sum is like a writer's complete works with crucial numbers missing. . . ." Thus the necessity for the informing imagination that enables John to recreate, with Judith's help, not only Moses's being and story but that of C. K., the latter's paternal grandfather.

John searches first for his father, whom he has always hated and known virtually nothing about. As if to insist that one is both an individual and a member of a race and of the human race, Moses Washington searched out his own past, particularly the involvement of his grandfather, Brobdingnag/ C. K., in the Chaneysville incident, in which fugitive slaves chose death rather than a return to slavery. When he found that past and understood death in the African sense, an act of imagination, he killed himself, but not before leaving a "spoor" to enable John to find both his own path and his family's.

John later recognizes the clues his father has left behind. At the funeral, he first hears the words of the song Moses has always hummed: "And before I'll be a slave I'll be buried in my grave, and go home to my Lord, and be free." John learns that it is the one sung by the slaves of the Chaneysville incident. Ultimately, he understands that, like other songs of slavery, it carries hidden meaning but in a much larger sense: freedom is death as it was conceived in the African mind. Moses killed himself when he pierced the heart of the Chaneysville incident—that C. K., his grandfather, killed the others, including the woman he loved, and himself in order to die and yet continue to be.

To point the way for John, Moses, shortly before his sui-

cide, added a third picture of himself to the family portrait gallery. In it, he stands on an unidentified hillside by a stone wall. John discovers that it is the site of the Chaneysville incident. A self-taught mason, Moses has built his house and his barbecue pit and surrounded every tree in his yard with triangular stones that point to that hillside. Had John been more susceptible to Black culture and its secret Masonic orders, instead of rebelling against them, he might have caught the clue earlier. Instead, his subconscious works on the material and drives him with such frightening dreams of his mother's trying to kill him and of Moses's kicking apart a triangular cairn and laughing at him that he tries to avoid sleeping. He does not see the point even when his mother tells him that Moses delighted in his persistence in tearing apart everything given him to learn its secrets.

John rejects "the Hill," the Black section of his small Pennsylvania hometown, as quickly as possible and makes it his business not to know about it. He also rejects the seemingly ideal role model, for although his maternal grandfather has a Ph.D. and is retired from Howard University, John hates him because he will not let his grandson read his books and, worse, does not read them himself. Further, he leaves his entire library to Howard in his will. With additional irony, John rebels, in a classic (and non-racial) stereotype, against his father and his mother, though for different reasons. His victory in his struggle with the former, whose suicide takes place when John is almost ten, is the key to the mystery at the heart of the novel and is a victory over self rather than over Moses Washington per se. The instrumentation of that victory is a recovered use of and appreciation for the imagination.

The elder of the Washingtons' children and the scholar, John is the opposite of his brother Bill in many ways. While both have dreamed of escaping the Hill, Bill has imagined visiting the world's great cities; John has thought only in terms of the various truck routes out of town. Although both hate their father, the manifestation of that hate distinguishes them and turns once more on imagination. Both have intensely resented working on Moses's barbecue pit and truck farm. After he dies, John simply rebels and will not return to the garden. Later, he learns to make nitroglycerin to blow up the barbecue. Bill tills the garden plot—but for flowers—and places a bouquet weekly on Moses's grave as an act of defiance.

Bill both conforms to and breaks stereotypes. He is the stereotypic jock who excels through sports; but, on the other hand, though he is Black, he has "'normal' American interests, hopes, characteristics, abilities. Not the bad ones . . . [but] the good things. . . ." He is the first Black in the county to have a pizza delivered to the Hill, for example. Unfortunately, he also becomes a more contemporary *Black* stereotype. Passed along from grade to grade because he can win trophies for the school, he is failed his senior year when his last sports have been played. With no high school diploma, he is drafted. When, breaking the *Black* stereotype at least, he flees to Canada and leaves behind a letter for the newspaper, his mother, a legal secretary, uses influence with her White bosses, Judge Scott and his son and partner Randall, to keep him out of jail and get him sent instead to Vietnam, where he is killed. John hates all who were involved in Bill's death, including their mother. He especially resents the suppression of the portion of Bill's letter that would have demonstrated his brother's greater rebellion: Bill had "want[ed] others like me to know they have a choice." After Bill's funeral, John does not return home until the phone call with which the book opens summons him to the death bed of his old mentor, Jack Crawley.

Bill was his father's son in being able to think like Whites and get along with them, but John accepts the utility and feasibility of such an approach only when he remembers that Moses made him fight anyone using racial slurs and when he begins to unravel his father's history and learns that Moses owned the Hill; he also finds that his father was a behind-the-scenes power in the town; had the imagination to predict the future for Judge Scott; and had the daring, though Black, to be a figure of legend. Moses, whose very successful moonshining business is based on a recipe of his grandfather, has thrived on a pattern of rebellion very different from that of his older son.

John's reaction to his mother's call with the news that Bill is dead is to take a shower and go on the date he has with a "special" woman, a White one. After his return from the funeral, he goes to see her and rapes her, as he latter tells Judith, who is also White. Again, in the midst of rebelliousness, he feeds on classic stereotypes: both the fascination between Black men and White women and the animosity between the Black and White races.

John's relation with Judith is central to *The Chaneysville Incident,* though he tries to keep her at a distance from what is really happening to him—the unfolding of his family's and his race's history and the placing of those experiences in the larger human context. At the last, when he is still nonplused about the facts he has accumulated on his color-coded notecards, she helps him recreate his great-grandfather's story and find the graves of the slaves in the Iames cemetery. At first, however, he rebels against the stereotype of Black male virility by having no sex with her for the first six months (and perhaps also atones for the earlier rape of the White woman). Yet, in spite of his hating Moses Washington, John is merely repeating—and diminishing—history here. His father went a year before consummating his marriage to Yvette Franklin Stanton; he waited until he and his only close friends, Jack Crawley and Josh White, completed a house for her.

John remains largely oblivious of the reason latent in his father's waiting: ritual—the husband transporting his bride from her father's house to *his* home for her. Hate blocks the requisite imaginative response and leaves John responding only to additional information to support a portrait of Moses as an individualistic, semi-Mafia figure who has buried his enemies in the masonry of his house and who, singlehandedly, murdered every revenue agent the government sent to investigate his trade in Black Lightning," the term itself another instance of rebellion. He finds obscenity in Moses's being only four years younger than his wife's father. While he alludes to Henri Christophe's Citadel, he cannot believe that Moses meant to consecrate his race's history with the house he has raised on the Hill. Similarly, its seven exits and its attic sanctuary for Moses raise no desire to probe symbolism and mystery but become additional evidence of his father's hateful obscurantism.

> **John's relation with Judith is central to**
> ***The Chaneysville Incident,* though he tries**
> **to keep her at a distance from what is**
> **really happening to him—the unfolding of**
> **his family's and his race's history and the**
> **placing of those experiences in the larger**
> **human context.**
> **—*Lynn Veach Sadler***

Though John recognizes the extremes: unyielding fact/history versus the romanticism of the novelist, he misses what is in between and what draws these extremes into a meaningful whole: everyday, individual experience that participates in the collective human experience. He grants that history is to be found more often in footnotes than in headlines, but that assessment demarks only his individual cleverness, as is true of his arch discourse on the sanitary facilities of airplanes, trains, and buses as a mode of differentiating the classes in America. If "the key to the understanding of any society lies in the observation and analysis of the insignificant and the mundane," imagination and creativity produced that observation in the first place and produced its examples. Yet John does not see their role.

He is ashamed, likewise, of the extravagant ritual, the would-be pomp and circumstance of Black life, but these mask the horrors of "dormant racism or well-meaning liberalism" and participate in the age-old and generally human rite of passage. As an example, at age thirty-one, he comes home to Jack to learn that old Bunk's Legion ceremonies prevented a Black boy's first haircut from becoming an introduction to racism. By the end of the novel, he understands the momentousness of receiving his first toddy from Jack, his first cup of coffee from his mother. He also understands why Jack and his own father have always insisted on putting things back where they belong; in ritual lies the key to the past and to continuity with it. Out of his imaginative and experiential response to the question of what makes a man, book-ignorant old Jack Crawley cycles back to a time when there was understanding of man's relationship to the external world. He reintroduces the four elements in teaching John that a man needs air, land, water, and the sun and that the last, which he connects with fire and power (and which the book connects with knowledge through the predominant image of the candle), gives a man "say" and keeps him from being an animal.

John Washington returns home because the man who taught him woodcraft calls for him. Jack is the only inhabitant of the far side of the Hill, and, at Moses Washington's request, he appeared the day of his friend's funeral, to take the nearly-ten-year-old John home with him to be initiated into the man's world of the woods and to be purged of the "woman" in him that will make him trust people (even Whites) and believe that there will always be somebody to help him "get through things." Initially, John rebels against Jack and hits him with his fist but later joins him when he realizes that no one really knows what Jack wants and that guessing is pointless, a manifestation of his growing rationalism. He curbs his fear of the boogey men purported to haunt the other side of the Hill by a similar act of reason: if others are changed to ghosts there, he will be, too, and will have nothing to fear from them. Simultaneously, however, his growth toward the use of his imagination also begins here because, as he makes his way to Jack's, he listens to the night for the first time.

Ultimately a sanguine work, *The Chaneysville Incident* is unforgiving of one legacy of slavery and racism but blames Blacks as well as Whites for it. The imposition of the White man's religion has killed the Black race in a special sense. Before slavery, Blacks did not die; death was but a translation into another form, and the dead remained among the living. The White man's religion brought literal death and, with it, the death of the imagination. Blacks can be faulted for accepting the White man's view of death and of themselves (for example, they could not believe that the man they have heard so much about, Moses Washington, "would turn out to be colored"). They are also faulted for accepting the denigration of the imagination. John Washington, the man of facts, is guilty on both counts but recovers.

The story turns on this view of death and the imagination. On his eleventh birthday, John realizes that Jack Crawley is adding something to Moses Washington's favorite story, the incident at Chaneysville. Only this time, Jack says that the slaves are not dead but are still here and that they are not ghosts because he has heard them panting as they run. The fact that John notices the addition proves him worthy of being retaught the values of the imagination, for, in contradis-

tinction to his disclaimers, he is not immune to it. He has, for example, heard the west wind sing. Angry with himself for experiencing an impossibility and refusing to believe Jack's claim that the wind's voices are the souls of Indians, he uses physics to account for the phenomenon. He goes to Jack's to exult in the "power of *knowing* what it was" and still hears singing and words:

> And so I had done what I had to do; I had gone away from the mountains, down to the flat land, . where there were no irregularities of surface. And I had promised myself I would never hear it again, that I would never go up into the mountains again. I had kept that promise, until now. Only now I knew where the lie had been: I had stopped hearing, but I had not stopped listening.

The book begins with John's hearing the telephone wire and its panting, his modern version of the fugitive slaves' panting in the mist near Chaneysville, a sound that his father Moses has also heard and the sound, John comes to understand, that he has formerly identified as the singing of the wind. Reactions to the telephone in turn link him to other characters in the novel and place additional emphasis on wholeness in a rebuke of his ironic treatise on its history. His mother and father, in agreement for once, recognize the negative features of the telephone, though she has one put in (as she buys a car and lets it sit for three years) to spite her husband. Later, the Judge takes a similar view, in a foreshadowing of the racial rapprochement that will come at the novel's end.

Many other examples of John's ultimate worthiness to follow his father and great-grandfather appear. In the opening pages, he finds that he has unwittingly taken on the attributes of Judith when she is not fully awake, another hint of the sharing that is to come and a tempering of another stereotype: that, because she is a White and a woman, she cannot understand him. As he goes to Jack's, he pictures what each of the inhabitants of the Hill is doing, though he denies that he has imagination. Once there, he can *hear* the walls of the cabin. While he perverts the old man's lessons on ritual—". . . even if [a man] claims to have no belief, no religion, no adherence to any formal or informal order of service, there is, somewhere within him, a hidden agenda. And he will respond to it without hesitation, without thought, almost without knowledge, certainly without will"—his acceptance of it prepares the way for his absorbing of the novel's teachings about death and imagination. He unconsciously pays homage to ritual in the antique flask he bought as a gift for himself. Even before he has worked through Moses's suicide and gone back through it to the death of great-grandfather C. K. and the fugitive slaves at Chaneysville, he anticipates what he will learn about them when he realizes that Judith does not understand about Jack: " . . . she thought that he was dead." He is worthy to receive this new insight into death, too, because his vision is larger than self and family. Thinking on the history of slavery, he says: " . . . when the wind is right, I think that I can smell the awful odor of eternal misery. And I know for certain that if I allow myself to listen, I can hear the sound of it. Oh, yes. Surely, I can hear." Again, before he has worked his way out of his hate for Moses, he goes to sit with the old Black men in the square as Moses had done before him.

John is also worthy to be his father's son and the descendant of his ancestors because he can learn from history. Although he succumbed to stereotype and vengeance in raping the White woman, he seems to have profited from Jack's account of Josh White's would-be miscegenation, despite the doubts that remain in the story. Jack's version is that the White girl entrapped Josh and that Moses lied to salvage Josh's ruined mind by telling him that Clydette really loved him and was forced to betray him by her father. Though Josh is never the same afterwards, never talks except when he must, the reason is unclear. Either he never recovered from losing the girl, or he never recovered from her betrayal. In any case, his spirit is spent prior to the Klansmen's stripping him and, in a reprise of stereotyping, holding a knife blade next to his genitalia.

The reader can infer that John, through such "histories," learns to cope with living in mystery and lack of resolution, to rely on the imagination. At the end of the novel, he, rather than Judith, makes the great leap of faith and imagination to the belief that the White mill owner, Richard Iames, rather than the Blacks who worked for the Underground Railroad, buried the dead slaves near Chaneysville. His father had shared Judith's interpretation of the story. John Washington has found his father and bested him. In so doing, he has laid down the Black man's burden: not to conform to stereotype. Yet neither did his father nor his great-grandfather.C. K. cast the deciding vote against Henry Highland Garnet, who proclaimed Denmark Vesey and Nat Turner patriots, and found a more creative way to combat slavery. Ironically, Chaneysville is in Southampton County, Pennsylvania, a piece of the South as much as Turner's Southampton County, Virginia. In lifting the stereotype from Richard Iames, John also redeems at least to a degree the history of slavery.

Martin Gliserman (essay date Summer 1986)

SOURCE: "David Bradley's *The Chaneysville Incident:* The Belly of the Text," in *American Imago,* Vol. 43, No. 2, Summer, 1986, pp. 97-120.

[*In the following essay, Gliserman analyzes the psychological importance of history in* The Chaneysville Incident, *focusing on the metaphorical implications of the repeated image of "the belly."*]

Introduction

David Bradley's *The Chaneysville Incident,* winner of the P.E.N. Faulkner Award in 1981, is a major novel by a Black American male. Bradley's novel builds on central themes in Black and white literary traditions, and creates a new dialectics both between and within these traditions. One sees Bradley's relation to Faulkner's "The Bear," Melville's *Moby Dick* and Hemingway's "The Old Man of the Sea" in his use of the hunt as a way to explore the relation of man and nature. Bradley's hero, John Washington, a professor of history, is a contemporary descendent of Faulkner's Ikkemotubbe; he knows the primal relation of man and animal, hunter and hunted. As Faulkner writes in the opening page of "The Bear": "It was of the men, not white not black not red but men, hunters, with the skill and hardihood to endure and the humility and skill to survive. . . ." But Bradley's hero also embodies a broader consciousness from the study of the written word. He hunts in the fields of language and history. Moreover, Bradley does not exclude women from his universe. His hero wants more than what is considered in "The Bear" "the best of all listening, the voices quiet and weighty and deliberate for retrospection and recollection and exactitude among the concrete trophies. . . ." For John Washington, the telling and listening to the telling of tales is a matter of spiritual life and death.

Bradley is also thematically related to Black writers, such as Baldwin, Ellison and Haley—in his hero's quest for identity as a Black man in America. John Washington's situation, however, is complicated by his mixed genetic heritage whose roots include African Black, American Indian and Anglo-Irish White—and his mixed education—apprenticed as a youngster to a Black back woodsman and later becoming a history professor. John Washington confronts the issue of racism (white and Black, external and internalized) through the family history he reconstructs, and in his intimate relationships with his childhood mentor (a dying Father) and the white woman with whom he has been living for five years. Bradley creates greater complexity than earlier writers—more splitting and density—in his hero's search for identity. Bradley's hero must endure new alienations, but he gains new unions and explores new possibilities.

Since the story is contemporary and its plot complex, an overview will be helpful. The novel is built on several temporal planes: a present time frame of nine days, and a past that includes both the history of the hero and the five generational history of the hero's paternal family line. As we move forward in the present, we also return to various dimensions of the past. For example, at the beginning of the novel, John's present life as a history professor is interrupted when he is asked to return to his rural place of birth to take care of his dying mentor and long time friend of his father, Jack Crawley. The spatial return sets John up to recall various aspects of his own growing up, his earlier search into his family history, and particularly his failure to resolve several problems in the historical reconstruction.

He began his historical researches in high school, working from documents his father had amassed and from the tales Jack Crawley told him about his father. He had put together a basic outline of the family history in America going back to the Cherokee brave and the Black slave woman who began it. There was, however, one crucial individual, John's great grandfather, whose death John could not account for. The great grandfather was a daring anti-slavery fighter who seems to have disappeared without a trace. John has a sense that the great grandfather's death is linked to the death of twelve runaway slaves—the Chaneysville Incident—that occurred at the time of his disappearance. But the connection is unclear and John is left with a "gap" in his history. He feels like a failure. His sense of failure provokes psychological symptoms—a coldness within, a kind of male frigidity, and a fear of the dreams that come with sleep. He stopped working on the history when he went away to college, and he kept his distance through graduate school and into his present career work; but the symptoms persist.

In the present time of the novel, John is living with Judith, a white woman, a psychiatrist; they have been together for five years. In the nine day period of the novel, John's relationship both to Judith and the unresolved history undergo radical changes. When John goes to take care of Jack Crawley, he begins retracing the history he has been avoiding. Thus, he opens up the psychological wound of his own failures and fears. His psychological pain increases with the recognition that his father committed suicide—it was not a hunting accident as the official story had it. In his pain, he withdraws from Judith and regresses into a suicidal state. Judith senses the danger John is in and goes to him, arriving shortly after Jack Crawley's funeral. Her presence and her love allow John to confront the "gaps." This time he is able to take a creative "burning leap."

The fleshed out version of the story sketched here is fascinating, and Bradley's way of developing it is even more so. The novel feels like an epic—not in the trivialized sense of being a long work that covers a long time. Bradley picks up the central thematic concerns of the *Iliad* and the *Odyssey,* to wit, the anger of Achilleus and the search (for the father) of Telemachos. Bradley's mode of story telling is also related to Homer—highly embedded, in the ways that John Barth playfully plays out in "The Menelaiiad" or the "Duniazadiad."

The Chaneysville Incident unfolds one new dimension af-

ter another—historical, political (micro- and macro-), linguistic, interpersonal, intrapsychic, spiritual. There is also an integral, unintrusive and illuminating consciousness of the process of "making" with language. There is the history John tells us, but also the histories of the history. Indeed, assembling and telling the history is what constitutes John's heroism. John's task involves all the processes of writing history—gathering and sorting information, reconstructing sequences and simultaneities, and confronting the gaps. The task also leads him to another modality of knowing—though to get there, he must drop his scientific/obsessional ways. The focus of the history itself is on racial conflict from slavery to the present as seen through the microcosm of one line of descent—that of John's father, Moses Washington. A central concern of the history is with Black rebellion and subversion, to be seen and treated as autonomous people. At the interpersonal level, the novel focuses on the tensions between generations, races and sexes. The history and present moments of John's relationship to Judith has its own distinct tensions; and these tensions are brought up against the origins of John's side of the antagonism and ambivalence: Jack Crawley, John's surrogate father, the last father in the line. Jack Crawley teaches John many invaluable skills; he tells two or three of the best stories in the novel (about the great trickster, Moses). At his funeral we learn how generous he has been—he without family. But he also prohibits John from the white world and the sexual world. John has entered both.

The world John grew up in, the one he now lives in and the one he returns to are fraught with tension. The focus of this paper is on how that tension manifests itself within the character, particularly how it is mapped onto his body. Specifically, I focus on the symptomatic pain in the belly of John Washington. The conflicts generating the pain and anxiety are rooted in the hero's historical quest, in the history he discerns, in the primitive rage developed within his family with its rage, and his fear of the gaps of history and relationships. The resolution of the symptomatic pain, the interpersonal knots and the historical problems emerge almost simultaneously, interdependently, precipitated by one another. The ending brings us to the birth of the narrative, the possible inception of new life, a new paternity, and an understanding of heroic suicide and spiritual birth. The hero, at least for the moment, succeeds in leaping the gaps between male and female, Black and white, past and present, present and future.

The working hypothesis of this essay is that in the present John is frigid, unable to "imagine" the resolution of the mysteries, unable to procreate; he is disabled by untold grief and the prohibitions of the Father. When Jack dies, John's mourning of that death effectively releases the grief embedded in the novel; it stops the voice of prohibition; and it clears John of his symptomatic pain. John is then free to love—he is able to procreate with Judith. His ability to love allows him to have a vision from which he creates the tale that resolves the mysteries.

The Belly

In *The Chaneysville Incident,* the most striking, i.e., redundant, bodily referent is to "the belly" of the narrator/hero, John Washington. Although the motif appears only eighteen times in a quarter of a million words, it is central to the layers of psychological patterning in the novel. The belly is the organ in which the hero's body, experience and generational history are inscribed; it reflects pain, need and desire. The belly is the locus of a symptom, a self attack—as John says "the place at the base my belly . . . never seemed to get enough warmth." Whenever John comes close to his particular psychological pain, he experiences a wave of cold in his gut—e.g., "a sudden chill at the base of my belly." We will track the symptom to its primal and generational roots, its crystallization and resolution. We will examine the "internal empire" of the belly—i.e., the establishment and creative transformation of the "glacier in his guts."

The belly is a dual location: A bowel and a womb. It is a place of excremental build up—deaths, grief, failure—and a place of creative ferment—generation, babies, tales. This duality is "syntactically" represented by the narrative structure. That is, the privileged loci in the novel—beginning, center and end—have this schema: [Birth [Death] Birth]. The novel opens and closes with birth, but right in the middle is a death and funeral—the symbolic father's. The strategic placement gives the dual thematics of the belly a significant redundancy: Death and birth are inscribed spatially by the privileged loci and temporally by the narrative. Death is in the belly of the novel as well as of the hero; but in the *end,* there is birth, as there was in the *beginning.*

In *The Chaneysville Incident,* the most striking, i.e., redundant, bodily referent is to "the belly" of the narrator/hero, John Washington. . . . The belly is the organ in which the hero's body, experience and generational history are inscribed; it reflects pain, need and desire.
—*Martin Gliserman*

We will examine the "internal empire" in a chronological fashion—reconstructed from the narrative sequence. The chronology of John's life, like the narrative, carries its own "syntax." In this case, we see another dual development— of primary relations, repeated twice. From age one to age nine, John has a bad mother/mad father; at age nine, he acquires a good father and at age 26 or so, he acquires a good mother. John's integrating of good and bad allows him to create and tell the story. The narrative shows the resolution of primitive and historic conflicts taking place in a relationship which could become a repetition, but instead evolves into maturity. In other terms, the oedipal configuration is played out twice—John with his mother and father, and John with Jack (his mentor) and Judith (his lover). When the two configurations are superimposed, seen as from the same temporal zone, we recognize splitting (i.e., good and bad mother and father); when seen as occurring successively, we recognize maturation and integration.

Birth, Weaning and Transitional Object

We can now turn to watch the evolution of the symptom. We begin with John's primary pain, represented in fragments of early bodily feelings of separation, shock and loss. The opening paragraphs are laden with images and sensations of separation—birth, weaning and death. There is a phone call from John's mother telling him about Jack Crawley's severe illness. The mother hangs up on John before answering all his questions; she will have nothing to do with Jack beyond conveying the message to John. A connection between mother and son is cut; while they were connected, the message concerned the pending death of John's father surrogate. The narrative continues to spiral from one separation to the next into a chasm five generations deep. As the hero gets deeper into the mysteries of the family, he actively withdraws from his intimate connection with Judith and moves into a suicidal position, a generational repetition.

Below the narrative surface of the opening are more primitive forms of similar thematics. The language asks us to hear, see and feel an older story, a conflation of fragmented moments. We are asked to feel the body—its cold, its shock. The sensory information intimates separation at birth and weaning. We feel an intrauterine space: "the night is deep and the room is dark." Into this comes the ringing of the phone, "slicing through . . . sleep." This brings a shock to the sensorium–there is "shivering," "the rasping of . . . breathing . . . and the hammering of . . . heartbeat." Most prominent is the image of the wire stretched between mother and son—the umbilical cord—the image recurs five times, is represented pronominally three times and is the implicit/ deleted head of nine other deep structure sentences. The image is associated with inarticulate sound—"crying, panting, humming, moaning like a live thing." The symbiotic connection breaks apart; we hear sounds of pain and struggle, the distress of waking into, being born into, the cold, the announcement of death. The voice of the mother has, *projectively,* a "little bite in it" and then a "real bite." She cuts the connection: leaves him with the scar of separation, omphalos; withdraws the breast at his bite.

The primary pain of birth and separation from the mother is

extended to the limits of John's tolerance by his father, Moses. Moses exploits the rage of John's frustration by manipulating John's transitional object. The "transitional object" delineated by Winnicott is a something—a blanket, a piece of string, a doll, etc.—the infant/child takes as not-me; it allows the child a bridge between self and other, helps to separate and clarify. The interaction of child and transitional object is a gauge of the mother-child interaction as felt by the child. Here is John as an infant/child, described by his mother: "I'd make you a toy and you'd . . . look at it for a long time . . . and then you'd pick it up and poke it and squeeze it and then you'd go to work and tear the stuffing out of it. And when you'd torn the thing to pieces, you'd sit there and giggle." She says he would "go crazy" when he couldn't figure out how to solve it. There is a disturbance in John's interactions with his toy. The fantasy of his action is one that Melanie Klein would recognize as a desire to open up the mother and tear out her insides (e.g., Mother is pregnant when John is 15 months old). It is a rageful fantasy, with sadistic pleasure—he giggles at the fragments. The motive for the rage is indicated by the separations noted above—from the body and the breast of the mother.

The rage and anguish expressed in relation to the transitional object could be soothed, but in fact they are encouraged by the father (whose mother died giving birth to him). The father "used to love" watching John tear things apart; he gives him objects increasingly difficult to tear:

> And one day he . . . got one that was too hard . . . and he sat there all day watching you while you tried to tear that thing apart. *You'd beat it and you'd bang it* until you were tired, and then you'd go to sleep, and then you'd wake up and *you'd beat it and bang it more* . . . [a]nd when it finally dawned on you that you weren't going to be able to tear that stuffing out of it, he sat there and laughed while you cried. . . . It almost made me wild, *the sound the two of you made, him laughing and you crying* . . . (my emphasis).

The hostility toward the bad breast is deepened by the father who teases the child into more sustained aggression and greater frustration. The father's sadism is partly motivated by his past. To turn Winnicott's phrase, the child functions as the father's transitional subject to whom he can transfer his historic frustration and rage. He wants John to repeat his history and get through it; he is teaching John a kind of crazy endurance.

The mother's desire to separate father and son stems from her intolerance of the madness of the scene—it seems a primal scene with hints of masturbation ("beating it"). The scene is sadistic, primal, maniacal, diabolic—"crazy making" as John says of another encounter with the father. The father's desire is to separate mother and son—for the higher purpose of solving the problem of family history. The theme of hostility to, and fears of dependency on, women is a strong one in the text. Jack Crawley conveys to John how Moses felt about women and particularly how he feared John's reliance on them—Moses "'was afraid your mama would do for you so much that you wasn't never gonna be able to do for yourself . . . an' end up the kind of fool that can't go to sleep lessen he knows 'xactly where he's gonna get his pussy an' his next pay.'" Moses weans John from the comforts of the breast/mother to focus him on tolerating frustration and confronting failure and death. Moses encourages the game of deconstruction in order to prepare John for his later life tasks. He is proud of John's development—Jack Crawley tells John that what Moses "'liked best'" was the way John "'hated him'"; Moses saw potential in that rage. The novel is the mark of John's success—the climactic moment resolves the puzzle, brings together the fragments and fills in the gaps. John breaks the repetition of madness, and makes reparation to the torn up breast.

History and Environment: The Negative Internalized

The primitive feelings of loss, separation and rage stay with John through his childhood. Thus he describes some photographs of himself: "I could look at a fading image of myself . . . at age seven or five or two, I had to be angry. No; furious." In his adolescence the complex of feelings finds a focus in history. Specifically, his father leaves for him a set of historical documents and problems concerning his line of descent. John intently studies the documents and maps out the history, but he reaches an impasse, as did Moses. There are "too many gaps," and the problem, like the transitional object his father gave him, is "crazy making." The intensity of the history culminates in a nightmare, the genesis of John's symptomatic inner cold. John hooks into the history; it replicates and amplifies his own primitive pain. He embeds it; it becomes impacted. In addition to internalizing the history, John is affected by his environment, another layer of redundancy. The environment, like John, is filled with death and excrement.

The negativity of John's history can be shown schematically in a genealogical sentence:

> [John Washington loses his father, Moses, at age 9; he also loses his brother, Bill, at age 20; and

> [Moses lost his mother, Cora Alice O'Reilly Washington, at birth; and

> [Moses' father, Lamen, lost his wife (Cora) and his father, C. K., at age 3, and

> [Lamen's father, named Brobdingnag but called

C. K., lost his father at age 8, his mother at age 18; he subsequently lost his wife (seven months pregnant), and after her a woman he loved deeply, and finally he loses his own life—in the service of the anti-slavery movement; and

[Zack, father to C. K., lost his life for trying to raise a rebellion against slavery; and

[Zack's mother, an unknown slave, lost her entire family and homeland; and his father, a Cherokee brave, belonged to a people who were being displaced in their own land.]]]]]]

As John studies his history, he internalizes it; he becomes the bearer of five generations of loss. His primitive rage is compounded by historic grief. He acquires "cold facts, and more cold facts," but they seem only to build up within—nothing is born from them.

In addition to this embedded grief, John grows up in a house marked by death. His father built the house from stones cut like the graveyard markers in a Chaneysville cemetery. The triangular stones of Moses' house are iconographic hints to John, so that when he discovers the Ur-stone, he will recognize it. John eventually discovers the graveyard—it is the scene of his father's suicide, and as it turns out it is the burial site of John's great grandfather as well as the twelve runaway slaves. Moses' house is a tomb for the living, a monument to the dead. John is permeated with death and living within its walls. The mother has a domestic habit that complements the system. She tends to pile things up such that no space "went . . . unfilled . . . until one day there wasn't any space . . . and the original shape of anything that had been there was lost under the piles." If the house is a symbolic body, its interior is a constipated bowel—piling things up within, burying them.

John is surrounded by death at home; the outside environment is also presented as psychologically toxic. For example: In the locale where he grew up, one would have "smelled a hundred and fifty years' worth of . . . shit"—i.e., the literal smell of the history of poverty created by slavery and racism. The excremental is strongly associated with death—corporeal, spiritual or moral decay—as we see from John's description of his feeling for the rural hollow where he grew up: "This place stinks. It makes me choke . . . a stench, like somebody buried something, only they didn't bury it quite deep enough, and it's somewhere stinking up the world." The external appearance of excrement in the "atmosphere" as well as in the literal pile, suggests an internal dimension—the grief, the cold, the death and the rage are all a form of withheld excrement, piled up within. Excrement is the physical analogue for unrelinquished generational grief.

Adolescent Nightmare of Cold

The fragments of pain—primitive, environmental and historic—crystallize in a nightmare of cold, leaving John with the symptomatic cold in his belly. The nightmare occurs when John is about seventeen and has been working for four years on the historical documents Moses left. The dream leaves John with "an all-encompassing sensation of icy coldness, and a visual image of total white . . . the coldness and the whiteness growing to envelop me, like an avalanche of snow . . . covering me, smothering me." The dream is precipitated by John's perception that he has failed to make something of all his labor on the puzzle of the family history. At the moment he senses his failure, he feels the cold of the attic—this is the first attack of coldness. One frightening thing about the dream is its similarity to those reported by schizophrenics just before they experience major episodes. The fear the dream engenders is not only maddening but lasts for the next fourteen years—it is a fear to sleep perchance to have the nightmare and suffocate in the cold.

John's analysis of his failure is that he has all the facts "but . . . could not discern the shape that they filled in", there are too many "gaps." He concludes that he "could not imagine" hence he could not solve the problem. Without being able to imagine "you will never know the truth." He will end up with something "full of cold, incontrovertible logic, never any of the burning inductive leaps that . . . let you really *understand* anything." The primitive problem is that there is a hole he cannot fill whose shape is beyond him (mother); he will fill himself up with cold things (excremental autocreation), until he learns to imagine and leap across the void, master the gap. The adolescent problem is more existential—focused on death, guilt and failure to make reparations. Johns says that "what a man's dying really means [is] his story is lost." Hence, if he cannot create the tale and tell the story, he has failed to keep Moses and C. K., in particular, alive, spirited through language.

In the dream, John is initially "burning"; his mother soothes him with "ice water." The fever turns to chills; he asks her to stop "but she kept on bathing me, and I realized she was trying to kill me." He escapes and she pursues; he reaches the crest of a hill and sees a "giant gorge, a hundred feet deep, with a stream of frothing white water. . . ." The gap in history, the gap of the mother, becomes "a giant gorge," which we meet again in the climactic tale. Here the gorge appears as the cold womb of certain death.

The image of death in the father's sector of the dream echoes the one in the mother's and translates "frozen" from coldness to stuckness, Sisyphean repetition. John sees Moses "naked to the waist despite the driving snow and horrible cold, building a cairn of giant triangular boulders." After he builds it, he kicks it down. John approaches the rocks and he builds them into one form, takes them down, puts them back, takes them down, etc. He knows "it would go on like that. Then I had tried to wake. But I could not. Something had shackled me in the dreaming state. . . ." In the mother's sector, we found the womb of death, here in the father's is the phallus of death—erected and deconstructed endlessly without creative power. John is frozen at the gap and shackled into narcissism. As devastating as the dream itself is the feeling of being stuck in its very universe—falling into some gap of the mind and going mad.

From the time John has this nightmare, he is unable to "take the risk to sleep" because he fears he won't awaken. He did not awaken spontaneously when he was living at home; his brother would wake him—"touching me lightly and waiting until the cries had stopped." Later, he sets his alarm clock to wake him at half-hour intervals. And when he begins living with Judith, she takes the role of the brother—she "slept with her hand on me, to feel the first shivering, and then . . . waking me and holding me. . . ." But as loving as Judith might be, she is tainted by the bad mother and proscribed by the father. John says, he "could never really trust her. Because some night she might not feel the shivering, and there would be nothing to wake me, and I would freeze." John's adolescent nightmare haunts him into adulthood; the cold it engenders won't be dispelled until he can accept the warmth of the other.

The Warm Belly—Good "Objects" and Creation: Jack Crawley—The Nurturing Phallus/Paternal Breast

Had John only internalized negativity—cold, death, grief and failure—he could not have begun to formulate the history he does, let alone resolve its conflicts. He may live on the edge of madness, of being frozen from within or smothered by the cold outer world, but he does not go over because there is something good within. The person identified with the good insides, the warm belly, is Jack Crawley who replaces Moses in John's life on the day of Moses' funeral. John acquires a mentor who is a good enough father, a master of tracking, nature, local history and telling tales. Jack teaches John a "know how" that goes beyond having skills to having a wisdom necessary to create.

By contrast, Moses knew a great deal but withheld everything. What Moses did not know was how to interrelate as a person. Moses releases what he knows when he dies; he leaves it in *writing*—documents and diaries he had collected in the search of his past. When John is growing up, the father spent much of his time in the attic—a *mad man* in the attic: "we knew that whatever he had been doing up there was bizarre and probably unfathomable and almost certainly crazy-making . . . a mystery. . . ." Moses is always intense, demanding instant attention, saying very little, making vis-

ceral assaults (e.g., as in his role with the transitional object).

From Jack, John obtains a good inside which is symbolized, metonymized, by the cup filled with hot toddy—the paternal breast, or the nurturant phallus. During their first meeting Jack makes a toddy in a cup for John—"in a minute," John says, "I could feel the *warmth growing in my stomach*" (my emphasis). With his second cup, he says, "All I knew was that the taste was strong and sweet and good, and that the *warmth of it moved through me like joy*" (my emphasis). Here is the first good breast of the novel, an antidote to the symptomatic cold engendered by John's toxic history. The antidote has an increased value for its association with Moses and C. K., both of whom had made and drank "'shine" to support their anti-slavery and anti-racist activities.

Jack teaches John how to order life space, but also indicates when rational order breaks down and one lets go of narrow intellect to assume a state of mediative action (hunting) or contemplation (listening to the voices in the wind). The paradigmatic lesson in ordering space is this: "'Always put things back where you found 'em so you'll know where they are when you need 'em again.'" The lesson is important to John for when he enters his father's inner (and upper) sanctum, he is able to recognize the order. Where John's brother only sees "a mess of old papers and books," John says "that 'mess' of things . . . put me in mind of Paradise." He has a profound respect for the order—"I realized that what I was looking at was perfect, and that anything I did, one false step, would destroy that perfection, would probably obscure whatever message might be in the scene."

John's reconstructive activities are obsessively ordered in comparison to Jack's mundane orderliness or the signifying order of Moses's study—John adds another layer of organization to the information. He develops separate notebooks for different sorts of facts; he "collected data" and "catalogued" it. Moreover, he says, "I developed a system of color-coded index cards on which I recorded events, and which I ordered by carefully noting the time of their occurrence, the time dating expressed as a string of numbers, year, month (in two digits), date (in two digits), and time of day (in a twenty-four-hour military-style expression), followed by the day of the week." The ordering is necessary but not sufficient; he must learn to see the data and get beyond it, as he does as a hunter—"Old Jack had marveled at the sudden ease with which I tracked, and commended me for finally *giving up trying to think my way to the game and allowing myself to feel my way to it*" (my emphasis). A similar process of giving up control will allow him to understand what happened to C. K. and the twelve runaway slaves. He will have to stop attending to the written word and learn to hear the wind.

The ordering is preliminary to the "burning . . . leap" John wants to make to a higher order, to the imaginative order he finally achieves in telling C. K.'s story. For John to make that leap, he must face death, mourn it and learn to see or hear its transformation into new life. The mourning is necessary because the quanta of familial grief blocks the possibility of letting go—of seed or story—or of understanding. In the very spatial-temporal center of the book—quite literally in its middle, its belly—is Jack's funeral. This funeral, being in the present and fully described, is a condensation of all the burials in the novel, where embedded grief is spoken and relieved. It is the only funeral that the reader attends. Grief has been suppressed in other places—C. K., most importantly, makes no note of his felt grief at the death of his wife, seven months pregnant. Moses could not have mourned his mother's death. And when Moses died John was too young to mourn; he says, "I had no idea how I should feel . . . laugh, cry, hate. . . ."

At Jack's funeral, after the formal services, the "amens" begin, testimony is offered. It was the one place in the book where my own feelings of grief opened up—the more I learned about Jack from the testimony, the deeper his loss became. The picture we have of Jack prior to the funeral comes largely from his stories about life in the hallow and about Moses; in these stories Jack always comes off behind Moses, who is made into a mythic hero. But at the funeral we learn another side of Jack, a local heroism. Neighbors testify to Jack's life saving generosity with food and his saving children in an epidemic. Even Evette Washington owns his importance—"'I had a husband,' she said, 'and I have a son. This man was a brother to my husband . . . Saved his life, more than once . . . And this man was a father to my boy. Taught him things I couldn't teach him . . . He taught him because he loved him.'" John, who concludes the ceremony, cites a passage from the Bible—"'In their descendants there remains a rich inheritance born of them. Their descendants stand by the covenants and, thanks to them, so do their children's children. Their offspring will last forever, their glory will not fade. . . .'" Just as Jack promised Moses to teach John, John here makes a promise to Jack, hence to Moses. John describes Jack's dying as "stories breaking up inside him; he coughed out fragments." John has to put the fragments together. The death and mourning of the father transforms the pattern of the novel from deathward toward birth—progeny and tales of heroic tragedy. The death of the Father frees John to love a woman and to know the past in a new way.

Judith—A Bridge

Judith serves as the bridge between past and present, bad and good objects, child and adult, male and female, black and white. She is a "transitional subject"—as John was for his father. She is John's only adult intimate, the only character with whom he has extensive interactions. His relationship with Judith allows him to submerge in and resolve the primitive and historical conflicts. Judith's role is often physical—she warms John in a variety of ways that enable him to see his vision, to hear his tale. Her warming is primitive, connected to his belly and hers. On another level, her role is that of a maturational agent. That is, she metacommunicates with John; she talks to him about his communications and behaviors. She urges him to talk, to tell the past; she draws him out. There are times that she fails, when her counterresistance gets the best of her—i.e., times when she does not want to hear John's story. Her persistent urging him to talk shuts him up the more; she goes on the offensive by offering him interpretations and telling him he is withholding. She is, however, conscious enough and loving enough to step out of the interdefensive knots they make with each other. Her metacommunications with John help to establish trust between them. Then they can face the mysteries of death, love and creating.

In the concluding segments of the novel one resistance after another gives way and the collective work of the body, the feelings and the words come to fruition. The sequence of resolutions begins in the following narrative setting: When John left Judith to tend to Jack, he intended to return. Once there he discovers, among other things, that his father did not have an accident but committed suicide. He writes to Judith saying that he is not returning. She decides to go to him, sensing he was in danger. He is not at Jack's shack when she arrives. When he comes in later from hunting he is frostbitten. The first interaction they have is symbolic of those to come—she warms him up. On previous occasions Judith tries to warm John up by "cupping" his belly—e.g., he says, she "slipped her hand inside my waistband . . . cupping my belly." But the belly never seems to get warm. On the day she arrives at Jack's shack she warms John's frostbitten hands: "She . . . thrust my hands into her armpits . . . I . . . felt the sensation come back, felt the warmth and pressure from her, the swell of her breasts against my wrists." Here the symptomatic cold is close to what it was in the nightmare but there is a good enough breast to warm him. He wants to feel that warmth in his belly and makes a toddy (daddy), but it fails him: "I wanted the toddy hot . . . [s]o hot it would burn." But having drunk it, he says, "The warmth hadn't made a dent on the cold in me."

After his body is thawed out, she pushes him to talk and he resists. Although he begins to talk, her resistance intrudes. Finally, she owns it: "'All the way up here I was waiting to talk to you. I was mad and I was worried and I was scared, but what I wanted was to talk to you. So I get here and all I can do is yell at you and badger you and act . . . like a Southern belle who can't have everything nice and neat and clean. . . .'" She was not prepared for all the "shit" she encountered on the hill and in the hollow. Moreover, she is ambivalent about hearing his past with all its grief: her white southern family may well have been involved with the slave trade. Her present communication is maturational. She owns her discomfort with the "smell" and the "dirt" of the place; she sees her defensiveness; and she declares her love by being loving. Her revelation is emotionally comforting to John—it warms him up; he feels loved—"'It's good to see you,'" he says in response.

John becomes trusting enough to tell her that he came to understand (on the day he wrote to her) that his father committed suicide, and he decided to stay here in order to understand that act of madness. Moses, it seems, was driven crazy by his inability to understand (or, by his understanding of) what happened to his grandfather, C. K. Judith is now closer to understanding why John had to "walk away from everything to come set up housekeeping in a one-room shack with a dirt floor." The revelation of Moses' suicide transforms them both.

In the very spatial-temporal center of the book—quite literally in its middle, its belly—is Jack's funeral. This funeral, being in the present and fully described, is a condensation of all the burials in the novel, where embedded grief is spoken and relieved.
—Martin Gliserman

At the moment of revelation, Judith becomes very powerful and he becomes a child: "She . . . pulled me up . . . undressed me quickly, efficiently, as if she were undressing a child. I did not resist her." She puts him to bed, undresses and joins him. In bed, she continues to hold him like a child—she "pulled me to her, her arms strong . . . holding me immobile . . . her body . . . unyielding." It is as if she had wrapped him in swaddling. He struggles, but she whispers "'Shhh'" and soothes him "until the keening of the logs . . . became a lullaby." Out of this quiet intensity comes an active intimacy; a symbiotic moment becomes a sexual one, likely a procreative one. Judith and John had talked of having a child shortly before he left—Judith said, "'I think I would like to have your child.'" But she feels that he would not—"'You as much as admitted that if I were pregnant, you'd leave me.'" In the shack, now, she takes his seed, he yields it.

Their intimacy occurs the night after Jack's funeral—the father is dead, all the fathers are dead. In the intimate moment, the biological fathers are to be re-generated: John is still in Judith's embrace: ". . . I thought I would fall asleep, fall away from her. And then, *just when I would have,* she gave one deep sigh and her breathing quickened, and I felt her thighs move, slipping around me below and above, and I *felt*

her belly against me and then the softness and heat and moistness that lurked below" (my emphasis). Judith "makes" him a child—follows him out of love and concern, warms him with her breasts, listens to his pain, undresses him, holds him in swaddling, merges with him ("just when I would have")—and then she makes a child with him in her belly. Her inner warmth, her creativity, her good insides, become his.

The regenerative act is powerful beyond the moment; this order of intimacy has not obtained in the family for long years. John's mother, for example, explains her marriage to Moses as being a kind of deal—"'He wanted two sons . . . after your brother was born, that was the end of . . . that part of things. Because he had what he wanted, and I had what I wanted.'" C. K. had conceived a child with a woman he loved, but she was killed in a white inspired race riot; he has a son, Lamen, with a woman whom he does not marry or particularly love as he loved his wife and later another woman, Harriette Brewer. Moses' mother dies in giving birth. Generative, emotional love carries with it a great danger in the family—the men are shocked by loss and fearful of contact. John has become frozen, suffering from a kind of male frigidity which Judith resolves. In loving her he has managed to fill in the gap, to cross the gorge.

The day after Judith and John are sexually intimate, they visit the graveyard where Moses killed himself and, John concludes, where C. K. and the runaways are buried. As in Moses' attic, John is able to read the scene of the graveyard—the layout of the stones tells who is related to whom. When they return to the shack, John begins explaining his hypothesis about Moses' death; it is a spiritual idea that Judith finds "crazy." But finally, she stops resisting, as she did the day before—she brings him a toddy for the first time: "'You don't think I understand. You're right; I don't understand. But I can believe in you . . . And if you say you need something that I can't give you, something you need a toddy to get, then I'll make a toddy for you.'" John gets what he wants and needs from Judith—basic support, belief, warmth from the female breast, and a sense of creative potency. With her good insides coming into him along with the good insides of the ancestral figures, he is intoxicated and enabled to follow Jack's tracking/hunting instructions: "'Quit tryin' to figure where he's at an' jest follow him.'"

John begins to hear the wind—as he heard the wire in the opening paragraph of the novel: he has a new symbiotic tie. In the wind he hears the breathing of the runaways; he is able to envision C. K. and reconstruct the two day ordeal he and the twelve runaways endure before dying. It is an important matter for him to tell the tale because of "what a man's dying really means: his story is lost." When Jack is close to death John says the "stories were breaking up inside him; he coughed out fragments." In telling the tale John offers reparation, becomes a progenitor and fulfills his promise.

By telling the tale, he also communicates with Judith: he tells her that her love for him has allowed him to leap the gorge, and has thawed him out. His metacommunications occur through the medium of the story. He tells her about a gorge, "a jagged gash in the mountainside," which C. K. will have to cross two times in order to shake his pursuers. This is the gorge of John's nightmare. It takes courage to jump, so C. K. "reached down into his guts and found a little more will, a little more determination" and he "leaped." Having shaken the bounty hunters he reaches the runaways among whom is his lost love, Harriette Brewer. John pauses and notes— "And then I realized that something strange was happening. Because I was no longer cold." The story is resumed, thus:

> "He was warm now," I said. "He was warm, and the feeling was strange. Because he had not realized how cold he had been. He had known that his hands and feet were cold . . . so numb he had lost the feeling . . . But he had not known about the other cold, *the cold inside, the glacier in his guts that had been growing and moving, inch by inch, year by year, grinding at him, freezing him . . . he could feel it melting. The heat that melted it did not come from the fire; it came from her arms . . . the warmth of her hand that cupped the base of his belly. . . .*"

Before Judith's arrival, John was on the brink of repetition, of suicide. Unable to speak, he would enact, reenact. What John figures out, or lets himself discover, is that C. K. and the twelve runaways were trapped by white slave catchers, but died rather than be taken. The song he imagines they sing when the slave catchers move in—the same sung at his father's funeral—tells the story—"'And before I'll be a slave I'll be buried in my grave, and go home to my God, and be free.'" Moses, enraged much of his life, is not able to love, is maddened and repeats the death he doesn't fathom. John is released from reenacting by telling the tale. He is free enough to risk living. In the description above we see that the cold in the belly is dissipated, and it is the "mother," with the good enough breast and insides, who has helped dissolve the ice. Judith brings him into new life; he brings Jack, Moses and C. K. back to life; and together Judith and John bring a new generation to life.

This paper has traced the history of a symptom portrayed as a part of a character's psychological make up. It has examined the evolution and transformation of the personal and transpersonal rage engendered by racism. It is the rage of the American Black—engendered by the external white world and internalized by the Black self, occasionally used against the Other in violence but invariably moved against the self, sometimes to the point of revolutionary or spiritual

suicide as the only escape from enslavement (one thinks of Richard in *Go Tell it on the Mountain* and Okonkwo in Achebe's *Things Fall Apart*).

The novel is a quest to complete history. Although arduous and painful, the quest is successful and liberating: the tale is told and the future becomes possible. The hero descends into the darkness of the past—slavery, post slavery racist destruction and the fight for political freedom—carrying with him the psychological pain of five generations. He emerges with a new understanding that enables him to be freed of psychological symptoms and to be generative as an artist and a man.

In the course of the quest, the racial frame that surrounds life for Blacks in America is confronted, but is not addressed in a simple fashion—white people enslaved Blacks and systematically cut off and destroyed routes of escape, physical and psychological; but, white people also fought against this system, and Black people, including John's own mother, sold out to it at great cost to others. Most significant to the present time in the novel is that John Washington has a long term relationship with a white woman whose family history is implicated in slave dealings, and this woman, Judith, helps John reach the understanding he is seeking. The rage that consumes John from within is the internalized bad object of racist (and sexist) perceptions, prescriptions and proscriptions. The intimacy offered by Judith neutralizes the rage and frees John's energy to focus on creation.

Resolution of racial conflict on a political level is not generalized. That John has an intimate relationship with Judith, that they might have an interracial child, does not suggest racial conflict is at an end. But on the aesthetic level and in the realm of creativity, there is a generative synthesis of Western white ways and African ways—e.g., scientific methodology and natural and spiritual in-touchness. We see the synthesis of narrative tradition and linguistic strains in Bradley's embedded way of telling the mesh of tales, and the ways he tells the individual tales. That is, Bradley gives us a range of voices—e.g., Jack Crawley's tales about Moses; C. K.'s various diaries and accounts (from his early literate period, through his educated period); John's tales to Judith and his monologues on such matters as a class analysis of toilet facilities in public transportation, the history of street names in his town, etc. It is in this range of voices that integration takes place.

Bradley sees it is possible for a Black man to make the synthesis of Black and white—he has done so. It is as Jack says of Moses several times, he can "talk like a white man." Knowing this other language allows an edge in the conflict as well as in creative and moral development. The question is whether a white man can do likewise—it will only be at that point that racial conflict will diminish because racial difference will be creatively appreciated instead of defended against out of fear, anxiety or guilt.

Paul Gilroy (review date 28 November 1986)

SOURCE: "Making History," in *New Statesman,* Vol. 112, No. 2905, November 28, 1986, p. 28.

[*In the following review, Gilroy identifies opposing representations of history in the African-American literary tradition, and discusses how these are merged in* The Chaneysville Incident.]

The experience of racial subordination has often been likened to living outside history. Slavery's suppression of temporal development and racism's capacity to represent blacks as 'people without a past' have bequeathed a distinct legacy to our storytellers. The best and most sensitive of them are prepared to confront a bitter obligation not just to validate black culture as a historical process, to restore to it the sense of being and belonging erased by slavery, but to bring blacks into history as active, cognitive beings—people who can think as well as feel.

A concern with history and the special importance of historical knowledge for blacks is at the centre of David Bradley's dazzling novel *The Chaneysville Incident.* This theme forms a vital link between him and the authors of the slave narratives, whose public acts of literary self-creation brought into being an expressive tradition and an interpretive community.

In a clever symbol for the syncretic processes which have shaped Afro-America, the book contrasts and eventually reconciles the two opposing modes of historical understanding which have formed its protagonist, Dr John Washington, a young black historian. One has been learnt by virtue of an elite education. The other is intuitive, a body of common sense acquired organically in his relationship to old Jack, a rogue bootblack who tutors him in the ancient rituals of masculinity which surround hunting and drinking. The young academic's mastery of these timeless skills connects his contemporary experience directly to the obsessive, emancipatory visions of his bootlegger father and great-grandfather. Supplementing the neatly colour-coded file cards on which he writes the dry details of his forebears' lives, this second model of historical knowledge encourages him to be open to the African voices of the past still audible in the Pennsylvania mountains.

In what often reads like a historical thriller, Bradley invites his readers to share in Washington's uses of these contrasting philosophies of science in pursuit of the explanation for a sequence of mysterious deaths. Via the complex interplay between public and private histories, the young scholar is led not just to self-discovery but also to a more profound understanding of the nature of the historical process itself. An understanding which generates its own special form of power in the struggle to resist and overcome the effects of racial subordination and terror. For both Washington and Bradley, it would seem that authority and authenticity are fundamentally intertwined.

Employing a variety of genres and literary techniques with great skill, not as pastiche but for the substantive value of each differing register of address, Bradley brings this story to life at an extraordinary intensity. He manages an epic, multi-layered narrative across four generations, uses all the technical tricks of detective fiction and, in his 'racial' dialogues, invokes the special forms of black meta-communication as well as any of his distinguished predecessors.

He possesses a refined sense of Afro-America's own traditions of fiction writing and, though his protagonist retreats up into an attic rather than downwards into Ralph Ellison's cellar or Richard Wright's sewers, the motif of withdrawal without retreat is a sign that Bradley recognises his own literary heritage. Washington's withdrawal into historical study is, however, less a period of preparation for action than a recognition of the need to create new kinds of understanding, new notions of historical causality and memory. Bradley is suggesting that these tasks are in themselves valid.

Black writers inevitably work in the field between the poles of protest and affirmation. Recently, this tension has come to be seen crudely along gender lines: on one side, the womanist heirs of Zora Neale Hurston affirming the vitality of down-home folk cultures; on the other, the nihilist descendants of Richard Wright supposedly demanding the subordination of literary autonomy and communal sentiment to the imperatives of their macho social realism. We may protest that this caricature is largely an effect of the political economy of publishing black authors, but it is rapidly acquiring the status of critical orthodoxy. *The Chaneysville Incident* is therefore doubly welcome, because its scope, humour and brilliant insights confound such facile generalisation. Its literary elegance, grace and sheer depth make concrete the means by which this disabling polarity can be left behind forever.

Matthew Wilson (essay date Spring 1995)

SOURCE: "The African American Historian: David Bradley's *The Chaneysville Incident,*" in *African American Review,* Vol. 29, No. 1, Spring, 1995, pp. 97-107.

[*In the following essay, Wilson analyzes the connections between history and imagination in* The Chaneysville Incident, *comparing Washington's role as historian in the novel to the interpreter's role in African oral tradition.*]

The figure of the African American historian in David Bradley's *The Chaneysville Incident* is almost the antithesis of the historian Hayden White delineates in "The Burden of History," a person who needs to be liberated from the burden of history. The African American historian, Bradley would argue, needs to take on and reconfigure that burden, but not by having recourse, as White suggests, to developments in Western culture, to literary modernism or even post-modernism. Bradley's historian, John Washington, goes outside the Western tradition and taps into the residue of African beliefs in African American culture (much as Paule Marshall's Avey Johnson does in *Praisesong for the Widow*) to create an alternative and heroic history. Washington's powerful narrative of the death of his forebear, C. K., and a group of escaped slaves is only made possible by history, and his groundwork as an historian bears much the same relation to his fiction as does Toni Morrison's relation to her research and her fiction *Beloved*. The ground of history and the work of the historian make possible fiction that fills in the historical gaps, but this effort, for the African American community, as the novel demonstrates, has more than an archival gravity. Historical consciousness, leavened by the imagination, allows us all, no matter what our experience and ethnicity, to know where we all stand in the present.

Hayden White, by contrast, has argued that in order for us to know where we stand in the present the "historical consciousness must be obliterated," particularly "if the writer is to examine with proper seriousness those strata of human experience which it is modern art's peculiar purpose to disclose." Using the figure of the "historian to represent the extreme example of repressed sensibility in the novel," novelists, White claims, have indicted historians either "for a failure of sensibility or will," and as a result, "the [fictional] historian's claim to be an artist appears to be pathetic when it does not appear merely ludicrous." Historians, both in and out of fiction, White contends, are seen as having no wisdom appropriate to the unique conditions of this century, and "contemporary Western man . . . is justifiably convinced that the historical record as presently provided offers little help in the quest for adequate solutions" to contemporary problems. White then pushes his analysis one step further, arguing that artists have come to believe that "'the historical imagination' . . . constitutes the fundamental *barrier* to any attempt by men in the present to close realistically with their most pressing spiritual problems" (emphasis added). White finds these assumptions at work in depictions of the figure of the historian in imaginative literature, but the writers that he alludes to in support of this contention are all male and,

with the exception of Edward Albee, all European. Using terms like "contemporary Western man," White is concerned with traditional history and with canonized male writers of fiction.

I would like to decenter his analysis of the historian in fiction by looking at an African American writer, David Bradley, and his African American historian John Washington from *The Chaneysville Incident.* If the figure of the white historian throughout this century is to be seen as a symptom of a large cultural failure in the "West," is the figure of an African American historian to be viewed any less pessimistically?

In discussing history and historians, White seems primarily concerned with the stranglehold that nineteenth-century historiography has had on the field, and how narrative history and the idea of objectivity in historical writing have vitiated history throughout this century. He wants histories attuned to what he perceives as our needs: "We require a history that will educate us to discontinuity more than ever before; for discontinuity, disruption, and chaos are our lot." By rejecting the influence of "modern art and modern science," contemporary history, White alleges, has chosen to remain blind to developments in this century, although since he first published this essay in 1966, one could argue that history has begun to take its blinders off. Significant changes have occurred from below, such as the rise of non-narrative history, oral history, the Annales school, and the merging of history and cultural studies in post-colonial studies. As Linda Hutcheon has observed, "There seems to be a new desire to think historically, and to think historically these days is to think critically and contextually."

Along with the desire to rehistoricize has come the desire to include the previously marginalized, what Hutcheon calls the "ex-centric," those who have previously fallen outside the purview of history. The attention to the once marginalized "be it in class, race, gender, sexual orientation, or ethnicity" is part of an "implied recognition that our culture is not really the homogeneous monolith . . . we might have assumed." David Bradley's historian John Washington is not only "ex-centric" in his experience, but also in his choice of academic specialization:

> "I specialize in the study of atrocities. . . . History
> is just one long string of atrocities. . . . You could
> say that history is atrocious. The best way to find
> out what they did is to find out where they hid the
> bodies."

As an academic specialist, Washington shares a sense of despair at the repetitiveness of history, and the phrase *history is atrocious* recurs in the novel. This feeling of despair only fuels his anger to find out "where they hid the bodies," an activity that is both metaphoric and literal. He conceives of his task as an historian as bringing to light, excavating, what's been buried—forgotten on purpose.

As a successful African American scholar, John Washington has adopted a stance toward history that is necessarily more complicated than that of a white historian. He realizes, of course, the degree to which African Americans have been constructed and negated by Western culture, and the degree to which much of African American experience remains undocumented and irrecoverable. As he says early in the novel, what's lost is often the "stuff of background, the material of understanding, the real power of history." Alienated by reason of experience and family history, he is driven by that very alienation to do history, to try to recover, to exhume. As he says to Judith, his white lover, being an historian means "'hating for things that still mean something. And trying to understand what it is they mean, so you can hate the right things for the right reasons.'" Clearly, Washington's alienation as an historian is quite different from the sense of cultural rupture experienced by Willa Cather's historian Godfrey St. Peter in *The Professor's House*. Washington, unlike St. Peter, cannot look back nostalgically to a period when the world seemed whole, for he is alienated from the narrative of mainstream American history and culture from the ground up. The areas that he investigates and writes about are directly connected to his own experience and the experience of other African Americans. Thus, he would probably disagree violently with White's contention that "historical studies" have to be transformed "in such a way as to allow the historian to participate positively in the liberation of the present from the burden of the past."

One might say, quite cynically, that mainstream American history has managed quite well throughout most of this century to liberate the present from this burden when it comes to the history of African Americans. Clearly, though, histories can be turned against History and can become weapons in the battle to pluralize our collective historical memory. Consequently, the "historical imagination" is not for Washington "the fundamental barrier" to understanding the present; rather, it is a tool needed to help understand the present as well as the past. Washington's position of "excentricity" would seem, then, to reverse White's formulation. Both see traditional History as an inadequate representation, and while White argues that historians must search for alternative encodings of history in literary modernism, Bradley consistently sees (and Washington sees at the end of the novel) that oral history and the African American vernacular tradition provide alternative ways to encode and represent. Washington can only understand his own position in the world by delineating the enduring conditions of oppression, and by grounding that understanding in African American vernacular culture.

If Bradley has created an historian who dramatizes the necessity of history for African Americans, Bradley himself seems to think of academic historians in rather negative terms—persons close to those described by White. In response to a question about how history is used in the novel, Bradley has remarked:

> I hate history on account of my father, because my father refused to have any fun with the stuff. And it's . . . a style of black history, name history; you read a biography or a book, it consists almost entirely of names, no faces, no events, and you don't know what's going on. I mean it's boring. It was boring to me. I like stories.

As Peter Levy has pointed out, the kind of historian Bradley describes here is something of a straw man, but it's also important to realize that Bradley is reacting to a particular style of "black history, name history," one that relies on research in primary sources, "the graveyards and the courthouses," a kind of history that bears more than a passing resemblance to traditional African oral histories as embodied in the figure of the griot. Name history also has some of the undernarrativized qualities that Hayden White has identified in the annals and the chronicle. Annals suggest narratives, but do not develop them; the chronicle, on the other hand, does narrativize, but it neither departs from the "order of chronology" nor does it conclude so much as "simply terminate." An example of this hybrid, name history is what Bradley's mother Harriet Bradley wrote about the evidence of the grave markers of the runaway slaves, on which the novel is based: "On the Lester Imes farm below Chaneysville one can still find the markers for twelve or thirteen graves of runaway slaves. Mr. Imes relates that when the slaves realized their pursuers were closing in on them, they begged to be killed rather than go back to the Southland and more servitude. Someone obliged." The next paragraph goes on to mention eight more unrelated names, none connected to what Imes told Mrs. Bradley. Clearly, although a ghost of a narrative is suggested, she is not interested in developing that suggestion. The point for this hybrid, name history is not to narrativize, but to collect data, data that consist in this case of the names of the early African American inhabitants of Bedford County, Pennsylvania.

As much as Bradley may hate this kind of history, he is indebted to it because it has conserved part of the historical record—the names and the suggestions of stories that would otherwise be lost. And although Bradley may hate name history as a form of historical discourse, I would suspect that he would acknowledge the theoretical function and importance of naming in African American discourse as a way of both affirming and negating experience and identity. Furthermore, Bradley's problematic relation to his mother's text—he hates name history, yet it provides him with the donnée of his novel—would seem to mirror his character's ambivalence toward his lover Judith, an ambivalence that is resolved only at the novel's end. Bradley's relation to his mother's text also might be seen as an expression of divided loyalties—an ambivalence toward both the Western literary tradition and a vernacular, oral African American tradition.

Bradley's impatience with this kind of history makes him want to create a story, and, as one of Bradley's interviewers, Susan Blake, has observed, he has mirrored the processes of his character. Both author and character discovered an "historical situation, researched it, and told a story about it." The third of these processes, the telling of the story, Hayden White has argued, is always interpretative. All historical narratives encode particular views of history, and the narrative patterns chosen by the historian are themselves interpretations.

The historian's ability to perceive patterns is literalized in the novel, and Bradley uses the word *pattern,* in the interview, in one particularly telling context. He says that, in finding and then interpreting the gravestones, Washington "discovers . . . the pattern, which allows him to reconstruct the family structure" of the escaped slaves. Discerning in the "pattern" of the physical objects a narrative pattern, Washington has not, as one of Bradley's interviewers suggests, liberated himself from "all that academic apparatus that stands between him and his ability to imagine, to imaginatively re-create history." Rather, as Bradley says, Washington has "to learn to do both things at the same time"—to use the ground of academic historical research to empower the imagination.

While Washington's faith in history contrasts sharply with White's characterization of fictional historians and with Bradley's disdain, the novel seems almost to brood over the problem of the imagination, for reasons that are directly connected to African American experience. Early in the novel, Washington says that, as a boy, he "had no imagination," and he apparently sees this lack of imagination as a crucial impediment to his ability to write narrative history. Even though Judith calls him a "superscholar," his own reflections on doing research and writing history are haunted by a failure seemingly made inevitable by this lack. For instance, Washington writes of his first real research as a failure:

> . . . I had seen the facts, there was no shortage of facts; but I could not discover the shape that they filled in. There were, it seemed, too many gaps. . . . I simply could not imagine what I should see. Could not imagine what it was I was looking at part of. I had everything I needed, knowledge and time and even, by then, a measure of skill—I could follow a fact through shifts and twists of history, do it and love it. But could not imagine. And if you cannot

imagine, you can discover only cold facts, and more cold facts; you will never know the truth.

Washington taught himself to be an historian by researching his father, Moses, who died when John was ten years old. What his father left him as a legacy was an attic full of books, newspapers, and notebooks—an archive—and the son "intuitively" realizes that his father had been "researching something." His research into his father's archive, throughout his teenage years, has come to have a dual focus. By trying to figure out what and why his father was researching, he is trying to understand his father. And he fails. He was unable to make "any of the burning inductive leaps that take you from here to there and let you really understand anything." Later, as an adult, "hot-shot historian," Washington returns to these materials only to experience the same sense of frustration. If, he says, ". . . I could learn to imagine just a little bit, I could understand. But I had no faith I would do it; I had never done it before." In the face of the "gaps," the lacunae in the historical record assembled by his father, and of African Americans in general, Washington feels impotent, unable to interpret, but he also feels continually impelled to interpret, to imagine.

According to Hayden White, the imagination plays an important role in the work of the historian, and he distinguishes two uses of the imagination in an historian's work. The first, which is "peculiar to the modern conceptualization of the historian's task," is "to enter sympathetically into the minds or consciousnesses of human agents long dead, to empathize with the intentions and motivations of actors impelled by beliefs and values that may differ totally from anything the historian might himself honor in his life, and to understand, even when he cannot condone, the most bizarre social and cultural practices." The second use of the imagination comes into play when the historian composes "a narrative in which to represent his findings," when "imagination is disciplined by its subordination to the rules of evidence which require that whatever is imagined be consistent with what the evidence permits one to assert as a 'matter of fact.'" In White's terms, then, Washington can neither enter into the consciousness of historical subjects nor can he write an historical discourse in which evidence empowers the imagination at the same time that it disciplines it. Although he is a "superscholar" by the account of his white lover Judith, his predicament as an historian is like that of Mr. Compson in Faulkner's *Absalom, Absalom!* who laments, "It's just incredible. It just does not explain. Or perhaps that's it: they don't explain and we are not supposed to know. . . . Judith, Bon, Henry, Sutpen. . . . They are there, yet something is missing; they are like a chemical formula. . . . you bring them together in the proportions called for, but nothing happens." Obviously, Mr. Compson lacks a crucial bit of recoverable knowledge—that of Charles Bon's parentage—but his interpretative problem is much the same as Washington's—that is, an inability to "to enter sympathetically into the minds or consciousnesses of human agents long dead." But what remains unknown for an African American historian signifies in a way that other historical unknowns do not, because where the bodies of the dead are buried was not an act of conscious evasion of the evidence of crime for the slaveholders—like the Soviets hiding the bodies of the Polish officers they killed in the Katyn Forest in 1941—but an act of not even deliberate forgetting—like burying an animal somewhere in the backyard. The graves of slaves are most often not worthy of mark or remark, and when Washington, as an historian, confronts their absence, and the presence of the slaveholders, his imagination must try to catalyze the relation of that absence to that presence.

In his meditations on his failings as an historian, however, Washington has almost obsessively linked the word *imagine* with the word *understand.* This connection is important because the word *understand* appears throughout the novel in still another context. John continually tells his white lover Judith that she cannot understand. As she says to him in one of their painful confrontations,

> "I was thinking all the time there was something wrong with you. But it's me, isn't it? I've got this horrible skin disease. I'm white. . . . That's it, isn't it?"

> "Yes," I said. "That's it exactly. Only you don't understand what it means."

Being unable to understand means, in the lexicon of this text, being unable to imagine, and Judith's imaginative failure through most of the novel makes her into the kind of historian Washington conceives of himself as being—one who is unable to formulate any satisfactory cross-cultural understanding. Judith is unable to cross the gap to understand what her whiteness means to him, and the gap is so wide that he is unable to cross it to let her know; together they have been unable to create a common discourse that would bridge that gap and create understanding. As he says late in the novel, "There was a lot that I needed that she would never understand. For she was a woman and she was white, and though I loved her there were points of reference that we did not share. And never would." So the novel would seem to arrive at a double impasse. His white lover (and by implication the white reader) cannot understand his or his people's experience, and he cannot understand the mystery that was part of his legacy from his father. Thus, he feels disabled as an historian.

This legacy/mystery is multifaceted: One aspect of it has to do with what his father was researching, while yet another is the mystery of Moses Washington's death and, even more remotely, what happened to his great-grandfather, C. K.

Washington. Moses Washington, an expert hunter, seemingly died in a hunting accident, while C. K. Washington simply disappeared. C. K., an escaped slave himself, planned and executed escapes of groups of slaves from the deep South, and he kept an extensive record of his activities, including a journal, while Moses himself had done extensive research. This archive has come down to John Washington, almost as patrimony.

C. K.'s journal simply breaks off on December 23, 1859, and as John says, "'That's the end of it; a period at the end of the sentence. That's the way history is sometimes. Sometimes you don't even get periods.'" Judith, though, in trying to understand what he asserts she is incapable of understanding, pushes him and refuses to accept that date as the terminus of all understanding of C. K. When John complains that "'there aren't any facts. . . ,'" she responds, "'So get more facts.'" And when he states that "'there aren't any more facts,'" she answers, "'Then forget the facts.'" The injunction with which she concludes is one that almost all historians would see as resulting in an abandonment of the "science" of history.

Despite his resistance and despite the absence of facts, John Washington finally creates understanding by using his imagination. Given all that cannot be known, he creates a fiction of C. K. Washington's last days, as if in acknowledgment of the limitation of the methods of history when it comes to the experience of African Americans. Early in the novel, Washington has characterized the historian as a "poor unimaginative fool," who is "really only a frustrated novelist," a person who "tries to put it all together. And fails." In the last astonishing pages of *The Chaneysville Incident,* the historian becomes a teller of stories, a fabulator, a griot almost, who accounts for, as a traditional historian cannot, what has gone unrecorded. As John says early in the novel, speaking as an academic historian, ". . . what a man's dying really means" is that "his story is lost." But for those capable of using the imagination, the absence of a first-person autobiographical narrative does not mean that the story is inevitably lost. In this novel, as Klaus Ensslen has written, "History can only become meaningful through active imaginative appropriation of its raw material, which is to say by an act of imaginative completion."

This imaginative completion, however, is more complicated than Ensslen's analysis allows for. I would argue that, while it is an imaginative completion of the story, it is also a rejection of Western assumptions about history. As James Baldwin wrote in *Just Above My Head:* "To be forced to excavate a history is, also, to repudiate the concept of history, and the vocabulary in which history is written; for the written history is, and must be, merely the vocabulary of power, and power is history's most seductively attired false witness." Excavating and then imagining a history, I would argue, is to repudiate a Western conception of history, and that repudiation does not leave one historyless, but rather it gives the historian the opportunity to make a kind of history less implicated in dominant discourses, and more open to other ways of structuring and organizing, ways that are collective and antithetical to the Western tradition. Repudiating the concept of Western history, Washington has appropriated an African concept of time, one that's been articulated by Woye Soyinka, who writes that "traditional thought" embodies "not a linear conception of time, but a cyclic reality." Soyinka knows that his conception of time is not unique either to

> the Yoruba or to the African world view. . . . the degree of integrated acceptance of this temporal sense in the life-rhythm, mores and social organisation of Yoruba society is . . . a reflection of that same reality which denies periodicity to the existence of the dead, the living and the unborn. The expression "the child is father to the man" becomes, within the context of this time structure, not merely a metaphor of development . . . but a proverb of human continuity which is not uni-directional.

Washington himself is aware of how porous the boundaries are that separate the living from the ancestors in traditional belief, and he realizes in this context that his father's suicide was a gesture of return, an act of faith in tradition, in cyclic African reality: He kills himself on the exact spot where C. K. died in the faith that he would join those ancestors. As Washington says, "'You don't throw your whole life away if you're not sure that the dead really are there, waiting for you.'" While Washington doesn't join the ancestors at the end of the novel, he does finish the story of C. K. in a locus of repetition: Old Jake's cabin, where he used to listen to the old man's stories. After coming to what seems to be a final impasse, John remembers the hunting advice of Old Jack: "'You figure too much, Johnny. . . . Quit tryin' to figure where he's at an' jest follow him.'" Immediately after this memory, John says to Judith, "'You want a story, do you?'" She replies, "'What? . . . I don't understand.'" "'Fetch the candle,'" John responds. In repeating exactly the words that Old Jack used to say to him, John not only recreates a ritual out of his childhood, but he also takes the position of Old Jack, his mentor, who educated him after his father's death, and Old Jack was a man whose wisdom was in his "stories." Taking Old Jack's role, John becomes almost a ritual storyteller, a bearer of collective wisdom, while Judith, conversely, assumes the role of John when he was young, a neophyte, an initiate.

Using the trope of hunting, John finishes the story of C. K. and tells how a famous slavecatcher used a group of escaped slaves to help catch a famous planner of slave escapes. C. K. is the hunted in the final section of the novel, and as the hunted, he realizes he must be doing more than "'gathering facts and ordering them'"; he must be "'really thinking, looking at the overall pattern of things and figuring out what the facts had to be.'" In order to survive, C. K. must imagine what the hunter, the slavecatcher Pettis, is trying to do; he must create his strategy out of his understanding of the hunter. In choosing, then, to tell the story from C. K.'s point of view, Washington, as historian/hunter, must understand both the hunted and the hunter. He must understand the hunter through the hunted; he must understand the white slavecatcher through the escaped slave.

But the trope of hunting also functions to describe Washington as an historian, and the failed deer hunt in the middle of the novel is a signal that he is still unable to give up completely his desire to "'figure'" (in the words of Old Jack) in favor of a more intuitive and subjective ability to "'feel'" and "'follow.'" He is unable to give up figuring until the moment he enters ancestral time and can translate the voices on the wind, the voices that Old Jack insisted he heard "'maybe five, six times in [his] whole life.'" The voices are those of the escaped slaves who, Old Jack asserts, "'ain't ghosts; they ain't dead. They're jest runnin' along. An' the sound you hear is the sound of 'em pantin','" a sound awaiting translation.

Moving into traditional time, John and Judith enter into a cycle and repeat (with a difference) the relationship of C. K. and Harriette Brewer. Judith has identified John with his ancestor ("'. . . you want to be just like him,'" she says), and while it may seem that there could be no convergence between a white psychologist and a woman who escaped from slavery before the Civil War, there is. The first form of convergence is Harriette's ancestry: She is half-white. Her mother fled "'because the child she was carrying belonged to her master.'" (There is a devastating pressure on the word *belonged*.) Although Judith has no African ancestors, she is implicated in the story by reason of her white ancestors (who owned slaves), and although Bradley says she's peripheral to the novel, her presence in the telling of the final story is absolutely crucial. She's not merely a stand-in for the white reader, because through discovering his love for her, Washington can explore the love of C. K. and Harriette, a conjunction that Bradley emphasizes by having Washington and C. K. simultaneously experience the same metaphoric thawing, one that indicates an opening up to the other. As Washington says, ". . . I realized something strange was happening. Because I was no longer cold." He's complained of his inability to get and stay warm throughout the novel, and when Washington resumes his story, Harriette physically warms C. K., but the gesture has more than physical resonance:

> ". . . he had not known about the other cold, the cold inside, the glacier in his guts that had been grow-

ing and moving, inch by inch, year by year, grinding at him, freezing him. He had not known that. But he knew it now. Because he could feel it melting. The heat . . . came from her, from . . . the warmth of her hands that cupped the base of his belly."

Through telling the story to Judith, John unfreezes his own glacier, and he discovers in ancestral time his love for her.

In order to tell the story, Washington must imaginatively assume several subject positions, and in order to tell a satisfactorily structured story, he must also imaginatively understand one other character—the white miller, Iiames. But this understanding only comes gradually during John and Judith's visit to the Iiames' family graveyard. Next to that graveyard they discover another, in exactly the same pattern as the white family's. At first, they believe that what they have uncovered in the snow (excavated almost?) are the graves of the slaves that Iiames owned, but ". . . as I shivered, the number of them came to me: one man, four women, seven children; twelve." John realizes he's found C. K.'s grave.

After John finishes the story, Judith returns to the interpretive problem of the graveyard, and she asks who buried them and, for the first time in the novel, drinks a hot toddy along with John. After rejecting a number of possibilities, John says:

> "They were buried next to a [white] family graveyard. They died there, but they didn't have to be buried there. They were buried with the same spacing as the family stones. . . ."

> "You're saying that the [white] miller—what's his name? Iiames?—you think he took the time to bury them like that, to figure out who loved who?"

> "Yes," I said. "That's what I believe."

> "But he was white," she said.

> "I know," I said.

> "Why would a white man . . . why would you think a white man. . . ?"

> I heard the soft squeaking of the chair as her body stiffened, as she turned to try and see my face.

Klaus Ensslen argues that John has, by interpreting "the very spacing and grouping of the graves," demonstrated the "empathy" of the white miller, Iiames, and "his ability to endorse imaginatively the value of their final gesture" of suicide, but what Ensslen fails to see is that, in asking her final question, Judith has not only "follow[ed] the example of Iiames," but transcended it. Entering the world of the story, Judith is speaking from within the experience and presuppositions of the African American community. As Bradley has said in an interview, her question here "indicates an absorption into John's point of view." Earlier, she would have been willing reflexively to insist on the existence of some whites of good will. Here, Iiames's burial of the "bodies of the fugitives as an act of atonement and love"—this act by a white man—is utterly incomprehensible to her, and her recognition of how far she has come in understanding is signaled by her body's "shifting." This act of "empathy" transcends Iiames's empathy because Judith is the only white character in the novel to succeed in empathetically understanding the other from the other's point of view. Her understanding, her entrance into the "minds or consciousnesses of human agents long dead" suggests the power of narrative to transform subject positions, to take a reader inside alien cultural assumptions. And the novel ends with John no longer asserting that Judith cannot understand, but with his hope that she will be able to continue to understand.

In entering ancestral time, John Washington becomes, as Jane Campbell has observed, a griot, a bearer of genealogies, a teller of tales. Although Campbell does not push the point, I would argue that the oral quality of Washington's narrative is an explicit challenge to Western conceptions of "objective" and "scientific" history. While Washington explicitly compares the historian to the Western novelist, he enacts a different set of cultural assumptions when he tells the story of C. K.'s death, assumptions which exist, he says, in all African Americans "independent of our volition." In having recourse to these alternative cultural assumptions, Bradley is employing what George Lipsitz has called (adapting and modifying a term from Foucault) counter-memory, which Lipsitz defines as

> a way of remembering and forgetting that starts with the local, the immediate, and the personal. Unlike historical narratives that begin with the totality of human existence and then locate specific actions and events within that totality, counter-memory starts with the particular and the specific and then builds outward toward a total story. Counter-memory looks to the past for the hidden histories excluded from dominant narratives.

What Bradley has done is to write a counter-history in this novel, one that resists dominant History and rewrites it in resolutely local terms. Although Bradley and Washington have at their fingertips local historical detail, it's only in the telling of the final story that the detail can begin to challenge "the hegemony of dominant discourse." As Lipsitz concludes, "Story-telling that combines subjectivity and objectivity, that employs the insights and passions of myth and folklore in the service of revising history, can be a powerful tool of contestation." Employing counter-memory as a way of moving into ancestral time, Washington has entered the tradition of African American writing, for as John M. Reilly has written: "It is the search for possibility, rather than reportage or protest, that distinguishes the African American writer's engagement with history."

Like other African American writers, Washington's completion of C. K.'s story is counter-writing, part of the extended effort of African Americans to write themselves rather than being written. Old Jack, early in the novel, reflects this awareness when he says, simply, "'. . . a man with no say is an animal.'" What Bradley has done is to give those fugitive slaves buried in Chaneysville their final say, because in Harriet Bradley's history they are victims: They "begged to be killed" and "someone obliged." David Bradley has created a powerful and terrible image of African American agency—a heroic mass suicide—an image as powerful and terrible in its own way as Sethe's killing Beloved in Morrison's novel. In both works, the writers transform the limitations of the historical documentation into "community legend," a community legend that finds its sources in Western conceptions of history and in the African American vernacular tradition, one that is made possible through the creation of a common discourse between John and Judith, a discourse powered by the agency of storytelling, a search "for one's origin in order to better understand oneself."

W. Lawrence Hogue (essay date June 1995)

SOURCE: "Problematizing History: David Bradley's *The Chaneysville Incident*," in *CLA Journal,* Vol. 38, No. 4, June, 1995, pp. 441-60.

[*In the following essay, Hogue demonstrates how Bradley's narrative techniques in* The Chaneysville Incident *undermine traditional concepts of history.*]

The Chaneysville Incident, by David Bradley, takes a novel approach to history and takes fictional liberties in resolving the modern and postmodern dilemmas of its protagonist. It resolves the modern and postmodern dilemmas of its protagonist by transforming, or imagining, aspects of the historical and cultural past into a contemporary constellation in order to validate, make coherent, and give history to certain modern and postmodern experiences. In the process of these transformations, these imaginings, *The Chaneysville Incident* problematizes, or undermines seriously, our modern traditional conception of history, which assumes that history seeks to explain what happened in the past by providing a precise and accurate reconstruction of the events reported

in the documents. It also liberates its protagonist from any external moral or transcendental authority. This liberation allows him to act purely on desire or want.

The Chaneysville Incident, in problematizing our sense of modern history and in issuing in a postmodern worldview, releases its protagonist from a metaphysical, absolute racial or cultural narrative, from an internally cohesive set of perceptions or formal conventions, and from a sanctioned notion of an ordered universe and of man's place in it. It revolts against the prevalent, representational style that views history and culture in universal, essential terms, that subordinates the individual's subjective experience to the consolidated values and the sociopolitical mechanisms of a metanarrative.

The kind of literature that *The Chaneysville Incident* represents is what Linda Hutcheon in *A Poetics of Postmodernism* calls "historiographic metafiction" or "postmodern historicism," which is "unwillingly unencumbered by nostalgia in its critical dialogical review of the forms, contexts, and values of the past." *The Chaneysville Incident* as historiographic metafiction is intensely self-reflexive and yet paradoxically also lays claim to historical events. It rewrites history yet calls history as a referent into question. It is aware of its own fictionalizing processes. It has a theoretical self-awareness of history and fiction as human constructs. This kind of fiction is not "realistic" in the nineteenth-century sense of asking the reader to assume that there is a one-to-one correspondence between the textual real and the social real. Neither is it radically nonreferential in the sense of experimental fiction, which attempts to escape realism. As historiographic metafiction, *The Chaneysville Incident* blurs the distinction between history and fiction. In the blurring of the two categories, the text aesthetically crosses the boundaries between modern and postmodern fiction.

> **As historiographic metafiction, *The Chaneysville Incident* blurs the distinction between history and fiction. In the blurring of the two categories, the text aesthetically crosses the boundaries between modern and postmodern fiction.**
> **—Matthew Wilson**

Unlike a modernist text such as Toni Morrison's *Song of Solomon, The Chaneysville Incident* does not want to exhume, or even preserve, a revered past. Nor does it want to deny the existence of the past as some critics of postmodern fiction have claimed. Rather, it wants, to use the words of Linda Hutcheon, "to revisit the past critically"; it wants to problematize the past's values, contents, conventions, and aesthetic forms. It wants a reevaluation of and a dialogue with the past that is informed by the present. Finally, it wants to arrive at a conscious, functional, and intentional truth about the past that is socially and ideologically conditioned.

John Washington, the protagonist in *The Chaneysville Incident,* is in a modern dilemma. He cannot overcome his alienation and fragmentation from, his lack of social identification with, and his lack of historical continuity with his father's, Moses Washington's, essentialist narrative, his values, conventions and definitions—values and definitions that are relevant to Moses Washington's existence but are incongruent with John's existence in the present. John Washington learns eventually that if he is going to find truth in history, he has to think of history critically and contextually. To achieve the freedom to live his life in the present, he has to accept the presupposition that history, like fiction, constitutes a system of signification by which we make sense of the past, that our readings and interpretations of the historical past are vitally dependent on our experience of the present.

At its opening, *The Chaneysville Incident* presents immediately John Washington's modern dilemma. His present living situation alienates him from the values and views of his father. John, who is a professor of history at a university in Philadelphia, has been living with Judith, a white psychiatrist, for the past five years. It appears to be a genuine relationship. They have developed the sort of esoteric codes of communication usually reserved for lovers. Judith has concern in her voice when she speaks to John, and the relationship is filled with human warmth, humor, and love.

Yet the five-year relationship has reached an impasse; it has not been finalized. John and Judith are not "legally espoused," and marriage does not appear imminent. Despite the fact that Judith's biological clock is running down, they have no children and there is no talk of children. John has not taken Judith home to meet his mother, and he refuses to discuss with her his childhood or his inability to reconcile his father's values—which he has adopted and internalized— with his present living situation. Why the failure at finalizing this relationship?

The five-year relationship has not been finalized because Judith is white, and interracial marriages and interracial babies are excluded from, or are repressed in, John Washington's conception of the social realm given to him by his father. What Judith's white skin represents for John is growing up with a father who had an essentialized narrative, a conception of time and space, that believes that a black man should be "natural," that he should not only be distrusting of white people, but also that he should be antithetical to a Judeo-Christian society. Basically, Moses Washington believed that man must be able to live in the

wilderness. He "has to be able to make a fire, has to know how to make it in the wind an' the rain an' the dark." Moses Washington believed that a man must know how to hunt, fish, curse, and drink whiskey. He must be independent— that is, not dependent on mother, Jesus, or the government.

After forty years of living naturally, or in nature, in the mountains and making and selling illegal whiskey, Moses Washington comes down into the small southwestern Pennsylvania town to live. But he does not become a conventional man; he continues to live by his own rules. He marries Yvette Stanton, the daughter of a prominent black historian in town. There is no love or companionship in this marriage. It is not a conventional marriage; it is a marriage between allies. She wants children and he wants two sons to carry on his legacy. But Moses Washington's marriage is not the only thing unconventional about his stay in society, where he remains a "natural" man. He continues to live by his own rules—totally disregarding the laws and mores of society. He pays bribes to the sheriff to sell his whiskey and keeps a "folio" of illegal doings by prominent white citizens for blackmail purposes. He has "far-reaching theological discussions" with preachers about "certain Christian assumptions concerning the afterlife." He continues to mistrust white people. Jack Crawley narrates to John: "Moses didn't have no love for whitefolks. He'd sell to 'em, an' he'd buy from 'em when he had to, an' he'd talk to 'em if there wasn't no way around it, but he sure as hell wasn't goin' to think too much of John fallin' in love with one of 'em."

This is the narrative or way of life that John Washington inherits from his father. On his death bed Moses solicits a promise from Jack Crawley that he would teach his son John "to be a man." Fulfilling his promise, Crawley teaches John how to be a "natural," independent man. He teaches him how to survive in the woods, how to aim a rifle, how to hunt and fish, how to "bring [his] breathing under control; to still [his] own fear, to be methodical; to accept [his] limitations and compensate." Like the men in his family who have come before him, John Washington is taught to be both rational and instinctive.

In asking Jack Crawley to teach his son how to be a "natural" man, Moses Washington is taking the necessary action to continue the universalization, or transcendence, of his particular definition of manhood—a definition which he receives from his grandfather C. K. and which he accepts uncritically and imposes upon his subjective, lived experiences. In Crawley's action, we see the process by which one notion of manhood gains power and authority over another. But we also see the limitations of this definition when we witness how it becomes ineffectual for John. It arrests John Washington emotionally, not allowing him to live his life in the present. It fails to explain John's contemporary, lived experiences and therefore represses his desires and wants.

For a while, Moses Washington's way of life, or vision of man, becomes what his son John Washington wants out of life: "to get up in the morning, build a fire and go the spring and pay a visit to the privy, and then cook my breakfast." In short, John accepts Moses Washington's definition of manhood or view of man as a part of an absolute racial or cultural narrative. At this moment in his life, John does not realize that Moses and C. K. have taken the raw material of history and made it relevant to them, or have imposed an external narrative upon their subjective, lived experiences.

But somewhere along the way John Washington abandons the natural, independent lifestyle of his father for the American success story. He accepts and internalizes some of the cognitive styles of the mainstream society. A "neat, clean-cut" appearance, the image of a "nice, gentle, shy Negro," and his passion for reading indicate that he has internalized the values of a secular American education and the behavior and appearance of middle-class America. John's competitive American spirit and his Protestant work ethic show as he reads the summer before college "the things that [his] soon-to-be classmates would have cut their intellectual teeth on." He becomes the local success story with his name and picture in the paper and his scholarship to college.

In addition to a father who held views and practiced values that are contradictory to his present living arrangement, John Washington's attitudes, especially about race, have also been shaped by his own experiences. He grows up in a small southwestern Pennsylvania town that was basically defacto segregated. He learns early "many of the little assumptions and presumptions that go with dormant racism or well-meaning liberalism." Although never understanding why, John and other black males had to travel forty miles to another town to get haircuts. They could not swim in the city's public swimming pool and they were not welcomed in the town's coffee shop. John is also aware that in this small southwestern Pennsylvania town blacks are buried in a segregated cemetery and black males are always drafted into the armed services before their white counterparts. More overt and more conscious are those incidents where John is "pursued by white boys from the town, shouting names and curses; [he] would make the climb imagining that all the house windows were eyes staring at [him]; that they knew, somehow, that that day someone had called [him] a name or threatened [him], and [he] had done nothing besides close [his] eyes and ears, trying to pretend it was not happening." Finally, there is the experience that John has with the white friend Robert from high school whose mother does not want John to visit the house anymore because he is black. These experiences of racism explain John's mistrust, or even hatred, at times, of whites. They also generate or affirm his father's racial views.

Lastly, John Washington's racial attitudes are further hard-ened by the circumstances surrounding his brother Bill's induction into the Army and his eventual death. Because of his athletic abilities in football and wrestling, Bill is passed academically through high school. When he has played out his four-year option and is of no more use to the school, he is flunked. Without school, Bill is eligible for the draft. Against John's advice and knowledge and through his mother's coercion, Bill is drafted into the Army and is sent to Vietnam, where he is killed. John never forgives his mother for Bill's death. In fact, after Bill's death, he cuts off all communication with her.

The racial incidents which he experiences in his hometown, along with the circumstances surrounding his brother's death and his obvious desire for a mainstream American type of lifestyle, make John want to escape from his family's past, particularly his father's definition of manhood. He comes to hate his mother, perhaps for her choice of Bill as her favorite; he hates his father and was never close to his brother. He "promised [himself] that someday [he] would go where [the trucks] were going." John does go away and does not return until he receives the call from his mother announcing Jack Crawley's sickness and impending death. In going away, he had hoped both to abandon his life on the hill and to repress his father's definition of manhood. Reflecting on this promise as he returns for Jack's death and funeral, John thinks: "I knew nothing about the Hill any longer, I had made it my business not to know."

Physically, John Washington is successful in escaping his family's past, but ideologically and psychologically he is still very much his father's son. He continues to accept uncritically Moses Washington's view of manhood as a part of an absolute racial or cultural narrative. His entrapment in many of the values and conventions of his father's essentialized narrative is amplified clearly in two poignant moments. The first moment comes after he has learned of Jack Crawley's illness. On the bus ride home, John grapples with the difficulty of abandoning his father's narrative: "And so I settled myself in my seat and took another pull on my flask and looked out the window at the mountainsides black with pine, and thought about how strange home is: a place to which you belong and which belongs to you even if you don't particularly like it or want it, a place you cannot escape, no matter how far you go or how furiously you run." The second moment comes in a conversation in which Judith asks him why he is with her if he hates white people: "You're the man with the logic," she said. "Here's some for you. You hate white people. I am a white person. Therefore you hate me. Only you say you don't; you say you love me. Which seems like a contradiction. So I guess you must be lying about something. Either you can't hate so much or you can't love—." John's response is that "it's not that simple." John still views the world through his father's lens and by the experiences of his personal past.

Judith, who takes a practical approach to the situation, does not understand the complexity of John's contradictory predicament. (Of course, she should, for she is a trained psychiatrist. This is one of four technical flaws in *The Chaneysville Incident.* The other three are the scaling of the catfish, the lack of an explanation for John's absence from his job, and Jack's talking, despite his sickness, without interruption or pause.) She does not understand how, on the one hand, John is in love with her, and how, on the other hand, he is tied or is entrapped, historically and ideologically, to a version of history or a racial narrative that mistrusts white people. For Judith, the situation is rather simple: either John loves her or he hates her. But because he is unable to articulate his complex, contradictory feelings to Judith, John becomes silent.

The event which forces John to confront and to eventually undermine his father's essentialized narrative and which forces him to confront his tenuous and unsettled relationship with Judith, who is growing impatient with him, comes with the illness and eventual death of Jack Crawley. After burying Jack, John becomes obsessed again with finding the truth about his father's life and death, which he has been pursuing since he was thirteen. Obviously, as a modern subject who needs a temporal unification between the past and future in the present, he needs answers from his family's past to function as a whole person in the present. He needs a historical line from the past to the present, and he hopes to find it in his father's past. John first pursues the truth of his father's life and death three years after Moses Washington's death. He enters his father's attic and finds "the chair, the table, the book, the lamp, the empty fireplace . . . the keys to a man's mind, laid bare to [him], clues to a mystery, the answer to every question there. All [he] had to do was interpret them. It was the greatest thrill [he] had ever known."

But this approach to history, as Hayden White argues in *The Content of the Form,* works from the assumption that history itself consists of a congeries of lived stories, individual and collective, and that the principal task of historians is to uncover these stories and to retell them in a narrative. John, the traditional novice historian, believes that history seeks to explain what happened in the past by providing a precise and accurate reconstruction of the events reported in the documents. In taking this approach to finding truth in history, John falls prey to one of the "greatest fallacies" that surrounds the study of the past: "the notion that there is such a thing as a detached researcher, that it is possible to discover and analyze and interpret, without getting caught up and swept away." In short, he refuses to accept the fact that our readings and interpretations of the historical past are vitally dependent on our experience of the present, or that history constitutes a system of signification by which we make sense of the past.

After John buries Jack, he returns again to his father's attic. This time his interest is sparked because he is bewildered by certain facts found in his father's portfolio. Again, he is seeking the objective truth of his father's life and death. Now, he is a professor of history who has been trained to order facts, to control data. John organizes his facts on color-coded index cards. The organization of Moses Washington's books, John surmises, indicates that Moses had been researching something, that what had happened was not, as everybody thought, that Moses Washington had given up hunting but rather that he had transferred his energies and efforts to a different pursuit.

The question that plagues John is: Why did Moses Washington then leave his books and take up his gun after ten years? For clues to his father's action, John traces his father's biblical research, examining all the facts and documents. But in acting still as a traditional historian who refuses to imagine, or to think of history critically and contextually, he is still unable to unravel "the whys and wherefores" of Moses Washington:

> I had put the facts together, all of them, everything
> I could cull from those books and his notebooks and
> my notebooks: everything. I had put it together and
> I had studied it until I could command every fact,
> and then I had stepped back and looked at the whole
> and seen . . . nothing. Not a thing. Oh, I had seen
> the facts, there was no shortage of facts; but I could
> not discern the shape that they fitted in.

Still, in his endless search to find the truth about his father's life and death, John seeks information and knowledge from other sources. He has a rare conversation with his mother and he talks with Judge Scott, his father's friend. His mother reaffirms his knowledge that his father's marriage was one of convenience and that he lived an unconventional life. From Judge Scott, John learns about his father's business, his payment of bribes, and the portfolio he used for blackmail purposes. John also learns from Judge Scott that Moses Washington was both methodical and instinctive. But neither John's mother nor Judge Scott is able to shed any additional insight into why Moses Washington killed himself.

John moves into Jack Crawley's cabin, which is innocent of modern appliances and of an indoor bathroom and which is literally very close to nature and the wilderness. He cleans the cabin of the "[stink] of dying," moves his belongings in from his mother's house, and adjusts to the meager comforts that Jack's cabin provides. Obviously, he has clear intentions of staying for a while in the cabin. The letter to Judith and the hunting trip in the woods indicate, argues Klaus Enssler, John's rejection of his present condition—his relationship with Judith and his job as a historian—and his return to, or reenactment of, Jack's and Moses Washington's natural way of life. But in absorbing the full implication of John's letter, Judith comes to the Hill and disrupts John's reenactment. Her arrival brings John back to the present, which includes his dealing with his own existential existence, his relationship with her, and the mystery of his father's suicide.

With Judith, John visits Chaneysville—the place where the twelve slaves are buried and where C. K. and Moses Washington committed suicide. But because he still refuses to be intuitive or imaginative—which is an integral part of interpreting history and which is a prerequisite for his giving "shape" and "pattern" to the facts in his possession—John still cannot find the truth about Moses Washington's suicide: "Bit by bit the thoughts came slipping in, the facts and the calculations, the dates and the suspicions. There was no pattern to them, nothing I could grab on to: it was just random cerebration; a mind checking itself." The provisionality and uncertainty of John Washington the historian do not cast doubt upon his seriousness. All of his actions indicate his complete devotion to finding the truth about his father. Rather, they define the new postmodern seriousness that acknowledges the limits and powers of writing about the past. He is forced to grapple with the possibility that we can only know the past through discursive systems.

Simultaneous with John Washington's search for the truth of his father's suicide are repeated flashbacks to his unrealized relationship with Judith. Obviously, resolving the historical dilemma concerning his father's and great-grandfather's past also means resolving his personal one. But Moses Washington's truth in history does not satisfy or explain adequately John's present wants and desires. In addition, John continues to view history as something that is objective, as something that is external to his subjective reality. Again in Judith's company, John recognizes her love and warmth. He also acknowledges his attraction to her:

> [S]he stepped closer to me and thrust my hands into her armpits and held them there with her own. Slowly I felt the sensation come back, felt the warmth and the pressure from her, the swell of her breasts against my wrists . . . seeing her cheek and belly and the faint hint of thigh beneath the material of her slacks, and I remembered how it felt to have the cheek against my chest, the belly and things solid and warm against mine.

Yet, despite the acknowledged love and warmth, John still refuses to tell Judith about himself or his family's past. He still refuses to give himself completely to the relationship.

But later, when Judith asks John how he got here, John, for the first time in their five-year relationship, begins to tell Judith about his family's past. He tells her about the history of the Hill where he grew up, about the role that the Meth-odist Church played in the slave trade. He tells Judith about the Underground Railroad. Then, in a radical turn of events, John, pulling his father's portfolio from the shelf, reconstructs for Judith the history of the Stantons, his mother's side of the family. Then he proceeds to reconstruct the history of the Washingtons, his father's side of the family.

In all of these stories about, and reconstructions of, the family's past, John is working only with facts. From the facts of his family's history, John sees a parallel in the lives of his father, Moses Washington, and his great-grandfather, C. K. Washington. Both C. K. and Moses were methodical and instinctive. For example, although C. K. is a "natural" man, he hunts the man down who killed his father and murders him. Likewise, Moses is a natural man but he also calculates how to manipulate the whites in town. Moses Washington had loved a woman because C. K. had loved a woman. Moses wanted sons because his grandfather had a son, Lamen Washington, who became "a fairly prominent black mortician." (Although *The Chaneysville Incident* does not consciously critique it, it shows unconsciously that John, like C. K. and Moses, sees women as objects. C. K. indifferently fathers a son. He "never ever mentions the fact that sometime during the winter she [Bijou, who is the mother of Lamen Washington] became his mistress." Moses also uses Yvette to bear him two sons; then he abandons her. John, even in his transformation in the end, still treats Judith as an object.) Both C. K. and Moses Washington had moved to the mountains of western Pennsylvania and had become bootleggers. By viewing Moses Washington's action outside the context of Christianity, John reasons that Moses's search was "to be sure that Christians were wrong." He also reasons that knowledge of death had a significance for Moses that it did not have for most men.

But the facts in John's possession do not lead to a complete satisfactory history for him. The facts, and the system of signification that presents them, do not give him a history that will allow him to explain his present living situation. John does not know why death is so significant for Moses and why Moses commits suicide; he does not know what happened to C. K., and that means he does not know anything. John does know that C. K.'s death and his father's death happened in Chaneysville, where twelve slaves are buried. He knows that C. K. was in love with Harriette Brewer, who was "educated and intelligent" and who helped to "take escapees [from slavery] who had made it as far as Philadelphia on north." But he does not know the "details of the affair." He also knows that F. H. Pettis, who might have known C. K., "had seen the lucrative possibilities represented by fugitive slaves, and he had begun to advertise in Southern newspapers, offering to track down and return fugitive property." But he does not know whether Pettis is the one who is responsible for C. K.'s murder.

In his visit to Chaneysville with Judith, John learns other things. He learns that Moses had killed himself in "close proximity" to Richard Iiames's remains and in a family graveyard belonging to a family named Iiames. He also discovers an unmarked thirteenth grave. "It was like the others, the same size and shape, and it had nothing written on it, but it was not in the pattern at all, it was above it, closer to the southeast corner of the Iiames family plot, almost exactly where [Moses] would have been when he killed himself." John knows the facts of the history he is trying to know. He knows names and places and people. In short, he knows "what Moses Washington [and C. K.] knew when [they] got this far." But what John does not know are the connections between these facts, between these names and places and people, and so he does not know their meaning. He does not know how to make these names and places and people relevant to his own subjective reality. He does not know how to establish a historical line from the past to the present—that is, until he takes a nonrational leap of faith.

As Judith gets the toddies, John begins to reconstruct imaginatively a historical past and a truth of his father's life and death that will be relevant to his own present living situation. He stops "wondering and worrying and start[s] doing what he should have been doing all along: thinking. Really thinking. Not just gathering facts and ordering them; not just trying to follow them along; *really* thinking, looking at the overall patterns of things and figuring out what the facts *had* to be." Unlike Moses Washington and C. K., when John Washington reaches the limit of his knowledge of his father's and great-grandfather's lives and deaths, he goes on beyond reconstruction into pure speculation. The signs of the narrative act fall away and with them all questions of authority and reliability: "Facts, I said. Don't you understand? There aren't any facts. All that about the runaway slaves and Moses Washington, that's extrapolation. It's not facts. I've used the facts."

In addition, John begins to trust Judith, who has stopped asking questions and is now just listening, and it is within this trust that he can "imagine" a truth of his father's and great-grandfather's life and death and resolve his unrealized relationship with Judith:

> [Judith] brought the cup to me and pressed it into my hands, letting her hands linger there for a moment, holding the warmth of the cup against mine. I knew then that I had underestimated her, and had done it in a way that cheated us both. . . . And then I realized that something strange was happening. Because I was no longer cold. . . . I saw that she was leaning forward, her eyes shining in the light, fixed on the candle. And I looked at it too, at the steady flame, hardly a flame at all now, but a round, warm,

even glow that seemed to grow as I looked at it, expanding until it filled my sight.

The shift from reconstructed history based on facts to speculation is manifested in the sounds and a voice that John, and not Judith, hears through the wind. These sounds put John squarely in the nonrational, non-Western, African tradition of C. K. and Moses. And just as C. K. and Moses, in committing suicide, had taken nonrational leaps, John takes a nonrational leap. With a drink and Judith's acceptance, John "imagines" and imposes a meaning on the historical past, on what happened to C. K. Washington and the slaves on the fateful night that they went running through the woods of South County. He has finally realized that the meaning and shape of history are not in the events or facts, but in the ideological or discursive systems that make these past events into present historical facts.

Therefore, he imagines that C. K.'s life had included a lost love, a woman named Harriette Brewer. C. K. had fallen in love with Harriette some years after his first wife was killed in a race riot. Before they could consummate the relationship, C. K. had gone back to the mountains to run his whiskey business, and Harriette, who believed not only in financing slave escapees but also in leading them out, had gone South. The discovery of her action led C. K. to his many daring rescues of slaves. Pursued by Pettis—whose business is catching runaway slaves—and half the men of South County, C. K. and Harriette, John imagines, are reunited a few hours before they face death together. C. K. arrives at their hiding place to bring them supplies and realizes that the slaves are "watching him" and "waiting for him to lead them." Cornered by Pettis and his men, C. K., Harriette, and the twelve slaves sing the song: "And before I'll be a slave I'll be buried in my grave and go home to my God, and be free." Then they kill themselves.

In John's "imagined" history, the warmth that C. K. experiences with Harriette and the warmth that John is simultaneously experiencing in his life with Judith are more than physical warmth. It is a human warmth of two people in love:

> But [John] had not known about the other cold, the cold inside, the glacier in his guts that had been growing and moving, inch by inch, year by year, grinding at him, freezing him. He had not known that. But he knew it now. Because he could feel it melting. The heat that melted it did not come from the fire, it came from her, from the warmth of her body that pressed against his back, the warmth of her arms around him, the warmth of her hands that cupped the base of his belly. He lay there, feeling the warmth filling him, feeling the fatigue draining from him, feeling the aching in his ribs easing, be-

coming almost pleasant, and wishing that he would never have to move.

As John nears the completion of C. K.'s imagined history, Judith's warmth begins the melting of his "other cold"—the cold that has prevented him from sharing his past, his present, and his future with her because she is white.

Completing his imagined history, John imagines other things. After the slaves kill themselves they are buried next to a family graveyard. Richard Iiames, a white man who had come to Chaneysville, the "oldest continuous settlement in the County," in 1728 had taken "the time to bury them like that, to figure out who loved who." This reconstructed event allows John to believe that there are some good white people, thereby undermining his father's essentialized narrative that black men cannot trust white people. John also concludes that Moses did not commit suicide, as C. K. had not committed suicide. Since he was sixteen, Moses had been on the search to prove the Christians wrong. John spends endless hours doing biblical research. He even goes to war because "he want[s] to understand dying," and he becomes a hero in the war because "he want[s] to take chances, [to] get closer to death." Finally, John reasons, Moses understands C. K.'s life and death. Going to Chaneysville, Moses was on a hunting trip—looking for his "Ancestors." Unlike Christians, C. K. and Moses saw death, John reasons, not as the end of life but as an extension of life. In "imagining" the historical past, John Washington recognizes that history depends as much upon intuition as upon analytical methods. He accepts the presupposition that the "shape" and "pattern" of history are informed by his experience of the present. Expressing his attitude toward history in an interview, David Bradley states: "History to me is raw material, the past is raw material. We can't be governed by it."

In "imagining," in rewriting and re-presenting the contents and events of C. K.'s and Moses's lives and deaths, John Washington produces a version of the past that validates and makes coherent his present existence. In producing his own narrative, John rejects the essentialist narrative and tradition of his father and great-grandfather and becomes postmodern. His narrative becomes what Lyotard in *The Postmodern Condition* calls a language game which has its own rules and has no recourse to a larger metanarrative or external principle of justice or authority. In this situation, the function of John's postmodern attitude, which is self-legitimating, is no longer truth but "performativity." He does what he does, not because there is an external truth or metanarrative to legitimate it but because that is what he wants to do; that is what he desires. In this instance, John's subjective experience is no longer subordinated to the consolidated values of his father's and great-grandfather's metanarrative. This postmodern attitude gives John the *option* of marrying Judith, which he hopes she understands:

As I struck the match it came to me how strange it would all look to someone else, someone from far away. And as I dropped the match to the wood and watched the flames go twisting, I wondered if that someone would understand. Not just someone; Judith. I wondered if she would understand when she saw the smoke go rising from the far side of the Hill.

In the conscious manipulation and interpretation of events from the past, John arrives at a truth that is socially and ideologically conditioned. It is a truth that is vitally dependent on his own subjective reality. In this truth, *The Chaneysville Incident* admits that the past is real and does exist, but it also suggests that there is no direct access to that past unmediated by the structures of our various discourses about it. John Washington has to use a discourse of his personal experience to make sense out of the past.

Therefore, as he and Judith prepare to leave Jack Crawley's cabin and return to Philadelphia, John seals the "folio up with candle wax, as [his] father had done for [him]" and puts it under his arm. Then he puts "the books and pamphlets and diaries and maps back where they belonged, ready for the next man who would need them." Finally, he burns all the "pads and cards" which he has accumulated. With the portfolio and the books and pamphlets and diaries and maps, *his* son (and hopefully his daughter), in years to come will have to rethink and rework the contents and facts of the past. He, like John, will have to make the raw material of history relevant to himself. It is this constant rewriting and rethinking of history that prevent it from being conclusive and teleological.

In moving beyond reconstruction of facts into "imagining" or pure speculation, *The Chaneysville Incident* passes from mimesis of facts, rumors, documents, information gathered from a graveyard visit, Moses Washington's "personal memoirs," and the various characters'—Jack Crawley's, Judge Scott's, and Yvette Washington's—accounts to what Brian McHale in *Postmodernist Fiction* calls "unmediated diegesis, from characters 'telling' to the author directly 'showing' us what happened" between the various characters. John Washington's mystery about his father's death and his great-grandfather's disappearance is solved not through epistemological processes of weighing evidence and making deductions—as traditional modern history is conceived and written—but through the imaginative projection of what could—and what *The Chaneysville Incident* insists, *must*—have happened. Abandoning the untraceable problems of attaining a reliable knowledge of the historical past, John Washington improvises a possible historical past. At this point, *The Chaneysville Incident* crosses the boundary between modernist and postmodernist writing.

In problematizing the entire notion of historical knowledge . . . *The Chaneysville Incident* puts into question the authority of any act of writing, by, to use the terms of Linda Hutcheon, "locating the discourses of both history and fiction within an ever-expanding intertextual network that mocks any notion of singularity." It also exposes the process by which C. K.'s and Moses Washington's notion of truth gained power and authority over others. Finally, the text makes us aware that historical truth is socially and ideologically conditioned. It shows that history itself depends on the conventions of narrative, language, discourse, and ideology in order to present what happened.

Edward Pavli (essay date Summer 1996)

SOURCE: "Syndetic Redemption: Above-Underground Emergence in David Bradley's *The Chaneysville Incident*," in *African American Review,* Vol. 30, No. 2, Summer, 1996, pp. 165-84.

[*In the following excerpt, Pavli examines the narrative method of* The Chaneysville Incident.]

Ralph Ellison's *Invisible Man* begins and ends with the narrator positioned in "black" *underground* space which can be seen as an expression of "white" modernist understandings of cultural process as a solitary and stationary exercise of mind. The narrator of Ellison's text, like his ancestor Fred Daniels in Richard Wright's "The Man Who Lived Underground," finds himself alienated from an *aboveground* reality which reacts to his black body by negating his mind, denying his voice, and limiting his physical movement. Both figures retreat into womb-like, solitary, underground space where their minds swirl, attempting to resist the assumptions of the white supremacist, aboveground world. Ellison's *Invisible Man* charts the territory, but his narrator's theorizing does not allow him to emerge from the hole and forge a viable connection between underground process and aboveground existence, black mind and black body.

In this essay I will explore how David Bradley's *The Chaneysville Incident* responds to these problems by creating a narrative structure which I will call the *emergence narrative* that redefines the patterns of hibernation and excavation described by Robert Stepto and Craig Werner. Demonstrating how the excavation of history can subvert inhibiting philosophical assumptions, Bradley's written text reveals how an oral, communal process can constitute an *above-underground mode* in which descendants and ancestors achieve living reciprocal relationships.

Robert B. Stepto's *From Behind the Veil: A Study of Afro-American Narrative* posits a kinetic theory of Afro-American narrative which culminates with Ellison's *Invisible Man* engaged in what Stepto calls a hibernation narrative. The Invisible Man's static and secluded position in hibernation reflects the profound difficulties experienced by black intellectuals as they attempt to use their "white" literacy and black communal or "tribal literacy" in the aboveground world. In *Playing the Changes: From Afro-Modernism to the Jazz Impulse*, Craig Werner refines Stepto's narrative of hibernation by contrasting the Afro-American narrative of excavation (James Baldwin, David Bradley, Gayl Jones, Ralph Ellison, Toni Morrison) with the Faulknerian narrative of repudiation. For Werner, excavation narratives attempt to redeem the complexity of formerly unknown or unacknowledged pasts. The failure to acknowledge the complexity of historical experience in Faulkner's narratives of repudiation points to the central importance of the process delineated in Baldwin's *Just Above My Head*:

> To be forced to excavate a history is also to repudiate the concept of history, and the vocabulary in which history, is written; for the written history is, and must be, merely the vocabulary of power. . . . Power clears the passage, swiftly: but the paradox, here, is that power, rooted in history, is also the mockery and the repudiation of history.

In *The Chaneysville Incident* Bradley draws on West African epistemologies to respond to the problems of power, history, and passage. John Washington struggles to enact ontological and epistemological shifts which enable him to use the ancestors' call in connection with his own present-day process in telling and knowing the familial tale. In terms of African-American literary ancestry, the emergence of John Washington's process can be read as a liberating extension of Ralph Ellison's narrator's underground process in *Invisible Man*.

A historian at a major American university, John Washington has "made it," and Bradley sets Washington on a quest to *know* whence he came. Through this process, he must get beyond blackness as an aboveground marker and struggle to create nuanced epistemological processes and ontological qualities requisite to *knowing* himself in connection with *all* of his ancestors. As the shifts leading from underground space to above-underground *mode* occur, several key questions facing African-derived creativity come to the fore. Can black-underground process be accomplished in stationary solitude? What effect do modern European epistemological assumptions have on the pursuit of African-American ancestry?

As Bradley's underground narrative emerges in above-underground *mode,* oral, mobile, and communal epistemic routes emerge from the print. This meta-narrative convergence pushes readers into confrontation with their own assumptions about their role in the above-underground narrative *mode*. The passage from Ellison's underground place to Bradley's above-underground *mode* requires three key shifts in the African-American response to "white" theoretical assumptions. These shifts attempt to identify and remedy conflicts between African-American cultural processes and theoretical assumptions based in stationary thought; linear, dialectical processes of cultural change; and solipsistic assumptions of dialogic communication.

In his 1990 essay "It's a Family Affair," Paul Gilroy adapts Manuel Castels's critique of understandings of identity stemming from static, origin-based myths of cultural life which become viable or "defensible" as a result of being "enclosed." Gilroy suggests that "one thing we might do is take a cue from Manual Castels, who describes the shift from an understanding of space based on notions of place and fixity to an understanding of space based on flows." Gilroy's 1993 work *The Black Atlantic* explicitly posits mobility—more specifically trans-national movement of "ships in motion across spaces between Europe, America, Africa, and the Caribbean"—as central to the creation of black Atlantic cultures. Gilroy's proposed shift calls for critics to recognize the centrality of mobile place, *mode,* in African-American aesthetics. This mobility of body *and* mind is essential to the emergence of Bradley's above-underground narrative, which engages the complex black/white experience of "double-consciousness."

In these mobile terms, Du Bois's appropriation of the Hegelian dialectic model can be construed as a mapping of flows which constitute African-American identity. Breaking from the premise of unilateral cultural influence as progress, Du Bois's Hegelian model of double-consciousness mapped African-American identity in terms of conflicting flows, similar to the cross-currents in Paule Marshall's *Praisesong for the Widow* which challenge Avey Johnson's passage in her "recuperative" journey *home*. While breaking the unilateral "one-way traffic" model, Du Bois's thinking articulated a multifaceted challenge to which we are heirs. Sandra Adell's *Double Consciousness/Double Bind: Theoretical Issues in Twentieth Century Black Literature,* David Levering Lewis's biography of Du Bois, and Anthony Appiah's *In My Father's House: Africa in the Philosophy of Culture* focus on various issues centered in the entanglement of Du Bois's thought with nineteenth-century German idealist philosophy. Gerald Early's edited collection *Lure and Loathing: Essays on Race, Identity and the Ambivalence of Assimilation* contains essays on the problematic nature of the Du Boisian convergence in contemporary African-American intellectual life. The dialectical underpinnings of double-consciousness call for assimilation or resolution of the conflicting flows of African-American identity and culture into a unified "true self-consciousness." In these terms, the Du Boisian model of African-American identity is synthetic,

whereas Bradley's above-underground *mode* points toward what scholars working with Yorùbá traditions have called a syndetic process.

Robert Plant Armstrong's work *The Powers of Presence: Consciousness, Myth, and Affecting Presence in Yorùbá Traditional Culture* situates Yorùbá creativity in an aesthetics of invocation in which modernist European conceptions of artifact, artist, and audience are redefined as parts of a fluid system based on reciprocity. In Armstrong's phrasing of the Yorùbá creative process, essences are not represented in artifacts which are valued for the fineness of their form. Rather, energies are invoked by artists and audiences who may use artifacts to facilitate connection with, or transfer of, deified energy between and among members of the earth-bound community. Egungun masks are artifacts of invocation through which ancestors assert their subjective presence in improvised connection with descendants. Anyone who has seen a movie in an all-black cinema has witnessed the communally improvised, fluid repudiation of the hierarchical division between artist, artifact, and audience. African-American audiences do not watch films; they invoke them in defiance of the out of place, formalist, "please observe silence" signal from the projectionist. This improvised, communal performance of film occurs to the dismay of any "white" audience members who may have mistaken the screen as the "enclosed and defensible space" in which movies are performed in cultures of invocation.

The inter-subjective and improvisational epistemics which underlie aesthetics of invocation depend on principles of cultural connection and combination which include but are not limited to linear, progressive, dialectical models. Armstrong's notion of a syndetic model of accretion describes how the cultural motion of Yorùbá aesthetics can not be limited to linear dialectics:

> Together with synthesis, syndesis constitutes the totality of those modes in which the human consciousness apprehends and enacts the world and the self—through a process of opposition and eventuation (synthesis) on the one hand, and through a process of accretion (syndesis) on the other. . . . The synthetic work owns inherent principles of *development*. It proceeds through the execution and resolution of opposites . . . insofar as successive phases grow out of prior ones, the synthetic work is linear. . . . The syndetic . . . growth is through repetition of the same inventory of similar units. It does not *develop*. . . .

By "it does not *develop*," Armstrong does not mean to suggest that Yorùbá cultural process is static. In these syndetic rituals, "past" moments are not objectified for synthesis with the next, by definition, oppositional, dialectical stage; the rituals' complexity "accretes." Present moments add to the *past-presence* of previous cycles without replacing them. The result is a process of cultural combination which does not require systematic resolution of "contradiction," since past moments (re)assert variable, at times problematic, meanings in an expanded "now." Phrasing double-conscious cultural process as syndetic empowers the African-derived aspects of consciousness, liberating them from "inevitable developmental synthesis" defined by a European, rational thesis, and encourages dynamic—not objectified—relationships with ancestors. A brief examination of the syndetic above-underground *mode* in contemporary black music makes it clear how, through respectful extension, ancestors are invoked in reciprocal, subjective relationship to descendants. Descendants learn from ancestors, and, in syndetic ritual, ancestors' complexity continues to accrete through the expanding consciousness of *all* performers. . . .

An awareness of how West African syndetic processes are present in contemporary African-American culture allows us to comprehend more fully the three epistemological shifts enacted in **The Chaneysville Incident.** The first shift involves questioning the relationship between the modernist stasis of Ellison's narrator and syndetic epistemology. What happens to African-American aesthetics when positioned in solitary performance spaces in which movement tends toward exercises of mind instead, or in spite, of body? To adopt Paul Gilroy's phrasing, does it entail the stationary meditation over cultural "roots," or the mobile, communal pursuit and, if necessary, "creation" of cultural "routes"? Concern with roots frequently leads to meditation on pre-dispersion African origins which often mirror Herderian conceptions of original cultural purity. Attention to routes of culture encourages analysis of mobile cultural change and hybridity as African cultures (re)form identities and traditions in response to diaspora conditions.

The second shift queries the connection between Du Bois's idea of double-consciousness and dialectical assumptions which drive progressive, generational historical models. Reliance on these dialectical models contributes to the static, objectified existence of ancestry in the modern world. Ancestors and past cultural moments become *dead* in these dialectical, historical models as new generations convert their living histories into "the inert totality of worked matter." Armstrong's description of syndetic aesthetics explains how prior generations are not left behind or "killed" by the dialectics of historical memory. As Bradley's adaptation of syndetic systems suggests, past ideas are not replaced by new ones, and the apparent contradictions need not be resolved in synthesis. Inter-generational and contemporaneous relationships do not always interact toward consensus unities, but exist in relation to each other, producing a complex mix of past and present, *past-presence.* These are the cultural processes which enabled the late Malcolm Shabazz, Toni Morrison, and Audre Lorde to envision communities of plu-

ralist unities, including contemporaneous and inter-generational relationships; Morrison names this syndetic tension "a conflict, not a problem." Through syndetic processes, . . . past generations *live* to (re)assert their influence through the consciousness of descendants in communal rituals involving drumming, dance, and oral narrative.

The third shift investigates the applicability of Bakhtin's ideas of dialogic variability in written language to oral, tonal African-American cultural processes. By this theoretical adaptation the potentially subversive power of Bakhtin's thought supports analysis of African-American cultural moments in which artist and audience cooperate toward "communal dialogics." "Communal dialogics" highlight the importance of an emergent African-American aesthetic *mode* in which tone links variable, improvised interpretations of language. Through antiphonal exchange which generates the terms of shared experience, black people such as John Washington and his ancestors—and, at least potentially, certain white people as well—*hear* each other through the cultural noise of Bakhtin's dialogic heteroglossia.

The final shift is particularly crucial to understanding the importance of Bradley's contribution to the rerouting of the diasporic quest. In *Marxism and the Philosophy of Language,* Volosinov/Bakhtin alludes to the danger of the process of reification and appropriation of subversive utterances which "inevitably [lose] force, denigrating into allegory and becoming the object not of live social intelligibility but of philological comprehension." Black underground cultural products, at least momentarily, *will* become commodities of mainstream culture. Given the modern communal dimensions of black life, this must play an integral role in the existence, or not, of above-underground *modes.* This process of rampant commodification and reproduction of the "signs of language," to Volosinov/Bakhtin, inevitably negates the improvised flexibility, the "multiaccentuality" of language into "uniaccentual" products at the service of dominant ideology. . . .

Ellison's narrator in *Invisible Man* progresses through the negative dialectics of the novel, systematically refusing to acknowledge the necessities for above-underground, communal subversion of historical order. Bledsoe, Brockway, Brother Jack, Tod Clifton, and others present the narrator with various versions of the lesson that above- and underground lives are separate and incompatible. The narrator's presence connects these realms, producing the sequence of explosions. Ellison's above-underground pedagogues—primarily Grandfather, Mary Rambo, Peter Wheatstraw, Rinehart, and Dupree—offer the narrator invaluable advice "routed" in his ancestry and present path. Rambo's blues, Wheatstraw's jazz vision of communal renewal through improvisations based on his collection of blue(s)prints, Rinehart's *hyper*-fluidity, and Grandfather's subjective *past-*

presence all offer alternatives to the strictly underground seclusion in which the alienated narrator opens and closes the novel.

In *The Chaneysville Incident,* John Washington slowly works through his reliance on ritual grounds located within enclosed, controllable, and solitary spaces. John's accreting consciousness incorporates mobile, communal, and oral/syndetic processes of invocation as he searches for connections to, and through, his ancestors. As John's syndetic sensibility accretes, he attains his ability to (re)voice the story of the ancestors. The underground process of Ellison's hibernating narrator emerges as the oral/syndetic process of John's ancestral invocation emerges in print. Through this *re*-construction, the supra-rational possibilities embodied in Peter Wheatstraw, Rinehart, Rambo, Dupree, and other *Invisible* above-underground pedagogues emerge in the aboveground presence of the body/community, while underground processes of the mind begin to combine in syndetic, improvised interrelation. . . .

Throughout *Shadow and Act,* Ellison argues the idea that African-American artists can and should choose their intellectual ancestry based on individual need, free from consideration of historical period, ideological predilection, or allegiance to essentialist racial identity. But without communal grounding, his narrator (who should not be confused with his creator) wanders through the modern landscape endangering himself and others, causing explosion after explosion. The haunting question at the heart of the ascent narrative Ellison's narrator pursues, which leads to limiting hibernation, raises crucial issues with [bell] hooks's understanding of isolation as a preparatory "context of autonomy." To what extent can personal growth occurring through isolated process be used "in public," toward communal goals? True, the personal self comprises part of the healthy communal whole, but the process of (re)establishing continuity between self and others becomes increasingly difficult as the period of seclusion lingers. Can significant steps toward what Judylyn Ryan calls the recuperation of double-consciousness, toward personal and communal "wholeness," take place in isolation? Through individual narrative quests, two of the most common and potentially debilitating modern, European cultural impositions are accented: first, the belief in the epistemological superiority of underground solitude; second, the flawed assumption that reflective subjectivity entails an immobile state of introspective concentration.

For African-Americans, these personal recuperative states often engage with "afrocentric" notions of a spiritual return to Africa. This accents the tension between hooks's faith in healing aloneness and attempts to recuperate a grounding with West African cultural identities founded on orally inflected, communal ways of being. The question, then, to hooks becomes: What do we mean by *alone?* Is it freedom

from burdens of communal responsibility which draws Ellison's narrator? Or is it a place for communion with ancestors and meditation on the present—and *past-presence* of—connections? In the case of the latter, "alone" does not seem an adequate phrasing.

While cautionary in framing his characters' ancestral and communal choices, David Bradley creates a character who starts in a state of deep alienation, reminiscent of Ellison's narrator, and, in part through denial of epistemological assumptions rooted in white modernist conceptions of solitude, grows toward meaningful contact with his ancestors. His process *moves* from solitary "underground" excavation based in historical methodology into a syndetic process in which his rationalist, historical process *interacts*—is not replaced—with oral/communal methods in the emergence *mode.* Enabled by the "accretion" of his own syndetic sensibility, which allows "previous" cultural cycles, to interact with "current" cycles, John Washington leads his ancestors and himself toward more meaningful understandings of the continuities between and within spirit-world and earth-bound communities. Importantly, Bradley gives detailed accounts of the micro-processes through which the connections are made.

By the end of the book, an undeniable process of growth is established but the text comes to no climactic resolutions. As in *The Autobiography of Malcolm X,* in which full identification with Malcolm through all of his phases and growth is impossible, Bradley forces the reader to acknowledge and accept, not resolve, the contradictions in the book in order to effect entry into the above-underground *mode.* The "resolution" of the emergence narrative need not find John Washington putting his newly constructed method and excavation to use in the above-underground. While it would add a dimension to the narrative, the absence of a fully realized image of social/political engagement simply calls for another syndetic cycle. As it is, Bradley's above-underground achievement establishes a detailed account of the generation of a syndetic process of oral, communal historical recovery embedded in print for readers to invoke. To those uneasy with the hanging potential of the novel's end, Jamaican dub poet Mutabaruka recalls the aesthetics of invocation. To reroute the words of Mutabaruka's "Dis Poem" (from *The Mystery Unfolds*), Bradley's novel will disappoint "because dis poem is to be continued in your mind." . . .

In *The Chaneysville Incident,* John Washington has dedicated his historical/professional life to studying the most condemnable aspects of American history. Old Judge Scott asks John how he handles frustration when "'searching for truth,'" and John indicates that, rather than seeking truth, he's "'trying to find out where the lies are. . . . I specialize in the study of atrocities.'" John's professional life, packed full of "atrocious" American history, and personal life—in the "filtered," not "distilled" company of Judith—protects him from the idea that his personal elders (Jack and his mother) and ancestors (especially, but not exclusively, Moses Washington) require from him more than historical method and appropriate scorn.

While in *Invisible Man,* the narrator's naïveté leads him toward uncritical adoption of aboveground positions in the city, leading to revelatory explosions which push him underground, John Washington has managed to freeze one of Ellison's dialectical explosions and carve within it a professional place for himself as an invisible historian in the American academy. Far from the self-revelatory but risky pursuit of familial ancestry which he abandoned before entering college, John has secluded himself in Stepto's "symbolic north" with a living and, he assumes, breathing symbol of the enemy ancestors. John rebukes Judith's early challenges to his protected professionalism:

> "Is that what being a historian means—hating for things that don't mean anything anymore?"

> "No," I said, "No, it means hating for things that still mean something. And trying to understand what it is they mean, so you can hate the right things for the right reasons."

As John's last remaining Black male elder, Jack, calls him to the healing vulnerability of contact with his ancestors, Bradley asserts the ambivalence of African-American ancestry, understood in expansive terms. While bringing the resulting paradox to consciousness, John faces a point of no return; with the scars at the surface, the need for recuperation becomes immediate; seclusion and denial are no longer alternatives. This realization alone illuminates no viable direction:

> . . . those of us who count black people among our ancestors (they are never *all* our ancestors) must live together with both. . . . It is not that we must choose between traditions. . . . It is not even that we are caught between some dialectical battle between African thesis and European antithesis. . . . No, the quandary is that there is no comfort for us either way. For if European knowledge is true, then death is cold and final, and one set of our ancestors had their very existence whipped and chained and raped and starved away, while the other set—a larger proportion than any of us would like to admit—forever burns in Hell for having done it to them. And if the African belief is true, then somewhere here with us . . . *all* of it . . . is still going on.

Here John faces the seemingly unresolvable frustration which African-American, double-conscious identity contains. Any

move toward a resolution of the dissonant, convergent flows of African-American ancestry results in a reduction of the complexity from which African-American experience emanates. Any synthetic system seeking resolution toward unitary, centered consciousness must here choose its amputations and accept only fragmented access to the ancestors' legacy. Through the syndetic, non-resolved model, however, the contradictions remain, moving in and out of conflict with each other as the descendant maintains contact with *all* dimensions of the story.

Even as Jack (rė)opens in John the space for the discovery of his familial ancestry, he, knowingly or not, sets John up. Having applied Moses's intellectual gifts in creating this sophisticated model of ancestry while still trapped in the racial and gender essentialisms which allowed Jack to survive—Jack manipulates but does not master his surroundings—John faces this seemingly inescapable ancestral paradox. The assimilation of the paradox into the syndetic process—the how of the healing puzzle—requires the dismantling of the binary structure which holds intellect and intuition; historical order and folk/mythic chaos; and, in the end, self, ancestors, and community, separate and mutually unknown. These theoretical separations hold the key to John's existential separations from his familial ancestors, including his father, and his earth-bound community, including Judith.

Before Judith's arrival in the underground, John's hunting trip signals the beginnings of the process in which the distinctions of Jack's world give way to the fluid syndetic sensibilities of Moses's plura-dimensional psyche. John's narration of the hunt expresses his understanding that, while intuiting—tracking or trailing—a deer, a man does not become an animal, but combines human intellect with animal intuition, since humans are, after all, simultaneously both. "I made my move without thinking. . . . I was working on a new question now, trying to sense how high up to go. . . . [U]sing a little logic too now . . . I found the right spot." But his syndesis of intellect and the natural world, inevitably partial, leads him to settle in a place where he "wait[s] for [the deer] to come within [his] range" while believing that his wait is "not a question of time. There was no time." John fails to recognize that in the absence of linear time, a watch and/or a deadline, "time" exists. More fluid, given to qualitative periods when "time flies"—or, in his case, "crawls"—this non-linear time compounds John's cold and static state to the point where it endangers the hunt by blurring the distinction between hunter and hunted:

> I waited. Awareness became discomfort. I waited. Discomfort turned to pain. I waited. The pain became boredom. Then it was dangerous.

As the hunt moves to culmination, John gives in to the ambiguity of solitude and cannot make the shot: "You might believe you're alone, but the truth is, you don't know." Faced with Judith's presence and the difficulty of putting progress made in solitude into communal practice, the rational, Western aspects of John's individual process (re)assert themselves upon his return to his/Jack's cabin.

Losing track of the subtle, fragile, work done "alone" in the woods, John confronts Judith's defensive prying by asserting his commitment to the fundamental separation between his underground process and his aboveground life, symbolized by his relationship with her. By concluding, "'What I'm doing here isn't because I hate you or because I love you. It has nothing to do with you at all,'" John gives Judith's defensive but justifiable indignation an opening where her point can register, or at least find useful voice. Behind her articulation of an undeniably basic level of connection, Judith invades John's intensely individual process where, from the inside, she continues to prod while his resistance grows feeble. In one of the last breaths of a failing solipsism, John shows his uncertainty: "'Struggling . . . is like defecation. It's natural and necessary, but it's vulgar, and ought to be done in private.'"

"Burdened" by having to explain to Judith, John begins first to recognize, then to overcome the limiting schisms in Jack's "natural" world, thereby freeing the syndetic, intuitive intellect of Moses in himself. An early stage of this process surfaces in John's interrogation of the authority of science, math and physics, over letters and history, proclaiming that ". . . Newton himself . . . in his later years, referred to mathematics and physics as 'recreations' and turned his mature attention to questions of history; in particular, to the fundamental problem of chronology." John deconstructs the hierarchy but leaves the structure in place. By the end of his interactive process, John knows that history is itself profoundly *re*creative. By finding that the lives of the ancestors mirror, parallel, and depend upon the lives of descendants and vice-versa, John's process shows how, as the *recreations* swirl, the ordering in syndetic processes of accretion becomes ambiguous. Because Bradley depicts underground process rather than translating to the aboveground audience via an omnipotent narrator, "trailing" John's incremental flow toward his ancestors becomes necessary.

Continuing to challenge barriers with the "help" of Judith's unnerving and, at times, downright annoying prodding, John takes another step toward facing his (re)creative historical task: "'Part of it is just deduction. . . . But there's more to it than reasoning. . . .'" "'Imagination?'" Judith responds. "'No,'" John answers, "'There's no imagination in it. You can't create facts. But you can discover the connections.'" John's most entrenched resistance concerns his conception of the sequential—essentially linear, chronological—process through which "connections" are made. John's notion that

discovery and connection constitute discrete acts mirrors Locke's idea of experience as the product of distinct, ordered acts of perception and reflection. John's commitment to this logocentric, one-two methodological combination inhibits his revelatory performance. While rightly accusing Judith of wanting him to subvert, or invert, this system, John resists the necessary, creative oral moment as well as the risky, uncontrollable level of honesty—"distilled," not "filtered"—produced via this inversion of rational process: "'. . . you want me to tell you things before I understand them.'" Twenty pages later, the struggle continues, but *not* in private: "'There's nothing to tell you,'" responds John.

"'That's the problem, I've got lots of facts and none of them connect.'" When Judith replies, "'And of course, you won't tell me until you know all the answers,'" John objects, "'Look . . . that's the way I am.'" The demise of John's logocentrism works out through spatial relocation of the increasingly less individual discovery process to the field. The implicit questioning of the epistemological viability of stationary solitude signals a change from conceptions of the underground as a fixed and defensible place of seclusion to the mobile and communal above-underground *mode.*

The initial word of the chapter "197903120400 (Monday)" reveals John's movement through the first syndetic cycle which will eventually lead to the redemption of his connection to his ancestry—the telling of "their" story. "*We* came slamming down off the Hill . . ." (emphasis added) signals that John has given in to the seemingly unpopular idea that pursuit of rites of passage do not have to be, in fact sometimes cannot be, performed in stationary solitude. When the method of recovery is oral, an audience, and an interactive one at that, constitutes an essential piece of the questing mission. Judith's specialized medical knowledge of the spread of epidemics allows her to contribute to the telling of John's story early in the process of collaboration. The accretion of the process, keyed by an important moment to follow, allows Judith to assume her role as an audience/community member and contribute in different, more effective ways to John's search for connections and words. In this epistemological process the story literally does not exist before it is told. The process of telling and the information told are mutually dependent. . . .

The margins of the audience, the community, those who are able to hear stories of dispersions and "track" their own—connected, *not* solitary—routes through communal histories are fluid, especially in undergrounds of "less" mediated communication, co-presence. Rituals which establish confidence and reciprocal responsibility between listeners and performers are enigmatic when they take place in the underground, and more so when mediated by aboveground market maximization. In mass-distribution market society, finding the listeners/readers who will respect the dialogic responsibility and invest in meaning, *any* meaning, becomes a task something akin to separating oxygen molecules from water in George Clinton's "Aqua Boogie," which invokes the possibility of "danc[ing] underwater without getting wet." The above-underground storyteller/writer must weave a context through which the story becomes *audible* to the listeners while simultaneously filtering the deafening incoherence of responses emanating from *supra*-communal consumers. In short, artists involved in this process need an audience, a critical Amen Corner which grounds the syndetic process in a democratic exchange between the impulse of the artist and the needs of the community.

Bound by audience to the dialogic epistemological and performance ritual, John must receive Judith into his community before he can free himself, his ancestors, and what he still conceives of as "his" story. John's telling the story to Judith should not be understood as a veiled message of inter-racial harmony on a macro-level; Bradley certainly acknowledges racial animosity. Judging by John's comments and Judith's reactions, the relationship probably developed out of John's need to abuse "a daughter of the confederacy" and flourished by his catering to Judith's sub-conscious need to repent for "her" ancestors' oppression of "John's." John's ability to "receive" Judith into his community/audience has ambiguous implications for their relationship to each other—it may signal the beginning or the end—but it surely has profound implications for John's relationship to himself and his ancestors. Whether their story is told through Jack's rooted, or Moses's routed, world view holds profound consequences for John's ability to tell and (re)tell the story based upon syndetic process. James Baldwin attested to the reciprocal prison which rigid (racial, gender, and otherwise) classification becomes, especially when employed on intimate, personal levels:

> There is a great instructive irony in this. That the image one is compelled to hold of another person—in order, as I have said, to retain one's image of oneself—may become that person's trial, his cross, his death. It may or may not become his prison: but it inevitably becomes one's own. . . . it is simply not possible for one person to define another. Those who try soon find themselves trapped in their own definitions.

Not at all in the abstract, John must "release" Judith in order to conceive of himself in a way which will enable him to subvert Jack's limited legacy and free Moses and the other above-underground ancestors from "death," indeed suicide, in the white world's historical narrative.

Frustrated with the search in the snow for the lost grave of his grandfather, C. K. Washington, John comes to the crucial decision about the dimensions of the fluid margins of community, and his story-process nearly succumbs to Jack's essentialist conceptions. For an instant, John wants to create the certainty, enact the repudiation, and corroborate the suspicions about Judith's ancestors' role in the slave trade. Then, he wants to tell her that she is, indeed, a contemptible descendant of slavers who has no business with him on this search. He pauses, and decides to go on. As he watches Judith's flailing attempts to aid in his search, he thinks:

> . . . just for a minute I wanted to tell her, tell her all about how Richard Iiames had come with Joseph Powell, grandson of Thomas, brother of John, captain of the *Seafoam;* for a minute I wanted to watch her face when I told her that. . . . She just went kicking across the slope, her feet throwing up frenzied clouds of snow. I didn't say anything, feeling the anger going out of me as she kicked, knowing what she was feeling, what it was like to go that way, searching, not knowing how, or for what. And I knew what it would be like for her when she failed to find anything at all.

But she didn't. She didn't fail.

Seeing his desperate, blind search mirrored in Judith's actions, John bridges Jack's essentialist—"'It's a *Black, Man's* thing, you wouldn't understand'"—divisions and allows Judith into his community, thus binding himself to the liberating responsibility of an audience. The effects of this bridged understanding are mutual, but not symmetrical, presence as an audience/community member allows Judith to trust John in ways before impossible. In Hurston's terms, if Judith's ears are still unknowing, at least they are "sympathetic." Judith puts herself in fairly rare white company; she knows that she doesn't know and she's still there. After preparing him for their journey by mixing John a toddy, an act, in Jack's mind, which would surely have poisoned the "drink," Judith voices her new-found trust as "'faith. . . . I know. . . . You don't think I understand. You're right; I don't understand. But I believe in you.'" After he accepts his responsibility as a griot, but before he tells the story, John attempts to get Judith to hear the ancestors' song in the wind. Judith responds: "'I can't. . . . I don't know how to listen that way. . . . I know they're there. . . . I can't hear them. But I know you can.'" Responding to the audience/community's acceptance, John Washington, griot, readies himself to track the ancestors. As a symbol of the ancestors' creative, syndetic freedom, as opposed to their Sartrian synthetic objectification—their *death*—Jack's precise words emanate from John as he begins his improvised telling: "'So you want a story, do you? . . . Fetch the candle.'" Prepared to do the work in the "candle light" of history, John begins: "'Yes,' I said, 'I can. I can hear them as they pass. I can't see them—it's misty. But I can hear them.'"

John's submission to the liberating convergence of his identity and process with those of his ancestors allows the underground to emerge through his narrative, creating the above-underground *mode.* In a subtle, and tremendously important, convergence, John's narrative forges a syndetic connection between C. K. Washington's intuitive sense and his own. As the syndetic process of identity exploration and creation subverts the linear historical model and synthetic evolutionary process, John runs out of facts and C. K. Washington leads John's creative telling of C. K.'s story. The ancestors' story takes shape as the descendant learns from the ancestor, animated through the descendant's voice. C. K. helps John overcome his logocentric methodological hang-up, allowing him to take his process past the point at which it was initiated, alone in his father's study and seemingly alone on the hunt. John runs out of *facts* in the telling just as C. K. runs out of *obvious alternatives* in his flight from the slave catchers in the story; the method of telling and the story being told merge into a syndetic, meta-narrative: Which is which and who is whom?

> "Then C. K. [or John?] stopped wondering and worrying and started doing what he should have been doing all along: thinking. Really thinking. Not just gathering facts and ordering them; not just trying to follow them along; *really* thinking, looking at the overall pattern of things and figuring out what the facts *had* to be."

After John and the ancestors achieve the methodological requisites, the two freely mix together. John's Grandmother Harriet's pose behind C. K. with "her hands cupped at the base of his belly" recalls Judith's posture with John at the beginning of the text: Her hand "found the place at the base of my belly." Harriet's story of struggle for control of her body in the face of a white man's sexual advances merges with the story of Mara, the daughter of the Madame who slept with John to avoid prostitution to white men:

> "She [Harriet] had been taken . . . to Alexandria . . . where she was purchased, at a premium because of her light skin, by a young blade . . . who wanted her for a concubine. But she escaped that fate by . . . telling the young man [that she was pregnant with a baby whose father was] as black as the ace of spades."

By this narrative technique, John completes the epistemological transition. He moves from an alienated consciousness rooted in rational processes to the interactive, fluid narration and invocation of communal/familial presence. Here, John takes steps toward de- or un-centered conceptions of personal, supra-individual identity not rooted in "empirically personal experience" but routed through the diverse energies of invoked syndetic familial narrative. By bridging the rational matrices of the literate, historical process, John's identity and the oral presence of his ancestors emerge from the underground of his alienated consciousness into print. The embedding of mobile oral processes in print establishes an important above-underground literary moment. . . .

But who came with him? That Bradley has created an empowering novel is without doubt. The costs, however, of the encoded complexity and the misogynist package are high. While the success resounds, Fredric Jameson's cautionary note rearticulates the need for ritualized pursuit of the goals which Bradley's novel offers to the scant few "individuals" with time, luxury, and inclination to excavate and enjoy it. Jameson's polemic challenges us to weigh theoretical complexity and dialogic coding in print against the restricted audience for these media, strangely revoicing the conclusion of Ellison's narrator—the "winner takes nothing." Jameson writes:

> And it is certain that there is a strange quasi-Sartrian—a "winner loses"—logic which tends to surround any effort to describe a "system," a totalizing dynamic. . . . What happens is that the more powerful the vision of some increasingly total system or logic . . . the more powerless the reader comes to feel. . . . Insofar as the theorist wins, therefore, by constructing an increasingly closed and terrifying machine, to that very degree he loses. . . .

In the dialogic aesthetics of syndetic invocation, the roles of theorist, critic, audience, and artist take on forms which Jameson's "totalizing paradox" does not neatly cover. Where Jameson portrays himself as forging new paths through the wilderness which readers attempt to follow, the present study engages another effort: to highlight and demystify the subtle epistemological and ontological shifts necessary to respond to the full complexity of African-American aesthetic systems. These systems often emerge in performance realms in which continuities *under* the rational matrices of the modern—race, class, genre, gender, dialectical generation—produce the intertextual, philosophical complexity of African-American aesthetics. These subtle shifts constitute a major source of the "dissonance" between the theoretical needs of African-derived and European aesthetics. Hopefully, the work above can aid in establishing productive continuities between theory and critique which make more room for renewed and enhanced engagement between artists and audiences. While Jameson meditates upon the potential alienation of the underground theorist, I hear the communal shifts of the emergence *mode* on the radio. *At least in Chicago.*

This merging of John, C. K., Judith, Harriet, and Mara across racial, spatial, and generational divides recalls exactly the syndetic ancestral presence offered by the Yorùbá systems of ancestor invocation. . . . The descendant acknowledges the complexity of the ancestor's path, honoring the positions in the suicide/liberation continuum.

By means of this process, Ellison's efforts emerge as they are deepened and extended by the next generation of writers. His "victory" has to do with the responses to his process, perceived through this system of aesthetics as an essential aspect of the process itself. Bradley's emergence narrative is not resolved; we all await the next syndetic, *not* dialectic, cycle of responses in print, film, and sound of which this essay intends to be a small part.

Codification, objectification, categorization are what they are. In aesthetics of invocation, grounded, subjective improvisations in syndetic respect of the ancestors create a critical discourse that, in the image of the Yorùbá òrìsà of aesthetic continuity, Èla and/or Òrúnmìlà, consumes itself in its own regeneration. The creative antiphonal exchange requires continuities between media through which the fluidity and integrity of Black expression thrives. By understanding these *modes* in terms of communal dialogic, above-undergrounds of exchange, we can discover and create continuities enhancing the living process itself.

Philip J. Egan (essay date Summer 1997)

SOURCE: "Unraveling Misogyny and Forging the New Self: Mother, Lover, and Storyteller in *The Chaneysville Incident*," in *Papers on Language and Literature,* Vol. 33, No. 3, Summer, 1997, pp. 265-87.

[*In the following essay, Egan traces the origin of narrator Washington's misogyny in* The Chaneysville Incident, *exploring the means by which the narrator is able to overcome it.*]

When David Bradley's *The Chaneysville Incident* appeared in 1981, it received mostly favorable reviews, became a Book-of-the-month Club selection, and won its author a Faulkner/PEN award. While many critics focus on the novel's treatment of history, only a few analyze one of its most important moral issues: misogyny. The prominence particularly of Old Jack Crawley, the protagonist's misogynous (but otherwise attractive) mentor, has earned *Chaneysville* the condemnation of one feminist critic ([Mary Helen] Washington), while the rehabilitation of the narrator has brought praise from another. Neither these nor other commentators, however, have taken the full measure of misogyny in this novel. *Chaneysville,* properly understood, does indeed dramatize one man's tortuous journey out of misogyny. But the tempting view that misogyny finds its source in Old Jack and its redeemer in Judith is only a partial truth; it does justice

neither to the complexity of John's misogyny nor to the means he uses to transcend it.

It helps first of all to establish *Chaneysville's* literary pedigree. Katherine Rogers in her survey of misogyny in literature, claims that male authors of this century, while continuing earlier attacks on domineering wives, old maids, and career women, introduce a new misogynous theme: "fear of Mom." Drawing upon Freud's insights about the Oedipus complex, Lawrence, Hemingway, Faulkner, and a host of other figures dramatize both attachment to the mother and resentment of her; furthermore, the mother's influence often proves so enduring that it haunts the son's adult attachments to women. In *Chaneysville* the prominence of both mother and lover (respectively Yvette Washington and Judith Powell) firmly anchors the novel in this tradition. Here and in other novels of this class, the son in some sort becomes a misogynist—i.e., acquires a deep and abiding distrust of women—from the experience of mother; the question implicitly posed is whether he can outgrow his misogyny later. Any complete treatment of misogyny in this type of work must engage Oedipal issues. Feminist commentary on *Chaneysville,* drawn to the lightning rod of Old Jack's obvious misogyny, tends to overlook the role Yvette Washington plays.

By introducing Old Jack as well as mother and lover, Bradley gives John's attitudes toward women three important sources; but, as important as Yvette, Judith, and Jack are, they remain separate. Apart from the brief sojourn of Old Jack's corpse in Yvette's parlor, they share no scenes with each other in the "present" of the novel. Still, these characters coexist and interact with each other as forces in John's own mind; and, as the novel progresses, they create oppositions and alignments that trace out John's progress against misogyny. Two of these three characters (Yvette and Old Jack) play an important role in the formation of John's misogyny; and two likewise (Judith and again Old Jack) play a role in his transcendence of it. The dual role of Old Jack particularly will surprise some critics; but, while Old Jack the misogynist is clearly a large part of John's problem, a careful reading of John's final tale reveals Old Jack the storyteller and spiritual visionary as a resource John uses for transcendence.

The "present" of *Chaneysville* constitutes only eight days, during which John offers us memories of his own life and stories of times well before that. John, who has raped a white woman in the past but now lives with one, has clearly left behind the worst of his misogyny before the novel begins, and there seems little danger that he will return to it. Still, *Chaneysville* suggests that outgrowing misogyny involves more than merely ceasing to do evil to women; one must *see* women differently. The "present" of the novel dramatizes the end of this process—the recovery of a psychic wholeness which allows him to see women as cosufferers of life's oppressions and coactors in liberation.

Rooted in the deep teachings of Old Jack and the still deeper imperatives to escape a threatening mother, John's misogyny requires both that he confront its sources and that he accept exterior help. Outgrowing misogyny in *Chaneysville,* then, has two large movements treated in the next two parts of this essay. The first of these examines the sources, effects, and resolution (such as it is) of John's problems with his mother. In this movement Bradley works the typical Freudian relationship in reverse: instead of simply representing the mother as blighting the man's adult attachments to women, Bradley has the lover help unravel the misogyny of which the mother is the source. The second part of the essay examines John's relationship with Judith and Old Jack and finds that he gradually brings these warring components of his life together; ultimately John represents these forces with elaborate narrative strategies and balances them in his created vision at the end. By creating his final story of C. K. Washington and Harriette Brewer, John, while using the components of his misogynous past, forges a non-misogynous self.

The discussion of Oedipal issues in a work of literature always runs the danger of reducing the tensions of the work to mere Freudian stereotype. In *Chaneysville,* however, Bradley obviates this danger by mixing Oedipal issues with other (often racial) matters and by allowing us to discover the Oedipal significance of some information only retrospectively. With this understanding, then, we can state that, in classic Freudian terms, John's problem amounts to castration anxiety. Normally centered on the father because of competition for the mother's love, John's castration anxiety reverts to Yvette after his father's suicide. Indeed, beginning with Moses's funeral, John increasingly finds his mother an oppressive presence, and he subsequently associates her with images of engulfment typical of a castration fear. Bradley's art in dealing with this fear is the gradually increasing depth it acquires and the different guises in which it appears. Ultimately, Oedipal tensions are significant largely because John is released from them; Yvette disappears at the end of the seventh chapter, after which John's unblocked creative powers can get beyond her. The Oedipal tensions of the first two-thirds of the novel, however, powerfully shape John's experience in ways that we need to recognize in order to understand Bradley's art in the final portion.

Bradley reveals the sources and depth of John's fear and resulting misogyny only gradually. At the beginning of the novel John clearly has a serious problem with his mother that amounts to a kind of hatred. Consciously, John experiences his mother-hate as a result of racial issues; even these, however, have Oedipal dimensions, and John's subconscious extends his fear to a much larger psychological realm. The most well-defined problem John has with Yvette is her too-ready submission to requirements of white society—her Uncle Tomism, in short. John presents one memory in which she wallops him across the head and subsequently warns, "so long as [white people are] teaching you what you need to learn, you have to be quiet and careful, and respectful. Because you've got your head in the lion's mouth." Yvette's crowning offense in this domain is convincing Bill, John's younger brother, to enlist in the army—John had primed him to flee to Canada—and then creating a flag-draped shrine in Bill's memory after his death in Vietnam. Since his brother's funeral, John has not been home; at the opening of the novel he is still bitter about Yvette's role in Bill's enlistment and death.

John, however, has a still deeper if less well-defined resentment of his mother: a fear of her unmaternal coldness. The scene in which she strikes John describes her face as "cold, determined, almost murderous" and echoes with the phrase *persona non grata,* which she applies to John. This fear becomes clearest, however, when John describes his recurring nightmare, which always begins with his mother bathing his head in ice water in apparent concern for a fever; soon, however, he realizes that she is trying to kill him, and he flees into a wintry landscape first to face the terror of an impassable gorge, then to encounter some warmth and comfort with Old Jack, and finally to engage in futile searches involving a buck and his father. The dream ends as John suffers "an all-encompassing sensation of icy coldness, and a visual image of total white" which engulf him "like an avalanche of snow" and from which he always has trouble awakening. If we concede that this final image—imprisonment in a cold womb-like existence—is a very negative female image, then the Wicked Mother and the Evil Female Principle become the alpha and omega of John's nightmare. The progression, moreover, gives the dream the power of psychological archetype and suggests that Yvette is the specific source of a more general fear of women—an indictment all the more powerful for being subconscious and therefore beyond rational dispute. Moreover, in this portion of the novel, several instances of Yvette's behavior, from her brisk conduct at Moses's funeral to her quick construction of Bill's patriotic shrine seem to confirm the indictment.

Obviously an important set piece, John's dream resonates with other important scenes that occur both before and after it. One of these is John's first meeting with Old Jack, in which, on the night after Moses's funeral, he slips out the window and makes his way to the other side of the Hill. At the funeral earlier that day, John tells us that his mother was dry-eyed, cool, and efficient; middle-aged women "of various shapes, sizes, and shades" dominate the proceedings at the funeral reception, and John feels oppressed by the odor of dying flowers and cheap perfume as well as by the image of desiccated masculinity his maternal grandfather presents; his brother Bill sits on the couch, "the soft pillows rising around him, seeming to swallow him"—a portentous image of engulfment in light of the blame John casts on Yvette later for Bill's death. When Old Jack, drunk, intrudes upon this pious group, he is expelled onto the street, where he remains "on all fours, his head hanging, his tongue lolling." Although Jack hardly presents an attractive image here, John, lying in bed later that night, thinks the group was "*wrong* [Bradley's emphasis]" to be frightened of him. By seeking Jack through the threatening dark, John expresses a profound dissatisfaction with the mother-dominated world of the funeral. Jack commences John's misogynous training almost at once, but even so Jack is not inscribing his misogyny on a blank slate. John senses that Old Jack, misogyny and all, fills an important need. The dream expresses with Gothic vividness the motives which the funeral scene hints at. In both scenes John flees the oppressions of women (led by his mother) to what looks at the time like safety or liberation. The greatest affront to feminism in *Chaneysville,* then, is not the role of Old Jack but of Yvette. Misogyny appears rooted in John's developmental imperative to escape the mother.

The novel, of course, does not allow matters to rest there. The subconscious operation of John's mother-hate, boosted by Old Jack's misogyny, poisons John's life even as it disguises his motives. When he explains to Judith that he has raped a white woman, John claims his reason is revenge against whites for Bill's death in Vietnam, leaving Yvette barely mentioned in the episode. However, John might have taken any of a variety of actions to express his outrage against whites. Why does he rape a woman who in fact shares his opposition to the war? And why does John treat this woman with consideration and deference before Bill's funeral only to return to rape her directly afterward? Surely John learns nothing new about the "white power structure" at Bill's funeral; Bradley subtly reveals, however, that John has reason at the funeral to see his mother in a new and horrifying light. John reveals this new vision in the "present" of the novel when he describes the shrine his mother had set up in Bill's honor:

> She had [set up the shrine] with a speed too great to be termed deliberate: she had received the telegram and long before whatever had been scraped out of the body bag and smeared into a coffin had been delivered to a local undertaker . . . long before she had informed me, she had taken the pictures [from both Bill's school and military years] and she had put them, together with the telegram (which she had framed) and the other nonsense that surrounded his dying and burying, on a flag-draped table at the far end of the dining room. . . . she deserved a lot of credit for having got him out of the family portrait gallery in the only decent way: she had got him

killed and then she had enshrined him. She had kicked him upstairs.

The bitter tone in this passage might almost make us overlook the importance of the information it conveys. Because Yvette sets up this shrine quickly, before informing John of his brother's death, it is in place for him to see when he goes home for the funeral. The passage furthermore suggests that Yvette not only accepts Bill's death but has directly caused it and indeed has somehow *willed* it. If John has ever felt castration anxiety toward his mother it would surely start to life again when he viewed this shrine. When John returns to his unfortunate dinner companion after the funeral, he undoubtedly does feel antipathy toward whites; but the rage that expresses itself *in rape* is more Oedipal than racial because his victim stands in for the woman he *really* hates but cannot do violence to directly. In the transfer of his mother-hatred to another woman, John's misogyny reaches its nadir. This Oedipal transfer, however, operates beneath his consciousness. By saying that he rapes this woman because she is white, John covers the deeper horror of mother-hatred with the more acceptable (because "political") motive of racial hatred. His still-recurring nightmare, however, reflects his real motive. At the most immediate level, women become for him the spoilers of masculine fun and inspiration. (Both Yvette and Judith, for example, favor coffee over liquor.) At the highest and most threatening level, however, women become the rather eager celebrants of masculine death.

Part of Bradley's art in *Chaneysville* is the subtlety with which events and revelations gradually dispute the threatening interpretation of Yvette and women suggested in John's nightmare. In order to outgrow misogyny, John must first discard the vision of his mother as an inhuman "force" and recover a sense of her humanity; and he begins to do so, despite his wariness, shortly after he relates the dream. In this process he experiences several views of her "for the first time." In one of her clumsy attempts to manipulate him, John discovers that "for the first time I could recall, she looked old." Later, Yvette surprises John by tearfully coming forward to eulogize Old Jack as a brother to her husband and a teacher to her son.

Even more important in this movement is that John reveals that he becomes cold in his own right. From very early in his life John has a general "desire to know." Moses often enjoyed watching John take apart toys to see how they worked; on the day of Moses's funeral John behaves in a numbed fashion, wanting only to be left alone so he could figure out "the what of it, so that I could then begin to figure out the why of it. Then I would understand it. So then I could figure out what I needed to do." During adolescence—the same time in which his nightmares begin—John discovers that, in opposing white racism, "[k]nowing nothing can get you humiliated and knowing a little bit can get you killed, but knowing all of it will bring you power." His quest to know "all of it," however, amounts to a broad philosophical conversion to rationalism that influences every aspect of his life. Not only does it allow him to refute cherished white notions of history and eventually to gain graduate degrees, but it also exacts an emotional price. At this point in his life John has an affair with Mara Jamison, the daughter of a prostitute for white men, who comes to John in hopes of avoiding her mother's destiny. Although he loves her, John reveals that at one point he "sat down with a piece of paper . . . and figured out" that in the long run she couldn't resist the economic temptations of her mother's profession, because decently-paying jobs didn't exist for black people. Acting somewhat like Hawthorne's Ethan Brand, he calculatedly withholds his commitment from Mara and simply observes as she first resists, and then slips into, the prostitution he had predicted for her. Also at this point John becomes alienated from Old Jack in part because he gains the knowledge to reject Jack's spiritual explanation of the sounds in the wind.

If the dream seems a powerful (and true) indictment of Yvette on first view in the fourth chapter of *Chaneysville*, it takes on a different significance in light of John's rationalism. At the same time he begins to suffer his recurrent nightmare, John is immersed in the quest to "know it all" through transcriptions of evidence to index cards, is involved with Mara from whom he deliberately withholds his love, and is preparing to reject Old Jack's spiritual values. Because John's own mind produces the nightmare, perhaps it is less an accusation of Yvette than a projection of blame onto her for a cold detachment in his life that is largely self-inflicted. Instead of telling the truth, perhaps John's dream is making excuses.

John completes the process of recovering his sense of his mother's humanity in the final scene with her, which in some ways hearkens back to both the nightmare and to Moses's funeral. One of the most important pivots on which the mother-and-lover theme turns, this scene has not gotten its due from academic critics. Just before this scene, John, having made love to Judith in Jack's cabin, rises in the predawn darkness, intending to walk out to the site of Moses's suicide in Chaneysville and to walk back. Worse than quixotic, John's intention reads like a parody of some "masculine" feat: with only a flask of whiskey for sustenance, he would travel forty-five miles, alone and on foot, in frigid, post-blizzard conditions. In following his father's footsteps out to Chaneysville, John takes a covertly suicidal action; if he does not consciously plan his death, his project clearly risks it. Before he is underway, however, he sees Yvette's house and cannot help reflecting that Moses did not "care enough about the effect of [his suicide] on his wife—and his children—to try to make it look like an accident; a man who showed her no mercy. And then I thought of Judith, waking in the morn-

ing to find me gone." This passage suggests that John himself recognizes the suicidal risk in his project; moreover, his analogy (Moses : Yvette : : John : Judith) causes him to enter his mother's house for the following conversation. (The final portion of the scene is quoted here at length because of its muted drama, its thematic importance, and its subtlety, which requires careful reading.) John asks Yvette, "Why did you marry [Moses]?"—which leads to the following exchange:

> "We were allies," she said. "We didn't want the same things, but what we each wanted was close enough. . . . I wanted children, he wanted sons. He wanted two sons. He said that at the very beginning. I said I hoped he knew you couldn't always control that kind of thing. He said he could. He had read and studied a lot of books and the Laws of the Old Testament, and he said that if we lived the way the children of Israel lived, then we would have sons. So we did. Part of the month he would sleep in the other room. And we had sons. And after your brother was born, that was the end of . . . that part of things. Because he had what he wanted, and I had what I wanted. . . ."

> "Didn't you ever want anything else?"

> "You mean love?" she said.

> I didn't say anything.

> "Yes," she said. "I wanted it. I suppose you could say I didn't get it. Moses didn't love the way most people would think a man should love. . . . I don't know. I had what he gave me. Maybe it was love, maybe it wasn't."

> "Was it worth it?"

> She didn't say anything. But suddenly I could hear her breathing, there in the darkness.

> "Was it?" I said. "Was it worth it?"

> I heard her move then, heard the bedsprings creak as she reached out and turned the radio back on. I heard it hum as the tubes warmed.

> I turned away from her then, and went into the powder room, wondering if I was doing the right thing, or even a kind thing; if Moses Washington's way had not been better; if she had not, when they came to tell her that her life with him was a finished incident, breathed, somewhere inside of her, a tiny sigh of relief. I stood there in the smell of the hair

pomade and stale perfume and wondered. But then the radio began to crackle again, and some insane insomniac began to chatter about the salvation of God, and I took the keys down and slipped them into my pocket and quietly went away.

The scene exposes the emotional barrenness of Yvette's life: Moses uses her for his narrow purpose, subjecting her all the while to bizarre and archaic beliefs about conception—and then he abandons her. His suicide leaves her alone in bed keeping company with a vulgar right-wing talk show. Despite all this, Yvette refuses the easy opportunity to whine a great deal about Moses's abuse of her; instead, she focuses on the ambiguity of it all: "I had what he gave me. Maybe it was love, maybe it wasn't." Typically, John doesn't give us his reaction to her statements, but it's a fair guess that, as a man of silences himself, he admires her stoicism. Furthermore, John's insistent question, "Was it worth it?" remains hanging in a haunting way because of the logic visible in Yvette's non-answer: she married Moses for children; one is dead and the other is John. Her unwillingness to say it was "worth it" amounts to a stinging critique of what her living son has become.

The final paragraph shows Bradley at his subtlest. Indeed, a first-time reader will scarcely recognize the nature of the decision John considers as he stands in the powder room. John, however, is still in the grip of the analogy between himself and Moses. In deciding whether or not to take the keys to Yvette's car, John is actually making the larger decision between "Moses Washington's way" and some other way. The car itself symbolizes the alternative; forbidden to own a car during Moses's lifetime, Yvette purchases it shortly after his death in an act of deferred defiance. John considers whether "Moses Washington's way had not been better" even for Yvette, who might well have felt relieved because of his suicide. While some critics consider it possible that John himself commits suicide at the end of the novel, he in fact confronts that threat even more directly in this passage: "Moses Washington's way," of course, was to offer no explanations to anyone but simply to walk out to Chaneysville and kill himself. Both Yvette (and by implication Judith) might feel relieved at John's own disappearance from their lives.

In different ways this scene evokes both the funeral scene and John's nightmare. The stale perfume of the powder room recalls the stifling atmosphere of the funeral scene and, by understanding her relief at Moses's suicide, John in essence forgives Yvette's cool and efficient behavior on that occasion. Because suspicion that a mother has wished the father's death can be a potent source of fear—and thus of misogyny—in male children, John's understanding of Yvette's "relief" at Moses's death unravels a major knot in his personal history. In addition to its allusions to the funeral, the

entire scene threatens to play out his earlier nightmare in reality. In the dream, his mother's hostility drives him out of the house into the cold, into a futile quest to decode his father's life, and into ultimate imprisonment in an "avalanche of snow." In this scene, John, in his mother's very bedroom, hears her refusal to say her life with Moses was "worth it" for his sake—and considers following Moses, risking literal death in the snow drifts surrounding Chaneysville.

What apparently sways John against his risky project, however, is the radio show Yvette has been listening to. Earlier in the scene Bradley makes clear that the show features bigoted callers expressing remarkably ignorant and racist opinions. (John overhears one outrageous reference to the middle passage: "My grandfather had to fight to get here, and [blacks] didn't have to do a thing.") By taking the keys to Yvette's car, John, by proxy, decides to break the analogy between himself and Moses. This means first that he must live; he must subordinate what seem to be the necessities of his personal quest to his responsibilities in a bigoted world. Second, this means that he must not treat Judith as Moses has treated Yvette. John takes the keys in the final words of the seventh chapter; the eighth chapter begins with John and Judith driving together to Chaneysville. While technically an act of theft, the taking of Yvette's car on this mission has a far different psychological significance: unlike his father or Old Jack, John has decided to accept the help of women in a matter that touches him most. Toward Judith, the decision amounts to an act of trust; toward Yvette it constitutes a peculiar recognition of sonship.

John's ride toward Chaneysville in his mother's car and his lover's company, full of the dangers of negotiating snowy conditions, might symbolize both the pleasures and perils of his new partnership. With the help of mother and lover, he conquers the very landscape that overwhelms him in his dream. His mother's contribution (the car) takes them only part way; but Judith camps with him in the snow and accompanies him into the very heart of the mystery. Whereas the dream reflects John's inability to solve the puzzle of his father's life and death, the trip to Chaneysville with Judith yields, albeit tentatively, the solution to that very puzzle. Indeed, Judith herself makes the key discovery when she stumbles upon what John takes to be C. K.'s grave.

Fruitful as it is, their joint trip to Chaneysville might never have taken place without John's final conversation with his mother. While Judith and Yvette never speak, this scene still in some sense makes these characters "overlap" in John's life: it is the only time John talks to Yvette *after* Judith has arrived. As Gliserman points out, Judith is, archetypally, a "good" mother who replaces the "bad" mother, Yvette; and indeed Judith plays something of a nurturant, even motherly, role in her sexual relations with John just before his final scene with Yvette. Her tender engulfment of John in their lovemaking opposes the images of threatening engulfment in his dream and in other associations with Yvette. But Bradley insists that Oedipal tensions be satisfied. Judith's warmth and sympathy, however regenerating they are, do not allow John to trust her immediately; rather, this tenderness enables John to hear his mother out. Only after seeing Yvette's life from Yvette's point of view and recovering his sense of her humanity, can he treat Judith equitably. Mother and lover, while ignorant of each other, become allied forces in John's psychic makeup; in complementary scenes, they unravel his mother-based misogyny.

While Judith and Yvette may seem natural allies in dealing with John's misogyny, Judith and Old Jack seem destined, from *Chaneysville's* opening pages, to be warring factions. Academic critics have given worthwhile treatments of both Judith and Old Jack, but they have not explained the relationship these characters develop as forces in John's psychic makeup or the way John synthesizes their influences. Although Judith and Jack never speak directly to each other, they do "converse" after a fashion within John's mind by means of juxtaposed scenes. Indeed, two such juxtapositions, one early in the novel and one late, mark the large second movement of the mother-and-lover theme. The early juxtaposition begins as John tries to convince Old Jack to go to the hospital, which leads to an acrimonious exchange on the virtues of "trustin' white people." At the end of this exchange, Jack alleges that John, in his long absence from home, has softened considerably, guesses that John is involved with a woman, and caps the conversation with a combined question, guess, and indictment: "This woman a yours. She's white woman, ain't she?" In embarrassment at Jack's canny guess, John leaves the cabin to stand out in the falling snow.

During this interlude, John supplies a memory that completes the juxtaposition. In this scene of several years earlier, Judith, unhappy that John fails to talk much about himself, defines (in somewhat clichéd terms) what she thinks is missing: "Trust, I guess. Sharing. Something between [us]." Perhaps to answer her request—or perhaps to punish her insistence by inflicting too much "trust"—John first takes her to his apartment and then reveals that he has raped a white woman out of racial revenge for his brother's death in Vietnam. Although John expects Judith to leave him at this admission, she surprises him by not walking out; the scene ends with Judith simply holding him.

Nor does the "conversation" between Jack and Judith end quite there. John's memory of Judith comes almost at the end of the second chapter; the next chapter contains what might be Old Jack's ultimate rebuttal: a story about a black man who loved and courted a white woman and who is nearly lynched for his efforts. Juxtaposed so obviously, these two scenes and Jack's subsequent story seemingly lock

Judith and Jack in a battle for John's soul: Jack holds out for the venerable old values of the woods, with all their imperatives toward independence, particularly from women; and Judith represents the humane-but-softening values of "trust," "sharing," and inclusion of women in matters of importance. But if the novel were so formulaic as this, its problem would be a false one because Judith has in a large degree already "won" before the story opens. Far from simply shedding Jack and accepting Judith, John's mind seeks something more complex and difficult: to integrate the influences of both in his own personality so that they may coexist with each other and perhaps even mutually support each other.

This movement, finally, gives *Chaneysville* its complexity as a psychological journey. It begins in good earnest with the second set of juxtaposed scenes at the beginning of the final chapter and continues through John's invented narrative of C. K.'s final hours. This time the juxtaposition begins with a conversation with Judith and ends with a memory of Jack. Judith and John have just returned from Chaneysville, where John discovers what he thinks is C. K. Washington's grave and the graves of twelve runaway slaves recorded in local legend. John at first irritably rejects Judith's attempt to prod him into telling her more, claiming that "[t]here *aren't* any more facts." Judith responds, "[t]hen forget the facts," and tries to stimulate his inspiration by bringing him a toddy. This is an important concession because Judith has earlier been wary of John's drinking.

John downs the toddy quickly, and, experiencing a drunken vertigo, he suddenly hears the voice of Old Jack and clearly recalls a particularly frustrating hunt. In this memory, John, believing that he had irrevocably lost track of a deer by miscalculating where it would be, is ready to give up the hunt. But Jack won't let him: "You figure too much," Jack tells him. "You ain't lost him. You jest lost your feel for him. He's still there. Quit tryin' to figure where he's at an' jest follow him." As many critics point out, the novel consistently compares hunting deer to John's historical researches. Here, both Judith and Jack pull John in the same direction; both implore him to give up his rationalism and to allow intuition to guide his quest. John responds to both by narrating his ultimate vision of C. K.'s fate. This invented tale further integrates the forces of Judith and Jack as they exist in John's mind; not only do they jointly inspire the story, they jointly influence both its structure and characterizations as well.

The final story's structure falls clearly into two parts. In the first part C. K. Washington diverts Pettis's dogs off the trail of the runaway slaves, intending to meet these slaves later at the mill. This part reaches its climax when, in order to escape Pettis, C. K. must make a daring leap across a gorge in front of his path. The second part of the story takes place at the mill where C. K. reunites with Harriette and at the nearby graveyard where the slaves collectively commit suicide. The story, then, *structurally* integrates the forces of Jack and Judith because its two parts are largely the product of these two characters' influence; jumping between the parts, moreover, requires in its way as much courage of the storyteller—and involves as much of its own kind of peril— as does C. K.'s leap across the gorge.

The first part of this final vision is a chase narrative, full of the logic and emotions of flight and pursuit. As such, this narrative is an homage to Old Jack because it incorporates so much of the knowledge he has passed on to John. Containing no women, this portion of the story presents the man-to-man battle of wits between Pettis and C. K. and involves considerations of the hunt such as scent, wind direction, weather conditions, topography, and backtrail—considerations readers will recognize from several other journeys, chases, and hunts related earlier in the novel, including a couple involving Old Jack himself. Through these earlier narratives Bradley brilliantly establishes the hunting idiom so that John can invoke it in his final vision of C. K. without giving the reader any difficulty. Moreover, as one critic perceptively points out, C. K.'s climactic "uphill" leap across the gorge revisits another aspect of the landscape of John's nightmare where he seems trapped by an impassable gorge with his murderous mother bearing down on him. By including a successful leap of the same gorge, John signals that he conquers a fear associated with both his search and his mother.

C. K.'s successful leap fulfills a second crucial function for C. K.'s narrator as well. When John finishes this portion of the story, he takes a brief break during which Judith makes him another toddy. John sees her "silhouette" as she makes the drink. When she brings the drink and tenderly offers it to him, John reflects that "I knew then that I had underestimated her, and had done it in a way that cheated us both." Resuming his story, he immediately cuts to the mill, where C. K. is looking in to see a female form "silhouetted against the glowing hearth, as she dipped a cup into a small kettle and then handed it to another woman." The silhouetted form, we later learn, is Harriette Brewer. We know from C. K.'s journal that Harriette had been his lover, had gone South to arrange a slave escape, and had simply disappeared, apparently killed or captured in the course of her mission. Her reappearance here is inspired by John's appreciation for Judith. During the narrative of the previous chapter, based upon C. K.'s journal, Judith highlights the romance between C. K. and Harriette. She applauds C. K.'s writing of love poetry for Harriette and speculates that, in planning his own missions to the South after her disappearance, C. K. was in fact looking for Harriette. In recognizing that he had "underestimated" Judith, John apparently decides at that moment to improvise the meeting between C. K. and Harriette, knowing, of course, that such a development would please Judith. The cinematic shift from the silhouette of Judith, making a

toddy to the silhouette of Harriette at the mill further implies Judith's inspiration.

John, in short, is crossing a narrative gap under Judith's influence. This narrative leap, however, is fraught with its own sort of peril. First, in introducing Harriette, John shifts from a narrative of flight and pursuit, which he finds quite natural because of his training in the woods and his frequent hunting, to a narrative of romance, at which John has shown little aptitude in his own life. Lovers sometimes do appear in the earlier narratives of *Chaneysville*—Josh White and Clydette, Zak and Hermia, and C. K. and Harriette—but we rarely see the details of courtship or the specific interactions of marriage. By cutting to Harriette at the mill, John takes the risk of leaping to a new genre.

The second peril posed by Harriette's appearance is a tactical one. Because she has disappeared into the South some years earlier and is unmentioned in the first portion of the story, Harriette's sudden appearance here constitutes the most improbable of coincidences. John risks the credibility of the entire narrative here—and pulls it off. Indeed the metaphor of "leaping a gap" comes naturally in this situation: the story to this point has enough "momentum" to carry the reader over the improbability; and once on the other side, John's story sustains the momentum by making Harriette far more than a mere romantic prop for C. K.

The characterizations of the final story—especially of the second part of it—constitute the second and more important way the story tracks John's progress against misogyny. While introduced by Judith's influence, Harriette in some ways celebrates Judith's qualities. Both Judith and Harriette, for example, exert a humanizing warmth on their lovers. In other ways, however, Harriette does not particularly resemble Judith but incorporates John's experience with women in a broader sense. While her magnificently dynamic character is something new for women in *Chaneysville,* her story, in its underlying forces, bears certain similarities to John's earlier narrative about his failure with Mara Jamison. Like Mara, Harriette Brewer is the daughter of a prostitute catering to white men who scorns her mother's trade; like Mara, she gives up her virginity to an intelligent man of her own race and uses that fact to discourage the attentions of white men; just as Mara saw her relationship with John as the chief escape route for her, so Harriette returns to C. K. upon escaping from slavery. As if to draw attention to this comparison, John gives the name of Mara to one of Harriette's children by her slave husband.

These similarities between Mara and Harriette make the differences stand out in high relief. Harriette and C. K. are much grander figures than either Mara or John—grander not just in their opportunities for courage, but in their aspirations and passions. At the mill Harriette tells an elaborate and heroic story of her past. Given in indirect discourse, it culminates in one of the novel's most startling passages as Harriette reveals that, in order to preserve her escape from betrayal, she cuts her slave husband's throat. This action foreshadows her role at the end and puts her on a par with the best and bravest in the novel. In addition, John postulates a C. K. Washington who has all of John's ability to think but who finally "[s]topped figuring the chances" when the runaway slaves were in danger. As we have seen, it is precisely because John *knows* so much and calculates the futility of Mara's resistance to such a nicety that he refuses to believe sufficiently in their love. In a sense, then, John can partly redeem the pettiness of his courage and the banality of his failure with Mara by imagining parallel characters stronger than he and Mara are: Harriette, notwithstanding an enormous temptation, never uses the lure of her beauty to gain favor with white men, as Mara finally does; and C. K., for volunteering to take all the risks with the runaways, proves to be the worthy Romeo that his great grandson is not.

Judith, then, influences John to create the character of Harriette through which John both celebrates Judith's warmth and revisits some of his own failures to love. Crucial both to the story and to John's reintegration, however, is Old Jack's influence, which persists even at this late moment. Not only does the first part of the story mention a helper on the underground railway named Crawley (Old Jack's grandfather), but John places a Jack-like figure among the runaway slaves as well. Both of his names ("Azacca" from his Haitian father and "Jacob" from his master) echo "Jack"; like Jack, he holds a position which is in some sense privileged while being extremely subordinate: Azacca tends the special gardens for growing flowers and vegetables for the master's family while Jack shines shoes of powerful whites in front of the courthouse. Both are old men who use stories to convey their wisdom. When the slaves are surrounded in John's final vision, even Harriette is reduced to whimpering in "a frightened voice, a cowered [*sic*] voice. A slave's voice." Azacca tells them the story that finally gives them the courage to commit mass suicide. In this story, an adaptation of an African myth, the Great Sky God sends a message to all people that Death "was not an ending of things, but a passing of spirit, a change of shape, and nothing more." Man, therefore, should not fear death. The message, however, is intercepted by a white man, who, along with others of his race, oppressively interprets the message for those with black skins, claiming that "their spirits would be cast into a lake of fire to burn in torment forever—unless they did exactly what the pale men said."

Clearly Azacca reflects John's own beliefs about the imperialistic nature of Christian religion. But Jack also disdains white man's religion and had much earlier said something similar about the runaways of the very legend John is now elaborating: "They're still here. . . . I know on accounta I

heard 'em. . . . they ain't ghosts; they ain't dead. They're jest runnin' along. An' . . . you hear the sound of 'em pantin'." While Azacca assures the slaves that they will not finally die, Jack, his spiritual grandchild, assures John that they are still alive. Or, stated in creative terms, John appropriates the theological beliefs of Old Jack, attributes them to Azacca, and makes them serve as Harriette's ultimate inspiration. After hearing Azacca's story, Harriette and C. K. recover their courage and lead the mass suicide.

Inspired by the voices of both Judith and Old Jack, John can harmonize the warring tendencies these characters bring out in him. In the story the wisdom of the old mentor, refined of its misogyny, combines with the passionate resolution of the younger woman to produce the heroic gesture of mass suicide in the graveyard of Chaneysville. But does this achievement really suggest an improvement in John's character or simply an advance in storytelling skill? Bradley himself suggests the answer in his account of how he became a writer. A story, says Bradley, should "cost" the artist the risk of unflattering emotional or moral revelation. In what amounts to a deeply romantic ethos, Bradley claims that the effort to create literary art involves becoming a better human being. John's own character reflects this faith. In responding to Judith's and Jack's joint inspiration, John must dethrone his rationalism to tell the story; then, in the novel's final action, he confirms and extends the coup by burning his index cards, which have been the sacred symbols of his rationalism for more than a decade. To create the grandeur of Harriette and C. K., he must recognize his own littleness; to make the necessary adjustments to reconcile Azacca with Harriette in his story, he must accommodate Old Jack and Judith in his mind. For this reason Bradley well earns the ending some critics see as "utopian" or "Edenic." The proof that John overcomes his misogyny for good lies in his life beyond the end of the novel. Nevertheless, by overcoming his mother-hate and reconciling his mentor with his lover, John has the new self that should be equal to that life.

FURTHER READING

Criticism

Bamforth, Iain. "The Case for Reconciliation." *Times Literary Supplement,* No. 4372 (16 January 1987): 56.
 Asserts that *The Chaneysville Incident* "could easily have shed half its length without losing dramatic impact, but at the expense of the marvellously hyperbolic vocabulary of some of its characters and all the vivid particulars that give it authenticity."

Barclay, Dolores. "Haunting Journey into His Story." *Black Enterprise* 11, No. 12 (July 1981): 10.

Discusses Bradley's journey in writing *The Chaneysville Incident.*

Brigham, Cathy. "Identity, Masculinity, and Desire in David Bradley's Fiction." *Contemporary Literature* 36, No. 2 (Summer 1995): 289-316.
    Traces the relationship between race, class, and gender in *South Street* and *The Chaneysville Incident.*

Campbell, Jane. "Ancestral Quests in Toni Morrison's *Song of Solomon* and David Bradley's *The Chaneysville Incident.*" In her *Mythic Black Fiction: The Transformation of History,* pp. 136-53. Knoxville: University of Tennessee Press, 1986.
    Analyzes the relationship between Judeo-Christian and African religions and the merging of personal and racial history in *The Chaneysville Incident* and Toni Morrison's *Song of Solomon.*

Ensslen, Klaus. "Fictionalizing History: David Bradley's *The Chaneysville Incident.*" *Callaloo* 11, No. 2 (Spring 1988): 280-97.
    Discusses the merging of history and storytelling in *The Chaneysville Incident.*

Kubitschek, Missy Dehn. "'So You Want a History, Do You?': Epistemologies and *The Chaneysville Incident.*" *Mississippi Quarterly* XLIX, No. 4 (Fall 1996): 755-74
    Discusses history's effect on the present in *The Chaneysville Incident.*

Additional coverage of Bradley's life and career is contained in the following sources published by Gale: *Black Literature Criticism; Black Writers,* Vol. 1; *Contemporary Authors,* Vol. 104; *Contemporary Authors New Revision Series,* Vol. 26; *Dictionary of Literary Biography,* Vol. 33; and *DISCovering Authors Modules: Multicultural.*

Sandra Cisneros

1954-

Mexican-American poet and short story writer.

The following entry provides an overview of Cisneros's career through 1997. For further information on her life and works, see *CLC,* Volume 69.

INTRODUCTION

With only a modicum of poetry and short story collections, Cisneros has attracted broad-based critical acclaim and popular success. Best known for *The House on Mango Street* (1984), a volume of loosely structured vignettes resisting any stable generic classification, Cisneros writes in an idiom that combines the prosaic and poetic syntax of both English and Spanish. Drawing heavily upon her childhood experiences and ethnic heritage as the daughter of a Mexican father and a Chicana mother, Cisneros's fiction and poetry address the impoverished conditions of *barrio* life, the cultural suppression of minorities in America, the struggle for self-identity in a pluralistic society, and the influence of culturally determined gender roles on the formation of character. Through dialogue and an emphasis on sensory imagery, Cisneros creates distinctly Latino characters who often exist along the margins of mainstream American culture, isolated because of their gender, ethnicity, or class origins. Most critics have commented on the multiple cultural perspectives exhibited by the themes, style, and language of Cisneros's writings, and others have commended her contributions to women's literature and gender studies.

Biographical Information

Born in 1954 at Chicago, Illinois, Cisneros is the only daughter of seven children. The family frequently moved between the United States and Mexico because of her father's homesickness for his native country and his devotion to his mother who lived there. Consequently, Cisneros often felt homeless and displaced; she sought comfort by reading extensively and occasionally wrote poetry and stories as a child and teenager. In 1976 Cisneros received a B.A. degree from Loyola University and a M.F.A. degree from the University of Iowa Writers' Workshop in 1978. Upon graduation, she returned to Chicago and taught at the Latino Youth Alternative High School until 1980, when she published her first poetry collection, *Bad Boys* (1980). Meanwhile, Cisneros began writing vignettes about the conflicted experiences of her youth that later became *The House on Mango Street.* In 1981 she took a position as college recruiter and counselor for minority students at

Loyola, and she received a NEA fellowship in 1982, which led to a year-long appointment as artist in residence at Foundation Michael Karolyi in Vence, France. In 1984 Cisneros went west to San Antonio, where she directed literary programs at the Guadeloupe Cultural Arts Center. She returned to poetry for her next book, *My Wicked, Wicked Ways* (1987). Since 1987, when she joined the faculty of California State University as a guest professor, Cisneros has held other visiting professorships at various American universities and has published another critically acclaimed prose collection, *Woman Hollering Creek* (1991), and *Loose Woman* (1994), her fourth book of poetry.

Major Works

Variously classified as either a short story collection or a series of prose poems, *The House on Mango Street* directly relates to Cisneros's upbringing and touches upon issues ranging from divided cultural loyalties, social alienation, and the humiliations of living in poverty. The work centers on a character named Esperanza (meaning "hope"), a poor Latina teenager who longs for a room of her own in a house of which she can be proud. Esperanza ponders the drawbacks of choosing marriage over education, the emotional liberation attained through writing words, and the sense of confusion associated with adolescence. In the piece "Hips," for instance, Esperanza agonizes over the repercussions of her body's physical changes. A collection of twenty-two narratives ranging from a few paragraphs to several pages, *Woman Hollering Creek* addresses issues concerning minority status in contemporary America. The stories in this volume contain the interior monologues of various Mexican-Americans living near San Antonio, Texas, who have assimilated into American culture but maintain fierce loyalty to their Mexican heritage. The title story, for instance, recounts the fantasy life of a Mexican woman, deluded by American soap operas, who recognizes that her marriage to a Texan bears little resemblance to those on television. In "Never Marry a Mexican," a young Latina begins to feel contempt for her Anglo lover when a sense of guilt and inadequacy overwhelms her since she cannot speak Spanish. *My Wicked, Wicked Ways,* a collection of sixty poems, describes Cisneros's native Chicago, her travels in Europe, and, as the title implies, the sexual guilt associated with her strict Catholic upbringing. Evincing Cisneros's penchant for merging various genres, these poems sometimes resemble short stories, and each one incorporates idiomatic Spanish, impressionistic metaphors, and social commentary that reveal the doubts and fears felt by many Hispanic women—traits common to all of Cisneros's writings. Through wry observations and extended metaphors, *Loose Woman* portrays a fiercely proud, independent woman of Mexican descent. In a review of *Loose Woman* Susan Smith Nash asserts that Cisneros "probes the extremes of perceptions and negotiates the boundary regions that define the self and the systems of knowledge required in constructing a notion of identity."

Critical Reception

The pieces in *The House on Mango Street* won praise for their lyrical narrative structures, vivid dialogue, and descriptive precision. "The reality of Hispanic life rarely enters mainstream American writing," remarked Jenny Uglow, adding that "Cisneros sets out to fill the blank page and let her people speak." Admiring the distinctive prose of *Woman Hollering Creek,* critics have described the characters in this volume as idiosyncratic, accessible individuals capable of generating compassion on a universal level. Attracted by themes that subvert conventional wisdom regarding gender roles and identity formation, commentators on Cisneros's fiction often note a relationship between the content and the form of her writing. "Cisneros is indeed skillful in utilizing long-established literary traditions for revolutionary purposes," wrote Laura Gutierrez Spencer, finding that Cisneros's writings show "how literature can challenge deeply inculcated values and change the ways in which we perceive the world." Although Cisneros is noted primarily

for her fiction, her poetry has also garnered attention, particularly for the way it tends to blur the distinction between literary genres. "What distinguishes Sandra Cisneros's poetry is also what makes categorizing it problematic," Nash observed, admitting that through her poetry "the reader gains the opportunity to celebrate the diversity of human experience and to participate in the reconfiguration of identity."

PRINCIPAL WORKS

Bad Boys (poems) 1980
The House on Mango Street (prose) 1984
The Rodrigo Poems (poems) 1985
My Wicked, Wicked Ways (poems) 1987
Woman Hollering Creek and Other Stories (prose) 1991
Hairs: Pelitos (juvenilia) 1994
Loose Woman (poems) 1994

CRITICISM

Ellen McCracken (essay date 1989)

SOURCE: "Sandra Cisneros's *The House on Mango Street:* Community Oriented Introspection and the Demystification of Patriarchal Violence," in *Breaking Boundaries: Latina Writing and Critical Readings,* edited by Asuncion Horno-Delgado, Eliana Ortega, et. al., University of Massachusetts Press, 1989, pp. 62-71.

[*In the following essay, McCracken asserts that* The House on Mango Street *is marginalized by four factors: its ideology, its language, its writer's ethnicity, and her gender. She argues that the book's treatment of patriarchal violence should move it, and others like it, toward being accepted as part of the canon.*]

Introspection has achieved a privileged status in bourgeois literary production, corresponding to the ideological emphasis on individualism under capitalism, precisely as the personal and political power of many real individuals has steadily deteriorated. In forms as diverse as European Romantic poetry, late nineteenth-century Modernismo in Latin America, the poetry of the Mexican Contemporáneos of the 1930s, the early twentieth-century modernistic prose of a Proust, the French *nouveau roman,* and other avant-garde texts that take pride in an exclusionary hermeticism, the self is frequently accorded exaggerated importance in stark contrast to the actual position of the individual in the writer's historical moment. Critical readers of these texts are, of course, often able to compensate for the writer's omissions, positioning the introspective search within the historical dimension and drawing the text into the very socio-political realm that the writer has tried to avoid. Nonetheless, many of us, at one time or another, are drawn into the glorified individualism of these texts, experiencing voyeuristic and sometimes identificatory pleasure as witnesses of another's search for the self, or congratulating ourselves on the mental acuity we possess to decode such a difficult and avantgarde text.

Literary critics have awarded many of these texts canonical status. As Terry Eagleton has argued, theorists, critics, and teachers are "custodians of a discourse" and select certain texts for inclusion in the canon that are "more amenable to this discourse than others." Based on power, Eagleton suggests metaphorically, literary criticism sometimes tolerates regional dialects of the discourse but not those that sound like another language altogether: "To be on the inside of the discourse itself is to be blind to this power, for what is more natural and non-dominative than to speak one's own tongue?"

The discourse of power to which Eagleton refers here is linked to ideology as well. The regional dialects of criticism that are accepted must be compatible, ideologically as well as semantically, with the dominant discourse. Criticism, for example, that questions the canonical status of the introspective texts mentioned above, or suggests admission to the canon of texts that depart from such individualistic notions of the self, is often labeled pejoratively or excluded from academic institutions and publication avenues.

We can extend Eagleton's metaphor to literary texts as well. How does a book attain the wide exposure that admission to the canon facilitates if it is four times marginalized by its ideology, its language, and its writer's ethnicity and gender? What elements of a text can prevent it from being accepted as a "regional dialect" of the dominant discourse; at what point does it become "another language altogether" (to use Eagleton's analogy), incompatible with canonical discourse?

The specific example to which I refer, Sandra Cisneros' ***The House on Mango Street,*** was published by a small regional press in 1984 and reprinted in a second edition of 3,000 in 1985. Difficult to find in most libraries and bookstores, it is well known among Chicano critics and scholars, but virtually unheard of in larger academic and critical circles. In May 1985 it won the Before Columbus Foundation's American Book Award, but this prize has not greatly increased the volume's national visibility. Cisneros' book has not been excluded from the canon solely because of its publishing circumstances: major publishing houses are quick to capitalize on a Richard Rodríguez whose widely distributed and reviewed *Hunger of Memory* (1982) does not depart ideologically and semantically from the dominant discourse. They

are even willing to market an Anglo writer as a Chicano, as occurred in 1983 with Danny Santiago's *Famous All Over Town.* Rather, Cisneros' text is likely to continue to be excluded from the canon because it "speaks another language altogether," one to which the critics of the literary establishment "remain blind."

Besides the double marginalization that stems from gender and ethnicity, Cisneros transgresses the dominant discourse of canonical standards ideologically and linguistically. In bold contrast to the individualistic introspection of many canonical texts, Cisneros writes a modified autobiographical novel, or *Bildungsroman,* that roots the individual self in the broader socio-political reality of the Chicano community. As we will see, the story of individual development is oriented outwardly here, away from the bourgeois individualism of many standard texts. Cisneros' language also contributes to the text's otherness. In opposition to the complex, hermetic language of many canonical works, ***The House on Mango Street*** recuperates the simplicity of children's speech, paralleling the autobiographical protagonist's chronological age in the book. Although making the text accessible to people with a wider range of reading abilities, such simple and well-crafted prose is not currently in canonical vogue.

> **Cisneros has socialized the motif of a house of one's own by showing its motivating roots to be the inadequate housing conditions in which she and others in her community lived.**
> **—*Ellen McCracken***

The volume falls between traditional genre distinctions as well. Containing a group of 44 short and interrelated stories, the book has been classified as a novel by some because, as occurs in Tomas Rivera's *...y no se lo tragó la tierra,* there is character and plot development throughout the episodes. I prefer to classify Cisneros' text as a collection, a hybrid genre midway between the novel and the short story. Like Sherwood Anderson's *Winesburg, Ohio,* Pedro Juan Soto's *Spiks,* Gloria Naylor's *The Women of Brewster Place,* and Rivera's text, Cisneros' collection represents the writer's attempt to achieve both the intensity of the short story and the discursive length of the novel within a single volume. Unlike the chapters of most novels, each story in the collection could stand on its own if it were to be excerpted but each attains additional important meaning when interacting with the other stories in the volume. A number of structural and thematic elements link the stories of each collection together. Whereas in *Winesburg, Ohio,* one important structuring element is the town itself, in ***The House*** *on Mango Street* and . . . *y no se lo tragó la tierra* the image of the house is a central unifying motif.

On the surface the compelling desire for a house of one's own appears individualistic rather than community oriented, but Cisneros socializes the motif of the house, showing it to be a basic human need left unsatisfied for many of the minority population under capitalism. It is precisely the lack of housing stability that motivates the image's centrality in works by writers like Cisneros and Rivera. For the migrant worker who has moved continuously because of job exigencies and who, like many others in the Chicano community, has been deprived of an adequate place to live because of the inequities of income distribution in U.S. society, the desire for a house is not a sign of individualistic acquisitiveness but rather represents the satisfaction of a basic human need. Cisneros begins her narrative with a description of the housing conditions the protagonist's family has experienced:

> We didn't always live on Mango Street. Before that we lived on Loomis on the third floor and before that we lived on Keeler. Before Keeler it was Paulina, and before that I can't remember. But what I remember most is moving a lot . . .

> We had to leave the flat on Loomis quick. The water pipes broke and the landlord wouldn't fix them because the house was too old. . . . We were using the washroom next door and carrying water over in empty milk gallons.

Cisneros has socialized the motif of a house of one's own by showing its motivating roots to be the inadequate housing conditions in which she and others in her community lived. We learn that Esperanza, the protagonist Cisneros creates, was subjected to humiliation by her teachers because of her family's living conditions. "*You live there?*" a nun from her school had remarked when seeing Esperanza playing in front of the flat on Loomis. "*There.* I had to look where she pointed—the third floor, the paint peeling, wooden bars Papa had nailed on the windows so we wouldn't fall out. *You live there?* The way she said it made me feel like nothing. . . . " Later, after the move to the house on Mango Street that is better but still unsatisfactory, the Sister Superior at her school responds to Esperanza's request to eat lunch in the cafeteria rather than returning home by apparently humiliating the child deliberately: "You don't live far, she says . . . I bet I can see your house from my window. Which one? . . . That one? she said pointing to a row of ugly 3-flats, the ones even the raggedy men are ashamed to go into. Yes, I nodded even though I knew that wasn't my house and started to cry. . . . " The Sister Superior is revealing her own prejudices; in effect, she is telling the child, "All you Mexicans must live in such buildings." It is in response to hu-

miliations such as these that the autobiographical protagonist expresses her need for a house of her own. Rather than the mere desire to possess private property, Esperanza's wish for a house represents a positive objectification of the self, the chance to redress humiliation and establish a dignified sense of her own personhood.

Cisneros links this positive objectification that a house of one's own can provide to the process of artistic creation. Early on, the protagonist remarks that the dream of a white house "with trees around it, a great big yard and grass growing without a fence" structured the bedtime stories her mother told them. This early connection of the ideal house to fiction is developed throughout the collection, especially in the final two stories. In **"A House of My Own,"** the protagonist remarks that the desired house would contain "my books and stories" and that such a house is as necessary to the writing process as paper: "Only a house quiet as snow, a space for myself to go, clean as paper before the poem." In **"Mango Says Goodbye Sometimes,"** the Mango Street house, which falls short of the ideal dream house, becomes a symbol of the writer's attainment of her identity through artistic creation. Admitting that she both belonged and did not belong to the "*sad red house*" on Mango Street, the protagonist comes to terms with the ethnic consciousness that this house represents through the process of fictive creation: "I put it down on paper and then the ghost does not ache so much. I write it down and Mango says goodbye sometimes. She does not hold me with both arms. She sets me free." She is released materially to find a more suitable dwelling that will facilitate her writing; psychologically, she alleviates the ethnic anguish that she has heretofore attempted to repress. It is important, however, that she view her departure from the Mango Street house to enable her artistic production in social rather than isolationist terms: "They will know I have gone away to come back. For the ones I left behind. For the ones who cannot get out."

Rather than the mere desire to possess private property, Esperanza's wish for a house represents a positive objectification of the self, the chance to redress humiliation and establish a dignified sense of her own personhood.
—*Ellen McCracken*

Unlike many introspective writers, then, Cisneros links both the process of artistic creation and the dream of a house that will enable this art to social rather than individualistic issues. In **"Bums in the Attic,"** we learn that the protagonist dreams of a house on a hill similar to those where her father works as a gardener. Unlike those who own such houses now, Esperanza assures us that, were she to obtain such a house, she would not forget the people who live below: "One day I'll own my own house, but I won't forget who I am or where I came from. Passing bums will ask, Can I come in? I'll offer them the attic, ask them to stay, because I know how it is to be without a house." She conceives of a house as communal rather than private property; such sharing runs counter to the dominant ideological discourse that strongly affects consciousness in capitalists societies. Cisneros' social motifs undermine rather than support the widespread messages of individualized consumption that facilitate sales of goods and services under consumer capitalism.

Another important reason why Cisneros's text has not been accepted as part of the dominant canonical discourse is its demystificatory presentation of women's issues, especially the problems low-income Chicana women face. Dedicated "A las Mujeres / To the Women," *The House on Mango Street* presents clusters of women characters through the sometimes naive and sometimes wise vision of the adolescent protagonist. There are positive and negative female role models and, in addition, several key incidents that focus the reader's attention on the contradictions of patriarchal social organization. Few mainstream critics consider these the vital, universal issues that constitute great art. When representatives of the critical establishment do accord a text such as Cisneros' a reading, it is often performed with disinterest and defense mechanisms well in place.

Neither does *The House on Mango Street* lend itself to an exoticized reading of the life of Chicana women that sometimes enables a text's canonical acceptance. In **"The Family of Little Feet,"** for example, Esperanza and her friends dress up in cast-off high heels they have been given and play at being adult women. At first revelling in the male attention they receive from the strangers who see them, the girls are ultimately disillusioned after a drunken bum attempts to purchase a kiss for a dollar. While capturing the fleeting sense of self-value that the attention of male surveyors affords women, Cisneros also critically portrays here the danger of competitive feelings among women when one girl's cousins pretend not to see Esperanza and her friends as they walk by. Also portrayed is the corner grocer's attempt to control female sexuality by threatening to call the police to stop the girls from wearing the heels. Cisneros proscribes a romantic or exotic reading of the dress-up episode, focusing instead on the girls' discovery of the threatening nature of male sexual power that is frequently disguised as desirable male attention and positive validation of women, though what is, in fact, sexual reification.

Scenes of patriarchal and sexual violence in the collection also prevent a romantic reading of women's issues in this Chicano community. We see a woman whose husband locks her in the house, a daughter brutally beaten by her father, and Esperanza's own sexual initiation through rape. Like the threatening corner grocer in **"The Family of Little Feet,"** the men in these stories control or appropriate female sexuality by adopting one or another form of violence as if it were their innate right. One young woman, Rafaela, "gets locked indoors because her husband is afraid [she] will run away since she is too beautiful to look at." Esperanza and her friends send papaya and coconut juice up to the woman in a paper bag on a clothesline she has lowered; metonymical-ly, Cisneros suggests that the sweet drinks represent the island the woman has left and the dance hall down the street as well, where other women are ostensibly more in control of their own sexual expression and are allowed to open their homes with keys. The young yet wise narrator, however, recognizes that "always there is someone offering sweeter drinks, someone promising to keep [women] on a silver string."

The cycle of stories about Esperanza's friend Sally shows this patriarchal violence in its more overt stages. Like Rafaela, the young teenager Sally is frequently forced to stay in the house because "her father says to be this beautiful is trouble." But even worse, we learn later that Sally's father beats her. Appearing at school with bruises and scars, Sally tells Esperanza that her father sometimes hits her with his hands "just like a dog . . . as if I was an animal. He thinks I'm going to run away like his sisters who made the family ashamed. Just because I'm a daughter. . . . " In **"Linoleum Roses,"** a later story in the Sally cycle, we learn that she escapes her father's brutality by marrying a marshmallow salesman "in another state where it's legal to get married before eighth grade." In effect, her father's violent attempts to control her sexuality—here a case of child abuse—cause Sally to exchange one repressive patriarchal prison for another. Dependent on her husband for money, she is forbidden to talk on the telephone, look out the window, or have her friends visit. In one of his fits of anger, her husband kicks the door in. Where Rafaela's husband imprisons her with a key, Sally's locks her in with psychological force: "[Sally] sits home because she is afraid to go outside without his permission."

A role model for Esperanza, Sally has symbolized the process of sexual initiation for her younger friend. Two stories in the cycle reveal Esperanza's growing awareness of the link between sex, male power, and violence in patriarchal society. In "The Monkey Garden," Esperanza perceives her friend Sally to be in danger when the older girl agrees to "kiss" a group of boys so that they will return her car keys; " . . . they're making her kiss them," Esperanza reports to the mother of one of the boys. When the mother shows no concern, Esperanza undertakes Sally's defense herself: "Sally needed to be saved. I took three big sticks and a brick and figured this was enough." Sally and the boys tell her to go home and Esperanza feels stupid and ashamed. In postlapsarian anguish, she runs to the other end of the garden and, in what seems to be an especially severe form of self-punishment for this young girl, tries to make herself die by willing her heart to stop beating.

In **"Red Clowns,"** the story that follows, Esperanza's first suspicions of the patriarchy's joining of male power, violence, and sex are confirmed beyond a doubt. She had previously used appellation throughout the first story in the Sally cycle to ask her friend to teach her how to dress and apply makeup. Now the appellation to Sally is one of severe disillusionment after Esperanza has been sexually assaulted in an amusement park while waiting for Sally to return from her own sexual liaison:

> Sally, you lied. It wasn't like you said at all . . . Why didn't you hear me when I called? Why didn't you tell them to leave me alone? The one who grabbed me by the arm, he wouldn't let me go. He said I love you, Spanish girl, I love you, and pressed his sour mouth to mine . . . I couldn't make them go away. I couldn't do anything but cry . . . Please don't make me tell it all.

This scene extends the male violence toward Esperanza, begun on her first day of work, when an apparently nice old man "grabs [her] face with both hands and kisses [her] hard on the mouth and doesn't let go." Together with other instances of male violence in the collection—Rafaela's imprisonment, Sally's beatings, and the details of Minerva's life, another young married woman whose husband beats her and throws a rock through the window—these episodes form a continuum in which sex, patriarchal power, and violence are linked. Earlier, Cisneros had developed this connection in the poem **"South Sangamon,"** in which similar elements of male violence predominate: "he punched her belly," "his drunk cussing," "the whole door shakes / like his big foot meant to break it," and "just then / the big rock comes in." *The House on Mango Street* presents this continuum critically, offering an unromanticized, inside view of Esperanza's violent sexual initiation and its links to the oppression of other women in the Chicano community.

Cisneros does not merely delineate women's victimization in this collection, however. Several positive female role models help to guide Esperanza's development. Minerva, for example, although a victim of her husband's violence, makes time to write poetry. "But when the kids are asleep after she's fed them their pancake dinner, she writes poems on little pieces of paper that she folds over and over and holds in her hands a long time, little pieces of paper that smell like a dime. She lets me read her poems. I let her read mine." Minerva's artistic production is reminiscent of Dr. Reefy in *Winesburg, Ohio*'s "Paper Pills," who scribbles words of wisdom on scraps of paper he crumples up, finally sharing them

with a patient. It is also similar to the character of Rosendo in Soto's *Spiks,* a barrio artist who can only find space to paint an idyllic scene on the crumbling wall of his tenement bathroom and whose wife, acutely aware of the pressing economic needs of their young children, cannot afford the luxury of appreciating this non-revenue-producing art. Like Dr. Reefy, but unlike Rosendo, Minerva succeeds in communicating through her art; exchanging poems with Esperanza, she contributes to the latter's artistic development while at the same time offering a lesson in women's domestic oppression and how to begin transcending it.

Also supportive of Esperanza's artistic creativity is her invalid aunt, Guadalupe: "She listened to every book, every poem I read her. One day I read her one of my own . . . That's nice. That's very good, she said in her tired voice. You just remember to keep writing, Esperanza. You must keep writing. It will keep you free. . . . " Although the aunt lives in squalid, poor surroundings and is dying from a disease that has disfigured her once-beautiful body, she listens to the girl's stories and poems and encourages Esperanza's artistic talent. The story, **"Three Sisters,"** recounts the wake held for the baby sister of Esperanza's friends Lucy and Rachel and is also the theme of Cisneros' earlier poem, **"Velorio,"** in the collection entitled *Bad Boys.* Expanding upon **"Velorio,"** however, this story introduces the figures of "the aunts, the three sisters, *las comadres,*" visitors at the *velorio* who encourage Esperanza to see her artistic production in relation to the community: "When you leave you must remember always to come back . . . for the others. A circle, you understand? You will always be Esperanza. You will always be Mango Street. . . . You can't forget who you are." Although Esperanza doesn't understand the women's message completely, the seeds of her socially conscious art have been planted here through the directives these women give her at the baby's wake.

Alicia, another positive role model who appears in **"Alicia Who Sees Mice"** and **"Alicia and I Talking on Edna's Steps,"** also counsels Esperanza to value Mango Street and return there one day to contribute to its improvement: "Like it or not you are Mango Street and one day you'll come back too." To Esperanza's reply, "Not me. Not until somebody makes it better," Alicia wryly comments "Who's going to do it? The mayor?." Alicia had previously appeared in the collection as a university student who takes "two trains and a bus [to the campus] because she doesn't want to spend her whole life in a factory or behind a rolling pin." Rebelling against her father's expectations of her, that "a woman's place is sleeping so she can wake up early . . . and make the lunchbox tortillas," Alicia "studies all night and sees the mice, the ones her father says do not exist." Fighting what the patriarchy expects of her, Alicia at the same time represents a clear-sighted, non-mystified vision of the barrio. As a role-model and advice-giver to Esperanza, she embodies both the antipatriarchal themes and the social obligation to return to one's ethnic community that are so central to Cisneros' text.

Cisneros touches on several other important women's issues in this volume, including media images of ideal female beauty, the reifying stare of male surveyors of women, and sex roles within the family. In an effort to counter the sexual division of labor in the home, for example, Esperanza refuses one instance of women's work: "I have begun my own quiet war. Simple. Sure. I am the one who leaves the table like a man, without pulling back the chair or picking up the plate." Although this gesture calls critical attention to gender inequities in the family, Cisneros avoids the issue of who, in fact, will end up performing the household labor that Esperanza refuses here. This important and symbolic, yet somewhat adolescent gesture merely touches on the surface of the problem and is likely, in fact, to increase the work for another woman in Esperanza's household.

The majority of stories in *The House on Mango Street,* however, face important social issues head-on. The volume's simple, poetic language, with its insistence that the individual develops within a social community rather than in isolation, distances it from many accepted canonical texts. Its deceptively simple, childlike prose and its emphasis on the unromanticized, non-mainstream issues of patriarchal violence and ethnic poverty, however, should serve precisely to accord it canonical status. We must work toward a broader understanding among literary critics of the importance of such issues to art in order to attain a richer, more diverse canon and to avoid the undervaluation and oversight of such valuable texts as *The House on Mango Street.*

Maria Elena de Valdés (essay date Fall 1992)

SOURCE: "In Search of Identity in Cisneros' *The House on Mango Street,*" in *The Canadian Review of American Studies,* Vol. 23, No. 1, Fall, 1992, pp. 55-72.

[*In the essay below, de Valdés examines the "highly lyrical narrative voice" of* The House on Mango Street *in relation to textual representations of "a poetics of identity" as a Chicana writer.*]

Sandra Cisneros (1954-), a Chicago-born poet of Mexican parentage, published her first novel in 1984. *The House on Mango Street* is written in the manner of a young girl's memoirs. The forty-four pieces are, however, not the day-to-day record of a preadolescent girl, but rather a loose-knit series of lyrical reflections, her struggle with self-identity and the search for self-respect amidst an alienating and often hos-

tile world. The pieces range from two paragraph narratives, like **"Hairs,"** to the four-page **"The Monkey Garden."**

There are a number of significant issues to be discussed concerning *The House on Mango Street* but I believe that the most pressing issue is the ideological question of a poetics of identity in the double materialization of a Chicana. I am opposed to any critical strategy which ignores the qualitative perspective of the lyric narrative voice, the referential situation from which she is writing, and the issues she is writing about. In this study, I shall present the highly lyrical narrative voice in all its richness of a "persona" to which my commentary will seek to respond.

Cisneros's literary persona, Esperanza, is the lyric narrative voice to whom the reader responds and who the reader eventually knows. My theoretical position is closely allied and, to a large extent, indebted to Naomi Black's social feminism, which she defines as "the argumentation and process in which feminism is able to use the doctrine of difference not to obliterate differences of kind, but to change a society that uses difference as a basis for exclusion." The feminist social criticism that I have developed over the last four years builds on the infrastructure of Black's work and the orientation of Julia Kristeva's writing, but also draws from Paul Ricoeur's hermeneutic mode of inquiry.

The plan of this paper is to move rapidly from a semiotic level to a semantic level of the text before attempting an intertextual interpretation of my reading. The final stage of my exposition is to present the significance of the reading experience in that dialogic relation between the text and the reader and the reader's community. The sensibility and feeling that the narrator captures from her experiences governs her relations with her world and its people, and is part of the long tradition of literature of the coming of age. As an aesthetic process, the apprehension of the world of Mango Street becomes a metaphor for identity. The consequence of this aesthetic process is that the reader is directed less toward the singularity of the places, events and persons of Mango Street than toward the eye/I that writes them. The protagonist, Esperanza, probes into her world, discovers herself and comes to embody the primal needs of all human beings: freedom and belonging.

I am aware that some feminists, especially in English-speaking North America, do not share my philosophical premises, but it is my conviction that they will listen and respond to this voice from the North American third world. The following passage from ["What Is Text"] by Ricoeur will serve as an intellectual paradigm for my commentary on Chicana identity as a part of the reading experience. Ricoeur writes: "What we want to understand is not something hidden behind the text, but something disclosed in front of it. What has to be understood is not the initial situation of discourse, but what points toward a possible world. . . . To understand a text is to follow its movement from sense to reference, from what it says, to what it talks about." The organization of the study is, therefore, a strategy of communication. The main semantic focus of the text is the presentation of the narrating self.

My commentary is aimed at establishing a historically based, critical model of reading for the presentation of self. The narrating presence is a composite of a poetic enunciating voice and a narrative voice, and this presence can best be described as a formal function within the literary structure who, as a speaker, is only knowable as a story-teller in her response to the extratextual, societal, and historical, determinate referents. Notions of self or voice are implicitly controlled by the spectrum of the world of action as known to the reader, and notions of character are explicitly linked to the notions of person in the world. The union of the self and person is the hallmark of the lyrical text. If voice or self is an impulse toward the world, person or character is a social structure of dispositions and traits. In brief, the text in *The House on Mango Street* presents the exterior and the interior of living in the world.

The narrative situation is a familiar one: a sensitive young girl's reflections of her struggle between what she is and what she would like to be. The sense of alienation is compounded because ethnically she is a Mexican, although culturally a Mexican American; she is a young girl surrounded by examples of abused, defeated, worn-out women, but the woman she wants to be must be free. The reflections of one crucial year in her life are narrated in the present from a first person point of view. This was the year of the passage from preadolescence to adolescence when she discovered the meaning of being female and Mexican living in Chicago, but, most of all, this was the year she discovered herself through writing. The girl who did not want to belong to her social reality learns that she belongs to herself, to others, and not to a place.

The frame for the short narratives is simple but highly effective. The family has been wandering from place to place, always dreaming of the promised land of a house of their own. When they finally arrive at the house on Mango Street, which is at last their own house, it is not the promised land of their dreams. The parents overcome their dejection by saying that this is not the end of their moving, that it is only a temporary stop before going on to the promised house. The narrator knows better. The conflict between the promised land and the harsh reality, which she always recognizes in its full force of rejection, violence, fear, and waste, is presented without compromise and without dramatization. This is just the way things are on Mango Street, but the narrator will not give up her dream of the promised house and will pursue it. The lesson she must learn is that the house she

seeks is, in reality, her own person. She must overcome her rejection of who she is and find her self-esteem. She must be true to herself and thereby gain control of her identity. The search for self-esteem and her true identity is the subtle, yet powerful, narrative thread that unites the text and achieves the breakthrough of self-understanding in the last pieces.

We can trace this search through some of its many moments. The narrative development begins in the first entry, **"The House"**: "I knew then I had to have a house. A real house. One I could point to. But this isn't it. The house on Mango Street isn't it. For the time being, Mama says. Temporary, says Papa. But I know how those things go." The narrator goes on to establish the family circle where she has warmth and love but is lonely and, most of all, estranged from the world outside. Her name, Esperanza, in English means hope: "At school they say my name funny as if the syllables were made out of tin and hurt the roof of your mouth. But in Spanish my name is made out of a softer something, like silver." Fear and hostility are the alienating forces she tries to understand. Why do people of other color fear her? And why should she fear others? That's the way it is. "All brown all around, we are safe." Changes are coming over her, she is awakening to sexuality and to an adult world. It is in **"Four Skinny Trees,"** that the identity question is explored: "They are the only ones who understand me. I am the only one who understands them."

> **The lesson she must learn is that the house she seeks is, in reality, her own person.**
> **—*Maria Elena de Valdés***

"A Smart Cookie" touches one of the most sensitive areas of the text: the mother-daughter relationship. Her mother remains nostalgic not for what was, but for what could have been: "I could've been somebody, you know?" Being somebody is full of unarticulated significance, but in its impact on Esperanza, it means primarily to be herself and not what others wanted her to be. Her mother tells her she had brains, but she was also self-conscious and ashamed not to look as well as other more affluent girls. She quit school because she could not live looking at herself in the mirror of the other girls's presence. She states forthrightly: "Shame is a bad thing, you know. It keeps you down." The syndrome is there; it is a closed circle. You are poor because you are an outsider without education; you try to get an education, but you can't take the contrastive evidence of poverty and "[i]t keeps you down." The constant movement of the narrative takes up one aspect after another of the circumstances of the emerging subject that is Esperanza Cordero.

There is a subtle sequential order to the short sections. The text opens with the description of the house and its significance to the narrator, moves on to a delicate image of the family group, and with the third piece, **"Boys and Girls,"** begins the highly lyrical exposition of the narrator's world, punctuated with entries of introspection in the narrator's struggle with her identity. **"My Name," "Chanclas," "Elenita, Cards, Palm Water," "Four Skinny Trees," "Bums in the Attic," "Beautiful and Cruel," "The Monkey Garden," "The Three Sisters,"** and **"A House of My Own,"** are the most significant pieces because they mark the narrative development of identity. The text ends with the anticipated departure from the house and the literary return to it through writing. Although each piece can be seen as a self-contained prose poem, there is the subtle narrative unity of the enunciating voice's search for herself as she observes and questions her world and its social, economic, and moral conventions.

Esperanza Cordero observes, questions, and slowly finds herself determined through her relationship to the others who inhabit her world. She is drawn to the women and girls as would-be role models; within her family, her mother and her younger sister Magdalena (Nenny) are characterized, but the most searching descriptions are of girls her own age or, as she says, a few years older. Marin from Puerto Rico is featured in **"Louie, His Cousin and His Other Cousin"** and **"Marin,"** Alicia in **"Alicia Who Sees Mice,"** Rafaela in **"Rafaela Who Drinks Coconut and Papaya Juice on Tuesdays,"** and, most important of all, Sally in **"Sally," "What Sally Said," "Red Clowns,"** and **"Linoleum Roses."** The older women are treated with a soft-spoken sympathy through imagery: Rosa Vargas in **"There Was an Old Woman She Had So Many Children She Didn't Know What to Do,"** Ruthie in **"Edna's Ruthie,"** the neighbour Mamacita in **"No Speak English,"** and her own mother in **"A Smart Cookie."**

The enunciating voice never breaks her verisimilar perspective. She speaks about what she sees and what she thinks. Her style is one of subtlety, understatement, and generosity. When she reflects on social hostility or the brutality of wife-beating, it is not with violence or rancour, but with a firm determination to describe and to escape the vicious circle of abused women: Rosa Vargas is the mother "who is tired all the time from buttoning and bottling and babying, and who cries every day for the man who left without even leaving a dollar for bologna or a note explaining how come"; Marin who is not allowed out and hopes to get a job downtown so that she "can meet someone in the subway who might marry and take you to live in a big house far away"; "Alicia, who inherited her mama's rolling pin and sleepiness" and whose father says that "a woman's place is sleeping so she can wake up early with the tortilla star"; "Rafaela, who is still young but getting old from leaning out the window so much, gets locked indoors because her husband is afraid Rafaela will run away since she is too beautiful to look at";

"Minerva is only a little bit older than me but already she has two kids and a husband who left . . . she writes poems on little pieces of paper that she folds over and over and holds in her hands a long time." And, there is Sally whose father hits her and "her mama rubs lard on all the places where it hurts. Then at school she'd say she fell. That's where all the blue places come from. That's why her skin is always scarred."

The first person moves effortlessly from observer to lyrical introspection about her place in the world. The language is basic, idiomatic English with a touch of colloquial speech and a few Spanish words. The deceptively simple structure of sentences and paragraphs has a conceptual juxtaposition of action and reaction where the movement itself is the central topic. For example, **"Those Who Don't,"** which consists of three short paragraphs, is about alienation and fear in a hostile society, but it is only fourteen lines in total. It begins with a direct statement about life as she sees it: "Those who don't know any better come into our neighborhood scared. They think we're dangerous. They think we will attack them with shiny knives. They are stupid people who are lost and got here by mistake." The second paragraph, five lines long, begins with the "we" that is the implicit opposite of the "they" of the preceding paragraph. "But we aren't afraid. We know the guy. . . ." With the economy of a well-written sonnet the third five-line paragraph brings the "they" and the "we" into an inverted encounter: "All brown all around, we are safe. But watch us drive into a neighborhood of another color and our knees go shakity-shake and our car windows get rolled up tight and our eyes look straight. Yeah. That is how it goes and goes." The description has been that of a keen observer, the composition is that of a poet.

This structure operates through a conceptual back and forth movement of images, like the action of the shuttle in the loom. An image appears which moves the reader forward, following the woof of the first-person through the warp of referential world, but as soon as the image takes shape it is thrust back toward the enunciator. The process is repeated again and again slowly weaving the tapestry of Esperanza's Mango Street. For example, in **"Those Who Don't,"** the initial image is about the others, "Those who don't know any better," but it reaches culmination with the observation that "they think we're dangerous." The counter-move is that "They are stupid people." The new thrust forward is the reassurance of familiarity with the ostensible menacing scene that greeted the outsiders and led them to fear they would be attacked. But, when the shuttle brings back the narrative thread, it presents the inversion. The "we" are the "they" in another neighborhood. The movement back and forth will go on, the narrator says, "That is how it goes and goes." The colour of the warp is different in each community, the woof keeps them next to each other, but their ignorance and fear keeps them separate. The tapestry that is being woven by this constant imagistic back and forth movement of the narrator's perceptions and thoughts is not a plotted narrative, but rather a narrative of self-invention by the writer-speaker. The speaker and her language are mutually implicated in a single interdependent process of poetic self-invention.

The poetic text cannot operate if we separate the speaker from her language; they are the inseparable unity of personal identity. There is no utterance before enunciation. There is a fictional persona, Esperanza Cordero, who will speak, and there is the implicit continued use of idiomatic American English. But the enunciation that we read is at once the speaker and the spoken which discloses the subject, her subjectivity, and ours. An inescapable part of this subject is what she is expected to be: "Mexicans, don't like their women strong." "I wonder if she [my great-grandmother] made the best with what she got or was she sorry because she couldn't be all the things she wanted to be. Esperanza. I have inherited her name, but I don't want to inherit her place by the window." This close reading of the text with attention to how it operates, suggests a movement and a counter-movement which I have described metaphorically as the movement of a loom weaving the presence of subjectivity. Subjectivity is always seen against the background of her community that is Chicago's changing neighbourhoods. This determinate background gives narrative continuation, or narrativity, to the narrator's thoughts. The narrative development of this text can be described as the elaboration of the speaker's subjectivity. The symbolic space she creates should not be abstracted from the writing, because the writing itself is the creation of her own space. The structure of this text, therefore, begins as a frame for self-invention and as the writing progresses so does the subject. She is, in the most direct sense of the word, making herself and in a space of her own.

There are numerous empirical and verisimilar truth-claims about the way of life in the neighbourhood. All of these references form a well-knit web of specific truth-claims about social reality. Simultaneous to these truth-claims is another kind of reference. The reference to the narrator's own sense of the world, her wonderment and search for answers of why things are the way they are for her and for those who are her family, friends, and neighbours: Minerva "comes over black and blue and asks what can she do? Minerva. I don't know which way she'll go. There is nothing *I* can do"; "Sally. What do you think about when you close your eyes like that? ... Do you wish your feet would one day keep walking and take you far away from Mango Street, far away and maybe your feet would stop in front of a house, a nice one with flowers and big windows." Esperanza meditates after her Aunt Lupe's death: "Maybe she was ashamed. Maybe

she was embarrassed it took so many years. The kids who wanted to be kids instead of washing dishes and ironing their papa's shirts, and the husband who wanted a wife again. And then she died, my aunt who listened to my poems. And then we began to dream the dreams." This quest for answers takes on an explicit tension because of the depth of the themes the narrator treats, but the manner in which she develops her search for answers is the fundamental dialectic of self-world. She describes what is around her, she responds to people and places, but, most importantly, she reflects on a world she did not make, and cannot change, but must control or she will be destroyed. She is a young, dark-skinned girl of Mexican parentage, born in Chicago, speaking English, and feeling alienated.

> **She describes what is around her, she responds to people and places, but, most importantly, she reflects on a world she did not make, and cannot change, but must control or she will be destroyed.**
> —*Maria Elena de Valdés*

The use of these determinate features is of primary importance, for it is through the interplay between the lyrical introspection and the truth-claims that the fusion of self (enunciating voice) and person (character) takes place. The power of the text lies precisely in the creation of this presence. It is this human presence that transcends the time, place, and condition of the composition to create a literary metaphor for a woman coming of age. Readers halfway around the world, who have never seen Chicago and have never experienced what it is to live with the fear expressed in "All brown all around, we are safe," can, nevertheless, understand what it is to be lonely and alienated and how difficult it is to come out free from an environment that enslaves.

The images evoked by the text all signal a subject: Esperanza Cordero, an adolescent Mexican American girl who wants to be a writer. As critical readers, we read in a manner that creates ourselves as recipients, our own self-invention as the sympathetic listeners of the tale, attentive to actualize the words into images clothed in the colors of our own experience. The subject that emerges from our reading is neither the author's nor ours; she is a unique construct of intersecting designs and paradigms, those of the author's structure of the text, and those of the larger cultural context we share, in part, with the author. But this construct can only be reconstructed from its effects on us, its readers. Thus, the subject I am dealing with in these pages is a deliberate reconstruction from the effects of reading.

In order to draw out the subject of this text I will comment on three of the numerous images which are part of this work. The imagery in this text functions on three levels, in the manner of prose poems. Images in this text are effective because they function at the level of form, of plot, and of symbolic significance. Each of these images serves, first, to establish the identity of the enunciating voice; this is primarily a poetic function of creating the lyric presence who experiences and speaks. But, the images also have a narrative function as a part of the plot line which is the search for the promised house. And, finally, each image takes on symbolic proportions because it participates in the rich intertextuality of literature.

"Four Skinny Trees" presents the most iconic image in the entire text. The trees are personified in the image of the narrator: "Four skinny trees with skinny necks and pointy elbows like mine," but the description is also markedly referential to the specific urban setting of the text: "Four who grew despite concrete." At the primary level of the enunciating voice's identity, the image evokes a powerful statement about belonging and not belonging to the place where they happen to have grown: "Four who do not belong here but are here." The narrative is composed of four short paragraphs. The first, with lyrical rhythm, establishes reciprocity between "I" and "they," "four skinny trees." The second completes the personification: "they" completely supplants "trees." The third paragraph introduces their function: "they teach"; and the fourth gives the lesson: to reach and not forget to reach and to "be and be."

At the level of plot, the trees serve as a talisman of survival in a hostile environment:

> Let one forget his reason for being, they'd all droop like tulips in a glass, each with their arms around the other. Keep, keep, keep, trees say when I sleep. They teach.
>
> When I am too sad and too skinny to keep keeping, when I am a tiny thing against so many bricks, then it is I look at trees. When there is nothing left to look at on this street. Four who grew despite concrete. Four who reach and do not forget to reach. Four whose only reason is to be and be.

Esperanza's survival amidst surroundings that are negative and a rejection of her sensibility is not a denial of where she is and who she is, but rather a continuous fight to survive in spite of Mango Street as Esperanza from Mango Street. It is, however, at the symbolic level that the image of the trees attains its fullest significance. There is a secret to survival that the trees make manifest—an unconquerable will to fight without respite in order to survive in an urban setting:

> Their strength is secret. They send ferocious roots beneath the ground. They grow up and they grow down and grab the earth between their hairy toes and bite the sky with violent teeth and never quit their anger. This is how they keep.

I want to emphasize that the visual aspects of the textual imagery engage the reader in the visual figuration of vertical movement in trees. Is this a form of intertextuality? I think it would be more appropriate to say that this visual imagery is a woman's prose painting.

The highly lyrical presentation of **"The Three Sisters"** evokes the fairy godmothers of fairy-tale lore, each with a unique image and gift for the heroine. Their gift is the gift of self: "When you leave you must remember to come back for the others. A circle, understand? You will always be Esperanza. You will always be Mango Street. You can't erase what you know. You can't forget who you are." This poempiece is unlike any of the others in form because it combines the prose-poem quality of the rest of the book with the most extended dialogue sequence. The three sisters speak to Esperanza. The speaking voices are of crucial importance for through their enunciation they become full participants in the story-telling evocation with Esperanza.

At the level of plot the sisters serve as revelation. They are the narrative mediators that enter the story, at the crucial junctures, to assist the heroine in the trial that lies ahead. It is significant that they are from Mexico and appear to be related only to the moon. In pre-Hispanic Mexico, the lunar goddesses, such as Tlazolteotl and Xochiquetzal, were the intermediaries for all women. They are sisters to each other and, as women, sisters to Esperanza. One has laughter like tin, another has the eyes of a cat, and the third hands like porcelain. This image is, above all, a lyrical disclosure of revelation. Their entrance into the story is almost magical: "They came with the wind that blows in August, thin as a spider web and barely noticed," for they came only to make the gift to Esperanza of her selfhood. At the symbolic level, the three sisters are linked with Clotho, Lachesis, and Atropos, the three fates. Catullus depicts them weaving their fine web of destiny: "These sisters pealed their high prophetic song, / Song which no length of days shall prove untrue." The tradition of the sisters of fate runs deep in Western literature from the most elevated lyric to the popular tale of marriage, birth, and the fate awaiting the hero or heroine. In Cisneros's text, the prophecy of the fates turns to the evocation of self-knowledge.

The last image I shall discuss is based on the number two, the full force of opposition between two houses, the one on Mango Street and the promised house which is now the projection of the narrator. Although this image runs through-

out the text, **"The House on Mango Street," "Alicia,"
"A House of My Own"** and "Mango Says Goodbye
Sometimes," are the principal descriptions. The imagery
of the house is in constant flux between a negative and a
positive, between the house the narrator has and the one she
would like to have: "I knew then I had to have a house. A
real house. One I could point to. But this isn't it. The house
on Mango Street isn't it." On the level of the narrative
voice's sense of belonging and identity, it is clear from the
first piece that the house is much more than a place to live.
It is a reflection, an extension, a personified world that is
indistinguishable from the occupant. The oppositional pull
and push continues throughout and reaches its climax in the
last three pieces. In **"Alicia and I Talking on Edna's
Steps,"** it is in the form of reported dialogue: "No, this isn't
my house I say and shake my head as if shaking could undo
the year I've lived here. I don't belong. I don't ever want to
come from here . . . I never had a house, not even a photograph . . . only one I dream of." Because the house has become an extension of the person the rejection is vehement.
She knows the person she is does not belong to the hostile ugly world she lives in.

"A House of My Own" expands on the promised house of
her dreams in subtle, yet evocative, intertextuality to Virginia
Woolf's *A Room of One's Own:* "Only a house quiet as
snow, a space for myself to go, clean as paper before the
poem." The house is now a metaphor for the subject and,
therefore, the personal space of her identity. The last piece
resolves the oppositional tension by transforming it into
writing, into the metaphor of going away from Mango Street
in order to return.

At the level of plot, the opposition of the house on Mango
Street and a house of her own provides the narrative thread
for the text. It is the movement implicit in the description of
hostility and poverty and the belief in a better life that gives
the story its inner cohesion and builds the consistency of
the narrator's reflections. The fact that this conflict between
alienation and the need to belong is common to persons of
all cultures and across history gives the text its thematic
link to world literature. There is a perfect circularity in the
plot insofar as the text ends when the writing begins. The
opening lines of the text are the closing. Esperanza has
made her tension a tension creative of her subjectivity.

The idea of creative tension is well known to us through
the work of Gaston Bachelard's *The Poetics of Space* and
The Poetics of Reverie as well as Paul Ricoeur's *The Rule
of Metaphor*; however, we must be reminded that this idea
was already implicit in Aristotle's discussion of representation as the tension between the object known to be represented and the means used to represent it. In my work, I
follow the theory that the image is not the residue of an impression, it is not an imprint that fades with time; on the

contrary, the image that is produced through speech gives
us the speaking subject and the subject spoken of, entwined
in a unity of expression. If we move from speech to the written text, the situation becomes richer with possibilities. The
text makes the image possible, the reader makes it actual and
the image is something new in our language, an entity of
reflection that was not there before; it is the poetic subjectivity in which we participate.

My commentary on these pages is reflective, aimed at participation and not at imposing closure on the text for other
readers. As readers, regarding the self-invention of writing,
we must respect the specificity of the self-invention, that
is, a Chicana coming of age. In all patriarchal societies, but
especially in this one, there is the imposition of the sign of
gender which serves to silence women, to force them to par-
ticularize themselves through the indirect means of the way
and style in which they serve others. This is the ideological
meaning of "a daddy's house." By writing, this young
woman has created herself as a total subject and not a gender role or a disembodied voice.

The symbolic level of the image of the house is the most
basic expression of existence. Everything about the house
on Mango Street repels the lyric narrator. This house is not
hers and does not reflect her presence. The house of her
dreams is first described in negative terms, by what it cannot be: "Not a flat. Not an apartment in back. Not a man's
house. Not a daddy's." This is followed by its attributes:
"A house all my own. With my porch and my pillow, my
pretty purple petunias. My books and my stories. My two
shoes waiting beside the bed." And it also excludes: "Nobody to shake a stick at. Nobody's garbage to pick up after." The problem is that she belongs to the house on Mango
Street and to deny it would be at the expense of herself, of
her identity. She belongs to a world that is not hers; it is an
opposition that will not be resolved in a synthesis or a compromise. The metaphor of a place of her own draws upon
the continuing tensional opposition. She learns not only to
survive but to win her freedom, and the text itself with its
title and its search for the promised house is the creative
tension of poetry. The semantic impertinence of belonging
and not belonging creates the metaphorical meaning of identity as one who does not forget to reach and to reach and
whose only reason is to "be and be."

The conclusion, **"Mango Says Goodbye Sometimes,"** is lyrical and meditative:

> Friends and neighbors will say, What happened
> to that Esperanza? Where did she go with all
> those books and paper? Why did she march so
> far away?

> They will not know that I have gone away to

come back. For the ones I left behind. For the ones who cannot out.

The liberation of Esperanza through her writing draws from a rich tradition of a writer's self-creation. Reflection, in this tradition, is the movement toward the very core of being. Not only does the past become the present through the act of writing, but, of more consequence, the projection into the self's future is predicated on the self-knowledge of this existentialized consciousness. To remember, therefore, is not just to go back in time, it is the recovery of the past that makes the future. Cisneros writes it in these words: "You must keep writing. It will keep you free, and I said yes, but at that time I didn't know what she meant."

Sandra Cisneros's text is a fictional autobiography of Esperanza Cordero. This is a postmodern form of fiction stitching together a series of lyrical pieces, "lazy poems" Cisneros calls them, into the narrativity of self-invention through writing. In her study on autobiography, Sidonie Smith establishes a theoretical position which is at once lucid and fully applicable to my endeavor in this essay. Esperanza's position as a woman gives a particularity to the writing itself in four instances: (1) the fiction of memory, (2) of self, (3) of the reader, and (4) of the narrativity itself. Her position of authority to interpret herself must be asserted by writing, but it must be done against the grain, for she lives in a patriarchal Mexican American culture where stories about women silence and subjugate them as in the case of her namesake, her great-grandmother. Finally, Esperanza's basis of authority—she knows what she has lived and felt better than anyone else—is vulnerable unless she asserts her presence in a specific everyday reality; in other words, it cannot slip into a daydream escape route which would be an evasion, not a liberation; she must make her presence, the presence of a woman writing.

Cisneros begins the end of her text with the affirmation of self-invention that displaces men's stories about women: "I like to tell stories. I am going to tell you a story about a girl who didn't want to belong." By writing, Esperanza has not only gained control of her past, she has created a present in which she can be free and belong at the same time. Her freedom is the fundamental freedom to be herself and she cannot be herself if she is entrapped in patriarchal narrativity. Mango Street will always be part of this woman, but she has taken the strength of trees unto herself and has found the courage to be the house of her dreams, her own self-invention.

Leslie S. Gutiérrez-Jones   (essay date 1993)

SOURCE: "Different Voices: The Re-*Bildung* of the Bar-

rio in Sandra Cisneros' *The House on Mango Street*," in *Anxious Power: Reading, Writing, and Ambivalence in Narrative by Women,* edited by Carol J. Singley and Susan Elizabeth Sweeney, State University of New York Press, 1993, pp. 295-312.

[*In the essay below, Gutiérrez-Jones discusses Cisneros's transformation of conventional elements of the* Bildungsroman *genre in* The House on Mango Street, *focusing on the link between communal and individual narrative strategies.*]

I

> The space of a tactic is the space of the other. Thus it must play on and with a terrain imposed on it and organized by the law of a foreign power.
> —de Certeau, *The Practice of Everyday Life*

Dreaming of a day when she might attain the "American dream" of home ownership, the young protagonist of Sandra Cisneros' ***The House on Mango Street*** promises herself that if that day comes, she will joyfully accommodate "passing bums" in her attic, because she "know[s] how it is to be without a house." Esperanza's lack of a "real house" to call her own repeatedly troubles this child of the barrio; when a nun from her school incredulously identifies the family's tenement lodgings, the little girl's sense of identity is devastated: "you live *there? The way she said it made me feel like nothing. There.* I lived *there.* I nodded. I knew then I had to have a house. A real house." The house of the title, which succeeds this apartment, still falls far short of Esperanza's dreams; it still "isn't it," not "a real house"— one with a yard and a fence and "real stairs, not hallway stairs, but stairs inside like the houses on T.V." Excluded from the suburban standard presented through her father's job and through television, Esperanza has available to her only external models—models she can "rent" but never own. Raised amid annual relocations, shared washrooms, and landlord-tenant battles, Esperanza also experiences her rootlessness on the most literal level; the house she searches for, she anxiously insists, must be one she "can point to." Acutely aware of the disempowerment that results from lacking "a home of one's own," she yearns to stake out an architectural space—one which she implicitly assumes will provide her with the "space" to develop a sense of identity and an artistic voice. But when architecture will not cooperate, she must look instead to her imagination in order to create a sense of place—one which can, in turn, provide a place for her writing.

Esperanza must learn to create for herself, and from herself, a "home" which will be truly hers. She finds—or creates—such a space for herself through her art, through the writing which her Aunt Lupe insists will keep her free.

Shifting from a literal to a metaphoric register, her "house" becomes not a structure she can point to, but a spiritual sanctuary she carries within: "only a house quiet as snow, a space for myself to go, clean as paper before the poem." During her year on Mango Street, Esperanza does develop a sense of place and identity: by the work's end, she has found peace and purpose in her writing; she has created for herself the "home in the heart" predicted by the local fortuneteller.

Just as Esperanza must leave behind her dependence on rented spaces and on standards external to her own experience, so Cisneros, a Chicana writer, is faced with the challenge of creating a home in the midst of a predominantly white, predominantly male, literary tradition: that of the *Bildungsroman*. Writer and character both face the conflict between desire for self-expression and fear of being co-opted by the very forms of self-expression available. The individual focus of writing, and particularly of the genre of the Bildungsroman, threatens to betray that aspect of identity which most calls out for expression: membership in a community. Only a fierce loyalty to this connection provides an adequate response, for Esperanza as for Cisneros, to the ambivalences generated by individual artistic achievement. Like her protagonist, who insists that the house of her own *cannot* be "a man's house"—especially "not a daddy's"—Cisneros must insistently remake the conventions and formulas of a patriarchal individualistic tradition, using them in order to transform them, tactically appropriating them in order to make them her own . . . and, by extension, her community's.

One model for understanding what is at stake in such an appropriation may be found in Michel de Certeau's analysis of the creative art forms of the disempowered, the "subtle, stubborn, resistant activity of groups, which, since they lack their own space, have to get along in a network of already established forces and relationships." For the marginalized writer, the "already established forces and relationships" are represented by the literary tradition of the dominant culture: the genre definitions, the intertextual "lineage," the theoretical frameworks, and the like. Such products of hegemonic culture are ubiquitous, and contact with them virtually inescapable; any writer, then, becomes a "consumer" of sorts. But consumption for de Certeau may become a form of production: creativity may thus be expressed in the Chicana writer's "ways of using," in her "innumerable and infinite small transformations of and within the dominant cultural economy in order to adapt it to [her] own interests and [her] own rules." Cisneros, in de Certeau's terms, "poaches" upon the supposedly private reserve of the white male Anglo-European literary tradition, moving like a nomad "across fields she did not write." Like Esperanza, she can neither purchase nor inherit a "ready-made" structure to call home, but instead creates from within a new space, a home in the heart where her fellow transients are welcome.

II

We advanced none to the rank of Masters but such as clearly felt and recognized the purpose they were born for, and had got enough of practice to proceed along their way with a certain cheerfulness and ease.
—Goethe, *Wilhelm Meister's Apprenticeship*

As a ready-made structure for a Chicana writer to inhabit, the Bildungsroman poses some serious problems, and so we should examine the literary territory Cisneros would occupy. On the most basic level, the controversy that surrounds any attempt to define this genre leaves the location of its "walls" quite uncertain. Among scholars of English literature, Jerome Buckley's *Season of Youth* remains the most popular touchstone for revision and debate; but perhaps Randolf Shaffner's study of the apprenticeship novel, which follows Buckley's analysis, illuminates most clearly the strain that would be involved in simply "inserting" a Chicana protagonist into Buckley's master plot. Shaffner begins his study with an explicit statement equating his use of the terms "Bildungsroman" and "apprenticeship novel"—an equation reinforced by his title. The concept of apprenticeship, however, by suggesting its senior counterpart, makes explicit the goals of normative—white, male—"development"; two items on Shaffner's "checklist" of the genre's distinguishing traits make glaringly apparent his model's essential incompatibility with Cisneros' project. According to Shaffner, the *Bildungsroman* presupposes "the belief that a young person can become adept in the art of life *and become a master*," as well as "the prerequisite of *potential for development into a master*" (emphasis mine). In Goethe's terms, he must be able to recognize the purpose he was born for. Esperanza may achieve a certain level of control over her life and art, even a certain (heavily circumscribed) sense of power and potential—but the society which constructs and sanctions the identity of "master" will nevertheless deny her this title based on her status as a Chicana. The issue of potentiality (and its corollary, another of Shaffner's presuppositions: "the key notion of choice") sets up the major tension for a female Bildungsroman: if *bildung* is the tradition whereby the "young male hero discovers himself and his social role," and if the sanctioned social role of women still precludes a true search for, or discovery of, an individual "self," how can this young *female* hero hope to experience a counterpart to bildung?

When Esther Labovitz tackles the problematic issue of defining a female Bildungsroman, she astutely identifies a number of the changes such a hybrid would entail, especially concerning distinctions between male and female parameters of rebellion; yet she assumes that the female Bildungsroman evolved naturally during the twentieth century in response to women's improved social conditions, developing belatedly as "cultural and social structures appeared to support women's struggle for independence." The degree to which the "cultural and social structures" cited by Labovitz as supporting women's independence are, in fact, in place for women of color (or more generally for women marginalized and oppressed on account of race, ethnicity, sexual orientation, or socioeconomic class) seems questionable; but, more critically, her analysis of the female Bildungsroman suggests a trajectory which would (and supposedly *should*) parallel the male version, presumably "catching up" at the projected point at which women's independence gains full social support: the point at which a young woman's rebelliousness, like a young man's, could be relegated to a simple and temporary "stage" preceding "mature" acceptance of the established social order. But while the Bildungsroman of a white western bourgeois male—or even, theoretically, of a "liberated" white western bourgeois female—might appropriately provide a dénouement stressing the achievement of "a proper balance between internal individual development and external submissions to group regulations," such a resolution would likely undercut the social critique of a politically self-conscious writer, or protagonist, of color.

Cisneros' narrator does finally achieve a sense of calm resolution, but it is not the resolution of surrender or acceptance; rather, Esperanza insists with quiet determination that she has "gone away to come back." She has left behind her selfish desire to escape, alone, from the barrio of Mango Street, not to return "until somebody makes it better." Realizing "Who's going to do it? The mayor?," Esperanza commits herself to changing, not accepting, the established order—to becoming that somebody who is emphatically not the mayor and who will indeed try to make it better. Esperanza's final determination to return to Mango Street "for the ones [she] left behind. For the ones who cannot [get] out" reflects a crucial point of difference from the sacred ground of the literary genre upon which Cisneros is poaching.

This shift from an individual to a communal perspective marks a significant turn upon the highly individualistic tradition Cisneros would "homestead." The Bildungsroman's emphasis on the individual reverberates with ethnocentric assumptions and political implications, as Susan Stanford Friedman notes, along with other feminist and cultural critics:

> Isolate individualism is an illusion. It is also the privilege of power. A white man has the luxury of forgetting his skin color and sex. He can think of himself as an "individual." Women and minorities, reminded at every turn in the great cultural hall of mirrors of their sex or color, have no such luxury.

A strong focus on the autonomous subject (exemplified by

Bildungsromane such as Joyce's *A Portrait of the Artist as a Young Man*) would betray Cisneros' political ideology in writing the life of a sexually, ethnically, and economically marginalized protagonist like Esperanza. As Esperanza's culture and experience little resembles Stephen Dedalus', so Cisneros' rendering of her narrative must distance itself from Joyce's; the Bildungsroman's privileging of the individual must not negate Esperanza's, and Cisneros', commitment to the community.

As narrator, Esperanza creates and chronicles her developing identity not through self-absorbed introspection, but by noting, recording, and responding to the lives around her—those lives for whom almost half of the collection's forty-four "prose poems" are named, and whose significance is underscored by Cisneros' title, which situates Esperanza not as a solitary loner but as she comes to perceive herself: a product and member of a particular community. Immune to the "privilege of power" associated with glorifying the individual, Esperanza comes to understand that the three strange sisters, and her friend Alicia, are right: Mango may say "goodbye *sometimes*," but even when set free from the physical locale, Esperanza "will *always* be Mango Street" (my emphases). Protagonists like Cisneros' might be outsiders vis à vis the dominant culture, yet they are emphatically not loners. Unlike the traditional "American" hero, who underscores his independence by isolating himself on the high seas (Captain Ahab), in the wilderness (Thoreau), in the "territories" (Huck Finn), or on the road (Jack Kerouac), Cisneros' hero has no such choice. Esperanza has already been symbolically cast out of mainstream "American" suburbia; her status as outsider is not chosen, but imposed. Yet she does not react to her exteriority by perceiving herself as "alone against the world." Rather, Esperanza defines herself as a member of a community—the community that is Mango Street.

III

> Let one forget his reason for being, they'd all droop like tulips in a glass, each with their arms around the other. Keep, keep, keep, trees say when I sleep. They teach.
>
> —Sandra Cisneros, *The House on Mango Street*

The reconceptualization of identity and individual development found in Cisneros' work radically transforms both the Bildungsroman and the standard wisdom of developmental psychology. Carol Gilligan takes issue with the traditional "developmental litany" which "intones the celebration of separation, autonomy, individuation, and natural rights." Gilligan cites Nancy Chodorow's claim for differences between female and male identity formation based on the child's recognition of similarity to (female) or difference from (male) the primary caretaker—most often maternal in our society—in order to examine both its empirical effects and its theoretical implications. Criticizing conventional notions that reduce development to a simple linear ordering based on separation, Gilligan instead envisions separation and attachment as a "reiterative counterpoint in human experience," recognizing both the "role of separation as it defines and empowers the self" and "the ongoing process of attachment that creates and sustains the human community." She sees a mature stage of development as one in which the individual recognizes her interconnectedness with the world, achieving a balance between responsibility to herself and responsibility to others.

Cisneros' Esperanza explores the difficulties—and the possibilities—inherent in the struggle for such a balance, as she learns that neither self nor community can sustain itself independently; each requires the other. For example, when she senses the difficulty of reconciling "femininity" with conventional notions of adulthood, she determines "not to grow up tame like the others" and instead practices her "own quiet war," "leav[ing] the table *like a man,* without putting back the chair or picking up the plate" (emphasis mine). But this strategy of male emulation only shifts the burden to her mother (whose sacrifices are described in the segment which immediately follows), and casts herself into the role of the "bad" woman, the villainess in the movies "with red red lips who is beautiful and cruel." Esperanza admires the selfishness of this woman whose "power is her own. She will not give it away," yet when she tries to envision such an identity for herself, the callousness of such power brings her to an abrupt—and disturbing—realization. When "the three sisters"—her friends' *comadres,* whose eerie clairvoyance suggests both the Fates and Macbeth's witches—order her to make a wish, she complies, thinking "Well, why not?" But when she is immediately reprimanded, "When you leave you must remember to come back for the others," she feels chastised and guilty: "Then I didn't know what to say. It was as if she could read my mind, as if she knew what I had wished for, and I felt ashamed for having made such a selfish wish."

The sisters recognize that Esperanza is "special," that "she'll go very far," and that she does therefore have a responsibility to herself and her talent, a responsibility which will necessitate her packing her "bags of books and paper." Esperanza likewise realizes the implications of her talents, acknowledging in her final vignette that she will indeed go far: "one day I will say goodbye to Mango. I am too strong for her to keep me here forever." And yet her power and freedom are both circumscribed and expanded through being shared. She will never be like the "tame" women "who lay their necks on the threshold waiting for the ball and chain"; but neither will she be like Stephen Dedalus, who

sees his art as a function of his own autonomy, necessitating his abandonment of home, fatherland, and church. Esperanza senses her ongoing responsibility: not toward the centers of (relative) power, the fathers and husbands who contribute to the oppression of Mango Street's women by demanding obedience and docility, but toward those to whom Cisneros has dedicated the work: "*A las Mujeres.*" Her loyalty is toward the less powerful, the less strong, the less articulate in the dominant language: toward those, the sisters remind her, "who cannot leave as easily as you." Although she recognizes in her closing statement that her achievements might be misunderstood by friends and neighbors, she reassures herself that all will be rectified: "They will not know I have gone away to come back. For the ones I left behind. For the ones who cannot get out." By the end of her narrative, then, Esperanza attains the balanced maturity described by Gilligan.

In order to reach this resolution, Esperanza must juggle her conflicting feelings toward suburban havens (**"Sally"** versus **"Those Who Don't"**); toward the onset of sexuality (**"Sire"** versus **"Red Clowns"**); toward marriage (**"Marin"** versus **"Linoleum Roses"**); and toward fathers (**"Papa Who Wakes Up Tired in the Dark"** versus **"What Sally Said"**). Throughout these struggles Esperanza continues to value connectedness; for example, although she first describes her younger sister Nenny as a burden ("Since she comes after me, she is my responsibility"), Nenny provokes more loyalty than resentment. When Nenny reveals her childish ignorance about the mystery of women's hips, Esperanza stubbornly stands by her:

> If you don't get them you may turn into a man. Nenny says this and she believes it. She is this way because of her age.
>
> That's right, I add before Lucy or Rachel can make fun of her. She is stupid alright, but she *is* my sister.

Putting her critical judgments aside, Esperanza asserts her familial loyalty above all. Similarly, her thoughts of her parents are filled not with the hostility and resentment of a sullen adolescent, but with tenderness and gratitude for the emotional security they provide:

> my mother's hair . . . sweet to put your nose into when she is holding you, holding you and you feel safe, is the warm smell of bread before you bake it, is the smell when she makes a little room for you on her side of the bed still warm with her skin, and you sleep near her, the rain outside falling and Papa snoring. The snoring, the rain, and mama's hair that smells like bread.

Likewise, she does her best to return such comfort, as she later sympathizes with her grieving father:

> my brave Papa cries. I have never seen my Papa cry and don't know what to do. . . .
>
> And I think if my own Papa died what would I do. I hold my Papa in my arms. I hold and hold and hold him.

The continuity between generations will remain unbroken; as her father weeps for the loss of his parent, Esperanza recognizes that some day she will in turn grieve his death—and will herself need to be held and held and held.

Esperanza's compassion extends beyond these ties to her immediate family, to the many abused or abandoned wives of Mango Street: to Rosa Vargas, "who is tired all the time from buttoning and bottling and babying and who cries every day for the man who left without even leaving a dollar for bologna or a note explaining how come," to Rafaela and Sally, whose husbands jealously lock them away, to Minerva, with whom Esperanza shares her poems. Her intuitive understanding of other, younger women—women closer to her own age—is especially striking, as she attains a sort of omniscience born of empathy:

> Marin, under the streetlight, dancing by herself, is singing the same song somewhere. I know. Is waiting for a car to stop, a star to fall, someone to change her life. Anybody. . . .
>
> Sally, do you sometimes wish you didn't have to go home? . . . You could close your eyes and you wouldn't have to worry about what people said because you never belonged here anyway and nobody could make you sad and nobody would think you're strange because you like to dream and dream . . . when all you wanted, all you wanted, Sally, was to love and to love and to love and to love and no one could call that crazy.

In such passages Esperanza's usually simple prose style reaches a lyrical intensity, as she gives voice to the longing for love and striving after dreams which breeds loneliness—and the seeds of dependency ("someone to change her life")—in these young women. In particular, Esperanza grasps Sally's unhappiness, and shares with her the anguish of a home that can never fulfill that term's promise—a home which is not her own, a home where she "never belonged . . . anyway."

Esperanza bonds with Marin and Sally over the sort of fantasies in which many residents of this barrio indulge; yet even more pervasive on Mango Street, when such escapism fails, is the sense of exclusion. Esperanza feels strongly for all her neighbors who "don't belong": the unhappy Mamacita who speaks no English, the eccentric Ruthie who "laughs all by herself," Esperanza's own Aunt Lupe "sick from the disease that would not go," and others. Through her sympathy for these individuals' plights, Esperanza comes to understand the nature of xenophobia, sexism, and bigotry—the fear of difference which excludes, and even ridicules, Mamacita, Ruthie, and Lupe, not for who they are but for how they look and how they speak. Esperanza has herself participated in such injustice, as when she joins her friends in mocking Lupe's infirmity. This cruelty, generated spontaneously from the obliviousness of a childhood game, is unintentional; Esperanza's simple defense is "We didn't know. She had been dying such a long time we forgot." But when her aunt does finally die, the girls take on responsibility for her death, and Esperanza unsparingly shoulders her share of the burden for their communal guilt:

> Most likely I will go to hell and most likely I deserve to be there. My mother says I was born on an evil day and prays for me. Lucy and Rachel pray too. For ourselves and for each other . . . because of what we did to Aunt Lupe.

Such painful experiences with "difference" elucidate Esperanza's encounters with racial prejudice: with misunderstanding and fear born of ignorance, and with the phenomenon of not belonging.

> Those who don't know any better come into our neighborhood scared. They think we're dangerous. . . . They are stupid people who are lost and got here by mistake.
>
> But we aren't afraid. . . .
>
> All brown all around, we are safe. But watch us drive into a neighborhood of another color and our knees go shakity-shake and our car windows get rolled up tight and our eyes look straight. Yeah. That is how it goes and goes.

Esperanza does not learn such lessons as an isolate individual, but rather shares them (as do the weird sisters), as part of a group: as one of three girlhood friends, in the case of mocking Lupe, or as part of a general "we" of Mango Street, in the case of **"Those Who Don't."** Her budding feminism, like this sensitivity to the dynamics of exclusion, is also gained through interaction and involvement with others. She recognizes the dangers of her gender and refuses the threatened "ball and chain" partly in response to the experiences and warnings of others (for example, her mother in **"A Smart Cookie"**) and partly in response to her own experiences with harassment and abuse, the majority of which either occur in the company of her friends (**"The Family of Little Feet"**), or result from a betrayal by more "sophisticated" classmates like Sally (**"The Monkey Garden"** and **"Red Clowns"**). Bearing out Gilligan's assertions, Esperanza does not experience—or narrate—the harsh lessons of growing up as an autonomous, self-absorbed individual, but as a sensitive and involved member of a community.

This more interactive model for development—what Gilligan refers to as a privileging of "identity as relationship"—may yet precipitate its own anxieties and ambivalences, especially in earlier stages of development, when, according to Gilligan, the sense of responsibility to others may overwhelm a sense of responsibility to oneself. At this stage Gilligan notes the emergence of a pattern of fears based on the "danger" of individual success. While an individual who privileges separation will experience relations with others in terms of a hierarchy, characters like Esperanza, who privilege attachment, may perceive her interaction with others in terms of a "web." These two metaphors imply contrasting goals (respectively, moving up versus staying centered) and contrasting dangers (entrapment born of intimacy versus isolation born of achievement). Rather than the more typically "male" anxiety—"the wish to be alone at the top and the consequent fear that others will get too close"—Esperanza must come to terms with "the wish to be at the center of connection and the consequent fear of being too far out on the edge." By determinedly marching away, yet with equal determination promising a return and reconciliation, Esperanza achieves a sense of balance between her own needs and the needs of her community—to the benefit of both.

IV

"Something" *different* speaks again and presents itself to the masters in the various forms of non-labor—the savage, the madman, the child, even woman.

—Michel de Certeau, *The Practice of Everyday Life*

Esperanza's narrative itself attains a similar balance between her needs and the community's. Just as she can understand and express the "voices" of silenced women like Marin and Sally, so too she "knows" and conveys experiences such as those of the anonymous hit-and-run victim, **"Geraldo No Last Name."** Geraldo died without having met Esperanza (she hears only the barest outlines of the episode, through her friend), and lived a life quite removed from her own, as a non-English-speaking (probably undocumented) immi-

grant. Yet she intuitively grasps—and communicates—aspects of his life otherwise closed off to acquaintances, doctors, police, and even his own family:

> They never saw the kitchenettes. They never knew about the two-room flats and sleeping rooms he rented, the weekly money orders sent home, the currency exchange. How could they?

> His name was Geraldo. And his home is in another country. The ones he left behind are far away. They will wonder. Shrug. Remember. Geraldo. He went north . . . we never heard from him again.

Esperanza speaks for the excluded, in de Certeau's terms "the various forms of non-labor": the sickly, the deranged, the abused, the anonymous dead and the disempowered; the simple poetry of her prose gives voice to the "cries of the People excluded from the written." She expresses herself as an artist by expressing the struggles of others, establishing her own identity as she conveys the identity of her neighborhood.

Esperanza does not experience—or narrate—the harsh lessons of growing up as an autonomous, self-absorbed individual, but as a sensitive and involved member of a community.
—Leslie S. Gutiérrez-Jones

Yet even with such a noble project, valorizing the lives of those not generally considered worthy of literary attention, Esperanza is still faced with the potentially alienating effects of artistic achievement: the more her identity becomes that of "the writer," the less she will be an ordinary member of her own community. As an intellectual and artistic enterprise, writing confers upon the writer a certain power: a certain autonomy, control, and *authority* which is likely to distance the writer from her own *dis*empowered community. De Certeau conveys just such a problematic when he associates the origins of written culture with the privileging of the autonomous individual, with the "mastery" of a hegemonic culture based on rationality, industry, and economic production. Powerless and placeless, the nonelite consumers of this master culture function as the oral disruption, the voices upon whose existence *and exclusion* the production of writing depends.

Esperanza (and, by extension, Cisneros) undercuts this alienating *authority,* evading its threatened division from the community by expressing herself and her subjects in prose which eschews the conventions of formal literary language.

The simple, childlike poetry of **Mango Street** does *not* stifle "the cries of the People excluded from the written" to provide a monologic narrative or an omnipotent narrator; rather, Esperanza gives expression to "a kind of speech" which emerges as "what 'escapes' from the domination of a sociocultural economy," from the tyranny of the written word. With the informal eloquence of a storyteller, she captures rhythms of speech and dynamics of conversation, conveying the oral element(s) of the barrio's voice(s). Quotation and explication are interwoven smoothly, with no quotation marks to isolate and contain other voices; for example, her own and her mother's voices are allowed to flow and alternate without interruption:

> Today while cooking oatmeal she is Madame Butterfly until she sighs and points the wooden spoon at me. I could've been somebody, you know? Esperanza, you go to school. Study hard. That Madame Butterfly was a fool. She stirs the oatmeal. Look at my *comadres.* She means Izaura whose husband left and Yolanda whose husband is dead. Got to take care all your own, she says shaking her head.

Similarly, free indirect discourse conveys the distressed and disjointed rhythms of Marin's narrative, even when Esperanza's retelling of it shifts pronouns into the third person.

> And how was she to know she'd be the last one to see him alive. An accident, don't you know. . . . And he was just someone she danced with. Somebody she met that night. That's right.
>
> That's the story. That's what she said again and again. Once to the hospital people and twice to the police.

At times Esperanza's narrative voice drops out altogether and she is heard faintly (even lost) among a chaotic chorus of children's voices, as in the segment made up entirely of dialogue (or multiple monologue) entitled **"And Some More"**:

> There's that wide puffy cloud that looks like your face when you wake up after falling asleep with all your clothes on.
>
> Reynaldo, Angelo, Albert, Armando, Mario . . .
>
> Not my face. Looks like your fat face.
>
> Rita, Margie, Ernie . . .
>
> Whose fat face?

> Esperanza's fat face, that's who. Looks like Esperanza's ugly face when she comes to school in the morning.

Such a blending of competing voices would elicit anxiety and resentment from a narrator like Stephen Dedalus, but for Esperanza this cacophony produces only light-hearted (and self-critical) humor, as Nenny's catalogue of cloud names finally intersects—and comments on—the bickering of the group:

> Your ugly mama's toes.
>
> That's stupid.
> Bebe, Blanca, Benny . . .
>
> Who's stupid?
>
> Rachel, Lucy, Esperanza, and Nenny.

The competing voices eventually blend to produce a sort of harmony—even a simple wry wisdom—in a way that a monologic narrative would not allow. Such rhetorical instances mark yet another aspect of Esperanza's unique development toward an artistic voice and a sense of self which would achieve an ongoing balance between connection and separation. Esperanza does not need either to indulge in self-imposed exile nor to inhabit externally-imposed, rented spaces that can never be her own; instead she creates a true home—a home in the heart—by absorbing and embracing the voices of her community.

The House on Mango Street, then, despite its apparently "single" narrator, expresses the multiplicity of focus found in many recent works of fiction by women: Alice Munro's *The Lives of Girls and Women,* Gloria Naylor's *The Women of Brewster Place,* Joan Chase's *During the Reign of the Queen of Persia,* Louise Erdrich's *Love Medicine,* Nicholasa Mohr's *Rituals of Survival,* Alison Lurie's *Only Children,* and Amy Tan's *The Joy Luck Club.* Telling a communal story diffuses the problematic ideology of individualism, and allows female writers the opportunity to explore (and potentially to resolve) tensions between group involvement and individual autonomy—tensions that cannot be addressed within a literary tradition glorifying a single protagonist. The genre of the Bildungsroman, then, provides a particularly treacherous, yet particularly rewarding, ground for Cisneros' "poaching." As the young Esperanza must create an identity for herself in a fictional world which denies selfhood to members of her sex, her class, and her ethnic group, Cisneros must create her own space, and assert her own voice, within a culture not historically open to her; her tactic of poaching upon the Bildungsroman provides an opportunity, as it were, to renovate and remodel the rented cultural space of this patriarchal genre, in order to make it her own.

Jean Wyatt (essay date Fall 1995)

SOURCE: "On Not Being La Malinche: Border Negotiations of Gender in Sandra Cisneros's 'Never Marry a Mexican' and 'Woman Hollering Creek,'" in *Tulsa Studies in Women's Literature,* Vol. 14, No. 2, Fall, 1995, pp. 243-72.

[In the following essay, Wyatt explores the transformations of feminine "icons" of Anglo and Mexican gender ideology by "borderland" cultural assumptions in "Never Marry a Mexican," "Woman Hollering Creek," and "Little Miracles, Kept Promises."]

Like many of the stories in **Woman Hollering Creek,** the title story and **"Never Marry a Mexican"** describe the advantages and the difficulties of "straddling two countries," as Cisneros describes the condition of living on the border between Anglo and Mexican cultures. In addition, these two stories deal with a problem specific to women: the female protagonists of **"Woman Hollering Creek"** and **"Never Marry a Mexican"** wrestle with Mexican icons of sexuality and motherhood that, internalized, seem to impose on them a limited and even negative definition of their own identities as women. In **"Never Marry a Mexican"** the protagonist, Clemencia, throws her energy into defying the model of La Malinche, a historical figure who over centuries of patriarchal mythmaking has become the representative of a female sexuality at once passive, "rapeable," and always already guilty of betrayal. In **"Woman Hollering Creek"** the protagonist, Cleófilas, must redefine La Llorona, the figure of traditional Mexican folklore who wanders wailing for her lost children, in order to redefine her own possibilities as a woman and a mother. On the one hand, the stories emphasize the tenacity of these icons' hold on Chicanas' and Mexican women's self-images. On the other hand, the protagonists inhabit a border zone between Anglo and Mexican cultures where the perpetual clash and collision of two sets of signifiers, two systems of social myth, can throw any one culture's gender ideology into question. **"Woman Hollering Creek"** dramatizes the positive aspect of border living—the possibilities it offers for transformation. But borderland existence can be disabling too: in **"Never Marry a Mexican"** the ambiguous space between cultures generates only confusion and, finally, a newly rigid gender definition. It is the dialectic between the fluidity of the borderland and the seeming intransigence of internalized icons of womanhood in **"Never Marry a Mexican"** and **"Woman Hollering Creek"** that this essay will explore.

It would seem, from what Chicana feminist writers report, that Mexican social myths of gender crystallize with special force in three icons: "Guadalupe, the virgin mother who has not abandoned us, la *Chingada* (Malinche), the raped mother whom we have abandoned, and la Llorona, the mother who seeks her lost children." According to the evi-

dence of Chicana feminist writers, these "three Our Mothers" haunt the sexual and maternal identities of contemporary Mexican and Chicana women. Cherríe Moraga, for instance, asserts that "there is hardly a Chicana growing up today who does not suffer under [La Malinche's] name." And Norma Alarcón, writing about the same legendary figure, says, "the pervasiveness of the myth is unfathomable, often permeating and suffusing our very being without conscious awareness." Cisneros speaks, in her interview with Pilar Aranda, of her own difficulties in growing up with a negative and a positive role model always held up before her—La Malinche and La Virgen de Guadalupe. These "ghosts" still haunt her, she says, and she writes not to exorcise them—that is impossible—but to "make [my] peace with those ghosts." In an interview with Reed Dasenbrock and Feroza Jussawalla, Cisneros claims that the narrative of Rosario in a third story in the collection, **"Little Miracles, Kept Promises,"** represents her own negotiation with the figure of the Virgen de Guadalupe. That story, which I will come back to at the end of this essay, makes it clear that Cisneros considers Mexican icons of femininity to be intimately bound up with individual Chicanas' and Mexican women's self-images and self-esteem; to live with them comfortably—and there is no way to run away from them—each woman has to "make her peace with them" in her own way.

> ... the protagonists inhabit a border zone between Anglo and Mexican cultures where the perpetual clash and collision of two sets of signifiers, two systems of social myth, can throw any one culture's gender ideology into question.
>
> —*Jean Wyatt*

A borderland offers a space where such a negotiation with fixed gender ideals is at least possible. Where cultures overlap, definitions become fluid. Cisneros draws attention to the shifting meaning of signifiers in the border zone by using the same "border" phrase to mean two different things: recurring in **"Never Marry a Mexican"** and **"Woman Hollering Creek,"** the phrase *"en el otro lado"*—"on the other side"—can mean either the U.S. or Mexico, shifting its referent according to where the speaker stands. Likewise, "Mexican" in the opening paragraph of **"Never Marry a Mexican"** means first a Mexican national, then a U.S. citizen of Mexican descent. Fixed definitions waver as the words in which they are moored lose their stability. Cisneros also puts the unitary definitions of things into motion by juxtaposing English and Spanish. For instance, in the story **"*Bien* Pretty"** in the same collection, the narrator ponders: "*Urracas.* Grackles. *Urracas.* Different ways of looking at the same bird."

The shift from one language to the other and back again implies a shift between cultural codes: the narrator is able to look at the bird from one side of the border, then from the other. And that "double vision" precludes a single authoritative definition of grackle. As with "grackle," so with "woman." A woman living on the border has a better chance of shaking off the hold of any single culture's gender definition because she has to move back and forth between Mexican and Anglo signifying systems, in, as Gloria Anzaldúa puts it, a "continual creative motion that keeps breaking down the unitary aspect of each paradigm."

In **"Woman Hollering Creek"** the word "Woman" (and therewith the gender role) becomes unstable as it is interpreted first within a Mexican symbolic system, then within a Chicana symbolic system. While the Mexican woman, Cleófilas, can hear in the sound of the river called Woman Hollering Creek only the wail of La Llorona, a Mexican figure of sorrowing womanhood, the Chicana Felice interprets the creek's sound—its "hollering"—as a "Tarzan hoot," and so gives both the word "Hollering" and the concept "Woman" a new definition. Felice can go back and forth between cultural paradigms, see things first from a Mexican perspective, then from an Anglo perspective, and take her choice of signifiers (and of mythic figures) from either side. Felice goes to *el otro lado*—the other side—of the gender border as well, appropriating Tarzan's cry from the territory of masculinity. If border living means that one can move back and forth across national boundaries—if one can choose to see birds as grackles or *urracas*—why should the border between genders remain inviolable? Why should Tarzan's expressive cry remain eternally and exclusively attached to an icon of masculinity if Felice can use it to express her own vision of womanhood? **"Woman Hollering Creek"** thus opens up gender definitions on all sides to the fluidity of border existence.

"Never Marry a Mexican," however, complicates the notion of subverting feminine gender roles by borrowing from masculinity: in reaction to the passive sexuality ascribed to La Malinche, Clemencia adopts the aggressive, violent sexual stance of the *"chingón,"* but that tactic fails to release her from the influence of the Malinche legend. Escaping the crippling polarities of gender is not so simple as appropriating the gestures of masculinity, then. (Clemencia's and Felice's subversions of gender—the one failed, the other successful—set up an interesting dialectic with Judith Butler's theory of gender as performance, a dialectic that I explore in the final section of this essay.) Likewise, **"Never Marry a Mexican"** tempers the optimism of **"Woman Hollering Creek"** about border existence. If shuttling back and forth between the standpoints of two different cultures can be creative, as it is in **"Woman Hollering Creek"**—if, as Anzaldúa says, thinking simultaneously through two divergent cultural paradigms can en-

gender a third way of looking at the world, a *mestiza* way—inhabiting a border zone can also mean getting caught between cultures. Clemencia in **"Never Marry a Mexican"** is stranded in the interstices, in "the space between the different worlds she inhabits," as Anzaldúa puts it. Both "alienated from her mother culture [and] 'alien' in the dominant culture," Clemencia does not fully grasp the meanings of either Mexican or Anglo signifying systems.

"Never Marry a Mexican"

The opening paragraph of **"Never Marry a Mexican"** introduces boundary living as Clemencia's heritage: "Never marry a Mexican, my ma said once and always. She said this because of my father. She said this though she was Mexican too. But she was born here in the U.S., and he was born there, and it's *not* the same, you know." As in *Woman Hollering Creek* generally, the ambiguity of border existence is immediately tied to the ambiguity of language. "Mexican" seems to mean two different things within the same paragraph: does Mexican mean a Mexican national or a U.S. citizen who identifies as Mexican? This sliding of "Mexican" from one side of the border to the other suggests the entitlement that Clemencia's birth position gives her to a vision that perceives things from both sides of the border at once. But the ambiguity of the word "Mexican" can also suggest confusion, and in Clemencia's story Cisneros explores the down side of being a *mestiza,* the discursive bewilderment that can result from living in the space where two cultural systems meet and conflict. As the focus of verbal ambiguity on the word "Mexican" implies, Clemencia's discursive confusion encompasses a confusion about her own identity and about her position in both Mexican and Anglo discourses.

In her interview with Aranda, Cisneros describes the discomfort of "being a Mexican woman living in an American society, but not belonging to either culture" as a kind of cultural "schizophrenia"—the negative version of Anzaldúa's double vision: "We're not Mexican and in some sense we're not American. I could not live in Mexico because my ideas are too . . . americanized. On the other hand, I can't live in America, or I do live here, but, in some ways, almost like a foreigner." In **"Never Marry a Mexican"** Cisneros dramatizes this double unbelonging through Clemencia's inability to function in either Anglo or Mexican discourse. "That's . . . water under the damn," she remarks, glossing her own speech: "I can't ever get the sayings right even though I was born in this country. We didn't say shit like that in our house." The disparity between the discourse "in this country" and the discourse "in our house" leaves Clemencia caught between, at home neither at home nor in "this"—her own—country.

Clemencia's response to bicultural indeterminacy is to

throw out the undecideable term—Mexican. In the following passage she is warming to her opening theme, "I've never married and never will," by listing the men she could never marry. But she is also negating the term "Mexican," apparently unaware of the implications for her own identity:

> Mexican men, forget it. For a long time the men clearing off the tables or chopping meat behind the butcher counter or driving the bus I rode to school every day, those weren't men. Not men I considered as potential lovers. Mexican, Puerto Rican, Cuban, Chilean, Colombian, Panamanian, Salvadorean, Bolivian, Honduran, Argentine, Dominican, Venezuelan, Guatemalan, Ecuadorean, Nicaraguan, Peruvian, Costa Rican, Paraguayan, Uruguayan, I don't care. I never saw them. My mother did this to me.

While Clemencia attributes her avoidance to her mother's advice, "Never marry a Mexican," she strays from her mother's discourse—where Mexican means a Mexican national, with Clemencia's father as prototype—into Anglo discourse. She borrows the Anglo habit of lumping all Latinos into a single monolithic identity—"Mexican"—a label that erases individual difference and distinct cultures to consign all brown-skinned persons to a single category. As in (racist) Anglo discourse, Clemencia's word choice blurs the distinction between race and class: "Mexican" here means busboys, butchers' assistants, bus drivers—working-class men lumped together under an ethnic label that in actuality designates a class—a class of servers. Clemencia dissociates herself from a Mexican or Mexican American discourse that would define these individuals differently.

But Clemencia has not mastered Anglo discourse either. And using that discourse without fully recognizing its racist values makes her miscalculate her own position in the sexual contract with Drew. To Drew, the white lover who abandoned her eighteen years before and who remains the obsessive center of her thinking, "Mexican" means Clemencia herself, as his own language makes clear when he breaks off their affair: "Hadn't I understood . . . he could *never* marry *me*. You didn't think . . .? *Never marry a Mexican. Never marry a Mexican* . . . No, of course not. I see. I see." What is a "Mexican"? An inappropriate other. But who that other is depends on where you stand; and Clemencia, caught between two discourses, has a foothold in neither. Although Clemencia of course means the term "Mexican" to apply only to men, only to potential suitors, the word is a shifter in this story, and its shifting does not stop at men, but moves on to designate Clemencia herself. Adopting the Anglo racist definition of "Mexican" ultimately means identifying against herself; and having emptied the term of value ("those weren't men . . . I never saw them"), she is left without resources when "Mexican" confronts her as the signifier of her own identity. The discursive naiveté that led Clemencia to misinterpret "Mexican," and her own social position, has tragic consequences; abandoned by Drew, she remains in an abstract space between cultures, isolated from both Anglo and Mexican American communities, where she replays in memory scenes from the sexual drama with Drew that took place eighteen years earlier.

Like her tactic of dismissing the signifier "Mexican" without examining her own implication in the cultural context she is throwing out, Clemencia deals with the influence of La Malinche on her sexuality not through introspection, but through outright repudiation of the passive, guilty sexuality that La Malinche models and through the definition of her own sexuality, in opposition, as active, violent, aggressive.

An Aztec princess sold into slavery, Malintzin, or Malinche, eventually became Cortez's translator; she was also his lover and the mother of their son, Don Martín, the first *mestizo*, of mixed Indian and Spanish parentage. Malinche not only translated for Cortez; she also advised him, giving away religious secrets of the Aztecs that allowed him to impose his authority on them. While the dignity and competence of the historical Malintzin were apparently respected by both Indians and Spanish, after independence Mexican storytellers pinned the blame for the Conquest on her complicity with Cortez and more specifically on her sexual complicity. As Cherríe Moraga explains, "Malintzin, also called Malinche, fucked the white man who conquered the Indian peoples of Mexico and destroyed their culture. Ever since, brown men have been accusing her of betraying her race, and over the centuries continue to blame her entire sex for this 'transgression.'" She is "slandered as La Chingada, meaning the 'fucked one,' or La Vendida, a sell-out to the white race." While it would seem that mastering several languages, giving successful strategic advice, negotiating between Indians and Spaniards, and enabling the Conquest imply an active competence, Malinche is characterized not as doing but as done to: "In the very act of intercourse with Cortez, Malinche is seen as having been violated. She is not, however, an innocent victim, but the guilty party—ultimately responsible for her own sexual victimization." Lack of agency together with guilt: according to Chicana feminists, contemporary Chicanas and Mexican women have to bear the full weight of this paradox. Norma Alarcón writes that "the myth contains the following sexual possibilities: woman is sexually passive, and hence at all times open to potential use by men whether it be seduction or rape. . . . nothing she does is perceived as a choice. Because Malintzin aided Cortés in the Conquest of the New World, she is seen as concretizing woman's sexual weakness . . . always open to sexual exploitation." By virtue of having female genitalia, then, woman is sexually guilty—guilty for being open to the world.

It is against this passive sexual identity that Clemencia defines herself. Although she accepted, laughing, the pet names Drew gave her—"Malinalli, Malinche, my courtesan"—apparently careless of the betrayal connoted by replaying the part of native courtesan to Drew's white conqueror, she rebels against the model of Malinche as sexually exploited victim, as "the *Chingada* . . . the Mother forcibly opened, violated." Octavio Paz elaborates all the meanings of *chingar* in an effort to understand "the strange permanence of Cortés and La Malinche in the Mexican's imagination." He argues, "The ultimate meaning always contains the idea of aggression. . . . The verb denotes violence, an emergence from oneself to penetrate another by force." When *chingar* is used in the narrowly sexual sense, "the *chingón* is the *macho,* the male; he rips open the *chingada,* the female, who is pure passivity, defenseless against the exterior world. The relationship between them is violent, and it is determined by the cynical power of the first and the impotence of the second." To Clemencia, apparently, one is either the *chingada* or the *chingón*—and she chooses to be the *chingón.* Describing sex with Drew, she says, "I leapt inside you and split you like an apple. Opened for the other to look and not give back." Clemencia not only takes the man's part—"I leapt inside you"—but she performs the violent actions attached to the verb *chingar:* "I split you like an apple" appropriates "the idea of breaking, of ripping open" attached to the usually masculine *chingar.* She imagines that this takeover puts Drew in her power: "You were ashamed to be so naked. . . . But I saw you for what you are, when you opened yourself for me." Following the logic of the violator, who pries open what is closed, peels back the protective surface to take possession of what is inside, Clemencia seeks to possess what is now revealed—Drew's private inner self—through her look; she thus appropriates the power of the male gaze to control, to possess ("to look and not give back").

Clemencia extends her sexual ravages to women's bodies, if only in fantasy. In the years since Drew left her, Clemencia has slept with other married men—often while their wives were giving birth. "It's always given me a bit of crazy joy to be able to kill those women like that. . . . To know I've had their husbands when they were anchored in blue hospital rooms, their guts yanked inside out." Now it is a woman's body that is opened up, exposed, vulnerable, while Clemencia, the "*gran chingón,*" pursues a bitter, vindictive sexual satisfaction—a kind of rape at one remove.

While Clemencia thus evades the stereotype of sexual victim, it is only by projecting it onto the other—the lover or the other woman—while leaving the gender dynamic of violence in place. And that dynamic imprisons her in a rigid sex role as surely as if the reversal had not taken place. In the cultural binary ascribed by Paz to the Mexican *macho,* "there are only two possibilities in life: either [one] inflicts the actions implied by *chingar* on others, or else [one] suffers them [oneself] at the hands of others." Having bought into this logic, which excludes any alternative to the pair violator/violated, Clemencia must live exclusively on the violator side of the equation; any hint of vulnerability would immediately situate her on the side of victim. Hence, perhaps, her emphatically one-sided self-definition—"I'm vindictive and cruel and I'm capable of anything"—and her equally emphatic determination to live outside the roles of wife and mother: "I'll *never marry* . . . I've never married and I never will." Having identified herself with the hard, ruthless, closed pole of the open-closed binary, she cannot admit desires to be loved or to nurture and protect, which would align her with the pole of open, vulnerable mother.

Yet it is just those desires that surface in the final lines of the story: "Sometimes all humanity strikes me as lovely. I just want to reach out and stroke someone, and say There, there, it's all right, honey. There, there, there." This expression of a desire to soothe and console—to mother, in a word—contradicts the ruthless tone of the whole preceding narrative. It would seem that positioning herself as *chingón,* "vindictive and cruel," makes Clemencia subdue maternal impulses to nurture and comfort that, if traditional, are unmistakably her own. This concluding return of a repressed desire for tenderness, while surprising, is only the last and most straightforward of eruptions from the underside of Clemencia's *macho* discourse. On the narrative surface Clemencia cares only about power, boasting of her power over Drew, whom she paints and repaints, choosing "to birth [him] on canvas. . . . And if that's not power, what is?" and of her power over women, whom she figuratively "kills" with adultery. Yet underneath runs a subtext of images drawn from maternal processes—conception, gestation, birth, nursing, even incest—which testify to desires for motherhood that Clemencia keeps hidden, even from herself.

On the night Drew's wife Megan gave birth to their son, for instance, Clemencia positioned herself parallel to the birth process: "While his mother lay on her back laboring his birth, I lay in his mother's bed making love to [Drew]." She has reenacted this imitation of birth many times, with other men: "And it's not the last time I've slept with a man the night his wife is birthing a baby. Why do I do that, I wonder? Sleep with a man when his wife is giving life, being suckled by a thing with its eyes still shut. Why do that?" It is at this point that she says, "It's always given me a bit of crazy joy to be able to kill those women like that. . . . To know I've had their husbands when they were anchored in blue hospital rooms, their guts yanked inside out, the baby sucking their breasts while their husband sucked mine." While sex is ostensibly the site of Clemencia's violence against women, the parallel with the suckling baby and mother suggests that sex functions, rather, as a poor substitute for maternity.

Addressing Drew's son mentally, Clemencia probes further into the workings of the maternal body: "Pretty boy. Little clone. Little cells split into you and you and you. Tell me, baby, which part of you is your mother. I try to imagine . . . her long long legs that wrapped themselves around this father who took me to his bed." Imagining back through the division of cells to the moment of conception, Clemencia here conflates her own body with the mother's body: "her long long legs" belong to Megan, but in the same phrase it is herself whom "this father took to his bed." She imagines herself into the very act of conception. Despite the avowed intention of Clemencia to injure Drew's wife for taking Drew away from her, it seems that Clemencia's rage reflects envy, not jealousy, in Jessica Benjamin's sense of the term: "Envy is about being, not having." The various images of maternity suggest that Clemencia does not so much want to *have* Drew as to be Megan, actively mothering. Hence her claim that she, not Megan, produced the son—from an abstract site of power divorced from the body: "Your son. Does he know how much I had to do with his birth? I was the one who convinced you [Drew] to let him be born. . . . I'm the one that gave him permission and made it happen, see."

Clemencia's use of gummy bears to mark her invasion of Megan's territory also demonstrates her ambivalence toward Megan. While Drew is cooking dinner, Clemencia finds a package of gummy bears in her back-pack and manages to put one in Megan's make-up jar, in her nail polish bottle, in her lipstick, even in her diaphragm. This is a language of signs legible to women on both sides of the race/class barrier: "I was here." Vengeance is hers, then—but again the act of the *chingón,* penetrating into all of Megan's most private places, carries a maternal subtext. Clemencia takes apart Megan's Russian babushka doll until she "got to the very center, the tiniest baby inside all the others . . . this [she] replaced with a gummy bear." Clemencia substitutes her own signifier for the "baby" in the doll-within-a-doll's innermost compartment, symbolically interrupting the clones of generational succession, each a replication of the same, with her own "difference." Then, borrowing motherhood, Clemencia puts the purloined "baby" into her pocket, where "all through dinner I kept . . . touch[ing] it, it made me feel good." But on the way home she throws the "baby" into a stagnant creek "where winos piss and rats swim. The Barbie doll's toy stewing there in that muck. It gave me a feeling like nothing before and since." The episode expresses the full range of Clemencia's ambivalence, an ambivalence shot through with feelings of racial exclusion: as Megan's baby in Clemencia's pocket, the doll evokes Clemencia's "borrowing" of her motherhood; as the toy of the "Barbie doll" (Clemencia's derisive label for Megan), the doll becomes metonymically identified with a Barbie doll, icon of white woman as idealized sex object. Clemencia's rage is directed not just against the woman who occupies the position she wants as Drew's lover and mother of his son, but against the principle that race determines desirability.

Now, some eighteen years later, Clemencia continues a process of revenge against Megan that is simultaneously an imitation of her motherhood. Namely, she has an affair with Drew and Megan's son:

> I sleep with this boy, their son. To make the boy love me the way I love his father. To make him want me, · hunger. . . . Come here, *mi cariñito.* Come to *mamita.* Here's a bit of toast.
>
> I can tell from the way he looks at me, I have him in my power. . . . Come to *mamita.* . . . I let him nibble. . . . Before I snap my teeth.

Again, Clemencia's ostensible motive is power—sexual power over the son, which gives her indirect power over his parents. But the rhetoric of nurturing and maternal endearment, which blends into the discourse of mastery, suggests that underneath she is continuing her peripheral relation to mothering. Clemencia seems to have taken a stand outside conventional marriage and family—"I've never married and never will"—only to force her way back in through the most enmeshed of family relations, incest: "You could be my son . . . ."

Just before the concluding upsurge of repressed maternal yearning directed to the world at large—"There, there, it's all right, honey. There, there, there"—Clemencia has a sudden insight into the physical life of the mother she has been imitating. She imagines how it feels to be Drew in bed "with that wife beside you, warm, radiating her own heat, alive under the flannel and down and smelling a bit like milk and hand cream, and that smell familiar and dear to you, oh." The wistful tone of Clemencia's description suggests that she glimpses the contrast between the concrete reality of the maternal body—warm, alive, smelling, radiating heat—and the insubstantiality of her own position in an abstract space.

The reader, misled for a time by the vividness of the questions and comments Clemencia addresses to Drew and his son, gradually comes to realize that there is no audience. Clemencia's narrative is a monologue that reflects her spiritual isolation. She is doubly marginalized. First, she exists in a margin of maternity, obsessed, but in the abstract, with maternal processes—metaphors, only, of conception, gestation, birth, nursing, and nurturing. Second, she occupies an uneasy position marginal to both Mexican and Anglo discourses. She is unable to grasp how race and gender discourses of Anglo culture situate her in relation to her white lover (she can't read the injunction, "Never marry a Mexican," from Drew's standpoint); and, having thrown out Mexican culture wholesale, she is too distanced to read the signs provided by traditional Mexican stories. For she remembers a scene she used to play with Drew fondly, apparently without realizing its implications:

> Drew, remember when you used to call me your Malinalli? It was a joke, a private game between us, because you looked like a Cortez with that beard of yours. My skin dark against yours. Beautiful, you said. . . .

> My Malinalli, Malinche, my courtesan, you said, and yanked my head back by the braid. Calling me that name in between little gulps of breath and the raw kisses you gave, laughing from that black beard of yours.

Clemencia calls attention to all the details—her hair, a braid in the style of an indigenous woman, her skin, dark against her lover's, her willing acceptance of the white man's sexual domination, even his violence—that place her squarely in the role of La Malinche, playing the part of traitor to her race in a white man's sexual games. Yet she does not see that she and Drew went on playing out the Malinche script: after exploiting her talents and her sexuality, Drew abandoned her as Cortez abandoned La Malinche after the Conquest.

Despite Clemencia's determination to throw out the Mexican ideology that ties her sexuality to La Malinche's, her life remains shackled to the Malinche story. Why? Clemencia's metaphor for her mother, whom she also denies, will perhaps throw light on what is wrong with Clemencia's tactic of repudiation. Clemencia says that she has not been able to mourn her mother's death because, before she died, her mother was to her what a crippled leg was to the little finch she used to have: the leg got twisted in a bar of the cage, then "dried up and fell off. My bird lived a long time without it, just a little red stump of a leg." Her memory of her dead mother is "like that": "like if something already dead dried up and fell off, and I stopped missing where she used to be." Her mother was "already dead" to her before she died: "where she used to be" was already an empty place. How can she mourn the absence of an absence? But if one follows the metaphor to completion—past what Clemencia intends—it seems that negation is insufficient to free her from the maternal connection. Clemencia has rejected her mother for marrying a white man and transferring her love, loyalty, and property to the new family. But denial of the mother—"like my ma didn't exist . . . Like if I never had a mother . . . Like I never even had one"—leaves her still attached, as the analogy with the bird's still connected stump suggests. The mother continues as a denied but still present appendage that spreads its deadness across Clemencia's living potentials. For although Clemencia sees her refusal to

marry as an independent stance, the insistent negatives, "I'll *never* marry. Not any man. . . . No. I've never married and never will. . . . those weren't men. Not men. . . . I never saw them," can be read as extensions of her mother's injunction, "Never marry a Mexican." The mother's negative spirit, encapsulated in the phrase, remains to frame the negative space where Clemencia lives, as it frames the text.

What is true for Clemencia's mother is true for the various signifiers of Mexican culture that Clemencia repudiates. The troubled identity of "Mexican" continues to plague Clemencia (as Drew's speech reminds us) in spite of her erasure of Mexicans as persons. She continues to act out La Malinche and Cortez—both sides, in fact—despite her willed repudiation of the gender ideology they embody. Because they are part of her social formation, they remain part of her inner life—dead remnants attached to her like stumps.

Are cultural icons then inescapable? **"Never Marry a Mexican"** seems to say they are. In **"Woman Hollering Creek"** Cisneros is more optimistic about the possibility of changing one's affiliation with damaging social myths. And hope for change rests precisely on the ground that seems so barren in **"Never Marry a Mexican,"** the ground of a Mexican American woman's consciousness where two cultures meet. Felice, the Chicana woman in **"Woman Hollering Creek,"** is a *mestiza* in Anzaldúa's sense—a woman who can balance the contradictory paradigms of Anglo and Mexican cultures in a single vision and out of their contradictions create "a new mythos—that is, a change in the way we perceive reality, the way we see ourselves." When Cleófilas, the Mexican protagonist, comes into contact with Felice's *mestiza* vision, the resulting "cultural collision" jolts Cleófilas into a new way of seeing Mexican myths of gender, liberating her from a debilitating identification with La Llorona.

"Woman Hollering Creek"

In **"Woman Hollering Creek"** Cisneros juxtaposes the heroines of contemporary Mexican *telenovelas* with the traditional figure La Llorona to imply that then, now, and always the ideals of femininity that Mexican popular culture presents to its women are models of pain and suffering. As the story begins, Cleófilas leaves her father and six brothers in Mexico to marry Don Pedro and move with him across the border to Texas. Cleófilas has been prepared for love and marriage largely by the *telenovelas* she watched as a girl growing up in a small Mexican town. "What [she] has been waiting for," single-mindedly, for years, is passion—"passion in its purest crystalline essence. The kind the . . . *telenovelas* describe when one finds, finally, the great love of one's life, and does whatever one can, must do, at whatever the cost." On the surface, the *telenovelas*' idealization of love ill prepares Cleófilas for the actualities of marriage: her new husband "doesn't look like the men on the *telenovelas*," and married life doesn't imitate their plots, either. More subtly, though, as Frances Restuccia has pointed out, the *telenovelas'* lesson that one must do "whatever one can . . . at whatever the cost," in order to keep on loving, prepares Cleófilas for the submissions of a beaten wife. The *telenovelas* glamorize pain as a necessary part of love, so that Cleófilas and her friends in Mexico adopt the idea of suffering and make it part of their life plans: "Somehow one ought to live one's life like that. . . . Because to suffer for love is good. The pain all sweet somehow."

While Cleófilas is shocked, when her husband beats her for the first time, to discover that the pains of love can be physical as well as emotional, the acceptance of suffering inculcated by the telenovelas—"the pain all sweet"—readies her for the part of beaten wife:

> The first time she had been so surprised she didn't cry out or try to defend herself. She had always said she would strike back if a man, any man, were to strike her.

> But when the moment came, and he slapped her once, and then again, and again; until the lip split and bled an orchid of blood, she didn't fight back, she didn't break into tears, she didn't run away as she imagined she might when she saw such things in the *telenovelas*. . . .

> Instead . . . she had been so stunned, it left her speechless, motionless, numb. She had done nothing but reach up to the heat on her mouth and stare at the blood on her hand as if even then she didn't understand.

Stunned into silence by the dissonance of the beating with all her beliefs about love and marriage, Cleófilas remains silent as the beatings continue because there is "no place to go," no one to talk to. Gone is the female community of her Mexican hometown whose shared values and gossiping intimacy are reflected in the narrative voice of the earlier, Mexican sections. In Texas, there is no female community—"no huddled whispering on the church steps each Sunday . . . here the whispering begins at sunset at the ice house instead"—and that is a gossiping among men, hostile to women. Cleófilas turns for companionship to the only female entity available, a creek named "La Gritona," or "the shouting woman": "The stream . . . a thing with a voice all its own, all day and all night calling in its high, silver voice. Is it La Llorona, the weeping woman? La Llorona, who drowned her own children. Perhaps La Llorona is the one they named the creek after, she thinks, remembering all the stories she learned as a child." Finding the heroines of the *telenovelas* useless as models for her present life situation,

Cleófilas falls back on an icon of Mexican tradition; but Mexican folklore joins with contemporary Mexican popular culture in offering Cleófilas only ideals of passive female suffering. "Pain is sweet," say the *telenovelas,* and the traditional figure of La Llorona is caught up in eternal sorrow, lamenting the loss of her children.

While the oral tradition to which La Llorona belongs is lively, generating ever new versions of what she suffered (three of my Chicana students related three different versions of the legend, told them by their mothers), what remains consistent through all the different versions is the sound of La Llorona's eerie wail. Usually, she is presented as a mother who has drowned her children and now roams searching for them. In one version, for instance, she kills her three children because they get in the way of her wild living; after her own death, God sends her back to seek them eternally. In another version, the figure is fused with La Malinche: when Cortez wanted to take their son back to Spain with him, Malinche killed the son, then herself, rather than be separated from her child; since then, her spirit roams, moaning "Aayy!" In other legends, La Llorona as the ghost of La Malinche mourns her lost children, the Indians whom she betrayed to Cortez. La Llorona's wail is sometimes said to have preceded Cortez, to have been one of the eight omens in Tenochtitlan that foretold the Conquest: in that case the children La Llorona grieves for are the Indians about to be slaughtered, and her cry continues through the centuries to mourn the loss of the indigenous civilization. Most often, La Llorona appears by the shore of a river or lake—she is said to have drowned her children—and sometimes she acts as siren, enticing men into the water to die. While the circumstances of her story change, La Llorona's cry of sorrow remains. That wail of inarticulate pain, reflected in the river's indeterminate *grito,* or shout—which Cleófilas reads as "pain or rage"—offers Cleófilas an analogue to her own inarticulate misery.

While Cisneros describes only Cleófilas first beating, she indicates that Cleófilas is baffled because she is caught in a classic cycle of domestic violence like the one that Lenore Walker describes, where the phase of intense battering is followed by a phase of loving contrition: "She could think of nothing to say, said nothing. Just stroked the dark curls of the man who wept and would weep like a child, his tears of repentance and shame, this time and each." Classic, too, are the obstacles to escape: a dependent child, a new pregnancy, a lack of money and mobility, a social climate that condones violence against women (the men who drink with her husband in the ice house joke about how one of them killed his wife), and, perhaps most debilitating, Cleófilas's isolation.

Drawing on Mexican culture for support, Cleófilas finds only a figure that reflects her helpless suffering: identifying with

La Llorona's frozen sorrow means accepting her lot as beaten wife, bound into a circle of uncomprehending pain, unable to articulate her experience or to find release through action. That identification offers a still more dreadful possibility: "La Llorona calling to her. She is sure of it. Cleófilas sets the baby's Donald Duck blanket on the grass. Listens. . . . The baby pulling up fistfuls of grass and laughing. La Llorona. Wonders if something as quiet as this drives a woman to the darkness under the trees." The juxtaposition of La Llorona, "who drowned her own children," with the baby laughing in its innocence creates the dread that Cleófilas will answer La Llorona's "call," drown her child, and so enter fully into La Llorona's mourning.

But a Chicana figure provides Cleófilas with a more positive role model. Cleófilas prevails on her husband to take her to a prenatal clinic. The reader is then privy to one side of a telephone conversation in which Graciela, a Mexican American nurse-practitioner at the clinic, describes Cleófilas bruised body and persuades her friend Felice to give Cleófilas a ride to the Greyhound station in San Antonio so she can take the bus back to her hometown in Mexico. Graciela's conversation contains a last reference to Cleófilas imprisonment in the Mexican iconography of suffering womanhood: "her name's Cleófilas. . . . One of those Mexican saints, I guess. A martyr or something." Graciela clearly sets herself apart from Mexican culture here, as in her condescension toward Cleófilas, whom she regards as "other"—"another one of those brides from across the border," who "doesn't even speak English."

The distance between Chicana and Mexican culture becomes even more apparent when her friend Felice drives Cleófilas and her small son across "La Gritona," or Woman Hollering Creek, on the way to San Antonio:

> But when they drove across the *arroyo*, the driver opened her mouth and let out a yell as loud as any mariachi. . . .
>
> Every time I cross that bridge I do that. Because of the name, you know. Woman Hollering, *Pues*, I holler. . . . Did you ever notice, Felice continued, how nothing around here is named after a woman? Really. Unless she's the Virgin. I guess you're only famous if you're a virgin. She was laughing again.
>
> That's why I like the name of that *arroyo*. Makes you want to holler like Tarzan, right?

Felice "said this in a Spanish pocked with English and laughed." The Chicana, who stands astride Anglo and Mexican cultures, is not captive to the myths of either culture: she can hear in the creek's voice either La Llorona's lament or Tarzan's cry, and take her pick. The creek is a "Woman," but unlike the landmarks named after the Virgin that annoy Felice, its name does not impose a single definition of femininity—nor is it confined to a single culture: the creek has both a Mexican and an English name. The indeterminacy of the creek's name, as of its sound, enables Felice to define "woman" for herself. When she hears the woman/creek's voice as a "Tarzan hoot," she appropriates for women the privileges of freedom and mobility usually associated with masculinity and comically exaggerated in Tarzan's hypermobility and freedom from all social constraints. Felice's *grito* may also be read as a call to arms, to the cause of female solidarity, which now rescues Cleófilas from domestic abuse, as in a Mexican general's *grito* to rally his troops or as in Tarzan's call to rally the elephants to Jane's rescue.

Cisneros does not problematize Felice's use of male codes to define a new female self, as she clearly does Clemencia's appropriation of the *chingón* persona. Felice drives a pickup truck; but rather than subject that symbol of masculine autonomy and power to doubts about the "gender trouble" involved in taking on the outward trappings of masculinity, Cisneros presents the pickup, through Cleófilas's admiring wonder, as the outward sign of Felice's independence, freedom of choice, and mobility—it is the vehicle, after all, of her effective action in the world, as she drives Cleófilas and her son to safety.

> Everything about this woman, this Felice, amazed Cleófilas. The fact that she drove a pickup. . . . when Cleófilas asked if it was her husband's, she said she didn't have a husband. The pickup was hers. She herself had chosen it. She herself was paying for it. . . .
>
> . . . Felice was like no woman she'd ever met. Can you imagine, when we crossed the *arroyo* she just started yelling like a crazy, she would say later to her father and brothers. Just like that. Who would've thought?
>
> Who would've? Pain or rage, perhaps, but not a hoot like the one Felice had just let go. Makes you want to holler like Tarzan, Felice had said.

To the Mexican woman whose sexual and maternal identity is imbricated with her culture's imagos of women, the Chicana's bicultural—and cross-gender—flexibility opens a new range of female possibilities. Not only does the *llorar* of the stream give way to a resounding *grito*, not only does Cleófilas see beyond the whimpering lamentation of the long-suffering woman to the possibility of a woman who shouts out triumphantly "a yell as loud as any mariachi," (p. 55), but the example of Felice's loud self-assertion apparently enables Cleófilas to regain her own voice. She shapes her experience into the story she will tell her father and brothers.

Beyond Cleófilas cognitive appreciation of women's alternatives in the paragraph cited above comes a leap into identification. The story ends: "Then Felice began laughing again, but it wasn't Felice laughing. It was gurgling out of [Cleófilas's] own throat, a long ribbon of laughter, like water." Cleófilas has a demonstrated talent for identification, first with the *telenovelas'* heroines, then with the creek and La Llorona. Here Cleófilas crosses over ego boundaries as well as national boundaries to identify with Felice. Her laughter, indistinguishable at first from Felice's, expresses in her own voice the female exuberance Felice has been modeling for her. The further description of her laughter as a "gurgle," a "ribbon of . . . water," suggests that this is a three-way merger. The promised identification with the creek has occurred—an identification no longer destructive now that the river's murmur can be heard as a celebration of female autonomy and mobility.

In this story where naming is so vital, there is even a hint (buried in Graciela's phone conversation with Felice) that Cleófilas might well use her gift for identification to imitate Felice's autonomy in choosing her own names, her own female models. Before the encounter with Felice Cleófilas could only wish for a name like the *telenovelas'* heroines—"somehow she would have to change her name to Topazio, or Yesenia, Cristal, Adriana, Stefania, Andrea, something more poetic than Cleófilas. Everything happened to women with names like jewels"; or she would have to name her mute suffering after La Llorona, thus squeezing her own experience into culturally validated categories, living "happily ever after" or mutely enduring one's suffering. Graciela's tongue-in-cheek remark on the phone to Felice—"When her kid's born she'll have to name her after us"—suggests the possibility of a naming that is less coerced by the ideological forces of myth and history, a naming that passes on to the next generation a more positive model of female autonomy ("Graciela" means graceful, and "Felice" means happy).

Just as the cycle of battering begins to seem inevitable to a woman captive to domestic violence, so the reader of this story feels increasingly trapped in a downward trajectory of events that appears to lead inevitably to more violence.

—Jean Wyatt

The narrative movement of the story imitates the abrupt change in Cleófilas's fortunes. Just as the cycle of batter-

ing begins to seem inevitable to a woman captive to domestic violence, so the reader of this story feels increasingly trapped in a downward trajectory of events that appears to lead inevitably to more violence. The intervention of the Chicana community in the last three pages, which frees Cleófilas from the helpless isolation of the battered woman, also release the reader from this narrative impasse. The very swiftness of the turn-around gives the reader a lift of spirit that enhances the text's celebration of the possibility that a Chicana perspective can transform Mexican cultural myths. What Felice does for Cleófilas is a synecdoche for what Cisneros is doing for the reader: rewriting a traditional Mexican story of gender to turn a lament into a shout of triumph or of joy.

Beyond the Borders of the Story: A Dialectic on Gender between "Never Marry a Mexican," "Woman Hollering Creek," and "Little Miracles, Kept Promises"

Felice is able to use the fluidity of the borderland creatively to produce a new vision of womanhood; Clemencia's effort at transformation fails: what is the difference between the two? Is Cisneros pointing to a specific psychological or social positioning that enables one to function well in a border situation? While one might wish for a clear and simple answer, Cisneros is not in the business of handing out morals for better border living or for managing traditional icons of womanhood; the two stories take their place with other stories in the collection to mark possible positions on a broad spectrum of accommodations to living between Anglo and Mexican cultures. Nonetheless, issues common to the two stories and to a third story, **"Little Miracles, Kept Promises,"** set up a dialectic that I would like now to explore.

Clemencia lives out the consequences of adopting a masculine role in **"Never Marry a Mexican."** She insists on being as far away as she can get from the pole of violable femininity, and so she leaps to the masculine pole just as narrowly defined, following Mexican tradition, as aggressive and violent. That masquerade leads to the self-deprivation that identification with any gender role does—to the denial of half her capacities and desires, the so-called "feminine" qualities of tenderness, comfort, and compassion. Susan Gubar argues that it does not strengthen female identity to leave it behind in favor of masculinity. Just the opposite: the necessity of abjuring womanhood in favor of masculine impersonation calls attention to the weakness of being a woman. And acting out masculinity leaves the underlying womanhood unaltered. Indeed, although Clemencia enjoys making the boasts of the *chingón*—"I'm guilty of having caused deliberate pain to other women. I'm vindictive and cruel"—she falls back on traditional "women's wiles" when she tries to act on the world outside her own sexual theater: waiting ("I've been waiting patient as a spider all these years"), jealous scheming against the "other woman," and manipulating men through giving and withholding sexuality. Clemencia's wholesale rejection of the sexuality associated with La Malinche neither redefines womanhood nor grants her possession of the power associated with masculinity, but leaves femininity and masculinity still standing as polar opposites, with Clemencia oscillating between.

In the light of Clemencia's failed appropriation of a masculine position, a reader may look askance, in retrospect, at Felice's imitation of Tarzan in **"Woman Hollering Creek."** Just as the *chingón* persona that Clemencia adopts exaggerates the aggressiveness conventionally associated with masculinity, so the figure of Tarzan enacts a construct of essential masculinity: muscular, mobile, masterful. Is not moving from La Llorona to Tarzan, from a stereotype of helplessly suffering femininity to an ideal of supermasculine agency, as much of a leap and as unavailing to women who have to function in the real world as the move from *la chingada* to *el chingón*? As I have argued, however, while Clemencia moves between the poles of a binary opposition, Felice positions herself on a border. That is, Felice goes back and forth across the gender border as freely as she goes across the border between Mexican and Anglo signifying systems, picking what she likes, selectively, from either side, as forms to express her own feelings. Looking to Tarzan for inspiration does not limit her to a masculine stance: while she hollers *like* a man, Tarzan, she does so *as* a woman, responding to the creek's invitation to imitate a "woman hollering." Similarly with her pickup: she adopts the masculine symbol of the pickup truck to enhance a woman's mobility—her own mobility and that of the woman she carries away from abuse. To the objection that Felice's adoption of a pickup is too easy or too unexamined a way of appropriating the freedom and mobility traditionally associated with masculinity, a biographical note will perhaps suggest a response. Cisneros herself drives a pickup, she said at a recent conference, and it is "menstrual blood red." Crossing the gender border and combining signifiers from both sides throws into question not Felice's (or Cisneros's) womanliness, but the gendered logic that assigns objects and gestures exclusively to one side or the other of a gender divide.

To put my analysis in terms of the ongoing feminist debate on gender construction and deconstruction: if gender is "performative," as Judith Butler argues—a temporal construct of gestures and speech acts infinitely repeated to give the illusion of a stable gender identity—if, in other words, gender is a discursive effect merely, then Felice's refusal to perpetuate the discourse of a unitary gender identity effectively deconstructs the "natural" category of exclusive femininity, and thus the feminine/masculine binary. Butler's theory seems useful on the level of social reality: that is, if many persons across a culture were performing disrup-

tive gender acts, then parody, displacement, and "proliferating gender configurations" like Felice's would be enough to make visible the imitative, constructed nature of gender and to suggest alternatives.

But the fact that gender is constructed does not make its hold less tenacious. Because Felice is on stage for only two pages, the reader is not privy to the struggles she went through to reach the point of masterful play with the signifiers of gender; Clemencia's example, meanwhile, throws into question the efficacy of acts and speech acts to shake the hold of gender on the individual consciousness. Clemencia embraces the performance of an alternative gender identity on every level: in gesture and speech act, in mental act too, she performs the *chingón*. Yet she remains caught in a cultural construction of gender, split between performing the male part and "acting like a woman." Butler's optimism about the ability of the subject to change through speech acts seems to be founded on a notion of the subject as produced exclusively by discourse: "To be constituted by language is to be produced within a given network of power/discourse which is open to resignification, redeployment, subversive citations from within and interruption and inadvertent convergence within such networks." In other words, the very iterability that produces the illusion of gender continuity also creates the possibility of slippage, opening up rigid gender structures to redefinition. But gender is both a discursive category to be contested and an integral element of a person's sense of who she (or he) is, as Stephen Frosh and Lynne Layton have recently argued. Gender ideology is intransigent because it produces the subject in question, so that conventional notions of gender ground not just cultural representations but self-representations as well. So an exclusive focus on the discursive possibilities for gender subversion minimizes both the complexity of gender identity acquisition and the cultural work required to change a gender identification. Some theory that takes the psychological production of subjectivity—both discursive and prediscursive—into account is necessary to bridge the gap that Butler's discourse theory leaves between the social signifying order and the individual psyche. Perhaps some attention to processes of identification can provide such a bridge.

Cisneros's tales of gender emphasize the force and tenacity of identificatory processes in the creation of gender identity; but **"Woman Hollering Creek"** also suggests the power of identification to change gender affiliations. Cleófilas's identification with the *telenovelas'* heroines leads her to absorb their attitudes toward life (love is everything, love is pain, pain is sweet). This identification with the image of the other on the screen is akin to mirror stage identification, when according to Lacan the ego is born out of the child's misidentification with the image in the mirror. Imaginary identification, then, carries the force of that early misrecognition and operates discursively, persuading Cleófilas to take on her culture's definition of womanhood as suffering. Here identification functions as interpellation, "the process whereby a social representation is accepted and absorbed by an individual as her (or his) own representation and so becomes, for that individual, real, even though it is in fact imaginary." But identification does not always operate hegemonically. Take Cleófilas's identification with Felice. If Cleófilas were constituted entirely by discourse, such that the identity of woman as loving and suffering for love were the only one that seemed "real" to her, then she would see Felice's gender position as bizarre and repellant. Yet she can identify with Felice and thus with a liberatory model of womanhood. What enables her to do this?

Identification is an archaic process that long predates the entry into language. In *Group Psychology and the Analysis of the Ego* Freud establishes identification as "the earliest expression of an emotional tie with another person" and specifies that "identification endeavors to mould a person's own ego after the fashion of the one that has been taken as a model." The two statements, taken together, imply that identification operates in the earliest stages of self-formation. In adult years, identification bears the mark of its primitive origins: when I identify with you, I do not make fine discriminations or choose selectively which traits to mimic, but experience identification as totalizing and immediate. I walk and talk and move like you and experience your beauty and power as my own. In "Sameness and difference: Toward an 'overinclusive' theory of gender development," Benjamin charts the gender identifications that take place over a child's first four years of life: until the oedipal stage (roughly the fourth year) the child identifies with both mother and father, elaborating these identifications in imitative play. Benjamin argues that the long developmental process of identifying with multiple roles creates as its (unconscious) legacy an adult capacity for identifying with various gender positions. Benjamin thus claims for identificatory processes the power to connect with difference and to undermine the rigidity of fixed gender roles. **"Woman Hollering Creek"** is a story about cultural influences and confluences rather than about psychosexual development, so there is no account of how Cleófilas acquired her capacity for identification. Whatever its origins, Cleófilas's aptitude for identification works counterhegemonically in the way that Benjamin suggests: her global identification with Felice (her laughter is Felice's laughter, her attitudes, at least for the moment, Felice's attitudes) bridges difference and springs Cleófilas free from the coercions of gender discourse as effectively as the identification with La Llorona and the *telenovelas'* heroines earlier imprisoned her in the position of inarticulately suffering woman.

Sometimes operating discursively, sometimes not, identi-

fication is representative of aspects of psychosexual development that have their origins in prelinguistic experience but must nevertheless be included in an account of gender identity acquisition and subversion. Indeed, **"Never Marry a Mexican"** implies that one's orientation to discursive pressures is formed by early psychosexual experience and that if one struggles against one's imbrication with cultural models of gender without dealing first with one's identifications within the family, one fails at transformation. Clemencia's attitude to cultural discourse—in particular, to the story of La Malinche—is conditioned by her identification with her mother, who apparently dealt with conflict by splitting, or polarizing: having trouble with a Mexican husband, she repudiated all Mexicans as a block. When Clemencia similarly repudiates all Mexican men and then rejects her mother, she is operating in a mimetic mode, thinking like her mother. She comes to discourse, and to the figure of La Malinche in particular, already identified with her mother's negativity, so that repudiation of La Malinche is her only defense. Fixed in the maternal conceptual habit of polarization, she is unable to think dialectically about the extremes of femininity and masculinity represented by the (mythical) Malinche and Cortez, so she can generate only more and more extreme versions (or inversions) of the gender binary she is trying to escape. And despite her conscious rejection of both her blood mother and her cultural mother, she remains identified with their stories: she undertakes the risky sexual liaison with the white man that she deplores in her mother's life, and she acts out La Malinche's story, experiencing the betrayal of both her mother and her white lover.

If identification plays a part in constructing a woman's gender identity, and if identification is as deep and tenacious as it proves to be in Clemencia's case—and as Alarcón and Moraga claim that identification with La Malinche is for many Chicana and Mexican women—then breaking free of these identifications may involve more than the invention of new speech acts. It may entail "a struggle at the roots of the mind," as Raymond Williams has said—"not casting off an ideology" (as Clemencia has done), "or learning phrases about it, but confronting a hegemony in the fibres of the self."

A character in **"Little Miracles, Kept Promises,"** a third story in *Woman Hollering Creek,* models such a struggle, thereby demonstrating the cultural and self-exploration that Clemencia's performance of gender lacks. The story also foregrounds the way that family and culture reflect and repeat a single gender definition, making a daughter's identification with the social ideal of womanhood seem inescapable. Because the final portion of this story comes close to a personal statement by Cisneros herself—"the last speaker, [Rosario] . . . That's me"—it can offer a quasi-autobiographical, metafictional commentary on Cisneros's project in the two stories under consideration. Rosario's "letter" to the Virgin models a border negotiation with a cultural icon: she goes back and forth between two cultures' constructions of the ideal woman—Indian and Mexican—and rather than settling on one side of the border or the other, she brings the two visions of sacred womanhood together in a single sentence.

Rosario has been raging, apparently for years, at the Virgen de Guadalupe for "all that self-sacrifice, all that silent suffering"—for modeling the passive endurance of misery and oppression that she sees reflected in her mother and grandmother. Her past warfare with the Virgen resembles Clemencia's outright repudiation of La Malinche and so makes the negative stand of that story seem like a stage in an ongoing dialectical process. "I wouldn't let you in my house. . . . Couldn't look at you without blaming you for all the pain my mother and her mother and all our mothers' mothers have put up with. . . . I wasn't going to be my mother or my grandma. . . . Hell no. Not here. Not me." The buildup of negatives, the determination not to "be" the cultural mother (or the blood mother either), the wholesale repudiation of a passive cultural icon, all recall Clemencia's one-dimensional strategy of rejection. But denial is only a stage; Rosario moves on to consider La Virgen from the standpoint of indigenous Indian culture. She acknowledges the Virgen's other face—the face of Tonantzín, the powerful Aztec fertility goddess who gives life to the crops and protects her Indian people: "No longer Mary the Mild, but our mother Tonantzín." Rosario does not, however, fix on this substitution of Tonantzín for "Mary the Mild"; she evokes the fierce Tonantzín side of the Virgen—the aspect that, because it represents all the Mexican people, Indian as well as Mexican, can rally everyone to fight against oppression—only to read the virtues of Mary the Mild through that vision:

> That you could have the power to rally a people when a country was born, and again during civil war, and during a farmworkers' strike in California made me think maybe there is power in my mother's patience, strength in my grandmother's endurance. Because those who suffer have a special power, don't they? The power of understanding someone else's pain.

Rosario does not settle on one side of the cultural border, then, not even on the side of power, but returns to read Mary's (and her own mothers') capacity for endurance through the strengths of Tonantzín. That encompassing vision, carried on down the page by a kind of triumphant border-crossing list of all Tonantzín's names—Aztec, Catholic, Mexican, American—enables the speaker to see her mother's and grandmother's strength as real and to embrace her own female potential. It is the Virgen de Guadalupe's biculturalism that gives her figure the capacity to empower different modes of being a woman.

This hard-won border dialectic points up by contrast Clemencia's imprisonment in a single culture's rigid dichotomy (*el chingón* versus *la chingada*), and it dramatizes the cultural labor that Clemencia avoids. It would seem, from the dialogue with the Virgen, that negotiating with and against the symbolic inheritance of Mexican culture involves an examination of how the cultural ideal works, both inside and outside: how the icon of La Virgen or La Malinche functions in the social world to maintain the hierarchy of gender relations; how it functions in the family to enhance and enforce mother-daughter identifications and so ensure the transmission of gender definitions from one generation to the next; and how it works in the internal world to limit and shape one's impulses and regulate one's behavior. Rosario follows the direction of her own anger to arrive at discursive analysis: La Virgen de Guadalupe has been used by the patriarchy to make her and women in general "docile and enduring." Rosario has to reconstruct La Virgen—has to retrieve her face of power, the face of Tonantzín, from her own Indian ancestry—in order to go forward with her life. It would seem that Clemencia has the opportunity to reconstruct Malinche through a similar act of sympathetic imagination: for Malinche, like Clemencia, came to occupy the untenable space between cultures—Indian and Spanish—and was abandoned there by a white lover. But rather than restore the historic dimension to Malinche (as contemporary Chicana revisionists are doing), Clemencia merely acts out against the Malinche of patriarchal tradition. To reject the cultural icon rather than reconstructing it does not work because Mexican cultural icons of womanhood are "part of you," as Cisneros says in her interview with Aranda: they "live inside you."

Viewed from the perspective of the collection as a whole, the three stories can be seen as parts of a dialectical process of negotiating with cultural icons that are both inalienable parts of oneself and limitations to one's potential as a woman. Accepting the ideals of womanhood as they are defined by Mexican culture does not provide a stage for ongoing development, as the example of Cleófilas demonstrates: identifying with La Llorona commits her to the long-suffering endurance of oppression, her powers of self-expression limited to a wail. Clemencia's strategy of repudiation cannot be a final solution either, because it locks her into a posture opposite to, and therefore defined by, the sexual victimization embodied in La Malinche: as Anzaldúa says, "all reaction is limited by, and dependent on, what it is reacting against." Rosario describes the stages of her negotiation with the Virgen de Guadalupe as a process that stretches over years and thus makes Cleófilas's and Clemencia's positions seem like two stages of an ongoing dialectic. Rosario rejects Guadalupe, re-examines her, embraces her, and finally reconstructs her as a figure that she can understand, live with, and use as a model. To revise the traditional icons is to empower oneself, as Rosario implies in her address to Guadalupe: "When I could see you in all your facets . . . I could love you, and, finally, learn to love me." Sandra Cisneros—unlike her character Clemencia—sees this reconstruction of the myths and the living identities tied to them as a communal process, shared with other Chicana writers, which she calls, following Alarcón, "'reinventing ourselves,' revising ourselves. We accept our culture, but not without adapting [it to] ourselves as women."

Harryette Mullen (essay date Summer 1996)

SOURCE: "'A Silence Between Us Like a Language': The Untranslatability of Experience in Sandra Cisneros's *Woman Hollering Creek*," in *MELUS*, Vol. 21, No. 2, Summer, 1996, pp. 3-20.

[*In the essay below, Mullen discusses Cisneros's representation of the conflict of Hispanic and Anglo cultures and their respective linguistic codes in terms of Latino tensions between race, class, gender, and ideology.*]

> . . . the cognitive level of language not only admits but directly requires recoding interpretation, that is, translation. Any assumption of ineffable or untranslatable cognitive data would be a contradiction in terms. But in jest, in dreams, in magic, briefly, in what one would call everyday verbal mythology, and in poetry above all . . . the question of translation becomes much more entangled and controversial . . . poetry by definition is untranslatable. . . . If we were to translate into English the traditional formula *Tradutore, traditore* as "the translator is a betrayer," we would deprive the Italian rhyming epigram of all its paronomastic value. Hence a cognitive attitude would compel us to change this aphorism into a more explicit statement and to answer the questions: translator of what messages? betrayer of what values?
>
> —Roman Jakobson

In jests, dreams, magic, poetry, and poetic prose, Sandra Cisneros finds abundant examples of the "everyday verbal mythology" of Mexican-American culture. Language and literacy as sites of cultural and class conflict, or what Paulo Freire and Donaldo Macedo describe as the "antagonistic" yet potentially "positive" relationship of minority to dominant linguistic and cultural codes, are critical matters in *Woman Hollering Creek*. The text includes frequent references to the specificity and difference coded into any and

all languages; to the violence of inadequacy of translation and interpretation; to the translator's and, by extension, the writer's unfaithful role as betrayer of the culture's inside secrets; and to the existence of encoded messages, which are more accessible to readers familiar with various insider codes and cryptographic devices deployed in the text.

These attributes Cisneros's text shares with texts by other Chicano, Latino, and minority writers, who implicitly or explicitly refer to their own ambiguous relationships to both dominant and subordinated cultures in their roles as translators and interpreters of minority experience. Novelists Arturo Islas in *The Rain God* and Ron Arias in *The Road to Tamazunchale* both refer to the surrender and resistance of the indigenous inhabitants of the Americas to Spanish conquistadors; both also refer to the resulting cultural conflict and inner division of those whose heritage comes from the mixing and mating of the Amerindian and the European, and those whose native culture straddles the border separating, yet also joining Mexico and the United States. The Mexican legend of the traitorous interpreter, La Malinche, an almost subliminal allusion in Ana Castillo's *The Mixquiahuala Letters*, is directly invoked in Cisneros's **"Never Marry a Mexican."** The sublimated or subliminal cultural script is yet another one of the insider codes that minority, ethnic, and feminist writers may deploy in their texts. The repression of subordinated cultures and languages by the dominant culture and language is paralleled by, and frequently associated metonymically with, other repressed elements that erupt from the "unconscious" of the text to disturb, contradict, or at least complicate its conscious signification.

> **The untranslatability of the beauty of Spanish, the unpronounceability of Spanish and Amerindian names on the gringo tongue, and the invisibility or discursive silencing of Chicanos are all figured in Cisneros's text.**
> —Harryette Mullen

That Spanish operates both as an insider code comprehensible to some but not to others, and also as a repressed language in its subordination to English as the dominant language in the U.S., might be read as the primary signification of the entire text of *Woman Hollering Creek*. The reader again and again confronts the untranslatability of the subordinated cultural discourse into the language of the culturally dominant other: "[The poem is] Pretty in Spanish. But you'll have to take my word for it. In English it just sounds goofy." The beauty of the Spanish language is as untranslatable into English as the beauty of Flavio Minguia in **"Bien Pretty"** or Chato (fat-face), aka Chaq Uxmal Paloquin in

"One Holy Night." Their masculine beauty, like the poetry of the Spanish language, is simply unreadable to anyone using a dominant Aryan standard of beauty, or whose perceptions are limited by a heterosexist male gaze. The untranslatability of the beauty of Spanish, the unpronounceability of Spanish and Amerindian names on the gringo tongue, and the invisibility or discursive silencing of Chicanos are all figured in Cisneros's text. Considering how Spanish is repressed in its subordination to English, Cisneros is also aware that Aztec, Mayan, Nahuatl, and other indigenous languages are repressed in turn by Spanish as Mexico's official language, its dominance a legacy of European colonial conquest. Amerindian words may enter the text of a Chicano writer as yet another insider code. The fact that even dictionaries, lexicons, and grammars of these languages are largely accessible only to readers of Spanish, means that the use of such words can create an insider discourse within an insider discourse, of educated Mexican and Mexican-American writers and readers who, in the process of exploring their own origins, have investigated Mexico's indigenous roots.

Of course Spanish itself operates in the text as a sign of insider status, particularly the bilingual Spanglish which, in the equivocal description of Castillo's poet-narrator, is spoken "with an outrageous accent splattered with Chicanismos, one could only assume was not done with some intention." One of Cisneros's characters, Cleófilas, calls the mixture "Spanish pocked with English," the latent metaphor, perhaps inadvertently, evoking disfigurement and disease. Particularly given "English Only" mandates, the backlash against bilingual education, and the resistance of U.S. publishers to bilingual texts, U.S.-born Chicanos sometimes express ambivalence about this language, while border-crossing Mexican-born artists, notably the poet Alurista and writer and performance artist Guillermo Gomez-Pena, apparently have felt freer to sample in their work the hybrid offspring of Spanish and English.

In a manner more subdued, given the pressure exerted by the audience of monolingual readers of English, the texts of Castillo, Cisneros, and other Chicano/Latino authors aesthetically and ideologically exploit the slippage of nonstandard dialects between error or deviation, and motivated or intentional differences arising from the historical and cultural distinctiveness of Spanglish, Tex-Mex, *Inglenol,* and Calo in relation to standard English as well as Castillian Spanish or standard Mexican Spanish. Like a joke or a Freudian slip of the tongue that reveals some unconscious truth, the linguistic "errors" of a character expose the repressed cultural conflict of the bilingual speaker: "But that's—how do you say it?—water under the damn? I can't ever get the sayings right even though I was born in this country. We didn't say shit like that in our house."

From this ideologically contested space of linguistic difference, error, mutual incomprehension and antagonism, these bilingual authors have the potential to construct what might be regarded as a third language, accessible to those whose linguistic experience, combined with their formal education, has produced a new and emancipatory literacy. This new literacy, with its syncretic aesthetic, embraces elements excluded by the dominant standardized languages used in Mexico and the U.S. Thus, it frequently incorporates what, in standard dictionaries of English and Spanish, would be labeled as slang, argot, colloquialism, or nonstandard usage; or what is often excluded from dictionaries because it is generally excluded from written, as opposed to spoken, discourses. For Cisneros and others, such elements include nicknames, diminutives relegated to "baby talk," the speech of children, and other intimate or familiar speech, nonstandard codes of subordinated minority cultures, folk references, obscenities, curses, as well as onomatopoeia, such as "¡zas!" and "rrr, rrr, rrr."

Signaling its intentionality in its exploration of the significance of linguistic codes, which both include and exclude, Cisneros's text incorporates obvious uses of cryptography, such as the poet's acrostic coding of the name of his beloved within the narrative text of **"Tin Tan Tan"**; in **"Little Miracles, Kept Promises"**; the use of a code substituting numerals for letters, that disguises the homoerotic content of a message included among other prayers—in Spanish, English, and Spanglish—inscribed as ex votos in a Mexican-American Catholic church; or, less obviously, the coded usage of Hispanic names one might (or because of cultural silencing perhaps might not) find stitched into the AIDS quilt in **"Remember the Alamo."** In this last story, the juxtaposition of a gay night club with perhaps the most famous Texas tourist site constructs a metonymical association of icons memorializing the massacre of celebrated heroes of Texas history on the one hand, and, on the other hand, obscure individuals who have died of AIDS during the ongoing epidemic of our own time. This juxtaposition further comments on the silencing of Mexicans in standard Texas histories as well as the silencing of linguistic and racial minorities in public discourses generated in the battle against the deadly virus.

Cryptic encodings of names and secret messages in the literary text privilege the literate over the illiterate, since they have no oral equivalent outside of literate discourses. Yet other encodings, while included in a literary discourse, refer to the "experience of the other." This discourse of the other includes illiteracy and orality, superstition and folk culture, ignorance and resistance. The conflict and potential dialogue of usually antagonistic domains, to which Cisneros is acutely sensitive, influence her approach, as a poet and fiction writer, in addressing an audience of bilingual readers of Spanish and English, as well as monolingual English readers.

> **As a highly educated writer, Cisneros is aware of the dominant canon from which her work deliberately and self-consciously deviates.**
> —*Harryette Mullen*

As a highly educated writer, Cisneros is aware of the dominant canon from which her work deliberately and self-consciously deviates. As a Chicana of working class background, she acknowledges and refers in her text to the linguistic and cultural practices of those usually excluded from dominant literate discourses. As "the daughter of a Mexican father" who gave her the language of tenderness ("*quien me dio el lenguaje de la ternura*") and "a Mexican-American mother" who "gave [her] the fierce language," Cisneros grew up exquisitely attuned to the vigor of ethnically inflected working class English and the emotional resonances and intimacies of colloquial, familial Spanish.

> *Ay*! To make love in Spanish. . . . To have a lover sigh *mi vida, mi precios, mi chiquitita,* and whisper things in that language crooned to babies, that language murmured by grandmothers, those words that smelled like your house, like flour tortillas, and the inside of your daddy's hat, like everyone talking in the kitchen at the same time. . . . *That* language. . . . Nothing sounded dirty or hurtful or corny. How could I think of making love in English again?

If, for J. Hillis Miller and Paul de Man, "deconstruction" and "unreadability" name "what is learned" and also, contrarily, the uncertainty or "undecidability" of determining any factual knowledge of cognitive data in a literary text, then for the ethnic text, what is learned—and what is never entirely fixed as certain, translatable knowledge—is always not only *who I am,* but also *who we are.* Thus, names and the process of naming, for individuals as well as communities, are thus fundamental to Cisneros's attempt to produce a culturally representative yet open and polysemous text.

Names, especially nicknames, and intimate forms of address, often diminutives, which circulate in private, usually oral, discourses operate in a similar way as insider codes in her stories. It is left to the reader to know or infer that "Chavela" is a nickname for "Isabel," as "Chayo" is short for "Rosario," and "Chucha" for "Jesua"; or to fathom the subtle distinctions enunciated by "Patty," "*la Patee,*" or "Patrrri-see-ah," as opposed to "Trish." Cisneros delights in the fact that even underpants, *calzones* in standard Spanish, have a baby talk nickname, *chones,* a word that, for those who know the

language, automatically signals the informality and intimacy of familiar speech. As in the stories titled "*La Fabulosa:* A Texas Operetta," "*Los* Boxers" and "*Bien* Pretty," the suggestive balancing of English and Spanish in the bilingual title of "My *Tocaya*" ("My Namesake") privileges the creative syncretism of the bilingual speaker's English-jangled Spanish and Spanish-entangled English, just as the signification of names and naming is privileged cultural discourse. While initially distancing herself from "Trish," the narrator considers her linguistic and cultural kinship with her *tocaya* reason enough to critique her behavior from a communal perspective.

Characters like Trish, the scandalous Carmen Berriozabal of "*La Fabulosa,*" Rosario, Clemencia, and Cleófilas, all attempt to escape narrow constraints defining women's experience. They are the wayward and wandering ones, whose names are mentioned in gossip, tabloid headlines, and prayers. The risk of waywardness is indicated by the unidentified dead girl in "My *Tocaya*." In contrast to Cisneros's first work of fiction, *The House on Mango Street,* which depicts a community of women restricted in their movements within the barrio, confined to interior spaces, and trapped in their domestic roles as daughters, wives, and mothers—with only the child narrator Esperanza (her name means Hope) escaping—*Woman Hollering Creek* offers stories of a variety of women trying various means of escape, through resistance to traditional female socialization, through sexual and economic independence, self-fashioning, and feminist activism, as well as through fantasy, prayer, magic, and art. Cisneros's most complex characters are those who, like adult Esperanzas, have left and returned to the barrio as artists. For them, art is a powerfully seductive way of "Making the world look at you from my eyes. And if that's not power, what is?" In "Little Miracles, Kept Promises" and "*La Fabulosa:* A Texas Operetta," characters who speak from within the community look askance at others who shed their "namesake" status and intimacy when they call themselves "Hispanic" or "Spanish" (rather than "Latino," "Mexican," or "Chicana") for the sake of assimilation, upward mobility, or winning government grants.

The inclusiveness or exclusiveness of the name "Mexican" is explored in "Never Marry a Mexican"; and the candies hidden by the Chicana protagonist inside the possessions of another woman constitute another cryptic communication. Like the perplexing advice of the narrator's mother, which gives the story its title, the candy bears are an example of the ambiguous signification of coded, hidden, or double messages. Clemencia hides candy "gummy bears" in intimate places where they are sure to be found and interpreted as a message from a sexual rival by the "scary Dallas type" wife of the narrator's lover. Clemencia's act of sabotage, a parody of insemination and impregnation, in which the seemingly impregnable complacency of the wife is penetrated, indicates the narrator's possessiveness toward her rival's husband and child, as well as Clemencia's ambivalent desire to escape representations of woman as sexual object, passive reproductive vessel, and compliant consumer, in favor of an alternative, self-authored, and subversive inscription as desiring subject and productive cultural agent.

Paradoxically, Clemencia is most "Mexican" when she acts out her rage in private rituals that connect her to cultural figures symbolizing women's destructive aspect. A gummy bear is substituted for the "tiniest baby inside" of Megan's nesting Russian "wooden babushka dolls." Clemencia symbolically drowns "the baby" in a muddy creek, as if re-enacting La Llorona's infanticide. At an extratextual level, the gummy bear has an idiosyncratic symbolic resonance for Cisneros. According to the author, "an upside-down gummy bear" resembles "a Mexican statute of Coatlicue." Thus, by inversion, the sugary sweet candy that the artist-protagonist plants like a poison pill in the boudoir of her rival connects her to the creative/destructive potential invested in the Aztec phallic mother goddess Coatlicue, as her cryptic communication resonates with the ambiguous signification of the traitorous translator Malintzin Tenepal/La Malinche/Dona Marina. Malintzin was betrayed by her own mother, who sold her daughter into slavery to protect her son's inheritance; and Malintzin, who served as *La Lengua* [the tongue] for Hernan Cortes, is silenced in Mexican and Spanish histories despite the extraordinary linguistic abilities that made her an agent of historical and cultural transformation. She who was active and indispensable as *La Lengua* becomes utterly passive and disposable as *La Chingada,* the one who got screwed: no virgin mother of immaculate conception, but mother of the new *mestiza* race and culture of Mexico.

As the meaning of childbearing gets gummed up when women's reproduction is defined and controlled within racist and patriarchal structures, a "gummy bear" candy signifies polyvalently, if not quite undecipherably. Clemencia subverts conventional social uses of candy as a means by which a (usually male) lover communicates affection to his beloved or as a gift given by a father to celebrate the birth of a daughter. Bearing a male child, being "white" and legally wed to Drew—and thus, by virtue of her birth, marriage, and reproductive labor, occupying a more secure class position—all make Megan an unforgivable enemy for the self-made woman Clemencia, whose refusal to marry signals both her rebellion and her search for autonomy as a woman unprotected by patriarchy, at the same time that it confirms her obedience as a daughter following her mother's counsel.

While on the surface it seems unequivocal, her mother's advice is actually cryptic, ambiguous, and certainly ironic, in part because "Mexican" frequently is used to refer not only to Mexican nationals but also to naturalized and native born U.S. citizens of Mexican descent. So it is uncertain who exactly are the "Mexicans" Clemencia's mother warned her against. Perhaps she meant only: Be sure not to marry a man like your father. Clemencia cannot forgive her mother for marrying an Anglo after her father's death. Her mother's advice might mean: Never marry a man born in Mexico. Clemencia herself is the offspring of a bourgeois Mexican father and a working class Mexican-American mother. In this story, "Mexican" operates chiefly as a sign of difference, whether it is a difference of nationality or national origin; of culture, language, or class; or even of gender, since (presumably) the "Mexicans" Clemencia is warned not to marry are all men. Yet the same term is also a sign of equivalence, since "Mexican" can be interpreted to include Clemencia and her mother, as well as the husband and father who was born in Mexico.

Then again, her mother's advice might mean: marry a man who is not of Mexican descent. Or more specifically: marry an Anglo, as the mother did when given a second chance. The erotically adventurous Clemencia behaves as if she had heard only the first two words of the admonition: never marry. Although she says she is "too romantic for marriage," she also prides herself on being something of a sexual outlaw, never a captive bride in the prison of marriage: have "Mexican" lovers, but refrain from marrying any of them. It is unlikely that is what her mother meant, but from a rebellious daughter's perspective, it is a plausible, if subversive, interpretation. The mother's advice to her daughter and her second marriage to an Anglo and Clemencia's own sexual independence, all point to a possible equation of "Mexican" with a set of culturally specific gender roles and rules, from which both mother and daughter, in different ways, seek to distance themselves.

When the U.S. born Clemencia considers her own sexual freedom and social mobility, the category "Mexican" excludes her, but expands to include any man of Latino heritage, particularly if he is working class. She dismisses from consideration the entire catalogue of Latino men. However, when it comes to her affair with a Texas yuppie, the meaning of "Mexican" suddenly doubles back to include Clemencia herself, thereby excluding her from the range of women suitable for marriage to Drew. She is blessed and cursed with fulfillment of her own rebellious wish: to be lover or mistress only, never a wife. As she contemplates her status as discarded lover in relation to Megan, her sexual rival, Clemencia imagines Drew explaining to his wife the trail of tell-tale gummy bears, with a fabrication about the superstitious Mexican house cleaner. Having believed that as an artist she was positioned outside of the hierarchical division of socio-economic classes, or possibly moved upward through her relationship with Drew, Clemencia gets her comeuppance by finding herself his servant. At most, she can hold onto her relationship to Drew only through her role as his son's instructor, a role she vengefully subverts by seducing the boy, as she herself had been seduced as Drew's student.

While the author insists that Drew is Anglo—clearly he is Anglo-identified—this reader sees nothing in the text that definitely fixes his ethnicity. Even Clemencia's statement, "I love it when you speak to me in any language," implying that Drew is not a native Spanish speaker, oddly echoes the narrator of **"Eyes of Zapata,"** who says to Emiliano, "you spoke to us in our language." While **"Eyes of Zapata"** is of necessity written in English, with a sprinkling of Spanish words evocative of the landscape and culture of Mexico, this statement reminds the reader that the text is not only the author's imaginative construction of the voice of Zapata's lover, but is also a translation of that imagined voice into a different language, since the narrator would actually address her lover, the Mexican revolutionary hero Emiliano Zapata, in Mexican Spanish. Ironically, her abandonment by her lover and isolation from her people, despite a common language and shared belief in the revolution, is echoed by the rejection and loneliness of the alienated Clemencia.

"Never Marry a Mexican" might be seen to reflect current debates concerning the proper naming of Mexican-Americans and other Latinos. Having largely jettisoned a prior designation as "Spanish" people, which seemed to signal a Eurocentric orientation while repressing indigenous Amerindian roots, the question remains whether U.S. Hispanics (a census category melding together people of diverse racial and national origins) desire to be counted as "white" people, and thus assimilable into the dominant culture of the U.S., as Linda Chavez counsels; or as a "brown" or "bronze" *raza,* and thus members of the global majority of "people of color," the identification preferred by many who designate themselves Chicanos or Latinos rather than Hispanics. At the least, the question of identity is a challenge for people whose culture resists Anglicization.

In addition to her portraits of the artist as a Chicana, Cisneros is concerned with representing the silenced and marginalized, including children, homosexuals, and working class and immigrant Chicanos and Mexicanos, whose stories have been untold or untranslated. Her particular focus on the silencing of women is signaled in the title story, **"Woman Hollering Creek."** The creek called "La Gritona" is reminiscent of popular folktales about "La Llorona," a nameless tragic woman who drowned herself and her children. The creek, the border, and the *telenovelas* define the mythic spaces given to Cleófilas in her fantasies of escape from a battering husband. The cultural scripts associated with each space offer her different escape fantasies: homicide and/or suicide, like La Llorona; dramatic border crossings, like the escape of an outlaw desperado from the U.S.

into Mexico, or the crossings of *mojados* and smuggler *coyotes*; or *telenovelas,* soap operas that provide the escape of entertainment. Cisneros creates a new destiny in a story that revises all three of these cultural scripts, allowing Cleófilas a realistic escape with the help of Chicana feminist activists. Translating from "La Llorona" (weeping woman) to "La Gritona" (shouting woman) to the English "Woman Hollering Creek" allows a greater set of possibilities for interpreting the cry of the restless spirit. With its haunting sound of wind and water, the creek speaks with an enigmatic voice—crying, weeping, wailing, shouting, hollering "like Tarzan," perhaps even laughing—a voice too often denied in traditional representations of Latinas. Paradoxically, "La Llorona," a woman silenced in life, wails her grief in death. Cleófilas learns to decode a feminist message of survival in the haunted voice of the creek that hollers with the rage of a silenced woman. Much as Chicana feminists have revised folklore, legend, and myth to open up possibilities for new representations of women, the activism of Felice and her *compañeras* helps Cleófilas to reinterpret the message of La Gritona, translating her voice from a wail, to a holler, to a shout, to laughter; from an *arroyo* associated with a tragic legend to "a creek . . . full of happily ever after."

Searching for and validating folk and popular articulations often excluded from "the literary," Cisneros employs throughout the entire text of **Woman Hollering Creek** a network of epigraphs taken, not from the literary traditions of the United States or Europe or Latin America, but instead from Mexican ballads and romantic popular songs that circulate throughout, and indeed help to constitute, Spanish-speaking communities through dissemination of recordings, through jukeboxes located in restaurants and nightclubs located (along with *tortillerias, mercados, cines,* and *botanicas*) in Latino neighborhoods, and through Spanish-language radio stations broadcasting to cities or geographic regions with large Spanish-speaking populations. Cisneros privileges such commercial/cultural sites in which commodities and services are aimed at a culturally specific clientele, such as the cinemas devoted to the showing of films from Mexico or *telenovelas,* soap operas, produced for Mexican television and syndicated in the U.S.

The church functions similarly, as a cultural as well as religious site: specifically as a site of origin for insider discourses specific to Mexican-American and other Latino cultures, through the exchange of prayers and religious services for offerings made and thanks given by devout Catholics whose religion syncretically embraces folk beliefs. Cisneros recognizes and acknowledges the prayers of ordinary people addressing the Christian God, Catholic saints fused with Aztec goddesses, and even African deities, as a folk discourse worthy of inclusion in a literary text of an emergent minority literature. As Rosario offers her braid to the

Virgin in thanks for the opportunity to become an artist rather than a mother, Cisneros offers her book (with its elaborate list of acknowledgments to family, friends, colleagues, *la Divina Providencia,* and *Virgen de Guadalupe Tonantzin*) as a kind of literary ex voto devoted to Chicano culture. Her text associates this folk genre with the religious articles and folk healing paraphernalia referred to in **"Anguiano Religious Articles," "Little Miracles, Kept Promises"** and **"*Bien* Pretty."** These religious or quasi-religious cultural sites, like such fixtures of U.S. commercial culture as Kwik Wash laundromats, K-Mart, Woolworth's, Kash N Karry, Luby's Cafeteria, and flea markets where fire-damaged Barbie doll Dream Houses can be purchased by families who could not afford to buy them even at K-Mart, are markers of class and gender, as well as sites for the reproduction of the dominant culture and the production of a resistant ethnic minority culture, which is neither entirely of the U.S. nor Mexico.

Permitting unstudied inscriptions of folk practice and entrepreneurial flair, associated with religious and secular sites of cultural production, to enter and influence her text is the author's conscious choice, signaling the intersection of aesthetic and ideological concerns. Cisneros asserts that selectively "allowing what comes in from the neighborhood" to inscribe itself within her own writing practice can change the course of a story as it is written. "The story was transformed" when the author incorporated into the manuscript of what became **"*Bien* Pretty"** the text of an advertising flyer left by a local exterminator, and Flavio Munguia, unschooled poet and slayer of cockroaches, was born. As a working-class organic intellectual, secure in his Mexican identity, he gently challenges the self-conscious Chicanismo of the narrator, Guadalupe (Lupe/Lupita), a new age bohemian artist. Her name invokes *La Virgen de Guadalupe* as a cultural symbol, as in the naming of San Antonio's Guadalupe Cultural Arts Center, a site of contact between artists and the local Mexican-American community.

Through the relationship of Flavio and Lupe, through the dialogue implied by the juxtaposition of **"Tin Tan Tan"** with **"*Bien* Pretty,"** as well as through the author's willingness to allow the barrio in some sense to collaborate in the writing of her text, Cisneros suggests a complex interaction of artist and community. Nourished by poetry, as Lupe is fed by her painting, Flavio represents the indigenous creativity and cultural "authenticity" of the barrio, on which the trained artist relies for inspiration. Perhaps attracted by the playful rhyme advertising the pest control services of *La Cucaracha Apachurrada* [The Squashed Cockroach], Lupe hires him as an exterminator, then offers him a job as artist's model, "Because you have such a wonderful. Face." Despite the threat that Lupe will objectify him, Flavio accepts, already imagining "what kind of story" he can make of the adventure. At first, he seems more committed to Lupe's project

than she herself. He arrives ahead of her at the garage studio, "like if he was the one painting me."

Like Chaq Uxmal Paloquin in **"One Holy Night,"** Flavio's Amerindian features seem to the narrator exotically, genuinely Mexican. "I'm thinking . . . you might be the perfect Prince Popo for a painting I've had kicking around in my brain." While Chaq, who bragged of descent from "an ancient line of Mayan Kings," turns out to be plain old Chato, with "no Mayan blood," Flavio has the "face of a sleeping Olmec . . . heavy Oriental eyes, thick lips and wide nose . . . profile carved from onyx." His bona fide Mexican identity, paradoxically indicated by Asian and African features, is partially confirmed for Lupe by the intimacies exchanged when they "make love in Spanish." However, the "true test" of authenticity is, significantly, a cry of pain: "When Flavio accidentally hammered his thumb, he never yelled 'Ouch!' he said '*Ay!*' The true test of a native Spanish speaker." Their tempestuous affair refigures, as it regenders, the dynamic encounter of the explorer artist with the indigenous creativity of the community. Here, the result is the artist's revisioning of an Aztec myth visualized in popular Mexican-American culture in countless velvet paintings, barrio murals, custom vans, and complimentary calendars "like the ones you get at Carniceria Ximenez or Tortilleria Guadalupanita." When Lupe learns that he has a wife in Mexico, she represses and sublimates her "uncontrollable desire to drive over to Flavio Munguia's house with [her] grandmother's *molcajete* and bash in the skull." Instead of pounding him with the stone mortar inherited from her abuelita's kitchen, she returns to her art work with a new inspiration, as well as an empowering feminist vision:

> Went back to the twin volcano painting. Got a good idea and redid the whole thing. Prince Popo and Princess Ixta trade places. After all, who's to say the sleeping mountain isn't the prince, and the voyeur the princess, right? So I've done it my way. With Prince Popocatepetl lying on his back instead of the Princess.

For middle-class characters, such as the narrators of **"*Bien* Pretty"** and **"Never Marry a Mexican,"** particular forms of identification with Mexican and Chicano cultures are indicated through specific modes of commodity consumption—as well as through self-conscious appropriations from working class, immigrant, and folk cultural production. The ironic humor with which they adorn themselves and decorate their homes with folk and kitsch artifacts signifies their middle class acculturation and privilege, as much as it indicates their attempt to escape or transcend class through self-fashioning: identifying as an artist, bohemian, new age hippie, or, like Gomez-Pena, an ethnically specific "hipiteca"; living in or near the barrio; patronizing local ethnic businesses; and blending culturally specific and syncretic spiritual practices with new age eco-feminist spiritualism. Cisneros's use of irony, humor, inversion, parody, deliberate transgression and strategic revision of cultural scripts, problematizes ethnic authenticity. Figuring the artist-intellectual as female, desiring subject, and the community as male, desired object also complicates the signification of identity, as gender further complicates the artist's cultural and class identification and inverts a previous gender coding found in the male-dominated cultural production of the emergent Chicano Movement of the late 1960s and 1970s.

"*Bien* Pretty" and **"Never Marry a Mexican"** are narrated by women artists, each pulled in a different direction by desire: Lupe toward the native intelligence of the community; Clemencia toward a seductive "Cortez" who introduces her to the world of "the rich, who come to [her] exhibitions and buy [her] work." While Clemencia describes her class position as "amphibious," Lupe stresses her activist credentials as a supporter of farmworkers: "[We] go back a long way. Back to the grape-boycott demonstrations in front of the Berkeley Safeway. And I mean the *first* grape strike." Clemencia regards her work as a translator as "a form of prostitution," while Lupe insists on the untranslatability of certain Spanish terms, like *la fulana,* and prefers the sound of the word *urracas* to its English equivalent "grackles." Each has faced a *gabacha* [nemesis]: the blonde whom Lupe calls "*la otra*" (inscribing the "white" woman as "the other"); and the "red-headed Barbie doll" who is the recipient of Clemencia's miniature Coatlicues.

For both women, art is revenge, therapy, magic, affirmation, and power. Clemencia obsessively paints and repaints portraits of her pale-skinned lover to gain power over something she "drew." Lupe's encounter with Flavio inspires her to confront her blank canvas; to challenge restrictive gender codes and cultural inscriptions; to possess, and inscribe her desire upon, the body of her lover, a body already imprinted with tattooed names of other women. Lupe "rewrites" her relationship to Flavio, as **"*Bien* Pretty"** rewrites **"Tin Tan Tan."** She boldly repositions herself in relation to the folk, who are both inscribers and themselves inscribed. Both Lupe, the proud Chicana, and Clemencia, the confessed Malinchista, perform art as *brujeria,* or "Mexican voodoo." Their powers link them to the spellbinding sorcery of the narrator of **"Eyes of Zapata,"** whose words "can charm" and "can kill," but who, nevertheless, is abandoned by her lover and the revolution. With their relative privilege and power offset by their gender and their marginal status in both Anglo and Hispanic cultures, Clemencia feels betrayed by "Cortez," Lupe by her "Prince Popo."

The implicit contradictions in the artist's appreciation of, and identification with, the folk culture of immigrants and work-

ing class Chicanos are demonstrated in these two stories; and the possible naïveté of such a position is explored. Clemencia self-consciously notes her idealization and possible infantilization of barrio culture, which she may have associated with her own childhood before she took on her adult identity of cosmopolitan artist-intellectual": "The barrio looked cute in the daytime, like Sesame Street." She is aware that she has romanticized the barrio where there are "more signs in Spanish than in English." As a painter, she cultivates an aesthetic appreciation for the popular culture and folk life of working class and immigrant Chicanos and learns, ambivalently and complexly, both to identify with and to dissociate herself from "Mexicans."

Lupe, the nomadic narrator of **"*Bien* Pretty,"** an artist turned arts administrator, humorously contrasts her own meager possessions with the grand inventory of cultural and aesthetic artifacts that contributes to the Frida Kahlo-inspired decor of the house she sublets from a successful Chicana artist. As a tenant, surrounded by someone else's possessions, in a house strategically located "where the peasantry lives—but close enough to the royal mansions" of a historic district—she measures her own poverty, or rather, her bohemian rootlessness and marginality. Confronted by Flavio, who forces her to admit to herself, "I was not Mexican," she feels her own inauthenticity, or rather her cultural hybridity. Yet she is rich in self-confidence once she makes the commitment to her painting.

If Rosario of the *milagritos* is the potential Chicana artist struggling from the cocoon of familial and communal expectations, Lupe and Clemencia are intense, brave butterflies, so deeply imbued with a sense of beauty and purpose that no heartache can deter them from their art. Such stories and characters, juxtaposed as they are with stories of poor, immigrant, and working class Chicanos and Mexicanos, draw the reader's attention, not only to the conflict of Hispanic and Anglo cultures and their respective linguistic codes, but also to tensions within Latino communities, of race, class, gender, and ideology; and of unequal access to education, bilingual instruction, literacy, class mobility, and the rights and privileges of U.S. citizenship.

Cisneros's text registers tensions implicit in a community where the border between the U.S. and Mexico is reproduced within the psyche of the individual, and where the "Mericans" are also the "Mexicans." The computer spell checker suggests "Mexican" as a substitute for "Merican," Cisneros's paragrammatic truncation of "American." The alteration, like translation, makes distinct signifiers equivalent. The words are equal in length if not identical in meaning. After all, Mexicans are Americans and, as the North American Free Trade Agreement reminds those who needed reminding, Mexico is part of North America. The spell checker also suggests "Moroccan" as a possible replacement for the unrecognized word, but that is another story.

Martha Satz (interview date Spring 1997)

SOURCE: "Returning to One's House: An Interview with Sandra Cisneros," in *Southwest Review,* Vol. 82, No. 2, Spring, 1997, pp. 166-85.

[*The following is a compilation of two interviews. In an author's note, interviewer Martha Satz states: "The first was conducted in 1985 under the auspices of the Dallas Public Library in a cable TV series titled "Conversations." The second took place on November 17, 1996, in connection with Cisneros's reading during the SMU Literary Festival. The conjunction provides an insight into the development of Cisneros's views and writing."*]

[*Satz:*] *Your book* **House on Mango Street** *has been marketed as a book for young people, but it isn't the sort of book that is usually produced for children. Would you talk about that?*

[Cisneros:] I'd like to comment on that. It seems to be marketed as a young people's book, but my readers range anywhere from second graders to university students to housewives. I like the fact that it has such a range. It's written, I suppose, with the intent that it can be read as single stories or as a novel. It does have one general theme.

I suppose the book is being marketed that way because the story is told from a child's point of view; the work is written in simple but very powerful language. It deals with an experience that's not usual for a young person's book.

My intent was to write stories that don't get told—my mother's stories, my students' stories, the stories of women in the neighborhood, the stories of all of those people who don't have the ability to document their lives.
—Martha Satz

It always surprises me when children like the story. When I have read it to children there are certain stories they understand and enjoy. My intent was to write stories that don't get told—my mother's stories, my students' stories, the stories of women in the neighborhood, the stories of all of those people who don't have the ability to document their lives. One of the reasons I dedicated the book to women was that there were so many people to whom I was indebted

because I stole their stories. That's how I put the book together. It's a young girl's diary in a sense. All the stories are told from the point of view of a woman-girl who is in that nebulous age between childhood and adulthood. Some days she's a child and for a few days she might be an adult. That always struck me as a kind of mysterious time, so I chose her as the persona for these stories.

I wanted to talk a little bit about the selection **"Hips,"** *just because it contains unusual material.*

It's fun to read that one out loud. I think the book has a wide range because some of the stories are very playful, and some are very sad and serious, and I guess **"Hips"** is a little bit of both. If I had to summarize the book, I guess I'd say it's a book about a young girl's discovery of her sexuality. I like to read it because I get to sing, which I don't get to do very often.

There are so many things in **"Hips"** *that don't usually appear in stories—all the jump rope rhymes, all the minutiae of the girl experience.*

I especially relish writing about all those little things no one ever writes about. I included all of the girl knowledge that you get. I had this storehouse of information—little nursery rhymes and jump rope songs—and I thought what can I do with these things? And finally, when I was writing this book, I thought I would throw them all into one story, and that's how that story came about.

It's unusual, too, in a book that is read sometimes by children, that the sun isn't shining and there's not a dog named Spot. There are rats.

It's very curious. I went to school at the Iowa Writers' Workshop, and everyone was writing about the sun shining and beautiful gardens, but those things weren't in my life. I think it was important for me to have the cultural shock I experienced at Iowa, for me to experience my otherness, in order for me to choose my subject intentionally.

I wanted to ask you about the girlhood that probably inspired **Mango Street.** *Tell me about what you were like as a small girl.*

We never owned books in my house, not because my mother didn't want us to have books. She loved books very much. We couldn't afford them, so I never knew you could own a book until I was about twelve. We did go to the public library, though, and our house was always filled with borrowed books. I think that was very important in nurturing me as a writer. My mother, of course, was instrumental in taking me there and bringing me back and making sure we had books and telling us stories.

What was your father's attitude toward the girl who had her head in a book?

I think in a way it's fortunate that I was a girl because my father thought it was all right that I was interested in writing and literature. He thought I was only a girl and therefore what harm could come of it? I would eventually get married and if I wanted to go to college and major in creative writing or literature, that was okay because I'd get married anyway. So he ignored it, whereas my mother, I think, lived through me vicariously, and she has supported me and is supporting me now. She is very happy about the choices I've made.

That attitude of your father, "she's only a girl . . ."

Well it's funny, I'm thirty-one and I've had quite a bit of success with my writing now. But my father never acknowledged my success until very recently—until last summer, in fact. Because he is from Mexico City, he reads in Spanish. Last summer I read at the Colegio de Mexico and several of my pieces, especially pieces from *House on Mango Street,* had been translated. It was the first time he read anything I wrote. He had a funny response. He kind of looked at it and said "mmm," and in Spanish he said, "Who wrote this?" I said, "I did." And he looked at it and said "Mmm, who helped you?" I think he's secretly been very pleased to see my name on books. And I'm very proud of it because I'm the only daughter of a family of six sons—very traditional sons at that—who always made me feel as if I was not a Cisneros because I was a girl and would forfeit my name at marriage. I'm very pleased to see that I'm the one who put the name on that book cover.

I read in an interview that you said men often write in a romanticized way about the barrio because they had a different experience from women.

That's true. I have lived in the barrio, but I discovered later on in looking at works by my contemporaries that they write about the barrio as a colorful, Sesame Street-like, funky neighborhood. To me the barrio was a repressive community. I found it frightening and very terrifying for women. The future for women in the barrio is not a wonderful one. You don't wander around "these mean streets." You stay at home. If you do have to get somewhere, you take your life in your hands. So I wanted to counter those colorful viewpoints, which I'm sure are true to some extent but were not true for me.

Tell me about your college experience.

It's very curious. I want to mention how fortunate it was for me to have gone the route that I did. I'm grateful to have had the opportunity to attend a university, unlike many

young writers I've met in the barrio and in the communities who work in isolation. I was born at a time when there were government grants that allowed me to pursue higher education. I was able to attend an undergraduate program that had a writer in residence, and he, of course, took great interest in my work and recommended me to the University of Iowa. At the time I entered rather naïvely, I had no idea that it was a prestigious workshop or that it was quite unusual that I got there. I was the only Chicano writer, and I believe the only Latina that has graduated from the program. But at the time I didn't have that consciousness. I just went there directly from undergraduate school, which may have been detrimental—to go so young in my life without having developed a voice of my own first. It was a bit of a shock to be in a program like the one at Iowa. It's a disciplined and rigorous program. I think I entered quite a different person from the one who left. I became very rebellious there. I never liked the work that my classmates were doing, and as an attempt to move far away from their style, I stumbled upon the voice that predominates in the *House on Mango Street,* which is a street child's voice.

What didn't you like about your classmates' work?

Well, theirs was a very distilled writing. I suppose it was a true voice for my classmates, but my attempt to try to imitate an esoteric style of writing was untrue to my experiences. I think everyone has to stumble around to find her voice. Coming from a working class background, an ethnic community, an urban community, a family that did not have books in the house, I just didn't have the same frames of reference as my classmates. It wasn't until I realized and accepted that fact that I came upon the subjects I wanted to write about.

So it was at Iowa that you understood you had a legitimate thing to write about and a legitimate way to write about it.

Right. I'm grateful for Iowa. If anything, it stirred me up, and that's good.

What did your classmates think when you began to produce this sort of material?

It's very funny. I think a workshop should not intimidate its students into not writing. Anything that silences you is dangerous. I didn't find it a supportive community, at first, and didn't write anything for a year. It wasn't until the second year that I decided I would write something no one else in the class could write about. I think it's an important thing to ask yourself: What can I write about that no one else can write about? For myself, since I was going through some traumatic experiences at the time, I chose to write about my past—my childhood experiences, my mother, and especially women in the community. So a great number of the stories in here are girl stories or women stories.

You write of women who are very powerful, in their own way—power disapproved of, but power nonetheless.

Yes. But in powerless circumstances, I think. It's true.

What do you make of your experience of woman and power? How do you use that material?

I think that growing up Mexican and feminist is almost a contradiction in terms. For a long time—and it's true for many writers and women like myself who have grown up in a patriarchal culture, like the Mexican culture—I felt great guilt betraying that culture. Your culture tells you that if you step out of line, if you break these norms, you are becoming anglicized, you're becoming the *malinche*—influenced and contaminated by these foreign influences and ideas. But I'm very pleased to be alive among the current generation of women. Many writers are redefining our Mexicanness and it's important if we're going to come to terms with our Mexican culture and our American one as well. So it's a dilemma. I think many of my stories come from dealing with straddling two cultures, and certainly it's something I'm going to deal with in future stories.

You spoke of your mother's pride in your work. What is her attitude, though, toward your strength and independence?

My mother is a very feisty, strong, and independent woman. It's too bad she was born when she was, because I think women were nurtured so much they were made helpless. She's very much the mother that is described in the story **"A Smart Cookie"**—a woman who can speak two languages and fix the TV and draw, but doesn't know how to get downtown because she doesn't know which train to take. She's a woman of contradictions. On the other hand, I'm sure if it weren't for her, my brothers and I would not be the creative individuals we are. So in a sense, we're living her dreams for her. I know she's very pleased with my stories, though she gets a little embarrassed about my writing about her. But so long as I read them in public when she's out of the room it's okay.

Do you feel that by writing her stories and other women's stories, you are redeeming her experience and giving her some strength?

Yes, very much so. I think my mother is always going to be a voice in my stories. She's very much the persona I use in these stories and in the poems. It's her voice I hear when I sit down and begin a piece.

*   *   *

[The second interview, conducted on November 17, 1996, begins here.]

Fifteen years have passed, and I must say I have been teaching **House on Mango Street** *for a number of years now, very happily too. And in the section called* **"My Name,"** *the protagonist ends by saying she'd like to baptize herself under a new name—ZeeZee the X. For me her chosen name seems to indicate a variable to be expressed, indicative of an identity to be shaped. Do you think the name may be seen as a metaphor for your life too, shaping the identity of a Latina, a feminist writer?*

Yes, I think so. Much of **Mango Street** I wrote on the blind, intuitively, and now when I read it out loud, it so much echoes my life that it's frightening. I did not intend it as autobiographical or as a mask for my own life, but it turns out that I'm living the fiction I created. ZeeZee the X came from my own love affair with the *Autobiography of Malcolm X.* I loved the X in Malcolm X and the idea of his choosing that as a name. I am and always have been enamored with exotic names and names that begin with letters of the alphabet like X or Y or Z, those strange letters. And so the name came out intuitively. But yes, you are right. I've had to be filling in that blank. And for Esperanza it's so nice to have a name with a Z in it because it lends a sense of flair. There's a zest to it. It sounds exotic and wild. So it's not just X. There's a wildness to Z.

And speaking of wildness, sex for women in **House on Mango Street** *is dangerous. In the section of Mango called* **"The Family of Little Feet,"** *when the little girls find high heels and try them on, the grocer Mr. Benny comments that the shoes are dangerous. And they prove to be so, because the shoes make the little girls objects of male sexual desire. Sexuality in the environment you describe brings oppression and confinement. But in your poetry, and especially in* **Loose Woman,** *you write female erotic poetry. Have you found this liberating?*

Well, you know what? I think **House on Mango Street** intimated that wherever there is a source of power for women, it is forbidden. Sex is forbidden by male society because men know that's where our nuclear reactors are, so to speak. These are Chernobyls in the making. And, of course, women venture into this dangerous space and then feel bad because patriarchy dictates they are dangerous. With **Loose Woman,** I entered a realm where I am writing from a dangerous fountainhead. But that book was never meant to be published. It was not even a book. It was what I call a box of poems. They were "poems I threw under the bed," metaphorically, thinking of Emily Dickinson, poems too dangerous to publish in my lifetime. And I had a very adverse reaction when *Loose Woman* came out in Texas. It received almost no reviews. The one or two reviews it received were so negative and so hurtful to me that I thought, why am I writing poetry for anyone? The reason I write it is not to publish it but to get the thorn out of the soul of my heart.

Do you think the negative reviews were a result of your being a daring woman writing about female sexuality?

Maybe that was true. I shouldn't imply there were that many reviews. They were just so vitriolic. I think the fact that I wandered into Texas with my awards rattling in my pocket threatened a lot of male poets—"How dare I?" So now in retrospect, I can see that it really wasn't about me, but about someone else's unhappiness, which is what a lot of bad reviews are about, I think.

Was publishing that book frightening for you because it was so personal?

Yes. I can go out and read the fiction and I'm on my little soap box, doing my politics, brandishing my sword. But poetry is not like that. Poetry doesn't have anything to do with the public. I can't even direct what I'm going to write about, it comes of its own accord. It's a little periscope that goes inside my psyche, and it's a frightening thing to have someone looking at your nightmares and dreams. Poetry has nothing to do with publishing. The idea that poetry must be published reminds me of the fallacy that because women have a uterus they must have children. That's how I felt about poetry when I saw my first book. I think Emily Dickinson was absolutely lucid to write so freely without thinking of the public or what the neighbors would say. She knew that the true reason one writes poetry and works at the craft is simply to write that poem. I learned this even before that bad review or before anybody said anything. All I needed was to see the picture on the cover of the small press edition with me sitting in a provocative pose, which was never supposed to be on a cover. It was an intimate picture that my photographer boyfriend and I took after we had been doing these traditional, close-cropped head portraits. Then we got wilder and wilder because I kept drinking glasses of wine as this photo session went on. When we saw the contact sheet, Ana Castillo said, "You should use this for the cover." I said, "Oh no, we can't use that." Of course then we did, and the photo is a metaphor for what's inside—seduction, playfulness, sassiness, everything revealed. I didn't like the idea of myself being exposed to that extent. I looked at it and realized that I don't have to publish. After that I decided to publish only my fiction and keep the poems private. A lot of my private life was being gobbled up by the public, and I wanted something for myself, and no one seemed to care about poetry anyway. It wasn't as if people were banging down the door for my poems.

So this is your decision as of now, not to publish your poetry?

No, that was then. What happened, though, was when Random House saw how successful I was (it wasn't that they loved poetry so much), they thought "Hey, we can sell this girl's books of poetry, too." And suddenly I was offered a deal. I didn't want them to have my book of poetry, but I wanted a small press, Third Woman Press, to benefit from my success. So the way we did it was give the paperback rights to Third Woman Press, which continues to this day, but sell the hardcover rights to Random House; therefore if someone wanted the book after the hardcover sold out they'd have to buy the paperback. In this way, the little press could piggyback on the big one. I'm very loyal to the editor of Third Woman and wanted to help her out. She's very loyal to me—a very, very dear friend. She didn't want to say no to this deal and keep me from having more success and distribution of my books. As for me, I didn't care if the book went out of print and no one ever saw the poems again. So what happens? I'm forced to go on a book tour to promote a book I wrote in my twenties.

Which is **My Wicked, Wicked Ways?**

Yes, and I don't even write like that anymore. I'm embarrassed because the poems are just my juvenilia. I don't like to read them. I tell the audiences this is akin to publishing your high school year book. What am I going to do? So what I do is this. I read the introduction, which is a poem. That is the only new thing in the book and a wonderful way to get out of reading the older poems. I read the introduction that talks about my position now and say, "Well, you can buy the book and read the rest of the poems. I'll read you some new poems." So that's how I pulled those poems out from under the bed. People used to come up to me after readings and say, "Where can I get that poem you just read?" And I'd say, "Oh that's not published." And so many people were asking for copies, it got to be a nuisance photocopying poems for friends and strangers. Eventually I gave them to Susan, my agent, thinking if we published them in a magazine, at least I could refer my audience to such and such journal, and they'd leave me alone and I wouldn't have to keep running to Kinko's, right? But as it turns out, Susan called me back immediately after I sent her the manuscript. It's really funny because the collection was in these different typefaces that kind of documented my poverty and my rise out of it. Some poems were composed on my junky little typewriter—the one that made little holes with the o; there were some on my little typewriter that was a step up, an electronic one; all the way finally to computers. So you could see these different typefaces over the years. Susan had counted the poems and said, "You have something like fifty-seven poems, and if you would write just a few more, you'd have a collection." I didn't want to publish a collection, but by then the poems were far enough removed from me that I said yes and I think the success of that book is partly because I wrote it as if it could not be published. It's looser in form. It's loose in every which way you can think of and I like that book of poetry. I don't read from the other one anymore.

There is an unusual poem in that collection called **"Down There,"** *which deals in part with menstruation.*

Yes. I wrote that for two of my male students when I was teaching at California State University. I had two freshmen in an introduction to creative writing class, and I couldn't make them understand. They would write these poems every class period to try to gross each other out. They were in a competition of picking gross subjects. You know, kind of locker room material.

Adolescent humor.

Right. My criticism was that these weren't poems. They thought I was being fastidious about subject matter and of course I was not. I was just saying that if you're going to use this, it has to be a poem. So when the class ended, I wrote that poem overnight as a gift to them, to show them what I meant. We had a class reunion at the end of the semester, which I always do with my workshops, and I read that poem to them as my response to their gross poems and I said, "Okay, I'm going to show you guys what I mean and I'll gross you guys out and yet at the same time make it a poem." That's why that poem is there.

I admire that kind of boldness in you. I've looked at your Ms. Magazine *article about Guadalupe the Sex Goddess.*

Yes. That's in the collection called *Goddess of the Americas.*

Yes. You talk quite explicitly about your sexuality.

I try to talk about the things that make me a little uncomfortable. Then I know I'm on the right track.

Do you mean uncomfortable for you, for your students, for your audience?

I make it an assignment to my students and myself to write about the things we don't talk about, because those are the things that are real gold mines.

Emotional gold mines? Poetic gold mines?

Both. Why would I want to write the same old thing about the Virgin of Guadalupe? I'm writing a novel. I don't have time to stop. If I'm going to stop my writing, it might as well be to discover something I've always wanted to say, something vital and necessary to the community. That piece for me is very important, and I wish it were in every sixth grader's textbook. Of course it never will be.

I read it for the first time a couple of days ago to prepare for this interview and I think I would like to make it part of my women's studies class curriculum.

Oh, I wish you would. There's so much that goes unspoken that I think the mainstream community needs to understand. For example, the whole idea of not having a bedroom with a door or not even having a separate bedroom makes the whole idea of yourself, your sexuality, and your awareness different. It is something that really needs to be taken into account. I don't see this in stories. I don't see this in children's books. These are the things I want to write about. There are kids that sleep on couches and how can you explore your body if you don't have privacy? How do you expect a girl to be a woman in the sixth grade and to know anything about her body—whether it's for pleasure, or to make choices about reproduction?

And no one has spoken about this?

That's right. Nobody talks about that. When I had the opportunity to write about the Virgin of Guadalupe, I said I'm not going to write anything unless it's something I've never said and no one else has written about. I do see the Virgin of Guadalupe as a very powerful, sexual goddess, a symbol of creative destructiveness.

As long as we are talking about powerful women, talk to me a little bit about the witch, the bruja, *in your story* **"Eyes of Zapata."**

Oh, I like that story.

I love it too.

I never get to read it because it's just as she says—her story's a thread and if you pull one string the whole plot comes undone. I have tried to read that, but you cannot pull out one part without the audience understanding the whole piece. But I was just talking to my friend who has a theater here in Dallas. I said that the story is meant as a play. He is going to take a look at it and think about performing it.

Where do you see this witch figure—in folklore, in women's lives?

In the mirror. When I see someone who is really wise and

in her power and really writing from her vulva, that's a witch.

What does writing from the vulva mean to you?

Well, you know how they say you have to write with balls. I really think that's not right, because for men, everything happens from the balls. Writing with balls is easy for men, and something I think they have to overcome. It's some sort of low-level shop work for them, and they've got to go beyond that. Women have to move away from the heart and go down just a little bit farther, don't you think? We have to go "down there." Writing from "down there" is difficult, again because there are all these restrictions. There are all these lead walls and vaults with doors—again I'm thinking of Chernobyl. We've got that nuclear power plant down there. It's very powerful.

And how does one get there? How have you gotten there?

I think one of the ways I've gotten there is the way I did **Loose Woman**—to pretend that what I'm writing is so dangerous that no one can see it in my lifetime. That's the way I could write from that place. I would be like Emily Dickinson. No one could see my writing in my lifetime. It allowed me, for the first time, to be absolutely free, to even say things that were not politically correct, things that I would be ashamed of saying.

When you say things that are not politically correct, you mean. . .?
Oh, things that are unsisterly or mean. I have written mean poems—vengeful, jealous, and ugly.

I wanted to ask you about your use of language. For example, in one of the poems you use the word cunt. *Many women see that word as a very negative, derogatory, male term. Do you think in your poem you have changed the usage of that word?*

I didn't even realize that book had so many bad words in it until one day . . .

I'm not offended by the dirty words.

I didn't even realize they were there until I had to read on the radio and they said, now you cannot use any of these words. I said, "My God, they're all in that book." But when I was writing it, I wasn't thinking in a sinister way. I was simply using the truest words I could to determine what I wanted to say with all of its richness and smells. It was what I wanted to say. There were no words that would say what I meant that didn't sound like I was in a doctor's office.

I understand and that's part of the progress we've made,

isn't it? Women writing from the vulva are going to create those words and those stories and that language.

Right. I've had to use the bad words in Spanish, too. Like *panocha* is a very bad word and I put it in my essay on the Goddess, and a lot of people were freaked out.

What does the word mean?

It would be like *cunt.* And people were freaked out when they heard that. In fact that essay could not find a home because people were so freaked out by it. The *New Yorker* wanted it but they cut out all of the goddess part. They just wanted the parts about going to high school. One of those bold, brassy magazines wanted it, but they wanted to clean it up. And then Susan, my agent, said no. This piece is exactly about fighting against all that. So we've got to leave it. *Ms.* was the only magazine that would take it just as it is. And they were brave enough to run it.

What has the MacArthur meant to you?

The MacArthur's meant some wonderful things, good and bad. The bad has been that I was in the middle of trying to still my life and settle it so that I could concentrate on my novel and it has stirred things up now. Everybody keeps bothering me and knocking on the door.

Now you're a certified genius.

I can imagine what it's like for someone like Toni Morrison or anyone who's gotten the bigger prizes. Man! It gets in the way of writing, which is a very solitary act. So it gets to the point where I was struggling with trying to quiet my life down and go underground when this MacArthur comes and stirs everything up again. On the other hand, it has allowed me something that I did not have without a great expense to myself, which is health insurance, because I'm an independent. I'm not associated with any university. It's given me five years in which I have security. I liken my job to a seamstress who sews a wedding dress before the wedding and has spent all the money already but still has to sew the dress. That's what my job is. So it's given me peace of mind. One of the other great things that it's done for me is give me my green card. Those who still had doubts about whether I was a real writer or not must be silent.

It's given you certification.

Right. I don't need the university anymore. Now I am a certified person. I am the real thing now as a writer. It has also meant that I don't need to work for awards anymore. The awards were important for me, for that credibility. When I was younger, they were important certainly for money to write with. Now awards for me are redundant. After this one, I don't need any more, psychologically.

Was it important for your confidence level, psychologically, or had you arrived at a place where you didn't need that external reinforcement?

No. There's something I needed. Dorothy Allison and I have talked about this. If you've been poor, you never get over the fear of being poor again. I've only had money for the last six years. People don't realize that I had a hard time paying my bills six years ago, and even though I earn more and more each year, much to my surprise, I'm always afraid there's going to be a time when I'll be poor again and won't be able to make the mortgage payment. All of these things are there, now. I think the MacArthur has given me a kind of security. Even after the money runs out, I can do lectures. It's built my self-confidence about all the ways I can make money to meet that mortgage. Like writing articles. I was very insecure about that when I was younger. I always thought about getting married to a university so that I could have the benefits, the security. Now I don't need that. The MacArthur has given me carte blanche to do whatever I want. The MacArthur is there for life, even if the money's not there. If I want to go teach anywhere or need reassurance that I have made it, there it is. And any other award now would just be redundant. It would just bring more fame, which I don't need. I need solitude to write.

When you say "get married to a university" . . . ?

Yes, because I think a university, academic life, for me has been like marriage. It's like giving up freedom.

You've always used this kind of language in talking about yourself as a poet. You've said that you've chosen a love of poetry over other kinds of love. You have insisted in your writing that you are not the wife of anyone, you are not the mother of anyone. Do you still think of writing and marriage as alternative paths?

Yes. It's still hard. I think as a writer I did things the reverse of the way some other writers have. I've been married to my writing and now I'm in a place where there's some security. So if I wanted to get married now I could. It's not my goal in life, but it's certainly feasible now. Children too, that's something I think of. I think, oh my God, will there be a day when my bio note will say she is someone's mother?

So it now becomes an option for you?

Well, it becomes an option as long as I earn the money. So in a way I wouldn't really be the mother, I'd be the father. And if I wanted to be the father, I'd have to invent that.

You've been inventing a lot of things.

I think so. That's why I have faith that I will come to something in the next ten years. If I want to have a child or if I want to have a partner, I'm confident that it's not going to be a traditional relationship or a traditional family life. At first I felt the pressure that it was something I had to do before I was forty-five. But now I know if I want a child I can adopt. There are lots of things I can do.

I have to tell you I've adopted two children, one when I was forty-three. I adopted my first child when I was in my twenties, he grew up, and then I adopted another one—a daughter.

I need to talk to you about that because it's something I've been thinking about. I don't want to have all these people coming to me and giving me their opinions. I don't think it's something other people can tell you, not even your partner because inevitably your partner's not going to be there when it comes to being the parent. I think women invariably, whether they're married or not, wind up being single parents. All mothers are single parents.

I adopted my children as a single person.

But even if you are married, you are still a single parent. Isn't that true? I know men who are the most politically correct, and they say I will be there and that's not true. They're not there.

They "babysit" their children.

I think in order to have a child, you have to have the father—the provider—and two mothers. Two nanas. I would be the father and I'd have to support two nanas. That I think is the way to do it. I would have to continue doing my writing to earn the money to support two nanas.

Would you find that a loss to yourself—the primary bond with the child?

I don't know because I've never been the mother. Maybe I would find that I would want to be the mother and the nanas would have to be the nanas. I still think it would take three women. I really think you have to hire the two and not take advantage of your family. I think I could earn enough money now so that I could have two nanas. My friend said you need a nana and *enano*—that's a midget. He was just being silly, but wouldn't that be funny if you had them like in the court of Velasquez? A nana, *enano,* and the mamma?

But this is part of you, you invent life.

Yes. I think it's like all the poems, and as I once said in a lecture, "Your life is like a rough draft." People see the final draft, which is the books, and so they expect you to be perfect. We, all of us, are just rough drafts.

Would you say of yourself that you inhabit the border-lands?

Yes, definitely, because there really isn't any other place for me to go. When I lived in the other world it was killing me. It killed my spirit.

The other world meaning . . . ?

The world that other men and women live in kills my spirit. It's so wonderful now, at this age, to get confirmation that living against the grain has taken me exactly where I wanted to go. I'm less fearful or maybe not less fearful, but fear is part of it and I expect it now. I know that I can get past it.

Have there been other women that you have looked to living in the borderlands, say Gloria Anzaldua?

Well I can't look at Gloria because Gloria's situation is a little bit different from mine. She's a lesbiana writer. We look at each other's work. But to live I find myself reading autobiographies and biographies to guide and inspire me at times when I'm really lost. The other women writers that I meet like Dorothy Allison, or film makers, people that come into my life as I meet them—we try to put our heads together. Very powerful women in film help me. In a sense, I think biographies help me a lot because I can know the end of the story.

So who, for example, strikes you in terms of biographies?
I like Maria Callas a lot. Of course I don't like her ending. I think she made some mistakes. Tina Modotti the photographer. I just finished reading her autobiography.

Powerful women always seem to be inventing their lives. In her book, Writing a Woman's Life, *Carolyn Heilbrun writes about how we don't have enough stories about women leading lives with alternative scripts.*

Yes. I look at the stories—Emily Dickinson, all of these biographies—and of course, I'm always reading between the lines. Jean Rhys, for example—a woman I love and adore. I love looking at her life and wonder how you can suffer so much and still make something wonderful by saying maybe you weren't great at living your life, but you were great at obsessing over it and coming out with a piece of fiction that is perfect even if your life is not. That kind of vindicates life. So I look at artists, at different movie stars . . . I'm always reading really bizarre people like Jean Harlow. I just finished reading her biography. It's really fascinating because people come to my house and they'll say "I don't have these books." It looks like a rather eclectic list but I read them because I must, I have to, I need a home.

And can you go back home?

You mean to my home?

I mean to your community, to your family? How does that work for you?

Well I have been going home because right now my father is very ill. So I am living half the time in my mother and father's home in my old bedroom. I say old even though it wasn't that old because we moved into the house when I was in college.

What is that like for you?

It's been really hard. I have moved there thinking I was going to stay the whole time my father was ill. My father has been diagnosed with a terminal illness. It's been too much, and yet I realize this is the household that created the writer. It's overwhelming to me to go back to the house where to be alone or to seek privacy is evil or anti-social, anti-family. A high school teacher recently told me her Latina students couldn't understand why Esperanza wanted to go off by herself, why she wanted to be alone. According to their perspective, to be alone, to be exiled from the family is so anti-Mexican. My family still finds my behavior rather strange. I'm pulled to be with them, and yet to be with them requires an inordinate amount of time in front of a television screen. So at the end of the day I feel bloated and sick, as if I've eaten a box of jelly donuts or something. To be with my father means to lie on the bed next to him and watch bad actresses weeping on *telenovela.*

Are you attempting to understand each other better now?

I understand them. I think my mother understands the tenor of my life. My father, I understand, I really feel I've made my peace with him in the last couple of years. One of the most wonderful things about the MacArthur has been that my father has recognized me as a writer.

When I interviewed you fifteen years ago, we talked about your relationship to your father. And I remember your telling a little story about your father reading **House on Mango Street** *for the first time and saying, "Who wrote this?"*

What he read was **"Tepeyac"**; he only read **House** recently because it came out in Spanish, which is also how he was able to read **"Tepeyac"**; it was translated. That one story came out in Mexico. He read **House** only because he is on dialysis, and he had to do something. He said, "This is all very fine, Sandra (he told me in Spanish), but couldn't you write something for adults?" I immediately thought of what I had written for adults, but there's nothing my father could see. **Woman Hollering Creek** just came out in Spanish, and I gave it to him. My father can't read because he's too sick. And even if he were well enough, he wouldn't read. He's not a reader. But my father understands what I do now, even if he doesn't read my stories. The novel I'm writing is about him. My agent asked me, when she found out my father was sick, if I was going to be reading chapters of the novel to him. No, he doesn't need to hear the book. He knows he's in the story. He has no curiosity about it. He doesn't have to read. Like Curie said about her own family, they don't need to read the book—they have me. I feel like that with my father.

So you have peace, you think, with each other?

Oh yes. That's the one blessing of my life, right now, with my father's illness. My father has lived long enough to understand what I do, without reading my work. He understands the level of my success, and he understands why I did it. It's so wonderful that he's lived long enough so that now he says *la novela*, the novel, instead of when are you going to get married? That's what he used to say. Now it's "Don't get married because they only want your money." That's what he advised recently.

That's a marvelous resolution.

I know. There's bitter sweetness to it. I just finished writing a letter to the MacArthur people saying that was the best gift the MacArthur gave me—my father. He's dying but this is what I always prayed for—that he would live long enough to see what I was doing, instead of introducing me like a high school teacher. When I won the MacArthur I had this horrible feeling that my father was going to die.

Now that all your wishes had been granted?

Yes. My father got sick last autumn and he had a quadruple bypass, and I was sure he was not going to survive it. It was a few months after the MacArthur, and I said well, here it comes. It didn't quite come then, it's coming now. Still, it was expected. His health has been failing. I believe there's something bigger, that a much more incredible Author than I'll ever be arranged all these things in an incredible pattern. I knew when the MacArthur came, that my father was going to be taken. It was just time.

And there's no more anger from you?

No. Actually, my anger hasn't been directed to my father in a long time. I think I was angry when I was an undergraduate. I had to tell my father everything, even if it hurt him. I insisted on being absolutely honest. I haven't had a relationship like that with my father in a long time. Now he has just let me go. It was more a frustration with my father not

understanding what I was doing with my life. But not anger.

You were not angry that the men in your family were protecting you from yourself and keeping you from your own power and sexuality?

They were. I also understood that part of the reason my father trapped me and kept my brothers protecting me, all of them telling me I was a princess, was that he loved me so much. He wanted me to be in a little bubble. But his overprotectiveness also allowed me to be who I am, so in a way he helped me to do things. You know how you always have this child that rebels against his parents and does the extreme opposite. So I don't think anger is the right word. There was that anger, I think, in my teens. I pretty much have done what I wanted. It was necessary that he be so protective because it allowed me to develop into who I am.

As you said in the selection **"Eleven"** *in* **Woman Hollering Creek,** *"what they never tell you when you're eleven, you're also ten, and nine, and eight, and seven, and six, and five, and four, and three, and two, and one." All of those contribute to the end.*

Yes. I think so.

Laura Gutierrez Spencer   (essay date 1997)

SOURCE: "Fairy Tales and Opera: The Fate of the Heroine in the Work of Sandra Cisneros," in *Speaking the Other Self: American Women Writers,* edited by Jeanne Campbell Reesman, University of Georgia Press, 1997, pp. 278-87.

[*In the essay below, Gutierrez Spencer analyzes the way Cisneros inscribes "feminine" motifs of fairy tales and librettos into her narrative art.*]

Within the Western narrative tradition, female characters are commonly presented within the narrow confines of polarized roles limited to either madonna or whore, villain or victim. In a similar fashion, the fate of these characters also tends to fall to extremes. Depending upon the narrative form, the female protagonist all too often finds either an early end in death or an equally premature, if metaphorical, "demise" as she conveniently disappears into a cloud of anonymity after the hero has come to the rescue and married her. In so many plots, the appropriate denouement of dramatic tension is the death of the heroine. Female characters who are adventurous, inquisitive, active, or otherwise rebel against patriarchal rules of female comportment are often killed in punishment for their disobedience. Unfortunately, the passive, pliant heroine often meets the same fate. Her death is portrayed as a valiant sacrifice for the life or comfort of the male hero. More simply stated, female protagonists, whether they are "good girls" or "bad girls" still die, in literal and metaphoric terms. Catherine Clément, in *Opera, or the Undoing of Women,* documents this tradition. Among the most famous operas for instance, the death toll includes "nine by knife, two of them suicides; three by fire; two who jump; two consumptives; three who drown; three poisoned; two of fright; and a few unclassifiable, thank god for them, dying without anyone knowing why or how. Still, that is just the first sorting. And with my nice clean slate in my hands, I examine all those dream names in their pigeonholes, like butterflies spread out on boards. All that is left is to write their names above them: Violetta, Mimi, Gilda, Norma, Brunhilde, Senta, Antonia, Marfa. . . ." The misogynistic effect of these plots, of course, is not limited to the world of opera. This tendency comes from the very wellspring of literature, myth.

The most common example of myth in modern times and the form that has had the most impact upon our society is the fairy tale. Many of the tales that we tell our children before they sleep include plots in which male heroes are rewarded for their audacity, courage, and curiosity. Demure princesses are praised for their beauty and kindness, while other female characters, like Goldilocks, are punished for their curiosity and active natures. The active female character in fairy tales is either vilified as a figure of evil or is punished for her audacity.

Throughout her work, Sandra Cisneros has critiqued the fate of the heroine in Western patriarchal literature. She accomplishes this, in part, through reference to popular fairy tales. Cisneros's first book includes a feminist analysis of the social and personal consequences for women who believe in fairy tales and wait for Prince Charming to fulfill their existence. In *The House on Mango Street,* Cisneros draws attention to the messages that fairy tales impart to females about the roles they should play, or not play, in life. This book contains glimpses of the lives of various women and the social, cultural, and economic forces that have entrapped them in stultifying circumstances. Although individual stories in *The House on Mango Street* include examinations of prejudice, poverty, domestic abuse, sexual harassment, sexual assault, and sexism, one of the central themes of the book is that the women of Mango Street have been limited in the opportunities available to them to develop their own agendas and talents. This repression serves to subordinate these women's lives to husband and home. The theme of limitation and restriction is represented by many images of trapped women. In these stories women lean out of windows, stand in doorways, stare at the seams between ceiling and walls, and envy other women who "throw green eyes easily like dice and open homes with keys."

The stories in *The House on Mango Street* that take the form of revisionist fairy tales feature characteristic elements of the classic children's stories but are set within a different context and have more specific outcomes for the female characters. They oppose the traditional marriage to the hero and "happily-ever-after" conclusion. Cisneros's version of these fables reveal the truer-to-life consequences for women who are socialized to live their lives waiting for the happy ending. The stories **"Rafaela Who Drinks Papaya and Coconut Juice on Tuesdays"** and **"The Family of Little Feet"** allude respectively to "Rapunzel" and "Cinderella." Cisneros's heroines are young girls and women in the housing projects of Chicago. They do *not* live happily ever after. Beautiful Rafaela, for instance, is locked in her own house by a jealous husband. She "leans out the window and leans on her elbow and dreams her hair is like Rapunzel's. On the corner there is music from the bar and Rafaela wishes she could go there and dance before she gets old." In **"The Family of Little Feet"** the little-girl protagonist and her friends are given a bag of used high-heeled shoes. The girls try on heels for the first time in their life and marvel at how the shoes make their legs look beautiful and long. They walk, dance, and strut around the neighborhood until they realize the power of the shoes. On this sojourn, the girls become the objects of leering glances, an angry rebuke, and the offer of a dollar for a kiss from a drunken bum. As if by magic, the shoes have drawn unwanted attention to the budding sexuality of the young girls. As opposed to the blushing Cinderella whose symbol of salvation is a shoe, these young heroines learn that high-heeled shoes "are dangerous." They learn that the power their sexuality holds in attracting attention from males often has negative consequences.

Cisneros's portrayals of fairy-tale heroines are revisionist only in the sense that she applies a feminist analysis to the underlying messages that fairy tales convey to women. In drawing attention to how male domination, denial of personal ambition, lack of education, abuse, and low expectations affect women's lives, Cisneros attacks the weak heroine of the fairy tale who is "unable to act independently or self-assertively; she relies on external agents for rescue; she restricts her ambitions to hearth and nursery." By revealing the concrete effects of waiting for someone to keep us "on a silver string," the author reveals the other side of the fate of the fairy-tale heroine..

Sandra Cisneros's use of operatic themes dates also to *The House on Mango Street.* Here, in a manner similar to her use of fairy tales, the author calls attention to the misogyny of patriarchal literature by way of reference to Puccini's *Madama Butterfly.* In a vignette entitled **"A Smart Cookie,"** the protagonist's mother laments her own lack of education and the life it might have brought her: "I could've been somebody, you know? my mother says and sighs. She has lived in this city her whole life. She can speak two languages. She can sing an opera. She can fix a T.V." In this quote, the mother's knowledge of opera serves as confirmation of her intelligence. However, as the story continues, it becomes evident that the author has featured the protagonist of Puccini's opera in the story to represent the patriarchal archetype of feminine virtue and sacrifice. The narrator talks about her mother, saying, "Today while cooking oatmeal she is Madame Butterfly until she sighs and points the wooden spoon at me. I could've been somebody, you know? Esperanza, you go to school. Study hard. That Madame Butterfly was a fool. She stirs the oatmeal. Look at my comadres. She means Izaura whose husband left and Yolanda whose husband is dead. Got to take care all your own, she says shaking her head." The mother in **"A Smart Cookie"** has seen through the sentimentalization of the heroine's sacrifice. The lives of her sisters and comadres serve as evidence of the foolishness of relegating the direction of one's life to another. The mother's disgust with Butterfly's sacrifice mirrors the disgust she feels over her own self-destruction: "Shame is a bad thing, you know. It keeps you down. You want to know why I quit school? Because I didn't have nice clothes. No clothes, but I had brains. Yup, she says disgusted, stirring again. I was a smart cookie then." Again, Cisneros reveals the danger for women of being more concerned with the opinions and impressions of others and allowing these concerns to dominate one's life. The mother does not perceive poverty but a lack of internal authority to be the source of her loss.

Even though the stories in *The House on Mango Street* fail to rewrite the tragic fate of the heroine, there is a foreshadowing of the desire to do so. For instance, in the story **"Beautiful and Cruel,"** the narrator claims as a role model a type of woman that she has seen in the movies. This woman is free, powerful, beautiful, and defiant:

> In the movies there is always one with red red lips who is beautiful and cruel. She is the one who drives the men crazy and laughs them all away. Her power is her own. She will not give it away.
>
> I have begun my own quiet war. Simple. Sure. I am one who leaves the table like a man, without putting back the chair or picking up the plate.

The narrator's gesture of defiance, leaving the table "like a man," signifies that she refuses to become a domesticated female. The heroine that Cisneros has created in this story will not self-destruct, nor will she give up control of her life. In the operatic realm, this character is most easily identified as Carmen. According to Catherine Clément's analysis of the ill-fated heroines of opera, the most feminist of these is "Carmen the Gypsy, Carmen the damned." Carmen indeed is an operatic manifestation of Cisneros's "one with red,

red lips," for Carmen "drives the men crazy and laughs them all away." Carmen, like the Medusa, the Sphinx, and the Minotaur, is a figure of paradox. The mere fact that she is a woman who acts like a man proves it, for within the symbolic order, the male occupies a position of active supremacy over the passivity of the female. To oppose that order is to invite disaster. Yet, what else could Carmen do? What Cisneros does not mention in **"Beautiful and Cruel"** is that according to the patriarchal literary tradition, the powerful and defiant female figure is inevitably punished for her audacity. That is why Clément refers to her as "Carmen the damned." The hierarchical structure upon which patriarchal societies are based cannot allow this carnivalesque figure to upset the social apple cart in which men are allowed more power and choices than women. According to Elisabeth Bronfen, the death of the female protagonist functions to eliminate a threat to the patriarchal order: "Countless examples could be given to illustrate how the death of a woman helps to regenerate the order of society, to eliminate destructive forces or serves to reaggregate the protagonist into her or his community." The defiant Carmen must be suppressed or die, and since she will never give her power away, she is killed.

The story **"La Fabulosa: A Texas Operetta"** appears in the collection by Sandra Cisneros entitled *Woman Hollering Creek and Other Stories.* This story at first reading is notable because of one salient and surprising element: the heroine does not die. Not only is she *not* punished for her freewheeling ways, but she flourishes and thrives. In this incongruous tale, the active, independent, and defiant woman is the one who "lives happily ever after." Upon closer examination, the reader discovers the subtext of this story. This is a revision of *Carmen.* The first clue Cisneros allows the reader is the title: **"La Fabulosa: A Texas Operetta."** The author gives an adulatory nickname to her protagonist, changes the context of the story from Spain to Texas, and calls the work an "operetta," a small opera.

In the first paragraph of the story Cisneros makes a tongue-in-cheek reference to the Spanish heritage of the original Carmen: "She likes to say she's 'Spanish,' but she's from Laredo like the rest of us—or 'Lardo,' as we call it. Her name is Berriozábal. Carmen." On one level, the narrator appears to be ridiculing this character, who, like many Mexican Americans, attempts to "whitewash" herself by ignoring her Indian heritage and eschewing the word "Mexican" in exchange for "Spanish." On another level, of course, Cisneros is associating her protagonist with the operatic figure.

The narrator continues with a description of the protagonist. Her most salient physical trait is her large breasts: "big *chichis,* I mean big." Carmen's other characteristic trait is her independent nature. "Carmen was a take-it-or-leave-it type of woman. If you don't like it, there's the door. Like that. She was something." While in some ways Cisneros's heroine is a quintessential feminist, unlike many authors, Cisneros avoids an idealization of her heroine. The narrator describes her as "not smart. I mean, she didn't know enough to get her teeth cleaned every year, or to buy herself a duplex." Although the protagonist is portrayed as a woman of limited attributes, this does not detract from her status as a heroine worthy of a happy end.

Cisneros's plot mirrors the opera in many ways. At the beginning of the Prosper Merimée plot, Carmen has taken as her lover a brigadier named Don José. The Chicana Carmen becomes involved with a corporal at Fort Sam Houston named José Arrambide. The Spanish Don José is engaged to a sweet young thing named Micaela who is waiting for him to marry her. In Cisneros's version, José's high school sweetheart "sold nachos at the mall, still waiting for him to come back to Harlingen, marry her, and buy that three-piece bedroom set on layaway." In the figure of Micaela, both plots include a reference to the classic fairy-tale heroine, the demure and passive one who waits for her prince to take charge of her life. She is often used in literature as the virtuous foil of the lecherous, adventurous "witches and bitches." According to Karen Rowe's analysis of fairy-tale figures, "Because cleverness, will-power, and manipulative skill are allied with vanity, shrewishness, and ugliness, and because of their gruesome fates, odious females hardly recommend themselves as models for young readers. And because they surround alternative roles as life-long maidens or fiendish stepmothers with opprobrium, romantic tales effectively sabotage female assertiveness." Another Micaela-like figure in opera is Alfredo's sister in *La Traviata*. This virginal character provides the motivation for the courtesan's sacrifice of her own happiness, in order that the other woman may make a financially and socially profitable marriage. Carmen, however, makes no sacrifice and fearlessly confronts her announced fate.

Again, according to Merrimée's story, Carmen entices Don José to abandon the army and join a group of smugglers, then leaves him for a toreador named Escamillo. Cisneros, on the other hand, has Carmen leave José for an ambitious Texas senator named Camilo Escamilla. In both stories, the besotted José is overcome with rejection and the realization that he has no control over Carmen. The opera ends as José confronts Carmen outside the bullring. Carmen defiantly proclaims her love for Escamillo before she is stabbed to death by her former lover. The violent death of the rebellious heroine is deemed as necessary in a symbolic system where the existence of a free and enterprising female is viewed as seditious and damaging to the social order. This tendency is as common, Rowe observes, in mythic tales as much as opera libretti: "By punishing exhibitions of feminine force, tales admonish, moreover, that any disruptive nonconformity will result in annihilation or social ostracism." While Western literature provides few examples of the rebellious feminine, these characters are necessarily punished in order to serve as an example to potential Carmens.

Catherine Clément has made an intriguing analysis of how Georges Bizet's score musically represents the conflict between the unfettered feminine versus the hierarchical rigidity of the patriarchal order. She identifies Bizet's use of tonality as a technique of representing the patriarchal social order in which the masculine has dominion over the feminine. Within this context, the term "tonality" refers to music written in a key according to the paradigm of a seven-tone scale. In its linear quality and the rigidity with which the tonal scale differentiates between notes considered harmonious and dissonant in each key, tonality could be said to correspond to the oppositional qualities of symbolic texts.

Sandra Cisneros is indeed skillful in utilizing long-established literary traditions for revolutionary purposes. Her versions of Cinderella and Rapunzel turn the classic versions inside-out to disclose the real consequences for women of patriarchal socialization.
—*Laura Gutierrez Spencer*

As Julia Kristeva has emphasized, in Western thought the "symbolic" is based upon the definition of elements of reality by means of restriction. These elements, then, are oriented according to mutual opposition, a system of opposition hierarchically organized in such a manner that good occupies a position superior to evil, light to dark, and male to female. It might be argued that the importance of the symbolic in patriarchal society is to maintain this hierarchical paradigm. The "semiotic" modality, on the other hand, is perceived to be seditious in its ignorance of phallocentric paradigms and traditions. It does not operate upon an epistemology of opposition and heirarchy. One of the primary characteristics of the semiotic modality is the figure of paradox. In its unification of disparate entities, the figure of paradox by definition defies the oppositional structure of the symbolic. The unclassifiable nature of paradox is, at the very least, threatening to the rational order of the symbolic, represented by mythic figures of opposition such as the male hero and the passive heroine. When paradox does enter into the realm of myth it is considered to be disruptive, even evil. In Western mythology at least, when a male hero confronts a figure of paradox, the hero inevitably prevails. This pattern is evident when one notes that in classical mythology Theseus slew the Minotaur and defeated an army of Amazons, Perseus beheaded the Medusa, and Hercules took the golden girdle of Ares from Hippolyte, the queen of the Amazons.

According to Clément, Bizet's use of chromaticism serves to challenge the supremacy of the tonal scale just as the semiotic modality challenges the patriarchal authority of the symbolic. Chromaticism, which came into common use in Western music during the end of the Romantic period, was used to stretch and blur the authoritative and restrictive quality of tonal music. Clément describes chromaticism as "the sultry, slippery, seductive female who taunts and entraps, who needs to be brought back under tonal domination and absorbed." The correlations between tonality and the symbolic order compared to those of chromaticism and the semiotic are remarkable. Within the domains of language and music, these modalities serve, respectively, to sustain and repudiate patriarchal epistemologies.

Within the text-score of *Carmen* we can see that chromaticism serves to disrupt a strict sense of tonality, just as the heroine diverts José from his militaristic discipline: as Clément remarks, "Carmen makes her first appearance with the slippery descent of her 'Habanera' and it is her harmonic promiscuity—which threatens to undermine Don José's drive for absolute tonal closure at the conclusion of the opera—that finally renders her death *musically* necessary." The predominance of the symbolic over the semiotic is made manifest by the defeat of the paradoxical figure of the active woman. Although Bizet's opera includes one of the most powerful of operatic heroines, her demise is as ignominious and inevitable as the rest. The Amazon is conquered again.

In her **"Texas Operetta,"** Sandra Cisneros acknowledges the literary tradition that punishes audacious heroines, yet she chooses to defy that tradition by rewriting millennia of literary history. Instead of imposing a finite conclusion upon the reader, Cisneros offers three possible endings from which to choose. The elective nature of the conclusion is created by the testimonial form of the narration: "According to who you talk to, you hear different." The first conclusion is similar to that of the opera in that José attacks Carmen with a knife: "José's friends say he left his initials across those famous chichis with a knife." The violence of this ending is mitigated by the skeptical attitude of the narrator: "but that sure sounds like talk, don't it?"

The second conclusion focuses on the male protagonist's pain: "*I* heard he went AWOL. Became a bullfighter in Matamoros, just so he could die like a man." The figure of Escamillo is alluded to with the reference to bullfighting. The expressed desire to "die like a man" represents the deleterious effect that Carmen's strength has upon the masculinity of the hero. This version of the conclusion turns the narrative violence of self-destructive tendencies toward the male

figure. Of course, this particular twist is quite rare in the operatic tradition, as women in opera are forever dying for, or because of, men. This option is provided in the following sentence: "Somebody else said *she's* the one who wants to die."

> **Through her revisions of fairy tales and**
> ***Carmen,*** **Sandra Cisneros's works**
> **demonstrate how literature can challenge**
> **deeply inculcated values and change the**
> **ways in which we perceive the world.**
> **Consequently, she tells stories that shake**
> **the roots of a literary tradition as old as the**
> **fairy tale.**
> **—*Laura Gutierrez Spencer***

The first two conclusions provided in **"*La Fabulosa:* A Texas Operetta"** fall into the register of the symbolic, under which only one of two opposing forces can prevail. Hélène Cixous deems it inappropriate for feminists to follow this traditional "rational" system in their writing. She observes: "Opposition, hierarchizing exchange, the struggle for mastery which can end only in at least one death (one master-one slave, or two nonmasters = two dead)—all that comes from a period in time governed by phallocentric values." In an effort to provide a literary space where resolution is not based upon unilateral annihilation, Cisneros provides another possible conclusion. Despite the discretionary quality presented by the inclusion of alternate endings, Cisneros uses the voice of the female narrator to give authority to the last and most felicitous conclusion. The narrator begins by denying the veracity of the first two denouements: "Don't you believe it. She ran off with King Kong Cárdenas, a professional wrestler from Crystal City and a sweetie. I know her cousin Lerma, and we saw her just last week at the Floore Country Store in Helotes. Hell, she bought us a beer, two-stepped and twirled away to 'Hey Baby Qué Pasó.'" Cisneros refuses to allow the suppression of the rebellious, chromatic feminine. This Carmen not only is not punished, but continues upon her adventurous path, finding love with a nurturing, masculine partner. The Tex-Mex hit "Hey Baby Qué Pasó" includes the only reference to the fate of José in this last version of **"*La Fabulosa*"**'s conclusion. The lyrics include the phrases: "Hey Baby, ¿qué pasó? / Porque me tienes el loco / No me dejes de ese modo." Cisneros uses this musical reference to create the background for Carmen's joyous exit from the story. Instead of the righteous and apocalyptic climax created by Bizet for the death of the heroine, the Chicana author employs a joyous polka by the Texas Tornados, appropriate for triumphant Carmen. In spite of the celebratory quality of the song, one can hear the echoes of José's incredulity in the chorus: "Hey baby, ¿qué pasó?"

Sandra Cisneros is indeed skillful in utilizing long-established literary traditions for revolutionary purposes. Her versions of Cinderella and Rapunzel turn the classic versions inside-out to disclose the real consequences for women of patriarchal socialization. Within her stories, Cisneros reveals the metaphoric death of the fairy-tale heroine. Although the princesses of the classic fairy tales supposedly go on to live "happily ever after," we never hear of their lives or paths of growth after the nuptials to the handsome prince. Cisneros picks up the tale and tells the *real* fate of the heroine who lives in patriarchy.

Within the operatic tradition there is no need to uncover the propensity for misogyny. On the contrary, scenes of women murdered at the hands of men or who commit suicide on behalf of men number among the most glorified moments in opera. In one salient characteristic, however, opera differs from the fairy tale. In the classic children's stories, the sweet, pliant princesses are rewarded by marriage to the prince, while the only active characters, witches and wicked stepmothers, are vilified and often punished with gruesome deaths. Opera libretti, on the other hand, tend to punish with remarkable regularity the passive heroine as well as the active, rebellious one. Sandra Cisneros defies this tradition in opera and other narrative forms by recreating the powerful female figure of Carmen and allowing her to live and thrive. Just as she retells the fairy tale in a more realistic light, Cisneros changes the context of the opera *Carmen* from nineteenth-century Seville to modern-day Texas. However, by altering the standard denouement of the tragedy in a way that contradicts the patriarchal necessity of opposition and the ultimate domination of the male, Cisneros dismisses the tradition of eliminating the paradoxical figure of a powerful woman. Through her revisions of fairy tales and *Carmen,* Sandra Cisneros's works demonstrate how literature can challenge deeply inculcated values and change the ways in which we perceive the world. Consequently, she tells stories that shake the roots of a literary tradition as old as the fairy tale.

FURTHER READING

Criticism

Herrera-Sobek, María. "The Politics of Rape: Sexual Transgression in Chicana Fiction." *The Americas Review* XV, Nos. 3-4 (Fall-Winter 1987): 171-88.

    Determines that the theme of the loss of innocence structures the rape scene of "Red Clowns."

Lee, A. Robert. "*Chicanismo* as Memory: The Fictions of Rudolfo Anaya, Nash Candelaria, Sandra Cisneros, and Ron Arias." In *Memory and Cultural Politics, New Approaches to American Ethnic Literatures,* edited by Amrijit Singh, Joseph T. Skerrett, Jr., and Robert E. Hogan, pp. 320-39. Boston: Northeastern University Press, 1996.

    Compares Chicana/o writers's representations of "memory," including Cisneros's use of female intimacy and "womanism."

Nash, Susan Smith. Review of *Loose Woman. World Literature Today* 69, No. 1 (Winter 1995): 145-46.

    Focuses on the deconstruction of patriarchal notions of "identity" in *Loose Woman.*

Uglow, Jenny. "A Local Universe." *Times Literary Supplement,* No. 4650 (15 May 1992): 20.

    Admires the domestic themes and "local" characters of *The House on Mango Street.*

Additional coverage of Cisneros's life and career is contained in the following sources published by Gale: *Authors and Artists for Young Adults,* Vol. 9; *Contemporary Authors,* Vol. 131; *Contemporary Authors New Revision Series,* Vol. 64; *Dictionary of Literary Biography,* Vols. 122, 152; *DISCovering Authors: Multicultural Authors Module; Hispanic Literature Criticism;* and *Hispanic Writers.*

Jorie Graham
1951-

American poet.

The following entry presents an overview of Graham's career through 1997. For further information on her life and works, see *CLC,* Volume 48.

INTRODUCTION

A Pulitzer Prize winning poet, Graham is considered to be one of the most innovative and intellectual poets alive today. Her efforts to restructure lyrical poetry, intensely personal style, and focus on metaphysical questions about self-knowledge and history have garnered her considerable attention and respect from critics, readers and colleagues.

Biographical Information

Graham was born in New York City on May 9, 1951, to Curtis Bill, a scholar of religion and theology, and Beverly Stoll Pepper, a noted artist. Raised in France and Italy, Graham's constant exposure to European churches and art would later influence her poetry and play a crucial role in her collection *Erosion* (1983). Graham was educated in French schools, which she credits with predisposing her to abstraction, and attended the Sorbonne. She returned to the United States as an adult and received a B.A. from New York University in 1973 and an M.F.A. from the University of Iowa in 1978. In 1983 she married James Galvin with whom she has a daughter, Emily. Since her graduation in 1978, Graham has held positions in English departments and writing workshops at numerous universities. Since 1983 she has been employed at the University of Iowa as a workshop instructor and professor of English. In addition to winning the Pulitzer Prize for Poetry in 1996 for *The Dream of the Unified Field* (1995), she has been awarded several grants, three Pushcart Prizes (1980, 1981, 1982), the American Academy of Poets Prize from the University of Iowa (1977), the American Poetry Review Prize (1982), the Morton Dauwen Zabel Award from the American Academy and Institute of Arts and Letters, as well as numerous other awards. In 1997 she was elected a Chancellor of the Academy of American Poets.

Major Works

Graham has written seven volumes of poetry, all of which reflect her intensely personal voice and her preoccupation with metaphysical questions. Throughout her career, Graham has been interested in the seamlessness of life and the way in which its structure is distorted by efforts to impose a narrative or history upon it. She has constantly striven to understand the meaning of an event while simultaneously feeling the experience of it. In her poetry she has focused on dichotomies: being and knowing, body and mind, beauty and ugliness, eternity and history. But while her poetic voice has remained distinct and recognizable, her writing style has evolved. Her first two collections, *Hybrids of Plants and of Ghosts* (1980) and *Erosion*, reflected the modernist tradition of Mark Strand and Amy Clampitt. Building on the work of Wallace Stevens, Graham deftly weaves images, ideas, and emotions while making intricate associations between such activities as writing, sewing, gardening, and, particularly in *Erosion,* painting. However, with *The End of Beauty* (1987), Graham marked a distinct shift in her work. More ambitious and indeterminate than in her earlier books, Graham introduces such devices as blank spaces and algebraic variables in the place of words to question the concept of the poem as a closed unit. Using mythical and historical figures, Graham examines self-knowledge and the nature of life. In her subsequent three volumes of new verse, she has built upon these changes. In *Region of Unlikeness* (1991) she juxtaposes common daily experiences with historical ones to explore the meaning and importance of events; in *Materialism* (1993) she responds to quotes from great thinkers in Western Civilization; and in *The Errancy* (1997) she focuses on angels, among other images. Throughout these works she continues to develop on unusual poetic style and to explore the nature of time, event, and self in modern society.

Critical Reception

From the first publication of her poems in journals, Graham has attracted the attention and praise of critics. Her efforts to self-consciously focus on the nature and purpose of poetry and her work in reshaping lyrical poetry by moving away from narrative have earned her respect from scholars and fellow writers. As Sanford Pinsker writes, "her work has been impressive, influential; indeed, it has so changed the landscape of what contemporary poetry is, and can be. . . ." Critics such as Mark Jarman and James Longenbach note the unusually distinct and personal style of writing Graham has developed, likening her to Emily Dickinson and T. S. Eliot. Longenbach states, "Graham has not simply forged a style; she is exploring the very notion of what it means for a poet to have a style. . . ." However, not all responses to Graham's work have been favorable. Critics such as William Logan found *Materialism* disappointing and Jonathan Holden thought the work too somber and melodramatic.

Many critics agree that Graham sets such difficult challenges for herself, as well as the genre, that she often falls short. Bonnie Costello criticizes Graham for using the same words too often, for replacing words with blanks, and for failing to hold the attention of her readers. However, these same critics agree that when Graham is successful she is unrivaled. As David Baker writes, "I can think of no other current American poet who has employed and exposed the actual mechanics of narrative, of form, of strategic inquiry more fully than she has—at least no other readable poet—and no other poet able to deploy so fruitfully and invitingly the diverse systems of philosophy, science, and history."

PRINCIPAL WORKS

Hybrids of Plants and of Ghosts (poetry) 1980
Erosion (poetry) 1983
The End of Beauty (poetry) 1987
Region of Unlikeness (poetry) 1991
Materialism (poetry) 1993
The Dream of the Unified Field: Selected Poems 1974-1994
     (poetry) 1995
The Errancy (poetry) 1997

CRITICISM

Elizabeth Frost (review date March 1984)

SOURCE: "Countering Culture," in *Women's Review of Books,* Vol. 11, No. 6, March, 1984, pp. 11-12.

[*In the following excerpt, Frost reviews* Materialism *and explores Graham's manipulation of Western philosophy, praising her handling of difficult ideas.*]

Jorie Graham, a Euro-American, ponders . . . dilemmas centered on the theme of cultural inheritance. Uncomfortable with the perceived gap between language and the material world, she wonders, "Is this body the one / I know as me. How private these words?" These two books diverge in tone and intent, but they share a concern central to women's lives: wresting a female identity from the vast store of white male traditions.

In this fifth collection [*Materialism*], Graham is even more rigorously philosophical than in her previous books—most recently, *Region of Unlikeness* (1992) and *The End of Beauty* (1987). At stake here is the whole body of Western thought. The "materialism" of her title refers not to American middle-class values (although Marx does make an appearance in one poem), but to the physical world—to matter

and life in their troubling otherness and flux, and to our attitude toward that world, including our own bodies. As in most Western philosophy, there is a marked distance in Graham's work between subjective experience and the objective world. Lines from the poem **"Subjectivity,"** in which she explains her use of the third person to refer to herself, capture this divide: "I say *she* because my body is so still / in the folds of daylight." Physicality can even become a mere afterthought. An aside in a poem called **"Invention of the Other"** runs: "(*the body!* she thought, as if she had forgotten it)."

Apparently we risk losing awareness of what is most basic to our existence—the body itself—and the culprit is rational thought, represented by the philosophical tradition, here given a voice. Graham has included passages from (among others) Plato, Bacon, Dante, Wittgenstein, Whitman, Benjamin and—only slightly out of place in this procession—McGuffey (from his *New Fifth Reader* of 1857). It is a bold gesture, one typical of Graham's restless poetry, to include landmarks of Western thought and then, in effect, talk back to them—to challenge even as she exploits the familiar mind/body split.

Although most of the quotations are separate from the poems, Graham does carry on a dialogue with them and the "great works" they stand in for. Excerpting can be a form of rewriting, and her selections often undermine the writer's original intentions. I was surprised to learn that the great nature-lover, Audubon, detailed the killing of "specimens" that served as excellent subjects for his sketches. One anecdote found here involves a buffalo—an ironic reminder to the contemporary reader of our destruction of this country's native inhabitants: "The head was cut off, as well as one fore and one hind foot. The head is so full of symmetry, and so beautiful, that I shall have a drawing of it to-morrow." In Graham's excerpt, Audubon's fine aesthetic sense supplies no regret for the animal's killing and dismemberment. Ethics and aesthetics, she implies, can remain dangerously disjunct.

Graham reflects on the artist's complicity in a similar act of violence in **"Subjectivity."** The speaker discovers a monarch butterfly whose beauty captivates her: it is "butter yellow, fever yellow, / yellow of acid and flax, / lemon and chrome." Finding the creature inert, she assumes that it's dead, and is preparing to "make it flat" and insert it into a collection when a friend tells her that the butterfly is still alive. The object of her gaze reclaims the poem:

> the yellow thing, the specimen,
> rising up of a sudden out of its
>   envelope of glances—
>
> a bit of fact in the light and then just

light.

The speaker manages to elude her own desire to possess, but the borders between preservation and destruction, artistic "appreciation" and imperialism, prove thin indeed.

This kind of moral dilemma leads Graham into territories she has explored in earlier work—the fields of myth and history. Juxtapositions of different narratives and historical periods within her poems suggest unexpected connections. **"Annunciation with a Bullet in It,"** for example, joins scenes from a Holocaust survivor's diary with an account of her dog's death following a shooting. In **"Concerning the Right to Life,"** descriptions of an abortion clinic during a protest alternate with descriptions of the speaker's concern for her fever-ridden daughter; the poem closes with excerpts from Christopher Columbus' diary, which remind us of colonization—also a trope for women's bodies.

For Graham, these connections are buried all too deeply in our culture. She presents a series of experiments by Sir Francis Bacon, the early scientist and preeminent humanist, that seems, in its very objectivity, to forecast our fatal disconnection from the material world and one another: "We took a glass egg, with a small hole at one end; we drew out the air by violent suction at this hole, and then closed the hole with the finger, immersed the egg in water, and then removed the finger." The pursuit of knowledge is mechanical and never-ending, as an ellipsis at the excerpt's conclusion (which occurs mid-sentence) indicates: "We took a leaden globe. . ." The "scientific method" involves a detachment of self from other that Graham also senses when she writes; in **"In the Hotel,"** she tries to bridge the gap between herself and the reader, between what she writes and what we feel: "What do you / want, *you,* listening here with me now? Inside the / monologue, / what would you insert? What word?"

Virtually all the poems in *Materialism* are painful meditations on why such efforts fail. **"Steering Wheel"** describes a moment in which the speaker, backing a car out of a driveway, notices a "veil of leaves / suctioned up by a change in current." While the poem seems to meditate on the most external of facts—leaves swirling, a hat caught by wind coursing down a street—the poem is finally about the fear of entrapment in one's own subjective experience. The final lines reflect on the meaning of the most basic rules of motion and gravity, "the law / composed of updraft, downdraft,"

> and angle of vision, dust, gravity,
>   solitude,
> and the part of the law which is the
>   world's waiting
> and the part of the law which is my
>   waiting,

and then the part which is my
    impatience—now; *now?*—

though there are, there really are,
things in the world, you must believe
    me.

The closing plea reveals the speaker's uncertainty about objective reality, "things in the world" other than the self. Graham charges her lines with longing for the "real" world. But how can we break through "solitude" to reach "the world's waiting"? Her answer seems to be that the observing eye, the poetic self that is aware of both the material and the spiritual, must remain utterly self-conscious. Acute observation is the closest we come to genuine knowledge—closer than speculative philosophy has taken us.

As in **"Steering Wheel,"** the most moving poems in the book use philosophical language with a double charge. In Graham's hands, the very diction of rational thought suddenly expresses intimacy, passion, longing. "The whole cannot exist without the parts," a speaker in one of the many sections of **"The Break of Day"** asserts. Then comes the voice of a different self, pleading for union: "Stay, stay." The "parts" are suddenly two people, full of need, and the philosophical dictum is transformed. The shift in tone bears witness to one of Graham's great gifts—turning rhetoric against itself and allowing a simple moment or utterance to unfold in all its nuances. In *Materialism,* an ambitious collage of the language of "great works" and the language of poetry, Graham responds to rational philosophy with the poet's rigorous and practiced vision.

Askold Melnyczuk (review date Spring-Summer and Fall-Winter 1985)

SOURCE: "The Mind of the Matter: CAT Scanning a Scat Singer," in *Parnassus,* Vols. 12-13, Nos. 2, 1, Spring-Summer and Fall-Winter, 1985, pp. 588-601.

[*In the review below, Melnyczuk compares* Erosion *to Graham's earlier writing and finds the poems in* Erosion *more urgent and arresting.*]

Fishing for subjects in her first book, ***Hybrids of Plants and of Ghosts,*** Jorie Graham casts a wide net. Her catch includes trees, birds, language, paintings, self-portraits, philosophers, wildflowers, recherché facts about the habits of squid and the like. The list is various enough to suggest a genuinely restive and curious sensibility. Better still, the play of the poet's mind over her *objets trouvés* is refreshingly idiosyncratic. In **"Self-Portrait"** the speaker faces a window instead of a mirror and describes the self in terms of what it sees:

After fresh snow I'll go up to the attic and look
  out.
My looking is a set of tracks—the first—
a description of the view
that cannot mar it.

The poem becomes a meditation on time, a theme that else-where elicits some of her best lines:

    The world we live in
is going to change, to more than disappear.
This is the light that blinds you by degrees
that it may always feel like sight.

(**"Harvest for Bergson"**)

If the passage doesn't exactly bid the rash gazer wipe his eye, it is because Graham is a stern helmsman who makes sure that most of the time the heart stays below deck.

She also shows signs of an ear subtly attuned to the sounds and native characters of the three languages (French, Italian, English) that shaped her childhood:

I Was Taught Three

names for the tree facing my window
almost within reach, elastic

with squirrels, memory banks, homes.
Castagno took itself to heart, its pods

like urchins clung to where they landed
claiming every bit of shadow

at the hem. *Chassagne,* on windier days,
nervous in taffeta gowns,

whispering, on the verge of being
anarchic, though well bred.

And then *chestnut,* whipped pale and clean
by all the inner reservoirs

called up to do their even share of work.

The characterizations—of the rambunctious, emotional Italian, the elegant, neurasthenic French, and the wholesome, energetic Yankee—are a witty variation on the game of cultural stereotyping. The poem recalls Rimbaud's *Vowels:* both reveal the poet as an initiate with insight into the mercurial soul of words. This early intimacy with the French language also explains why, in her fondness for abstractions, Graham has more in common with many French poets than with her peers.

Too often, however, the work in this first book leaves this reader annoyed and disappointed. Graham seems to be testing out ways of making poems that will support a content yet to surface. Only rarely does the voice speak from an urgency deep enough to justify breaking that cardinal rule of the Pythagoreans: be silent, or say something better than silence. For all the poems' intelligence, evident in the patterns of recrudescent ideas and words, in the complicated images (see, for example, the creation, through cross-hatching, of a shadow tree in **"Still Life"**), the tone is monochromatic, the voice regular as rain, impartial as the sky. As is often the case, in her weakness lies her strength. The "coolness" of the voice suggests a poet capable of casting a cold eye where less steely spirits would blush and shudder.

Let me focus my objections. In **"Pearls"** Graham suggests something of her approach toward speech and poetry:

    To be saved
is to keep finding new solutions to the problem,
like scat

singing or improvisation where you're never
  wrong
as long as you keep on.

But scat singing is no mere jabberwocky of vowels and consonants strutting about in self-celebration. In mimicking an instrument, the scat singer also resembles a child in the preverbal stage, gleefully spitting out syllables which are anything but meaningless, which convey, sometimes better than could words, the singer's emotions. I remember playing a game with a friend (I believe he said it was used by actors to limber tongue and lips) in which we took passages from well-known poems (Shakespeare's sonnets, say) and replaced the words with nonsense syllables improvised on the spot. We were astonished at how frequently we recognized the originals beneath their disguises. Doubtless intonation and rhythm had something to do with it. But was there more? Was there something in the strength of feeling underlying a great poem, a feeling existing beyond, or below, the surface value of words which could be neither suppressed nor masked—what Aristotle called "the pulse of the blood?" In *Hybrids* the supporting pylons seem to be more words which have smothered all feeling. Graham certainly has the gestures of a poet: she spins out similes more easily than most poets spell: "Perhaps it is a daughter who practices the piano, practices / slow and overstressed like the train. . ."; "like the crickets"; "tight at first like crickets and ivories"; "Like taffeta, the song. . ."; "Like pennies we pushed / into the soil." These from one poem (**"Girl at the Piano"**) thirty-two lines long. Sometimes the images are layered so thickly they overwhelm the poem's occasion. But what do they add up to?

The first poem in the book heralds the poet's resurrection from the grave of youthful solipsism and declares her faith in the pungent accuracy of the world outside her consciousness:

> The way things work
> is that we finally believe
> they are there,
> common and able
> to illustrate themselves.

The pragmatic optimism reminds one of Whitman. She takes pains to reaffirm the credo:

> A miracle
> would seem to be
> what builds itself
> in spite of us—white cells gone mad or syllables
> be
> coming thought

("Lourdes: Syllables for a Friend")

Such avowals bring with them duties. These include composing with an awareness that words are not fungible.

In this regard *Hybrids'* weaknesses are partly the product of the prevailing intellectual climate. The generation of writers currently enshrined in the Academy came of age under the shadow of Auden's strange lines about poetry making nothing happen. It was a pithy restatement of the symbolist creed (sonnets are made of words, Dégas, not ideas; later: no ideas but in things, etc.), one which Yeats, whose death Auden elegizes, had long since disowned. Auden himself wrote that "insofar as poetry, or any other of the arts can be said to have an ulterior purpose, it is, by telling the truth, to disenchant and disintoxicate." (Try squaring *that* with Nietzsche.) Surely telling the truth is not nothing. Recently another monolith has risen in the desert and it bears this inscription:

> What is poetry which does not save
> Nations or people?
> A connivance with official lies,
> A song of drunkards whose throats will be cut in a
> .moment,
> Readings for sophomore girls.

("Dedication")

Although the words belong to Milosz, I may as well have chosen lines by Pablo Neruda or Adrienne Rich or any writer who still believes poetry is capable of nourishing more than the lives and careers of specialists. Poetry may not always be called on to save nations; but it may fairly be expected

to do as much for individual souls. These doubts arise when Graham writes lines like the following:

> Indeed the tulips
> change tense
> too quickly

("Strangers")

and:

> Every morning and every dusk like black leaves
> the starlings cross,
> a regular syntax on wings.

("Syntax")

and:

> The bird is an alphabet.

("A Feather for Voltaire")

The lines sound nice enough—it is passably pretty to pretend tulips and birds behave according to the laws of grammar—but they add nothing to our understanding of either birds, tulips, or language. Language may well be the world's double, its soul, but the equation is not reversible. Transformations which take place at the level of words alone, without reference to internal changes in the poet's psyche, or external shifts in the world, do injustice to both the visible and invisible universe. At its worst, figurative language is merely ornamental. Used properly it can delight us by disclosing a similarity between such disparate elements as two lovers and a compass; and/or indirectly underscore a poet's attitude toward his subject, as when Donne declares his lover is "all states to him." When Herbert compares a sweet and virtuous soul to seasoned timber, we come away feeling we've gotten more than fictions and false hair for our money.

Graham in her deepest self must be aware of the dangers of treating language like a lever on a slot machine. In **"On Why I Would Betray You,"** she writes:

> Because this is the way our world goes under:
> white lies, the snow,
> each flake a single instance of
> nostalgia. Before you know it
> everything you've said
> is true.

The premise is that "I" can rewrite the world, revise the past (and, by implication, the present and future) according to my desires. But poetry exists in order to assert the opposite.

Graham's book, to its credit, has helped revive a generation's interest in the poetic uses of abstractions:

> To have experienced joy
> as the mere lifting of hunger
> is not to have known it
> less.

("Over and Over Stitch")

And:

> For some of us the only way of knowing we are
> here at all, going
> across and going down,
> exquisitely temporal though at no point believable;
> fragile; tragic.

("Mirror")

Not long ago such bald statements would have been attacked as hallmarks of bad writing: the poet was telling instead of showing. But fashions change: as John Crowe Ransom put it, "Because of the foolishness of idealists, are ideas to be taboo for the adult mind?" I mentioned earlier I suspect it's Graham's French side that's behind her fluency with abstractions. Paul Auster points out in an introduction to his superb anthology, *The Random House Book of Twentieth Century French Poetry,* that literary French, "the language of essences," has periodically pollinated English verse ever since Chaucer translated *Le Roman de la Rose.* It is good to see the tradition continuing.

If *Hybrids of Plants and Ghosts* seems like apprentice work, then few first volumes proceed with such confidence:

> The way things work
> is that eventually
> something catches.

That "eventually" comes with *Erosion.* In the new book, the poet's net is less finely woven than in the first; as a result, some things slip through. But that is exactly what Graham intends, because here she is after bigger fish.

Erosion is brilliantly wrought: the individual poems work together like the citizens of a harmonious and self-contained little republic. The book yields most when read as one long poem, by turns an argument and a meditation, on appearance and reality, and on the self exploring the volatile boundaries between them. Graham's talent has grown in every way. Her voice has deepened, matured. Her images have progressed from the idiosyncratic to the urgent. She's capable now of arresting music: "So here you are, queen of the chiaroscuro, black girl, / black girl, / backstitching on us . . ." (The

long *e*'s play against the short vowels like light and shadow; the consonants and consonant clusters *q, ch, bl, ck* echo resonantly in the one word *backstitching.*) And the questions she takes on would not have embarrassed the masters (Plato, Keats, Berryman, Masaccio) whose work she invokes. In her vision, which contains more than a few gnostic elements, the world is perceived as a wound: "I think the world is a desperate / element. It would have us / calm it / / receive it." It is up to the self to heal that wound: "The self, too / / is an act of / rescue. . . ." Graham would like to declare this world, even with its "architecture of grief," equal to Eden, but the desire is undermined by the many grim verities she forces herself to confront: idealism struggles with realism, and the victory is poetry's.

***Erosion* is brilliantly wrought: the individual poems work together like the citizens of a harmonious and self-contained little republic.**
—*Askold Melnyczuk*

From the very first poem we find ourselves in the presence of a skilled cicerone—haunted, breathless, intense—with an eye (and ear) for the dramatic:

> In this blue light
> I can take you there,
> snow having made me
> a world of bone
> seen through to.

("San Sepolcro")

The tone implies she can tell us things nobody else could. The lines about the snow are puzzling in the way that Eliot can often be ("Lady, three white leopards sat under a juniper-tree."). As we read on, the idea of "seeing through" gathers resonance: the poet has indeed "broken through" and this book is in a sense her transcript of the experience. Gone are the facile similes that clotted the earlier work with their facsimile insights. There's a new sensuality to her descriptions: "There's milk on the air, / ice on the lemonskins." It's a delectable atmosphere, pristine and innocent. Part of its strangeness is simply a matter of weather: we don't associate snow with Italy. We're still obliged to scramble to keep up with the characteristic Graham fidgetiness, her refusal to look at any one thing for very long. She is far more interested in chronicling the leaps of her own consciousness. But this time the voice is rich and multivalent enough to hold us.

The landscape suggests itself as a metaphor for the mind:

"How clean the mind is, / holy grave." She moves to a painting of the pregnant Virgin:

> It is this girl
> by Piero
> della Francesca, unbuttoning
>   her blue dress,
> her mantle of weather,
>   to go into
>
> labor. Come, we can go in.
>   It is before
> the birth of god.

At birth we enter the world, and we repeat and renew that entrance with every breath. So also, through contemplation, do we enter a work of art, and a book. Faulkner remarked that life is tragic because we can admire a sunset only in retrospect: while looking at it, we're likely to be worrying about an unpaid phone bill. We understand the meaning, appreciate the power of the landscape we've walked through, only in memory. In its closing lines, as each breath unbuttons us in time, bringing us closer to death and birth, the duet of images builds to a crescendo, when suddenly Graham changes figures and we are again in the company of an improvisatory musician, who this time knows her trade.

"San Sepolcro" opens at dawn; by the end, however, linear time has collapsed. The poem reminds me of paintings by certain contemporaries in which figures of Osiris and Daphne about against lawns mowers and barca loungers, as if to document that the "acceleration of history" has indeed created a time machine: all periods are contemporaneous, and all is always now. When Graham writes: "It is before / the birth of god," possibly we're to infer the poet's vision is pagan. On the other hand, the poem's title, **"Holy Grave,"** evokes the cave in which Christ's body was laid after the crucifixion. Analogy, Octavio Paz observed, is the lifeblood of poetry and survives both paganism and Christianity.

Cézanne and Rothko were the two painters invoked in *Hybrids.* Here Graham has reached back for tutelary spirits to the early Renaissance masters della Francesca, his student Luca Signorelli, and Masaccio. Yeats exalted Byzantium for its successful fusion of art, religion, and the demands of dailiness—the integration earned the citizens that "unity of being" Yeats so coveted. The Renaissance serves as a similar touchstone for Graham: the self shuts its eyes on the purely interior vision, surrendering the Middle Ages' absorption in the supernatural, and opens them with new wonder on the natural world. But "unity of being" for Graham involves a far greater tolerance for the fluid transactions between the world and the self than Yeats could have accepted: her mask is considerably more porous. And her work reminds one less of Rothko or della Francesca than of Turner,

where edges between elements blur. All is in flux: the self is swallowed by mist, fishermen wading into a river are seen as "trying to slip in / and pass / / for the natural world." The lines themselves race and hover like dragonflies. The self, so uncertainly present in the earlier book ("when will the self become a permanent mirage?"), remains an undefined element:

> We live up here
>   by blurring the boundaries, calling it *love, the*
>   *present moment, or the beautiful.*
>
> We live a harsh fecundity, it seems to me, the
> symbol
>   tripping much too freely
>   over everything
>   it signifies.

Here our carelessness with words and the definitions by which we understand ourselves and the world disturbs the poet, while elsewhere Graham delights in the discovery that the self cannot be pinned and anatomized:

> I know it's better, whole, outside, the world—
>   whole
> trees, whole groves—but I
> love it in here where it blurs and nothing starts or
>   ends, but all is
> waving, and colorless,
> and voiceless. . . .

The passage limns the pleasures of the contemplative, who is not in retreat from reality but rather rapt in a different one. At times this inwardness allows her to see the outside world as though no one had ever looked at it before; her images remain even when the lines themselves (the curse of free verse!) do not: the waterstrider devouring the bee, the bird letting ants crawl over its body, a piano thrashing about on the hook of a baton, Luca Signorelli conducting an autopsy on his dead son. These are a long way from the grammar of flowers.

The effects Graham achieves with her free verse, however, can be masterly. In **"Updraft"** the pneumatic drive of the aspirates "who . . . hush . . . heady . . . hum" enforces the feeling of the wind breathing through New York City, and the fluctuations in the length of the lines evoke something of the city's relentless unpredictability, its impersonality and hallucinatory whirl:

> You who are not different,
> let the hush and click of the heady leaves, the
>   avenues
>   announcing rain
> and the hum of the neon

and the miraculous ropings of spittle and dead
leaves and urine
and new rain
in the gutters
stick to You.

Graham also knows how to refuse the more standard gambits of the age. **"Patience"** promises to be a poem of nostalgia. Graham begins by sketching a morning from childhood which might have been transformed into a Norman Rockwell painting. All the elements seem to agree: a young girl and a woman (Maria) are ironing a shirt for the girl's father. An open door admits "a perfect shaft / of light," there's a smell of wisteria, and the comforting sound of someone raking gravel. The moment appears ordained for canonization by memory into one of those chapels of respite to which we can retreat from the chaos of the present. "Tell me / where that room is now, / that stubborn / fragrant bloom?" Graham asks. But the question, perhaps because it is a cliché, becomes a key unlocking the door of deeper memory. She recalls that Maria, so beat "even the sweetness of / wisteria / hurts," was crying while ironing—she had just lost her son—and the girl, far from helping, was fumbling around "the ugly twistings of / the wicker / hamper. . . ." A pretty fiction has crumbled like a house of sand. But by reclaiming depth, the moment has gained durability.

The republic is not quite a utopia. Every poet deploys a vocabulary of favorite words and images and metaphysical preferences. Graham, for better or worse, seems to be hooked on sewing imagery. It's everywhere: a boy catches "his lost stitch of breath"; an exhumed saint is said to be "backstitching" on us; for a wolf pacing a cage "minutes stitch shut"; lovers are dispatched as "lost stitches." Finally the reader grows suspicious. Poetry relies on the multiple meanings and secret relations between words, and one wouldn't want to pin Graham down. Of course the world is a wound which needs to be sutured. We know that. But is the poet really looking and thinking and feeling when she sees this community of invisible seamstresses hemming the skirts of the world, or is she merely repeating phrases which have worked for her before?

The Eros poems in *Erosion* (**"Kimono," "I Watched a Snake," "Salmon"**) are eccentric but only partly satisfying. Their virtues include a kind of Mediterranean sanity toward sensuality that reminds us Graham's home is near the birthplace of the Troubadors. In the best of these the speaker is in her garden brushing her hair. She knows a small boy is watching her from behind an evergreen. Each time she moves, the landscape printed on the kimono alters slightly so that "reeds are suddenly / ravines." Its beautifully sexy conclusion not only resolves the narrative, but also reminds us we've glimpsed an initiation ritual older than and every bit as mysterious as Eleusis. The poem falters twice for me.

Once when the first-person speaker modestly refers to herself as "the style of the world"—itself an attractive locution, which ought to be used again, with more discretion. In the second instance, a downpour of particularly dreary adjectives (Graham is abundantly adjectival)—"green scrim," "open door," "small spirit," "new ice," "gentle limbs"—almost drowns the seventh stanza.

"We live," wrote Emerson, "amid surfaces and the true art of life is to skate well on them." But Graham's obsession is with penetrating below them, in reaching after essences and sounding depths. Like Rilke she is an archeologist of the buried life. Variations on the theme of "breaking through" recur in poem after poem: "come, we can go in"; "trying to slip in"; "weak enough to enter"; "how far is true enough?". What are we to make of all this? What is the poet's intended destination?

At the heart of *Erosion* lies an experience which must be called mystical or visionary: it is the center from which all the lines radiate. Whatever else it might mean to the poet, it has made it impossible for her to rest at ease amid appearances:

Finally I heard
into music,
that is, heard past
the surface tension . . .

("**In What Manner the Body
Is United with the Soule**")

In good democratic fashion Graham immediately qualifies her claim: "Not that I heard / very deep." She wishes to remain a woman addressing other women and men. Now the mystic's experience often carries certain restrictions. What Pascal calls "the prudence of God" proscribes direct communication of the revelation, and this partly accounts for Graham's lateral approach to her subjects. In a poem unabashedly titled **"In What Manner the Body Is United with the Soule"** Graham gives us an image meant to satisfy expectations raised by the title. We watch a waterstrider devour a bee which it shares with the insect's reflection in the water ("the back-swimmer"). Although the analogy is deliberately ambiguous (paraphrasing a Graham poem is like trying to whittle a sprawling rhododendron into chopsticks), she seems to suggest that body and soul (the waterstrider and its double) intersect in their reliance on the quotidian, on the outside world that nourishes both: the gold bee. Elsewhere, probing appearances, the poet asks:

How far is true
enough?
How far into the
earth

can vision go and
    still be

love?

          ("The Age of Reason")

How far (into ourselves, into others, into the objects around us) can we gaze before matter and identity dissolve and we find ourselves peering into the empty spaces between molecules? How long before a glimpse of the abyss changes love into terror? It doesn't matter, the poem concludes: our desire would not shrink by an inch or an ounce. To extend for a moment the analogy with physics, Martin Gardner writing in the *New York Review of Books* described a recently discovered cache of subatomic particles and suggested that space might not be as permeable as we thought. In her meditation over the exhumed (and, we assume, severely decomposed) body of Santa Chiara, Graham speculates on the endless divisibility of matter: "As if this were always / what flesh is a declension of: more flesh".

But the burden of infinite desire bears a darker aspect. Unreasonable in its demands, like Saul Bellow's Henderson "the Rain King" who keeps hearing a voice crying I WANT! I WANT!, it seems not to care how it is placated. At times it seems the echo of curiosity gone mad, its refrain the promise of incrementally acuter insights into reality. When Graham describes Luca Signorelli, in an access of Renaissance zeal, dissecting his own son, we draw a relationship between his action and the voice inquiring where soul and body meet *and* the voice urging a young man to murder his girlfriend: "our / desire hissing Tell me / your parts / that I may understand your body." Signorelli's operation, however, appears successful:

    It took him days
        that deep
    caress, cutting,
        unfastening,

    until his mind
        could climb into
    the open flesh and
        mend itself.

We are left to decide for ourselves whether he has reached that peace which passeth understanding or lapsed into the lassitude that follows mental and physical exhaustion. In the book's last poem Graham offers lines that sound like a synthesis and a conclusion: "Because the body must open / for its world / so that we know there is a wall / beyond which we can't go." By insisting on the need for staking out the boundaries human reason should not expect to cross, Graham has not allied herself with Emerson. Appearances share

a world with "true being" but the two have not merged. Her position is rather closer to that of Plato's durable explorer who on returning to the cave must readjust to a society in which the blind man is king while still keeping faith with the vision vouchsafed him. One way of achieving this is by writing poems, as Jorie Graham does, in which images of the world remain "afloat in solution / unsolved."

Marianne Boruch (review date March-April 1987)

SOURCE: A review of *The End of Beauty,* in *American Poetry Review,* Vol. 16, No. 2, March-April, 1987, p. 22.

[*In the following excerpt, Boruch praises Graham's poems for their mystical, abstract quality.*]

In *Recitative*'s interview with Donald Sheehan, Merrill makes the distinction between Eliot, whose poems put "civilization under glass," and Stevens, who "continues to persuade us of having had a private life." Jorie Graham in her astonishing third collection, ***The End of Beauty,*** manages both. Like many of Dunn's poems, these are loose meditations, flung onto the page, staged accidents. Yet they are often enactments—frightening and ceremonial as the myths they shadow: Penelope, Orpheus, Eve, Daphne, all drawn with such fierce private light that abruptly it's clear why these stories have been prized for centuries. "But a secret grows, a secret wants to be given away," Graham writes of Eve's lethal plan. "For a long time it swells and stains its bearer with beauty." Miraculous things weight this book, from a real visit to the shrine of St. Claire up a "birthcry" road in Montefalco, where a woman "presses her beautiful nowhere / against the face-sized grille repeated speech / has oxidized green . . ." ("You say you've come to see / the saint"), to the more contemporary jolt of photographs for which the poet recasts the Hopi belief that they steal the spirit. "Rather that *being-seen* will activate that soul / until the flesh / is something that can be risen through." One feels in fact something rising through these poems, something terrible and wonderful, past control, certainly past the conscious truce in Graham's earlier collections between the autobiographical and the philosophical. It is the visionary gift of the child in **"Imperialism,"** the final poem here, who is taken to bathe with thousands in the Ganges so she might "know the world" and finds instead horror, finds in her mother who would comfort only ". . . a plot, a / shape, one of the finished things, one of the / *beauties* . . . a thing / completely narrowed down to love . . . all / arms no face at all dear god, all arms—"

Helen Vendler (review date 21 November 1991)

SOURCE: "Mapping the Air," in *New York Review of Books,* Vol. 38, No. 19, November 21, 1991, pp. 50-6.

[*In the following excerpt, Vendler argues that Graham expands on her earlier work, pushing forward her style of lyrical poetry.*]

Like [Adrienne] Rich, Jorie Graham, a younger poet now teaching at the University of Iowa, uses vignettes and anecdotes, but to raise metaphysical, more than ethical, questions. Graham's grand metaphysical theme is the tension between existence and death. These are its ultimate terms; but the tension is also expressed as that between other polarities, such as continuity and closure, indeterminacy and outline, being and temporality, or experience and art. Graham sees human beings as creatures capable both of "intentionality"—directedness of aim—and of suspension in moments of pure being without aim.

These two inherent, inescapable capacities are fatal to each other. Nothing goes nowhere, however much we might want it to. Courtship presses toward commitment, idea toward its enactment, sensation toward exhaustion. For the artist especially, the passion to impose a determinate shape on experience is at war with the passion to live suspended within experience. The Graham muse sings two siren songs: the one says, "Hurry: *name* it"; the other says, "Delay: *be* it."

In her earlier work (*Hybrids of Plants and of Ghosts,* 1980; *Erosion,* 1983; and *The End of Beauty,* 1987) Graham was already sketching the crucial intersection of the passional and the philosophical from which the poems radiate. The metamorphoses of the theme, even in early work, were numerous and inventive—and yet this is the wrong way to put it. Rather, experience kept leading Graham back, by way of formal discoveries, to her central theme of what one could call openness versus shape. At first, each moment of experience tended to have its own single poem, in which the tension between being and interpretation was named rather than shown, as in **"Strangers":**

> . . . Dusk,
>
> when objects lose their way, you
> throw a small
> red ball at me
> and I return it.
> The miracle is this:
> the perfect arc
>
> of red we intercept
> over and over
> until it is too dark
> to see, reaches beyond us

> to contemplate
> only itself.

(From *Hybrids of Plants and of Ghosts*)

Later, the moment of suspension—imagined in the poem **"Updraft"** as an upward motion bearing us temporarily away from gravity—begins to be shown in action rather than described, and Graham's use of the present tense and long unfolding sentences keeps us afloat in the updraft for a long time. The actual moment of suspension itself becomes the center of the poem, as in **"San Sepolcro"** from her second volume, *Erosion,* we see the Madonna unbuttoning her dress before labor:

> . . . It is this girl
>   by Piero
> della Francesca, unbuttoning
>   her blue dress,
> her mantle of weather,
>   to go into
>
> labor. Come, we can go in.
>   It is before
> the birth of god. . . .
>
> . . . .This is
> what the living do: go in.
>   It's a long way.
> And the dress keeps opening
>   from eternity
>
> to privacy, quickening.
>   Inside, at the heart,
> is tragedy, the present moment
>   forever stillborn,
> but going in, each breath
>   is a button
>
> coming undone, something terribly
>   nimble-fingered
> finding all of the stops.

These poems often end in a standoff between suspension and finality: **"Wanting a Child"** (from *Erosion*) ends with the force of the ocean pushing up into the tidal river meeting the force of the river draining into the ocean.

The ecstasy of the state of suspension itself, however, had finally to be analytically examined as well as sensually rendered; and this became the (partly chilling) achievement of Graham's third book, *The End of Beauty* (with its intended pun: the aim of beauty and the termination of beauty are one). Graham's technique in *The End of Beauty* was to anatomize the moment of suspension in being by isolating each of its successive seconds in its own numbered freeze-frame. Here, for instance, is Eve, tired of the stasis of Paradise, deciding to eat of the apple and give it to Adam.

> 15
> so that she had to turn and touch
>   him to give it away
> 16
> to have him pick it from her as the
>   answer takes the question
> 17
> that he should read in her the rigid
>   inscription
> 18
> in a scintillant fold the fabric of
>   the daylight bending
> 19
> where the form is complete where
>   the thing must be torn off
> 20
> momentarily angelic, the instant
>   writhing into a shape,
> 21
> the two wedded, the readyness
>   and the instant,
> 22
> the extra bit that shifts the scales
>   the other way now in his hand,
> the gift that changes the balance,
> 23
> the balance that cannot be broken
>   owned by the air until he
>   touches,
> 24
> the balance like an apple held up
>   into the sunlight
> 25
> then taken down, the air changing
>   by its passage . . .

("Self-Portrait as the Gesture between Them")

Here motion no longer is absorbed in a swirl of impulse, but is broken down and minutely studied, its progress almost halted in the slow-motion inching forward of the film, frame by frame.

But we are still concerned here with a single action, a moment of fateful impulse given a mythological shape. Poems on subjects like this are the defining poems of *The End of Beauty,* where archetypal moments of relation (Apollo and Daphne, Orpheus and Eurydice, Demeter and Persephone) are isolated, unsparingly (even cruelly) investigated, magnified, slowed down, and understood.

Now, in *Region of Unlikeness,* Graham has taken what seems, with hind-sight, an inevitable step. She has made the demanding leap to a practice of connecting together moments widely separated in time and space and occurring on disparate mental levels (usually the autobiographical, the historical, and the mythical). Each of these moments is important, each has its own unintelligibility, each demands to be both recorded and comprehended. But even more, the hidden connections among them in the writer's sensibility (and perhaps in the culture at large) have to be exhumed. The mode of comprehension derives from the, at first unintelligible, connection of separate stories in the writer's mind. As she understands why she has intuitively connected them, she can compose a poem juxtaposing and interacting them.

For instance, Graham's maternal grandmother appeared in *Erosion* (1983) in an unremarkable poem showing her consigned to a nursing home. The image occurring to the poet as corresponding to her grandmother's confinement was the myth of Daphne enclosed in bark. The link between the autobiographical and the mythical is the speaker recalling a tree in her grandmother's "tiny orchard." "She looks," says the poet (fusing grandmother and Daphne), as if she could outrun anything,

> . . . although of course
>   she's stuck
>
> for good here in this
>   memory,
> and in the myth it calls
>   to mind,
> and in this late interpretation
>   stolen from
> a half-remembered tree
>   which stands
> there still like some god's
>   narrow throat
>
> or mind nothing can slit her
>   free of.

("At the Long Island Jewish Geriatric Home")

The rather heavy-handed transition here ("in the myth it calls / to mind, / and in this late interpretation") gives the story of the grandmother temporal priority, makes the myth secondary and decorative, and places interpretation in the place of honor, closing the poem.

The grandmother appears in the new book in two far more complex poems, one called **"From the New World"** (and another called **"Chaos"**), both containing a visit from the granddaughter to the nursing home. To see one of the later poems against the earlier one is to see a writer returning to troubling material to do it over, do it better, do it—if such a thing is possible—right. No longer are the autobiographical, the mythical, and the intellectual on three different planes.

"From the New World" splices together three stories, two of them historical, one autobiographical (as I have earlier noted). The first is a 1940s story of a young girl "who didn't die / in the gas chamber, who came back out asking / for her mother." The second is the story of the 1987 trial, in Israel, of a man identified as the concentration camp worker who ordered the rape of the young girl before she was sent back into the gas chamber. The third story is the personal one—the last chapter of the life of the author's grandparents:

> We put him in a Home, mother
>   paid.
>   There wasn't one that would
>   take both of them we
> could afford.
>   We were right we put him down
>   the road it's all
> there was,
>   there was a marriage of fifty
>   years, you know this
>
> already don't you fill in the blanks,
>   they never saw each other
>   again . . .
>
>   we put her in X, she'd fallen out
>   we put her back in,
>   there in her diaper sitting with her
>   purse in her hands all
>   day every
>   day, asking can I go now
>   meaning him, meaning the
>   apartment by them long since let
>   go you know this

The moral of this story is not explicitly drawn, but we are intended to see the parallel between the helpless "Please" of the girl in the camp and the equally helpless "can I go now" of the grandmother. The granddaughter's place in the story is revealed at the crucial moment of the grandmother's shocking amnesia:

> The one time I knew something
>   about us
> though I couldn't say what
>
> my grandmother then already ill
>   took me by the hand asking to be
>   introduced.
> And then no, you are not Jorie—

but thank you for
  saying you are. No, I'm sure. I
    know her you
see.

The granddaughter flees into the nursing-home bathroom and acknowledges, for the first time, the certain extinction of everyone in the world. Yet she realizes at the same time how nature's infinite desire for life presses more and more beings into existence, although all of them are headed for death. The bathroom becomes a surreal gas chamber:

> they were all in there, I didn't
>   look up,
> they were all in there, the coiling
>   and uncoiling
> billions,
>
> the about-to-be-seized,
>   the about to be held down,
>
> the about to be held down, bit
>   clean, shaped,
>   and the others, too, the ones
>   gone back out, the ending
> wrapped round them,
>   hands up to their faces why I
>   don't know,
>
> and the about-to-be stepping in. . . .
>
> Without existence and then with
>   existence.
> Then into the clearing as it
>   clamps down
> all round.
>   Then into the fable as it clamps
>   down.

Even in this abbreviated quotation, the two cruelties—the intended cruelty of the camp and the "necessary" cruelty of the confinement of the senile, both ending in extinction—can be seen. But the poem cannot stay "in existence" ("the clearing") or in history ("the fable"); it must examine itself as consciously shifting between the close perspective of living and the detached focus of telling. There is a rapid montage of the familial (the grandfather talking to his wife, nursing home to nursing home, on the telephone), the historical (the guard in the dock), and the personal (the horrified granddaughter watching her grandmother nervously and pleadingly clasping her pocketbook with its "forties sunburst silver clasp")—all of this bequeathed by time to the grown-up granddaughter, now the poet, who has in her keeping these fragments of history:

and Ivan (you saw this) offering
  his hand, click, whoever
he is, and the old man getting a
  dial-tone, friend,
  and old whoever clicking and
    unclicking the clasp the
silver knobs,
  shall we end on them? a tracking
    shot? a

  close-up on the clasp a two-headed
    beast it turns out
    made of silvery
leaves?

The montage and the self-conscious, formal questions are steps toward the overwhelming metaphysical question: Why, if these are the conditions of existence, do we want life? What is Being *like*? In what words, what symbols, can it be made intelligible?

  Like what, I wonder, to make the
    bodies come on, to make
  room,

  like what, I whisper,

  like which is the last new world,
    like, like, which is the thin

  young body (before it's made to go
    back in) whispering please.

The story can finally end only if satisfactory words can be found to encompass the facts—the facts of man's inhumanity to man, of senility, and of death, but equally the fact of the subversive, persistent, and random energies of life. I have here flattened out and made logical the tissue of language which, in the poem itself, comes to us in a zigzag of half-articulated suspicions, invocations, silences, hints, glimpses, stumblings, and contradictions—the very picture of the mind making meaning.

Graham now uses the lyric to connect things widely disparate in time and space by means of metaphor and simile. The dramatic, even theatrical sweeping of the searchlight of the artist asking, "What is like this?" or "Why do I feel that these things or stories are alike?" provides the tension of the poem, as it leaps from past to present to past again, from passively absorbed personal history to intellectual self-consciousness, from confusion to mythological or metaphysical clarification. Underneath the parallel layers of autobiography, history, myth, and philosophical interpretation lies the faith that "the storyline" (as Graham has often called it) is not linear but a "coil" (the name she gives it in **"From the New World"**).

This means that resemblances spiral over resemblances with each turn of the coil of time. Deciphering the coiled sequencing of memory on different planes is the artist's task- finding (or inventing) likenesses in a region of unlikeness.

Insofar as the artist's materials lie in the half-forgotten events of her childhood and youth, she has to describe those events, reclaim them from partial amnesia, in order to explain why later impressions (from history, literature, experience) seem urgent, meant, revelatory, demanding. To catch, accurately, the impressions undergone by a child twenty years ago is a strange endeavor, brought most vividly into literary representation by Wordsworth in *The Prelude.* Like Wordsworth. Graham "sees by glimpses" and must capture a past almost uncapturable. In the title poem, **"The Region of Unlikeness,"** we are shown the flight home of a thirteen-year-old girl, in the dawn, from the bed in a man's apartment where she has had her first sexual experience. The artist makes herself maintain a trance-state between sleep and waking, staying in the longpast memory:

  Don't wake up. Keep this in black
    and white. It's

  Rome. The man's name. . .? The
    speaker
    thirteen. Walls bare. Light like a
    dirty towel.
  It's Claudio. He will overdose
    before the age of
  thirty. . . .

  A black dog barks. Was it more
    than

  one night? Was it all right? Where
    are
    the parents? Dress and get to the
    door.

Each sense impression of the girl's flight roots itself into her flesh, "the field where it will grow." Each impression is "a new planting—different from all the others—each planted fast, there, into that soil." Later, the artist will have to find an exact word for each memory-planting, or she will not reach the essential psychic assuagement for her adolescent violation:

  Later she will walk along, a word
    in
  each moment, to slap them down
  onto the plantings,
  to keep them still.

For twenty years the artist has been in bondage to the

memory, twenty years in which the thirteen-year-old has not stopped running, twenty years in which the right words have not been found to "slap down" on the plantings and lay the ghost. Life lies "entombed in being" (**"Immobilism"**). But the mind's search for the adequate expression of the past is arduous and tormenting—

> It darts, it stretches out along the
> dry hard ground,
> it cannot find the end, it darts, it
> stretches out—

("Immobilism")

When Augustine awoke after a vision of God's "unchangeable light" to say he found himself "far from You in a region of unlikeness," he suggested that the region of likeness would be a place where no metaphors would be needed, where thing, thought, memory, imagination, and language would all coalesce in the oneness of eternity. But in temporality, as we yearn forward and the object of desire or the object of memory perpetually recedes, we are shaped by the absence of the object of our longing. Graham quotes Augustine and Heidegger (*What Is Called Thinking*) among her epigraphs, but she could as well have quoted Coleridge's "Constancy to an Ideal Object," where "the enamoured rustic" does not realize that it is his own shadow, cast before him on the morning mists, that he worships as a divine presence: "Nor knows he makes himself the shadow he pursues." The concept of desire fulfilled is always deduced from desire unfulfilled, and yet we give it ontological priority in our imaginings of original perfection.

Graham is a poet of strong polarities, playing in the space between male and female, being and ceasing to be, sense and thought, ritual and eschatology, veiling and apocalypse, matter and interpretation, immobilism and shape-making, nesting and flying free.

—Helen Vendler

Graham is a poet of strong polarities, playing in the space between male and female, being and ceasing to be, sense and thought, ritual and eschatology, veiling and apocalypse, matter and interpretation, immobilism and shape-making, nesting and flying free. Her music is that of the traditional lyric in its highs and lows, its accelerations and ritardandos, but the new poems are so long in themselves and so stretched-out in their elastic and "illogical" lines that it is difficult to master, measure, or enclose them, especially at first reading. Eventually one can map them, connect the dots, see the "coil"—but by their arabesques of language on different

planes they frustrate this desire both at first and in the long run, however much one grasps the underlying map. The reader must, to remain "in" the poem, stay with the poet, going deeper and deeper down, not knowing whether or not the labyrinth has an exit.

The expansion of the poetic line visible in both Rich and Graham (and in other contemporary poets from Ginsberg to Wright and Ashbery) means that many poems are coming to resemble cloud chambers full of colliding protons rather than well-wrought urns. Many particles of experience and history are put into play; they are bombarded by more particles of thought and feeling as both imagination and analysis are exerted on the materials at hand; the excited states resulting from the collisions are registered by the poem as a new field of energy, rather than as a linear "result" or "conclusion." Rich argues that we have to compile an atlas of the whole difficult world"; Graham wants us to find words for the whole "region of unlikeness." Rich said years ago, in the person of a woman astronomer, "I am bombarded yet I stand." This could be the motto of both of these new volumes, which ask lyric poetry to take on epic dimensions. As if to temper their breadth and earnestness, however, both poets end their volumes with a short poem. Graham closes, in **"Soul Says,"** with cosmic laughter enveloping human mortality:

> Now then, I said, I go to meet that
> which I liken to
> (even though the wave break and
> drown me in laughter)
> the wave breaking, the wave drown-
> ing me in laughter—

And Rich ends, in "Final Notations," with a prophecy about the poem of the future:

> it will not be simple, it will not be
> long
> it will take little time, it will take all
> your thought
> it will take all your heart, it will
> take all your breath
> it will be short, it will not be simple

Even the new poetry of the force field, it seems, cannot forget its origins in simple song.

Bonnie Costello (review date 27 January 1992)

SOURCE: "The Big Hunger," in *The New Republic,* January 27, 1992, pp. 36-9.

[*In the review below, Costello argues that while Graham's style has changed in her first four books, her philosophical quest remains the same.*]

"Poetry implicitly undertakes a critique of materialist values," Jorie Graham argued in her introduction to *The Best American Poetry 1990*. It competes with the comforts of "story," which sprays "forward over the unsaid until it [is] all plot," and it competes with the power of images, our culture's "distrust of speech and of what is perceived as the terminal 'slowness' of speech in relation to the speedier image as a medium of sales." Poetry has responded too timidly, she believes, to the challenges of commercial culture, and retreated into a narrow realm of trivial reflections, decorative forms, and platitudes.

Graham has taken it upon herself in her recent work to confront the power of plot and image head on. She has always been a philosophical poet. First she tested her metaphysics in a quiet, lyric space of nature and art, but lately she has plunged into the rush of history, memory, and contemporary life. Frequently she takes the artist and her own creative acts as the subject of her poems. What is the relation of language to its objects? How might language make a place for the spiritual rather than covering it over? How can poetry engage the world without succumbing to limitation? Increasingly such questions of poetic authority have become, for Graham, a matter of moral accountability, a question even of salvation, with the broadest cultural implications. Restless with the answers she found before, her vision has become more ecstatic, more omnivorous, more abstraction in each of her four books. It has also become looser and more notational, less concerned with shapeliness and eloquence.

Graham has explained herself in rather urgent terms:

> I feel like I'm writing as part of a group of poets—
> historically—who are potentially looking at the end
> of the medium itself as a vital part of their culture—
> unless they do something to help it reconnect itself
> to mystery. . . . We need to recover a high level of
> ambition, a rage if you will—the big hunger.

She has identified her ambition with John Ashbery's, James Tate's, and Michael Palmer's—writers who approach their work not as artifacts or statements, but as performances. She has also cited the theatrical work of Robert Wilson as an inspiration, and she is translating Rimbaud. It is not hard to find structural and rhetorical similarities to these artists in Graham's recent work: darting images without explicit connections; a digressive, decentered approach to thought; the fragmentation of linear plots and arguments; indeterminate allegory; parodic language; fragmented allusion and misquotation.

These are all qualities commonly identified with post-modernism. But Graham has a fundamentally different orientation. She is much less interested in randomness and indeterminacy, in the material and the dynamic field of language. Her theatrically—the poem as drama, in which the poet is suffering protagonist before the chaos of the world— engages her in a search for meaning. For Ashbery or Tate, poetry is not a matter of metaphysics, of sustaining the rigor of truth or opening words to ecstatic vision. Poetry, for them, goes on inside language, where our clichés and routines are rearranged in tragic and hilarious new combinations that reveal our ways of knowing and relating. Graham's work is still driven by ideas, however subverted, and by metaphors of the spiritual.

Her first two books sit quite comfortably on the shelf alongside the late progeny of modernism: Mark Strand, Amy Clampitt, Charles Simic, Charles Wright, all of whom use sensual images to pursue the invisible. Like these writers, Graham eschewed the psychological and political emphasis of much poetry of the 1970s, focusing instead on the meditating mind and taking her cues from Keats, Rilke, Stevens. In her early work she limited meditation to individual objects of nature or art around which her thoughts could circle to form twisting, elegant designs:

I WATCHED A SNAKE

    hard at work in the dry grass
      behind the house
    catching flies. It kept on
      disappearing.
    And though I know this has
      something to do
    with lust, today it seemed
      to have to do
    with work

Since then she has been working toward a new music of meditation that involves a deep skepticism and a constant check on the impulse toward story and interpretation. The poems raise questions, for reader and author alike, about the purpose of poetry: "And what is poetry now? What is it going to keep in life that life is ready to shake off?"

Not meaning, anymore, or order, or beauty, certainly not a story line or a controlling metaphor. Rather, poetry "wants to stick to the skin of the beast as it shakes," to register the force of being "until it is not a randomness anymore" but "a wave, making the whole love fit into its body." But sometimes one feels that the pleasures of poetry (its shapeliness, its precision) are neglected by Graham in the name of the higher conceptual risk of encountering the world without design, without the aid of a story or a statement about it. And sometimes one cannot help feeling that Graham's dedication to that risk may be a little disingenuous: that this poet, for all her commitment to the unmediated encounter, has in fact relinquished very little poetic authority.

In *Hybrids of Ghosts and of Plants* (1980), her first book, Graham didn't worry at all about fending off the lure of plot or the mesmerizing buzz of sound bites. Her hybrids of thought and image thrived in a well-weeded lyric garden. Many of her poems compared thought to nature, appreciating in the former all the fluency of the latter:

> A bird re-entering a bush,
> like an idea regaining
> its intention, seeks
> the missed discoveries
> before attempting
> flight again.

Contemplation offered occasions for epigram, gestures into the unknown that even in their ambiguity often had a certain verbal crispness: "only perfection can be kept, not its perfect instances"; "they say the eye is most ours / when shut, / that objects give no evidence / that they are seen by us." Large questions of perception, meaning, and identity could be stimulated by small things, taken one at a time, with little symbolic reserve: an artichoke, a chestnut tree, her mother's sewing box. If they lacked intellectual discipline, the cerebral notions in these poems were still a part of the experiment of seeing. We trusted this poet's move toward "pure idea" for the move was always made with a knowledge of its antithesis: "we have no mind in a world without objects."

In *Erosion* (1983), Graham's confidence in the authority of art was at its peak. She understood more clearly the iconic and sacramental nature of her mind, as she showed in coming to terms with the landscape of her childhood. (She was raised in Rome by an artist mother on the objects of ancient and high culture.) In these poems, art and sacred objects replace nature as the reigning muse. So often the detached observer, even the voyeur poking through blinds and noting neighbors' movements, Graham's stance as a beholder of works of art is an honest one, not just a device as with other poets. It leads her to many of her central themes: the dialogue of the body and the soul, the boundary between the eternal and the temporal, the mental and the natural.

The monumental works and the sacred objects are approached with simplicity and intimacy ("come, we can go in. / It is before / the birth of god"). The focus may shift, but we know where we are (sometimes down to the address: the Piazza di Spagna, the Quinta del Sordo, "down here this morning in my white kitchen"), even as the poetry complicates that concreteness. Especially after the casual assertiveness of *Hybrids,* the reflections that these precise images inspire are often puzzled and paradoxical ("As if

flesh were the eternal portion after all, / here it is, your blunt modesty, pure, / even after a ton of dirt"). History, especially the Holocaust, begins to seep into the sacred ground of these poems, but it is absorbed rather than rooted out, or allowed to overwhelm the meditation. Although Graham risks sensationalism with some of her references to atrocity, most often she succeeds in presenting an honest tension between aesthetic patience and moral rage.

In *The End of Beauty,* which appeared in 1987, Graham largely abandoned the metaphoric and iconic methods, as well as the slow, winding syntax. In their place is a more immediate, urgent contemplation of figures from classical and biblical myth. Steeped in Milton, Keats, and Rilke, big hungerers all, Graham takes myths as allegories of consciousness, in fact as "self-portraits." These self-portraits render the lyric poet's psyche not as an integrated unit, but as a variety of dramatic tensions and repeated gestures (Eve taking the apple and offering it to Adam, Apollo pursuing the elusive Daphne, Orpheus longing for Euridyce, Demeter relinquishing Persephone, Penelope weaving and unweaving to avoid her suitors). Within these paradigms, Graham explores questions of freedom and necessity, of desire and resistance, in fresh ways.

The use of myth also allowed her to deal more directly with an idea that has always preoccupied her: the sense of an abiding wholeness behind a "veil" or "shroud" that is ripped to form a "storyline," to divide experience into "minutes," to frame it in limited "points of view." Myth helps us to understand that fragmentation of the world into discrete "finished things," constrained by shapes and boundaries, and helps us to think beyond it into a sacred, unfinished dimension. The poet of myth is more concerned to represent intense vision than achieved wisdom. And this intensity is typographically expressed: questions, dashes, ellipses, parentheses abound, and lines reach into margins.

The problem with *The End of Beauty* was that Graham had not found the formal or the linguistic means to sustain her prophetic project. Her mythic meditations aim for the intensity of *The Spiritual Exercises,* but the imagery is spare and non-pictorial. The poems are too infused with redundant abstractions and attenuated allegories to take physical or conceptual hold of us. Terms such as "gap," "delay," "plot," "rupture," constantly repeated, begin to sound like predictable buzzwords rather than like insights. The poet's language sags and loses direction: it can't sustain the ecstatic level. Too often it sounds like a bad translation of a Greek chorus ("why this sky why this air why these mountains why this sky"). Without a formal design to direct this stream of consciousness, the current dissipates. The aversion to "finished things" at the thematic heart of this book does not justify Graham's constant use of blanks ("that which sets the — in motion"; "mud, ash, —, —"). The poet's job, after all, is to give us the words and the pictures, however tentative, qualified, or figurative, for what we cannot name or see ourselves. Graham's blanks represent a poetic failure—honest, perhaps, but hardly satisfying, and certainly not redemptive.

Still, the major poem in *The End of Beauty,* called **"Breakdancing,"** proved that Graham has aesthetic power equal to her prophetic ambition. A youth breakdancing on television gives the poet an image she can compare first to our own edgy, fragmented twentieth-century lives, but then also to Christ himself, who showed himself "in pieces" to St. Teresa. The poet manages to shift her rhetoric brilliantly, to chart her emotional flux and roving focus through media time, human time, sacred time. Her language can be jive ("What / is poverty for, Mr. Speed, Dr. Cadet, Dr. Rage, / Timex"), technical ("The robot-like succession of joint isolations / that stimulate a body in reaction to electric shock"), even homiletic ("staying alive is the most costly gift you have to offer Him"). These words rise to a poetic as well as a local rhetorical purpose.

Region of Unlikeness, Graham's new book, takes up many of the concerns of **"Breakdancing,"** particularly its attention to the textures of contemporary life, to the media blitz and the terrorism that threaten our humanity and invade the quiet space of the lyric, demanding its renovation. As in **"Breakdancing,"** the TV hums in many of these poems, the poet's own attention darting from image to image as if to compete with its mediating presence. Indeed, the poems seem at times like a grazing of channels, a desperate effort to forestall the reader's lapse of attention.

Where nature, painting, and myth each inspired previous volumes, the movie camera is the ambivalent muse now, both a threat to our sense of reality and an opportunity for new poetic strategies. Graham studied film at New York University, and her interest in the medium has surfaced in her verse before. But its overwhelming affect on contemporary consciousness—on our sense of history, of time and space, our conception of suffering—becomes a dominant theme in *Region.* Graham records the constant "click, click" of the mind taking up the world "in pieces." The mind inhabits a region of temporality, history, and representation "unlike" the wholeness and the presence that it longs to unveil.

Graham's poetic strategies are aimed at expressing and overcoming this condition. The poems cut, splice, fast forward, play, reverse, replay, and shift back and forth between independent scenes without making connections explicit. "Can I from down there, please, from Later On, / have a shot of a) the mall, b) flying the kite late August choppy wind, c) the men having fast to beat the rain?" Ideas are like voiceovers, never quite meshing with images. The poet stars in and directs these movies, which are at least partly about their own making.

"Manifest Destiny," for instance, works like cinema montage, a pastiche of images outpacing narrative and argument. It begins, like so many movies, with a drive along a dusty, golden road (this one near Rome) through "shafts of morning light." The poet/director gives a visionary cast to the scene as the dust and the light mingle to throw up allegorical shapes, "all the contortions of the human form," anticipating subsequent images—"dusty money" and "gold bars," which later connect to prison bars, bills being paid in a restaurant, whores calling out of prison windows, meats on sale in a marketplace arcade. These are set against an ancient background of stone:

> —colonnades, promenades, porticoes,
> shadows of warriors, lovers and the various
> queens of heaven—
>   arms raised holding stone fruit, lips
> parted uttering the stone word—the stone
> child in the stone arms.

A set of implicit prophetic themes emerges: an assault on materialist values in the face of "change," an anguished glimpse of human life reduced to "a handful of cloth, cash, skin," a criticism of the poet's own desire for "meaning" as a form of currency.

Dissatisfied with the narrow corner to which poetry has retreated, Graham seeks to achieve the stillness of the private, metaphysical vision within the harried institutions of our time: cities, nursing homes, extermination camps, prisons, psychiatric wards. The titles alone suggest something of her level of ambition and its increasingly ideological inflection (**"Short History of the West," "Manifest Destiny," "From the New World"**). Graham identifies history not only in images of the marketplace, but in riots and arrests, suicides and assassinations. Yet her effort to cut these images loose from sensational journalism can seem a little facile. The effect too often is merely to display a politically engaged and righteous sensibility, without attempting much historical scrutiny or political reflection. Though South African children, Holocaust victims, and AK-47s may flash in and out of her field of attention, the poems have less to do with events on the news (or even with history) than with the problems of consciousness that Graham loosely suggests may result in such events, or that go into shaping "the news."

Graham's "big hunger," then, has led her to somewhat contradictory impulses: to a confrontation with history and to a passion for the "imperial invisible," the wholeness behind the veil. Plenty of poets—Yeats, Pound, Eliot—have preceded her in this double vision, but in Graham it has resulted in some unsatisfying shifts of ground. Not wanting to reduce her images from history and experience to a political or psychological narrative (a "plot" or "story"), she swerves away from their implications. **"Picnic,"** a poem that traces the fall from childhood innocence into the web of adult deceptions, abruptly turns at the end to become a poem contemplating being and truth ("the predicate—'is, is, is.'"). **"From the New World,"** which begins with images of the gas chamber and hunted Nazis and which turns to maudlin images of her grandmother in a nursing home, ends up as a meditation on "like," on the problem of resemblance and naming, the wish for words that will not smother being. We are meant to feel that language and representation, unless constantly renewed, are—like the nursing home, like the gas chamber—forms of extermination. But surely distinctions in the order of being and the degree of atrocity ought to be made, if we are not to feel that all of this history really serves only as a trope.

> **Dissatisfied with the narrow corner to which poetry has retreated, Graham seeks to achieve the stillness of the private, metaphysical vision within the harried institutions of our time: cities, nursing homes, extermination camps, prisons, psychiatric wards.**
>
> *—Bonnie Costello*

We are prepared for these shifts to metaphysical questions, though, because they have preoccupied her in earlier books. A sequence of epigraphs—from Augustine, Heidegger, the Bible, Melville—serves as a "foreword" to *Region of Unlikeness.* They tell, in philosophic terms, a story of desire to recover lost presence, of thinking as a drawing toward what withdraws. The influence of the late Heidegger is especially strong, giving the poems an all too discursive and derivative character, despite the poet's suspicion of meaning ("The whole time looking for limitation, the place / without promise, where the adventure is finally over / and shape grips down"). This is nothing new in Graham. What is new is her effort to bring her desire for and resistance to meaning, interpretation, and judgment right up to the surface of the poems, to make that struggle their whole matter. Yet as she repeatedly treats the same themes, the digressions seem more to illustrate than to enact this struggle: matter "wants to remain asleep," change tries to arouse matter as she "lifts and drops each veil" of form, and matter continues to refuse her.

Still, some of the best poems in her new book tell a story of refusing the lure of narrative continuity in a way that centers the restless thought and sensation without reducing it to a discursive point. The parallel syntax and the often jerky, pounding, repetitive lines that portray the mind in motion can break out of abstraction when sufficiently imploded with metaphor, as in **"What is Called Thinking."** The poem opens simply enough: on a walk, the poet, listening to a Walkman, glimpses a deer. This initiates a mediation on the mind's relation to nature, and also an enactment of that relation. The "self-reflective strings of the / eighteenth century" heard from the Walkman become metaphors for our interpretive "voice-over" of observed reality, our wish to "brand" reality with our own identities. Graham then expands her explorations of the mind. The mind is a "transparent unmoving frenzy" that includes raw sensation and the desire to shape. An angel appears, a Promethean spirit of imagination and desire who converts nature into objects of thought, yet who laughs at his own error, is indeed robed in error. As Graham darts back and forth among images of the deer and her natural setting, the poet's "strings" of interpretation (the tape going on in her mind), and the daemonic angel that is larger than either, an exhilarating drama unfolds.

One feels the need to hear these poems read. Their force is performative, and they are very difficult to quote. Yet they are so burdened with doubts about eloquence in this age of distraction that moments of visual and linguistic pleasure are rare. When even seeing is upstaged by self-consciousness, when every act of perception or meaning becomes a noun ("my looking up"), a thing that blocks the view, it is difficult for the reader to enter the poem's world, despite the brusque imperatives ("Sit," "Blink," "Feeling OK?"). The abstractions begin to take on a life of their own ("the now," "the about," "the thing-in-us-which-trials-behind"), yet the allegories (with the exception of the Kafkaesque **"At the Cabaret Now"**) lack either pictorial or intellectual vitality ("mother Matter—the opposite of In-/ terpretation: his consort"). The poems seem to be about so much that they are about nothing at all.

What is the purpose of poetry? To stop and hold the hurry without extinguishing it, to put the world in parentheses and then let it out again, is Graham's current answer. It is not always a satisfying answer, nor is it an entirely honest one. History is not really embraced in its randomness in these poems. It seems, rather, to be selectively imported from the media for its emotional punch. And nature is rarely more than mere shorthand—mother bird and eggs, garden and secret lovers—a designation rather than a true evocation of raw being.

Graham's volume ends with Prospero laying down his magical garment. But how much poetic authority has Graham really relinquished in her project to encounter the world without the aid of a preconceived story or statement about it? Has she bravely stepped aside to let in the big vision, or are her tactics an abdication of a truly ambitious poetic project? She repeatedly interrupts her movies with protestations that she is only a camera: "Where would you go now?"; "shall we end on them?"; "a tracking shot?" But such interactive features of her poems are too often rhetorical, glib illustrations of the familiar point that we must oppose the "silky swerve into shapeliness" in the name of larger vision.

The poetics of failure that Graham constantly invokes has grown stale by now. Poetry must indeed sustain a reach beyond its grasp if it is to matter, and Graham's "big hunger" represents an inevitable, laudable shift away from the timid appetite of the much-spurned "workshop poem." Still, the reader's own big hunger should not be satisfied when it is served up imitations of Heidegger and allusions to the Holocaust in place of the poet's independent struggle to wrest beauty and meaning—howevertentative and qualified—from the abyss of language and the randomness of experience.

Bonnie Costello (essay date Summer 1992)

SOURCE: "Jorie Graham: Art and Erosion," in *Contemporary Literature,* Vol. 33, No. 2, Summer, 1992, pp. 373-95.

[*In the following essay, Costello considers the visual images at the center of the poetry in* Erosion.]

Jorie Graham emerged in the 1980s as a major poet, distinguished for her philosophical depth, her sensuous vision, the grandeur of her style and themes. In a decade of poetry stigmatized for its shrunken ambition, or sidetracked by politics and ideology, she celebrated the spiritual and metaphysical reach of art. In her first book, *Hybrids of Plants and of Ghosts* (1980), Graham limited her meditation primarily to tentative reflections based on natural objects. *Erosion* (1983) marked a striking maturity for this poet in finding a focus to the roving eye of *Hybrids,* and in understanding the iconic and even sacramental nature of her mind. Her language in this volume is marked by eloquence and sententious boldness, and she identifies her project more directly with that of monumental artists from the past. While ordered around a passion for mystery, the poems themselves aspire to the unity and completeness of an artifact rather than the residue of a process. Whatever twists of thought may arise in the poems end in a tied, integrated imagery, a tense unity.

Graham's emphasis on iconic representation and visual design in *Erosion* expresses at once her strong sense of the body and her resistance to the force of erosion. Painting rather than nature becomes her primary model for how we can pursue the invisible in the visible, how we can shape our limitations into a form that can surpass them. In relation to the word, the visual icon seems inexhaustible, infinitely deep, yet centered. Art is the implicit answer to Graham's query, "in what manner the body is united with the soule." It forms an alternative space to the world of erosion, a form of "rescue" from the flux, a means of centering vision and restoring unity beyond the grasp of reason and the word. In this celebration of beauty over knowledge, and art over history, *Erosion* is essentially a modernist text, whereas Graham's later work may be characterized as post-modern.

Erosion, loss, grief, the past, history, evolution, dispersion—these central facts of our world pervade the poetry. But they are almost always set against their opposite—the aesthetic transformation of the world as iconic design. The title poem, **"Erosion,"** asserts:

> I would not want, I think, a higher intelligence,
>   one
> simultaneous, cut clean
> of sequence. No,
> it is our slowness I love, growing slower,
> tapping the paintbrush against the visible,
> tapping the mind.

The mind of the painter "tapping the paintbrush against the visible" and of the beholder may be sequenced, but the work of visual art is not. Indeed, its major distinction from literary art is its simultaneity, its spatial rather than sequential presentation. Graham sets her intelligence toward images detached from their surroundings, held in a private, contemplative space and made timeless through aesthetic transformation, even as she remains in a dimension of history. It is not surprising, then, that eight of the poems in *Erosion* describe established masterpieces of visual art. Ecphrasis is her chief rhetorical strategy. The word is approach and commentary; the icon holds out a promise of presence. Even as Graham questions the value of design or acknowledges the "tragic" aspect of the pursuit of the eternal, hers is an essentially optimistic view of art. "The beautiful," the centering of images into an order where mystery is held and glimpsed, is *Erosion*'s highest value.

In more recent work Graham has begun to decenter the image, thrusting it out of controlling aesthetic form and into personal and public history, unpacking and deconstructing its narrative and discursive implications. Film rather than painting has become her sister art. *Erosion* was a significant book for the eighties, however, because it boldly reasserted modernist values and ambitions which she has never entirely surrendered—the pursuit of the timeless, the impersonal, the beautiful over the brutality and flux of history, the desire of the mind for the eternal and the drive of art to pursue it. Now, however, vision occurs in moments wrested from chaos rather than preserved in sequestered icons.

Graham's strong pull toward an iconic center apart from the flux finds expression in both **"Mist"** and **"Reading Plato."** In each she conceives of a figure by which the transient world is arrested even as it is evoked. In **"In What Manner the Body is United with the Soule,"** Graham pursues a single figure beneath the surface of the stream, which can be drawn out and elevated as art. The symbolist imagery of the poem presents the mutuality of body and spirit central to *Erosion*'s idea of art. Graham's iconic imagination often forms a permeable inside/outside opposition as well. In **"Still Life with Window and Fish"** the interrupted and reassembled images of the external world define an inner space, a new dynamic unity in still form. In other poems (**"To a Friend Going Blind," "Kimono," "The Lady and the Unicorn and Other Tapestries," "At the Exhumed Body of Santa Chiara, Assisi"**) Graham imagines design in terms of fabric—the world securely woven into a tapestry or sewn into a garment. The complex metaphor of stitching suggests that art is a means of mending a world we experience as broken, uniting the horizontal and the vertical, the temporal and the eternal, in its movement. This tapestried nature also clothes a mystery, giving a sense of depth to the physical world, a vanishing point in the design. The numinous is not dispersed, then, but hidden and disclosed in art.

Several poems in *Erosion* deal directly with a masterpiece of visual art—by Piero della Francesca, Luca Signorelli, Masaccio, Gustav Klimt. In these poems Graham poses as beholder, in the world of erosion, reflecting on the work, its relation to her world, and the creative process of the artist. Graham's preoccupation with Christian subjects (the Resurrection, the expulsion from the garden of Eden, the birth of Christ), which will continue in later volumes, suggests the importance of her analogy between Christian paradoxes and the mysteries of art. In her treatment of modern works Graham continues to conceive of art as a process of drawing off and transforming the given to a fabric that will enclose something infinite as its secret center. But she no longer takes for granted the nature of the mystery and the purpose of its aesthetic covering.

In **"Mist"** Graham describes the condition of consciousness ("this quick intelligence") we live in and act on. In our hungry rationality we are "blind" but "forever trying to finger the distinctions" between being and becoming, essence and existence. The mist represents the mind "making everything / part of itself," seeking "the whole idea" which eludes it. Our "geography" is better than our "history" as we try to map out a world in flux. But the mist also suggests, more traditionally, the condition of erosion in which we live and think.

The rational mind pursuing absolutes in a world of erosion ("the rose inside the rose that keeps on opening") fails, but the creative will provides an alternative:

> and then
> this other still
> wherein it is a perfect rose
> *because* I snap it

from the sky,

because I want it,

another, thicker, kind of sight.

In a world opening, being consumed, swimming, and waving good-bye, that is, the poet chooses an icon, not out of reason but out of desire. To counteract erosion she "snaps" a different mode of seeing, one thicker and thus more stable than the swimming, blind/deaf world of thought she has characterized throughout most of the poem. The rose is "perfect" not because it realizes a Platonic truth, but "*because*" her imagination draws it out from "the sky."

Similarly, in **"Reading Plato"** Graham describes her friend making lures. This action is a "beautiful lie" because it is based on the representation of a "good idea" of forms "past death, past sight," suspended from the world of erosion. Graham is anti-Platonic, believing not in ideal, rational forms but in "the body // they were all once / a part of." But she admires these lures, initiating here a distinction she will make frequently, between the beautiful (the forms of art, which may surpass reason in their importance to us) and the true (which eludes the forms of reason). While constructed of fragments of nature we experience as broken, the lures have a unifying force. "A hook / under each pair / of wings," they reunite body and spirit as they are cast into the stream. Graham contrasts our dispersed, sensuous "knowledge of / the graceful // deer" to the fly made out of deer hair because it is "hollow / and floats" (the form of our dissecting, abstract knowing). But the iconic lure, cast into the stream, has led her to imagine back to the whole. We will see in other poems that the dismemberment of reality is redeemed by the construction of forms that permit a glimpse of numinous wholeness.

The relation of the icon to the stream is again the focus of the three-part poem **"In What Manner the Body is United with the Soule."** This time what floats above the stream is not an artifact but an agency, a self, in the figure of a "miraculous / water-strider" which can "measure ripples / for meaning." Graham's connection of this invisible "meaning" with art is explicit from the beginning. The first section of the poem considers, through the metaphor of the stream, the effect of music. The sounds, their "surface tension / which is pleasure" lead to the sounding of "meaning / —small, jeweled, deep-water— / flash." At the outset of the poem, then, the soul is understood in terms of the aspirations and effects of art. But music, the most abstract and temporal of the arts, must give way to iconic symbols for Graham. Indeed, in the next section that "flash" turns out to be "manuscripts / illuminated by monks" which are unearthed from "the mud / of the Arno." These verbal icons release their "gold" into the "lush browns" in which "all the difficulties / of the passage

/ of time" are caught and held. Thus they "illuminate" the mud as the mud preserves them through time. "The self" is the center of this reciprocity:

> an act of
>   rescue
> where the flesh has risen,
>   the spirit
> loosened. . . .

In the final section of the poem Graham writes only of the natural world, but her symbolist images mirror and unite earlier images of art. The stream which has run through each section is here "smaller, / almost still," as if made ready for creation, a "delay" in the "hurry" of life and erosion that allows for artistic vision. The "jewels" of meaning in section 1 are now held as "tiny insect / life" which the waterstrider-self consumes. The "gold bee," an image perhaps of the inspiration or food of art, parallels the gleam on the ice over the mud that holds the manuscripts. The golden eggs of the waterstrider-self are the creative expression of this insight:

> Of silence, mating striders make
>   gold eggs
> which they will only lay
>   on feathers
>
> dropped by passing birds
>   or on the underside
> of a bird's tail
>   before it wakens and
> flies off, blue and white and host
>   to a freedom
>
> it knows nothing of.

The final movement here is clearly out of the stream, into the freedom of the disembodied spiritual, but the body is made, by the self, the vehicle of transcendence even as its direction may be elsewhere.

Each of the poems I have discussed deals with a condition of flux or erosion (figured as mist or stream), from which something iconic is constructed or fathomed, a "perfect rose," a "lure," an "elaborate gold frame," isolated parts that can evoke a whole. Along with this relation of icon and flux Graham frequently poses a relation of outside world and inside mind or art. Our minds want to draw the "outside" world into the "inside" structures of thought and representation. Graham presents this as a natural and positive impulse when driven by a regard for mystery, for the beautiful, rather than for rational meaning. The aesthetic, iconic "inside," while it is walled off from the world, evokes and transforms that world. This iconic space has its own indeterminate movement even as it resists temporality.

"Still Life with Window and Fish" is a celebration of aesthetic space and a study of its attractions. Fragments of the world "outside" the window (of her room, of her mind) are brought "inside," "dismembered" but also "remembered." They enter as shadows made when objects interrupt the passage of light—as what is seen in the window, held in the mind, or represented in ornamental designs. The "inside" forms a space where things are simplified and reassembled.

> The whole world outside
> wants to come into here,
> to angle into
> the simpler shapes of rooms, to be broken and
> rebroken
> against the sure co-ordinates
> of walls.

The "sure co-ordinates of walls," like the frames of art, designate a boundary in which images are sequestered from reality. But within the walls relations "blur" and "nothing starts or / ends," unlike the eroding world outside. Graham emphasizes that the space "inside" is partial and "broken," yet its delights are clear. The shadows, designs, and other images of the world outside are loosed from their physical boundaries:

> Here is a fish-spine on the sea of my bone china
> plate. Here is a fish-spine on the sea of my hand,
> flickering, all its freight
> fallen away.

The fish image returns here to suggest the transfiguration of the flux into an "indelible / surf," the surf-ace of art or imaginative transformation of reality. The self is drawn into this surf where the restless imagination can sustain itself against the tide of erosion:

> If I should die
> before you do,
> you can find me anywhere
> in this floral, featureless,
> indelible
> surf, We are too restless
> to inherit
> this earth.

This interior, formal space of "still life" provides a kind of rescue, then, from the world of erosion. Its very limitations and interruptions transfigure and save.

The same sense of an "inside" space which may "block the view" of the outside world but which, at the same time, may rescue us from erosion arises in **"To a Friend Going Blind."** The complete integration of many associative links in this poem is testimony to art's power to unify. The poem begins with a description of walking:

> I had to walk this town's entire inner
> perimeter to find
> where the medieval walls break open
> in an eighteenth century
> arch.

Graham here recognizes both limitation and the artistic transformation of limitation which designs an inner space to be permeable to the outside, even to reveal it. The poet shifts abruptly to an apparently unrelated issue. "Bruna," a local seamstress, "is teaching me / to cut a pattern." Bruna is linked to the medieval town when her measuring tapes are described as "corn-blond and endless, / from her neck" — like Rapunzel's hair. Bruna is an artist, who, judging her "material" "for texture, grain, the built-in / limits," turns those limits into something useful and, incidentally, beautiful. As a kind of Rapunzel she can teach the poet, who can teach her imminently blind friend, to get imaginatively beyond the walls. We may remember that Rapunzel's lover was blinded by the witch until Rapunzel's tears fell upon his eyes and cured them. Bruna teaches how the outside world might come inside, transfigured, how limitation might provide access since the whole world itself seeks "interruption." Thus the poet's journey through the walled town is an imitation of the lesson from Bruna: "I wandered all along the street that hugs the walls, / a needle floating / on its cloth." Bruna teaches the usefulness of art: enclosed as we are within our tower, art can help us escape as Rapunzel's prince could not:

> When Bruna finishes her dress
> it is the shape of what has come
> to rescue her. She puts it on.

The controlling metaphor of **"To a Friend,"** stitching, binds its two images (Bruna's sewing, walking the town's wall) into a kind of New Critical verbal icon. The metaphor informs nearly half the poems in *Erosion.* Stitching involves several varied but related desires for Graham: we desire to make of the world's raw material (and our own built-in limits) something that can "rescue" us from flux and that can give form to the numinous. We would bind together what is broken (the temporal and the eternal, life and death, the individual and the whole) and penetrate the gaps and cracks in our norms in order to create new wholes. Finally, we respond to the "beautiful," for the pleasure it gives and the mystery it shrouds. Stitching is an act of love, something that seeks to draw the objects of this world into a more permanent, shaped, beautiful "fabric" of art.

Graham expresses her measured faith in "stitching" in **"The Lady and the Unicorn and Other Tapestries."** The ephemeral world is woven into the permanent fabric of the tapestry:

> If I have a faith it is something like this: this
> ordering
>   of images
> within an atmosphere that will receive them, hold
> them
>   in solution, unsolved.

That "unsolved" is importantly double—undissolved by erosion, yet perpetually mysterious (the tapestry is a "still moment"), unapproachable by the interpretive invasion of the word.

The title is curious since the poem never mentions the central subjects of the famous tapestry series. The Cluny tapestries depict the Lady and the Unicorn in various postures that symbolize the five senses. In certain of these and other unicorn tapestries quail are shown settled on or rising from a tree, but they are more decorative than functional in the pictures. Even in the famous hunt tapestry (at the Cloisters in New York), it is the unicorn, not the quail, which is pursued. But it is precisely the decorative impulse, the impulse to design rather than to symbolism, that interests the poet. Graham's strategy of peripheral vision in response to classic works of art allows her the freedom to invent new meanings for these overdetermined works and to explore the nature of art itself as an aesthetic rather than a symbolic activity. The opening lines of the poem (quoted above) might well apply, implicitly, to the effect of the tapestries as a whole, however, since the tapestries depict a mysterious "ordering of images" in which lady and unicorn stand as paradoxical companions (chastity and virility).

The quail provide the link between the artwork and the familiar natural world and allow the poet to imagine that world itself in terms of design: "the quail / over the snow // on our back field run free and clocklike, briefly safe." Art makes that moment of "safety" more enduring. Yet in the next breath she qualifies "the beautiful" as "our whitest lie," white because of its benevolence, a lie because its orders do not represent the realities of erosion. Art gives us a way of looking at the world, allows us to see the hunt itself as design— the quail's role that of "prey." The "ancient tree their eyes map out" is the tree of Eden (symbol of our erosion from the ideal) as well as the tree on which the quail are perched in the tapestries. In response to the Fall we slaughter the quail but also preserve them as decorative feast, as art:

> the quail are woven
> into tapestries, and, stuffed
> with cardamon and pine-nuts
>
> and a sprig of thyme.

The sprig of thyme is our memento of our fall, our temporality, marked within atemporal form. The tapestry artist holds these paradoxes "in solution, unsolved," unlike the hunter who would possess and destroy.

More often Graham's stitching metaphor connects with her imagery of clothing, with the idea of a numinous center within or behind the aesthetic pattern. Art is not only an ordering of images but a shroud of the infinite; its surface is arranged around a vanishing point. Graham returns repeatedly to the metaphor of the garment which wraps the eternal invisible. Whether "the invisible" is itself an effect of art rather than a separate reality is not a question Graham raises in *Erosion,* though many poems in the volume invite it.

"Kimono" combines the ideas of art as design and as garment. The fluency and pictorial richness of fabric allow Graham to imagine the world of erosion in an aesthetic space. Stitched in visual delight with "valleys, clear skies, / thawing banks / narcissus and hollow reeds," the kimono's fabric represents our knowledge of the world. A boy depicted in this garden becomes our innocence, in which we mistake our knowledge for reality: "It means the world to him, this flat / archaic fabric / no weather worries." But formed into a garment, this limited knowledge becomes art and suggests something real and whole within it. The poet, wearing the kimono, identifies herself with a permanent spirit of the world that moves it:

> What he sees,
> in my garden, is the style
> of the world
> as she brushes her hair
> eternally beyond
>
> the causal crumbling forms
> of boughs.

If the world is a kimono, erosion is the "style / of the world" where "reeds are suddenly / ravines" but not its essence. Something whole stands "eternally beyond" it as well, which we may glimpse through the "open door" of the shifting "green scrim." It is "late" in the evolution of our knowledge, the poet tells us often, for any transparency of truth. Yet even in this lateness, the human spirit, "a sacred store / of dares," glimpses the disrobing of nature, the disclosure of a unifying presence.

What makes this vision "late" and modernist rather than romantic is the self-conscious mediation of art. It is art, not nature, that allows us this glimpse into the whole. As a work of art, this fabric, this "beautiful lie," can wrap a "reality" which is an otherwise unknown "something"—its mystery. It is not our knowledge of the world but our knowledge

transfigured as garment, our world transfigured as art, with its "abstract" branches, that allows, even intends, the glimpse suggested at the end of the poem into "something most whole," beyond erosion. Indeed, that "something" may only have identity through art.

The poet, through the metaphor of the kimono, gives herself a privileged position. She is caught in the "archaic fabric" like the boy but also takes the position of the object beheld, the spirit-woman inside the aesthetic surface. The switching pronouns, in which "I'm / wearing valleys" and "she brushes her hair" coincide in the subject, suggest a double stance of penetration and disclosure. Again the artist affirms the reality beyond art's "archaic fabric" only by positing that reality within art, as a place of unveiling.

In **"Kimono"** Graham apparently follows a traditional romantic paradigm of male consciousness as desire toward veiled female nature. She modernizes this paradigm by showing how art fosters it. And without subverting this paradigm she does complicate it by shifting her identity from object to beholder. In Graham the icon as clothed female figure represents a reciprocal aspect of art in which the beholder "going in" experiences a sense of mystery yielding itself, without a complete consummation. In **"San Sepolcro,"** about Piero della Francesca's image of the laboring virgin, the aesthetic mediation is explicit and the paradigm of vision as male desire is more clearly transfigured. But this basic reciprocity in the figure remains. This poem about a monumental work of art (conveyed in humble language) opens the volume *Erosion,* suggesting that the mediation of iconic representation controls many of the poems in their understanding of the relationship between the body and the spirit.

"San Sepolcro" again works with a contrast between the world outside and the more private, contemplative space of iconic representation. And again the representational space is associated with penetration and disrobing. But here art is not merely a matter of male desire extended by an inexhaustible, yielding female image. The sexuality implicit in **"Kimono"** (where the peeping Tom climbs the "gentle limbs" of a tree and observes nature as she "loosens her stays") is displaced by a metaphor of birthing. Graham is "one of the living," Mary a symbol of the mind's power to conceive eternity beneath the temporal, the "blue . . . mantle of weather"—thus partaking of both male and female mythology. Male and female stereotypes (penetrating mind and desired object) are transcended. The beholder-self of the poet is a transparent vessel ("snow having made me / a world of bone / seen through to"), but also active ("I can take you there"), enabled by this receptivity. This structure is repeated in the presentation of Mary, whose figure paradoxically unites immaculate male mind ("How clean / the mind is, // holy grave. It is this girl") and female body waiting "to go into // labor." Mary's dress represents the threshold nature of the icon itself.

"San Sepolcro" begins with an invitation to move from the outside temporal world into, first, the interior world of the walled house, then to a picture whose colors evoke an idea of eternity. Thus again an apparent narrowing into limits allows for a sense of expansion. Graham opens like a tour guide but, in the manner of Elizabeth Bishop, goes on from the literal to the symbolic, and hence to the beautiful and the mysterious, from the profane ("Etruscan") place of San Sepolcro (with its assembly lines and open-air markets) to the elusive, undefined, "sacred" space of art, from the public to the private. The pivotal figure is the rooster, Christian symbol of betrayal and sacrifice, who stands between the world of "mist outside the walls," the unclear world of erosion, and the disclosure of the icon, "before the birth of god." Just here Graham defines the limits, the "tragedy" of art, which awakens in the beholder a desire for presence. The icon is not an incarnation; the "still moment" is "forever still-born." "The living," approaching the icon, "go in" but never "arrive." Yet art's power to awaken our thoughts of the infinite insures its hold on us:

> but going in, each breath
>   is a button
>
> coming undone, something terribly
>   nimble-fingered
> finding all of the stops.

The model of veiled female as icon arises once more in **"At the Exhumed Body of Santa Chiara, Assisi."** She is "pure even after a ton of dirt," in the world of erosion but not of it. Again the model of contemplation is one of desire fore-stalled. The poet's own worldly desire ("whether I leave him / or not") is delayed, as was the worldly desire of the earthly Chiara ("So and so you loved, / so and so you left"). These are left to the world of disappearances, replaced by a spiritual desire, a "deep[er] delay" in the contemplation of "nowhere" marked by the clothed, iconic figure.

Graham views the exhumed body of Santa Chiara, "queen of the chiaroscuro," almost as a work of art, a figure dark against a background of contemporary "blue." "Blue over your body in its afterlife / on its back in its black dress with gold trim." The phenomenon of Chiara's exhumed body is itself parallel to the phenomenon of art "as if the flesh were the eternal portion after all." This is not a Christian but a modern notion of the icon, recalling Wallace Stevens's secular reversal: "Beauty is momentary in the mind—The fitful tracing of a portal; / But in the flesh it is immortal." Graham, too, approaches art as a means to approach the infinite rather than escape the body. The reciprocity of the icon rests in the paradox of the veil placed "in order / to be seen."

In *Erosion,* I have argued, Graham treats the icon as a form of rescue from the flux and as a veil which shrouds but also discloses the infinite. Her constant return to Christian images and subjects reveals an important analogy. But her secular treatment of these subjects also reveals a distinctly modernist cast to the analogy, one which erases ideas of transcendence to a spiritual other realm. Art itself becomes the redeemer, though the terms of redemption are not in arrival but in the "going in." Eternity is redefined so that it is bound to the earthly ("beneath motion, more flesh") even as it is released from flux.

Two of Graham's ecphrastic poems, **"At Luca Signorelli's Resurrection of the Body"** and **"Masaccio's Expulsion,"** make this shift from Christian to modernist iconicity especially clear. Graham's return to the rhetorical strategy of ecphrasis emphasizes the aesthetic nature of the "nowhere" which absorbs her meditation.

The figures resurrected in Signorelli's painting are not raised by God but by art, drawn up "into the weightedness, the color, / into the eye / of the painter," and hurry toward "distance" and "perspective," the limitations of human timespace defined in terms of painting. The notion that these figures never wholly arrive, that "there is no entrance, only entering," itself derives from the experience of painting rather than from the painting's illusion and its Christian promise of resurrection. The still moment of figures caught in action and held into that action is never complete. There remains an inherent "gap," to use Graham's favorite word, between the painting and presence, between representation and desire.

Signorelli's frescoes, of which "The Resurrection" (the emphasis on "the body" is Graham's addition) is one of several at the cathedral in Orvieto, represent the pinnacle of his career. Graham has captured in this poem the central power of motion and bodily impact which is often celebrated in his work. She begins her poem by focusing the reader's attention immediately on the dramatic subject of the bottom half of Signorelli's fresco—bodies rising from openings in the earth, transformed from skeletons to fleshed figures:

> See how they hurry
>   to enter
> their bodies,
>   these spirits.
>
> . . . .
>
>   From above
> the green-winged angels
>   blare down
> trumpets and light. But
>   they don't care,

they hurry to congregate,
    they hurry
into speech, until
    it's a marketplace,
it is humanity.

It is not quite true that the figures in Signorelli's fresco ignore the angels above them (who make up the top half of the fresco and are considerably larger and more prominent than the human figures). Many gaze in awe and ecstasy at these figures. But it is their resumption of human activity—dancing, bartering, debating—that interests the poet. "Hurry" is a key word for Graham, used six times in this poem and denoting our temporal nature (its paired term is "delay," involving the gap between our temporal natures and the eternal dimension we desire, the dimension opened by art). Art holds that hurry in its still moment.

By shifting from subjects to beholders Graham makes an important qualification to her idealization of art's beautiful lie, the same qualification she makes in **"San Sepolcro,"** where the desire for arrival, for presence of the infinite (the birth of God), meets "tragedy." (The "at" in the title **"At Luca Signorelli's Resurrection of the Body"** emphasizes, as it does in **"At the Exhumed Body of Santa Chiara,"** the threshold between history and art.) Unlike the Christian believer, Graham, as beholder of the icon, recognizes no "arrival," no complete presence. The ecphrastic poet fails by definition, as she yearns to approach the condition of presence evoked by the visual icon. For Graham this verbal/visual difference simply reveals the inherent limits of art to provide the arrival we yearn for. Thus "there is no entrance, / only entering," addressed to the figures in Signorelli's paintings as they "hurry" into representation, applies reciprocally (as it did in **"San Sepolcro"**) to the condition of the beholder before the visual image.

Graham's next major shift in the poem is to the artist himself and his creative process. Whereas the figures in "The Resurrection" depicted the "hurry" of our temporal natures, the emphasis here is on patience and slowness. That patient penetration of the "wall / of the flesh" (like the opening garment in **"San Sepolcro"**) is demonstrated in Signorelli's practice of studying anatomy through autopsy. This literal breaking into the body in search of "arrival," in search of its essential aspect, yields to a transformation from the fleshly to the iconic where it becomes inexhaustible, where "the flesh / opens endlessly, / its vanishing point so deep / and receding // we have yet to find it." This absorption in the flesh as icon has a counterpart in a movement "from the symbolic" (where the flesh might simply serve to convey an unearthly message) "to the beautiful" (where the flesh is itself cast in an eternal dimension).

This idea of the "beautiful" defines the redemptive charac-

ter of art, counterpoint to the "tragedy" of elusive presence. Graham may have drawn from Vasari the apocryphal anecdote of Signorelli painting the body of his dead son. Vasari suggested that the son was the model for the pietà in "The Deposition"; actually Antonio probably died of the plague, and it is unlikely that Signorelli used his body as a model. But the legend suits Graham's vision of the redemptive power of art. Signorelli's act of drawing his dead son is implicitly parallel to the resurrection depicted in his famous fresco and described in the first part of the poem. But it is not the resurrection of the dead son so much as of the bereaved artist that we are left with, for Signorelli's mind enters the "open flesh" just as the spirits hurried into their bodies in his picture:

It took him days
    that deep
caress, cutting,
    unfastening,

until his mind
    could climb into
the open flesh and
    mend itself.

Like Bruna cutting and sewing in **"To a Friend Going Blind,"** Signorelli forms, from the broken flesh, an icon, the shape which will rescue him if he puts it on. Visual art, more than poetry, involves this pursuit of the timeless through an immersion in the body.

"At Luca Signorelli's Resurrection of the Body" concerns a reciprocal need: the body's need for art to lift it out of the world of erosion, the mind's need for the body, for embodiment of its idea of the infinite. We see a similar compensatory and reciprocal principle at work in Graham's poem **"Masaccio's Expulsion."** The poem describes one in a continuous series of frescoes Masaccio painted in Florence, arranged so that the Expulsion clearly leads into the other images of biblical history, to which the poem alludes collectively. As in **"Resurrection,"** Graham emphasizes the pictorial nature of the space as well as the illusion of reality. The poem begins with the grief of the figures and the common notion that the condition of representation is a fall, a loss of presence:

Is this really the failure
    of silence,
or eternity, where these two
    suffer entrance
into the picture
    plane[.]

The poem goes on to revise this negative judgment. Like Keats's "still unravished bride of quietness," art is not the failure of silence but the triumph of the visual. Graham goes on to find in the world of the paint, not just of the illusion, certain compensatory features. Having lost presence and immortality, these figures emanate their loss, and this "price" can "live forever" as art.

Graham begins with the figures of Adam and Eve refusing sight: "a man and woman / so hollowed / by grief they cover / their eyes / in order not to see." But the poet's position depends on looking, and her poem is, as it goes on, an appeal to redemptive features of sight. Art makes a "garden" of this fallen world, this "inexhaustible grammar" of history, "its dark and light" objects and shadows. This space of the "picture / plane" represents a narrowness in which the fullness of live being is reduced to "symbols, // balancing shapes in / a composition," yet art provides a compensation for the loss of freedom it represents, a commemorative and aestheticizing power that rises up out of these limits. The pivot of this compensatory view is not in the central, symbolic subject matter of the frescoes but, as in **"The Lady and the Unicorn,"** in a decorative detail:

> And perhaps
> it is a flaw
>
> on the wall of this church, or age,
> or merely the restlessness
> of the brilliant
> young painter,
> the large blue bird
> seen flying too low
> just where the trees
> clot.

This bird, "the gift of / the paint," appears on the fresco as a wing-like blotch at the edge near Eve's thigh, incomplete as a bird shape but close enough for Graham to figure it as such. It becomes her image of the imagination, driven to seek form, to enter "a space too small / to fit in" but also hovering above that space.

That narrowing into embodiment has a reciprocal effect of expansion on the beholder. Graham's eye moves down from Adam and Eve to various figures "in the foreground" (more central in the alcove) who represent biblical history. But their pictorial power in "the gold air" of art raises them from their passage into the narrowness of history:

> There isn't a price
> (that floats up
> through their miraculous
> bodies
> and lingers above them
> in the gold air)
> that won't live forever.

Art assures this immortality and causes the figures to "float up" from history and form. It provides the countermotion to the down-ward glance of Adam and Eve and the general lines of the fresco they occupy.

In the poems described above Graham affirms the triumph of the beautiful, the power of the aesthetic to raise the spirit above not only the flux of history but also the weight of symbolism, the mere interpretation of history. But as Graham turns her attention to art of the modern age and to the pressures of modern history, she begins to approach aesthetic value with more uncertainty. The weight of modern history carries a moral imperative that is hard to reconcile with aesthetic pleasure or notions of art's "beautiful lie" against time. While such issues revise Graham's thoughts about the role of the icon, however, they do not finally change her faith in its value or understanding of its structure.

The beholder in **"Two Paintings by Gustav Klimt"** brings to the fin de siècle works a knowledge of subsequent history which she cannot help but impose on what she views (history is not, here, "hopelessly even"). She uses the juxtaposition of two paintings as if to corroborate her own archaic vision. Behind the idealized icon, a space of eternal beauty, lies a scream, the juxtaposition seems to say. Yet such an unveiling is by itself too simple; it is the relation between the veil and what lies behind it, the relation of desire, that interests Graham and determines the value of the aesthetic for her.

> **Graham affirms the triumph of the beautiful, the power of the aesthetic to raise the spirit above not only the flux of history but also the weight of symbolism, the mere interpretation of history.**
> *—Bonnie Costello*

The first painting is a landscape, a "buchen-wald," or beech forest. Klimt painted a number of such landscapes, which expressed his spiritually and sexually symbolic vision in a network of prominent verticals and high horizontals. *Gustav Klimt* by Alessandra Comini is the probable source of many details in **"Two Paintings by Gustav Klimt."** Comini describes "Beech Forest I" as a "rhythmic grouping of elemental verticals and horizontals." The beholder's vision of the landscape stands between Klimt and twentieth-century history, so that his meaning-saturated environment takes on the meanings that postdate it, in which the term "buchen-wald" is forever blighted. Graham introduces the issues that have concerned her throughout the book—the aesthetic transformation of "flaws" into "the beautiful":

> Although what glitters

on the trees
row after perfect row,
  is merely
the injustice
  of the world,

the chips on the bark of each
  beech tree
catching the light, the sum
  of these delays
is the beautiful, the human
  beautiful,
body of flaws.

The "injustice / of the world" is very broadly defined here as erosion itself because the word "buchen-wald" has not been introduced. Despite the opening disclaimer, the poem clearly presents the world depicted, the world of erosion— "leafrot," "mottled shadows," "broken skins"—caught in art, as evoking an elusive ideal of "something to lean on / that won't / give way." "The dead / in their sheer / open parenthesis" at this point simply stand as a contrast of the mortal world to the abidance of landscape and art. But these "dead" are the victims not only of our mortal but of our moral nature—the anonymous dead of the Holocaust, for whom the trees soon stand as symbols, not opposites. The continuities of landscape and art, and the aesthetic balance achieved in art, come into tension in the poem with the poet's knowledge of human brutality, the weight of the word "buchenwald." For the post-Holocaust observer "late / in the twentieth / century," the yellow light is a "gaseous light." But against this view the poet holds out another, amoral view, inaccessible to her but embodied in the beautiful landscape, where

To receive the light
  and return it

and stand in rows, anonymous,
  is a sweet secret.

The air, like the male gaze, would penetrate this mysterious image of the trees, with "little hooks" that "poke," anticipating the pornographic image in the second painting. The "sweet secret" of the trees is, of course, their inhumanity, their innocence of history, the idea of the infinite they embody.

Graham's poem may in one sense describe a transformation in seeing from the nineteenth to the twentieth century, in which the idealization of the landscape is no longer possible and an unveiling of the moral horror beneath the masks of aestheticism is inevitable. But I think Graham's vision, and her view of art in particular, is too complex for this simple

contrast. The beautiful holds its place, drawing us into mystery.

The tension between the moral and the aesthetic and the aestheticizing of the moral comes to a focus in the second half of the poem, in which Graham considers a very different painting by Klimt, an incomplete, pornographic rendering of the female body, clothed only in a transparent garment. The woman's genitalia form a "mouth" "something like / a scream." Her facial expression remains "bored, feigning a need / for sleep." For Klimt she is a figure of Freudian desire and repression, for Graham a figure perhaps of public indifference to the known horror of fascism.

Certainly the "scream" Graham identifies with this mouth establishes the parallelism between the two paintings through the idea of a violence beneath tranquil surfaces. The major interest of the poem, however, is not in the genital "mouth" (or the issues it raises about the male gaze in Western art), or in the bored face of the woman (with its political implications). Graham's central interest is, as always, in the garment, which is not merely condemned as the cover up for brutal obscenity. "The fabric // defines the surface, / the story, / so we are drawn to it."

Graham directly compares the "feathery garment" that Klimt had begun to paint over the figure to his rendering of landscape in the other painting, describing "its blues / and yellows glittering / like a stand // of beech trees." She remains ambiguous about how we are to evaluate this analogy or the placement of the garment itself. But the resemblance of this garment to other images of clothing in Graham suggests that she approves of it. Through the garment of art we glimpse what is otherwise unrepresentable.

But rather than pursue this metaphor (garment/story), Graham abruptly returns to the first painting by Klimt: "In // the finished painting / the argument / has something to do / with pleasure." In one sense the juxtaposition of the two paintings, weighted in favor of the unfinished one and the Holocaust allusion, turns pleasure into decadence or even cruel obscenity. Yet that "surface tension / which is pleasure" (in **"In What Manner"**) "holds / the self // afloat" and draws us toward the unknown and unspeakable. Thus "pleasure" may become a vehicle of insight, beauty a route to unfathomable truth (whatever its moral register). **"Two Paintings by Gustav Klimt"** is finally not an exposé but an assertion of the value of the veil. Still, "pleasure" stands as a highly vulnerable term by the end of the poem, as the "argument" of the second painting is inevitably grafted onto the first.

"Two Paintings by Gustav Klimt" repeats the erotic structure of the icon implicit in other poems I have discussed. Graham does not condemn, in fact she seems in sympathy with, this structure. The addition of the Holocaust imagery does not undermine this fundamental vision of art; it simply changes the character of the "secret" dimension of the icon and turns the promised wholeness behind the surface into an abyss. But this shift, and Graham's vagueness—which is not clearly ambivalence—about "pleasure" and elsewhere in *Erosion* about "the beautiful," may account for the dramatic change in her style and approach to the image in her next volume, *The End of Beauty* (1987).

For this ambitious poet each book is a critique of the one before. The very titles she has chosen map this out. Where *Erosion* imagines the construction of an integrated, centered eternal space set apart from the flux, even rescuing us from its absolute effects, *The End of Beauty* concerns itself with edges, boundaries, origins and ends, images unraveling into "minutes" and splitting into dialogue, the still moment dissolving into narrative. Graham has pursued this shift in recent work. Her focus is increasingly on the hurry of this world (this "region of unlikeness" no icon can transfigure) and the struggle to sustain a visionary stance within it rather than with drawing into a contemplative one. The darting, temporally unstable images of cinema and television rather than the static images of painting have become her gauge. Digression rather than integration is the dominant aesthetic effect.

These and other qualities represent Graham's move from a spatial, modernist to a temporal, postmodern aesthetic, one that subscribes less to art as artifact than to art as process. One needn't make a value judgment to comprehend the necessity of this shift for the poet (one needn't, that is, see a plot in her development). But whatever place *Erosion* may take in the evolution of Graham's work, its value to us as achieved vision will remain.

Mark Jarman (review date Fall 1992)

SOURCE: "The Grammar of Glamour: The Poetry of Jorie Graham," in *New England Review,* Vol. 14, No. 4, Fall, 1992, pp. 252-61.

[*In the review below, Jarman compares* The End of Beauty *to* Region of Unlikeness, *praising the former but finding the form and content of the poems incompatible with those of the later collection.*]

"The serpent beguiled me, and I did eat." Eve's famous excuse suggests that she has not only been tricked but charmed. To use an old Scottish word, a *glamour* has been thrown over her eyes, in her case, the allurement of knowledge. For Jorie Graham, the beguiling serpent is time; its succession and linearity give birth to history. Her poetry seeks to break the spell that holds us in time, requiring that history have a be-

ginning, middle, and end, and that art, especially literature and particularly poetry, be mimetic and made up of similitude, metaphor, and narrative or "storyline" as she calls it. Her response to these conventions is to cast a counter spell, to throw one glamour over another, or so it has been in her last two books, *The End of Beauty,* published in 1987, and her new collection, *Region of Unlikeness,* published in 1991.

There is another sort of glamour that might be associated with her poetry and it is the one we usually think of as allurement and fascinating personal attractiveness, which are both exciting and romantic, but may be illusory. This glamour is rooted in the material she uses from her own life, setting poems in Italy, for example, where she grew up in proximity to works of art that had their own sheen of definite beauty. As she implies in her poem **"I Was Taught Three"** from her first book, *Hybrids of Plants and of Ghosts,* she grew up knowing three names, in English, French, and Italian, for the chestnut tree. She had, as Nabokov once remarked about his own life, a perfectly normal trilingual childhood. The matter of such a life is innately interesting. Glamourous, if you will. In a grosser sense, the very packaging of her last two books, including their glossy cover art and the striking photographs of the author, proffer glamour.

> Jorie Graham's recent poetry, with its special vocabulary or lexicon, with its spellbinding repetition, with its passionate energy, not to say urgency, reads like a near frenzied search for the magic words, the open-sesame, that will allow entrance to a world before time, a world which may be paradise.
>
> *–Mark Jarman*

But I am interested in the other kind of glamour, which is associated with enchantment and is also a form of the word *grammar.* Jorie Graham's recent poetry, with its special vocabulary or lexicon, with its spellbinding repetition, with its passionate energy, not to say urgency, reads like a near frenzied search for the magic words, the open-sesame, that will allow entrance to a world before time, a world which may be paradise. Its glamour has a grammar, which is to say it has a structure. Perhaps her most impressive achievement in a decade of writing is to create a new style. No mean feat.

She certainly did not spring fully formed from her own mind equipped with her now identifiable way of writing. Her change of manner has included a change of heart. Her present concerns are similar to those in her first book, but her attitude towards them has altered one hundred and eighty degrees. **"The Way Things Work"** and **"A Feather for**

Voltaire," the poems that respectively begin and end *Hybrids of Plants and of Ghosts,* tell us much, now, in retrospect. The poet who wrote that "the way things work / is by solution" and that she believed "forever in the hooks," who averred,

> The way things work
> is that eventually
> something catches . .

now regards that catching to be the sort of closure that ends possibility and locks us into history. She has become apocalyptic with this knowledge; for her the world ends not with a bang or a whimper but with a *click.* Still, in **"A Feather for Voltaire"** she acknowledges that reality inheres in languages: "The bird is an alphabet." Graham's poetry has usually been about language and often about her own poetic composition. Her recent epiphany has been to discover that language itself, "the key to the kingdom" in **"A Feather for Voltaire,"** is also a prison. The double-bind, the way she wants to have her cake and eat it, too, may be to make poetry out of what, in her recent *New Republic* essay on Graham's work, Bonnie Costello calls "the failures of poetry." Yet I do not think Costello has quite grasped Graham's project. It is even more ambitious than that.

Graham wants to make poetry out of the moment before poetry is made. To do this does require that she acknowledge the failures of poetry, much as T.S. Eliot does often in his work. At the same time, what she manages to affix to the page identifies her aim, even if it does not accomplish it.

Erosion, Graham's second book, contains many fine things that have been accomplished because doubt, the catalyst for her change, has not yet taken hold and made her feel bound by an evil spell. In **"I Watched a Snake,"** the image that symbolizes linear succession in her recent poetry here represents an admirable quality. She associates the snake's hunting with work, and work, like the making of art, is related to desire and passion. Graham has always shown a gift for moving facilely among large abstractions, defining them in almost believable ways or in ways we might wish to believe. Having taken her moral lesson from the snake, she writes, "Passion is work . . ."

> It makes a pattern of us,
>   it fastens us
> to sturdier stuff
>   no doubt.

But *Erosion* concludes with **"The Sense of an Ending,"** an artful look ahead to her future methods and a skeptical examination of that "sturdier stuff." Graham imagines human souls "in a frenzy / to be born" pressing into her "human frame." She imagines they feel it would be better to enter "this skin, this line / all the way round and sealed into the jagged island // form, the delicate / ending, better, even for an instant, even if never brought / further than term. . . ." Their desire to be born, according to Graham, is also a desire to fall. And though another poem in *Erosion* is called **"Wanting a Child"** and one of the most moving poems of the book describes Luca Signorelli dissecting the body of his dead son, Graham comes in **"The Sense of an Ending"** to suspect the urge, "the procreant urge of the world" as Whitman called it, because it initiates the trap, the spell, the glamour she abjures: history with its beginning, middle, and end.

The End of Beauty, her third book and I believe her most original along with being one of the most important books of the 1980s, seems to be by another poet altogether, one whose mind has changed. Her execution is as close to success as we might expect for one who wishes to capture an instant that is almost ontologically impossible to grasp: the moment before form is born and sealed into its fate with a click.

I do not think it is appropriate to consider the ambiguous possibilities of the book's title. As it is represented in these poems, beauty is not an instrument of utility or an aim, because the end or ends to which beauty might be employed are not given. The title must be read as it first announces itself: this book will show the destruction of beauty and, by analogy, hint at the end of the world. The reason for this reading, and the one ambiguity we can entertain, is that in Graham's lexicon *end* and *beauty* are synonymous. Both occur in time, and time is what she would be free of. The title phrase occurs in a poem called **"The Lovers."**

> Here it is, *here,* the end of beauty, the present.
> What the vista fed into. What it wants to grow
>   out of, creeping, succulent. . . .
> No No says the voice pinpointing the heart of
>   these
> narrows.

Here is the heart of her dialectic, her spell against the spell of time, glamour versus glamour. The poem tries to hold a moment of decision, when the lovers commit themselves to one another and time continues. Time, "the vista," is said to be "creeping, succulent," and you can hear the serpentine suggestiveness of both those words. In other poems the verb *hiss* is given as the voice of form, beauty, time, etc.

A number of poems in *The End of Beauty* depict fatal moments in myth: the eating of the apple, Orpheus losing Eurydice, Demeter losing Persephone, Apollo losing Daphne. Some of them, like **"Self-Portrait as Apollo and Daphne,"** draw attention to the controlling hand of the poet. At the instant before the god Apollo can capture her and before she will be transformed into a laurel tree, Daphne is described by Graham in a kind of suspension.

> She stopped she turned,
> she would not be the end towards which he was
>   ceaselessly tending,
> she would not give shape to his hurry by being
>   its destination,
> it was wrong this progress . . .

Here Graham shows the moral authority of her vision. The end of beauty or when beauty is the end is "wrong" because it is a product of "progress."

The beauty brought to an end in these poems is the conventional one that exists in time. Mimetic, finished, it is the sort of beauty we can hold and contemplate, much as Erich Auerbach holds the works of literature he describes with such relish in his book *Mimesis.* Graham's desire is to locate beauty not in the finished product but in the process of composition, which includes the nervous and at times anxious mind in the act of finding not only what will suffice, in Wallace Stevens's terms, but what it will create. The most exact expression of this desire in *The End of Beauty* is **"Pollock and Canvas."** Here she depicts the abstract expressionist painter leaning over his canvas as God leaned over the earth in the act of creation.

> When he leaned down over
>   the undefeated soil
> to make it end somewhere,
>   to make it beautiful . . .
>
> what he chose
>   through the see-no-evil, through the eye for
> the eye,
>   choosing to no longer let the brushtip touch,
> at any point,
>   the still ground,
> was to not be trans-
>   formed but to linger
> in the hollow, the about-to-be . . .

She chooses this, too—not to be transformed and thus finished, but to "linger in the hollow." The hook she loved for the way it caught in **"The Way Things Work"** and that she describes in the poem **"Reading Plato"** in *Erosion* as part of a lure made of deer hair evoking the graceful deer in its transformation, now she admires as if it were a drop of Pollock's flung paint not yet adhering to the canvas.

> 3
>
> here is the hook before it has landed, before
>   it's deep in the current

> 4
>
> the hovering—keeping the hands off—the gap
> alive,
>
> 5
>
> the body of talk between the start and beauty

Graham's use of numbers to separate single lines both suggests sequence and allows her to interrupt sequence with *non sequitur.* The numbers are part of the spell, the glamour thrown over our eyes. But they are beguiling, too, alluring, so that it hardly matters if they are illusory, part of a slippery veil of meaninglessness.

Graham's new aesthetics are exciting. And in so far as she manifests them in poem after poem in *The End of Beauty,* I wonder facetiously if the book could also be thought of as *The Beauty of Beauty.* Yet she is not satisfied to be merely the purveyor of a new way to look at language and poetry. There is a moral dimension to her realization about the trap of time and it has given her a vision of history, too. **"What the End Is For"** is her most apocalyptical poem and, in its structure, resembles many of the poems in her new book, *Region of Unlikeness.* The poet narrates a personal event, in this case being shown in Grand Forks, North Dakota, SAC bombers on alert on a runway. She juxtaposes this with a small domestic drama in which she and a "you" have trouble communicating in a darkening kitchen. She concludes the poem by alluding to the slaughter of Orpheus by the Maenads. We know that the SAC bombers, had they ever gone into action, would have brought our world to an end. The kitchen drama Graham relates also seems to represent an ending—the "you" will not hold the speaker. And though Orpheus's head went on singing after his dismemberment, Graham imagines it floating out into the dissolving noise of the ocean, a noise very like the sound of the B-52s on the runway. This vision is based on a belief that time as it has been understood in Western culture has led us to the brink of thermonuclear holocaust. It is a compelling vision, or was a compelling vision. The end of the Cold War seems to suggest that if time, or Western time, has an end, it will not be what any of us, least of all Jorie Graham, expected. I am reminded of Sandra McPherson's poem "Eschatology," which states:

> I am glad when doom fails. Inept apocalypse
> is a specialty of the times . . .

The End of Beauty may be the last major book of poetry to show the influence of the Cold War.

Graham seems to know this, too, for none of the many stories told in *Region of Unlikeness* has quite the eschatological flavor of poems in *The End of Beauty.* This is not to say they do not have historical contexts. They do, indeed, and each has the sense that at this moment in the poet's life she has understood what history is all about. Most of them are like the last poem in *The End of Beauty,* **"Imperialism,"** in that a title claiming an enormous amount, usually in historical or political or mythical terms, is attached to an anecdote, often an event from the speaker's life. Before going on to *Region of Unlikeness,* it might be helpful to look at what happens in **"Imperialism."**

The poem relates a story from the speaker's childhood. It is being told for some reason not only to the reader but to a "you" with whom the speaker appears to have reached an impasse similar to the one in **"What the End Is For."** The story is about a nine year old child in India with her mother who takes her to the banks of the Ganges. Mother exposes the child to various life-enriching scenes there, like the cremation pyres whose grilles "covered with ash and cartilage" are rinsed off in the river. The daughter is forced to immerse herself in the filthy water and experiences a vision of the void, the other bank, which appears "utterly blank," as "a line drawn simply to finish // the river." This makes her ill and hysterical. The poem ends with an awful memory of Mother comforting her. And with it a variable of Graham's aesthetic equation is completed.

> And as for her body . . .
> it became nothing to me after that, or something
>   less,
>   because I saw what it was, her body, you see—a
>   line
> brought round, all the way round, reader, a plot, a
>   shape, one of the finished things, one of the
>
> *beauties,* (hear it click shut?) a thing
> completely narrowed down to love—all arms, all
>   arms
>   extended in the
>   pulsing sticky heat, fan on, overhead on, all
> arms no face at all dear god, all arms—

I fail to see what this has to do with imperialism, unless we really stretch the situation to some understanding of post-colonial India being analogous to the relationship between the mother and the child. But I do see what this has to do with Graham's aesthetics and her historical vision. This image of the Mother as an oppressive presence, even as she comforts, is equated with form, beauty, and the clicking shut of possibility. The vision Graham presents to us is deeply rooted, like all visions, in a personal obsession. This personal obsession, murky, dynamic, and finally elusive, is the catalyst for poem after poem in *Region of Unlikeness.* But the stories she tells are overwhelmed by a style or grammar

not really suited for them. The spell is broken. The glamour falls from the eyes.

The most successful thing in *Region of Unlikeness* is the Foreword. It is a masterful compilation of related passages from Augustine, Heidegger, Isaiah, John of Patmos, and Melville, recapitulating the project Graham completed in *The End of Beauty.* Separation from God is the theme that links them, especially in this timebound world with its inadequate mimetic forms. Augustine certainly felt this separation. Heidegger was aware of the ontological barrier to connection with the transcendent. Isaiah, in the passage Graham quotes, offers God's typical Old Testament demurral to being embodied in language or the flesh. In the lengthy passage Graham quotes from *Revelation,* John of Patmos describes his vision of Israel giving birth to Christ; this may be Graham's Yeatsian acknowledgment that modern history begins with Christ's birth. But the final quote from *Moby Dick* offers the most telling, most accurate analogue for Graham's ambition: "'Swim away from me, do ye?' murmured Ahab." Indeed, Graham's ambitions are great.

But her project, as I said, was finished in *The End of Beauty. Region of Unlikeness,* if not a false step, is certainly an overextension, especially since the form she has done so much to demonize—storyline or narrative—is central to these new poems. However, if a new idea has been introduced in this book, and I am not sure it has been, it is that in this world, this region of unlikeness, where metaphor is unworkable even provisionally, the only way to represent human experience is through story. I think there is a very good argument for this idea, but I do not think Graham is making it. Still, she employs the very poetic conventions she abjures—narrative, metaphor, mimesis. They separate her poetry from the dreary linguistic bits of the Language Poets with whom she has been compared. There is a further thing, too, not to be underestimated, that separates her from poets like John Ashbery and Michael Palmer with whom she has also been grouped. And that is her passion. Their poetry is marked by a world-weary knowingness, a cool that is terminally hip. Graham may be cynical at times, with her representation of convention in variables—the x, the y, the _____, particularly when she realizes she is once again in the grip of storyline, that snake. But the strength of her feeling cannot be doubted and at times it is actually possible to feel it, too, despite the mannerisms which convey it.

When she embodies her idea in the mythic moments of *The End of Beauty* or even in a scene fraught with Cold War anxiety, she not only makes a point, but her grammar works toward its proper end; the anxious repetition, the search for a way out or in or a way of holding this instant in place before time starts again and brings about the end, her glamour, her very act of spell-casting, are tragic. But when, in the first poem of *Region of Unlikeness,* she tells us where

she was when she heard the news that Kennedy had been
shot, the same portentousness does not apply. In fact, it is
sentimental to believe that if Kennedy had lived, the last 25
years of history would have been different. It is not sentimental to reinhabit the moment when one first heard the
news of his assassination. Everyone of Graham's generation
or older knows where he or she was when the news broke
and just how it felt. The speaker of **"Fission"** was watching
a matinee showing of "Lolita." How the title, the movie, and
the horrible news go together, except in their surreal inex-
plicability, is as puzzling as anything in this book, where
many similar juxtapositions occur. But was Kennedy's assassination on the order of atomic fission? Was the lust of
Humbert Humbert, depicted gigantically on the screen, part
of it? A motif reintroduced from *The End of Beauty* is the
veil, "the layers of the / real," here shown as the movie
screen, the interruption of its light by the houselights, then
daylight, and the man down front who is frantically announcing the event to the crowd. Graham manages to end the poem
on the passionate wish that the news not be true, that the inevitable can be forestalled:

> what is, what also is, what might be that is,
> what could have been that is, what
>   might have been that is, what I say that is,
> what the words say that is,
> what you imagine the words say that is—Don't
>   move,
> don't
>
> wreck the shroud, don't move—

"Fission" sprawls over half a dozen pages; a number of the
24 poems in the book are as long or longer. The Shroud of
Turin itself is introduced in a later poem, one of more modest scope and hearkening back to *Erosion.* I think the problem with **"Fission"** is that for an experience so many of us
share, Graham has claimed for her own experience more than
history will allow.

"Fission" and the other poems like it are monumentally ambitious, but they are rather like hearing a Wagnerian soprano
singing a Mozart aria about the end of the day. **"Manifest
Destiny"** is another example of a poem whose title is disproportionate to its subject matter. The poem includes a
moving portrait of a friend, apparently a drug addict, who
has died; the feelings are elegiac. But the central event is a
day in Rome when the speaker and her friend pause outside
of Rebbibia, which a note tells us "is the name of the
women's jail in Rome." The two watch and listen to the
women calling and gesturing from their barred windows. The
poem ends with an exhortation of humanity.

> Oh why are you here on this earth, you—*you*—
> swarming,

> swirling
> carrying valises, standing on line,
> ready to change your name if need be—?

If questions are remarks, as Wallace Stevens said they were,
then this one suggests that humanity's existence is out-
weighed by the friend's death. As intense as that feeling is,
it does not convey the intenser tragedy that the friend's death
is insignificant.

"From the New World" comes closer to justifying its
claims, although once again, a personal matter is juxtaposed
with a larger historical one. The trial of John Demanjuk, the
so-called Ivan the Terrible of Treblinka, is recounted along
with a story of two elderly grandparents being put into separate nursing homes. Presumably, "the New World" has meant
a kind of incarceration for both Demanjuk and the grandparents. But there is a third element in the poem and that is
the anecdote of a child in a German death camp who, instead of remaining in a gas chamber, somehow got out and
was found looking for her mother. This sort of moment, this
suspension of the inevitable, now bears Graham's signature.
She is at her best, responding to it in her reflexive mode, at
once identifying her motivation and casting her spell.

> God knows I too want the poem to continue,
> want the silky swerve into shapeliness
>   and then the click shut
> and then the issue of sincerity, the glossy
>   diamond-backed
> skin—

Of course, nothing she can do can change the facts or save
the particular child she has in mind. It is a curious consequence of Graham's aesthetic vision that she should blame
the tragedy she describes on a poem's "shapeliness" rather
than on Nazi Germany.

That metonymic reference to the snake of storyline ("the
glossy diamond-backed / skin") comes again later in **"Who
Watches from the Dark Porch,"** one of the book's most
interesting poems and most compelling. The poet produces
an event: she is sitting in a rocking chair on her porch in
the evening and hears a cry, perhaps the cry of a child, coming from her neighbor's house. "Now I will make a sound
for you to hear," she writes and goes on to describe the
sound, which is the beginning of a speculative story, as "a
shriek? no? a laugh?— // lung-stuff, flinty, diamond-backed,
floating through / the layer of flesh, the layer of house. . . ."
She suggests that there are all sorts of ways to mask such a
sound, a sound that may require a response. One way is to
turn on the TV and channel surf. The passage in which she
describes the surreal montage of changing channels is dazzling and illuminating, as well. Is it possible that TV itself
is the mimetic source of these poems? Whereas the number-

ing and repetition of the poems in *The End of Beauty* were ways to bind a spell and stop time, in *Region of Unlikeness,* the excess verbiage and the onslaught of stimuli from a kind of word-noise, not unlike the imagery and sound that emanate from the TV, the reality of which is, as she says, "dots, dots / roiling up under the golden voice—"

> Now: connect the dots, connect the dots,
> connect the dots, connect the dots,
> connect the dots, connect the dots,
> connect the dots, connect the dots—
>
> Feeling okay?

Graham is never funny, but here one is inclined to give a small, exhausted, but real laugh. We *have* learned to make reality into an infinitely variable fiction through the medium of television. But is language itself the culprit? Are the conventions of poetry to blame? Well, questions *are* remarks, and so are mine. I don't think so.

There are two passages in *Region of Unlikeness* that are more moving as poetry than any others in the book. Both occur in the book's best poem, **"The Phase After History."** They seem to occur almost in spite of Graham's usual grammar, but as part of poetry's capacity for metaphor and for making everyday speech into poetry. The poem, which is 11 pages long and occupies its own section in the book, concerns in part the attempt of a young man, a student, to cut off his own face. His parents must be notified and their child committed to a mental institution. The poet reports the student's mother's remark.

> We called him the little twinkler
> says his mother at the commitment hearing,
>
> because he was the happiest.

That is as unadorned as anything we might find in the recent poetry of Louis Simpson. Later, Graham describes the young man,

> His wrists tied down to the sides of the bed.
> And the face on that shouldn't come off.
> The face on that mustn't come off.
> Scars all round it along the hairline under the chin.
> Later he had to take the whole body off
>
> to get the face.

And that is a moment of insight, conveyed metaphorically ("take the whole body off // to get the face"), as penetrating as anything in poetry or literature. Except for the repetition that charts her progress toward enlightenment, it is also an exceptional passage in this poet's recent poetry.

"The Phase After History" also includes some of the portentous and inappropriate language that overinflates many of the other poems. Trying to locate a bird trapped in her house, the poet asks, "Which America is it in? / Which America are we in here?" That hardly seems to be the question to ask. And yet woven into the poem are also allusions to Shakespeare's *Macbeth.* In reference to Stuart, the young man who tries to cut off his face, she writes: "Who would have imagined a face / could be so full of blood." And to encourage herself to go on with her anecdote, she says wittily, "Oh screw thy story to the / sticking place." But the clincher comes when she tries to put the anecdote of the trapped bird, the suicide, and *Macbeth* together: "Lady M. is the intermediary phase. / God help us." Somehow Lady Macbeth's attempt to wash the blood from her hands is another image, for Graham, of the deadliness of form, story, shape, what you will, all that destroys innocence or, as she says, "the free." But that's just a guess.

The last poem in the book, **"Soul Says,"** is subtitled "(Afterword)." A note says it is spoken by Prospero. Aside from the presumption of speaking as Prospero, Graham does appear to say something about all of this.

> (This is a form of matter of matter she sang)
>
> (Where the hurry is stopped) (and held) (but not
> extinguished) (no)
>
> (So listen, listen, this will soothe you) (if
> that is what you want)

Though Graham's poetry, at its best, is an imitation of stopped or held "hurry," the speed of the mind trying to find its place, it does not soothe me. But soothing is not what I want. I want a poetry in which the subject matter and the means of conveying it are equal to each other. When that occurs in Jorie Graham's poetry, the grammar of glamour turns invisible with its exactitude. It does so in *The End of Beauty,* but not in this new book.

Helen Vendler (review date 11 July 1994)

SOURCE: "Ascent into Limbo," in *The New Republic,* July 11, 1994, pp. 27-30.

[*In the following review of* Materialism, *Vendler discusses Graham's rhythm structure and the connection between structure and subject in these poems.*]

Jorie Graham, brought up in Italy by American parents and educated in French schools, has published five books of verse, beginning with *Hybrids of Plants and of Ghosts*

(1980) and continuing with *Erosion* (1983), *The End of Beauty* (1987), *Region of Unlikeness* (1991) and her newest book, *Materialism*. The poetry has always been strikingly ambitious in subject matter, genre-exploration and metrical invention. Like all new poets, Graham has mostly been discussed in terms of themes, which range, in her work, from notes on the reality of the self to the inflictions of history, from mutual corrections of identity in marriage to the nature of modern war.

For me, it is fundamentally Graham's rhythms that are irresistible. Here she is, riding with other passengers on the New York subway:

> 1982 on the downtown Express just out
>   of 72nd Street,
> having found a seat in what is like a dream,
>   the sideways-rocking
>   mixed-in with the forward
> lunge making me slightly
>   sleepy, watching the string of white
> faces lined up across from
>   me—
> the interlocking vertebrae
>   of the endless twisting creature's
>   spine—
>
>   watching it lob to absorb the shocks—
> watching it twist all one way to wreathe
>   the rudderless turns—
> watching the eyes in it narrow, widen, as
>   the tunnelling forwardness
>   cleaved to its waiting like flesh—
> widen and narrow—blinking—the whole
>   length of the train (I thought)
>   this dynamism of complex acceptance,
> sleepy, staring out. . . .

There is a startling ratio of unaccented syllables to accented ones in such lines; and though the lines are full of trisyllabic feet, Graham's metrical feet do not evoke the galloping effect of classical anapests and dactyls, mostly because she regularly interrupts trisyllabic feet with shorter ones. Sooner or later, too, she checks her rapid hurrying long lines with a brief one, like the one that closes the passage above.

This is one of Graham's characteristic rhythms—the cascading or tumbling one of urgent presentness followed by a lapse into pause or exhaustion. Another is an abrupt, strongly marked spondaic rhythm of disorientation, where in rapid succession the reader may see italics, an ellipsis, a dash, a question or a command:

> *First* this. *Then* this . . . Oh, glance—
>   gnawing the

> overgrowth,
> criss-crossing the open for broken spots,
>   leaks—
> what is there? what is
> the object? Look: see the face without eyes.
>   Don't be
> afraid—twitch, lisp, slur—. . . .

Of course, this rhythmic urgency on the page would be fruitless unless there were a corresponding urgency of subject.

Urgency of subject, while it can compel an inexperienced reader into a piece of verse, has no power over someone thirsty for a real poem—and the thirst for a poem is a parching one, as real as acute physical thirst or the longing for sleep. A compelling rhythm is the first sign of a tide of utterance rising to expression. The thirst will be slaked by anything—a dance rhythm, a sly rhythm, a peremptory rhythm, a hesitant rhythm—but only a rhythm will do. And in Graham it finds many such tidal motions.

Then the reader's thirst wants to know what the rhythm itself is athirst for, what it is bent on finding, where the drive of the poem is sending it. If the quest of the poem turns out to be trivial or shopworn or unintelligent, everything collapses and the rhythmic trance is broken. A rhythm makes the experienced reader's ears come alive: an orchestra is turning up, where will it lead? Does Graham earn her cascades of words, her Dickinsonian dashes, her questions, her italics, her present participles vibrating in the ether of the poem? And if so, how?

She stops, literally, at nothing. Her voice can even move, at a climactic moment, into the tone of biblical prophecy:

> Thou didst divide the sea by thy
>   strength: thou breakest
> the heads of the dragons
>   in the waters:
> thou driest up the mighty river:
>   the day is thine. . . .

By what authority does she assume this tone, invading literature in its most sacred quarters, raiding it, appropriating it for her poem? Such a posture must be earned, or it will become absurd.

The recent modest circumscription of lyric poetry to the personal voice has made most of our poets forget that the lyric can also be magisterially impersonal. (Within the "personal" I include the "class-personal," the voice that says "I, a woman" or "I, a black.") The personal lyric represents the socially marked self; but the impersonal lyric represents what used to be called the soul, but might better, in Graham, be called consciousness. Personal circumstance is acknowledged to underlie the awakening of consciousness, and Graham's poems often begin in individual autobiographical circumstance—but their restless search drives them to ranges of feeling and speech where it really does not matter whether one is male or female, young or old, black or white.

A Graham poem may recall, for instance, a point where a boy starts firing a gun in your car of the subway, where until this moment you have been noting only the serpentine rocking of the train:

> light and blood swirling—us down
>   here
> on our knees in
>   secret, living, living,
> *my portion of time,*
>   *my portion, full,*
> (can you stand it?)
>   (get down and hide). . . .
>
> all things can happen,
> wave after wave. . . .

This moment—in which everyone is huddled on the floor, afraid to die—is one illustration of Graham's metaphysical moment, an instant when human beings, no matter what their social identities may be, breathe with one breath, feel one collective horror, think one apocalyptic thought. Another such moment is the time of unendurable physical pain—as it is preserved, for example, in the bite-marks on a Civil War bullet seen in a Memphis museum. Yet another is the moment of transition from one kind of perception to another, as when someone who has been lost in listening to music suddenly, with the ending of the music, becomes aware of the light:

> When the music ended she noticed
>   the light.
> *The music has ended* it said all over the
>   things.

This is a transition that on one can have failed to experience—a sudden crossing from the attentiveness of one sense, to the attentiveness of another sense. After the construction of human possibility implicit in identity politics, it is like coming into light and air to move in Graham's enormous world of multifarious change, where import lies in any circumstance, and the import is general to all.

There are five poems in *Materialism* entitled **"Notes on the Reality of the Self"**—five separate poems scattered throughout the book, each bearing this title. Whitman speaks, in "There Was a Child Went Forth," of "the sense of what is real, the thought if after all it should prove unreal"; and with the vanishing of a theological sanction for reality (in the no-

tion of the participation of the material world in "the image and likeness of God"), the necessity to redefine "reality" has become a continuing and pervasive effort of modernity, around which Graham has structured her book.

The twentieth-century self inquired into by means of Graham's poems is not primarily defined by personal or social detail. Graham's task is to make the voice of metaphysical and moral consciousness as strong a source of language as the voice of the socially inflected self, which is rooted in nationality, ethnicity, social class, age and gender. The soul— the old lodging for the metaphysical and moral consciousness—was defined by its opposition to body, matter, dust. Graham proposes that the soul, on the contrary, must be materially definable, and she situates her poetry in the wake of the great philosophical crisis about the nature of reality provoked by the scientific advances of the Renaissance.

Since the poet, as Wordsworth said, must create the taste by which he is to be enjoyed, Graham creates the context in which her poems are to be understood by interspersing among them, in *Materialism,* various central texts from the history of the material understanding of nature, from Leonardo da Vinci on "Movement and Weight" ("Weight, force, a blow and impetus are the children of movement because they are born from it") to Sir Francis Bacon on scientific method ("We must bring men to particulars and their regular series and order, and they must for a while renounce their notions and begin to form an acquaintance with things") down to Wittgenstein ("Objects, the unalterable, and the subsistent are one and the same") and Benjamin ("The angel of history . . . sees one single catastrophe that keeps piling wreckage on wreckage and hurls it in front of his feet"). These are merely illustrative snippets from the pages—about thirty of them to 110 pages of poetry—that confront us with the intellectual axes of Graham's present imaginative world.

Prefacing all of this—as frontispiece and jacket—is a preliminary drawing for Mantegna's *Descent into Limbo,* showing Christ, seen strikingly from the back, his garments swirled about him by the infernal wind, as he descends to fetch from the depths of the earth all those who, since Adam's fall, have been waiting for salvation. By choosing as her emblem a Christ who is intent on his descent into the earth, his face turned toward death and the depths as he passes into matter, Graham declares that the spiritual can arrive at its realization only through the gate of materiality.

How is this to be accomplished in poetry? Graham suggests, quoting from "Sun-Down Poem" (later called "Crossing Brooklyn Ferry"), that Whitman is her predecessor in this venture:

> We *realize* the soul only by you, you faithful
>   solids and fluids;

Through you color, form, location,
sublimity, ideality;
Through you every proof, comparison, and
all the suggestions and determinations of
ourselves.

You have waited, you always wait, you
dumb, beautiful ministers! . . .
We fathom you not—we love you.

Whitman's rapturous immersion in "faithful solids and flu-
ids" is an aspect of American romanticism that cannot be
repeated. Graham's landscapes of material perfection are almost always broken in on by historical catastrophe. Yet catastrophe itself is only the social version of the biological
catastrophe that is organic dynamism, always pressing toward its end. The material soul is mortal; and when Graham
wholly inhabits a material phenomenon—say, the blooming
of an amaryllis—it is the ineluctable curve toward death that
the poem follows, even though it is called **"Opulence"**:

The self-brewing of the amaryllis rising
before me . . .
stepping out of the casing
outstretched,
high-heeled—
something from underneath coaxing the
packed buds up . . .
till the four knots grow loose in their
armor,
and the two dimensions of their perfect-fit
fill out and a third,
shadow, seeps in . . .
the four of them craning this way then that
according to
the time
of day, the drying wrinkled skins of the
casing
now folded-down beneath, formulaic,
the light wide-awake around it—or is it the
eye—
yes yes yes yes says the mechanism of the
underneath tick tock—
and no footprints to or from the place—
no footprints to or from—

Since nothingness both precedes and follows being, and there
is no risen Jesus to leave footprints behind as he walks away
from the sepulcher, the soul, defining itself from what it sees
of the various beings "outside" it, learns the lesson, from the
amaryllis, of its own essence, its perishable nature, as the
very "tick tock" of "the mechanism of the underneath"—
"evolutionary progress itself"—impersonally extinguishes
what it has evolved.

Graham's **"Notes on the Reality of the Self"** confront not
only the transience of the materially constituted metaphysical self, but also its radical incompleteness. Just as the
bushes in her backward bending under the force of the
wind—utterly responsive to its force—are wholly unresponsive to a nearby force—the sound (strong, urgent, metallic)
of a brass band practicing nearby—so human consciousness
can respond to, and draw its own sense of itself from, only
a limited range of phenomenological stimuli available to it.
Here are Graham's backyard bushes, deaf to the band-sound
that deluges them:

For there is not a sound the bushes
will take
from the multitude beyond them, in the
field, uniformed—
(all left now on one heel) (right) (all fifty
trumpets up
to the sun)—not a molecule of sound
from the tactics of this glistening beast,
forelimbs of silver (trombones, french
horns)
(anointed by the day itself) expanding,
retracting,
bits of red from the surrounding foliage
deep
in all the fulgid
instruments—orient—ablaze where the
sound is released—
trumpeting, unfolding—
screeching, rolling, patterning,
measuring—
scintillant beast the bushes do not know
exists
as the wind beats them, beats in them, beats
round them,
them in a wind that does not really even
now
exist,
in which these knobby reddish limbs that
do not sway
by so much as an inch
its arctic course
themselves now sway—

In this, the most brilliant of the **"Notes,"** with its untrammeled natural energies of light and wind, and its equally untrammeled human energies of band music, all focused on the
bending bushes unconscious of the band, Graham adopts a
voice of such piercing responsiveness that one wants to call
it "subjectivity" and a voice of such pellucid reportage that
one wants to call it "objectivity." It is this interpenetration
of spirit and matter, so that each is known only by the con-
tour it gives the other, that Graham means by both "materialism" and "subjectivity." And Graham's emblematic wind

of fate and anthropomorphized swaying bushes are such highly conventional emblems that they do not compromise the impersonal identity of the narrator.

Perceptual spirit, even fated spirit, Graham tacitly argues, can find itself indistinguishable from matter, must construct itself out of the forces and fortunes of matter, can find its predicate only in the predicaments of matter. Not that this is an easy thing to bring about convincingly in poetry—but Graham makes it happen, with her passionate conviction that it must be done.

Perceptual spirit, fated spirit: that, indeed, can be shown finding itself in matter. Ethical spirit, however, is another story. If we realized ourselves, as Whitman thought, in those "dumb, beautiful ministers," silent phenomena, can they be the means through which we "realize" ourselves as moral agents? In moral cognition about the self, yes, insofar as it is a fundamental moral act to admit circumstance rather than to deny it—and this is the grounding moral act of art, to see, as Stevens said, "nothing that is not there and the nothing that is." Several of Graham's poems concern this fundamental accuracy of moral observation, in which evaluation keeps shifting because life does. In the first of the self's **"Notes,"** a thawing spring river, at first swollen, turbid, choked with leaves ("all content no meaning"), brings the question,

> Is there a new way of looking—
> valences and little hooks—inevitabilities,
>   proba-
> bilities? It flaps and slaps. Is this body the
>   one
> I know as me?

The giant body of the river gradually becomes invested as an adequate locus for the self as it rearranges the meaningless leafy flotsam of the past year into new, released motion:

> thawing then growing soggy then
> the filaments where leaf-matter accrued
>   round a
> pattern, a law, slipping off, precariously, bit
>   by bit,
> and flicks, and swiftnesses suddenly more
>   water than not.

Graham looks so scrupulously at the earth that the scrim between her will and the river's will vanishes and she sees the dissolution of her own old patterns enact itself in the river's freed throat. That is a practice of inner cognitive morality.

Social morality, on the other hand, is carried in Graham's poetry by narrative, with extended reference in ***Materialism*** to incidents from the Holocaust, colonial exploration, the Russian Revolution, novelistic practice (*Madame Bovary*),

Tiananmen Square and local American life (the gun-wielding boy in the subway car). The poet is sometimes an attender to social history, sometimes a participant in it. Though the encapsulated short narrative has often served Graham well, I found some of the historical incidents here, notably the Holocaust narrative forming nine of the seventeen sections of **"Annunciation with a Bullet in It,"** too long for the proportions of the lyric. And some of Graham's attempts at collage (**"The Break of Day,"** for instance) seem strained. There is a limit, after all, to how many disparate things can be made to hang together: and a poem bringing into mutual relation Plato and *The Golden Bough* and Heidegger and Marx and *Madame Bovary* seems to me in danger of incoherence. Yet such a poem can contain pieces of dazzling writing. Here is the poet speaking as Adam, out of whose rib God will tear Eve (created matter):

> I feel the skin tighten like Saran Wrap now,
>   the god finishing up
>
> the form—privacies are added—the starry
>   dizziness
>   rammed into the eyepits—deep in—
>
> the symmetry like a forked shriek
>   effected—two and then
>   two—His thumbs
> smoothing it out—
> and Balance struck through the top of
>   me—down through—
> steel rod—slicing the parts of the visible
>   forever from—
>
> severing the front from that parched earth
>   behind me now—
> cramping me in,
> the sill of nothing to nothing,
> this propane forwardness now swelling
>   up, starched—a cancellation but
>   of what I
>
> can't say—and mended (*whoosh*)
> muddled. . . .

Keats wrote that "The Imagination may be compared to Adam's dream—he awoke and found it truth." In the gap between Keats's idealized dream and waking, on the one hand, and Graham's tortured and violent separation of self from being, on the other, we can see the gap between a naturalized supernaturalism and a late, disbelieving materialism.

"We are *in a drama,*" says Graham, and her rendition of the dramatic force of aesthetic attention and choice ("What am I / supposed // to take, what?") restores to poetry, if in a different vein, the impassioned idealism of Shelley. The combat against nostalgia in Graham is especially fierce in this new volume. As she encounters, on her way through life, the various clichés of our moment—abortion-clinic protests, drug addicts, television, the commemoration of 1492—she makes of them something that claws out toward a larger order, a more comprehensive view, while maintaining the coursing emotions proper to poetry and missing from conventional metaphysics.

Perhaps the most congenial single philosopher for her verse is Wittgenstein, in the passage she quotes from the *Tractatus:*

> 2.026 There must be objects, if the world is to have an unalterable form.
>
> 2.027 Objects, the unalterable, and the subsistent are one and the same.
>
> 2.0271 Objects are what is unalterable and subsistent; their configuration is what is changing and unstable.
>
> 2.0272 The configuration of objects producers states of affairs.
>
> 2.03 In a state of affairs objects it into one another like the links of a chain. . .
>
> 2.04 The totality of existing states of affairs is the world.

What would a poetry be that took as its theory these passages? It is the poetry that Graham has invented in *Materialism*—philosophically stern in spite of its verbal opulence, morally severe in spire of its allusive spangles. It is not what has generally been thought of as "women's poetry." Graham's fierce sense of the philosophic universal may help remind American poets that there is a dimension of the lyric that goes beyond the merely personal, the merely social. It is a dimension we find in Emily Brontë and in Emily Dickinson—austere, renunciatory, far-seeing, but also detailed, intimate, saturated with phenomena.

Graham relies on a prolonged moment of phenomenological observation to spin out her poems; and she has become perhaps a prisoner of the present participle, hovering over the ground of perception. Through the present participle she hopes to hold at bay both the temptations of the historical past, threatening lyric with narrative, and the abyss of the unknown future, threatening lyric with closure. In keeping with this desire to prolong the lyric moment, Graham was originally attracted to paintings as vehicles of suspended attention. Now, she has substituted the senses as more primary vehicles, bending over nature as the mind once bent over art. In each case her aim has been to suspend closure while

appearing to hurry toward it. What will happen to her poetry when death is taken, not as an inevitable end to be held off as long as possible, but as the condition of all existence?

Peter Sacks (review date 5 May 1996)

SOURCE: "What's Happening?," in *New York Times Book Review,* May 5, 1996, p. 16.

[*In the following review of* The Dream of the Unified Field, *Sacks praises Graham as a writer who is pushing poetry in new directions.*]

"Man has already begun to overwhelm the entire earth and its atmosphere, to arrogate to himself in forms of energy the concealed powers of nature, and to submit future history to the planning and ordering of a world government. This same defiant man is utterly at a loss simply to say what is; to say what this is—that a thing is." By the time Heidegger wrote those words, soon after the first use of nuclear weapons, he had turned his attention increasingly to poets, for it was they, he felt, who might not only reveal what is but do so with the sentient charge and the clarifying beauty needed to turn mankind from ignorant predators to thoughtful custodians of one shared life.

Half a century later, Jorie Graham is one of the contemporary writers most open to this call for revelatory poetic thinking. Her poems are philosophically and historically alert, and their acts of thought arise with almost instinctual urgency from an astonished responsiveness that in itself becomes part of what she names "the vivid performance of the present." Chosen from five volumes, *The Dream of the Unified Field: Selected Poems 1974-1994*—which won a Pulitzer Prize this year—allows followers of her rapid and ever-startling development to review her achievement to date.

Take the first poem as a way in. It opened her first book, *Hybrids of Plants and of Ghosts,* and its title, **"The Way Things Work,"** signals the young writer's intent not simply to address "things" themselves—one of her great gifts—but to give an account of reality-as-process, perceived with some degree of generality. Like many of her early poems, this one tracks down the page in brief lines, resembling a pathway. Its first words lead on directly from the title:

> is by admitting
> or opening away.
> This is the simplest form
> of current: Blue
> moving through blue;
> blue through purple;
> the objects of desire

opening upon themselves
without us;
the objects of faith.

Fluid yet tautly reined, measuring and releasing their own initiatory energy, these phrases navigate by minute distinctions of wavelength and line length. They also pulse far ahead, the focus on current revealing an interest not in fixities but in the forces that will make up Ms. Graham's "dream of the unified field" (her version, perhaps, of the project of theoretical physics to seek a single theory to account for all the forces of universal nature). And the inclusive flow of mind swiftly reaches other enduring themes—the limits of subjectivity in relation to "objects of desire," and the question of faith:

The way things work
is that we finally believe
they are there,
common and able
to illustrate themselves.

To judge from the late poem **"Steering Wheel"** ("though there are, there really are, / things in the world, you must believe me"), the poet's commission does not become easier. And if we check the end of **"The Way Things Work,"** we may begin to see why: "I believe / forever in the hooks. / The way things work / is that eventually / something catches." What are the hooks? How do they catch? Ms. Graham's career is in part a self-renewing attempt to answer such questions while giving eloquent voice to her ethical ambivalence about what the various modes of capture might involve.

Can words "catch" anything at all? If so, can they avoid coming between us and the world's work of self-illustration? Another early poem, **"The Age of Reason,"** asks, "Isn't the / honesty / of things where they / resist?" Sharing that resistant honesty, stressing the artificial relation between word and thing, Ms. Graham reaches with quickened sensitivity for poetry's supply of the associative, sonic and formal properties rustling beyond mere denotation. Never losing sight of the screens of representation, she also develops a genius for apprehending and scrutinizing human perceptions, reflections and desires, whose links to language are somewhat less arbitrary, since they are themselves partly shaped and made available to us by words ("we need to seize again / the whole language / in search of / better desires"). And she constantly reminds us of the resurgent "blizzard of instances" that enliven us all even as they exceed our mental grasp.

"There is a feeling the body gives the mind / of having missed something," Ms. Graham writes, and few poets match the precision with which she finds words for the sensory sub-

soil that is too often neglected by the intellect. Massed B-52 bombers

sound like a sickness of the inner ear,
where the heard foams up into the noise of
listening,
where the listening arrives without being extinguished.
The huge hum soaks up into the dusk.

Minutely observing the visible soil, she writes:

If I look carefully, there in my hand, if I
break it apart without
crumbling: husks, mossy beginnings and endings,
ruffled
airy loambits,
and the greasy silks of clay crushing the pinerot
in. . . .

Straining to register "how the invisible roils," she asks:

Is there a new way of looking—
valences and little hooks—inevitabilities, proba-
bilities? It flaps and slaps.

Scenting, tasting, feeling the touch even of time ("the spike-headed minutes pushing up round her, / up under the thighs, there at the elbows the hips"), Ms. Graham's poetry is among the most sensuously embodied and imaginative writing we have, its added power stemming from the fact that sensation in her work not only registers what is immediately present but also remains tensely and restlessly attuned to whatever may still emerge

A further distinctive and evolving feature of Ms. Graham's work is its stress on delay and between-ness. Poetic form itself, of course, shifts between acceleration and sudden braking, or breaking, between enlargement and arrest. **"The Geese"** suspends its wavering between the traveling lines of migratory birds and the retentive meshes of spider webs by discovering: "And somewhere in between / these geese forever entering and / these spiders turning back, / this astonishing delay, the everyday, takes place." Two books later, **"Noli Me Tangere"** begins:

You see the angels have come to sit on the delay
for a while,
they have come to harrow the fixities, the sharp
edges of this open
sepulcher,
they have brought their swiftnesses like musics
down
to fit them on the listening.

And a still later poem ends: "Is hisses the last light on the reddish berries, is is the much / blacker shadows of spring now that the leaves are / opening, now that they're taking up / place."

With the more aerated reach of these lines, whose roving, irregular lengths mark Ms. Graham's later work, poetry remains the space in which she can best attend to what might otherwise never be made manifest. A source of excitement, even suspense, as one reads through this book is the developing brilliance and volatility, wedded to further innovations (particularly her braidings of myth, anecdote, meta-narrative and commentary), with which she presents a more complex and frequently troubled sense of just what it is that takes place.

What happens, for example, when her wariness about the possible mismatch between word and world, or between selective acts of mind and "the fizzing around the diagram," grows to include a sense of humanity's violent colonizing of the earth? Or when authentic human curiosity (including that of the poet) is seen to slide over into the urge to dominate and possess? What happens when an intense openness to sensory experience, allied to a fierce regard for the liberty of individuals, confronts the fixed gaze of another's point of view (**"Self-Portrait as Apollo and Daphne"**) or suffers the affliction of another's sexual or political designs (**"From the New World"**)?

> **Ms. Graham's poetry is among the most sensuously embodied and imaginative writing we have, its added power stemming from the fact that sensation in her work not only registers what is immediately present but also remains tensely and restlessly attuned to whatever may still emerge.**
>
> *—Peter Sacks*

To watch Ms. Graham rise to the lure and challenge of such questions is to see her break through to her extraordinarily inventive later work. Poems from her third volume, *The End of Beauty,* introduce a cinematic freeze-frame technique to reimagine and reorient the paradigmatic stories of couples ranging from Eve and Adam to Penelope and Ulysses, Mary Magdalene and Jesus, mother and daughter. Magically, the events appear to unfold for the first time:

1

The gesture like a fruit torn from a limb, torn swiftly.

2

The whole bough bending then springing back as if from sudden sight.

3

The rip in the fabric where the action begins, the opening of the narrow passage.

These stories are chopped and stylized partly to create magnifying lenses of attention, partly to subvert all narrative simplifications and to rebel against the enforcements of plot and closure. Eve resists God's ordinance so that something unpredictable can occur; Eurydice eludes the familiar reifying gaze of Orpheus. There is both exhilaration and pathos in all these poems (several of which are oblique, triadic self-portraits). With a strange, almost telepathically compassionate candor, the poet reveals people who wish to be seen and loved—but without delimitation, almost without features, as if each merited the unrepresentable ineffability otherwise reserved for God.

A brief review cannot trace the ramifications of event, memory, speculation, history, myth and allusion that make up the later poems. **"The Phase After History,"** a poem from Ms. Graham's fourth and darkest book, *Region of Unlikeness,* interweaves a description of birds trapped in the house of the writer (she would like to "get the house out of their way") with fragments from *Macbeth,* as well as with an account of a student who tries to cut off his face and who eventually kills himself. The effect on the reader is a terrifying experience of crisis and of the tragically engaged compulsions for release, for renewal or for the capacity to face and survive one's own implication in stories of entrapment and unredeemable pain. In **"Picnic,"** what is flickers through a child's memory of adult sexual deceit, a memory bound to that of a frightening makeup session in which the mother refigures the child's face in the mirror—leaving the speaker in a temporally as well as spatially fractured state of between-ness. Can any surface be trusted? What is a face? Is the very fixing of features the object of a lie? Would a fuller regard for the self and the other resist delineation altogether? No wonder the speaker hovers on the very threshold of predication: "'is is is is' I thought."

However vertiginous, that last phrase may be Ms. Graham's ontological counterpoint to Sylvia Plath's psychological "ich, ich, ich, ich / I could hardly speak." It marks her distance from Plath's "barb wire snare" of confessionalism (or from the fashionable compounds of identity-based ideologies). And it points to the liberating embrace of her fifth book, *Materialism.* After the tragic cast of *Region of Unlikeness,* we could call this embrace comedic. Or taking a cue from the afterwords to her preceding collection, which she borrows from Prospero ("the wave drowning me in laughter"), we could say that *Materialism* has the character of late romance. Radiant and manifold, reveling both in language and in the bristling world within and around them, these poems celebrate the thawing romance between "the river of my attention" and that current of reality that has flowed through Ms. Graham's work from the beginning: "I say iridescent and I look down. / The leaves very still as they are carried."

Jonathan Holden (review date Winter 1997)

SOURCE: Review of Materialism, in *Prairie Schooner,* Vol. 71, No. 4, Winter, 1997, pp. 170-72.

[In the excerpt below, Holden praises Graham's use of intellectualism and tone in Materialism.]

Jorie Graham, in *Materialism,* runs the same risks as [Patricia] Goedicke—higher risks because her poetry is pronounced from an Olympian height. Graham is the Henry James of our poets, dramatizing time and again how language and ultra-sophisticated European civilization both tantalize and obscure what Stevens refers to in the final line of "The Man On the Dump" as "the truth: The the." Paradigmatic of a Graham poem would be, from the earlier book *Erosion,* "Two Paintings by Gustav Klimt," a poem in which "Buchenwald" (birchwood) becomes a name for how the most civilized people could have turned out to be, in the Holocaust, the least. In books that follow, *Land of Unlikeness* and *The End of Beauty,* Graham becomes increasingly philosophical, worrying the various epistemological issues that have been the concern of literary theorists: what is a text, what is an author, and (picking up on Heidegger) on what ground do they exist? In both learning and intellect, Graham is probably the equal of T.S. Eliot. Indeed, the very name of Graham's collection *Materialism* echoes *The Waste Land. Materialism* is Graham's homage to *The Waste Land* and, like that poem, explicitly prophetic. Like the Eliot poem, Graham's book teems not just with quotes but with long "adaptations" from such famous writers as Sir Francis Bacon (*Novum Organum*), Wittgenstein (the *Tractatus*), Dante (Canto XI of the *Inferno*) Walter Benjamin, Plato (*Phaedo*), Brecht ("A Short Organum of the Theatre"), Benjamin Whorf (*Language, Thought, and Reality*), Audubon (*Missouri River Journals*), and others. (The Audubon quote runs to five pages.) Graham's strategy recalls Eliot's famous dictum, "Bad poets borrow, good poets steal," and the way in which Eliot stuffed *The Waste Land* with quotations. The quotations are all from the most crucial parts of the texts quoted. They demonstrate for me that of all our poets, Graham has not only the most eclectic but the *best* intellectual taste. There is a danger, though. Some of the quotations may be *too* interesting.

They compete with Graham's poetry, not always to her advantage.

Materialism evinces structure. It begins, in **"Notes On the Reality of the Self,"** with a river (probably Heraclitian) and returns to that river at the end. **"Notes"** is ominous and beautiful: when Graham allows herself to be imagistic and descriptive (which is seldom), nobody can exceed her:

> Watching the river, each handful of it closing over
> 　the next,
> brown and swollen. Oaklimbs,
> gnawed at by waterfilm, lifted, relifted, lapped-at
> 　all day in
> this dance of non-discovery, All things are
> possible. Last year's leaves, coming unstuck from
> 　shore,
> rippling suddenly again with the illusion,
> and carried, twirling, shiny again and fat,
> towards the quick throes of another tentative
> conclusion, . . . Is this body the one
> I know as me?. . . .

The issues Graham is dealing with are the same as Goedicke's, but Graham's tone is uniformly grave and, at certain points, melodramatic. "Melodrama," etymologically, is "drama" with the rhetoric of music (*melos*) added to augment the effect of the drama. The connotations of the word "melodramatic" are slightly invidious, suggesting that which is adventitious: emotional excess. In *Materialism,* melodrama, when it is present, happens at two levels. The first—the corny kind—when it occurs happens in Graham's diction. The second—the inventive kind—happens at the level of structure. Graham's poem **"The Dream of the Unified Field"** is sometimes melodramatic in diction. The event that starts the poem, "bringing you the leotard / you forgot to include in your overnight bag," leads to excess:

> Starting home I heard—bothering, lifting, then
> 　　　　　　bothering again—
> the huge flock of starlings massed over our
> 　　　　　　neighborhood
> these days; heard them lift and
> swim overhead through the falling snow
> as though the austerity of a true, cold thing, a
> verity,
> the black bits of their thousands of bodies
> swarming
> 　　　　　　then settling

The poem is filled with such moments, in which everything in a scene is dwelt upon as if in slow motion, with a violin accompaniment: the kind of quotidian observation that Emily Dickinson would have dispatched with a firecracker has been bloated into something akin to "The 1812 Overture."

At the structural level, however, Graham's "melodrama" is thrilling. The "music" added to the "drama" consists of the long quotations, and of the juxtapositions between verse and prose quotation, such as the decision to follow the poem **"Concerning the Right to Life"** with Graham's adaptation "from Sir Francis Bacon's NOVUM ORGANUM" or her placement of a passage "from Jonathan Edwards DOC-TRINE OF ORIGINAL SIN" between "from Walt Whitman's CROSSING BROOKLYN FERRY" and **"The Break of Day,"** are telling.

In the penultimate poem, **"Existence and Presence,"** we are reminded of the underlying epistemological problematic of the book—wherein is the ground of being and of the self?

> And how shall this soliloquy reverberate
> over the hillside? Who shall be
> the singleness over the yawning speckled lam-
> bency?
> I think I feel my thinking-self and how it
> stands—its condensation, its voice-track . . .
> An alphabet flew over, made liquid syntax for a
> while,
> diving and rising, forking, a caprice of clear
> meanings,
>   right pauses . . .

The "condensation" of "my thinking-self" is the poem we are reading. "I think I feel" is Cartesian. All Graham can be sure of is Mind. But the world, on whatever ground it stands, she finds to be fascinating, even lovely at times. At the conclusion of *Materialism,* we are returned to the river:

> It has a hole in it. Not only where I
>   concentrate.
> The river still ribboning, twisting up,
>   into its re-
> arrangements, chill enlightenments, tight-knotted
>   quickenings
> and loosenings—whispered messages dissolving
>   messengers—
> . . .
> and the river of my attention laying itself down—
>   bending,
> reassembling—

Perhaps the Mind, through language, through poetry, can penetrate the world. *Materialism* is a daring and splendid book.

James Longenbach (review date 21 July 1997)

SOURCE: "Identity, Vision, Style," in *The Nation,* Vol. 265, No. 3, June 21, 1997, pp. 40-2.

[In the review below, Longenbach praises Graham's writing in The Errancy *as mature and argues that it is her best work to date.]*

Jorie Graham stands among a small group of poets (Dickinson, Hopkins, Moore) whose styles are so personal that the poems seem to have no author at all: They exist as self-made things. Each of her books has interrogated the one preceding it, and *The Errancy* feels like a culmination. It is her most challenging, most rewarding book. Graham has not simply forged a style; she is exploring the very notion of what it means for a poet to have a style—an exterior mark of an inner vision.

> **Jorie Graham stands among a small group of poets (Dickinson, Hopkins, Moore) whose styles are so personal that the poems seem to have no author at all: They exist as self-made things.**
> **—James Longenbach**

"It has a fine inner lining but it is / as an exterior that you see it—a grace." Graham makes this remark about the coat in which Pascal was buried: A note containing his unrevealed proof of the existence of God was sewn into its sleeve. The remark also describes Graham's notion of the self: Whatever we know about it we know as purely external sensation. In **"Easter Morning Aubade"** a woman attempts to "clench the first dawnlight *inside her skull*," but the world refuses to stand still. The woman looks past sleeping soldiers to a boy dropping a pebble into a river; the stone enters the water just as the scene enters the woman's mind, but the stone is immediately lost. No fathomable depth exists beneath the surface.

> . . . as he stares I can see
> that the place of disappearance has
>   disappeared,
> it cannot be recovered, his eyes darting
>   over the moving waters,
> and how a life cannot be lived therefore,
>   as there is no place,
> *in which the possibility of shapeliness*
>   *begins to rave,*
> and the soldiers awakening, of course, to
>   the blazing *not-there,*
> and the 30,000 mph of the sun's going,
> rubbing its disappearance now all over
>   this,
> and the hand going back into the dirt at
>   one's feet, fingers feeling around
> for another perfect stone, wanting to see
>   it once again, that opening.

These lines are in part a response to Piero della Francesca's *Resurrection:* The soldiers awake to find that Jesus's body has disappeared just as the stone disappears beneath water, just as the place of disappearance disappears before it can be preserved in the mind. Graham suggests that revelation cannot happen only once; we need the continuing experience of an exterior world if we are to imagine an interior. Yet the precise nature of that space—the space within the skull, beneath the river, beyond the body—remains obscure to us. The result is a poetry of what Graham calls "intractable thereness," a poetry both vividly sensuous and enticingly elusive. "No back-of-the-mind allowed," she says in **"Little Requiem,"** insisting that the surface of things is all we know. In **"The Guardian Angel of Self-Knowledge,"** an angel looks down at people scraping away their surface characteristics in order to reveal their inner truth. This supposed act of self-revelation is in fact an act of self-annihilation: "who will they be when they get to the bottom of it? . . . Who will they resemble when they're done with resemblance?"

Graham's own integrity is on the surface: The difficulty of *The Errancy* consequently feels earned, essential to the texture of its language. The poems rush irresistibly forward, and like sparrows unspooling above the parking lot in **"Untitled Two,"** they "quote each other endlessly." Metaphors used to describe Pascal's coat ("its raveling hem") reappear in other poems to characterize a river or a shadow; metaphors of "folding" or "pleating," inspired by the philosopher Gilles Deleuze, appear in various contexts to describe the coat, the body or the relationship of surface and depth. In addition, two sequences of linked poems are spread throughout the book: One consists of aubades, or poems addressing dawn, the other of poems spoken by angels. While these repetitions do not give *The Errancy* anything like a systematic wholeness, they allow us to participate in the difficult process of making and remaking sense.

As the title of her Pulitzer Prize winning *The Dream of the Unified Field* suggests, Graham has always been interested in this process. But throughout much of her earlier work, she was suspicious of ordering devices—story, closure and plot; in the opening poem in *The End of Beauty,* for instance, Eve disrupts the divine "plot" and finds that she likes "that error, a feeling of being capable *because* an error." Throughout *The Errancy,* in contrast, Graham depends upon a more complex and more precarious sense of error. "The point is not that there would be no error if there were no truth," remarks Jacques Lacan, meditating on the notion that all human knowledge begins with errancy—with the infant's misrecognition of its reflection as another person: "Error is the usual manifestation of truth itself." Similarly, Graham's poems now suggest that there is no human experience outside of discursive structures like plot and closure; we are capable of knowing ourselves only because we resemble other selves. Errancy is no longer the discovery of world elsewhere, but rather our very state of being.

Graham emphasizes this point in several ways. In **"The Guardian Angel of Point-of-View,"** she says that "truth" simply is "the path without the crumbs"—a wandering with no hope of return. In many poems, words like "storyline" or "programming" are used to describe natural processes, suggesting that it is not possible to break through the structures of human understanding. These poems are not less formally disruptive than Graham's earlier work; but now that freedom may be found within (rather than beyond) discursive structures, the disruptiveness feels like something we want to live with rather than move past. In **"Le Manteau de Pascal"**—one of several long poems—Graham presents Réne Magritte's painting of the coat as an image of formal transgression. Because the coat is "ripped," "distracted," open to "abandonment," willing to be "disturbed," one might think that it merely disrupts or occludes truth; in fact, it is precisely because the coat is ripped that we are able to see the "starpocked" sky behind it.

> The sky shivers through the coat because
>   of the rips in it.
>
> The rips in the sky ripen through the rips
>   in the coat.
>
> There is no quarrel.

The Errancy is marked by Graham's interest in philosophy and literary theory, but the poems have none of the arid consistency one might associate with these modes of writing. Graham's older notion of error as a deviation from truth occasionally resurfaces, and such inconsistencies are crucial to her dramatization of the errant processes of thought itself. While she insists that there can be "no back-of-the-mind," she nonetheless honors our insatiable need to imagine a world beneath the surface. In **"Emergency,"** the most harrowing and beautiful poem in the book, Graham walks beside a river at night, imagining a world beneath the black surface, imagining that she could join that world. The river talks back:

> why are you still here the house of cards
>   *will fall it slushes*
> struggle, get up and be, climb back onto
>   *the walkway the city has provided,*
> the little path, good-bye, catch-up with
>   *the story, where you left off,*
> *that is the only subject of your poem,*
> *you have no other form but story,*
> and various assortments of cause and
>   *effect—publicity, existence,*
> *how to travel faster at night—*

go—repeat where was I? where was I?—
drifting thoughtfully towards common
  knowledge,
the war is over, the stars are in me. . .

If part of Graham longs for transcendence—for a world of lush interiority, a world beyond discursive structures—the river resists her desires, sending her back to the city's world of story and plot.

Unlike her last entirely new book of poems, *Materialism,* which begins and ends with poems set beside the river, *The Errancy* begins and ends with poems set within the city: It is only here, Graham insists, that we might find "*liberty* spooring in the evening air." Still, by imagining an inner consciousness for the river in **"Emergency,"** Graham has already violated the river's wisdom. And as **"Emergency"** unfolds, the city becomes a place where the "war" is far from over: A woman strikes her baby and waits for it to breathe, her own identity dissipated by the horror of what she's done. "Let us pray," intones Graham. "Let us pray to be a torpid river, Lord." Having forced herself not to indulge in fantasies of interiority or escape, Graham nonetheless reaches for those fantasies—the proof of God's existence hidden in the fold of Pascal's coat.

Recently, Graham remarked that poets seem to be "yearning for permission to break past their own remarkably sophisticated understanding of the ideological premises of their enterprise." Graham does exactly that: These poems offer sophisticated meditations on identity, language and culture, but the poems are deeply moving because they turn against their own best discoveries, refusing to settle for the consolation of what is merely right. *The Errancy* provides all the satisfactions we expect from poetry—aural beauty, emotional weight—along with an intellectual rigor we don't expect. No one but Jorie Graham could have written it.

FURTHER READING

Criticism

Bedient, Calvin. "Postlyrically Yours." *The Threepenny Review* XV, No. 2 (Summer 1994): 18-20.
  Compares Graham's poetry to that of Jane Miller and Carolyn Forché.

D'Evelyn, Thomas. "Two Contemporary Poets." *The Christian Science Monitor* (12 August 1987): 17.
  Compares the theoretical abstract poetry of Graham's *The End of Beauty* with the traditional, concrete poetry of Elizabeth Jennings.

Isaacson, Lisa. "Ad Interim: 2000—A Delayed Reading Lightly Attended." *Denver Quarterly* 28, No. 4 (Spring 1994): 136-41.
  Considers *Materialism* in relation to Graham's earlier collections.

Redmond, John. "Accidents of Priority." *London Review of Books* 18, No. 16 (22 August 1996): 25-6.
  Compares Graham's *The Dream of the Unified Field* to John Ashbery's writing.

Additional coverage of Graham's life and career is contained in the following sources published by Gale: *Contemporary Authors,* Vol. 111; *Contemporary Authors New Revision Series,* Vol. 63; and *Dictionary of Literary Biography,* Vol. 120.

Philip Levine
1928-

American poet.

The following entry presents an overview of Levine's career through 1997. For further information on his life and works, see *CLC*, Volumes 2, 4, 5, 9, 14, and 33.

INTRODUCTION

Philip Levine has published poetry collections regularly since *On the Edge* was published in 1961. One of the most respected contemporary American poets, he has received numerous grants and prizes and was awarded a Pulitzer Prize for *The Simple Truth* (1994) in 1995. His primary poetic device is that of narration. Employing the idioms and cadences of normal speech, Levine seeks to write about the ordinary people and events of everyday life. Often called a working-class poet, he writes with particular intensity of the socially and economically deprived, and champions those who have little voice in the social hierarchy. One of the most dominant features of his poetry is the pervasive feeling of human dignity and justice. Though a keen and often bitter observer of class and economic wrongs and inequities, his working-class subjects are generally brave, spirited, and willful. Suffused with the dream of freedom, they do not quit. Richard Hugo has observed that Levine's themes revolve around what is most fundamental to humanity and that his poetry heightens compassion and understanding in readers.

Biographical Information

Levine was born in Detroit, Michigan, in January, 1928, the child of Russian-Jewish emigrants. His father died when he was young, and Levine was reared in an impoverished household. He attended Wayne State University from which he graduated with a B.A. and an M.A., in 1950 and in 1954 respectively. During the early 1950s Levine also worked at a number of factory jobs, an experience that strengthened his interest in working-class issues. Many of these issues figure prominently in his poetry. In 1954 he married Frances Artley, a marriage that produced three sons, Mark, John, and Theodore. Having refused to serve in the Korean War, Levine attended the University of Iowa where John Berryman and Robert Lowell were among his teachers. Levine graduated with a M.F.A. in 1957. He then spent time at Stanford University on a fellowship where he came into contact with Yvor Winters. In 1958 Levine became a professor at California State University, Fresno. He has also taught and lectured at numerous universities both at home and abroad. He has lived for extended periods in Spain, a

country that has influenced some of his political and social beliefs as well as provided themes for a number of poems. In particular, he has identified very strongly with the anti-fascist and anarchist factions in the Spanish Civil War. Levine has received grants from such agencies as the Guggenheim Foundation, the National Endowment for the Arts, and the National Institute of Arts and Letters. Among the honors he has received are the American Book Award, the National Book Critics Circle Award, the National Book Award for Poetry, and the Pulitzer Prize.

Major Works

The major themes of Levine's poems, from his first collection *On the Edge* through his subsequent volumes, have remained largely unchanged. Much of his poetry reveals his frustration and anger with the manifold problems of contemporary society. Themes of defiance, indignation, and anger are especially frequent in such early collections as *Not This Pig* (1968) and *They Feed They Lion* (1972). He is particularly concerned with social, political, and ethnic topics. Also called an "urban" poet, Levine sets many of his poems in the working-class environment of such cities as Detroit and Fresno, and he writes feelingly of the problems and abuses of American society and of the strong spirit of American urban dwellers. His subjects are invariably ordinary working folk. He writes, in the words of David St. John, "of the universal struggle of individuals ignored and unheard by their societies." Levine identifies with those in dead-end jobs and was influenced by the menial, mainly industrial jobs at which he worked during the early fifties in Detroit. Richard Chess sees Levine's sympathy for the unsung workers and the victims of a materialistic and commercial world as stemming in part from experiences growing up as a Jew in Detroit. However, though there are clearly many autobiographical elements in Levine's poetry, it is also important to recognize that he enjoys a consummate ability to employ, as Carol Frost puts it, "artistic reality." Levine is praised for his strength at imagining and empathizing "with invented characters to the point that readers assume they are acquaintances or relatives." Yet much of his work is realistic, and his poems are liberally sprinkled with dates, times, people's and places' names. While this is natural in poems dealing with such specific historical topics as Hiroshima, the Holocaust and the Spanish Civil War, he is also careful to supply many of his other poems with realistic detail. The Spanish people, history, and countryside are also frequent themes in his poetry. Particularly prominent is his strong regard for the anti-Franco faction in the Spanish Civil War, which reflects his resolute leftist leanings. For example, the 1930s Spanish anarchist movement is well treated in his 1976 collection *The Names of the Lost*. Levine's later collections of poetry continue to chronicle the lives of ordinary working class citizens, and to champion the cause of the underprivileged and downtrodden.

Critical Reception

Levine is a prolific writer who has published regularly since 1961. The quality of this large oeuvre has been deemed somewhat inconsistent. Some have seen his distinctly proletarian image as responsible for producing calculated, studied poetry. Nevertheless, critical assessment of his poetry over the decades has been overwhelmingly positive. In 1977 Richard Hugo asserted that Levine "is deservedly destined to be one of the most celebrated poets of the time," and many critics agree that Levine has emerged as one of America's preeminent poets. Fred Marchant wrote that Levine has produced "a rich and important body of work." David St. John considered that Levine's early work "remains some of the most highly-crafted and imaginatively powerful poetry of the time." Critics have noted a mellowing of Levine's anger in his later poems. Though remaining a keen chronicler of the wrongs inflicted on society's marginalized, his poetry becomes more tender and optimistic. While rage and sadness are still evident, there is also hope and celebration. Edward Hirsch has observed, "What starts as anger slowly deepens

into grief and finally rises into joy." A much greater acceptance of what cannot be changed is evidenced in Levine's later poems. Hirsch has compared Levine's poetry to that of William Carlos Williams, Hart Crane, and Theodore Roethke.

PRINCIPAL WORKS

On the Edge (poems) 1961
Silent in America: Vivas for Those Who Failed (poems) 1965
Not This Pig (poems) 1968
5 Detroits (poems) 1970
Thistles (poems) 1970
Pili's Wall (poems) 1971
Red Dust (poems) 1971
They Feed They Lion (poems) 1972
1933 (poems) 1974
The Names of the Lost (poems) 1976
On the Edge & Over (poems) 1976
Ashes: Poems New and Old (poems) 1979
Don't Ask (collection of interviews with Levine) 1979
7 Years from Somewhere (poems) 1979
One for the Rose (poems) 1981
Selected Poems (poems) 1984
Sweet Will (poems) 1985
A Walk with Tom Jefferson (poems) 1988
New Selected Poems (poems) 1991
What Work Is (poems) 1991
The Bread of Time: Toward an Autobiography (essays) 1994
The Simple Truth (poems) 1994
Unselected Poems (poems) 1997

CRITICISM

Ricard Hugo (review date May-June 1977)

SOURCE: "Philip Levine: Naming the Lost," in *American Poetry Review*, May-June, 1977, pp. 27-8.

[*In the following review, Hugo lauds Levine's poetry collection,* The Names of the Lost, *stressing in particular the poems' emotional depth.*]

Philip Levine knows a few things so well that he cannot forget them when he writes a poem, no matter what compositional problems might arise. He seldom tells us anything we don't already know but what he tells us is basic to the maintenance of our humanity, and fundamental to perpetuating our capacity for compassion. If I were dictator of the world long enough to pass a few laws, two of those laws would be: (1) at least once a year, everyone must view the films taken at Hiroshima immediately after the bombing; (2) at least once every six months, everyone must read a book of Philip Levine's poems aloud. That wouldn't necessarily make us better people, but it might make us hope we won't get any worse, and want to be the best we can be. . . .

Here are a few things Levine knows well: to the heart, in time relationships transcend values (**"On the Birth of Good and Evil During the Long Winter of '28."** Levine's world is at least as old as religion. The professional is outlawed. It is the amateur who discovers "7000 miles from home" that she who "bruised his wakings" can, on this cold day after her death, be forgiven for the wool cap she knitted long ago, whose very color once seemed despicable.

We did not return love when it was needed. When we realize that failure it is too late and we must live with the resultant regret. We did not accept the essential relationships that provided our sense of self. When we understand that, it is too late and self-acceptance remains painfully difficult (**"The Secret of Their Voices"**).

People hurt each other in lasting ways. The ways we help each other seem trivial and transitory in contrast. Time and memory and accumulated experience make the helpful acts as permanent as the hurtful ones (**"No One Remembers"**).

Levine's poems seldom fail to remind us of important things about ourselves we should not forget. *The Names of the Lost* is the third powerful book Levine has given us in the past five years. Give him a saliva test. The title might be so-so for some poets, but it is ideal for Levine. He has been naming the lost for a long time. Not just lost people but lost associations and feelings.

Levine's method of writing depends to some extent on the ear of the reader to get into the poems. Few of his first lines are grippers: "Nine years ago, early winter," "Beyond that stand of firs," "In a coffee house at 3 a.m.," "It is Friday, a usual day," but they are immediate enough that we faintly sense something is going on, and we faintly sense that feelings are involved in the terse sounds of the words even when the words seem to be only narrating, conveying information or setting the scene. In a lesser poet this would be starting too far upstream, at the beginning of things rather than in the middle. For the reader it seems like getting a running start, then becoming aware that the race has already begun, long ago. The feeling seems to precede its source.

In a way, Levine's technique corresponds with his vision of the world in which grief is presumed the perpetual condition of humanity, there long before the individual has experienced anything to grieve. When something happens that causes us grief, we are already in good grieving condition because we have been practising a long time.

> **Levine's poems seldom fail to remind us of important things about ourselves we should not forget.**
> **—*Ricard Hugo***

Since Levine can write as if feeling precedes experience, he can command a wider range of subjects than many poets. By wider range, I mean his subjects can vary in the intensity of their relationship to him. (In their natures, his subjects are similar). He can invest as much feeling in poems about the poets of Chile or a man killed in Spain when Levine was eight years old in Detroit, as he can in poems involving relatives, friends and personal experience.

No poem in this fine collection is disappointing and almost every poem seems to be the best when reading it. My favorite, **"And the Trains Go On,"** is a poem of great faith and it immediately precedes the final poem, **"To My God in His Sickness,"** a somewhat grim parody of John Donne's "Hymne to God my God in my sicknesse." If Levine is solely responsible for the arrangement of the book, he may still consider the faith he has found in the power of words, in the power of naming, secondary to the religious faith he has lost in the face of an unjust world. If that is necessary to keep poems of such emotive force coming, let's not try to set him straight.

"And the Trains Go On" is a sort of microscopic Odyssey. The speaker is on the run from a self and a situation he could not bear, "The run from a war no one can win," and finds himself in a bizarre, cruel and despairing world. At first he and a companion are "at the back door / of the shop" and a "line of box cars / or soured wheat and pop bottles / uncoupled and was sent creaking down our spur. . . ." Already what is given ("was sent") is a world used, empty ("pop bottles") and spoiled ("soured wheat"). The old man who steps from the box car certifies the negative heritage with mock gentility—". . .and tipped his hat. 'It's all yours, boys!'" The speaker wonders "whose father / he was and how long he kept / moving until the police / found him, ticketless, sleeping in a 2nd class waiting room / and tore the card-board box / out of his hands and beat him / until the ink of his birth smudged / and surrendered its separate vowels." So the speaker has no doubt about the outcome. In this brutal world we lose not only our meagre possessions but our beginnings and our names to civilization's authority. Though the speaker never sees the man again, his vision is so relentless and fixed that the man's fate is determined in detail.

With the mention of "2nd class" the scene has shifted to Europe. Levine senses in the more immediate heritage, the historical heritage. He writes in some historical depth anyway, despite the immediacy of emotions and images. What civilized authority can do to the mind is revealed in the next event in the poem. A dog is wandering in the Milan railyard. A boy makes a perfectly reasonable explanation: the dog is "searching for his master." But the boy's grandfather "said, 'No. He was sent by God / to test the Italian railroads.'" The boy can still believe in the desirability and need for affectionate and supportive relationships. The grandfather has cynically accepted a bizarre explanation, involving phony religiosity, the deity's direct interest in the state, and a presumed unimportance of humanity.

This unimportance of humanity on the scale of civilization's values is reinforced by the next image. The speaker sleeps in a "box car of coffins bound / for the villages climbing north" and wonders if he will waken when "women have come to claim" dead husbands, sons, lovers, "what is left of glory." Or will he sleep through that and not waken again until he is back in the States, crossing the Mystic River, which is in Massachusetts?

Levine takes the poem out beautifully, "back the long / tangled road that leads us home," but now his companion is you, and me, and it is also him, the self he ran from, "in a dirty work-shirt that says *Phil*," (the only person named in the poem). And if we, you, I, Levine, can "lean way out / and shout out the holy names / of the lost neither of us is scared / and our tears mean nothing." We can go home (accept the self we ran from) with the certainty, the poet's certainty, that our words (their names and ours) are all we can give, and if we can share in that, then we have transcended our grief and redeemed our loss.

This is one of the most moving poems I've seen. In its capacity to touch and affect, I believe it rivals Yeats' "Easter, 1916," and like "Easter, 1916," we find ourselves in a world where 'motley is worn' or if not motley, then its industrial work-shirt counterpart. It is a world that doesn't hear and doesn't care. Levine's poems are important because in them we hear and we care. They call us back to the basic sources of despair: the dispossession, the destitution, the inadequacy of our love for each other. And they call back again that we can triumph over our sad psychic heritage through language and song.

Given the emotional depth of Levine's poems, one is inclined to avoid prolonged explorative analysis. Not that it would be ruinous, the poems are too tough for that, but that it would seem secondary, if not trivial—like program notes to a splendid concert. But at least one poem in this collection lends itself to discussion because it is somewhat revelatory of Levine's psychic process involved in the act of writing. More

than most of his poems, it shows how his writing grows out of ways he feels about himself and his relations with the world.

Let It Begin

Snow before dawn, the trees asleep.
In one window a yellow light—someone
is rising to wash and make coffee
and doze at the table remembering
how a child sleeps late and wakens
drenched in sunlight. If he thinks
of a street, he knows it has gone,
a dog has died, a tulip burned
for an hour and joined the wind.
With the others I drift, useless,
in the parking lot while the day-shift
comes on, or I stand at the corner
as the sun wakens on a gray crust.
The children pass by in silent knots
on the way home from the burial
of the birds. The day has begun.
I can put it away, a white shirt,
unworn, at the back of a drawer,
but my hands are someone else's—
stained, they shine like old wood
and burn in the cold. They have joined
each other in the fellowship
of the shovel. I stood in the temple
of junk where the engine blocks
turned and the nickle-plated grills
dripped on hooks, and though
steel rang on the lip of the furnace
and fire rose out of black earth
and rained down, in the end
I knelt to cinders and ice. I stared
into the needle's dark eye
so the peddler could mend his elbow
and gasp under his sack of rags.
Now the cat pulls on his skullcap
of bones and bows before the mouse.
Light that will spread the morning glory
burns on my tongue and spills
into the small valleys of our living,
the branches creak, and I let it begin.

Levine feels that loss, like the imagination, is the final equalizer. The man "thinks of a street" and knows three losses, the street, a dog and a tulip, equal in value now they are gone, equal *because* they are gone. In a world where loss predominates, the yellow light in the window is as good a beginning as dawn which comes now, not to waken the child but to wake itself on the gray industrial crust of the city. The speaker is "useless" (dawn does not need him), one of the many third shift workers who "drift in the parking lot." The aimlessness of their existence is as gratuitous as the snow that starts this poem, this day. You come off shift and it's just there: "Snow before dawn, the trees asleep."

The workers are "children" bound together in "knots" of an innocence they've inherited. The innocence of an existence that dims the senses, minimizes experience and limits possibilities. They are silent as the birds who are buried in silence once dawn is complete and their song is ended. When childhood is over and they could no longer wait for sunlight to drench them awake, but had to obey the call of the alarm clock, their impulse to song (poetry?) drained away.

The speaker can't be part of the middle class and knows it. His white shirt can be put away, unworn, for good. In Levine's case, very much for good, his and ours. But neither is he part of the working class. His hands are worker's hands, but they are not his, even though "they have joined each other in the fellowship of the shovel," a union (labor union?) of dubious worth. The sentimentality seemingly built into certain "of" constructions is ideal for nailing down a sarcastic phrase—my garden book of memories.

He is not of the working class because he cannot identify with accomplishment; the engine blocks, the grills, the steel and fire of the plant, that "temple of junk." Given the deterioration of religious values by industrial values that in turn are inadequate substitutes, the poet kneels not to abandoned Gods of the past, nor to the gods of the present, progress, civilization, the end products of manufacturing. He kneels to the end products of the whole process, cinders and ice, the two ways it can end, according to Frost. Levine will not break off his love affair with the finality of loss.

He stares into the "needle's dark eye" not for mystical purposes, the try for "inscape," but to prolong and perpetuate the suffering of the forlorn, the deprivation of humanity, the quotidian despair. The eye of the needle could be the gate of the biblical city, "dark" suggesting what cities have become, but the word "mend" suggests that whatever its metaphorical past it is now just a needle.

If that were all Levine was saying in this passage, he would be guilty of no more phoniness than is normal to a poet. He would be saying, I'll keep you patched together, your elbow mended, so you can gasp under your sack of rags and I can write "and gasp under his sack of rags." In a way that *is* what he is saying. But of course he is also trying to save the rag man (and you, and me) from oblivion. By prolonging our suffering, Levine is giving himself a chance to finish the poem, but he is also prolonging us.

The cat bows to the mouse because the cat needs the mouse just as the poet needs the rag man. The "skullcap of bones" suggests the death of religion and the act of kneeling is not a religious act, but an aesthetic one. Because the poet has insight, he is not part of what he sees and realizes a certain powerful advantage, the advantage of the cat over the mouse. He gives up the advantage to write the poem.

Levine has remained a child and kept alive his impulse to sing. The dawn that drenched him awake, still burns in him, on his tongue, in his words. The "it" he lets begin is the dawn, the life that belongs to all of us and is all we have, the poem itself. He not only shouts out the holy names of the lost, he shouts out the holy names of the living. And we are not lost. That's a big beautiful cat at our mousy feet.

Levine may very well believe that imagination and loss are not just close allies or forces that mutually trigger each other, but one and the same. One of our able critics should enlighten us on this in the years ahead. Those of us who are not critics should read Levine not for whatever literary advance he could be making but because he reminds us of what we are in a time it is important that we don't forget. And whatever we are, hopeful hurt, angry, sad, happy, we should forget least of all Philip Levine's poems. They attend us and our lives in profound, durable ways. I believe he is deservedly destined to be one of the most celebrated poets of the time.

Emily Grosholz (review date Summer 1982)

SOURCE: A review of *One for the Rose,* in *Hudson Review,* Vol. XXXV, No. 2, Summer, 1982, pp. 331-33.

[*In the following excerpt, Grosholz discusses Levine's focus on and praise of the ordinary.*]

. . . Philip Levine's poems in *One for the Rose* often begin in the midst of the ordinary: "This is an ordinary gray Friday after work / and before dark in a city of the known world." Not just anything, however, can count as ordinary, for it is an honorific term which Levine uses to bless things. Bus stations in Ohio are one of his paradigms, and so are small shops, bars and hotels in midwestern cities crossed off with rows of small, shoddy trees and polluted rivers. His people are working people, his times of day the gray mornings before we go to work and the gray dusk we come back home in. The ordinary is what social and literary convention passes over as transient and meaningless; Levine criticizes these norms through a poetic act of redemption which remembers certain lost places and people, exhibits their significance, calls them by name.

His strategy of redemption is to move back and away from his specific ordinary, viewing it from a great height as someone lifting off in an airplane would, or from the distanced perspective of memory. Thus **"Salt"** begins with a woman weeping alone in an airport late at night, between a porter mopping the floor and an old cleaning lady emptying the ashtrays. Then up and out: we follow the airplane of the man who has left her, flying from Cleveland to Chicago over cloud banks and the Lakes, as he returns to his wife and children through a light drizzle, and dreams of "the rain that hangs / above the city swollen with red particles / of burned air" or of tears:

> tears which must always fall
> because water and salt were given us
> at birth to make what we could of them,
> and being what we are we chose love
> and having found it we lost it over and over.

Or, again, from a room in the back of Peerless Cleaners, where a little pants presser is telling a child about revolution and the dignity of labor, Levine draws back thirty-eight years, over the conflagration of World War II, the theaters of Europe and the Pacific, and addresses his old instructor.

> Come back, Cipriano Mera, step
> out of the wind and dressed in the robe
> of your pain tell me again that this
> world will be ours. Enter my dreams
> or my life, Cipriano, come back
> out of the wind.

Encompassing his ordinary creatures in a wider vision, Levine shows them riding upon the thousands of days of history, the breast of earth which itself rides on the dark abyss of space. This vision might lead to the wisdom of Silenus, for such expanses engulf and dwarf the pinpoints of light. But Levine, looking back on our small illuminated places, observes that we have nothing except (of course, what else?) each other.

When Levine is moving out in a poem, so that we can see the gold edges of our local cloud, the signs of this transformation are usually wind or water. For someone who believes that the center of creation would like to listen to our music, but can't, that god will not rise from the stone of his cathedrals, wind is a natural replacement for spirit. Wind animates the forlorn geometry of earth, and lifts even the impacted deadliness of our cities. And the sea is threshold and freedom for a city kid brought up landlocked in the heart of America, "the sea / rocking the deep cradle of all / of us and water and salt without end . . . " The sea is the tide in our veins, our blood which is mostly salt water, and our tears. When the wind is tangled in the small, shoddy trees of Ohio, it sounds like the sea.

Richard Tillinghast (review date 12 September 1982)

SOURCE: "Working the Night Shift," in *New York Times Book Review,* September 12, 1982, Sec. 7, p. 42.

[*In the following review, Tillinghast applauds the poetry in* One for the Rose *for its readability and declares that "Belief" is one of the age's outstanding poems.*]

"A good poet," according to Randall Jarrell, "is someone who manages, in a lifetime of standing out in thunderstorms, to be struck by lightning five or six times." Among the poems in *One for the Rose,* the latest of Philip Levine's 10 books of poetry, the lightning strike is unmistakable in **"Belief."** This poem asserts by denying—using the recurring motif, "No one believes," to capture the ambivalent attitude we take toward things we somehow believe while "knowing" they cannot be true. While insisting upon denial, the poem creates a detailed, compelling vision:

> No one believes that to die
> is beautiful, that after the hard pain
> of the last unsaid word I am swept
> in a calm out from shore
> and hang in the silence of millions
> for the first time among all my family.

If no other single poem in the book quite matches the achievement of **"Belief"**—one of the outstanding poems of our time—there is much to like in *One for the Rose.* Philip Levine's poems have the rare and laudable virtue of readability; they carry the charm and vitality of the poet's distinctive speaking voice, which is by turns assertive and tough or humorously self-deprecatory.

Mr. Levine has been called a blue-collar poet, and it is true that he typically presents himself as a young man from the poor streets of Detroit, working the night shift at some place like "Detroit Transmission." But even among scenes like "the oily floors / of filling stations where our cars / surrendered their lives and we called / it quits and went on foot," the speaker is never a bluecollar caricature, but someone with brains, feelings and a freewheeling imagination that constantly fights to free him from his prosaic environment, as in these first lines from **"I Was Born in Lucerne":**

> Everyone says otherwise. They take me
> to a flat on Pingree in Detroit
> and say, up there, the second floor. I say,
> No, in a small Italian hotel overlooking
> the lake.

Levine's poems are notable for his quick eye and deft turn

of phrase, as when he notices "the dew that won't wait long enough / to stand my little gray wren a drink."

The other side of this poet's accessibility is a frequent flatness of diction and an overreliance on the line break for emphasis, but those are practically generic faults in contemporary American poetry. The repetitive rhetorical device that is so effective in **"Belief"** is unconvincing in some other poems. Another weakness is his reliance on easy rhetorical clinchers such as "Somewhere I am a God. / Somewhere I am a holy / object. Somewhere I am." But even his least successful efforts have their appeal. No reader of poetry would want to do without these gritty, funny, deeply engaged poems that take on the world as it comes. As Philip Levine describes the events of his life, "each one smells like an overblown rose, / yellow, American, beautiful, and true."

Fred Marchant (essay date Winter 1984)

SOURCE: "Cipriano Mera and the Lion: A Reading of Philip Levine," in *Imagine*, Vol. 1, No. 2, Winter, 1984, pp. 148-54.

[*In the following essay, Marchant discusses the spirit of anarchism in Levine's poetry.*]

Not many people in the United States would call themselves anarchists, but the poet Philip Levine does. In so doing he does not mean to invoke the image of a terrorist, a bomb in hand. Instead, he wants to acknowledge his passionate opposition to any soul-destroying forces in our social relations. His anarchism means that he does not believe in "the validity of governments, laws, charters" because they "hide us from our essential oneness." Levine has also said that his anarchism is "an extraordinarily generous, bountiful way to look at the universe," and that it has to do with "the end of ownership, the end of competitiveness, the end of a great deal of things that are ugly." And while one can debate the practicality of these ideas, it is clear that they have been enormously valuable to Philip Levine's poetry. In eleven books over the past twenty years he has made a rich and important body of work, all rooted in the generous, radical faith that human beings are essentially one.

One early benefit of this faith was an intuitive sympathy with the victims of a predatory, commercial society. Take, for example, **"Animals Are Passing from Our Lives,"** in *Not This Pig* (1968). The ostensible speaker of this poem is a pig on its way to market. Excited, his senses heightened with fear, the pig smells the blade and block, and can picture the flies and consumers landing on his re-arranged parts. Not only does this pig have a lively imagination, he also has a

profound sense of his own dignity. The pig thinks that the boy driving him along expects:

> that any moment I'll fall
> on my side and drum my toes
> like a typewriter or squeal
> and shit like a new housewife
>
> discovering television
> or that I'll turn like a beast
> cleverly to hook his teeth
> with my teeth. No. Not this pig.

Levine himself has explained that the poem celebrates the quality of digging in one's heels, and that this fastidious pig has resolved to act with more dignity than the human beings he will feed. But as fine as pigs are, they are not the subject of this poem. This pig represents a type of human being, those who have sacrificed their bodies in the marketplace. In "No. Not this pig," one hears the echo of every person who has ever resolved to be as dignified as possible as he or she marched into an office, factory, mine, or war. In this vein it seems right to recall that this poem was composed in the mid-1960's, when non-violent resisters as well as dutiful soldiers were passing from our lives.

And if it seems right to recall that era in relation to **"Animals,"** it seems necessary to do so in regard to **"They Feed They Lion."** Levine has said that this poem is his response to the black "insurrection" in Detroit in 1967, calling it a "celebration of anger." But it is also an explanation of the causes and the legitimacy of a fury that has found its expression:

> From the sweet glues of the trotters
> Come the sweet kinks of the fist, from the full
>   flower
> Of the hams the thorax of caves,
> From "Bow Down" come "Rise Up,"
> Come they Lion from the reeds of shovels,
> The grained arm that pulls the hands,
> They Lion grow.

Given **"Animals,"** it is not surprising that pigs have nourished this lion, or that labor has hardened its muscles. What is surprising is the way that this lion of anger has swept up all before it, black and white alike. The last stanza suggests that the speaker is a white man:

> From my five arms and all my hands
> From all my white sins forgiven, they feed,
> From my car passing under the stars,
> They Lion, from my children inherit,
> From the oak turned to a wall, they Lion,
> From they sack and they belly opened

And all that was hidden on the oil-stained earth
They feed they Lion and he comes.

In fear and exhilaration, the speaker has imaginatively embraced "They," and done it in defiant Black English gram-
matical constructions. And along with its African
connotation, the lion suggests a literary antecedent: probably
it is descended from Yeats' rough beast slouching toward
another city to be born.

One might naturally wonder how a poet whose vision is
based on our essential oneness could turn and celebrate the
anger of an insurrection. Levine's response to such a question would be to point out that the world of his poetry is
not a pastoral setting. Many of his poems are set in the factory world of Detroit, where Levine grew up, and all are
grounded in a realist's commitment to depict our actual lives.
As such, he is a poet of conflict, whose vision always has a
hard edge, and whose poems always stand in some degree
of opposition to the dominating powers that be. For example,
in *One for the Rose* (1981), in a poem he titled **"The Fox,"**
Levine says that he thinks he must have been a fox in a prior
life. This, he says, would explain a lot: his nose, the hair at
the base of his spine, the loathing he feels whenever he sees
ladies and gents mounted on horseback. He sees himself
standing in the middle of a horsepath in Central Park, rock
in hand, shouting and refusing to budge, "feeling the dignity / of the small creature menaced / by the many and
larger."

But such anger and defiance have their limitations, and one
of the great pleasures of reading Levine's recent *Selected
Poems* comes in watching his lyric expressions of anger lead
him to new emotional terrain. In 1974 he opened up that new
terrain in his sixth book, titled *1933.* The title refers to the
year when Levine's father died, when Levine himself was
barely six years old. Most of the poems in the book are elegiac, and the book as a whole seems an exploration of sorrow and the poet's memories of the dead. It is not as if either
memory or sorrow had been absent prior to *1933,* but now
these became at least as important as his anger and defiance.

"Hold Me" is the best example of the new tone and material in *1933.* What follows are the first four stanzas of that
seven stanza poem:

> The table is cleared of my place
> and cannot remember. The bed sags
> where I turned to death, the earth fills
> my first footsteps, the sun drowns my sight.
>
> A woman turns from the basket
> of dried white laundry and sees the room
> flooding with the rays of my eyes,
> the burning of my hair and tongue.

> I enter your bedroom, you look up
> in the dark from tying your shoes
> and see nothing, your boney shoulders
> stiffen and hold, your fingers stop.
>
> Was I dust that I should fall?
> Was I silence that the cat heard?
> Was I anger the jay swallowed?
> The black elm choking on leaves?

As with **"Animals Are Passing from Our Lives,"** and with
"They Feed They Lion," the first thing one notes about this
poem is the disconcerting, ambiguous nature of the persona.
Who is this speaker? He may be a dead man, or at the very
least a man imagining himself dead. He seems to have come
back to haunt a familiar place, possibly a familiar "woman,"
and what is certainly a familiar "you." Although he can see
them, they don't quite register his specific presence, and they
are clearly going about the business of their lives without
thinking of him. The rhetorical questions of stanza four
sound frustrated, annoyed, and maybe angry. We get the
sense that he is disappointed that no connections are made.
These are about as many inferences as one can reasonably
make from the opening stanzas, and the reader, like the
speaker, feels frustrated, on the outside of the situation and
in need of some connection.

When we turn to the last three stanzas, we become delighted
to discover the crystalline imagery of a clearly formulated
memory:

> In May, like this May, long ago
> my tiny Russian Grandpa—the bottle king—
> cupped a stained hand under my chin
> and ran his comb through my golden hair.
>
> Sweat, black shag, horse turds on the wind,
> the last wooden cart rattling down
> the alley, the clop of his great gray mare,
> green glass flashing in the December sun . . .
>
> I am the eye filled with salt,
> his child climbing on the rain, we are
> all the moon, the one planet, the hand
> of five stars on the night river.

The images of stanzas five and six are models of memory
and love. As the grandfather held the boy's face in his hands,
so too the speaker holds the image of the grandfather in his
mind's eye. When the table did not remember the speaker's
place, and when the "you" looked up into the darkness and
saw nothing, the spirit of the speaker withered into those
querulous questions. Now, with the memory of the grandfather and his kinship alive in his mind, the speaker soars into
the images of the last stanza. As the tears well up, the hand

that had been recalled, that stained hand of the grandfather, now becomes an image which spans the universe. In another age it might have been called the hand of God holding these lights of life as they drift on the dark river. Without the memory of that stained hand, the speaker would have nothing to hold onto, and no one to hold onto him.

Levine had always had an elevated sense of memory, but in and after *1933,* its precious connection with the beloved dead made it a matter of primary importance in his poetry. This did not mean he lulled his vivid, anarchist's conscience to sleep. Instead, memory and its attendant sorrows and joys deepened his poetry. It made his speakers more complex, vulnerable, and in the end, more believable. If in **"Animals Are Passing from Our Lives"** one hears a voice utterly and justly confident in its moral perspective, one hears a more tentative voice in the first stanzas of **"Hold Me."** If in **"They Feed They Lion,"** one hears a voice reminiscent of Biblical prophecy, one hears in the last stanzas of **"Hold Me"** a voice aware of what can be and has been lost. And although there are exceptions, it seems generally true that the speakers in Levine's poetry in and after *1933* seem more vulnerable because they know a great deal more about loss.

A very moving example of this is **"To Cipriano, in the Wind,"** a poem from *One for the Rose* (1981). It begins:

> Where did your words go,
> Cipriano, spoken to me 38 years
> ago in the back of Peerless Cleaners,
> where raised on a little wooden platform
> you bowed to the hissing press
> and under the glaring bulb the scars
> across your shoulders—"a gift
> of my country"—gleamed like old wood.
> "Dignidad," you said into my boy's
> wide eyes, "without is no riches."
> And Ferrente, the dapper Sicilian
> coatmaker, laughed: What could
> a pants presser know of dignity?
> That was the winter of '41, it
> would take my brother off to war,
> where you had come from, it would
> bring great snowfalls, graying
> in the streets, and news of death
> racing through the halls of my school.

The lessons in idealism and death continued on into the spring, when wild phlox leaped in the field, the Germans rolled into Russia, and some cousins died, presumably in battle. The speaker recalls that he

> walked alone in the warm spring winds
> of evening and said, "Dignity." I said
> your words, Cipriano, into the winds.

> I said, "Someday this will all be ours."
> Come back, Cipriano Mera, step out
> of the wind and dressed in the robe
> of your pain tell me again that this
> world will be ours. Enter my dreams
> or my life, Cipriano, come back
> out of the wind.

The last lines of this poem are a song of experience. One feels how hard it is to sustain a decent faith in the possibilities of mankind. One hears how hard it is to sustain even the little bit of innocence that this faith implies.

Who was Cipriano Mera? When an interviewer asked Levine about the origins of his anarchism, he recalled that when he was growing up in Detroit there were "two Italians who ran a cleaning and dyeing operation down on my corner who were anarchists, and whom I used to talk to all the time." Naturally one thinks that this must have been Cipriano Mera. But, reading on in the interview, one learns of Levine's boyhood interest in the Spanish Civil War, an interest that has lasted all his life and no doubt introduced him to the tradition of political poetry in Spanish. His fascination with the Spanish Civil War could also have been the source of the name, for there was a Cipriano Mera commanding an anarchist militia in Barcelona in 1936. Probably Levine has merged these people under one name, and such a merger is not so much poetic license as it is an example of that innocent, anarchist faith. The militia commander and the pants presser were but two faces of the same volatile spirit.

As with most of Philip Levine's poetry, **"To Cipriano, in the Wind"** enacts and embodies the spirit of anarchism's ability to survive in this world. Cipriano Mera does step out of the wind and into the words of the poem. So too in **"They Feed They Lion."** The white speaker and the black rage merge into a chant that implies a sense of oneness could exist at least in some hearts. The prayer to Cipriano is a more complicated and less confident assertion, but despite the difference in mood and meaning, the spirit of both poems is the same. Cipriano Mera and the Lion are one.

David St. John (essay date Spring 1986)

SOURCE: "Where the Angels Come Toward Us: The Poetry of Philip Levine," in *Antioch Review,* Vol. 44, No. 2, Spring, 1986, pp. 176-91.

[*In the following essay, St. John considers Levine's career and asserts that his poetry "has become both the pulse and conscience of American poetry."*]

The publication of Philip Levine's most recent collection of poetry, *Sweet Will,* following by only a year his superbly edited *Selected Poems,* presents an excellent opportunity to consider the twenty years of work these two volumes represent.

Throughout his career, Philip Levine has looked for an American voice, a voice that could stand comfortably in the tradition of Whitman and William Carlos Williams. Levine's primary impulse is narrative, and his poems are often narratives of human struggle—of the particularly American struggle of the immigrant, and of the universal struggle of individuals ignored and unheard by their societies. Levine's poetry gives voice to these "voiceless" men and women who he feels have been too rarely recognized and honored in our literature.

Philip Levine's poetry, known for being urban and "angry," is also filled with great naturalistic beauty and great tenderness.
—David St. John

Philip Levine's poetry, known for being urban and "angry," is also filled with great naturalistic beauty and great tenderness. His poems present a poetic voice that is both as colloquial and unliterary as daily speech and as American as jazz. Levine has always desired a relatively "invisible" and unadorned style, one that could allow the voices of his speakers and the details of their stories to fully command the reader's attention. Yet the technical achievements and the formal underpinning of his poetry are too often neglected. The *Selected Poems* makes clear that the metrical and rhymed poetry of Levine's early books, as well as his superb syllabic verse, remains some of the most highly-crafted and imaginatively powerful poetry of the time.

For Levine, poetry is almost always the powerful poetry of witness. Here is his requiem for the silent fifties, and the title poem of his first collection, **"On The Edge"**:

> My name is Edgar Poe and I was born
> In 1928 in Michigan.
> Nobody gave a damn. The gruel I ate
> Kept me alive, nothing kept me warm,
> But I grew up, almost to five foot ten,
> And nothing in the world can change my weight.
>
> I have been watching you these many years,
> There in the office, pencil poised and ready,
> Or on the highway when you went ahead.
> I did not write; I watched you watch the stars
> Believing that the wheel of fate was steady;
> I saw you rise from love and go to bed;

> I heard you lie, even to your daughter.
> I did not write, for I am Edgar Poe,
> Edgar the mad one, silly, drunk, unwise,
> But Edgar waiting on the edge of laughter,
> And there is nothing that he does not know
> Whose page is blanker than the raining skies.

The poem's speaker, with his refrain, "I did not write," was born—like Levine—in 1928, in Michigan. His name recalls, with a wry wit, one of America's more famous outsiders. Here are the elements of what will remain at the core of many of Levine's poems: a disenfranchised voice, often American, solitary yet resilient, self-ironic, accusing, compassionate, steadily proclaiming his or her role as observer from the harsh recesses of the working world. Since any real "power" to this voice, even in a democracy that promises the equal importance of *all* of its citizens' voices, has been neutralized, the speaker has seized instead the voice of this poem. In this way, in spite of the speaker's insistence upon his own silence, we find, in fact, that this silence has been *spoken.* That is, it has been written, and it is a silence that becomes both testimony and inscription.

"The Horse," another of the poems drawn from *On The Edge,* illustrates the moral outrage that will steadily inform Levine's work. This poem, dedicated to a survivor of Hiroshima, establishes two of Levine's recurring concerns—the earth's constant ravishing and destruction by man, and the capacity of the natural world to regenerate and renew itself. It is this same power of resurrection, earthly resurrection, that Levine finds and champions in the oppressed men and women who people many of his poems, one of the most memorable of these victorious losers being the boxer of the poem **"A New Day"**:

> The headlights fading out at dawn,
> A stranger at the shore, the shore
> Not wakening to the great sea
> Out of sleep, and night, and no sun
> Rising where it rose before.
>
> The old champion in a sweat suit
> Tells me this is Chicago, this—
> He does not say—is not the sea
> But the chopped grey lake you get to
> After travelling all night
>
> From Dubuque, Cairo, or Wyandotte.
> He takes off at a slow trot
> And the fat slides under his shirt.
> I recall the Friday night
> In a beer garden in Detroit
>
> I saw him flatten Ezzard Charles
> On TV, and weep, and raise

Both gloved hands in a slow salute
To a God. I could tell him that.
I could tell him that those good days

Were no more and no less than these.
I could tell him that I thought
By now I must have reached the sea
We read about, or that last night
I saw a man break down and cry

Out of luck and out of gas
In Bruce's Crossing. We collect
Here at the shore, the two of us,
To make a pact, a people come
For a new world and a new home

And what we get is what we bring:
A grey light coming on at dawn,
No fresh start and no bird song
And no sea and no shore
That someone hasn't seen before.

The delicate and powerful syllabics of **"The Horse"** and the iambic tetrameter lines (with gorgeous variations) of **"A New Day"** provide supple examples of Levine's technical grace and of the coupling of formal exactitude with unfamiliar subjects that is one of his many gifts. Even with its wink at Keats, **"A New Day"** remains unforced and unliterary.

It was in his second book, *Not This Pig,* that Levine first brought to maturity the line that would serve as the basis for his narrative ambitions in the poems to come. One of the several poems of seven-syllable lines in this volume, **"The Cemetery at Academy, California,"** best represents this solidifying of voice in Levine's poetry. Here is the central stanza of that poem:

I came here with a young girl
once who perched barefoot on her
family marker. "I will go
there," she said, "next to my sister."
It was early morning and
cold, and I wandered over
the pale clodded ground looking
for something rich or touching.
"It's all wildflowers in the spring,"
she had said, but in July
there were only the curled cut
flowers and the headstones blanked out
on the sun side, and the long
shadows deep as oil. I walked
to the sagging wire fence
that marked the margin of the
place and saw where the same ground,
festered here and there with reedy

grass, rose to a small knoll
and beyond where a windmill
held itself against the breeze.
I could hear her singing on
the stone under the great oak,
but when I got there she was
silent and I wasn't sure
and was ashamed to ask her,
ashamed that I had come here
where her people turned the earth.

Levine loves to braid strands of narrative, visual, and meditative detail into a unified poetic whole. He often uses details of the present to stitch together fragments of memory, pieces of the past (both public and private histories), to give texture and relief to the surface fabric of a poem. This technique, which helps lend narrative unity and historical resonance to his poems, is one Levine will echo and refine throughout his career.

"Not This Pig," with its superb air of defiance, is often seen as the poem most clearly embodying the strengths of Levine's work of this period; yet I think a far more representative poem, one more indicative of the directions he would take, is the delicate and moving **"Heaven."** The poem reflects Levine's ever-present questioning of individual and society, of the relationship between conscience and law. The poem has a basis in Levine's own refusal to serve in the Korean War, but its central figure is not Levine; he is *anyone* with beliefs:

If you were twenty-seven
and had done time for beating
your ex-wife and had
no dreams you remembered
in the morning, you might
lie on your bed and listen
to a mad canary sing
and think it all right to be
there every Saturday
ignoring your neighbors, the streets,
the signs that said join,
and the need to be helping.
You might build, as he did,
a network of golden ladders
so that the bird could roam
on all levels of the room;
you might paint the ceiling blue,
the floor green, and shade
the place you called the sun
so that things came softly to order
when the light came on.
He and the bird lived
in the fine weather of heaven;
they never aged, they

never tired or wanted
all through that war,
but when it was over
and the nation had been saved,
he knew they'd be hunted.
He knew, as you would too,
that he'd be laid off
for not being braver,
and it would do no good
to show how he had taken
clothespins and cardboard
and made each step safe.
It would do no good
to have been one of the few
that climbed higher and higher
even in time of war,
for now there would be the poor
asking for their share,
and hurt men in uniforms,
and no one to believe
that heaven was really here.

One of the valid conventional wisdoms about Philip Levine is that he is one of the few urban—as opposed to suburban—American poets. He is, certainly, our most gripping poet of the city. Perhaps this is because he sees the used and abused city, the working city, not the city of galleries, museums, and restaurants. He sees and records the workings of the ravaged and exhausted city; he witnesses the blood and courage of those who live and work within it.

Perhaps the most compelling aspect of Levine's poetry is the place that anger is granted in his work. One of the few sources of power left to many of his speakers is to touch their own frustration and rage, and it is that current that electrifies their presence in these poems. The daily injustices that build into a larger sense of outrage accrue in Levine's poems much as they do in his speakers' lives—slowly and inexorably. It is an especially clarifying anger that we find at work throughout Levine's poetry, an anger that grants us the perspective of the real, and not a literary, world. It is an anger that we experience as a relief, the same relief we feel when the lens of a movie projector finally comes into focus; it is the clarity of truth that provides our sense of relief. No other American poet so clearly acknowledges the place and necessity of anger—in our lives and in our country—and it gives Levine's poetry an energy and an unkempt integrity that is unique.

In Levine's search for an authentic American voice, we can see the influence of daily speech, as well as the echo of black speech. It's not simply Levine's empathy with the oppressed and victimized that gives rise to a poem like **"They Feed They Lion."** It is also his desire to unleash the full power that he sees latent in American speech, in *all* of America's

voices. We can hear it crashing forward in this poem, along with echoes of Whitman, Yeats, and Christopher Smart:

> Out of burlap sacks, out of bearing butter,
> Out of black bean and wet slate bread,
> Out of the acids of rage, the candor of tar,
> Out of creosote, gasoline, drive shafts, wooden
>   dollies,
> They Lion grow.
>   Out of the gray hills
> Of industrial barns, out of rain, out of bus ride,
> West Virginia to Kiss My Ass, out of buried
>   aunties,
> Mothers hardening like pounded stumps, out of
>   stumps,
> Out of the bones' need to sharpen and the
>   muscles' to stretch,
> They Lion grow.

One facet of Levine's special genius is that those "literary" influences are always an internal fuel for his poems, never an exterior decoration. **"They Feed They Lion"** concludes with this extraordinary verbal surge:

>   From the sweet glues of the trotters
> Come the sweet kinks of the fist, from the full
>   flower
> Of the hams the thorax of caves,
> From "Bow Down" come "Rise Up,"
> Come they Lion from the reeds of shovels,
> The grained arm that pulls the hands,
> They Lion grow.
>   From my five arms and all my hands,
> From all my white sins forgiven, they feed,
> From my car passing under the stars,
> They Lion, from my children inherit,
> From the oak turned to a wall, they Lion,
> From they sack and they belly opened
> And all that was hidden burning on the oil-stained
>   earth
> They feed they Lion and he comes.

Just as Philip Levine chooses to give voice to those who have no power to do so themselves, he likewise looks in his poems for the chance to give voice to the natural world, taking—like Francis Ponge—*the side of things,* the side of nature and its elements. And Levine is in many ways an old-fashioned troubadour, a singer of tales of love and heroism. Though it comes colored by the music of his world, what Levine has to offer is as elemental as breath. It is the simple insistence of breath, of the will to live—and the force of all living things in nature—that Levine exalts again and again. At the conclusion of his exquisite love poem, **"Breath,"** he says:

> Today
> in this high clear room
> of the world, I squat
> to the life of rocks
> jewelled in the stream
> or whispering
> like shards. What fears
> are still held locked
> in the veins till the last
> fire, and who will calm
> us then under a gold sky
> that will be all of earth?
> Two miles below on the burning
> summer plains, you go
> about your life one
> more day. I give you
> almond blossoms
> for your hair, your hair
> that will be white, I give
> the world my worn-out breath
> on an old tune, I give
> it all I have
> and take it back again.

The startling and memorable poems of *They Feed They Lion* first brought Levine to national prominence, yet it's his next book, *1933,* that most clearly reflects the realm of loss that touches all of his work. The title refers to a year of great personal loss (the death of his father) as well as to a world on the verge of radical change. It is a world seen from the perspective of innocence, the perspective of a child. The poems form a loose family album of portraits of people and events culled from memory and given a unified shape. The spirit—the emblem of the sparrow that inhabits these and other of Levine's poems—bears witness to these losses and to this changing world of industrial explosion, an ending depression, and a growing war. Each day brings only the barest hope, but hope exists. It is in this book that Levine, in confronting the vanished past and his father's death, first confronts the image of his own mortality. And it is, he says in one of his interviews, his "urge to memorialize details" that helps him to stay the loss of places and people.

In the poem **"Goodbye,"** about the funeral of a child (seemingly a relative, perhaps a cousin, of Levine's), the poet sees in his own reckoning with this death (a feared, mirror-death for the child-speaker) that it is this occasion that enacts a shift from childhood to young adulthood. The sparrow—both messenger and angel—is seen here as the embodied spirit of the lost child. Notice the double meaning of the conclusion of **"Goodbye":**

> In the first light
> a sparrow settled outside
> my window, and a breeze woke

> from the breathing river,
> I opened my eyes
> and the gauze curtains
> were streaming.
> "Come here," the sparrow said.
> I went. In the alley below
> a horse cart piled with bags,
> bundles, great tubs of fat,
> brass lamps the children broke.
> I saw the sheenie-man pissing
> into a little paper fire
> in the snow, and laughed.
> The bird smiled. When I unlatched
> the window the bird looked back
> three times over each shoulder
> then shook his head.
> He was never coming back inside,
> and rose in a shower
> of white dust above
> the blazing roofs
> and telephone poles.
>
> It meant a child
> would have to leave the world.

Almost all of the poems of this volume become entries and notations of homecoming and return. The title poem, **"1933,"** seems to me one of Levine's finest. Surreal, gnarled, emotionally charged, and—in some ways—collapsing under the pressure of its own intensity, the poem rises to an elegiac beauty that allows the poet an essential recovery of his childhood. It is also a profound declaration of loss. The poem brings together again the son and the lost father (as will the later poems **"Starlight"** and **"The Face"**) in the most elemental of meetings. The voiceless father, whose voice arises in his son, the poet, and the details of their mutual loss will continue to thread their way through other of Levine's poems. It is the poem **"1933"** that freed Levine to write two of his most astonishing poems, also poems of sons and fathers, **"New Season"** and **"My Son and I."**

The poem **"New Season"** represents the culmination of Levine's work to this stage. It is personal and yet public; it concerns both the private matters of his life (the daily events in the life of one of his sons and the occasion of his mother's seventieth birthday) and the public past (the Detroit race riots that occurred when Levine was fifteen). In spite of its length, let me quote in full **"New Season"** in order to show the "braided" narrative movement the poem employs, a movement that occurs in many of Levine's best poems:

> My son and I go walking in the garden.
> It is April 12, Friday, 1974.
> Teddy points to the slender trunk
> of the plum and recalls the digging

last fall through three feet
of hard pan and opens his palms
in the brute light of noon, the heels
glazed with callus, the long fingers
thicker than mine and studded with
silver rings. My mother is 70 today.
He flicks two snails off a leaf
and smashes them underfoot
on the red brick path. Saturday,
my wife stood here, her cheek cut
by a scar of dirt, dirt on her bare
shoulders, on the brown belly,
damp and sour in the creases
of her elbows. She held up a parsnip
squat, misshapen, a tooth pulled
from the earth, and laughed
her great white laugh. Teddy talks
of the wars of the young, Larry V.
and Ricky's brother in the movies,
on Belmont, at McDonald's,
ready to fight for nothing, hard,
redded or on air, "low riders,
grease, what'd you say about my mama!"
Home late, one in the back seat,
his fingers broken, eyes welling
with pain, the eyes and jawbones
swollen and rough. 70 today, the woman
who took my hand and walked me
past the corridor of willows
to the dark pond where the one swan
drifted. I start to tell him
and stop, the story of my 15th spring.
That a sailor had thrown a black baby
off the Belle Isle Bridge was
the first lie we heard, and the city
was at war for real. We would waken
the next morning to find Sherman tanks
at the curb and soldiers camped
on the lawns. Damato said he was
"goin downtown bury a hatchet
in a nigger's head." Women
took coffee and milk to the soldiers
and it was one long block party
till the trucks and tanks loaded up
and stumbled off. No one saw
Damato for a week, and when I did
he was slow, head down, his right arm
blooming in a great white bandage.
He said nothing. On mornings I rise
early, I watch my son in the bathroom,
shirtless, thick-armed and hard,
working with brush and comb
at his full blond head that suddenly
curled like mine and won't
come straight. 7 years passed

before Della Daubien told me
how three white girls from the shop
sat on her on the Woodward streetcar
so the gangs couldn't find her
and pull her off like they did
the black janitor and beat
an eye blind. She would never
forget, she said, and her old face
glows before me in shame
and terror. Tonight, after dinner,
after the long, halting call
to my mother, I'll come out here
to the yard rinsed in moonlight
that blurs it all. She will not
become the small openings
in my brain again through which the wind
rages, though she was the ocean
that ebbed in my blood, the storm clouds
that battered my lungs, though I hide
in the crotch of the orange tree
and weep where the future grows
like a scar, she will not come again
in the brilliant day. My cat Nellie,
15 now, follows me, safe
in the dark from mockingbird
and jay, her fur frost tipped
in the pure air, and together we hear
the wounding of the rose, the willow
on fire—to the dark pond
where the one swan drifted, the woman
is 70 now—the willow is burning,
the rhododendrons shrivel
like paper under water, all
the small secret mouths are feeding
on the green heart of the plum.

This melding of the narrative line with present and recollective detail is a crucial feature of Levine's later poetry. The narrative voice, with its measured intelligence and quiet confidence, shares a kinship with the voice of **"The Cemetery at Academy, California"** and other earlier poems. It has been a natural progression from the seven-syllable syllabic line to the primarily three-beat "free verse" line that characterizes these later poems. The conversational ease of this voice is always remarkable, and Levine seems closest here to one of his ambitions—to bring forward a body of poetry that is accessible to *all* readers. It's instructive to look again at what Levine himself has to say about the development of this aspect of his poetry, in particular about his use of the three-beat line. In a passage from an interview with David Remnick, he says:

> I think I developed that line from my favorite line,
> which is Yeats's trimeter line. I think it comes from
> an attempt to find a free verse equivalent. He can

use it in a song-like way or mold it into long paragraphs of terrific rhythmic power. I was very early awed by the way he could keep the form and let the syntax fall across it in constantly varying ways, the way certain sixteenth-century poets could with pentameter. The short line appeals to me because I think it's easier to make long statements that accumulate great power in short lines. You can flow line after line, and the breaks become less significant because there are so many of them, and they build to great power.

It is equally important to consider the issue of Philip Levine's political beliefs, which he calls "anarchist" and which are, in fact, quite simple: he believes an individual human being is of more value than any government; he believes human freedom and dignity are the world's most precious resources (as opposed to say, gold and oil); he believes that faith in the individual and the truthful (poetic) use of language are both political acts. In the preface to his book of interviews, *Don't Ask,* Levine writes:

> When I refer to myself as an anarchist I do not mean to invoke the image of a terrorist or even a man who would burn the deed to his house because "property is theft," which I happen to believe is true. I don't believe in the validity of governments, laws, charters, all that hide us from our essential oneness. "We are put on earth a little space," Blake wrote, "That we may learn to bear the beams of love." And so in my poems I memorialize those men and women who struggled to bear that love. I don't believe in victory in my lifetime, I'm not sure I believe in victory at all, but I do believe in the struggle and preserving the names and natures of those who fought, for their sakes, for my sake, and for those who come after.

And in an interview with Arthur Smith, he adds: "I think the writing of a poem is a political act. We now exist in the kind of a world that Orwell was predicting, and the simple insistence upon accurate language has become a political act. Nothing is more obvious than what our politicians are doing to our language, so that if poets insist on the truth, or on an accurate rendition, or on a faithful use of language, if they for instance insist on an accurate depiction of people's lives as they are actually lived—this is a political act."

Philip Levine has always written poetry that is also more overtly political, and much of the best of it in his *Selected Poems* is drawn from the volumes *The Names of the Lost* and *7 Years from Somewhere:* "Gift for a Believer"; "On the Murder of Lieutenant Jose Del Castillo by the Falangist Bravo Martinez, July 12, 1936"; "On a Drawing by Flavio"; "Francisco, I'll Bring You Red Carna-

tions"; and two exceptionally powerful poems of domestic politics, **"Ask the Roses"** and **"To My God in His Sickness."** In these poems, as always in his work, Levine is giving voice to those without, as he returns "names" and presence to those whose names have been taken from them or erased by history. There is often a barely restrained passion in these poems; for those who prize decorum above all else in their poetry, Levine's poems will seem ill-mannered in their fierce convictions and desires. Like few other American poets, Levine forces us to consider our own moral values and, more generally, the place of moral values in any body of poetry. Levine's ethics are often the true refrain of his poems.

Levine managed, in his book *One for the Rose,* to disconcert some of his readers and to delight the rest with the kaleidoscope of voices and the fragments of self given full stage there. There is an imaginative range to these poems that remains pleasing and surprising even after many readings, and a mad, rakish quality that is invigorating. Levine's humor is at its most relaxed and open; the characters in these poems are full of extravagant and playful gestures, impossible histories, and biting commentaries. A sampling of these exuberant speakers includes: the world's first pilot; **"The Conductor of Nothing,"** who rides trains endlessly back and forth across the country; a man who believes he once lived as a fox (and behaves accordingly); and a foundling who may well be the embodiment of the Second Coming! They are the most appealing gallery of rogues and impostors and saints of any book of American poetry in recent years. Still, perhaps the most powerful works of this period are the more typically, "Levine" poems, **"Having Been Asked 'What Is a Man?' I Answer"** and **"To Cipriano, in the Wind."** Both of these poems address the nature of human dignity. The former considers courage in the face of serious illness; the latter celebrates the fierce beliefs of man from Levine's past:

> Where did your words go,
> Cipriano, spoken to me 38 years
> ago in the back of Peerless Cleaners,
> where raised on a little wooden platform
> you bowed to the hissing press
> and under the glaring bulb the scars
> across your shoulders—"a gift
> of my country"—gleamed like old wood.
> *"Dignidad,"* you said into my boy's
> wide eyes, "without is no riches."
> And Ferrente, the dapper Sicilian
> coatmaker, laughed. What could
> a pants presser know of dignity?

In Levine's most recent collection, *Sweet Will,* he uses as an epigraph to the book a passage from Wordsworth that concludes, "Ne'er saw I, never felt, a calm so deep! / The river glideth at his own sweet will. . . ." *Sweet Will* has been seen by some reviewers as a transitional volume, a book that takes up past concerns of Levine's poetry. Yet *Sweet Will* strikes me as an especially autobiographical collection, more nakedly so than any other of Levine's books. Like the river in the passage from Wordsworth, Levine glides ever forward, carrying with him his own past. The poems here carry with them the great freedom of voice won by the work of *One for the Rose*. It's my own feeling that *Sweet Will* is both a reckoning with past themes and concerns and also a sequence of highly personal and revealing annotations to those *Selected Poems.* Levine addresses his own past in the most direct manner of his career. Once again, he examines the current of politics in his poetry as it's expressed in the context of the crushing American workplace and in the history of European anarchism. But he announces most explicitly what he considers the real continuity of purpose in all of his poetic works—that he is, first and foremost, a storyteller, a moral storyteller. The poem that serves as a centerpiece for *Sweet Will,* **"A Poem with No Ending,"** begins, "So many poems begin where they / should end, and never end. / Mine never end, they run on / book after book, complaining / to the moon that heaven is wrong / or dull, no place at all to be. / I believe all this." And it's true that all of Levine's work can be seen as being of a piece; like **"To Cipriano, in the Wind,"** all of his poetry seems, whether public or private, to revolve around the questions of human freedom and human dignity. A poem that exhibits this force in Levine's poetry as dramatically as any is the title poem of this volume, **"Sweet Will."** A paradigm of the complex braiding of concerns that occurs in all of Levine's work, this poem is another of the defiant celebrations of the individual that distinguish his poetry. **"Sweet Will":**

> The man who stood beside me
> 34 years ago this night fell
> on to the concrete, oily floor
> of Detroit Transmission, and we
> stepped carefully over him until
> he wakened and went back to his press.

> It was Friday night, and the others
> told me that every Friday he drank
> more than he could hold and fell
> and he wasn't any dumber for it
> so just let him get up at his
> own sweet will or he'll hit you.

> "At his own sweet will," was just
> what the old black man said to me,
> and he smiled the smile of one
> who is still surprised that dawn
> graying the cracked and broken windows
> could start us all to singing in the cold.

> Stash rose and wiped the back of his head

> with a crumpled handkerchief and looked
> at his own blood as though it were
> dirt and puzzled as to how
> it got there and then wiped the ends
> of his fingers carefully one at a time
> the way the mother wipes the fingers
> of a sleeping child, and climbed back
> on his wooden soda-pop case to
> his punch press and hollered at all
> of us over the oceanic roar of work,
> addressing us by our names and nations—

> "Nigger, Kike, Hunky, River Rat,"
> but he gave it a tune, an old tune,
> like "America the Beautiful." And he danced
> a little two-step and smiled showing
> the four stained teeth left in the front
> and took another suck of cherry brandy.

> In truth it was no longer Friday,
> for night had turned to day as it
> often does for those who are patient,
> so it was Saturday in the year of '48
> in the very heart of the city of man
> where your Cadillac cars get manufactured.

> In truth all those people are dead,
> they have gone up to heaven singing
> "Time on My Hands" or "Begin the Beguine,"
> and the Cadillacs have all gone back
> to earth, and nothing that we made
> that night is worth more than me.

> And in truth I'm not worth a thing
> what with my feet and my two bad eyes
> and my one long nose and my breath
> of old lies and my sad tales of men
> who let the earth break them back,
> each one, to dirty blood or bloody dirt.

> Not worth a thing! Just like it was said
> at my magic birth when the stars
> collided and fire fell from great space
> into great space, and people rose one
> by one from cold beds to tend a world
> that runs on and on at its own sweet will.

This poem, like the body of Philip Levine's poetry, makes one simple demand of us—that we read it by the light of human compassion. Quietly, dramatically, with growing power and beauty, the poetry of Philip Levine has become both the pulse and conscience of American poetry. He is one of our few essential poets, and in his eloquent voice he reminds us of the courage required to sing the most worthy songs.

Frederick J. Marchant (review date June 1988)

SOURCE: A review of *A Walk with Tom Jefferson*, in *Boston Review*, Vol. 13, No. 3, June, 1988, pp. 28-9.

[*In the following review, Marchant considers Levine's humanistic faith and the nature of spirituality in his poetry.*]

In a dozen books over the last twenty-five years, one of Philip Levine's most significant achievements has been to extend the province of the lyric to include the world of the blue-collar laborer. In Levine's poetry the smell of garlicky lunchboxes and greasy machinery have always had a place. There has also been a place for the description of mind-numbing work, and most important of all, his poetry has given voice to the angers that so easily well up after such labor has taken its toll. Levine was born in Detroit in 1928 and came of age working in a number of automotive factories there. He has been a full-time poet for many years now, but his poetry still holds an imaginative landscape centered on this working-class experience. As with Robert Frost's relation to his Derry farm, Philip Levine's imagination has never totally abandoned his youthful workplace, and it has in many ways become Levine's root metaphor for life in our time and place.

> **In Levine's poetry the smell of garlicky lunchboxes and greasy machinery have always had a place.**
> **—Frederick J. Marchant**

One of the most important and revealing blue-collar incidents in Levine's new book, *A Walk with Tom Jefferson,* comes toward the end of the long poem from which the book takes its title. The poem concludes with a speaker reminiscing about a time in his youth when he "worked nights" on a milling machine in a factory which turned out Cadillac transmissions. He recalls that

> another kid just up
> from West Virginia asked me
>   what was we making
> and I answered, I'm making
>   2.25 an hour,
> don't know what you're
>   making, and he had
> to correct me, gently, what was
>   we making out of
> this here metal, and I didn't know.

An epiphany for the speaker of the poem, the recollection here is like fingering an old scar, and it forcefully brings to the speaker's mind the real cost of living and working as an appendage to a machine. His consciousness had been shrunk to the size of his hourly wage, and the important questions had somehow been banished by the din and clatter.

What are we making here? That is the question which haunts both the title poem and the book as a whole. In some poems in this volume it prompts Levine to sound like a Biblical prophet damning a nation which would allow its cities to become "block after block / of dumping grounds" with the streets littered with everything from "old couches and settees / burst open, the white innards / gone gray" to "whole market counters / that once contained the red meats / we couldn't get enough of." The prophet's tone, however, more often gives way to the elegiac note which characterizes Levine's best work. In **"Buying and Selling,"** for instance, Levine recalls a time in his youth when he worked as a purchasing agent for buyers ("my waiting masters" he calls them) of Army surplus automotive parts. He remembers once going into "the wilderness of warehouses" and cutting into the crates which held driveshafts and universal joints packed in preservative cosmoline. The parts were perfect, the bids made, the deal consummated. As the truck pulled away from the warehouse, however, the speaker found himself in the grip of a profound sadness:

> The great metal doors
> of the loading dock crashed down, and in
> the sudden aftermath I inhaled a sadness
> stronger than my Lucky Strike, stronger
> than the sadness of these hills and valleys
> with their secret ponds and streams unknown
> even to children, or the sadness of children
> themselves, who having been abandoned
>   believe
> their parents will return before dark.

These lines have the characteristic Levine rhythms. The mostly enjambed lines cascade down the page and give the ending an aura of arrival and inevitability. The sadness of these lines also seems inevitable. It is part of the product of the poem's slowly accumulating anger at the meaninglessness of buying and selling. The speaker of this poem feels like an abandoned child precisely because in the wilderness of warehouses he is bereft of any transcendent meaning. No God the Father here to lay down the laws, just the commerce in the so-called "goods" and services. Such commerce, the poem seems to want to say, might well be our daily glimpse into a small corner of the abyss.

There is, however, another side to Levine's imagination. His darker thoughts and intuitions are balanced at times by a genuinely humanistic faith. The character Tom Jefferson can be thought of as this book's most obvious representative of the more affirmative streak in Levine's work. Tom has "the same name as the other one," but this Jefferson is a black man surviving in the urban wasteland of Detroit. Having emigrated from Alabama prior to World War II, Tom Jefferson owns and lives in one of the few houses left standing amid the vacant lots and debris. It is late autumn in the poem, and he is tidying up what's left of his summer vegetable garden. Stoic, tenacious, and resolved, he is planning what he will plant next year. He will not quit the place. What he represents is a life-affirming spirit of rootedness, commitment, and nurture. He knows precisely what he is making with his work. He is making something decent and useful out of what the city of automobile manufacture has offered and given him.

Levine calls him a "believer," and there are other believers in this book. For instance, the speaker of one poem imagines his dead father as preceding him into the darkness, "burning the little candle / of his breath, making light of it all." In another poem, **"For the Country,"** Levine imagines an elderly woman living alone, nearing her death, filled with memories that seem more real than anything else around her. In her last moments, death becomes for her a "dark sister" with whom she stays up late, playing with her in bed, as if both were little girls again. Imaginings such as these are all acts of faith in the spirit that Tom Jefferson represents. Probably the most affirmative poem in the collection is called **"The Whole Soul."** Here the speaker wonders if the soul is like an onion, the same as one moves toward the core. "That would be suitable," he says, for the soul is "the human core and the rest / meant either to keep it / warm or cold depending / on the season." The whole soul, however, is more than just the individual. It is, in this poem, the larger, perhaps impersonal interconnectedness between self and creation. The poem ends with the speaker on the seashore, taking a few handfuls of water in his hands and thinking:

> I speak in a tongue hungering
> for salt and water without salt,
> I give a shape to the air going
> out and the air coming in,
> and the sea winds scatter it
> like so many burning crystals
> settling on the evening ocean.

That is Levine's idea of the "whole soul," transpersonal, transcendent, ultimately absorptive in death. For this poet whose work is so rooted in working-class American life, it is perhaps ironic to think that he so firmly believes that there is a spiritual component to life on earth. But there is another truth about the human soul which Levine's poetry dramatizes. It is the sense that our souls can pass away long before our bodies. Human consciousness can shrink down to practically nothing, and without nurture, the soul will wither away. Like Keats, Levine would say that the world we live in, like it or not, is a vale of soul-making. Or, to be more accurate, that

is what our world ought to be, even as we tie ourselves to our machines and the wages we get paid for so doing.

Edward Hirsch (essay date Spring 1989)

SOURCE: "Naming the Lost: The Poetry of Philip Levine," in *Michigan Quarterly Review,* Vol. XXVIII, No. 2, Spring, 1989, pp. 258-66.

[*In the following essay, Hirsch considers the evolution of Levine's poetry and its gradual change in themes and attitudes. He declares it begins in rage, grows into elegy, and culminates in celebration. He stresses Levine's growing belief in human acceptance and possibility.*]

> I force myself
> to remember
> who I am, what I am, and
> why I am here.
> Silent in America"

In his seminal postmodern meditation, "Thinking Against Oneself," the philosopher E. M. Cioran argues that "We measure an individual's value by the sum of his disagreements with things, by his incapacity to be indifferent, by his refusal as a subject to tend toward the object." Philip Levine's poetry is characterized by just such a profound disagreement with things as they are, by an incapacity for indifference and a rage against objectification. Throughout his work his first and most powerful commitment has been to the failed and lost, the marginal, the unloved, the unwanted. His primary impulse has been to memorialize the details and remember the exploitations. The dedicatory seventh section of his poem, **"Silent in America"**—his largest and most summary early poem—is explicit:

> For a black man whose
> name I have forgotten who danced
>   all night at Chevy
>   Gear & Axle,
>   for that great stunned Pole
> who laughed when he called me Jew
>   Boy, for the ugly
>   who had no chance,
>   the beautiful in
> body, the used and the unused,
>   those who had courage
>   and those who quit—
>   Rousek and Ficklin
> numbed by their own self-praise
>   who ate their own shit
>   in their own rage;

> for these and myself
> whom I loved and hated, I
> had presumed to speak
> in measure.

Levine is a poet of the night shift, a late ironic Whitman of our industrial heartland, a Romantic anarchist who repeatedly proclaims, "Vivas for those who have failed. . . ." His life's work is a long assault on isolation, an ongoing struggle against the enclosures of suffering, the private, hermetic, sealed-off nature of our lives; indeed, he is a poet of radical immanence who has increasingly asserted a Keatsian faith in the boundlessness of human possibility. One might say that his work begins in rage, ripens towards elegy, and flourishes in celebration. All three moods—rage, sorrow, and a kind of wry hopefulness—appear and reappear in his work, sometimes in complex tonal combinations. One lyric points forwards, another backwards, and yet the overall drift and progress of the poems is clear. What starts as anger slowly deepens into grief and finally rises into joy.

Levine's early work follows a stylistic and thematic arc from *On the Edge* (1963) to *They Feed They Lion* (1972). These poems are written under the sign of the thistle and the fist, what one poem invokes as the "bud of anger, kinked tendril of my life" (**"Fist"**). Levine has always written with a special concentrated fury about the so-called "stupid jobs" of his youth and his first books established and developed his working-class loyalties and themes. They evoke three distinct but related cities: Detroit, Fresno, and Barcelona, all of which are defined as landscapes of desolation, rugged cities of the enraged, the exhausted, the exploited. Levine began as a relentlessly urban writer and one of the motivating premises of his early work was his determination to center that work around the city, to create a poetry of the urban landscape. In this regard, the poem which reverberates through all of his work is Wordsworth's sonnet, "Composed Upon Westminster Bridge, September 3, 1802," which eventually provided the title for his book, *Sweet Will.* Wordsworth's last line—"And all that mighty heart is lying still!"—has a special resonance in Levine's case because his work begins in silence and failure: indeed, one of the persistent themes of the early books is voicelessness, the desperate silence of **"Silent in America,"** the failure of poets who don't write in **"My Poets."** He increasingly insists on the defiant transformation of blankness into speech, and refuses to be quieted. This theme of the necessity of violently breaking silence peaks in the furious incantatory rhythms of **"They Feed They Lion,"** a poem which celebrates the communal insurrection of the Detroit riots of 1967. All that mighty heart is no longer lying still.

Levine's first volume, *On the Edge,* published when he was thirty-five years old, was a book of free-floating despair, hampered by its own formalism, alienated even from itself.

Levine himself has said that these were the poems of someone on the verge of despair and breakdown, on the edge of his own culture, even of his own life. One of the formal problems of the poems is that they are too tightly-controlled; they are rhyming iambic pentameter lyrics whose underlying subject matter is mostly suppressed and in conflict with the tradition of "pure poetry" out of which they emerge. The sole exception is **"The Horse"**—a devastating poem about the survivors of Hiroshima—which anticipates the idiomatic and controlled free verse style of Levine's later work. The title poem is a skillful eighteen-line lyric which sounds a brooding note of defiance from the poet's alter ego: "My name is Edgar Poe and I was born / In 1928 in Michigan. / Nobody gave a damn." The poem projects a certain hip bravado but also suggests the depth of the writer's alienation: "I did not write, for I was Edgar Poe, / Edgar the mad one, silly, drunk, unwise. . . ." *On the Edge* was a striking debut stymied by its own pent-up rage: it is about being on the margins, close to breakdown, hedged in by despair.

Levine's second book, *Not This Pig* (1968), exchanged despair for determination, furiously digging in its heels. It is a volume of well-wrought lyrics where the urban furies reign. In this world no one wants to remember who he is, happiness and despair are a "twinight doubleheader," the eight o'clock factory whistle comes "blasting from heaven," and there are no fresh starts. Edgar Poe has been replaced by "Baby Villon," an underdog who is everywhere victimized but continues to fight back, a version of the poet as outlaw. But the book's key figure is a self-conscious pig being driven to market who staunchly refuses to squeal or break down. The pig in **"Animals are Passing from our Lives,"** a Bartleby of the animal world, can already smell "the sour, grooved block," the blade "that opens the hole / and the pudgy white fingers / that shake out the intestines / like a hankie," but he refuses to fall down in terror, to turn futilely "like a beast" against the boy who drives him along, resolutely keeping his dignity, proclaiming "No. Not this pig." In a way, the pig is a tough, metaphorical stand-in for his human counterpart, the worker who refuses to give up his dignity or to be objectified.

The bud of anger blossoms into full flower in *They Feed They Lion,* the culminating book of Levine's early work. In his two previous small-press books, *Red Dust* and *Pili's Wall* (both published in 1971), Levine began to abandon his early formalism, developing an increasingly narrative and supple free verse style, a more open and self-questioning approach to the dramatic lyric. He linked a Spanish surrealist imagery to a street-wise American idiom. **"Clouds"** is representative:

> Morning is exhaustion, tranquilizers, gasoline,
> the screaming of frozen bearings,
> the failures of will, the tv talking to itself.

The clouds go on eating oil, cigars,
housewives, sighing letters,
the breath of lies. In their great silent pockets
they carry off all our dead.

In these poems Levine has turned from a descendant of Poe into a grandson of Whitman. Thereafter his poems seem to have grown directly from the gritty soil of William Carlos Williams. They became larger and more inclusive, representing the rugged, impure, democratic side of our poetry.

They Feed They Lion reaps the fruit of that labor. It is Levine's most eloquent book of industrial Detroit, evoking the world of Dodge Main and Wyandotte Chemical, grease shops and foundries, the city "pouring fire." The poems remember the "unburned" Detroit of 1952 (**"Saturday Sweeping"**) as well as the "charred faces" of Detroit in 1968 (**"Coming Home, Detroit, 1968"**). Some are set in California (**"Renaming the Kings"**), some in Spain (**"Salami,"** **"To P. L., 1916-1937"**), but all record a nightmare of suffering, what **"To a Fish Head Found on the Beach near Málaga"** calls "the burned essential oil / seeping out of death." Yet their author is also capable of thorny affirmations, of celebrating his own angels of Detroit. The magisterial title poem—with its fierce diction and driving rhythms influenced by Biblical language, Dylan Thomas's poetry, and colloquial Black speech—is Levine's hymn to communal rage, to acting in unison. The poem has a sweeping musical and rhetorical authority, a burning sense of "the acids of rage, the candors of tar," a psychological understanding of what drives people to move from "Bow Down" to "Rise Up," and it builds to an apocalyptic conclusion:

> From my five arms and all my hands,
> From all my white sins forgiven, they feed,
> From my car passing under the stars,
> They Lion, from my children inherit,
> From the oak turned to a wall, they Liown,
> From they sack and they belly opened
> And all that was hidden burning on the oil-stained
> earth
> They feed they Lion and he comes.

Both in stylistic and in thematic terms, Levine's next two books, *1933* (1974) and *The Names of the Lost* (1976) are a single unit, a major turning point in his work, the books where he becomes a poet absorbed by memory and preoccupied by the deep past. *1933* is first and foremost a book haunted by the death of the father, ritualizing its suffering, asking the question, "Where did my father go in my fifth autumn?" (**"Zaydee"**) The fundamental psychological shock at the heart of Levine's work—its first reverberating loss— is the death of the father: indeed, the dead father stands as the authoritative absence at the heart of all his poetry. Thus the year 1933 is not—as so many have assumed—the date

of his own birth, but the year of his father's death, his true baptism into the world. The title poem is simultaneously a letter to a man who died long ago ("Father, the world is so different in many places" and "you would not know me now") and a Roethkean elegy to a man who "entered the kingdom of roots / his head still as a stone" when the poet was only a child. The poem typifies much of Levine's most recent work in the way it alternates between the present tense ("I go in afraid of the death you are") and an irretrievable past ("I would be a boy in worn shoes splashing through rain"). As a book, *1933* powerfully evokes what is for the speaker "the blind night of Detroit" in the 1930s. It enlarges the first loss of the father to include a series of family elegies: **"Zaydee," "Grandmother in Heaven," "Goodbye," "Uncle,"** and the centerpiece, **"Letters for the Dead."** Thereafter Levine will always be a poet who relies heavily on long-term memory. His poems become less protected and defended, more open and exposed, emotionally riskier.

As Levine's work has progressed, a predominant tone of ferocious anger has slowly evolved into a more vulnerable and elegiac tenderness. His poems have developed a softer edge while maintaining their brooding intensity. Almost everything he has written has been characterized by a determination to witness and remember, to memorialize people who would otherwise be forgotten. His middle work begins neither with outrage nor with an Adamic impulse to name the swarming fullness of things; it begins not with *presence* but with *absence,* with a furious determination to remember what is already lost. These are books more concerned with memory than with imagination, defining the poet as someone who names and recovers, who recalls the victimized, the disenfranchised, the fallen. Nowhere is this sense of the writer's task more clearly defined than in his book *The Names of the Lost.* In these poems, Levine explicitly links the people of his childhood whom "no one remembers" with his doomed heroes from the Spanish Civil War. As a lyric like **"Gift for a Believer"** makes clear, the poems originate with a personal oath to remember ("When old Nathan Pine / gave two hands to a drop-forge / at Chevy, my spit turned to gall / and I swore I'd never forget"), but they also take up the anarchist dream of freedom and justice, the chant of "We shall inherit," the world that Durrutti said "is growing here / in my heart this minute." The anarchist struggle for a new world as well as the romantic sense that "the human is boundless" provided Levine with a political as well as a personal way to understand the past.

Levine's next book, *Ashes: Poems New and Old* (1979), is in some ways a transitional volume that looks back toward the two previous books of death as well as forward to the new poems of regeneration. It begins by addressing the dead father, "a black tooth planted in the earth / of Michigan," asking him not to return (**"Father"**). The whole book is animated by the simple factual recognition that certain losses are final, death and childhood. And yet the book ends on the resolutely optimistic note that "for now / the lost are found" and that father and son, the living and the dead, can enter the world together (**"Lost and Found"**). Thus what began with the death of the father has been converted into a dream of possibility. The silence and failure of people turning away from each other has been transformed into an idea of communal inheritance. Out of the ashes, the names are given back to the lost.

The motif of regeneration and rebirth resounds through Levine's next three books: there is a plaintiveness in *7 Years from Somewhere* (1979) that turns into a dark optimism and even hopefulness in *One for the Rose* (1981) and a bittersweet acceptance in *Sweet Will* (1985). These books begin with the playful assertion, "I could come to believe / almost anything" (**"I Could Believe"**) and conclude on the image of the late sunlight "promising nothing" and overflowing "the luminous thorns of the roses," catching fire "for a moment on the young leaves" (**"Jewish Graveyards, Italy"**). In these books Levine becomes a Wordsworthian poet of humanistic naturalism, a poet of joy as well as of suffering.

Many of the poems in *7 Years from Somewhere* have the intimate character of prayers half-addressed to the interior self, half to the darkness. Poems such as **"I Could Believe," "Hear Me," "Let Me Begin Again," "Words,"** and **"Let Me Be,"** have the tone of a man talking—in his own words—either "to no one or myself," disavowing wisdom, asking unanswerable questions. The old angers burn and crackle in **"You Can Have It,"** perhaps the book's single greatest poem, but most of the poems turn away from the hard fury of such a renunciation, in actuality accepting the flawed earth as it is, returning to the here and now, celebrating a world "drowning / in oil, second by second" (**"The Life Ahead"**). The speaker in **"Francisco, I'll Bring You Red Carnations"** returns to the grave of a fallen Spanish Civil War hero not only to remember the dream of a city "where every man and every woman gives / and receives the gift of work / and care," but also to affirm that the dream "goes on in spite of all / that mocks it" and to celebrate "the unbroken / promise of your life that / once was frail and flesh."

This more celebratory mood of acceptance—self-questioning, darkened by doubts—continues to animate many of the more playful and narrative poems of *One for the Rose* and *Sweet Will.* In these books Levine weaves fuller and larger stories, mixing imagination and memory, creating alternative lives for himself, phantasmagorias of the past. He announces with wry irony, "I was born in Lucerne," and "I think I must have lived / once before, not as a man or woman / but as a small, quick fox pursued / through fields of grass and grain / by ladies and gentlemen on horseback" (**"The Fox"**). We may say that this sly, quick fox is a metonymic cousin not only to the courageous pig of *Not This Pig* and the lion of *They Feed They Lion,* but also a metaphoric relative of the anarchists, Francisco Ascara and Cipriano Mera, the emblematic Spanish immigrant in the poem, **"To Cipriano, in the Wind."** Cipriano worked in the back of Peerless Cleaners and enunciated the word "Dignidad" for the young poet. He told him, "Some day the world / is ours" and "Spring, spring, it always comes after." Levine's politics are utopian and the final hardwon affirmation of his work is a Keatsian faith that the poet's breath can be passed on "to anyone who can / believe that life comes back / again and again without end /and always with the same face . . ." (**"Belief"**). His vision is humanistic; he concludes by embracing the earth as his own home (**"The Voice"**).

Levine's recent work struggles against the incapacities of the word, the gulfs of language and experience. This is one of the reasons that it has increasingly tended toward rhetorical narrative, toward the healing coherence of story. His work is neither logocentric nor disjunctive, but asserts a semi-objectivist, semi-visionary faith in the radical capacity of language to render up our world. His thirteenth collection to date, *A Walk with Tom Jefferson* (1988), is a book of radiant memories that ramify outward to tell a recurrent story of buying and selling, of how we work (and don't) in America. "I am in my element," he tells us in one poem, "urging the past / out of its pockets of silence," recalling with a certain comic relish his depressing early jobs (in the book's first poem he remembers selling copper kitchenware, Fuller brushes, American encyclopedias), ferociously condemning the brutality of so much of our working lives, speaking out with genuine indignation and moral authority against what is most corrupting and exploitative in American life. He also celebrates the gritty heroism of people who manage to survive against the odds.

The long title poem is the book's narrative centerpiece, the memory of an emblematic walk through Detroit with an unsung black man, a retired factory worker who shares, in Levine's words, "the fierce spirit of independence and originality of his namesake." Tom Jefferson acts as the poet's Virgilian guide—tough, unbowed, faithful, humane—leading him through a neighborhood that had been devastated in the late sixties. In the aftermath of the destruction, amidst the vacant lots and condemned property, the poet discovers that people are leading quasi-rural lives—keeping gardens and animals, mustering their resources, rooting in, making do, cultivating new life. Their triumphs are small but real: they have the courage of survivors. As Levine said in a recent interview in *The Paris Review,* "The poem is a tribute to all these people who survived in the face of so much discouragement. They survived everything America can dish out." Here, as elsewhere in his work, Levine's great subject is the sustaining dream of freedom, the stubborn will of the dispossessed to dig in and endure.

Philip Levine's work is still evolving, still growing and changing. And yet it has already earned a rightful place in an American Romantic lineage that includes Hart Crane's *The Bridge,* William Carlos Williams's "Asphodel, that Greeny Flower," Theodore Roethke's "North American Sequence," Robert Hayden's "Middle Passage," and Galway Kinnell's "The Avenue Bearing the Initial of Christ into the New World." Levine's life's work sounds what Wallace Stevens called "the No that precedes the final Yes," and for all its furious renunciations it ends by being a poetry of praise "for a world that runs on and on at its own sweet will."

Linda Gregerson (review date December 1989)

SOURCE: A review of *A Walk with Tom Jefferson,* in *Poetry,* Vol. CLV, No. 3, December, 1989, pp. 236-39.

[*In the following review, Gregerson considers some of the major themes in Levine's poetry, both in this collection and elsewhere.*]

New York, Detroit, Fresno, Medford: from a shifting home front, the poet at sixty files his report on "God's Concern / for America." The evidence is not such as to make the poet sanguine. The walls that keep the darkness out are everywhere paper-thin. The news from above is mostly of ourselves: the autumnal sunset brilliant with pollutants, "all the earth we've pumped / into the sky," makes a pageant of doom from the by-products of human hope and industry (**"A Walk with Tom Jefferson"**). In Fresno, just this side of the fault line, the poet dreams the end of the world (**"Waking in March"**). The news arrives, bad joke that it is, from the glow above Los Angeles, and the poet can do no more than "go from bed / to bed bowing to the small damp heads / of my sons. . . ." Outside the dream, the children have long since left home, but every parent knows those rounds by heart, knows the fault line panic opens beside the beds and their sweet burdens. The children have fallen asleep imagining that it is safe to do so; the parent, standing for safety, knows that safety is illusion. Who's in charge here? "If I told you that the old woman / named Ida Bellow was shot to death / for no more than $5 and that a baby / of eighteen months saw it all from / where she wakened on the same bed / but can't tell because she can't speak / you'd say I was making it up" (**"These Streets"**).

While America goes to the dogs, the poet with America stuck in his throat rehearses the lessons of his American masters, of Stevens and Whitman (**"I Sing the Body Electric"**), of Williams (**"A Theory of Prosody"**), of the carping Yvor Winters (**"28"**). Levine writes, as the good ones do, to save his life. He also writes a revisionist esthetic of Decline and Fall, retrieving poetry from frontier bravado ("Rexroth /

reminiscing on a Berkeley FM station in the voice / God uses to lecture Jesus Christ"). To Whitman's triumphant corporal embrace, to Stevens's pungent oranges and extended wings, Levine replies with the echoing actuarials of Hartford on a Sunday morning ("In my black rain coat I go back / out into the gray morning and dare / the cars on North Indemnity Boulevard / to hit me, but no one wants trouble / at this hour"). To Williams's manifesto on the modernist poetic line ("As the cat / climbed over / the top of // the jamcloset . . . "), Levine replies with feline Nellie, who "would sit behind me / as I wrote" and paw at the hand that extended a line too far. "The first / time she drew blood I learned / it was poetic to end / a line anywhere to keep her / quiet." To Winters, for whom meter was morality and syntax a hedge against chaos, Levine replies with loopy numerology: the poet at 56 traces the numbered highways of America, the enumerated rehearsals of oblivion (14 hours of fevered sleep, 3 close encounters with death), and the domestic plenum (2 opposing families of 5) back to himself at 28, just half the age of the century, half the age of his newfound mentor (Winters in Los Altos), half the age of the older self who writes this poem. Winters titled his collected prose *In Defense of Reason.* Levine's bittersweet critique of reason records the patent incapacity of form to structure meaning, all the while making meaning of vaporous coincidence.

Escaping the dead end of swing-shift Detroit for sumptuous California, the artist as a young man delivered himself into the hands of one who, all but forgotten among younger writers now, was a name to conjure with in the middle decades of this century: a poet who came to believe that free verse led to madness, a critic who represented the far right fringe of the canon police, a teacher, bless him, who fostered most passionately those protégés most certain to defect. While Winters presided in the hills of Los Altos and the gentlemen's club of Stanford, the young Levine kept house with two kids and a pregnant wife in East Palo Alto, Stanford's shadow ghetto, an unincorporated stretch of cinderblock and prefab for the un- and the underemployed. For the apprentice poet, California's royal way—El Camino Real—was a divider strip between the good life and real life, a place for poaching lilacs. The poaching has stood him in good stead, evolving a poetry whose range of consciousness and conscience, whose capacity for anger and debunking and sweet recuperation lends heart to the embattled republic, or to those of its citizens with leisure to read.

In the title poem of his new book, Levine takes a mentor of another sort. Brought up from Alabama on the dream of $5 a day, Tom Jefferson, grown old now, tends a garden in the gutted Promised Land, "Between the freeway / and the gray conning towers / of the ballpark" in post-industrial Detroit. Having lost his youth to the auto plant and his son to Korea, Tom Jefferson quotes scripture and pushes a shopping cart through abandoned lots. Tom Jefferson "is a believer. / You can't plant winter vegetables / if you aren't. . . ." Tom Jefferson takes his name from the slave-holding theorist of liberty and "property," revised to the pursuit of happiness. Walking with Tom Jefferson, Levine recalls his own first part in capitalism's long last coma:

> when I worked nights
>   on the milling machines
> at Cadillac transmission,
>   another kid just up
> from West Virginia asked me
>   what was we making,
> and I answered, I'm making
>   2.25 an hour,
> don't know what you're
>   making, and he had
> to correct me, gently, what was
>   we making out of
> this here metal, and I didn't know.

What he ultimately made, of course, was work of another sort. The thirteen bound volumes of that work to date, remarkable intersections of private memory and political fable, will not, unaided, cure what ails us. But in an age more notable for overflowing landfills than for neighborhood renewal, it is much to make poems that heal the breach between ignorance and understanding, labor and wage.

Richard Chess (essay date Fall 1990)

SOURCE: "In the Tradition of American Jewish Poetry: Philip Levine's Turning," in *Studies in American Jewish Literature,* Vol. 9, No. 2, Fall, 1990, pp. 197-214.

[*In the following essay, Chess discusses the Jewishness of Levine's poetry. He contends that when Levine tackles an explicitly Jewish topic, the result is often cliché. However, when he writes sincerely of general social and political justice, a genuine Jewish voice emerges.*]

The discussion of American Jewish poetry has remained limited at best. On one hand, occasional book reviews have drawn attention to the treatment of Jewish subjects by this poet or that. On the other, there has been a virtual dismissal of the subject as one worthy of extensive investigation by critics like Harold Bloom and Herbert Levine, both of whom criticize the work of American Jewish poets on the grounds of their religious shortcomings.

But the fact is that this century's American poetry includes, and has been deeply influenced by, the work of dozens of American Jewish poets, most of whom have little or no in-

terest in the Jewish religious experience. This is not to say they have no interest in the Jewish cultural experience. Indeed, sensitive reading of the poetry, especially those poems that on the surface appear to have little to do with the Jewish experience, often reveals how profound the influence of Jewish experience has been on a poet's vision and aesthetic. This essay will examine the work of Philip Levine, one of the better living American poets, identifying the particular ways Jewish experience shapes his poetry, as well as the ways he translates that experience in the poems.

Philip Levine's poetry is famous for its portraits of working-class and political heroes, victimized survivors of a brutal world, rendered in short-lined free verse. The characteristic rhythmic intensity of his poems comes from long sentences of parallel phrases, composed of a blend of colloquial and biblical diction, that build toward dramatic climaxes. This style in part reflects the universalization of Levine's experience as an American-Jewish working-class male from Detroit.

Levine is no stranger to work, as he insistently reminds us in the biographical note to many of his books: "After a succession of stupid jobs he [Levine] left the city for good . . . " (*7 Years from Somewhere*). This terse biographical note implicitly warns readers against regarding Levine's poems about workers as a liberal's sentimental portait of the proletariat. For a significant portion of his youth Levine suffered the same life as the workers about whom he regularly writes. The black man "who danced all night at Chevy Gear & Axle" of **"Silent in America"** (*Not This Pig* 1968); the angel Bernard, a factory worker, **"The Angels of Detroit"** (*They Feed They Lion* 1972); Eddie of **"Making Soda Pop"** (*One for the Rose* 1981); Stash, the punch-press operator of **"Sweet Will"** (*Sweet Will* 1985)—these and other unsung workers are the realistic heroes of Levine's poems. Even when not portraying men at work, Levine is conscious of man laboring without relief. "[E]ach man has one brother . . . and . . . together they are only one man sharing a heart that always labors," Levine writes in **"You Can Have It"** (*Years*).

In section VII of the powerful early poem **"Silent in America,"** Levine dedicates his work, his poetry, to the workers and other victims he met at one or another of his "stupid jobs":

> For a black man whose
> name I have forgotten who danced
>   all night at Chevy
>   Gear & Axle,
>   for that great stunned Pole
> who laughed when he called me Jew
>   Boy, for the ugly
>   who had no chance
>
>   (*Pig*)

His sympathy for the underdog originates, in part, in his experiences as a Jew growing up in Detroit:

> We were a people scattered all over the world who knew what it was to be scattered all over the world. We knew what it was to be underdogs and to survive in the face of enmity and disrespect of others. We knew we were a noble people no matter what anyone told us to the contrary. Our great cultural heritage was that we could feel the suffering of any people and know that any people was as good as any other.
>
> *(Don't Ask)*

Levine's particular experience of Jewish suffering enables him to act compassionately toward anyone who suffers; it also helped him discover in the Jew a universal symbol of suffering, of exile. Consequently, Levine's portraits of the Jew and other underdogs share realistic as well as mythological characteristics.

"Baby Villon" (*Pig*) for instance, depicts an encounter between the poet and an imaginary other—an outcast, marginal figure who survives the cruelty of the world by fighting back:

> He tells me in Bangkok he's robbed
> Because he's white; in London because he's black
> In Barcelona, Jew; in Paris, Arab;
> Everywhere and at all times, and he fights back.

This protean creature is never transformed into a member of the dominant race; he's the international suspect, the mythological alien who refuses to give in, who in fact is strengthened by his pain. Though he could be angry at the world that despises him, there is "no anger / In the flat brown eyes flecked with blood"; though he could be enraged by his lowly status, "he's rated seventh in the world, / And there's no passion in his voice."

There is a marked resemblance between the poet and his imaginary brother:

> And he points down at his black head ridged
> With black kinks of hair. He touches my hair,
> Tells me I should never disparage
> The stiff bristles that guard the head of the fighter.

There are also characteristics that distinguish the two men from each other; the poet is graced with an untroubled fair and smooth face; Baby Villon, hardened by his travails, is "stiff, 116 pounds, five feet two, no bigger than a girl." The encounter concludes as Baby Villon "holds my shoulders, / Kisses my lips, his eyes still open, / My imaginary brother, my cousin, / Myself made otherwise by all his pain."

The hero of this excellent poem, Baby Villon, is presented in terms that assure we will sympathize with his predicament. He is unjustly victimized, yet he remains level headed while defending his dignity. He is a fighter, but not a ruthless fighter; he is sensitive, loving, and kind. He is a family man, saddened by the loss of his father, his brother, to the war or worse. Not only does he defend his own human rights, but because of his composite nature he defends the rights of all marginal men and women. In particular he struggles for the right to his past, his uncensored past: "He [Baby Villon] asks me to tell all I can remember / Of my father, his uncle."

Of course, this poem is as much about the poet as it is about Baby Villon. Through the encounter with his "imaginary brother," an encounter made more dramatic by its uniqueness—"We stand to end this first and last visit"—the poet undergoes a profound transformation; he is "made otherwise by all his [Villon's] pain." In fact, Baby Villon is a reflected image of the poet, the victimized Jew as well as the fatherless son. In addition to the vulnerability they share as Jews, Baby Villon's desire, his need to know all he can of his dead father, is Levine's need, reflected in poem after poem, to know all he can of his own father who died when Levine was five.

The poem **"Baby Villon,"** then, records a moment in which life and myth converge—the life of the poet, the myth of Baby Villon—a moment in which Levine intuitively perceives the universality of his particular experiences as a Jew. I say intuitively because it was only some time after publication, upon questioning by Abraham Chapman, editor of *Jewish-American Literature: An Anthology,* that Levine consciously recognized the essentially Jewish nature of the poem:

> To him [Chapman] **"Baby Villon"** was a Jewish poem. I saw what he meant: it was a celebration of courage and integrity and the difficulty of life wherever it takes place.
>
> *(Don't Ask)*

Aside from Levine's belated recognition of **"Baby Villon"** as a Jewish poem, we can identify traces of a biblical story that contribute further to the Jewish nature of the poem: the enigmatic, transformative encounter on the bank of the Jabbok river between Jacob and a man, an angel, or God (the text is ambiguous). Though Levine certainly did not have this story in mind when composing **"Baby Villon,"** there are several poignant parallels between the two texts. Levine describes Baby Villon, his "imaginary brother," as a "stiff," rugged fighter. Esau, Jacob's brother—a hunter, a sportsman, a fighter—is also characterized by his ruggedness. And Jacob, like the speaker of **"Baby Villon,"** is shy and fair skinned.

Furthermore, both Jacob and Levine are profoundly changed by their respective encounters. Though the identity of the figure with whom Jacob wrestled is ambiguous, some rabbinical interpreters have argued convincingly that the struggle occurs between two aspects of Jacob's personality, the heroic (a characteristic that prior to this event had only asserted itself in Jacob's dreams) and the mediocre, the unassuming. At Peniel, Jacob's day-time personality defends itself victoriously; Jacob discovers the strength to behave heroically in his waking life. In **"Baby Villon"** Levine, too, undergoes a transformation; his fair, sheltered side is toughened through his encounter with the fighter-for-justice Villon, a representative of the heroic side of Levine's personality.

In this case, the correspondence between the two texts is probably no more than coincidental—coincidence, however, grounded in Levine's familiarity with Hebrew scriptures. Indeed, on many other occasions Levine deliberately draws on biblical characters and episodes to lend mythological weight to his subjects. *On the Edge,* Levine's first book, is full of biblical allusions, even if the contemporary world depicted seems at odds with the biblical world. **"Berenda Slough"** (*Edge*), for instance, is an anti-Genesis poem: "Earth and water without form, / change, or pause: as if the third / day had not come, this calm norm / of chaos denies the Word." Thus the poem begins with a vision that seems to deny creation. But, as the poem instructs and warns us, the viewer who "denies this is creation . . . shall find nothing he can comprehend." The warning stated, the poem concludes with its apocalyptic vision: "Here the mind beholds the mind / as it shall be in the end." This vision of creation and the end of time is a particularly metaphysical one, characteristic of Levine's earliest work. Looking out on the landscape, the viewer witnesses not "stumps," "clumps," and "rushes," but a vision of his own mind.

In its use of biblical allusions to intensify a rejected lover's despair, **"Green Thumb,"** another poem from the first book, becomes unintentionally comic. "Shake out my pockets! Harken to the call / Of that calm voice that makes no sound at all!" the poem begins, imitating the form of a prayer (*Edge*). But to whom is this bereaved lover calling? God? No, to the great, mysterious "Green Thumb." The poem goes on to describe the love affair at the height of its passion.

> My blood was bubbling like a ten-day stew;
> It kept on telling me the thing to do.
> I asked, she acquiesced, and then we fell
> To private Edens in the midst of hell.
> For forty days temptation was our meal,
> The night our guide, and what we could not feel
> We could not trust.

In bed the couple is in Eden, though they are surrounded by hell. The affair endures, apparently, for 40 days, the length

of time the Israelites wandered the desert on their Exodus from Egypt, led by a pillar of fire and clouds to Mount Sinai and the divine revelation. But this couple will not survive until the revelation, for at the start of the next stanza we are informed, "At last we parted, she to East Moline, / I to the service of the great unseen." The speaker wanders about, lost, trying to interpret the "great unseen's" portents, until he learns, by mail, that his departed beloved is pregnant. Guilt ridden, "heartsick and tired," the poet begs for relief:

> . . . to you, Green Thumb, I prayed
> For her reprieve and that our debt be paid
> By my remorse. "Give me a sign," I said,
> "Give me my burning bush." You squeaked the
>   bed.
> I hid my face like Moses on the hill,
> But unlike Moses did not feel my will
> Swell with new strength; I put my choice to
>   sleep.
> That night we cowered, choice and I, like sheep.

This failed Moses can attain no comfort from the traditional religious order of experience. The biblical motif, used in this way, overwhelms the poem. The gap between the sacred and the profane is too great, creating one comic effect after another. If Levine wants to mythologize his experience, he must find a way other than overlaying the mundane with the biblical.

The presence of the biblical remains strong even in Levine's most recent work. In **"A Walk with Tom Jefferson,"** Tom, a black man whose family moved from Alabama to Detroit, where he lives in a burned-out neighborhood growing vegetables in the least likely squares of earth, sees life around him as if it were biblical:

> A father puts down a spade, his son
>   picks it up,
> "That's Biblical," he [Tom] says,
>   "The son goes off,
> the father takes up the spade
>   again, that's Biblical." (57)

Jefferson is so persistent in perceiving the biblical resonance in the life about him that the speaker too begins to share this perception, until finally he asks, "What commandment / was broken to bring God's / wrath down on these streets, / what did we do wrong, going / about our daily lives." Here Levine speaks within a covenantal framework as if he believes that God's wrath was brought on by some human violation of one of the commandments. He then goes on to sum up the season in nature, the season in American life. "It's Biblical, this season / of color coming to its end," Levine writes, referring at once to autumn and the dominant racial theme of the poem. Levine has absorbed the Hebrew Bible. In the Tom

Jefferson poem, the title poem of his most recent book, Levine seems to be proclaiming that his work is biblical, a point that most critics and reviewers of Levine have either ignored or overlooked.

The biblical character and moment that figure most often in Levine's work is Adam and his banishment from the garden of Eden. **"For Fran,"** one of the best poems in *On the Edge,* describes Levine's wife, a gardener, working "on the hard ground where Adam strayed, / where nothing but his wants remain. . . . " While Fran gardens, Levine strays on the hard ground, book after book, suffering the frustration of his and his heroes's unfulfilled desires.

In **"In a Vacant House,"** a less-successful poem in which the poet in his privacy attempts to distinguish between the facts and illusions of his existence, Levine comes to the realization that "No one can begin anew / naming by turn beast, fowl, / and bush with the exact word" (*Edge*). Adam, the first poet, experienced the unique freedom to name the things of the world. All poets since Adam have had to face the challenging prospect of writing about a world in which everything has already been named. Adam was cursed with exile, the poets after Adam have been cursed with the diminished possibilities of language.

Adam is a natural character for Levine to select as his biblical other. As Adam was cursed with toiling the earth all the days of his life, so too Levine has suffered the curse of hard labor. As Adam wandered forever in exile, so too Levine suffers the homelessness of exile. And as Adam named things with exact words, so too Levine strives, though sometimes unsuccessfully, to find the exact words to describe his world. In **"The Face,"** Levine, "[t]ired and useless," resigns himself to silence (a deadly gesture for a poet). Instead of speaking, he listens to the street cries of Barcelona "as though one word mattered more / than another in this world, / in this city, broken and stained, / which is the home of no one, / though it shouts out all / our names" (*Years*). Levine the poet must bring himself to believe that "one word matter[s] more than another" if he is to continue writing. Levine the son of Adam knows that the post-Edenic world is not his home, despite the fact that his name is among those shouted out during roll call. When Levine does go home, as in **"Coming Home, Detroit 1968,"** he finds his home "charred" and "boarded up" and "dirtied with words" (*Lion*). It is not that Eden, guarded by an angel with a flaming sword, is off limits. Eden is burned, destroyed, written.

Perhaps the most startling and revealing use of the figure of Adam appears in **"The Turning"** from *On the Edge:*

> Unknown faces in the street
> And winter coming on. I
> Stand in the last moments of

> The city, no more a child,
> Only a man,—one who has
> Looked upon his own nakedness
> Without shame, and in defeat
> Has seen nothing to bless.
> Touched once, like a plum, I turned
> Rotten in the meat, or like
> The plum blossom I never
> Saw, hard at the edges, burned
> At the first entrance of life,
> And so endured, unreckoned,
> Untaken, with nothing to give.
> The first Jew was God; the second
> Denied him; I am alive.

Here the embodiment of the exiled Adam is complete. The shameless, defeated poet stands alone at the edge of a dying world: the city behind him is dying, fall is collapsing into winter, the promise of childhood has been replaced with the depletion of manhood.

The poem concludes by tracing the poet's lineage, a common device in the Bible (a begot b, b begot c, c begot d, and so on): "The first Jew was God; the second denied him; I am alive." It is the concluding two lines that startle. Traditionally, one does not think of the God of the Hebrew Bible as a Jew, but as the God of all humankind. Abraham is customarily considered the father of Judaism. Nor does one regard Adam as a Jew. Adam is the mythological father of all humankind. By identifying Adam as a Jew, Levine particularizes a universal character, the obverse of his customary universalization of Jewish experience. Furthermore, in aligning himself with Adam the second Jew (according to Levine), a Jew who denied God, Levine expresses a sharply ambivalent relation to his Jewish heritage: he is a Jew, but he rejects the central tenet of Judaism, belief in God. Through Adam, Levine locates himself within and without the Jewish tradition.

Not only does **"The Turning"** articulate Levine's divided Jewish identity, it also characterizes a poet who is in part defined by what he rejects, whose very life originates in an act of opposition: the first Jew was God, the second denied him; I am alive. To the extent that Levine stands in opposition to Judaism, he is defined by Judaism.

As he is empowered by the Judaism he rejects, Levine paradoxically is sustained by a Bible he simultaneously embraces and rejects. This is clearly evident in **"My Son and I,"** a poem in which Levine masterfully intertwines the biblical with the mundane in a strikingly personal and mythological manner. "In a coffee house at 3 am / and he believes / I'm dying," the poem begins (*The Names of the Lost*). Levine's poems are almost never set in the middle of the day. Usually they are set at dawn, a time of hope—often false hope—

or at twilight, the hour of despair. This poem, however, is set during the dead and hopeless hours of the night. The location is New York City, where "the wind / moves along the streets / . . . picking up / abandoned scraps of newspapers / and tiny messages of hope / no one hears." The efficacy of prayer is lost; written communication is cheap and readily discarded. His son is the same laborer Levine once was. The son is "dressed / in worn corduroy pants / and shirts over shirts, / and his hands are stained / as mine once were / with glue, ink, paint."

Seated in the coffee house, with the fallen world about them, the son is deeply saddened by the belief that his father is dying: "For forty / minutes he's tried not / to cry." Had we not already uncovered some of the biblical motifs underlying many of Levine's poems, we might simply dismiss the "forty minutes" as an ordinary report of factual information. Indeed, there is pathos suggested in the detail; forty minutes is a long time to hold back tears. But the number forty, as we have seen elsewhere in Levine, is biblically resonant: forty days the Jews wandered the desert until they reached Sinai and were blessed with divine revelation. Levine draws on this legend later in the poem.

Faced with the loss of his father, the son is concerned with the condition of the rest of his family:

> . . . How are his brothers?
> I tell him I don't know,
> they have grown away
> from me. We are Americans
> and never touch on this
> stunned earth where a boy
> sees his life fly past
> through a car window.

The sociological phenomenon of contemporary American life registered, the American myth of the automobile invoked, Levine again echoes a biblical theme: "stunned earth": "cursed be the ground because of you," God tells Adam in Genesis 3:17.

And Levine continues in the biblical spirit, telling his son about his mother.

> She is deaf and works
> in the earth for days, hearing
> the dirt pray and guiding
> the worm to its feasts.

Finally the son asks the question he has been wanting to ask all along.

> . . . Why
> do I have to die? Why

do I have to sit before him
no longer his father, only
a man? Because the given
must be taken, because
we hunger before we eat,
because each small spark
must turn to darkness.
As we said when we were kids
and knew the names of everything
. . . just because.

As Levine changes in his son's eyes from father to man, he changes in his own eyes. He seems to have outgrown Adam. "When we were kids" we "knew the names of everything." When we were kids, Levine suggests, we were all like Adam, acquiring language and naming the world anew with each word acquired. But now Levine has entered a new stage of life, the Mosaic stage, as it were, a stage in which language fails to say what needs to be said, a stage in which he helplessly replies "just because" to his son's question. Just as Levine finally fails to find the language to give his son a satisfactory answer, he also fails to find a blessing for his son:

> . . . I reach
> across the table and take
> his left hand in mine.
> I have no blessing.

Levine would like to be able to reenact the biblical scenes, the blessing of Isaac by Abraham, and Jacob by Isaac. But try as he might, he cannot find the words. He has absorbed the biblical vision only to realize the bankruptcy of that vision. He has learned to speak the language of the Bible only to learn that he cannot say what must be said, and so, here, as in other poems, Levine careens toward silence.

> . . . I can
> tell him how I found
> the plum blossom before
> I was thirty, how once
> in a rooming house in Alicante
> a man younger than I,
> an Argentine I barely understood,
> sat by me through the night
> while my boy Teddy cried out
> for help, and how when he slept
> at last, my friend wept
> with thanks in the cold light.
> I can tell him that his hand
> sweating in mine can raise
> the Lord God of Stones,
> bring down the Republic of Lies,
> and hold a spoon. Instead
> I say it's late, and he pays

I can tell him this, I can tell him that, I can tell him the other thing, Levine tells us, as he considers moments in his personal as well as collective history that he believes might be of some importance to his son. But, defeated, the father, the poet opts for silence:

> . . . Instead
> I say it's late and he pays
> and leads me back
> through the empty streets
> to the Earl Hotel, where
> the room sours with the mould
> of old Bibles dumped down
> the air shaft.

Aha, we might say, Levine has finally freed himself from the influence of the Bible. And, in part, we would be right, since Levine spends much of his time in poems in which the Bible figures, however subtly, denying its relevance. But Levine is not yet through with the Bible:

> . . . In my coat
> I stand alone in the dark
> waiting for something,
> a flash of light, a song,
> a remembered sweetness
> from all the lives I've lost.
> Next door the TV babbles
> on and on, and I give up
> and sway toward the bed
> in a last chant before dawn.

Despite his failure to find sustenance in the Bible, Levine has arrived at Sinai, awaiting revelation. The revelation, of course, does not come, and he despairs. Is his final gesture one of a man who has dumped the Bible down the air shaft for the last time? Absolutely not. It's the traditional gesture of a praying Jew: "I . . . sway toward the bed in a last chant." At the same time he gives up, he prays, he chants his prayer, he chants his poem. This is Levine, within and without the Hebrew biblical culture, the Jewish culture, at his best.

It is through the integration of biblical archetypes and language with the colloquial speech patterns of an American man from Detroit that Levine transforms his personal lyric into a communal form of address. But despite his success in integrating the biblical with the colloquial, the historical with the contemporary, the past with the present, the communal with the private, the extent of Levine's Jewish vision remains limited.

Explicit references to Jews or Jewish life can be found throughout Levine's work. In **"Saturday Sweeping"** (*Lion*) Levine alludes to the legend of "the great talking dogs that saved the Jews," a legend, he informs us in an interview, he learned from his grandfather (*Ask*); in **"Uncle"** (*1933*) he writes of an uncle who "argued the Talmud under his nails"; in **"Letters for the Dead"** (*1933*) he mentions going off to work "with bloodless [kosher] sandwiches"; **"My Name"** (*One for the Rose*) concludes with an irreverent boy smoking a cigarette or picking his nose "just when the cantor soars before him into a heaven of meaningless words;" in **"Salts and Oils"** (*Sweet Will*) Levine alludes to the imaginary "final, unread book of the Midrash." In short, Levine's work is salted with casual references to essentially American-Jewish cultural experience. But in proportion to the totality of Levine's work, these kinds of specific Jewish references appear only infrequently and feel almost incidental to the heart of the work, as if the references themselves were thoroughly assimilated into the larger world of Levine's poetry. The image that occurs with the greatest frequency is that of the Jew as victim, the Jew as an object of discrimination. **"Making Soda Pop"** begins, "The big driver said / he only fucked Jews" (*Rose*). The poem **"Sweet Will"** celebrated Stash, a Polish-American punch-press operator who

> hollered at all
> of us over the oceanic roar of work,
> addressing us by our names and nations—
> "Nigger, Kike, Hunky, River Rat,"
> but he gave it a tune, an old tune,
> like "America the Beautiful."

As he set out to do in **"Silent in America,"** Levine continues to celebrate the outcast, the overlooked, the discriminated against, the ignored—and without dramatizing that he includes himself as a member of that group.

Of course, growing up as a Jew in Detroit Levine had the unfortunate opportunity to experience anti-Semitism firsthand:

> . . . Detroit was an extraordinarily anti-Semitic city.
> I don't know if you're aware of a man named Father Coughlin, who was on the radio every Sunday from Royal Oak, which is a suburb of Detroit. He had a huge church out there and he preached Hitler every Sunday. I spent most of my childhood and adolescence fighting with people who, you know, wanted to beat me up because I was Jewish. I didn't enjoy it at all. Even winning wasn't very satisfying, you weren't winning anything.
>
> (*Ask*)

Clearly, these childhood and adolescent experiences had a profound impact on Levine, inspiring him to take up the cause of the "failed and lost, the marginal, the unloved, the unwanted," the black, the worker, the Spanish anarchist— and occasionally even the Jew, which he does either in passing references or in more extended form, as in his poems on the Holocaust.

His two poems on the Holocaust are **"The Survivor,"** an elegy for a cousin; and **"On a Drawing by Flavio,"** a poem on a drawing of the Rabbi of Auschwitz. In the latter, Levine comes to the startling recognition that he and the rabbi portrayed in the drawing hanging over his desk are the same man. This is the second character from Jewish life with whom Levine strongly identifies.

"Above my desk / the Rabbi of Auschwitz / bows his head and prays / for us all," the poem begins (*Ashes*). It is both personal and communal: Levine confronts the image of the rabbi in the privacy of his study; at the same time he recognizes profoundly that the image he sits before is one of a man whose concern is for all humankind. Not surprisingly, God does not play a leading role in the poem. If there is a mysterious force in the world, it is centered in nature: ". . . the earth / which long ago inhaled / his last flames turns / its face toward the light."

The arrival of dawn and the "first gray shapes" of the day cause Levine to question, as he sits before the drawing and the window:

> At the cost of such
> death must I enter
> this body again,
> this body which is
> itself closing on
> death? (*Ashes*)

Again, the answer to his question comes not from God but from nature:

> . . . Now the sun
> rises above a stunning
> valley, and the orchards
> thrust their burning
> branches into the day.
> Do as you please, says
> the sun without uttering
> a word.

Nature speaks, though not with a verbal language. A man divided against himself, a man torn between his moral allegiance to the Rabbi of Auschwitz and his own physical nature, Levine confesses his dilemma—he cannot do as he pleases:

> . . . But I can't.
> I am this hand that
> would raise itself
> against the earth

and I am the earth too.

It is as if Levine has identified the earth as the rabbi's enemy, not other men. Perhaps his failure to direct his rage at the true enemies of the rabbi and the Jews is an indication of Levine's utter despair over the moral condition of the human race; certainly the rage Levine might have directed at a God who could allow such horrors as the Holocaust to occur has been ineffectually directed toward the earth. This leads Levine to a state of paralysis, moral and physical:

> I look again and closer
> at the Rabbi and at last
> see he has my face
> that opened its eyes
> so many years ago
> to death. He has these
> long tapering fingers
> that long ago reached
> for our father's hand
> long gone to dirt, these
> fingers that hold
> hand to forearm,
> forearm to hand because
> that is all that God
> gave us to hold.

This closing passage moves from the communal vision with which the poem opens to a wholly private, personal perspective. Looking at the rabbi, Levine is reminded of his own father and the death of his father. Whereas for Levine the tragedy of his life centers around the death of his father, the tragedy in the rabbi's life is the death or failure of God, father of us all. Finally, having personalized the rabbi and sunk to the depth of his own misery, Levine redirects his anger away from earth toward God, a God who in His cruelty has given man nothing on which to depend, onto which to hold.

Considering its subject matter, this poem remains remarkably quiet, lacking the kind of moral outrage and energy of a poem such as **"They Feed They Lion"** or any of Levine's poems for the fallen Spanish anarchists he loves to heroize. **"On a Drawing by Flavio"** fails to sustain any real sense of moral conviction and urgency. It wavers between the personal (and at times, perhaps, selfish) and the communal and works itself into a state of moral paralysis, a problem that does not arise in other poems on political and moral subjects. Levine's recognition of himself in the Rabbi of Auschwitz is, finally, willed and not sincere. The rabbi is nothing if not a man of God; Levine, a man of the earth—in this poem and others—cannot possibly have the kind of sincere identification with him that he does with Adam (a Hebrew word meaning "earthy"), the character who denied God.

This poem provides us a sharp image of the limitations of the Jewishness of Levine's poems. In particular, Levine cannot adequately engage the central belief of Judaism as a religion, the belief in one God. Of course, as a secular American Jew, Levine cannot be expected to write passionately about God. But when he does tackle a subject, such as the Rabbi of Auschwitz, that demands some engagement with theological issues, Levine must be able to address God or the absence of God with a clear and forceful voice. Instead, Levine backs away from the terrifying theological implications of the Holocaust and speaks finally only of the local, personal loss that has troubled his days.

It would be wrong to criticize Levine harshly for failing to do something he has no intention of doing. It is not wrong, however, to note the weakening of Levine's poetry when he approaches explicitly Jewish subjects, as in **"Jewish Graveyards, Italy"** (*Sweet Will*), for instance. That these graveyards are specifically Jewish is of some import to the poet—it must be or else he would not have bothered to identify them as such in the title. The poem, however, avoids exploring the subject the title's specificity suggests. For the most part, this is a nature poem, divided into three sections under the headings of "dust," "shade," and "rain." The first section establishes the setting in language that is neither overly exciting nor engaging:

> it is summer, and even before noon
> the heat is rising to stun us all,
> the crickets, salamanders, ants.
> The large, swart flies circle slowly
> in air around something I can't see
> and won't be waved away.

There is a hint at an encounter with the mysterious in this passage, though this subject is never fully engaged as the poem unfolds. After a fuller presentation of the locale, the speaker finally performs his ritual, the ritual for which he has apparently come to this graveyard:

> I . . . bend to the names
> and say them as slowly as I can.
> Full, majestic, vanished names
> that fill my mouth and go out
> into the densely yellowed air
> of this great valley and dissolve

Once again Levine has come to record the names of the lost, the Jewish lost, though these Jews were neither victims nor martyrs but ordinary citizens of a once thriving Italian-Jewish culture. One hopes that the poem will intensify from here, fully engaging the subject with Levine's customary visionary passion, the same passion we encounter in Levine's masterful elegies, such as **"To P. L., 1916-1937: a soldier of the Republic"** and **"On the Murder of Lieutenant Jose**

Del Castillo By The Falangist Bravo Martinez, July 12, 1936." Sadly, this is not what we get, for just as soon as Levine has engaged what could have become the heart of the poem, he backs away from it, returning to the rather romantic and unintentionally comic depiction of nature that dominates the poem's second part.

In "shade," Levine again approaches what should be the true center of the poem as he identifies the grave of "Sofia Finzi Hersch, who died / in New Jersey and rests / among her Italian relatives." What are we to make of this information? Unfortunately, Levine hasn't given us a clue. Finally, in section three, "rain," Levine confesses, "whatever truth falls from the sky / as slowly as dust settling in / morning light or cold mist rising / from a river, takes the shape / I give it, and I can't give it any." The poet is the shaper of truth, a Keatsian notion perhaps, but here Levine is admitting to his failure: neither truth nor beauty can be found here. It is not that the subject has overpowered him and gotten away from him. Rather, Levine has simply shied away from the true subject of the poem, knowingly or unknowingly. Though **"On a Drawing by Flavio"** fails, it approaches its subject with greater courage and directness. **"Jewish Graveyards, Italy"** dissolves into philosophical reflections on nature, missing the opportunity to present an elegy for people who might well fulfill Levine's requirements for ordinary heroes.

Levine's difficulty writing strong poems on overtly Jewish subjects is perhaps a reflection of his acknowledged ambivalence toward his Jewish identity, an ambivalence based on his rejection of God as well as his discomfort with the concept of Jewish exclusivity:

> I thought it [Judaism] was a religion that preached exclusiveness. In every sense. I'm talking about the culture more than the faith. I was told that people who weren't Jewish hated me, and I ought to hate them, and no matter how I kidded myself sooner or later they'd get me. I was supposed to be somehow superior to them either because I did let them get me or I didn't—I could have my choice.
>
> *(Ask)*

As a source of sympathy for other victims, national and international, however, Levine's Jewishness helps him produce inspired poetry, empowered by a deep sense of human justice and dignity. Indeed, the relatively few poems on overtly Jewish subjects may be less an indication of the minimal effect Jewishness has had on Levine's poetic vision than an indication of Levine's desire to avoid the potential charge of Jewish exclusivity. And he does avoid the charge by essentially abandoning Jewish life as subject matter and embracing in its stead the lives of other marginal characters and groups. Levine himself draws the connection between his Jewish past and his interest in the Spanish Civil War:

It began [his interest in the Spanish Civil War] because it was apparent to me . . . coming from a Jewish household, I had a very heightened sense of what fascism meant. It meant anti-Semitism; it meant Hitler. I mean he was like the king fascist. And then there were these minor league fascists, but they essentially meant the same thing. And I saw the threat reaching right into my house and snuffing me out if something wasn't done to stop the advance of fascism.

(Ask)

Thus, Levine's poems on the Spanish Civil War can be regarded as a displaced or, perhaps, universalized expression of his concerns as a Jew. This alone is evidence of the extent to which Levine's Jewish past continues to influence him precisely in the ways in which he rejects that past.

"Gift for a Believer," dedicated to the artist responsible for the portrait of the Rabbi of Auschwitz, may best exemplify the way Levine is able to incorporate powerful Jewish experience in a poem that addresses a subject that is not overtly Jewish. **"Gift for a Believer"** recounts a pledge not to forget atrocities perpetrated against man by systems political or economic. And the poem records the failure to honor that pledge. But the poem does not end on a note of utter despair:

> It is Friday, a usual day
> in Italy, and you wait. Below
> the street sleeps at noon.
> Once the Phoenicians came that way,
> the Roman slaves on foot,
> and later the Nazis.
> <flushrt(*Lost*)

The poem moves quickly from the present to the past, the historical perspective:

> . . . To you came
> the Anarchists chanting, 'We shall inherit,'
> and among them Santo Caserio
> who lost his head for knifing
> the President of France, the ambassador
> to hell.

As we have seen, Levine will not be trapped by what he perceives as the exclusivity of Judaism. Therefore, he does not express his moral outrage at crimes committed against Jews but finds a substitute, equivalent crime toward which to direct that moral outrage, which in this case is fascism and the Spanish Civil War.

> . . . Came little Ferrer
> in his long gown who taught

the Spanish children to question.
His fine hands chained behind
his back, his eyes of a boy
smeared, he swings above the stone trench
of Montjuich. The wind came
to blow his words away, then snow
that buried your childhood
and all the promises, that rusted
out the old streetcars and humped
over your fathers' graves.

Montjuich, as we learn in the poem of the same title, is translated variously as "Hill of Jews," "named for a cemetery long gone," or "Hill of Jove" (*Ashes*). It is in that cemetery that Ferrer and other anarchists and martyrs are buried. This is as close as Levine can come to linking the fate of the Jews with the fate of the Spanish anarchists. Consistent with Levine's other poems, this dutifully records a vision of the shattered, post-Edenic world—a world of wind that blows words away, and snow that buries one's childhood and obscures the graves of one's ancestors, cutting one off from one's past. Each time a hopeful vision is offered, it is immediately shattered:

> In your vision Durruti whispered
> to an old woman that he would
> never forget the sons and daughters
> who died believing they carried
> a new world there in their hearts,
> but when the doctor was summoned
> and could not stop his wounds
> he forgot. Ascaso, who fled
> with him to Argentina, Paraguay,
> Bruxelles, the first to die
> storming the Atarazanas Barracks,
> he forgot. The railyards of Leon
> where his father doubled over
> and deafened, forgotten. That world
> that he said is growing here
> in my heart this minute
> forgotten. (*Lost*)

Clearly, Levine, by writing this poem, is resisting the pressures of an unjust world that caused Durruti to forget his vision for a just society, though Levine himself records with regret his own failure to remember tragedies witnessed in the workplace:

> . . . When old Nathan Pine
> gave two hands to a drop-forge
> at Chevy, my spit turned to gall
> and I swore I'd never forget.
> When the years turned to a gray mist
> and my sons grew away without faith,

the memory slept, and I bowed
my head so that I might live.

Resigned, humbled by the destructive forces of the world around him, Levine again adopts the pose of a penitent, the pose of prayer, and then turns to a passage resonant with biblical overtones:

On the spare hillsides west
of here the new lambs stumble
in the fog and rise. My wife kneels
to the cold earth and we have bread.

All the basic biblical (pastoral, as well) ingredients are present: lambs, earth, bread, etc. But as elsewhere in Levine's work, the promise of return to a biblically centered world affords no comfort:

I see and don't believe. Farther
west the ocean breaks
on cold stones, the great Pacific
that blesses no one breaks
into water. So this is what
I send you, friend, where you wait
above a street that will waken
into dark shops, sellers of flour
and onions, dogs, hawkers
of salt, iron, lies. I send
water to fill your glass
and overflow, to cool your wrists
in the night ahead, water
that runs like a pure thread
through all my dreams
and empties into tears, water
to wash our eyes, our mother's last wine,
two palm-fulls the sky gave us,
what the roots crave, rain. (*Lost*)

In this exalted, visionary conclusion, Levine is able, momentarily, to overcome his despair, to identify at least one pure thing in the world, water. He is able to cry and to be nourished and to offer a gift, from a non-believer who has not yet given up on the world to a believer who has not given up yet either.

This poem modulates perfectly between a private voice—the voice that remembers Nathan Pine, the voice that dedicates the poem to a friend, and a public voice—the voice of history, the voice of the Bible. The poem brilliantly offers its gift, a bridge that joins believer to non-believer, Jewish historical experience to non-Jewish historical experience, the personal to the universal. Levine's despair, finally, is a representative despair; Levine's modest hope is our hope as well.

Indeed, when Levine attempts to write a poem about an explicitly Jewish subject his power is diminished. When he flavors his poems with images collected from Jewish cultural life, the images come closer to cliché than to anything authentic, original, true. But when Levine applies his sense of social justice, which he understands as having derived from his experiences as a young Jew growing up in Detroit, to atrocities beyond the circumscribed pale of Jewish life, he is able to write with absolute power and conviction, he is able to pour his Jewish and biblical sensibility into his language, and he is able to write unforgettably rich poems that may not speak exclusively to Jews, but that do speak to the Jew in each of us.

Andrew Hudgins (review date Winter 1992)

SOURCE: Review of *New Selected Poems* and *What Work Is* in *Hudson Review,* Vol. XLIV, No. 4, Winter, 1992, pp. 681-682.

[*In the following review, Hudgins considers Levine's* New Selected Poems *and* What Work Is. *He is particularly complimentary of the latter work, declaring that it is a brilliant collection and that Levine is a superb poet.*]

Except for the addition of fifteen poems culled from *Sweet Will* (1985) and *A Walk with Tom Jefferson* (1988), Philip Levine's *New Selected Poems* is identical with his *Selected Poems* (1984), right down to pagination and typeface. *New Selected Poems,* which serves to consolidate the poet's move from his previous publisher to Knopf, will be of interest primarily to readers new to Levine's poetry. *New Selected Poems* was published simultaneously with *What Work Is,* a frequently brilliant collection of new poems. The book's recurrent metaphor for work is burning, a metaphor that is introduced in the first poem, **"Fear and Fame."** After cleaning pickling tanks with a "burning stew" of acids, a worker emerges from the tanks and removes his protective gear: "Ahead lay the second cigarette, held in a shaking hand, / as I took into myself the sickening heat to quell heat, / a lunch of two Genoa salami sandwiches and Swiss cheese / on heavy peasant bread baked by my Aunt Tsipie, / and a third cigarette to kill the taste of the others." Perhaps speaking for the poet too, the vat cleaner returns to his work "stiffened / by the knowledge that to descend and rise up / from the other world merely once in eight hours is half / what it takes to be known among women and men." The ending is evocative, but opaque. To attain fame, this Orpheus who returns from his eight-hour shift in the burning underworld will require something beyond his labor, but what is it—talent, luck, something else?

In another fine poem, **"Fire,"** a father thinks of his son who is off fighting a forest fire and he, the father, vicariously experiences "on my skin, a light oil, a sweat / born of some forgotten leaning into fire." Fire turns to smoke again in **"On the River,"** in which the speaker's brother once a week uses his lunch hour ("his only free time") to row out onto the Detroit River so he can look "with a painter's eye" at the industrial landscape and see "beneath the shadows / of concrete and burned brick towers / the flickering hints of life." The speaker speculates that his brother performs this weekly ritual so he can "behold his own life / come into view brick by dark brick, / bending his back for all its worth, / as the whole thing goes up in smoke." The metaphorical equation of work with burning becomes tendentious in **"Burnt,"** a long poem that constitutes the third section of the book. Though the poem contains some of the best, most compelling writing in the book, as a whole it inclines toward slackness; and the weaker sections, which could easily have been omitted, undermine the good ones.

Occasionally Levine goes on auto-pilot and becomes Philip Levine, tough-guy poet and voice of the common man. You can hear this voice clearly in the title of the book: *What Work Is.* He knows, you don't, and he's going to tell you. A poem in this mode might begin with an abrupt tough-guy self-righteousness that asserts the speaker's superior sensitivity to the travails of the worker ("Take this quiet woman, she has been / standing before a polishing wheel / for over three hours, and she lacks / twenty minutes before she can take a lunch break. Is she a woman?") and end with heart-of-gold sentimentality (". . . she places the five / tapering fingers of her filthy hand / on the arm of your white shirt to mark / you for her own, now and forever"). Another tough-guy ending is the tossed-off cheap shot, such as the conclusion of **"Gin,"** which takes a gratuitous swipe at "the military and political victories / of Dwight Eisenhower, who brought us / Richard Nixon with wife and dog. / Any wonder we tried gin." But such easy preaching to the converted is largely absent from *What Work Is.* The book is full of lovely, powerful, surprising poems that reaffirm Levine as one of poetry's contemporary masters and the inventor of a distinctive verse line that riffs off of an iambic rhythm while its crisp line breaks derive from Levine's early work with syllabics. The poems in the book's fourth and final section are uniformly superb. Especially incisive, unflinching, funny and compassionate is **"The Sweetness of Bobby Hefka."** The poem begins with Bobby Hefka sitting in a high school classroom "admitting to Mr. Jaslow / that he was a racist and if Mr. Jaslow / was so tolerant how come he couldn't tolerate Bobby?" Through a funny, heartbreaking series of turns that never seem contrived, the poem manages to end "Bobby Hefka loved me." In *What Work Is* Philip Levine is a superb poet working at the top of his form.

Carol Frost (review date Fall 1992)

SOURCE: "Philip Levine at Work," in *New England Review,* Vol. 14, No. 4, Fall, 1992, pp. 291-305.

[*In the following review of* New Selected Poems *and* What Work Is, *Frost not only considers the poems of these two books, but also ranges over the spectrum of Levine's wider output and poetic career.*]

Exceptional poets come in two kinds: those whose territory is small (the neighborhood or garden, privately walled, perhaps) and those who speak for a wider locale. Both—like mapmakers, blues singers, and revolutionaries—are remarkable in their reinventions of common ground. It comes down to an act of mind, the imagination's ability to inhabit a place and time so deeply that the names for it are transformed. Philip Levine is a poet of wide territory, primarily interested in portraying the lives of ordinary working class people in America, shore to shore (Detroit, Gary, Pasadena, New York City, Dubuque, Akron, Baltimore, Wheeling, L.A.), in Spain (Barcelona, Malaga, Valladolid), and, with more passing reference, in Italy, Thailand, France, Hungary, Poland, Russia, Mexico, Canada, and Germany.

The Midwest exerts the strongest pull on his imagination, with its auto industry and its foundries, fertile ground for his treatment of the American work ethic, human will, and fatedness. Such places as Detroit and Belle Isle take on a nearly mythic glow, lit by the iron-colored fires of the transmission and chemical factories. "We burn the city every day," he says in **"Coming Home,"** and references to fire and iron appear again and again throughout the 292 pages of his *New Selected Poems* and in *What Work Is.* Levine's poetry forges, out of a wide and common geography, terms for a new understanding of late-twentieth-century experience, rooted in the lives of second- and third-generation immigrants who continue their manual labors for a living and for their sense of dignity. But for all of that interest in the lives of others, Levine's poems are strongly personal; he so thoroughly empathizes with his characters, remembered and invented, that their experience becomes his own, and ours.

Levine's ideal is similar to Whitman's, who talks about his preference for the common over the heroic in notes for a lecture under the heading *Beauty:*

> [N]ot the beautiful girl or the elegant lady . . . but the mechanic's wife at work . . . not the scenery of the tourist, picturesque, but the plain landscape, the bleak sea shore, or the barren plain, with the common sky and sun.

Everywhere in Levine's new collections are touches of a nearly journalistic plainness. Other features of Levine's work underscore his affinities with Whitman: colloquial speech, oratorical devices (in such poems as **"They Feed They**

Lion"), parallel sentence structure, enumeration, very direct presentation of human experience, and the exclusion of conventional literary subjects. Levine has stated that Garcia Lorca's poetry offered him a model for "all the eloquence and fury a poet could master" (**"The Poet in New York in Detroit"**), and that Keats's poetry and theory, "being in uncertainties," added to his evolving sense of how to write a poetry no one else could write. The influences, one comes to understand as one reads through all the poems in the *New Selected Poems,* are numerous. Levine's mature line, for instance, is most closely related to the free verse of William Carlos Williams—a much less oceanic phrasing and a thinner profile on the page than Whitman or Lorca, less sensual than Keats. Furthermore, his imagery, rather than being exclusively realistic, is sometimes highly surreal, particularly in the poems selected from his earlier books, where the pressure of statement and emotion cause a more extravagant crafting of the poem, as in some of Dickinson and in Stephen Crane, and certainly in Lorca.

To mention Whitman, Emily Dickinson, and Stephen Crane in this context is to open up for myself one chapter in literary history out of which Levine's work seems surely to come, and which, therefore, helps to explain the thematic development in these chronologically arranged selections of poems, as well as Levine's methods. His belonging to the continuum of realism-to-naturalism and his affinities with late-nineteenth-century poetry hardly make his work seem old-fashioned, narrowly American, or derivative. Levine's poetry is most notable for its freshness and originality. A freshness so apparent misdirects you, and you take the poems for granted as individual specimens of formally heightened emotion at its best; but then as the weight of your interest in the poems increases and you want to know what makes them tick and where they come from, common sense points to earlier poets, both like and unlike the one you are reading now, for new ways into the work. Levine writes what he writes not only because of his experiences in the "real world," but also because he has read what he has read and because of his accord in temperament, method, and theme with some of those poets. Fully invented as they are, the poems were not written in a literary vacuum.

II

The literary territory that Levine stakes out for himself is largely realistic, both in method and attitude. Verisimilitude is one of his virtues, and many of his poems present journalistic detailing: dates, place names and addresses, the exact time ("he woke at 3," "40 miles from Malaga," "Detroit, 1951, Friday night," and, in speaking of Barcelona, "Here / is the Plaza of San Jaime, here the Rambla / of San Pedro"). Even his most fantastic poems are faithful to realistic detail, as in a poem like **"Angel Butcher,"** where the angel hoses out the abattoir prior to receiving Christophe, who asks

the angel for "all the names of / all the tools and all / their functions," then "lifts / and weighs and / balances, and runs a long / forefinger down the tongue / of each blade" prior to his being stunned for slaughter. The surreal scene is made to appear tangibly true—as if in heaven such a place exists. Perhaps the clearest statement of Levine's method is made in **"Silent in America,"** a poem which depicts the speaker's feelings of inadequacy ("Fresno's / dumb bard, America's last / hope") to speak for the downtrodden and the beautiful: Jews, Poles, the fated, and "those who had courage"— a full range of Americans. "Surely I have failed," he says. In section five, the speaker explains that what he surely knows about the world comes from a close scrutiny of physical details:

> I tell time
> by the sunlight's position
>   on the bedroom wall:
> it's 5:30, middle June.
>   I rise, dress,
>   assume my name
>
>   and feel my
> face against a hard towel.
>   My mind is empty;
> I see all that's here to see:
>   the garden
>   and the hard sky;
>
>   the great space
> between the two has a weight,
>   a reality
> which I find no burden,
>   and the height
>   of the cot tree
>
>   is only
> what it has come to deserve.
>   I have not found peace,
> but I have found I am where
>   I am by
>   being only there,
>
>   by standing
> in the clouded presence of
>   the things I observe.

This section of the poem goes on to take note of the fact that there is an unobservable force in the air which "moves / when it is still" and "speaks / of being alive." It is in part in response to the unknowable, the answers to questions— why, for instance, there is little "to choose / but failure" (**"Lights I have seen Before"**) for the ordinary people who populate the cities and neighborhoods of the America Levine talks about, why "half / the men in this town / are crying in the snow," why fathers die young ("the mouth asking everybody and nobody / *Why Why*" in **"Letters for the Dead"**), why people want earth to be heaven and for there to be a heaven, and why "the earth / would let the same children die day / after day, let the same women curse / their precious hours, the same men bow / to earn our scraps" (**"Ashes"**)—that Levine's realism shades into naturalism.

The details of the lives that Levine depicts, particularly in the selections of poems from his first eight books, are grim, and the speaker's tone frequently angry. As with Emily Dickinson, Levine's close observation of natural detail results in poems which sound naturalistic. It seems not to be his intention (or hers) to follow the tenets of the naturalists as much as it is the objective outcome of such close scrutiny of the physical world which makes him doubt human ability to overcome the difficulty ordinary living provides.

The seeds of Levine's naturalistic view appear early in his work in his references to fate, the incontrovertible nature of death, and the "failures of will" he finds all around him. He also early expresses anger toward what he perceives as an indifferent universe. In one early poem, **"Noon"** (*Red Dust*), in a landscape of abandoned bicycles, "ripening dirt," and washerwomen slapping the life out of laundry with worn hands, the speaker says, "At such times / I expect the earth / to pronounce." He seems to expect some benevolent word from the natural world, and gets none. In **"Clouds,"** another early poem, Levine expresses his anger at a similar silence, this time from the clouds. Below them the wreckage of civilized living—abandoned cars, "the TV talking to itself," pollution, war, and death—is met by silence from the clouds who "have seen it all." In a characteristic statement which carries with it the presumption of nature's power and the notion that nature ought to be benevolent, the speaker says that the clouds

> . . . should be punished every morning,
> they should be bitten and boiled like spoons.

This bitterness is reminiscent less of Dickinson than of Stephen Crane, although many of Dickinson's ironies concerning the absence of an intervening God or universe when one faces death (in fact, nature's complicity suggested in such lines as "The blonde Assassin passes on— / That Sun proceeds unmoved / To measure off an Approving God" and "When Winds take Forests in their Paws— / The Universe— is still") seem to mock the conventions of nature and God. In Crane, however, particularly in "The Open Boat," a reader finds a rationale for a bitterness toward nature, a bitterness that matches Levine's. Crane writes, "When it occurs to a man that nature does not regard him as important, and that she feels she would not maim the universe by disposing of him, he at first wishes to throw bricks at the

temple, and he hates deeply the fact that there are no bricks and no temples."

There are expressions of anger toward nature's indifference throughout the first half of the *New Selected Poems,* but the greatest concentration of this attitude occurs in the selections from *The Names of the Lost.* Speaking to his dead uncle in "No one remembers," the speaker says, "The earth is asleep, Joe, it's rock, steel, ice, / the earth doesn't care / or forgive." In **"Gift for a Believer,"** speaking to a patriot who still believes in a dream of goodness, in politics righting political and social wrongs, despite historical evidence to the contrary, the speaker tells how the wind and the snow obliterate "your childhood / and all the promises." Then, near the end of the poem, the speaker describes the earth as cold and says "on cold stones, the great Pacific / that blesses no one breaks / into water." In *Ashes* there are several other such references to a cruelly indifferent world. In **"On a Drawing by Flavio,"** though the Jews have been incinerated in Auschwitz, the sun seems to say, "Do as you please," and the implication is that it ought somehow to have put a stop to the killing. In **"Ashes,"** the speaker wonders why the earth allows children to hunger and men to sacrifice their dignity for the little that they can earn and provide.

Levine also expresses anger at a god and a heaven which, if they existed, ought to provide solace and answers. God, it seems, does not care and probably doesn't exist, which is why in **"Fist"** (*Red Dust*) a fist is described as "a flower / that hates God," why in **"Blasting from Heaven"** (*Not This Pig*) the sounds issuing from heaven in response to the sad lives of a little family are the 8 o'clock whistle, and why in **"Angel Butcher"** (*They Feed They Lion*) at least one of the seraphim is responsible for the slaughter of the good and innocent who "come up the long climb." In a later poem, **"Uncle"** (*1933*), Levine mocks religious faith when he has the speaker remember that his uncle "taught / the toilet the eternal." There seems to be nothing substantial to be found in the pursuit of religious faith, for, as Levine tells us, "heaven was nowhere" (**"On the Murder of Lieutenant Jose del Castillo by the Falangist Bravo Martinez, July 12, 1936"**). If God has given people anything, it is each other and it is the corporeal.

And while realism turns Levine to a scrutiny of the common particulars of our experience, it also turns him to certain unhappy truths. The conflict that is presented through the first half of the *New Selected Poems* is between the ideals of human will, aspiration, and hard work on the one hand—all that represents promise—and reality on the other. Levine is angry about broken promise, about the discrepancy between the wish "for a new world and a new home" (**"A New Day"**) and people's willingness to work for it, "putting their lives / into steel" (**"The Helmet"**), working until they are often too tired to stand up; and he is angry about the reality of poverty, the essential uselessness of work.

In **"Hear Me,"** Levine says that the notion that work presents "salvation" is laughable. Men work hard, and get nowhere; children seem to follow in their fathers' footsteps. The poems in *1933* are poems about the real or imagined lives of parents and other relatives whose lives are repeated in the lives of their children. "The lie is retold in the heart," the speaker says in **"Letters from the Dead,"** a poem which tells the story of a young man's remembrances of his family, the father a drunk who dies young, the mother vain and disappointed. The events of the father's life are reflected in the son's. He too leaves home, traveling on a hot bus to "the dawn of a new world," which provides nothing. As the speaker remembers this journey and then his father's death by suicide, he feels the air that "crackles with their angers," and later recalls his violence toward his "strange tall son." Disappointments seem generational, if not hereditary; in the unpromising environment depicted in these poems, children are caught up in a fate they do not quite understand. More particularly, the premature death of the father, "himself a child," ensures his son's loneliness. How can the future be anything more than the "scar" the grown child with his own nearly grown son calls it in **"New Season"**? Violence leads naturally and generationally to violence. A working class father spawns a working class son, and neither seems able to control his environment; neither seems fully to understand what forces are at work to prevent the promise of something wonderful.

> **It is only after his first eight books that Levine comes to an understanding which allows him, if not to love the experiences of living, at least to accept what can't be altered.**
>
> —*Carol Frost*

In **"No One Remembers,"** the speaker, addressing his uncle, indicts him for his violence toward his own wife—"She'll cry like always / when you raise your voice / or your fist." The speaker says it is his hand, not the uncle's, that the woman will take and will "feel / slowly finger by finger / like so many threads back / to where the blood dies / and our lives met / and went wrong, back / to all she said she'd be, / woman, promise." The identification with the uncle by the speaker shows the essential relationship of the generations to the conflict I mentioned earlier between promise and doomed hopes. In these poems the family is not presented without fondness: a grandfather in **"Zaydee"**—small and vulgar, a dandy, card cheat, cigar smoker, thief, ex-con, sensualist—is presented as wise and loving, for instance. A war veteran and a woman, who in the context of the other po-

ems seem to be the speaker's relatives, fall in love at a dance in **"At the Fillmore,"** and their illusions, "the promises again," are presented with a sweet regard. But the poems clearly set out the notion that the past traps the future.

It is only after his first eight books that Levine comes to an understanding which allows him, if not to love the experiences of living, at least to accept what can't be altered. The pivotal poem in *New Selected Poems* is **"Lost and Found"** (*Ashes*). Levine's quarrel with the world is partly resolved in this poem, which has the speaker take responsibility for his boyhood and the familial past, so that "father and child / hand in hand, the living and / the dead, are entering the world." What has allowed the speaker to reach this point of maturity is stated in the beginning of the poem:

> How long it takes to believe
> the simplest facts of lives—
> that certain losses are final,
> death is one, childhood another.

As a consequence of his acceptance of the unalterable nature of the starkest realities, Levine's speaker is able to escape the angers and victimizations of experience. He has "come home from being lost, / home to a name I could accept, / a face that saw all I saw / and broke in a dark room against / a wall that heard all my secrets / and gave back nothing." That becoming aware of the limitations of life is an act of adulthood is echoed in **"Salts and Oils"**; the speaker says that his fully digesting the "filth and glory / of the palatable world" happens "because I have to grow up."

In both these poems the moment of mature understanding occurs in the morning—"one quiet morning" in **"Salts and Oils,"** and at the end of "the night which seemed so final" in **"Lost and Found."** There are seventy references to dawn or a new day in the 292 pages of *New Selected Poems,* as well as a few references to a new world or season as a part of the same thematic indication. In the poems before **"Lost and Found,"** dawn is most often symbolic of nature's cheat. The expectations for nature's benevolence are shown as illusory in such lines as "A gray light coming on at dawn, / no fresh start and no bird song" (**"A New Day"**) and "has anyone fallen on his knees / and begged the dawn to reconsider" (**"Ask the Roses"**). However, starting with **"Lost and Found,"** dawn's symbolic value changes. Nature is no longer seen as cruelly indifferent or even malignant, and the new light of day more often shines on a world worth calling home. For instance, in **"Rain Downriver,"** the speaker says, "the earth gives each of us / a new morning," and in the end he is able to declare that "the world is mine." This is a reversal of the earlier sentiment, as expressed in **"Told,"** where the speaker says that the world "was not home." When Levine comes to accept that the experience of living is a mixture of good and bad news, the new sun, the new day, the new light, and the new season are much less often treated ironically. Overall, the positive and negative references to dawn are about equal, thirty-six to thirty-four—but it is most interesting to note that in the one hundred sixty-nine pages before **"Lost and Found,"** the ratio of positive to negative is 1:3, and with that poem the ratio reverses itself.

A similar shift occurs in Levine's numerous references to tears. That the world gives people ample reason to cry is made clear by the variety of those who weep (grown men, children, mothers, wives, fathers, lost souls, an angel, laborers), and the inanimate objects that also do (the hills, the sea, the radio). These are tears of despair for the most part, the sadness relating to Levine's sense of injustice and hopelessness, and there is no shame in them. Still, when Levine's change of heart occurs in **"Lost and Found,"** the expressions of sadness diminish considerably, even if the reasons for tears don't entirely alter. There are fifty-five early references to tears and only eighteen after *Names of the Lost.* The nature of tears changes slightly, with four of the later references suggesting stoicism: "He didn't like to cry" (**"Nitrate"**), "cry without a sound" (**"A Poem with No Ending"**), "the tears held back so long" (**"28"**), "She's not going to cry about it" (**"These Streets"**).

The thematic shift in Levine's work from a strong emphasis on the sad realities of a hostile world, wherein humanity is fated to failure through no fault of its own, to an acceptance of the natural world (a shift not accompanied by any shift in his method of closely observing and recording the physical world) is consistent with a major strain of the American literary tradition. Where for a romantic the ideal dominates—nature and God are benevolent and an individual can affect his or her fate—for the naturalist physical reality dominates. Many naturalists eventually look for consolation. For Dickinson, the same forces that beheaded flowers bring the consolations of summer and autumn ("Summer makes her light escape / Into the Beautiful") and for Hemingway the consolation is how human beings perform in the face of danger and death; the conditions of his world are naturalistic, but his characters face them, so they seem idealized, even in failure. For Levine, the conditions of the world are bleaker than for either of the two writers mentioned, so it might be argued that his need for consolation is even greater. He introduces several: nature, courage in the face of impossible odds, love—"each other" (**"Sources"**)—and, as in Whitman and Stephen Crane, camaraderie. The fellowship between the shipmates in Crane's "The Open Boat" is similar to the camaraderie that factory workers and other laborers share in **"And the Trains Go On," "Sweet Will,"** and **"An Ordinary Morning."**

In Levine's later poems, a kind of comfort comes through realizing that nature's indifference, which once seemed cruel, is benign, even when its natural processes result in death.

The speaker in **"The Face,"** for instance, notes that the streets of the "battered" Spanish city are "filled with dirty children," but still listens for the "one word" from his dead father, who he imagines tells him "of why the earth takes / back all she gives." Knowing that earth does this, and having imagined his father's voice, "even that," he says, "comes to be enough." Imagining himself as dead in **"Let Me Begin Again,"** the speaker says, "Let / me come back to land after a lifetime / of going nowhere." He wants to begin again in the world he knows is nothing more than "salt water and dark clouds" because, despite the "black wastes," his life is like no other. In **"Snow,"** the "foolishness of the world" and "the filthy waters of their river" are givens, but what is left over from those who have died, their tears (snow), "given their choice chose then / to return to earth." Earth, the speaker in **"Voice"** says, "is my one home, as it always was," echoing the last lines in **"Rain Downriver"**: "The fall of evening / glistens around my shoulders that / also glisten, and the world is mine." Once death is seen as a part of living, a reality that is painful ("No one believes that to die is beautiful"), an understanding and even a little joy are possible: "Do you hear the wind / rising all around you? That comes / only after this certain joy."

Perhaps the most complete statement of this new attitude occurs in **"The Poem of Flight,"** spoken by the Wright brother who was the first to fly. Concerning his flight, he has this to say:

> . . . the time has come to say something
> to a world that largely crawls, forwards
> or backwards, begging for some crust
> of bread or earth, enough for a bad life
> or a good death. I've returned because
> thin as I am there came a moment
> when not to seemed foolish and difficult
> and because I've not yet tired
> of the warm velvet dusks of this country
> of firs and mountain oak. And because
> high above the valleys and streams
> of my land I saw so little of what is here,
> only the barest whiff of all I eat each day.
> I suppose I must square my shoulders,
> lean back, and say something else,
> something false, something that even I
> won't understand about why some of us
> must soar or how we've advanced beyond
> the birds or that not having wings
> is an illusion that a man with my money
> refuses to see. It is hard to face
> the truth, this truth or any other,
> that climbing exhausts me, and the more
> I climb, the higher I get, the less I
> want to go on, and the noise is terrible,
> I thought the thing would come apart,

and finally there is nothing there.

As this poem makes clear, the truth for Levine is that earth—with the fouled lakes, broken bottles, and shoddy trees, wrong turns, sulking gray factories, mentally deranged and violent people we continue to be reminded of—is what we've got, and as his own acceptance grows, he begins to be able to treat the notion of perfecting the world with some humor, as in **"The Suit."** As his zoot suit tatters from overwearing and abuse, so do the speaker's "other hopes for a singular life in a rich / world of a certain design: / just, proportioned, equal and different / for each of us and satisfying like that flush / of warmth that came with knowing / no one could be more ridiculous."

Levine is less and less apt to be furious, or to demand change, in the face of the bad he continues to see in American experience; the good he now allows. The earth is "amazing," according to the poor black man Tom Jefferson in **"A Walk with Tom Jefferson,"** despite racism, plunder, and his neighborhood—the "dumping ground" for "mangled chifforobes" and "ice boxes / yawning at the sky." Tom Jefferson is "six feet of man, unbowed." There are other heroes in Levine's universe, stoics most of them—old boxers, uncomplaining peasants, and especially political idealists from the same war Hemingway idealized in *For Whom the Bell Tolls.* In **"Francisco, I'll Bring you Carnations,"** the conditions of the working people for whom the leftists fought during the Spanish Civil War have not, the speaker says, improved. The Barcelona which Francisco knew is gone, "swallowed / in industrial filth"; the "smiling masters" and the police remain, but despite the slums and Francisco's early death (half his life before that spent in prison), "that dream / goes on," the dream "where every man / and every woman gives / and receives the gifts of work / and care." Those who manage to believe in a better future despite evidence to the contrary, who keep on with the belief even in quiet ways, are worthy of our admiration, Levine tells us in **"To Cipriano, in the Wind,"** where the speaker praises a simple man's dignity. Cipriano, who presses pants, believes that "Some day the world / is ours," just as he believes spring follows the icy winter. Addressing Cipriano at the end of the poem, the speaker asks him to "enter my dreams / or my life" because he also would like to believe that "this / world will be ours." And he would like to live with dignity. Just as Hemingway's essentially nihilistic vision is repeatedly modified by his assertion of the possibility of living with courage, so in this poem is Levine's; but it isn't until after working through the journalistically recorded grimness of working class life and a period of youthful anger and wishful thinking—the position that the universe needs to be amended and God or nature was to blame for the lack of change, Crane's position—that Levine comes fully to appreciate the idea of grace under pressure, a faithfulness to the ordeal of living and dying. Two earlier poems featuring political heroes, **"Gift for a Believer"** and **"On the Murder of Lieutenant Jose del Castillo by the Falangist Bravo Martinez, July 12, 1936,"** early as they are in Levine's thematic evolution, are basically negative; the characters' ideals turn into gray mist and smoke when they die, reality defeating promise.

During the twenty-five years it took for the books from *On the Edge* to *A Walk with Tom Jefferson* to be published, Levine's themes evolved in ways similar to the evolution of realism through seventy-five years. Faithfully recording the physical, social, and psychological facts of the American working class, Levine moves from a youthful anger at the way things are, at the machine of the natural universe which seems to grind up essentially innocent people, toward an acceptance of palpable reality, inimical nature, including the certainty of death he earlier railed against. In the last poems his attitude seems to be that human beings can persevere in the face of such realities, and that they have a responsibility toward the "amazing" planet that is home (**"A Walk with Tom Jefferson"**).

This development is hardly casual; it is a growing process, a maturing of vision, and it is large. It is as if more than seventy-five years of American literary history have been telescoped into Levine's twenty-five years of writing and publishing poems, twenty-five years of living and seeing blended into what he has read and what he creates out of it—poems impressionistic, paradoxical, often ironic, and highly original.

III

The Levine line to which his readers have become accustomed is an orthodox free verse line, broken syntactically. He has a knack for rising action and for succinct detail, and can quickly establish the tone of narration, as in **"Sweet Will,"** the title poem of a book published in 1985:

> The man who stood beside me
> 34 years ago this night fell
> on to the concrete, oily floor
> of Detroit Transmission, and we
> carefully stepped over him until
> he wakened and went back to his press.
> It was Friday night, and the others . . .

Most of Levine's mature poems are informed by a similar strong narrative impulse, and it would seem that he is remembering events from his personal past, so that the story of his life is made to stand for the story of many. There are, however, so many exceptions to this that it would be a mistake to label Levine's *oeuvre* as narrowly autobiographical. An early example of a Levine poem which sounds like a personal narrative is **"The Midget"** (*Not This Pig,* 1968). In a quickly unfolding drama in a bar "lined with factory work- ers" who are drinking alone and heavily, Levine describes a midget with a potbelly and a cummerbund who singles out the speaker, asking him to verify his manhood by feeling part of his anatomy. The poem is so carefully detailed that it is reasonable for a reader to think that Levine has depicted an event from his own life, and that the *I* is Levine himself. The question might simply be where the real event stopped and the poet's imagination took over, perhaps at the point where the midget climbs into the speaker's lap, or when the speaker begins to sing a lullaby to him, "this late-born freak / of the old world swelling in my lap." It's a surprising poem, and when I mentioned it to Levine this fall, he told me there wasn't a midget, that he hadn't existed. What matters, of course, is the semblance of existence, *artistic* reality. One of Levine's particular strengths as a writer is his ability to imagine and empathize with invented characters to the point that readers assume they are acquaintances or relatives.

"On my Own," a poem from his tenth book *One for the Rose* (1981), further illustrates Levine's empathic powers. The piece also has intertextual significance, inasmuch as it serves to amplify and lend clarity to those of the older po- ems which own a debt to the surreal. In **"On my Own,"** a supernatural being describes his entry into the ordinary stream of life on earth as a seven-year-old. Having chosen the house of an old woman who "opened her door expect- ing milk" and instead got the youngster with plastered-down hair and a suitcase filled with earthly paraphernalia (children's books, clothing, a stuffed toy), he must choose a name and go off to school for the first time, as if he's just moved into the neighborhood:

> I chose Abraham Plain
> and went off to school wearing a cap
> that said "Ford" in the right script.

The boy slowly gets used to the simple pleasures of earth, "the beauty of sleep" and being able to dream of "seascapes / at the other end of the world," and it is in the guise of this fictive character that Levine reveals his belief in the "infi- nite" powers of the imagination to enliven reality. The boy addresses the reader as if he had been present as a crossing guard:

> Sure, now you
> know, its obvious, what with the light
> of the Lord streaming through the nine
> windows of my soul and the music of rain
> following in my wake and the ordinary air
> of fire every blessed day I waken with the world.

Though it has been argued that Levine's poetry is more con- cerned with his personal life than with the life on the imagi- nation, the two together seem equally to inform his poems.

Indeed, Levine claims imaginary, idealized truths as his pre- rogative in **"I was born in Lucerne"** (*One for the Rose*): to have had a beautiful young woman as his mother, "A woman of independence and courage / who sang the peas- ant songs of her region," who turned the past of his father and other male relatives into myth, and helped protect the speaker from the facts about poverty and war. Balanced against the grayer truths "in the fields or in the factories" is Levine's sun-touched and, strangely, more defiant idea of reality:

> Look in my eyes!
> They have stared into the burning eyes of the
>   earth,
> molten metals, the first sun, a woman's face,
> they have seen the snow covering all
> and a new day breaking over the mother sea.
> I breathed the truth, I was born in Lucerne.

The act of articulation resides in imagining the scene as viv- idly as memory, in careful reformulations of the way things are or seem to be. Levine's many references in the *New Se- lected Poems* to silence are accompanied by his personae's expressions of fear that he, and others, and reality itself, might lie. His strategy for telling the truth involves stepping bodily into the lives of all sorts of people—boxers, rabbis, stone-cutters, young girls (*Pili's Wall*), fathers, sons, wives— who experience the weight of disappointment and death, as well as joy. In the best of his poems, the stories of their lives unfold swiftly through a series of precise images which de- lineate mood and tone and psychological motivation. In some of the weaker poems—under the influence of the style of the time, perhaps—the images are more vivid and easily asso- ciated with a feeling or attitude but the reason for the feel- ing exists off the page. A few of the poems in *Red Dust* (1971) contain exotic images of anger. The mood poem **"Fist,"** for instance, suffers from a lack of context. A reader knows the terrible power of the speaker's anger in similes for his clenched hand, "a flower / that hates God, the child / tearing at itself," but would have to try to guess at the mo- tivation for the anger unless he or she had read more of Levine's work.

If in a few poems Levine creates riddles while talking of real things, making impossible combinations of them, normally he ascribes to the ideals of style articulated in Aristotle's *Poetics*. His narratives and lyrics use the "regular words for things," but his language also varies from the "common el- ement," largely in his use of metaphor, though also by chang- ing the traditional value of a word by altering the syntax of his sentences, as in **"They Feed They Lion."** Anaphoric, syntactically parallel and at the same time syntactically wrenched, the poem makes use of high and low speech and a mixture of ordinary and extreme metaphors. Here are the first lines:

Out of burlap sacks, out of bearing butter,
Out of black bean and wet slate bread,
Out of acids of rage, the candor of tar,
Out of creosote, gasoline, drive shafts, wooden
    dollies,
They lion grow.
    Out of gray hills
Out of industrial barns, out of rain, out of bus ride,
West Virginia to Kiss My Ass, out of buried
    aunties,
Mothers hardening like pounded stumps, out of
    stumps,
Out of the bones' needs to sharpen and the
    muscles' to stretch,
They lion grow.

In **"A Theory of Prosody"** (*A Walk with Tom Jefferson*), Levine refuses to reveal his poetic intentions as they relate to the line, and the poem establishes, humorously (the tone that he employs with greater and greater frequency in his later poems), that chance is at least as operative in his decisions about line breaks as theory. Of the cat Nellie, the speaker says

She would sit behind me
as I wrote, and when the line
got too long she'd reach
one sudden black foreleg down
and paw at the moving hand, the offensive one.
    The first
time she drew blood I learned
it was poetic to end
a line anywhere to keep her
quiet.

Though she is described as "alert," the speaker says it is the artist's pretense to say that nothing is left to chance. The poem's charm is a mixture of hyperbole and modesty. In lines which communicate Levine's refusal to acknowledge the skill that attends an intuitive sense of how a line should sound, the poem illustrates the simple authority of a well-schooled writer of free verse in the tradition of Williams. None of the lines in this particular poem are by themselves memorable, but overall they get the job done, with an occasional modest gesture in the direction of form repeating content. In a poem that is about accidental line breaks, Levine writes such a line as "quiet. After all, many morn-," yet he seems to be ribbing the theorist who would expect such a break. The authority of his lines often appears to derive solely from establishing a length and staying with it. Their integrity is related to narrative image; the poem unfolds, the details of the story are interesting, and the line carries those details with no visible show of artistic adornment. The rhythms of language and life grow out of one another. Despite Levine's rigorous schooling in the tradition (as a student he wrote son-

nets for John Berryman), and despite evidence throughout the anthology of syllable- and accent-counting, it might be as simple as that.

IV

What Work Is (1991) is a continuation of Levine's dual attempt to give voice to the complicated lives of men and women and to make that voice something closer to simple song than ordinary speech. The reasons for song are not the usual—happy, happy love or the beauties of nature—although Beauty does matter in the world Levine creates, and love is redemptive. Whistling in the dark is, perhaps, a better description of the kind of song sung by the people of whom Levine tells us. Life, he says, is not easy, not even for children, who in **"Among Children"** are asleep "so as to be ready for what is ahead, / the monumental boredom of junior high / and the rush forward tearing their wings / loose and turning their eyes forever inward." Their fathers "work at the spark plug factory or truck / bottled water"; the children's backs already "have thickened," and their hands are "soiled by pig iron." The speaker would like to

sit down among them and read slowly
from the Book of Job until the windows
pale and the teacher rises out of a milky sea
of industrial scum, her gowns streaming
with light, her foolish words transformed
into song, I would like to arm each one
with a quiver of arrows so that they might
rush like a wind there where no battle rages
shooting among the trumpets, Ha! Ha!

What this poem contends is that the teacher's lessons on history, math, and civics will be of less importance to the children of Flint, Michigan, than laughter and song in the face of the stupefying boredom and difficulties of working people. The songs are the songs of grandfathers who sing themselves to sleep (**"Burned"**), of jazzmen like John Coltrane "playing his music with such joy / and contained energy and rage" that a woman twice his age, who has heard the solo in a dream, recognizes it as a gift that she passes along to her son, of hymns sung by women on a bus returning from church (**"Coming Home from the Post Office"**); of a boy at his first job at the soap factory, "singing / my new life of working and earning" (**"Growth"**); and of the blue morning glories along a fence whose existence is described as both music and laughter. "They blared all day," Levine tells us, "though no one could score their sense or harmony / before they faded in the wind and sun."

There are harmonies in these people's confrontations with reality—the daily labors of the workplace, where who you are and "what it takes to be known among women and men" (**"Fear and Fame"**) is revealed by the normal effort expended at work, the dirt and grime associated with work, the hunger for a better position, the meals prepared and eaten, the rise and fall of day and season and man and woman, familial ties and personal histories out of which the rational and irrational hopes for the future come. It is work to find these harmonies, Levine tells us, work to "enter the fires of your own making, naked / day after day, until the burning becomes / a sweetness" (**"Burned"**). To transform a life, and life itself, into more than its angry and sad bits of experience, into "the final truth" of the same poem, one must enter the fires of the past, "stare into fire," and risk burning:

> I have to climb
> the slag hills again, but this time not
> as a child, and look out over the river of iron,
> and hold it all in my eyes,
> the river, the iron mountains, the factories
> where our brothers burned. I have to repeat
> the prayer that we will all go back
> to earth one day soon to become earth,
> that our tears will run to the sea
> a last time and open it, and our fires
> light the way back home for someone.

This is the work of living, and it exists as a monumental task. It includes "the mythology of boys growing into men," "girls fighting to be people" (**"Coming of Age in Michigan"**), and the lies attending the relationships between young men and women:

> We even lied back in return, inventing squadrons
> of blondes and serious brunettes driven by love
> to wait on our doorsteps until we returned
> by bus, filthy and broken by the long days
> of breaking the earth, women with new cars
> and old needs content to take their turns. (**"Innocence"**)

"It isn't easy," the speaker says in **"On the River,"** to "get a better / look" at one's "own life" through the smoke "of our own making," and even though this smoke is really the dirty residue from factories, it also seems to be representatives of all that we allow to get in our way—fears, "false Gods" (**"Burned"**), facts, "foolish hopes" (**"My Grave"**), and forgetfulness, "an old pillow of forgetting, / a way out before the world got in" (**"Perennials"**).

Levine's attempt to find out truth, to work for it and make it work for him, is accompanied by modest demurrals throughout the book. "I don't have the answer," he says in **"Scouting"** in reply to the question "What is it Like?" When in **"Snails"** the speaker is at the point of saying "something final" about the autumn beauty, he says he "kept quiet." By listening to the ticking of the leaves, and watching the shadows, letting the world "escape / to become all it's never

been," Levine practices the art of the poet who has made a tangible commitment to truth; he lets the world speak for itself.

The bright, sung conversations of the earth and the earthbound are what the poems in *What Work Is* records. If these are nearly the same stories, about trying to live with dignity in a very difficult century, that he told in *New Selected Poems,* they are worth their retelling. They continue Levine's quest for ways to understand the paradoxes of isolation and community, Godlessness and spirituality, death and beauty, tears and "deep song" (Lorca's phrase) which are synonymous with the experience of living. Firemen, steelworkers, boxers, women, dead poets and other ghosts, young and old, get a say. What they have in common he simultaneously turns into myth and demythifies. How they are different he acknowledges. The territory of this poetry keeps coming back to a center—praise for the common person, an American, probably with immigrant parents, who having gotten "off the bus / at the bare junction of nothing / with nothing" (**"Scouting"**) manages to find a way home.

Richard Eder (review date 16 January 1994)

SOURCE: "The Riot That Found Its Threnody," in *Los Angeles Times Book Review,* January 16, 1994, pp. 3, 9.

[*In the following review of* The Bread of Fire: Toward an Autobiography, *Eder discusses some of the prominent aspects of Levine's life.*]

"I don't understand. I don't understand," Federico Garcia Lorca exclaimed when he arrived in New York. Out of the bewildered encounter between the finely surreal singer of slain gypsies and flowers that bleed, and Manhattan's stink and clangor, came "Poet in New York." A poet can write out of any state of spirit as long as he trusts it. Lorca trusted his dismay.

And he taught Philip Levine to trust his. Levine came to poetry in the course of a dozen years alternately spent studying and working in the hot-metal foundries of Detroit's auto industry. Illegitimate, not knowing who his father was, raised in near-poverty by a keen-spirited mother, he wore his blue collar with pride; particularly when he took a course from the languidly patrician Robert Lowell, whom he loathed. He also wore it with a sense of artistic constriction. Had he lived in the '30s, he might have settled into Socialist Realism. In the supremely disengaged '50s, his proletarian condition, leftist convictions and passion for the old Spanish Republic had no place to lodge. But there was more to it than that.

After working the overnight shift at Chevrolet Gear & Axle,

he would try to write, he tells us in one of these autobiographical essays. It didn't work. What stopped him was not weariness or unfashionability. It was his own sensibility. How could you write poetry about the gritty reality of America's working life? His rage was rhetoric-sized but he despised rhetoric. He loved Whitman, but there can be no other Whitman. He loved Keats, Stevens, William Carlos Williams and the fine, shining craft.

In this doubt, he tells us, he came upon "Poet in New York." Outrage shatters the sheer heaviness of things—derricks, subways, office-buildings—and the heaviness of outrage is lifted in turn, by the childlike joyfulness of Lorca's imagery. "A wooden wind from the south," Levine quotes from a dockside passage, "slanting through the black mire / spits on the broken boats and drives tacks into shoulders. / A south wind that carries / tusks, sunflowers, alphabets, / and a battery with drowned wasps."

"Never in poetry written in English had I found such a direct confrontation of one image with another or heard such violence held in abeyance and enclosed in so perfect a musical form," Levine writes. "What in my work had been chaotic rant was in his a stately threnody circling around a center of riot." It validated Levine's own rioting center; it told him that he might find a threnody of his own to circle it. It took years, he tells us. It was achieved—though he doesn't tell us—in his great collection *What Work Is,* published two years ago.

The pieces in *The Bread of Time* are a series of experiments in remembering rather than a whole organized act of memory. In suggesting the present simultaneity of discrete past images, Levine sometimes introduces bits that don't very clearly fit. He can strut his blue collar, as in his mockery of a young academic who "pranced before us reading some sprightly little paper for 'Notes and Queries'." *He* prefers bowling, he lets us know.

His wandering method works perfectly, though, in his portrait of his mother. She lived in Europe for a while, worked for years and in near-poverty in Detroit to raise her children and, when they were grown, skipped to California. Philip visits her when she is 80; she is sardonic and free. She shows an odd familiarity with the Italian poet Gabriele d'Annunzio—Levine pauses to wonder if *he* could be his father—and translates one of his poems for him. "It's a lot worse than it sounds," she assures him. "It loses a lot in the original." Truly, a poet's mother.

After sketching a mannered professor who taught him James Joyce at college, Levine touches upon various aspects of his own life and his growing sense of aging. Suddenly the professor is back, no longer caricatured but a contemporary in Levine's own autumnal process. The professor ends his course with Joyce's injunction that a reader should spend a lifetime reading what it took him, Joyce, a lifetime to write.

"I am that reader," Professor Prescott tells his departing students, "and I can tell you that it was a wasted life."

The three best pieces are about Levine's poetic mentors. He portrays John Berryman as a man stretched past his own long gawkiness in his passion to impart what poetry must be. His voice went so high that "it seemed that only a dog could hear it." His class was a battlefield; Berryman would tear the poems apart or praise them; either way, the students were goaded to make them better. "Levine, this will never do," still rings in the writer's ears, along with, "One must be ruthless with one's own writing or someone else will" and—when one student turned in a magnificent sonnet—"Say that better in 1,000 words and you're a genius."

Levine's young passion for the Spanish Republic led him to spend a sabbatical, years later, in Barcelona. He evokes the mid-'60s when the Franco regime still oppressed, but with a shaky hand. There is a wonderful encounter with two members of the once-feared Guardia Civil taking refuge from the rain in a bar. One of them showed Levine a cork stuck in the muzzle of his carbine to keep the water out, and launched into a sardonic political skit: "This is what they have given me to defend the sacred shores of Spain from the communist fleet. I haven't a chance. The string on the cork is broken; one shot and I'm through."

Out of his sketch comes the shadowy figure of Antonio Machado, modern Spain's greatest poet. Levine takes Spanish lessons from a young poet; he in turn introduces his pupil to Machado's grave, seemingly plain and magically haunted work. It has all but defied translation. Levine's efforts to translate a poem, and his irritation over a set of translations by Robert Bly, produce a comically frank image of a poet's work and prickles. Finally there is a beautiful tribute—virtually a prose poem—to Machado's spiritual oneness with the gaunt landscape of Castille. Levine calls it "soul" and his writing strips the word of millennia of lofty and sentimental associations and delivers it plain.

It is also the key word in his portrait of Ivor Winters. Freed from factory work by a fellowship to Stanford, Levine spent a year studying with the bristly and resolutely unfashionable poet and critic. In almost every respect they were opposites. Levine was young and new; Winters was old and even his contemporaries considered him a stylistic reactionary. Levine depicts a man whose passion for what he considered real poetry—he insisted that an obscure Georgian poet, T. Sturge Moore, was superior to Yeats—had isolated him both aesthetically and personally. Yet Levine manages to let us see what burned beneath the crust. Through long afternoons Winters read old French and Breton poetry to him, laying out imagery and etymology. In the passion for craft it recalled Berryman; and in another way it recalled Machado. "Philip," Winters told him once, "we must never lie or we shall lose our soul."

Dana Gioia (review date 20 February 1994)

SOURCE: "Stanzas in a Life," in *New York Times Book Review,* February 20, 1994, p. 14.

[*In the following review, Gioia considers* The Bread of Time, *Levine's collection of autobiographical essays. Though Gioia praises certain facets of the work, he also criticizes it for certain shortcomings both as an autobiography and as a book of essays.*]

The last few years have witnessed a changing of the guard in American poetry. The influential generation of writers born in the 1920's has reached retirement. It's hard to imagine this vigorous bunch, which includes Adrienne Rich, Donald Justice, Robert Bly, Richard Wilbur and Louis Simpson, as senior citizens. It seems like yesterday they were barnstorming the nation to oppose the war in Vietnam, redefine feminism or champion Surrealism. But the evidence is indisputable: they have begun publishing their memoirs. The last 12 months have seen the appearance of *A Different Person* by James Merrill and Donald Hall's *Life Work* as well as Adrienne Rich's autobiographical literary essays, *What Is Found There.* To those personal testimonies, one can now add *The Bread of Time* by Philip Levine.

Born in Detroit in 1928, Mr. Levine has assiduously cultivated the image of a tough working-class poet. His 15 volumes of feisty, chip-on-the-shoulder verse alternately celebrate and elegize a gritty world of lonely highways, aging factories and dead-end jobs. Although Mr. Levine's rebellious proletarian persona has always made for lively reading, it has also occasionally seemed studied and self-conscious. Something important was missing from his story. *The Bread of Time* explains the special circumstances that created this unusual writer.

"Although I was born into the middle class," he confides, "my father died before I was old enough to enjoy my station." After the poet's businessman father passed on without adequate insurance, the family began a slow economic descent into "a series of ever-shrinking apartments." Money became the nagging topic of mealtime conversation. The crummy jobs that the young Philip Levine agonizingly endured would have seemed natural to most working-class kids. To him, they opened up the nightmare of downward mobility, the middle-class terror of becoming poor. His outsider's perspective on working-class existence became his defining

imaginative vision. The way genuine artists do, he took bad luck and made it inspiration.

The Bread of Time collects nine overlapping but independent personal essays, each of which focuses on a particular person or place important in the author's life. The subtitle, *Toward an Autobiography,* however, suggests the problem inherent in the volume's subjective and unchronological organization. Although it contains many compelling episodes, the book never quite coheres. It lacks the narrative unity of an autobiography but seems too repetitious and self-regarding to be a satisfactory book of essays.

Mr. Levine's natural medium is lyric poetry: the vivid and subjective expression of a particular moment. *The Bread of Time* sometimes reveals the strain of an artist working in an unfamiliar form. (Mr. Levine's only previous prose collection, *Don't Ask,* consists entirely of interviews.) A lyric poem need not present a balanced view of experience; it must only be true to the moment's insight. A memoir, however, raises a different set of imaginative challenges. There needs to be a cogent overall design that credibly connects past action and present reflection. Since the author is both the observer and the observed, the narrator's motives are always open to question. If a memoir seems too self-serving, the reader loses confidence in its veracity. Although every author is entitled to be the hero of his own story, an autobiographer must earn a reader's trust with at least a modicum of embarrassing candor and self-criticism.

> **Mr. Levine's natural medium is lyric poetry: the vivid and subjective expression of a particular moment.**
> **—Dana Gioia**

While Mr. Levine's lyrical prose usually captures the emotional intensity of past experience, his inspired subjectivity aggravates the problems inherent in the book's episodic structure. For all its energy, *The Bread of Time* never develops much narrative momentum. What Mr. Levine offers instead is personal myth-making: the working-class anarchist from Depression-era Detroit who struggles to the top of American poetry. There are moments when his self-dramatization brings the book uncomfortably close to a celebrity autobiography. He is savvy enough to recognize his temptation to self-mythologizing, but he doesn't control it, probably because the strategy has worked so well in his poetry. Equally troubling is his obsession with settling old scores. One essay, **"Class With No Class,"** seems to exist for no other reason than to smear a well-to-do family that briefly employed the 18-year-old writer to tutor their "exceedingly rat-faced" son. Perhaps this nasty clan was really as dreadful as Mr. Levine claims, but what the story mostly conveys is stereotypical class hatred.

In an introductory note Mr. Levine admits that his "original intent was not to write an autobiography" but to celebrate the memory of people who had helped shape his life. *The Bread of Time* works best when it sticks closest to the author's original vision. The high points of the volume are portraits of his poetic mentors, John Berryman and Yvor Winters. These two brilliant but difficult men touched a sympathetic nerve in Mr. Levine when he was young. His portrait of Berryman is particularly fine. As he recounts his arrival at the University of Iowa Writers' Workshop, he captures the passionate intensity of a young writer struggling to define his own identity in the intellectual and artistic ferment that followed World War II. If there ever was a place and a time to enlist in a graduate writing program, it was Iowa in 1953, when Robert Lowell and then Berryman were instructors and the entering class included Mr. Levine, Donald Justice, W. D. Snodgrass, Henri Coulette, Jane Cooper and several other notables. In Berryman Mr. Levine found the demanding but democratic teacher he needed to challenge his imagination. Mr. Levine's memoir makes no pretense of fairness; it is an overt celebration of a man he loved and revered. It may be prose, but it displays the irresistible force of poetry.

The finest moments in this volume mostly share the emotional quality of the Berryman episode. Love is the passionate and enduring attentiveness that incites Mr. Levine's imagination most vividly. Whether his subject is famous, like the eccentric, domineering and penetrating Winters, or forgotten, like Cipriano, the Detroit anarchist who worked in the neighborhood dry cleaners, the people Mr. Levine admires come alive on the page while the objects of his derision lie inert. "What will survive of us is love," Philip Larkin once wrote. He could have been reviewing *The Bread of Time*.

Philip Levine with Chris Wyrick and Others (interview date Winter 1995/1996)

SOURCE: "A Conversation with Philip Levine," in *TriQuarterly*, No. 95, Winter, 1995/1996, pp. 67-82.

[*In the following interview, conducted in Harry Thomas's English class at Davidson College on April 25, 1995, Levine answers questions about the sources and subject matter of his poetry as well as his writing style. He also discusses such topics as the nature of contemporary American poetry, some of its movements and practitioners, and the poetic process in general.*]

[*Chris Wyrick:*] *Congratulations on the big prize! [The Pulitzer Prize in Poetry for* **The Simple Truth** *(1994)]*

[Philip Levine:] Well, thank you. Yes. It's been a long time coming. But, you see, patience does pay off. Actually, I think it's better to get it when you're old. Ah, I'm happy to win it.

[*George Weld:*] *I think now especially a lot of young writers feel a tension between the feeling that they need to be activists in their work for social change and a feeling that, as Auden says, "Poetry makes nothing happen," that poetry is irrelevant or elitist, and I'm wondering whether you feel this tension yourself.*

Well, frankly, I think that Auden is wrong. Poetry *does* make things happen. And I think that if a young person is troubled by the idea that he or she is practicing an elitist art, then he ought to do something else. I mean, if you have grave doubts about being a poet because you will thereby not achieve your social ambitions, then don't write poetry. Poetry will make it without you. And the question you have to ask yourself is, "Can I make it without poetry?" And if the answer is fuzzy and hazy, do something else. The answer had better be very loud and very clear: "I *can't* make it without poetry." Because there's so much in a life of poetry that can defeat you. And the apparatus for rewarding you is so abysmal, and the rewards themselves, aside from the writing of the poems, so small, that there's no point in doing it unless you're utterly confident that that's your vocation, that's your calling. I was very lucky when I was your age. T. S. Eliot came to see me. He said, "American poetry just needs you, Phil." He took the bus. In Detroit. I was surprised to see him in a Jewish neighborhood, but there he was. I said, "You're Tom Eliot." He said, "Say Sir, son." Of course, I'm kidding. It was a long bus ride from London, from Faber and Faber.

When I was your age I had no doubt. I also had social goals, and I was naive enough at eighteen or nineteen to think that poetry or fiction could have a vast social influence because it had a vast influence on the way I felt and thought. It wasn't very long before I realized that if I wasn't being read I wasn't going to influence many people through my writing. I was aware of the fact that while I was reading poets like Eliot, Auden, Spender, Wilfred Owen, Lowell, Stevens, and Hart Crane, my neighbors weren't. They wouldn't have known who the hell I was talking about, so I didn't talk about them. I'd guess much of my family was puzzled. They must have thought, "What is this infatuation and how long will it last?" I was the only member of my family ever to finish college. There's a Yiddish expression that translates, "For this you went to college?" That's exactly what my grandfather said to me when I graduated from college and told him I wanted to be a poet. He told me about this man who lived in his village back in Russia before he left in '04 to come to the

United States. This guy was some sort of lunatic who went from house to house; people fed him and listened to his terrible poems. My grandfather said, "At least he didn't go to college. Why did you go, for this?" I tried to explain to him that I didn't go to college to become a poet, that while I was there my romance with poetry deepened. He just shrugged.

But poetry does make things happen. You know that already. It changes all of us who read it. But it will not change legislation.

[*Rachel Newcomb:*] *I have another question that's along those same lines. In an interview in 1988 you said that perhaps American poetry had stopped believing in itself, and I was wondering if you felt that contemporary American poetry has become marginal and, if so, how can poetry attract a wider audience?*

I don't know why I said that in '88. I can't recall the occasion. Perhaps I was reading a lot of boring poetry. I talk to a lot of younger poets and most of them don't seem to feel their generation has found itself as yet. I had a conversation for publication recently with a wonderful younger poet, Kate Daniels—she must be thirty-eight or so—and she felt her generation hadn't yet found what it wanted to do, but she felt that my generation had to assert itself early because we were under the shadows of the giants. If you looked at the magazines in which I first published, you'd see I'm in there with Stevens, Marianne Moore, Williams. I wasn't awed by them. I knew how good they were, I knew they were writing far better than I, but I thought, given enough time, they will vanish from the earth in their bodily incarnations and then maybe my writing will get as good as theirs. Well, the first part did happen, and I'm still waiting for the second.

You asked about the audience for poetry in our country. I think it's the largest it's ever been. I know we're told otherwise. There's this "expert," Joseph Epstein, who published something like "Who Killed Poetry?" or something like that. Nobody killed poetry. Guys like Epstein like to hearken back to some dreamland America in which people got up in the morning and opened their windows to the birds singing and when they felt their souls elevated they recited American poetry to the waiting world. Bullshit! If you go back to the time when Stevens, Eliot, Williams were first publishing, exactly the same things were being said in the middlebrow press: "Look at this generation of turkeys. You can't understand a word they write. They're so obscure and so negative. Give us back our uplifting verse!" That was the middlebrow response to one of the great outpourings of poetry in the history of the English language, which took place early in this century. What happened in American poetry was extraordinary: Frost, Stevens, Williams, Pound, Moore, Eliot, all writing at the same time, E. A. Robinson, the whole Imagist thing. And the Epsteins of that hour were griping

just as they are now. My guess is that today it still has something to do with class; they can't stand the idea of all these poets coming out of Turkey Tech and Fresno State and Puma J. C. They're from the fancy places that once owned our poetry. We had the same response from the Eastern lords when the Beats hit the press.

I think poetry now is very healthy. There is no such thing as an official style. It's open house. It doesn't matter how tall or short you are, what color you are or what sex you are or what nine sexes, you can put anything in your work.

You can write about anything. No matter how badly you write you can find somebody who'll publish you. Time will sift the good stuff from the bad. As far as readership goes it's the largest it's ever been. I know, we're told no one is reading it, but that's nonsense. Go back and discover how large, say, an edition of William Carlos Williams was in 1944. His last book, *The Wedge,* was published in fewer than 500 copies. In '54 his great book, *The Desert Music,* was published by Random House; I'd be surprised if they did more than 1,200 copies. How big was the first edition of Lowell's incredible *Lord Weary's Castle?* One thousand copies? Berryman's *The Dispossessed?* I'd bet fewer than 1,000. The first edition of my new book is 7,500. And Sharon Olds and Adrienne Rich outsell me; they must do 10,000 of theirs. My editor told me the other day that Galway Kinnell's *The Book of Nightmares* had sold 60,000 copies and is still selling. I remember a year ago reading with Galway in Portland, and afterwards they had a book-signing, and for over an hour people kept lining up with old battered copies of his books. Those books had been read, God knows by how many people. There is a huge readership. We're told otherwise by the naysayers, but it's not true.

[*Patrick Malcor:*] *You said that there is no specific style of poetry right now. Do you think poetry is beyond the point where it can have a movement, a certain mass style, or do you think that it needs that?*

There will always be movements. We have one right now that began in California, the Language Poets. Do you know their work? [Blank looks.] You don't, God bless you. Young poets begin movements to have something to belong to, something potentially exciting: "We're going to change American poetry!"

Ever since I began writing I've noticed that certain movements are there mainly to help people without talent write something they can pass off as poetry. If you can't tell a decent story, denounce poems that tell stories. If you can't create characters, denounce poems with people in them. If you can't create images, write boring generalities. If you have no sense of form, imitate the formlessness of the sea. If you have no ear, disparage music. If everything you write is ugly and senseless, remind your readers that the world is ugly and senseless. Bad poets are incredibly resourceful. But those are movements that are easily forgotten. About fifteen years ago we had something called the New Formalism, and it seems to have vanished already. Very curious movement, a sort of nostalgia for the poetry of the fifties and perhaps for the decade itself, and it occurred at a time when the best formal poets of the fifties—Wilbur, Merrill, Hecht, Nemerov—were still writing incredibly well. The important movements change the way we see poetry or poetry sees us.

When I was your age a poet friend of mine, Bernie Strempek, and I founded a revolutionary poetry movement. We called it The New Mysticism; that was Bernie's idea. I believe he truly believed in the majesty and burning of the invisible whereas I was about as mystical as a sofa. Clearly we didn't change anything, not even the way we saw ourselves, but for a few weeks we had great fun talking about how we were going to change the country. Both the Language poets and the New Formalists strike me as less interesting than the New Mystics, though I am hardly objective. They're such conservative movements: neither seems in the least interested in shouldering a social or spiritual or political agenda. Both are academic and largely praised by academic critics and by the poets themselves, but perhaps they will have a healthy impact on our writing. They probably find my work and the contemporary work that resembles it garbage, which is fine. What's important is there is not a single official, accepted style. Today someone entering poetry can take any number of directions and find other poets who will validate his or her work. I hate the notion that any style, mine or anyone else's, is *the* style.

We have had very important, essential movements in this century. For me the most important one was the Imagist movement, which included such poets as Williams, Pound, Ford Madox Ford, D. H. Lawrence, and profoundly changed both English and American poetry. One in England right after the end of World War II changed the entire focus of their poetry. It was labeled "The Movement" and was something of a repudiation of the high-flown rhetoric of poets like George Barker, Dylan Thomas and Henry Treece. Suddenly we got these hard-assed poems from poets like Thom Gunn and Philip Larkin. They seemed more interested in what went on in a department store than what went on after you died and went to heaven. They'd write about trying to pick up a girl or spinning out on your motorcycle or finding a pair of pants that made you look sexy. In their poems people sound like people and not holy texts. In "Church Going" Larkin writes about a man with no religious faith who goes into an empty church and wonders what the hell it's for. At one point in the poem he says "up at the holy end"; he can't think of the name for that part of the church, if he ever knew it. It's a marvelous poem about the need for religious feelings in people without religious feelings.

And then in the late fifties we had the Beat or Black Mountain thing, all the poets represented in Donald Allen's anthology *The New American Poetry*. If you can still find that book have a look at it. You'll find it contains some of the best American poets of the second half of the century: Gary Snyder, Creeley, Ginsberg, Robert Duncan, Denise Levertov. All of us who write poetry owe those poets a great debt for ending the absolute domination of the official Eastern establishment; that was a great service. Maybe you folks would like to start a movement: the Davidson Suicide Squad or the North Carolina Stompers. It couldn't do any harm, and it might enliven things. They're a little dull right now.

[*Todd Cabell:*] *You mention in the first essay in your book,* **The Bread of Time,** *that anybody can become a poet, that we have democratized poetry, and then you mention creative-writing classes in colleges and high schools. I wonder, being a teacher yourself, what exactly do you view as bad in that movement?*

Nothing. I think it's a wonderful thing. When I started writing there was not the sense that everybody could become a poet. Chicano poetry did not exist, Asian-American poetry did not exist, such giants as Robert Hayden and Sterling Brown were not represented in the official anthologies. I'm having fun in that essay, and I'm also being serious because I do think there are too many writing programs and many are staffed by people who can't write themselves. I visit places where poetry writing is taught in graduate programs, and I can't believe the level of writing. Then I see the poetry the teachers write, and I know why. And you visit a class, and everything is praised: the MO seems to be, "Let's pretend all this writing is poetry." Once you create a program you require students, so you let everyone in and you keep them in by making them happy. I also visit writing programs in which real standards are operating, the students have talent and are reading and working like mad; the teachers are dedicated, demanding, fair, and they are gifted and productive poets themselves. There are two things you must have for a valuable writing program: first and most importantly, the right students. Then the teachers. You could have mediocre teachers if you had great students because the students will teach each other and inspire each other. The problem is great students rarely gravitate to mediocre teachers.

[*Chris Wyrick:*] *I'd like to ask a question about your method of writing. In* **What Work Is,** *in the poem* **"Scouting,"** *you say, "I'm scouting, getting the feel of the land," and in the poem* **"What Work Is,"** *"Forget you. This is about waiting, shifting from one foot to another." And I want to ask you if you could tell us more about this process of scouting that you engage in your poems.*

That's a difficult and interesting question. How do you research a poem, which is what scouting is? Or at least that's one of the things I'm scouting for in the poem, the poem itself. You know you're constantly obliged when you apply for grants or things like grants to describe the specific steps you're going to take to write the book you're asking for financial support to write, and of course you rarely know exactly what you'll have to do. If you've been doing it as long as I, you have some idea, and I'd call it a kind of scouting. It's a circling and circling, quite literally—a cityscape, a landscape, a subject, an emotional obsession. I'll give you an example. I have this fascination with Spanish anarchism, so back in the seventies I went to one of the great collections of anarchist literature, The International Institute for Social Study in Amsterdam. The records of the CNT and the FAI—the National Workers Confederation and the Iberian Anarchist Federation—were stored there. Most of the stuff is in Spanish, and at the time my Spanish was good enough to read it. The people who worked in the library there were very helpful and generous; they brought me whatever I wanted to see, old newspapers, posters, memoirs, manifestoes, anything I asked for, and I sat there for hours, day after day, reading. The poetry I finally got had nothing to do with Spanish anarchism, though I have written many poems out of that obsession; this "scouting" produced poems that had to do with being in a library. They had to do with the quality of light, the sadness that invades a library late in the afternoon when you've been there all day from 9:00 in the morning until 5:30 and suddenly you realize the light has changed and the day is ending. In Amsterdam the weather can change very suddenly, and I would glance out the window and dark clouds were blowing in from the North Sea, and the day was totally different from the one I left when I entered the library. My heart was always yearning to go out in the streets and to be in Amsterdam; it's such a beautiful and lively city. I learned a hell of a lot about Spanish anarchism and I wrote about my hours in the library, the people I met there, the yearning for the city, the shocking realization of how quickly time was passing and the light going.

And **"Scouting,"** the poem itself, is about my days in North Carolina, your dear state, where I lived the summer of 1954 in a mountain town called Boone. I thought I'd made a drastic step that might mean I would never become the amazing poet I had seemed destined to become. I had just gotten married. I had fallen in love with a woman who had a young child, and so we married. I thought, "Look what a foolish thing love has driven me to do. I must now be a responsible human being. I'm only twenty-six years old and I've thrown my young life away." You know, men at twenty-six are total idiots. I would go for long walks most days. I didn't have to work, my new wife was working and supporting all of us. I was supposed to be writing poems, but my mother-in-law had come for the wedding, and no one can write with his mother-in-law in the house, even, as in my case, if she's a lovely woman. So I went on these long walks and began to discover the landscape of those mountains and the people.

I'd knock on doors of these little cabins and say, "Could I have a drink of water?" And besides the water, which I always got, I'd get different responses. "Where you from, son?" "What are you doing here?" They'd hear my accent and know I was not local, these gracious country people sharing their water with me, their time; we'd have wonderful conversations. It was a kind of scouting. As I got further and further into it I realized I was carrying out research, I was researching myself as well as these people and their place. My mother-in-law left, so in the mornings I'd work for hours on poetry; I found Saintsbury's *History of English Prosody* in the local library, never had been read, pages uncut, and I poured over that. I'd been trying to write poetry for ten years, and I still didn't know how to do it and knew I didn't know. But I was getting clues and I was also learning how to research poems: you keep your eyes open, your ears open, all your senses open. The world responds to you, and you respond to the world. It goes on that way, it never ends.

Keats has a late letter to Shelley. I don't think he ever truly cared for Shelley. It might have been a class problem, Shelley coming from the rich and famous family and living his "spontaneous" life. Like Byron, Shelley wrote all the time. Keats had long bouts of silence, what we too easily call writer's block. He suggests to Shelley that his poetry might be richer if he "loaded every rift with ore," if he wrote less and did it with more intensity. He goes on to say that he has sat as long as six months without writing. I think Keats believed, as I have come to believe, that not writing is part of the process of writing. Not in the beginning—for first you have to learn what the hell it is you're doing—then you must write, as Berryman said to me, everything that occurs to you.

I've been very lucky. I've never had one of those terrible droughts. Three or four months is the longest I've ever gone without writing poetry or something I could regard as poetry. I've come to think part of the process, an essential part, is waiting, being patient, and avoiding what one might call busy work. There's the temptation to construct what you secretly know is second-rate and keep working at it because it beats not working at anything. I think you're better off not writing at all than just soothing yourself with busywork. I'm not talking about beginning writers; they have no idea where anything will go and should plow ahead with whatever comes to them. By the time you've been at it fifteen years you know when you're just imitating yourself.

"Scouting" is also about that dreadful moment here in North Carolina when I said to myself, "Philip, you have o'erstepped your usual timidity and entered upon marriage." You know I was just like any other jerk my age. No one had told me how to become a poet, and I'd figured out that if you didn't have money there were two ways to live: you can have a family or you can write poetry, but you ain't going to do both. How the hell are you going to take care of kids, help dress and feed them, get them off to school, and then write a poem? What kind of nonsense is that? I figured I should have someone coming into my study with toast and tea, I should have silence interrupted at intervals for wonderful meals. Wasn't that how Rilke lived? How many nights do you think he sat up with a sick kid? You know at one point or another in your life you have to wake up and become a person. The irony of all this is I was incredibly lucky. I was marrying a woman who had a profound regard for poetry and this kid I adopted turned out to be one of my best friends. It was probably one of the three or four intelligent decisions I've made in my whole life. Another was buying the house I work in in Fresno. Another was not going to the Korean War. I can't think of another one, but there must be a fourth.

[*Mary Stephens:*] *I'm interested in how memory works in the writing process because so many of your poems are retrospective. How does this process differ from poems that are observed at the moment of conception? And how important is looking back, not only on your own experiences, but on your earlier writing?*

I don't know if I can answer the second part. It seems to me that you made a distinction between writing a poem that would come out of memory and one that would come out of an experience that was before you. But you'll notice that in my poems it almost doesn't seem to matter what's before me: I go back into memory and try often to twine what I remember with what I'm observing. And I'm not sure why I do this, although it's obviously something that I do. I think that a lot of it has to do with the fact that I feel an urgency to record things because they seem so transitory. And I am now a kind of archive of people, places and things that no longer exist. I carry them around with me, and if I get them on paper I give them at least some existence. And that seems like a legitimate thing to be doing with poetry. To be granting some form of permanence—I mean, however permanent the poems are—to the things, to a way of life and the people who made up that way of life.

As far as looking back at my own writing, I try not to. I purposely don't memorize my poems. When I'm on the brink of memorizing a poem I stop using it at readings. I wait for time to erase it because I don't want to memorize it. I don't mind memorizing other people's poems, but I'm not going to sit down and write a poem that I've memorized by Hardy or Wyatt or Dylan Thomas. I'm not going to do that. Whereas a poem that's my own may haunt me if I go back to it. I don't want to go back to it. I don't want to look at it. And sometimes when I look at them I'm a little depressed by the fact that they're better than what I'm writing now. That's another thing: I believe some of the older poems have

more imagination, more vitality. I know that these last two books have won all these honors, but I actually prefer some of the older books.

People ask me, for example, what's the book I'm working on now, what's it about, and when I tell them the truth they think I'm putting them on. I say, "I don't know yet. I won't know until I'm done." But that's the truth. That's happened with every book I've ever written. I didn't know what the book was about until I finished it or got close to finishing it. And then I saw, "Oh, that's what I've been obsessed with!" For example, in writing the last book, *The Simple Truth,* I saw at a certain point that there were three poems I needed. I had taken out a group of poems that either weren't good enough or didn't belong. I said to myself, "I need three poems to go right there," and in the next month I wrote them. That was very rare for me.

With the book *What Work Is,* I suddenly realized I needed a long poem at the center, so I revived a poem I'd been working on for at least a dozen years and had failed to finish, **"Burned."** I looked at what I had and knew the time had come to finish it. And I got it. I didn't get it right, but I think I got it as right as I would probably ever get it. Sitting over it another year wouldn't have made it any better, so I let it out into the world. And it was well treated. Have I answered your question?

[*Geordie Schimmel:*] *What if not poetry? If not the dialogue with stars and trees at thirteen, what would you have chosen?*

It would have been the dialogue at fourteen. That's what I was going to do. I don't have the least doubt about it. Before I was ten I was utterly fascinated with language, with the shape and flavor of words. And I got so much pleasure out of using language, and I used it with snap. Besides, there weren't that many other options. I couldn't have been a dancer, I'm too awkward. I can't draw so I couldn't have been a painter. Maybe an Abstract Expressionist, except my sense of color stinks. I can't carry a tune worth a damn, so although I love music it wasn't for me. I might have become a critic. No, never a *cricket,* as Mark Twain calls them. Better to be an honest huckster and sell Buicks. I might have become a novelist. When I was in college I worked as hard at fiction as I did at poetry, but back then my temperament wasn't suited for it; I hadn't yet developed the incredible patience a novelist requires.

[*William Robert:*] *I'd like to return to your works for a minute and ask you a question about them. Pretty consistently, from the earliest ones to the ones that just came out in* **The Simple Truth,** *you develop many philosophical threads. And one of the most fundamental seems to me to be the lack of, the impotency of, even the impossibility of,* *true communication between individuals. Do you see this as an ironic stance for a poet, namely one who depends on communication, to take?*

No, no, I don't. Failing to communicate is part of what we live with, part of our condition. Poetry is about as good as we can get at communicating without the aid of gestures, without the aid of our bodies. Rilke wrote somewhere that without our bodies we cannot love. Also with our bodies, with our gestures, with our facial expressions, we can communicate far more fully than with merely words on the telephone or words in a letter. Poetry is as close as we can get to complete communication with words alone. And I think it's good enough. I believe that when I'm reading Keats or Hardy—another of my favorite poets—I'm getting it, the essence of what they have to say and even more than the essence, lots of the particulars. Obviously I'm not getting it all. There's no such thing as perfect communication. Hardy's experience of the world is not mine, though our lives overlapped by some months. Keats's experience of the London of his era is not mine; their experience with the words they use is so different from mine. But the miracle of poetry is that it can cross so many of these barriers. Approximate communication seems so amazing itself when you consider how separate we are or how separate we have conceived of ourselves. I believe that we aren't nearly as separate as we think we are. If, for example, someone in this room were running a fever we would all heat up a bit, we'd feel it even though we might not know we felt it. Our eyes tell us we're more separate than we actually are, and our conscious experience tells us, and we've conditioned ourselves to believe we're more separate. But to get back to poetry, given who we've created out of ourselves, poetry is miraculous.

But you're right: there is an obsession in much of my work with the failures of people to communicate, but those failures are usually very specific. I'm usually concerned with a few people, perhaps only two, and how they fail to communicate. A book that moved me enormously when I was young, maybe eighteen, was *Winesburg, Ohio.* I remember a story about two very lonely people, a man and a woman, who have no one to communicate with and whose experience of love is very limited. As I recall—I haven't read the story in ages—they get together and they discover they have these mutual needs and they could be dear friends. As I recall the man oversteps the bounds of this budding friendship; while the woman is trying to speak out of her joy that she has a listener he shuts her up by kissing her. There's this awful and wonderful irony that he has chosen to communicate his love or joy in the occasion this way, and she wants to communicate it another way and you can't do both at the same time. She says something like, "But, Harold, let me tell you what it was like to be six and a solitary girl," and he goes smack, smack, as if to say, "Let me show you what it's like to be twenty-seven and a man in the company of a

woman." I thought Anderson had captured something amazing: how even when we fail each other the miraculous happens, they cross that great divide that separates one person from another. I believe it's possible. I believe I've done it, totally. I try to record it in my poem **"The Escape."** The communication between the speaker and the woman is total, and he becomes a creature endowed with two sexes, an angel with no wings. They don't do it merely with words, but they do it. He touches the woman and discovers he's also touching himself because they've become one being.

[Kristina Nevius:] Through this interview you've mentioned languages. What effect have foreign languages and cultures had on your poetry?

When I go to a foreign country where I don't speak the language I usually make no effort to learn it. I'm just "The Ugly American," as Eugene Burdick called us in his novel years ago. I enjoy the ignorance, I use it. Say I go into the Campo Fiori, the great open market in Rome. I stop and listen to two people standing in line to buy eggs. The man says to the woman, "Was there ever a more perfect shape than an egg? And the luminosity! The amazing delicacy of the color, the way it takes the hues of the air. Not only does the egg contain sustenance for us, for our bodies which feed our souls, but within each egg is the potential of a creature that can fly." Amazing, they say such rare things in such common places in Rome; Italians are angels. Of course that's not what they're saying at all. The guy has turned to his cousin Elfonzina and said, "Holy shit, the bastard raised the price again!" Because I don't speak Italian I've endowed him with poetry, and I say to myself, "How fortunate you are, Philip, to be living among such profound people when in fact they're saying the same trivial things they'd be saying in Fresno or Detroit."

One invaluable thing I learned from studying Spanish was how great our own poetry is, how many things it can do that Spanish poetry hasn't done. We appear in American poetry and we speak in our daily voices. It gave me a new regard for American poetry. Discovering the great poetry written in Spanish in this century was intoxicating. There's also much more awful poetry written in Spain than in the U.S. because anyone who goes to the university in Spain publishes a book of poetry. The dentist will hand you a beautifully printed book of poems—each dentist has one—all about the perfume of flowers, the brightness of the moon, the tenderness of kisses, the sweetness of the night air of Andalusia, the kindness of wild herbs. The poetry of love, dreams, moonlight, fantasy. Absolute garbage. It's so bad they couldn't even sing it in Nashville, and they can sing anything in Nashville. The great poetry is able to use the same vocabulary and break all the silly conventions and astonish you.

Even though I had to work like a demon on my Spanish, I got a great kick out of being able to speak it and understand it. I also found it exhausting to speak it for hours on end. One day I got so tired I went into a little park near the *futbol* stadium in Barcelona, flopped on a bench and slept for hours. Once I started dreaming in Spanish I got scared I'd lose my American English, so I would go down to the port and speak to American sailors and marines off the ships.

I think, too, it's very good to read poetry in another language to discover the immense possibilities we're not taking advantage of in our poetry. I know you can discover much of that reading translations, say of Zbigniew Herbert or Tomas Tranströmer, but I think you get an even keener sense when you read someone like García Lorca or César Vallejo in the original. And you're inspired in the same way you're inspired when you read Whitman or Dickinson or Williams. I can still recall struggling with the poems of Miguel Hernández in the original and those sudden glimpses of how astonishing the poetry was, how brutal and lyrical at exactly the same moment. I'd never read anything like it; it reconfirmed my belief in the power and beauty of poetry in the face of the worst life can dish out. These are poems that grew out of the most tragic circumstances. They are full of indescribable pain, which he foresees. They are very great and very difficult poems; I had to work hours, and then I would get this glimpse of their majesty. Going to Spain, living there, was a wonderful experience for me. I owe the discovery of the poetry mainly to Hardie St. Martin, the poet and translator I met in Barcelona. He was working on his great anthology, *Roots and Wings,* and generously took me into his stable of translators.

[*Alex Crumbley:*] *Did it take you long to become comfortable writing persona poems? And when you do, do you have trouble with people assuming you're the narrator when you're not?*

First thing, it didn't take long at all. Once I decided I wanted to do it, I just did it. I had written a lot of fiction, at least a dozen stories and large chunks of two novels, so I was used to the problem of getting into the heads of other characters and getting them to speak in my writing.

As far as people misreading, I don't much care. I remember a review I got, I think it was in the *Village Voice,* in which a woman wrote that one of my poems from *7 Years from Somewhere* was very curious. The poem, **"I Could Believe,"** is in the voice of a guy who has come back from the Spanish Civil War. This woman wrote something like, "Levine is an autobiographical poet, so it's amazing to discover that he fought in the Spanish Civil War, which ended when he was eleven." She mused over this, and then wrote, "Perhaps he's trying something different." Perhaps if I'd written in the voice of someone coming back from the American Civil War she wouldn't have missed it, but you can't be sure. If you're troubled by being misunderstood then you'd better not publish.

Even our fellow poets and friends read our poetry differently. I remember going to a class at the University of Minnesota and having a conversation with them; it was much like today. At the end someone asked if I would read one poem. I said, "Sure, let me read something I'm working on and we'll see what you think of it." I read **"Listen Carefully"** in an early draft. After I was done a young woman asked me if I would publish the poem. I said, "Yeah, if I ever get it right." "But if your sister read it, how would she feel?" I said, "I don't have a sister." She was shocked. My host, Michael Dennis Browne, an English poet who has become a fine American poet, then told an interesting story.

He said, "You know, Sharon Olds was sitting in that same chair last year, and for some reason she got on the subject of Phil's poetry. She told us how she had asked Phil where she might get 'chocolate cookies in the shape of Michigan,' cookies Phil refers to in one of his poems. To Sharon's surprise Phil said he just made it up." Michael quoted her in a surprised voice, "He made it up!" as though that were unheard of. Sharon is a dear friend of mine, and my guess is she was having fun. It's very possible it's not something she would do in her own poems, but I'm sure she knows it's something I do all the time. To me it's always open house; if you want it and it doesn't exist, just make it up. This poem with the cookies in it is about an amazing kid, a kid so amazing he's not human and yet he is. He's what human beings would be if human beings were totally themselves. Now how would I know what human beings would be if they were totally themselves? I'll tell you how; I've been totally myself. I've experienced it. That's what you become when you're inspired, you become totally yourself. We pray to the muse and all the rest of that. Poets tell us, Coleridge and Keats for example, that they wrote some of their most inspired works when they were invaded by a force not their own. Maybe they're right, but I have a different notion: I don't believe there is this outside force. I believe that we are so rarely totally ourselves that when we are we don't know who we are. I think it's similar to what athletes refer to as being "in the zone."

That's what poets live for, those days when we are totally ourselves. I know when I'm there. I awaken in the morning, and I know I'm there, that today it's going to happen. I've been working toward that day for ages, and when it comes I'm in no hurry. I learned from Alberto Giacometti to take my time when *the* day comes. I think it was in 1968 I read a book called *A Giacometti Portrait,* by James Lord. One chapter describes a day on which Alberto knows he's going to do great work, he just has it, so he just goes about his day very slowly. He wants to touch and perhaps bless as much of his daily life as he possibly can, the people and the places and the things that make up his daily life. He takes a long walk, he visits his usual haunts, he talks to people, and then he gets down to work. I had no idea you could do that until I was forty or forty-one; I didn't know the poem wouldn't run away from me. When you're inspired there's no rush; it's who you've become. Take your time, move around, absorb all you can, reach out as far as possible. You're not going to lose it. It's there. It's you.

Kevin Stein (essay date 1996)

SOURCE: "Why 'Nothing is Past': Philip Levine's Conversation with History," in *Private Poets, Worldly Acts: Public and Private History in Contemporary American Poetry,* Ohio University Press, 1996, pp. 71-89.

[*In the following essay, originally published in* Boulevard, *Volumes 25 and 26, Stein discusses Levine's historical consciousness. He analyzes Levine's insistence that the past is in constant dialogue with the present and that people and events of the past continue to mold those of today and of the future.*]

Three-quarters of the way through Philip Levine's **"The Present,"** a poem recounting the bloody memory of what happened when "Froggy Frenchman" fell from a high pallet at work, Levine shares a secret with his readers, "I began this poem in the present / because nothing is past." On a rhetorical level, Levine addresses his readers merely to let them know why, given the possibilities available to him, he chose present tense for a poem devoted to events long past. It's a way of saying, "Here's how this poem works," and though the remark surprises, it hardly smacks of the memorable. However, on an aesthetic plane, these lines reveal Levine's fundamental attitude towards the way the past impinges upon the present, enlivening, deepening, and sometimes haunting our lives. The past has never truly left us, Levine implies, and we can never flee from it.

In this larger sense, then, Levine has staked out a position on the interplay of history and the poet's own historical consciousness, insisting on a kind of dialogue with the people and events that compose the past and continue to shape the present. No solipsist, Levine is looking for an understanding of self that transcends the self, one that takes into account both the individual's place in history and history's place within the individual. In this way, Levine's thinking resembles Hans-Georg Gadamer's conception of the individual's relationship to history and its texts. Like Levine, Gadamer regards this process as a dialogue between the past and the present. In his *Truth and Method,* Gadamer makes this encounter an even more intimate affair, describing it as

a "conversation," ideally one in which a person comes "to experience the 'Thou' truly as 'Thou,' i.e. not to overlook his claim and listen to what he has to say to us." It was Gadamer, after all, who once called history itself "the conversation that we are." Still, while Gadamer concerns himself mostly with how one reads and interprets a text, Levine demonstrates how this process applies as well to the creation of an artistic text, to the making of a poem.

Moreover, Levine apprehends one aspect of this conversation that Gadamer complacently overlooks: that often the dialogue excludes the disempowered, the poor and the marginalized, those who have by some intentional or unintentional means been silenced by the exercise of power. Recorded history is rarely written by or about those individuals disenfranchised from the realms of political or economic power. Levine's poetry, compelled by moral and aesthetic urgency, therefore directly engages those individuals in poetic conversation. Whereas James Wright often spoke *for* the silenced, Levine instead speaks directly *to* and *with* them. What most interest me are those poems in which the speaker addresses an historical "you" in a kind of dialogic act. Sometimes that "you" says nothing in the conversation, other times a dialogue ensues, and occasionally the reader is the "you" the poem addresses. These poems provide a forum for Levine both to intermingle the private and the cultural and to interact with history—offering, in the process, an aesthetic means for him to personalize the historical and historicize the personal.

Gadamer regards this process as a "fusion" of historical "horizons": that which the individual brings to the subject and that of the subject which speaks to him. In fact, Gadamer believes only a fool would consider these horizons as separate. Our individual horizon, what he calls "everything that can be seen from a particular vantage point," always exists within "one great horizon that moves from within," always remains part and parcel of "a single horizon that embraces everything contained in historical consciousness." Understanding takes place when our own personal horizon of historical meanings and assumptions comes to be seen as "only something laid over a continuing tradition" and when our horizon fuses with that of the historical subject we are examining, whether it is a text, an event, or a person. Gadamer refers to this simultaneous projection and removal of horizons as "effective-history."

This may be a somewhat fancified way of saying that we come to see history as part of us and ourselves as part of history. Once we realize that "the present is being continually formed" by our "encounter with the past," as Gadamer asserts, we come to see how these horizons which we thought to be discrete actually define, inform, and shape each other. Because the present requires the past to give it depth and perspective, and vice versa, understanding always issues from a "fusion" of these horizons which we imagine to exist by themselves. Levine's version of this is simply: "nothing is past."

Frequently these poems that converse with history examine the process by which human beings, burdened by oppressive economic and political forces and often nearly broken by them, still retain their essential human dignity. This idea surges like an undercurrent beneath much of Levine's poetry. Because it is a belief continually submitted to questioning, prodding, and belligerent testing, it charges his poems with poles of joy and anger, faith and despair, affirmation and resignation. For many poets such a compulsion might remain unfocused, a theme that inadvertently crosses wires and brings forth occasional sparks. Levine, however, claims both a personal source and an historical focus for his attentions: the Spanish Civil War. In his youth, Levine found in the Spanish anarchist's politics a system that promised to avoid the abuses of capitalism, fascism, and communism, a way of life he describes to an interviewer as having "to do with the end of ownership, the end of competitiveness, the end of a great deal of things that are ugly." Levine goes on to say that his "obsession" with the war gained poignancy while he was growing up Jewish in the "extraordinarily anti-Semitic city" of Detroit, largely because the Spanish anarchists seemed to be the only ones willing to fight the fascism already spreading like plague through Europe and potentially, he feared, "reaching right into my house and snuffing me out."

If, as in the poem **"To P. L., 1916-1937,"** originally published in ***They Feed They Lion*** (1972), the historical figure remains silent, a conversation takes place just as surely as though the two were sitting face to face, over a cup of coffee, in a kitchen dark but for the light above the sink. And perhaps Levine did converse with P. L. before the man's death, for Levine reveals to Studs Terkel that P. L. was the "older brother of my closest friend," one of those men from Levine's Detroit neighborhood who "went off to fight for a free Spain and didn't come home." Vividly imagining the soldier's death, the speaker fashions a kind of dialogue with the dead man in which one of the parties (necessarily) remains silent in much the same way as the Russian theorist M. M. Bakhtin describes below: "Imagine a dialogue of two persons in which the statements of the second person are omitted. . . . The second speaker is present invisibly. . . . We sense that there is a conversation, although only one person is speaking, and it is a conversation of the most intense kind, for each present, uttered word responds and reacts with its every fiber to the invisible speaker. . . ."

The poem opens by graphically recounting P. L.'s lonely death in the snow, with "one side of your face / frozen to the ground," and then describes the casual way "they . . . bundled you / in canvas, and threw you away." It's interesting to note that the poem begins with P. L. already dead, his sacrifice on the altar of democracy as complete as it was apparently futile. What the speaker focuses on in this conversation, and what he in effect thinks P. L. ought to know, is what happened *after* his sacrificial death for the republic.

Here the speaker envisions, in the person of an "old country woman / of the Aragon," an utterly pragmatic way in which good comes out of such abject defeat. The woman relieves the dead man of his Wellington boots, his hunting socks, and a knife he had worn on his right hip, laughing ambivalently at the thought of the knife even "though she had no meat to cut." In her poverty, caught in the middle of a violent and pitiful battle for freedom, the woman comes to see the dead man as an angel who has, through his passing, delivered unto her a tangible means of sustenance more valuable than mere rhetoric. Believing she "understood" the true nature of P. L.'s sacrifice, the old woman wears the boots and socks, and then passes them down to her nephew in a trail of inheritance which extends the traditional notion of family.

It's worth mentioning that Levine and P. L. share initials, for their identities tend to mingle by the poem's end. Like P. L., described here as "a soldier of the republic," Levine sees himself as a kind of soldier in the cause of social equality, as his many poems of the working class demonstrate. Moreover, the Spanish Civil War, which Levine calls "the most meaningful war I can remember," embodies all of the qualities most evocative in his world view: the pugnacity of the little guy against overwhelming odds, the obstinate human will for social democracy, and the unrelenting force used to squash such citizen rebellions. Levine wants P. L. to know simply that, despite his death and the anarchists' defeat, the human spirit remains fiercely unbroken. What's more, the dead man's inheritance proffers to this day a tangible as well as spiritual utility:

> The knife is still used, the black handle
> almost white, the blade
> worn thin because there is meat to cut.

Here the battle knife becomes the table knife—enacting a transformation as regenerative as the more familiar conversion of swords into ploughshares. In a larger sense, the poem achieves Gadamer's "fusion" of historical horizons; simply put, the poem's conversation with history asserts that the past is not past. Certainly not for the old woman, who years later sees in her mind's eye the dead man's "tight fists / that had fallen side by side" and must turn in grief from her bread and soup. Surely not for Levine, who, even after the woman's death, memorializes the spot where the man lay dead:

> Without laughter she is gone
> ten years now,

and on the road to Huesca in spring
there is no one to look for you
among the wild jonquils, the curling
grasses at the road side,
and the blood red poppies, no one
to look on the farthest tip
of wind breathing down from the mountains
and shaking the stunted pines you hid among.

To say the poem is political is no revelation, though the terms of its rebellion have less to do with overthrowing governments than with freeing the human heart. Its politics are implicit, inherent to Levine's conception of writing, for "just the writing of a poem is a political act. . . . if a man or a woman insists on depicting the truth, that in itself is a kind of political act." In **"Gift for a Believer,"** a poem addressed to the anarchist artist Flavio Costantini, Levine labors to depict such "truth," linking the fates of Jews under Nazism and all those who suffered under Spanish fascism.

The poem surveys the pitiable results of the Spanish anarchists'—and his own—dream for a "new world." It offers a cracked litany of those who were in one way or another defeated by the fascist system, including "Santo Caserio / who lost his head for knifing / the President of France, the ambassador / to hell," Ferrer Guardia, the leader of a Spanish free school that taught the "children to question" fascism, and Francisco Ascaso, killed during the "storming" of a fascist barracks. Troubled by the broken promise of these lives, the speaker dwells on a dream of Costantini's in which the anarchist Durruti voices his most solemn pledge:

> In your vision Durruti whispered
> to an old woman that he would
> never forget the sons and daughters
> who died believing they carried
> a new world there in their hearts,
> but when the doctor was summoned
> and could not stop his wounds
> he forgot.

Remembering those victimized by systems political or economic is perhaps the cornerstone of Levine's poetry, the sacred act of memorializing upon which all of his art is built. If Durruti's failure to remember receives rebuke here, the speaker's real argument is with the system that violently snuffed out the anarchist's dream. But lest he too easily let himself off the hook, the speaker recalls his own forgotten vow:

> When old Nathan Pine
> gave two hands to a drop-forge
> at Chevy, my spit turned to gall
> and I swore I'd never forget.
> When the years turned to a gray mist

and my sons grew away without faith,
the memory slept, and I bowed
my head so that I might live.

This fusing of the personal and the historical gives the poem emotional depth and historical sweep. It shows Levine's readiness to interpolate his own historical presence within the broader scope of history, a practice which, as we shall see, only intensifies as his work matures.

In *7 Years from Somewhere,* three years after the publication of **"Gift to a Believer"** in *The Names of the Lost* (1976), Levine still stubbornly mulls over the complex interrelationship of his own past and the broader movements of history, particularly the Spanish Civil War. If Levine broods, he does so not to satisfy some yearning for self-pity, or to feed the self-congratulatory conviction that he is indeed more sensitive than most. Instead, he ponders the past as a way to give proportion and perspective to the present, as a way to make sense of what it is to be human and caught up in the spiralling of larger forces against which our grandest designs have so little effect. Levine appears stolidly intent upon contradicting Heidegger's advice to the poet residing in a period such as ours, the "time of the world's night": "To be a poet in a destitute time means: to attend, singing, to the trace of the fugitive gods." Levine purposefully neglects the godly in favor of the human. He turns his eyes not to heaven but to the dirt beneath his feet, to the horizon he moves through and which moves through him.

It's no wonder, then, that Levine throughout his career makes frequent pilgrimages to cemeteries, locales that hold the last physical traces of those whose lives have ended but whose influence may doggedly persist. For example, in **"Francisco, I'll Bring You Red Carnations,"** a poem addressed to the anarchist Ascaso, the speaker wanders the "great cemetery / behind the fortress of Barcelona," among the graves of poor and rich alike, all of them finally equal in the blank, earthly brotherhood of death. The poem quickly moves to Levine's characteristic themes: poverty, economic and political oppression, and testing of the human spirit's will to endure. But the poem also marks a clear departure from the earlier **"Gift for a Believer,"** for in it the speaker regains his confidence in himself and the greater cause:

> While the streets are echoing
> with victory and revolution,
> Francisco Ascaso will take up
> the hammered little blade
> of his spirit and enter for
> the last time the republics
> of death. I remember
> his words to a frightened
> comrade who questioned
> the wisdom of attack: "We

have gathered here to die, but we
don't have to die with dogs,
so go."

There again is that knife blade, the knife of battle and of table, glinting with the promise for which Ascaso and P. L. and others gave their lives. There again is the dream of a "city / of God, where every man / and every woman gives / and receives the gifts of work / and care." This time, however, the speaker discovers that dream of social democracy "here / growing in our hearts, as / your comrade said." This time he asserts the dream will not end with their "last / breaths," for someone else will "gasp it home to their lives" and revivify its faltering spirit. This time, he vows to uphold that promise in word and deed:

> we will be back,
> across an ocean and a continent,
> to bring you red carnations,
> to celebrate the unbroken
> promise of your life that
> was once frail and flesh.

The startling transition that has taken place between *They Feed They Lion* (1972) and *7 Years from Somewhere* (1979) signals a transformation in Levine's attitude toward the persistence of the dream of social change. Just as remarkably, his personal horizon and the larger historical horizon have begun both to question and to define each other within these poems. It's arguable that the most compelling of these conversations with history appears in *One for the Rose* (1981), **"To Cipriano, in the Wind,"** a piece that deftly conflates the personal and the historical.

Here, for the first time in these dialogic poems, the historical figure's own words take preeminence over the poet's, serving as both catalyst for the poem and object of the poet's need:

> Where did your words go,
> Cipriano, spoken to me 38 years
> ago in the back of Peerless Cleaners,
> where raised on a little wooden platform
> you bowed to the hissing press
> and under the glaring bulb the scars
> across your shoulders—'a gift
> of my country'—gleamed like wood.
> 'Dignidad,' you said into my boy's
> wide eyes, 'without which is no riches.'
> And Ferrente, the dapper Sicilian
> coatmaker, laughed. What could
> a pants presser know of dignity?

"*Dignidad.*" That which makes even the poorest human being rich. That which cannot be bought or stolen or wrenched

by force from a man or woman who truly owns it. This, in a word, is the fullest expression of Levine's humanism. In the battle against political or economic oppression, Levine tells us, using Mera's words, we may be destroyed but never truly defeated if we retain our human dignity. Later in the poem Mera says it more succinctly, in stately though broken English, with subtle Biblical overtones:

> . . . 'Some day the world
> is ours, someday you will see.'

And still later,

> 'Spring, spring, it always come after.'

After the winter's "worst snow," of course, when "within a week wild phlox leaped / in the open fields" surrounding Detroit. And after, Levine must also be thinking, P. L.'s death, after the old woman had liberated his boots, socks, and knife, soon came the spring and its "blood red poppies." Looking for a way to reaffirm his own beliefs, the speaker turns to Mera's words for emotional and intellectual succor. That out of apparent defeat, victory may come—this is what he sorely needs to be reminded of. He finds it not only in the person and words of Mera, but also in a host of personal memories that gain broader, historical perspective when associated with these remarks. Notice how the speaker personalizes the historical and, in turn, historicizes the personal:

> That was the winter of '41, it
> it would take my brother off to war,
> where you had come from, it would
> bring great snowfalls, graying
> in the streets, and the news of death
> racing through the halls of my school.
> I was growing. . . .
>   That was the winter
> of '41, Bataan would fall
> to the Japanese and Sam Baghosian
> would make the long march
> with bayonet wounds in both legs,
> and somehow. . .
> he would return to us and eat
> the stale bread of victory.

This lesson of eventual "victory" in the long fight echoes the Biblical promise that the meek shall indeed inherit the earth. It is Mera's sustaining gift to Levine, a gift of belief equal to Costantini's and Ascaso's and more than enough to counter the ironic "gift" of scars Mera received from his country. Even more significant is what occurs near the close of the poem, when the poet, the supposed master of language, rejects his own words and instead appropriates Mera's. Levine speaks "Dignity" and "Some day this will all be ours" into the "winds" that surely blew across P. L.,

Ascaso, Durruti, his own dead Russian "cousins," as well as the inhabitants of Barcelona's cemetery, in the end imploring the past to enter his present:

> Come back, Cipriano Mera
> . . . . Enter my dreams
> or my life, Cipriano, come back
> out of the wind.

Levine's insistence on immersing himself in such dialogue with history brings with it a commensurate receptivity to the voice of the Other. By the publication of *A Walk with Tom Jefferson* (1988), Levine's conversation becomes a true dialogue. Moreover, Levine shows a striking willingness to cede the remarkable lines of his poems, those lines most resonant of meaning and most memorable to the ear, to the voice of that Other. In the case of the title poem, it is Tom Jefferson, a black man scraping out a meager existence amidst a nearly abandoned neighborhood devastated by the 1967 riots in Levine's native Detroit. Levine offers a clue to the source of the poem, and a key to its manner, when he tells Mona Simpson: "I discovered in some of the areas that had been burned out back in '67 . . . almost a semi-rural life. . . . Lots of empty spaces, vacant lots, almost like the Detroit I knew during the war. . . . I met a guy who lived in one of these houses. He didn't own or rent it, and in fact he didn't even know who owned it. He described his life there, and the poem rose out of the conversation we had."

By the time **"A Walk with Tom Jefferson,"** a poem of nearly six hundred lines, appears in print, the "conversation" to which Levine alludes has grown considerably. It embraces not only the original two characters and their respective histories, but also the history of Detroit, as well as a broad gauge history of race relations in America. And clearly Levine ups the ante when he names the character Tom Jefferson, "[s]ame name as the other one," for this man carries with him the powerfully charged associations of the "other" Jefferson's conflicting roles as defender of individual rights, president, plantation owner, and slave holder.

Given this range of characters, the poem's conversation with history can be expected to build and follow its own momentum, to veer off haphazardly in the manner such conversations take in the real world of late afternoon walks. In fact, the "walk" itself becomes a fitting metaphor for the process of dialogue, as the men amble over an ever-changing terrain, a wasteland, really, whose presence is both mental and physical. Gadamer recognizes this unpredictable quality of any conversation and clearly relishes it: "We say that we 'conduct' a conversation. . . . Rather, it is generally more correct to say that we fall into a conversation, or even that we become involved in it. The way in which one word follows another, with the conversation taking its own turnings and reaching its own conclusion, may well be conducted in some way, but the people conversing are far less the leaders of it than the led. No one knows what will 'come out' in a conversation."

When the narrator discovers that Tom Jefferson was a schoolmate of the boxer Joe Louis, the conversation quickly accelerates. Louis, who knocked out Max Schmeling and thereby debunked at once the myths of Nazi superiority and black inferiority, serves as public symbol of the private fight for dignity Tom Jefferson and others like him have fought within our society. Like Louis, Tom's father was "up from Alabama" and its cotton fields, "lured" to the good life expressed piquantly by the delicious phrase, "the $5 day." Like so many African-Americans, his family came to Detroit to seek factory work, as others migrated north for the same reason to Cleveland, Gary, Indianapolis, Chicago, and a score of Midwestern industrial sites, changing, in the process, the literal and figurative complexion of these cities. Thomas, of Rita Dove's *Thomas and Beulah,* came to Akron for similar reasons. . . .

Tom Jefferson embodies that transformation and its sullied promise. "We all come for $5 / a day and we got *this!*" Tom says, as he opens his arms, gesturing to both narrator and reader, upon a Whitmanian catalogue detailing the "dumping ground" of the broken and the lost. Here's a sampling:

>   old couches and settees,
> burst open, the white innards
>   gone grey, cracked
> and mangled chifforobes
>   that long ago gave up
> their secrets, yellow wooden
>   ice boxes yawning
> at the sky, their breath
>   still fouled with years
> of eating garlic sausage
>   and refried beans. . .

It's clear the narrator is touched by the sight of such desolation, especially in a neighborhood once familiar to him, and his choice of pronouns reveals his agitation and *angst*. He sails Tom's story amidst a heaving sea of pronouns, "he," "you," and "I" tossing on waves of emotion, sometimes allowing Tom to tell his story in his own words, sometimes paraphrasing him, and occasionally interjecting his own perspective on things, as he does below, when he links Tom, his readers, and himself in the inclusive embrace of "we":

> We feel it as iron
>   in the wind. We could escape,
> each of us feels in
>   his shuddering heart,
> take the bridge south to Canada,
>   but we don't.

The narrator realizes "escape," whether real or imagined, remains impossible. Even though snow will soon transform the assembled junk into a strangely beautiful "new world," he refuses its easy enticements. More importantly, he again seems to refuse the larger possibility of the "new world" Durruti spoke of, the city Ascaso dreamed of where everyone receives "the gifts of work / and care." The narrator's previous sense of unity momentarily disintegrates as he recognizes what differentiates Tom from himself: While the narrator "won't believe" in such change, Tom Jefferson "is a believer. / You can't plant winter vegetables / if you aren't."

Not surprisingly, Jefferson's garden, planted out of the need to feed his family, then becomes the focus of conversation. It's one means of "making do" with diminished resources, of course, an expression of undaunted human will to survive, as the narrator smartly points out Tom was planting his "before the Victory Gardens" occasioned by World War II or those made popular among the genteel classes by the PBS television series. This garden, by necessity, values sustenance over beauty or hobby. But, as Gadamer remarks, "no one knows what will 'come out' in a conversation," and Jefferson's garden abruptly gains symbolic and Biblical overtones. Gradually the metaphor blossoms and spreads, entwining the narrator's and Jefferson's lives.

When Jefferson went off to World War II, his son "took over the garden," and later when his son went off to the Korean War and died there, Tom resumed his duties:

> 'That's Biblical,' he says,
>   'the son goes off,
> the father takes up the spade
>   again, that's Biblical.'

This sense of cycle and loss, as well as the corresponding need for someone to pick up the fallen flag and carry it forward, suddenly permeates the conversation. In Tom's eyes everything is "Biblical," and the word recurs, repeated like the chorus of a gospel hymn, each time more resonant and encompassing, each repetition more compelling. Tom relies on it to describe his relationship with his wife after their son's death, the story of David and Saul and Absalom, "[m]aybe even" war and the fighting of poor whites and poor blacks for the same "gray" jobs and housing. It's not clear in the poem whether the last two remarks are made by Tom or by the narrator, for as Richard Jackson points out, the narrator "seems to absorb some of Jefferson's vocabulary and images," so much so that a "gradual fusion of points of view" occurs in the poem. Such fusion began fitfully, as I've noted, with the narrator's use of the pronoun "we," and it suggests a key to the poem's structure.

Levine's melding of viewpoints resembles the fusing of historical horizons Gadamer describes in *Truth and Method*,

and the poet nicely gathers these perspectives into a complex but unified whole. Jefferson's belief that we "need / this season" of winter cold to fulfill Biblical and natural cycle persuades the narrator himself to believe that "the heart / of ice is fire waiting," that "the new seed / nestles in the old, / waiting, frozen, for the land to thaw." These sentiments surely echo Mera's belief in eventual "victory" in the long fight, in the coming birth of a moral state, in his conviction that "some day this will all be ours."

Here the poem's true dialogic structure reasserts itself. As a conversation can take unexpected swerves, so does the poem, for the dialogue sheers away to the narrator's memory of working, as a "kid," at Cadillac transmission (where Levine, it should be noted, once worked himself):

> When I worked nights
>   on the milling machines
> at Cadillac transmission,
>   another kid just up
> from West Virginia asked me
>   what was we making,
> and I answered, I'm making
>   2.25 an hour,
> don't know what you're
>   ' making, and he had
> to correct me, gently, what was
>   we making out of
> this here metal, and I didn't know.
>   Whatever it was we
> made, we made of earth. Amazing earth. . .

And with it the cycle continues, ineluctably, as another kid like Tom, "just up" from the South, sets to work in the factories. But if Tom knows what he makes out of earth, his beets and cabbages and tomatoes, these men have no idea what they are making on the assembly line. If ever the time were ripe for Levine to issue forth Marxist dogma, this is it. The dissociation of maker from the thing made begs the question of commodity reification, a process Fredric Jameson describes as the "way in which, under capitalism, the older forms of human activity are instrumentally reorganized and . . . reconstructed according to various rational models of efficiency." The result, Jameson argues, is that "all forms of human labor" lose their qualitative differences as human acts of making and come to be judged solely "under the common denominator of money."

Instead, through the voice of his narrator, Levine abjures such dogma, much as James Wright does, in favor of Jefferson's belief in the ultimate efficacy and dignity of human labor. Jefferson's example persuades the narrator to "half-believe" he was indeed making transmission parts all those years ago. Moreover, Jefferson's argument about the value of "making do," which pervades the poem, proves, in the end, more convincing than the fact it said "Chevrolet Gear & Axle / right on the checks they paid / us with." Through Jefferson's example, the narrator recognizes human dignity can endure, if not elude, enslavement by the "common denominator of money." He comes to understand that, no matter what he was in fact making on the assembly line, he was truly "making do"—the most blessed expression of human endeavor. Tom Jefferson's example bespeaks the full measure of Mera's "*Dignidad,*" and as such, these two men (plus Jefferson's presidential namesake) blend race, nationality, and time in a kind of global/historical humanism.

One curious aspect of these conversations with history is the role of the reader, who has, for the most part, remained a passive witness to the proceedings. True enough, Levine occasionally refers to the reader as "you" in **"A Walk with Tom Jefferson,"** and his use of the pronoun "we" further acknowledges the reader's presence. Still, the narrator's own ruminations and his interaction with Jefferson direct the poem's development through distance and time.

Many of Levine's most recent conversations with history change all of that. In ***What Work Is,*** winner of the 1991 National Book Award, Levine often reaches out to yank the reader into the poem, in the process decentering the speaker as the focus of attention and replacing him with the reader. One example of this is **"Coming Close,"** where the speaker serves merely as guide for the reader's encounter with a brass polisher—one of those disempowered "historical" voices that Gadamer too conveniently overlooks. Once passive observer, the reader now becomes active participant, dirtied by the grimy reality of industrial labor. The poem's opening tugs its readers by the lapels into a dehumanizing factory setting that renders even gender questionable:

> Take this quiet woman, she has been
> standing before a polishing wheel
> for over three hours, and she lacks
> twenty minutes before she can take
> a lunch break. Is she a woman?

The speaker asks the reader to consider what this kind of work has done to the woman, to note her "striated" triceps, the "dusting of dark brown" above her lip, even the sweat that spills beneath the "red / kerchief across the brow" and the "darkening" wrist band she uses to wipe it away. Everything is open to question, everything subject to debate, the speaker implies. What's more, when this distance proves too great to ascertain the facts, the speaker insists,

> You must come closer
> to find out, you must hang your tie
> and jacket in one of the lockers
> in favor of a black smock. . .

This merging of identities, this willingness to "experience the 'Thou' truly as 'Thou,'" as Gadamer argues, undergirds true historical consciousness: the ability to see, from our perspective in the present, the fusing of our personal horizon within the larger horizon of history. Precisely this understanding is available to the reader who grunts to lift heavy loads with the woman and who ferries her "new trays of dull, / unpolished tubes," experiencing, if only imaginatively, the bludgeoning repetitiveness of her work. To learn to see this woman as an individual, not as a nondescript face among masses of workers, this at once serves as the speaker's goal for the reader and the reader's unspoken, and perhaps unwilling, quest.

If in the past these conversations primarily involved the poet, history, the poem, and a reader whose role in the dialogue was rarely acknowledged, now this reader actively engages both text and history. Even though poetic form, of course, prevents the reader from actually speaking words within the text, that reader's response is what gives the poem its urgency and communion, its full historical vitality. Without the reader's active mental presence and rhetorically implied physical presence, the poem would falter. Its conversation would fall ineffectually silent. Similarly, although the reader cannot answer the woman when she asks "why" her life and work must be like this, that reader is marked for life by the encounter:

> Even if by some magic
> you knew, you wouldn't dare speak
> for fear of her laughter, which now
> you have anyway as she places the five
> tapering fingers of her filthy hand
> on the arm of your white shirt to mark
> you for your own, now and forever.

What's striking about the final gesture is the way the woman just as well marks the reader for *her* own, the dirt of her hand serving as outward sign of the reader's inward experience. Thus, Levine's rhetorical decision to engage the reader in the poem's dialogue introduces the reader to a person inhabiting a different historical circumstance. In the poem **"What Work Is,"** as well as the poem above, that historical circumstance separating reader from Other has more to do with class than with temporal distance. If in **"Coming Close"** the reader merely assists the narrative's main figure, here the reader becomes the poem's central character. Note how the poem's opening pronouns forcefully merge speaker and reader, as the speaker's "we" pulls the reader's "you" into the line of men seeking work:

> We stand in the rain in a long line
> waiting at Ford Highland Park. For work.
> You know what work is—if you're
> old enough to read this you know what

work is, although you may not do it.
Forget you. This is about waiting,
shifting from one foot to another.
Feeling the light rain falling like mist
into your hair, blurring your vision
until you think you see your own brother
ahead of you, maybe ten places.

"Forget you," the speaker commands the reader. Forget you are reading poetry in an overstuffed chair and instead become the "you" standing in line, in light mist, "waiting" for an offer of work that odds say won't be forthcoming. Refocus your "vision" so radically that you see not a clump of men wearing flannel shirts and baseball caps but "your own brother" among those looking for work. Fuse your horizon with this "you" so as to become him, this Other "you."

Thereafter, the speaker's use of the word always carries a double meaning, so that the "you" experiencing the poem's narrative is joined with the "you" reading it. The effect is a compelling fusion of poem and reader, especially when "you" discover that, even though it is "someone else's brother" standing in line, that man shares your brother's "stubbornness, / the sad refusal to give in" to the cold reality of "No, / we're not hiring today" which awaits both of you. In fact, your brother is lucky; he has a job. He's home sleeping off "a miserable night shift" so he can awaken to study German and "can sing / Wagner . . . / the worst music ever invented."

The thought of your brother's refusal to be defeated by the economics of hard labor and thus his yearning for self-betterment, even through something as questionable as Wagnerian opera, floods "you" with an emotional torrent. In him, Mera's dream of "*Dignidad*" still breathes. Unlike so many of the workers Herbert Marcuse describes in *Eros and Civilization* (1955), your brother has not been psychologically victimized by mind-numbing factory labor, denuded of any individual qualities by the assembly line. But perhaps "you" have—not by work, but by the lack of it. The poem moves to climax as a result of this sudden recognition, which prompts an overwhelming urge to tell your brother you love him and "maybe" kiss his cheek:

You've never
done something so simple, so obvious,
not because you're too young or too dumb,
not because you're jealous or even mean
or incapable of crying in
the presence of another man, no,
just because you don't know what work is.

The poem's final line *cleaves* the poem's "you" and the readerly "you," both unifies and separates them in keeping with the word's double meaning. On one hand, the line em-

phasizes the importance given to work in our culture, so much so that being without it strikes at the core of a man's sense of maleness, his acceptance of the stereotypical burden to support himself and his family. To "know what work is," to have a job, is to know one's place in the culture and thus to know one's self. On the other hand, the line carries an accusatory tone, particularly if one keeps in mind that the poem originally appeared in *The New Yorker*. Most of the magazine's upscale readers, one assumes, have never known standing in line for work at "Ford Highland Park," or better, have never known the debilitating wound that lack of work can inflict upon one's psyche. Remember, also, that much of Levine's best work has appeared in *The New Yorker,* and he has been known to suggest at poetry readings that he frequently considers the response such a poem will generate among its readers.

One final poem, **"On the Meeting of Garcia Lorca and Hart Crane,"** a poem which also appeared in *The New Yorker* and which opens Levine's 1995 Pulitzer Prize-winning *The Simple Truth,* exemplifies the tendencies discussed thus far. The poem concerns the speaker's cousin, Arthur Lieberman, a former "language student at Columbia" who, on his deathbed, told the speaker of his having brought together Lorca and Crane in Brooklyn in 1929. Not only does Arthur facilitate such historical dialogue, he also, because he "knows both Spanish and English," acts as its interpreter. He would therefore seem to be the perfect embodiment of Gadamer's "effective-history."

Surprisingly, not a word of the conversation between the two "poetic geniuses" appears in the poem. Neither Arthur nor the speaker is "frivolous" enough to try to recapture it or to "pretend" it bore "wisdom." Neither is foolish enough to attempt to "invent a dialogue of such eloquence / that even the ants in your own / house won't forget it." No doubt theirs was a conversation like all others, fraught with misunderstanding and peril and surprise. No doubt theirs was no better or worse than the conversations each of these poems has pursued. What does come to Arthur as a result of this encounter is a "double vision" which fuses his historical horizon with theirs, shocking him with a premonition of the poets' untimely deaths: Crane's suicide from a ship at sea in 1932 and Lorca's at the hands of a firing squad during the Spanish Civil War (returning us to the wellspring of Levine's work). The speaker asks his reader:

Have you ever
had a vision? Have you ever shaken
your head to pieces and jerked back
at the image of your young son
falling through open space, not
from the stern of a ship bound
from Vera Cruz to New York but from
the roof of the building he works on?

Have you risen from bed to pace
until dawn to beg a merciless God
to take these pictures away? Oh, yes,
let's bless the imagination. It gives
us the myths we live by. Let's bless
the visionary power of the human
(the only animal that's got it) . . .

Levine acknowledges this perilous aspect of imagination, the way that we humans, by imagining the life of others, may come face to face with the "horror" as well as the beauty of our own existence. This "double vision" issues from an assiduous attention to the intersection of our lives with that of the Other, and it orders our sense of place and value in a world divided along historical, social, and racial lines. Through their conversations with history, these poems seek to enlarge both the poet's and the reader's individual horizons, to extend what we can see from our "particular vantage point," as Gadamer puts it. These poems ask readers to chance a "vision" of ineffable loveliness and equal ugliness, a vision of what it is to be human. If we take Levine's word that "nothing is past," then we readers follow this vision toward a future always in dialogue with the past and the evanescent moment of our present.

Jeff Parker Knight (review date Summer 1997)

SOURCE: Review of *The Simple Truth* in *Prairie Schooner,* Vol. 71, No. 2, Summer, 1997, pp. 179-82.

[*In the following excerpt, Knight briefly considers the role of truth and reality in Levine's poems and also mentions Levine's "mastery of craft."*]

There's just no reason for anyone to continue believing the old maxim that poets will have done their best work by middle age. Following the example of Robert Penn Warren, a number of American poets—among them A. R. Ammons, Maxine Kumin, and Donald Hall—are writing excellent poems past age sixty. For the reader who has watched a poet's literary life unfold, reading a first-rate collection of new poems from a longtime favorite is deeply satisfying. So it is with the . . . most recent [book] from Philip Levine. . . .

Philip Levine . . . is interested in the holiness of daily life, the beauty of bare existence. American poets have spent a good deal of the twentieth century reminding us how complex reality is, how we see only "truth" or "truths," never Truth. We are forever getting poems written from Medusa's point of view, or Hitler's, or Nixon's, showing us that perspective is everything. The concrete poets, and more recently the language poets go out of their way to draw attention to the way the words were put on the page by someone at some-

time, to de-familiarize the style, reminding the reader that it's all just another representation. Reality can never be known. There is no privileged place to stand above it all and say what's what. In this kind of poetic context, it's worth asking why Levine chose to call his latest volume *The Simple Truth.* Part of the answer comes from the uneasiness of what Lawrence Ferlinghetti called "constantly risking absurdity" as the poet strives to find something worthwhile to say, along with an interesting way to say it. More than one poet has the frequent and uneasy feeling that it would be better just to shut up, that we miss the obvious in stretching for some grand trope. Certainly that's the sense I get in the first of these poems, **"On the Meeting of Garcia Lorca and Hart Crane."** In the meeting, if it happened (and in the poem in any case), neither man speaks the other's language. They have been brought together by a graduate student, who interprets. Levine writes that the meeting was uneventful, that the young man stared out the window at the river, bored, and "Something flashes across his sight," his eye and imagination play some kind of trick on him, and he sees a horrible vision of some kind. Levine writes:

Let's not be frivolous, let's
not pretend the two poets gave
each other wisdom or love or
even a good time, let's not
invent a dialogue of such eloquence
that even the ants in your own
house won't forget it. The two
greatest poetic geniuses alive
meet and what happens? A vision
comes to an ordinary man staring
at a filthy river.

There's more to the poem, but this sloughing off of poetic expectations keys us to one dimension of Levine's provocative title: the simple truth isn't going to live up to the grandeur of myth. In **"The Trade"** we see a man who's had enough of the latter make a choice to embrace the former. If Levine weren't such a good writer, this would seem heavy-handed, whether or not the events actually took place. Levine, traveling in Genoa, takes a man up on his offer of two lemons and a knife ("A grape knife, wooden handled, / fattened at one end like a dark fist, the blade / lethal and slightly rusted") for Levine's pocket edition of T. S. Eliot's *Selected Poems*! Levine tells us, protesting too much, that he hadn't meant to rid himself "of the burden / of a book that haunted me," a book that was a gift, a book he had carried "all those years until the words, memorized, / meant nothing." Eliot represents the power of the imagination, what art can accomplish, and Levine swaps all that for a simpler tool. The title poem, placed in the center of the book, takes this idea as far as it can go:

Some things

you know all your life. They are so simple and true
they must be said without elegance, meter and
    rhyme,
they must be laid on the table beside the salt
    shaker,
the glass of water, the absence of light gathering
in the shadows of picture frames, they must be
naked and alone, they must stand for themselves.

But of course, the poems are poems. They are not the things standing for themselves. It is Levine's very mastery of craft that enables him to suggest its lack, in lines like these (also from **"The Simple Truth"**):

I bought a dollar and a half's worth of small red
    potatoes,
took them home, boiled them in their jackets
and ate them for dinner with a little butter and salt.
Then I walked through the dried fields
on the edge of town.

In the subsequent pieces, many of which touch on issues of identity and family, Levine finds himself backsliding from the view expressed in **"The Simple Truth."** Relationships are complex, after all, and it's hard to know the truth, much less tell it. In trying to give each other some idea of how things seem to us, it turns out, all we have are these words, just these words, and we are back on that high wire, risking absurdity. There are no answers in the back of the book. *The Simple Truth* is a fine poet's engagement with tough issues of representation, perception, memory, love, and language. . . . Levine . . . remind(s) us, in poem after poem, that literature (like love) has pleasures to offer beyond the fire

and passion of youth: there is perspective, the way your history led you to this moment, which is already the seed of the next, and the next. Without making too much of "old poets," let me close with this: . . . [this book] rewards the reader with a careful and loving focus on the details of life-as-lived, the particulars of any given moment, the perspective gained from an attentive lifetime.

FURTHER READING

Criticism

Disch, Thomas M. "The Occasion of the Poem." *Poetry* CLX, No. 2 (May 1992): 94-107.
    Praises *What Work Is* as a tight and consistent work.

Jackson, Richard. "The Long Embrace: Philip Levine's Longer Poems." *Kenyon Review* XI, No. 4 (Fall 1989): 160-69.
    Explores the resurgence of long poems by examining some of Levine's longer poems.

Mariani, Paul. "Keeping the Covenant." *Kenyon Review* XI, No. 4 (Fall 1989): 170-77.
    In depth review of *A Walk with Tom Jefferson.*

Saner, Reg. "Studying Interior Architecture by Keyhole: Four Poets." *Denver Quarterly* 20, No. 1 (Summer 1985): 107-17.
    Describes *Selected Poems* as a "book one must have."

Additional coverage of Levine's life and career is contained in the following sources published by Gale: *Contemporary Authors,* Vols. 9-12R; *Contemporary Authors New Revision Series,* Vols. 9, 37, and 52; *Dictionary of Literary Biography,* Vol. 5; *DISCovering Authors Modules: Poets;* and *Poetry Criticism;* Vol. 22.

Antonine Maillet

1929-

Canadian dramatist, novelist, short story writer, non-fiction writer, and author of children's books.

The following entry presents an overview of Maillet's career through 1996. For further information on her life and works, see *CLC,* Volume 54.

INTRODUCTION

Maillet was the first author to write in the Acadian vernacular, a language derived from seventeenth- and eighteenth-century French. Her body of work helped define the Acadian culture, a culture which, over two hundred years, successive governmental powers have tried to destroy. Her best-known work, *Pélagie-la-Charrette* (1979) dramatizes the exodus that occurred in Canada after the British destroyed a settlement of French-speaking Acadians in 1755 and dispersed the people along the eastern coast of North America. Some, such as the Cajun in Louisiana, formed new settlements, but many surreptitiously made their way back to Canada.

Biographical Information

Maillet was born May 10, 1929, in Bouctouche, New Brunswick, Canada. Both her father, Leonide, and her mother, Viriginie, were schoolteachers. She was educated at various religious schools before obtaining a B.A. from College Notre Dame d'Acadie in 1950. Over the next several years, alternating between periods of teaching and study, Maillet wrote her first two plays—*Entr'Acte* (1957) and *Poire-Acre* (1958)—before obtaining her M.A. from the University of Mocton in 1959, a LL.D. from the University of Montreal in 1962, and a Ph.D. from Laval University in 1970. Her doctoral dissertation examined the influences of François Rabelais in Acadian folklore, especially his earthy humor.

Major Works

Maillet's first novel, *Pointe-aux-coques* (1958), is a semi-autobiographical story about her youth in New Brunswick and was awarded the Prix Champlain. Her next novel, *On a mange la dune* (1962), is seen by many as an extended metaphor for the isolation of the Acadian experience. The main character is a young Acadian girl whose perspective of the world is limited to the dunes surrounding her small village. Maillet's interest in Acadian folklore can be seen in her short story collection *Par derrière chez mon père* (1972) and the

novel *Don l'Orignal* (1972), both of which are adaptations of Acadian folk tales. In *Mariaagélas* (1973) and *Crache-à-pic* (1984) Maillet presents larger-than-life female main characters, both who are Acadian bootleggers. Many see these women as refutations of the retiring, submissive Evangeline, the Acadian heroine of Henry Wadsworth Longfellow's epic poem of that name. Maillet confronts Longfellow's Evangeline head-on in her play *Evangéline Duesse* (1976), wherein her heroine openly scoffs at the actions of the poet's character. In *Pélagie-la-Charrette* (1979), Maillet uses the title metaphor (translated as *Pélagie: The Return to a Homeland* in 1982) to present a story of Acadian exodus. Pélagie, an Acadian uprooted in the dispersal of 1755, decides to return to her homeland after fifteen years of working the fields in Georgia. The novel depicts her epic journey, spanning over two thousand miles and ten years, as she leads a growing band of Acadians and other refugees to their northern promised land. Pélagie herself is the cart as she carries her clans along on this exodus with wit, courage, determination, and love.

Critical Reception

Maillet's is the first writer living outside France to receive the Acadèmie Goncourt annual prize for literature. She has generally enjoyed the favor of critics throughout her career and her initial body of work, written in the Acadian dialect and focusing on the Acadian experience, is praised as new and authentic. Her protagonists are poor, illiterate, and in some ways naive, yet portrayed with a folksy wisdom and persevering spirit. Maillet skillfully incorporates the folktales of Acadia in her storylines and uses multiple narrators to recreate the feeling of the oral story-telling experience. As her body of work developed, many of her characters reappeared in subsequent stories. This led some critics to suggest that her work was becoming predictable and repetitive, limited to the small scale of the Acadian experience. But the grand scope of *Pélagie the Cart* showed that Maillet is capable of painting on a larger canvas. The novel rises to the level of historical saga, encompassing the ten years of Pélagie's return to her homeland, as well as the issues of slavery in the South and the beginnings of the American Revolution. The novel operates on several levels: an adventure, an Acadian folktale, and an allegorical tale about the triumph of the spirit. Several critics see the earthy humor of Rabelais in the novel, as well as a revisitation of the Bible's story of Exodus, with Pélagie as Moses (and his wife). Paul G. Socken says, "*Pélagie-la-Charrette,* like the Bible, operates on two levels—those of sacred text and historical document; that is, the novel affirms elements of faith which are shared by a people and purports to be historically accurate. As sacred text, both are imbued with ritual, embody symbolism and imply a mission or destiny. As historical document, they are rooted in time and place and chronicle real events." *Pélagie* begins Maillet's process of expanding the Acadian experience in a manner that speaks to universal truths.

PRINCIPAL WORKS

Entr'Acte (play) 1957

Poire-Acre (play) 1958

Pointe-aux-coques (novel) 1958

Bulles de Savon (play) 1959

Les Jeux d'enfants sont faits (play) 1960

On a mange la dune (novel) 1962

Les Crasseux (novel) 1968

*La Sagouine (radio script) 1970-1971

Don l'Orignal (novel) 1972 [translated by Barbara Godard as *The Tale of Don l'Orignal,* 1978]

Par derrière chez mon père (short stories) 1972

La Sagouine (play) 1972

L'Acadie pour quasiment rien [with Rita Scalabrini] (essays) 1973

Gapi et Sullivan [translated by Luis Cespedes as Gapi and Sullivan] (novel) 1973

Mariaagélas (novel) 1973; (play) 1973 [translated by

Ben-Zion Shek as *Mariaagelas: Maria, Daughter of Gelas,* 1986]

Les Crasseux (play) 1974

Emmanuel a Joseph a Davit (novel) 1975

Evangeline Deusse (novel) 1975; (play) 1976

Les Cordes-de-bois (novel) 1977

La Veuve enragée (novel) 1977; (play) 1977

Le Bourgeois Gentleman (novel) 1978; (play) 1978

Pélagie-la-Charrette (novel) 1979; translated by Philip Stratford as *Pélagie: The Return to a Homeland* 1982

Cent ans dans les bois (novel) 1981

La Contrebandiere (novel) 1981)

Les Drolatiques, Homfiques et Epouvantables Aventures de Panurge, ami de Pantagruel, d'après Rabelais (novel) 1983

Panurge (play) 1983

Crache-à-pic (novel) 1984; translated by Stratford as *The Devil Is Loose!* 1986

Garrochés en paradis (novel) 1986 (play) 1986

Le Huitième jour (novel) 1986

*Also published as a novel in 1971 (translated by Luis de Cespedes, 1979); a play, 1972; and adapted for television, 1975

CRITICISM

Ben-Z Shek (review date March 1980)

SOURCE: "Antonine Maillet and the Prix Goncourt," in *Canadian Modern Language Review,* Vol. 36, No. 3, March 1980, pp. 392-96.

[*Shek provides an overview of Maillet's work, praising her style and use of language.*]

Late in November, 1979, the Académie Goncourt announced that its prestigious annual prize for literature had been awarded to Antonine Maillet, the prominent Acadian novelist, playwright and short-story writer. This was the first time that the coveted honor, created in 1874 by the will of Edmond de Goncourt, (who, with his brother Jules, was a pioneer of the naturalist novel) was offered to a writer living outside France. Antonine Maillet won it for her novel *Pélagie-la-charrette* published in Montreal by Leméac and in Paris by Grasset.

Before having affixed to her name the label "Prix Goncourt", Antonine Maillet was best known as the author of the brilliant, moving and expressive series of dramatic monologues, *La Sagouine,* written in the rhythmic and colorful Acadian dialect of the Bouctouche region of New Brunswick, where she was born. This ancient speech (only slightly sprinkled with anglicisms and names of commercial products by La

Sagouine), nearly extinct today, was brought to North America in the 16th and 17th centuries by the *colons* of Poitou and Touraine. Its peculiar morphology, phonetic system and lexicon were rendered inimitable by the outstanding interpretation of actress Viola Léger.

Maillet's writing career began more than 20 years ago. Her first book was ***Pointe-aux-Coques,*** a novel, published in 1958, and was followed by five other novels: ***On a mangé la dune*** (1968), ***Don l'Orignal*** (winner of the Governor General's Award, 1972), ***Mariaagélas,*** (1973), ***Emmanuel à Joseph à Dâvit*** (1975) and ***Les Cordes-de-bois*** (1977). Besides ***La Sagouine*** (1971), she has published six other plays, the short-story collection ***Par derrière chez mon père*** (1972), and her doctoral dissertation, ***Rabelais et les traditions populaires en Acadie*** (1971).

Antonine Maillet is both a product of, and a catalyst for, the cultural renewal among New Brunswick francophones.
—Ben-Z Shek

Antonine Maillet is both a product of, and a catalyst for, the cultural renewal among New Brunswick francophones. Her creative activity grew out of the burgeoning cultural and political awakening of the 1960's during which time the Université de Moncton was created, there took place the struggles of that city's one-third French-speaking population against the bigoted Mayor Leonard Jones, and, eventually, the Parti acadien was formed. Her books were published in parallel with the release of Pierre Perrault's film, *L'Acadie, L'Acadie* (1971), the records of Edith Butler, Calixte Duguay and Angèle Arsenault (who is from P.E.I.) and those of the musical group, "1755". Some feel that these movements of cross-fertilization have come too late to stem the tide of assimilation in New Brunswick, which has had a history of turbulent struggles to maintain the "French fact". Yet Antonine Maillet and the other creative forces of the Acadian renewal are determined to carry on. It should, however, be noted that they depend a great deal on material support from the institutions and public of Quebec, which certainly acts as the *foyer* of French-language culture in Canada, and whose own cultural flowering and growing self-confidence have been fundamental supports for the Acadian revival.

Maillet's novel, ***Pélagie-la-charrette,*** is in fact linked to a capital moment of her people's history, namely the expulsion in 1755 of the Acadians, mainly grouped then in Nova Scotia, by the British forces, and their scattering throughout the southern colonies of the Atlantic seaboard. This traumatic reference point is variably (and sometimes, euphemistically) called in the novel, La Déportation, le Grand Dérangement, l'Evénement, La Grande Echouerie, La Dispersion.

The novel is indelibly marked by the rhythm of continuity, which is its lifeblood and heart-beat. The dedication by the author is to her mother, Virginie Cormier, an identically named ancestor of whom is one of the characters, and the book ends with the inscription, "Bouctouche, le 23 juin, 1979, en cette année du 375e anniversaire d'Acadie". The very title, named after the heroine who will lead a ragamuffin band of remnants of her people back to Acadia during a 10-year-long trek on foot and in carts of all sizes and shapes, also underlines the dominant theme of continuity: "C'était coutume en Acadie d'apporter en dot une charrette à son homme, la charrette, signe de pérénnité."

The narrative structure, based on a lineage of chroniclers re-telling the saga at a distance of 100 years (at the end of the 19th century and today, at the end of the 20th) is, too, one of continuity. The unobtrusive primary narrator in the present (who says symbolically "moi, qui fourbis [nettoie] chaque matin mes seize quartiers de charrette", relates most of the events of the epic return of the Acadians between 1770 and 1780 as they are told to her by her cousin, "le vieux Louis à Bélonie, dit le jeune", who himself had them passed down from his grandfather, Bélonie, a story-teller of the late 19th century, who used to argue about the fine points of the heroic feat with Pélagie-la-Gribouille, both of the latter descendants, respectively, of the nonaganerian Bélonie and the original Pélagie, who actually lived the saga of the arduous homecoming. Continuity is also syncopated by the recurrence of names of typically Acadian families, such as Bastarache, Le Blanc, Landry, Gaudet, Doucet, Maillet and others, and by the Acadian fashion of designating the lineage of male characters through their male line: e.g. "Pierre à Pierre à Pierrot."

Pélagie-la-charrette has other important rhythmic devices that give cohesion and unity to the novel, and fuse its form and content into a whole. One of the most vital of these is the *dédoublement* between the oxen-led *charrette* of Pélagie, that of life, of hope, of optimism, and the ghostly *charrette de la mort,* that of destruction, despair and fatalism, with its six black horses constantly evoked and perceived by the wizened Bélonie, as travelling alongside, and sometimes in the very ruts of, Pélagie's vehicle. The two *charrettes* "compete" mercilessly throughout the narrative. Old man Bélonie, too, is the source of other elements of fantasy, as he recounts tales of visions of Black Beard, of flaming pirate ships, of the White Whale, and the hallucinatory ringing of the church-bells of Grand-Pré, the village razed to the ground by the British, during sea storms.

The story is structured, too, by the refrain of the traditional Acadian folk-song, "Le Grain de Mil" ("Et j'ai du grain de mil, et j'ai du grain de paille, et j'ai de l'oranger, et j'ai du tri, et j'ai de tricoli . . . ") which is sung on the relatively few happy occasions that broke the suffering of the exiles. Another refrain is that of the expletive, "et merde au roi d'Angleterre", evoked when the burning of the church at Grand-Pré or other tribulations at the hands of British commanders Lawrence, Winslow and Monckton are recalled. Also, there is frequent repetition, with variation, of the phrase, "N'éveille pas l'ours qui dort . . . " This reference to the Loyalist majority of New Brunswick is evoked at the very outset of the novel, in the prologue: " . . . surtout pas l'ours qui dort sur le marche-pied de ton logis. C'est pourquoi l'Acadie qui s'arrachait à l'exil, à la fin du XVIIIe siècle, est sortie de ses langes tout bas . . . Elle est rentrée au pays par la porte arrière et sur la pointe des pieds." It echoes at the end of the novel, too: "Surtout, n'éveillez pas l'ours qui dort. Rentrez chacun à votre chacunière sur la pointe des pieds et attendez le temps qu'il faut." In her commentaries on *La Sagouine,* Maillet had already explained her views on the passive resistance of the Acadians to discrimination and inequality and the importance of patience and subterfuge in their struggles to redress ancient ills.

While the British troops of the 1755 events and their aftermath are often the butt of Maillet's irony and bitterness, she creates a counter-movement by linking to the Acadian exiles a host of episodic characters belonging to other wronged peoples: Micmac Indians, a Scottish woman miracle-healer, a freed Black slave (sometimes treated a touch paternalistically), the witches of Salem, and, finally, the American rebels of 1776. Yet the rancour of the past gives way to forgiveness, in the hope of starting life anew on Acadian soil: ". . . le printemps qu'on lui avait volé, à la Pélagie, vingt-cinq ans auparavant, l'attendait sur les rives de la baie Française. Plus rien que ces cent lieues et elle oublierait, et elle pardonnerait, et elle bâtirait son logis incendié."

The language of *Pélagie-la-charrette* is largely that of the spoken word. Antonine Maillet has given it a more stylized form than she did in *La Sagouine,* to which she appended a glossary, still keeping its essential flavour while making her text more accessible to the average reader. The oral flavour is present in the "huhau" shouted to the oxen, in the stories within the story recounted mainly by old man Bélonie, in the songs and refrains, and in the constant interpellations to the reader-listener.

The texture of the language is also richly poetic in many instances. Most of the images grow out of the maritime topography of Acadia, e.g.: "Une belle île, celle-là . . . aux abords déchirés par des anses et des baies, comme si les baleines depuis des temps reculés avaient mordu dans les côtes à belles dents." The poetry inundates the prose towards the end of the novel, in the springtime of the return to Acadia in 1780, and the end of "le plus long hiver de leur vie . . .

un hiver d'un quart d'un siècle", and especially during Pélagie's pilgrimage to the desolate Grand-Pré of her childhood and youth. Poetic, too, and effectively so, is the personification throughout the work of inanimate objects, especially *la charrette,* and abstract concepts, especially l'Acadie, which are infused with life, joy, sobs, murmurs, cries.

The language is often humorous, as laughter interrupts the tears of the exile and painful return. The humor is earthy, Rabelaisian, *démesuré,* and is found especially in the tales within the tale recounted by old man Bélonie. Sometimes it is ironic, as in the scenes of the slave auction in Charleston, North Carolina; often it is outrageously hyperbolic as in the tale told by Beausoleil of his crew's having their speech frozen in the Polar region until a hail storm showered them with their own words some six months later, thus giving them back their speech; or that told by another Acadian storyteller a century later, of urine turned into instant icicles at 55 below zero!

Maillet's *Pélagie-la-charrette* is not without weaknesses, sometimes suffering from *rembourrage* as in her other works, occasionally turning melodramatic, or presenting historical episodes without sufficient aestheticization. Nevertheless, together with *La Sagouine, Pélagie* has helped build a corpus which has already left its vital mark on the francophone literature of Canada and beyond.

In an interview with *Le Devoir* on December 1, 1979, Antonine Maillet stressed the following significance of her Goncourt prize:

> Il y a plus important encore: le Goncourt est une reconnaissance universelle. Et c'est un statut qu'on donne à notre langue. C'est important, pour tous les écrivains d'ici qui se sont battus et pour ceux qui nous suivent, de savoir que la langue qu'ils parlent, les idées qu'ils émettent, les personnages qu'ils créent, le monde qu'ils font, sont universels. Depuis le temps qu'on nous disait: 'Vous parlez patois . . . ou le dialect acadien . . . ou le dialect québécois . . .' Il me semble qu'on ne peut plus maintenant entendre ces phrases! Le jour où une académie donne un prix de cette envergure à une oeuvre, c'est qu'elle reconnaît le statut de cette langue aussi.

(There is much one could say on this aspect of the rehabilitation of one of the major dialects of Canadian French, but space does not permit it.) Another key point made by Antonine Maillet in the same interview is that she sees herself as a *sujet transindividuel,* or *sujet collectif,* in the terms of the late French critic and sociologist, Lucien Goldmann:

> L'écriture, c'est grand. De toute façon, *La Sagouine*

est plus grande que moi, *Pélagie* est plus grande que moi. Elles valent mieux que moi. Elles sont les produits de tout un peuple qui me les a passées. Et moi, je ne fais que les rendre aux autres. Mais je suis plus petite que mes personnages: ils ont été fait par 375 ans d'histoire. J'ai été tributaire de ces personnages que j'ai rendus au monde. Mais d'autres Jes ont faits avec moi.

In her typically modest fashion, Antonine Maillet nevertheless thus describes a profound truth: the intersection of a people and a creative spirit.

Pierre Gobin (review date March 1982)

SOURCE: "Space and Time in the Plays of Antonine Maillet," in *Modern Drama,* Vol. XXV, No. 1, March, 1982, pp. 46-59.

[*Gobin analyzes the recurring themes in Maillet's plays, emphasizing the author's written word, rather than the production of the plays.*]

Antonine Maillet's dual careers, as novelist and playwright, have been developing in parallel for some twenty years now. She began as a novelist with *Pointe-aux-Coques* in 1958, and also achieved her greatest success with a novel, *Pélagie-la-Charrette,* which won the Goncourt Prize in 1979. However, her most memorable character, La Sagouine, was created for the stage, and around her a mythical universe has developed. The stage has also provided the medium which enabled Maillet to articulate most coherently a complex *Weltanschauung.* For the stage she has created a concert of voices and characters (as Godin has shown to be the case in *Évangéline Deusse*), as well as a succession of monologues in which the narrator/performer explores her memories and her perceptions just as one sight-reads a score—rehearses them, redefines and modulates them. She has also developed a dual intertextual network: the external, explicitly referred to by the author writing as critic; and the internal, reaching from one play to another, with echoes and allusions, or reworking the same "score" in successive versions.

Maillet's dramatic corpus is actually broader and more ambitious than her *oeuvre* as a novelist. Thus in 1978, with *Le Bourgeois Gentleman,* "a comedy inspired by Molière," she introduces settings, characters, and problems entirely different from the Acadian background of her other works. Here she devotes her attention primarily to external intertextuality and transposes ideological concerns from relations between classes to relations between national groups in a colonial context (Albert Memmi's *Portrait du colonisé* may well have served as a source text). But while this latest undertaking is of considerable interest (though not altogether successful), I shall here consider only her Acadian dramatic works (not including three early, unpublished attempts from 1957, 1958 and 1960): that is, the five plays which have been performed and published. Three of these—*Les Crasseux* (1968/1972), *La Sagouine* (1971/1974), *Gapi et Sullivan,* with its expanded version, *Gapi* (1973/1976)—have been considerably reworked. I shall not consider this aspect of intertextuality here, and shall use the final versions, as well as the other two Acadian plays: *Évangéline Deusse* (even though it takes place in Montréal, the chief character is Acadian, a demystified successor to Longfellow's archetypal heroine), and *La Veuve enragée,* published in 1977.

In order to attempt a definition of drama as a specific mode of writing or textual production, I shall, however, make use of the novels, since, by and large, their fables or narrative lines, their sets of characters, and even their locales are similar to what we find in the plays. One can, for instance, draw obvious parallels between *Les Crasseux* and *Don l'Orignal, La Veuve enragée* and *Mariaagélas* as well as *Les Cordes-de-bois.* The presentation of time and space in the novels thus refers to the same setting as that of the plays, but does not take into account the contingencies of stage production which appear as a significant variable in the comparison.

At one further remove, I shall also consider Maillet's non-fiction writing; i.e., her guide to Acadia and her critical essays (excluding, however, her thesis on Rabelais, which contributes to the external intertextuality); such non-fiction writings indeed make us aware of what I should like to call a referential galaxy, which includes objective systems, ideological complexes, constellations of myths, and whose elements may or may not be consciously developed. These texts involve Maillet only as *écrivant,* to use Barthes's terminology, or as "transitive writer," whereas the novels and the plays are the work of an *écrivain,* transmuting into a poetic universe not only the message, but also its spatial and temporal co-ordinates. The referential galaxy claims to represent a world; the poetic universe is a creation in words manifest through the "casting" of "distributed" discourse, and through the relay of speech articulated by the playwright but forever "to be proffered." "The haunting concern with time and space in the Acadian works of Antonine Maillet" was pointed out a few years ago by Hans Runte, who also suggested some of its political and ideological implications.

My aim is to study how the specifically dramatic expression of this concern has developed, not only with the growth of Maillet's corpus (in a syntagmatic extension, so to speak), but also by the reinforcement of a number of paradigmatic connections, through additions or corrections, and by a focussing or adjustment that define a specific style of writing for the stage. However, rewarding though it would be, for lack of space—and of competence—I shall not attempt a study of the "second production," the actual staging leading to and including the performance, and shall limit my remarks to what is inscribed in Maillet's text as part of the "first production." I shall simply note that Maillet, who seems little concerned with the definition of the "performance space" in her early works, and provides but few stage directions and virtually no comments on the pragmatic conditions of performance, becomes more precise and more explicit as she becomes experienced and familiar with the actual conditions of the "second production." This development, I believe, gives a measure of her humility, flexibility, and good sense. On the other hand, what Anne Ubersfeld describes as "*hors-scène*" (that is, all the events that can be assumed to take place off-stage), growing by metonymy out of what can actually be represented on stage, and "*extra-scène*" (what may be evoked—through allusion or metaphorical expansion—in the text that is spoken on stage), have all along been extremely important in Maillet's dramatic texts. One may indeed consider that her works are a projection of what Souriau describes as a "sphere"—an expression of the mental universe assigned to the characters—rather than an attempt to meet the contingencies of the "cube" provided by the actual playing area; or, to use another one of Souriau's distinctions, it is clear that in her plays, dramatic time and space are paramount, while scenic reductions, streamlining "the complex interplay between the senses of time" (to use Ubersfeld's description), and, of course, simplifying the presentation of space, are left to the initiative of future directors and producers.

Thus, I have not discovered in the Acadian plays any case where "the performance reinvests in the text its own contingencies." Maillet pioneers the development of a "national" repertoire in a country with very limited resources for staging that repertoire: she conceived the character of the Sagouine for radio, and later had her plays produced in Montréal by the Rideau Vert—a company which, in spite of its flair for discovering new material, is not noted for its propensity to experiment with staging. One should therefore not be surprised if the codes of the stage production are less important for Maillet than the "symbolization of socio-cultural perceptions of space," and if the definition of markers to indicate the passage of time means less than the transposition of a "true story" into an exemplary development. The text, and what it says, is therefore paramount. (It tends to be, at any rate, when it comes to conveying the sense of time, except in the rare cases when a stage device cleverly emphasizes the passing of time [for instance, the tree "covered with leaves" in the second act of *Godot*] or the arbitrary release from the passing of time [for instance, the clock that strikes twenty-odd times at the beginning of *The Bald Soprano*].)

All the same, Maillet makes use of a few fairly simple stage conventions, and sometimes defines space and time with the setting or with the props. Thus in **Les Crasseux,** the rail-

way tracks define an area and relegate the characters to a "wrong side" with powerful sociological connotations, whereas in **Don l'Orignal,** its novelistic counterpart, the "hay island" is a floating, utopian territory that is not anchored to any objective geographic co-ordinates nor connected to any specific historical situation. In **La Sagouine,** the scrubbing pail (*le seau à "forbir"*), which, while collecting the grime left by others, is a vessel where the protagonist's hands are "purified" and her wrinkled face mirrored, offers a clever visual symbol of the ambiguous status of the character: she is a socially dispossessed and physically broken type, and yet she has soft, white hands, and possesses a magic mirror with which she can engage in dialogue, like the powerful queen of a fairy-tale. In **Évangéline Deusse,** the stop-sign carried by the guard at the crosswalk and the young, tender fir-tree the heroine wishes to transplant not only offer a contrast between (present) urban space and a (past, nostalgic) rural scene, or a jerky, choppy perception of time (the stop/go of traffic) and a continuous sense of growth that transcends seasons (the evergreen), but also act as powerful reminders of the exile of all the characters, and of their pathetic efforts to grow new roots.

What is more, in all the plays the set or the props can offer a starting-point, a kind of cue to the dialogue, which in turn makes their suggestions explicit. For instance, at the beginning of **La Veuve enragée,** Old Patience sits in front of her shack in "Cordwood Town": she thus asserts both her own position in the play and the central issue that will be dealt with in the play's action; she plays on her own (magic) name and recites an incantation. The place that she occupies physically, her powerful "all-pervasive laughter" (which she nevertheless keeps under strict control), the performative value of her words, all contribute to the creation, from the outset, of a carnival atmosphere that will modify the normal perception of space and time (as Bakhtin has pointed out) and of a number of symbolic relationships that will define the conditions of the action (in the way, for instance, that the opening of the gates in the prologue of Claudel's *The Tidings Brought to Mary* or the scrubbing of the doorsteps by the maids in *Pelléas et Mélisande* suggest a ritualistic process of initiation). Here is the opening of **La Veuve enragée:**

> *A huge burst of laughter from Patience, which begins as the curtain rises, and is kept up until the audience join in . . . if possible. Then a sharp cut-off.*
>
> PATIENCE You jest set and the time bide
> On the stoop in front of your dwelling
> Then you'll see them by the bye
>
> The corpse of your foe carrying
>
> *She returns to carding her wool and sings*

My Father had a house built . . . .

In *Gapi,* the insults the character hurls at the gulls ("just shut up you goddam tarnation of little picked chickens!") evoke a space wholly devoid of human presence—at the moment—but capable of being defined through ecological sharing: "—There's room for all of us fishin' folk right here." The lighthouse in the setting thus provides a focus and a boundary, and by sweeping this territory with its beam of light, creates another human rhythm, establishes another language, engages in dialogue with the old fisherman. But the effect of the settings and the props is maximal at the beginnings of the plays. In the body of the drama, the *hors-scène* and *extra-scène* evoked through the dialogue are indeed by far the most significant modes of presentation of space and time.

Unfortunately, we lack suitable methods to analyse such modes. Ubersfeld, adapting some of Yuri Lotman's ideas, suggests an inventory of the conflictive effects and the binary opposition systems which determine space patterns. This can be done effectively for plays like **Les Crasseux** or **La Veuve,** strongly polarized characters defining their own space, but the patterns of relationships between characters are not always of an emotive/conative nature. In **La Sagouine,** the confrontation between the narrator and her community on the one hand (first person *je*/I, *nous*/we), and the third persons bourgeois on the other (*eux*/they), is only reported or alluded to; moreover, it is often mediated by an appeal to the second person (*vous*/you). Recourse to the phatic function, a notable feature of plays with a single character on stage (**La Sagouine** can be compared in this respect with Beckett's *Not I,* or Cocteau's *Le Bel indifférent* or *The Human Voice*), postulates a constant shift in the spatio-temporal framework. In **Gapi,** the opposition between the protagonist and Sullivan, his one-time drinking pal and secret rival, appears only in the second part of the play. The entire beginning is made up of the dreamy speculations (the *jonglerie*) of a lonely man who transcends the constraints of his increasingly narrow present space by flights into the realm of memory. Whatever conflict there is takes place only within the succession of figures of the protagonist, past and present, as with Vauthier's *Le Personnage combattant* (The Struggling Protagonist), or Beckett's Krapp (*Krapp's Last Tape*) and Winnie (*Happy Days*).

One might of course use Lotman's suggestion and restore a paradigm of oppositions between the living and the dead, and consider that the first part of the play deals with the lasting love—alive but not truly valued—of Gapi for the late Sagouine, while the second part, after Sullivan's arrival and the revelation of his love for the same woman, presents an actual conflict in which La Sagouine's value is enhanced ("A treasure, Gapi, is not always buried in a sea-chest"), but her husband's comforting memories of her are shattered. Such an interpretation would make the temporal model congru-

ent with the spatial opposition Gapi/Sullivan: he who remains/he who travels, the keeper of the lighthouse/the sailor who visits exotic lands. However, the "dramatic" conflict remains virtual and undeveloped ("*the two men eye each other and clench their fists*"). There is no "crossing of the frontier," and the "*movement* from one space to another," which according to Ubersfeld is a significant feature of dramatic conflict, is not actualized. Should one then return to Lotman's hypothesis concerning the exclusivity of each character's space and time, and the inherent lack of mutual penetration? Alternatively, should a large portion of the Maillet corpus be considered not in terms of dramatic interaction, but only as a variety of modulated narrative? I do not believe that either such exclusivity or such an exclusion is warranted.

What constitutes the dramatic tension may well take place not between different characters, but within a given character: this occurs whenever the system of actantial functions is not actualized into explicit roles developed on stage. For instance, in *Krapp's Last Tape or Happy Days,* there is very little physical (on-stage) indication of movement; yet the text, the words assigned to the character, evoke off-stage (*hors-scène*) conflicts and provide genuine clues not only to the passage of time but to a change in the kind of space considered. This evocation takes place also in those of Maillet's plays which assume the form of a soliloquy or tend towards that form. Indeed, Maillet's repertoire offers an important clue to the workings of the kind of soliloquy which does not take stock of a situation; that is, which does not follow the pattern one finds most commonly in dramatists who make the soliloquy ancillary to the presentation of conflicts on stage. The opposition to be found then is not between spaces of a similar nature which could be actualized in actions within the cube, to use Souriau's description, but between the heterogeneous spaces that develop within the cube and within the sphere. In fact, this opposition—which may or may not be entirely coterminal between that of the "world" and the "universe" of a protagonist—is probably an important feature of the world's most deservedly famous soliloquies, in Corneille, Calderón, or Shakespeare.

In Maillet's plays, this opposition takes the form of what Québécois or Acadian French describes, in a very felicitous phrase, as "*jonglerie.*" This is not a mere "juggling" with thoughts, but a complex interplay of fantasies, memories, and dreams; it involves a move to a "somewhere else," a transposition of conflicts within a realm of myths, an escape from the grid of "positive" categories. What takes place then is not a conative action (of the kind analysed by Ubersfeld), but the development of a poetic relationship to time and space conveyed through a phatic implication of the public who then must, through the exercise of imagination, substitute for the absent partner(s) of the character engaged in *jonglerie.* This *jonglerie* is never entirely absent from

Maillet's dramatic works. Often, along with the action, in the time and space of the cube, which develops in syntagmatic fashion, it presents a series of reactions (one might even venture the psychoanalytic term of abreactions) and of phantasmal interactions.

In **Les Crasseux,** for instance, in spite of the injunction of his father, the old "realistic" chief Don l'Orignal ("Listen to your father, Noume, don't act crazy [. . .] listen to your granddad and all your line of ancestors who spent their lives in this spot and had [. . .] very little time for fool-juggling [*pour jongler*]"), young Noume persists in his *jonglerie*. But in this way Noume (*Nomen est numen:* he is a paradigm of the "houme," the man of the shabby settlers on the wrong side of the tracks, who by the act of "nommer," of naming, turns them into thinking subjects and potential heroes) "kind of figures a plan" to provide a new space for the evicted squatters. He will "overturn the tables of the law" (and set them right side up!) and volunteer to clear the dump as a project for improving the environment so as to receive a clear deed to the site. His "thinking crazy" is a prelude to a "crazy act" which turns out to be the extreme of wisdom, and establishes a space and a historical "base time" for a renewed community. While his father equates *jonglerie* with madness, Noume turns it into the mode of actualization of an idea that can change the world for him and for his society. While Don l'Orignal is concerned mostly with "making ends meet"—a pathetic spatial image of mere survival in the cube—and "not dying before your last hour has come"—its translation in time, the young hero draws from his dream sphere the vision that can unite myth (the founding of a "city") and reality. He can then reinvest the tension of the sphere/cube contest in a properly scenic situation: the decision to occupy the dump site leads to a clearly dramatic confrontation of the squatters with the solid burghers who wanted to cheat and exclude them from the time and space of the city.

In **La Veuve enragée,** the "juggling" (in this case made visible by step-dancing) of the marginal women of *Cordes-de-bois* takes place inside the time and space of the carnival, which belong to the order of the sphere ("Mardi Gras does it again!" exclaims la Piroune at the end of the play, to affirm the victory of her laughing cohorts over the solemn widow champion of the sober establishment). The merry wenches, the jolly witches and their ally the Irish sailor, Tom Thumb—leprechaun and circus performer, teller of tall tales, spinner of dream epics—will also at the end translate their poetic time and space into a conative action, and take renewed possession of the ancestral hillock where they have been squatters. This renewal is made very clear in the text:

> ZELICA Here it is, our home and native land. It ain't ready to die yet, the hilltop our old ancestor

has cleared (*la butte qu'a défrichetée l'ancêtre Mercenaire*).

It is also represented by the action on the stage:

> *La Piroune leads her people in a merry round. The widow is driven from the stage and runs away screaming.*

> *The End.*

In the less "scenic" plays, *jonglerie* alone must evoke conflicts and tensions, and define the dramatic style. In order to study those plays, the procedure suggested by Ubersfeld to analyze the treatment of the time and space needs to be somewhat adapted. Of course, the study of spatial paradigms, the definition of semic and scenic categories, and the distribution of characters and objects into polarized classes remain necessary tasks. But in this case, stage directions (or *didascalies*) offer little help: in **La Sagouine,** they have to be deduced from the character's words; in *Gapi* and ***Évangéline Deusse,*** they are often, if not redundant, at least subordinated to the text:

> ÉVANGÉLINE You should not need to tell them who try and shoot roots in foreign soil when they're getting on in years . . . how raucous the shriek of sea-gulls can be . . .

> *One hears faintly at first, then gradually louder the call of sea birds. (Évangéline,* final scene)

> GAPI . . . There's no one left . . . no one . . .

> *Shrieks of the sea-gulls, all agitated.*

> No, not a one! Now you just shut up, you up there! I want to be left alone.

Spatial and temporal models are dependent less upon the (conative) representation of actions and conflicts than upon the (poetic) evocation of conflicts in the tales or the recitatives of the protagonists. Binary patterns that could be used to define sets of characters or objects are constantly modified as the speakers proceed with their *jonglerie*. For instance, in **La Sagouine,** the group of *us* is sometimes split up, and we have an opposition between *I* and *you;* within the *I,* one may even at times distinguish between an individual *I* (or somatic self) and a representative *I,* who speaks on behalf of the community and is apt to use a mixed singular/plural form (*j'avons*). The opposition of the first-person character(s) to the third person is fairly constant. But some *they*—who are incapable of speech, within expression, the "poor slaves"—are occasionally subsumed by *us.* In addition, there are beyond expression, a group of *they* that I have called *tiers abstraits* (the abstract third parties) who have no existential correlative. Their voice is that of non-people and is heard through the media (the "gazettes" or newspapers); it takes the form of officialese ("newspeak"), or of clericalese ("oldspeak"), and expresses the "*machino-fichier*" (the power of machines and files). That *tiers abstrait* which uses what Gobard would call a "referentiary language" is the cold arch-enemy of the vernacular; it even distorts and dehumanises the vehicular. In order to escape it, one must travel through the looking-glass of the theater and reach the realm of the living imagination where comforting old myths still hold sway, where one is free to create personal mythologies and even to tinker with an individual, idiosyncratic expression, with idiolects and "idiomytholects."

This multiplicity of levels and the constant creative interplay among them are to be found not only in the distribution of voices, characters and objects, but also as major characteristics of the treatment of time and place by Maillet. The author of **La Sagouine** is clearly of the same generation as Armand Gatti, the generation that has become aware of the necessity to accommodate scientific relativity into its experience of life. She does not establish the kinds of precise relationships among four-dimensional systems that can be found in *Thirteen Suns (Les Treize Soleils)* or *The Stork (La Cigogne)*. But beyond the chronicle of familiar events which provides the framework of the narrator's discourse in **La Sagouine**—the seasons and feast-days of Christmas (*Nouël*), Happy New Year (*La Boune Ânnée*), Springtime (*Le Printemps*); the recurring activities that establish the cycles of human existence, such as one's life-work (*le métier*), youth (*la jeunesse*), death (*la mort*)—she also establishes the presence of historical events: war, the census. These events proceed according to mysterious laws, and their comprehensible order often appears in the guise of arbitrariness. Nevertheless, the heroine connects them with realities she has experienced; she reads some sense into their absurdities and naïvely reveals ironies without necessarily perceiving them in herself. The economic crash becomes *crache écumunique* (ecumenical spit), a description which invests it with religious dignity—Christ suffering insult, the efforts to unify churches—enhancing its world-wide character; the fates that are "in the cards" are connected to existential patterns. Moreover, beyond such human contingencies, the heroine is aware of cosmic horizons: the moon can be brought within reach, in the same way as heaven, and La Sagouine believes in space travel, by an act of faith which Gapi, ever critical, refuses to accomplish.

It would therefore be rewarding to develop the study of the *jonglerie* plays not only as poetic explorations, but also as mythical constructs. A systematic mythocritique ought to detect in them the workings of imagination, be it collective or individual. In spite of the cultural starvation imposed on the characters by their poverty and their comparative isolation, an active interplay of memories and speculations, a resourceful weaving together of vernacular and mythical languages (in Gobard's terminology), as well as the occasional bold leap into the *hors-dit* (that postulated treasure which dramatizes the *non-dit* and complements the *hors-scène*) make such plays extremely rich. I am unfortunately not in a position to present a developed proposal for such a mythocritique, both because of the limitations of this paper, and because of the methodological problems I still have to work out (including the techniques for dealing with the heterogeneous, in spite of Bataille's seminal suggestions; or the relationship between mental categories and verbal equipment, although Benveniste's observations on "categories of language and categories of thought" may well provide a starting-point). But I would like to submit here a few samples, the result of a rapid and somewhat subjective survey rather than of a systematic and thorough investigation, and to venture a few hypotheses and suggestions for future research.

Among the most obvious problems raised by Antonine Maillet's corpus are those of the relationships between her plays and her stories which could often be analysed in parallel from the point of view of the plot lines, the characters, the techniques of actualization and the mediations of the emotive function. The plays' originality could be assessed also by a study of the strong sociological and heterological polarization of their spatial features. One could also draw attention to the tendency of Maillet the dramatist towards a deconstruction of history and the redistribution of its elements. These elements are manifested as day-to-day history (*petite histoire*), emphasizing anecdotes and extending them in the direction of parable and/or exempla; in other words, transposing time sequences into a symbolic construct and offering a commentary based on folk wisdom and *doxa,* thus offering thumb-nail sketches of morality plays. But time sequences may also be reorganized in cyclical patterns or in epic or pseudo-epic narratives—again with commentary—thus providing a different proto-Brechtian kind of epic theater whose protagonists are again held to be in the oral tradition since most of them are functionally illiterate. Finally one could consider, as the starting-point for a definition of Maillet's theatricality, her use of paradigmatic disjunctions, the valorization of certain terms and their dual role as syntactic shifters and as semantic terms of reference.

I have briefly discussed the relation between the plays and the stories, as well as the spatial polarizations and the temporal deconstructions, and shall return to them in other studies now in progress. But the fourth problem seems particularly relevant to our overall project here, and indeed is considered to be crucial by several theoreticians, whether they deal with drama (Ubersfeld) or with other projections of the imaginative faculties (Gobard). I shall therefore concentrate on it as best I can with the limited theoretical equipment now available.

The obligatory focus, which establishes contact at the present time of the actual performance (re-presentation), at the point of emission of the spoken work (whether or not it is perceived as a transposition, a final term in a succession of relays, a speech act grounded in experience, with referential and / or metalingual co-ordinates), is the here and now vehicular: *ici et maintenant* with their variants in vernacular: "*icitte,*" "*là où je suis*" (where I am), "*où je sons*" (combining singular speaker and collective awareness), etc. This base point must always be considered in its poetic function in the text of the play but, whenever enunciated, it also involves all participants in the dramatic experience, be they internal to the play or external, identified or removed (*verfremdet*). From this base point radiate revolving semantic beams which reveal for a brief moment a particular experience and make it possible to share it.

The lighthouse in the set for *Gapi,* firmly established in a given point in space, offers a metaphor and an analogue of the here and now in Maillet. It constitutes a landmark, but at the same time emits signals which reveal other areas (and reveal it as far as the eye can see) and which must be interpreted in relation to a rhythmic, temporal pattern superimposed upon natural rhythms such as those of the tide or the phases of the moon. The place of and the part played by this emitter of signals offer a visible correlative of the way the text and its dramatic production are associated. The here and the now are not, however, any more punctual than the speaking *I* of a character, which can, as we have noted, be considered at any moment under a variety of guises, and which of course evolves as the play progresses. But they can serve as anchoring points for paradigmatic series arranged according to modes or aspects, and include terms which are more or less strongly marked. For instance, starting from *now,* one finds the vehicular *tomorrow* and *yesterday, soon, shortly* (à l'instant), *still* (aspect of duration), *again* (iteration), but also the vernacular *still and all* (toujours ben), *as of tomorrow* (dès demain), which often convey a charge of emotion and imply an existential urgency.

The mythical horizon is conveyed by expressions even more idiosyncratic and with a faintly archaic flavor to evoke the time of origins—*once upon early days* (sus l'empremier)— or the eschatological horizon—*some fine day* (un beau jour). These two later terms recur in all of Maillet's plays and might establish a kind of teleology of *jonglerie.* But Maillet (or her characters) seems to shy away from the absolute: the Creation and the Last Judgement are dealt with by the very human, very Acadian agents. God Himself is very much in the image of a neighborly, jolly old fellow (La Sagouine would feel happy in Heaven if ". . . God the Father could come over to call the square dances 'pon a Saturday night

. . .") Eternity is conceived of as a development of experience: "a real Spring, that won't stop, but that will last, and then that will last, and then . . . why, *that* will be Heaven, and on that there day (*c'te jour-là*) I do believe I shall be dead and right inside Paradise."

On the other hand, if the absolute is made relative, the relative is durable: provisional and precarious conditions provide the basis for lasting ideologies and for a world-view based on the desire to "hang on tight." The important characters in Maillet's plays (with the notable exception of Citrouille and the Merchant's daughter in **Les Crasseux,** humble modern counterparts of Romeo and Juliet, even though social conflicts are more important in their tragedy than feudal pride) refuse to die. When they are taken from life, it is after a tough battle against hardship **(La Sagouine),** or even when they have weathered the worst storms and are within sight of a safe harbor (the old Breton of *Évangéline*). Their ability to "surge up again" (*ressoudre*), their physical and moral resourcefulness, is indeed their most remarkable feature: each individual takes up the collective fight of the Acadian nation and, without illusion, refuses to give in to time and its grim ally, death:

> you must not come and tell old folks what's what, it's no use coddling them, it's definitely no use trying to pull the wool over their eyes . . . Old folks and those who have been deported . . . That's on account of their being the only ones (*par rapport qu'i' sont les seuls*) I have ever met who know all about life, since they are the only ones who have started over several times, and who have kept going to the very end . . . to the very end . . .

as Évangéline puts it before the curtain falls.

Among those poor and thrifty people who are used to mending nets and patching old clothes, the effort to negate the wear and tear of time leads to a patient reconstruction of sequences. While history has been unkind, with its succession of spoliations and uprootings, a complementary counter-history must be wrought from the little shreds that have been treasured by individuals. In that respect, the work of the *défricheteuses de parenté*—the careful genealogists who at the same time, in a complex metaphor, untangle confusing skeins, clear areas which are overgrown with weeds, and restore the continuity of "lines" in the vegetation of family trees, in the weaving of family "tapestries"—is exemplary. In fact, the work of restoring the chronicle may well mean more than the reconstructed chronicle itself. The Acadian descent, although it is patrilineal according to the common Western pattern, often takes its virtue from the tracing up (through the work of women) of a lineage from the individual ("he is Thomas, born of Jos, born of Samuel") rather than from proceeding in the Biblical style down from the (male) ancestor ("Samuel begat Jos, who begat Thomas") who established a root or "stirps." The family is ascent, not descent, and an effort to evolve. Thus, a tension against time is created, and that too is a factor of dramatization.

The tension against space is quite as notable, and what is more, in its most crucial form, the inherited fight against displacement (which in *Évangéline Deusse* actualizes the deportation into a personal experience of collective deportation), is part of the same struggle, of the same agon. Generally speaking, the Acadian characters stay in their places but will not be pushed around: should anyone attempt such an abuse, he would arouse a popular movement, such as that which takes place at the end of *Les Crasseux* at the instigation of Noume, the juggler-hero. Any individual who breaks ranks and tries to move apart (or believes he/she can move up) is punished by ridicule (La Sainte, in the episode of the church pews in *La Sagouine*) or visited with some more obscure retribution from within or without the group. But this tenacity cannot be equated with immobilism: the characters are active and mobile inside the space which they define.

These all too brief remarks in no way exhaust even one aspect of a complex set of issues. I hope, nevertheless, that they provide some clues to the originality of a remarkable corpus. Maillet's dramas are very specific: they offer the defense and illustration of a national theater for a nation that is still as much in limbo as Poland was in Jarry's *Ubu*. They are the representative voice of a social group that is still not heard publicly, of a sex that is still often relegated to the status of "other." But at the same time, this Acadian repertoire, whose major protagonists are old, poor women, is universal in its topoi and its structures: it constitutes in many respects a paradigm for the study of general ideology, of cultural patterns, of the layering of language. It would therefore be rewarding to use it as a basis for further research, dealing for instance with mythopoetic *jonglerie* and other extensions of the dramatic into the *hors-scène*. But such extensions are most often reinvested in the scenic cube, even if this return, this new surging up, carries with it the strange atmosphere of myth or carnival, of a different truth, a different time, a different space. Perhaps this is an example of the theater of the oppressed at work. Perhaps it is the expression of a general rule of any theater which establishes reality against reality by a process of denial.

Antonine Maillet with Martine Jacquot (interview date 3 November 1985)

SOURCE: "Last Story-Teller," in *Waves,* Vol. 14, No. 4, Spring, 1986, pp. 93-95.

[*In the following interview conducted on November 3, 1985, on the occassion of the Canada-in-Commonwealth conference held at Acadia University, Jacquot talks with Maillet about her background and motivation for writing.*]

Looking at the Grand-Pré dikes, Antonine Maillet says: "I was here when the Acadians were deported, I was in the blood of my ancestors." And she has decided to write their story because they had no way to do so.

Antonine Maillet is the last of a generation of story-tellers and the first one of a generation of writers. It is because of that deeply rooted need to tell that her books are stories. She has published 20 books including novels, plays and stories for children. She has received 13 honorary doctorates and many literary awards, namely the prestigious Prix Goncourt in 1979 with *Pélagie la Charette.* I interviewed her a few miles from Grand-Pré, on her land, as she put it, on the occasion of the Canada-in-Commonwealth conference held at Acadia University on November 3, 1985, to which she had been invited to read from her works.

[*Jacquot:*] *Is it because you consider yourself as the last story-teller that you are so much attracted to the past?*

[Maillet:] I am not that much attracted to the past. I mean, the past becomes important to me when I can find something in it which inspires me and reflects my present, something which stimulates me. In all my stories set in the past, there is a small cell in each of my characters which developed into the person I am. So the past is part of me, but I don't consider that I look back.

So when you write, you develop a slice of your personality?

Yes, my characters are all my different possibilities. When I write, I multiply myself, I live one million lives, which I could not do otherwise because life is too short and the world is too small.

The main characters of your books are generally women. Is it a deliberate choice?

No, it is an unconscious and necessary one. A writer does not really choose: the choices are ready-made, somehow. When I was born, I had not decided to be born that year, in that village, and so on. Those choices had been made for me. Automatically, I gathered in my surrounding a series of characters which were going to be developed in my books. The fact that my characters are women does not even come from the fact that I am one, but because I lived that life, in an Acadian environment, during the war and depression years in which feminine values were predominant. So it is because of my story, my biography, as well as my personality that my characters are women.

You are an artist, a woman, an Acadian and you are French-speaking. You seem to represent most of the minorities . . .

Yes, but I'd like to give to the word minority a positive connotation, because minorities should be valorized as being more precious and fragile because unique. The artist is, in a way, the small voice. Women, even though superior in number, are just starting to speak up. L'Acadie is small and its survival is still insecure. So the position of all these minorities and the urgency for them to be protected gives me the strength to write. I am a multi-minority, but my basic elements are rare pearls.

Would it be difficult to write if you came back to New Brunswick? People say that you are turning into a Montrealer . . .

No, I did not leave l'Acadie. It is not a place, it is a culture. I can live in Montreal and stay Acadian. If I were living in Acadie, I would fundamentally be the same. The milieu would just be smaller. I live in Montreal because it is the cultural capital city for me.

Have you ever thought of publishing a book in Acadie?

Yes, and long before all the other Acadian writers. But when I wrote my first book in 1958, there were no publishing houses there. I had already published at least 8 books when les Editions d'Acadie were founded. Then, I had a kind of moral contract with my publisher. Moreover, I live off my craft, and books are better distributed in Montreal. So historical reasons prevented me from getting published in Acadie. In a way, it is because people like me looked for a publisher elsewhere that les Editions d'Acadie were born.

The world that you create in your books can be defined as South-East Acadian as far as themes, language and settings are concerned. Is not there a danger to limit yourself to one genre?

There are always dangers, but I try to prevent to get stuck in a ditch. It is the danger of repeating one's first book, especially if it has been a success. I refuse to be dominated by that kind of danger and I know I can avoid it. I think that there has been a constant evolution in my works with each new book. When I wrote **Les Crasseux** I stepped away from **On a mangé la dune.** The same happened with **La Sagouine,** which became a kind of wave with **Gapi** and **Les Crasseux.** I opened a new phase with **Les Cordes de Bois.** It was a new way of looking at things, a new technique of writing. Then there was a new stage which could probably look like the previous one, but to me it consists in a conti-

nuity. Now I am building a bridge to leave the period of **Pélagie, Cent Ans dans les Bois** and **Crache à Pic.** It is going to be a continuity of the same world, because I cannot escape from my own world, but I will reveal new facets of it.

You won the Prix Goncourt in 1979 thanks to **Pélagie la Charette.** *Is it your favorite book?*

I always have a favorite book, but it changes every day! **Pélagie** was important in my life, not only because of the Goncourt which was the outside significance. But it meant something special for me because I realized I was writing a kind of epic poem in the Acadian fashion. **Pélagie** is a reverse epic poem, and I love to do things upside down. The epic poem is the story of a people in the minute which precedes its birth. The return of **Pélagie** represents the 10 years during which it was going to be decided whether l'Acadie was going to go on existing or not. The cart would decide. As opposed to the classical epic poem in which the hero rides a horse, here the heroine is walking. As opposed to the official language, here the characters speak the everyday language of the people. Those who speak the official language are making history: the States are receiving a constitution, becoming independent. Meanwhile, **Pélagie** goes back home through the back yard of America, unaware that *she* is making history. So **Pélagie,** in spite of me, became an epic in the sense that it tells of the story of the boat-people of that time, but it is a reverse one because it tells of their return.

You write a lot for the theater. Do you get a chance to work with actors?

It is true, I have always been very fond of theater and whenever one of my plays is being acted, I participate back stage. I attend the rehearsals, I help as much as I can, I give advice for the costumes, the stage setting, I see the play evolve. Yes, I feel I am part of the company.

Have you ever worked with Viola Léger?

Many times: Whenever Viola acts in one of my plays, which has happened more than once, I am always there.

How did you meet?

We were teaching in the same school a long time ago. At that time, we used to stage plays with our students: I was writing them, and she was staging them. I realized at once she was very gifted for the theater. When I wrote **La Sagouine** she was in Paris studying drama. I sent her my manuscript to know what she thought of it. She answered that she was coming back right away to perform it. It was the beginning of her fame.

One of your major themes is genealogy. It is important for you in your life, too.

Yes, I already knew that my Maillet ancestor, Jacques, came from Paris, and not from the east of France like all the other Acadians. But I recently discovered that the name Maillet was given in 1163 to three brothers who were building cathedrals, namely Notre-Dame-de-Paris. One of them was my ancestor.

Marjorie A. Fitzpatrick (essay date 1985)

SOURCE: "Antonine Maillet and the Epic Heroine," in *Traditionalism, Nationalism, and Feminism: Women Writers of Quebec,* edited by Paula Gilbert Lewis, Greenwood Press, 1985, pp. 141-55.

[*In the following essay, Fitzpatrick examines the female roles in several of Maillet's novels.*]

Traditionalist, feminist, nationalist—how is one to classify the broad range of Antonine Maillet's important female characters? The answer has to be: partly each, yet not exclusively any of the above. At the risk of offending partisans of all three groups, I suggest that the wonderfully gifted Maillet—surely one of the best storytellers writing in French today—has simultaneously transcended the confining stereotypes of traditionalism, the humorlessness of some feminism, and the narrow vision of fanatic nationalism. At the same time, no author currently writing has created women who are at once more classically feminine, more liberated . . . and more Acadian.

> **I suggest that the wonderfully gifted Maillet—surely one of the best storytellers writing in French today—has simultaneously transcended the confining stereotypes of traditionalism, the humorlessness of some feminism, and the narrow vision of fanatic nationalism.**
> **—*Marjorie A. Fitzpatrick***

How has Maillet achieved this remarkable synthesis? One thinks, of course, of her humor and her narrative genius, but in addition there is the striking use she makes of female protagonists. When one examines their characters, personalities, objectives, and actions, it is clear that many of these women have much in common with the typically male epic hero. Indeed, "heroine" seems almost too derivative a word to apply to these strong, memorable figures. They come closer

to the powerful but unquestionably feminine women that Maya Angelou refers to as "she-roes."

Although Maillet's best known character is doubtless la Sagouine, the kind of epic heroine (let us resign ourselves to the traditional word) alluded to above is better exemplified in her narrative works, of which three will be considered here: *Mariaagélas, Les Cordes-de-Bois,* and—obviously—*Pélagie-la-Charrette.* Two of these sparkling novels proclaim the centrality of their women protagonists right in their titles. The third, *Les Cordes-de-Bois,* in fact does so as well, since the title refers to the entire clan of extraordinary women known as the Mercenaires, whose most impressive (and central) figures are la Piroune and her daughter la Bessoune.

The strictures that threaten the freedom and self-fulfillment of these redoubtable Mercenaire women are reflected spatially in the setting of the novel: a stifling, hypocritical, "well-ordered" village called le Pont after its most prominent physical feature, standing cheek by jowl with the rakishly timber-covered butte called les Cordes-de-Bois, home of and synonym for the Mercenaires. The entire novel will revolve around the opposition between these two microcosmic universes and the principles they represent.

More specifically, however—in a major departure from much feminist literature—the struggle will pit la Piroune and la Bessoune against another woman, Ma-Tante-la-Veuve, a fire-breathing, witch-hunting virago who has become the self-appointed guardian of the morals of le Pont. In this novel, as in *Mariaagélas* and more subtly in *Pélagie,* we thus find both the forces for "good" (the struggle for freedom, the refusal to bow to convention, the determination to conquer obstacles) and the forces of "evil" (self-righteous hypocrisy, adherence to convention, the cult of personal power for its own sake) led by women. Maillet virtually suggests that only another woman would have the boldness, the shrewdness, the energy to serve as a worthy adversary for the likes of the world's Pirounes and Bessounes. The latter, seen as personal scourges by Ma-Tante-la-Veuve, give scandal precisely because they refuse to be bound by the traditional limits on their freedom to which the "respectable" village ladies docilely adhere. If the continuous dust-ups between the Mercenaires and Ma-Tante-la-Veuve owe more to the *héroï-comique* tradition of Boileau's *Lutrin* than to the epic heroism of Roland facing the Saracens, the fact remains that the two courageous Mercenaire women, relying only upon their own resources and wile, overcome numerous and often apparently insurmountable obstacles strewn in their path by an implacable foe.

The same pattern emerges in *Mariaagélas.* The young heroine, Maria, born into a family known for its rejection of the petit bourgeois norms of village society, has as chief antagonist the female incarnation of that society in all its hypocritical rectitude: la veuve à Calixte. In many ways the struggle between these two is even more sharply etched (though narrower in its feminist implications) than the conflict between the Mercenaires and Ma-Tante-la-Veuve, since Maria and la veuve à Calixte seem to take their greatest satisfaction from out-smarting each other. While the Mercenaires and Ma-Tante-la-Veuve symbolize irreconcilable mores that necessarily come into confrontation, the unending fight between the outlaw Maria and the ambitious veuve à Calixte has more the quality of a personal grudge match. In both cases, however, the author's—and therefore the reader's—sympathies clearly lie with the renegade women, who willingly forgo comfort, respectability, acceptance, and even legality in exchange for freedom and self-fulfillment.

Has Maillet set up these female antagonisms for the sake of symmetry, or are Ma-Tante-la-Veuve and la veuve à Calixte simply surrogates for men in what is essentially a male-ordered universe? Can we make a case for the latter by noting that both women are identified only by titles that define them in terms of their relationship to men? One might take such an argument one step further and observe that both these dragons, while serving as champions of the most benighted traditionalism, are freed from some of its more oppressive routine aspects by their very widowhood.

As tempting as it is to pursue this line of thought, a better explanation may in fact be the one suggested earlier. While the heroines and their antagonists find themselves (the latter willingly, the former most involuntarily) in a world whose parameters have been largely shaped by authoritative men, the fundamental struggle as they conceive it seems not to be between male and female, but between institutional constraint and individual freedom. Women are lined up against women, not in some mutual self-destructive loathing, but because they make worthy and *interesting* adversaries. Indeed, as the narrator points out in one sardonic passage in *Mariaagélas,* both heroine and villain are so accustomed to coping mainly with men that they occasionally underestimate each other:

> La veuve à Calixte connaissait tout ça [that most rumrunners were eventually caught and jailed by the authorities], et savait par conséquent qu'un jour ou l'autre le sort tomberait sur Mariaagélas comme sur les autres contrabandiers. Mais la veuve à Calixte avait oublié une chose: Mariaagélas n'était pas un contrabandier, mais une contrabandière.

> De son côté, Mariaagélas avait négligé de reconnaître les attributions de la veuve, s'imaginant que sa fonction se limitait à de petits commérages de bénitier ou de bureau de poste. Depuis belles

années, pourtant, la veuve à Calixte débordait chaque saison son rôle et étonnait tout le monde.

Pélagie-la-Charrette, for all its good humor and savory Acadian epithets, comes closer than either of the other novels to being a true epic. The struggles played out in mischievous fun between the Mercenaires and Ma-Tante-la-Veuve, between Maria the bootlegger and la veuve à Calixte, are repeated in deadly earnest by Pélagie and her prime adversary, no less a figure than Death herself (feminine in French). Pélagie's quest is not merely for personal freedom but for the very life of Acadia, the Promised Land whence she was expelled during the Great Dispersion and to which, against all the wiles of the Foe, she is determined to lead her little remnant of survivors. Death takes many forms along Pélagie's route, all of them female or identified by feminine nouns. At one particularly desperate moment in the journey she is *la Faucheuse,* the Grim Reaper, whom Pélagie bests only through exhausting and heroic efforts. Be it noted, however, that Pélagie's triumph depends on her moral force rather than physical strength, for which she unhesitatingly relies upon the men in the company. As *la Faucheuse* lurks impatiently nearby, Pélagie's Cart, symbol of life and hope, is sinking inexorably into the Salem swamp. While the men bend every ounce of their strength to extricate the wagon, Pélagie wages her titanic struggle out of the depths of her soul:

> Les chroniqeurs du dernier siècle ont juré que Pélagie n'avait pas bougé durant toute la scène, qu'elle se tenait droite comme un peuplier, la tête au vent. Elle n'aurait pas crié, ni prié, ni montré le poing au ciel comme l'on a prétendu. Personne ne l'a vue se jeter à genoux et se lamenter, ce n'est pas vrai. Personne ne l'a entendue hucher des injures aux saints, ni les supplier pour l'amour de Dieu.

> "Et alors, son cri?"

> "Elle a dit un seul mot, un seul. . . ."

> "Ma vie!" qu'on entendit monter des marais de Salem et rouler sur les roseaux jusqu'au pont de bois.

> La charrette a dû l'entendre, car elle a grincé de toutes ses pentures et de tous ses essieux. Deux fois en un jour on s'en venait impudemment lui barrer la route? Qui osait?

Another female manifestation of Death on Pélagie's path is the phantasmagoric black cart, the *charrette noire,* which attaches itself to Pélagie's companion Bélonie-le-Vieux and is visible only to him. While Pélagie imbues her own cart with her vibrant sense of life, hope, purpose, and freedom, Bélonie's cart seems instead to define him as it rumbles mockingly along with the pilgrims like a malevolent shadow, sapping energy and provoking despair. As Pélagie is to her Cart of Life (alive, active, generative of hope), so the Cart of Death is to Bélonie (resigned, passive, prepared to be trundled to his death). Only with the discovery of a living grandson, long thought dead, does Bélonie truly, totally, join in the communion of Pélagie's joyous will to survive, to reach Acadia again. Robbed of its essence, Bélonie's death cart then disappears, never to return. The epic heroine, wielding as sole weapons her own vitality (maternal as well as personal) and the wagon that embodies it, has faced down the greatest adversary of humankind, won the race against doom, and saved her less hardy friend. Though the nature of her struggle and the mode of her triumph are, as we shall see, defined by her womanhood, she thinks of them not as primarily a victory of Woman over Man, but of Life over Death.

This is not to say that the gender of Maillet's protagonists is irrelevant to their struggles—quite the contrary! In every case the fact that a struggle is necessary at all is a consequence at least partly of their sex, and both the nature of the obstacles they face and the weapons they use in overcoming them are tied to it as well.

The linkages in *Mariaagélas* are multiple but quite clear. At eight years of age the profit-minded preschooler Maria was out cornering the village market in returnable bottles while she was thought to be safely at home, like a good little girl, with her grandmother. At fourteen she was destined, like other girls of similarly humble circumstances, to be shipped off by her father to work in the shops, or to go into domestic service, but Maria was not about to accept either option. With scornful disregard for her future employability in any "respectable" home, she settled a perceived insult by the schoolmistress to her younger sister by storming into the schoolhouse one day, "avant que personne n'eût pu prévoir le coup, et sous le regard ébarroui des petits de la petite classe, . . . avait administré à M'zelle Mazerolle le plus formidable poing dans l'oeil de mémoire scolaire."

Moreover, Maria was not the first woman of her family to reject the traditional destiny: her Aunt Clara, much admired by the adolescent Maria, had become a prostitute and a vagabond in preference to remaining in the horrid conditions of a succession of sweat-shops. In her last such job Clara had even organized the other women in a short-lived mutiny, torched the shop, and spent time in prison. Despite the cost, Maria was deeply impressed by Clara's refusal to conform and looked to her as a model in her own budding life of outlawry. Nor did she aspire to the "respectable" women's roles as dependent wife, doting mother, pious parishioner, and loyal good citizen. No one—not her father, the priest, the schoolmarm, or tradition—was about to tell Mariaagélas what she must do or what she must become, or not become.

Fortified by her natural taste for adventure and her business acumen, she therefore seemed to fall almost by fate into a highly profitable profession—bootlegging—that made her a moral, social and legal outlaw.

From then till the end of her days, Maria took mischievous pleasure not only in running the most successful bootlegging operation in her area during those dangerous Prohibition days, but in carrying out her feats under the very nose of the sanctimonious veuve à Calixte. In one supremely ironic ruse, Maria played upon two of the most deeply entrenched stereotypes of her society. Disguising herself as a nun, she had a bootlegging partner drive her and a full cargo of illegal liquor in her own Buick across the American border, counting accurately upon the gallantry of the *québécois* border guards towards her sex and the respect of the Irish-American guards for her habit to protect her from the usual close search. Her contempt for the limitations placed upon her free choice by tradition and prejudice inspired her to use them as weapons in the service of her own illegal ends.

The outlawry of la Piroune and la Bessoune in *Les Cordes-de-Bois* was more social than statutory, but as disruptive of local society as that of Mariaagélas. Like Maria, they were members of a renegade family whose women were known for flouting the conventions (in this case principally sexual) established by their "betters." Again the battle lines were drawn early, and again a small act of defiance signaled the charge. The bourgeois society of le Pont was centered, typically, around the parish church, whose Angelus bells called all right-thinking townspeople (notably innocent young girls) to pious meditation. The Mercenaires, however, worshiped at a shrine belonging to a very different myth. The nubile Piroune, in particular, was drawn to the quay instead of the church, and one fateful evening she jingled the little bells on the buoy at the very moment the Angelus was sounding. Though Ma-Tante-la-Veuve would not have believed it, the narrator claims that this was not a gesture of contempt, but one of affirmation:

> [L]a Piroune, à cette époque de sa vie, ne cherchait dans les bateaux que des souvenirs, une sorte de mémoire-hommage à l'ancêtre. Elle se rendait au quai comme Marie-Rose et Jeanne-Mance [two of Ma-Tante-la-Veuve's many respectable nieces] à la niche de Marie-Immaculée: en pèlerinage. Cette orpheline de père et de mère semblait s'accrocher à son passé, faute d'avenir, à son lignage tout plein de mystère et de faits glorieux qu'elle revivait là sur sa bouée.

Indeed, the first of the Mercenaires had surfaced generations before in some mysterious fashion from the sea, had braved nature and the local owner to establish his brood permanently on top of the butte, and had passed down both his affinity for the sea and his rejection of conventions to his many descendants, now mostly women. As her male progenitor had emerged from the sea, la Piroune's own mother, Barbe-la-Jeune, had disappeared into it after saving the lives of some sailors stranded on ice floes by a sudden thaw.

The motif of the sea is all-pervasive in this novel (and prominent in the two others), but in contradictory ways. It gives birth and brings death. It promises hope (the vigil of la Piroune at the quay, where passing sailors come to meet her and often stay), and inflicts despair (la Bessoune's efforts to drown herself after her young priest/lover has apparently done just that). It beckons to far-off lands (the Irish sailor, "Tom Thumb," finds it an almost irresistible lure), and validates the regeneration of the entrenched Mercenaires (la Bessoune is born nine months after her mother, la Piroune, heroically saves a child snared in some ship's rigging and celebrates with the cheering assembled sailors). Neither exclusively male nor female in its symbolism, it is a self-complete, eternal, mystical life force, permeating all Acadian myth and legend. La Bessoune, twinless twin of an unknown father, is indeed a child of the sea, whose wildness and freedom she fully incarnates. Like the rest of her line, she will not be mastered by mere ordinary mortals and their silly laws, any more than they can dictate to the restless waves of the unending sea.

As a child la Bessoune puts up with the discipline of Church and school only as much and as long as she pleases, then abandons both. With adolescence she steps easily into the footsteps of her mother, selling contraband liquor and offering the bounty of her own sensuous nature to passing sailors. La Piroune and la Bessoune do not so much challenge the institutions of le Pont as ignore them, with an insouciance that often leaves Ma-Tante-la-Veuve in a state of spluttering frustration. The mere existence of the Mercenaires is an intolerable affront to the well-ordered universe of le Pont, whose futile efforts to control them result in constant, inevitable confrontation.

While the Mercenaire women thwart Ma-Tante-la-Veuve mainly by attracting most of her potential male allies to their side through sheer joyous sensuality, their ultimate ironic triumph comes on the widow's own supposed home ground: the domain of the spirit. Like everything else in le Pont, charity has been institutionalized. At a yearly "auction" held by the parish church, the destitute are assembled and farmed out to whatever families bid the lowest amount and promise to provide for them. One year, a truly pathetic case disturbs the smug rhythm of the auction: Henri à Vital, a once-popular local *raconteur* who had gone off for adventure to the States and was now back, a poor paralytic wreck, finds no takers. Ma-Tante-la-Veuve and the others are willing enough to do their Christian duty for the elderly and sickly, who can be counted upon not to survive beyond a

decent interval. But who, the sweating auctioneer suddenly realized, would take on the wheelchair-bound Henri à Vital, "pas un vieillard encore, ni tout à fait un déshérité, qui mangerait ses trois repas par jour et pouvait vivre encore des années?"

Into the silence that follows steps la Piroune, prodded by la Bessoune, who offers to take Henri à Vital—for nothing. Ma-Tante-la-Veuve, nearly apoplectic, tries to sidetrack this scandalous turn of events, but the new young curate, overriding his stunned pastor, vigorously supports the right of the poor to go off with whomever they choose. Henri à Vital, predictably, heads right for the Cordes-de-Bois, as do a pair of orphans who have clung instinctively to la Piroune's welcoming skirtfolds.

The narrator describes the sweet taste of vengeance the whole affair leaves in the mouths of the Mercenaires as they savor the discomfiture of their archenemy:

> Effectivement, le vicaire avait le pied sur celui de son curé, c'est la Bessoune qui l'a vu. Et elle sourit, la Bessoune. Un sourire qu'elle flanqua sous le nez de la Veuve en plein mitan de l'estrade de l'encan des pauvres. Tout était à l'envers, ce jour-là: les chenapans et les vieux renards qui faisaient leurs Pâques à la Trinité occupaient la tribune de l'église: les filles à matelots narguaient le Tiers-Ordre et les confréries; les pauvres achetaient les pauvres; et voilà que le vicaire marchait sur les pieds de son curé.

> On a dit que la Bessoune avait été saisic alors d'un tel élan d'éblouissement et de reconnaissance, qu'elle aurait sauté au cou du jeune prêtre, là, à la face de toute la paroisse qui en amait fait: aah!

This incident, with its climactic position near the end of the novel, underscores an interesting aspect of the question of womanhood in this particular Maillet universe. For Ma-Tante-la-Veuve the sexual behavior of the Mercenaires is a thing apart, a sin-in-itself, a violation of all the old guilt-inducing strictures of Church and polite society. For la Piroune and la Bessoune, however, sexual gratification is not an avenue into which they are reluctantly channeled for want of freedom, but a perfectly natural manifestation of the freedom they already joyously feel. As human beings, and specifically as women, they are whole beings of free-spirited openheartedness, no more self-conscious about the sharing of their bodies than they are about sharing family loyalty or the maternal warmth to which the poor and the abandoned are instinctively drawn. The struggle they are forced to wage is not within themselves, but against an embittered foe who cannot even understand, much less successfully prevent, the totality of their freedom, both defined by and expressed through their specific nature as women.

We see in Pélagie-la-Charrette the same harmony between a passion for freedom and strong womanly traits of the most traditional sort. Survivor (unlike her husband) of the sack of Grand-Pré at the time of the Great Acadian Dispersion, she has seen friends and relatives strewn all up and down the Atlantic coast and has spent fifteen years tied alongside black slaves to the plough of a Georgia planter. When she finally decides she has had enough, her revolt is inspired in equal measure by heroism of soul—strong, brave, decisive, bent on action—and by a vivid belief in her critical role as surviving mother of a whole race. The Cart of Life that she sets plunging northward on the path to liberty is also a warmly enveloping rolling home, full of the weak and defenseless, crammed with pots and pans, sheltering the pitiful remnants of a nearly exterminated generation. Hopelessness and suffocation are not, however, related to the dark interior of Pélagie's wagon, but to the monotonous closed circle traced by the Georgia planter's plough, the mud that nearly sucks the wagon under in Salem, and the frenetic, aimless charge of Bélonie's Cart of Death. Pélagie's womanhood is as traditional as a tigress fighting to save her cubs and as liberated as the warrior hero who saves a nation. It is the essential context of her being, the condition that gives form and meaning to her epic quest for life and freedom—not a contradiction but an affirmation.

The only power strong enough to distract Pélagie even momentarily from her relentless drive northward is the call of the nearby sea—here, as elsewhere in Maillet, a mysterious atavistic force of compelling power for all Acadians. Both progenitor and protective mother, master of nature and alluring mistress, proof of freedom and assurance of continuity, the sea links man and woman, past and future, life and eternity. Tempted as she sometimes is to divert her route towards its magical embrace, Pélagie sees it as above all a guaranteeing sign of her odyssey's ultimate success: "La mer restait leur plus sûr lien avec l'Acadie du Nord. On peut s'égarer dans la forêt, ou se cogner le front aux monts; mais la mer du nord ne saurait aboutir qu'aux pays."

We have seen the strength of Maillet's assertive women, but what of the men in their worlds? In all three novels the important role of chief antagonist is given to another woman (though in **Les Cordes-de-Bois** and **Mariaagélas** these women may, through their widowhood, represent an institutionalized, bourgeois, male-dominated society). There are, however, several important male characters in these novels, and there are—perhaps surprisingly—very few instances of hostility in the relations between them and the epic heroines. A few of the men are subjects of mild scorn, like the simple-minded soldier Bidoche and the informer Ferdinand in *Mariaagélas,* or the strait-laced pastor in **Les Cordes-de-Bois.** Some are sympathetic but clearly secondary characters, such as Maria's bootlegging partner le Grand Vital and the stream of men captivated and lured to the butte by the Mercenaires.

Of greatest interest, however, are the examples of genuine respect and affection between the epic heroines and certain men around them. Hinted at in the family loyalty of Mariaagélas, which extends even to her rough-spoken father, this kind of warm relationship blossoms more clearly in **Les Cordes-de-Bois.** Two of la Bessoune's "conquests" are most unlikely partners: "Tom Thumb," the homesick Irish sailor always going back off to sea—except the last time—and the earnest young curate.

The latter, first drawn to the butte by the desire to convert the lawless Mercenaires, soon falls under their spell. They, and particularly la Bessoune, seem to possess already all the joy, selflessness, and freedom that he has come to preach. After long months of pleasure on the butte and scandal in the village, the priest is reported one night to have stepped off the bridge into the dark sea. As reported by Catoune, another Mercenaire and the only witness, his parting words are a confession of guilt to the village charge that for all his natural virtues he has not led a single soul to God: "C'est Ma-Tante-la-Veuve qu'avait raison . . . qu'il a dit." To this Catoune adds her own assessment: "Fallit qu'il mettit l'océan entre lui pis le monde . . . fallit qu'il éteignit le feu . . . le feu qui y brûlait les boyaux." When the heartbroken Bessoune tries soon thereafter to join her lost lover at the bottom of the sea, she is saved by Tom Thumb, now a permanent inhabitant of the Cordes-de-Bois. His healing compassion, inspired by the Mercenaires' own rough-hewn love, thus completes the redemptive cycle. In a final, gentle benediction, a report later filters back that the curate did not drown after all but has been spotted on a ship bound for Rome.

Tom Thumb, as we have noted, comes to rest at the Cordes-de-Bois only after innumerable short stays followed by renewed sea voyages. The narrator's commentary on his ultimate decision to stay explains what the spirit of the Mercenaires, and the Acadia they symbolize for him, has come to mean in his life:

> Vous aviez ciu, vous, qu'il allait partir comme ca, le Tom Thumb? quitter un pays qui lui rendait son Irlande transposée et transfigurée, pour une Irlande réelle et misérable qui mourait de faim? Allez donc! C'est en Amérique que l'Irlande est belle. Et c'est en Acadie que Tom Thumb pourrait en rêver à son aise.
>
> Il s'ébroua, le petit matelot, et offrit sa plus splendide grimace à la Bessoune.

"Moi pis le grand Brendan," qu'il dit, "on ira par terre et mer chercher les héros: les géants, les saints, les navigueux, les sorciers, les holy men . . . et on juchera tous ces salauds sur le faît des Cordes-de-Bois. Pis ça sera là le centre du monde," qu'il fit.

La Bessoune ne répondit pas. Mais Charlie Boudreau jure qu'elle a mis sa main dans celle de Tom Thumb, et qu'ils sont partis tous les deux par les dunes vers les Cordes-de-Bois.

The end of Tom Thumb's lifelong search for mythical Celtic heroes has come in the undemanding affection of the outcast Mercenaires, for whom love is sharing, not dependency. Like freedom and heroism, it is not to be found in some distant, inaccessible place, but within the soul.

No one could be less dependent than the determined Pélagie-la-Charrette, who takes her vocation as epic heroine very seriously. Others defer to her natural leadership without question, as when, on a day when she decides to give her flagging troup a pep talk. "I'Acadie entière lève des yeux bleus suppliants sur son chef qui déjà s'empare de la tribune." When she has finished, "elle redescend de la tribune en se drapant dans sa cape comme un consul romain dans sa toge." The narrator notes the stirring effect of her speech on the little band of travelers: "Ce jour-là, on l'aurait couronnée de lauriers, la Pélagie, si on avait été en saison." Her admiring friend, Captain Broussard dit Beausoleil, characterizes her thus: "Quelle femme, cette Pélagie! capable à elle seule de ramener un peuple au pays. De le ramener à contre-courant."

Yet the two most cherished friends of this Pélagie—heroine, leader, object of admiration—are men. Though her relationships with Bélonie-le-Vieux and with Captain Broussard dit Beausoleil are very different, each is rooted in love of a very special kind. Bélonie, noted *croniqueur* described as already old at the outset of the trek, brings out Pélagie's protective instincts: "maternal" would not be too strong a word. Her youth contrasts with his age, her strength and vigor with his feebleness, his black cart of despair—of resignation to death—with her Cart of Life. Pélagie, who must have strength enough for them both, refuses to leave Bélonie behind: "Pélagie n'aurait pas eu le coeur de laisser derrière le doyen des déportés, même s'il devait traîner avec lui jusqu'à la Grand' Prée [sic] sa charrette fantôme."

Onwards she prods and encourages him, mile after mile, until at last along the coast of Massachusetts the miracle occurs. The *Grand' Goule* (formerly the deportation ship, *Pembroke*, seized from the English by the exiles themselves) intercepts Pélagie's wagon near Salem. Captain Beausoleil hails the straggling band and proudly presents one of his crew: young Bélonie, grandson of Bélonie and unsuspected survivor of the Great Dispersion. Pélagie's obstinate determination to keep the old man alive is now abruptly vindicated; the death wagon becomes a pointless relic, and Bélonie-le-Vieux joins the ranks of Life. Maillet, through her narrator, uses an astonishingly effective reversed sex-role image to convey the intensity of Bélonie's joy at that moment:

Le ciel lui-même a dû ce jour-là enregistrer le cri du capitaine Beausoleil-Broussard, puis le renvoyer rebondir à la tête de Bélonie-le-Vieux qui le reçut comme un coup de pied au ventre. Si jamais un homme depuis le début des temps, a éprouvé l'ombre d'une douleur de l'enfantement, c'est le Bélonie de la charrette. A cent ans, ou presque, il venait de mettre au monde sa lignée.

Pélagie and the gallant Beausoleil have a very different sort of relationship. She often turns to him for the same sort of strength and moral support that Bélonie seeks from her. The first meeting of Pélagie and Beausoleil after the Dispersion, when the *Grand' Goule* comes into port as Pélagie's wagon is passing through Charlestown, shows the depth of their mutual affection:

Le front du capitaine se déride et ses joues éclatent dans un large rire à l'ancienne comme Pélagie n'en a point entendu depuis le temps. Alors les bras de cette femme éperdue se referment sur son coeur pour le garder au chaud et l'empêcher de bondir hors du coffre: ce rire vient du passé, mais point de l'Au-delà. Et de la poitrine de cette veuve d'Acadie qui traîne depuis tant d'années une plaie ouverte, s'arrache un cri que même les morts auront entendu:

"Il est en vie!"

From then on Beausoleil is Pélagie's guiding star, paralleling at sea the route of her wagon on land. Their reunions at a succession of coastal points are so many marks of progress along Pélagie's path to Acadia. Beausoleil helps save her foundering cart in the Salem swamp and cheers her when her courage wavers. At their last rendezvous before her final push through Maine, Pélagie measures the extent of her debt to Beausoleil and the depths of her affection and gratitude:

Il était là, son capitaine, son chevalier, son héros, l'homme qui avait par trois fois risqué sa vie pour elle, qui avait calé dans la vase mouvante pour la troisième fois qui est toujours la dernière, pour elle, pour les siens, et à la fin pour sa charrette. C'est lui à la fin qui l'avait sauvée, sa charrette, lui qui s'était agrippé aux ridelles, à la vie, à la mort.

Et elle se serra contre lui, se berça la tête au creux

de ses épaules en murmurant des gloussements et des mots qu'il n'entendait pas.... Il avait risqué sa vie pour elle qui en échange avait offert la sienne. Leur double vie en otage l'un pour l'autre. Plus rien n'effacerait ça dans le ciel. La charrette à jamais en serait le gage.

The bond suggested here is beyond the sexual, though it involves mutual self-giving, profound union, and regeneration. The same is true of the love that links Pélagie with Bélonie—clearly not sexual, yet bursting with the seed of rebirth, of new life. Both Bélonie and Beausoleil disappear at the end—Bélonie into the forest, Beausoleil out to sea—and thus quickly pass into the domain of legend. Pélagie herself is the source and inspiration of that legend as she and her Cart of Life at last go to their final rest in the soil of the new Acadia. Thus Acadia itself becomes the heaven of the emerging myth, the medium of ultimate union between Pélagie and the two men she loves. Pélagie is the brightest star in the new constellation, neither diminishing Bélonie by offering him her strong protection nor herself diminished by accepting the same from Beausoleil. She is the epic heroine whose quest for life and freedom has given significance to the lives of the others, and it is her womanhood that shapes that quest. Her triumph is in defining the roles of the others without limiting them.

> **All the heroines in these Maillet novels could in some sense be symbols of Acadia—a small nation, weak in the eyes of a world that knows only physical force, but strong in her desire to live and flourish despite all obstacles.**
> —*Marjorie A. Fitzpatrick*

Pélagie herself asserts the primacy she attaches to womanhood by selecting her daughter Madeleine rather than one of her sons to carry on after her death. Near Pélagie's grave in the new Acadia, Madeleine takes up the challenge to renew the race and "refaire l'Acadie":

C'est tout près, dans la vallée de Memramcook, qu'elle abattrait son premier arbre, Madeleine LeBlanc, sous le regard ahuri de son homme et de ses frères qui n'en croient point leurs yeux.... Allez, flancs mous, c'est icitte que je nous creusons une cave et que je nous bâtissons un abri! ... Madeleine, digne rejeton de la charrette par la voie des femmes.

"La voie des femmes"—the royal road to the rebirth of Acadia! All the heroines in these Maillet novels could in some sense be symbols of Acadia—a small nation, weak in

the eyes of a world that knows only physical force, but strong in her desire to live and flourish despite all obstacles. Refusing the right of others either to condemn her to death or to dictate the conditions of her life, this Acadia triumphs over her foes by courage, boldness, humor, shrewdness, and nobility of spirit. There is heroism in her struggle, but also a saving mischievousness that excludes excessive solemnity. She is Maria the bootlegger, refusing the life of the shops, thumbing her nose at the fate others have reserved for her. She is la Piroune, using the buoy bells to broadcast the invitation of a generous heart across the open sea. She is above all Pélagie, hitching up her hem and setting off in a dilapidated wagon towards life and liberty. Her traditionalism does homage to a past born in the Celtic mists of the sea and tempered in the fire at Grand-Pré; her liberation creates a nation that determines its boundaries by the location of its soul; her nationalism is a reflection of the universal human quest for life and freedom. One may smile at her indulgently, but always with admiring affection, for Acadia is still living her epic—glorious, and, in its way, consummately female.

Bernard Arésu (essay date 1986)

SOURCE: "*Pélagie-la-Carrette* and Antonine Maillet's Epic Voices," in *Explorations: Essays in Comparative Literature*, edited by Makoto Ueda, University Press of America, 1986, pp. 211-226.

[*In the following essay Arésu traces the development of Maillet's artistic voice and vision.*]

In 1979, Antonine Maillet, the Canadian novelist, playwright and critic, received the French establishment's most prestigious literary award, the Prix Goncourt. This award was the capstone of a series of widely acclaimed and brilliantly crafted works that had preceded her last book, *Pélagie-la-Charrette.* It may first be appropriate to remark that her first novel was not, as the ethnocentric publisher of *Pélagie* may lead the unsuspecting reader to believe, *Mariaagélas,* actually her ninth volume. As of 1973, the date of *Mariaagélas'* first edition, Mrs. Maillet had indeed already three other novels in print, as well as a collection of short stories, two plays, a humoristic presentation of the history and civilization of Acadia in the form of a very unconventional tourist guide, not to mention her published doctoral dissertation on Rabelais and the oral traditions of Acadia. Between *Mariaagélas* and *Pélagie-la-Charrette,* the author published another three plays, one of which the now famous *La Sagouine,* and three novels. One of the latter, *Les Cordes-de-Bois* narrowly missed, in 1978 the Prix Goncourt which Mrs. Maillet was awarded the following year.

Published on both sides of the Atlantic, the Canadian writer has thus been recognized as a major voice in world literature and contributed much needed rejuvenation to a contemporary French fiction perhaps too often mired in the type of formal solipsism generated by the New Novel. Mrs. Maillet's works also attest to the most significant development in post-1950 French literature, that of francophonic writings and their relevance not only to academic study but in the very terms of their universal implications and concerns. Hers is thus a complex and rich production which gained the recognition it deserves only belatedly and perhaps for sadly well-known reasons: too many francophonic works still have to take the inevitable detour of French publishing houses, the sole guarantee of prestigious exposure; it is significant that Antonine Maillet's fame spread only *after* the publication of four of her works by Grasset. Moreover, the traditional focus, in studies on francophonic Canadian literature, on "Québécoise" production, often fails to take into consideration such brilliant creations as those Maillet has woven around the history, civilization and legends of Acadia.

Over such two richly productive decades of literary endeavors, a thematic evolution seems to emerge, from the early novels of individual quest to the epic narrations of the more recent works. Between the opposite poles of this creative trajectory, moreover, another two phases clearly stand out: Mrs. Maillet's masterful adaptation, on the one hand, of the infinite resources of the folk-tale in such novels as **Don l'Orignal** and in the short stories of **Par Derrière chez mon père,** and, on the other hand, a series of plays, among which the internationally acclaimed **La Sagouine** and the lesser-known but equally important **Evangeline Deusse** represent prominent landmarks. A rapid survey of these various productive stages helps delineate the unique kind of epic and mythic aura Mrs. Maillet's last novel exudes.

In **Pointe-aux-Coques** (1958) and **On a mangé la dune** (1962), the author set out to explore the sociological, thematic, and, above all, linguistic parameters within which her subsequent works would develop. Very much like the **Pélagie-la-Charrette** of seventeen years later, **Pointe-aux-Coques** deals with the theme of self-discovery and the symbolic journey of returning. The heroine of the novel, a young American school-teacher of Acadian ancestry, discovers in a small Canadian village the rich and complex fabric of a society in transition. Love, death, cultural identity, the conflict between tradition and modernism, especially in the inexorably changing area of social realities, the lucid and quietly humorous analysis of human foibles, the gripping dramas of everyday life, all coalesce into a fictional tableau already foreshadowing many of the preoccupations of works to come. The novel's stylistic hesitancy, however, stems from the author's too uniform a reliance on an academic language frequently at odds with the reality of the milieu depicted.

The lyrical and poetic tone at work in the first novel will

nevertheless and again permeate the prose of **On a mangé la dune,** a nostalgic and appollonian evocation of childhood and adolescence. Focusing as it does on the passage from adolescence into adulthood, the novel does not only concern itself with the problem of spiritual integrity and maturation, with metaphysical realities apprehended through the initiatory experience of growing, but also represents a step toward artistic development, the strengthening of inspiration and form within an ever sturdier framework of fictional creativity to which the fictional mode of the dionysian tale will bring full blossoming.

In her **Rabelais et les traditionals populaires en Acadie** (1971), Antonine Maillet had conducted an ethnological analysis of the oral structures of Acadian popular traditions. The concurrent integration of the "parlure acadienne" in her creative works constituted an important turning point: the author was now fully apprehending the fictional and linguistic appropriateness of oral traditions to her subject matter as well as to her own artistic temperament. **Par Derrière chez mon père** and **Don l'Orignal,** both published for the first time in 1972, best exemplify the coming of age of her narrative mode. The short pieces of **Par Derrière chez mon père,** which sketch out in concisely self-contained fashion many of the plots and characters of subsequent works, now unfold with solid serenity within the timeless creative mode of ancestral tales. But nowhere as in **Don l'Orignal,** a story of socio-economic rivalry set in the microcosmic universe of a tiny island, and inspired by both Rabelais and Voltaire, does the art of the tale reach such consummate perfections: comedy, literary parody, humor, farce, social and moral satire intermingle in thirty-five short chapters seething with the enlightening effervescence of philosophical laughter. The book constitutes what can easily be considered Mrs. Maillet's first masterpiece, a novel that also established the epic mold in which many subsequent works will be cast.

It was inevitable that the narrative vivaciousness of Rabelaisian prose would find an even more spontaneous outlet in the dynamic universe of the stage. **Les Crasseux,** first published in 1968, adapted with considerable dramatic strength the plot of **Don l'Orignal.** In the absence of the novel's pervasive satirical point of view, the play ludically focuses on the dynamics of confrontation between two rival groups whose characterization makes for unforgettable social comedy. But more significantly, the author's artistic endeavors now point to novel preoccupations. Quasi "engagés," her writings have become strategically conscious of their audience. And the stage's dionysian outbursts underscore more and more the socio-philosophical meaning of laughter. While steering clear of the ponderous strictures of political moralizing, Mrs. Maillet's dramas display, indeed, persistent shades of Brechtian determinism.

By the time **Mariaagélas** was published, in 1973, the seeds of Mrs. Maillet's best creations were blossoming into superb prose epics. This richest phase of her creative evolution yielded four novels in which her affinities with Rabelais, her epic and ritualistic apprehension of human destiny and her masterly characterization of female protagonists won her international recognition and the courtship of Canada's and France's most prestigious publishing houses.

By the time *Mariaagélas* was published, in 1973, the seeds of Mrs. Maillet's best creations were blossoming into superb prose epics.
—*Bernard Arésu*

Mariaagélas represented her first full-fledged novelistic portraiture of the heroine as rebel, a grown-up and pugnacious avatar of Radi, the adolescent protagonist of *On a mangé la dune*. The book merits critical attention not only for its magnificent fresco of ancestral traditions, but also for the brilliant mordancy of its social satire, its humanistic ideology and comico-dramatic characterization of a fiercely independent woman during the rum-running days of Prohibition.

Emmanuel à Joseph à Dâvit (1975), tonally autonomous from the novels of this period, harks back to the quiet inspiration of *Par Derrière chez mon père,* but symbolically juxtaposes, in the North-South axis of two neighboring villages, the quietly traditional life of the land and that of the sea, the latter suddenly threatened by the relentless encroachments of modern industrial interests. Peacefully counterpointing this conflict, a nativity story unfolds, ostensibly patterned on the Biblical model, but whose mythical undertones throw a new light on Mrs. Maillet's use of religious themes, and significantly counterbalances her abrasive satire, in other works, of unbending and dotardy religion.

Les Cordes-de-Bois centers on the truculent and sympathetically caricatural portraiture of a matriarcal bevy (the Mercenaire family,) and chronicles its hilariously eventful *démêlés* with the religious clan of contentiously prude Ma-Tante-la-Veuve. The gay satire and exhilarating lustfulness of the novel gave way, two years later, to *Pélagie-la-Charrette* (1979) and its dramatic account of the journey of dispersal and return of a group of Acadian exiles during the momentous years of 1755-1780. Immersed anew in the ancestral and historical traditions of her people, the narrator retraces, with phenomenal immediacy and Steinbeckian vigor their joys and sorrows, commingling history, legend, popular tales and age-old beliefs in a breathtaking succession of seventeen episodes. But in the last resort, the most impressive achievement of *Pélagie-la-Charrette* may be its mythic

vision, its ritualization of historical awareness and its figurative appropriation of primitive legends.

In dwelling on the dispersal of the Acadian people and the epic diaspora of a group of exiles, the novel's wider historical perspective thus subsumes and amplifies many of the key themes of previous works. More successfully than any of these works, though, *Pélagie-la-Charrette* exemplifies brilliant formal unity and linguistic autonomy, a triumphal "aboutissement" in light of the author's earlier inner struggle with the problem of language and cultural identity. Antonine Maillet once confided in an interview: "(Mon) premier (roman), *Pointe-aux-Coques,* est un petit roman que j'ai écrit en faisant tous les efforts pour ne pas écrire à l'acadienne, presque pour éteindre la personalité que chacun pouvait avoir . . . je m'efforçais d'écrire 'en francais'." It is precisely the opposite attitude, the pervasive reliance on the "parlure acadienne" and its spontaneous amalgamation into the historical but above all legendary and mythical strata of the novel that gives Maillet's narration such powerful impact.

Told from the point of view of oral tradition, the narrative of *Pélagie-la-Charrette* covers twenty-five years of exile of a group of Acadians, from 1755, the date of their systematic deportation and dispersal, to 1780, the date of their stealthy but victorious return. While one of Antonine Maillet's concerns is obviously to set the historical record straight, she does not choose to do so through the medium of purely politico-historical narration but through that of the popular epic chronicle, retracing historical events through the joys and tribulations and the collective consciousness of a whole people. While 1755 signalled the beginning of the dispersal, a central thematic motif referred to as "l'exil", "la Déportation", "le Grand Djéangement", or the euphemisitc "l'événement", the novel's narrative structure revolves around the homecoming journey to the promiscd land of the ancestors, la Grand' Prée, a journey of grief and sorrow as well as joy and self-discovery, above all an eventful experience of coming together and of recreation of group identity: "les gens, au départ, sont une famille, à l'arrivée, un peuple" Maillet recently remarked.

Two voices harmoniously blend in the narration of this oral chronicle, intermingling everyday occurrences, historical events, popular legends, dialogues and interpersonal conflicts into the flow of a strikingly dynamic epic. The ageless, earthily dialectal voice of an Acadian narrator-participant in the journey, in turn Pélagie herself, in turn a "conteux et défricheteux" without whom "l'histoire aurait trépassé à chaque tournant de siècle", pervades the whole novel. To this voice periodically responds the omniscient voice of a modern narrator, a voice nonetheless tonally and thematically in keeping with the storyteller's voice of popular tradition. *Pélagie-la-Charrette* owes its structural unity precisely to the narrative equilibrium that such a dual, complementary perspective provides. Moreover, the expressive dovetailing of two stylistic registers, actualizing as it does past experience, projects it into the realm of modern collective consciousness and opens the gate to the type of universalizing myth-making that successfully transcends the immediate socio-historical framework of reference.

By the time *Pélagie* was completed, Antonine Maillet's position on the validity of French Acadian as an artistic medium had radically changed. Of this coastal language, separate from the "joual" and distinct from the French-English "chiac" of the Moncton area, she avers: "Premierement je dis que c'est une langue. Je ne crois pas que l'acadien soit un patois. C'est une langue ancienne, désuète. On n'a rien inventé chez nous: tous les mots que j'emploie dans *Pélagie-la-Charrette,* à 99.5", sont des mots français, mais des mots d'ancien francais; Si je dis callouetter, si je dis aveindre, si je dis cobbi, si je dis chacunière, allez tout vérifier ça, c'est dans Rabelais, dans Villon, dans Marguerite de Navarre, et même dans Molière". Of *La Sagouine* and the lesser known play *Les Crasseux,* she had already indicated: "Je n'ai pas choisi la langue de *La Sagouine* ou des *Crasseux,* j'ai choisi la Sagouine et les crasseux. Ceux-là n'avaient pas le choix: ils devaient parler leur langue. Tout au plus en ai-je fait une transposition littéraire; comme est transposition toute langue écrite".

This notion of literary transposition perhaps best explains the kind of epic immediacy Maillet so successfully achieves in the novel. Early in the book, when admonishing her troops at the beginning of the journey of return, Pélagie's ostensibly unfelicitous choice of words elicits a tellingly vigorous vindication on the narrator's part, and one wonders to what extent such textual intrusions (for they are numerous in the novel) do not aim at the strategic pre-emption of the inflexible censorship of traditional stylistic propriety: "Elle avait mal choisi son image, Pélagie, et aurait mieux fait de parler de tabac ou de coton. Mais Pélagie ne choisissait pas ses images, elle les traînait avec elle depuis le pays. Un pays de mâts et de haubans, encadré de baies, balafré de fleuves, et tout emmuré d'aboiteaux. Les aboiteaux! Ce seul mot la mit en rut, Pélagie-la Charrette, et elle fouetta les boeufs".

Elsewhere Maillet states: "Trois-quarts des Acadiens sont nés les pieds dans l'eau," later adding: "vous me permettrez quand-même de vous donner en deux mots les raisons historiques qui ont fait se peupler les abords des rivières. Premièrement, les Acadiens ne disposaient que de bateaux pour tout moyen de transport; deuxièmement, ils vivaient de la pêche; troisièmement, ils devaient pouvoir se déplacer rapidement à l'approche des Anglais qui leur ont fait la chasse pendant plusieurs décennies après l'exil. A l'époque, les rivières étaient les grand' routes qui reliaient la forêt à la mer".

Summing up the historical condition of Maillet's characters, the narration of the endless journey from forest to sea and from sea to forest shows compulsive delving into the treasures of natural and animal tropes, as well as authorial predilection for symbolic evocations of a cosmic nature. Frequent assimilation of the characters' experience with animal or forest life pervade the novel, as in the characterization of the orphaned and lonesome Catoune: "la Catoune me pouvait s'égarer dans les bois, les bois qui avaient abrité et nourri sa prime enfance. Elle avait dans la peau le nord absolu, Catoune, comme d'autres le diapason. Et si l'on en croit Bélonie, elle aurait été la seule, ce jour-là, avec la boussole dans l'oeil." The frequent recurrence of "humer" and "flairer," likewise, graphically depicts the protagonists' ever so cautious progress throughout the forests of exile, and suggestively evokes the animalistic determination moving Pélagie's companions: "Mais pendant les joyeuses funérailles de cette Acadie du Nord, auxquelles trinquaient si joyeusement Lawrence, Winslow, Monckton, et le roi George dans toute sa joyeuse majesté, des lambeaux d'Acadie du Sud remontaient, tête entre les jambes, piaffant, suant et soufflant des deux narines, une Amérique qui n'entendit même pas grincer les essieux de la charrette."

While the "grincement" of poverty and suffering effectively points out, throughout the novel, the jarring note of quiet uphcaval and stubborn progress of the protagonists, the animal metaphor of the ox simultaneously conveys not only humorous self-mockery but a concurrent sense of dogged resolution and robust obstinancy. The novel's long march of joys and sorrows, likewise, remains closely associated with meteorological phases and natural cataclysms, as if cosmic moods were made to echo and dramatically underscore the whims of historical adversity. But perhaps most telling is the metaphorical designation of "défricheteux" or "défricheteux-de-parenté", ubiquitous under Maillet's pen and playing a central role in the vast fresco of her writings. For the expression, which designates those of the elders who keep track of the complex genealogical ramifications of various clans, figuratively and earthily comingles the function of oral tradition and that of attachment to the land, *sine qua non* conditions of Acadian survival.

In *On a mangé la dune* and in the tales of *Par derrière chez mon père,* Maillet had already revealed significant glimpses of the rich framework of inspiration that the reality and legends of Acadian coastal life were to represent in her fiction. Significantly, in the 1979 epic, the return to the land of the ancestors originates on an island, the Isle of Hope in northern Georgia, and the focus of the narration frequently shifts to the fate of Captain Beausoleil, to his sea adventures along the eastern coast during the American revolution: "Pendant qu'elle (Pélagie) dressait, barreau par barreau, les ridelles d'une charrette qui la ramèenait avec les siens au pays, là-bas en mer, une goéleete chargeait les restes d'un peuple, des côtes de la Nouvelle-Angleterreaux rives de la Nouvelle-France." The continuous superimposition of such realities reinforces that sense of idiolectal allegiance Maillet had once emphasized: "Il existe aussi (in Acadian French) des termes marins adaptés au language terrien: on va 'amarrer' ses souliers, on 'grée' une mariée, on 'frête' une voiture." "Et pour tout bâtiment Pélagie *gréa* une charrette" says the narrator in the first chapter of the novel (our emphasis); Pélagie herself will later announce "Demain au petit jour, je mettons le cap sur l'Acadie du Nord", and again later we are told that: "Après toutes ces années le coeur au sec, Pélagie laissa la brise du large lui minatter les joues et la peau de l'âme", in metaphorical constructs firmly anchoring human experience in the symbolic fabric of cosmic awareness.

The journey northward thus becomes both a historical occurrence and an experience of self-discovery, an assertion of cultural identity through the dialectical code of the group. On this subject, Maillet had already warned her reader, with delightfully incisive humor: "Ne vous méprenez pas (l'Acadien) parle francais; mais le sien. C'est une question de nuance." This archaic French of the late Middle Ages and of Rabelais symbolizes, in a sense, a striking phenomenon of cultural resistance, fighting as it does, unlike the joual and chiac dialects, against the encroachments of the language of the conquerors. To the modern reader, it provides not only a rich insight into the cultural and historical development of an ethnic group but, above all, the narrative expressiveness of numberless stylistic surprises, such as the phonetic evocativeness of "hucher" for "crier", "pigouiller" for "chatouiller", "sourlinguer" for "secouer", "tétines de souris" to designate an indigenous plant. Such stylistic particularities make for countless humorous episodes in the novel, and, more importantly, reinforce one of Mrs. Maillet's most fundamental creative impulses, the use of language as play, of words as ludic or agonistic structures textually re-enacting or mirroring individuals or collective trials and experience.

The following observations concerning two young men's brash but unsuccessful advances to the beautiful Catoune crisply illustrate, in the light vein, the author's superb manipulation of language to such ludic ends: "Les deux rescapés des Sauvages, durant ce temps-là, flairaient et humaient les cotillons, lançaient des phrases équivoques et pigouillaient à tort et à travers. A travers surtout. Et le jour où le beau Maxime, qui avait cru avec la disparition de son rival Jean retrouver le champ libre autour de Catoune, voulut traverser l'étoffe épaisse d'un corsage qui gardait le fruit défendu, il comprit qu'il venait de pigouiller à tort."

Beside such sonorous notations as "des huchements de Pélagie à ses commères d'exil," which evokes to this reader the jarring cacophony of a screeching flock of exotic birds, Maillet's prose teems with crisp and vivid comments, brisk observations amounting to unforgettable one shot portraits. "Et le vieux radoteux de Bélonie reprit son récit là même où le pied bot de Celina avait planté son point d'orgue," for instance, instantaneously and hilariously captures the perennial conflict between the incorrigibly garrulous characters of Bélonie the patriarch and Celina the limping midwife. The abrupt failure of Bourgeois' demands before Pélagie's fierceful determination are likewise expressed in a beautifully caricatural combination of onomatopeia, halting rhythm, and equine metaphor: "—Et je veux plus en entendre parler. Le Bourgeois se cabra, fit heu! puis se tut." Most memorable, however, is the phrasing of old Bélonie's patriarchal but rather rusty and mechanic progression toward Pélagie in the twelfth chapter of the novel, where "il fit jouer sur leurs gonds ses os quasi centenaires, et se dirigea vers Pélagie."

Typographically isolated as autonomous paragraphs, such statements naturally take on incisive theatrical expressiveness. Insofar as they display the dynamism and graphicness of Maillet's prose, its quickness to seize upon the humorous and the caricatural, the question of Rabelais's influence poses itself. While it is not within the scope of this paper to analyze Maillet's indebtedness to the sixteenth-century writer, some salient formal and thematic *affinities* deserve mention: the didactic role and causticity of laughter, the compulsive use of the burlesque, the grotesque and the scatological, the inclusion of the structures of the chronicle and of folk tale, the parodic nature of encyclopedic accumulations (of which we have numerous examples in ***Pélagie***), and above all the fictional reliance on folkloric and legendary material, as shown in gigantean characterization. All of these constitute not only the hallmark of Maillet's felicitous resurrection of a hallowed literary tradition, but also of effective incorporation of a larger framework of imagination, that of myth.

If, in its modern sense, myth symbolically projects a people's collective values and attempts to articulate its reality, Maillet's reliance on the rich legendary traditions of Acadia and her revival of ancient folk traditions attest to her imaginative propensity to mythically transcend historical reality and to strike roots in the rich humus of a pre-industrial consciousness made of "bribes d'images restées dans toutes les mémoires." The tale of the white whale and the golden ring, for instance, both scatological and initiatory, intertwines legendary and historical experience, that of intestinal engulfment and of entrapment in the dark, mazelike corridors of a Charleston prison. In turn, myth sacralizes historical experience, as does the Acadian "empremier," a term that effectively associates memories of early Acadian history and, from an etymological point of view, *ab origine* times. "Je m'inspire beaucoup de la tradition orale, mais dans la mesure où elle est vivante. La littérature orale a transmis des mythes, des croyances, des gestes, des drames, des héros populaires:

tout cela est la plus riche matière litéraire" significantly re-marked the writer.

At a higher degree of symbolization, her last novel ritual-izes historical experience into mythical visions of unusual lyrical quality. Primordial creation, rebirth and salvation from water and from fire, the mythical dance of Life and Death are central preoccupations that deserve indeed full critical recognition. As mythical a figure as Brecht's Pelagea Vlassova or Steinbeck's Ma Joad, with whom she shares so many features, Pélagie enacts, throughout her clan's initia-tory and reconstructive journey, many of the ritual gestures of an archetypal mother. In the end, the nocturnal symbol of her metonymic wagon, "logis primitif" and "signe de perénnité," triumphs over the most dramatic of all trials, the nyctomorphous threat of ruthless marshes, of "cette boue mouvante qui cherche à l'aspirer comme un gouffre béant."

The luxuriance of Antonine Maillet's literary imagination and of her textual strategies is indeed stupendous.
—*Bernard Arésu*

The luxuriance of Antonine Maillet's literary imagination and of her textual strategies is indeed stupendous. As this survey suggests, incorporation of oral traditions, ludic didac-ticism, socio-historical awareness, linguistic revivalism and universal myth-making constitute some of the more salient foundations of her works, and because of a rich career ex-tending now over twenty-three years, it is easier to appreci-ate the eminence of her contribution to the world of letters, what a critic has recently termed an "imposing presence." Very similar to that of other illustrious regionalists" (Faulkner's, Gionos's and Steinbeck's especially come to mind,) her vision is able to transcend the immediate sphere of native sources and, through the optimistic medium of self-derisive laughter, the catharsis of insane comedy and the overriding power of humanistic concerns, to explode in the type of pan-human statements of which only true art can par-take.

David Homel (review date June 1986)

SOURCE: "Antonine Maillet's Eternal Return of the Acadian Character," in *Quill & Quire,* Vol. 52, No. 6, June, 1986, p. 37.

[*In the review below, Homel praises* The Devil is Loose, *the English translation of* Crache-à-pic.]

Beginning in 1755 an event occurred that the Acadians, with

wry understatement, call *le grand dérangement*—"the big disruption"—their expulsion from their homeland in eastern Canada. Was the action directed from Britain, or was it a local initiative? Antonine Maillet, Acadia's best-known writer, is unsure which of the two versions is correct. But the themes of exile and return nourished her writing through-out her career as novelist and playwright. Two more of her novels were published in English translations last month: *The Devil Is Loose* by Lester & Orpen Dennys and *Mariaagélas* by Simon & Pierre. Though *Mariaagélas* was first published—in French—13 years before *Devil,* both books use the stuff of legend and oral tradition to express timeless Acadian themes.

Maillet lives on the avenue Antonine-Maillet in Montreal's Outremont district. Few writers in this country can boast of streets named on their behalf. "It was a product of circum-stances," she explains. "Six or seven years ago there was a drive to find French names for some of the streets in this part of town. I had just won the Prix Goncourt, so some neighbor mentioned my name." Having your street named after you while you're still living on it may be partly an em-barrassment and partly an honor; Maillet takes it mostly not as a personal triumph but as a blow struck for literature.

These triumphs and others—including a dozen honorary doc-torates to add to the Ph.D. in literature she earned from Université Laval—have come to a writer from Bouctouche, New Brunswick, a town on the Northumberland Strait, fac-ing Prince Edward Island. She attended school in Bouctouche and in the late 1940s became one of the first students at Collège Notre Dame d'Acadie in Moncton. Her schooling included reading both Racine and Shakespeare in the original, and today Maillet says that she largely learned to write through reading. She still has a residence in Bouctouche—fittingly, a lighthouse—where she spends the summers eating lobster, sailing, and writing.

Though her first novel was set in Acadia, it was not specifi-cally Acadian in subject-matter or style. Only since the 1971 publication and staging of *La Sagouine,* the story of a char-woman who was memorably interpreted for the stage by Viola Léger, has Maillet come to the forefront as the voice of Acadia. She has been followed by an entire wave of Acadian novelists and poets. Maillet's country, by her own admission, exists more in time than in space. After the loss of the Acadian territory in 1755, Maillet points out, there was no land to identify with; there was a sense of nation-hood, an ideology, a mentality, but no territory.

Enter the only figure capable of making a country out of all this once more: the writer. "Perhaps there may be little chance for Acadia's survival, perhaps her virtues are ex-hausted. But when I write, the old Acadia surfaces again." Certainly Maillet has given us a dreamed Acadia in her books, but perhaps this invented land is truer than the one we can see today on a drive along the coast from Caraquet to Shédiac. But all writers are in the business of transforming our vision of the place they come from, and in that area Maillet excels, for she has made her readers believe that Acadia really is those legendary figures and goings-on between the covers of her books.

There's no shortage of legendary characters and occurrences in her latest novel *The Devil Is Loose,* first published in French in 1984 and now available in Philip Stratford's English translation, published by Lester & Orpen Dennys. It's an old-fashioned story with real and concocted ghosts, raging seas, mysterious portents, village gossips, wise fools: the entire village microcosm. The book is set during American Prohibition, a time when Acadians (and not only Acadians) were fighting hard times by providing contraband liquor to their thirsty neighbours to the south. At one point the novel's swashbuckling heroine Crache-à-pic (literally, "straight-spitter") dresses up as a nun to cross the United States border on a mercy mission, an event that happened just that way, according to Crache-à-pic's creator. The heroine has sworn to operate her own family-run bootlegging operation, flying in the face of Dieudonné, supplier for the Mob in the States, including Al Capone, whom she hopes will turn up one foggy night off the Acadian shores. There are marvelous portraits of village life as Crache-à-pic and Dieudonné try to outfox each other under the indulgent eye of the local constable. But then Quicksilver, an officer who wants to make the law stick, arrives on the scene, and the inevitable happens: the untameable Crache-à-pic and the intensely upright Quicksilver fall in love. Their idyll enchants the village, and all goes well until a shotgun blast from the Dieudonné gang's boat puts an end to the unlikely couple's happiness. "It's a lot like Acadia's history," Maillet muses. "There's a lot of clowning and buffoonery and nonsense, but it turns out badly in the end."

The book gives Maillet's most typical Acadian characters a stage on which to strut their stuff. Never ones to be rushed, they are nevertheless equipped with a strong sense of timing and a tenacious patience. Their humor is like that of underdog peoples everywhere: a little defensive, never loud, always wry. And though they might be distrustful of outsiders at the start, they jump at the chance to roll up the rug and celebrate. *Mariaagélas* (translated by Ben-Zion Shek) tells a similar story about Maria, the daughter of Gélas, who turns to smuggling during Prohibition when she loses her job after punching a schoolteacher in the nose (the teacher had failed to give her kid sister the part of the Virgin Mary in the school play). It explores similar themes but without the love interest. There are boot-leggers, ghosts, and ersatz nuns, though with less of the appeal to tradition than in *The Devil Is Loose.* But in both books, the evil-doer is brought to justice in a particularly Acadian fashion.

In *Devil* Dieudonné and his cronies are brought to trial, but the villagers, including those closest to Crache-à-pic, suddenly lose the faculty of speech and forget where they were the night of the crime. The trial is made a shambles; justice, at least of the conventional variety, is roundly mocked. But this seeming non-co-operation by the villagers is actually designed to give Crache-à-pic the right occasion to set her trap. She inflicts a much more apt punishment on Dieudonné (which will not be wholly revealed here) based on the Acadian themes of exile both abroad and in one's own land. The village has spoken; the popular will has been done. That's the genius of Acadia, Maillet says. "An outlawed people will put themselves above the law."

> **Winning the prize [the Prix Goncourt in 1979] opened the European continent for Maillet and raised her to the status of a fully accepted French-language writer.**
> *—David Homel*

Antonine Maillet won the Prix Goncourt in 1979 for *Pélagie-la-charette* (Doubleday published the English translation by Philip Stratford, *Pélagie: The Return to a Homeland,* in 1982). It was the first time France's most prestigious literary award had been won by someone not a native of France. Winning the prize opened the European continent for Maillet and raised her to the status of a fully accepted French-language writer. "The Goncourt gave me the assurance that I had really written a book in French!" Maillet laughs. "It was also a seal of approval for the Acadian language." This *lettre de noblesse* is especially important, for it chased away any question that Acadian writing and language were merely quaint, folkloric leftovers from an earlier time. Even if she has received approval from Paris, Maillet is no less Acadian now than before the Goncourt. There's a moral in the story: she won this internationally prestigious prize by being as resolutely local as possible.

Getting her language into English has been no small task, and we have Stratford to thank for delivering her two memorable heroines, Pélagie and Crache-à-pic, into lively English. Recalls Stratford, "Maillet didn't want a literal translation. She would tell me, 'Go ahead, be free.' That invitation to freedom let me be more inventive." What Stratford did with that freedom was to go back to what he calls his "treasure-hoard of past expressions" gathered from years of reading sea stories by C. S. Forester, Conrad, Kipling, and other sources, and create a salty, slightly archaic style that would recall the Atlantic provinces in the 1930s while avoiding the trap of a "dialect" translation.

After completing *The Devil Is Loose,* Maillet took a year off from writing to teach, read, travel, and lecture. Getting back to the grindstone proved difficult. She wanted to resume writing but it took another full year before she could completely limber up. But when her writer's block broke, it broke with a vengeance. Recently she completed a play and currently is finishing off a novel for fall 1986 publication with Leméac in Montreal.

Maillet works in a converted attic in her house, and a glance into her studio reveals the absence of a usual piece of equipment: there is no typewriter. She writes with a pencil in large notebooks of graph paper, a more effective way, perhaps, to reach back to the mythical Acadia and make it live for us again.

Paul G. Socken (essay date Summer 1987)

SOURCE: "The Bible and Myth in Antonine Maillet's *Pélagie-la-Charrette,*" in *Studies in Canadian Literature,* Vol. 12, No. 2, Summer, 1987, pp. 187-98.

[*In the following essay, Socken delineates in great detail the mythical elements and biblical parallels in Maillet's* Pélagie-la-Charrette.]

The parallels between Pélagie's return to Acadia from exile in Georgia and events in the Hebrew Bible are striking and revealing. The story is the Biblical account of the exodus in a modern context enhanced and reinforced by elements of mythology.

The many similarities to the Biblical account are in some cases direct, in others, indirect. I propose to make these parallels clear and to suggest associations with some major motifs of world mythology in order to show how the dominant theme and images confer a larger—possibly universal—meaning on the narrative.

The novel represents the fusion of chronological time (Acadian history) and mythical time (the eternal cycle of perpetual life), and of Biblical imagery and that of ancient mythology. So too there is fusion on a spiritual level of the profane and the sacred, as the Acadians are portrayed as deceptively irreverent, for their rebirth reaffirms the principle of destiny and divine mission.

The general structure of the narrative loosely follows the Biblical text. The first chapters introduce us to Pélagie, Bélonie and the other characters, describe their situation, and establish the purpose of their journey, just as Genesis describes the Patriarchs and their times and points to an historical mission. The novel then proceeds to chronicle the journey itself including the fighting and rebellion, corresponding to the "deliverance" and "apostasy" of Exodus. The remainder of the novel, except for the last two chapters and the epilogue, concerns the consolidation of the wanderers into a people, paralleling the same phenomenon in Leviticus and Numbers. The final part narrates Pélagie's address to the people, her death and her people's arrival in Acadia, as Deuteronomy recounts Moses' invocation to the Israelites, his death, and the arrival in the Promised Land.

Pélagie-la-Charrette, like the Bible, operates on two levels—those of sacred text and historical document; that is, the novel affirms elements of faith which are shared by a people and purports to be historically accurate. As sacred text, both are imbued with ritual, embody symbolism and imply a mission or destiny. As historical document, they are rooted in time and place and chronicle real events.

In the novel, credibility is established on an historical level. Bélonie is the "historian" whose recollections and story-telling form an important link between the Acadians and their past. Pélagie III, called La Gribouille, insists on the historical accuracy of the account of the Acadian return as the basis of the people's revival: "la seule histoire qui compte . . . c'est celle de la charrette qui ramenait un peuple à son pays."

In the Bible, too, great pains are taken to establish the authority and veracity of the text. The tone is one of unquestionable fact and historical record: "These are the stages of the children of Israel, by which they went forth out of the land of Egypt . . . and Moses wrote their goings forth, stage by stage" (Numbers 33:1-2).

In addition, both texts rely on lineage to validate their claim to historical accuracy. Throughout, parentage, descendants and ancestors are a constant preoccupation: "Il n'avait rien perdu de son vieux fonds gaulois, le Bélonie, sorti de Jacques, sorti d'Antoine, sorti de Paris au temps des chansons et contes drôlatiques." The words *génération, lignée, ancêtre* and *aïeul* all appear on a single page. Enumerations concerning lineage abound in the Bible. Genesis 10 lists the generations of the sons of Noah; Genesis 22:20-24, those of Abraham's family; Genesis 25:19, the generations of Isaac; and Genesis 36, the generations of Esau. This is an important device that runs through both narratives to authenticate the stories and lend them verisimilitude.

The Acadians are explicitly compared to the Israelites ("les Hebrews ont bien eux, traversé le désert") and the historical link between the two peoples is taken for granted: "Depuis quatre mille ans que la terre roulait sa bosse, combien y avait-il eu de générations entre Adam, Abram, Moise et le premier des Bélonie sorti d'un dénommé Jacques à Antoine, sorti de France au mitan du siècle précédent?" In addition, the expelled Acadians all have their eyes "rivés sur cette terre promise." Finally, Girouard accuses the Bourgeois family "de traîner dans la charrette de Pélagie un ménage capable de rebâtir Jérusalem."

The historical and the sacred are aspects of the same phenomenon for the Acadians and the Israelites. Both cultures view ordinary events symbolically, with the result that historical reality is seen to transcend the mundane and to enter into the realm of the sacred. It is through ritual that this transformation occurs.

Because of the Acadians' and the Israelites' reverence for life and their attachment to their past, burial ceremonies represent moments of poignant emotion. A landowner surprises the Acadians who are burying the Cormier boy and demands to be paid for the use of his field, just as Abraham had to pay the children of Heth in order to bury Sarah. This material payment symbolizes a spiritual commitment to the memory of those who are laid to rest.

The issue of leadership is vital to the Acadians and the Israelites. The leader symbolizes the people and its survival. There is an implicit parallel between Pélagie and Moses, for the two function similarly as peacemakers. Pélagie stands between the Bourgeois family and the others when they quarrel over bringing the chest filled with their possessions, she breaks up a fight between her son, Jeannot, and Maxime Basque. Moses, too, was constantly having to repair rifts and rally the people (Exodus 6:9, 14:11).

In addition, the two leaders symbolize the unity and ideals toward which their peoples aspire. Pélagie tries to keep the group together when some decide to leave for Louisiana and Moses does the same when the children of Reuben and Gad prefer not to cross the river Jordan (Numbers 32).

Pélagie, like Moses, is responsible for the safety of her people. She sends her twin sons scouting to gather news of Baltimore, and they return with a great deal of information, reminding the reader of Numbers 13 in which Moses dispatches twelve men to explore the land, to learn its character and that of its inhabitants.

Prophecy is an aspect of leadership in both stories. Pélagie sends off some of her group for water, saying that after "le règne des vaches maigres vient cestuy-là des grasses," recalling Joseph's interpretation of Pharoah's dream in Genesis 41. In Virginia, they work the fields in exchange for food, "par rapport qu'il faut bien garder le meilleur pour le pire," as did that other leader of the Israelites, Joseph. For both the Acadians and the Hebrews, there were to be hard times in store, and their leaders were invested with the power to forsee those events.

Symbolic changes of name are common to the novel and the Bible and reflect the importance of the respective leaders.

"Pélagie Bourg, dite led Blanc," becomes Pélagie-la-Charrette just as Jacob is renamed Israel (Genesis 32:29). In both texts, the main characters function as models for their societies and for successive generations. The change of name suggests that they are "reborn" to embody their people. Jacob *is* Israel. Pélagie *is* the cart that symbolizes the return to Acadia.

The two leaders are both individuals and symbols representing a people. They are mortal and fallible, yet greater than the average person, a part of history, and instruments of a destiny which transcends historical reality.

In addition to the symbolic attributes of the leaders discussed above, there are symbolic acts which link the historical and sacred levels of the narratives. The first of the acts concerns Rebekah. Rebekah personally offers water to Abraham's servant, demonstrating her quality of heart and worthiness to be Isaac's wife and thus one of the matriarchs of her people (Genesis 24). So, too, Pélagie performs the same act for the lost militiamen, thereby proving her merit and justifying her as the matriarch of her own people: "elle se dirigea droit sur ses hôtes et de ses propres mains leur offrit à boire dans la tasse dite de l'hospitalité, un goblet *rituel* (emphasis added) rescapé du Grand Dérangement. Et pour accompagner le geste, aussi la phrase *rituelle* (emphasis added):—Faites comme chez vous." Pélagie's literal, factual, gesture represents a more important spiritual truth that identifies her with her Biblical forerunner.

Both cultures acknowledge a mysterious aspect to human life that springs from primal sources. This acknowledgement finds expression in rituals of various sorts. One of Pélagie's oxen is killed for food, but the vocabulary surrounding the ritual suggests a kind of religious sacrifice: "immoler"; "on accomplit le sacrifice dans les rites, comme si l'on retrouvait d'instinct ou par une sorte de mémoire involontaire les origines primordiales de l'immolation"; "les lieux du sacrifice." Catoune is said to kill as if she were a high priestess. In the Hebrew Bible, after the Ten Commandments are given, God commands that sacrifices be offered, and sheep and oxen are specified (Exodus 20:21). In addition, the Israelites ratify the Covenant with a sacrifice of oxen (Exodus 24:5-6).

In this instance, the Acadians' killing is for food and the Israelites' is not, but the unconscious link with the Biblical rite is prominently and repeatedly mentioned. The Acadians' physical act is clearly replete with symbolic meaning that binds them to the Israelites. The Acadians assuring their corporal nourishment and physical survival (killing for food) finds its reflection in their spiritual nourishment and sacred mission (sacrificial rite).

The playing of music and singing, too, are ritual acts that

are associated with dramatic and significant events in the life of both peoples. They function ceremonially. Since the arrival of the Basques, "le violon avait comme assourdi le grincement de la charrette." The Acadians mourn the loss of the Cormier child with lamentations and the playing of a violin. Maxime Basque pulls out a reed flute and "casts a spell" over his Indian captors. Bélonie's death is lamented in song—"mille complaintes à la mémoire du barde centenaire"—and the group's final entry into Acadia is accompanied by music and song—"L'Acadie tout entière rentrait en chantant." Music is accorded an equally prominent role in the Bible. Moses and the Israelites sing a hymn of praise after the parting of the Red Sea (Exodus 15:1-18), they sing a song of triumph after their victory over the Canaanites (Judges 5), and the song of Moses in Deuteronomy 32, which Moses sings before his death, is the dramatic culminating point of the Biblical narrative.

In addition to symbolic acts, there are symbolic objects which link the historical and sacred levels of the texts. Beausoleil appeals to Pélagie for some certainty and reassurance about their future by using the Biblical image of the dove: "J'allons-t-i' point un jour voir apparaître une colombe dans le ciel, Pélagie? Une colombe avec sa branche d'olivier dans le bec?" recalling the dove and olive branch of Genesis 8:8-12, which meant that the inhabitants of the Ark would be safe and secure. Beausoleil's desire for a secure relationship expresses itself in a Biblical image of universal peace.

The two ships in the following passage, the one Acadian, the other American, represent attempts at self-determination:

> Ce sont des frères de souche, sortis ensemble des chantiers navals de Liverpool, destinés aux mêmes déboires et à la même lutte, à la même gloire devait dire plus tard la chronique de chaque pays. L'un et l'autre ayant réussi un coup dont peu de naivres purent se vanter en cette fin du XVIIIe siècle: décocher un caillou en plein front à cette toute-puissante Albion, maitresse des mers, comme David à Goliath. Les quatre-mâts jumeaux avaient tous deux, à un quart de siècle de distance, fait un pied de nez à la marine anglaise.

The Acadians' return occurs during the American Revolution of 1776. Acadia's struggle, like America's, is compared to that of David in the Bible. The ships serve not only a military and logistical purpose but, more importantly, are instruments of the universal quest for freedom of which Acadia is a part.

The people of Acadia themselves become ultimately more than a mere group whose drama is played out in a limited historical framework. They come to symbolize the possibility that a disparate group of exiles may become a people. They explicitly do not qualify as a people at the beginning of their journey: "Pas encore un people, non. . . . la troupe n'était constituée que de lambeaux de parenté et de voisinage." However, by chapter fourteen, when they unite in an effort to save the cart, they have become indissolubly linked: "Astheur, les hommes, faisez une chaîne. . . . " They do join together ("on fait une chaîne") and become "Des pavés humaines." Pélagie is proud to witness the development: "son peuple. Pour la première fois, Pélagie s'aperçut que sa famille de Géorgie dans une charrette, rendue en Acadie était devenue un peuple." So it is, too, in the Biblical narrative. At the end of the forty years of wandering, it is said of what had been a "mixed multitude" (Exodus 12:38), "this day thou art become a people unto the Lord thy God" (Deuteronomy 27:9).

Their struggle, as well, takes on symbolic proportions. Theirs is not simply a long trek to return home, but a conscious choice to survive as a people. They decide to live on in spite of the odds against them. The novel explicitly and repeatedly pits the forces of life against the forces of death. The narrator points to "une conversation qui s'était déroulée d'âme à âme entre deux patriarches jouant à colin-maillard avec la Vie et la Mort." Death always stalks the travellers: "Car nul n'est dupe au pays, c'est la Mort en personne qui est entrée en lice ce jour-là et qui a tiré l'épée contre la Vie." In the final analysis, Bélonie, who is associated with the "charrette de la mort," chooses life. He bargains with Death and saves Beausoleil. The Bible, too, asks the people to choose life: "I have set before thee life and death, the blessing and the curse; therefore choose life" (Deuteronomy 30:20).

To sum up this part of the study, *Pélagie-la-Charrette* and the Bible present themselves as part of history, for they tell stories that purport to be about real people at a point in time, yet they participate in the world of the sacred, as their undertaking clearly has meaning that transcends the literal. The leaders in both the Bible and the novel, the events that take place, and the objects that are named all exist for a purpose; that is, the people of Acadia and Israel are portrayed as participating in a mission. That they survive is no accident but the manifestation of their destiny.

* * *

The Biblical framework is augmented by additional archetypes associated with mythology. In the second stage of this study, I shall show how the dominant images of the circle and the "charrette" in the novel reflect ancient and primitive symbolic patterns. These images enhance the Biblical parallels and suggest that the Acadians are participating in a cycle of perpetual renewal and regeneration.

Before examining the implicit and regenerative imagery of the circle, let us first note some of the explicit references to rebirth. The reader's indulgence is invoked to witness "par quel miracle . . . des rejectons surgissent même d'une race éteinte." Pélagie is confident that just as spring returns—"le printemps reviendrait avec les outardes, brisant les glaces, ouvrant les champs"—so the people will be reborn. The birth of each new child is a triumphant reaffirmation: "La sage-femme rendait un enfant aux Cormier, un nouveau Frédéric en remplacement de l'autre. La vie avait en réserve des pièces de re-charge et pouvait se refaire, par en dedans."

Like all Acadians, it is incumbent upon Charles-Auguste "d'être digne fils de son père et des aïeux. Il lui faudrait réincarner toute la lignée à lui seul". Even Bélonie, who is associated with the "charrette de la mort", and who thought his entire family was lost, is part of this renewal when his grandson is discovered.

In addition to the references to rebuilding and rebirth, there is an ongoing "dialogue" between the past, present, and future, from the very beginning to the very end of the novel. (Characters repeat statements first uttered a century before by other characters, and questions posed during one generation are answered several generations later.) The reader is informed that "Pélagie-la-Gribouille, un siècle plus tard, devait servir toute la phrase au descendant de Bélonie" and, later, that "C'est le Bélonie contemporain de la Gribouille qui devait le répéter un siècle plus tard." This kind of interchange is very frequent: it suggests that the past is never dead and lost, but is rather constantly present in a process of perpetual becoming.

Symbols reinforce the meaning of the text as representing a people's return to life. Images of the circle—including that of the sun and the wheel—and images of the "charrette" are indispensable to the development of the central theme.

Pélagie herself is associated with the circle in its many forms. Pélagie enters "en plein mitan [centre] du *cercle* et d'un seul coup de front fit taire tout le monde." She is in the middle of the circle, her place is at the hub of the wheel, that is, at the centre of her people. Beausoleil "prit dans ses mains le visage de cette femme (Pélagie) comme s'il fut sa *boussole*". Pélagie, like a compass, guides her people and gives them direction. After the fire in Boston destroys one cart, Pélagie prevents Jeanne Aucoin from "auctioning off" the survivors to the other carts: "Ce jour-là, on l'aurait eu *couronnée de lauriers,* la Pélagie, si on avait été en saison." The image of Pélagie crowned queen serves to confirm her authority and leadership. Through the image of the circle Pélagie is represented as the undisputed head of her people.

However, the image appears independently of her. The Acadians are identified with it, too. They are determined to return and "*renoueront* le passé à l'avenir", associating them with the "dialogue" between the past and the present discussed earlier, and suggesting their survival into the future. Jailed in Charleston after they stormed the slave market to free Catoune, they are subsequently released from prison:

> Et rendus à l'*anneau* d'or, ils ouvrirent toutes grandes les portes cochères, après avoir fait passer le peuple de la charrette par les couloirs et labyrinthes puants de la prison de Charleston.

The act of securing their freedom is associated with a circular form, the ring. Finally, captured by the Indians, one of the Acadians gives an Indian woman a crucifix, "transformant un chapelet acadien en *collier* sauvage". The transformation of the Acadian rosary to the Indian necklace links the Acadian experience to its primitive origins just as the "sacrifice" of the oxen linked Acadia with its Biblical roots.

The journey of the Acadians is expressed through circular images. The voyage is a long one, "oui, mais *la boucle se refermait.*" The wheels of the cart carrying them home are mentioned. The caravan is said to have thirty-six wheels and Acadia itself is compared to the spokes of a wheel: "Comme *une roue de charrette,* comme *le timon* [steering wheel, another circle] d'un bâtiment [here, meaning a ship], l'Acadie nouvelle avait lancé aux quatre coins du pays les rayons de *sa rose des vents* [wind chart in circular form], sans s'en douter."

Thus Pélagie, her people, and their journey are associated with the image of the circle, the symbol of perpetual beginnings, constant renewal and eternal regeneration: it is implied that the death of Acadia is out of the question, that survival and good fortune await them.

The sun is yet another circle, by far the most dominant and suggestive. J. Chevalier points out that "le soleil est chez beaucoup de peuples une manifestation de la divinité . . . Le soleil apparaît ainsi comme un symbole de résurrection et d'immortalité." Furthermore, there is an important link between the sun and the wheel imagery in ancient societies:

> Le soleil comme coeur du monde est parfois figuré au centre de la roue du Zodiaque . . . . Si le symbole universel du char solaire est généralement en relation avec le mouvement cyclique, la roue de ce char . . . est elle-même avant tout le symbole du soleil rayonnant.

The circle, and its most powerful expression, the sun, therefore, suggest the very center of life, the guarantee of immortality, and, for Acadia, return and rebirth.

The sun is omnipresent in the novel. When things are going badly for the wanderers in *Pélagie-la-Charrette,* it is said that "la terre tournait à l'envers du *cadran solaire.*" Beau*soleil,* whose very name is tied to the solar imagery, cannot die:

> La chronique du temps en avait conclu qu'aucun Beausoleil jamais ne disparaîtrait sous l'eau, mais passerait son éternité à voguer loin au large, entre les algues géantes qui amarrent l'horizon au soleil couchant.

Because he is associated with the sun, he becomes a symbol of immortality.

The caravan is guided by the sun as well: "Quand les charrettes reçurent la nouvelle avec les premiers rayons de l'aube . . . . Et les charrettes prirent le chemin de l'est, franc est, là où se lève le soleil."

The religious dimension to the solar image is recalled as the sun is associated with an implied church bell: "Mais au petit matin, le soleil sauta à l'horizon et fit sonner le ciel comme un gong." Virginie's miraculous recovery takes place in the presence of life-giving sun: "La fièvre s'éteignit d'elle-même et l'enfant sortit de l'ombre comme un champignon de la nuit, en dressant la tête au soleil." The people of Acadia are urged: "venez prendre votre place au soleil." They return home in May, during springtime, under a resplendent sun.

The symbolism of the "charrette" is second in importance only to that of the circle. The word "charrette" is a metonymy for the Acadians: "les charrettes reçurent", "les charrettes prirent". The people themselves are referred to as "les descendants de la charrette". And Pélagie herself *is* the cart—Pélagie-*la-Charrette.*

The cart had been handed down for one hundred years and played a central role in Acadian society: "C'était coutume en Acadie d'apporter en dot une charrette à son homme, la charrette, signe de pérennité." We note also the religious aspect of the image when Pélagie wishes the wood of the cart to serve as a cross for her grave.

G. Durand finds that the juxtaposition, and even the coupling of the two images, the circle and the "charrette," is highly evocative:

> Il est tout naturel de rapprocher de ces techniques du cycle, de la mise en "joug" des contraires, le char traîné par les chevaux. Bien entendu la liaison est facile à établir entre la roue et le char qu'elle porte ou le voyage qu'elle suscite. Les dieux et les héros "fils," Hermès, Héraklès, et même notre Gargantua avec son "rude chariot" sont de grands voyageurs.

Le char constitue d'ailleurs une image fort complexe, car il peut consteller avec les symboles de l'intimité, la roulotte et la nef. Mais il se rapproche cependant nettement des techniques du cycle lorsqu'il fait porter l'accent mythique davantage sur l'itinéraire, le voyage que sur le confort intime du véhicule. Enfin le symbolisme de l'attelage, de la mise au "joug" vient surdéterminer souvent le symbole cyclique de fusion des contraires. Dans la *Gîtâ le "conducteur du char" et Arjuna, le passager,* représentent les deux natures, spirituelle et animale, de l'homme. "Les deux personnages montés sur le char d'Arjuna n'en forment en réalité qu'un seul." Dans l'épopée védique, comme plus tard chez Platon, le char est le "véhicule" d'une âme à l'épreuve, il porte cette âme pour la durée d'une incarnation. Les conducteurs de char sont les messagers, les ambassadeurs symboliques du monde de l'au-delà, "un tour de char symbolise soit la durée d'une existence humaine, soit la durée d'une existence planétaire, soit la durée d'un univers." Ces chars flamboyants renvoient également au symbolisme du feu. . . .

Ainsi technique du tissage comme technique du voyage se chargent l'une et l'autre, dès leur origine, de la riche mythologie du cercle. L'on peut même avancer que la roue et toutes ses variantes, mouvement dans l'immobilité, équilibre dans l'instabilité, avant d'être techniquement exploitée et de se profaner en simple instrument utilitaire, est avant tout engrenage archétypal essentiel dans l'imagination humaine.

This brings us back to the harmonization of the circle and the "charrette" imagery which, together, combine to animate the novel with the theme of regenerative, eternal life.

This union, combined with the Biblical model, lend the novel an impressive authority. It is clear that, in *Pélagie-la-Charrette,* the cumulative effect of the two kinds of imagery is to convey the idea that Acadia's return is part of an eternal cycle of rebirth given expression in the imagination by established mythic patterns. It can be seen, therefore, as part of destiny that the people of Acadia, and Pélagie as one of the "conducteurs . . . ambassadeurs symboliques" mentioned by Durand, realize the dream of an Acadia reborn.

Pélagie-la-Charrette won the Prix Goncourt of France in 1979 and has met with wide acclaim in French Canada. The novel's success can be attributed, in part at least, to the fact that it is extraordinarily rich in the diversity of the traditions upon which it draws and in its ability to assimilate them into a coherent narrative.

Michèle Lacombe (essay date Spring 1988)

SOURCE: "Narrative, Carnival, and Parody: Intertextuality in Antonine Maillet's *Pélagie-la-Charrette,*" in *Canadian Literature,* No. 118, Spring, 1988, pp. 43-56.

[*In the following essay, Lacombe examines the references to Longfellow and Rabelais in Maillet's novel.*]

According to Linda Hutcheon, the intertext is generated by a reader who recognizes, responds to, and activates the textual referents brought into alignment by the author in a contract with the reader. As with any self-reflexive text, Antonine Maillet's epic novel ***Pélagie-la-Charrette*** (1979) is brought into being, in the reader's mind or experience, by the interplay of three factors: text (in this case the unique combination of story and narrative that is signalled by the hyphenated title); context (historical referents, here specifically pertaining to the survival of the Acadians); and intertext (the sum total of allusions, influences, parallels, and comparisons, both implicit and explicit, with other texts). The foregoing quotations from the novel suggest that the relation of identity to fiction is a central paradox explored by ***Pélagie;*** according to Maillet, in a comment which echoes both Jacques Ferron and Gilles Vigneault, "mon pays c'est un conte." Into this known equation she introduces a new element: if Acadie survives primarily through its storytellers, and if Maillet literally finds herself situated at the transition point between orality and writing, then her text enacts or translates for the reader the simultaneous birth and death of history, culture, and language.

> **Acadians have survived, rather paradoxically, through their silence, that is to say through the growth of a strong oral tradition in the face of ever-present threats—illiteracy, expropriation, assimilation. . . .**
> —*Michéle Lacombe*

Acadians have survived, rather paradoxically, through their silence, that is to say through the growth of a strong oral tradition in the face of ever-present threats—illiteracy, expropriation, assimilation: "Apres ça, venez me dire á moi, qui fourbis chaque matin mes seize quartiers de charrette, qu'un peuple qui ne sait pas lire ne saurait avoir d'Histoire." ***Pélagie's*** reader must therefore confront the presence in the intertext of a considerable body of Acadian legend, myth, and folklore in addition to echoes of the Bible (specifically Exodus), the *Odyssey,* Rabelais' *Gargantua,* and Longfellow's *Evangeline,* among other texts. Simple folk elements include songs ("Et j'ai du grain de mil"), proverbs ("N'éveille pas l'ours qui dort"), and oaths ("Et merde au roi d'Angleterre"), leit-motifs that illustrate the billingsgate aspect of popular speech located by Bakhtin at the heart of Rabelais' work and of the linguistic marketplace. These tags are also used to punctuate folk narratives based on Acadian legend, narratives which begin by interrupting the action only to merge with major episodes in the story: Bélonie's traditional tale of the white whale, for example, is significantly altered by the exiles' escape from Charlestown prison, "the belly of the beast," while an Acadian variant of the Flying Dutchman legend is radically revised by Beausoleil's capture and rechristening of an English ship used to deport the Acadians. In both cases the oral tradition rescues the action but is irrevocably changed in the process. For Maillet, this complex, shape-shifting relation between signifier and signified is further complicated by the added movement from oral to written forms of discourse. The oral tradition becomes part of the canon questioned by subsequent generations of chronicler-storytellers, and joins the classical texts (all epics traditionally situated at the margins of the oral and the written) parodied by the author through her primary narrator.

This playful treatment of the oral tradition situates ***Pélagie*** within the domain of fantasy rather than historical realism as a more appropriate genre for exploring the relation of myth to history. The model for this fabulous blurring of story and narrative, the real and the imaginary, writing and the oral tradition, does not come from Latin American fiction so much as from Mikhail Bakhtin's work on the carnivalesque in Rabelais and popular culture. For Bakhtin, Rabelais is of consequence precisely because he bridges the gap between medieval and Renaissance world-views:

> The primitive and naive coexistence of languages and dialects had come to an end [with the Renaissance]; the new consciousness was born not in a perfected and fixed linguistic system but at the intersection of many languages and at the point of their most intense interorientation and struggle . . . . In these exceptional conditions, linguistic dogmatism or naivety became impossible. The language of the sixteenth century, and especially the language of Rabelais, are sometimes described as naive even today. In reality the history of European literature presents no language less naive.

Creating the illusion of orality, Maillet is in fact writing at a stage of Acadian culture which reproduces these conditions: ". . . au dire du vieux Louis, cette Acadie-là qui sortait du bois en riant des yeux et en roulant les rrr . . . ne se serait point marié en blanc." Maillet's approach to narrative, carnival, and especially parody, a term which Linda Hutcheon has recently expanded to displace the notion of plagiarism, are the three aspects of ***Pélagie's*** language that I will address as part of its self-reflexive strategy for subverting the lapses of history.

Narrative voice and the multiplication of narrators through a combination of framing and Chinese box effects are those aspects of the novel which, despite their complexity, have received the most critical attention to date. René LeBlanc has recognized that the novel's action, constituting the return of the heroine and her people to their devastated homeland and encompassing a fifteen-year journey by oxcart from Georgia to Grand Pré, is relatively simple, while the narration of that journey, filtered through many generations of conflicting storytellers, is extremely complex. Kathryn Crecelius, focusing on doubling motifs and patterns of repetition, argues that these serve to underline "une narration en abyme," and describes the novel as "le récit de la (re) création d'un passé à la fois vrai et imaginaire." James Quinlan, addressing the novel as poetry, identifies the dual function served by the title's personification—Pélagie-the-Cart is both "object and subject, vehicle and sign." In this context I am reminded of Craig Tapping's reading of George Lamming's *In the Castle of My Skin* as a post-colonial text—citing Kristeva, his comments could easily apply to *Pélagie:* "the novel *is* the truth about which it writes, embodies and unfolds the process it describes."

If Maillet's response to the injustices of history seems to substitute poetry for politics, it is because she recognizes the strong links between language and freedom. The breastcloth/handkerchief which Pélagie opens to the winds and folds into her apron pocket is a dominant symbol for the relation between what Naim Kattan terms "desire and power." At once empty and full, it is a female emblem of potentiality, a "country of the heart" or realm of possibility never finally denied/fulfilled. This "uncertain country" is nonetheless *linguistically* embedded in a world that is fully realized and fully Acadian:

> Et dans sa poche de devanteau, elle enfouit aussi des mots, des mots anciens aveindus à cru de la goule de ses pères et qu'elle ne voulait point laisser en hairage à des gots étrangers; elle y enfouit des légendes et des contes merveilleux, horrifiques ou facétieux, comme se les passait son lignage depuis le début des temps; elle y enfouit des croyances et coutumes enfilées à son cou comme un bijou de famille qu'elle laisserait à son tour en héritage à ses descendants; elle enfouit l'histoire de son peuple commencée deux siècles plus tôt, puis ballottée aux quatre vents, et laissée moribonde dans le ruisseau ... jusqu'au jour où un passant la ramasserait, et la ravigoterait, et la rentrerait de force au pays ...

This passage follows the climactic moment when Pélagie faces the double realization that she is dying and that home no longer exists in Grand Pré, and as such it locates Acadia within the ever-renewable world of fiction. The narrator's identity finally merges totally with that of her ancestor and namesake; this dual Pélagie in turn is closely identified with Maillet herself, in keeping with Hutcheon's recognition of the author's role in the reader/text interface, and clarifying this author's insistence that "je suis parole." In the breakdown of subject-object distinctions that accompanies the verb made flesh, history is personified, feminized, and appropriated. Rather than quietly containing her tears, Pélagie's hankie amplifies sentiment, making room for the deluge: it is large enough to accommodate the white whale metamorphosed into the sleeping giantess. Because the tale is never ended, the quest can go on.

At this juncture a double diagram might clarify *Pélagie*'s form: the first represents the two conflicting story lines, and focuses on narrative; the second represents the triple odyssey, focusing on story.

***

It should be noted that in Diagram I, Pélagie Leblanc is the name of the novel's primary narrator. The multiplication of narrators is now seen to be marked by circularity as well. The fact that Bélonie I descends from a Parisian immigrant named Antoine Maillet, really the author's ancestor, like the dedication of the novel to the memory of Virginie Cormier, the name of Maillet's mother but also of the character who becomes the cart of life's mascot, underscores the interpenetration of real and imaginary observed by Crecelius. The use of repetition with difference in the prologue and epilogue which frame the novel marks the distance which the *reader* has traveled in the interim: with the ritual chanting of family names at the end, a form of greeting in the imperative mode, we are now informed and prepared to enter the narrator's carnivalesque world. The playful recognition and celebration of identity is complete as soon as the reader acquires the knowledge for bringing it to life, a context which only the novel and its reading can provide:

> —Grouillez-vous, bande de flancs mous! Personne viendra vous nourrir à la louche ni vous border au lit. Aveindez-vous de vos trous et venez prendre votre place au soleil.

Our entry into the text is facilitated, for example, once we are familiar with the events signalled and assumed by Diagram I: 1880 is the date of the first Acadian national conference in Memramcook, when the people literally and metaphorically emerged from the woods and entered recorded history/writing. This was an occasion for Rabelaisian feasts of storytelling, and for Maillet every reading of the chronicling tradition, however contentious, becomes another such occasion. As the first to *write* the feast, however, she has had to invent a new, "nonexistent" language, one which I have already indicated convinces us that it is not writing at all but true Acadian speech. The power of this illusion is such that my first complete reading of the novel, on December 25, 1979, was while seated at my mother's feet: for the first time since my childhood, she quite naturally adopted the highly formal role of storyteller, decoding the text by uncritically breaking into song in a way that I, the would-be bearer of gifts, could not. Maillet at once suspends an endless number of layers between the reader and the truth/past, and recreates "original" events by conferring upon them the immediacy of an archetypal fairytale endlessly repeated. Citing Bakhtin, Linda Hutcheon reminds us that parody (here directed to the oral tradition) can celebrate as well as satirize: "through the paradox of its authorized transgression, the parodic appropriation of the past reaches out beyond textual introversion and aesthetic narcissism to address the 'text's situation in the world.'"

The multiplication of narrators evident in Diagram I is matched by the multiplication of carts in Diagram II, first and foremost by the hyperbolic growth of the original cart into a caravan and ultimately an entire people. The circularity emphasized by my diagram of the narrative structure, however, is not reproduced here, but rather is replaced by the parallel lines of the three principal players' movements. These intersect at several crucial moments and in one crucial locale, Salem marsh, to explode the illusion sustained throughout that their journeys progress independently. Pélagie's quest is at once threatened and renewed by her predilection for the wily captain, as it is by the haunting presence of Bélonie, the chinwagger who at first appears to embody the dead past. The point of intersection, when the Cart of Life is rescued from the "slough of despond," occurs when Broussard's phantom ship defeats Bélonie's phantom cart by bringing with him into battle Bélonic II, the centenarian's last living relative, long presumed dead. However, Broussard wins only because Bélonie agrees to stave off the Grim Reaper, and because Pélagie offers up her life in exchange for that of her lover. It is at this point that my two diagrams also come into alignment: "car sans ces conteux de Bélonie, fils de Bélonie, l'Histoire aurait trépassé à chaque tournant de siècle."

In addition to summarizing the broad outlines of the story, Diagram II serves to introduce the topic of intertextuality as yet another layer of the novel's action, leading us to the related issues of carnival and parody. The diagram provides the main textual points of reference for the three protagonists, referents in all cases supplemented by historical and legendary material, real or imagined, attributed to the oral tradition. Bélonie is repeatedly compared to an Old Testament prophet leading the chosen people into the promised land, or recording that quest for their descendants. Broussard Beausoleil, whose name associates him with pagan sun-worship and fertility gods, blends the characteristics of king and outlaw, earning him the nickname "Robin Hood of the Seas" and creating a parallel with Homer's Ulysses, while his crew, particularly the giant P'tite Goule and the dwarf fool Pierre à Pitre, belong to the world of Rabelais' *Gargantua*. Finally Pélagie, accompanied by the ghost of Evangeline in the form of the silent, war-scarred orphan Catoune, is of course contrasted with the heroine of Longfellow's epic.

The parallels with biblical events are fairly straightforward; these provide epic analogues that situate *Pélagie* within an old and honourable tradition. Even when the allusions possess ironic overtones, "repetition with difference" serves to recontextualize and demystify both scriptural and Acadian episodes in a parodic enterprise that Linda Hutcheon sees as clearly distinct from mere "ridiculing imitation." Maillet plays with the limits of her text's relation to its precursors, even occasionally mocking intertextuality itself in order to privilege "pure" story—for example, when the narrator informs us that if the twins Charlécoco had been literate "ils se seraient pris eux-mêmes pour de petits Pharaons" but that their ignorance of any history other than their own fortunately saved them from such a fate, tradition and education would seem to be a burden. The insertion of "eux-mêmes," however, implies the presence of an other/observer; here the reader is in collusion with the narrator in recognizing the relative merits of textual innocence and experience. The original Pélagie, like Charlécoco, is confined to story (the myth of action), while the latest one is restricted to narrative (the myth of signification).

The allusions to Homer are also fairly straightforward. References to the double odyssey of "l'Acadie du Nord" and "l'Acadie du Sud," like that of Pélagie and Broussard, captains on land and on sea, emphasize general similarities and specific differences in order to confer legitimacy upon the Acadian inheritance without deprecating the parodied text. The connection between Pélagie and Longfellow's heroine, however, is more complex and more central than the foregoing; it comes closer to what Hutcheon terms parodic satire, marked by a contesting rather than a respectful or playful (neutral) ethos. According to Renate Usmiani, virtually all of Maillet's plays create anti-types of Evangeline, and the author has repeatedly indicated that such a reversal also takes place in the novel:

> Pour moi, les femmes de *Pélagie-la-Charrette* sont justement plus près de ce qu'a été l'Acadienne que la fameuse Evangéline de Longfellow. J'ai donc pris une petite revanche sur cette Evangéline qu'on a toujours trouvée plutôt mièvre. Il y a un paragraphe dans "Fanie" qui explique tout ça: "La voilà, votre véritable Evangéline! une courageuse, astucieuse gueuleuse, mère de onze garçons. Lâchez-là au milieu d'un poème, et elle saura bien en faire une

épopée. Une épopée étoffée non plus de vierges-symboles et de femmes éternelles, mais de tante Zélica, de maraine Maude, de Mariaagélas, de Fanie."

As early as 1971, when Maillet seems to have been at work on a new play combining the eventual approaches to *Evangéline Deusse* and *Pélagie-la-Charrette,* she articulated her concept of the relation between Longfellow and Acadian writing:

> Ma prochaine pièce ... tentera de faire *la parodie historique* [emphasis mine] d'Evangéline première, l'héroïne de Longfellow. Cette nouvelle Evangéline qui se présentera comme la seule authentique femme acadienne offrira à son homologue le contraste amusant d'une femme d'un certain âge, mère de dix-sept enfants, à l'allure d'une Mère Courage ou d'une Dulle Griet beaucoup plus que la virginale héroïne figée sur un certain socle. Et c'est cette nouvelle Evangéline qui, supplantant l'autre, devra faire face à l'armée anglaise, à la Déportation et à l'Histoire .... C'est un genre de pièce qui tentera de forcer le temps, l'Histoire et le théâtre à se démêler dans les lois nouvelles.

Longfellow is not easily exorcized, however, and Maillet's feminist discourse, embodied in a matriarchal story and matrilinear narrative structure, pays its grudging respects to the old man. Even the redoubtable Pélagie-la-Gribouille joins the narrator in silencing the "conteurs-chroniqueurs de la mauvaise lignée" who would query the heroine's intentions in admitting certain passengers to her cart. The reader might doubt the narrator's claim that Pélagie "ne pouvait pas se prêter, dans les circonstances, à une telle gymnastique de mauvaises intentions," but it cannot be denied that if the cart shelters the midwife Célina because she possesses no other family, it must accommodate the patriarch Bélonie for the same reasons. We are clearly confronted with what Hutcheon, in her chapter on Bakhtin, terms "the paradox of parody" when dealing with the question of origins and Longfellow as fictive father.

Maillet's solution, if any solution to such a paradox can be found, lies in the substitution of Rabelais for Longfellow in her quest for origins. As her "true" father, he emerges in the personification of Acadian legend in the form of the ship which Broussard has reappropriated from the English and named the Grand' Goule in a personal attempt to rescue history. The importance of Rabelais to *Pélagie* is manifold. First, Maillet's reading of his books and her Ph.D. dissertation on their direct links with Acadian speech and folk culture prepared her for the eventual benign imitation which Hutcheon locates at the centre of parody. The novel's many allusions to the *Gargantua,* combined with the generation

of new giants' tales, are a "riposte" to the foreign vision and language of Longfellow, who cannot help but be belittled in the process. As we have noted, Diagram II associates Bélonie with death and the past, Broussard with rebirth; in the end it is Broussard who saves Bélonie by restoring to him his true heir. Yet it would not do to establish too close a liaison between Bélonie and Longfellow; rather, Broussard and his crew embody and emphasize by contrast that Rabelaisian/Acadian "joie-de-vivre," resilience and generous capacity for lying which contribute their share to survival and the success of the epic:

> Car telle restera jusqu'au bout la différence entre les deux plus grands conteurs de l'Acadie du retour: alors que Bélonie, durant près de cent ans, devait transmettre fidèlement à son lignage un répertoire de contes et légendes sorti du temps des Grandes Pluies, Pierre à Pitre, le Fou du peuple, allait verser dans ce répertoire des versions, variantes, improvisations, élucubrations de son cru qu'il est bien malaisé aujourd'hui de distinguer de l'authentique ancien.

If Longfellow dramatized the Deportation, together Bélonie and Pierre address "l'Acadie du retour"—the former preserves the facts of the return, the latter provides the artful touches which transform it from tragedy to epic romance.

The inventiveness and occasional foolhardiness of Broussard and his crew bring us to our second major point: beyond specific debts to Rabelais, *Pélagie* is marked by a more general use of and dependence on the carnivalesque. The narrator, in the first of many such comments, poses the following key rhetorical question about the nature of the enterprise: "Les Basques étaient-ils en quête d'un pays ou d'une promenade par les terres d'Amérique entre une fête et un carnaval?" It would seem that the very episodes which confer interest upon the action are interludes that as entertainment threaten to imperil as well as to prolong the quest. Thus "la Gribouille" would dearly love to relive the Charleston escape/party interlude, described by the primary narrator as "une nuit de carnaval en prison" but is repeatedly forced back to the main story line: "la seule histoire qui compte, dans tout ça, c'est celle de la charrette qui ramenait un peuple à son pays."

Yet the pauses which punctuate the journey are an integral part of the story; like the tale of the white whale with which Bélonie entertains the carts, the Baltimore striptease and the celebrations surrounding Madeleine's wedding serve more than just a decorative purpose. The cart only stops to accommodate life, whether in the form of the birth of Virginie Cormier or the arrival of new pilgrims from the bayous. Speaking of the women in her fiction, Maillet has stated that "si Longfellow avait dressé l'une de ces femmes en face des troupes anglaises, je ne dis pas qu'il aurait sauvé l'Acadie de l'exil, mais il aurait donné au Grand Dérangement un certain ton de vérité qui nous l'aurait rendu plus réel et, qui sait? moins tragique." Carnival thus marks the difference between the perspectives of Longfellow and of Maillet on the response of Acadians to official history. Although the love of Pélagie and Broussard, like that between Evangeline and Gabriel, is denied permanence, the narrator uses their first meeting to emphasize that Acadians recognize each other through the quality of their *laughter.* Speaking of Rabelais as both scientist and humanist, Maillet approves of his philosophy that if you can't cure the patient, you can make him laugh long enough to forget/ accept his ills. Such is the function of carnivalesque interludes during the pilgrimage, and of Rabelaisian allusions "during" the narration, as my two final examples will try to make clear.

Bakhtin views carnival as the popular or literary expression of laughter which parodies or inverts official culture, which flaunts the religious and political rules of the waking, everyday world. It is marked by ritual spectacles, comic verbal compositions, billingsgate, and an absence of distinctions between actor and spectator. For him, carnival is a second, festive life, based on laughter:

> . . . as opposed to the official feast, one might say that carnival celebrated temporary liberation from the prevailing truths and from the established order; it marked the suspension of all hierarchies, rank, privileges, norms and prohibitions. Carnival was the true feast of the time, the feast of becoming, change and renewal. It was hostile to all that was immortalized and complete.

In the struggle for survival, the carts do not stop for law, convention, or propriety, whether finding food for orphans or husbands for widows, although they continue to hold dear their traditions and to preserve folk wisdom. Thus the Bourgeois' chest (a parody of the ark of the covenant), the Basques' violin, and the Allains' crucifix paradoxically emerge as emblems of identity and symbols of what must, despite sentimental attachments, be abandoned in order for the journey to continue and the quest to succeed. Speaking of grotesque realism, Bakhtin reminds us that "degradation digs a bodily grave for a new birth; it has not only a destructive, negative aspect, but also a regenerating one," and that by "breaking up false seriousness, false historic pathos, [Rabelais] prepared the soil for a new seriousness and for a new historic pathos."

Madeleine's wedding and the celebrations, poetic and bodily, which accompany it, set against the violent backdrop of the American revolution, illustrate Maillet's attitude to carnival as the expression of temporary liberation and a form of change, becoming, and renewal. In the "unfortunate" absence

of priests and patriarchs following the deportation, the women must evolve new traditions to replace the old ways "before the fall":

> Sa fille Madeleine n'avait point connu les moeurs anciennes d'avant le Dérangement. La plupart des chefs de familles avaient péri dans la tourmente, emportant au fond des bois ou des mers leur bâton d'autorité reçu au paradis terrestre. Les femmes avaient dû par la suite se dresser seules face à l'ennemi et à l'adversité, et ramasser elles-mêmes le sceptre de chef de famille. Madeleine en avait été témoin, enfant posthume de son père et de ses aieux. Pélagie pouvait compter sur sa fille pour continuer sa lignée.

In the absence of the Basques' violin, Célina invents the "reel dit de la boiteuse," and although "toutes les mélodies ne sont pas sorties de la lyre d'Orphée," the primary narrator claims that this wedding alone must have enriched the oral tradition with half of its refrains and a quarter of its "ravestans." Maillet's characterizations and choice of incidents thus serve at once to reproduce and to deconstruct Acadian folklore; the fictive fabrication of origins for such folklore is joined by pointed alterations and inversions of established custom. This example illustrates what Hutcheon means by "the authorized transgression of norms": parody cannot help but posit the order which it transgresses. At the same time, Madeleine's wedding also underlines the difference between Rabelaisian and modern parody; Maillet is much closer to the former than to the existential art examined in Hutcheon's study of postmodernism:

> We must stress, however, that the carnival is far distant from the negative and formal parody of modern times. Folk humor denies, but it revives and renews at the same time. Base negation is completely alien to folk culture.

Maillet's unique perspective as an Acadian and a woman enables her to narrow the gap between Rabelaisian carnivalesque and postmodern parody; the myth of the fortunate fall acquires new meaning and poetic resonance in her iconoclastic treatment of "le grand dérangement."

The novel's multiplication of amorous encounters, both legitimate and determined by circumstance, includes Célina's with the fool-poet, Jeanne Girouard's with her brother-in-law, Jean's with his Indian princess, and of course Pélagie's with Broussard as well as Madeleine's wedding. They all serve to contrast with the tragic tale of Gabriel and Evangeline; clearly the official order superseded for Maillet by Rabelais is the static Acadia/Arcadia pastoral vision "immortalized" by Longfellow. Maillet does not object to the poem itself so much as to the institutionalization of

Longfellow's vision by a conservatively nationalistic clerical élite out of touch with the people and their traditions:

> Mais, entendons-nous bien, le but de l'élite qui propose une nouvelle idéologie faite d'un mélange d'assomption, de tricolore étoilé, de loyalisme envers la langue, la religion et la terre des aieux, idéologie que nous qualifierions d'évangélisme, si nous osions, n'a rien à voir avec la conservation des véritables traditions populaires d'Acadie.

It is through art, that is to say through the politics of parody, that this "evangelism" can best be exploded: the spokesman's loyalty to the Acadian flag, language, and religion is replaced, for Maillet, by an allegiance to the Rabelaisian trinity of "conte, roman, épopée."

Two passages from the novel emphasize the relation between writing and freedom mentioned in my introduction: Ti-Jean Fourteen's quest for the three magic words that will allow him to marry and to live happily ever after; and Captain Beausoleil's second, exaggerated account of his ship's miraculous rebirth and rechristening. The first involves Bélonie's tale of the white whale transformed, on the eve of the storyteller's death, into that of the sleeping giantess. At first this never-ending tale seems to be the literal embodiment of Bakhtin's "unfinished and open body (dying, bringing forth and being born) . . . not separated from the world by clearly defined boundaries." When the Acadian everyman Jean Leblanc ("John Smith") half-emerges from the bowels of his ancestor clutching the three magic words which constitute the legendary buried treasure of his clan, he joins his latest creator Bélonie in partaking of the grotesque body which, according to Bakhtin, swallows the world and is swallowed by the world. Maillet's contribution consists of the emphasis on language as the jewel buried in the dungheap: culture and identity emerge from the rediscovery of the word and its elusive, un/limited powers of renewal.

Just as the secretion of language in the grotesque body's nether regions mockingly celebrates Acadian dialects at the expense of codified French, Captain Beausoleil's involvement in the "Charleston Whiskey Carnival," explicitly contrasted with the Boston Tea Party, elevates Acadian history at the expense of American experiments and the high seriousness of their chroniclers. As Broussard repeats to the carts the tale he told the crew of his ship's twin, an English vessel taken over by American rebels, he simultaneously defers to and deflates his American host's exploits. Foreign ears are opened and Broussard's tongue unfrozen by the contraband Irish whiskey; his English gradually improves during the course of his tale about how the Pembroke/Grand' Goule came to speak only French. This process of translation invertedly mirrors the story itself, in which his crew is frozen alive when chased to northern climes by talking whales,

only to return to life a quarter of a century later upon drifting south. When a melting hail of French words finally assaults the decks, we are once more confronted with a carnivalesque celebration that blurs distinctions between subject and object, signifier and signified, story and narrative.

The reader joins an ever-expanding audience composed of the Virginian's crew, the caravan of carts, and the Acadians seated around the hearth a century later. Even in Philip Stratford's English translation, a version that the text seems to anticipate, we run the risk of becoming Acadian under the influence. The text's seduction of the reader, followed by a rude awakening from the illusion of freely flowing speech, is in this instance accompanied by one of several literal explosions. The tower of Babel vies with a keg of gunpowder in a verbal revolution or artifice of fireworks:

> La réserve de whisky d'Irlande fit un tel effet sur l'équipage de la Grand' Goule, que bientôt l'arsenal de Charleston se mit à résonner de mots sortis de tous les pays jalonnant l'Atlantique. On était en pleine Pentecôte. Ou à mardi gras. Un véritable carnaval des mers qui vidait les tonneaux et striait le ciel de feux d'artifice.
>
> . . . Un feu trop proche des poudres, à vrai dire: une partie de l'arsenal sauta.
>
> On a accusé à tort la Grand' Goule: elle n'avait fait que fêter ses retrouvailles avec le temps des mortels.

The return to the land of the living, correctly translated by Stratford as "the land of *mortal* men," is signalled by the breaking of a very long silence. "Frozen words" suggest the sterile canonization of Acadian life by Longfellow; the melting torrent of words in Broussard's tale and in the telling of it suggests not a return to pure primordial speech so much as the birth of Acadian writing and the acknowledgment of its debt to Rabelais' *Gargantua* as well as to the popular tradition. Maillet's repeated emphasis upon narrative, carnival, and parody adds poignancy to her text, because these are not techniques so much as conscious strategies for denying the ravages of time in the eternal struggle between the phantom cart and the Cart of Life.

Eloise A. Brière (essay date 1996)

SOURCE: "Antonine Maillet and the Construction of Acadian Identity," in *Postcolonial Subjects: Francophone Women Writers,* edited by Mary Jean Green, Karen Gould, Micheline Rice-Maximin, Keith L. Walker, and Jack A. Yeager, University of Minnesota Press, 1996, pp. 3-21.

[In the essay below, Briere argues the case for interpreting Pélagie-la-charrette *as a feminist epic.]*

Although North American historical and literary discourse has spoken about Acadians, only in this century have Acadians begun to speak about themselves, in their mother tongue. The silencing of Acadians is a project that began with the Treaty of Utrecht in 1713. With its signing, Acadie became Nova Scotia, ushering in attempts to eradicate the French presence in the colony. French-speaking Acadians would be assimilated by the British colonizer; failing that, they would be deported. The novels of Antonine Maillet are part of a project by the French of North America to construct a language-based identity that defines their New World experience. No longer silent objects of discourse, Maillet's Acadian characters become speaking subjects. Moreover, Antonine Maillet has created not only a linguistic homeland for Acadians but a space for the emergence of feminine discourse, contesting genealogies of gender on which supremacy has rested. Thus, with Maillet's works a new space of cultural significance opens up within the Canadian national discourse.

Antonine Maillet's novels generally exhibit traits rooted in Acadian oral culture; none, however, so clearly attempts to recreate that culture and the gender-based dynamics of its transmission as does *Pélagie-la-charrette.* Recreating the time when word, raconteur, and audience were one, Maillet's novel affirms primal Acadian culture while it contests the hegemony of North American Anglo culture. In depicting her people's baptism of fire, Maillet creates an American epic that establishes the Acadian people's claim to North American history. Now written down, the Acadian vernacular and the story of the "Grand Dérangement" become tools for the decolonization of Acadian historical and literary discourse. In a radio interview in 1985 Maillet reminded the audience of the epistemological shift that her works represent: "Don't forget that I'm the first one in history to have written down the Acadian language in books that were sold outside of Acadia . . . which means that it's about fifteen years ago."

Maillet's book is based on a collective epic generated at different moments by different authors/tellers who, through the generations, were unaware of each other's retellings. Until her novel, the Grand Dérangement story was the work of the entire community, a collective form of orature, produced through the binding force of the vernacular. Acadian French played a key role in this collective production, providing the affective link between the audience and its history of resistance to the British attempt to annihilate Acadie.

True or false, original or copy, the story has been the basis for a shared feeling of community among the Acadian diaspora of North America (the Canadian Maritime Prov-inces, Louisiana, and New England) from 1755 to modern times. Its significance lies in the collective death and rebirth it embodied. A communal experience that sealed the bond between language and collective emotion, the retellings of the Grand Dérangement provided a basis for Acadian identity. The Grand Dérangement thus predetermined the way each member of the community conferred significance on the Acadian past and interpreted the Acadian encounter with the British colonizer.

As Acadian society changed, the relationship between tellers of tales and their audience lost the intimacy of shared ancestry and known bloodlines. Modern means of communication widened the rift between author and audience, transforming the latter into an anonymous group of readers. As a result, the modern writer would be quite incapable of reciting the genealogy of any one of her readers, whereas the Acadian teller of tales would most probably have known the lineage of each listener sitting around the hearth. In turn, each of the listeners would probably already have heard at least one version of the Grand Dérangement story, the expulsion of Acadians by the British having been, up until Maillet's book, collectively generated.

> **Thus in the case of Maillet, writing not only rescues the Acadian language from oblivion but also nurtures and shields the revived Acadian identity from the "othering" implicit in the British control of Acadie.**
> *—Eloise A. Briére*

As the Canadian nation took shape after the 1867 confederation, francophone minorities of the Canadian Maritime Provinces were educated into the written English tradition and moved into employment where French was not used. As a result, Acadian national legends and myths were no longer functional in structuring the nascent Canadian national identity. Although collective orature would be practiced well into the twentieth century, it could no longer give significance to the larger Canadian national history. Thus, the textual authority of written English and historiography replaced collective oral history in French; the new language and written tradition were pressed into service to spawn a Canadian national identity that perpetuated British colonial objectives. Such a strategy inevitably led to the deconstruction of Acadian identity. Forgetting—a common strategy in the forging of national identities—is implicit in the use of the English language and the British imperial perspective. Longfellow's *Evangeline* conveniently filled the void left by the forgetting, distancing Acadians still farther from their past and their culture.

Thus in the case of Maillet, writing not only rescues the Acadian language from oblivion but also nurtures and shields the revived Acadian identity from the "othering" implicit in the British control of Acadie. The effects of alienation from othering were clearly shown in *La Sagouine,* Maillet's first work in the Acadian vernacular. The protagonist knows she is Acadian, yet she discovers that there is no "national" context into which this survival of early French colonial America will fit. Based on what the government census taker tells her, she concludes that Acadie is not a country nor is Acadian a nationality, because nothing has been written about it in "Joe Graphy's books." In order to qualify as reality, existence must be grounded in written texts. Because Acadian identity had no such guarantee, Acadians were denied the comfort of social belonging, the powers of political affiliation, and a clear sense of social order. *La Sagouine* thus defines the problem of the postcolonial subject in a nation whose discourse—like an ill-fitting garment—is a constant reminder of the subject's otherness. As in much of the colonial and postcolonial literature, the congruence between identity and national discourse will remain elusive for la Sagouine.

Maillet's writing down of the Acadian language is, however, more than an attempt to counter the voices that deny Acadian claims to culture, language, and justice. Not only is her novel a form of resistance to British and North American Anglo hegemonic discourse, but it aims to give voice to those who have had the least access to such discourse: Acadian women. *Pélagie* is unique in its attempt to create a space in North American French writing for Acadian women. It is, then, a program that aims to counter three centuries of silence, which in Acadie were punctuated only by birthing screams or the soft, sweet sound of convent voices, raised in prayer, to His everlasting power. *Pélagie-la-charrette* is an attempt to confer power on women's voices by erasing the boundaries relegating Acadian women outside the margins of the North American nation-space as determined by male British/North American Anglo narratives. Maillet's epic narrative restores Acadian women to history.

Gynocentric history has not always figured so prominently on Maillet's agenda, however. Years before the novel's publication, she made it clear that she had no intention of telling the story of the Grand Dérangement. No need to tell a story already told by men, a story written down in history books:

> Mais ne vous énervez pas; je ne vous raconterai pas l'histoire de la Déportation. Il existe bien trop de gros livres sur la question. Tous plus savants les uns que les autres. On a tout dit, épuisé le sujet, épuisé raide mort.

> [Don't worry; I'm not going to tell you the story of the Deportation. There are too many fat books about

it, each more authoritative than the other. Everything has been said, the subject has been exhausted, exhausted to death.]

Here the writer is clearly defining her turf. No, she will not touch the monument to the Acadian holocaust; men have said all that need ever be said about the expulsion and its sequels. The Grand Dérangement is surely not the theater Maillet will use for the Acadian woman to recover her voice, for—as we shall see—writing about the expulsion is where the "anxiety of influence" weighs most heavily.

Thus for twenty years, Maillet remained within the boundaries of the kitchen, so to speak, writing about girlhood, schoolteachers, charwomen, nuns, prostitutes, and religious bigots, maintaining a respectful distance from the "fat history books" and their account of the Grand Dérangement. Why then did Maillet suddenly take leave of the kitchen in 1979? Perhaps this was, as the narrator of *Cent ans dans les bois* states, a time for unearthing the past: "Le temps était venu pour défricher."

In Acadian, "défricher" means not only unearthing, clearing the land, but also examining bloodlines, determining one's genealogy, one's ancestry. If women are to be a part of contemporary Acadie, female genealogy must be made clear. It can best be clarified through a reexamination of the moment when the identity of Acadian woman—like Acadie itself—was ripped apart by English rule. In deporting Acadians from their land, families were split, with women becoming pawns in the imperialistic conflict between France and England. The successful rape of Acadie by the British plunged the land and its people into silence; hegemonic discourse would henceforth be in the King's English.

Pélagie-la-charrette is not the account of events as one would find them in history books: it is a return to an epic moment in the Acadian past. A common New World attempt, the journey back to the kernel of national origins, by laying claim to the past, is a means of reclaiming the foundation on which identity will be (re)built. It is only when this knowledge is whole that the poet's words can envision the future.

Maillet views history with some suspicion because none of the "fat history books" have succeeded in stoking the fires of Acadie's soul. Her view is typical of those about whom historiography has spoken, but who have been unable themselves to articulate the written record of their own past: women, minorities, and the colonized. Her suspicion is evident in the opening chapter of *Cent ans dans les bois:*

> La différence entre le menteurx, dans mon pays, est la même qu'entre l'historien et le conteur: le premier raconte ce qu il veut; l'autre, ce que vous

voulez. Mais au bout d'un siècle, tout cela devient de la bonne pâte à vérité.

[The difference between the liar and the fibber, in my country, is the same as between the historian and the teller of tales: the first one recounts what he will and the other tells you what you want to hear. But after a century or so, it all becomes fodder for truth.]

What Maillet is interested in is not official archival history but the mechanism that makes a people create oral epics from their history and how the production of orature is related to their survival. The seeds of such concern can be seen in Maillet's early work *Par derrière chez mon père* (1972), where she states that at a time when it was forgotten by history itself, Acadie was forging its own new soul, so filled with vitality that historiography would be quite incapable of containing it. It is precisely out of this vital legendary period, pregnant with life, that Maillet will forge Acadie's epic: *Pélagie-la-charrette.*

Language, especially the affirmation of mother tongue, is at the epicenter of Maillet's novel. No one will deny Maillet's pride, delight, and skill in exploring the resources of her language as she uses it to shape a North American legend. Although Maillet was schooled in standard English and later learned to write standard French, neither of these is her first language. Both are far removed from the speech of the people she writes about. At the risk of being unintelligible to the reading majority, Maillet has rejected European languages for her mother tongue: the Acadian variant of New World French.

Such a choice is highly significant: the expulsion from Acadie and subsequent exile caused the vernacular to become the "carrier" of *Acadiénitude,* for as Vossler has stated: "If a man is robbed of his earthly home he finds a spiritual home in his mother tongue, which is everywhere and always present to his senses, and can, therefore, at some time again become concrete and have an earthly 'home.'"

Reclaiming the mother tongue is much more than reproducing a dialect or marshaling archaic vocabulary; it is an allegory of national rebirth, a strategy for finally producing congruence between language, geographic space, and time.

Through the use of the sounds of Acadie and the rich oral tradition in which women have participated, Maillet makes *Acadiénitude* palpable. Acadians now have a crystal through which the culture can be refracted. It is through linguistic consciousness that the writer can gather up the dispersed pieces of Acadie's past to create an epic, just as Pélagie fills her wagon with exiles who will form a new Acadian nation. The following statement from *Pélagie-la-charrette,* often repeated by the narrator's informant, exemplifies the stirrings of ethnic consciousness that precede national rebirth:

Les gens du pays se reconnaissent sans s'etre jamais vus, à de tout petits signes: la voix rauque, l'odeur de sel sous la peau, les yeux bleus et creux qui regardent par en dedans comme par en dehors, le rire enfin, qui vient de si loin qu'il a l'air de dégringoler de quelques cieux perdus.

[Our countrymen could recognize one another without ever having met before, by certain small signs: a hoarseness in the voice, the smell of salt under the skin, the hollow blue eyes that look inside as well as out, and last but not least the laugh that comes from so far away it seems to have tumbled down from some seventh heaven.]

Small details perhaps, but the rebuilding of ethnic identity rests also on the recognition of such common traits.

Thus, Maillet has chosen to exploit a historical theme not for its content but for the opportunity it offers her as a crafter of words to use Acadian French, and to introduce Acadian otherness within the Canadian national dialogue. Such a stance signals that Acadian culture has clearly entered a postcolonial phase, questioning the old British cultural hegemony, adding its voice to the Canadian national cultural dialogue. Maillet's attitude toward language is an indication of this newfound stance: she is no longer bound, as she was, by standard Euro-French, the only French once recognized by Anglo-Canadians. Maillet has used Acadian syntax and vocabulary since the production of her highly successful radio play *La Sagouine* in 1971. Such a shift must be considered against the backdrop of Quebec's Quiet Revolution and the subsequent experiments among writers with the use of "joual" as a medium of literary expression and national self-affirmation.

There is more, however, that motivates the creation of Pélagie against the backdrop of the Grand Dérangement, for any number of heroines/heroes from the past could have been created for the purpose of demonstrating the renaissance and viability of Acadian culture and language. Maillet chose the story of Pélagie because, as she says, "J'ai grandi avec ce bouchon dans la gorge: un compte à régler avec mes premiers parents" (I grew up with this lump in my throat: a need to get even with my ancestors).

This "bouchon," or primordial lump in the writer's throat, impedes self-expression and comes from a score she feels she must settle with her ancestors. They are responsible for the pervasive existential anguish that prevented her from finding her true voice. It is clear, though, that at least part of the lump in Maillet's throat is due less to existential malaise than to the particular ordering of her gender and history that has been imposed from without—from the United States, and in a foreign tongue besides. Writing is therefore Maillet's way of setting things aright, of reordering the world, and of getting even with her forebears, who were unable to ensure that Acadian genealogy was inscribed in history.

By the time Maillet was old enough to read, an American myth at the root of such dispossession had firmly taken hold in the popular culture of the Maritime Provinces, where she spent her childhood. From the patriotic song "Evangeline," performed at most school and religious functions to the name of the province's daily newspaper, *Evangeline,* the presence of Longfellow's saintly submissive—and silent—heroine was pervasive.

Published in 1846, Henry W. Longfellow's cantos in hexameter met with immediate acclaim; within a century there had been over 270 different editions and at least 130 translations of *Evangeline.* Maillet settled on the story of the Grand Dérangement and chose to develop a legendary female protagonist as part of a strategy not only to repatriate Acadian discourse but also to reshape the perennial evangelinian myth that glorifies patriarchal values. If Longfellow's poem transformed living, acting Acadian women into "objects," mere reflections of an already written history, Maillet's work would regenerate them as performers in a national story.

John Nickrosz noted some time ago that all of Acadian literature is written in reaction to the Evangeline myth. Although such a sweeping generalization may be difficult to maintain today, it does apply to Maillet's work: there is an ongoing dialectic between Longfellow's heroine and the women characters Maillet has developed, most notably in *Pélagie-la-charrette* and *Evangeline Deusse.*

In Maillet's early novel *Pointe-aux-coques* (1958) Evangeline is no more than a reference to the name of the Acadian daily newspaper. In *L'Acadie pour quasiment rien,* however, her nonfiction book on Acadie from the same period, we see Maillet's first attempt at replacing the Longfellow myth with a homegrown version:

> Et au lieu d'Evangeline Bellefontaine, assise au bord du puits, vous verrez passer une femme qui s'en va éteindre avec son seau l'incendie de l'église; et au lieu de Gabriel, l'angélique, vous verrez le capitaine maîtriser l'équipage anglais.

> [And instead of Evangeline Bellefontaine, sitting on the edge of the well, you would see a woman with her bucket, going to put out the fire of the burning church; and instead of Gabriel, the angelic one, you

would see captain Belliveau gain control of the English crew.]

The passage demonstrates an obvious desire to replace the passive acceptance of calamity with energetic resistance. This short paragraph contains the seeds of Maillet's revolt against the Longfellow myth, a revolt which in *Pélagie-la-charrette* will produce an energetic foil for the meek Evangeline and one for Gabriel as well: the sea captain Broussard, dit Beausoleil. In the quoted passage, Belliveau's overpowering of the English crew signals not only the writer's first attempt at rewriting Longfellow but also her wish to counter English language domination as well.

Given Maillet's own experience of being forced to use English as a schoolgirl in New Brunswick, linguistic domination is no doubt also part of the lump in the writer's throat, propelling her to reorder the world. In *Pélagie-la-charrette,* the name change of the British ship, the *Pembroke,* can be seen as a figure for linguistic decolonization. Pélagie's male counterpart, the sea captain Beausoleil-Broussard is captured by an English navy commander near Charleston during the Revolutionary War. Expecting to discover American rebels on board, the British captor is stunned to find that what had been a British ship twenty years before had become a French vessel.

Beausoleil-Broussard glibly explains that the British crew became French after having lost its ability to speak because of the extreme cold in the northern seas. The crew sailed in total silence for six months; it regained the power of speech during a hailstorm, as it was pelted by the frozen French words it has been using since. The British *Pembroke* now bears the appropriately rabelaisian name "La Grand' Goule." It is precisely through his own "grande gueule" that Beausoleil-Broussard fabricates the story that extricates him from difficulty.

Beausoleil's decolonization of the *Pembroke* is the equivalent of "merde au roi d'Angleterre," the blithe refrain from a traditional French folksong that punctuates all of *Pélagie.* The use of words to outsmart the British tormentor is not a futile exercise, for as the narrator states, at the bottom the plight of the Acadians was really a matter of words:

> Une parole est une parole; et son peuple avait déjà payé assez cher une parole donnée au Roi d'Angleterre qui, sur une clause controversée d'un serment d'allégéance, l'expédiat à la mer sans plus de cérémonie.

> [A man's word is his word, and Beausoleil's people had already paid dear enough for the word they gave the King of England who, over a controversial

clause in the oath of allegiance, had packed them all off to sea without standing on ceremony.]

The renaming of the *Pembroke* is then part of the scheme for national rebirth. Exactly as the British had erased the French name of the province and its villages from the map, the writer removes the British name from the ship that captain Beausoleil will use to repatriate countless numbers of Acadians.

The linguistic revenge implicit in the ship's renaming is essential to Maillet's program. The metaphor is based on knowledge that no real emotional integration of identity— of *Acadiénitude*—is possible as long as those in charge of administration, law enforcement, business, and industry communicate in a language that the Acadian masses do not share. Such linguistic alienation began to change in New Brunswick with the election of the Acadian Prime Minister Louis Robichaud in 1960 and the province's subsequent adoption of official bilingualism in 1969; thus the stranglehold of English in New Brunswick began to wane.

Maillet's vernacular Acadian French is primal cultural self-affirmation. For the rebuilding of identity to be effective, however, not only must language domination end but so must the hegemony of the older debilitating Evangeline myth. Maillet sensed that Evangeline had to be replaced by a character that could energize Acadie. Such energy was waiting to be exploited in the myth of death and rebirth contained in the Grand Dérangement. It could be said that in this respect *Pélagie-la-charrette* exemplifies Fanon's thesis on the creation of a national culture:

> La culture nationale est l'ensemble des efforts faits par un peuple sur le plan de la pensée pour décrire, justifier et chanter l'action à travers laquelle le peuple s'est constitué et s'est maintenu.

> [National culture is constituted by all of the conceptual efforts made by a people to describe, justify, and celebrate the actions through which it became and maintained itself as a people.]

Evangeline's foil is quite a different character from other feminine protagonists in Maillet's works. La Sagouine, Mariaagelas, la Bessoune, and even Evangeline Deusse are all clearly socially determined. Their strong nature and aspiration for a more just social order are in a dialectical relationship to Acadian society's prescriptions for women in the twentieth century. Although we know that Pélagie has worked alongside black slaves in cotton fields, this detail has little import in determining the character herself. In *La Sagouine*, on the other hand, exploitation of the main character as a "fille de joie," then as a charwoman are significant elements in her social determination, making it

impossible for her to heed the inner voice of rebellion, too faint to spur her to action.

Pélagie is a character freed from the societal constraints that govern Maillet's earlier female characters. She has already fulfilled the requirements prescribed for her gender: motherhood and marriage. With Pélagie's husband dead and her children grown, Maillet sets the scene for the development of a protagonist who is not at odds with society and who is at the same time free to embody a new myth. As Carolyn Waterson has stated, "Pélagie embodies the most important individual myth Maillet has been striving to generate in the majority of her works . . . the myth of the heroic Acadian woman."

Thus it is this liberated woman who will lead her people along the freedom trail, through the obstacles of exile to rebirth. Although the rebirth quest or journey is commonplace in literature, in women's fiction it is an expression of women's awakening to selfhood. Quest in this novel, however, is not that of individual rebirth: it is intended to encompass a collective phenomenon. As Colin Partridge has explained, "The narrative device of journeying bridges the enormous gap between the internal socio-historical phenomena that shaped the culture and the artist's inward vision seeking to encompass new proportions."

These new proportions bear the distinctive trait of women's culture; Pélagie, a powerful, integrative mother figure, is assisted in the rebirth journey by Celina the midwife. The narrator of *Pélagie-la-charrette* conflates Celina's skill at delivering babies with her mastery of oral history. The theme of the interplay between verbal creativity and cultural survival is emphasized as the midwife—"sage-femme"—becomes the saga woman, a "défricheteuse" or teller of tales.

Celina knows everyone's genealogy. Her own ancestry is significant because it is the very embodiment of the new society being created in North America. With the arrival of the Europeans, races that had never before met began to blend. With a father who was a Micmac Indian and a French mother, "coureuse des bois" and part sorceress, Celina's genealogy certainly fits no typical evangelinian pattern of Acadian femininity or racial "purity."

The blending of races, and the attendant verbal transmission of Native American lore and medicine, contributes to the revival of the Acadians in exile. Celina presides over this renaissance, bringing countless numbers of babies into the world. Significantly, the first of these births on the trek engages Celina as no other had before. Not only does she deliver the baby, but she feels the birth physically as if she herself were the mother: "Une crampe l'envahissait, une crampe retenue durant trente ans, trente ans de sa vie de femme délaissée." ("A cramp invaded her body, a cramp held back for thirty years, thirty years of her life as a neglected woman.")

The birth is clearly part of the attempt to rewrite history, to revise the evangelinian myth that had frozen Acadian women in time. Unfreezing past history, the women characters have decided to give birth without the help of their men. The best of them, an aging chronicler enthralled with the past, is clearly not a comrade with whom to build the future. Thus the female characters in *Pélagie* unite in a fierce rebirthing of Acadie that the men can only witness but not participate in.

Significantly, the first birth on the trek back to Acadie turns out to be a girl. Her naming takes on special significance: the first Acadian ever to bear the American name of Virginie, she will start a new lineage. The women borrow the name itself, Virginia, from the American state where the birth occurs. It suggests a new virgin beginning where all is possible because old myths are wiped away to make room for new dynamic ones. At the same time the name calls to mind manly strength ("vir") borne by a woman ("gyn"). The fundamental act of naming, as Partridge states, responds to a basic need in a new culture: "the first need is to name: . . . the bestowal of names is comparable to the axe-blow of the pioneer in the silent forest."

Narration in *Pélagie-la-charrette* is Maillet's strategy for encompassing continental space and immemorial time. The verbal equivalent of a pioneering axe-blow, narration will enable the writer to retrace a history that was to have left no trace. Thus, in *Pélagie-la-charrette* the reader sees the origins of the oral tradition that stretches from the characters who participated in the Grand Dérangement—modern Acadie's founding myth—to the contemporary narrator who retells the story. Narration clearly shows how the common thread binding one generation to the other was initially spun in 1780, several years after deportation. From such emanations of popular culture, the Acadian ethnic group will be reborn.

In the penultimate chapter of *Pélagie-la-charrette,* as the ragged band of exiles at last reaches Acadie, it meets its other half: a group of Acadians who avoided deportation by hiding in the woods. Both groups are of common stock, yet their history, their past, has diverged over the course of an entire generation. Now reunited, they are faced with the task of building bridges between the history of those who were exiled and those who sought refuge in the woods.

Their reunion echoes an encounter that occurred ten years before, reuniting the passengers of Pélagie's carts and the crew of Beausoleil-Broussard's ship, la Grand' Goule. At this earlier reunion, family members eagerly sought information about the missing. We do not yet see, however, the formal emergence of a "story" that allows the deportees to make sense of the holocaust. An oral history of the deportation will emerge later, through the consciousness of Belonie-the-younger, grandson of Belonie, the chronicler of the carts. At this juncture, however, it is too soon to sift through the events, to reorder them into a unified chronology.

The reordering of history occurs at the journey's end when the two halves of Acadie begin to fill the void that has separated them. As they reconstitute their existence as a whole people, the reader sees how a common discourse about an epic event emerges in an "oral" setting. The novel details the initiation of Belonie-the-younger—grandson of the Belonie who made the journey in Pélagie's cart—into the art of telling oral history, as he recounts, for the benefit of those who had remained in the woods, the story of the carts. His counterpart from the woods, Bonaventure dit Bellefontaine, then takes up the young tale-teller's verbal thread to spin the parallel story of those whose clandestine existence was concealed from the British by the woods of the territory that had lost its French name to become Nova Scotia.

We thus have Maillet's account of how an oral epic tradition is born. As the two tale-tellers mend the rent in the whole cloth of the Acadian past, each supplying a different version of the cataclysmic event, the reader composes the scene of rebirth not through the sound of the teller's voice but by means of a solitary reading of the printed word.

Thus the immediacy and the intensity of the act performed by the teller of tales recede. We no longer hear the modulation of the teller's voice, see the dramatic gestures of his hands, the contortions of his face as he mimics pain, terror, joy, and sorrow. Writing represses the immediacy of this experience into the unconscious layers of *Pélagie-la-charrette,* constituting its oral subtext. No longer is group solidarity reinforced by the sharing of an aesthetic experience.

Despite this, Maillet deliberately reconstitutes certain paradigms of such an experience, which is why *Pélagie* acts as a catalyst that reconstitutes the sentimental links between Acadians today and their counterparts in epic time. Thus the reader has the distinct impression of witnessing the gathering of fragmented Acadian collective consciousness. As Edward Saïd has remarked about such texts, Maillet "deliberately conceives the text as supported by a discursive situation involving speaker and audience; the designed interplay between speech and reception, between verbality and textuality, *is* the text's situation, its placing of itself in the world."

The most typical device to this end is the "placing" of the

audience around the "macoune," the hearth of la Gribouille's kitchen, which is periodically repeated throughout the novel. The narrative strategy in *Pélagie-la-charrette* functions in a way that recreates the illusion of the moment in time when word, raconteur, and audience were one. In another admirable example of this, the reader "sees" Belonie's audience come out from under the tale-teller's spell:

> Toutes les têtes sortent du conte l'une après l'autre, laissant le conteur Belonie ralentir ses phrases, freiner, puis semer dans l'air du temps trois ou quatre points de suspension, avant de baisser les yeux sur son auditoire qui déjà s'affaire et court aux quatre horizons.

> [One by one the heads pull out of the tale, leaving storyteller Belonie to slow down his phrases, brake, then cast three or four points of suspension out into the waiting air, before lowering his eyes to his audience who are already busily dashing hither and thither.]

Not only does Maillet tie the otherwise silent text to the world of orality, but *Pélagie-la-charrette* contains several variants of the Grand Dérangement oral tradition. As the two halves of Acadie are reunited in 1780, each has a different story to tell the other. Not only do the different parts of Acadie carry on a synchronic dialogue, but the different Acadies through time pursue diachronic dialogue in the narrative symphony Maillet develops in *Pélagie-la-charrette.* Such a strategy allows the reader to see the Grand Dérangement story from multiple perspectives and along several time lines. The reader sees the story take root as a formal oral performance in Belonie-the-younger's initial telling in 1880. His is not the only version of the story, however, because the narrative strategy Maillet develops gives the illusion of hearing subsequent retellings, each a century apart from the other.

The first of these occurs in 1880, a date considered to be a watershed in Acadie's rebirth, because this is when Acadians began to speak for themselves, ending what Maillet has called elsewhere "a century of silence and incubation." At the end of this period, several Acadians were invited to participate in Quebec's Société St Jean-Baptiste congress in 1880. In a deliberate attempt to create a unified vision and group ideology, Acadians held a series of similar "national" conventions before the turn of the century. Like the Acadians who participated in these "national" conferences, the narrators Maillet places in 1880 begin the tentative process of conscious reflection on the past, melding multiple points of view to create a national history.

The second retelling of Pélagie's return from exile occurs in 1979, the year the novel was completed; this time the teller is the narrator/writer's cousin, Louis à Belonie. The three renditions of the cart story—1780, 1880, and 1979—are not sequential nor chronological but rather woven as a tapestry, with the threads of one story interrupting those of the other as they pass through the narrative focal point provided by the "je/I" narrator-writer of 1979. The latter and his informant share bloodlines with previous tellers of the tale, signaling the durable nature of the cart story, reaching the reader via the narrator who is genealogically linked to the oral source of the first telling. Such a device is the narrator's guarantee of authenticity required for the reader's willing suspension of disbelief, and for the creation of a founding myth.

The narrator's voice is heard throughout, interrupting the diegesis to sum up, make a point, or ensure that the reader has grasped the causal relationship between the oral tradition and cultural survival. For instance, Belonie's tale of the quest of the golden ring leading the protagonists through the innards of a white whale parallels the cart people's escape from the bowels of the Charleston jail. The narrator of the 1880 retelling concludes his story in this way: "Et c'est comme ça que je sons encore en vie, nous autres les exilés, par rapport que j'ons consenti à sortir d'exil et rentrer au pays par le cul d'une baleine" ("And that's why we're still alive today, those of us who were exiled, because we ended our exile and returned home through the arse end of a whale"). We then hear the narrator of 1979, who tells us how the white whale story was added to Acadie's repertoire of tales, passed down in front of the hearth.

As this example illustrates, the diachronic narrative voices do not exist as separate entities, but they speak in counterpoint with each other across the centuries, completing each other as the modern narrator provides information not available to the 1880 narrator. In addition, the narrator provides the contemporary reader with information that establishes yet another type of dialogue, this one being synchronic.

When a name must be chosen for the baby girl born in Virginia, for instance, the group considers the name Frédérique; then the narrator adds the following comment enclosed within dashes: "pas Frédérique, mais non, en 1773 personne n'aurait songé à confondre les sexes à ce point-là" ("not Frédérique, why of course not, in 1773 no one would have dreamed of confounding the sexes to that extent"). Such a comment implies that the reader has participated in the protagonists' debate over the name and has supplied the inappropriately modern "Frédérique," thus causing the narrator to intervene for the sake of historical authenticity!

In view of the fact that *Pélagie-la-charrette* is Maillet's attempt to create a "feminine epic" that would recover the voices of Acadian women occulted by patriarchy and the evangelinian myth, questions arise about narrative choices made by the writer. Pélagie's story is filtered through the male voices of the Belonie line of tale-tellers, clearly highlighting the generative powers of male discourse. Moreover, the narrator in the prologue to *Pélagie-la-charrette* states that were it not for male chroniclers, History would have died long ago. This narrative seems to stand in conflict with what Maillet herself has stated about her novel. She sees it as a tribute to the generative powers of women rather than to the masculine forces of destruction common in male-generated epics of conquest.

Adding to the contradiction, the narrator of 1979 continually reminds the reader of the weighty patriarchal voice s/he is transmitting, and that s/he is merely relating the words of Belonie-the-younger, as they have come down through the centuries. This narrative strategy is a rhetorical triumph over silencing by death and the passage of time for it produces multiple layers of imagined listeners, metaphors for the durability of the Acadian nation through time. However, does it not show storytelling and the attendant cultural regeneration to be men's work? Does this narrative device not perpetuate the kind of situation Maillet has risen up against in her desire to blaze an empowering new path? Like the Acadians silenced by Longfellow's account of their history, women in the novel must first pass through male consciousness before they can exist, rather than speaking for themselves as the principal actors in the Grand Dérangement story.

Such attention is not accepted calmly by Pélagie's descendant, Pélagie-la-Gribouille, however; throughout the novel this contemporary of Belonie (the 1880 tale-teller) contests his version of her ancestress's story. Belonie cannot take seriously la Gribouille's repeated attempts at telling Pélagie's story on the cold wintry nights when listeners gather round the hearth. These are times—the narrator tells us—when Belonie laughs at la Gribouille's amateurish attempts to recreate the past. He is in effect deauthorizing her story, sending the putative verbal artist back to her kitchen and proper women's work. The constant joshing of la Gribouille and her vain attempts to produce her own version of Acadian women's history illustrates the fact that although women may have been important actors in the central Acadian epic, they could not be entrusted with its telling, at least not in 1880.

La Gribouille's numerous protests nonetheless contain the suggestion that despite the existence of several male versions of the story, hers is the "correct," yet unheard, one. Her conviction is such that she swears to the scoffers sitting in front of her hearth that she will write the story of her family herself, just to set the record right. Her intention is an ironic reminder that the making of the narrative, as constructed by the reader through Belonie's account, is still man's work. Does Pélagie's descendant's powerlessness before male narrators indicate that Maillet—a student of folklore herself—

has fallen into the trap that has plagued folklorists who traditionally have ignored women as the producers of oral literature and history?

Perhaps the male narrative voice simply illustrates the point where Maillet's revisionism in *Pélagie-la-charrette* falls short, opting instead to reflect the patriarchal aspects of Acadian reality. Or is she telling us something else? Is she implying that women are the true builders of society (pelagi/*agir* = to act) whereas men are the passive spinners of yarns; does she want us to read "baloney" into Belonie? After all, when the reader follows the thread handed to him by *Pélagie-la-charrette*'s narrators, the thread that enables him to weave his way back through the meanderings of the path already taken, whose powers do we admire? The man who tells tales or the woman who weaves the living threads of Acadie back together?

The information the narrator tells us would have been inscribed on Belonie's tomb provides a key to the enigma of the male narrative voices in *Pélagie.* The fictional inscription would have stated that Belonie was the "son of Antonine Maillet," making it at last clear that the Belonie and Maillet lines are one and the same. Thus, like Antonine Maillet herself, the 1979 narrator is a direct descendant of this Maillet as is her informant and cousin Louis-à-Belonie. Because of this genealogical information, the 1979 narrator can thus be conceived of as Antonine Maillet's "double": a woman.

The strictures of dominant mores in 1880 defeated Pélagie-la-Gribouille's attempts to tell Pélagie's story; control of narration could not yet be wrested from Belonie. A century later, however, Maillet seems to be saying women need no longer accept such hegemony. The female narrator of 1979 is invested with all of the power inherent in the verbal creativity formerly held by the Belonie line. Thus not only does Maillet create a dynamic protagonist, but she places a woman at the helm of the story's telling. In so doing, Maillet subverts Acadian male oral creativity as represented by the Belonie "tradition." Moreover, Maillet has reversed the terms of Longfellow's poem, in which male discourse framed feminine action, creating the myth of Acadian submissiveness. Maillet's double, recycling myth and transposing gender, reverses the evangelinian tradition of female passivity inscribed in the dominant scripts of the Acadian legacy. *Pélagie* then counters the cultural displacement inherent in Longfellow's powerful narrative, which had so conveniently slipped into the void created by British colonial discourse after the Grand Dérangement.

Through this skillful representation of the recuperation of narration, Maillet has succeeded in giving the Acadian past and women's history cultural significance within the context of Canadian national identity. Recognition of the Acadian past and women's creation of history is not just a substitu-

tion of terms: Acadian for Anglo, Acadian French for Canadian English, female narrators for male narrators. The new
strategies for identity, language, myth, and narration produce
forms of meaning from an Acadian feminine perspective,
something North America had not heard before Antonine
Maillet.

FURTHER READING

Criticism

Weiss, Jonathan M. "Acadia Transplanted: The Importance
of *Evangéline Deusse* in the Work of Antonine Maillet."
Colby Literary Quarterly XIII, No. 3 (September 1977):
173-85.
>   Discusses the development of Acadian themes in
>   Maillet's works leading up to *Evangéline Deusse* and
>   examines how Maillet broadens the Acadian exile ex-
>   perience to a universal view.

**Additional coverage of Maillet's life and career is contained in the following sources
published by Gale:** *Contemporary Authors,* **Vols. 115, and 120;** *Contemporary Authors
New Revision Series,* **Vol. 46;** *Dictionary of Literary Biography,* **Vol. 60; and**
DISCovering Authors: Canadian.

August Wilson

1945-

American playwright.

The following entry provides an overview of Wilson's career through 1997. For further information on his life and works, see *CLC,* Volumes 39, 50, and 63.

INTRODUCTION

Wilson emerged in the 1980s as a significant voice in American theater. His dramas, for which he has variously received such coveted prizes as the Tony Award, the New York Drama Critics Circle Award, and the Pulitzer Prize, are part of a planned play-cycle devoted to the story of black American experience in the twentieth century. "I'm taking each decade and looking at one of the most important questions that blacks confronted in that decade and writing a play about it," Wilson explains. "Put them all together and you have a history." The leisurely pace and familial settings of Wilson's dramas have evoked comparisons to Eugene O'Neill's works. Praised for their vivid characterizations, Wilson's plays often center upon conflicts between blacks who embrace their African past and those who deny it. His rich yet somber explorations of black history prompted Samuel G. Freedman to describe Wilson as "one part Dylan Thomas and one part Malcolm X, a lyric poet fired in the kiln of black nationalism."

Biographical Information

Wilson grew up in a Pittsburgh, Pennsylvania ghetto called the Hill. He gained an early pride in his heritage through his mother, who worked as a janitor to support her six children. Frustrated by the rampant racism he experienced in several schools, Wilson dropped out in the ninth grade, thereafter deriving his education from his neighborhood experiences and the local library. In a collection of books marked "Negro," he discovered works of the Harlem Renaissance and other African-American writers. After reading works by such authors as Ralph Ellison, Langston Hughes, and Arna Bontemps, Wilson realized that blacks could be successful in artistic endeavors without compromising their traditions. In his early writings, Wilson was so heavily influenced by other styles that it was difficult for him to find his own. In 1968, inspired by the civil rights movement, Wilson co-founded Black Horizon on the Hill, a community theater aimed at raising black consciousness in the area. The playhouse became the forum for his first dramas, in which Wilson purposely avoided the study of other artists in order to

develop his own voice. Wilson's first professional breakthrough occurred in 1978 when he was invited to write plays for a black theater in St. Paul, Minnesota. In this new milieu, removed from his native Pittsburgh, Wilson began to recognize poetic qualities in the language of his hometown. While his first two dramas garnered little notice, his third, *Ma Rainey's Black Bottom* (1984), was accepted by the National Playwrights Conference in 1982, where it drew the attention of Lloyd Richards, the artistic director of the Yale Repertory Theater. Upon reading the script, Richards recalls, "I recognized it as a new voice. A very important one. It brought back my youth. My neighborhood. Experiences I had." He directed *Ma Rainey* at the Yale Theater and later took the play to Broadway. Since then, with Richards in the role of mentor and director (with the exception of *Seven Guitars* (1995) with which Richards was unable to be involved due to illness), all of Wilson's plays have had their first staged readings at the Playwrights Conference followed by runs at the Yale Repertory Theater and regional theaters before opening on Broadway.

Major Works

Set in the 1920s, *Ma Rainey's Black Bottom* is an exploration of the effects of racism. It is based on an imaginary episode in the life of legendary black singer Gertrude (Ma) Rainey, regarded by some artists as the mother of the blues. The action takes place in a recording studio and focuses mainly on four musicians who are waiting for Ma's arrival. As the details of the musicians' lives unfold, the audience becomes aware of the racism that these successful black performers have had to face throughout their careers. The attitudes of the group's white manager and the owner of the studio reveal continuing exploitation of Ma and her band. The play climaxes when one of the musicians, Levee, vents his frustrations on the others. In his next play, *Fences* (1985), Wilson again examines the destructive and far-reaching consequences of racial injustice. Set in the late 1950s, on the eve of the civil rights movement, *Fences* revolves around Troy Maxson, an outstanding high school athlete who was ignored by major league baseball because of his color. Struggling through middle age as a garbage man, Troy's bitterness results in family conflicts. His son, who also aspires to an athletic career, must battle his father's fear and envy of him, and Troy's wife is humiliated by his adultery. *Joe Turner's Come and Gone,* (1986) debuted while *Fences* was still running on Broadway. *Joe Turner,* which is regarded as more mystical than Wilson's other works, centers upon the struggles of migrants in the post-Civil War North. The play takes place in 1911 in the Pittsburgh boardinghouse owned by Seth and Bertha Holly. Following seven years of illegal bondage, Herald Loomis, a black freedman, travels to Pennsylvania in search of the wife who fled north during his enslavement. The critical issue of white oppression is symbolized in Herald's haunted memories of Joe Turner, the infamous Southern bounty hunter who captured him. His sojourn ends at the Holly boardinghouse, where the black residents are also searching for some kind of connection and wholeness in their lives. Partially assimilated to white America, they nevertheless embrace the African traditions of their past. At the play's end, the boarders sing and dance a *juba,* an African celebration of the spirit. Their shared joy represents an achievement of unity, having come to terms with the trauma of slavery and the harsh reality of white persecution. *The Piano Lesson* (1987), which examines the confrontation of black heritage with the possibilities of the future, won the Pulitzer Prize before appearing on Broadway. A piano serves as a major element in this play, which is set in 1936 in Doaker Charles's Pittsburgh home. Decades earlier, the white master of the Charles family traded Doaker's father and grandmother for the piano, and the grief-stricken grandfather carved African totems of his wife and son in the piano's legs. Later, Doaker's older brother was killed in a successful conspiracy to steal the piano, which now sits in Doaker's living room untouched and revered. Conflict arises when Boy Willie, the son of the man who stole the piano, wants to sell it to purchase the land on which his ancestors were slaves. *Two Trains Running* (1990)

opened on Broadway in 1992; this play is set in a run-down diner on a single day in 1969 and concerns the reactions of the diner's regular patrons to the imminent sale of the diner as well as the burial preparations occurring across the street at a funeral parlor. *Seven Guitars,* which is set during the 1940s, debuted in 1995 and relates the tragic undoing of blues guitarist Floyd Barton. At the opening of the play, Floyd's friends have gathered to mourn his untimely death. The action flashes back to Floyd's last week of life, revealing that Floyd recently recorded his first hit record and has another opportunity to make a recording if he can travel to a studio in Chicago. Floyd tries to acquire the money for his trip to Chicago and also seeks to reconcile with his former girlfriend, Vera.

Critical Reception

The numerous awards and accolades Wilson has received reflect the widespread critical appreciation of his mastery of poetic language, humor, and tragic realism in his dramatic works. Wilson's treatment of his subject matter—a first-hand history of black people in twentieth-century America—has also been highly praised by critics, who assert the various ways in which Wilson's brilliance as a playwright illuminates the complex nuances and themes encompassed by his characters' experiences. In an interview, Wilson's long-time friend Nick Flournoy summed up the playwright's career: "August Wilson is on a trek. He's saying who you are and what you are are all right. It's all right to be an angry nigger. It's all right to be whatever you are. It's what the great Irish writers did. They took that narrow world and they said, 'Here it is.' Here it is and its meaning is universal."

PRINCIPAL WORKS

The Homecoming (drama) 1976
The Coldest Day of the Year (drama) 1979
Fullerton Street (drama) 1980
Black Bart and the Sacred Hills (drama) 1981
Jitney (drama) 1982
Ma Rainey's Black Bottom (drama) 1984
Fences (drama) 1985
Joe Turner's Come and Gone (drama) 1986
*The Piano Lesson (drama) 1987
Two Trains Running (drama) 1990
Seven Guitars (drama) 1995

---

*The Piano Lesson was adapted for television and broadcast as part of the "Hallmark Hall of Fame" series on CBS in 1995.

CRITICISM

August Wilson with Kim Powers (interview date Fall/Winter 1984)

SOURCE: "An Interview with August Wilson," in *Theater,* Vol. 16, No. 1, Fall/Winter, 1984, pp. 50-5.

[In the following interview, Wilson discusses various aspects of his works, including themes, symbols, and characters.]

August Wilson's play **Ma Rainey's Black Bottom** garnered rave reviews at the Yale Rep last Spring. It met with even greater success this Fall in New York, where the play opened at the Cort Theatre on October 11, with the same production staff, including director Lloyd Richards, and a majority of the original Rep cast. Wilson leapt from virtual obscurity as a playwright to the leading ranks with only this one play. **Ma Rainey,** originally produced at the Eugene O'Neill National Playwrights Conference in 1982, is, in part, an examination of race relationships in America, set in 1927 against the backdrop of one of the legendary blues singer's recording sessions at a "race division" of Paramount Records. The battling egos of the musicians, and the transitory status of the blues itself, become metaphors for rage and injustice.

At our interview, conducted in New Haven in mid-May, 1984, Wilson had just returned from the O'Neill's "Pre-Conference", during which each playwright reads his or her play aloud. August had read his play *Mill Hand's Lunch Bucket* (retitled *Joe Turner's Come and Gone* during the summer), and was both exhilarated by the new creation and alerted to the hard revisions ahead. Our focus on this play in the interview is indicative of his excitement. **Joe Turner** is set in a boardinghouse in Pittsburgh in 1911 and uses a sort of "Grand Hotel" strategy to take in a number of characters who are searching for a racial and spiritual identity. As Wilson explains in the interview, the play has a more mystical and less realistic base than **Ma Rainey.** The Yale Rep has already optioned **Joe Turner** for its 1985-86 season. (Wilson is quickly becoming a sort of resident playwright at the Rep. His play **Fences,** read at the 1983 O'Neill Conference, will be directed by Lloyd Richards at the end of the 1984-85 season.)

August Wilson says he came to playwriting out of arrogance and frustration, certain he could write just as well as other playwrights about the Black experience in America. He didn't use other plays as a primer on how to write, but combined his poetry background with fledgling efforts as a director at a small theater in Pittsburgh, which devoured the plays from the early 70's anthologies of Black drama. His first play written for that theater was called **Jitney:** it concerned a group of jitney cab drivers, two of whom are involved in a pivotal father/son conflict. The play was an SRO success; a large portion of the black audience going to the theater for the first time refused to leave when told the show was already sold out. The play came back the next year to satisfy the demand. In his second play, Wilson deliberately tried to expand the dramatic world from the rather narrow "slice" of the first play. Although Wilson considers the play a failure, it did lay the groundwork for the expanded fictional realm and overlapping scenes of **Ma Rainey.**

August Wilson was born in Pittsburgh, Pennsylvania and now lives in St. Paul, Minnesota. He is a member of New Dramatists, and an Associate Playwright at the Playwrights Center in Minneapolis. Mr. Wilson is the recipient of Bush, Rockefeller, and McKnight Foundation Fellowships in playwriting. In addition to his summers at the O'Neill National Playwrights Conference (1982, '83, and '84), Mr. Wilson's poetry has been published in various magazines and anthologies.

[Powers:] You've written other plays before **Ma Rainey's Black Bottom,** *but is that the one you wanted to hit the public first? Did you instinctually know it might be a bigger play?*

[Wilson:] Oh, no—I wanted to hit the public with all of them. But about **Ma Rainey** I felt that I was growing as a playwright and moving toward learning more about the craft and how to articulate my ideas dramatically. I had submitted a couple of other plays to the O'Neill, but I'm glad they weren't selected. I'm glad my exposure was with **Ma Rainey** because I think it is a stronger play than the others I had submitted.

You've mentioned a cycle of history plays you have in the works. What is that?

As it turns out, I've written plays that take place in 1911, 1927, 1941, 1957, and 1971. Somewhere along the way it dawned on me that I was writing one play for each decade. Once I became conscious of that, I realized I was trying to focus on what I felt were the most important issues confronting Black Americans for that decade, so ultimately they could stand as a record of Black experience over the past hundred years presented in the form of dramatic literature. What you end up with is a kind of review, or re-examination, of history. Collectively they can read, certainly not as a total history, but as some historical moments.

Why did you switch from writing poetry to playwriting? Did you need something as "big" as a play?

I would describe my poetry as intensely personal. I needed something as big as a play because my ideas no longer fit in the poems, or they fit in a different way, for myself only. I needed a larger canvas that would include everyone.

Your concern with history hasn't been evidenced by many other American playwrights. Although there is a contemporary tone to your historical plays, what would you write in a 1984 play, a play without a past framework?

I don't know. But if, as you pointed out, my historical plays are contemporary in tone, I think you can write a play set in 1984 that is historical in tone. A play set in 1984 would still have to contain historical elements—as the lives of the people do not exist in a vacuum. The importance of history to me is simply to find out who you are and where you've been. It becomes doubly important if someone else has been writing your history. I think Blacks in America need to re-examine their time spent here to see the choices that were made as a people. I'm not certain the right choices have always been made. That's part of my interest in history—to say "Let's look at this again and see where we've come from and how we've gotten where we are now." I think if you know that, it helps determine how to proceed with the future.

What is your response to some of the **Ma Rainey** *reviews that said you were just repeating incidents and attitudes from the past that people already knew existed?*

I would hope that the play as a whole provides a different view—which is what art and literature are about—to present the familiar with a freshness and in a manner never quite seen before. What I tried to do in *Ma Rainey,* and in all my work, is to reveal the richness of the lives of the people, who show that the largest ideas are contained by their lives, and that there is a nobility to their lives. Blacks in America have so little to make life with compared to whites, yet they do so with a certain zest, a certain energy that is fascinating because they make life out of nothing—yet it is charged and luminous and has all the qualities of anyone else's life. I think a lot of this is hidden by the glancing manner in which White America looks at Blacks, and the way Blacks look at themselves. Which is why I work a lot with stereotypes, with the idea of stripping away layer by layer the surface to reveal what is underneath—the real person, the whole person.

What do you think of the angry young Black playwrights of the early 70's—Ed Bullins, Leroi Jones, Papp's people?

I think it was an absolutely great time, much needed, and I'm sorry to see it dissipated. It was a response to the time, the turbulence of the 60's. I think it goes back to a person like Malcolm X, who began to articulate for the first time what the masses of Black people were saying on the street corners. It was all a part of the people's lives; they had been given a platform, and there was an explosion of Black art and literature comparable to the Harlem Renaissance.

When you write your 60's play, will you write about a real

historical figure such as Malcolm X or Martin Luther King, or will you use that as a background for imagined characters?

So much has been written about them that I don't think I would attempt it. Here again, I would try to find the major idea of the decade and examine that. The play I write about the 60's will be about what happened prior to the 60's, its historical antecedents. I think the ideas of the 60's are rooted in the morality of American society of the 50's. I would try to uncover what made the 60's a troubled, turbulent and violent decade not only for Black but for White society as well.

Let's start with your historically earliest play, **Joe Turner's Come and Gone,** *set in 1911. You pervade the storytelling with alien folklore, or mysticism.*

I set the play in 1911 to take advantage of some of the African retentions of the characters. The mysticism is a very large part of their world. My idea is that somewhere, sometime in the course of the play, the audience will discover these are African people. They're Black Americans, they speak English, but their world view is African. The mystical elements—the Binder, the ghosts—are a very real part, particularly in the early 20th century, of the Black American experience. There was an attempt to capture the 'African-ness' of the characters.

And yet there are characters, such as Seth and Bertha, who own the boarding house, who seem very 'American.'

Well, they are of African descent though their experiences in America have been different. Seth is a Northern free man. His father was not a slave. His grandfather was not a slave. He was born in the North. So his experiences are totally different from the rest of the characters who have come up from the South, whose parents have been slaves. The fact that he owns the boarding house and that he is a craftsman, that he has a skill other than farming, sets him apart from the other characters. That was also a part of the Black experience.

There is a part of the character of Loomis that is similar to Levee from **Ma Rainey***—an anger or drive, a sense of something not being accomplished.*

I don't know if Levee's angry. For some reason I don't like that word. Levee is trying to wrestle with the process of life the same as all of us. His question is, "How can I live this life in a society that refuses to recognize my worth, that refuses to allow me to contribute to its welfare—how can I live this life and remain a whole and complete person?" I think Loomis and Levee are very similar in some elements of their character, as you pointed out, but Levee has a firmer sense of who he is—where Loomis is more clearly on a search for identity, on a search for a world that contains his image.

How did you get the ideas for the characters of the People Finder and The Binder in **Joe Turner***?*

Well, the first title of the play was the title of a painting by Romare Bearden, *Mill Hand's Lunch Bucket.* It's of a boarding house in Pittsburgh in the 20's. There is a figure in the painting that my attention was drawn to. The figure of a man sitting at a kitchen table in a posture of defeat or abandonment. And I wondered, "Who is this man and why is he sitting there and what are the circumstances of his life?" That became Herald Loomis. It occurred to me that at the time and particularly after slavery there was a lot of dispersement among Blacks. Families were separated. I had been working on a series of poems called "Restoring the House" in which a man set out in search of his wife who had been sold from Mississippi to a family in Georgia maybe five years before the Emancipation. Of course, when he finds her, all kinds of things have happened in the interim. That idea of people leaving each other, of people being separated—there has to be someone who wants to heal them and bind them together. So that's how the idea of the Binder came about. I gave him the name Bynum, which was my grandfather's name, and which seemed appropriate. The People Finder is almost the same concept, but it's a White application of it. Rutherford Selig is a peddler of pots and pans. He travels about knocking on people's doors, and as a result he's the only one who knows where everybody lives. So if the people were looking for someone, it's only logical they would ask Selig. I don't think he called himself the People Finder—this is something the people of the community called him.

Do you see him as more evil than Bynum?

Oh, no, he's not evil at all. In fact, he's performing a very valuable service for the community. The fact that his father was a "People Finder" who worked for the plantation bosses and caught runaway slaves has no bearing on Selig's character. That was his job. That was something he did and got paid for. His grandfather was a "Bringer" working on a slave ship. Selig doesn't make any apologies for any of this. It's not his fault. It was his grandfather's job. It was hard work. His grandfather got married and had some kids. This contact with Blacks, of being paid for performing some service that involved Blacks, has been going on in his family for a long time. Selig is the guy who opens up a hardware store in a Black community. He's got a long history of involvement.

What about the story of Joe Turner, who took slaves and kept them for seven years?

Joe Turner was a real person. He was the brother of Pete Turner who was the Governor of Tennessee. Joe Turner would press Blacks into peonage. He would send out decoys who would lure Blacks into crap games and then he would swoop down and grab them. He had a chain with forty links to it, and he would take Blacks off to his plantation and work them. The song "Joe Turner" was a song the women sang down around Memphis. "Joe Turner's got my man and gone."

When I became aware of this song somehow it fit into the play. Because the seven years Loomis is with Joe Turner, seven years in which his world is torn asunder and his life is turned upside down, can in fact represent the four hundred years of slavery, of being taken out of Africa and brought to America. At some point someone says, "Okay, you're free." What do you do? Who are you, first of all, and what do you do now that you're free, which is Loomis' question. He says, "I must reconnect and reassemble myself." But when he goes to the place where he lived, his life is no longer there. His wife and daughter aren't there. He is, in effect, a foreigner to the place. So he goes off on a search. He searches for a woman to say goodbye to and to find a world that contains his image, because there's nothing about the world that he finds himself in that speaks to the thing that's beating inside his chest. And in the process of that search he falls into an ancestral drove and is witness to bones rising up out of the ocean, taking on flesh and walking up on the land. This is his connection with the ancestors, the Africans who were lost during the Middle Passage and were thrown overboard. He is privileged to witness this because he needs most to know who he is. It is telling him, "This is who you are. You are these bones. You are the sons and daughters of these people. They are walking around here now and they look like you because you are these very same people. This is who you are." This is what Bynum tries to guide him toward. And the scene where Loomis reveals his vision can be read as a baptism, as a naming. Loomis' recognition of that, his "learning to sing his song", and his acceptance of that is what makes him luminous.

When did you find the end of the play, with Loomis slashing his own chest?

When I wrote it. It's something that just happened. I said to myself, "What was that?" and I looked and examined it. At first it read as a liberation, a severing of the bonds, a bloodletting rite. But I think its larger meaning especially in relation to the Christian context, is that Loomis accepts the responsibility for his own presence in the world, and the responsibility for his own salvation. It says, "I don't need anyone to bleed for me, I can bleed for myself." Because your god should resemble you. When you look in the mirror you should see your god. If you don't, then you have the wrong god.

Were you conscious that **Ma Rainey** *also ended with a knife?*

There are knives in the two, but that's the only similarity. In *Joe Turner* it's accepting the responsibility for your own salvation. In *Ma Rainey,* it's a transference of aggression from Sturdyvant to Toledo, who throughout the play has been set up as a substitute for the White man. It happens in a kind of blind rage as opposed to something that comes from an inner life. When Loomis slashes himself, he's conscious of all the meanings. He knows he must do it. The thing he's been looking for those four years he finds in that moment.

Are you consciously writing religious symbols in the plays?

I don't try to. I write whatever's there. Whatever comes out of me.

As we've said, one of the aspects of your plays is a sort of looking back at history, or even a contemporary involvement in that history. (For example, in compiling program notes for **Ma Rainey,** *you didn't want primary source documents from the Harlem Renaissance writers of the 20's and 30's, but rather contemporary writing examining that period.) In* **Joe Turner,** *the integrations of both worlds seems particularly complete, even forging an unknown sort of "otherworld" through an elevation of language and ideas.*

I think you just said it—the ideas are universal ideas. When I started I knew it wasn't like my other plays. I knew I wanted to create the sense of a whole other world. It's a blending together, an overlap. You're looking at the familiar in a new way.

Do you have a total stage picture from the audience's perspective as you write, or do you write from the viewpoint of each character, dropping into each voice as you write?

The characters actually do what they want to do. It's their story. I'm like Bynum in *Joe Turner:* walking down a road in this strange landscape. What you confront is part of yourself, your willingness to deal with the small imperial truths you have accumulated over your life. That's your baggage. And it can be very terrifying. You're either wrestling with the devil or Jacob's angel, the whole purpose being that when you walk through that landscape you arrive at something larger than you had when you started. And this larger something should be illuminating and as close to the truth as you can understand. I think if you accomplish that, whether the play works or not, you've been true to yourself and in that sense you're successful. So I write from the center, the core, of myself. You've got that landscape and you've got to enter it, walk down that road and whatever happens, happens. And that's the best you're capable of coming to. The characters do it, and in them, I confront myself.

The characters in your plays are each trying to find their songs, or they receive a gift from someone who perceives what their songs might be. In your 50's play, **Fences,** *the father has a beautiful speech that sums up his life, his song. Would you quote that?*

"I come in here every Friday. I carry a sack of potatoes and a bucket of lard. You all line up at the door with your hands out. I give you the lint from my pockets. I give you my sweat and blood. I ain't got no tears. I done spent them. We go upstairs to that room at night and I fall down on you and try to blast a hole into forever. I get up Monday morning . . . find my lunch on the table. I go out. Make my way. Find my strength to carry me through to the next Friday. That's all I got. That's all I got to give. I can't give nothing else."

Hilary DeVries (essay date January 1987)

SOURCE: "A Song in Search of Itself," *American Theatre,* Vol. 3, No. 10, January, 1987, pp. 22-5.

[*In the following essay, DeVries examines the recurring themes in Wilson's cycle of plays regarding the black experience. She identifies the most pervasive theme as "the need for black Americans to forge anew their identity, an identity that is at once African and American."*]

In August Wilson's most recent play, *The Piano Lesson,* the young protagonist Boy Willie declares: "That's all I wanted. To sit down and be at ease with everything. But I wasn't born to that. When I go by on the road and something ain't right, then I got to try and fix it." The speaker is the son of a slave determined to transform his family's racial legacy into a self-determining future; but the words also bear witness to their author's aspirations as one of this country's leading black playwrights.

In the black American theatrical tradition, often distinguished as much by political circumstance as individual accomplishment, August Wilson has emerged as a compelling new voice. Chronicling the history of black Americans through the 20th century, Wilson draws on his background as a poet to enrich his more recently honed talents as a dramatist. His three best-known plays, *Ma Rainey's Black Bottom, Fences* and *Joe Turner's Come and Gone,* evince both their author's fecund use of language and a storyteller's narrative touch.

The plays' cumulative intent, however, is as pedagogic as it is expository. Wilson describes his artistic agenda as an attempt to "concretize" the black American tradition, to demonstrate how that tradition "can sustain a man once he has left his father's house." Indeed, the theme that surges through

Wilson's work is the need for black Americans to forge anew their identity, an identity that is at once African and American.

In the seven years he has been writing plays—his first efforts resulted in a handful of seldom if ever produced one-acts—Wilson has undertaken an ambitious, systematic project: each work is to be set in a different decade from 1900 to the present. "I'm taking each decade and looking back at one of the most important questions that blacks confronted in that decade and writing a play about it," says Wilson. "Put them all together and you have a history."

The dramatic chronicle that has resulted thus far is peopled by striking protagonists earmarked by the eras in which they lived: Levee, the impetuous young trumpeter of *Ma Rainey,* struggles to survive in a white entertainment world during the '20s; Loomis, the forbiddingly Dickensian protagonist of *Joe Turner,* fights to regain his identity after seven years of forced labor in the early 1900s; Troy, the tyrannical patriarch of *Fences,* rages at social injustice prefiguring that of the explosive '60s. Collectively they constitute Wilson's overt literary intent: "You should be able to see a progression through the decades from Loomis to Levee to Boy Willie [in *The Piano Lesson*] to Troy. Says drama critic Ernie Schier, "August is a better chronicler of the black experience in this country than Alex Haley. In 40 years, he will be the playwright we will still be hearing about."

Ironically, Wilson is emerging at a time when few black American playwrights are finding and keeping a national audience, when politically and artistically the country is more attuned to the racial injustices of South Africa than to the dilemmas of its own black population. Nonetheless, after nearly two decades of writing both poetry and drama and four years of almost exclusive collaboration with director Lloyd Richards at the O'Neill Theater Center and Yale Repertory Theatre, Wilson is entering a new and broader arena.

The Piano Lesson received its first staged reading at the O'Neill this past summer. A trio of Wilson's other plays are currently crisscrossing the country. *Fences,* starring James Earl Jones, is set to open in New York in March after runs last season at the Goodman Theatre in Chicago and (with a different cast) at Seattle Repertory Theatre. The Yale production of *Joe Turner* has just completed the first of its regional theatre stopovers at Boston's Huntington Theatre Company. And—although *Ma Rainey* never recouped its investment during its commercial New York run two years ago, despite its critical heralding and a 1984 Tony nomination—Wilson is tilting anew at Broadway. In addition to the upcoming New York run of *Fences,* Wilson has just completed the book for a new musical about black jazz musician Jelly Roll Morton, which is to star Gregory Hines and open on Broadway in the spring under Jerry Zaks's direc-

tion. "I consider this a jazz-blues folk opera," says Wilson, "an encapsulation of the history of black music until 1928."

The undertaking is further evidence of Wilson's commitment to his delineated literary turf—history, that individual and collective process of discovery that, as the author says, "becomes doubly important if someone else has been writing yours for you." His plays maintain a contemporary involvement with the past, and punctuate each era with its own particular totems. By mining black American music, which Wilson sees as one of the few traditionally acceptable venues for black American culture, Wilson is able to reveal the cumulative history informing his protagonists: nearly all his characters are in search of their individual songs of identity. Wilson describes Loomis's meta-physical journey in *Joe Turner,* for example, as a "song in search of itself."

Its musical allusions aside, Wilson's writing is a poetic melding of African and Western imagery. His use of ethnographically specific folklore borders on the mystical and reinforces the distinctively non-linear narrative style which the playwright ascribes to an "African storytelling mode." While some have been slow to warm to this non-traditional dramatic structure, others have praised it as indigenous to the black oral tradition, a heritage that embraces African as well as Bible Belt oral patterns and serves as Wilson's own palimpsest. "It is writing based on centuries of 'hearing'," says director Claude Purdy, who staged Wilson's *Fences* at GeVa Theatre in Rochester, N.Y.

Wilson describes his work as an attempt to confront "the glancing manner in which white America looks at blacks and the way blacks look at themselves." By probing the sociological archetype with sufficient metaphor but without conspicuous didacticism, Wilson has set himself apart from many of the so-called angry young black playwrights, including Ed Bullins and Amiri Baraka, whose work proliferated during the late '60s. "I can only do what I do because the '60s existed," Wilson reasons. "I am building off that original conflict."

Although he maintains that "the one thing that has best served me as a playwright is my background in poetry," Wilson first came to the theatre out of a search for a broader forum in which to voice his social concerns; initially he thought about a legal career. But after a boyhood spent on the streets of Pittsburgh—Wilson dropped out of school at age 15—the playwright says "my sense of justice [became] very different from what the law says. It just happened that my talent lies with words." Claude Purdy, now director-in-residence at St. Paul's Penumbra Theatre, confirms Wilson's motives: "August came out of the '60s with a responsible attitude, eager to explore his community's culture and do something for his people."

As a co-founder of Pittsburgh's Black Horizons Theatre, Wilson wrote his early one-acts during the height of the black power movement as a way, he says, "to politicize the community and raise consciousness." Today Wilson prefers the label of "cultural nationalist."

"An interviewer once asked me if having written these plays I hadn't exhausted the black experience. I said, 'Wait a minute. You've got 40,000 movies and plays about the white experience, and we don't ask if you've exhausted your experience.' I'll never run out of material. If I finish this cycle, I'll just start over again. You can write forever about the clash between the urban North and the rural South, what happened when [blacks] came to the cities, how their lives changed and how it affected generations to come."

It is an outspoken assertion from this usually reserved 41-year-old Pittsburgh native now residing in St. Paul. Wilson's conversational style only hints at his transplanted Midwest roots. With his soft-spoken affability and almost old-fashioned politeness, he hardly appears the source for the chorus of vibrant voices—by turns soft and genial, angry and defiant—one hears in his plays.

"After I turned 20, I spent the next 10 to 15 years hanging out on streetcorners, following old men around, working odd jobs. There was this place called Pat's Cigar Store in Pittsburgh. It was the same place that Claude McKay mentioned in his book *Home to Harlem.* When I found out about that, I said, 'This is a part of history,' and I ran down there to where all the old men in the community would congregate."

Although Wilson originally channeled his literary efforts into poetry, his move to Minnesota in the early 1970s served as a catalyst, permitting those colloquial voices and his own skills as a dramatist to come into their own. Initially working as a script writer for the local science museum's children's theatre while firing off "five plays in three years" to the O'Neill, Wilson did not conceive of himself as a playwright until he received the first of several writing grants. After submitting *Jitney* to Minneapolis's Playwrights' Center, Wilson was awarded a Jerome Foundation fellowship in the late 1970s. (He has subsequently received Bush, Rockefeller, McKnight and Guggenheim fellowships.) "I walked in and there were 16 playwrights," Wilson remembers about that encounter with the Playwrights' Center. "It was the first time I had dinner with other playwrights. It was the first time I began to think of myself as one."

It was this "two hundred bucks a month for a year" that afforded Wilson the opportunity to rework a one-act about a blues recording session into what became the full-length *Ma Rainey,* his first play accepted by the O'Neill and the most naturalistic of his dramas. Set in a Chicago recording studio in 1927, the play is a garrulous and colloquially accurate look at the exploitation of black musicians. Through Wilson's carefully orchestrated verbal riffs, the characters' struggle for identity slowly escalates to a violent conclusion.

In *Ma Rainey,* the struggle is predicated not only upon friction between the white recording executives and the black musicians but also upon subtle conflicts within the black community itself. Ma, the recording star, knows the limits of her commercial success, admitting, "It's just like I been a whore"; the elderly pianist, Toledo, is an African nationalist who argues, "We done sold ourselves to the white man in order to be like him"; Levee, the headstrong trumpeter, is intent on making it in the white world, on seeing his name in lights. Unable to confront his white oppressors, Levee fatally lashes out at his own. Wilson describes Levee's condition·in a rhetorical question: "How can I live this life in society that refuses to recognize my worth, that refuses to allow me to contribute to its welfare?"

It is a question that Wilson probes again in *Fences,* written partly as a response to criticism of *Ma Rainey*'s bifurcated focus. "*Fences* was me sitting down saying, 'Okay, here is a play with a large central character.'" It was also the writer's attempt to create a protagonist who, unlike the impatient and intransigent Levee, had achieved a grudging parity with his times, albeit a smoldering suppression of desire suitable to the political realities of the 1950s. "Unlike Levee, Troy didn't sell his soul to the devil," says Wilson.

A former Negro League ballplayer past his prime by the time Jackie Robinson broke the color barrier, Troy Maxson can be considered Wilson's most overtly didactic character. "I had to write a character who is responsible and likes the idea of family," says the playwright. This sense of responsibility—for one's own destiny as well as one's own family—is pivotal for Wilson, not only in its metaphysical ramifications but in its more pragmatic applications as well. "We have been told so many times how irresponsible we are as black males that I try and present positive images of responsibility," says the writer. "I started *Fences* with the image of a man standing in his yard with a baby in his arms."

It is this sense of individual accountability that Wilson's other protagonists—Loomis in *Joe Turner* and Boy Willie in the yet-to-be-produced *Piano Lesson*—confront in more mystical terms. "In *Ma Rainey* and *Fences,*" Wilson explains, "the two roads into white American society traditionally open to blacks, entertainment and sports, fail the characters." As a result, the leading figures in the subsequent plays do not establish their identities relative to the white world; they rediscover themselves as Africans. "If black folks would recognize themselves as Africans and not be afraid to respond to the world as Africans, then they could make their contribution to the world as Africans," says Wilson.

Set in 1911 in order to get closer to this "African retentiveness," *Joe Turner* is infused with so much non-Western mysticism and folklore—ghosts, myths, chants and spells—that the narrative can be seen as a spiritual allegory. Based partly on a painting by black artist Romare Bearden, "Mill Hand's Lunch Bucket," as well as the legend of the actual slave hunter Joe Turner, the play is rife with historical detail as well as religious feeling. Loomis's search for his own past after seven years of bondage symbolizes the quest of an entire race. "As a whole, our generation knows very little about our past," explains Wilson. "My generation of parents tried to shield their children from the indignities they'd suffered."

For Loomis, the journey towards self-knowledge includes two apocalyptic moments—baptismal exorcisms that bracket the play's two acts and reverberate with violence. In the first of these cathartic steps, Loomis confronts his vision of "bones walking on top of water," a mythic image of ancestral suffering. In the final scene, Loomis faces both Christianity and African myth, and with a single symbolic act, finds himself purged from his past and a free man. As Loomis states, "I don't need anyone to bleed for me, I can bleed for myself."

It is a moment of individual transmogrification that Wilson examines again, and to even stronger effect, in *The Piano Lesson.* Although Wilson intends to rewrite this latest entry in his historical cycle next summer, the play's inherent dramatic conflict—a brother and sister argue over their shared legacy, the family piano—and its crisp scenic construction bode well for its arrival on stage. The piano itself is Wilson's clearest, most fully realized symbol, one that resounds with African and Western significance while forming the fulcrum of the play's metaphysical debate. "The real issue is the piano, the legacy. How are you going to use it?" says Wilson.

There are two choices, one taken up by Berneice, who wants to preserve the blood-stained piano as a totem to the family's violence-wracked past. Her brother, Boy Willie, however, is intent on literally capitalizing on the family's history to create a new future; he wants to sell the piano and buy the land which their father originally farmed as a slave. "I ain't gonna be no fool about no sentimental value," Boy Willie says. "With that piano I get the land and I can go down and cash in the crop." As Wilson describes his character's position, "I often wonder what the fabric of American society would be like if blacks had stayed in the South and somehow found a way to [economically] develop and lock into that particular area. That's what Boy Willie is articulating. He wants to put his hands to better use."

Willie's desire encapsulates the playwright's overall intent. "I think it's largely a question of identity. Without knowing your past, you don't know your present—and you certainly can't plot your future," Wilson says. "You go out and dis-cover it for yourself. It's being responsible for your own presence in the world and for your own salvation."

Margaret E. Glover (essay date Summer-Fall 1988)

SOURCE: "Two Notes on August Wilson: The Songs of A Marked Man," in *Theatre,* Vol. 19, No. 3, Summer-Fall, 1988, pp. 69-70.

[*In the essay below, Glover examines the role of blues music in Wilson's plays.*]

A black man walks into a bar. The words "for whites only" do not hang over the neon sign in the window, but as he enters he senses that the bartender and his patrons wish he were not there. He is thirsty and does not know the city well enough to look for another bar where he would be welcome. He takes a seat at the bar and orders a drink. The bartender serves him; the next song begins to play on the juke box. He recognizes the music as the same music he would hear coming out of a juke box on the other side of town. He begins to breathe more deeply; he stops trying to make himself invisible; he rests his arms firmly on the bar; he moves the beer bottle to the right, his glass to the left and marks out his space at the bar. "If they are playing my music, this is where I belong."

The man is August Wilson. The year is 1987. The voices of his characters come back to him. Ma Rainey in Sturdyvant's Chicago recording studio. "Wanna take my voice and trap it in them fancy boxes with all them buttons and dials . . . and then too cheap to buy me a coca-cola." Bynum to Jeremy in Seth Holly's boarding house [in *Joe Turner's Come and Gone*]. "You ought to take your guitar and go down to Seefus . . . That's where the music at . . . The people down there making music and enjoying themselves. Some things is worth taking the chance going to jail about." And Wining Boy at one of the stops along his road [in *The Piano Lesson*].

> You look up one day and you hate the whiskey, you
> hate the women, and you hate the piano. But that's
> all you got. You can't do nothing else. So all you
> know is how to play that piano. Now, who am I?
> Am I me . . . or am I the piano player? Sometimes
> it seem like the only thing to do is shoot the piano
> player 'cause he's the cause of all the trouble I'm
> having.

This is the dilemma. His music gave the black man a place in the white man's world, but at the cost of losing his right to that music and the part of himself he put in it. Ma Rainey knows that once Sturdyvant and Irvin have gotten what they want from her music, "then it's just like I'd been some whore and they roll over and put their pants on." But the same music she sold to make a name for herself was the blues that "help you get out of bed in the morning. You get up knowing you ain't alone. There's something else in the world . . . You get up knowing whatever your troubles is you can get a grip on them 'cause the blues done give you an understanding of life." Ma Rainey chooses to believe that the blues from which she took the melodies for her own songs will always be there, just as the blues has always been there waiting for the people to find their own songs in its fullness.

But does that music remain whole and free when strains of it are sold to the white man? Berneice and Boy Willie struggle to resolve a similar question in *The Piano Lesson.* Berneice argues that to sell the piano for a stake in a new life is to sell one's soul. Boy Willie counters that to guard the piano as a shrine to those who died for it is to bind him to the slavery and homelessness of the past.

The underlying agony is between the personal freedom that the music and its songs provide and the fact that just singing the music for one's self is not enough to live free in the white man's world. It is through music that Levee seeks a way to tell the stories that gnaw at him [in *Ma Rainey's Black Bottom*], but he is denied the right to tell people how to play it. Where is the law preventing him from leaving his mark on the world by playing his own music? Others have left their mark on him while exercising what they called their "Freedom." For Levee, as for the other marked men in August Wilson's plays, personal freedom is not enough.

In *Joe Turner's Come and Gone* Bynum tells the story of how he found his Binding Song as a lesson to Loomis. "All you got to do is sing it. Then you'll be free." But Joe Turner took Loomis' song to fill his own emptiness, and Herald Loomis may never get it back. In *The Piano Lesson* Wining Boy calls his music an albatross. It has become a way for others to name him without knowing him. He looks at the piano and sees something the white man gives him to play on.

Others hear what they want to, but do not really listen to what the words, the rhythms and the melodies of Levee's songs of the city or Wining Boy's and Doaker's songs of the road tell them about the souls of these men.

There is something frightening in this music "that breathes and touches. That connects. That is in itself a way of being, separate and distinct from any other." (August Wilson) It frightens the white man because it is something the characters in August Wilson's plays are not only willing to go to jail for but to fight each other for. It frightens the singers because they know they can neither control nor contain it.

To find their songs they must open themselves to be consumed by this music.

> Its warmth and redress, its braggadocio and roughly poignant comments, its vision and prayer . . . instruct and allow them to reconnect, to reassemble and gird up for the next battle to which they could claim both victim and ten thousand slain.

Sandra G. Shannon (essay date Fall 1989-1990)

SOURCE: "The Good Christian's Come and Gone: The Shifting Role of Christianity in August Wilson Plays," in *MELUS,* Vol. 16, No. 3, Fall, 1989-1990, pp. 127-42.

[In the following essay, Shannon examines Wilson's treatment of Christianity in his plays.]

The center of African American playwright August Wilson's growing theatrical universe is conspicuously occupied by African American men. They are the thinkers, the doers, the dreamers. Revolving around them in seemingly expendable supporting roles are wives, mistresses, sisters, children and other relatives. As characters such as Levee (*Ma Rainey's Black Bottom*), Troy Maxson (*Fences*), Herald Loomis (*Joe Turner's Come and Gone*), and Boy Willie (*The Piano Lesson*), impose their authority, they overshadow the concerns of others. Most noticeable in their blind quest for omnipotence and wealth is that they place no stock in Christian dogma, adapting instead a purely secular ideology. Consequently, what emerges from their abandonment of Christianity is a more convenient, self-serving religion—one totally unaligned with the cultural reservoir provided by what many African Americans have traditionally referred to as "good old-fashioned religion." While this good old-fashioned religion has, for centuries, provided inspiration, strength and moral principles for African Americans, Wilson's men affirm that it has not and will not suit their needs. Therefore, they demonstrate their disavowal by challenging and withdrawing from the religion of their ancestors.

August Wilson has apparently chosen to focus on the African American man's oppression in this country to symbolize the collective struggles of all African Americans. Since the early 1980s, Wilson has committed himself to writing ten plays chronicling the history of his people in each decade of their existence in the United States. Often depicted on the verge of an emotional breakdown, Levee, Herald Loomis, Troy Maxson, and Boy Willie dominate center stage and become Wilson's primary spokesmen. Although the African American woman appears in various supporting roles—devoted wife and mother, cranky blues singer, docile sex object, stubborn sister, etc.—the actions of the African American man clearly convey the themes of each of the four plays Wilson has completed toward his ten-play mission.

What is the place of Christianity in the lives of Wilson's African American men? What has caused them to abandon this previously vital ingredient in their culture? Despite Wilson's frequently quoted belief that "God does not hear the prayers of blacks," his probing treatment of each African American man's personal modification of Christianity begs a far less simplistic analysis. The African American man's shift from devout Christian reverence to outright blasphemy may be partially explained by examining one of many effects of continued racism in America—what Joseph Washington labels as "folk religion" in his study *Black Religion.* This religion of the folk, per se, was the African American's communal response to economic, social and racial oppression. Noting that their white oppressors often quoted the scriptures to them to justify so-called "ordained" subjugation, many African Americans rationalized that the Bible did not serve their interests. According to folk religion, ethics and morals were determined by adhering to group consensus and by adapting as righteous certain accepted practices within the African American community; the Bible was not the focal point of "folk religion."

From Reconstruction to the Civil Rights Movement, African Americans who were once Christians met discrimination and violence with a bitter mixture of Christian humility and human dignity. According to Washington, who disputes the existence of a so-called "Negro Church," the

> common suffering of segregation and discrimination is the crucible out of which the folk religion was created in the past. . . . The folk religion is not an institutional one. It is a spirit which binds Negroes in a way they are not bound to other Americans because of their different histories. Here and there this folk religion may be identifiable with a given congregation, yet, wherever and whenever the suffering is acute, it transcends all religious and socio-economic barriers which separate Negroes from Negroes.

This communal spirit among mutually oppressed African Americans was a generic response to the too restrictive commandments of the Christian faith. Unfortunately, as is the case with Wilson's African American men, it is also a thin veil between agnosticism and outright atheism.

Among Christians the Old Testament's *Book of Job* remains one of the most typical lessons in "good" Christian behavior. However, few objective readers can deny that Job appears to be unfairly victimized by a God who tests his faithfulness by initiating one catastrophe after another—each

one more crippling than the preceding one. It is not difficult, therefore, to see the parallels in the levels of misfortune between Wilson's characters and the long-suffering Job in this classic work of victimization. Yet Wilson's characters have lost the patience of Job. Worn thin by centuries of disappointments and delays, their patience has fermented into extreme cynicism and destructive behavior. Consequently, they act out those previously repressed desires to respond to their misfortunes, even though they cannot alter them.

> **It is not difficult . . . to see the parellels in the levels of misfortune between Wilson's characters and the long-suffering Job. . . .**
> *–Sandra G. Shannon*

Wilson's introduction to the "big-league" among the American theater circuit came with his much hailed production of *Ma Rainey's Black Bottom* (1981). Set in 1927, the play depicts the vulnerable state of African American jazz musicians creating music in a decade when the majority of the country's African American population was pre-occupied with relocating to crowded urban areas during what is now known as the Great Migration. Unfortunately, this mass exodus of African Americans from southern farmland to city dwellings extended into the Depression Era. Not only did African Americans from the South buckle to the poverty and racism that awaited them in northern cities, but those who were already in the North also experienced increasing injustice. For example, while African American performers were often denied access to public facilities, their white fans were welcome in the Jim Crow-separated or exclusively white entertainment halls where blacks crooned, danced or played their jazz before them. Frequently, in the recording industry especially, opportunistic white promoters lined their pockets from ticket and album sales from the music of unsuspecting African American artists. This often proved to be a precarious business arrangement, for such artists had no protection against being surreptitiously discarded at the slightest signs of waning popularity or disfavor with the promoter.

Detained by a freak car accident, Ma Rainey comes late to a recording studio where she is scheduled to sing several of her popular works for an album. Already irritable because of her tardiness, Sturdyvant and Irvin, her white promoters, grumble as she continues to stall by demanding a Coca Cola, by complaining about the chilly studio and by insisting that her stuttering nephew Sylvester be allowed to announce her on the album before she sings.

While Ma Rainey tries the patience of her two promoters, her musicians waiting in the basement band room, all of whom are African American men, bicker and taunt each other in deceptively simple banter. Their conversations, which slip from the correct spelling of "music" to an existentialist discussion of African American history, gradually intensify and unexpectedly erupt in a fatal stabbing. The self-made philosopher Toledo inadvertently steps on the new Florsheim shoes of Levee, the trumpet player, and, apparently for that, he is murdered. Still sulking because of Sturdyvant's recent refusal to pay him fairly for songs which he had composed, the trumpet player turns an otherwise commonplace incident into a justification for homicide.

Contrary to its title, **Ma Rainey's Black Bottom** is not really about Ma Rainey. Even though the play revolves around the life of the one-time blues legend Ma Rainey, Wilson includes her not as a leading lady but rather as a less conspicuous though uninhibited commentator on the callous, white-controlled music industry. Instead, it is the trumpeter, Levee, who ultimately conveys Wilson's more powerful message of the veritable "rape" of black blues performers whose talents were exploited by greedy white promoters.

The most latent and ultimately the most destructive form of victimization is exemplified by Levee, the band's ambitious trumpet player. Instead of directly confronting his nemesis, he transfers his aggression to a colleague. Apparently he has channeled his hostility inward for quite some time—so much so that at the moment of Toledo's death, Levee appears totally out of control. In him one may note shades of Richard Wright's Bigger Thomas or flashes of Amiri Baraka's cynical antiheroes Walker Vessels and Rochester. As the play strongly suggests, Levee kills another African American man in a bloody ritual that provides a temporary catharsis for his hatred of Sturdyvant. Under the guise of retaliation for a temporarily soiled pair of Florsheim shoes, Levee wields a blade into another African American man with a fury that seems to be a gross over-reaction to a misplaced foot.

Although Levee's action may seem impetuous, one may note in dialogue throughout the play reasons for his pre-existing cynicism. He brings with him to the recording session a history of victimization that spans his entire life. For example, as an eight-year-old, he watched his mother as she was raped by white men:

> I didn't know what they were doing to her . . . but I figured whatever it was they may as well do it to me too. My daddy had a knife that he kept around there for hunting and working and whatnot. I knew where he kept it and I went and got it.

Levee is further victimized when his business arrangement with Sturdyvant does not proceed as he had hoped. After agreeing to promote lyrics composed by Levee, Sturdyvant squashes the trumpet player's ambitions to start a band of his own and play his own brand of jazz.

Yet Levee's cynicism is not restricted to the white man. Like other Wilson African American men, Levee has concluded that God is on the side of the white man. Reasoning as such, he simultaneously rails against the white man for a history of abuse and against his now alien God for allowing it to persist. For example, Levee is quick to question the whereabouts of the white man's God as he recalls when the black minister Reverend Gates missed his train to Atlanta one night and was surrounded by a group of jeering whites who stripped him of his cross and Bible and made him dance until they grew tired of watching him.

> What I wants to know is . . . if he's a man of God, then where the hell was God when all of this was going on? Why wasn't God looking out for him? Why didn't God strike down them crackers with some of this lightning you talk about to me?

Further enraging fellow band members Cutler and Toledo with his vituperative blasphemy, Levee comes to the conclusion that August Wilson suggests in each of his four published chronicles of African American life in America:

> . . . he a white man's God. That's why! God ain't never listened to no nigger's prayers. God take a nigger's prayers and throw them in the garbage. God don't pay niggers no mind. In fact . . . God hate niggers! Hate them with all the fury in his heart. Jesus don't love you, nigger!

Even after Cutler hurls Levee to the floor and bludgeons his face for this sacrilegious attack on his God, Levee presses his point further, but this time armed with a knife:

> We gonna find out whose God He is! . . . Come on and save him [Cutler] like you did my mama! . . . I heard her when she called you! I heard her when she said, "Lord, have mercy! Jesus, help me!"

No longer convinced that the Christian God is an ally, Levee resorts to annihilating a member of his own race to appease his frustration. Implicit in this homicidal tendency is an enigmatic love-hate relationship with whites. Although Levee must know that it is the whites who pose the greatest obstacle to his career, he uses his African American colleagues as scapegoats in order to vent his frustrations. Consequently, he self-deludes himself into thinking that he is in the white man's favor while his colleagues appear naive. After failing to negotiate a more lucrative deal for his songs with Ma Rainey's capitalistic white business manager, Levee, like many once ambitious, creative young African Americans, becomes disillusioned, self-defeating, and ultimately violent.

The frequency with which Wilson emphasizes the bleak prospects of African American men who do not embrace

Christianity suggests that little good comes to those who totally abandon their God, regardless of how they perceive Him. In the wake of his offensive anti-Christian rhetoric— "Jesus hate your black ass!" (*Ma Rainey*)—Levee seems destined to a dead-end career, and, as Toledo's murderer, he faces certain long-term incarceration. Yet Wilson also suggests the fatalistic outlook that those who do aspire to the Christian faith still encounter overwhelming odds and frequently utter failure or an abrupt death. Thus, the various misfortunes that plague the lives of Wilson's African American men (violent deaths, forced peonage and exile, family strife, or irreparably damaging business deals) are not necessarily divine punitive measures against them. They could simply be the dealings of fate.

Fences is even more indicative of the waning significance of Christianity in the lives of modern African American men. Set in the 1950s, the play is a domestic drama that examines the psychological battles of the secular "blues man" in a Christian oriented African American society. Although the overbearing but essentially frustrated African American garbage collector, Troy Maxson, still grapples with the effects of quitting school early to help his father at farming, of robbing and serving time for murder, and of being passed over in his bid for a baseball career, this cynical black man does not lay his burdens down at the church's altar. As is the case with each of Wilson's men, Christianity plays no role in Troy's search for comfort and direction.

Fences opens as two middle-aged African American men make their way home to celebrate another end of the work week. Troy, the more vocal one, comes in complaining of the blatant discrimination he faces on his job. He is upset that only white men drive the garbage trucks while the job of hoisting the huge trash-filled receptacles and emptying them into the compactors belongs to the African American workers. His frustration, which goes back as far as the 1920s Negro League, an unfulfilled career in major league baseball, and several years spent in jail for murder, affects his relationship with his wife Rose, his son Cory and his brain-damaged brother Gabriel.

Despite a seemingly loving and passionate relationship with his wife, an extra-marital affair with the "big-legged Florida gal" Alberta is Troy's only real joy. From this affair a daughter is born, yet Alberta dies in childbirth leaving Troy with no option but to ask his wife to become a surrogate mother to the child. He also succeeds in alienating his son by standing in the way to his playing professional football, preferring instead that Cory keep his job at the local A&P and get a good education.

Troy's often re-enacted fight against Death personified, which he describes in baseball terminology, finally becomes a reality. He dies one day while batting the rag ball he has tied to a tree in the yard. This final scene takes place at the dawn of the 1960s—a decade which will bring significant changes for African Americans. On the day of Troy's funeral, the Maxson family members tighten their bonds; Rose gently convinces their son Cory to tear down the emotional fences that have long separated him and Troy.

Troy finds his greatest solace in the blues, not Christianity. As a matter of fact, some of his most memorable lines in the play come at moments when he is most vulnerable to self pity: "Rose, I'm standing here with my daughter in my arms. She ain't but a wee bittie little old thing." The blues is more than a pastime for Wilson's characters. It is their universal means of communicating on the one hand and a means of healing emotional wounds on the other. Wilson recently explained this crucial cultural element:

> The blues are important primarily because they contain the cultural response of blacks in America to the situation that they find themselves in. Contained in the blues is a philosophical system at work.

> [Bill Moyers, *A World of Ideas: Conversations with Thoughtful Men and Women about American Life Today and the Ideas Shaping Our Future*, 1989.]

For Troy, this philosophical system apparently may not coexist with Christianity, which sanctions neither his marital infidelity nor the extortion of his brother's money.

Unlike Levee and Loomis, Troy does not openly blaspheme against God for his misfortunes, yet his obvious disregard for the saving grace of the church still reflects his less vocal form of atheism. While Christianity does not interest Troy, he adopts the game of baseball as a more relevant metaphor for his life. In addition to this sport, the play features several other substitutes for Troy's spiritual life, all of which prove futile in offering him any sort of lasting consolation.

For Troy, life is a baseball game riddled with fast balls, curve balls, sacrifice flies and sometimes strikeouts, yet too few homeruns. Although the conflict of the ball game lasts for only nine innings, Troy sees himself as being constantly at bat for much of his life. From keeping Death at bay to announcing a "full count" against his defiant son Cory, Troy adopts the language of the only game he knows. The various rules of the game become the basis for his own code of ethics—his Bible, his religion. Understandably, then, as a result of his allegiance to the laws governing a traditionally male-oriented sport stigmatized by raw competition and sauntering egos, Troy lacks candor in handling the more delicate relationships in his life. In one of the most intense moments of the play, Troy struggles to explain to his wife that he has not only been unfaithful to her but has also fathered a child outside of their marriage bed.

> I fooled them, Rose. I bunted. When I found you and Cory and a halfway decent job . . . I was safe. Couldn't nothing touch me. I wasn't gonna strike out no more. . . . I stood on first base for eighteen years and I thought . . . well, goddamn it . . . go on for it!

Thus, baseball jargon and traditional ethics of the game substitute for what might have been a prayer to God to save his marriage. Troy completely alienates both his son and his wife by forcing upon them his very narrow view of life. Consequently, he cannot see past immediate self gratification. He cannot compromise, nor can he ask for forgiveness.

Yet another clue to understanding Troy's secular philosophy is his rather heroic perception of his own mortality. Clearly undaunted by ideas of the life hereafter, Troy grapples with death by placing it comfortably within the context of his convenient baseball metaphor. Death, as Troy boasts, is "a fastball on the outside corner." Seen this way, its hold becomes less ominous when the victim has a role in determining his own fate.

Not only does Troy challenge death's omnipotence by likening its drama to the conflict of baseball, but he also defuses it, first, by personifying it and, second, by engaging it in a wrestling match:

> We wrestled for three days and three nights. I can't say where I found the strength from. Every time it seemed like he was gonna get the best of me, I'd reach way down deep inside myself and find the strength to do him one better.

In giving form to the Grim Reaper, Troy is able to further exert his machismo and remain precariously in control of his destiny. As Mei-Ling Ching asserts in "Wrestling Against History," [*Theater,* Vol. 19, 1988,] "Through his intentional mockery of death, [Troy] cleanses himself of his deepest fear and reaffirms his claim to life."

In addition to the stark contrast he provides to the rowdy, domineering Troy, his brother Gabriel is yet another manifestation of Troy's futile search to fill his spiritual void. After a World War II head injury leaves Gabriel virtually mentally retarded, he is convinced that he is, in fact, Archangel Gabriel, whose task is to open the Pearly Gates in Heaven and to chase away hell hounds. The conversations of this gentle man, therefore, are exclusively devoted to religious images associated with his imagined calling. When certain of Gabriel's irreversible condition, Troy claims the

$3,000 compensation awarded him and uses it to purchase a home.

Although Gabriel Maxson bears the name given to him by his parents, Wilson, no doubt, invites parallels to the Archangel of the Old Testament (see St. Luke 1:11 and 1:26; Daniel 8:16 and 9:21). Appearing throughout as a spokesman for God, Archangel Gabriel enjoys a direct line of communication with Him. Thus, by examining the many opposite features of Troy's relationship with Gabriel, one may measure the extent to which he has fallen from grace. Clearly, Gabriel is Troy's alter ego. While Troy is brash and overbearing, Gabriel is gentle and docile. While Troy is consciously manipulative, Gabriel is dishearteningly naive. While Troy is completely alienated from any sense of Christian ethics, Gabriel is consumed by it (albeit as a result of a mental disorder) to the point of self-delusion.

Despite Gabriel's apparent mental retardation, one should not dismiss his significance to the play because of his distorted sense of reality. Despite being the object of patronizing tolerance, community harassment, and Troy's suspicious handling of his finances, Gabriel maintains a self-assuredness uncharacteristic of any of the supposedly sane individuals around him. Moreover, he proves to be the purest representation of those Christian virtues that Troy lacks. Not even the long suffering Rose or her justifiably defiant son Cory emphasize as much as Gabriel how utterly blurred Troy's morals have become.

Wilson does not give much insight into the fraternal relationship between Troy and Gabriel. During the few times when Troy does engage in conversation with him, he does so with obvious indifference:

> GABRIEL: Troy . . . St. Peter got your name in the book. I seen it. It say . . . Troy Maxson. I say . . . I know him! He got the same name like what I got. That's my brother!
>
> TROY: How many times you gonna tell me that, Gabe?

Troy's somewhat less than enthusiastic tolerance of Gabriel betrays a very strained fraternal relationship. Although the supposedly guilt-ridden man seems to display admirable compassion for Gabriel (especially while in the company of Rose or his older son Lyons), it is Cory who touches an exposed nerve by acknowledging his father's ulterior motives: "You took Uncle Gabe's money he got from the army to buy this house and then you put him out."

The most lasting effect of Troy's egocentric philosophy comes from his extramarital relationship with Alberta. Even after he admits to the affair and the illegitimate daughter it produces, he displays a persistent self-righteousness in acknowledging his actions. He is just as blatant about upholding his obligations to both the mother and child as he is about explaining to Rose why he cheated on her: "I can sit up in her house and laugh. Do you understand what I'm saying. I can laugh out loud . . . and it feels good. It reaches all the way down to the bottom of my shoes."

Alberta provides a respite for Troy away from his pressing responsibilities as a family man. With her he does not have to walk the marital tightrope, nor does he feel obliged to give her any more than himself. Obviously content to let Troy come and go as he pleases, Alberta is the antithesis of Rose, who wishes to fence him in. While Gabriel provides Troy with a financial base, Alberta offers him an unconditional physical and emotional relationship. Troy understandably thinks he does not need any divine inspiration when such human substitutes are available.

How, then, does Rose fit into Troy's self-serving scheme? Is she no more than an expendable commodity—a scapegoat for his insensitive antics? Outwardly, Troy is robust in professing his love for her around his friend Bono, yet he allows himself to be consumed by an extra-marital affair. Indeed, to the disinterested observer, Rose could be perceived as merely someone who cooks Troy's food, does his laundry, gives him sex and acts as mediator in the spats between him and his two sons. Although he boasts to his life-long protegé Bono how much he loves Rose and insinuates a healthy sexual relationship with her, Troy apparently is not satisfied with just her. Consequently, Gabriel, Alberta and Rose appear to be private pawns in Troy's game of life. His relationships with each of them noticeably lack the degree of genuine compassion found in an otherwise morally conscious man. For the most part, Troy's self-conscious tirades, his apologies, his explanations, and his excuses seem to be more rhetorical exercises to bolster his own self-righteousness than attempts to communicate with those whom he loves.

Troy Maxson came to manhood in a poor urban industrialized environment where Christianity somehow did not seem to blend with what many struggling African Americans saw as necessary survival tactics. Although Troy openly laments the many bad decisions he has made in his life, he somehow remains unchanged, unconvinced that there is a better way. Clearly, Troy's opportunism is an extension of his personal code for survival and further indication of his anti-Christian sentiments. Like that of many African American men having to provide for themselves and their families in the Pittsburgh steel mill environment of the 1950s, Troy's religion is a practical religion with the haunting overtones of Social Darwinism—survival of the fittest and self-preservation. This secular perspective on life was the only means of sustaining their very crucial masculine egos in the face

of dehumanizing poverty and failed careers. When African American men like Troy did fall into the pits of depression, they did not reach for the Bible. They created their own convenient laws of behavior.

In his play *Joe Turner's Come and Gone,* Wilson concentrates upon cultural fragmentation; that is, the emotional and physical effects associated with the displacement of newly Americanized African Americans following the Civil War. Herald Loomis, the "prodigal son" of *Joe Turner's Come and Gone,* is a native son of this unstable environment. Among Wilson's four disillusioned African American men, the restless vagrant Herald Loomis perhaps best epitomizes the devastating alienation that influenced all aspects of the African American man's existence in this country. While just beginning to become accustomed to the bittersweet freedom afforded by the Emancipation Proclamation, Loomis is again enslaved—this time by the legendary white Tennesseean, Joe Turner, who forces him to labor on his plantation for seven years. As Wilson explains in a 1984 interview [with Kim Powers, in *Theater*],

> Joe Turner would press Blacks into peonage. He would send out decoys who would lure Blacks into crap games and then he would sweep down and grab them. He had a chain with forty links to it, and he would take Blacks off to his plantation and work them.

Once released, Loomis returns, disillusioned by the long separation from his wife and daughter.

But when Loomis seeks shelter at a boardinghouse, he learns that his wife Martha Pentecost has become saved and no longer wishes to be his wife. Left with the custody of his daughter Zonia, Loomis, like Troy, feels especially incomplete now that he is without his wife. Frustrated, disillusioned, heartbroken, Loomis slashes his chest in a ritualistic act of exorcism, declaring "I don't need nobody to bleed for me! I can bleed for myself." Loomis's final gesture is one of frustration rather than reverence. This obviously inverted religious gesture parodies the Judeo-Christian belief that Jesus Christ's crucifixion was the ultimate sacrifice. Although extreme in its example, the blood shed by Loomis undermines the crucifixion of Jesus as a broken agreement. Sensing abandonment and betrayal by his God, Loomis assumes responsibility for his own salvation in one quick stroke of his own knife. Thus, Loomis's self-sacrificing bloodletting offers an unmistakable commentary upon the African American man's frustrations with the inherent "lie" of traditional religion within the framework of this country's society.

Herald Loomis's personal quest to find his wife, Martha Pentecost, becomes more than a desire to locate a lost mate. Indeed, his predicament strongly suggests allegorical parallels to the entire race of African Americans who have been separated from their past. Driven by an obsession to reconnect with his family, Loomis enlists the services of the self-proclaimed "People Finder," Rutherford Selig. In one of several highly emotional displays, the melancholy Loomis notes,

> I just wanna see her face so I can get me a starting place in the world. The world got to start somewhere. That's what I been looking for. I been wandering a long time in somebody else's world. When I find my wife that be the making of my own.

Once re-united with the now "saved" Martha, Loomis resists her attempts to convert him, having lost all faith in her God.

In clinical psychologists' terms, Loomis's drastic behavior may be explained away as symptoms of a nervous breakdown. However, such a neat assessment ignores the play's larger message concerning the root causes of the African American man's rage against himself, other African Americans, and—as evidenced by the sustained pattern in Wilson's plays—against God and religion. Joseph T. Washington, author of an extensive re-examination of the role racial segregation has played in shifting theological significance in African Americans and whites alike, notes:

> The ethical preoccupation in the religion of the Negro has been accepted by many as merely a one-sided emphasis; with the decrease of social problems and the increase in educated Negro leaders, it is assumed that the slightly askew religion of the Negro will be corrected. Rather than being diagnosed and treated as a symptom of a critical malignancy, the religious expressions of the Negro have been dismissed as understandable nervous disorders. (viii)

Quite noticeable in each of August Wilson's plays is the cynical regard for Christianity as a positive force in the lives of his African American men. In Loomis's case, a dollar bill given to a so-called "People Finder" substitutes for what might have been a fervent prayer for God's assistance. Moreover, displays of religious devotion are met with biting cynicism. For example, during a scene in which the doubting Loomis and the saved Martha finally confront each other, he reveals that Jesus Christ, to him, has become not more than a "Great big old white man":

> Your Mr. Jesus Christ. Standing there with a whip in one hand and tote board in another, and them niggers swimming in a sea of cotton. And he counting. He tallying up the cotton.

Loomis's disgust for the Deity as well as religious rituals rep-

resents a complete reversal from his earlier pious life as a Deacon in the Abundant Life Church. Once concerned about saving the lost souls of gamblers, he now wants no part of "the white man's God." Consequently, this total abandonment of Christianity may be seen as the cause of his obsessive dependence upon a mortal (his wife Martha) for direction.

The harsh undertones implied by Loomis's blasphemy and bloodletting represent an extreme denunciation of Christian belief by an African American and an extreme act to compensate its loss. Herald Loomis is, no doubt, a tormented African American man, yet, instead of renewing his faith in God, he not only viciously blasphemes Him but also resorts to self-inflicted bloodletting as a measure of his disgust. Loomis's self-flagellation forces one to examine this man and others like him within the entire context of their sufferings—internal and external. They each stagger from the weight of antagonistic forces around them, which seem to favor their being nomads rather than the crucial cohesive element in their families. Indeed, the sardonic tone of Loomis's language as well as his willingness to draw his own blood reflect a kind of exasperation that is relatively new to African American theater.

Wilson's latest published play, *The Piano Lesson,* gives numerous lessons on the dreams of one African American man. As he does in two other plays featuring bitter confrontation within the black family (*Joe Turner's Come and Gone* and *Fences*), Wilson examines the divisive forces which the African American man has to expel in order to achieve the American Dream. This recent addition to Wilson's ten-play mission also prominently features an African American man having to devise and abide by his own code of ethics.

Central to *The Piano Lesson*'s conflict, an old piano simultaneously functions as an emblem of both African folk tradition and American capitalism. The pictorial history carved into its surface by the great grandfather of the currently embattled siblings, Berneice and Boy Willie, appreciates both its monetary and sentimental values. Thus, it becomes just as endearing to Berneice's memory of her family's past as it is valuable to her brother's future security.

Despite his sister's refusal to sell the family heirloom, Boy Willie maintains that he can reap more practical good from the otherwise useless object by investing his share of the sale in a small plot of land. With impeccable logic, he rationalizes against Berneice's less forcibly argued need to preserve the common link with their family's history. Like the obsessed Walter Lee of Lorraine Hansberry's *Raisin in the Sun,* who extorts a reward to which he has only partial birthright, Boy Willie wants to use the family heirloom to purchase a piece of the American Dream. Unfortunately, Boy Willie's sincerity distinguishes him only marginally from his character's antecedent—the hot-headed, impetuous Walter Lee—who risks and loses his family's cash reserve in his bid to purchase a liquor store.

In much the same way as Troy Maxson, Boy Willie challenges the family's unity as well as Christian ethics by his desire to advance his station in life. He does not buy into Berneice's more nostalgic regard for the musical instrument, nor is he moved by the Christian rhetoric of his aspiring brother-in-law and minister Avery. Boy Willie confronts Berneice, her boyfriend Avery, as well as their indifferent Uncle Doaker Charles, with the single-minded intent of actualizing his ambition to own land. If this means forcibly removing the piano from his sister's home, sawing it in half, facing possible bodily harm or risking alienation from his family, Boy Willie is prepared to endure the consequences.

When romantic idealists (such as Berneice) unconditionally embrace their African heritage and Christians (such as the would-be minister Avery) advise humility, the African American man seems to have no better alternative than to formulate a separate consciousness. For Boy Willie, therefore, this resulting eclectic philosophy is necessarily part survivalist, part self-made moralist, and, most noticeably, part agnostic or atheist. Thus, what may seem like over-ambition to some could more aptly be described by others as heeding opportunity's onc and only knock.

For Boy Willie, heeding opportunity involves neither naiveté nor passivity. He is fully aware of the moral and cultural forces that oppose his efforts and knows that his success depends upon his ability to exorcise each of them. To do this, he must transcend the heavy emotional bonds that consume his sister. Consequently, he replaces accepted rules of good Christian behavior with roughshod "street smarts." This having been done, the choice between revering symbols of African ancestry and converting them to functional use becomes less of an issue to him.

One such opposing force which Boy Willie must exorcise in order to accomplish his goal is the pesky ghost of the piano's former owner, Robert Sutter. Also apparently obsessed with retrieving the controversial piano, Sutter's ghost makes several appearances in Berneice's home. According to Doaker Charles, who relates the rather dubious legend of Sutter's ghost, the white man's spirit that haunts Berneice's home was once the grandson of their family's original slave master. As a result of a barter to acquire slaves from Sutter's grandfather, another white slave owner offered a piano as collateral. The result of this deal was the transferred ownership of Doaker's father and grandmother. Thus, the piano came to represent not only the memory of Doaker's immediate relatives but also the spirit of each extended family member from Africa to America.

Boy Willie sees the separation of the spiritual from the physical world as imperative to his mission and ultimately convinces Berneice of this. Frustrated with Avery's use of awkward religious incantations to exorcise the ghost, Boy Willie intercedes by simply sprinkling the air with water from a pan on the stove and shouting profanity: "All this old preaching stuff. Hell, just ask him to leave. (He grabs a pot of water off the stove and begins to fling it about the room.) Hey Sutter! Sutter! Get your ass out this house!" Once he succeeds in bringing Sutter's image into view, both he and his sister instinctively collaborate in two final symbolic rituals of liberation: Berneice plays the once shunned piano, and Boy Willie engages Sutter's ghost in "a life and death struggle fraught with perils and faultless terror."

This apparent reconciliation between agents of two distinct ideologies resounds with didactic importance. What Wilson suggests in the play's resolution is a call to fellow blacks to renounce ties with the spiritual world and to cultivate a healthier awareness of the more immediate, more tangible features of their lives. As exemplified in the stubborn spirit of Sutter's ghost which attaches itself to the piano, the African American man's African heritage is, by design, a mixture of nightmare and reverence. Only through sensible adaptations of the more pragmatic virtues of his past can he succeed. Although this preference for the here and now runs counter to Christian ideals of the life hereafter, the world in which Berneice and Boy Willie live demands a reassessment of tradition.

Berneice's boyfriend Avery could very well be considered as Boy Willie's alter ego. He becomes an important part of a dialectical lesson on the advantages and/or disadvantages of being a good Christian as well as a proud African American man. At odds are his more immediately successful survival tactics and the less measurable benefits of Christianity. Exhibiting paradoxically similar ideals, the con artist and the minister go about achieving their goals with equal persistence. While Boy Willie is set on selling the piano to purchase land, Avery is determined to borrow enough from the local white-owned bank to erect his own church. Their common desire to drum up capital to support investments prompts impressive emotional appeals. Both are masters of persuasive rhetoric—Avery, by quoting the scriptures and Boy Willie, by citing street logic.

Avery is a toned-down version of the frequently caricatured Baptist minister. Although not as extreme as similar examples in James Baldwin's *Go Tell It on the Mountain* or Amiri Baraka's *The Baptism,* he does exemplify familiar tendencies toward passivity. He prefers going through the frequent frustration and delay of proper channels to get what he wants rather than assuming a more direct, assertive approach. From finance to romance, each attempt to improve himself is met with lukewarm reception.

As seen through the eyes of the play's other African American men, Avery is a shyster. They refuse to believe that he was "called" to the ministry, choosing instead to believe that, like them, Avery has found a lucrative scheme to support himself. Boy Willie casually cajoles him at their initial encounter: "How you get to be a preacher, Avery? I might want to be a preacher one day. Have everybody call me Reverend Boy Willie."

With a foreboding resonance, each of Wilson's four published plays addresses the difficulties the African American man has had in accepting Christianity as a moral frame of reference. Levee, Herald Loomis, Troy Maxson and Boy Willie do not stop short of lambasting white society for their misfortunes. They blaspheme against Christianity with ease and run roughshod over any obstacle to their respective ambitions. But they are not above acknowledging themselves as villains. Having conceded this, they choose to pass over Christianity as practiced by fellow African Americans in favor of less restrictive adaptations of their own brand of survival. Consequently, the language and actions associated with their makeshift ideals reflect a new means of compensating for their previously unquestioned belief in God.

Quite unlike the sorely tried though patient Job of the Old Testament, Wilson's African American men have given up on their God. No longer content to "wait on the Lord," they make impetuous, often foolhardy decisions about their lives. They are no longer so easily appeased by spewing profanity and threats at white America or by finding solace in the word of God. Neither are they intimidated by the moral consequences of their infidelity. Where once the sanctity of Christianity may have been reinforced by a heavy hand like that extended by Hansberry's uncompromising Lena Younger: "In my mother's house there is still God" (*Raisin,* Act I.i), its ethics are being either challenged or totally ignored. Consigned to a life of subjugation, the African American men who dominate Wilson's plays discard Christianity in favor of more flexible, man-made commandments.

Lisa Wilde (essay date Winter 1990)

SOURCE: "Reclaiming the Past: Narrative and Memory in August Wilson's *Two Trains Running,*" in *Theater,* Vol. 22, No. 1, Winter, 1990, pp. 73-4.

[*In the following essay, Wilde studies how Wilson gives expression to the memories of African Americans in* Two Trains Running.]

"All I do is try to live in the world but the world done gone crazy. I'm sorry I was ever born into it" —Sterling

May, 1969. The corner of Fullerton and Wylie Street in Pittsburgh. A small restaurant, long forgotten by the general crowds and now being readied for demolition. Outside, the world moved convulsively towards the future. But within the walls of the restaurant, the regulars spin webs of refuge: they spend hours philosophizing, telling stories, debating politics, competing to prove each other wrong. In their profuse yet precise recombinations of image and phrase, they rebuild the past.

In his newest play, *Two Trains Running,* August Wilson summons up the people and circumstances of this world from his own memory, reclaiming stories from the obscurity into which so much of the oral storytelling tradition has passed. The audience enters into the intimacy of the routine of these characters—stopping by for their morning coffee, checking on the numbers, commenting on the events on the street—just as Sterling Johnson, newly released from prison, breaks into the closed circle of the restaurant and provokes new performances of the stories and debates shared by Memphis and Holloway.

Both of these older men remain distrustful of the sound and fury surrounding the civil rights movement. Memphis, the restaurant's owner, recalls that he's seen movements and demonstrations over and over again that haven't led to reforms, haven't changed anything: "Soon as they finish with one rally they start planning for the next. They forget about what goes in between. You rally to spur you into action. . . . I want to see if it last three years." All these attempts by black men to gain justice and equality are almost predoomed to end in martyrdom. They are fighting both fate as determined by the white man and the uselessness of trying to play by rules not written for them. Their struggle goes back beyond this specific crisis and movement; it extends back through centuries of suffering which can only be expiated by reclaiming that past. Memphis has fled the destruction of his farm in Jackson, Mississippi to make a new life in Pittsburgh. The possibility of a new loss forces him to narrate and confront that original dispossession.

The insistent rhythm of time and mortality pulses through the play. The restaurant is across the street from Lutz's Meat Market and West's Funeral Home—the characters travel between these three primitive sites of slaughter, consumption and decay. People speculate about the last days of the world. The block the restaurant is on is scheduled to be levelled. West, the undertaker, goes about the ancient rituals of preparing the dead for the afterlife. He is a modern high priest officiating over the ceremonies of grief and valediction. Yet an impulse towards action emerges out of this desolation. Risa, Holloway, Sterling and Memphis try to find their own ways to envisage a future through consulting prophets and oracles, playing with chance. Wolf, the numbers runner, offers new lives and different endings for the price of a ticket.

Playing the numbers is a way to try to control fate and get enough money to get ahead. There is no logic to the world: getting ahead happens only through a lucky number or a sudden contract. Working, particularly working according to standards imposed by white America, yields up only a slight variant on slavery. The real battle is revealed to be one not of language or attitude but of economics. Wilson tells stories of people inadequately recompensed for the work they've done, legal clauses written so a property owner can be bought out for a fraction of the price he paid, even lottery winnings that are cut in half. The only way to recover what has been lost or stolen is by following the dominant culture's tactics: robbery, burning buildings for insurance, carrying guns to assert power. But these people are arrested and imprisoned for actions that in the marketplace would be considered shrewd business. Wilson's characters are not innocent: they have already tried to make their lives work as the world dictates and lost. Their need to reclaim what has been taken from them, either in actual or symbolic terms— Herald Loomis' lost wife in *Joe Turner's Come and Gone,* the piano bought with a father's blood in *The Piano Lesson,* Memphis' farm—becomes the truest form of revolution and affirmation.

In each of Wilson's plays, this liberating moment comes through communicating with the supernatural or occult mysteries. Troy Maxson in *Fences* wrestles with Death and ultimately loses; his brother Gabriel sends him off to the hereafter with a blast of sound and an outpouring of light. *Joe Turner*'s Bynum helps Loomis discover his hidden song through a ritual purging. Boy Willie must wrestle with Sutter's ghost as his sister Berneice exorcises the suffering from the piano by touching it in *The Piano Lesson.* In *Two Trains Running,* travelers seeking answers are sent to the red door at 1839 Wylie Street to consult Aunt Ester, a three hundred and twenty-two year old prophetess. Like the Cumaean Sibyl or the Sphinx, she provides her pilgrims not with answers but with riddles and parables, divinations that they themselves must interpret. Specifically, she offers them the choice of remaining passive or moving towards their fate—if they are ready to walk through fire to reach it. She may extend healing but the comfort comes with a knife's edge. Her presence, reaching back to precolonial days, represents African American memory: the choice is to ignore it or to retrieve it. As Memphis says of his own travels, "I'm going back there one day. . . . They've got two trains running every day."

Both Wilson and Director Lloyd Richards have often spoken of how their collaborations on four previous plays have allowed them both to recover their own personal histories, to retell stories they heard in their childhood. August Wilson has written his plays so that each expresses some aspect of the African American experience in each decade of the twentieth century: *Joe Turner's Come and Gone* at the turn

of the century; *Ma Rainey's Black Bottom* in the Jazz Age; *The Piano Lesson* during the Depression; *Fullerton Street* during World War II and *Fences* in the 1950s. These plays create their own context and history for *Two Trains Running.* The characters and events do not exist merely as distinct dramatic moments; they are woven into the fabric of remembrance August Wilson summons up in his chronicle of the African American experience. Memory has been given a voice.

Frank Rich (review date 14 April 1992)

SOURCE: "August Wilson Reaches the '60s With Witnesses from a Distance," in *The New York Times,* April 14, 1992, pp. 139-40.

[*In the following review, Rich offers a largely favorable assessment of* Two Trains Running.]

In *Two Trains Running,* the latest chapter in his decade-by-decade chronicle of black American life in this century, August Wilson arrives at a destination that burns almost too brightly in memory to pass for history. *Two Trains Running* is Mr. Wilson's account of the 1960's, unfurling at that moment when racial conflict and the Vietnam War were bringing the nation to the brink of self-immolation.

Yet Mr. Wilson's play, which opened last night at the Walter Kerr Theater, never speaks of Watts or Vietnam or a march on Washington. The Rev. Dr. Martin Luther King Jr. is mentioned only once. The garrulous characters, the regulars at a Pittsburgh ghetto lunch counter in 1969, are witnesses to history too removed from the front lines to harbor more than the faintest fantasies of justice. They invest their hopes in playing the numbers, not in distant leaders sowing lofty dreams of change.

So determined is *Two Trains Running* to avoid red-letter events and larger-than-life heroes that it is easily Mr. Wilson's most adventurous and honest attempt to reveal the intimate heart of history. In place of a protagonist that a Charles Dutton or James Earl Jones might play is a gallery of ordinary people buffeted by larger forces that they can join or gingerly battle but cannot begin to promote or control. While such 60's props as a gun and cans of gasoline do appear in *Two Trains Running,* the evening's most violent dramatic event causes no serious injury and takes place offstage. Even so, a larger, national tragedy is spreading underfoot.

As might be expected in a work that departs from every Wilson effort except *Joe Turner's Come and Gone* in its experimental will to demolish the manufactured confrontations of well-made drama, *Two Trains Running* is not without blind alleys. And it is compromised by a somewhat bombastic production, staged by the author's longtime collaborator Lloyd Richards, that sometimes takes off running in a different direction from the writing. But the play rides high on the flavorsome talk that is a Wilson staple. The glorious storytelling serves not merely as picturesque, sometimes touching and often funny theater but as a penetrating revelation of a world hidden from view to those outside it.

> **The glorious storytelling [in *Two Trains Running*] serves not merely as picturesque, sometimes touching and often funny theater but as a penetrating revelation of a world hidden from view to those outside it.**
> *—Frank Rich*

Much of the talk is prompted by two deaths that filter into Memphis Lee's restaurant, itself doomed to be demolished. The sole waitress, Risa (Cynthia Martells), grieves for Prophet Samuel, an evangelist whose attainments included a cache of jewelry, a white Cadillac, a harem and a huge flock that is viewing his open casket down the street. The one stranger to visit Memphis Lee's, a newly released convict named Sterling (Larry Fishburne), is latently preoccupied with the 1965 assassination of Malcolm X, not out of any deep ideological convictions but because a rally in the fallen radical's name at the local Savoy Ballroom gives him a pretext to ask Risa for a date.

Though the issue is never articulated, Mr. Wilson's characters are starting to compare the prophets who offer balms for their poverty and disenfranchisement, and no two representative prophets could be more different than Malcolm X and Samuel. But the play's real question may be, as one line poses it, "How we gonna feel good about ourselves?" The liveliest talkers in *Two Trains Running* are members of an older generation skeptical of all externally applied panaceas, secular and religious.

Memphis (Al White), who is negotiating a price for the city's demolition of his restaurant, is confident he can beat the white man at his own game as long as he knows the rules. To him, those who argue that "black is beautiful" sound like "they're trying to convince themselves." Holloway (Roscoe Lee Browne), a retired house painter turned cracker-barrel philosopher, is not only scathing about white men who exploit black labor but also about any effort by what he calls "niggers" to fight back. He sends anyone with a grievance to a mysterious, unseen prophet, the supposedly 322-year-old Aunt Ester, the neighborhood's subliminal repository of its buried African identity and a magical universe of faith and superstitions.

In some of the richest and most hilarious arias, the marvelously dyspeptic Mr. Browne encapsulates the whole economic history of the United States into an explosive formula and reminisces scathingly of a grandfather so enthralled by the plantation mentality he could not wait to die and pick heaven's cotton for a white God. Even nastier gallows humor is provided by West (Chuck Patterson), an undertaker whose practical view of death has made him perhaps the community's keenest social observer and certainly its wealthiest entrepreneur.

As conceived by Mr. Wilson, the monologues, musical in language and packed with thought and incident, are not digressions; they are the play's very fiber. Such plot as there is involves the fate of a symbolic mentally unbalanced man named Hambone (Sullivan Walker) who pointedly "ain't willing to accept whatever the white man throw at him" and the rising political consciousness and romantic ardor of Sterling, whose sincere efforts to cobble a post-penitentiary life and livelihood are constantly frustrated.

Along with the usual Wilson repetitions and the heavy metaphorical use of Hambone (who is a hammier version of the mentally disturbed Gabriel in *Fences*), the flaws of *Two Trains Running* include its inability to make more than a thematic conceit out of its lone woman, Risa, who enigmatically bears self-inflicted razor scars, and its failure to delve far below Sterling's surface, despite a searching performance by Mr. Fishburne. Mr. Wilson's reticence about his two youngest and most crucial characters turns up most glaringly in the pivotal but underwritten Act II scene that brings them together to the music of a previously dormant jukebox.

Mr. Fishburne, who greets each of Sterling's defeats with pride and heroic optimism, and Mr. Browne, an orator of Old Testament fire, are the jewels of the production. The rest of the cast is at most adequate, with Mr. White's ranting Memphis, whose longer soliloquies punctuate both acts, inflicting the greatest damage. The uneven casting is compounded by the harsh, bright lighting, the flatly realistic set and the slam-bang choreography of a text that needs to breathe rather than hyperventilate. Instead of looking like a production that has been polished during its long development process through the country's resident theaters, *Two Trains Running* sometimes seems the battered survivor of a conventionally grueling road tour.

The play fascinates anyway and makes its own chilling point. Just as this is the Wilson work in which the characters are the furthest removed from both Africa and the Old South (to which the untaken trains of the title lead), so it is also the Wilson play closest in time to our own. "You take something apart, you should know how to put it together," says Sterling early on, referring to a wristwatch he hesitates to dismantle. Rough in finish and unresolved at the final curtain, *Two Trains Running* captures a racially divided country as it came apart. That Mr. Wilson's history bleeds so seamlessly into the present is testimony to the fact that the bringing together of that America is a drama yet to unfold.

Mary L. Bogumil (essay date December 1994)

SOURCE: "'Tomorrow Never Comes': Songs of Cultural Identity in August Wilson's *Joe Turner's Come and Gone*," in *Theatre Journal,* Vol. 46, No. 4, December, 1994, pp. 463-76.

[*In the following essay, Bogumil explores Wilson's handling of his characters experiences with identity, culture, ethnicity, and displacement in* Joe Turner's Come and Gone.]

The subject of displacement in all its psychological vicissitudes is dramatized in August Wilson's *Joe Turner's Come and Gone,* a play in which the African American residents of a boarding house in Pittsburgh Pennsylvania in 1911 attempt to rediscover, repossess, and redefine themselves historically and socially as free citizens. These children of newly freed slaves, like others who came before them, attempt to make a place for themselves in this polyethnic, and certainly hostile, environment.

In order to contrast and magnify the sense of displacement each of these characters of Southern origin experiences in the North, Wilson in his preface personifies many elements of the setting. For example, the fires of the steel mill rage, the barges trudge up the river, and the city of Pittsburgh flexes it muscles "with a combined sense of industry and progress." Simply put, the environment Wilson depicts is metaphorically combative.

Into this environment

> [wander] [f]rom the deep and near South the sons and daughters of newly freed African slaves.... Isolated, cut off from memory, having forgotten the names of the gods and only guessing at their faces, they arrive dazed and stunned, their hearts kicking in their chest with a song worth singing. They arrive carrying Bibles and guitars, their pockets lined with dust and fresh hope, marked men and women seeking to scrape from the narrow, crooked cobbles and the fiery blasts of the coke furnace a way of bludgeoning and shaping the malleable parts of themselves into a new identity as free men of definite and sincere worth.

Foreigners in a strange land, they carry as part and parcel of their baggage a long line of separation and dispersement which informs their sensibilities.

Outsiders in a strange land, these characters attempt to "reconnect" and "reassemble" themselves as free citizens of "definite and sincere worth." Moreover, Wilson asserts that they want "to give clear and luminous meaning to the [their ethnocentric] song [a voice whether collective or individual] which is [comprised of] both a wail and a whelp of joy." But why is their song both a wail and a whelp of joy? In this essay, I shall explore this question, situating the experiences and traumas of several of Wilson's characters within a historical and cultural context that will explain each character's attempt to "reconnect" and "reassemble" (often out of conflicting or contradictory influences) his or her identity as an African American living in twentieth-century America.

As a result of the Reconstruction period in the South—and after the 1896 Supreme Court Decision Plessy *vs.* Ferguson, which declared the "separate but equal" doctrine—the Southern states vehemently began to impose segregation and to enforce Jim Crow laws by rewriting each state's constitution, legislating an exclusionist policy toward African Americans. By 1907 many African Americans had moved to Northern industrial cities to escape the impact of this constitutional discrimination and to find work other than that of itinerant sharecroppers and docile servants. With the massive migration came feelings of displacement for many of those who were former slaves and for the sons and daughters of those slaves. These feelings were symptomatic reactions to their new social climate. While the African Americans were now free men and women in the North, their freedom unfortunately often took the form of a self-imposed isolation, perhaps a vestige of their marginalization as a culture in the antebellum South. It is this sense of displacement, particularly but not exclusively of black males, which is dramatized in several ways in Wilson's play: in the "religiomagical" plantation dance, the juba; in what I will refer to as Zonia's song; in Wilson's inclusion of the blues song "Joe Turner's Come and Gone"; and especially in the central characters, Bynum Walker and Herald Loomis.

In his poem, "Afro-American Fragment," Langston Hughes describes the significance of an individual's "song" and, in turn, the African American's collective sense of displacement—a fragmented sense of self and of community within a culture:

> So Long,
> So far away,
> Is Africa.
> Not even the memories alive
> Save those that history books create,

Save those that songs
Beat back out of blood with words sad sung
In strange un-Negro tongue—
So long,
So far away
Is Africa.

Subdued and time-lost are the drums—
And yet, through some vast mist of race
There comes this song
I do not understand
The song of atavistic land,
Of bitter yearnings lost, without a place—
So long,
So far away
Is Africa's
Dark face.

This "song of [an] atavistic land" is captured in the "juba," a dance that routinely begins after Sunday suppers in Seth and Bertha Holly's boarding house. The boarders' participation in the dance evokes Herald Loomis's surrealistic vision of a people's barbarous captivity, displacement, and virtual destruction. The juba signifies the recurrence (in memories, in deeds, and in visions) of remote ancestral ties—a paternal, cultural legacy from the characters' African forefathers. Yet as scholarship on this subject indicates, the juba's origins and the interpretations surrounding the motivation for its practice are somewhat difficult to delineate. For example, [in "Africanisms and the Study of Folklore," *Africanisms in American Culture,* edited by Joseph E. Holloway, 1990] Beverly J. Johnson analyzes one possible origin of the dance:

> One of the earliest records of the term *juba* dates back to American minstrelsy. Both Juba and Jube consistently appeared as names of enslaved Africans who were skilled musicians and dancers. The father of a celebrated black artist who was popular outside the minstrelsy circuit, Horace or Howard Weston, was named Jube.

Johnson elaborates upon the myriad etymological origins of the word "juba": *juba* or *diuba* in Bantu "means to pat, beat time, the sun, the hour"; linguistically the word comes from the African *giouba,* referring to a sacred polyrhythmic African step dance whose secular origins trace back to South Carolina and the West Indies, and juba was a word referring to both a mixture of leftovers consumed by the plantation slaves and a song they created to prepare them psychologically to eat what she terms "slop." Johnson also includes lines from the "Juba Song," which she attributes to Besse Jones, along with her own explication, which appears on the right:

Juba up, Juba down,   That means everywhere,
                        all around the
Juba all around the town. whole country . . .
                        everybody had
Juba for ma, Juba for pa, juba. And they made a
                        play out of it.
Juba for your brother-in-law. So that's where this
                        song came from;
                        they would get all this kind of
thing
                        off their brains and minds.

If we take Jones's explication of juba as a purgative incantation and couple it with the following explication of the term in the *Oxford English Dictionary,* the cause of Herald Loomis's mental breakdown (or epiphany) and the juba's purgative effect upon him become clear. Like Johnson, the *OED* defines "juba," sometimes spelled "juber" or "jouba," as a species of dance that often included the reenactment of a mental breakdown. But unlike Johnson, the *OED* definition implies that the juba's origin was exclusively American despite its African ritual dance elements. More precisely, it was a dance performed by the antebellum plantation slaves in the deep South—a dance whose choreography consisted of the clapping of hands, the patting of knees and thighs, the striking of feet on the floor, and the singing of a refrain where the word "juba" was repeated, a refrain that acted as an incantation to the Holy Ghost or an invocation to manifest a transcendent being. Marshall and Jean Stearns state [in *Jazz Dance: The Story of American Vernacular Dance,* 1979] that this version of the juba is commonly called the "patting juba" and elaborate upon the choreographed movements of the dancers:

> Patting Juba, which started as any kind clapping with any dance to encourage another dancer, became a special routine of clapping of the hands, knees, thighs and body in a rhythmic display. (In Africa, of course, this function would be performed by drums, but in the United States where drums had frequently been forbidden for the fear of slave revolts, the emergence of the patting seems to have been inevitable.)

The Stearns also note that the words and the steps were performed in a call-and-response fashion. Certainly, this mode of call-and-response communication was a major vehicle in sustaining a sense of community—not unlike the call-and-response spirituals that were sung by slaves on one plantation to communicate with those on another nearby plantation—in an environment where a sense of community was systematically undermined by the institution of slavery. In addition, it seems that the dance was invested with elements of the unreal and the grotesque. The Stearns trace "juba" to "mane," a loose thread-like beard which hangs at the end of husks of corn. No doubt, this interpretation of the word "juba" illustrates why the juba was performed by many of the slaves during corn harvesting time.

When we encounter the character of Herald Loomis, whose paroxysmal breakdown is prompted by his adverse reaction to the other characters' participation in the dance, we are initiated into a world where the natural and supernatural co-exist and impinge upon one another. As Loomis says to Bynum Walker, "The ground's starting to shake. There's a great shaking. The world's busting half in two. The sky's splitting open. I got to stand up." The juba—as song, as dance, with all its competing cultural resonances—plays a significant role in Wilson's play. Specifically, in the final scene of act 1, all the residents of the boarding house converse after Sunday dinner, except for Herald Loomis, who is not there. As they retire to the parlor, Seth and Jeremy want to juba, and the two wake Bynum Walker, who is half asleep, to join them in the dance. Instantly, the atmosphere is jubilant as the others join in. Then Loomis enters and cries out for them to stop. He blasphemes the Holy Ghost, the greatness of God's grandeur, and then unzips his pants. All are devastated as Loomis suddenly begins to speak in tongues and dance frenetically around the kitchen. Without a moment's hesitation, Walker runs after him, while Seth shouts out that Loomis is crazy, and Bertha tells her husband to be quiet. "Thrown back," or stunned by his vision, Loomis then tells of a horrific vision: bones walking upon the water; bones sinking into the depths of the water; and bones washing up upon the land, where they transform into flesh, black flesh. Walker attempts to crawl closer to Loomis, and Loomis, who is nearly out of breath, tries to stand, but cannot. Loomis knows that he must stand up to break the spell of his vision; he says that he must "get upon the road" like the others, but cannot, and collapses onto the floor.

We should pay close attention to August Wilson's stage directions in this scene, where he describes particularities of the juba, and compare it to Herald Loomis's disturbing reaction to all those involved in the dance:

> *The Juba is reminiscent of the Ring Shouts of the African slaves. It is a call and response dance. BYNUM sits at the table and drums. He calls the dance as others clap their hands, shuffle and stomp around the table. It should be as African as possible, with performers working themselves up unto a near frenzy. The words can be improvised, but should include some mention of the Holy Ghost. In the middle of the dance HERALD LOOMIS enters.*

LOOMIS: (*In a rage.*) Stop it! Stop it! (*They stop and look to him.*) You all sitting up here singing about the Holy Ghost? You singing and singing. You think the Holy Ghost is coming? You sing for

the Holy Ghost to come? What he gonna do, huh? He going come with tongues of fire to burn up your woolly heads? You gonna tie onto the Holy Ghost and get burned up? What you got then? Why God got to be so Big? Why he got to be bigger than me? How much big is there? How much big do you want? (*LOOMIS starts to unzip his pants.*)

Perhaps what disturbs Herald Loomis about the characters' participation in the dance is that sense of community, of solidarity, of an atavistic legacy of Africa, but sadly also of the bondage still in the consciousness of the post-Civil War generation—all of which are in sharp contrast to his desire for autonomy. Why do they laud it over him? Why do they wish to be reminded of their cultural past? Is the dance and all that it represents more important than an individual's efforts to become American?

Ronald Takaki writes that most blacks of the post-Civil War generation walked away from anything that recalled their servitude in the South, "the racial etiquette of deference and subordination." Takaki claims that many who traveled north were "restless, dissatisfied, unwilling to mask their true selves and accommodate to traditional roles." Is not the juba a connection to that unwanted past or tradition? In Herald Loomis's mind, to re-establish such a connection is unbearable and dangerous. Takaki says that compared to the "older class of colored labor," men who were "pretty well up in years" and who constituted a "first rate class of labor," the blacks of the "younger class" were "discontented and wanted to be roaming."

When Loomis tells Walker of his vision, he describes a wave that transforms the bones of their ancestors into flesh, then reiterates his desperate desire for individual autonomy: "They got flesh on them! Just like you and me! . . . They black. Just like you and me. Ain't no difference. . . . They ain't moved or nothing. They just laying there. . . . I'm going to stand up. I got to stand up. I can't lay here no more. All the breath coming into my body and I got to stand up." Listening to this apostasy, Walker recognizes that Loomis is a victim of Joe Turner. As he later tells him:

> Now I can look at you, Mr. Loomis, and see you a man who done forgot his song. Forgot how to sing it. A fellow forget that and he forget who he is. . . . See, Mr. Loomis, when a man forgets his song he goes off in search of it . . . till he find out he's got it with him all the time. That's why I can tell you one of Joe Turner's niggers. 'Cause you forgot how to sing your song.

Walker sees that the traces of enslavement in Loomis's vision are a form of personal hegemony in which the song of the individual—that is, the individual's ties to the past as well as his or her place in the world—is negated; and this was the goal of Joe Turner:

> What he wanted was your song. He wanted to have that song to be his. He thought by catching you he could learn that song. Every nigger he catch he's looking for the one he can learn that song from. Now he's got you bound up to where you can't sing your own song. Couldn't sing it them seven years 'cause you was afraid he would snatch it from under you. But you still got it. You just forgot how to sing it.

During this scene, the others present seem aware of their autonomy as individuals apart from their identity as a race; they can participate in this dance as a form of celebration, for they can acknowledge their songs (words and actions) as signatures of their autonomy as individuals and as members of a race. All of them can embrace this legacy of their culture both of Africa and America, but Herald Loomis cannot, due to his haunting Joe Turner nightmare of imprisonment.

Although the same atavistic "ghost" is within him, Loomis believes that his autonomy as an individual, as a man, is at best tenuous. In an interview, August Wilson explains the haunting presence of the white plantation owner from Tennessee and its effect upon the African American male: "Joe Turner would press Blacks into peonage. He would send out decoys who would lure Blacks into crap games and then he would sweep down and grab them. He had a chain with forty links to it, and he would take Blacks off to his plantation and work them."

According to William W. Cook, the direct result of the institution of slavery upon African Americans was a deprivation of the coadunate elements within their native African culture. Consequently, the practice of religions, languages, and customs became convergent and were expressed in art. Cook states [in "Change the Joke and Slip the Yoke: Traditions of Afro-American Satire," *Journal of Ethnicity,* Vol. 13, No. 1, 1985] that the African descended from an "absorptive culture, meaning a culture in which certain divisions do not exist." He further elaborates that within an "absorptive culture" which implements the call-and-response pattern, there is no line drawn between performer and audience as there is in western theatre; moreover, words and dance are of equal importance in dances like the juba, as are vocals and instrument in the blues. Thus, in the play when Herald Loomis attempts to stop the juba, he disrupts this call-and-response pattern, this cultural tradition—something which [Cook explains] is not tolerated in African societies: "African societies discourage face-to-face confrontations and pull in line those who were out of line. This vent of feelings obviates the possibility that private grievances will fester and become a community problem. The great and powerful are in a sense leveled with the weak."

Moreover, the juba, and African ritual dance in general, is "earth oriented," an expression of a kinship with the earth. This kinship is initially demonstrated in act 1 during the sacrificial ritual enacted by Bynum Walker near the Hollys's vegetable garden. In contrast, the choreographic movements of classical European dance reflect a pull away from the earth, according to Cook. Herald Loomis, a member of the post-Civil War generation, attempts to sever that native African connection to the earth and to break free from that past American connection to Joe Turner enslavement in order to become Americanized in post-Emancipation Proclamation America.

Surrounded by what he perceives as a conspiratorial group, Loomis even degrades his own ancestry with his vociferous attack against the religiomagical elements of his African American ethnicity, including physical and sexual stereotypes, to further his insult upon others present. And even though he and Bynum Walker have a verbal exchange, they are not exchanging "dozens"—a contest of call-and-response verbal combat highly regarded as a skill in African societies; Loomis's verbal attack is against his culture and results in his breakdown and collapse.

In Wilson's play, an acute displacement, which is actually the African American's disenfranchisement in white America, is reflected in each character's desire to participate in the synergistic dance called the juba—a dance of cultural mutability in America and of traditional immutability in their "atavistic land." That disenfranchisement is further illustrated in some of the key male characters' need to wander or to turn away from that which is familiar, thereby causing the Joe Turner "syndrome"—a cultural idiom that refers both to the convict-lease system, which was devised as a post-Reconstruction socioeconomic advantage for white southern landowners to further exploit black labor and to an individual's desire to wander away from a sense of community or home, itself a sociological vestige of the institution of slavery. The central characters are in search of their voice, a "song" which will enable them to articulate their individual and cultural identities, a song that, perhaps, will lead them down the "right road" and not down the behavioral road to aversion, a song that signifies these feelings of displacement, which are referred to as "Joe Turner."

Beyond its direct reference to peonage, "Joe Turner" is a blues song that alludes to the African American's sense of imprisonment in a white world. Bynum Walker sings it in the play:

> They tell me Joe Turner's come and gone
> Ohhh Lordy

They tell me Joe Turner's come and gone
Ohh Lordy
Got my man and gone
Come with forty links of chain
Ohhh Lordy
Come with forty links of chain
Ohh Lordy
Got my man and gone.

According to Leroi Jones [in *Blues People: Negro Music in White America,* 1963], the African American's place in post-slave society was nonexistent, because the only place or role that she or he knew—and that white America knew—was on the periphery, as a slave even in the new "separate but equal" America: "Blues did begin in slavery, and it is from that 'peculiar institution,' as it is known euphemistically, that the blues did find its particular form. And if slavery dictated certain aspects of blues form and content, so did the so-called Emancipation and its subsequent problems dictate the path blues would take." Essentially, the blues reflect that displacement and engender an African American vision or, as Jones claims, a legal subterfuge of his or her role as a disenfranchised American in this new, free America—the America in August Wilson's *Joe Turner's Come and Gone*—where antebellum sentiments have not been erased.

Houston Baker has explored the importance of the blues in the African American experience and has concluded [in *Blues, Ideology, and Afro-American Literature: A Vernacular Theory,* 1984] that the blues are as difficult to define as the cultural experience of African Americans: "Afro-American blues constitute such a vibrant network. They are what Jacques Derrida might describe as the 'always already' of African American culture. They are the multiplex, enabling *script* in which Afro-American cultural discourse is inscribed." Thus, any attempt to separate the codes inscribed in the culture from the codes inscribed in the blues song is futile, for the song signifies the culture through referents, and the culture is inscribed in the song through referents: "The blues matrix is a 'cultural invention': a 'negative symbol' that generates (or obliges one to invent) its own referents." As Baker explains, if we look for a fixed coda—a coda that will be invested with a mutual, exclusive signifier—the text of song and culture will erupt semantically through the process of interpretation. This complex, intertextual, culturally inscribed discourse that informs the blues is apparent in Wilson's play. It is a cultural discourse that entails Christian elements alongside native African nature-religious elements, a discourse that entails a longing for family and a sense of belonging as well as the desire to wander, and a discourse that entails the opportunities and obligations of freedom in conjunction with the lingering traces of slavery.

Some in Wilson's cast of characters reflect these complexities as well as the issue of displacement and the difficulties arising from each character's attempt at acculturation. Even some of the characters' names exemplify their internal and external struggles. The Hollys's longtime boarder is Bynum Walker, a man who often speaks in parables and whose name epitomizes the wanderer, the Joe Turner type. Walker is a man in his early 60s who is described as a rootworker: a conjure man who is known as "the Binding Man," for he is the glue which sticks everyone together or, more precisely, those who wish to be bound. Bynum Walker is described as the voodoo, heebee jeebee, mumbo jumbo, root man and the conjure man who is looking for the shiny man. Walker, like his late father, has special powers. And like his father before him, a plantation shaman who was known as the "Healing Man," Walker, the boarding house's resident shaman, is known as the "Binding Man." In fact, Walker's purpose, his song, is inscribed in both his names: "Bynum," the one who binds people together so that they discover a sense of truth within themselves; "Walker," the one who wanders, a seeker.

Like characters in stories of Charles Chesnutt such as "The Goophered Grapevine" and "The Conjurer's Revenge," Bynum Walker embodies a strong sense of separateness between the world of the African American and that of the European American like Rutherford Selig. Selig, "the People Finder," is a descendant of those who captured, bound, and enslaved those who appear in Loomis's horrific vision. He is the European American trickster, an amicable con man who transports blacks for a fee and then charges other blacks to locate them. His father was a man who captured escaped slaves for money, his grandfather a man who captured and transported slaves aboard ship for money. And Bertha notes that Selig is actually no different from his ancestors:

> You can call him a People Finder if you want to. I know Rutherford Selig carries people away too. He done carried a whole bunch of them away from here. Folks plan on leaving plan by Selig's timing. They wait till he get ready to go, then they hitch a ride on his wagon. Then he charge folks a dollar to tell them where he took them. Now, that's the truth of Rutherford Selig. This old People Finding business is for the birds. He ain't never found nobody he ain't took away.

Bynum Walker has binding skills of another kind. He is endowed with a powerful insight into the human condition, as demonstrated by his clairvoyant interpretation of Herald Loomis's vision—in which Loomis envisions bones with black flesh arising from the sea—indicates. And ultimately, Walker's skills will lead to the reunion of Herald Loomis, Zonia, and Martha Pentacost Loomis in the play's final scene.

Walker also performs conjurations or "goophers" in his rituals with the blood of pigeons and with curative concoctions—like the one he gives to the heartbroken Mattie Campbell—to enable himself and others to overcome the sociological and psychological difficulties in an arbitrary white world. For example, Bertha Holly, a churchgoer who nevertheless expresses a faith in folk beliefs, respects Walker for his shamanistic or spiritual powers. She is not perturbed by Walker's mumbo jumbo. More than tolerating him, she defends Walker against Seth's mockery in the opening scene: "You don't say nothing when he bless the house. . . . Seth, leave that man alone." Bertha's response to Walker exemplifies this separation between the African American and the European American even further in that she can incorporate elements of both Christian (European) and African religions. Even though she practices the Christian religion, she nonetheless sprinkles the boarding house with salt and lines pennies across the threshold to ward off evil spirits.

Throughout the play, Bynum Walker is always looking for the shiny man, a modernday shaman, and to assist him in this quest he has requested the services of Rutherford Selig. On the road one day, Walker met the shiny man, who seemed hungry and lost, but the shiny man had a "voice" in his head that told him where to go. And that man said that he would reveal to Walker the "Secret of Life."

Walker recalls his mystical journey on the road with this man, who, Walker says, initially paused at the bend and then told Walker to rub his hands together. When Walker did so, his hands began to secrete blood, which he was told to rub all over his body in order to "clean" himself. Herald Loomis performs a similar act at the end of the play when he slashes his chest and rubs the blood on his face. At this moment, Loomis is freed from his ties to Joe Turner, and, in contrast to his inability to stand after his vision in act 1, is able to stand on his own. Wilson reveals the importance of Loomis's epiphany in the stage directions:

> *Having found his song, the song of self-sufficiency, fully resurrected, cleansed and given breath, free from any encumbrance other than the workings of his own heart and the bonds of the flesh, having accepted the responsibility for his own presence in the world, he is free to soar above the environs that weighed and pushed his spirit into terrifying contractions.*

Herald Loomis then becomes the shiny man whom Bynum Walker has been searching for for so long, "shining like new money!"

In his earlier encounter with the shiny man, Walker noticed that he and the shiny man seemed to be transported to somewhere else, a place where everything was magnified in size and where his fellow traveler suddenly had a brightness coming out of him. At that moment, the light the shiny man emit-ted was so bright that it almost blinded Walker. Then, suddenly, the shiny man vanished—just as Herald Loomis does at the end of the play.

Shortly thereafter, Bynum's father appeared: his stature was normal, but his mouth was enormous and his hands as big as hams. He beckoned Walker to draw near and told him he grieved that his son was in a world where he carried other people's songs around, not having a song of his own. Then, magically, he "carried" Walker to the ocean, where he showed him how to find his song, a song whose luminous meaning would be powerful, a "binding song" (just as the juba evoked a vision that carried Herald Loomis to the ocean and revealed his ancestral ties to slavery). Walker asks his father about the shiny man's purpose and whereabouts; his father's response simply is to herald the shiny man as "One Who Goes Before and Shows the Way." Before he directs Walker back to the road, the father tells Walker that if he ever encounters a shiny man again, he will know that his song has served its purpose and he can die a happy man, for he would be a man who has left his mark on life not just one of those marked men.

The word "mark" is significant, for the motif of "mark" in various contexts is explored throughout the play: "marked men and women"; "mark out"; "mark on life"; "mark down life"; "Joe Turner done marked me"; "got a mark on me"; "marked man"; "you mark what I'm saying"; and "made them marks." Essentially, this word and its meanings refer to the struggle of African Americans with the status quo, the struggle of those "marked," who, like Cain, are banished from the chosen people.

There must, of course, be an antagonist in the play, but this antagonist just may be, ironically, also the protagonist—an ex-convict appropriately named Herald Loomis. He will become the *Herald,* the shiny man, the one who knows all that came before, as the ghost of Walker's father foretold. It appears, though, that Herald Loomis possesses a "looming quality" and is perceived by all others—with the exception of Zonia, his daughter, and Bynum Walker, his fellow boarder—to be someone who is threatening, as a menace. Even his attire, a long dark wool coat and hat, is ominous. When any character sees Loomis's face, Loomis is always described as wild eyed and mean looking. However, most of the characters, even Reuben Scott (Mercer), know that Loomis is distraught because he cannot find his wife, Martha "Pentecost" Loomis, who has been gone nearly ten years.

Loomis's vision of the world and of himself is at odds with reality. At times, he claims that he is a deacon of a church, and at times he claims he previously had worked on a farm. Whether he is a deacon or a farm laborer, or both, as he claims—or a gambler or a murderer, as others speculate; whether the farm was a prison farm and he a leased convict or a family farm he maintained with his wife Martha—these aspects of Loomis's narrative are left somewhat suspect in Wilson's play. Undoubtedly, they must remain suspect so that Wilson can accentuate Loomis's internal struggle over his identity, as the character's dream or nightmare demonstrates. It seems that Loomis is an unwilling, self-imposed Joe Turner, despite the fact that he cannot understand the significance of his vision until Walker interprets it. In many ways, Herald Loomis as the shiny man, whom Bynum Walker has sent Selig to locate, is the blind prophet who sees more than he knows, as Bynum Walker eventually will discover.

Despite the fact that "August Wilson has apparently chosen to focus on the African American man's oppression in this country to symbolize the collective struggles of all African American males," as Sandra G. Shannon asserts [in "The Good Christian's Come and Gone: The Shifting Role of Christianity in August Wilson Plays," *MELUS,* Fall, 1989-1990], some of Wilson's female characters become a means of their salvation, their sense of identity. Bynum Walker explains the significance of a woman to Jeremy:

> When you grab hold to a woman, you got something there. You got a whole world there. You got a way of life kicking up under your hand. That woman can take and make you feel like something. I ain't just talking about in the way of jumping off into bed together and rolling around with each other. Anybody can do that. When your [*sic*] hold to that woman and look at the whole thing and see what you got . . . why, she can take and make something out of you.

One of the most significant female characters in Wilson's play in Zonia Loomis. As voiced by a child on the verge of adolescence, her unique rendition of the blues is encoded with or "constitute[s]" what Baker calls "the amalgam" of purposes of the blues. Her songs represent the "always becoming, shaping, transforming, displacing the peculiar experience of Africans in the New World." Zonia represents a mark of intersection. She acts as Loomis's guide in his interaction with other characters; and, in turn, she serves them as a guide into her father's enigmatic character. The following is the song that Zonia sings:

> I went downtown
> To get my grip
> I came back home
> Just a pullin' the skiff
>
> I went upstairs
> To make my bed
> I made a mistake
> And bumped my head

> Just a pullin' the skiff
>
> I went downstairs
> To milk the cow
> I made a mistake
> And I milked the sow
> Just a pullin' the skiff
>
> Tomorrow, Tomorrow
> Tomorrow never comes
> The marrow the marrow
> The marrow in the bone.

This song describes Loomis's departure from his life with his wife Martha, from his labor on Henry Thompson's farm, and from reality into a phantasmagoric self-imposed exile. This exile led Loomis inevitably to his incessant atavistic visions—such as the one in the parlor during the juba—of the African American's horrific journey to America and the African-American's experience in America, which is reflected in the line "the marrow and the bone." It is not until Loomis can confront his own demons that his non-temporal state of limbo, or "tomorrow never comes" attitude, can change.

The lines to this song are also emblematic of Zonia's relationship with her father, for she must accompany him on his travels in search of Martha. Zonia wants to remain Loomis's little girl forever. Despite the fact that she is growing up, Zonia attempts to remain small and slight, "a spider," even at age eleven. Zonia realizes that one day they will find Martha and that she will have to stay with her mother forever. Her interaction with the little boy who lives near the boarding house only exemplifies her dream that things remain the same, that "tomorrow never comes." Zonia's song, then, is about her life.

Zonia's playmate is Reuben Scott (Mercer) who lives with his grandfather next door to the boarding house and who clings to the past as well. Reuben and Zonia are kindred spirits. Zonia is deeply fond of her father, and never wants to leave his side, wants to stay his little girl forever. Reuben refuses to relinquish his relationship with his dead friend by keeping up the pigeon coop as a sort of a shrine or memento mori. Both children try to hold on to the past—Zonia through her behavior, Reuben through the pigeon coop. The spell is broken when Reuben has a vision of this past: Miss Mabel, Seth Holly's mother who has long since died, tells Reuben to set the pigeons free. When Reuben tells Zonia about the vision, and that he heard that she and her father will be leaving soon, their sense of the world about them changes. A sense of the present and the future dispels the childrens' sense of the past. Amidst their childlike reverie, Reuben subverts the past by flirting with Zonia and by proposing marriage to her—thus signifying a shift in the level of their games and simultaneously a shift in their behavioral codes from childhood to adolescence to adulthood.

While Zonia dreads and longs to put off that day when she will have to start her life anew, Mattie Campbell sees such new beginnings as a recurring and inescapable aspect of life, as she tells Herald Loomis: "I ain't never found no place for me to fit. Seem like all I do is start over. It ain't nothing to find no starting place in the world. You just start from where you find yourself." Mattie Campbell is one female character who represents a composite portrait of the dissolution of a myth—the socially inscribed, traditional roles to which all African American women had unwillingly acquiesced. Mattie met Jack Carper, a Joe Turner, in Texas while picking peaches with her mother, who dies before Mattie moves in Carper. Carper left because he considered Mattie to be a cursed woman, a post-lapsarian Eve. Consequently, Mattie moves north and into the Hollys's boarding house, where she eventually moves in with Jeremy Furlow, another Joe Turner, whose brief encounters with those whom he meets—whether at work on the road crew, at the local bar, or at the boarding house render his last name a pun. Of course, Furlow will leave Mattie too, and she will linger on in the hope that someday Carper will return—until Bynum Walker tells her otherwise. What is interesting about Mattie's character is that she rushes out the door after Herald Loomis at the end of the play because both characters at that moment come to the realization that tomorrow does come and that people do (or can) change.

Three of the female characters—Zonia, Mattie, and even Martha—represent the dissolution of a myth: the simplified, traditional, dichotomous portrait of women as merely doting mothers or conniving Mata Haris. Simply stated, each woman is more psychologically complex than the creatures who dwell within such a mythic construct. Each woman's interaction with the Joe Turners, those who also are disenfranchised African Americans in this play, elicits a change to some extent within each one of them, resulting in a song of self that each woman must discover for herself.

Thus, August Wilson clearly addresses the issue of uprooted African Americans, for they as a culture have been "enslaved" both physically and psychologically. The need to dispel or shake off an identity as a non-man (or non-person) is an important theme in this play. The play has been described as a panoramic and insightful view of Black America and as a spiritual allegory. Its author, who grew up in a poor family, describes his view of the African American experience in this way: "My generation of blacks knew very little about the past of our parents . . . They shielded us from the indignities that they suffered" [*Black Writers*, Gale, 1989, p. 605]. Although he was shielded from them while growing up, the indignities Wilson mentions are nonetheless a part of the African American's experience, as Ishmael Reed explains [in

"Is Ethnicity Obsolete?," *The Invention of Ethnicity*, edited by Werner Sollors, 1989]:

> As long as such public attitudes about "Black America" are maintained, ethnicity will never become obsolete. By blaming all its problems on blacks, the political and cultural leadership are able to present the United States as a veritable utopia for those who aren't afraid of "hard work." A place where any goal is possible, for the "strong hearted" and "the brave," and other cheerleading myths. And, so, instead of being condemned as a "problem," the traditional view of the "black presence," the presence of "blacks" should be viewed as blessing. Without blacks taking the brunt of the system's failures, where would our great republic be?

When asked to define his role in the theatre, Wilson defined himself [in *Black Writers*] as a "cultural nationalist [a playwright who is] trying to raise consciousness through theater." Wilson's play must and does contain complex themes and complex characters. To a varying extent, the characters of Bynum Walker, Herald Loomis, Mattie Campbell, and Zonia Loomis each experience his or her own private purgation, a sense of displacement or disenfranchisement, which each character expresses through song. Whether this song is the juba, a blues song like "Joe Turner's Come and Gone," or a voice to express his or her troubles, each character's song enables him or her to find strength, to begin life anew, and, for August Wilson, to leave the "mark" of African American culture on the American stage.

James Robert Saunders (essay date December 1995)

SOURCE: "Essential Ambiguities in the Plays of August Wilson," in *The Hollins Critic*, Vol. XXXII, No. 5, December, 1995, pp. 1-12.

[*In the following essay, Saunders overviews Wilson's life and career in order to illuminate the playwright's use of ambiguous and often paradoxical characters, details, and themes in his works.*]

In a 1984 interview, August Wilson intimated that the "importance of history . . . is simply to find out who you are and where you've been," a task made all the more difficult for African Americans because of our history of enslavement and subsequent years of slow economic advancement. Even as we struggle to find our place in the mainstream culture, we carry the added burden of color. For Wilson, that burden was further exacerbated because as was the case with James Weldon Johnson's troubled protagonist in *The Auto-*

biography of an Ex-Coloured Man (1912), Wilson himself was the offspring of an interracial relationship. As had been the case with Johnson's narrator, Wilson suffered the consequences of having a white father who reneged on his parental responsibility. The future playwright grew up in a two-room apartment at the back of a grocery store without the benefit of a telephone, hot water, or even respect enough from teachers to keep him from being expelled when he turned in a superb essay that they thought he had plagiarized.

After a barrage of distressing events, *Ex-Coloured Man*'s nameless narrator finally decided to "pass," desert the black race, and live out his life as a white man. Wilson, on the other hand, immersed himself in African American culture with the aim of reconciling himself with both a turbulent history and the contemporary racial situation. Though he seems to have burst suddenly on the scene with his award-winning play, **Ma Rainey's Black Bottom** (1985), it is useful to trace a fuller development of those years that led up to his fame. From the mid-1970s to the early 1980s, he was busily honing his playwrighting skills, producing, among other things, scripts such as **The Homecoming** (1976)—about blues singer Blind Lemon Jefferson who died of exposure in Chicago, and **Fullerton Street** (1980)—about a group of African Americans struggling against the odds in the urban North. Prior to that phase of his literary endeavors, several of his poems appeared in periodicals such as *Negro Digest, Black World,* and *Black Lines.* He experimented with literary forms and pursued what he, in the 1984 interview, referred to as the "need" for African Americans to "re-examine their time spent here to see the choices that were made as a people."

In her biography, *Mother of the Blues: A Study of Ma Rainey* (1981), Sandra R. Lieb says:

> Ma Rainey's life symbolizes the confrontation between the black rural South and the changes wrought by industrialization, urban migration, and the development of modern mass communications. She represents a collision between the unchanging aphorisms of folk poetry and the nervous rhythms of modern life.

Born in 1886, in Columbus, Georgia, Rainey was privy to the work songs, field hollers, and ballads out of which the classic blues tradition grew. By 1900, she had begun her stage career with the Bunch of Blackberries Revue, and for the next two decades she would perform with many black minstrel troupes, including the Florida Cotton Blossoms, Shufflin' Sam from Alabam', and her most famous of these shows, the Rabbit Foot Minstrels. In those early days, her repertoire included songs such as "I Ain't Got Nobody" and "See, See Rider," the latter a song she would become the first singer ever to record.

Though she was not the first blues singer to make a recording, she was part of the "race" record phenomenon of the 1920s that saw blues singers rise to a level of popularity that had heretofore never been achieved. Columbia, Victor, and Paramount were but a few of the companies that rushed to record the great blues singers, oftentimes drawing them up out of the South to record in the Northern studios. One such studio comprises the 1927 Chicago setting for Wilson's play. Rainey arrives late for the recording session only to discover that one of her band members, Levee, has substituted his own more sophisticated version of "Ma Rainey's Black Bottom" for the version she knows to be closer to its black folk roots. Prior to Rainey's arrival, Levee had persuaded the other band members and the two white promoters to accept his rendition. When Rainey arrives and hears the band practicing Levee's version, she berates them: "What you all say don't count with me. You understand? Ma listens to her heart. Ma listens to the voice inside her. That's what counts with Ma."

Lieb, in comparing Rainey to other blues artists, describes how she "performed in a rougher, more down-home style." The poet Sterling Brown once said, "She would moan, and the audience would moan with her. . . . Ma really *knew* these people; she was a person of the folk; she was very simple and direct." It is significant that Paramount was the only company for which Rainey recorded. That company's acoustic methods were crude even by the standards of that time, which explains the difference in quality of product between Rainey's recordings and those of her contemporary, Bessie Smith, whose recordings have a clearer, more pungent sound. One is reminded of the point in Wilson's play where Rainey tells the two promoters that "Levee ain't messing up my song with none of his music shit. Now, if that don't set right with you and Sturdyvant. . .then I can carry my black bottom on back down South to my tour, 'cause I don't like it up here no ways."

Lieb further observes that the song "Ma Rainey's Black Bottom" has a dual meaning: it refers both to a black person's backside and to the quintessential all-black section of a small Southern town. However, Sandra Shannon, in her essay "The Long Wait: August Wilson's **Ma Rainey's Black Bottom**" (1991), gives a different, albeit intriguing interpretation. By that critic's account, Rainey is telling all those who would exploit her, or distort her music forms, that they can "kiss her ass." She sought out no better sound studio for her recordings because she recognized that the music industry was exploitative. "They don't care nothing about me," she tells Cutler, another member of her band. "As soon as they get my voice down on them recording machines, then it's just like if I'd be some whore and they roll over and put their pants on. Ain't got no use for me then." In essence, Rainey never accepted the recorded music form as a legitimate means of conveying Southern country blues. For her, the process of recording was as much a struggle against cooptation as it was an act of submitting to a necessary communications medium.

And this is the paradox we are left with by the end of the play. However much we are inclined to admire Rainey in her attempt to contend with the rapidly developing music industry, we know that her efforts will fail. By 1929, her recording career was over, supplanted by new musical trends, particularly "swing." Big bands became the craze. And blues singers who survived were able to do so by means of accomplishing the very thing that Rainey had rejected in Levee. Singers and musicians such as Ethel Waters and Louis Armstrong prospered only in proportion to the degree that they were willing to commercialize their art. Perhaps Levee's haunting words ring truer than the music that Rainey was so inclined to protect. "You got to move on down the road from where you sitting," Levee tells Cutler, "and all the time you got to keep an eye out for that devil who's looking to buy up souls. And hope you get lucky and find him!"

In *Fences* (1987), Troy Maxson claims to have encountered the devil who assumed the guise of an ordinary man offering credit for a furniture purchase. "Now you tell me," Maxson jabs at his audience, "who else that could have been but the devil?" Of course we know that it was no devilish fiend who extended the offer of credit, but a mere mortal doing his earthly job. Rose characterizes her husband's tale-telling habits as she issues the simple retort, "Troy lying." Maxson and his friend, Jim Bono, derive great pleasure from the act of sitting around telling each other tales. In fact, the very first dialogue of the play consists of Bono's exclamation, "Troy, you ought to stop that lying!" In that instance, Maxson had just finished telling the story of a black man who hid a watermelon under his coat because he was too ashamed to let a white man know that he liked eating watermelon. The protagonist in Maxson's story felt bound to deny what he perceived as a negative stereotype.

In telling the tale and criticizing the protagonist's feelings of embarrassment, Maxson shows himself to be someone who has already learned what it took Ralph Ellison's Invisible Man (*Invisible Man,* 1952) twenty years to discover—that within the deep recesses of certain stereotypes lie valuable truths about African American culture. We will recall the exhilaration that Ellison's narrator felt upon acknowledging that chitterlings and hog maws were nothing to be ashamed of so much as they were foods he should embrace on the road to self-knowledge.

As it turns out, the black man in Maxson's watermelon story is a version of a worker at the sanitation department where Maxson himself is employed. Historian Lawrence Levine, in *Black Culture and Black Consciousness* (1977), writes that during slavery "it did not take much for . . .common

events to become embroidered into more elaborate and fanciful tales." Now a century or more later, Maxson is still employing that slavery-time technique of revealing certain truths through a "fanciful" style. The meekness of the black man in the watermelon story is the reticence of Maxson's black coworker, who is troubled that Maxson would complain about no blacks being allowed to drive the garbage trucks. "Embroidered" though he may be, the watermelon man is, in an important sense, actually real. Similarly, it is not so very difficult to comprehend how the imaginary devil of Maxson's furniture story is indeed a "devil" in the lives of poor blacks who are enslaved to financial indebtedness. Though Maxson is frequently called a liar, we must consider what his tales reveal about African American life.

The most problematic of Maxson's stories is the one concerning his prowess as a baseball player. He is 53 years old as the play opens, set in 1957. 10 years earlier, Jackie Robinson had broken the color barrier and begun playing in the modern major leagues. It is ironic that at the point of Robinson's groundbreaking accomplishment, Maxson was too old to partake of the glory in terms of playing in the majors himself. As players followed Robinson's suit, crossing from the Negro Leagues over into the majors, Maxson could only watch those others taking advantage of the opportunity he never had. "Times have changed, Troy," says Bono, appreciative about the historic turn of events. "You just come along too early." Maxson rails back at him, "There ought not never have been no time called too early!" As proud as Bono is of Robinson's accomplishment, therein also lies a tragedy.

The year before Robinson broke into the majors, an extraordinarily gifted baseball player, James "Cool Papa" Bell, was playing out his final year of top Negro League competition. He was 41 years old and still one of the fastest players in the game. But at the point of baseball integration he, like Maxson, was too old to benefit personally. Satchel Paige once said of Bell that in his prime he "was so fast that he could turn off a light switch and jump into bed before the room got dark." That sounds like a Maxson-type exaggeration. Nevertheless it is an appropriate testament to the skills of a baseball phenomenon. In his book *Only the Ball Was White* (1970), a comprehensive study of the Negro Leagues, Robert Peterson acknowledges that "Bell was probably the fastest runner who ever played baseball." Bell himself claimed to have stolen 175 bases in 1933, which presumably would have made him not only better than Ty Cobb but also better than more modern-day base stealing champions including Lou Brock and Ricky Henderson. But since Bell was not allowed to play in the majors, we will never know how good he was.

What are the psychological effects of such an injustice? At one point, Maxson's son, Cory, informs him that Hank Aaron has hit his 43rd home run. Maxson responds bitterly, "Hank Aaron ain't nobody. . . . Hell, I can hit forty-three home runs right now!" Keep in mind that Maxson is 53 years old, "over the hill" by baseball standards. It is highly unlikely that he at this age can keep pace with the man who eventually will break Babe Ruth's home run record. But how about Maxson in his prime? Could he have been as good as Hank Aaron if only he had not "come along too early?"

And Maxson holds special venom for Jackie Robinson:

> I done seen a hundred niggers play baseball better than Jackie Robinson. Hell, I know some teams Jackie Robinson couldn't even make! What you talking about Jackie Robinson. Jackie Robinson wasn't nobody.

Notwithstanding Maxson's proclivity for storytelling, we are made to consider the possibility that there were 100 Negro League players who were better than Robinson. Negro League rosters that Robinson could not have made? It sounds inconceivable. Yet Peterson cites several players who indeed were not impressed with Robinson's skills. Walter (Buck) Leonard, known during the 1930s and 1940s as the black Lou Gehrig, expressed surprise at the Robinson selection and explained, "We thought we had other ballplayers who were better players than he." The first black man in the modern major leagues had to be a certain type of person. In addition to being athletically gifted, he had to be willing to withstand the inevitable barrage of racial epithets. Representatives from the majors had been searching for decades for just the right man. How many were overlooked in the process? Maxson was perhaps one.

In a 1987 *Hudson Review* article, theater critic Richard Hornby praised James Earl Jones's Broadway performance:

> He still has the physical strength and agility he had twenty years ago in *The Great White Hope,* and although, like the character he played in **Fences,** he shows his age, he also convinced you of his underlying athletic ability, which is so important to the role. When Troy insisted that he "can hit forty-three home runs right now!" Jones made you believe it.

As improbable as it might sound that Maxson could hit 43 home runs at the age of 53, it was important for Jones to convince us that Maxson could possibly have done it. Buck Leonard played professionally until he was 48 years old. Baseball historians argue over whether or not Satchel Paige was actually 48 years old when he broke into the majors one year after Robinson. Whatever his age, he was still able to amass a pitching record of 28 victories and 31 defeats. He had been cagey about his age in order to increase his base-

ball longevity, anticipating that his talents would linger long enough for him to get a shot at playing in the majors.

Such was not to be the case for the man many refer to as the best ever (black or white) to play the game of baseball. Josh Gibson was said to have hit 89 home runs in one season and 75 in another. Babe Ruth's record was 60. However, some of the teams Gibson played against were only semi-professional. And how does one compare two players who did not even play against the same competition? As was the case with "Cool Papa" Bell, Gibson was also closing out his career the year before Robinson broke the color barrier. Another player who "come along too early," Gibson is said to have died of a broken heart the year after Robinson got the opportunity to do what players like Gibson had been denied their entire athletic careers.

In some ways, Maxson epitomizes Gibson's tragic plight. Both men were powerful hitters, deprived of occupational opportunity. Consequently, Maxson now can only think of life in baseball terms, saying at one point, "You born with two strikes on you before you come to the plate." He equates his own extramarital affair with trying to "steal second." Even death, as far as he is concerned, "ain't nothing but a fastball on the outside corner." By comparison, baseball was so substantially a part of Gibson's life that once his playing days were over, he quite likely lay down and died. Just as we cannot know how good Maxson was in his prime, we will never know how good Josh Gibson was, or hundreds of others who were barred from the majors in the pre-Jackie Robinson era.

Cory of course belongs to a different sports era. Gifted at football, it is at the point where he is being recruited by a North Carolina college that his father demands he quit the football team because "the white man ain't gonna let you get nowhere with that football noway." Maxson is so trapped in the tragedy of his own athletic experience that he cannot believe things will be any different for his son. One is tempted to conclude immediately that Maxson is doing Cory a disservice, depriving him of not only an athletic but also an educational opportunity. Or is he sparing Cory a heartache that is reminiscent of what past black athletes had to endure? In his essay entitled "The Black Athlete on the College Campus" (1969), Harry Edwards characterized the process of college recruiting as the "modern-day equivalent of the slave trade." Specifying low graduation rates and social alienation, Edwards renders a portrait of college athletics that is as fraught with tragedy as Maxson's own pre-integration athletic experience. How can we say the father does not have his son's best interests at heart as he forbids any further participation?

Not altogether different from her husband, Rose wants a fence built to keep out all would-be intruders. This goal, however, is as much destined to failure in *Fences* as it is in Wilson's next play, *Joe Turner's Come and Gone* (1988). Wilson elucidates in a 1984 interview:

> Joe Turner was a real person. He was the brother of Pete Turner who was the Governor of Tennessee. Joe Turner would press Blacks into peonage. He would send out decoys who would lure Blacks into crap games and then he would swoop down and grab them. He had a chain with forty links to it, and he would take Blacks off to his plantation and work them.

Actually, Tennessee is not the only state where this sort of atrocity occurred. In Toledo, Ohio, during the 1980s, I met a woman from Mississippi who recounted the tale of how her son was kidnapped and made to pick cotton for a period of several years before he was finally released. She, in fact, had come to Toledo to escape the bad memories. Wilson's play is set in 1911. The woman I met insisted that such things were going on well into the 1950s.

In Wilson's play, Herald Loomis is the victim who has been wrested from his family and made to work on Joe Turner's plantation for seven years. When he is finally freed, he discovers that his world has been, as Wilson says in his interview, "torn asunder and his life is turned upside down." He no longer knows where his wife and daughter are, and thus begins the search. Wilson actually uses the seven-year imprisonment period as a metaphor for the long centuries during which legal slavery existed. The process whereby slaves were transported from Africa resulted in extreme alienation. As the conjure man Bynum (binder) tells Loomis, "You forgot how to sing your song." The song that Loomis has forgotten how to sing is indicative of how he is no longer connected with his wife. The song that African Americans in general have forgotten is a consequence of forced separation from their African roots.

In this play is a rather intriguing character, Rutherford Selig, who is a peddler of pots and pans. Also known as the People Finder, he, by virtue of his occupation, knows how to find everybody. For a fee, he will even find Loomis's wife. He succeeds in this, but the reunion between husband and wife is ambiguous. "Now that I see your face," Loomis says to his long lost wife, "I can say my goodbye and make my own world." Wilson seems to be telling us that 400 years of separation from Africa is too long to hope now for any ultimate reconnection. After seven years, Loomis cannot put the pieces back together to make his life what it once was. Similarly, African Americans will have to reconcile themselves to the task of creating a culture that may or may not resemble what exists on the African continent.

Selig finds people. As he tells Loomis, "We been finders in my family for a long time. Bringers and finders." In using the term "bringers," the peddler alludes to the fact that his great-grandfather "used to bring Nigras across the ocean on ships." Selig's father hunted runaway slaves. And now that slavery is over, Selig himself finds black people who were separated from their relatives during the "peculiar institution." From our perspective, Selig's work is much more palatable than the jobs held by his great-grandfather and father. Yet the youngest Selig is inextricably linked to the family tradition. His skills are grounded in the duties that his ancestors undertook. The fact that he, of all people, is the one who finds Loomis's wife poses a major dilemma, for we are left to wonder if blacks will ever evolve from the shadow of slavery. And if we do, will we ever be able to overcome the influence of whites who have profited from the centuries-long period of black subjugation?

Human bondage continues as an issue in Wilson's next play, *The Piano Lesson* (1990). Though the setting is 1930s Pittsburgh, the play concerns a piano that, generations earlier, had been the "currency" used to purchase two slaves. The slaves that had been sold were the father and grandmother of the elderly Doaker Charles who now lives with his niece (Berneice) who adamantly refuses to play the piano but just as adamantly refuses to let her brother, Boy Willie, sell it. Boy Willie wants to sell it for money towards the purchase of the same tract of land upon which their ancestors were slaves.

When his wife and child were sold. Doaker's grandfather was ordered to carve their pictures into the newly acquired piano. Doaker explains. "Miss Ophelia got to missing my grandmother . . .the way she would cook and clean the house and talk to her and what not. And she missed having my daddy around the house to fetch things for her." After the grandfather had finished the carvings. Miss Ophelia "had her piano and her niggers too." But the grandfather did more than just carve the two images that had been required of him. He carved his family's whole history—birthdates, marriages, deaths, the sales of individual family members. This in part is why Berniece cannot bring herself to sell the piano. And the no longer plays it because, as she declares, "I don't want to wake them spirits."

We sympathize with Berniece's position. The piano is an heirloom rife with meaning. Yet Boy Willie is determined to sell it. Michael Morales, in his essay "Ghosts on the Piano" (1994), characterizes Boy Willie as "the consummate materialist." That brother seems not to comprehend the piano's spiritual significance. Berniece accuses him of selling his soul, whereupon the brother retorts, "I ain't talking about selling my soul. I'm talking about trading that piece of wood for some land. . . . You can always get you another piano." Those do indeed sound like the words of a person who cares only about the "bottom line."

Still, it is important to consider what Richard Hornby had to say in yet another *Hudson Review* article (1990). There, he addressed the issue of how relatives can respond to crucial phenomena in different, yet equally vital ways. Said Hornby:

> The controversy over selling the piano is not just a simple conflict between sentimentality and practicality. The piano is a symbol for Berniece. . . . On the other hand, for Boy Willie, selling the piano is not just a means of getting some cash. Buying a hundred acres of the old plantation is a way of getting control over the family's terrible past. The land for him functions as the carvings on the piano did for his great-grandfather. Taking something that belonged to the master and making it into his own is a means to power, a way to go on record and be somebody.

In the final analysis, the piano is not sold. But Hornby's comparison of Boy Willie with his great-grandfather still merits some evaluation. What would that great-grandfather have wanted? He might very well have thrilled at the prospect that one of his offspring could own the very land upon which he was a slave. Nevertheless, the great-grandfather did go to great lengths, carving his family's history into the wooden structure. The dilemma is a difficult one, made no less problematic by the passage of time since that original unspeakable deal.

Wilson's latest play, ***Two Trains Running*** (1993), also takes place in Pittsburgh, and while this time the year is 1969, the issue remains one of how blacks should best proceed in their struggle for basic human dignity. Memphis is the owner of an inner city restaurant scheduled to be razed as part of an urban renewal plan. He and several others are engaged in conversation about various subjects of concern to the African American community.

When Sterling, just released from prison, announces that there is going to a rally to celebrate Malcolm X's birthday, Memphis declares, "Malcolm X is dead. . . . Dead men don't have birthdays. . . . I ain't going to no party for no dead man." It is not that Memphis cannot comprehend the validity of celebrating the birthday of a deceased great man. It is just that he does not feel Malcolm X is deserving of such respect. "That's what half the problem is," Memphis insists, "these black power niggers. They got people confused."

It is Memphis who first invokes the name "Martin." "They killed Martin," he says. "If they did that to him you can imagine what they do to me or you. If they kill the sheep you know what they do to the wolf." This equating of Martin Luther King with "sheep" must be juxtaposed with the long held view of Malcolm X as a person who was determined to achieve a certain victory, even if violence was the necessary means.

Contrast in perspectives becomes further evident as another customer, Holloway, tells his version of what happened to Hambone. The former tells how nine and a half years earlier, the owner of Lutz's Meat Market promised Hambone a ham for painting his fence. Once the fence was painted, however, Lutz was only willing to give Hambone a chicken.

Immediately, Memphis objects:

> That ain't how it went. Lutz told him if he painted his fence he'd give him a chicken. Told him if he do a good job he'd give him a ham. He think he did a good job and Lutz didn't. That's where he went wrong—Letting Lutz decide what to pay him for his work: If you leave it like that, quite naturally he gonna say it ain't worth the higher price.

Memphis's explanation is an attempt to ameliorate the injustice. He advances the most brutal techniques of the marketplace as a legitimate basis for one-on-one human interaction. What Memphis has temporarily forgotten is that almost four decades earlier, he was in a situation similar to what Hambone had suffered one decade ago. In 1931, that entrepreneur was summarily chased off his farm in Jackson, Mississippi, because such acts were facilitated by a racist climate. He, like Hambone, knows what it means to be socioeconomically violated. A question, however, concerns who between the two of them has the appropriate response.

In a 1992 interview, Wilson stated rather bluntly, "Hambone shows us that a new black man was created in the 1960's who would not accept a chicken." And indeed for nine and half years, Hambone has stood outside Lutz's market demanding his ham, rejecting Lutz's insistence that he just take a chicken. Ironically, Memphis has the potential to be just as demanding. "One of these days," he says, "I'm going back and get my land." He still has the deed, but will he be moved to action?

Memphis may not know how to get back to Jackson. Yet, he maintains, "I ain't even got to know the way." What he does know is that at the depot, "They got two trains running every day." Lisa Wilde, in her essay "Reclaiming the Past: Narrative and Memory in August Wilson's ***Two Trains Running***" (1990), interprets the phrase "two trains" to be symbolic of a choice incumbent upon blacks to either bypass or retrieve the essential elements of their history. Wilson for his part has chosen retrieval, and in creating these plays, he has left us to ponder the question: Now where do we go from here?

Yvonne Shafer (essay date 1995)

SOURCE: "Breaking Barriers: August Wilson," in *Staging Difference: Cultural Pluralism in American Theatre and Drama,* edited by Marc Maufort, Peter Lang, 1995, pp. 267-85.

[*In the following essay, Shafer analyzes Wilson's life and his techniques as a playwright, and chronicles the stage productions of his plays.*]

August Wilson is one of only seven American playwrights to win two Pulitzer Prizes, and one of only three black playwrights to receive the prize. Unlike many black playwrights he has written plays which appeal to both black and white audiences. When *Ma Rainey's Black Bottom* opened in 1984, Wilson was completely unknown in the theatre. In the following ten years he achieved such success that, as critic Paul Taylor has noted, "Wilson is the only contemporary dramatist, apart from Neil Simon, who is assured a Broadway production and his have been the pioneer black works at many regional theatres" ["Emptying the Contents of His Bag," *Independent* (London), October 21, 1993]. He has won Bush, McKnight, Rockefeller, and Guggenheim Foundation fellowships in playwriting, and Tony awards and Drama Critics Circle Awards. In 1988 he achieved the distinction of having two plays running on Broadway, *Fences* and *Joe Turner's Come and Gone.* His plays have been described as "powerful," "thrilling," and "explosive." Critic Richard Christiansen noted the unusual quality of Wilson's work which has contributed to his popularity, saying, "Wilson's genius for translating common language into poetry through rhythm, repetition and telling imagery reveals a world of myth, religion, and folk spirit" ["'Two Trains' Has Ticket to Amazing Trip," *Chicago Tribune,* January 26, 1993]. Remarkably, Wilson has been able to explore and communicate the black experience in America in a way which seems particular to blacks and also achieves a universality which has drawn the white audiences needed for a commercial success in the American theatre. He explores small lives in very particular places, but as Taylor commented, "They're small people in a small space but in *Two Trains Running* they summon up a universe." An analysis of Wilson's background, his approach to playwriting, and the stage history of his plays reveals a unique experience in the American theatre.

Wilson was born Freddy August Kittel in 1945 in Pittsburgh, Pennsylvania. His mother's maiden name was Wilson. His background seems an unlikely one to produce either a poet or a playwright who has achieved "widespread acclaim as the most invigorating new voice in our theatre" [Sid Smith, "Playwright: Blacks Should Look Back, Go South," *Chicago Tribune,* February 23, 1993]. His white father was a German baker named August who "was at best an infrequent and sporadic presence in the household" [Samuel G. Freedman "A Voice from the Streets," *New York Times Magazine,* March 15, 1987]. Young August's mother (who supported the children by a janitorial job and money from welfare), however, was determined that her children would have a chance to compete in society. As Wilson says, "My mother taught me how to read. She had six kids and taught us all how to read. I learned how to read when I was four. She kept books around the house; it was very important. We had a time that we would all sit down and she would read a few pages and then she would let us go out and play" [quoted in Yvonne Shafer's "An Interview with August Wilson," *Journal of Dramatic Theory and Criticism,* Fall, 1989].

As a child Wilson suffered the effects of racism in America: when his family tried to move into a mostly white neighborhood, bricks were thrown through the windows and when he went to a largely white high school, white students left ugly, racist notes on his desk. He left one school, tried another, and at the age of fifteen dropped out of school. However, his education did not end: he spent part of his days in the library reading—especially books in the section marked "Negro." He recalls, "Those books were a comfort, Just the idea black people would write books. I wanted my book up there, too. I used to dream about being part of the Harlem Renaissance" (Freedman).

When he wasn't in the library, Wilson was hanging around bars and pool halls—his was the archetypal black American experience. From the streets he learned a rich, vibrant argot which he has transmuted into powerful, striking language in his poems and plays. He began his career by writing poetry for more than twenty years. His poems appear in numerous journals and anthologies including *The Poetry of Black America.* Unlike many black playwrights, his own experience and his knowledge of the history of blacks in America has not resulted in bitter, vituperative dramas. Particularly in the sixties, some black playwrights were so militant against white culture that they literally drove white audiences out of the theatre. Claude Purdy (director-in-residence at the Penumbra Theatre in St. Paul, Minnesota) knew Wilson in Pittsburgh, and encouraged his playwriting. He has commented, "August came out of the '60s with a responsible attitude, eager to explore his community's culture and do something for his people" [Hilary De Vries, "A Song in Search of Itself," *American Theatre,* January, 1987]. Wilson's plays both inform audiences about the cruelties of the past and indicate the possibilities in the future for blacks in America. He is keenly committed to the idea of demonstrating to white audiences the reality of African culture.

Wilson turned to playwriting during the black power movement in the United States. He began writing one-act plays to raise the consciousness of his community. He was co-founder of the Black Horizons Theater Company in Pittsburgh. In 1978 he was invited by Claude Purdy to join him in the Penumbra Theatre. In this period Wilson produced some plays at Penumbra and became a member of the Playwrights Center of Minneapolis. He began to receive grants which enabled him to focus entirely on writing plays. Although he has been closely related to the Eugene O'Neill Theater Center's National Playwrights Conference in recent years, at first he had little success there. He submitted five plays which were all rejected. However, he persevered and in 1982 his play *Ma Rainey's Black Bottom* was accepted. He traveled to Connecticut from his home in St. Paul and his work with director Lloyd Richards began.

Wilson is writing a play for each of the decades of this century depicting the black experience throughout the years. So far he has written five plays which are a representation and summation of a particular decade. When asked if he would start over, once he had finished, he responded, "Then I'll start over, sure. There's more than one story to tell" [quoted in Shafer interview]. In fact, Wilson takes umbrage at the suggestion that he could use up his material:

> An interviewer once asked me if having written these plays, I hadn't exhausted the black experience. I said, "Wait a minute. You've got 40,000 movies and plays about the white experience and we don't ask you if you've exhausted your experience." I'll never run out of material. I'll just start over again. You can write forever about the clash between the urban North and the rural South, what happened when blacks came to the cities, how their lives changed and how it affected generations to come. [quoted in DeVries]

Part of the recent controversy which revolves around Wilson's work is the charge by Robert Brustein, artistic head of the American Repertory Theatre in Cambridge, Massachusetts, that Wilson is limiting his development by writing about the black experience. He further stated that he had been fatigued by "Wilson's essays on racism" ["The Lesson of 'The Piano Lesson'," *New Republic,* May 21, 1990]. Asked to expand his remarks for *The New York Times,* Brustein wrote, "I feel he's explored that [the black experience] in four plays. I want to see another theme. And therefore something like that can become self-limiting" (quoted in Mervyn Rothstein, "Passionate Beliefs Renew Theater Fight over Art and Profit," *New York Times,* May 15, 1990]. Wilson responded to Brustein's remarks by indicating once again his amazement that someone could feel the black experience was exhausted after a few plays, and concluded, "Has anyone ever told a white playwright to write about blacks? There's no idea that cannot be contained in black life. It's full and it's flourishing. How can that be limiting? Was it limiting to Chekhov to write about his people?" [quoted in Rothstein]

The plays Wilson has written about his people include *Joe Turner's Come and Gone,* set in 1911, *Ma Rainey's Black Bottom,* set in 1927, *The Piano Lesson,* set in 1936, *Fences,* set in 1957, and *Two Trains Running* set in 1969. As he has said, "I've got a very large story—the four hundred year biography of the black experience in America" [quoted in Janice Arkatov, "August Wilson: His Way," *Los Angeles Times,* June 7, 1987].

Wilson's plays were first performed in staged readings at the Eugene O'Neill Theater Center's National Playwrights Conference. Wilson worked closely with Lloyd Richards, then Dean of the Yale School of Drama and Artistic Director of the Playwrights Conference. (Richards came to prominence as director of the first Pulitzer Prize winning play by a black playwright, *A Raisin in the Sun.*) Wilson's fruitful relationship with Richards has continued to the present. Wilson says that they have developed a way of working together which calls for very little dialogue because Richards has an intuitive understanding of the overall arc of his work and what he is trying to accomplish.

Wilson slowly moved from his work as a poet to the profession of playwriting. Although he had read many plays, the did not see a professional play until he was thirty-one. Being a poet is still important in his writing. He has commented on this aspect of his work, saying in one interview, "I think the idea of metaphor comes into the plays because I'm a poet. Writing a poem you have a very small space to work in, you compress a lot of ideas in a small space, and it is the process of thinking that allows you to do that. . . . Now the play is a big space, but you still think the same way" [quoted in Shafer].

Turning from Wilson's background and his approach to playwriting to an analysis of his plays, one is struck by the themes and archetypal elements which have made them engrossing both to blacks and whites in the audience. The question of self-identity seems to be the major force in his plays. *Ma Rainey's Black Bottom* centers on black musicians who are exploited by white managers and record producers. Cutler and Sturdyvant represent white society, responsible in the blacks' view for their unhappy lives, yet the final arbiters of their actions. In a dispute over the arrangement of the music the blacks cease to argue only when the white man says what he wants. The piano player, Toledo, chides the others, saying, "As long as the colored man looks to white folks to put the crown on what he says . . . as long as he looks to white folks for approval . . . then he ain't never gonna find who he is and what he's about."

The title of the play is a type of pun; the Black Bottom was a dance popularized by Ma Rainey's song, but, of course, Ma Rainey also has a black bottom and she and the other blacks are at the bottom of society because of their color.

The play explores their position through a simple story line: the black musicians and the white managers are waiting for the famous singer, Ma Rainey. When she finally arrives she initially refuses to make the records, then finally agrees. She makes it clear throughout the play that she feels used by the white men who run the business. Saying that they care nothing about her, she concludes, "As soon as they get my voice down on them recording machines, then it's just like if I'd be some whore and they roll over and put their pants on."

A young black trumpeter, Levee, is attracted to Ma Rainey's sexy young gal, but is warned by the other musicians to keep away from her or Ma Rainey will be jealous. Throughout the play tensions are high because of the frustration the black performers feel: their aspirations are meaningless given the impotence inherent in their positions. At the end of the play, as Ma leaves with her gal after firing Levee, the frustrations turns to rage—the senseless rage of black against black. Toledo accidentally steps on Levee's new shoe and this minor act sets off an explosion of emotion in Levee:

> (All the weight in the world suddenly falls on Levee and he runs at Toledo with his knife in his hand.)
>
> LEVEE: Nigger, you stepped on my shoe!
>
> (He plunges the knife into Toledo's back up to the hilt. Toledo lets out a sound of surprise and agony. Cutler and Slow Drag freeze.)
>
> He . . . stepped on my shoe. He did. Honest Mr. Cutler, he stepped on my shoe. What he do that for? Toledo, what you do that for? Cutler, help me.
>
> He stepped on my shoe, Cutler.

In the published play the white man is taking charge and from the blacks the only sound is heard from Levee's trumpet: "a muted trumpet struggling for the highest of possibilities and blowing pain and warning." However, in the excellent 1994 production at the Denver Center Theatre Company only the blacks were onstage. This undercuts the point of the white men controlling the lives of the blacks, but the ending was still dramatically effective. At the end of the play, the largely white audience rose to its feet and shouted approval.

Ma Rainey's Black Bottom reflects Wilson's belief in the value of the blues to American blacks and the inability of whites to comprehend either the blues or black people. (Wilson has pointed out the irony that on most recordings the notes about the music are written by white men.) The blues become a metaphor for the differences between the two races. For Wilson music, the blues in particular, are a part of the black legacy and an important element of life. He frequently states that the blues are an integral part of black people's lives, so in all of his plays he uses music both for theatrical effect and as a true element of African-American culture. Critics often note, too, the "jazz rhythms" in Wilson dialogue.

The critics greeted *Ma Rainey's Black Bottom* with outstanding notices. Jack Kroll spoke of the "rich and resonant work," in "this extraordinary Broadway debut by a new playwright, August Wilson" ["So Black and Blue," *Newsweek,* October 22, 1984]. Frank Rich wrote in *The New York Times,* "Mr. Wilson articulates a legacy of unspeakable agony and rage in a spellbinding voice. . . . He makes [the characters'] suffering into art that forces us to understand and won't allow us to forget" ["Wilson's 'Ma Rainey's Opens," October 12, 1984]. Critics praised the direction by Lloyd Richards and the ensemble acting in general. For actor Charles S. Dutton, a recent graduate from the Yale School of Drama, critics used the terms "red hot," "magnificent," and "astonishing." All aspects of the production received praise from the critics. The *Downbeat* critic summed things up by saying,

> Simply put, *Ma Rainey's Black Bottom* works. The language is rich, the emotions ring true and the direction by Lloyd Richards is right on target. Black playwright August Wilson is being hailed by critics everywhere as a major new voice in the theatre. It is rare that a black drama makes it to Broadway. One only hopes that *Ma Rainey's Black Bottom* stays around for a long time to come. ["'Ma Rainey's Black Bottom' Is a Winner on Broadway," March, 1985]

In contrast to many works by black playwrights which could not draw enough whites into the theatre to sustain a long run on Broadway, Wilson's play "stayed around" for a run of ten months and won the New York Drama Critics Circle Prize.

In his next play, *Fences,* Wilson is dealing with the polarities of loving and dying. In *Beyond the Pleasure Principal* Freud noted Eros and the death wish as the elementary powers whose counterpoint governs all the puzzles of life. Wilson establishes these two forces as governing factors in the life of the protagonist. *Fences* deals with the failed dreams of Troy Maxon, a black ball player who played in the minority black leagues, but was barred from the major (all white) leagues because of his race. Set in the 1950s, *Fences* presents conflicts familiar to blacks in the audience—indeed, one critic wrote that he was moved to tears because he seemed to see his own life on stage [Brent Staples, "'Fences': No Barrier to Emotion," *New York Times,* April 5, 1987].

The central metaphor in the play is that of fences: fences between the races, fences to keep people out, fences to keep people in, futile attempts at fencing in life. Troy Maxon was fenced in when he was in prison. He is literally building a fence around his house to please his wife, Rose, although he sees no use for it. Unable to fence in Troy's love, Rose is crushed when he informs her that he has another woman who is expecting a child. When the woman dies in childbirth, Troy challenges Mr. Death, and says he will fence in the yard so he can't sneak up on him again. In the following scene he enters the yard carrying the child which he asks Rose to take care of. She agrees, but tells him that he is now "womanless."

Juxtaposed with the threat of death is the attempt to find life and some meaning in life through sex. Troy's life has been blighted, and in a speech he describes an existence familiar to both blacks and whites:

> I come in here every Friday. I carry a sack of potatoes and a bucket of lard. You all line up at the door with your hands out. I give you the lint from my pockets. I give you my sweat and my blood. I ain't got no tears. I done spent them. We go upstairs to that room at night and I fall down on you and try to blast a hole into forever. I get up Monday morning . . . find my lunch on the table. I go out. Make my way. Find my strength to carry me through to the next Friday. That's all I got to give. I can't give nothing else.

Another major motif which is familiar to blacks and whites is the difficult relationship between fathers and sons. Although Troy criticizes his own father, he gives him credit for raising him and feeding him. When Troy criticizes his grown son by a previous marriage, the son responds, "If you wanted to change me, you should have been there when I was growing up." With Cory, his son by Rose, Troy is hard and demanding, and in a strong scene between the two, grills him about his housing, his food, and his clothing, concluding, "I done give you everything I had to give you, I gave you your life. . . . And liking your black ass wasn't part of the bargain." Early in the play he tells Cory that he is in the batter's box and has one strike. Finally, Troy says Cory has struck out, and following an intense confrontation Troy ejects his son from his home.

In the final scene of the play Cory returns for Troy's funeral. The play ends with a climactic event as Troy's deranged brother Gabriel initially fails in his attempt to blow his horn so Troy can get into heaven, then does a "slow, strange dance, eerie and life-giving. A dance of atavistic signature and ritual." As he finishes his dance the stage is diffused with light as "the gates of heaven stand open as wide as God's closet." Gabriel has succeeded in playing Troy into heaven and states with satisfaction, "That's the way that go!"

Fences has been Wilson's most successful play to date. It broke the record for non-musical plays by grossing $11 million during the first year in New York. First presented at the Yale Repertory Theater (a pattern for Wilson's first five plays), the play subsequently moved to Broadway in 1987 where it was hailed by the critics as an outstanding play. Howard Kissel wrote, "Wilson is one of the few American playwrights you can call a poet. His characters are simple but deeply felt, and his language ennobles their troubling live" ["One Man's Failure Is Another Man's Smash," *Daily News* (New York), March 27, 1987]. William A Henry III said, "Wilson's greatest gift is his ability to make sense of anger: he writes naturalistic scenes of genial humor turning into an explosive violence that flows from his characters and from the warping effect racism has had upon them" ["Righteous in His Own Backyard," *Time,* April 6, 1987]. In his review entitled "Fiery Fences," Clive Barnes stated, "It is the strongest, most passionate American dramatic writing since Tennessee Williams" [*New York Post,* March 27, 1987]. Several critics commented on Wilson's ability to depict the black American experience but extend the field of interest beyond that specific area. Edwin Wilson remarked, "Another impressive quality of Mr. Wilson's play is that it is not a polemical piece. Because the play is set in the late '50s, just before the civil-rights movement exploded, racial discrimination is very much a part of the fabric of the play, affecting the situation of every character. As important as it is, however, that is not the main focus. Rather it is the universal quality of the people ["Theater: Wilson's 'Fences' on Broadway," *Wall Street Journal,* March 31, 1987].

Fences won both the Pulitzer Prize and the New York Drama Critics Circle Award. It also won four Tony awards including best play, best direction of a play (Lloyd Richards), best performance by an actor in a play (James Earl Jones), and best performance by a featured actress in a play (Mary Alice). The play has enjoyed enormous success in regional theatres as well.

Following *Fences* came *Joe Turner's Come and Gone* in which the question of identity is central. Into a boarding house in Pittsburgh comes a strange lost man with a child seeking his wife. Almost everyone in the play is seeking someone, and they appeal for assistance to two wondrously mythic types—similar in many ways to the Rat Wife in Ibsen's *Little Eyolf*—the People Finder and the Binder of What Clings. The white man, Selig, is in a line of People Finders, but in contrast to his father who found runaway slaves for the plantation bosses, he is a beneficent figure who finds black people separated after the end of slavery and reunites families. Bynum is in a line of African conjure men and works spells. He, however, is in search of his own song; in a vision his father revealed to him that if he could find a "shiny man"—a man who is One Who Goes Before and Shows the Way—"I would know that my song had been accepted and worked its full power in the world and I could lay down and die a happy man." In the course of the play it is revealed that the stranger, Loomis, was entrapped into seven years of indentured servitude by the notorious Joe Turner (an actual historical figure) and thereby lost not only his wife, but his whole sense of the world and his place in it.

In an electrifying climax to the first act Loomis speaks like a crazy man of a vision of bones which rose out of water and walked on top of it, speaks in tongues, dances, and ultimately collapses, unable to stand up, skittering wildly across the floor. The play as a whole concludes with a number of people finding themselves or being found. The People Finder returns with Loomis' missing wife and Loomis turns their daughter over to her. Still lost, Loomis laments the past and the attempts people have made to bind him, "Well, Joe Turner's come and gone and Herald Loomis ain't for no binding. I ain't gonna let nobody bind me up!" The play rises to a climax as his wife prays and tells him he must be washed with the blood of Jesus, "You got to be something, Herald. You can't just be alive. Life don't mean nothing unless it got a meaning." But Loomis suddenly finds himself and responds, "I don't need nobody to bleed for me! I can bleed for myself. . . . You want blood? Blood make you clean? You clean with blood? (Loomis slashes himself across his chest.) I'm standing! I'm standing. My legs stood up! I'm standing now!" Having found his song, the song of self-sufficiency, and accepting the responsibility for his own presence in the world, Loomis is free. And Bynum, the Binder, has found his song because he has found his shiny man. He cries, "Herald Loomis, you shining! You shining like new money!"

The critics received the play enthusiastically. Noting that Wilson had two plays running on Broadway, "an unprecedented feat for a black playwright," Jack Kroll stated, "'Joe Turner' is Wilson's best play to date and a profoundly American one. Like all of his plays it resonates far beyond its explicit details" ["August Wilson's Come to Stay," *Newsweek,* April 11, 1988]. This was noted by several other critics including David Patrick Stearns who wrote, "There are flashes of profundity—Loomis is universal enough that he could be a Vietnam vet or anyone else who has suffered dehumanization. Indeed, the rooming house is in many ways a metaphor for the splintering of modern society. Characters reel about like pinballs, bouncing off their own self-perpetuating neuroses" ["'Turner' Comes to a Near Halt," *USA Today,* March 29, 1988]. Ron Cohen praised the play saying, "Playwright August Wilson is at the crest of his power in *Joe Turner's Come and Gone* at the Ethel Barrymore Theater. . . . The interaction of his people builds to a stunning climax that resonates with the power to overcome. *Joe Turner* is as evocative as Wilson's Pulitzer Prize-winning *Fences* and more original in scope."

The power of the climax was noted by a number of other critics including Douglas Watt who praised the play and the performance: "The cast of 11 is exceptionally directed by Lloyd Richards right up to the orgiastic climax, as striking a moment of theater as our stage has to offer" ["Second Thoughts on First Nights," *Daily News* (New York), April 8, 1988]. Describing the impact of the climax, Jack Kroll offers insight into Wilson's process of playwriting:

> When he was writing the climactic scene in *Joe Turner,* in which Loomis slashes himself across the chest [Wilson says], "I had no idea where it was going. When Loomis cut himself it was a surprise to me. I looked down at the page and said, "Where did that come from?" I was drained. I was limp. But I felt good. I knew I had something." ["August Wilson's Come to Stay"]

Wilson's next play, *The Piano Lesson,* was first performed at Yale and then in a number of other regional theatres before opening on Broadway in April 1990. The setting is again a boarding house in Pittsburgh. A group of blacks who live there are displaced from their roots and their acquaintances in Mississippi. Doaker and his niece Berniece are surprised by the unexpected arrival of Berniece's brother, the high-spirited Boy Willie, and his friend Lymon who have driven from Mississippi with a load of watermelons. Boy Willie hopes to make a large amount of money from selling the watermelons so he will have part of the money he needs to buy a farm. He also hopes to persuade his sister Berniece to sell the family piano so that he can get the rest of the money he needs. The play becomes a struggle over the family inheritance, an elaborately decorated piano with pictures of family members carved on the legs. As critic Michael Billington noted in his review of the London production, "a bitter family dispute becomes a powerful social metaphor . . . in a play about the need to acknowledge the past without being in thrall to it" ["Family Discord," *Guardian* (London), October 9, 1993].

A history of tragedy is connected with the piano and each of the characters relates to it in a different way. The great-grandfather of Berniece and Boy Willie carved the piano for a white man. Later he was murdered and burned in a railroad car on the Yellow Dog Line by several white men. Each of these men has subsequently died mysteriously. Berniece claims that she has seen the latest, Sutter, standing upstairs in a blue suit. Boy Willie is alarmed, but claims she has made the story up as a means of getting him out of the house.

The play examines both the significance of death and the struggle in which blacks from Mississippi attempt to acclimatize themselves in the North. There is a powerful mood of the past which keeps a hold on the characters, and the voices of the dead are likened to the wind. It is not clear if the playwright intends the audience to accept the actuality of a struggle with a ghost or whether the implication is that the struggle is against the past history of the blacks in America. The present generation cannot disassociate itself from the past struggle against "the man." Even in Pittsburgh, the "ghost" of "the man" pursues Boy Willie. But in the final moments he and Berniece achieve a closeness which seemed impossible early in the play and the mystical ending gives the audience a sense of elevation and hope.

Several critics noted the increased ambiguity and complexity of this play by Wilson. Mimi Kramer noted,

> The central object in this play—the piano, a beautifully carved upright, decorated with faces and scenes—means something different to everyone. To Boy Willie, who wants to use money from the sale of the piano to buy the land his family worked as slaves and sharecroppers, the piano means the future and his spiritual emancipation. To his widowed sister Berniece whose father died stealing it from the man who owned it, the piano means a heritage of grief and bitterness and women without men. ["The Theatre," *New Yorker,* April 30, 1990]

Some American critics and several British critics objected to the supernatural element in the play and to its length. However, Michael Billington commented that because of the inherent vital theatricality, "I can easily forgive Wilson's wordiness and the play's final descent into the supernatural in which the ghost of the slave-owning Sutter is noisily exorcised." Critics in general noted the preeminent position Wilson had reached with this play. The critic for *Time Magazine* wrote, "In just over five years, since his first professionally produced play, *Ma Rainey's Black Bottom,* reached Broadway, Wilson has established himself as the richest theatrical voice to emerge in the U.S. since the post-World War II flowering of Tennessee Williams and Arthur Miller. Just as significant, he has transcended the categorization of 'black' playwright to demonstrate that his stories, although consistently about black families and communities, speak to the entire U.S. culture" ["Two-Timer," April 23, 1990].

Wilson has established himself as the richest theatrical voice to emerge in the U.S. since the post-World War II flowering of Tennessee Williams and Arthur Miller.
—*Yvonne Shafer*

Critics also noted the powerful use of music throughout the play. Frank Rich concluded his rave review by saying, "That haunting music belongs to the people who have lived it, and it has once again found miraculous voice in a play that August Wilson has given to the American stage" ["A Family's

Past in Wilson's 'Piano Lesson,'" *New York Times,* April 17, 1990].

It was no surprise that Wilson's **The Piano Lesson** garnered the major prizes for the year. First, the Pulitzer Prize, then the Drama Critics Circle Award. At this stage in his career critics began to ask, "How long can he keep it up?" Wilson responded with a new play which opened in New Haven while **The Piano Lesson** was running. Concluding his praise for **The Piano Lesson,** *Time Magazine* critic commented on the newest play by Wilson, "The episodic structure and comedic tone differ radically from **The Piano Lesson** and **Fences.** The main thing the newest play has in common with them is that it, too, is terrific" ("Two-Timer").

With his play **Two Trains Running,** Wilson explored the decade of the '60s. The play opened at Yale, then toured for two years to regional theatres, then in April 1992, opened on Broadway. Although some critics felt the critical political and social events of the period were too removed from the play, in fact, they are constantly in the air and from the underpinning of a period of great change, some of it good, some of it bad for the blacks. The play is set in Memphis' small diner in a section of Pittsburgh which has disintegrated and is scheduled for demolition. The decay of the inner cities is reflected in the conversation about the black businesses which have closed and the absence of opportunity for the blacks. Another change is in the world view of blacks. Holloway the 65 year-old neighborhood philosopher says he has lasted this long because he stayed out of other people's business. His allegiance is to Aunt Ester, a seer who claims to be 322 years old. The waitress Risa believed in the Prophet Samuel who is lying in state in West's funeral parlor across the street. In contrast, Sterling, the wild young man just out of the penitentiary and looking for some chance in life, hands out posters about a rally in memory of Malcom X. Risa will have no part of it because there might be a riot. In the event, she is wooed by Sterling and does go to the rally. The characters discuss it the next day and bring out the daily events of the '60s:

> Wolf: I saw you all down at the rally last night. Wasn't that something? Everybody was down there Even the niggers that swear up and down on two sacks of Bibles that they ain't black . . . they was down there. Ain't but five hundred chairs and three thousand people. Wasn't no fight or nothing. It was real nice.
>
> Sterling: The police was down there taking people's pictures.
>
> Wolf: I seen that. Wasn't that something? They don't go out there where the white folks at and take their pictures. . . . It's hard to live in America.

Wolf is content to run the numbers which he feels is a legitimate operation offering the blacks hope. But Memphis has been run off his farm in the South by a white man named Stovall and is determined to take pragmatic action to better his life. He hires a white lawyer who knows the white man's rules, and demands a fair price from the city before they tear down his building. He refuses to display a poster for the rally, saying:

> I don't want this up in my place. I ain't putting no sanction on nothing like that. That's what the problem is now. All them niggers wanna do is have a rally. Soon as they finish with one rally they start planning for the next. They forget about what goes in between. You rally to spur you into action. When it comes time for action these niggers sit down and scratch their heads. They had that boy Begaboo. The police walked up and shot him in the head and them same niggers went down there to see the mayor. Raised all kind of hell. Trying to get the cop charged with murder. They raised hell for three weeks. After that it was business as usual. That's the Sterling boy bringing that stuff in here. Something wrong with that boy. That boy ain't right. (To Risa:) If I was you I'd stay away from him. He ain't gonna do nothing but end up right back down there in the penitentiary.

In fact, Risa intends to stay away from Sterling and from all men. Through her character, Wilson subtly introduces another element of change in the '60s, the attitude of black women about themselves. Risa, a beautiful woman, has deliberately scarred her legs so that men will not consider her as a sex object, but will look deeper into her character.

Although several critics felt the social matter of the period was too much in the background, Frank Rich said the play "makes its own chilling point" and quoted Sterling's line relating to the pointless destruction in cities like Detroit and Watts, "You take something apart, you should know how to put it back together" ["August Wilson Reaches the '60s," *New York Times*, April 14, 1992]. Some critics commented that there was no central struggle in the diffuse, three-hour-long play which, as Edwin Wilson wrote could "give the play focus and move the plot forward" ["Two Trains Running," *Wall Street Journal*, April 20, 1992]. These critics were correct insofar as the structure involves the interweaving of all the characters, each of whom relates to the past and present in different ways, and each of whom tells a story. For example, Hambone is a man cheated out of a ham nine years earlier and whose mental state has deteriorated so much that he can only say, "He gonna give me my ham. I want my ham." Sterling tries to help him by teaching him to say "Black is beautiful" and "Malcolm lives." As Davin Ansen summed up the play,

As thematically rich as it is dramatically discursive, *Two [Trains] Running* isn't organized around any single dramatic event. It unfolds as a succession of street-wise arias, and the monologues, in Lloyd Richards's impressively acted production, often rise to musical eloquence. Wilson leaves it to the audience to pull together his interlocking themes of economics, self-esteem and spirituality. What we witness is not a play *about* the '60s, but a form of oral history, in which we're invited to eavesdrop on the timeless continuum of the African-American experience. These are the stories *behind* the political slogans, Wilson implies: listen and learn. ["Of Prophets and Profits," *Newsweek*, April 27, 1992]

Ultimately, Wilson ties up all the stories. Sterling has finally lured Risa out of her nun-like existence and they have what seems to be a meaningful relationship. Memphis enters in the last moments, drunk and hilarious, having got $35,000 from the city. On Aunt Ester's advice, he plans to settle his feelings about the past by going back to see about his farm: "I'm going back to Jackson and see Stovall. If he ain't there, then I'm gonna see his son. He enjoying his daddy's benefits he got to carry his daddy's weight. I'm going on back up to Jackson and pick up the ball." Finally, Hambone gets his ham. Although he has died and the white grocer Lutz refused to the end to give it to him, Sterling breaks into the store, takes a ham and the play ends as follows: "(Sterling enters, carrying a large ham. He is bleeding from his face and his hands. He grins and lays the ham on the counter.) Say, Mr. West . . . that's for Hambone's casket."

Many critics noted that the play ended happily and that there was a great deal of comedy throughout. (The comedy is present in all of Wilson's plays, but critics have not given it much attention.) David Patrick Stearns observed, "this is Wilson's most moving play in years. While his writing can often be diffuse, *Trains* is well-focused and intermingles extremes of comedy and tragedy with breathtaking elegance" ["Wilson's 'Trains' On Track," *USA Today*, April 14, 1992]. Much of the comedy is just tossed off in causal conversations. Talking about bad luck reminds Holloway, "A man was driving a truck . . . hauling a whole truck full of mirrors . . . lost the brakes and ran into a telephone pole. He wasn't hurt or nothing. He looked back there and saw all them mirrors broke . . . he was staring at two hundred years of bad luck. They had to carry him away in a straitjacket." As John Beaufort noted, "***Two Trains Running*** seems the most comic of the Wilson cycle thus far. Wilson doesn't write jokes. But he finds constant humor in the speech patterns and verbal idiosyncracies of his characters" ["Wilson's 'Two Trains Running' Scores," *Christian Science Monitor*, April 28, 1992]. Critics of the regional theatre performances of the play, too, noted the comedy and its obvious appeal for audiences. In Chicago, Julian Frazin wrote:

Once again under the sensitive direction of Lloyd Richards, *Trains* is a tale built upon almost 350 years of disappointment and shattered dreams; yet little of the bitterness emerges in this story of joy, laughter and the continual hope for change. . . . Unlike many of the recent films of Spike Lee and others depicting rage and violence in the African-American neighborhoods, Wilson's play is one of little heroes who survive and prevail in spite of life's calamities. ["'Two Trains' Runs Faster than An Alleycat," *Chicago Lawyer,* March, 1993]

While not all the critics in New York or throughout the country were satisfied with this play, a number felt it was his best to date. In it he explores the interaction of life and death, his title indicating the literal two trains which run down to Jackson every day, and, as Wilson wrote in a program note, there are "always and only two trains running. There is life and there is death. Each of us rides them both. To live life with dignity, to celebrate and accept responsibility for your presence in the world is all that can be asked of anyone" [quoted in Linda Winer, "Grappling with Their Stations in Life," *New York Newsday,* April 14, 1992]. Writing in *Time,* William A. Henry III called the play "Wilson's most delicate and mature work" ["Luncheonette Tone Poem," April 27, 1992]. The critic John Simon, notoriously difficult to please, wrote a long thoughtful review in *New York* in which he said,

> What I find a step forward here in Wilson's stagecraft is the ability not to rely on such obvious dramatics as onstage violence, supernatural phenomena, vicious heavies, mysterious strangers, ponderous symbols, and the rest. Indeed, the play's eponymous symbol, the place to and from which only two trains are running, is mentioned but once, and left open to several interpretations—my own being that you can live your life blindly forward, or go back into the past and try to mend the old mistakes. ["Two Trains Running," April 27, 1992]

During the pre-Broadway tour the play Wilson was awarded the American Theatre Critics Association 1990-91 New Play Award. The play itself did not receive any major awards after the New York opening, but Larry Fishburne won a Tony Award for his dynamic portrayal of Sterling.

In the 1994-95 season, Wilson's first play after a break of several years will be presented at the Goodman Theatre in Chicago, directed by Lloyd Richards. *Seven Guitars,* Wilson says, is about a jazz musician whose death is explored in a series of flashbacks. "The point is not who killed him but the content of his life. Barton was in and out of jail and a vagrant in some ways. But one of the issues I find fascinating is the separate relationships between these '40s mu-

sicians and the black and white communities" [quoted in Smith].

August Wilson is only 48 and as a playwright he is still developing and perfecting his art. Compared to someone like Eugene O'Neill his body of work is small. Yet, he is already one of the most honored playwrights in America. It is inevitable that his work will be compared to that of Eugene O'Neill as there are many similarities. In fact, Clive Barnes called his review of *Joe Turner's Come and Gone* "O'Neill in Blackface," writing, "Wilson starts his play with the leisureliness of a Eugene O'Neill slowly pinpointing this family—a boarding house in industrial America, filled with transients. . . . The mood, however, is funny, odd, eccentric . . . very cozy, very O'Neill himself in blackface" [*New York Post,* March 28, 1988]. Reviewing *The Piano Lesson* in London, Michael Billington wrote "As in Ibsen or O'Neill, the past constantly informs the present." Wilson is associated with O'Neill in critics' minds in part because his first opportunities occurred at the Eugene O'Neill Theatre Center. Just as O'Neill provided great roles for black actors including Charles Gilpin and Paul Robeson, so Wilson has provided great roles for black actors including James Earl Jones, Yaphet Kotto, Charles S. Dutton, Mary Alice, and Larry Fishburne. Both playwrights have won the Pulitzer Prize more than once. Like O'Neill, Wilson envisions a cycle of plays about the history of America. But more important than these similarities are their shared viewpoints about the seriousness of writing. Like O'Neill, Wilson writes about serious subjects but mixes comedy and tragedy. As O'Neill wrote about matters which disturbed him emotionally, Wilson says he is writing plays "about the stuff that beats in my head" [quoted in Arkatov]. Critics rarely commented on the comedy in such plays as O'Neill's *The Iceman Cometh* in which, as in Wilson's plays, each of the characters has stories to tell, and many of them are very funny. Although critics occasionally comment on the comic element in Wilson's plays, not enough attention is given to his ability to create strong, memorable comic characters and speeches. A final similarity with O'Neill is that both playwrights are motivated by the urge to create works of art, rather than by financial gain. Wilson said once, "All I ever needed was a few dollars for cigarettes and beer" quoted in William A. Henry III, "Exorcising the Demons of Memory," *Time,* April 11, 1988]. Although he quit his four-pack-a-day habit, he has changed little else. In 1993 he told a critic that he prefers smaller cities to New York's glamour, doesn't drive, and prefers a simple life, "Give me my books and records and I'm happy" [quoted in Misha Berson, "The Story Weaver," *Seattle Times,* April 11, 1993]. He presently lives in Seattle and has continued his connection with O'Neill Center working with a young playwright as Lloyd Richards worked with him.

At a time when many American playwrights write about transitory problems Wilson seeks the great themes. When asked about his opinion about the state of playwriting in America, he responded that he thinks the present generation of American playwrights has been spoiled by a childhood spent with television rather than literature. Of those he has met, "There were not very many who knew authors and writers, who had read novels: they were actually in a very small world. They talked about TV and movies." He says that most of the playwrights he knows have little to say and nothing beating in their hearts that drives them. Making a distinction between the artist and the craftsman, he cast his lot with the former, saying, "I think that plays should be considered a part of literature. . . . I aspire to the highest art" [quoted in Shafer]. However, he regards his own work with modesty, and commented amusingly about his slow process of work on his latest play. It took him a long time to complete the play which was initially called *Moon Going Down* and was set in a turpentine camp down South: "The more I got into it, the more I realized I didn't know much about turpentine camps" [quoted in Peter Vaughan, "After Three Year Break from Writing," *Star Tribune* (Minneapolis), April 30, 1993]. His modesty is also expressed in his reaction to theatre critics' comments about his work: "I read all my reviews, of course I do. I think writers who say they don't aren't being entirely honest. And I learn something from every review" [quoted in Berson].

August Wilson occupies an unusual position in American theatre. Although he feels very passionate about the historical treatment of blacks in American society, his characters break through the barriers of race and speak to both whites and blacks because they relate to archetypal themes and questions: What is true freedom? What is it to be a man or woman? How does a family relate? What is the nature of responsibility? What, ultimately, is the purpose of life and how does one "find one's own song?" How does one become (or find) a "shiny man"? In plays filled with poetic images, Wilson explores these questions. So far his record is amazing: in the terminology of baseball which occurs in *Fences,* Wilson has never struck out, he is batting a thousand, and there is nobody else in his league. One critic wrote, "He is the playwright that in forty years we will still be hearing about" [De Vries]. He has a long career ahead and looks forward to it with zest. He has recently agreed to write a play to premiere at the Alliance Theatre Company in Atlanta during the Olympic Arts Festival in 1996. He looks forward with pleasure to completing his cycle of plays: "I think I'll do the 80s and 90s first and then go back to the first decade. It would really be something to have all ten finished" [quoted in Vaughan]. Wilson's fans and many of the critics share that feeling. Writing in 1993, Misha Berson summed up Wilson's achievements so far:

> Wilson will leave behind his own record. At age 47, the largely self-educated author has racked up a rare achievement: five plays successfully produced on

Broadway and nationwide, two Pulitzer Prizes, and the forging of a distinctive voice, a sensibility, a style not to be mistaken for that of any other taleteller.

Regina Taylor (essay date April 1996)

SOURCE: "That's Why They Call It the Blues," *American Theatre,* Vol. 13, No. 4, April, 1996, pp. 18-23.

[*In the following essay, Taylor illustrates how Wilson uses blues music and blues artists to enhance his depictions of the African American experience in his works.*]

Seven Guitars begins with a blues refrain: "*Does anybody here want to try my cabbage. . .?*" The lyrics could have dropped out of the insinuating mouth of Bessie Smith herself. "All the attitudes of my characters come straight out of the blues," says August Wilson, without equivocation. "'The blues' is the bedrock."

It was when Wilson was 20 years old and living in a boarding house in Pittsburgh, across the street from a second-hand store where he could buy 78-RPM records for a nickel apiece, that he came across a bootleg copy of "Bessie Smith: Empress of the Blues."

> "*Nobody in town can bake a sweet jelly roll like mine. . .*"

He had more than 2,000 records up in his room and could sing the lyrics of Walter Huston and Patti Page by heart, but "I had never heard a sound like that," Wilson remembers. After listening to Bessie, he began to view those around him differently. "Somehow there was something about them that came through in Bessie that I had never known." Of Bessie's music, Wilson thought: "This is mine." Unknowingly, he had found his voice as a writer.

Wilson's *speaking* voice is a soft lilting hum combined with a rapid-fire delivery, a mixture, perhaps, of inflections from his North Carolina-born mother and his own Pittsburgh Hill District upbringing. His speech becomes more staccato and explosive as a tidewater of images and ideas flood through him.

"The blues," he intones, "is simplicity and profundity at the same time. It's a cultural response to the world that contains our world view and our ideas of life. If we disappeared and someone found these recordings, they could tell about our pain, our pleasure, our God, our devil."

Wilson begins to sing/speak—"'*If the train don't hurry /*

There'll be some walking done'"—then cuts off the tune to say, "People think it's just a song. It sounds funny." Just as abruptly, he continues with—"*'I'm leaving in the morning walkin' / Take a chance that I may ride.'*" From Wilson's perspective, you can cast an "anthropological eye" on the blues and piece together a time and a place. You can mend fractured histories, heal the souls and psyches of characters who must embrace their past to be made whole.

Born from the "field hollers" and "sorrow songs" that got black people through slavery, the blues slapped disappointment off the face of freedom. It dared fate to mete out yet another blow. The early blues singers were anonymous wanderers carrying their songs from town to town, mixing despair with humor—an American invention in (literal) blackface. Their stories and indomitable spirits passed from mouth to mouth, and have been reclaimed for another era in Wilson's music-infused theatre works.

The title character of Wilson's first Broadway drama, *Ma Rainey's Black Bottom,* is one of the earliest professional blues singers; the white man pays her to "trap her voice in a box." In *Fences,* the spirit of Troy Maxson survives in the passing of his song to his children. Joe Loomis of *Joe Turner's Come and Gone* is a man "who done lost his song" during his illegal slavery in a chain gang. The object of conflict in *The Piano Lesson* is an actual relic of slavery—Boy Willie and Berniece's inherited piano, evoking painful memories but also offering possible barter for a piece of land. In *Two Trains Running,* set in 1969, the tide of the Civil Rights Movement (swelling during *Fences*) is at a standstill: the restaurant's jukebox has fallen silent.

In *Seven Guitars,* which began previews last month on Broadway, the blues are a source of power and transcendence. This new play (which debuted in early 1995 at Chicago's Goodman Theatre under Walter Dallas's direction, then moved on to Boston's Huntington Theatre Company, San Francisco's American Conservatory Theater and Los Angeles's Ahmanson Theatre under the reins of Wilson's longtime collaborator, director Lloyd Richards) is set in post-World War II Pittsburgh, where a group of friends have gathered after burying Floyd "Schoolboy" Barton. Floyd's life was cut short just as he was on the verge of "making it" in the cutthroat world of the urban music industry, and his friends talk about the black-hatted angels who appeared at the gravesite and carried Floyd away. To the sounds of his first hit recording. "That's Alright," the play jumps back in time to piece together the final days of Floyd's life.

While coming home from his mother's funeral, Floyd is stopped with empty pockets by the police and arrested for vagrancy. ("Men are arrested for vagrancy, for worthlessness," says Wilson. "Worthlessness is a crime in America.") In the workhouse, Floyd discovers that he has a hit record

. . . but no hit record money. Upon release he gets a letter from his white producers inviting him back to Chicago to cut yet another record. Floyd sees the summons as a promise that he will become a star—all he has to do is find a way to get enough money together for his band to return to Chicago.

In what may be Wilson's most masculine play, the men of Floyd's band strut around the backyard in their Pittsburgh neighborhood like roosters scratching for territory. They crow in unison, each with his own unique voice. They riff off each other. The solos fly.

Hedley, dying of tuberculosis, dreams that the legendary New Orleans trumpeter Buddy Bolden will come down and give him money for a plantation; Red would happily return to Chicago (if Floyd could only get his drums out of hock); Canewell, a harmonica player who's tired of the road, still hungers for fame but would like to put down roots. The women of the play, a bit worn around the edges, sing of love gone wrong. Vera, Floyd's girlfriend, takes him back after he left her for another woman; Louise, the landlady, claims she doesn't want anyone knocking on her door anymore; Ruby, Louise's fast niece, has just fled Alabama where one man killed another over her. "All the characters," Wilson points out, "are living the blues."

In *Seven Guitars,* history is viewed with blacks as the spiritual center: a whole world is encompassed in the characters' backyard. Wilson describes that yard as an arena, a killing field, a cemetery and "a garden where something is growing—it's new life." It is the pulse-point of black culture in 1948: "The situation of blacks was hopeful after the war. We thought, 'When we fight and die for our country, we will no longer be second-class citizens.' But we quickly found that we remained stigmatized by color and culture."

Wilson emphasizes that it is not as much skin color but "what you do" that sets African Americans apart. "The fact is, we act differently, we think differently, we face the world differently—and it is our difference that makes us unique. We must embrace our culture or we will lose ourselves and disappear."

Wilson says that while the exploitation of early blues musicians was a central subject of *Ma Rainey,* here exploitation is a given: "*Seven Guitars* is about people battling society and themselves for self-worth." The black characters' new urban challenge is symbolized by Miss Tillery's rooster—her neighbors loudly complain that the Alabama rooster's crowing at odd times has no usefulness in Pittsburgh. "This the city. Roosters belong in the country. Miss Tillery needs to get rid of that thing," complains Floyd. Later, Hedley justifies killing the rooster by explaining that it was too good to live among those who do not appreciate its song.

Through Floyd, Wilson comments on the discrepancy between black lives and the American Dream: "Now here's what I don't understand. If I go out there and punch a white man in the mouth, they give me five years even if there ain't no witnesses. Joe Louis beat up a white man in front of a hundred thousand people and they give him a million dollars. Now you explain that to me." Tired of being on the bottom, Floyd declares, "All I want is you to get out my way. I got somewhere to go. See, everybody can't say that . . . They don't wanna go nowhere. Time done got short and it getting shorter everyday. The only thing I want you to do is get out my way."

> **Wilson is redefining, reaffirming and reclaiming the moral personality of black Americans. He does not place the blame on society's racism and claim that African Americans are victims—he states the facts and lets the indictments fall where they may.**
>
> —*Regina Taylor*

Wilson's characters are trying to change their situations—to make luck happen. To even the odds, they arm themselves—Floyd carries a .38, Red a .32 and Canewell a pocketknife. Wilson sees their stance as political and revolutionary. "They are about black power, self-determination. 'Black power'—the combination of the words feels right. People refer to the Civil Rights Movement, but Black Power means we can alter relationships to society to gain power. We can alter how we see ourselves."

In *Seven Guitars,* both Hedley and Floyd understand the potential of their music as a means to gain power. While Hedley anticipates Buddy Bolden's descent, Floyd is unwilling to wait for divine intervention, and he ends up, as Wilson puts it, "standing there in the yard, in this time in history, with blood on his hands."

Wilson is redefining, reaffirming and reclaiming the moral personality of black Americans. He does not place the blame on society's racism and claim that African Americans are victims—he states the facts and lets the indictments fall where they may. Without pulling his punches, Wilson shows black life in all its richness and fullness, its wit and rage. His plays are peopled with those who are constantly reassembling and reinventing themselves, "to give clear and luminous meaning to the song which is a wail and a whelp of joy."

Ralph Ellison discovered the materialization of poetry in the blues, and Wilson himself becomes visible as an Ellisonian figure. His words—thick with the poetry, rhythm and mother-wit of the blues—give shadow, substance and heartbeat (as well as time, place and voice) to an invisible people. His six plays to date, each set in a different decade, turn on thousands of lightbulbs, illuminating the presence of African Americans through the 20th century. It is an American history turned on its ear, seen through the eyes of a black man.

Douglas Anderson (essay date June 1997)

SOURCE: "Saying Goodbye to the Past: Self-Empowerment and History in *Joe Turner's Come and Gone*," in *CLA Journal,* Vol. XL, No. 4, June, 1997, pp. 432-57.

[*In the following essay, Anderson explores how* Joe Turner's Come and Gone *is a play which illustrates that "in reclaiming the self by recovering the past, the individual becomes capable of constructing a future."*]

A character in August Wilson's play *Joe Turner's Come and Gone* tells a story about how he was "cure[d]" of playing in guitar contests. Called out to play his guitar for an unspecified prize offered by a white man, Wilson's character does his best to demonstrate his skill against his two black opponents until he realizes that the white man is tone deaf and cannot distinguish the quality of each man's music. All three players finally substitute volume for skill, and the white judge, unable to declare a winner, pronounces "all three . . . the best guitar player" and divides a paltry prize of twenty-five cents between the contestants with a "penny on the side."

The anecdote related by Wilson's character serves as a reminder that white efforts to understand the products of black cultures can be attended by arrogance and insensitivity, a tendency to hear one essentialized black voice speaking of a single black experience. White readers of Wilson's play should want to avoid both the arrogance of the tone-deaf white man who assumes that economic and social privilege qualify him to judge a black culture, and his insensitivity to the different voices within that culture. This insensitivity, as the anecdote makes clear, always renders the same leveling judgment, a judgment of unimportance or non-worth.

The anecdote and Wilson's play as a whole, however, are not primarily about an insensitive, indifferent or hostile white society but about the process of recovering and recreating black voices after the white judge has turned individual music into noise. The premise of the play, and the focus of my argument about the play, is that this recovery and re-creation can only occur with the recognition that Joe Turner, the personification of white oppression of African Americans, has "come and gone." Joe Turner is part of a past that, acknowledged and appropriated for the self, loses its power to determine the future. Consigning Joe Turner to the past does not mean naively believing that white oppression is at an end. Wilson's play depicts ongoing efforts by white society to deflect and misdirect black progress toward community and individual identity. But if white oppression extends into the present, its power to diminish or impugn the self is denied when the history of that oppression is confronted and countered with the collective and personal memory that grounds identity. In reclaiming the self by recovering the past, the individual becomes capable of constructing a future.

A play about recovering the past and leaving it behind, *Joe Turner's Come and Gone* appropriately treats a transitional phase in African-American history: the Great Migration. Over a period of twenty years, from 1910 to 1930, some one and a half million African Americans, a sixth of the nation's black population, left rural and urban areas of the South for industrial cities of the North—New York, Chicago, Philadelphia, Detroit, and, the city that is the setting for August Wilson's play, Pittsburgh. What the migrants left behind, what they hoped to find and what kind of life greeted them in the North are questions of fact that historians of this period generally agree on. The migrants left racial violence, segregation, and disfranchisements in the South. They also left a Southern economy hurt by a boll weevil invasion that reduced cotton yields, low cotton prices, and a pattern of Northern investment that turned the South into a dependent colony with a shrinking labor market. They were drawn to the North by the promise of higher wages and, after 1916, by the employment possibilities created when World War I stopped the flow of European immigrant labor. In leaving for the industrialized cities of the North, the migrants hoped to find not only higher wages but also economic and political equality, educational opportunities, and social justice. What the migrants found in the North was something less: voting rights that did not translate into political power, discriminatory hiring and promotion practices that kept them at the bottom of the employment ladder, segregated and substandard housing and education. Some gains were made in economic well-being, political rights, and opportunities in education. But, as James Grossman suggests in *Land of Hope: Chicago, Black Southerners, and the Great Migration*, "the dreams embodied in the Great Migration eventually collapsed under the weight of continued racial oppression and the failure of industrial capitalism to distribute its prosperity as broadly as the migrants expected." In Carole Marks's succinct summary in *Farewell—We're Good and Gone*, reality never matched the dream of the Great Migration."

Though Grossman and Marks agree about many of the facts surrounding the Great Migration and though both find that the migration achieved little in the way of concrete economic, social and political gains, they do not agree about the meaning of this mass movement of people, particularly

its meaning for those who made the journey. For Marks, the Great Migration was a drama in which the migrants themselves were "minor actors." The real stars of this drama were economic forces: the declining Southern economy, the need of Northern industrialists for cheap and expendable labor after World War I ended European immigration and, at the most abstract level, an economic order in which developed, capital-rich cores draw natural resources and cheap labor from undeveloped peripheries (Marks). Though the migrants created many of their own lines of communication and institutional supports for the move, labor agents were pivotal in inducing them to leave, and "much of the mobilization of the migration was orchestrated in the board rooms of Northern industrial enterprises" (Marks).

> **Wilson's play depicts ongoing efforts by white society to deflect and misdirect black progress toward community and individual identity. But if white oppression extends into the present, its power to diminish or impugn the self is denied when the history of that oppression is confronted and countered with the collective and personal memory that grounds identity.**
> —*Douglas Anderson*

In a review essay of Marks's and Grossman's books ["The Beginnings of a Renaissance: Black Migration, the Industrial Order, and the Search for Power," *Journal of Urban History*, May, 1991], Earl Lewis observes that Marks's claim for the primacy of economic forces will be disconcerting to "social historians who have dared to understand how African Americans empowered themselves during the industrial age. As one of these social historians, James Grossman rejects historical accounts that portray migrants as objects of economic and social forces and suggests that we can better understand the Great Migration by viewing it "as a conscious and meaningful act rather than as a historical imperative." This act, Grossman suggests, grew out of migrants' consciousness of their identity as black Americans and their willingness to adapt and recreate that identity in a new urban, industrial context. The same pride in racial heritage and identity that Marcus Garvey drew on in the twenties, he suggests, was central to the "ideology of the Great Migration." By migrating to industrialized cities of the North, black Southerners affirmed their power to make themselves, just as they had proved their freedom through spatial mobility of a more limited kind following emancipation (Grossman).

As a "second emancipation," the Great Migration represented a break with the past but also its preservation and adaptation (Grossman). Though migration entailed the abandonment of a long-standing ideal of land ownership as the route to independence and the ability to recast the self as industrial worker and city dweller, "the migrants," as Grossman puts it, "did not leave their cultural baggage at the train station." This cultural heritage informed the decision to migrate and the migrants' response to the institutions and social forms that they found in the North, at the same time that it changed that environment and was changed by it, a mutual reshaping evident, Grossman suggests, in "the aromas of southern cooking . . .; the sounds of New Orleans jazz and Mississippi blues; styles of worship; patterns of speech . . . ."

However, not all differences of cultural heritage or of interest were reconciled in quite so harmonious a way, and in focusing on the Great Migration as a historical process in which African Americans asserted a common heritage and identity, Grossman does not assume a monolithic African-American culture. As Lewis points out in his review of *Land of Hope,* Grossman recognizes the intra-ethnic conflicts that frequently marked relations between the "Old Settlers" and the new arrivals, conflicts generated by differences of class as well as region and that were often manifested as the fear that the newcomer's rural lack of sophistication in dress, manner, or religious expression would injure community image. In spite of these differences, however, migrants and the established black community shared a sense of ethnic identity which synthesized much of the experience of both groups and redefined African-American cultural identity both North and South. It is as a process of cultural self-creation that Grossman sees the Great Migration's chief significance and promise. Viewed from the perspective of subjects recreating themselves, from "forward" rather than "backward," the Great Migration, he suggests, was not a failure, for in this singular reversal of the historian's perspective, we see the migrants not as the objects of historical forces and the histories written about them but as agents in their own history (Grossman).

Grossman's analysis of the Great Migration as a process in which African Americans drew on the past to remake themselves is close to August Wilson's dramatic interpretation of the migration in *Joe Turner's Come and Gone.* Like Grossman, Wilson see[s] the Great Migration not merely as a demographic or geographical shift but a historical transition to a new identity, and in his play the image of movement, of traveling the roads, serves as an apt metaphor for the search for self. *Joe Turner's Come and Gone* represents this search as both personal and collective. Though Wilson's characters seek an individual "song" that will guide them along the road into the future, they are enabled to recover this song only through recovery of a collective as well as a personal past. Recovery of one's song, however, is not easy, and, as Jeremy's anecdote of the guitar contest suggests, that song is in continual danger from the effects of white racism.

Before I go to look more closely at what the search for self or "song" entails, I think it is important to understand something of the conditions and the world in which Wilson portrays that search. The world depicted in Wilson's drama consists of material and spiritual parts or aspects which must be brought into meaningful synthesis, a synthesis in which each is informed by or exists through the other. The search for self or "song" can be viewed as a personal version of this broader task of creating a world in which the spiritual and the material infuse one another. Or, again, since Wilson suggests the individuals, couples and communities can be worlds of their own, the two tasks are substantially the same task. Recovering the unique self of one's song is also the creation of a world in which the material and spiritual are in harmony.

Both interdependence of the material and the spiritual and the need to bring them into fuller relation are suggested in the opening scene of *Joe Turner's Come and Gone.* The setting for this scene and for the rest of the play is a Pittsburgh boardinghouse in 1911. When the play opens, the owner of this boardinghouse, Seth Holly, is watching one of his tenants, a "rootworker" or shaman named Bynum, perform a religious ritual or rite. Seth reports the progress of this ritual to his wife, Bertha, while she cooks breakfast and they exchange comments about Seth's work in a Pittsburgh steel mill and his efforts to get a loan to finance a small shop for the manufacture of pots and pans.

The staging of this scene, dialogue, and characterization suggests that the material and spiritual aspects of the world are in intimate contact but somehow not fully integrated. On the one hand, the staging dramatizes separation. The material world of everyday concerns, of seeking business loans and baking biscuits, is located inside the boardinghouse, where it can be directly witnessed by the audience. The spiritual realm is outside and offstage, accessible to the audience only through Seth's description of it. This description, moreover, is made by a man who is somewhat scornful of what he witnesses. A skilled craftsman and a property owner, a practical man accustomed to dealing in the materials of his craft and the economic realities of running a boarding house and resisting exploitation in his work life, Seth is prone to see the ritual performed by Bynum as "mumbo jumbo nonsense," as something not quite civilized. Watching a ritual in which Bynum kills a pigeon and pours some of its blood into a cup, Seth speculates: "I believe he drink that blood."

Bertha's immediate reproach to her husband for this fantasy suggests that Bynum is not so far outside social norms as Seth likes to believe:

> "Seth Holly, what is wrong with you this morning?
> . . . You know Bynum don't be drinking no pigeon blood."

"I don't know what he do."

"Well, watch him, then. He's gonna dig a little hole and bury that pigeon. Then he's gonna pray over that blood . . . pour it on top . . . mark out his circle and come on into the house."

Yet Bynum does function as a foil for Seth. Described in the play's notes as a man "lost in a world of his own making and [able] to swallow any adversity or interferences with his grand design," Bynum represents a spiritual world that is antagonistic to the material and practical one, but different from and somewhat indifferent to it. This indifference and the potential for tension between Bynum's spirituality and Seth's materialism are humorously represented in Bynum's apparent unconcern for the vegetable garden in which he conducts his ritual, unconcern that leads Seth to yell, "Hey Bynum . . . Watch where you stepping!" from his station by the window.

While characterization and staging tend to present the material and the spiritual as separate realities, they do not present this separation as absolute or even as clearly marked. Though the vegetable garden provides bodily sustenance and ostensibly belongs to Seth, it is also the site of Bynum's ritual and the place where Bynum grows plants for use in magical preparations. The division of "Seth's" garden, moreover, reflects a similar division (or amalgamation) in Seth's character, for though he calls Bynum's rituals "mumbo jumbo," he has the conjure man bless his house. Likewise, though Bynum represents the claims and needs of the spirit, he is no enemy of the material world or of pragmatic, commercial realities that Seth deals in. He both relishes Bertha's biscuits and accepts payment for spiritual services. In a similar way, the staging suggests the intimate connection as well as separation of the material and spiritual. Though the spiritual world is off stage, it is connected to the material, the practical and the everyday by a window, and Seth's report on that world while Bertha bakes biscuits suggests that these two realities exist in close relation. Indeed, Bertha's matter-of-fact response to Seth's sacrilegious speculation about how Bynum will use the pigeon's blood suggests that, in some fundamental way, the spiritual or extramundane is part of everyday, pragmatic reality. Bertha knows the course of Bynum's ritual without looking because she has seen it many times, because it is a regular part of everyday existence.

The first scene's dialogue continues a pattern of showing the material and spiritual to be separated and interrelated, but it also shows how their integration can be subverted. Seth's commentary on Bynum's off-stage ritual is interspersed with discussion of more material, pragmatic concerns—his unsatisfying work on the night shift at a mill and his desire to start his own business with the financial help of white businessmen. Despite the practicality of Seth's plan, however, the white men he approaches refuse to lend him the money he needs unless he signs his house over to them. It is here that we begin to see why Seth's house needs to be blessed and in what way the spiritual and material may become not integrated and complementary but opposed realities. At least part of the material, pragmatic, and everyday world inhabited by Wilson's characters, that part dominated by whites, opposes their spiritual being because it is organized to oppress them.

Much of the oppression experienced by Wilson's characters might be described as material or economic. Thus, Seth's guitar-playing tenant, Jeremy, is jailed without cause and fined two dollars and later fired from his job on a road crew when he refuses to pay a white coworker fifty cents in protection money. Steady work and home ownership give Seth a certain financial security, yet he too is vulnerable to a white society bent on extracting what it can from him and limiting his opportunities for economic advancement. Commenting on the hopes of black migrants for prosperity in Pittsburgh, Seth notes that though he has lived in Pittsburgh all his life, white European immigrants have "come over and in six months got more than what I got."

Though the oppression encountered by Wilson's characters may seem to be solely economic or material, that oppression is spiritual as well in its capacity to deprive the individual of a sense of himself or of his unique "song." Since the play presents the material and the spiritual as interwoven or integrated, material oppression necessarily has an effect on the individual spirit, denying it value and even existence. The individual spirit or song, in Wilson's play, can only exist as a manifestation in the world, as an act or *expression* of self that "marks" or makes the world. This expression, in a sense, uses the self up to create the world, translates the spirit into material form. Bynum's song, for example, consists in the act of binding people together, but this use of his song "cost[s] me a piece of myself every time I do it." The use of self to create the world does not really entail the sacrifice or loss of self, however, but leads rather to that self's realization. As Bynum puts it at one point, "[I] got so I used all of myself up in the making of that song. Then I was the song in search of itself." Because the world created through the individual's song is a place in which the self is reflected, a place in which the individual is able to see and know how to identify himself, to use the self in the expression of one's song is also to create and affirm that self.

Material oppression as it is depicted in Wilson's play denies this essential bond with the world of one's creation and, consequently, the being of the subject who creates the world. To be defrauded of the products of one's labor, or to see that creation diminished (as that of Jeremy and the other musicians is in the guitar contest), is to be denied a reflection of individual worth and identity in the world. It is to be exiled from self and world together. This alienation and displacement of the individual, moreover, is accompanied by the severing of relationships and the fragmentation of community. "People cling to each other out of the truth they find themselves," Bynum says at one point. Hence, if they have been separated from this truth through the operation of oppression, their capacity to bond with one another, to form friendships, couples, families, or a people, is undermined. The social effects of the alienation felt by Wilson's characters are expressed in their stories of broken relationships and in the uncertainty or suspicion that they feel toward one another. As Seth puts it, "Anybody liable to be anything as far as I'm concerned."

The connection between oppression, alienation from self and inability to form bonds with others is clearest in the character of Herold Loomis, the hero of Wilson's play. Accompanied by his young daughter, Loomis arrives at Seth's boarding house while searching for his wife, Martha. Loomis became separated from his wife ten years earlier when he was imprisoned and forced to work on a chain gang for seven years by a white man named Joe Turner. When Loomis was finally released, he returned to the farm where he had been a sharecropper to find that little remained of his former life. Though he found his daughter in the home of his wife's mother, his wife had gone to the North with the church. Taking his daughter with him, Loomis went in search of his wife, but he also sought himself and the ability to connect with others. Joe Turner had separated Loomis not only from his family and the life in which he knew himself but, in a more fundamental way, from his sense of self-worth and identity. Turner's ability to oppress Loomis carried a judgment of non-worth which a guard made explicit: "He told me I was worthless." This judgment of worthlessness, which Loomis was forced to accept by the reality of the white man's power, has "marked" Loomis as "one of Joe Turner's niggers" at the same time that it has caused him to forget "how he's supposed to mark down life." It has, in other words, transformed Loomis from a subject into an object, a condition in which he remains bound to Joe Turner even after he has been released.

Marked by Joe Turner as a worthless object without agency or power, Loomis is not only alienated from himself but displaced from his relation to the world, for the world is home only to selves able to create it in their own image. He is unable to establish bonds with people around him ("I done forgot how to touch," he tells Mattie Campbell), and he wanders without a clear sense of either his origin or destination. Asked where he is from, Loomis replies: "Come from all over. Whicheverway the road take us that's the way we go." Deprived of a place in the world through oppression, Loomis is "bound up to the road." By finding the wife he has lost, Loomis hopes to reconnect with the past life which had grounded his identity and, in this way, to find a "starting place" for remaking the self in the future. As Loomis tells Martha when he finally sees her, "now that I see your face I can say my goodbye and make my own world."

In his search for the past and himself, Loomis enlists the services of a white traveling salesman or trader named Selig, who, besides selling pots and pans he purchases from Seth, hires himself as a "people finder" to blacks looking for lost loved ones. For a dollar fee, Selig writes down the name and description of the missing person and watches for that person as he travels around the country selling his wares. If one of the purchasers of his goods happens to be on Selig's list of missing persons, then that person has been "found" and can be reunited with Selig's client. By performing this service for African Americans in search of one another, Selig follows a calling he has inherited from his father and grandfather. As he tells Loomis,

> [W]e been finders in my family for a long time. Bringers and finders. My great-grandaddy used to bring Nigras across the ocean on ships. . . . My daddy, rest his soul, used to find runaway slaves for the plantation bosses. . . . After Abraham Lincoln give you all Nigras your freedom papers and with you all looking all over for each other . . . we started finding Nigras for Nigras.

In a recent interview in which he was asked if Selig is an evil figure, Wilson replied, "[H]e's not evil at all. In fact, he's performing a very valuable service for the community." Given the continuity between Selig's "finding" and that performed by his father and grandfather, Wilson's defense of his character and his commercial sideline seems disingenuous. And the play presents Selig's people finding in quite another light.

In order to be "found" by Selig, a black man or woman must first buy something from him, must, that is, enter the market economy as customer. While this leveling of identity within economic relations does not reproduce quite the radical denial of intrinsic human worth entailed in the professions of Selig's ancestors, the parallel nevertheless seems clear. The economic system represented by Selig, a system which exploits and excludes blacks, is one that they can be "found" in only as "Nigras." And to be found in this way is to experience the same alienation from self and community that created the need for Selig's services in the first place. As Bertha Holly informs Loomis after he has hired Selig to find his wife,

> You can call him a People Finder if you want to. I know Rutherford Selig carries people away too. . . . Folks plan on leaving plan by Selig's timing. They wait till he get ready to go, then they hitch a ride on his wagon. Then he charge folks a dollar to tell

them where he took them. Now, that's the truth of Rutherford Selig. He ain't never found nobody he ain't took away.

Selig represents economic forces which not only exploit African Americans but deny their intrinsic worth as persons, in the terms of the dichotomy discussed above, as spirit. Though these forces may not be self-consciously "evil," the injury they inflict through indifferent exploitation resembles that inflicted by Joe Turner's more direct oppression.

If the search for the past and self through the economic system represented by Selig seems to be doomed to failure, a second possibility for self-recovery is presented through Bynum's account of how he learned "the Secret of Life" and discovered his essential self or "song." Bynum's experience of revelation and self-recovery is described in terms of a spiritual journey. While walking along a road, Bynum met a man who, saying he has not eaten for three days, asked him for food and for information about the road Bynum had come by. The stranger then offered to show Bynum "the Secret of Life" and led him back the way he, Bynum, had come. The stranger was able to serve as guide on this unfamiliar road because he had "a voice inside him telling him which way to go." After cleansing Bynum's hands with blood, the stranger led him to a place where "everything was bigger than life" and there left him, disappearing in a light streaming from his body so that Bynum "had to cover up my eyes to keep from being blinded." After the "shiny man" left, the spirit of Bynum's father appeared and took over his instruction, taking him to an ocean where he witnessed "something I ain't got words to tell" and teaching him how to find his song. Bynum chose "the Binding Song," he tells Selig, "because that's what I seen most when I was traveling . . . people walking away and leaving one another." Possession of this song conferred on Bynum both a new identity and a unique task in the world: "Been binding people ever since. That's why they call me Bynum."

Bynum's narrative of revelation and self-recovery resembles Afro-Baptist conversion narratives. In these narratives, according to Michael Sobel [in *Trabelin' On: The Slave Journey to an Afro-Baptist Faith*], a "seeker" makes a journey that leads him not only to rebirth in Christ but to recovery of his essential self, "the 'little me' in the 'big me.'" Though unique, this self is also a manifestation of a collective spirit that, Sobel suggests, "the Black had brought . . . with him from Africa, not as a deity but in his own inner self.'" By recovering the 'little me,' the convert is both reborn in Christ and "brought . . . back to his African heritage." As in Afro-Baptist conversion, the self recovered by Bynum was both unique (his personal "song") and already there and waiting for him as part of his African heritage, a self related to an ancestral or ethnic past. Thus, the place where Bynum was taught "the Secret of Life" and learned how to find his song

was one that lay on a road Bynum had already traveled, and he received instruction from an ancestor, the spirit of his father. As "the One Who Goes Before and Shows the Way," the shiny man was potentially both spiritual guide and spiritual ancestor.

Elements of Bynum's narrative of revelation and self-recovery evoke the Biblical story of Saul's transformative encounter with a risen Christ on the road to Damascus. Reading Bynum's story through the Biblical one suggests that the shiny man who guided Bynum toward his song and then disappeared in blinding light was a Christ figure from whom Bynum received a new identity, just as Saul, the persecutor of Christians, was transformed into Paul, the great preacher of the gospel. Bynum himself, according to this paradigm, would be a reborn Paul and his "binding song" the task of uniting African Americans in anticipation of a returning savior or messiah. Bynum does, in fact, hope to see the shiny man again, but the person and the advent he waits for do not have quite the meaning that they have in the Biblical paradigm. If the shiny man is a messiah figure, he is not an otherworldly or even exceptional individual. As Bynum tells Selig, "I ain't even so sure he's one special fellow. That shine could pass on to anybody. He could be anybody shining." The shiny man is an ordinary man who, possessing his song as "a voice inside him telling him which way to go," is able to guide others toward repossession of their songs, toward becoming shiny men in their own right. And since "that shine could pass on to anybody," the shiny man is also the individual who has not yet found his song, one who searches for himself. That search takes place in the world, and for Bynum to see the shiny man "again" means assisting that search by acting as the shiny-man guide to another. Seeing the shiny man again does not entail Bynum's deliverance from the world but confirmation of his contribution to it. As Bynum's father told him, "There was lots of shiny men and if I ever saw one again before I died then I would know that my song had been accepted and worked its full power in the world . . . ."

The shiny man is an ordinary individual who seeks himself or is sought by others in the world, so it is not entirely strange that Bynum engages Selig's help in this search, paying him a dollar to find that shiny man for him. Given that this search is for an individual's self, song or soul, however, Bynum's use of Selig's services is highly ironic, and his greetings to the "People Finder" carry more than a hint of sarcasm:

Bynum: If it ain't the People Finder himself.

Selig: Bynum, before you start . . . I ain't seen no shiny man now.

Bynum: Who said anything about that? I ain't said

nothing about that. I just called you a first-class People Finder.

Selig cannot find the shiny man because neither he nor the economic system he represents is able to recognize African Americans as persons or individuals. Bynum's description of the shiny man as "anybody shining" is an affirmation of the intrinsic value of each individual. The shiny man could be anybody because each individual possesses the potential for self-realization which the shiny man represents. Selig's observation that "there's lots of shiny Nigras," by contrast, implies that African Americans are indistinguishable from one another, that they are, in fact, not individual subjects but bodies that are ultimately the same body: "The only shiny *man* I saw was the Nigras working on the road gang with the sweat glistening on them" (emphasis added).

Though the economic system which Selig represents cannot see black persons, the shiny man cannot be found wholly outside that system since persons realize themselves in a world of concrete material relations. Bynum acknowledges the material basis of the search for self in his employment of Selig and in his description of the shiny man as one who "shine like new money." The shiny man's spiritual or inner shine cannot be divorced from the material or economic world, but it also transforms it, makes it serve the expression of soul, self, or song. Bynum uses Selig, then, but he does not rely on him, and the real "People Finder," as Bynum hints at one point, is Bynum himself: "I binds them [people] together. Sometimes I help them find each other."

Bynum can act as "People Finder," however, only to people who carry within themselves a sense of their own humanity. He can act as a spiritual guide only to the "anybody" who already searches for himself. As a man cut off from self and community, seeking himself through the recovery of the past, Herold Loomis is that anybody, as Seth unconsciously reveals when he voices suspicions about Loomis's identity: "Anybody can tell anybody anything about what their name is. That's what you call him . . . Herald Loomis. His name liable to be anything." Though Seth's distrust expresses the fragmentation of community that accompanies the self-alienation of its members, a community of anybodies is also one that might cohere as its members find their own identities through a past that is collective. Since Loomis is the anybody who could be the shiny man, his search and Bynum's are the same. Loomis is searching for himself through recovery of the past, and Bynum is searching for the man whom he can guide to himself and whose self-recovery will validate the efficacy of Bynum's own song, its "power in the world." The search for the shiny man is a collaborative and, indeed, a collective project, for the self that is its object can be found only in a past that is held in common with others.

Searching for the self in the past presupposes that the past is one which can ground a self, that it was made by other selves whose agency can function as the precedent for and promise of one's own. Initially, Loomis is unable to see the collective African-American past in this way, as can be observed in a powerful scene that begins when the lodgers of Seth's boarding house perform a variant of the "ring shout," an Afro-Christian ritual in which frenzied dance and ecstatic shouts mediated an experience of possession or inspiration by the Holy Ghost (Sobel). When Loomis walks in on this dance, he is angrily contemptuous of the boarders' evocation of a past which he clearly considers to have been marked by passive suffering and useless piety: "You singing for the Holy Ghost tocome? What he gonna do huh? He gonna come with the tongues of fire to burn up your wooly heads?" Loomis, however, is fundamentally connected to the past and people he scorns, and his own challenge, giving way to dance, glossolalia and a visionary trance, merges with and continues the act of the collective memory which he has interrupted. The lodgers' ecstatic ritual, in fact, produces precisely the state of trance and vision which it was originally intended to, and the vision which Loomis witnesses is given expression in a collective act, a call-and-response exchange between Loomis and Bynum:

Bynum: What you done seen, Herald Loomis?

Loomis: I done seen bones rise up out of the water. Ride up and walk across the water. Bones walking on top of the water.

Bynum: Tell me about them bones, Herald Loomis. Tell me what you seen

Asking questions, prompting, repeating images and phrases, interpreting earlier lines, Bynum is essential to the realization of Loomis's vision as more than a private experience.

The past evoked in Loomis's vision is one which affirms the possibility of agency Loomis has defined. Briefly, Loomis's vision records two journeys. The first is a journey of bones traveling across a body of water, a journey symbolizing the trans-Atlantic voyage in which Africans, enslaved and taken from their homes, both died by the thousands and were treated as mere bodies without identity of human worth: "Wasn't nothing but bones and they walking on top of the water." The enslaved Africans of Loomis's vision do not remain insentient bones however. The bones sink into the ocean from which they are then resurrected as bodies with flesh and restored to life by a wind that fills them with breath or spirit. Resurrected, the Africans then begin a second journey which requires individual agency and decision. Standing up from the shore of the New World where a wave has thrown them, the Africans bid each other goodbye and leave the place to pursue their different paths: "They shaking hands and saying goodbye to each other and walking every whichaway down the road."

Loomis's vision is one which affirms the presence of agency in the African-American past, suggesting that it is not one of victimization alone, but of agency and self-empowerment. The vision suggests, moreover, that even the history of victimization can be and has been redeemed. The people of Loomis's vision exercise agency not only in the present following their resurrection, but in relation to the past that brought them to the New World. By beginning a second journey which parallels or repeats the first but adds the new dimension of choice and self-determination, the people of the vision change the meaning of the past, remake it retrospectively. This re-creation of the past might be called an act of transformative repetition such as is embodied in the call-and-response form itself. Moving from statement to repetition and restatement, the call-and-response exchange shared by Loomis and Bynum continually remakes itself as it develops, symbolically remaking the events which are its theme.

This history of self-empowerment is Loomis's by right of inheritance, for the people of his vision are his people: "They black. Just like you and me. Ain't no difference." But the connection that justifies the claim of copossession of historical agency seems to go beyond inheritance and precedent, as Loomis becomes not simply like his ancestors but one of them:

> Loomis: They ain't moved or nothing. They just laying there.
>
> Bynum: You just laying there. What you waiting on, Herald Loomis?
>
> Loomis: I'm laying there . . . waiting.
>
> Bynum: What you waiting on, Herald Loomis?
>
> Loomis: I'm waiting on the breath to get into my body.

Here the collapse of differences of time and identity would seem to open the possibility of re-entering and enacting the past in order to fully claim its legacy of self-empowerment. Loomis, however, is not yet able to claim this legacy by standing up with the people of his vision. The part of the vision in which the Africans stand up, say goodbye to one another, and depart on their different journeys is recounted by Bynum alone, suggesting that this part of history does not yet exist for Loomis and cannot exist until he realizes it through an act of his own.

Before Loomis can claim the legacy of empowerment left him by his ancestors, he must confront and understand his own experience of oppression: seven years of false imprisonment and forced labor on the chain gang of Joe Turner, brother to the governor of Tennessee. Though this experience is part of Loomis's personal past, it is not one that he has suffered alone, but with the men imprisoned with him, those who lived in fear of imprisonment and the families deprived of their men. Loomis's experience, then, is once again part of a collective past, a past preserved for collective memory in a song. The refrain of this song is, "They tell me Joe Turner's come and Gone." As sung by "the women . . . down around Memphis" who "made up that song," the song is a testimony of loss. If "Joe Turner's come and gone," then husbands, sons, fathers and brothers have been taken away from their families. By singing this song, Bynum uses collective memory to confront Loomis with his personal loss and with the way this loss still affects him:

> Now, I can look at you, Mr. Loomis, and see you a man who done forgot his song. Forgot how to sing it. A fellow forget that and he forget who he is. Forget how he's supposed to mark down life. . . . See, Mr. Loomis, when a man forgets his song he goes off in search of it . . . till he find out he's got it with him all the time. That's why I can tell you one of Joe Turner's niggers. 'Cause you forgot how to sing your song.

Bynum's suggestion that a song of loss and victimization has displaced Loomis's own song and that Loomis is still in bondage to Turner, still "one of Joe Turner's niggers," provokes first violent denial, then implicit acknowledgement as Loomis recounts the story of his imprisonment, his release to find nothing left of his former life and his efforts to see his wife once more so that he can begin again: "I just wanna see her face so I can get me a starting place in the world." By acknowledging the past, Loomis is enabled to confront the judgment of worthlessness which keeps him bound to Joe Turner and counter it with his own truth. Joe Turner did not catch and keep him for seven years because he was "worthless": "Worthless is something you throw away. . . . I ain't seen him throw me away." Rather, it was envy of Loomis's song that led Joe Turner to imprison him. As Bynum puts it, "What he [Joe Turner] wanted was your song. He wanted that song to be his. . . . But you still got it. You just forgot how to sing it."

Once Loomis has understood the past in which he was victimized and has rejected the judgment of worthlessness which oppression forced upon him, it remains for him to say "goodbye" to what he has lost and reclaim the self that Joe Turner has not been able to take away. What Loomis has lost is the life he had with his wife, Martha, before Joe Turner entered it. He cannot reclaim that life except as a past he confirms by seeing Martha again: "I just wanted to see your face to know that the world was still there. Make sure everything still in its place so I could reconnect myself together." Loomis must "say goodbye" to Martha and the world they made, but this goodbye is everything. By relinquishing the past, Loomis also reclaims it as his own, in a sense, nullifying Joe Turner's expropriation. Loomis's declaration, "Well, Joe Turner's come and gone and Herald Loomis ain't for no binding," transforms the meaning of the words sung by women whose men had been taken away. The words no longer communicate present loss but consign Joe Turner to a history of which Loomis is the subject. Repossessed of the past, Loomis is no longer its victim but the measure of its meaning, free to judge it and reject what seems false, including the Christian faith that Martha tries to lead him back to:

> Great big old white man . . . your Mr. Jesus Christ. Standing there with a whip in one hand and a tote board in another, and them niggers swimming in a sea of cotton. And he counting. He tallying up the cotton. "Well, Jeremiah . . . what's the matter, you ain't picked but two hundred pounds of cotton today? Got to put you on half rations." And Jeremiah go back and lay up there on his half rations and talk about what a nice man Mr. Jesus Christ is 'cause he give him salvation after he die. Something wrong here. Something don't fit right!

Loomis rejects Christian promises of salvation as complicit with African Americans' historical oppression and, declaring that "I don't need nobody to bleed for me!" slashes himself across the chest. This declaration of self-sufficiency and of break with the pieties of the past is also one in which Loomis reconnects with a collective identity and a heritage of self-empowerment: he finds that "I'm standing now" just as the ancestors in his vision had stood up. Reclaiming himself and translating a collective past to the present, Loomis becomes indeed the shiny man who knows his own song and, "shining like new money," shows the way (94).

FURTHER READING

Criticism

Barnes, Clive. "'Trains' Doesn't Run." *New York Post* (14 April 1992): 138.
    Mixed assessment of *Two Trains Running*.

Bergesen, Eric, and William W. Demastes. "The Limits of African-American Political Realism: Baraka's *Dutchman* and Wilson's *Ma Rainey's Black Bottom*." In *Realism and the American Dramatic Tradition*, edited by William W. Demastes, pp. 218-34. Tuscaloosa: University of Alabama Press, 1996.

Contrasts Amiri Baraka's *Dutchman* and Wilson's *Ma Rainey* as examples of two divergent styles of approaching African-American subjects.

Birdwell, Christine. "Death as a Fastball on the Outside Corner: *Fences'* Troy Maxson and the American Dream." *Aethlon* VII (Fall 1990): 87-96.
    Surveys *Fences*, illustrating Wilson's use of baseball as subject, symbol, and metaphor in the play.

Bissiri, Amadou. "Aspects of Africanness in August Wilson's Drama: Reading the *Piano Lesson* through Wole Soyinka's Drama." *African American Review* 30, No. 1 (Spring 1996): 99-113.
    Examines *The Piano Lesson* in order to "trace aspects of Africanness" and to "probe the overall significance of Wilson's dramaturgic interest in Africanness."

Ching, Mei-Ling. "Wrestling Against History." *Theater* XIX, No. 3 (Summer/Fall 1988): 70-1.
    Explores history and spiritual issues in Wilson's dramas.

Elam, Harry J. "*Ma Rainey's Black Bottom:* Singing Wilson's Blues." *American Drama* 5, No. 2 (Spring 1992): 76-99.
    Illustrates the significance and role of blues music in *Ma Rainey* and in the interpretation of African-American history.

Grant, Nathan L. "Men, Women, and Culture: A Conversation with August Wilson." *American Drama* 5, No. 2 (Spring 1992): 100-22.
    Interview in which Wilson discusses politics and culture and their effects upon his dramatic works.

Hornby, Richard. Review of *Fences*, by August Wilson. *The Hudson Review* XL, No. 3 (Autumn 1987): 470-72.
    Laudatory assessment of *Fences*.

———. Review of *Joe Turner's Come and Gone*, by August Wilson. *The Hudson Review*, XLI, No. 3 (Autumn 1988): 518.
    Offers high praise for *Joe Turner's Come and Gone*.

Shannon, Sandra G. "The Role of Memory in August Wilson's Four Hundred Year Autobiography." In *Memory and Cultural Politics: New Approaches to American Ethnic Literatures*, edited by Amritjit Singh, Joseph T. Skerrett, Jr., and Robert E. Hogan, pp. 175-93. Boston: Northeastern University Press, 1996.
    Delineates the function of memory in Wilson's dramas.

Smith, Philip E., II. "*Ma Rainey's Black Bottom:* Playing the Blues as Equipment for Living." In *Within the Dramatic Spectrum*, edited by Karelisa V. Hartigan, pp. 177-86. University Press of America, 1986.

Discusses the historical background of *Ma Rainey's Black Bottom* and the major themes of the play.

Weales, Gerald. Review of *Ma Rainey's Black Bottom,* by August Wilson. *The Georgia Review* XXXIX, No. 3 (Fall 1985): 622-23.
    Mostly favorable review of *Ma Rainey,* with some reservations about some matters involving theme and plot.

————. Review of *Joe Turner's Come and Gone,* by August Wilson. *The Georgia Review* XLII, No. 3 (Fall 1988): 599-600.
    Brief positive review of *Joe Turner's Come and Gone.*

Additional coverage of Wilson's life and career is contained in the following sources published by Gale: *Authors and Artists for Young Adults,* **Vol. 16;** *Black Literature Criticism; Black Writers; Contemporary Authors,* **Vols. 115, and 122;** *Contemporary Authors New Revision Series,* **Vols. 42, and 54;** *DISCovering Authors; DISCovering Authors: British; DISCovering Authors: Canadian; DISCovering Authors Modules: Dramatists, Most-Studied, and Multicultural; Drama Criticism,* **Vol. 2;** *Major Twentieth-Century Writers;* **and** *World Literature Criticism Supplement.*

☐ Contemporary Literary Criticism

Indexes

Literary Criticism Series
Cumulative Author Index
Cumulative Topic Index
Cumulative Nationality Index
Title Index, Volume 118

How to Use This Index

The main references

Camus, Albert
1913-1960 . . . . . . .CLC 1, 2, 4, 9, 11,
14, 32, 69; DA; DAB; DAC; DAM
DRAM, MST, NOV; DC2; SSC 9;
WLC

list all author entries in the following Gale Literary Criticism series:

BLC = *Black Literature Criticism*
BLCS = *Black Literature Criticism Supplement*
CLC = *Contemporary Literary Criticism*
CLR = *Children's Literature Review*
CMLC = *Classical and Medieval Literature Criticism*
DA = *DISCovering Authors*
DAB = *DISCovering Authors: British*
DAC = *DISCovering Authors: Canadian*
DAM = *DISCovering Authors Modules*
 DRAM = *dramatists;* *MST* = *most-studied
 authors;* *MULT* = *multicultural authors;* *NOV* =
 novelists; *POET* = *poets;* *POP* = *popular/genre
 writers;* *DC* = *Drama Criticism*
HLC = *Hispanic Literature Criticism*
LC = *Literature Criticism from 1400 to 1800*
NCLC = *Nineteenth-Century Literature Criticism*
PC = *Poetry Criticism*
SSC = *Short Story Criticism*
TCLC = *Twentieth-Century Literary Criticism*
WLC = *World Literature Criticism, 1500 to the Present*
WLCS = *World Literature Criticism Supplement*

The cross-references

See also CA 89-92; DLB 72; MTCW

list all author entries in the following Gale biographical and literary sources:

AAYA = *Authors & Artists for Young Adults*
AITN = *Authors in the News*
BEST = *Bestsellers*
BW = *Black Writers*
CA = *Contemporary Authors*
CAAS = *Contemporary Authors Autobiography Series*
CABS = *Contemporary Authors Bibliographical Series*
CANR = *Contemporary Authors New Revision Series*
CAP = *Contemporary Authors Permanent Series*
CDALB = *Concise Dictionary of American Literary
Biography*
CDBLB = *Concise Dictionary of British Literary
Biography*

DLB = *Dictionary of Literary Biography*
DLBD = *Dictionary of Literary Biography
Documentary Series*
DLBY = *Dictionary of Literary Biography Yearbook*
HW = *Hispanic Writers*
JRDA = *Junior DISCovering Authors*
MAICYA = *Major Authors and Illustrators for
Children and Young Adults*
MTCW = *Major 20th-Century Writers*
NNAL = *Native North American Literature*
SAAS = *Something about the Author Autobiography
Series*
SATA = *Something about the Author*
YABC = *Yesterday's Authors of Books for Children*

Literary Criticism Series
Cumulative Author Index

20/1631
See Upward, Allen
A/C Cross
See Lawrence, T(homas) E(dward)
Abasiyanik, Sait Faik 1906-1954
See Sait Faik
See also CA 123
Abbey, Edward 1927-1989 .... **CLC 36, 59**
See also CA 45-48; 128; CANR 2, 41
Abbott, Lee K(ittredge) 1947- .... **CLC 48**
See also CA 124; CANR 51; DLB 130
Abe, Kobo 1924-1993**CLC 8, 22, 53, 81; DAM NOV**
See also CA 65-68; 140; CANR 24, 60; DLB 182; MTCW 1
Abelard, Peter c. 1079-c. 1142 ...... **CMLC 11**
See also DLB 115, 208
Abell, Kjeld 1901-1961 .... **CLC 15**
See also CA 111
Abish, Walter 1931- .... **CLC 22**
See also CA 101; CANR 37; DLB 130
Abrahams, Peter (Henry) 1919- ....**CLC 4**
See also BW 1; CA 57-60; CANR 26; DLB 117; MTCW 1
Abrams, M(eyer) H(oward) 1912- ... **CLC 24**
See also CA 57-60; CANR 13, 33; DLB 67
Abse, Dannie 1923-..**CLC 7, 29; DAB; DAM POET**
See also CA 53-56; CAAS 1; CANR 4, 46, 74; DLB 27
Achebe, (Albert) Chinua(lumogu) 1930-**C L C 1, 3, 5, 7, 11, 26, 51, 75; BLC 1; DA; DAB; DAC; DAM MST, MULT, NOV; WLC**
See also AAYA 15; BW 2; CA 1-4R; CANR 6, 26, 47, 73; CLR 20; DLB 117; MAICYA; MTCW 1; SATA 40; SATA-Brief 38
Acker, Kathy 1948-1997 .... **CLC 45, 111**
See also CA 117; 122; 162; CANR 55
Ackroyd, Peter 1949- .... **CLC 34, 52**
See also CA 123; 127; €ANR 51, 74; DLB 155; INT 127
Acorn, Milton 1923- ....**CLC 15; DAC**
See also CA 103; DLB 53; INT 103
Adamov, Arthur 1908-1970**CLC 4, 25; DAM DRAM**
See also CA 17-18; 25-28R; CAP 2; MTCW 1
Adams, Alice (Boyd) 1926-**CLC 6, 13, 46; SSC 24**
See also CA 81-84; CANR 26, 53, 75; DLBY 86; INT CANR-26; MTCW 1
Adams, Andy 1859-1935 .... **TCLC 56**
See also YABC 1
Adams, Brooks 1848-1927 .... **TCLC 80**
See also CA 123; DLB 47
Adams, Douglas (Noel) 1952- .... **CLC 27, 60; DAM POP**
See also AAYA 4; BEST 89:3; CA 106; CANR 34, 64; DLBY 83; JRDA
Adams, Francis 1862-1893 .... **NCLC 33**
Adams, Henry (Brooks) 1838-1918 **TCLC 4, 52; DA; DAB; DAC; DAM MST**
See also CA 104; 133; DLB 12, 47, 189
Adams, Richard (George) 1920-**CLC 4, 5, 18; DAM NOV**

See also AAYA 16; AITN 1, 2; CA 49-52; CANR 3, 35; CLR 20; JRDA; MAICYA; MTCW 1; SATA 7, 69
Adamson, Joy(-Friederike Victoria) 1910-1980 **CLC 17**
See also CA 69-72; 93-96; CANR 22; MTCW 1; SATA 11; SATA-Obit 22
Adcock, Fleur 1934- ....**CLC 41**
See also CA 25-28R; CAAS 23; CANR 11, 34, 69; DLB 40
Addams, Charles (Samuel) 1912-1988**CLC 30**
See also CA 61-64; 126; CANR 12
Addams, Jane 1860-1945 .... **TCLC 76**
Addison, Joseph 1672-1719 .... **LC 18**
See also CDBLB 1660-1789; DLB 101
Adler, Alfred (F.) 1870-1937 .... **TCLC 61**
See also CA 119; 159
Adler, C(arole) S(chwerdtfeger) 1932-..**C L C 35**
See also AAYA 4; CA 89-92; CANR 19, 40; JRDA; MAICYA; SAAS 15; SATA 26, 63, 102
Adler, Renata 1938- .... **CLC 8, 31**
See also CA 49-52; CANR 5, 22, 52; MTCW 1
Ady, Endre 1877-1919 .... **TCLC 11**
See also CA 107
A.E. 1867-1935 .... **TCLC 3, 10**
See also Russell, George William
Aeschylus 525B.C.-456B.C. ..**CMLC 11; DA; DAB; DAC; DAM DRAM, MST; DC 8; WLCS**
See also DLB 176
Aesop 620(?)B.C.-564(?)B.C. .... **CMLC 24**
See also CLR 14; MAICYA; SATA 64
Affable Hawk
See MacCarthy, Sir(Charles Otto) Desmond
Africa, Ben
See Bosman, Herman Charles
Afton, Effie
See Harper, Frances Ellen Watkins
Agapida, Fray Antonio
See Irving, Washington
Agee, James (Rufus) 1909-1955 **TCLC 1, 19; DAM NOV**
See also AITN 1; CA 108; 148; CDALB 1941-1968; DLB 2, 26, 152
Aghill, Gordon
See Silverberg, Robert
Agnon, S(hmuel) Y(osef Halevi) 1888-1970 **CLC 4, 8, 14; SSC 30**
See also CA 17-18; 25-28R; CANR 60; CAP 2; MTCW 1
Agrippa von Nettesheim, Henry Cornelius 1486-1535 .... **LC 27**
Aherne, Owen
See Cassill, R(onald) V(erlin)
Ai 1947- .... **CLC 4, 14, 69**
See also CA 85-88; CAAS 13; CANR 70; DLB 120
Aickman, Robert (Fordyce) 1914-1981 .**C L C 57**
See also CA 5-8R; CANR 3, 72
Aiken, Conrad (Potter) 1889-1973**CLC 1, 3, 5, 10, 52; DAM NOV, POET; SSC 9**

See also CA 5-8R; 45-48; CANR 4, 60; CDALB 1929-1941; DLB 9, 45, 102; MTCW 1; SATA 3, 30
Aiken, Joan (Delano) 1924- .... **CLC 35**
See also AAYA 1, 25; CA 9-12R; CANR 4, 23, 34, 64; CLR 1, 19; DLB 161; JRDA; MAICYA; MTCW 1; SAAS 1; SATA 2, 30, 73
Ainsworth, William Harrison 1805-1882 **NCLC 13**
See also DLB 21; SATA 24
Aitmatov, Chingiz (Torekulovich) 1928-**C L C 71**
See also CA 103; CANR 38; MTCW 1; SATA 56
Akers, Floyd
See Baum, L(yman) Frank
Akhmadulina, Bella Akhatovna 1937-**CLC 53; DAM POET**
See also CA 65-68
Akhmatova, Anna 1888-1966**CLC 11, 25, 64; DAM POET; PC 2**
See also CA 19-20; 25-28R; CANR 35; CAP 1; MTCW 1
Aksakov, Sergei Timofeyvich 1791-1859 **NCLC 2**
See also DLB 198
Aksenov, Vassily
See Aksyonov, Vassily (Pavlovich)
Akst, Daniel 1956- .... **CLC 109**
See also CA 161
Aksyonov, Vassily (Pavlovich) 1932-**CLC 22, 37, 101**
See also CA 53-56; CANR 12, 48
Akutagawa, Ryunosuke 1892-1927 **TCLC 16**
See also CA 117; 154
Alain 1868-1951 .... **TCLC 41**
See also CA 163
Alain-Fournier .... **TCLC 6**
See also Fournier, Henri Alban
See also DLB 65
Alarcon, Pedro Antonio de 1833-1891**NCLC 1**
Alas (y Urena), Leopoldo (Enrique Garcia) 1852-1901 .... **TCLC 29**
See also CA 113; 131; HW
Albee, Edward (Franklin III) 1928-**CLC 1, 2, 3, 5, 9, 11, 13, 25, 53, 86, 113; DA; DAB; DAC; DAM DRAM, MST; WLC**
See also AITN 1; CA 5-8R; CABS 3; CANR 8, 54, 74; CDALB 1941-1968; DLB7; INT CANR-8; MTCW 1
Alberti, Rafael 1902- .... **CLC 7**
See also CA 85-88; DLB 108
Albert the Great 1200(?)-1280 ...... **CMLC 16**
See also DLB 115
Alcala-Galiano, Juan Valera y
See Valera y Alcala-Galiano, Juan
Alcott, Amos Bronson 1799-1888 .... **NCLC 1**
See also DLB 1
Alcott, Louisa May 1832-1888 . **NCLC 6, 58; DA; DAB; DAC; DAM MST, NOV; SSC 27; WLC**
See also AAYA 20; CDALB 1865-1917; CLR 1, 38; DLB 1, 42, 79; DLBD 14; JRDA;

MAICYA; SATA 100; YABC 1

Aldanov, M. A.
See Aldanov. Mark (Alexandrovich)

Aldanov, Mark (Alexandrovich) 1886(?)-1957 **TCLC 23**
See also CA 118

Aldington, Richard 1892-1962 .... **CLC 49**
See also CA 85-88; CANR 45; DLB 20, 36, 100, 149

Aldiss, Brian W(ilson) 1925- . **CLC 5, 14, 40; DAM NOV**
See also CA 5-8R; CAAS 2; CANR 5, 28, 64; DLB 14; MTCW 1; SATA 34

Alegria, Claribel 1924-**CLC 75; DAM MULT**
See also CA 131; CAAS 15; CANR 66; DLB 145; HW

Alegria, Fernando 1918-................... **CLC 57**
See also CA 9-12R; CANR 5, 32, 72; HW

Aleichem, Sholom .... **TCLC 1, 35; SSC 33**
See also Rabinovitch, Sholem

Aleixandre, Vicente 1898-1984 ... **CLC 9, 36; DAM POET; PC 15**
See also CA 85-88; 114; CANR 26; DLB 108; HW; MTCW 1

Alepoudelis, Odysseus
See Elytis, Odysseus

Aleshkovsky, Joseph 1929-
See Aleshkovsky, Yuz
See also CA 121; 128

Aleshkovsky, Yuz .... **CLC 44**
See also Aleshkovsky, Joseph

Alexander, Lloyd (Chudley) 1924- .. **CLC 35**
See also AAYA 1, 27; CA 1-4R; CANR 1, 24, 38, 55; CLR 1, 5, 48; DLB 52; JRDA; MAICYA; MTCW 1; SAAS 19; SATA 3, 49, 81

Alexander, Samuel 1859-1938 .... **TCLC 77**

Alexie, Sherman (Joseph, Jr.) 1966- **CLC 96; DAM MULT**
See also CA 138; CANR 65; DLB 175, 206; NNAL

Alfau, Felipe 1902-............................ **CLC 66**
See also CA 137

Alger, Horatio, Jr. 1832-1899 .... **NCLC 8**
See also DLB 42; SATA 16

Algren, Nelson 1909-1981**CLC 4, 10, 33; SSC 33**
See also CA 13-16R; 103; CANR 20, 61; CDALB 1941-1968; DLB 9; DLBY 81, 82; MTCW 1

Ali, Ahmed 1910-............................. **CLC 69**
See also CA 25-28R; CANR 15, 34

Alighieri, Dante
See Dante

Allan, John B.
See Westlake, Donald E(dwin)

Allan, Sidney
See Hartmann, Sadakichi

Allan, Sydney
See Hartmann, Sadakichi

Allen, Edward 1948-........................ **CLC 59**

Allen, Fred 1894-1956.................... **TCLC 87**

Allen, Paula Gunn 1939- ....**CLC 84; DAM MULT**
See also CA 112; 143; CANR 63; DLB 175; NNAL

Allen, Roland
See Ayckbourn, Alan

Allen, Sarah A.
See Hopkins, Pauline Elizabeth

Allen, Sidney H.
See Hartmann, Sadakichi

Allen, Woody 1935- **CLC 16, 52; DAM POP**

See also AAYA 10; CA 33-36R; CANR 27. 38, 63; DLB 44; MTCW 1

Allende, Isabel 1942-. **CLC 39, 57, 97; DAM MULT, NOV; HLC; WLCS**
See also AAYA 18; CA 125; 130; CANR 51, 74; DLB 145; HW; INT 130; MTCW 1

Alleyn, Ellen
See Rossetti, Christina (Georgina)

Allingham, Margery (Louise) 1904-1966**C L C 19**
See also CA 5-8R; 25-28R; CANR 4, 58; DLB 77; MTCW 1

Allingham, William 1824-1889 ...... **NCLC 25**
See also DLB 35

Allison, Dorothy E. 1949- ....**CLC 78**
See also CA 140; CANR 66

Allston, Washington 1779-1843 .... **NCLC 2**
See also DLB 1

Almedingen, E. M. ....**CLC 12**
See also Almedingen, Martha Edith von
See also SATA 3

Almedingen, Martha Edith von 1898-1971
See Almedingen, E. M.
See also CA 1-4R; CANR 1

Almodovar, Pedro 1949(?)-.............. **CLC 114**
See also CA 133; CANR 72

Almqvist, Carl Jonas Love 1793-1866 **N C L C 42**

Alonso, Damaso 1898-1990 ....**CLC 14**
See also CA 110; 131; 130; CANR 72; DLB 108; HW

Alov
See Gogol, Nikolai (Vasilyevich)

Alta 1942-...**CLC 19**
See also CA 57-60

Alter, Robert B(ernard) 1935- ....**CLC 34**
See also CA 49-52; CANR 1, 47

Alther, Lisa 1944-......................... **CLC 7, 41**
See also CA 65-68; CAAS 30; CANR 12, 30, 51; MTCW 1

Althusser, L.
See Althusser, Louis

Althusser, Louis 1918-1990 .... **CLC 106**
See also CA 131; 132

Altman, Robert 1925- .... **CLC 16, 116**
See also CA 73-76; CANR 43

Alvarez, A(lfred) 1929- .... **CLC 5, 13**
See also CA 1-4R; CANR 3, 33, 63; DLB 14, 40

Alvarez, Alejandro Rodriguez 1903-1965
See Casona, Alejandro
See also CA 131; 93-96; HW

Alvarez, Julia 1950- ....**CLC 93**
See also AAYA 25; CA 147; CANR 69

Alvaro, Corrado 1896-1956............. **TCLC 60**
See also CA 163

Amado, Jorge 1912- **CLC 13, 40, 106; DAM MULT, NOV; HLC**
See also CA 77-80; CANR 35, 74; DLB 113; MTCW 1

Ambler, Eric 1909-1998 .... **CLC 4, 6, 9**
See also CA 9-12R; 171; CANR 7, 38, 74; DLB 77; MTCW 1

Amichai, Yehuda 1924- ... **CLC 9, 22, 57, 116**
See also CA 85-88; CANR 46, 60; MTCW 1

Amichai, Yehudah
See Amichai, Yehuda

Amiel, Henri Frederic 1821-1881 .... **NCLC 4**

Amis, Kingsley (William) 1922-1995**CLC 1, 2, 3, 5, 8, 13, 40, 44; DA; DAB; DAC; DAM MST, NOV**
See also AITN 2; CA 9-12R; 150; CANR 8, 28, 54; CDBLB 1945-1960; DLB 15, 27, 100,

139; DLBY 96; INT CANR-8; MTCW 1

Amis, Martin (Louis) 1949-**CLC 4, 9, 38, 62, 101**
See also BEST 90:3; CA 65-68; CANR 8, 27, 54, 73; DLB 14, 194; INT CANR-27

Ammons, A(rchie) R(andolph) 1926-**CLC 2, 3, 5, 8, 9, 25, 57, 108; DAM POET; PC 16**
See also AITN 1; CA 9-12R; CANR 6, 36, 51, 73; DLB 5, 165; MTCW 1

Amo, Tauraatua i
See Adams, Henry (Brooks)

Amory, Thomas 1691(?)-1788 .... **LC 48**

Anand, Mulk Raj 1905- .. **CLC 23, 93; DAM NOV**
See also CA 65-68; CANR 32, 64; MTCW 1

Anatol
See Schnitzler, Arthur

Anaximander c. 610B.C.-c. 546B.C.**CMLC 22**

Anaya, Rudolfo A(lfonso) 1937- ..... **CLC 23; DAM MULT, NOV; HLC**
See also AAYA 20; CA 45-48; CAAS 4; CANR 1, 32, 51; DLB 82, 206; HW 1; MTCW 1

Andersen, Hans Christian 1805-1875**NCLC 7; DA; DAB; DAC; DAM MST, POP; SSC 6; WLC**
See also CLR 6; MAICYA; SATA 100; YABC 1

Anderson, C. Farley
See Mencken, H(enry) L(ouis); Nathan, George Jean

Anderson, Jessica (Margaret) Queale 1916- **CLC 37**
See also CA 9-12R; CANR 4, 62

Anderson, Jon (Victor) 1940-..**CLC 9; DAM POET**
See also CA 25-28R; CANR 20

Anderson, Lindsay (Gordon) 1923-1994**C L C 20**
See also CA 125; 128; 146

Anderson, Maxwell 1888-1959**TCLC 2; DAM DRAM**
See also CA 105; 152; DLB 7

Anderson, Poul (William) 1926- ...... **CLC 15**
See also AAYA 5; CA 1-4R; CAAS 2; CANR 2. 15. 34, 64; DLB 8; INT CANR-15; MTCW 1; SATA 90; SATA-Brief 39

Anderson, Robert (Woodruff) 1917-**CLC 23; DAM DRAM**
See also AITN 1; CA 21-24R; CANR 32; DLB 7

Anderson, Sherwood 1876-1941 **TCLC 1, 10, 24; DA; DAB; DAC; DAM MST, NOV; SSC 1; WLC**
See also CA 104; 121; CANR 61; CDALB 1917-1929; DLB 4, 9, 86; DLBD 1; MTCW 1

Andier, Pierre
See Desnos, Robert

Andouard
See Giraudoux, (Hippolyte) Jean

Andrade, Carlos Drummond de .... **CLC 18**
See also Drummond de Andrade, Carlos

Andrade, Mario de 1893-1945 .... **TCLC 43**

Andreae, Johann V(alentin) 1586-1654**LC 32**
See also DLB 164

Andreas-Salome, Lou 1861-1937 ... **TCLC 56**
See also DLB 66

Andress, Lesley
See Sanders, Lawrence

Andrewes, Lancelot 1555-1626 .... **LC 5**
See also DLB 151, 172

Andrews, Cicily Fairfield
See West, Rebecca

Andrews, Elton V.
See Pohl, Frederik
Andreyev, Leonid (Nikolaevich) 1871-1919
   TCLC 3
   See also CA 104
Andric, Ivo 1892-1975 .... **CLC 8**
   See also CA 81-84; 57-60; CANR 43, 60; DLB
   147; MTCW 1
Androvar
   See Prado (Calvo), Pedro
Angelique, Pierre
   See Bataille, Georges
Angell, Roger 1920- .... **CLC 26**
   See also CA 57-60; CANR 13, 44, 70; DLB 171,
   185
Angelou, Maya 1928-CLC 12, 35, 64, 77; BLC
   1; DA; DAB; DAC; DAM MST, MULT,
   POET, POP; WLCS
   See also AAYA 7, 20; BW 2; CA 65-68; CANR
   19, 42, 65; CLR 53; DLB 38; MTCW 1;
   SATA 49
Anna Comnena 1083-1153 .... **CMLC 25**
Annensky, Innokenty (Fyodorovich) 1856-1909
   TCLC 14
   See also CA 110; 155
Annunzio, Gabriele d'
   See D'Annunzio, Gabriele
Anodos
   See Coleridge, Mary E(lizabeth)
Anon, Charles Robert
   See Pessoa, Fernando (Antonio Nogueira)
Anouilh, Jean (Marie Lucien Pierre) 1910-1987
   **CLC 1, 3, 8, 13, 40, 50; DAM DRAM; DC
   8**
   See also CA 17-20R; 123; CANR 32; MTCW 1
Anthony, Florence
   See Ai
Anthony, John
   See Ciardi, John (Anthony)
Anthony, Peter
   See Shaffer, Anthony (Joshua); Shaffer, Peter
   (Levin)
Anthony, Piers 1934- ..... **CLC 35; DAM POP**
   See also AAYA 11; CA 21-24R; CANR 28, 56,
   73; DLB 8; MTCW 1; SAAS 22; SATA 84
Anthony, Susan B(rownell) 1916-1991 **T C L C
   84**
   See also CA 89-92; 134
Antoine, Marc
   See Proust, (Valentin-Louis-George-Eugene-)
   Marcel
Antoninus, Brother
   See Everson, William (Oliver)
Antonioni, Michelangelo 1912- .... **CLC 20**
   See also CA 73-76; CANR 45
Antschel, Paul 1920-1970
   See Celan, Paul
   See also CA 85-88; CANR 33, 61; MTCW 1
Anwar, Chairil 1922-1949 .... **TCLC 22**
   See also CA 121
Apess, William 1798-1839(?)NCLC 73; DAM
   MULT
   See also DLB 175; NNAL
Apollinaire, Guillaume 1880-1918TCLC 3, 8,
   51; DAM POET; PC 7
   See also Kostrowitzki, Wilhelm Apollinaris de
   See also CA 152
Appelfeld, Aharon 1932- .... **CLC 23, 47**
   See also CA 112; 133
Apple, Max (Isaac) 1941- .... **CLC 9, 33**
   See also CA 81-84; CANR 19, 54; DLB 130
Appleman, Philip (Dean) 1926- .... **CLC 51**
   See also CA 13-16R; CAAS 18; CANR 6, 29,

56
Appleton, Lawrence
   See Lovecraft, H(oward) P(hillips)
Apteryx
   See Eliot, T(homas) S(tearns)
Apuleius, (Lucius Madaurensis) 125(?)-175(?)
   CMLC 1
Aquin, Hubert 1929-1977 .... **CLC 15**
   See also CA 105; DLB 53
Aragon, Louis 1897-1982 ..CLC 3, 22; DAM
   NOV, POET
   See also CA 69-72; 108; CANR 28, 71; DLB
   72; MTCW 1
Arany, Janos 1817-1882 .... **NCLC 34**
Aranyos, Kakay
   See Mikszath, Kalman
Arbuthnot, John 1667-1735 .... **LC 1**
   See also DLB 101
Archer, Herbert Winslow
   See Mencken, H(enry) L(ouis)
Archer, Jeffrey (Howard) 1940- ..... **CLC 28;
   DAM POP**
   See also AAYA 16; BEST 89:3; CA 77-80;
   CANR 22, 52; INT CANR-22
Archer, Jules 1915- .... **CLC 12**
   See also CA 9-12R; CANR 6, 69; SAAS 5;
   SATA 4, 85
Archer, Lee
   See Ellison, Harlan (Jay)
Arden, John 1930-CLC 6, 13, 15; DAM DRAM
   See also CA 13-16R; CAAS 4; CANR 31, 65,
   67; DLB 13; MTCW 1
Arenas, Reinaldo 1943-1990 . CLC 41; DAM
   MULT; HLC
   See also CA 124; 128; 133; CANR 73; DLB
   145; HW
Arendt, Hannah 1906-1975 .... **CLC 66, 98**
   See also CA 17-20R; 61-64; CANR 26, 60;
   MTCW 1
Aretino, Pietro 1492-1556 .... **LC 12**
Arghezi, Tudor 1880-1967 .... **CLC 80**
   See also Theodorescu, Ion N.
   See also CA 167
Arguedas, Jose Maria 1911-1969 CLC 10, 18
   See also CA 89-92; CANR 73; DLB 113; HW
Argueta, Manlio 1936- .... **CLC 31**
   See also CA 131; CANR 73; DLB 145; HW
Ariosto, Ludovico 1474-1533 .... **LC 6**
Aristides
   See Epstein, Joseph
Aristophanes 450B.C.-385B.C.CMLC 4; DA;
   DAB; DAC; DAM DRAM, MST; DC 2;
   WLCS
   See also DLB 176
Aristotle 384B.C.-322B.C. ... CMLC 31; DA;
   DAB; DAC; DAM MST; WLCS
   See also DLB 176
Arlt, Roberto (Godofredo Christophersen)
   1900-1942TCLC 29; DAM MULT; HLC
   See also CA 123; 131; CANR 67; HW
Armah, Ayi Kwei 1939- . CLC 5, 33; BLC 1;
   DAM MULT, POET
   See also BW 1; CA 61-64; CANR 21, 64; DLB
   117; MTCW 1
Armatrading, Joan 1950- .... **CLC 17**
   See also CA 114
Arnette, Robert
   See Silverberg, Robert
**Arnim, Achim von (Ludwig Joachim von
   Arnim)** 1781-1831 ...... NCLC 5; SSC 29
   See also DLB 90
Arnim, Bettina von 1785-1859 .... **NCLC 38**
   See also DLB 90

Arnold, Matthew 1822-1888NCLC 6, 29; DA;
   DAB; DAC; DAM MST, POET; PC 5;
   WLC
   See also CDBLB 1832-1890; DLB 32, 57
Arnold, Thomas 1795-1842 .... **NCLC 18**
   See also DLB 55
Arnow, Harriette (Louisa) Simpson 1908-1986
   CLC 2, 7, 18
   See also CA 9-12R; 118; CANR 14; DLB 6;
   MTCW 1; SATA 42; SATA-Obit 47
Arouet, Francois-Marie
   See Voltaire
Arp, Hans
   See Arp, Jean
Arp, Jean 1887-1966 .... **CLC 5**
   See also CA 81-84; 25-28R; CANR 42
Arrabal
   See Arrabal, Fernando
Arrabal, Fernando 1932- .... CLC 2, 9, 18, 58
   See also CA 9-12R; CANR 15
Arrick, Fran .... **CLC 30**
   See also Gaberman, Judie Angell
Artaud, Antonin (Marie Joseph) 1896-1948
   TCLC 3, 36; DAM DRAM
   See also CA 104; 149
Arthur, Ruth M(abel) 1905-1979 ...... **CLC 12**
   See also CA 9-12R; 85-88; CANR 4; SATA 7,
   26
Artsybashev, Mikhail (Petrovich) 1878-1927
   TCLC 31
   See also CA 170
Arundel, Honor (Morfydd) 1919-1973CLC 17
   See also CA 21-22; 41-44R; CAP 2; CLR 35;
   SATA 4; SATA-Obit 24
Arzner, Dorothy 1897-1979 .... **CLC 98**
Asch, Sholem 1880-1957 .... **TCLC 3**
   See also CA 105
Ash, Shalom
   See Asch, Sholem
Ashbery, John (Lawrence) 1927-CLC 2, 3, 4,
   6, 9, 13, 15, 25, 41, 77; DAM POET
   See also CA 5-8R; CANR 9, 37, 66; DLB 5,
   165; DLBY 81; INT CANR-9; MTCW 1
Ashdown, Clifford
   See Freeman, R(ichard) Austin
Ashe, Gordon
   See Creasey, John
Ashton-Warner, Sylvia (Constance) 1908-1984
   CLC 19
   See also CA 69-72; 112; CANR 29; MTCW 1
Asimov, Isaac 1920-1992 CLC 1, 3, 9, 19, 26,
   76, 92; DAM POP
   See also AAYA 13; BEST 90:2; CA 1-4R; 137;
   CANR 2, 19, 36, 60; CLR 12; DLB 8; DLBY
   92; INT CANR-19; JRDA; MAICYA;
   MTCW 1; SATA 1, 26, 74
Assis, Joaquim Maria Machado de
   See Machado de Assis, Joaquim Maria
Astley, Thea (Beatrice May) 1925- ...CLC 41
   See also CA 65-68; CANR 11, 43
Aston, James
   See White, T(erence) H(anbury)
Asturias, Miguel Angel 1899-1974 CLC 3, 8,
   13; DAM MULT, NOV; HLC
   See also CA 25-28; 49-52; CANR 32; CAP 2;
   DLB 113; HW; MTCW 1
Atares, Carlos Saura
   See Saura (Atares), Carlos
Atheling, William
   See Pound, Ezra (Weston Loomis)
Atheling, William, Jr.
   See Blish, James (Benjamin)
Atherton, Gertrude (Franklin Horn) 1857-1948

MTCW 1; SATA 2, 31, 79

Blunden, Edmund (Charles) 1896-1974 **C L C 2, 56**
See also CA 17-18; 45-48; CANR 54; CAP 2; DLB 20, 100, 155; MTCW 1

Bly, Robert (Elwood) 1926-**CLC 1, 2, 5, 10, 15, 38; DAM POET**
See also CA 5-8R; CANR 41, 73; DLB 5; MTCW 1

Boas, Franz 1858-1942 .... **TCLC 56**
See also CA 115

Bobette
See Simenon, Georges (Jacques Christian)

Boccaccio, Giovanni 1313-1375 .. **CMLC 13; SSC 10**

Bochco, Steven 1943- .... **CLC 35**
See also AAYA 11; CA 124; 138

Bodel, Jean 1167(?)-1210 .... **CMLC 28**

Bodenheim, Maxwell 1892-1954 .... **TCLC 44**
See also CA 110; DLB 9, 45

Bodker, Cecil 1927- .... **CLC 21**
See also CA 73-76; CANR 13, 44; CLR 23; MAICYA; SATA 14

Boell, Heinrich (Theodor) 1917-1985 **CLC 2, 3, 6, 9, 11, 15, 27, 32, 72; DA; DAB; DAC; DAM MST, NOV; SSC 23; WLC**
See also CA 21-24R; 116; CANR 24; DLB 69; DLBY 85; MTCW 1

Boerne, Alfred
See Doeblin, Alfred

Boethius 480(?)-524(?) .... **CMLC 15**
See also DLB 115

Bogan, Louise 1897-1970 . **CLC 4, 39, 46, 93; DAM POET; PC 12**
See also CA 73-76; 25-28R; CANR 33; DLB 45, 169; MTCW 1

Bogarde, Dirk .... **CLC 19**
See also Van Den Bogarde, Derek Jules Gaspard Ulric Niven
See also DLB 14

Bogosian, Eric 1953- .... **CLC 45**
See also CA 138

Bograd, Larry 1953- .... **CLC 35**
See also CA 93-96; CANR 57; SAAS 21; SATA 33, 89

Boiardo, Matteo Maria 1441-1494 .... **LC 6**

Boileau-Despreaux, Nicolas 1636-1711 **LC 3**

Bojer, Johan 1872-1959 .... **TCLC 64**

Boland, Eavan (Aisling) 1944- .. **CLC 40, 67, 113; DAM POET**
See also CA 143; CANR 61; DLB 40

Boll, Heinrich
See Boell, Heinrich (Theodor)

Bolt, Lee
See Faust, Frederick (Schiller)

Bolt, Robert (Oxton) 1924-1995 ..... **CLC 14; DAM DRAM**
See also CA 17-20R; 147; CANR 35, 67; DLB 13; MTCW 1

Bombet, Louis-Alexandre-Cesar
See Stendhal

Bomkauf
See Kaufman, Bob (Garnell)

Bonaventura .... **NCLC 35**
See also DLB 90

Bond, Edward 1934- **CLC 4, 6, 13, 23; DAM DRAM**
See also CA 25-28R; CANR 38, 67; DLB 13; MTCW 1

Bonham, Frank 1914-1989 .... **CLC 12**
See also AAYA 1; CA 9-12R; CANR 4, 36; JRDA; MAICYA; SAAS 3; SATA 1, 49; SATA-Obit 62

Bonnefoy, Yves 1923- .. **CLC 9, 15, 58; DAM MST, POET**
See also CA 85-88; CANR 33, 75; MTCW 1

Bontemps, Arna(ud Wendell) 1902-1973**C L C 1, 18; BLC 1; DAM MULT, NOV, POET**
See also BW 1; CA 1-4R; 41-44R; CANR 4, 35; CLR 6; DLB 48, 51; JRDA; MAICYA; MTCW 1; SATA 2, 44; SATA-Obit 24

Booth, Martin 1944- .... **CLC 13**
See also CA 93-96; CAAS 2

Booth, Philip 1925- .... **CLC 23**
See also CA 5-8R; CANR 5; DLBY 82

Booth, Wayne C(layson) 1921- .... **CLC 24**
See also CA 1-4R; CAAS 5; CANR 3, 43; DLB 67

Borchert, Wolfgang 1921-1947 .... **TCLC 5**
See also CA 104; DLB 69, 124

Borel, Petrus 1809-1859 .... **NCLC 41**

Borges, Jorge Luis 1899-1986**CLC 1, 2, 3, 4, 6, 8, 9, 10, 13, 19, 44, 48, 83; DA; DAB; DAC; DAM MST, MULT; HLC; PC 22; SSC 4; WLC**
See also AAYA 26; CA 21-24R; CANR 19, 33, 75; DLB 113; DLBY 86; HW; MTCW 1

Borowski, Tadeusz 1922-1951 .... **TCLC 9**
See also CA 106; 154

Borrow, George (Henry) 1803-1881 **NCLC 9**
See also DLB 21, 55, 166

Bosman, Herman Charles 1905-1951 . **T C L C 49**
See also Malan, Herman
See also CA 160

Bosschere, Jean de 1878(?)-1953 ... **TCLC 19**
See also CA 115

Boswell, James 1740-1795 . **LC 4; DA; DAB; DAC; DAM MST; WLC**
See also CDBLB 1660-1789; DLB 104, 142

Bottoms, David 1949- .... **CLC 53**
See also CA 105; CANR 22; DLB 120; DLBY 83

Boucicault, Dion 1820-1890 .... **NCLC 41**

Boucolon, Maryse 1937(?)-
See Conde, Maryse
See also CA 110; CANR 30, 53, 76

Bourget, Paul (Charles Joseph) 1852-1935 **TCLC 12**
See also CA 107; DLB 123

Bourjaily, Vance (Nye) 1922- .... **CLC 8, 62**
See also CA 1-4R; CAAS 1; CANR 2, 72; DLB 2, 143

Bourne, Randolph S(illiman) 1886-1918 **TCLC 16**
See also CA 117; 155; DLB 63

Bova, Ben(jamin William) 1932- ......**CLC 45**
See also AAYA 16; CA 5-8R; CAAS 18; CANR 11, 56; CLR 3; DLBY 81; INT CANR-11; MAICYA; MTCW 1; SATA 6, 68

Bowen, Elizabeth (Dorothea Cole) 1899-1973 **CLC 1, 3, 6, 11, 15, 22, 118; DAM NOV; SSC 3, 28**
See also CA 17-18; 41-44R; CANR 35; CAP 2; CDBLB 1945-1960; DLB 15, 162; MTCW 1

Bowering, George 1935- .... **CLC 15, 47**
See also CA 21-24R; CAAS 16; CANR 10; DLB 53

Bowering, Marilyn R(uthe) 1949- ....**CLC 32**
See also CA 101; CANR 49

Bowers, Edgar 1924- ....**CLC 9**
See also CA 5-8R; CANR 24; DLB 5

Bowie, David ....**CLC 17**
See also Jones, David Robert

Bowles, Jane (Sydney) 1917-1973 **CLC 3, 68**

See also CA 19-20; 41-44R; CAP 2

Bowles, Paul (Frederick) 1910- **CLC 1, 2, 19, 53; SSC 3**
See also CA 1-4R; CAAS 1; CANR 1, 19, 50, 75; DLB 5, 6; MTCW 1

Box, Edgar
See Vidal, Gore

Boyd, Nancy
See Millay, Edna St. Vincent

Boyd, William 1952- .... **CLC 28, 53, 70**
See also CA 114; 120; CANR 51, 71

Boyle, Kay 1902-1992**CLC 1, 5, 19, 58; SSC 5**
See also CA 13-16R; 140; CAAS 1; CANR 29, 61; DLB 4, 9, 48, 86; DLBY 93; MTCW 1

Boyle, Mark
See Kienzle, William X(avier)

Boyle, Patrick 1905-1982 .... **CLC 19**
See also CA 127

Boyle, T. C. 1948-
See Boyle, T(homas) Coraghessan

Boyle, T(homas) Coraghessan 1948-**CLC 36, 55, 90; DAM POP; SSC 16**
See also BEST 90:4; CA 120; CANR 44, 76; DLBY 86

Boz
See Dickens, Charles (John Huffam)

Brackenridge, Hugh Henry 1748-1816**N C L C 7**
See also DLB 11, 37

Bradbury, Edward P.
See Moorcock, Michael (John)

Bradbury, Malcolm (Stanley) 1932- **CLC 32, 61; DAM NOV**
See also CA 1-4R; CANR 1, 33; DLB 14, 207; MTCW 1

Bradbury, Ray (Douglas) 1920-**CLC 1, 3, 10, 15, 42, 98; DA; DAB; DAC; DAM MST, NOV, POP; SSC 29; WLC**
See also AAYA 15; AITN 1, 2; CA 1-4R; CANR 2, 30, 75; CDALB 1968-1988; DLB 2, 8; MTCW 1; SATA 11, 64

Bradford, Gamaliel 1863-1932 ...... **TCLC 36**
See also CA 160; DLB 17

Bradley, David (Henry), Jr. 1950- .. **CLC 23, 118; BLC 1; DAM MULT**
See also BW 1; CA 104; CANR 26; DLB 33

Bradley, John Ed(mund, Jr.) 1958- . **CLC 55**
See also CA 139

Bradley, Marion Zimmer 1930-**CLC 30; DAM POP**
See also AAYA 9; CA 57-60; CAAS 10; CANR 7, 31, 51, 75; DLB 8; MTCW 1; SATA 90

Bradstreet, Anne 1612(?)-1672**LC 4, 30; DA; DAC; DAM MST, POET; PC 10**
See also CDALB 1640-1865; DLB 24

Brady, Joan 1939- .... **CLC 86**
See also CA 141

Bragg, Melvyn 1939- .... **CLC 10**
See also BEST 89:3; CA 57-60; CANR 10, 48; DLB 14

Brahe, Tycho 1546-1601 .... **LC 45**

Braine, John (Gerard) 1922-1986**CLC 1, 3, 41**
See also CA 1-4R; 120; CANR 1, 33; CDBLB 1945-1960; DLB 15; DLBY 86; MTCW 1

Bramah, Ernest 1868-1942 .... **TCLC 72**
See also CA 156; DLB 70

Brammer, William 1930(?)-1978 ...... **CLC 31**
See also CA 77-80

Brancati, Vitaliano 1907-1954 .... **TCLC 12**
See also CA 109

Brancato, Robin F(idler) 1936- .... **CLC 35**
See also AAYA 9; CA 69-72; CANR 11, 45; CLR 32; JRDA; SAAS 9; SATA 97

Brand, Max
  See Faust, Frederick (Schiller)
Brand, Millen 1906-1980 ....**CLC 7**
  See also CA 21-24R; 97-100; CANR 72
Branden, Barbara .... **CLC 44**
  See also CA 148
Brandes, Georg (Morris Cohen) 1842-1927
    TCLC 10
  See also CA 105
Brandys, Kazimierz 1916- .... **CLC 62**
Branley, Franklyn M(ansfield) 1915-**CLC 21**
  See also CA 33-36R; CANR 14, 39; CLR 13;
    MAICYA; SAAS 16; SATA 4, 68
Brathwaite, Edward Kamau 1930- **CLC 11;**
    BLCS; DAM POET
  See also BW 2; CA 25-28R; CANR 11, 26, 47;
    DLB 125
Brautigan, Richard (Gary) 1935-1984**CLC 1,**
    3, 5, 9, 12, 34, 42; DAM NOV
  See also CA 53-56; 113; CANR 34; DLB 2, 5,
    206; DLBY 80, 84; MTCW 1; SATA 56
Brave Bird, Mary 1953-
  See Crow Dog, Mary (Ellen)
  See also NNAL
Braverman, Kate 1950- .... **CLC 67**
  See also CA 89-92
Brecht, (Eugen) Bertolt (Friedrich) 1898-1956
    TCLC 1, 6, 13, 35; DA; DAB; DAC; DAM
    DRAM, MST; DC 3; WLC
  See also CA 104; 133; CANR 62; DLB 56, 124;
    MTCW 1
Brecht, Eugen Berthold Friedrich
  See Brecht, (Eugen) Bertolt (Friedrich)
Bremer, Fredrika 1801-1865 .... **NCLC 11**
Brennan, Christopher John 1870-1932**TCLC**
    17
  See also CA 117
Brennan, Maeve 1917-1993 .... **CLC 5**
  See also CA 81-84; CANR 72
Brent, Linda
  See Jacobs, Harriet A(nn)
Brentano, Clemens (Maria) 1778-1842**NCLC**
    1
  See also DLB 90
Brent of Bin Bin
  See Franklin, (Stella Maria Sarah) Miles
    (Lampe)
Brenton, Howard 1942- .... **CLC 31**
  See also CA 69-72; CANR 33, 67; DLB 13;
    MTCW 1
Breslin, James 1930-1996
  See Breslin, Jimmy
  See also CA 73-76; CANR 31, 75; DAM NOV;
    MTCW 1
Breslin, Jimmy .... **CLC 4, 43**
  See also Breslin, James
  See also AITN 1; DLB 185
Bresson, Robert 1901-........................ **CLC 16**
  See also CA 110; CANR 49
Breton, Andre 1896-1966**CLC 2, 9, 15, 54; PC**
    15
  See also CA 19-20; 25-28R; CANR 40, 60; CAP
    2; DLB 65; MTCW 1
Breytenbach, Breyten 1939(?)- . **CLC 23, 37;**
    DAM POET
  See also CA 113; 129; CANR 61
Bridgers, Sue Ellen 1942- .... **CLC 26**
  See also AAYA 8; CA 65-68; CANR 11, 36;
    CLR 18; DLB 52; JRDA; MAICYA; SAAS
    1; SATA 22, 90
Bridges, Robert (Seymour) 1844-1930**TCLC**
    1; DAM POET
  See also CA 104; 152; CDBLB 1890-1914;

  DLB 19, 98
Bridie, James .... **TCLC 3**
  See also Mavor, Osborne Henry
  See also DLB 10
Brin, David 1950- .... **CLC 34**
  See also AAYA 21; CA 102; CANR 24, 70; INT
    CANR-24; SATA 65
Brink, Andre (Philippus) 1935- **CLC 18, 36,**
    106
  See also CA 104; CANR 39, 62; INT 103;
    MTCW 1
Brinsmead, H(esba) F(ay) 1922- .... **CLC 21**
  See also CA 21-24R; CANR 10; CLR 47;
    MAICYA; SAAS 5; SATA 18, 78
Brittain, Vera (Mary) 1893(?)-1970 . **CLC 23**
  See also CA 13-16; 25-28R; CANR 58; CAP 1;
    DLB 191; MTCW 1
Broch, Hermann 1886-1951 .... **TCLC 20**
  See also CA 117; DLB 85, 124
Brock, Rose
  See Hansen, Joseph
Brodkey, Harold (Roy) 1930-1996 .... **CLC 56**
  See also CA 111; 151; CANR 71; DLB 130
Brodskii, Iosif
  See Brodsky, Joseph
Brodsky, Iosif Alexandrovich 1940-1996
  See Brodsky, Joseph
  See also AITN 1; CA 41-44R; 151; CANR 37;
    DAM POET; MTCW 1
Brodsky, Joseph 1940-1996 **CLC 4, 6, 13, 36,**
    100; PC 9
  See also Brodskii, Iosif; Brodsky, Iosif
    Alexandrovich
Brodsky, Michael (Mark) 1948- .... **CLC 19**
  See also CA 102; CANR 18, 41, 58
Bromell, Henry 1947-........................ **CLC 5**
  See also CA 53-56; CANR 9
Bromfield, Louis (Brucker) 1896-1956**TCLC**
    11
  See also CA 107; 155; DLB 4, 9, 86
Broner, E(sther) M(asserman) 1930- **CLC 19**
  See also CA 17-20R; CANR 8, 25, 72; DLB 28
Bronk, William 1918-........................ **CLC 10**
  See also CA 89-92; CANR 23; DLB 165
Bronstein, Lev Davidovich
  See Trotsky, Leon
Bronte, Anne 1820-1849 .... **NCLC 71**
  See also DLB 21, 199
Bronte, Charlotte 1816-1855 **NCLC 3, 8, 33,**
    58; DA; DAB; DAC; DAM MST,NOV;
    WLC
  See also AAYA 17; CDBLB 1832-1890; DLB
    21, 159, 199
Bronte, Emily (Jane) 1818-1848**NCLC 16, 35;**
    DA; DAB; DAC; DAM MST, NOV, POET;
    PC 8; WLC
  See also AAYA 17; CDBLB 1832-1890; DLB
    21, 32, 199
Brooke, Frances 1724-1789 .... **LC 6, 48**
  See also DLB 39, 99
Brooke, Henry 1703(?)-1783 .... **LC 1**
  See also DLB 39
Brooke, Rupert (Chawner) 1887-1915 **T C L C**
    2, 7; DA; DAB; DAC; DAM MST, POET;
    PC 24; WLC
  See also CA 104; 132; CANR 61; CDBLB
    1914-1945; DLB 19; MTCW 1
Brooke-Haven, P.
  See Wodehouse, P(elham) G(renville)
Brooke-Rose, Christine 1926(?)- .... **CLC 40**
  See also CA 13-16R; CANR 58; DLB 14
Brookner, Anita 1928-**CLC 32, 34, 51; DAB;**
    DAM POP

  See also CA 114; 120; CANR 37, 56; DLB 194;
    DLBY 87; MTCW 1
Brooks, Cleanth 1906-1994 **CLC 24, 86, 110**
  See also CA 17-20R; 145; CANR 33, 35; DLB
    63; DLBY 94; INT CANR-35; MTCW 1
Brooks, George
  See Baum, L(yman) Frank
Brooks, Gwendolyn 1917- **CLC 1, 2, 4, 5, 15,**
    49; BLC 1; DA; DAC; DAM MST, MULT,
    POET; PC 7; WLC
  See also AAYA 20; AITN 1; BW 2; CA 1-4R;
    CANR 1, 27, 52, 75; CDALB 1941-1968;
    CLR 27; DLB 5, 76, 165; MTCW 1; SATA 6
Brooks, Mel .... **CLC 12**
  See also Kaminsky, Melvin
  See also AAYA 13; DLB 26
Brooks, Peter 1938-........................... **CLC 34**
  See also CA 45-48; CANR 1
Brooks, Van Wyck 1886-1963 .... **CLC 29**
  See also CA 1-4R; CANR 6; DLB 45, 63, 103
Brophy, Brigid (Antonia) 1929-1995 . **CLC 6,**
    11, 29, 105
  See also CA 5-8R; 149; CAAS 4; CANR 25.
    53; DLB 14; MTCW 1
Brosman, Catharine Savage 1934- ..... **CLC 9**
  See also CA 61-64; CANR 21, 46
Brossard, Nicole 1943-...................... **CLC 115**
  See also CA 122; CAAS 16; DLB 53
Brother Antoninus
  See Everson, William (Oliver)
The Brothers Quay
  See Quay, Stephen; Quay, Timothy
Broughton, T(homas) Alan 1936- ..... **CLC 19**
  See also CA 45-48; CANR 2, 23, 48
Broumas, Olga 1949- .... **CLC 10, 73**
  See also CA 85-88; CANR 20, 69
Brown, Alan 1950- .... **CLC 99**
  See also CA 156
Brown, Charles Brockden 1771-1810 **N C L C**
    22, 74
  See also CDALB 1640-1865; DLB 37, 59, 73
Brown, Christy 1932-1981 .... **CLC 63**
  See also CA 105; 104; CANR 72; DLB 14
Brown, Claude 1937- **CLC 30; BLC 1; DAM**
    MULT
  See also AAYA 7; BW 1; CA 73-76
Brown, Dee (Alexander) 1908-.. **CLC 18, 47;**
    DAM POP
  See also CA 13-16R; CAAS 6; CANR 11, 45,
    60; DLBY 80; MTCW 1; SATA 5
Brown, George
  See Wertmueller, Lina
Brown, George Douglas 1869-1902 **TCLC 28**
  See also CA 162
Brown, George Mackay 1921-1996**CLC 5, 48,**
    100
  See also CA 21-24R; 151; CAAS 6; CANR 12,
    37, 67; DLB 14, 27, 139; MTCW 1; SATA
    35
Brown, (William) Larry 1951- .... **CLC 73**
  See also CA 130; 134; INT 133
Brown, Moses
  See Barrett, William (Christopher)
Brown, Rita Mae 1944-**CLC 18, 43, 79; DAM**
    NOV, POP
  See also CA 45-48; CANR 2, 11, 35, 62; INT
    CANR-11; MTCW 1
Brown, Roderick (Langmere) Haig-
  See Haig-Brown, Roderick (Langmere)
Brown, Rosellen 1939-...................... **CLC 32**
  See also CA 77-80; CAAS 10; CANR 14, 44
Brown, Sterling Allen 1901-1989 **CLC 1, 23,**
    59; BLC 1; DAM MULT, POET

See Leonard, Hugh
See also CA 102; INT 102
Byron, George Gordon (Noel) 1788-1824
**NCLC 2, 12; DA; DAB; DAC; DAM MST,
POET; PC 16; WLC**
See also CDBLB 1789-1832; DLB 96, 110
Byron, Robert 1905-1941 .... **TCLC 67**
See also CA 160; DLB 195
C. 3. 3.
See Wilde, Oscar
Caballero, Fernan 1796-1877 .... **NCLC 10**
Cabell, Branch
See Cabell, James Branch
Cabell, James Branch 1879-1958 .... **TCLC 6**
See also CA 105; 152; DLB 9, 78
Cable, George Washington 1844-1925 **T C L C
4; SSC 4**
See also CA 104; 155; DLB 12, 74; DLBD 13
Cabral de Melo Neto, Joao 1920- ... **CLC 76;
DAM MULT**
See also CA 151
Cabrera Infante, G(uillermo) 1929- ..**CLC 5,
25, 45; DAM MULT; HLC**
See also CA 85-88; CANR 29, 65; DLB 113;
HW; MTCW 1
Cade, Toni
See Bambara, Toni Cade
Cadmus and Harmonia
See Buchan, John
Caedmon fl. 658-680 .... **CMLC 7**
See also DLB 146
Caeiro, Alberto
See Pessoa, Fernando (Antonio Nogueira)
Cage, John (Milton, Jr.) 1912-1992 . **CLC 41**
See also CA 13-16R; 169; CANR 9; DLB 193;
INT CANR-9
Cahan, Abraham 1860-1951 .... **TCLC 71**
See also CA 108; 154; DLB 9, 25, 28
Cain, G.
See Cabrera Infante, G(uillermo)
Cain, Guillermo
See Cabrera Infante, G(uillermo)
Cain, James M(allahan) 1892-1977**CLC 3, 11,
28**
See also AITN 1; CA 17-20R; 73-76; CANR 8,
34, 61; MTCW 1
Caine, Mark
See Raphael, Frederic (Michael)
Calasso, Roberto 1941- .... **CLC 81**
See also CA 143
Calderon de la Barca, Pedro 1600-1681 . **L C
23; DC 3**
Caldwell, Erskine (Preston) 1903-1987**CLC 1,
8, 14, 50, 60; DAM NOV; SSC 19**
See also AITN 1; CA 1-4R; 121; CAAS 1;
CANR 2, 33; DLB 9, 86; MTCW 1
Caldwell, (Janet Miriam) Taylor (Holland)
1900-1985**CLC 2, 28, 39; DAM NOV, POP**
See also CA 5-8R; 116; CANR 5; DLBD 17
Calhoun, John Caldwell 1782-1850**NCLC 15**
See also DLB 3
Calisher, Hortense 1911-**CLC 2, 4, 8, 38; DAM
NOV; SSC 15**
See also CA 1-4R; CANR 1, 22, 67; DLB 2;
INT CANR-22; MTCW 1
Callaghan, Morley Edward 1903-1990**CLC 3,
14, 41, 65; DAC; DAM MST**
See also CA 9-12R; 132; CANR 33, 73; DLB
68; MTCW 1
Callimachus c. 305B.C.-c. 240B.C. **CMLC 18**
See also DLB 176
Calvin, John 1509-1564 .... **LC 37**
Calvino, Italo 1923-1985**CLC 5, 8, 11, 22, 33,**

39, 73; DAM NOV; SSC 3
See also CA 85-88; 116; CANR 23, 61; DLB
196; MTCW 1
Cameron, Carey 1952- .... **CLC 59**
See also CA 135
Cameron, Peter 1959- .... **CLC 44**
See also CA 125; CANR 50
Campana, Dino 1885-1932 .... **TCLC 20**
See also CA 117; DLB 114
Campanella, Tommaso 1568-1639 ...... **LC 32**
Campbell, John W(ood, Jr.) 1910-1971 **C L C
32**
See also CA 21-22; 29-32R; CANR 34; CAP 2;
DLB 8; MTCW 1
Campbell, Joseph 1904-1987 .... **CLC 69**
See also AAYA 3; BEST 89:2; CA 1-4R; 124;
CANR 3, 28, 61; MTCW 1
Campbell, Maria 1940- .... **CLC 85; DAC**
See also CA 102; CANR 54; NNAL
Campbell, (John) Ramsey 1946-**CLC 42; SSC
19**
See also CA 57-60; CANR 7; INT CANR-7
Campbell, (Ignatius) Roy (Dunnachie) 1901-
1957 .... **TCLC 5**
See also CA 104; 155; DLB 20
Campbell, Thomas 1777-1844 .... **NCLC 19**
See also DLB 93; 144
Campbell, Wilfred .... **TCLC 9**
See also Campbell, William
Campbell, William 1858(?)-1918
See Campbell, Wilfred
See also CA 106; DLB 92
Campion, Jane .... **CLC 95**
See also CA 138
Campos, Alvaro de
See Pessoa, Fernando (Antonio Nogueira)
Camus, Albert 1913-1960**CLC 1, 2, 4, 9, 11, 14,
32, 63, 69; DA; DAB; DAC; DAM DRAM,
MST, NOV; DC 2; SSC 9; WLC**
See also CA 89-92; DLB 72; MTCW 1
Canby, Vincent 1924- .... **CLC 13**
See also CA 81-84
Cancale
See Desnos, Robert
Canetti, Elias 1905-1994**CLC 3, 14, 25, 75, 86**
See also CA 21-24R; 146; CANR 23, 61; DLB
85; 124; MTCW 1
Canfield, Dorothea F.
See Fisher, Dorothy (Frances) Canfield
Canfield, Dorothea Frances
See Fisher, Dorothy (Frances) Canfield
Canfield, Dorothy
See Fisher, Dorothy (Frances) Canfield
Canin, Ethan 1960- .... **CLC 55**
See also CA 131; 135
Cannon, Curt
See Hunter, Evan
Cao, Lan 1961- .... **CLC 109**
See also CA 165
Cape, Judith
See Page, P(atricia) K(athleen)
Capek, Karel 1890-1938 ... **TCLC 6, 37; DA;
DAB; DAC; DAM DRAM, MST, NOV; DC
1; WLC**
See also CA 104; 140
Capote, Truman 1924-1984**CLC 1, 3, 8, 13, 19,
34, 38, 58; DA; DAB; DAC; DAM MST,
NOV, POP; SSC 2; WLC**
See also CA 5-8R; 113; CANR 18, 62; CDALB
1941-1968; DLB 2, 185; DLBY 80,84;
MTCW 1; SATA 91
Capra, Frank 1897-1991 .... **CLC 16**
See also CA 61-64; 135

Caputo, Philip 1941- .... **CLC 32**
See also CA 73-76; CANR 40
Caragiale, Ion Luca 1852-1912 ...... **TCLC 76**
See also CA 157
Card, Orson Scott 1951-**CLC 44, 47, 50; DAM
POP**
See also AAYA 11; CA 102; CANR 27, 47, 73;
INT CANR-27; MTCW 1; SATA 83
Cardenal, Ernesto 1925- ....**CLC 31; DAM
MULT, POET; HLC; PC 22**
See also CA 49-52; CANR 2, 32, 66; HW;
MTCW 1
Cardozo, Benjamin N(athan) 1870-1938
TCLC 65
See also CA 117; 164
Carducci, Giosue (Alessandro Giuseppe) 1835-
1907 .... **TCLC 32**
See also CA 163
Carew, Thomas 1595(?)-1640 .... **LC 13**
See also DLB 126
Carey, Ernestine Gilbreth 1908- .... **CLC 17**
See also CA 5-8R; CANR 71; SATA 2
Carey, Peter 1943- .... **CLC 40, 55, 96**
See also CA 123; 127; CANR 53, 76; INT 127;
MTCW 1; SATA 94
Carleton, William 1794-1869 .... **NCLC 3**
See also DLB 159
Carlisle, Henry (Coffin) 1926- .... **CLC 33**
See also CA 13-16R; CANR 15
Carlsen, Chris
See Holdstock, Robert P.
Carlson, Ron(ald F.) 1947- .... **CLC 54**
See also CA 105; CANR 27
Carlyle, Thomas 1795-1881 . **NCLC 70; DA;
DAB; DAC; DAM MST**
See also CDBLB 1789-1832; DLB 55; 144
Carman, (William) Bliss 1861-1929 **TCLC 7;
DAC**
See also CA 104; 152; DLB 92
Carnegie, Dale 1888-1955 .... **TCLC 53**
Carossa, Hans 1878-1956 .... **TCLC 48**
See also CA 170; DLB 66
Carpenter, Don(ald Richard) 1931-1995**C L C
41**
See also CA 45-48; 149; CANR 1, 71
Carpenter, Edward 1844-1929 .... **TCLC 88**
See also CA 163
Carpentier (y Valmont), Alejo 1904-1980**CLC
8, 11, 38, 110; DAM MULT; HLC**
See also CA 65-68; 97-100; CANR 11, 70; DLB
113; HW
Carr, Caleb 1955(?)- .... **CLC 86**
See also CA 147; CANR 73
Carr, Emily 1871-1945 .... **TCLC 32**
See also CA 159; DLB 68
Carr, John Dickson 1906-1977 .... **CLC 3**
See also Fairbairn, Roger
See also CA 49-52; 69-72; CANR 3, 33, 60;
MTCW 1
Carr, Philippa
See Hibbert, Eleanor Alice Burford
Carr, Virginia Spencer 1929- .... **CLC 34**
See also CA 61-64; DLB 111
Carrere, Emmanuel 1957- .... **CLC 89**
Carrier, Roch 1937-**CLC 13, 78; DAC; DAM
MST**
See also CA 130; CANR 61; DLB 53; SATA
105
Carroll, James P. 1943(?)- .... **CLC 38**
See also CA 81-84; CANR 73
Carroll, Jim 1951- .... **CLC 35**
See also AAYA 17; CA 45-48; CANR 42
Carroll, Lewis ...... **NCLC 2, 53; PC 18; WLC**

See also Grindel, Eugene
Elyot, Sir Thomas 1490(?)-1546 .... **LC 11**
Elytis, Odysseus 1911-1996 **CLC 15, 49, 100;**
DAM POET; PC 21
See also CA 102; 151; MTCW 1
Emecheta, (Florence Onye) Buchi 1944-**C L C**
14, 48; BLC 2; DAM MULT
See also BW 2; CA 81-84; CANR 27; DLB 117;
MTCW 1; SATA 66
Emerson, Mary Moody 1774-1863 **NCLC 66**
Emerson, Ralph Waldo 1803-1882 .**NCLC 1,**
38; DA; DAB; DAC; DAM MST, POET;
PC 18; WLC
See also CDALB 1640-1865; DLB 1, 59, 73
Eminescu, Mihail 1850-1889 .... **NCLC 33**
Empson, William 1906-1984**CLC 3, 8, 19, 33,**
34
See also CA 17-20R; 112; CANR 31, 61; DLB
20; MTCW 1
Enchi, Fumiko (Ueda) 1905-1986 .... **CLC 31**
See also CA 129; 121; DLB 182
Ende, Michael (Andreas Helmuth) 1929-1995
CLC 31
See also CA 118; 124; 149; CANR 36; CLR
14; DLB 75; MAICYA; SATA 61; SATA-
Brief 42; SATA-Obit 86
Endo, Shusaku 1923-1996 **CLC 7, 14, 19, 54,**
99; DAM NOV
See also CA 29-32R; 153; CANR 21, 54; DLB
182; MTCW 1
Engel, Marian 1933-1985 .... **CLC 36**
See also CA 25-28R; CANR 12; DLB 53; INT
CANR-12
Engelhardt, Frederick
See Hubbard, L(afayette) Ron(ald)
Enright, D(ennis) J(oseph) 1920-**CLC 4, 8, 31**
See also CA 1-4R; CANR 1, 42; DLB 27; SATA
25
Enzensberger, Hans Magnus 1929- . **CLC 43**
See also CA 116; 119
Ephron, Nora 1941- .... **CLC 17, 31**
See also AITN 2; CA 65-68; CANR 12, 39
Epicurus 341B.C.-270B.C. .... **CMLC 21**
See also DLB 176
Epsilon
See Betjeman, John
Epstein, Daniel Mark 1948- ..,.........**CLC 7**
See also CA 49-52; CANR 2, 53
Epstein, Jacob 1956- .... **CLC 19**
See also CA 114
Epstein, Joseph 1937- .... **CLC 39**
See also CA 112; 119; CANR 50, 65
Epstein, Leslie 1938- .... **CLC 27**
See also CA 73-76; CAAS 12; CANR 23, 69
Equiano, Olaudah 1745(?)-1797 **LC 16; BLC**
2; DAM MULT
See also DLB 37, 50
ER .... **TCLC 33**
See also CA 160; DLB 85
Erasmus, Desiderius 1469(?)-1536 ..... **LC 16**
Erdman, Paul E(mil) 1932- .... **CLC 25**
See also AITN 1; CA 61-64; CANR 13, 43
Erdrich, Louise 1954- ..... **CLC 39, 54; DAM**
MULT, NOV, POP
See also AAYA 10; BEST 89:1; CA 114; CANR
41, 62; DLB 152, 175, 206; MTCW 1;
NNAL; SATA 94
Erenburg, Ilya (Grigoryevich)
See Ehrenburg, Ilya (Grigoryevich)
Erickson, Stephen Michael 1950-
See Erickson, Steve
See also CA 129
Erickson, Steve 1950- .... **CLC 64**

See also Erickson. Stephen Michael
See also CANR 60. 68
Ericson, Walter
See Fast, Howard (Melvin)
Eriksson, Buntel
See Bergman, (Ernst) Ingmar
Ernaux, Annie 1940- .... **CLC 88**
See also CA 147
Erskine, John 1879-1951 .... **TCLC 84**
See also CA 112; 159; DLB 9, 102
Eschenbach, Wolfram von
See Wolfram von Eschenbach
Eseki, Bruno
See Mphahlele, Ezekiel
Esenin, Sergei (Alexandrovich) 1895-1925
TCLC 4
See also CA 104
Eshleman, Clayton 1935- .... **CLC 7**
See also CA 33-36R; CAAS 6; DLB 5
Espriella, Don Manuel Alvarez
See Southey, Robert
Espriu, Salvador 1913-1985 .... **CLC 9**
See also CA 154; 115; DLB 134
Espronceda, Jose de 1808-1842 ..... **NCLC 39**
Esse, James
See Stephens, James
Esterbrook, Tom
See Hubbard, L(afayette) Ron(ald)
Estleman, Loren D. 1952-**CLC 48; DAM NOV,**
POP
See also AAYA 27; CA 85-88; CANR 27, 74;
INT CANR-27; MTCW 1
Euclid 306B.C.-283B.C. .... **CMLC 25**
Eugenides, Jeffrey 1960(?)- .... **CLC 81**
See also CA 144
Euripides c. 485B.C.-406B.C.**CMLC 23; DA;**
DAB; DAC; DAM DRAM, MST; DC 4;
WLCS
See also DLB 176
Evan, Evin
See Faust, Frederick (Schiller)
Evans, Caradoc 1878-1945 .... **TCLC 85**
Evans, Evan
See Faust, Frederick (Schiller)
Evans, Marian
See Eliot, George
Evans, Mary Ann
See Eliot, George
Evarts, Esther
See Benson, Sally
Everett, Percival L. 1956- .... **CLC 57**
See also BW 2; CA 129
Everson, R(onald) G(ilmour) 1903-..**CLC 27**
See also CA 17-20R; DLB 88
Everson, William (Oliver) 1912-1994 **CLC 1,**
5, 14
See also CA 9-12R; 145; CANR 20; DLB 5,
16; MTCW 1
Evtushenko, Evgenii Aleksandrovich
See Yevtushenko, Yevgeny (Alexandrovich)
Ewart, Gavin (Buchanan) 1916-1995**CLC 13,**
46
See also CA 89-92; 150; CANR 17, 46; DLB
40; MTCW 1
Ewers, Hanns Heinz 1871-1943 ..... **TCLC 12**
See also CA 109; 149
Ewing, Frederick R.
See Sturgeon, Theodore (Hamilton)
Exley, Frederick (Earl) 1929-1992 **CLC 6, 11**
See also AITN 2; CA 81-84; 138; DLB 143;
DLBY 81
Eynhardt, Guillermo
See Quiroga, Horacio (Sylvestre)

Ezekiel, Nissim 1924- .... **CLC 61**
See also CA 61-64
Ezekiel, Tish O'Dowd 1943- .... **CLC 34**
See also CA 129
Fadeyev, A.
See Bulgya, Alexander Alexandrovich
Fadeyev, Alexander .... **TCLC 53**
See also Bulgya, Alexander Alexandrovich
Fagen, Donald 1948- .... **CLC 26**
Fainzilberg, Ilya Arnoldovich 1897-1937
See Ilf, Ilya
See also CA 120; 165
Fair, Ronald L. 1932- ....**CLC 18**
See also BW 1; CA 69-72; CANR 25; DLB 33
Fairbairn, Roger
See Carr, John Dickson
Fairbairns, Zoe (Ann) 1948- .... **CLC 32**
See also CA 103; CANR 21
Falco, Gian
See Papini, Giovanni
Falconer, James
See Kirkup, James
Falconer, Kenneth
See Kornbluth, C(yril) M.
Falkland, Samuel
See Heijermans, Herman
Fallaci, Oriana 1930- .... **CLC 11, 110**
See also CA 77-80; CANR 15, 58; MTCW 1
Faludy, George 1913- .... **CLC 42**
See also CA 21-24R
Faludy, Gyoergy
See Faludy, George
Fanon, Frantz 1925-1961 ... **CLC 74; BLC 2;**
DAM MULT
See also BW 1; CA 116; 89-92
Fanshawe, Ann 1625-1680 .... **LC 11**
Fante, John (Thomas) 1911-1983 ..... **CLC 60**
See also CA 69-72; 109; CANR 23; DLB 130;
DLBY 83
Farah, Nuruddin 1945-**CLC 53; BLC 2; DAM**
MULT
See also BW 2; CA 106; DLB 125
Fargue, Leon-Paul 1876(?)-1947 ... **TCLC 11**
See also CA 109
Farigoule, Louis
See Romains, Jules
Farina, Richard 1936(?)-1966 .... **CLC 9**
See also CA 81-84; 25-28R
Farley, Walter (Lorimer) 1915-1989 **CLC 17**
See also CA 17-20R; CANR 8, 29; DLB 22;
JRDA; MAICYA; SATA 2, 43
Farmer, Philip Jose 1918- .... **CLC 1, 19**
See also CA 1-4R; CANR 4, 35; DLB 8; MTCW
1; SATA 93
Farquhar, George 1677-1707 ...**LC 21; DAM**
DRAM
See also DLB 84
Farrell, J(ames) G(ordon) 1935-1979 **CLC 6**
See also CA 73-76; 89-92; CANR 36; DLB 14;
MTCW 1
Farrell, James T(homas) 1904-1979**CLC 1, 4,**
8, 11, 66; SSC 28
See also CA 5-8R; 89-92; CANR 9, 61; DLB 4,
9, 86; DLBD 2; MTCW 1
Farren, Richard J.
See Betjeman, John
Farren, Richard M.
See Betjeman, John
Fassbinder, Rainer Werner 1946-1982**CLC 20**
See also CA 93-96; 106; CANR 31
Fast, Howard (Melvin) 1914- **CLC 23; DAM**
NOV
See also AAYA 16; CA 1-4R; CAAS 18; CANR

CDALB 1917-1929; DLB 54; DLBD 7;MTCW 1; SATA 14

Froude, James Anthony 1818-1894 **NCLC 43**
See also DLB 18, 57, 144

Froy, Herald
See Waterhouse, Keith (Spencer)

Fry, Christopher 1907- **CLC 2, 10, 14; DAM DRAM**
See also CA 17-20R; CAAS 23; CANR 9, 30, 74; DLB 13; MTCW 1; SATA 66

Frye, (Herman) Northrop 1912-1991 **CLC 24, 70**
See also CA 5-8R; 133; CANR 8, 37; DLB 67, 68; MTCW 1

Fuchs, Daniel 1909-1993 .... **CLC 8, 22**
See also CA 81-84; 142; CAAS 5; CANR 40; DLB 9, 26, 28; DLBY 93

Fuchs, Daniel 1934- .... **CLC 34**
See also CA 37-40R; CANR 14, 48

Fuentes, Carlos 1928- **CLC 3, 8, 10, 13, 22, 41, 60, 113; DA; DAB; DAC; DAM MST, MULT, NOV; HLC; SSC 24; WLC**
See also AAYA 4; AITN 2; CA 69-72; CANR 10, 32, 68; DLB 113; HW; MTCW 1

Fuentes, Gregorio Lopez y
See Lopez y Fuentes, Gregorio

Fugard, (Harold) Athol 1932- **CLC 5, 9, 14, 25, 40, 80; DAM DRAM; DC 3**
See also AAYA 17; CA 85-88; CANR 32, 54; MTCW 1

Fugard, Sheila 1932- .... **CLC 48**
See also CA 125

Fuller, Charles (H., Jr.) 1939- **CLC 25; BLC 2; DAM DRAM, MULT; DC 1**
See also BW 2; CA 108; 112; DLB 38; INT 112; MTCW 1

Fuller, John (Leopold) 1937- .... **CLC 62**
See also CA 21-24R; CANR 9, 44; DLB 40

Fuller, Margaret .... **NCLC 5, 50**
See also Ossoli, Sarah Margaret (Fuller marchesa d')

Fuller, Roy (Broadbent) 1912-1991 **CLC 4, 28**
See also CA 5-8R; 135; CAAS 10; CANR 53; DLB 15, 20; SATA 87

Fulton, Alice 1952- .... **CLC 52**
See also CA 116; CANR 57; DLB 193

Furphy, Joseph 1843-1912 .... **TCLC 25**
See also CA 163

Fussell, Paul 1924- .... **CLC 74**
See also BEST 90:1; CA 17-20R; CANR 8, 21, 35, 69; INT CANR-21; MTCW 1

Futabatei, Shimei 1864-1909 .... **TCLC 44**
See also CA 162; DLB 180

Futrelle, Jacques 1875-1912 .... **TCLC 19**
See also CA 113; 155

Gaboriau, Emile 1835-1873 .... **NCLC 14**

Gadda, Carlo Emilio 1893-1973 .... **CLC 11**
See also CA 89-92; DLB 177

Gaddis, William 1922-1998 **CLC 1, 3, 6, 8, 10, 19, 43, 86**
See also CA 17-20R; 172; CANR 21, 48; DLB 2; MTCW 1

Gage, Walter
See Inge, William (Motter)

Gaines, Ernest J(ames) 1933- **CLC 3, 11, 18, 86; BLC 2; DAM MULT**
See also AAYA 18; AITN 1; BW 2; CA 9-12R; CANR 6, 24, 42, 75; CDALB 1968-1988; DLB 2, 33, 152; DLBY 80; MTCW 1; SATA 86

Gaitskill, Mary 1954- .... **CLC 69**
See also CA 128; CANR 61

Galdos, Benito Perez
See Perez Galdos, Benito

Gale, Zona 1874-1938 **TCLC 7; DAM DRAM**
See also CA 105; 153; DLB 9, 78

Galeano, Eduardo (Hughes) 1940- ... **CLC 72**
See also CA 29-32R; CANR 13, 32; HW

Galiano, Juan Valera y Alcala
See Valera y Alcala-Galiano, Juan

Galilei, Galileo 1546-1642 .... **LC 45**

Gallagher, Tess 1943- ...... **CLC 18, 63; DAM POET; PC 9**
See also CA 106; DLB 120

Gallant, Mavis 1922- ... **CLC 7, 18, 38; DAC; DAM MST; SSC 5**
See also CA 69-72; CANR 29, 69; DLB 53; MTCW 1

Gallant, Roy A(rthur) 1924- .... **CLC 17**
See also CA 5-8R; CANR 4, 29, 54; CLR 30; MAICYA; SATA 4, 68

Gallico, Paul (William) 1897-1976 ..... **CLC 2**
See also AITN 1; CA 5-8R; 69-72; CANR 23; DLB 9, 171; MAICYA; SATA 13

Gallo, Max Louis 1932- .... **CLC 95**
See also CA 85-88

Gallois, Lucien
See Desnos, Robert

Gallup, Ralph
See Whitemore, Hugh (John)

Galsworthy, John 1867-1933 **TCLC 1, 45; DA; DAB; DAC; DAM DRAM, MST, NOV; SSC 22; WLC**
See also CA 104; 141; CANR 75; CDBLB 1890-1914; DLB 10, 34, 98, 162; DLBD 16

Galt, John 1779-1839 .... **NCLC 1**
See also DLB 99, 116, 159

Galvin, James 1951- .... **CLC 38**
See also CA 108; CANR 26

Gamboa, Federico 1864-1939 .... **TCLC 36**
See also CA 167

Gandhi, M. K.
See Gandhi, Mohandas Karamchand

Gandhi, Mahatma
See Gandhi, Mohandas Karamchand

Gandhi, Mohandas Karamchand 1869-1948 **TCLC 59; DAM MULT**
See also CA 121; 132; MTCW 1

Gann, Ernest Kellogg 1910-1991 ...... **CLC 23**
See also AITN 1; CA 1-4R; 136; CANR 1

Garcia, Cristina 1958- .... **CLC 76**
See also CA 141; CANR 73

Garcia Lorca, Federico 1898-1936 **TCLC 1, 7, 49; DA; DAB; DAC; DAM DRAM, MST, MULT, POET; DC 2; HLC; PC 3; WLC**
See also CA 104; 131; DLB 108; HW; MTCW 1

Garcia Marquez, Gabriel (Jose) 1928- **CLC 2, 3, 8, 10, 15, 27, 47, 55, 68; DA; DAB; DAC; DAM MST, MULT, NOV, POP; HLC; SSC 8; WLC**
See also AAYA 3; BEST 89:1, 90:4; CA 33-36R; CANR 10, 28, 50, 75; DLB 113; HW; MTCW 1

Gard, Janice
See Latham, Jean Lee

Gard, Roger Martin du
See Martin du Gard, Roger

Gardam, Jane 1928- .... **CLC 43**
See also CA 49-52; CANR 2, 18, 33, 54; CLR 12; DLB 14, 161; MAICYA; MTCW 1; SAAS 9; SATA 39, 76; SATA-Brief 28

Gardner, Herb(ert) 1934- .... **CLC 44**
See also CA 149

Gardner, John (Champlin), Jr. 1933-1982 **CLC 2, 3, 5, 7, 8, 10, 18, 28, 34; DAM NOV, POP; SSC 7**
See also AITN 1; CA 65-68; 107; CANR 33, 73; DLB 2; DLBY 82; MTCW 1; SATA 40; SATA-Obit 31

Gardner, John (Edmund) 1926- **CLC 30; DAM POP**
See also CA 103; CANR 15, 69; MTCW 1

Gardner, Miriam
See Bradley, Marion Zimmer

Gardner, Noel
See Kuttner, Henry

Gardons, S. S.
See Snodgrass, W(illiam) D(e Witt)

Garfield, Leon 1921-1996 .... **CLC 12**
See also AAYA 8; CA 17-20R; 152; CANR 38, 41; CLR 21; DLB 161; JRDA; MAICYA; SATA 1, 32, 76; SATA-Obit 90

Garland, (Hannibal) Hamlin 1860-1940 **TCLC 3; SSC 18**
See also CA 104; DLB 12, 71, 78, 186

Garneau, (Hector de) Saint-Denys 1912-1943 **TCLC 13**
See also CA 111; DLB 88

Garner, Alan 1934- **CLC 17; DAB; DAM POP**
See also AAYA 18; CA 73-76; CANR 15, 64; CLR 20; DLB 161; MAICYA; MTCW 1; SATA 18, 69

Garner, Hugh 1913-1979 .... **CLC 13**
See also CA 69-72; CANR 31; DLB 68

Garnett, David 1892-1981 .... **CLC 3**
See also CA 5-8R; 103; CANR 17; DLB 34

Garos, Stephanie
See Katz, Steve

Garrett, George (Palmer) 1929- **CLC 3, 11, 51; SSC 30**
See also CA 1-4R; CAAS 5; CANR 1, 42, 67; DLB 2, 5, 130, 152; DLBY 83

Garrick, David 1717-1779 .... **LC 15; DAM DRAM**
See also DLB 84

Garrigue, Jean 1914-1972 .... **CLC 2, 8**
See also CA 5-8R; 37-40R; CANR 20

Garrison, Frederick
See Sinclair, Upton (Beall)

Garth, Will
See Hamilton, Edmond; Kuttner, Henry

Garvey, Marcus (Moziah, Jr.) 1887-1940 **TCLC 41; BLC 2; DAM MULT**
See also BW 1; CA 120; 124

Gary, Romain .... **CLC 25**
See also Kacew, Romain
See also DLB 83

Gascar, Pierre .... **CLC 11**
See also Fournier, Pierre

Gascoyne, David (Emery) 1916- ...... **CLC 45**
See also CA 65-68; CANR 10, 28, 54; DLB 20; MTCW 1

Gaskell, Elizabeth Cleghorn 1810-1865 **NCLC 70; DAB; DAM MST; SSC 25**
See also CDBLB 1832-1890; DLB 21, 144, 159

Gass, William H(oward) 1924- **CLC 1, 2, 8, 11, 15, 39; SSC 12**
See also CA 17-20R; CANR 30, 71; DLB 2; MTCW 1

Gasset, Jose Ortega y
See Ortega y Gasset, Jose

Gates, Henry Louis, Jr. 1950- **CLC 65; BLCS; DAM MULT**
See also BW 2; CA 109; CANR 25, 53, 75; DLB 67

Gautier, Theophile 1811-1872 .. **NCLC 1, 59; DAM POET; PC 18; SSC 20**
See also DLB 119

Gawsworth, John
See Bates, H(erbert) E(rnest)
Gay, Oliver
See Gogarty, Oliver St. John
Gaye, Marvin (Penze) 1939-1984 .... **CLC 26**
See also CA 112
Gebler, Carlo (Ernest) 1954- .... **CLC 39**
See also CA 119; 133
Gee, Maggie (Mary) 1948- .... **CLC 57**
See also CA 130; DLB 207
Gee, Maurice (Gough) 1931- .... **CLC 29**
See also CA 97-100; CANR 67; SATA 46, 101
Gelbart, Larry (Simon) 1923- .... **CLC 21, 61**
See also CA 73-76; CANR 45
Gelber, Jack 1932- .... **CLC 1, 6, 14, 79**
See also CA 1-4R; CANR 2; DLB 7
Gellhorn, Martha (Ellis) 1908-1998 **CLC 14, 60**
See also CA 77-80; 164; CANR 44; DLBY 82
Genet, Jean 1910-1986**CLC 1, 2, 5, 10, 14, 44, 46; DAM DRAM**
See also CA 13-16R; CANR 18; DLB 72; DLBY 86; MTCW 1
Gent, Peter 1942- .... **CLC 29**
See also AITN 1; CA 89-92; DLBY 82
Gentlewoman in New England, A
See Bradstreet, Anne
Gentlewoman in Those Parts, A
See Bradstreet, Anne
George, Jean Craighead 1919- .... **CLC 35**
See also AAYA 8; CA 5-8R; CANR 25; CLR 1; DLB 52; JRDA; MAICYA; SATA 2, 68
George, Stefan (Anton) 1868-1933**TCLC 2, 14**
See also CA 104
Georges, Georges Martin
See Simenon, Georges (Jacques Christian)
Gerhardi, William Alexander
See Gerhardie, William Alexander
Gerhardie, William Alexander 1895-1977 **CLC 5**
See also CA 25-28R; 73-76; CANR 18; DLB 36
Gerstler, Amy 1956- .... **CLC 70**
See also CA 146
Gertler, T. .... **CLC 34**
See also CA 116; 121; INT 121
Ghalib .... **NCLC 39**
See also Ghalib, Hsadullah Khan
Ghalib, Hsadullah Khan 1797-1869
See Ghalib
See also DAM POET
Ghelderode, Michel de 1898-1962**CLC 6, 11; DAM DRAM**
See also CA 85-88; CANR 40
Ghiselin, Brewster 1903- .... **CLC 23**
See also CA 13-16R; CAAS 10; CANR 13
Ghose, Aurabinda 1872-1950 .... **TCLC 63**
See also CA 163
Ghose, Zulfikar 1935- .... **CLC 42**
See also CA 65-68; CANR 67
Ghosh, Amitav 1956- .... **CLC 44**
See also CA 147
Giacosa, Giuseppe 1847-1906 .... **TCLC 7**
See also CA 104
Gibb, Lee
See Waterhouse, Keith (Spencer)
Gibbon, Lewis Grassic .... **TCLC 4**
See also Mitchell, James Leslie
Gibbons, Kaye 1960-**CLC 50, 88; DAM POP**
See also CA 151; CANR 75
Gibran, Kahlil 1883-1931 . **TCLC 1, 9; DAM POET, POP; PC 9**
See also CA 104; 150

Gibran, Khalil
See Gibran, Kahlil
Gibson, William 1914- .. **CLC 23; DA; DAB; DAC; DAM DRAM, MST**
See also CA 9-12R; CANR 9, 42, 75; DLB 7; SATA 66
Gibson, William (Ford) 1948- ... **CLC 39, 63; DAM POP**
See also AAYA 12; CA 126; 133; CANR 52
Gide, Andre (Paul Guillaume) 1869-1951 **TCLC 5, 12, 36; DA; DAB; DAC; DAM MST, NOV; SSC 13; WLC**
See also CA 104; 124; DLB 65; MTCW 1
Gifford, Barry (Colby) 1946- .... **CLC 34**
See also CA 65-68; CANR 9, 30, 40
Gilbert, Frank
See De Voto, Bernard (Augustine)
Gilbert, W(illiam) S(chwenck) 1836-1911 **TCLC 3; DAM DRAM, POET**
See also CA 104; SATA 36
Gilbreth, Frank B., Jr. 1911- .... **CLC 17**
See also CA 9-12R; SATA 2
Gilchrist, Ellen 1935-**CLC 34, 48; DAM POP; SSC 14**
See also CA 113; 116; CANR 41, 61; DLB 130; MTCW 1
Giles, Molly 1942- .... **CLC 39**
See also CA 126
Gill, Eric 1882-1940 .... **TCLC 85**
Gill, Patrick
See Creasey, John
Gilliam, Terry (Vance) 1940- .... **CLC 21**
See also Monty Python
See also AAYA 19; CA 108; 113; CANR 35; INT 113
Gillian, Jerry
See Gilliam, Terry (Vance)
Gilliatt, Penelope (Ann Douglass) 1932-1993 **CLC 2, 10, 13, 53**
See also AITN 2; CA 13-16R; 141; CANR 49; DLB 14
Gilman, Charlotte (Anna) Perkins (Stetson) 1860-1935 .... **TCLC 9, 37; SSC 13**
See also CA 106; 150
Gilmour, David 1949- .... **CLC 35**
See also CA 138, 147
Gilpin, William 1724-1804 .... **NCLC 30**
Gilray, J. D.
See Mencken, H(enry) L(ouis)
Gilroy, Frank D(aniel) 1925- .... **CLC 2**
See also CA 81-84; CANR 32, 64; DLB 7
Gilstrap, John 1957(?)- .... **CLC 99**
See also CA 160
Ginsberg, Allen 1926-1997**CLC 1, 2, 3, 4, 6, 13, 36, 69, 109; DA; DAB; DAC; DAM MST, POET; PC 4; WLC**
See also AITN 1; CA 1-4R; 157; CANR 2, 41, 63; CDALB 1941-1968; DLB 5, 16, 169; MTCW 1
Ginzburg, Natalia 1916-1991**CLC 5, 11, 54, 70**
See also CA 85-88; 135; CANR 33; DLB 177; MTCW 1
Giono, Jean 1895-1970 .... **CLC 4, 11**
See also CA 45-48; 29-32R; CANR 2, 35; DLB 72; MTCW 1
Giovanni, Nikki 1943- **CLC 2, 4, 19, 64, 117; BLC 2; DA; DAB; DAC; DAM MST, MULT, POET; PC 19; WLCS**
See also AAYA 22; AITN 1; BW 2; CA 29-32R; CAAS 6; CANR 18, 41, 60; CLR 6; DLB 5, 41; INT CANR-18; MAICYA; MTCW 1; SATA 24
Giovene, Andrea 1904- .... **CLC 7**

See also CA 85-88
Gippius, Zinaida (Nikolayevna) 1869-1945
See Hippius, Zinaida
See also CA 106
Giraudoux, (Hippolyte) Jean 1882-1944 **TCLC 2, 7; DAM DRAM**
See also CA 104; DLB 65
Gironella, Jose Maria 1917- .... **CLC 11**
See also CA 101
Gissing, George (Robert) 1857-1903**TCLC 3, 24, 47**
See also CA 105; 167; DLB 18, 135, 184
Giurlani, Aldo
See Palazzeschi, Aldo
Gladkov, Fyodor (Vasilyevich) 1883-1958 **TCLC 27**
See also CA 170
Glanville, Brian (Lester) 1931- .... **CLC 6**
See also CA 5-8R; CAAS 9; CANR 3, 70; DLB 15, 139; SATA 42
Glasgow, Ellen (Anderson Gholson) 1873-1945 **TCLC 2, 7**
See also CA 104; 164; DLB 9, 12
Glaspell, Susan 1882(?)-1948**TCLC 55; DC 10**
See also CA 110; 154; DLB 7, 9, 78; YABC 2
Glassco, John 1909-1981 .... **CLC 9**
See also CA 13-16R; 102; CANR 15; DLB 68
Glasscock, Amnesia
See Steinbeck, John (Ernst)
Glasser, Ronald J. 1940(?)- .... **CLC 37**
Glassman, Joyce
See Johnson, Joyce
Glendinning, Victoria 1937- .... **CLC 50**
See also CA 120; 127; CANR 59; DLB 155
Glissant, Edouard 1928- . **CLC 10, 68; DAM MULT**
See also CA 153
Gloag, Julian 1930- .... **CLC 40**
See also AITN 1; CA 65-68; CANR 10, 70
Glowacki, Aleksander
See Prus, Boleslaw
Gluck, Louise (Elisabeth) 1943-**CLC 7, 22, 44, 81; DAM POET; PC 16**
See also CA 33-36R; CANR 40, 69; DLB 5
Glyn, Elinor 1864-1943 .... **TCLC 72**
See also DLB 153
Gobineau, Joseph Arthur (Comte) de 1816-1882 .... **NCLC 17**
See also DLB 123
Godard, Jean-Luc 1930- .... **CLC 20**
See also CA 93-96
Godden, (Margaret) Rumer 1907-1998 **C L C 53**
See also AAYA 6; CA 5-8R; 172; CANR 4, 27, 36, 55; CLR 20; DLB 161; MAICYA; SAAS 12; SATA 3, 36
Godoy Alcayaga, Lucila 1889-1957
See Mistral, Gabriela
See also BW 2; CA 104; 131; DAM MULT; HW; MTCW 1
Godwin, Gail (Kathleen) 1937- **CLC 5, 8, 22, 31, 69; DAM POP**
See also CA 29-32R; CANR 15, 43, 69; DLB 6; INT CANR-15; MTCW 1
Godwin, William 1756-1836 .... **NCLC 14**
See also CDBLB 1789-1832; DLB 39, 104, 142, 158, 163
Goebbels, Josef
See Goebbels, (Paul) Joseph
Goebbels, (Paul) Joseph 1897-1945 **TCLC 68**
See also CA 115; 148
Goebbels, Joseph Paul
See Goebbels, (Paul) Joseph

Goethe, Johann Wolfgang von 1749-1832
   NCLC 4, 22, 34; DA; DAB; DAC; DAM
   DRAM, MST, POET; PC 5; WLC
  See also DLB 94

Gogarty, Oliver St. John 1878-1957 TCLC 15
  See also CA 109; 150; DLB 15, 19

Gogol, Nikolai (Vasilyevich) 1809-1852 NCLC
   5, 15, 31; DA; DAB; DAC; DAM DRAM,
   MST; DC 1; SSC 4, 29; WLC
  See also DLB 198

Goines, Donald 1937(?)-1974 CLC 80; BLC 2;
   DAM MULT, POP
  See also AITN 1; BW 1; CA 124; 114; DLB 33

Gold, Herbert 1924- .... CLC 4, 7, 14, 42
  See also CA 9-12R; CANR 17, 45; DLB 2;
   DLBY 81

Goldbarth, Albert 1948- .... CLC 5, 38
  See also CA 53-56; CANR 6, 40; DLB 120

Goldberg, Anatol 1910-1982 .... CLC 34
  See also CA 131; 117

Goldemberg, Isaac 1945- .... CLC 52
  See also CA 69-72; CAAS 12; CANR 11, 32;
   HW

Golding, William (Gerald) 1911-1993 CLC 1,
   2, 3, 8, 10, 17, 27, 58, 81; DA; DAB; DAC;
   DAM MST, NOV; WLC
  See also AAYA 5; CA 5-8R; 141; CANR 13,
   33, 54; CDBLB 1945-1960; DLB 15, 100;
   MTCW 1

Goldman, Emma 1869-1940 .... TCLC 13
  See also CA 110; 150

Goldman, Francisco 1954- .... CLC 76
  See also CA 162

Goldman, William (W.) 1931- ...... CLC 1, 48
  See also CA 9-12R; CANR 29, 69; DLB 44

Goldmann, Lucien 1913-1970 .... CLC 24
  See also CA 25-28; CAP 2

Goldoni, Carlo 1707-1793 LC 4; DAM DRAM

Goldsberry, Steven 1949- .... CLC 34
  See also CA 131

Goldsmith, Oliver 1728-1774 . LC 2, 48; DA;
   DAB; DAC; DAM DRAM, MST, NOV,
   POET; DC 8; WLC
  See also CDBLB 1660-1789; DLB 39, 89, 104,
   109, 142; SATA 26

Goldsmith, Peter
  See Priestley, J(ohn) B(oynton)

Gombrowicz, Witold 1904-1969 CLC 4, 7, 11,
   49; DAM DRAM
  See also CA 19-20; 25-28R; CAP 2

Gomez de la Serna, Ramon 1888-1963 CLC 9
  See also CA 153; 116; HW

Goncharov, Ivan Alexandrovich 1812-1891
   NCLC 1, 63

Goncourt, Edmond (Louis Antoine Huot) de
   1822-1896 .... NCLC 7
  See also DLB 123

Goncourt, Jules (Alfred Huot) de 1830-1870
   NCLC 7
  See also DLB 123

Gontier, Fernande 19(?)- .... CLC 50

Gonzalez Martinez, Enrique 1871-1952
   TCLC 72
  See also CA 166; HW

Goodman, Paul 1911-1972 ...... CLC 1, 2, 4, 7
  See also CA 19-20; 37-40R; CANR 34; CAP 2;
   DLB 130; MTCW 1

Gordimer, Nadine 1923- CLC 3, 5, 7, 10, 18, 33,
   51, 70; DA; DAB; DAC; DAM MST, NOV;
   SSC 17; WLCS
  See also CA 5-8R; CANR 3, 28, 56; INT CANR-
   28; MTCW 1

Gordon, Adam Lindsay 1833-1870 NCLC 21

Gordon, Caroline 1895-1981 CLC 6, 13, 29, 83;
   SSC 15
  See also CA 11-12; 103; CANR 36; CAP 1;
   DLB 4, 9, 102; DLBD 17; DLBY 81; MTCW
   1

Gordon, Charles William 1860-1937
  See Connor, Ralph
  See also CA 109

Gordon, Mary (Catherine) 1949- CLC 13, 22
  See also CA 102; CANR 44; DLB 6; DLBY
   81; INT 102; MTCW 1

Gordon, N. J.
  See Bosman, Herman Charles

Gordon, Sol 1923- .... CLC 26
  See also CA 53-56; CANR 4; SATA 11

Gordone, Charles 1925-1995 CLC 1, 4; DAM
   DRAM; DC 8
  See also BW 1; CA 93-96; 150; CANR 55; DLB
   7; INT 93-96; MTCW 1

Gore, Catherine 1800-1861 .... NCLC 65
  See also DLB 116

Gorenko, Anna Andreevna
  See Akhmatova, Anna

Gorky, Maxim 1868-1936 TCLC 8; DAB; SSC
   28; WLC
  See also Peshkov, Alexei Maximovich

Goryan, Sirak
  See Saroyan, William

Gosse, Edmund (William) 1849-1928 TCLC 28
  See also CA 117; DLB 57, 144, 184

Gotlieb, Phyllis Fay (Bloom) 1926- .. CLC 18
  See also CA 13-16R; CANR 7; DLB 88

Gottesman, S. D.
  See Kornbluth, C(yril) M.; Pohl, Frederik

Gottfried von Strassburg fl. c. 1210- . C M L C
   10
  See also DLB 138

Gould, Lois .... CLC 4, 10
  See also CA 77-80; CANR 29; MTCW 1

Gourmont, Remy (-Marie-Charles) de 1858-
   1915 .... TCLC 17
  See also CA 109; 150

Govier, Katherine 1948- .... CLC 51
  See also CA 101; CANR 18, 40

Goyen, (Charles) William 1915-1983 CLC 5, 8,
   14, 40
  See also AITN 2; CA 5-8R; 110; CANR 6, 71;
   DLB 2; DLBY 83; INT CANR-6

Goytisolo, Juan 1931- . CLC 5, 10, 23; DAM
   MULT; HLC
  See also CA 85-88; CANR 32, 61; HW; MTCW
   1

Gozzano, Guido 1883-1916 .... PC 10
  See also CA 154; DLB 114

Gozzi, (Conte) Carlo 1720-1806 .... NCLC 23

Grabbe, Christian Dietrich 1801-1836 N C L C
   2
  See also DLB 133

Grace, Patricia 1937- .... CLC 56

Gracian y Morales, Baltasar 1601-1658 LC 15

Gracq, Julien .... CLC 11, 48
  See also Poirier, Louis
  See also DLB 83

Grade, Chaim 1910-1982 .... CLC 10
  See also CA 93-96; 107

Graduate of Oxford, A
  See Ruskin, John

Grafton, Garth
  See Duncan, Sara Jeannette

Graham, John
  See Phillips, David Graham

Graham, Jorie 1951- .... CLC 48, 118
  See also CA 111; CANR 63; DLB 120

Graham, R(obert) B(ontine) Cunninghame
  See Cunninghame Graham, R(obert) B(ontine)
  See also DLB 98, 135, 174

Graham, Robert
  See Haldeman, Joe (William)

Graham, Tom
  See Lewis, (Harry) Sinclair

Graham, W(illiam) S(ydney) 1918-1986 C L C
   29
  See also CA 73-76; 118; DLB 20

Graham, Winston (Mawdsley) 1910- CLC 23
  See also CA 49-52; CANR 2, 22, 45, 66; DLB
   77

Grahame, Kenneth 1859-1932 TCLC 64; DAB
  See also CA 108; 136; CLR 5; DLB 34, 141,
   178; MAICYA; SATA 100; YABC 1

Granovsky, Timofei Nikolaevich 1813-1855
   NCLC 75
  See also DLB 198

Grant, Skeeter
  See Spiegelman, Art

Granville-Barker, Harley 1877-1946 TCLC 2;
   DAM DRAM
  See also Barker, Harley Granville
  See also CA 104

Grass, Guenter (Wilhelm) 1927- CLC 1, 2, 4, 6,
   11, 15, 22, 32, 49, 88; DA; DAB; DAC;
   DAM MST, NOV; WLC
  See also CA 13-16R; CANR 20, 75; DLB 75,
   124; MTCW 1

Gratton, Thomas
  See Hulme, T(homas) E(rnest)

Grau, Shirley Ann 1929- .. CLC 4, 9; SSC 15
  See also CA 89-92; CANR 22, 69; DLB 2; INT
   CANR-22; MTCW 1

Gravel, Fern
  See Hall, James Norman

Graver, Elizabeth 1964- .... CLC 70
  See also CA 135; CANR 71

Graves, Richard Perceval 1945- ...... CLC 44
  See also CA 65-68; CANR 9, 26, 51

Graves, Robert (von Ranke) 1895-1985 C L C
   1, 2, 6, 11, 39, 44, 45; DAB; DAC; DAM
   MST, POET; PC 6
  See also CA 5-8R; 117; CANR 5, 36; CDBLB
   1914-1945; DLB 20, 100, 191; DLBD 18;
   DLBY 85; MTCW 1; SATA 45

Graves, Valerie
  See Bradley, Marion Zimmer

Gray, Alasdair (James) 1934- .... CLC 41
  See also CA 126; CANR 47, 69; DLB 194; INT
   126; MTCW 1

Gray, Amlin 1946- .... CLC 29
  See also CA 138

Gray, Francine du Plessix 1930- ..... CLC 22;
   DAM NOV
  See also BEST 90:3; CA 61-64; CAAS 2;
   CANR 11, 33, 75; INT CANR-11; MTCW 1

Gray, John (Henry) 1866-1934 ...... TCLC 19
  See also CA 119; 162

Gray, Simon (James Holliday) 1936- CLC 9,
   14, 36
  See also AITN 1; CA 21-24R; CAAS 3; CANR
   32, 69; DLB 13; MTCW 1

Gray, Spalding 1941- CLC 49, 112; DAM POP;
   DC 7
  See also CA 128; CANR 74

Gray, Thomas 1716-1771 LC 4, 40; DA; DAB;
   DAC; DAM MST; PC 2; WLC
  See also CDBLB 1660-1789; DLB 109

Grayson, David
  See Baker, Ray Stannard

Grayson, Richard (A.) 1951- .... CLC 38

See also CA 85-88; CANR 14, 31, 57
Greeley, Andrew M(oran) 1928- ..... **CLC 28;
    DAM POP**
    See also CA 5-8R; CAAS 7; CANR 7, 43, 69;
    MTCW 1
Green, Anna Katharine 1846-1935 **TCLC 63**
    See also CA 112; 159; DLB 202
Green, Brian
    See Card, Orson Scott
Green, Hannah
    See Greenberg, Joanne (Goldenberg)
Green, Hannah 1927(?)-1996 .... **CLC 3**
    See also CA 73-76; CANR 59
Green, Henry 1905-1973 .... **CLC 2, 13, 97**
    See also Yorke, Henry Vincent
    See also DLB 15
Green, Julian (Hartridge) 1900-1998
    See Green, Julien
    See also CA 21-24R; 169; CANR 33; DLB 4,
    72; MTCW 1
Green, Julien .... **CLC 3, 11, 77**
    See also Green, Julian (Hartridge)
Green, Paul (Eliot) 1894-1981**CLC 25; DAM
    DRAM**
    See also AITN 1; CA 5-8R; 103; CANR 3; DLB
    7, 9; DLBY 81
Greenberg, Ivan 1908-1973
    See Rahv, Philip
    See also CA 85-88
Greenberg, Joanne (Goldenberg) 1932- **C L C
    7, 30**
    See also AAYA 12; CA 5-8R; CANR 14, 32,
    69; SATA 25
Greenberg, Richard 1959(?)- .... **CLC 57**
    See also CA 138
Greene, Bette 1934- .... **CLC 30**
    See also AAYA 7; CA 53-56; CANR 4; CLR 2;
    JRDA; MAICYA; SAAS 16; SATA 8, 102
Greene, Gael ....**CLC 8**
    See also CA 13-16R; CANR 10
Greene, Graham (Henry) 1904-1991**CLC 1, 3,
    6, 9, 14, 18, 27, 37, 70, 72; DA; DAB; DAC;
    DAM MST, NOV; SSC 29; WLC**
    See also AITN 2; CA 13-16R; 133; CANR 35,
    61; CDBLB 1945-1960; DLB 13, 15, 77,
    100, 162, 201, 204; DLBY 91; MTCW 1;
    SATA 20
Greene, Robert 1558-1592 .... **LC 41**
    See also DLB 62, 167
Greer, Richard
    See Silverberg, Robert
Gregor, Arthur 1923- .... **CLC 9**
    See also CA 25-28R; CAAS 10; CANR 11;
    SATA 36
Gregor, Lee
    See Pohl, Frederik
Gregory, Isabella Augusta (Persse) 1852-1932
    TCLC 1
    See also CA 104; DLB 10
Gregory, J. Dennis
    See Williams, John A(lfred)
Grendon, Stephen
    See Derleth, August (William)
Grenville, Kate 1950- .... **CLC 61**
    See also CA 118; CANR 53
Grenville, Pelham
    See Wodehouse, P(elham) G(renville)
Greve, Felix Paul (Berthold Friedrich) 1879-
    1948
    See Grove, Frederick Philip
    See also CA 104; 141; DAC; DAM MST
Grey, Zane 1872-1939 .. **TCLC 6; DAM POP**
    See also CA 104; 132; DLB 9; MTCW 1

Grieg, (Johan) Nordahl (Brun) 1902-1943
    TCLC 10
    See also CA 107
Grieve, C(hristopher) M(urray) 1892-1978
    CLC 11, 19; DAM POET
    See also MacDiarmid, Hugh; Pteleon
    See also CA 5-8R; 85-88; CANR 33; MTCW 1
Griffin, Gerald 1803-1840 .... **NCLC 7**
    See also DLB 159
Griffin, John Howard 1920-1980 ..... **CLC 68**
    See also AITN 1; CA 1-4R; 101; CANR 2
Griffin, Peter 1942- .... **CLC 39**
    See also CA 136
Griffith, D(avid Lewelyn) W(ark) 1875(?)-1948
    TCLC 68
    See also CA 119; 150
Griffith, Lawrence
    See Griffith, D(avid Lewelyn) W(ark)
Griffiths, Trevor 1935- .... **CLC 13, 52**
    See also CA 97-100; CANR 45; DLB 13
Griggs, Sutton Elbert 1872-1930(?)**TCLC 77**
    See also CA 123; DLB 50
Grigson, Geoffrey (Edward Harvey) 1905-1985
    CLC 7, 39
    See also CA 25-28R; 118; CANR 20, 33; DLB
    27; MTCW 1
Grillparzer, Franz 1791-1872 .... **NCLC 1**
    See also DLB 133
Grimble, Reverend Charles James
    See Eliot, T(homas) S(tearns)
Grimke, Charlotte L(ottie) Forten 1837(?)-1914
    See Forten, Charlotte L.
    See also BW 1; CA 117; 124; DAM MULT,
    POET
Grimm, Jacob Ludwig Karl 1785-1863**NCLC
    3**
    See also DLB 90; MAICYA; SATA 22
Grimm, Wilhelm Karl 1786-1859 .... **NCLC 3**
    See also DLB 90; MAICYA; SATA 22
Grimmelshausen, Johann Jakob Christoffel von
    1621-1676 .... **LC 6**
    See also DLB 168
Grindel, Eugene 1895-1952
    See Eluard, Paul
    See also CA 104
Grisham, John 1955- ..... **CLC 84; DAM POP**
    See also AAYA 14; CA 138; CANR 47, 69
Grossman, David 1954- .... **CLC 67**
    See also CA 138
Grossman, Vasily (Semenovich) 1905-1964
    CLC 41
    See also CA 124; 130; MTCW 1
Grove, Frederick Philip .... **TCLC 4**
    See also Greve, Felix Paul (Berthold Friedrich)
    See also DLB 92
Grubb
    See Crumb, R(obert)
Grumbach, Doris (Isaac) 1918-**CLC 13, 22, 64**
    See also CA 5-8R; CAAS 2; CANR 9, 42, 70;
    INT CANR-9
Grundtvig, Nicolai Frederik Severin 1783-1872
    NCLC 1
Grunge
    See Crumb, R(obert)
Grunwald, Lisa 1959- .... **CLC 44**
    See also CA 120
Guare, John 1938- . **CLC 8, 14, 29, 67; DAM
    DRAM**
    See also CA 73-76; CANR 21, 69; DLB 7;
    MTCW 1
Gudjonsson, Halldor Kiljan 1902-1998
    See Laxness, Halldor
    See also CA 103; 164

Guenter, Erich
    See Eich, Guenter
Guest, Barbara 1920- .... **CLC 34**
    See also CA 25-28R; CANR 11, 44; DLB 5,
    193
Guest, Judith (Ann) 1936- .**CLC 8, 30; DAM
    NOV, POP**
    See also AAYA 7; CA 77-80; CANR 15, 75;
    INT CANR-15; MTCW 1
Guevara, Che .... **CLC 87; HLC**
    See also Guevara (Serna), Ernesto
Guevara (Serna), Ernesto 1928-1967
    See Guevara, Che
    See also CA 127; 111; CANR 56; DAM MULT;
    HW
Guild, Nicholas M. 1944- .... **CLC 33**
    See also CA 93-96
Guillemin, Jacques
    See Sartre, Jean-Paul
Guillen, Jorge 1893-1984 .... **CLC 11; DAM
    MULT, POET**
    See also CA 89-92; 112; DLB 108; HW
Guillen, Nicolas (Cristobal) 1902-1989 .**C L C
    48, 79; BLC 2; DAM MST, MULT, POET;
    HLC; PC 23**
    See also BW 2; CA 116; 125; 129; HW
Guillevic, (Eugene) 1907- .... **CLC 33**
    See also CA 93-96
Guillois
    See Desnos, Robert
Guillois, Valentin
    See Desnos, Robert
Guiney, Louise Imogen 1861-1920 **TCLC 41**
    See also CA 160; DLB 54
Guiraldes, Ricardo (Guillermo) 1886-1927
    TCLC 39
    See also CA 131; HW; MTCW 1
Gumilev, Nikolai (Stepanovich) 1886-1921
    TCLC 60
    See also CA 165
Gunesekera, Romesh 1954- .... **CLC 91**
    See also CA 159
Gunn, Bill .... **CLC 5**
    See also Gunn, William Harrison
    See also DLB 38
Gunn, Thom(son William) 1929-**CLC 3, 6, 18,
    32, 81; DAM POET**
    See also CA 17-20R; CANR 9, 33; CDBLB
    1960 to Present; DLB 27; INT CANR-33;
    MTCW 1
Gunn, William Harrison 1934(?)-1989
    See Gunn, Bill
    See also AITN 1; BW 1; CA 13-16R; 128;
    CANR 12, 25, 76
Gunnars, Kristjana 1948- .... **CLC 69**
    See also CA 113; DLB 60
Gurdjieff, G(eorgei) I(vanovich) 1877(?)-1949
    TCLC 71
    See also CA 157
Gurganus, Allan 1947- .. **CLC 70; DAM POP**
    See also BEST 90:1; CA 135
Gurney, A(lbert) R(amsdell), Jr. 1930- .**C L C
    32, 50, 54; DAM DRAM**
    See also CA 77-80; CANR 32, 64
Gurney, Ivor (Bertie) 1890-1937 ... **TCLC 33**
    See also CA 167
Gurney, Peter
    See Gurney, A(lbert) R(amsdell), Jr.
Guro, Elena 1877-1913 .... **TCLC 56**
Gustafson, James M(oody) 1925- .. **CLC 100**
    See also CA 25-28R; CANR 37
Gustafson, Ralph (Barker) 1909- ..... **CLC 36**
    See also CA 21-24R; CANR 8, 45; DLB 88

Helvetius, Claude-Adrien 1715-1771 . **LC 26**
Helyar, Jane Penelope Josephine 1933-
See Poole, Josephine
See also CA 21-24R; CANR 10, 26; SATA 82
Hemans, Felicia 1793-1835 .... **NCLC 71**
See also DLB 96
Hemingway, Ernest (Miller) 1899-1961 **C L C 1, 3, 6, 8, 10, 13, 19, 30, 34, 39, 41, 44, 50, 61, 80; DA; DAB; DAC; DAM MST, NOV; SSC 1, 25; WLC**
See also AAYA 19; CA 77-80; CANR 34; CDALB 1917-1929; DLB 4, 9, 102; DLBD 1, 15, 16; DLBY 81, 87, 96; MTCW 1
Hempel, Amy 1951- .... **CLC 39**
See also CA 118; 137; CANR 70
Henderson, F. C.
See Mencken, H(enry) L(ouis)
Henderson, Sylvia
See Ashton-Warner, Sylvia (Constance)
Henderson, Zenna (Chlarson) 1917-1983 **S S C 29**
See also CA 1-4R; 133; CANR 1; DLB 8; SATA 5
Henley, Beth .... **CLC 23; DC 6**
See also Henley, Elizabeth Becker
See also CABS 3; DLBY 86
Henley, Elizabeth Becker 1952-
See Henley, Beth
See also CA 107; CANR 32, 73; DAM DRAM, MST; MTCW 1
Henley, William Ernest 1849-1903 .. **TCLC 8**
See also CA 105; DLB 19
Hennissart, Martha
See Lathen, Emma
See also CA 85-88; CANR 64
Henry, O. .... **TCLC 1, 19; SSC 5; WLC**
See also Porter, William Sydney
Henry, Patrick 1736-1799 .... **LC 25**
Henryson, Robert 1430(?)-1506(?) ..... **LC 20**
See also DLB 146
Henry VIII 1491-1547 .... **LC 10**
See also DLB 132
Henschke, Alfred
See Klabund
Hentoff, Nat(han Irving) 1925- .... **CLC 26**
See also AAYA 4; CA 1-4R; CAAS 6; CANR 5, 25; CLR 1, 52; INT CANR-25; JRDA; MAICYA; SATA 42, 69; SATA-Brief 27
Heppenstall, (John) Rayner 1911-1981 . **C L C 10**
See also CA 1-4R; 103; CANR 29
Heraclitus c. 540B.C.-c. 450B.C. ... **CMLC 22**
See also DLB 176
Herbert, Frank (Patrick) 1920-1986 **CLC 12, 23, 35, 44, 85; DAM POP**
See also AAYA 21; CA 53-56; 118; CANR 5, 43; DLB 8; INT CANR-5; MTCW 1; SATA 9, 37; SATA-Obit 47
Herbert, George 1593-1633 ..... **LC 24; DAB; DAM POET; PC 4**
See also CDBLB Before 1660; DLB 126
Herbert, Zbigniew 1924-1998 ..... **CLC 9, 43; DAM POET**
See also CA 89-92; 169; CANR 36, 74; MTCW 1
Herbst, Josephine (Frey) 1897-1969 **CLC 34**
See also CA 5-8R; 25-28R; DLB 9
Hergesheimer, Joseph 1880-1954 ... **TCLC 11**
See also CA 109; DLB 102, 9
Herlihy, James Leo 1927-1993 .... **CLC 6**
See also CA 1-4R; 143; CANR 2
Hermogenes fl. c. 175- .... **CMLC 6**
Hernandez, Jose 1834-1886 .... **NCLC 17**

Herodotus c. 484B.C.-429B.C. ...... **CMLC 17**
See also DLB 176
Herrick, Robert 1591-1674 **LC 13; DA; DAB; DAC; DAM MST, POP; PC 9**
See also DLB 126
Herring, Guilles
See Somerville, Edith
Herriot, James 1916-1995 **CLC 12; DAM POP**
See also Wight, James Alfred
See also AAYA 1; CA 148; CANR 40; SATA 86
Herrmann, Dorothy 1941- .... **CLC 44**
See also CA 107
Herrmann, Taffy
See Herrmann, Dorothy
Hersey, John (Richard) 1914-1993 **CLC 1, 2, 7, 9, 40, 81, 97; DAM POP**
See also CA 17-20R; 140; CANR 33; DLB 6, 185; MTCW 1; SATA 25; SATA-Obit 76
Herzen, Aleksandr Ivanovich 1812-1870 **NCLC 10, 61**
Herzl, Theodor 1860-1904 .... **TCLC 36**
See also CA 168
Herzog, Werner 1942- .... **CLC 16**
See also CA 89-92
Hesiod c. 8th cent. B.C.- .... **CMLC 5**
See also DLB 176
Hesse, Hermann 1877-1962 **CLC 1, 2, 3, 6, 11, 17, 25, 69; DA; DAB; DAC; DAM MST, NOV; SSC 9; WLC**
See also CA 17-18; CAP 2; DLB 66; MTCW 1; SATA 50
Hewes, Cady
See De Voto, Bernard (Augustine)
Heyen, William 1940- .... **CLC 13, 18**
See also CA 33-36R; CAAS 9; DLB 5
Heyerdahl, Thor 1914- .... **CLC 26**
See also CA 5-8R; CANR 5, 22, 66, 73; MTCW 1; SATA 2, 52
Heym, Georg (Theodor Franz Arthur) 1887-1912 .... **TCLC 9**
See also CA 106
Heym, Stefan 1913- .... **CLC 41**
See also CA 9-12R; CANR 4; DLB 69
Heyse, Paul (Johann Ludwig von) 1830-1914 **TCLC 8**
See also CA 104; DLB 129
Heyward, (Edwin) DuBose 1885-1940 **T C L C 59**
See also CA 108; 157; DLB 7, 9, 45; SATA 21
Hibbert, Eleanor Alice Burford 1906-1993 **CLC 7; DAM POP**
See also BEST 90:4; CA 17-20R; 140; CANR 9, 28, 59; SATA 2; SATA-Obit 74
Hichens, Robert (Smythe) 1864-1950 . **T C L C 64**
See also CA 162; DLB 153
Higgins, George V(incent) 1939- **CLC 4, 7, 10, 18**
See also CA 77-80; CAAS 5; CANR 17, 51; DLB 2; DLBY 81; INT CANR-17; MTCW 1
Higginson, Thomas Wentworth 1823-1911 **TCLC 36**
See also CA 162; DLB 1, 64
Highet, Helen
See MacInnes, Helen (Clark)
Highsmith, (Mary) Patricia 1921-1995 **CLC 2, 4, 14, 42, 102; DAM NOV, POP**
See also CA 1-4R; 147; CANR 1, 20, 48, 62; MTCW 1
Highwater, Jamake (Mamake) 1942(?)- **C L C 12**

See also AAYA 7; CA 65-68; CAAS 7; CANR 10, 34; CLR 17; DLB 52; DLBY 85; JRDA; MAICYA; SATA 32, 69; SATA-Brief 30
Highway, Tomson 1951- **CLC 92; DAC; DAM MULT**
See also CA 151; CANR 75; NNAL
Higuchi, Ichiyo 1872-1896 .... **NCLC 49**
Hijuelos, Oscar 1951- **CLC 65; DAM MULT, POP; HLC**
See also AAYA 25; BEST 90:1; CA 123; CANR 50, 75; DLB 145; HW
Hikmet, Nazim 1902(?)-1963 .... **CLC 40**
See also CA 141; 93-96
Hildegard von Bingen 1098-1179 . **CMLC 20**
See also DLB 148
Hildesheimer, Wolfgang 1916-1991 . **CLC 49**
See also CA 101; 135; DLB 69, 124
Hill, Geoffrey (William) 1932- **CLC 5, 8, 18, 45; DAM POET**
See also CA 81-84; CANR 21; CDBLB 1960 to Present; DLB 40; MTCW 1
Hill, George Roy 1921- .... **CLC 26**
See also CA 110; 122
Hill, John
See Koontz, Dean R(ay)
Hill, Susan (Elizabeth) 1942- ... **CLC 4, 113; DAB; DAM MST, NOV**
See also CA 33-36R; CANR 29, 69; DLB 14, 139; MTCW 1
Hillerman, Tony 1925- .. **CLC 62; DAM POP**
See also AAYA 6; BEST 89:1; CA 29-32R; CANR 21, 42, 65; DLB 206; SATA 6
Hillesum, Etty 1914-1943 .... **TCLC 49**
See also CA 137
Hilliard, Noel (Harvey) 1929- .... **CLC 15**
See also CA 9-12R; CANR 7, 69
Hillis, Rick 1956- .... **CLC 66**
See also CA 134
Hilton, James 1900-1954 .... **TCLC 21**
See also CA 108; 169; DLB 34, 77; SATA 34
Himes, Chester (Bomar) 1909-1984 **CLC 2, 4, 7, 18, 58, 108; BLC 2; DAM MULT**
See also BW 2; CA 25-28R; 114; CANR 22; DLB 2, 76, 143; MTCW 1
Hinde, Thomas .... **CLC 6, 11**
See also Chitty, Thomas Willes
Hindin, Nathan
See Bloch, Robert (Albert)
Hine, (William) Daryl 1936- .... **CLC 15**
See also CA 1-4R; CAAS 15; CANR 1, 20; DLB 60
Hinkson, Katharine Tynan
See Tynan, Katharine
Hinton, S(usan) E(loise) 1950- **CLC 30, 111; DA; DAB; DAC; DAM MST, NOV**
See also AAYA 2; CA 81-84; CANR 32, 62; CLR 3, 23; JRDA; MAICYA; MTCW 1; SATA 19, 58
Hippius, Zinaida .... **TCLC 9**
See also Gippius, Zinaida (Nikolayevna)
Hiraoka, Kimitake 1925-1970
See Mishima, Yukio
See also CA 97-100; 29-32R; DAM DRAM; MTCW 1
Hirsch, E(ric) D(onald), Jr. 1928- .... **CLC 79**
See also CA 25-28R; CANR 27, 51; DLB 67; INT CANR-27; MTCW 1
Hirsch, Edward 1950- .... **CLC 31, 50**
See also CA 104; CANR 20, 42; DLB 120
Hitchcock, Alfred (Joseph) 1899-1980 **CLC 16**
See also AAYA 22; CA 159; 97-100; SATA 27; SATA-Obit 24
Hitler, Adolf 1889-1945 .... **TCLC 53**

See also CA 117; 147

Hoagland, Edward 1932- .... **CLC 28**
See also CA 1-4R; CANR 2, 31, 57; DLB 6;
SATA 51

Hoban, Russell (Conwell) 1925- . **CLC 7, 25;
DAM NOV**
See also CA 5-8R; CANR 23, 37, 66; CLR 3;
DLB 52; MAICYA; MTCW 1; SATA 1, 40,
78

Hobbes, Thomas 1588-1679 .... **LC 36**
See also DLB 151

Hobbs, Perry
See Blackmur, R(ichard) P(almer)

Hobson, Laura Z(ametkin) 1900-1986**CLC 7,
25**
See also CA 17-20R; 118; CANR 55; DLB 28;
SATA 52

Hochhuth, Rolf 1931- ...**CLC 4, 11, 18; DAM
DRAM**
See also CA 5-8R; CANR 33, 75; DLB 124;
MTCW 1

Hochman, Sandra 1936- .... **CLC 3, 8**
See also CA 5-8R; DLB 5

Hochwaelder, Fritz 1911-1986**CLC 36; DAM
DRAM**
See also CA 29-32R; 120; CANR 42; MTCW 1

Hochwalder, Fritz
See Hochwaelder, Fritz

Hocking, Mary (Eunice) 1921- .... **CLC 13**
See also CA 101; CANR 18, 40

Hodgins, Jack 1938- .... **CLC 23**
See also CA 93-96; DLB 60

Hodgson, William Hope 1877(?)-1918 **T C L C
13**
See also CA 111; 164; DLB 70, 153, 156, 178

Hoeg, Peter 1957- .... **CLC 95**
See also CA 151; CANR 75

Hoffman, Alice 1952- ... **CLC 51; DAM NOV**
See also CA 77-80; CANR 34, 66; MTCW 1

Hoffman, Daniel (Gerard) 1923-**CLC 6, 13, 23**
See also CA 1-4R; CANR 4; DLB 5

Hoffman, Stanley 1944- .... **CLC 5**
See also CA 77-80

Hoffman, William M(oses) 1939- ..... **CLC 40**
See also CA 57-60; CANR 11, 71

Hoffmann, E(rnst) T(heodor) A(madeus) 1776-
1822 .... **NCLC 2; SSC 13**
See also DLB 90; SATA 27

Hofmann, Gert 1931- .... **CLC 54**
See also CA 128

Hofmannsthal, Hugo von 1874-1929**TCLC 11;
DAM DRAM; DC 4**
See also CA 106; 153; DLB 81, 118

Hogan, Linda 1947- ... **CLC 73; DAM MULT**
See also CA 120; CANR 45, 73; DLB 175;
NNAL

Hogarth, Charles
See Creasey, John

Hogarth, Emmett
See Polonsky, Abraham (Lincoln)

Hogg, James 1770-1835 .... **NCLC 4**
See also DLB 93, 116, 159

Holbach, Paul Henri Thiry Baron 1723-1789
LC 14

Holberg, Ludvig 1684-1754 .... **LC 6**

Holden, Ursula 1921- .... **CLC 18**
See also CA 101; CAAS 8; CANR 22

Holderlin, (Johann Christian) Friedrich 1770-
1843 .... **NCLC 16; PC 4**

Holdstock, Robert
See Holdstock, Robert P.

Holdstock, Robert P. 1948- .... **CLC 39**
See also CA 131

Holland, Isabelle 1920- .... **CLC 21**
See also AAYA 11; CA 21-24R; CANR 10, 25,
47; JRDA; MAICYA; SATA 8, 70; SATA-
Essay 103

Holland, Marcus
See Caldwell, (Janet Miriam) Taylor (Holland)

Hollander, John 1929- .... **CLC 2, 5, 8, 14**
See also CA 1-4R; CANR 1, 52; DLB 5; SATA
13

Hollander, Paul
See Silverberg, Robert

Holleran, Andrew 1943(?)- .... **CLC 38**
See also CA 144

Hollinghurst, Alan 1954- .... **CLC 55, 91**
See also CA 114; DLB 207

Hollis, Jim
See Summers, Hollis (Spurgeon, Jr.)

Holly, Buddy 1936-1959 .... **TCLC 65**

Holmes, Gordon
See Shiel, M(atthew) P(hipps)

Holmes, John
See Souster, (Holmes) Raymond

Holmes, John Clellon 1926-1988 ...... **CLC 56**
See also CA 9-12R; 125; CANR 4; DLB 16

Holmes, Oliver Wendell, Jr. 1841-1935**T C L C
77**
See also CA 114

Holmes, Oliver Wendell 1809-1894 **NCLC 14**
See also CDALB 1640-1865; DLB 1, 189;
SATA 34

Holmes, Raymond
See Souster, (Holmes) Raymond

Holt, Victoria
See Hibbert, Eleanor Alice Burford

Holub, Miroslav 1923-1998 .... **CLC 4**
See also CA 21-24R; 169; CANR 10

Homer c. 8th cent. B.C.- ... **CMLC 1, 16; DA;
DAB; DAC; DAM MST, POET; PC 23;
WLCS**
See also DLB 176

Hongo, Garrett Kaoru 1951- .... **PC 23**
See also CA 133; CAAS 22; DLB 120

Honig, Edwin 1919- .... **CLC 33**
See also CA 5-8R; CAAS 8; CANR 4, 45; DLB
5

Hood, Hugh (John Blagdon) 1928-**CLC 15, 28**
See also CA 49-52; CAAS 17; CANR 1, 33;
DLB 53

Hood, Thomas 1799-1845 .... **NCLC 16**
See also DLB 96

Hooker, (Peter) Jeremy 1941- .... **CLC 43**
See also CA 77-80; CANR 22; DLB 40

hooks, bell ....**CLC 94; BLCS**
See also Watkins, Gloria

Hope, A(lec) D(erwent) 1907- ...... **CLC 3, 51**
See also CA 21-24R; CANR 33, 74; MTCW 1

Hope, Anthony 1863-1933 .... **TCLC 83**
See also CA 157; DLB 153, 156

Hope, Brian
See Creasey, John

Hope, Christopher (David Tully) 1944- **C L C
52**
See also CA 106; CANR 47; SATA 62

Hopkins, Gerard Manley 1844-1889 .. **N C L C
17; DA; DAB; DAC; DAM MST, POET;
PC 15; WLC**
See also CDBLB 1890-1914; DLB 35, 57

Hopkins, John (Richard) 1931-1998 .. **CLC 4**
See also CA 85-88; 169

Hopkins, Pauline Elizabeth 1859-1930**T C L C
28; BLC 2; DAM MULT**
See also BW 2; CA 141; DLB 50

Hopkinson, Francis 1737-1791 .... **LC 25**

See also DLB 31

Hopley-Woolrich, Cornell George 1903-1968
See Woolrich, Cornell
See also CA 13-14; CANR 58; CAP 1

Horatio
See Proust, (Valentin-Louis-George-Eugene-)
Marcel

Horgan, Paul (George Vincent O'Shaughnessy)
1903-1995 .... **CLC 9, 53; DAM NOV**
See also CA 13-16R; 147; CANR 9, 35; DLB
102; DLBY 85; INT CANR-9; MTCW 1;
SATA 13; SATA-Obit 84

Horn, Peter
See Kuttner, Henry

Hornem, Horace Esq.
See Byron, George Gordon (Noel)

**Horney, Karen (Clementine Theodore
Danielsen)** 1885-1952 .... **TCLC 71**
See also CA 114; 165

Hornung, E(rnest) W(illiam) 1866-1921
TCLC 59
See also CA 108; 160; DLB 70

Horovitz, Israel (Arthur) 1939-**CLC 56; DAM
DRAM**
See also CA 33-36R; CANR 46, 59; DLB 7

Horvath, Odon von
See Horvath, Oedoen von
See also DLB 85, 124

Horvath, Oedoen von 1901-1938 ... **TCLC 45**
See also Horvath, Odon von
See also CA 118

Horwitz, Julius 1920-1986 .... **CLC 14**
See also CA 9-12R; 119; CANR 12

Hospital, Janette Turner 1942- .... **CLC 42**
See also CA 108; CANR 48

Hostos, E. M. de
See Hostos (y Bonilla), Eugenio Maria de

Hostos, Eugenio M. de
See Hostos (y Bonilla), Eugenio Maria de

Hostos, Eugenio Maria
See Hostos (y Bonilla), Eugenio Maria de

Hostos (y Bonilla), Eugenio Maria de 1839-
1903 .... **TCLC 24**
See also CA 123; 131; HW

Houdini
See Lovecraft, H(oward) P(hillips)

Hougan, Carolyn 1943- .... **CLC 34**
See also CA 139

Household, Geoffrey (Edward West) 1900-1988
CLC 11
See also CA 77-80; 126; CANR 58; DLB 87;
SATA 14; SATA-Obit 59

Housman, A(lfred) E(dward) 1859-1936
**TCLC 1, 10; DA; DAB; DAC; DAM MST,
POET; PC 2; WLCS**
See also CA 104; 125; DLB 19; MTCW 1

Housman, Laurence 1865-1959 .... **TCLC 7**
See also CA 106; 155; DLB 10; SATA 25

Howard, Elizabeth Jane 1923- ..... **CLC 7, 29**
See also CA 5-8R; CANR 8, 62

Howard, Maureen 1930- .... **CLC 5, 14, 46**
See also CA 53-56; CANR 31, 75; DLBY 83;
INT CANR-31; MTCW 1

Howard, Richard 1929- .... **CLC 7, 10, 47**
See also AITN 1; CA 85-88; CANR 25; DLB 5;
INT CANR-25

Howard, Robert E(rvin) 1906-1936 **TCLC 8**
See also CA 105; 157

Howard, Warren F.
See Pohl, Frederik

Howe, Fanny (Quincy) 1940- .... **CLC 47**
See also CA 117; CAAS 27; CANR 70; SATA-
Brief 52

Howe, Irving 1920-1993 .... **CLC 85**
See also CA 9-12R; 141; CANR 21, 50; DLB
67; MTCW 1

Howe, Julia Ward 1819-1910 .... **TCLC 21**
See also CA 117; DLB 1, 189

Howe, Susan 1937- .... **CLC 72**
See also CA 160; DLB 120

Howe, Tina 1937- .... **CLC 48**
See also CA 109

Howell, James 1594(?)-1666 .... **LC 13**
See also DLB 151

Howells, W. D.
See Howells, William Dean

Howells, William D.
See Howells, William Dean

Howells, William Dean 1837-1920TCLC 7, 17,
41
See also CA 104; 134; CDALB 1865-1917;
DLB 12, 64, 74, 79, 189

Howes, Barbara 1914-1996 .... **CLC 15**
See also CA 9-12R; 151; CAAS 3; CANR 53;
SATA 5

Hrabal, Bohumil 1914-1997 .... **CLC 13, 67**
See also CA 106; 156; CAAS 12; CANR 57

Hroswitha of Gandersheim c. 935-c. 1002
CMLC 29
See also DLB 148

Hsun, Lu
See Lu Hsun

Hubbard, L(afayette) Ron(ald) 1911-1986
CLC 43; DAM POP
See also CA 77-80; 118; CANR 52

Huch, Ricarda (Octavia) 1864-1947TCLC 13
See also CA 111; DLB 66

Huddle, David 1942- .... **CLC 49**
See also CA 57-60; CAAS 20; DLB 130

Hudson, Jeffrey
See Crichton, (John) Michael

Hudson, W(illiam) H(enry) 1841-1922TCLC
29
See also CA 115; DLB 98, 153, 174; SATA 35

Hueffer, Ford Madox
See Ford, Ford Madox

Hughart, Barry 1934- .... **CLC 39**
See also CA 137

Hughes, Colin
See Creasey, John

Hughes, David (John) 1930- .... **CLC 48**
See also CA 116; 129; DLB 14

Hughes, Edward James
See Hughes, Ted
See also DAM MST, POET

Hughes, (James) Langston 1902-1967CLC 1,
5, 10, 15, 35, 44, 108; BLC 2; DA; DAB;
DAC; DAM DRAM, MST, MULT, POET;
DC 3; PC 1; SSC 6; WLC
See also AAYA 12; BW 1; CA 1-4R; 25-28R;
CANR 1, 34; CDALB 1929-1941; CLR 17;
DLB 4, 7, 48, 51, 86; JRDA; MAICYA;
MTCW 1; SATA 4, 33

Hughes, Richard (Arthur Warren) 1900-1976
CLC 1, 11; DAM NOV
See also CA 5-8R; 65-68; CANR 4; DLB 15,
161; MTCW 1; SATA 8; SATA-Obit 25

Hughes, Ted 1930-1998 ..CLC 2, 4, 9, 14, 37;
DAB; DAC; PC 7
See also Hughes, Edward James
See also CA 1-4R; 171; CANR 1, 33, 66; CLR
3; DLB 40, 161; MAICYA; MTCW 1; SATA
49; SATA-Brief 27

Hugo, Richard F(ranklin) 1923-1982 **CLC 6,
18, 32; DAM POET**
See also CA 49-52; 108; CANR 3; DLB 5, 206

Hugo, Victor (Marie) 1802-1885NCLC 3, 10,
21; DA; DAB; DAC; DAM DRAM, MST,
NOV, POET; PC 17; WLC
See also DLB 119, 192; SATA 47

Huidobro, Vicente
See Huidobro Fernandez, Vicente Garcia

Huidobro Fernandez, Vicente Garcia 1893-
1948 .... **TCLC 31**
See also CA 131; HW

Hulme, Keri 1947- ....**CLC 39**
See also CA 125; CANR 69; INT 125

Hulme, T(homas) E(rnest) 1883-1917 **T C L C
21**
See also CA 117; DLB 19

Hume, David 1711-1776 .... **LC 7**
See also DLB 104

Humphrey, William 1924-1997 ....**CLC 45**
See also CA 77-80; 160; CANR 68; DLB 6

Humphreys, Emyr Owen 1919- ....**CLC 47**
See also CA 5-8R; CANR 3, 24; DLB 15

Humphreys, Josephine 1945- ..... **CLC 34, 57**
See also CA 121; 127; INT 127

Huneker, James Gibbons 1857-1921TCLC 65
See also DLB 71

Hungerford, Pixie
See Brinsmead, H(esba) F(ay)

Hunt, E(verette) Howard, (Jr.) 1918- .**CLC 3**
See also AITN 1; CA 45-48; CANR 2, 47

Hunt, Kyle
See Creasey, John

Hunt, (James Henry) Leigh 1784-1859N C L C
1, 70; DAM POET
See also DLB 96, 110, 144

Hunt, Marsha 1946- ....**CLC 70**
See also BW 2; CA 143

Hunt, Violet 1866(?)-1942 .... **TCLC 53**
See also DLB 162, 197

Hunter, E. Waldo
See Sturgeon, Theodore (Hamilton)

Hunter, Evan 1926- .CLC 11, 31; DAM POP
See also CA 5-8R; CANR 5, 38, 62; DLBY 82;
INT CANR-5; MTCW 1; SATA 25

Hunter, Kristin (Eggleston) 1931- ....CLC 35
See also AITN 1; BW 1; CA 13-16R; CANR
13; CLR 3; DLB 33; INT CANR-13;
MAICYA; SAAS 10; SATA 12

Hunter, Mollie 1922- ....CLC 21
See also McIlwraith, Maureen Mollie Hunter
See also AAYA 13; CANR 37; CLR 25; DLB
161; JRDA; MAICYA; SAAS 7; SATA 54

Hunter, Robert (?)-1734 .... **LC 7**

Hurston, Zora Neale 1903-1960CLC 7, 30, 61;
BLC 2; DA; DAC; DAM MST, MULT,
NOV; SSC 4; WLCS
See also AAYA 15; BW 1; CA 85-88; CANR
61; DLB 51, 86; MTCW 1

Huston, John (Marcellus) 1906-1987 CLC 20
See also CA 73-76; 123; CANR 34; DLB 26

Hustvedt, Siri 1955- ....CLC 76
See also CA 137

Hutten, Ulrich von 1488-1523 .... **LC 16**
See also DLB 179

Huxley, Aldous (Leonard) 1894-1963 CLC 1,
3, 4, 5, 8, 11, 18, 35, 79; DA; DAB; DAC;
DAM MST, NOV; WLC
See also AAYA 11; CA 85-88; CANR 44;
CDBLB 1914-1945; DLB 36, 100, 162, 195;
MTCW 1; SATA 63

Huxley, T(homas) H(enry) 1825-1895 N C L C
67
See also DLB 57

Huysmans, Joris-Karl 1848-1907TCLC 7, 69
See also CA 104; 165; DLB 123

Hwang, David Henry 1957-...CLC 55; DAM
DRAM; DC 4
See also CA 127; 132; CANR 76; INT 132

Hyde, Anthony 1946- .... **CLC 42**
See also CA 136

Hyde, Margaret O(ldroyd) 1917- .... **CLC 21**
See also CA 1-4R; CANR 1, 36; CLR 23; JRDA;
MAICYA; SAAS 8; SATA 1, 42, 76

Hynes, James 1956(?)- .... **CLC 65**
See also CA 164

Ian, Janis 1951-.............................. **CLC 21**
See also CA 105

Ibanez, Vicente Blasco
See Blasco Ibanez, Vicente

Ibarguengoitia, Jorge 1928-1983 ..... **CLC 37**
See also CA 124; 113; HW

Ibsen, Henrik (Johan) 1828-1906 TCLC 2, 8,
16, 37, 52; DA; DAB; DAC; DAM DRAM,
MST; DC 2; WLC
See also CA 104; 141

Ibuse, Masuji 1898-1993 .... **CLC 22**
See also CA 127; 141; DLB 180

Ichikawa, Kon 1915- .... **CLC 20**
See also CA 121

Idle, Eric 1943- .... **CLC 21**
See also Monty Python
See also CA 116; CANR 35

Ignatow, David 1914-1997 ..CLC 4, 7, 14, 40
See also CA 9-12R; 162; CAAS 3; CANR 31,
57; DLB 5

Ihimaera, Witi 1944- .... **CLC 46**
See also CA 77-80

Ilf, Ilya .... **TCLC 21**
See also Fainzilberg, Ilya Arnoldovich

Illyes, Gyula 1902-1983 .... **PC 16**
See also CA 114; 109

Immermann, Karl (Lebrecht) 1796-1840
NCLC 4, 49
See also DLB 133

Ince, Thomas H. 1882-1924 .... **TCLC 89**

Inchbald, Elizabeth 1753-1821 ...... **NCLC 62**
See also DLB 39, 89

Inclan, Ramon (Maria) del Valle
See Valle-Inclan, Ramon (Maria) del

Infante, G(uillermo) Cabrera
See Cabrera Infante, G(uillermo)

Ingalls, Rachel (Holmes) 1940- .... **CLC 42**
See also CA 123; 127

Ingamells, Reginald Charles
See Ingamells, Rex

Ingamells, Rex 1913-1955 .... **TCLC 35**
See also CA 167

Inge, William (Motter) 1913-1973 CLC 1, 8,
19; DAM DRAM
See also CA 9-12R; CDALB 1941-1968; DLB
7; MTCW 1

Ingelow, Jean 1820-1897 .... **NCLC 39**
See also DLB 35, 163; SATA 33

Ingram, Willis J.
See Harris, Mark

Innaurato, Albert (F.) 1948(?)- .. **CLC 21, 60**
See also CA 115; 122; INT 122

Innes, Michael
See Stewart, J(ohn) I(nnes) M(ackintosh)

Innis, Harold Adams 1894-1952 .... **TCLC 77**
See also DLB 88

Ionesco, Eugene 1909-1994CLC 1, 4, 6, 9, 11,
15, 41, 86; DA; DAB; DAC; DAM DRAM,
MST; WLC
See also CA 9-12R; 144; CANR 55; MTCW 1;
SATA 7; SATA-Obit 79

Iqbal, Muhammad 1873-1938 .... **TCLC 28**

Ireland, Patrick

See O'Doherty, Brian
Iron, Ralph
  See Schreiner, Olive (Emilie Albertina)
Irving, John (Winslow) 1942-**CLC 13, 23, 38, 112; DAM NOV, POP**
  See also AAYA 8; BEST 89:3; CA 25-28R; CANR 28, 73; DLB 6; DLBY 82; MTCW 1
Irving, Washington 1783-1859 . **NCLC 2, 19; DA; DAB; DAC; DAM MST; SSC 2; WLC**
  See also CDALB 1640-1865; DLB 3, 11, 30, 59, 73, 74, 186; YABC 2
Irwin, P. K.
  See Page, P(atricia) K(athleen)
Isaacs, Jorge Ricardo 1837-1895 ... **NCLC 70**
Isaacs, Susan 1943- .... **CLC 32; DAM POP**
  See also BEST 89:1; CA 89-92; CANR 20, 41, 65; INT CANR-20; MTCW 1
Isherwood, Christopher (William Bradshaw) 1904-1986.... **CLC 1, 9, 11, 14, 44; DAM DRAM, NOV**
  See also CA 13-16R; 117; CANR 35; DLB 15, 195; DLBY 86; MTCW 1
Ishiguro, Kazuo 1954-..**CLC 27, 56, 59, 110; DAM NOV**
  See also BEST 90:2; CA 120; CANR 49; DLB 194; MTCW 1
Ishikawa, Hakuhin
  See Ishikawa, Takuboku
Ishikawa, Takuboku 1886(?)-1912 **TCLC 15; DAM POET; PC 10**
  See also CA 113; 153
Iskander, Fazil 1929- .... **CLC 47**
  See also CA 102
Isler, Alan (David) 1934-................... **CLC 91**
  See also CA 156
Ivan IV 1530-1584 .... **LC 17**
Ivanov, Vyacheslav Ivanovich 1866-1949 **TCLC 33**
  See also CA 122
Ivask, Ivar Vidrik 1927-1992 .... **CLC 14**
  See also CA 37-40R; 139; CANR 24
Ives, Morgan
  See Bradley, Marion Zimmer
J. R. S.
  See Gogarty, Oliver St. John
Jabran, Kahlil
  See Gibran, Kahlil
Jabran, Khalil
  See Gibran, Kahlil
Jackson, Daniel
  See Wingrove, David (John)
Jackson, Jesse 1908-1983 .... **CLC 12**
  See also BW 1; CA 25-28R; 109; CANR 27; CLR 28; MAICYA; SATA 2, 29; SATA-Obit 48
Jackson, Laura (Riding) 1901-1991
  See Riding, Laura
  See also CA 65-68; 135; CANR 28; DLB 48
Jackson, Sam
  See Trumbo, Dalton
Jackson, Sara
  See Wingrove, David (John)
Jackson, Shirley 1919-1965 . **CLC 11, 60, 87; DA; DAC; DAM MST; SSC 9; WLC**
  See also AAYA 9; CA 1-4R; 25-28R; CANR 4, 52; CDALB 1941-1968; DLB 6; SATA 2
Jacob, (Cyprien-)Max 1876-1944 .... **TCLC 6**
  See also CA 104
Jacobs, Harriet A(nn) 1813(?)-1897**NCLC 67**
Jacobs, Jim 1942- .... **CLC 12**
  See also CA 97-100; INT 97-100
Jacobs, W(illiam) W(ymark) 1863-1943 **TCLC 22**

See also CA 121; 167; DLB 135
Jacobsen, Jens Peter 1847-1885 ..... **NCLC 34**
Jacobsen, Josephine 1908-........ **CLC 48, 102**
  See also CA 33-36R; CAAS 18; CANR 23, 48
Jacobson, Dan 1929- .... **CLC 4, 14**
  See also CA 1-4R; CANR 2, 25, 66; DLB 14, 207; MTCW 1
Jacqueline
  See Carpentier (y Valmont), Alejo
Jagger, Mick 1944- .... **CLC 17**
Jahiz, al- c. 780-c. 869 .... **CMLC 25**
Jakes, John (William) 1932-..**CLC 29; DAM NOV, POP**
  See also BEST 89:4; CA 57-60; CANR 10, 43, 66; DLBY 83; INT CANR-10; MTCW 1; SATA 62
James, Andrew
  See Kirkup, James
James, C(yril) L(ionel) R(obert) 1901-1989 **CLC 33; BLCS**
  See also BW 2; CA 117; 125; 128; CANR 62; DLB 125; MTCW 1
James, Daniel (Lewis) 1911-1988
  See Santiago, Danny
  See also CA 125
James, Dynely
  See Mayne, William (James Carter)
James, Henry Sr. 1811-1882 .... **NCLC 53**
James, Henry 1843-1916 **TCLC 2, 11, 24, 40, 47, 64; DA; DAB; DAC; DAM MST, NOV; SSC 8, 32; WLC**
  See also CA 104; 132; CDALB 1865-1917; DLB 12, 71, 74, 189; DLBD 13; MTCW 1
James, M. R.
  See James, Montague (Rhodes)
  See also DLB 156
James, Montague (Rhodes) 1862-1936**T C L C 6; SSC 16**
  See also CA 104; DLB 201
James, P. D. 1920-......................... **CLC 18, 46**
  See also White, Phyllis Dorothy James
  See also BEST 90:2; CDBLB 1960 to Present; DLB 87; DLBD 17
James, Philip
  See Moorcock, Michael (John)
James, William 1842-1910 .... **TCLC 15, 32**
  See also CA 109
James I 1394-1437 .... **LC 20**
Jameson, Anna 1794-1860 .... **NCLC 43**
  See also DLB 99, 166
Jami, Nur al-Din 'Abd al-Rahman 1414-1492 **LC 9**
Jammes, Francis 1868-1938 .... **TCLC 75**
Jandl, Ernst 1925- .... **CLC 34**
Janowitz, Tama 1957- ... **CLC 43; DAM POP**
  See also CA 106; CANR 52
Japrisot, Sebastien 1931-................... **CLC 90**
Jarrell, Randall 1914-1965**CLC 1, 2, 6, 9, 13, 49; DAM POET**
  See also CA 5-8R; 25-28R; CABS 2; CANR 6, 34; CDALB 1941-1968; CLR 6; DLB 48, 52; MAICYA; MTCW 1; SATA 7
Jarry, Alfred 1873-1907 . **TCLC 2, 14; DAM DRAM; SSC 20**
  See also CA 104; 153; DLB 192
Jarvis, E. K.
  See Bloch, Robert (Albert); Ellison, Harlan (Jay); Silverberg, Robert
Jeake, Samuel, Jr.
  See Aiken, Conrad (Potter)
Jean Paul 1763-1825 .... **NCLC 7**
Jefferies, (John) Richard 1848-1887**NCLC 47**
  See also DLB 98, 141; SATA 16

Jeffers, (John) Robinson 1887-1962**CLC 2, 3, 11, 15, 54; DA; DAC; DAM MST, POET; PC 17; WLC**
  See also CA 85-88; CANR 35; CDALB 1917-1929; DLB 45; MTCW 1
Jefferson, Janet
  See Mencken, H(enry) L(ouis)
Jefferson, Thomas 1743-1826 .... **NCLC 11**
  See also CDALB 1640-1865; DLB 31
Jeffrey, Francis 1773-1850 .... **NCLC 33**
  See also DLB 107
Jelakowitch, Ivan
  See Heijermans, Herman
Jellicoe, (Patricia) Ann 1927-............ **CLC 27**
  See also CA 85-88; DLB 13
Jen, Gish ....**CLC 70**
  See also Jen, Lillian
Jen, Lillian 1956(?)-
  See Jen, Gish
  See also CA 135
Jenkins, (John) Robin 1912- .... **CLC 52**
  See also CA 1-4R; CANR 1; DLB 14
Jennings, Elizabeth (Joan) 1926-.. **CLC 5, 14**
  See also CA 61-64; CAAS 5; CANR 8, 39, 66; DLB 27; MTCW 1; SATA 66
Jennings, Waylon 1937- .... **CLC 21**
Jensen, Johannes V. 1873-1950 ...... **TCLC 41**
  See also CA 170
Jensen, Laura (Linnea) 1948- .... **CLC 37**
  See also CA 103
Jerome, Jerome K(lapka) 1859-1927**TCLC 23**
  See also CA 119; DLB 10, 34, 135
Jerrold, Douglas William 1803-1857**NCLC 2**
  See also DLB 158, 159
Jewett, (Theodora) Sarah Orne 1849-1909 **TCLC 1, 22; SSC 6**
  See also CA 108; 127; CANR 71; DLB 12, 74; SATA 15
Jewsbury, Geraldine (Endsor) 1812-1880 **NCLC 22**
  See also DLB 21
Jhabvala, Ruth Prawer 1927-**CLC 4, 8, 29, 94; DAB; DAM NOV**
  See also CA 1-4R; CANR 2, 29, 51, 74; DLB 139, 194; INT CANR-29; MTCW 1
Jibran, Kahlil
  See Gibran, Kahlil
Jibran, Khalil
  See Gibran, Kahlil
Jiles, Paulette 1943- .... **CLC 13, 58**
  See also CA 101; CANR 70
Jimenez (Mantecon), Juan Ramon 1881-1958 **TCLC 4; DAM MULT, POET; HLC; PC 7**
  See also CA 104; 131; CANR 74; DLB 134; HW; MTCW 1
Jimenez, Ramon
  See Jimenez (Mantecon), Juan Ramon
Jimenez Mantecon, Juan
  See Jimenez (Mantecon), Juan Ramon
Jin, Ha 1956- .... **CLC 109**
  See also CA 152
Joel, Billy ....**CLC 26**
  See also Joel, William Martin
Joel, William Martin 1949-
  See Joel, Billy
  See also CA 108
John, Saint 7th cent. - .... **CMLC 27**
John of the Cross, St. 1542-1591 .... **LC 18**
Johnson, B(ryan) S(tanley William) 1933-1973 **CLC 6, 9**
  See also CA 9-12R; 53-56; CANR 9; DLB 14, 40

Johnson, Benj. F. of Boo
See Riley, James Whitcomb
Johnson, Benjamin F. of Boo
See Riley, James Whitcomb
Johnson, Charles (Richard) 1948-**CLC 7, 51, 65; BLC 2; DAM MULT**
See also BW 2; CA 116; CAAS 18; CANR 42, 66; DLB 33
Johnson, Denis 1949- .... **CLC 52**
See also CA 117; 121; CANR 71; DLB 120
Johnson, Diane 1934- .... **CLC 5, 13, 48**
See also CA 41-44R; CANR 17, 40, 62; DLBY 80; INT CANR-17; MTCW 1
Johnson, Eyvind (Olof Verner) 1900-1976 **CLC 14**
See also CA 73-76; 69-72; CANR 34
Johnson, J. R.
See James, C(yril) L(ionel) R(obert)
Johnson, James Weldon 1871-1938 **TCLC 3, 19; BLC 2; DAM MULT, POET; PC 24**
See also BW 1; CA 104; 125; CDALB 1917-1929; CLR 32; DLB 51; MTCW 1; SATA 31
Johnson, Joyce 1935- .... **CLC 58**
See also CA 125; 129
Johnson, Judith (Emlyn) 1936-.... **CLC 7, 15**
See also CA 25-28R; 153; CANR 34
Johnson, Lionel (Pigot) 1867-1902 **TCLC 19**
See also CA 117; DLB 19
Johnson, Marguerite (Annie)
See Angelou, Maya
Johnson, Mel
See Malzberg, Barry N(athaniel)
Johnson, Pamela Hansford 1912-1981**CLC 1, 7, 27**
See also CA 1-4R; 104; CANR 2, 28; DLB 15; MTCW 1
Johnson, Robert 1911(?)-1938 .... **TCLC 69**
Johnson, Samuel 1709-1784**LC 15; DA; DAB; DAC; DAM MST; WLC**
See also CDBLB 1660-1789; DLB 39, 95, 104, 142
Johnson, Uwe 1934-1984 .. **CLC 5, 10, 15, 40**
See also CA 1-4R; 112; CANR 1, 39; DLB 75; MTCW 1
Johnston, George (Benson) 1913-.... **CLC 51**
See also CA 1-4R; CANR 5, 20; DLB 88
Johnston, Jennifer 1930- ....**CLC 7**
See also CA 85-88; DLB 14
Jolley, (Monica) Elizabeth 1923-**CLC 46; SSC 19**
See also CA 127; CAAS 13; CANR 59
Jones, Arthur Llewellyn 1863-1947
See Machen, Arthur
See also CA 104
Jones, D(ouglas) G(ordon) 1929- ..... **CLC 10**
See also CA 29-32R; CANR 13; DLB 53
Jones, David (Michael) 1895-1974**CLC 2, 4, 7, 13, 42**
See also CA 9-12R; 53-56; CANR 28; CDBLB 1945-1960; DLB 20, 100; MTCW 1
Jones, David Robert 1947-
See Bowie, David
See also CA 103
Jones, Diana Wynne 1934- .... **CLC 26**
See also AAYA 12; CA 49-52; CANR 4, 26, 56; CLR 23; DLB 161; JRDA; MAICYA; SAAS 7; SATA 9, 70
Jones, Edward P. 1950-..................... **CLC 76**
See also BW 2; CA 142
Jones, Gayl 1949- ... **CLC 6, 9; BLC 2; DAM MULT**
See also BW 2; CA 77-80; CANR 27, 66; DLB 33; MTCW 1

Jones, James 1921-1977 ...... **CLC 1, 3, 10, 39**
See also AITN 1, 2; CA 1-4R; 69-72; CANR 6; DLB 2, 143; DLBD 17; MTCW 1
Jones, John J.
See Lovecraft, H(oward) P(hillips)
Jones, LeRoi .... **CLC 1, 2, 3, 5, 10, 14**
See also Baraka, Amiri
Jones, Louis B. 1953- ....**CLC 65**
See also CA 141; CANR 73
Jones, Madison (Percy, Jr.) 1925-.......**CLC 4**
See also CA 13-16R; CAAS 11; CANR 7, 54; DLB 152
Jones, Mervyn 1922- .... **CLC 10, 52**
See also CA 45-48; CAAS 5; CANR 1; MTCW 1
Jones, Mick 1956(?)- .... **CLC 30**
Jones, Nettie (Pearl) 1941- .... **CLC 34**
See also BW 2; CA 137; CAAS 20
Jones, Preston 1936-1979 ....**CLC 10**
See also CA 73-76; 89-92; DLB 7
Jones, Robert F(rancis) 1934- .... **CLC 7**
See also CA 49-52; CANR 2, 61
Jones, Rod 1953-............................... **CLC 50**
See also CA 128
Jones, Terence Graham Parry 1942- **CLC 21**
See also Jones, Terry; Monty Python
See also CA 112; 116; CANR 35; INT 116
Jones, Terry
See Jones, Terence Graham Parry
See also SATA 67; SATA-Brief 51
Jones, Thom 1945(?)- .... **CLC 81**
See also CA 157
Jong, Erica 1942- **CLC 4, 6, 8, 18, 83; DAM NOV, POP**
See also AITN 1; BEST 90:2; CA 73-76; CANR 26, 52, 75; DLB 2, 5, 28, 152; INT CANR-26; MTCW 1
Jonson, Ben(jamin) 1572(?)-1637 .. **LC 6, 33; DA; DAB; DAC; DAM DRAM, MST, POET; DC 4; PC 17; WLC**
See also CDBLB Before 1660; DLB 62, 121
Jordan, June 1936-**CLC 5, 11, 23, 114; BLCS; DAM MULT, POET**
See also AAYA 2; BW 2; CA 33-36R; CANR 25, 70; CLR 10; DLB 38; MAICYA; MTCW 1; SATA 4
Jordan, Neil (Patrick) 1950-............ **CLC 110**
See also CA 124; 130; CANR 54; INT 130
Jordan, Pat(rick M.) 1941- ....**CLC 37**
See also CA 33-36R
Jorgensen, Ivar
See Ellison, Harlan (Jay)
Jorgenson, Ivar
See Silverberg, Robert
Josephus, Flavius c. 37-100 .... **CMLC 13**
Josipovici, Gabriel 1940- .... **CLC 6, 43**
See also CA 37-40R; CAAS 8; CANR 47; DLB 14
Joubert, Joseph 1754-1824 .... **NCLC 9**
Jouve, Pierre Jean 1887-1976 ....**CLC 47**
See also CA 65-68
Jovine, Francesco 1902-1950 .... **TCLC 79**
Joyce, James (Augustine Aloysius) 1882-1941 **TCLC 3, 8, 16, 35, 52; DA; DAB; DAC; DAM MST, NOV, POET; PC 22; SSC 3, 26; WLC**
See also CA 104; 126; CDBLB 1914-1945; DLB 10, 19, 36, 162; MTCW 1
Jozsef, Attila 1905-1937 ....**TCLC 22**
See also CA 116
Juana Ines de la Cruz 1651(?)-1695**LC 5; PC 24**
Judd, Cyril

See Kornbluth, C(yril) M.; Pohl, Frederik
Julian of Norwich 1342(?)-1416(?) .... **LC 6**
See also DLB 146
Junger, Sebastian 1962- .... **CLC 109**
See also CA 165
Juniper, Alex
See Hospital, Janette Turner
Junius
See Luxemburg, Rosa
Just, Ward (Swift) 1935- .... **CLC 4, 27**
See also CA 25-28R; CANR 32; INT CANR-32
Justice, Donald (Rodney) 1925- .. **CLC 6, 19, 102; DAM POET**
See also CA 5-8R; CANR 26, 54, 74; DLBY 83; INT CANR-26
Juvenal..**CMLC 8**
See also Juvenalis, Decimus Junius
Juvenalis, Decimus Junius 55(?)-c. 127(?)
See Juvenal
Juvenis
See Bourne, Randolph S(illiman)
Kacew, Romain 1914-1980
See Gary, Romain
See also CA 108; 102
Kadare, Ismail 1936-........................ **CLC 52**
See also CA 161
Kadohata, Cynthia .... **CLC 59**
See also CA 140
Kafka, Franz 1883-1924**TCLC 2, 6, 13, 29, 47, 53; DA; DAB; DAC; DAM MST, NOV; SSC 5, 29; WLC**
See also CA 105; 126; DLB 81; MTCW 1
Kahanovitsch, Pinkhes
See Der Nister
Kahn, Roger 1927- .... **CLC 30**
See also CA 25-28R; CANR 44, 69; DLB 171; SATA 37
Kain, Saul
See Sassoon, Siegfried (Lorraine)
Kaiser, Georg 1878-1945 .... **TCLC 9**
See also CA 106; DLB 124
Kaletski, Alexander 1946- .... **CLC 39**
See also CA 118; 143
Kalidasa fl. c. 400- .... **CMLC 9; PC 22**
Kallman, Chester (Simon) 1921-1975 **CLC 2**
See also CA 45-48; 53-56; CANR 3
Kaminsky, Melvin 1926-
See Brooks, Mel
See also CA 65-68; CANR 16
Kaminsky, Stuart M(elvin) 1934- .... **CLC 59**
See also CA 73-76; CANR 29, 53
Kane, Francis
See Robbins, Harold
Kane, Paul
See Simon, Paul (Frederick)
Kane, Wilson
See Bloch, Robert (Albert)
Kanin, Garson 1912-......................... **CLC 22**
See also AITN 1; CA 5-8R; CANR 7; DLB 7
Kaniuk, Yoram 1930- .... **CLC 19**
See also CA 134
Kant, Immanuel 1724-1804 ..... **NCLC 27, 67**
See also DLB 94
Kantor, MacKinlay 1904-1977 ....**CLC 7**
See also CA 61-64; 73-76; CANR 60, 63; DLB 9, 102
Kaplan, David Michael 1946- .... **CLC 50**
Kaplan, James 1951-........................ **CLC 59**
See also CA 135
Karageorge, Michael
See Anderson, Poul (William)
Karamzin, Nikolai Mikhailovich 1766-1826

NCLC 3
See also DLB 150

Karapanou, Margarita 1946- .... **CLC 13**
See also CA 101

Karinthy, Frigyes 1887-1938 .... **TCLC 47**
See also CA 170

Karl, Frederick R(obert) 1927- .... **CLC 34**
See also CA 5-8R; CANR 3, 44

Kastel, Warren
See Silverberg, Robert

Kataev, Evgeny Petrovich 1903-1942
See Petrov, Evgeny
See also CA 120

Kataphusin
See Ruskin, John

Katz, Steve 1935- .... **CLC 47**
See also CA 25-28R; CAAS 14, 64; CANR 12; DLBY 83

Kauffman, Janet 1945- .... **CLC 42**
See also CA 117; CANR 43; DLBY 86

Kaufman, Bob (Garnell) 1925-1986 **CLC 49**
See also BW 1; CA 41-44R; 118; CANR 22; DLB 16, 41

Kaufman, George S. 1889-1961 **CLC 38; DAM DRAM**
See also CA 108; 93-96; DLB 7; INT 108

Kaufman, Sue .... **CLC 3, 8**
See also Barondess, Sue K(aufman)

Kavafis, Konstantinos Petrou 1863-1933
See Cavafy, C(onstantine) P(eter)
See also CA 104

Kavan, Anna 1901-1968 .... **CLC 5, 13, 82**
See also CA 5-8R; CANR 6, 57; MTCW 1

Kavanagh, Dan
See Barnes, Julian (Patrick)

Kavanagh, Patrick (Joseph) 1904-1967 **C L C 22**
See also CA 123; 25-28R; DLB 15, 20; MTCW 1

Kawabata, Yasunari 1899-1972 **CLC 2, 5, 9, 18, 107; DAM MULT; SSC 17**
See also CA 93-96; 33-36R; DLB 180

Kaye, M(ary) M(argaret) 1909- .... **CLC 28**
See also CA 89-92; CANR 24, 60; MTCW 1; SATA 62

Kaye, Mollie
See Kaye, M(ary) M(argaret)

Kaye-Smith, Sheila 1887-1956 .... **TCLC 20**
See also CA 118; DLB 36

Kaymor, Patrice Maguilene
See Senghor, Leopold Sedar

Kazan, Elia 1909- .... **CLC 6, 16, 63**
See also CA 21-24R; CANR 32

Kazantzakis, Nikos 1883(?)-1957 **TCLC 2, 5, 33**
See also CA 105; 132; MTCW 1

Kazin, Alfred 1915- .... **CLC 34, 38**
See also CA 1-4R; CAAS 7; CANR 1, 45; DLB 67

Keane, Mary Nesta (Skrine) 1904-1996
See Keane, Molly
See also CA 108; 114; 151

Keane, Molly .... **CLC 31**
See also Keane, Mary Nesta (Skrine)
See also INT 114

Keates, Jonathan 1946(?)- .... **CLC 34**
See also CA 163

Keaton, Buster 1895-1966 .... **CLC 20**

Keats, John 1795-1821 **NCLC 8, 73; DA; DAB; DAC; DAM MST, POET; PC 1; WLC**
See also CDBLB 1789-1832; DLB 96, 110

Keene, Donald 1922- .... **CLC 34**
See also CA 1-4R; CANR 5

Keillor, Garrison .... **CLC 40, 115**
See also Keillor, Gary (Edward)
See also AAYA 2; BEST 89:3; DLBY 87; SATA 58

Keillor, Gary (Edward) 1942-
See Keillor, Garrison
See also CA 111; 117; CANR 36, 59; DAM POP; MTCW 1

Keith, Michael
See Hubbard, L(afayette) Ron(ald)

Keller, Gottfried 1819-1890 **NCLC 2; SSC 26**
See also DLB 129

Keller, Nora Okja .... **CLC 109**

Kellerman, Jonathan 1949- ... **CLC 44; DAM POP**
See also BEST 90:1; CA 106; CANR 29, 51; INT CANR-29

Kelley, William Melvin 1937- .... **CLC 22**
See also BW 1; CA 77-80; CANR 27; DLB 33

Kellogg, Marjorie 1922- .... **CLC 2**
See also CA 81-84

Kellow, Kathleen
See Hibbert, Eleanor Alice Burford

Kelly, M(ilton) T(erry) 1947- .... **CLC 55**
See also CA 97-100; CAAS 22; CANR 19, 43

Kelman, James 1946- .... **CLC 58, 86**
See also CA 148; DLB 194

Kemal, Yashar 1923- .... **CLC 14, 29**
See also CA 89-92; CANR 44

Kemble, Fanny 1809-1893 .... **NCLC 18**
See also DLB 32

Kemelman, Harry 1908-1996 .... **CLC 2**
See also AITN 1; CA 9-12R; 155; CANR 6, 71; DLB 28

Kempe, Margery 1373(?)-1440(?) .... **LC 6**
See also DLB 146

Kempis, Thomas a 1380-1471 .... **LC 11**

Kendall, Henry 1839-1882 .... **NCLC 12**

Keneally, Thomas (Michael) 1935- **CLC 5, 8, 10, 14, 19, 27, 43, 117; DAM NOV**
See also CA 85-88; CANR 10, 50, 74; MTCW 1

Kennedy, Adrienne (Lita) 1931- **CLC 66; BLC 2; DAM MULT; DC 5**
See also BW 2; CA 103; CAAS 20; CABS 3; CANR 26, 53; DLB 38

Kennedy, John Pendleton 1795-1870 **NCLC 2**
See also DLB 3

Kennedy, Joseph Charles 1929-
See Kennedy, X. J.
See also CA 1-4R; CANR 4, 30, 40; SATA 14, 86

Kennedy, William 1928- ..**CLC 6, 28, 34, 53; DAM NOV**
See also AAYA 1; CA 85-88; CANR 14, 31, 76; DLB 143; DLBY 85; INT CANR-31; MTCW 1; SATA 57

Kennedy, X. J. .... **CLC 8, 42**
See also Kennedy, Joseph Charles
See also CAAS 9; CLR 27; DLB 5; SAAS 22

Kenny, Maurice (Francis) 1929- ..... **CLC 87; DAM MULT**
See also CA 144; CAAS 22; DLB 175; NNAL

Kent, Kelvin
See Kuttner, Henry

Kenton, Maxwell
See Southern, Terry

Kenyon, Robert O.
See Kuttner, Henry

Kepler, Johannes 1571-1630 .... **LC 45**

Kerouac, Jack .... **CLC 1, 2, 3, 5, 14, 29, 61**
See also Kerouac, Jean-Louis Lebris de
See also AAYA 25; CDALB 1941-1968; DLB 2, 16; DLBD 3; DLBY 95

Kerouac, Jean-Louis Lebris de 1922-1969
See Kerouac, Jack
See also AITN 1; CA 5-8R; 25-28R; CANR 26, 54; DA; DAB; DAC; DAM MST, NOV, POET, POP; MTCW 1; WLC

Kerr, Jean 1923- .... **CLC 22**
See also CA 5-8R; CANR 7; INT CANR-7

Kerr, M. E. .... **CLC 12, 35**
See also Meaker, Marijane (Agnes)
See also AAYA 2, 23; CLR 29; SAAS 1

Kerr, Robert .... **CLC 55**

Kerrigan, (Thomas) Anthony 1918- **CLC 4, 6**
See also CA 49-52; CAAS 11; CANR 4

Kerry, Lois
See Duncan, Lois

Kesey, Ken (Elton) 1935- **CLC 1, 3, 6, 11, 46, 64; DA; DAB; DAC; DAM MST, NOV, POP; WLC**
See also AAYA 25; CA 1-4R; CANR 22, 38, 66; CDALB 1968-1988; DLB 2, 16, 206; MTCW 1; SATA 66

Kesselring, Joseph (Otto) 1902-1967 **CLC 45; DAM DRAM, MST**
See also CA 150

Kessler, Jascha (Frederick) 1929- .... **CLC 4**
See also CA 17-20R; CANR 8, 48

Kettelkamp, Larry (Dale) 1933- .... **CLC 12**
See also CA 29-32R; CANR 16; SAAS 3; SATA 2

Key, Ellen 1849-1926 .... **TCLC 65**

Keyber, Conny
See Fielding, Henry

Keyes, Daniel 1927- **CLC 80; DA; DAC; DAM MST, NOV**
See also AAYA 23; CA 17-20R; CANR 10, 26, 54, 74; SATA 37

Keynes, John Maynard 1883-1946 **TCLC 64**
See also CA 114; 162, 163; DLBD 10

Khanshendel, Chiron
See Rose, Wendy

Khayyam, Omar 1048-1131 **CMLC 11; DAM POET; PC 8**

Kherdian, David 1931- .... **CLC 6, 9**
See also CA 21-24R; CAAS 2; CANR 39; CLR 24; JRDA; MAICYA; SATA 16, 74

Khlebnikov, Velimir .... **TCLC 20**
See also Khlebnikov, Viktor Vladimirovich

Khlebnikov, Viktor Vladimirovich 1885-1922
See Khlebnikov, Velimir
See also CA 117

Khodasevich, Vladislav (Felitsianovich) 1886-1939 .... **TCLC 15**
See also CA 115

Kielland, Alexander Lange 1849-1906 **T C L C 5**
See also CA 104

Kiely, Benedict 1919- .... **CLC 23, 43**
See also CA 1-4R; CANR 2; DLB 15

Kienzle, William X(avier) 1928- ..... **CLC 25; DAM POP**
See also CA 93-96; CAAS 1; CANR 9, 31, 59; INT CANR-31; MTCW 1

Kierkegaard, Soren 1813-1855 ...... **NCLC 34**

Killens, John Oliver 1916-1987 .... **CLC 10**
See also BW 2; CA 77-80; 123; CAAS 2; CANR 26; DLB 33

Killigrew, Anne 1660-1685 .... **LC 4**
See also DLB 131

Kim
See Simenon, Georges (Jacques Christian)

Kincaid, Jamaica 1949- **CLC 43, 68; BLC 2; DAM MULT, NOV**

35
See also DLB 168
Leimbach, Martha 1963-
See Leimbach, Marti
See also CA 130
Leimbach, Marti .... **CLC 65**
See also Leimbach, Martha
Leino, Eino .... **TCLC 24**
See also Loennbohm, Armas Eino Leopold
Leiris, Michel (Julien) 1901-1990 .... **CLC 61**
See also CA 119; 128; 132
Leithauser, Brad 1953- .... **CLC 27**
See also CA 107; CANR 27; DLB 120
Lelchuk, Alan 1938- .... **CLC 5**
See also CA 45-48; CAAS 20; CANR 1, 70
Lem, Stanislaw 1921- .... **CLC 8, 15, 40**
See also CA 105; CAAS 1; CANR 32; MTCW
1
Lemann, Nancy 1956- .... **CLC 39**
See also CA 118; 136
Lemonnier, (Antoine Louis) Camille 1844-1913
TCLC 22
See also CA 121
Lenau, Nikolaus 1802-1850 .... **NCLC 16**
L'Engle, Madeleine (Camp Franklin) 1918-
CLC 12; DAM POP
See also AAYA 1; AITN 2; CA 1-4R; CANR 3,
21, 39, 66; CLR 1, 14; DLB 52; JRDA;
MAICYA; MTCW 1; SAAS 15; SATA 1, 27,
75
Lengyel, Jozsef 1896-1975 .... **CLC 7**
See also CA 85-88; 57-60; CANR 71
Lenin 1870-1924
See Lenin, V. I.
See also CA 121; 168
Lenin, V. I. .... **TCLC 67**
See also Lenin
Lennon, John (Ono) 1940-1980 . **CLC 12, 35**
See also CA 102
Lennox, Charlotte Ramsay 1729(?)-1804
NCLC 23
See also DLB 39
Lentricchia, Frank (Jr.) 1940- .... **CLC 34**
See also CA 25-28R; CANR 19
Lenz, Siegfried 1926- .... **CLC 27; SSC 33**
See also CA 89-92; DLB 75
Leonard, Elmore (John, Jr.) 1925-**CLC 28, 34,
71; DAM POP**
See also AAYA 22; AITN 1; BEST 89:1, 90:4;
CA 81-84; CANR 12, 28, 53, 76; DLB 173;
INT CANR-28; MTCW 1
Leonard, Hugh .... **CLC 19**
See also Byrne, John Keyes
See also DLB 13
Leonov, Leonid (Maximovich) 1899-1994
CLC 92; DAM NOV
See also CA 129; CANR 74, 76; MTCW 1
Leopardi, (Conte) Giacomo 1798-1837**NCLC
22**
Le Reveler
See Artaud, Antonin (Marie Joseph)
Lerman, Eleanor 1952- ....**CLC 9**
See also CA 85-88; CANR 69
Lerman, Rhoda 1936- .... **CLC 56**
See also CA 49-52; CANR 70
Lermontov, Mikhail Yuryevich 1814-1841
NCLC 47; PC 18
See also DLB 205
Leroux, Gaston 1868-1927 .... **TCLC 25**
See also CA 108; 136; CANR 69; SATA 65
Lesage, Alain-Rene 1668-1747 .... **LC 2, 28**
Leskov, Nikolai (Semyonovich) 1831-1895
NCLC 25

Lessing, Doris (May) 1919-**CLC 1, 2, 3, 6, 10,
15, 22, 40, 94; DA; DAB; DAC; DAM MST,
NOV; SSC 6; WLCS**
See also CA 9-12R; CAAS 14; CANR 33, 54,
76; CDBLB 1960 to Present; DLB 15, 139;
DLBY 85; MTCW 1
Lessing, Gotthold Ephraim 1729-1781 **LC 8**
See also DLB 97
Lester, Richard 1932- .... **CLC 20**
Lever, Charles (James) 1806-1872 . **NCLC 23**
See also DLB 21
Leverson, Ada 1865(?)-1936(?) ...... **TCLC 18**
See also Elaine
See also CA 117; DLB 153
Levertov, Denise 1923-1997 **CLC 1, 2, 3, 5, 8,
15, 28, 66; DAM POET; PC 11**
See also CA 1-4R; 163; CAAS 19; CANR 3,
29, 50; DLB 5, 165; INT CANR-29; MTCW
1
Levi, Jonathan .... **CLC 76**
Levi, Peter (Chad Tigar) 1931- .... **CLC 41**
See also CA 5-8R; CANR 34; DLB 40
Levi, Primo 1919-1987 .. **CLC 37, 50; SSC 12**
See also CA 13-16R; 122; CANR 12, 33, 61,
70; DLB 177; MTCW 1
Levin, Ira 1929- .... **CLC 3, 6; DAM POP**
See also CA 21-24R; CANR 17, 44, 74; MTCW
1; SATA 66
Levin, Meyer 1905-1981 . **CLC 7; DAM POP**
See also AITN 1; CA 9-12R; 104; CANR 15;
DLB 9, 28; DLBY 81; SATA 21; SATA-Obit
27
Levine, Norman 1924- .... **CLC 54**
See also CA 73-76; CAAS 23; CANR 14, 70;
DLB 88
Levine, Philip 1928-**CLC 2, 4, 5, 9, 14, 33, 118;
DAM POET; PC 22**
See also CA 9-12R; CANR 9, 37, 52; DLB 5
Levinson, Deirdre 1931- .... **CLC 49**
See also CA 73-76; CANR 70
Levi-Strauss, Claude 1908- .... **CLC 38**
See also CA 1-4R; CANR 6, 32, 57; MTCW 1
Levitin, Sonia (Wolff) 1934- .... **CLC 17**
See also AAYA 13; CA 29-32R; CANR 14, 32;
CLR 53; JRDA; MAICYA; SAAS 2; SATA
4, 68
Levon, O. U.
See Kesey, Ken (Elton)
Levy, Amy 1861-1889 .... **NCLC 59**
See also DLB 156
Lewes, George Henry 1817-1878 ... **NCLC 25**
See also DLB 55, 144
Lewis, Alun 1915-1944 .... **TCLC 3**
See also CA 104; DLB 20, 162
Lewis, C. Day
See Day Lewis, C(ecil)
Lewis, C(live) S(taples) 1898-1963**CLC 1, 3, 6,
14, 27; DA; DAB; DAC; DAM MST, NOV,
POP; WLC**
See also AAYA 3; CA 81-84; CANR 33, 71;
CDBLB 1945-1960; CLR 3, 27; DLB 15,
100, 160; JRDA; MAICYA; MTCW 1; SATA
13, 100
Lewis, Janet 1899-1998 .... **CLC 41**
See also Winters, Janet Lewis
See also CA 9-12R; 172; CANR 29, 63; CAP
1; DLBY 87
Lewis, Matthew Gregory 1775-1818**NCLC 11,
62**
See also DLB 39, 158, 178
Lewis, (Harry) Sinclair 1885-1951 . **TCLC 4,
13, 23, 39; DA; DAB; DAC; DAM MST,
NOV; WLC**

See also CA 104; 133; CDALB 1917-1929;
DLB 9, 102; DLBD 1; MTCW 1
Lewis, (Percy) Wyndham 1882(?)-1957**T C L C
2, 9**
See also CA 104; 157; DLB 15
Lewisohn, Ludwig 1883-1955 .... **TCLC 19**
See also CA 107; DLB 4, 9, 28, 102
Lewton, Val 1904-1951 .... **TCLC 76**
Leyner, Mark 1956- .... **CLC 92**
See also CA 110; CANR 28, 53
Lezama Lima, Jose 1910-1976**CLC 4, 10, 101;
DAM MULT**
See also CA 77-80; CANR 71; DLB 113; HW
L'Heureux, John (Clarke) 1934- .... **CLC 52**
See also CA 13-16R; CANR 23, 45
Liddell, C. H.
See Kuttner, Henry
Lie, Jonas (Lauritz Idemil) 1833-1908(?)
TCLC 5
See also CA 115
Lieber, Joel 1937-1971 .... **CLC 6**
See also CA 73-76; 29-32R
Lieber, Stanley Martin
See Lee, Stan
Lieberman, Laurence (James) 1935- . **CLC 4,
36**
See also CA 17-20R; CANR 8, 36
Lieh Tzu fl. 7th cent. B.C.-5th cent. B.C.
CMLC 27
Lieksman, Anders
See Haavikko, Paavo Juhani
Li Fei-kan 1904-
See Pa Chin
See also CA 105
Lifton, Robert Jay 1926- .... **CLC 67**
See also CA 17-20R; CANR 27; INT CANR-
27; SATA 66
Lightfoot, Gordon 1938- .... **CLC 26**
See also CA 109
Lightman, Alan P(aige) 1948- .... **CLC 81**
See also CA 141; CANR 63
Ligotti, Thomas (Robert) 1953-**CLC 44; SSC
16**
See also CA 123; CANR 49
Li Ho 791-817 .... **PC 13**
Liliencron, (Friedrich Adolf Axel) Detlev von
1844-1909 .... **TCLC 18**
See also CA 117
Lilly, William 1602-1681 .... **LC 27**
Lima, Jose Lezama
See Lezama Lima, Jose
Lima Barreto, Afonso Henrique de 1881-1922
TCLC 23
See also CA 117
Limonov, Edward 1944- .... **CLC 67**
See also CA 137
Lin, Frank
See Atherton, Gertrude (Franklin Horn)
Lincoln, Abraham 1809-1865 .... **NCLC 18**
Lind, Jakov .... **CLC 1, 2, 4, 27, 82**
See also Landwirth, Heinz
See also CAAS 4
Lindbergh, Anne (Spencer) Morrow 1906-
CLC 82; DAM NOV
See also CA 17-20R; CANR 16, 73; MTCW 1;
SATA 33
Lindsay, David 1878-1945 .... **TCLC 15**
See also CA 113
Lindsay, (Nicholas) Vachel 1879-1931 **T C L C
17; DA; DAC; DAM MST, POET; PC 23;
WLC**
See also CA 114; 135; CDALB 1865-1917;
DLB 54; SATA 40

Malabaila, Damiano
    See Levi, Primo
Malamud, Bernard 1914-1986CLC 1, 2, 3, 5,
    8, 9, 11, 18, 27, 44, 78, 85; DA; DAB; DAC;
    DAM MST, NOV, POP; SSC 15; WLC
    See also AAYA 16; CA 5-8R; 118; CABS 1;
    CANR 28, 62; CDALB 1941-1968; DLB 2,
    28, 152; DLBY 80, 86; MTCW 1
Malan, Herman
    See Bosman, Herman Charles; Bosman, Herman
    Charles
Malaparte, Curzio 1898-1957 .... TCLC 52
Malcolm, Dan
    See Silverberg, Robert
Malcolm X .... CLC 82, 117; BLC 2; WLCS
    See also Little, Malcolm
Malherbe, Francois de 1555-1628 .... LC 5
Mallarme, Stephane 1842-1898 NCLC 4, 41;
    DAM POET; PC 4
Mallet-Joris, Francoise 1930- .... CLC 11
    See also CA 65-68; CANR 17; DLB 83
Malley, Ern
    See McAuley, James Phillip
Mallowan, Agatha Christie
    See Christie, Agatha (Mary Clarissa)
Maloff, Saul 1922- .... CLC 5
    See also CA 33-36R
Malone, Louis
    See MacNeice, (Frederick) Louis
Malone, Michael (Christopher) 1942-CLC 43
    See also CA 77-80; CANR 14, 32, 57
Malory, (Sir) Thomas 1410(?)-1471(?)LC 11;
    DA; DAB; DAC; DAM MST; WLCS
    See also CDBLB Before 1660; DLB 146; SATA
    59; SATA-Brief 33
Malouf, (George Joseph) David 1934-CLC 28,
    86
    See also CA 124; CANR 50, 76
Malraux, (Georges-)Andre 1901-1976CLC 1,
    4, 9, 13, 15, 57; DAM NOV
    See also CA 21-22; 69-72; CANR 34, 58; CAP
    2; DLB 72; MTCW 1
Malzberg, Barry N(athaniel) 1939- .... CLC 7
    See also CA 61-64; CAAS 4; CANR 16; DLB
    8
Mamet, David (Alan) 1947-CLC 9, 15, 34, 46,
    91; DAM DRAM; DC 4
    See also AAYA 3; CA 81-84; CABS 3; CANR
    15, 41, 67, 72; DLB 7; MTCW 1
Mamoulian, Rouben (Zachary) 1897-1987
    CLC 16
    See also CA 25-28R; 124
Mandelstam, Osip (Emilievich) 1891(?)-1938(?)
    TCLC 2, 6; PC 14
    See also CA 104; 150
Mander, (Mary) Jane 1877-1949 ... TCLC 31
    See also CA 162
Mandeville, John fl. 1350- .... CMLC 19
    See also DLB 146
Mandiargues, Andre Pieyre de .... CLC 41
    See also Pieyre de Mandiargues, Andre
    See also DLB 83
Mandrake, Ethel Belle
    See Thurman, Wallace (Henry)
Mangan, James Clarence 1803-1849NCLC 27
Maniere, J.-E.
    See Giraudoux, (Hippolyte) Jean
Mankiewicz, Herman (Jacob) 1897-1953
    TCLC 85
    See also CA 120; 169; DLB 26
Manley, (Mary) Delariviere 1672(?)-1724 L C
    1, 42
    See also DLB 39, 80

Mann, Abel
    See Creasey, John
Mann, Emily 1952- .... DC 7
    See also CA 130; CANR 55
Mann, (Luiz) Heinrich 1871-1950 ... TCLC 9
    See also CA 106; 164; DLB 66, 118
Mann, (Paul) Thomas 1875-1955 TCLC 2, 8,
    14, 21, 35, 44, 60; DA; DAB; DAC; DAM
    MST, NOV; SSC 5; WLC
    See also CA 104; 128; DLB 66; MTCW 1
Mannheim, Karl 1893-1947 .... TCLC 65
Manning, David
    See Faust, Frederick (Schiller)
Manning, Frederic 1887(?)-1935 ... TCLC 25
    See also CA 124
Manning, Olivia 1915-1980 .... CLC 5, 19
    See also CA 5-8R; 101; CANR 29; MTCW 1
Mano, D. Keith 1942- .... CLC 2, 10
    See also CA 25-28R; CAAS 6; CANR 26, 57;
    DLB 6
Mansfield, KatherineTCLC 2, 8, 39; DAB; SSC
    9, 23; WLC
    See also Beauchamp, Kathleen Mansfield
    See also DLB 162
Manso, Peter 1940- .... CLC 39
    See also CA 29-32R; CANR 44
Mantecon, Juan Jimenez
    See Jimenez (Mantecon), Juan Ramon
Manton, Peter
    See Creasey, John
Man Without a Spleen, A
    See Chekhov, Anton (Pavlovich)
Manzoni, Alessandro 1785-1873 .... NCLC 29
Map, Walter 1140-1209 .... CMLC 32
Mapu, Abraham (ben Jekutiel) 1808-1867
    NCLC 18
Mara, Sally
    See Queneau, Raymond
Marat, Jean Paul 1743-1793 .... LC 10
Marcel, Gabriel Honore 1889-1973 .. CLC 15
    See also CA 102; 45-48; MTCW 1
Marchbanks, Samuel
    See Davies, (William) Robertson
Marchi, Giacomo
    See Bassani, Giorgio
Margulies, Donald .... CLC 76
Marie de France c. 12th cent. - CMLC 8; PC
    22
    See also DLB 208
Marie de l'Incarnation 1599-1672 ...... LC 10
Marier, Captain Victor
    See Griffith, D(avid Lewelyn) W(ark)
Mariner, Scott
    See Pohl, Frederik
Marinetti, Filippo Tommaso 1876-1944TCLC
    10
    See also CA 107; DLB 114
Marivaux, Pierre Carlet de Chamblain de 1688-
    1763 .... LC 4; DC 7
Markandaya, Kamala .... CLC 8, 38
    See also Taylor, Kamala (Purnaiya)
Markfield, Wallace 1926- .... CLC 8
    See also CA 69-72; CAAS 3; DLB 2, 28
Markham, Edwin 1852-1940 .... TCLC 47
    See also CA 160; DLB 54, 186
Markham, Robert
    See Amis, Kingsley (William)
Marks, J
    See Highwater, Jamake (Mamake)
Marks-Highwater, J
    See Highwater, Jamake (Mamake)
Markson, David M(errill) 1927- .... CLC 67
    See also CA 49-52; CANR 1

Marley, Bob .... CLC 17
    See also Marley, Robert Nesta
Marley, Robert Nesta 1945-1981
    See Marley, Bob
    See also CA 107; 103
Marlowe, Christopher 1564-1593 LC 22, 47;
    DA; DAB; DAC; DAM DRAM, MST; DC
    1; WLC
    See also CDBLB Before 1660; DLB 62
Marlowe, Stephen 1928-
    See Queen, Ellery
    See also CA 13-16R; CANR 6, 55
Marmontel, Jean-Francois 1723-1799 . LC 2
Marquand, John P(hillips) 1893-1960CLC 2,
    10
    See also CA 85-88; CANR 73; DLB 9, 102
Marques, Rene 1919-1979 ..... CLC 96; DAM
    MULT; HLC
    See also CA 97-100; 85-88; DLB 113; HW
Marquez, Gabriel (Jose) Garcia
    See Garcia Marquez, Gabriel (Jose)
Marquis, Don(ald Robert Perry) 1878-1937
    TCLC 7
    See also CA 104; 166; DLB 11, 25
Marric, J. J.
    See Creasey, John
Marryat, Frederick 1792-1848 .... NCLC 3
    See also DLB 21, 163
Marsden, James
    See Creasey, John
Marsh, (Edith) Ngaio 1899-1982 CLC 7, 53;
    DAM POP
    See also CA 9-12R; CANR 6, 58; DLB 77;
    MTCW 1
Marshall, Garry 1934- .... CLC 17
    See also AAYA 3; CA 111; SATA 60
Marshall, Paule 1929- .. CLC 27, 72; BLC 3;
    DAM MULT; SSC 3
    See also BW 2; CA 77-80; CANR 25, 73; DLB
    157; MTCW 1
Marshallik
    See Zangwill, Israel
Marsten, Richard
    See Hunter, Evan
Marston, John 1576-1634LC 33; DAM DRAM
    See also DLB 58, 172
Martha, Henry
    See Harris, Mark
Marti, Jose 1853-1895NCLC 63; DAM MULT;
    HLC
Martial c. 40-c. 104 .... PC 10
Martin, Ken
    See Hubbard, L(afayette) Ron(ald)
Martin, Richard
    See Creasey, John
Martin, Steve 1945- .... CLC 30
    See also CA 97-100; CANR 30; MTCW 1
Martin, Valerie 1948- .... CLC 89
    See also BEST 90:2; CA 85-88; CANR 49
Martin, Violet Florence 1862-1915 TCLC 51
Martin, Webber
    See Silverberg, Robert
Martindale, Patrick Victor
    See White, Patrick (Victor Martindale)
Martin du Gard, Roger 1881-1958 TCLC 24
    See also CA 118; DLB 65
Martineau, Harriet 1802-1876 .... NCLC 26
    See also DLB 21, 55, 159, 163, 166, 190; YABC
    2
Martines, Julia
    See O'Faolain, Julia
Martinez, Enrique Gonzalez
    See Gonzalez Martinez, Enrique

Martinez, Jacinto Benavente y
  See Benavente (y Martinez), Jacinto
Martinez Ruiz, Jose 1873-1967
  See Azorin; Ruiz, Jose Martinez
  See also CA 93-96; HW
Martinez Sierra, Gregorio 1881-1947 **TCLC 6**
  See also CA 115
Martinez Sierra, Maria (de la O'LeJarraga)
  1874-1974 .... **TCLC 6**
  See also CA 115
Martinsen, Martin
  See Follett, Ken(neth Martin)
Martinson, Harry (Edmund) 1904-1978 **C L C
  14**
  See also CA 77-80; CANR 34
Marut, Ret
  See Traven, B.
Marut, Robert
  See Traven, B.
Marvell, Andrew 1621-1678 ... **LC 4, 43; DA;
    DAB; DAC; DAM MST, POET; PC 10;
    WLC**
  See also CDBLB 1660-1789; DLB 131
Marx, Karl (Heinrich) 1818-1883 . **NCLC 17**
  See also DLB 129
Masaoka Shiki .... **TCLC 18**
  See also Masaoka Tsunenori
Masaoka Tsunenori 1867-1902
  See Masaoka Shiki
  See also CA 117
Masefield, John (Edward) 1878-1967 **CLC 11,
    47; DAM POET**
  See also CA 19-20; 25-28R; CANR 33; CAP 2;
    CDBLB 1890-1914; DLB 10, 19, 153, 160;
    MTCW 1; SATA 19
Maso, Carole 19(?)- .... **CLC 44**
  See also CA 170
Mason, Bobbie Ann 1940- **CLC 28, 43, 82; SSC
    4**
  See also AAYA 5; CA 53-56; CANR 11, 31,
    58; DLB 173; DLBY 87; INT CANR-31;
    MTCW 1
Mason, Ernst
  See Pohl, Frederik
Mason, Lee W.
  See Malzberg, Barry N(athaniel)
Mason, Nick 1945- .... **CLC 35**
Mason, Tally
  See Derleth, August (William)
Mass, William
  See Gibson, William
Master Lao
  See Lao Tzu
Masters, Edgar Lee 1868-1950 **TCLC 2, 25;
    DA; DAC; DAM MST, POET; PC 1;
    WLCS**
  See also CA 104; 133; CDALB 1865-1917;
    DLB 54; MTCW 1
Masters, Hilary 1928- .... **CLC 48**
  See also CA 25-28R; CANR 13, 47
Mastrosimone, William 19(?)- .... **CLC 36**
Mathe, Albert
  See Camus, Albert
Mather, Cotton 1663-1728 .... **LC 38**
  See also CDALB 1640-1865; DLB 24, 30, 140
Mather, Increase 1639-1723 .... **LC 38**
  See also DLB 24
Matheson, Richard Burton 1926- .... **CLC 37**
  See also CA 97-100; DLB 8, 44; INT 97-100
Mathews, Harry 1930- .... **CLC 6, 52**
  See also CA 21-24R; CAAS 6; CANR 18, 40
Mathews, John Joseph 1894-1979 .. **CLC 84;
    DAM MULT**

See also CA 19-20; 142; CANR 45; CAP 2;
  DLB 175; NNAL
Mathias, Roland (Glyn) 1915- .... **CLC 45**
  See also CA 97-100; CANR 19, 41; DLB 27
Matsuo Basho 1644-1694 .... **PC 3**
  See also DAM POET
Mattheson, Rodney
  See Creasey, John
Matthews, Greg 1949- .... **CLC 45**
  See also CA 135
Matthews, William (Procter, III) 1942-1997
  CLC 40
  See also CA 29-32R; 162; CAAS 18; CANR
    12, 57; DLB 5
Matthias, John (Edward) 1941- .... **CLC 9**
  See also CA 33-36R; CANR 56
Matthiessen, Peter 1927- **CLC 5, 7, 11, 32, 64;
    DAM NOV**
  See also AAYA 6; BEST 90:4; CA 9-12R;
    CANR 21, 50, 73; DLB 6, 173; MTCW 1;
    SATA 27
Maturin, Charles Robert 1780(?)-1824 **N C L C
  6**
  See also DLB 178
Matute (Ausejo), Ana Maria 1925- .. **CLC 11**
  See also CA 89-92; MTCW 1
Maugham, W. S.
  See Maugham, W(illiam) Somerset
Maugham, W(illiam) Somerset 1874-1965
    **CLC 1, 11, 15, 67, 93; DA; DAB; DAC;
    DAM DRAM, MST, NOV; SSC 8; WLC**
  See also CA 5-8R; 25-28R; CANR 40; CDBLB
    1914-1945; DLB 10, 36, 77, 100, 162, 195;
    MTCW 1; SATA 54
Maugham, William Somerset
  See Maugham, W(illiam) Somerset
Maupassant, (Henri Rene Albert) Guy de 1850-
  1893 **NCLC 1, 42; DA; DAB; DAC; DAM
    MST; SSC 1; WLC**
  See also DLB 123
Maupin, Armistead 1944- **CLC 95; DAM POP**
  See also CA 125; 130; CANR 58; INT 130
Maurhut, Richard
  See Traven, B.
Mauriac, Claude 1914-1996 .... **CLC 9**
  See also CA 89-92; 152; DLB 83
Mauriac, Francois (Charles) 1885-1970 **C L C
    4, 9, 56; SSC 24**
  See also CA 25-28; CAP 2; DLB 65; MTCW 1
Mavor, Osborne Henry 1888-1951
  See Bridie, James
  See also CA 104
Maxwell, William (Keepers, Jr.) 1908- **CLC 19**
  See also CA 93-96; CANR 54; DLBY 80; INT
    93-96
May, Elaine 1932- .... **CLC 16**
  See also CA 124; 142; DLB 44
Mayakovski, Vladimir (Vladimirovich) 1893-
  1930 .... **TCLC 4, 18**
  See also CA 104; 158
Mayhew, Henry 1812-1887 .... **NCLC 31**
  See also DLB 18, 55, 190
Mayle, Peter 1939(?)- .... **CLC 89**
  See also CA 139; CANR 64
Maynard, Joyce 1953- .... **CLC 23**
  See also CA 111; 129; CANR 64
Mayne, William (James Carter) 1928- **CLC 12**
  See also AAYA 20; CA 9-12R; CANR 37; CLR
    25; JRDA; MAICYA; SAAS 11; SATA 6, 68
Mayo, Jim
  See L'Amour, Louis (Dearborn)
Maysles, Albert 1926- .... **CLC 16**
  See also CA 29-32R

Maysles, David 1932- .... **CLC 16**
Mazer, Norma Fox 1931- .... **CLC 26**
  See also AAYA 5; CA 69-72; CANR 12, 32,
    66; CLR 23; JRDA; MAICYA; SAAS 1;
    SATA 24, 67, 105
Mazzini, Guiseppe 1805-1872 .... **NCLC 34**
McAuley, James Phillip 1917-1976 .. **CLC 45**
  See also CA 97-100
McBain, Ed
  See Hunter, Evan
McBrien, William Augustine 1930- .. **CLC 44**
  See also CA 107
McCaffrey, Anne (Inez) 1926- **CLC 17; DAM
    NOV, POP**
  See also AAYA 6; AITN 2; BEST 89:2; CA 25-
    28R; CANR 15, 35, 55; CLR 49; DLB 8;
    JRDA; MAICYA; MTCW 1; SAAS 11; SATA
    8, 70
McCall, Nathan 1955(?)- .... **CLC 86**
  See also CA 146
McCann, Arthur
  See Campbell, John W(ood, Jr.)
McCann, Edson
  See Pohl, Frederik
McCarthy, Charles, Jr. 1933-
  See McCarthy, Cormac
  See also CANR 42, 69; DAM POP
McCarthy, Cormac 1933- **CLC 4, 57, 59, 101**
  See also McCarthy, Charles, Jr.
  See also DLB 6, 143
McCarthy, Mary (Therese) 1912-1989 **CLC 1,
    3, 5, 14, 24, 39, 59; SSC 24**
  See also CA 5-8R; 129; CANR 16, 50, 64; DLB
    2; DLBY 81; INT CANR-16; MTCW 1
McCartney, (James) Paul 1942- . **CLC 12, 35**
  See also CA 146
McCauley, Stephen (D.) 1955- .... **CLC 50**
  See also CA 141
McClure, Michael (Thomas) 1932- **CLC 6, 10**
  See also CA 21-24R; CANR 17, 46; DLB 16
McCorkle, Jill (Collins) 1958- .... **CLC 51**
  See also CA 121; DLBY 87
McCourt, Frank 1930- .... **CLC 109**
  See also CA 157
McCourt, James 1941- .... **CLC 5**
  See also CA 57-60
McCoy, Horace (Stanley) 1897-1955 **TCLC 28**
  See also CA 108; 155; DLB 9
McCrae, John 1872-1918 .... **TCLC 12**
  See also CA 109; DLB 92
McCreigh, James
  See Pohl, Frederik
McCullers, (Lula) Carson (Smith) 1917-1967
    **CLC 1, 4, 10, 12, 48, 100; DA; DAB; DAC;
    DAM MST, NOV; SSC 9, 24; WLC**
  See also AAYA 21; CA 5-8R; 25-28R; CABS
    1, 3; CANR 18; CDALB 1941-1968; DLB
    2, 7, 173; MTCW 1; SATA 27
McCulloch, John Tyler
  See Burroughs, Edgar Rice
McCullough, Colleen 1938(?)- **CLC 27, 107;
    DAM NOV, POP**
  See also CA 81-84; CANR 17, 46, 67; MTCW
    1
McDermott, Alice 1953- .... **CLC 90**
  See also CA 109; CANR 40
McElroy, Joseph 1930- .... **CLC 5, 47**
  See also CA 17-20R
McEwan, Ian (Russell) 1948- .... **CLC 13, 66;
    DAM NOV**
  See also BEST 90:4; CA 61-64; CANR 14, 41,
    69; DLB 14, 194; MTCW 1
McFadden, David 1940- .... **CLC 48**

NCLC 14
See also DLB 99
Mooney, Edward 1951-
See Mooney. Ted
See also CA 130
Mooney, Ted .... **CLC 25**
See also Mooney. Edward
Moorcock, Michael (John) 1939-**CLC 5, 27, 58**
See also AAYA 26; CA 45-48; CAAS 5; CANR
2, 17, 38, 64; DLB 14; MTCW 1; SATA 93
Moore, Brian 1921- **CLC 1, 3, 5, 7, 8, 19, 32,**
90; DAB; DAC; DAM MST
See also CA 1-4R; CANR 1, 25, 42. 63; MTCW
1
Moore, Edward
See Muir, Edwin
Moore, G. E. 1873-1958 .... **TCLC 89**
Moore, George Augustus 1852-1933**TCLC 7;**
SSC 19
See also CA 104; DLB 10, 18, 57, 135
Moore, Lorrie .... **CLC 39, 45, 68**
See also Moore. Marie Lorena
Moore, Marianne (Craig) 1887-1972**CLC 1, 2,**
4, 8, 10, 13, 19, 47; DA; DAB; DAC; DAM
MST, POET; PC 4; WLCS
See also CA 1-4R; 33-36R; CANR 3, 61;
CDALB 1929-1941; DLB 45; DLBD 7;
MTCW 1; SATA 20
Moore, Marie Lorena 1957-
See Moore, Lorrie
See also CA 116; CANR 39
Moore, Thomas 1779-1852 .... **NCLC 6**
See also DLB 96, 144
Morand, Paul 1888-1976 .... **CLC 41; SSC 22**
See also CA 69-72; DLB 65
Morante, Elsa 1918-1985 .... **CLC 8, 47**
See also CA 85-88; 117; CANR 35; DLB 177;
MTCW 1
Moravia, Alberto 1907-1990**CLC 2, 7, 11, 27,**
46; SSC 26
See also Pincherle, Alberto
See also DLB 177
More, Hannah 1745-1833 .... **NCLC 27**
See also DLB 107, 109, 116, 158
More, Henry 1614-1687 .... **LC 9**
See also DLB 126
More, Sir Thomas 1478-1535 .... **LC 10, 32**
Moreas, Jean .... **TCLC 18**
See also Papadiamantopoulos, Johannes
Morgan, Berry 1919- .... **CLC 6**
See also CA 49-52; DLB 6
Morgan, Claire
See Highsmith, (Mary) Patricia
Morgan, Edwin (George) 1920- .... **CLC 31**
See also CA 5-8R; CANR 3, 43; DLB 27
Morgan, (George) Frederick 1922- . **CLC 23**
See also CA 17-20R; CANR 21
Morgan, Harriet
See Mencken, H(enry) L(ouis)
Morgan, Jane
See Cooper, James Fenimore
Morgan, Janet 1945- .... **CLC 39**
See also CA 65-68
Morgan, Lady 1776(?)-1859 .... **NCLC 29**
See also DLB 116, 158
Morgan, Robin (Evonne) 1941- .... **CLC 2**
See also CA 69-72; CANR 29, 68; MTCW 1;
SATA 80
Morgan, Scott
See Kuttner, Henry
Morgan, Seth 1949(?)-1990 .... **CLC 65**
See also CA 132
Morgenstern, Christian 1871-1914 . **TCLC 8**

See also CA 105
Morgenstern, S.
See Goldman. William (W.)
Moricz, Zsigmond 1879-1942 .... **TCLC 33**
See also CA 165
Morike, Eduard (Friedrich) 1804-1875**NCLC**
10
See also DLB 133
Moritz, Karl Philipp 1756-1793 .... **LC 2**
See also DLB 94
Morland, Peter Henry
See Faust, Frederick (Schiller)
Morley, Christopher (Darlington) 1890-1957
TCLC 87
See also CA 112; DLB 9
Morren, Theophil
See Hofmannsthal, Hugo von
Morris, Bill 1952- .... **CLC 76**
Morris, Julian
See West, Morris L(anglo)
Morris, Steveland Judkins 1950(?)-
See Wonder. Stevie
See also CA 111
Morris, William 1834-1896 .... **NCLC 4**
See also CDBLB 1832-1890; DLB 18, 35, 57,
156, 178, 184
Morris, Wright 1910-1998**CLC 1, 3, 7, 18, 37**
See also CA 9-12R; 167; CANR 21; DLB 2,
206; DLBY 81; MTCW 1
Morrison, Arthur 1863-1945 .... **TCLC 72**
See also CA 120; 157; DLB 70, 135, 197
Morrison, Chloe Anthony Wofford
See Morrison, Toni
Morrison, James Douglas 1943-1971
See Morrison, Jim
See also CA 73-76; CANR 40
Morrison, Jim .... **CLC 17**
See also Morrison, James Douglas
Morrison, Toni 1931-**CLC 4, 10, 22, 55, 81, 87;**
BLC 3; DA; DAB; DAC; DAM MST,
MULT, NOV, POP
See also AAYA 1, 22; BW 2; CA 29-32R;
CANR 27, 42, 67; CDALB 1968-1988; DLB
6, 33, 143; DLBY 81; MTCW 1; SATA 57
Morrison, Van 1945- .... **CLC 21**
See also CA 116; 168
Morrissy, Mary 1958- .... **CLC 99**
Mortimer, John (Clifford) 1923-**CLC 28, 43;**
DAM DRAM, POP
See also CA 13-16R; CANR 21, 69; CDBLB
1960 to Present; DLB 13; INT CANR-21;
MTCW 1
Mortimer, Penelope (Ruth) 1918- .... **CLC 5**
See also CA 57-60; CANR 45
Morton, Anthony
See Creasey, John
Mosca, Gaetano 1858-1941 .... **TCLC 75**
Mosher, Howard Frank 1943- .... **CLC 62**
See also CA 139; CANR 65
Mosley, Nicholas 1923- .... **CLC 43, 70**
See also CA 69-72; CANR 41, 60; DLB 14, 207
Mosley, Walter 1952- **CLC 97; BLCS; DAM**
MULT, POP
See also AAYA 17; BW 2; CA 142; CANR 57
Moss, Howard 1922-1987 **CLC 7, 14, 45, 50;**
DAM POET
See also CA 1-4R; 123; CANR 1, 44; DLB 5
Mossgiel, Rab
See Burns, Robert
Motion, Andrew (Peter) 1952- .... **CLC 47**
See also CA 146; DLB 40
Motley, Willard (Francis) 1909-1965 **CLC 18**
See also BW 1; CA 117; 106; DLB 76, 143

Motoori, Norinaga 1730-1801 .... **NCLC 45**
Mott, Michael (Charles Alston) 1930-**CLC 15,**
34
See also CA 5-8R; CAAS 7; CANR 7, 29
Mountain Wolf Woman 1884-1960 .. **CLC 92**
See also CA 144; NNAL
Moure, Erin 1955- .... **CLC 88**
See also CA 113; DLB 60
Mowat, Farley (McGill) 1921-**CLC 26; DAC;**
DAM MST
See also AAYA 1; CA 1-4R; CANR 4, 24, 42,
68; CLR 20; DLB 68; INT CANR-24; JRDA;
MAICYA; MTCW 1; SATA 3, 55
Mowatt, Anna Cora 1819-1870 ...... **NCLC 74**
Moyers, Bill 1934- .... **CLC 74**
See also AITN 2; CA 61-64; CANR 31, 52
Mphahlele, Es'kia
See Mphahlele, Ezekiel
See also DLB 125
Mphahlele, Ezekiel 1919-1983 **CLC 25; BLC**
3; DAM MULT
See also Mphahlele, Es'kia
See also BW 2; CA 81-84; CANR 26, 76
Mqhayi, S(amuel) E(dward) K(rune Loliwe)
1875-1945**TCLC 25; BLC 3; DAM MULT**
See also CA 153
Mrozek, Slawomir 1930- .... **CLC 3, 13**
See also CA 13-16R; CAAS 10; CANR 29;
MTCW 1
Mrs. Belloc-Lowndes
See Lowndes, Marie Adelaide (Belloc)
Mtwa, Percy (?)- .... **CLC 47**
Mueller, Lisel 1924- .... **CLC 13, 51**
See also CA 93-96; DLB 105
Muir, Edwin 1887-1959 .... **TCLC 2, 87**
See also CA 104; DLB 20, 100, 191
Muir, John 1838-1914 .... **TCLC 28**
See also CA 165; DLB 186
Mujica Lainez, Manuel 1910-1984 .. **CLC 31**
See also Lainez, Manuel Mujica
See also CA 81-84; 112; CANR 32; HW
Mukherjee, Bharati 1940-**CLC 53, 115; DAM**
NOV
See also BEST 89:2; CA 107; CANR 45, 72;
DLB 60; MTCW 1
Muldoon, Paul 1951-**CLC 32, 72; DAM POET**
See also CA 113; 129; CANR 52; DLB 40; INT
129
Mulisch, Harry 1927- .... **CLC 42**
See also CA 9-12R; CANR 6, 26, 56
Mull, Martin 1943- .... **CLC 17**
See also CA 105
Muller, Wilhelm .... **NCLC 73**
Mulock, Dinah Maria
See Craik, Dinah Maria (Mulock)
Munford, Robert 1737(?)-1783 .... **LC 5**
See also DLB 31
Mungo, Raymond 1946- .... **CLC 72**
See also CA 49-52; CANR 2
Munro, Alice 1931- .... **CLC 6, 10, 19, 50, 95;**
DAC; DAM MST, NOV; SSC 3; WLCS
See also AITN 2; CA 33-36R; CANR 33, 53,
75; DLB 53; MTCW 1; SATA 29
Munro, H(ector) H(ugh) 1870-1916
See Saki
See also CA 104; 130; CDBLB 1890-1914; DA;
DAB; DAC; DAM MST, NOV; DLB 34, 162;
MTCW 1; WLC
Murdoch, (Jean) Iris 1919-**CLC 1, 2, 3, 4, 6, 8,**
11, 15, 22, 31, 51; DAB; DAC; DAM MST,
NOV
See also CA 13-16R; CANR 8, 43, 68; CDBLB
1960 to Present; DLB 14, 194; INT CANR-

Parnell, Thomas 1679-1718 .... **LC 3**
See also DLB 94
Parra, Nicanor 1914- ...... **CLC 2, 102; DAM MULT; HLC**
See also CA 85-88; CANR 32; HW; MTCW 1
Parrish, Mary Frances
See Fisher, M(ary) F(rances) K(ennedy)
Parson
See Coleridge, Samuel Taylor
Parson Lot
See Kingsley, Charles
Partridge, Anthony
See Oppenheim, E(dward) Phillips
Pascal, Blaise 1623-1662 .... **LC 35**
Pascoli, Giovanni 1855-1912 .... **TCLC 45**
See also CA 170
Pasolini, Pier Paolo 1922-1975 . **CLC 20, 37, 106; PC 17**
See also CA 93-96; 61-64; CANR 63; DLB 128, 177; MTCW 1
Pasquini
See Silone, Ignazio
Pastan, Linda (Olenik) 1932- **CLC 27; DAM POET**
See also CA 61-64; CANR 18, 40, 61; DLB 5
Pasternak, Boris (Leonidovich) 1890-1960
CLC 7, 10, 18, 63; DA; DAB; DAC; DAM MST, NOV, POET; PC 6; SSC 31; WLC
See also CA 127; 116; MTCW 1
Patchen, Kenneth 1911-1972 ... **CLC 1, 2, 18; DAM POET**
See also CA 1-4R; 33-36R; CANR 3, 35; DLB 16, 48; MTCW 1
Pater, Walter (Horatio) 1839-1894 .. **NCLC 7**
See also CDBLB 1832-1890; DLB 57, 156
Paterson, A(ndrew) B(arton) 1864-1941
TCLC 32
See also CA 155; SATA 97
Paterson, Katherine (Womeldorf) 1932-**C L C 12, 30**
See also AAYA 1; CA 21-24R; CANR 28, 59; CLR 7, 50; DLB 52; JRDA; MAICYA; MTCW 1; SATA 13, 53, 92
Patmore, Coventry Kersey Dighton 1823-1896
NCLC 9
See also DLB 35, 98
Paton, Alan (Stewart) 1903-1988 **CLC 4, 10, 25, 55, 106; DA; DAB; DAC; DAM MST, NOV; WLC**
See also AAYA 26; CA 13-16; 125; CANR 22; CAP 1; DLBD 17; MTCW 1; SATA 11; SATA-Obit 56
Paton Walsh, Gillian 1937-
See Walsh, Jill Paton
See also CANR 38; JRDA; MAICYA; SAAS 3; SATA 4, 72
Patton, George S. 1885-1945 .... **TCLC 79**
Paulding, James Kirke 1778-1860 ... **NCLC 2**
See also DLB 3, 59, 74
Paulin, Thomas Neilson 1949-
See Paulin, Tom
See also CA 123; 128
Paulin, Tom .... **CLC 37**
See also Paulin, Thomas Neilson
See also DLB 40
Paustovsky, Konstantin (Georgievich) 1892-1968 .... **CLC 40**
See also CA 93-96; 25-28R
Pavese, Cesare 1908-1950 ... **TCLC 3; PC 13; SSC 19**
See also CA 104; 169; DLB 128, 177
Pavic, Milorad 1929- .... **CLC 60**
See also CA 136; DLB 181

Payne, Alan
See Jakes, John (William)
Paz, Gil
See Lugones. Leopoldo
Paz, Octavio 1914-1998 **CLC 3, 4, 6, 10, 19, 51, 65; DA; DAB; DAC; DAM MST, MULT, POET; HLC; PC 1; WLC**
See also CA 73-76; 165; CANR 32, 65; DLBY 90; HW; MTCW 1
p'Bitek, Okot 1931-1982 .... **CLC 96; BLC 3; DAM MULT**
See also BW 2; CA 124; 107; DLB 125; MTCW 1
Peacock, Molly 1947- .... **CLC 60**
See also CA 103; CAAS 21; CANR 52; DLB 120
Peacock, Thomas Love 1785-1866 . **NCLC 22**
See also DLB 96, 116
Peake, Mervyn 1911-1968 .... **CLC 7, 54**
See also CA 5-8R; 25-28R; CANR 3; DLB 15, 160; MTCW 1; SATA 23
Pearce, Philippa .... **CLC 21**
See also Christie, (Ann) Philippa
See also CLR 9; DLB 161; MAICYA; SATA 1, 67
Pearl, Eric
See Elman, Richard (Martin)
Pearson, T(homas) R(eid) 1956- .... **CLC 39**
See also CA 120; 130; INT 130
Peck, Dale 1967- .... **CLC 81**
See also CA 146; CANR 72
Peck, John 1941- .... **CLC 3**
See also CA 49-52; CANR 3
Peck, Richard (Wayne) 1934- .... **CLC 21**
See also AAYA 1, 24; CA 85-88; CANR 19, 38; CLR 15; INT CANR-19; JRDA; MAICYA; SAAS 2; SATA 18, 55, 97
Peck, Robert Newton 1928- ..... **CLC 17; DA; DAC; DAM MST**
See also AAYA 3; CA 81-84; CANR 31, 63; CLR 45; JRDA; MAICYA; SAAS 1; SATA 21, 62
Peckinpah, (David) Sam(uel) 1925-1984 **C L C 20**
See also CA 109; 114
Pedersen, Knut 1859-1952
See Hamsun, Knut
See also CA 104; 119; CANR 63; MTCW 1
Peeslake, Gaffer
See Durrell, Lawrence (George)
Peguy, Charles Pierre 1873-1914 ... **TCLC 10**
See also CA 107
Peirce, Charles Sanders 1839-1914 **TCLC 81**
Pena, Ramon del Valle y
See Valle-Inclan, Ramon (Maria) del
Pendennis, Arthur Esquir
See Thackeray, William Makepeace
Penn, William 1644-1718 .... **LC 25**
See also DLB 24
PEPECE
See Prado (Calvo), Pedro
Pepys, Samuel 1633-1703 **LC 11; DA; DAB; DAC; DAM MST; WLC**
See also CDBLB 1660-1789; DLB 101
Percy, Walker 1916-1990 **CLC 2, 3, 6, 8, 14, 18, 47, 65; DAM NOV, POP**
See also CA 1-4R; 131; CANR 1, 23, 64; DLB 2; DLBY 80, 90; MTCW 1
Percy, William Alexander 1885-1942 **TCLC 84**
See also CA 163
Perec, Georges 1936-1982 .... **CLC 56, 116**
See also CA 141; DLB 83
Pereda (y Sanchez de Porrua), Jose Maria de

1833-1906 .... **TCLC 16**
See also CA 117
Pereda y Porrua, Jose Maria de
See Pereda (y Sanchez de Porrua), Jose Maria de
Peregoy, George Weems
See Mencken, H(enry) L(ouis)
Perelman, S(idney) J(oseph) 1904-1979 **C L C 3, 5, 9, 15, 23, 44, 49; DAM DRAM; SSC 32**
See also AITN 1, 2; CA 73-76; 89-92; CANR 18; DLB 11, 44; MTCW 1
Peret, Benjamin 1899-1959 .... **TCLC 20**
See also CA 117
Peretz, Isaac Loeb 1851(?)-1915 .. **TCLC 16; SSC 26**
See also CA 109
Peretz, Yitzkhok Leibush
See Peretz, Isaac Loeb
Perez Galdos, Benito 1843-1920 .... **TCLC 27**
See also CA 125; 153; HW
Perrault, Charles 1628-1703 .... **LC 2**
See also MAICYA; SATA 25
Perry, Brighton
See Sherwood, Robert E(mmet)
Perse, St.-John
See Leger, (Marie-Rene Auguste) Alexis Saint-Leger
Perutz, Leo(pold) 1882-1957 .... **TCLC 60**
See also CA 147; DLB 81
Peseenz, Tulio F.
See Lopez y Fuentes, Gregorio
Pesetsky, Bette 1932- .... **CLC 28**
See also CA 133; DLB 130
Peshkov, Alexei Maximovich 1868-1936
See Gorky, Maxim
See also CA 105; 141; DA; DAC; DAM DRAM, MST, NOV
Pessoa, Fernando (Antonio Nogueira) 1898-1935 .... **TCLC 27; HLC; PC 20**
See also CA 125
Peterkin, Julia Mood 1880-1961 ...... **CLC 31**
See also CA 102; DLB 9
Peters, Joan K(aren) 1945- .... **CLC 39**
See also CA 158
Peters, Robert L(ouis) 1924- ....**CLC 7**
See also CA 13-16R; CAAS 8; DLB 105
Petofi, Sandor 1823-1849 .... **NCLC 21**
Petrakis, Harry Mark 1923- ....**CLC 3**
See also CA 9-12R; CANR 4, 30
Petrarch 1304-1374 **CMLC 20; DAM POET; PC 8**
Petrov, Evgeny .... **TCLC 21**
See also Kataev, Evgeny Petrovich
Petry, Ann (Lane) 1908-1997 ... **CLC 1, 7, 18**
See also BW 1; CA 5-8R; 157; CAAS 6; CANR 4, 46; CLR 12; DLB 76; JRDA; MAICYA; MTCW 1; SATA 5; SATA-Obit 94
Petursson, Halligrimur 1614-1674 .... **LC 8**
Peychinovich
See Vazov, Ivan (Minchov)
Phaedrus 18(?)B.C.-55(?) .... **CMLC 25**
Philips, Katherine 1632-1664 .... **LC 30**
See also DLB 131
Philipson, Morris H. 1926- .... **CLC 53**
See also CA 1-4R; CANR 4
Phillips, Caryl 1958- . **CLC 96; BLCS; DAM MULT**
See also BW 2; CA 141; CANR 63; DLB 157
Phillips, David Graham 1867-1911 **TCLC 44**
See also CA 108; DLB 9, 12
Phillips, Jack
See Sandburg, Carl (August)

CLC 1, 2, 3, 4, 5, 7, 10, 13, 18, 34, 48, 50, 112; DA; DAB; DAC; DAM MST, POET; PC 4; WLC
See also CA 5-8R; 37-40R; CANR 40; CDALB 1917-1929; DLB 4. 45, 63; DLBD 15; MTCW 1
Povod, Reinaldo 1959-1994 .... **CLC 44**
See also CA 136; 146
Powell, Adam Clayton, Jr. 1908-1972 CLC 89; **BLC 3; DAM MULT**
See also BW 1; CA 102; 33-36R
Powell, Anthony (Dymoke) 1905-CLC 1, 3, 7, 9, 10, 31
See also CA 1-4R; CANR 1, 32, 62; CDBLB 1945-1960; DLB 15; MTCW 1
Powell, Dawn 1897-1965 .... **CLC 66**
See also CA 5-8R; DLBY 97
Powell, Padgett 1952- .... **CLC 34**
See also CA 126; CANR 63
Power, Susan 1961- .... **CLC 91**
Powers, J(ames) F(arl) 1917-CLC 1, 4, 8, 57; **SSC 4**
See also CA 1-4R; CANR 2, 61; DLB 130; MTCW 1
Powers, John J(ames) 1945-
See Powers, John R.
See also CA 69-72
Powers, John R. .... **CLC 66**
See also Powers, John J(ames)
Powers, Richard (S.) 1957- .... **CLC 93**
See also CA 148
Pownall, David 1938- .... **CLC 10**
See also CA 89-92; CAAS 18; CANR 49; DLB 14
Powys, John Cowper 1872-1963 CLC 7, 9, 15, 46
See also CA 85-88; DLB 15; MTCW 1
Powys, T(heodore) F(rancis) 1875-1953 **TCLC 9**
See also CA 106; DLB 36, 162
Prado (Calvo), Pedro 1886-1952 .... **TCLC 75**
See also CA 131; HW
Prager, Emily 1952- .... **CLC 56**
Pratt, E(dwin) J(ohn) 1883(?)-1964 **CLC 19; DAC; DAM POET**
See also CA 141; 93-96; DLB 92
Premchand .... **TCLC 21**
See also Srivastava, Dhanpat Rai
Preussler, Otfried 1923- .... **CLC 17**
See also CA 77-80; SATA 24
Prevert, Jacques (Henri Marie) 1900-1977 **CLC 15**
See also CA 77-80; 69-72; CANR 29, 61; MTCW 1; SATA-Obit 30
Prevost, Abbe (Antoine Francois) 1697-1763 **LC 1**
Price, (Edward) Reynolds 1933-CLC 3, 6, 13, 43, 50, 63; **DAM NOV; SSC 22**
See also CA 1-4R; CANR 1, 37, 57; DLB 2; INT CANR-37
Price, Richard 1949- .... **CLC 6, 12**
See also CA 49-52; CANR 3; DLBY 81
Prichard, Katharine Susannah 1883-1969 **CLC 46**
See also CA 11-12; CANR 33; CAP 1; MTCW 1; SATA 66
Priestley, J(ohn) B(oynton) 1894-1984 CLC 2, 5, 9, 34; **DAM DRAM, NOV**
See also CA 9-12R; 113; CANR 33; CDBLB 1914-1945; DLB 10, 34, 77, 100, 139; DLBY 84; MTCW 1
Prince 1958(?)- .... **CLC 35**
Prince, F(rank) T(empleton) 1912-.. **CLC 22**

See also CA 101; CANR 43; DLB 20
Prince Kropotkin
See Kropotkin. Peter (Aleksieevich)
Prior, Matthew 1664-1721 .... **LC 4**
See also DLB 95
Prishvin, Mikhail 1873-1954 .... **TCLC 75**
Pritchard, William H(arrison) 1932- CLC 34
See also CA 65-68; CANR 23; DLB 111
Pritchett, V(ictor) S(awdon) 1900-1997 C L C 5, 13, 15, 41; **DAM NOV; SSC 14**
See also CA 61-64; 157; CANR 31, 63; DLB 15. 139; MTCW 1
Private 19022
See Manning, Frederic
Probst, Mark 1925- .... **CLC 59**
See also CA 130
Prokosch, Frederic 1908-1989 ..... **CLC 4, 48**
See also CA 73-76; 128; DLB 48
Propertius, Sextus 50(?)B.C.-15(?)B.C. **CMLC 32**
Prophet, The
See Dreiser. Theodore (Herman Albert)
Prose, Francine 1947- .... **CLC 45**
See also CA 109; 112; CANR 46; SATA 101
Proudhon
See Cunha, Euclides (Rodrigues Pimenta) da
Proulx, Annie
See Proulx, E(dna) Annie
Proulx, E(dna) Annie 1935-... **CLC 81; DAM POP**
See also CA 145; CANR 65
Proust, (Valentin-Louis-George-Eugene-) Marcel 1871-1922 **TCLC 7, 13, 33; DA; DAB; DAC; DAM MST, NOV; WLC**
See also CA 104; 120; DLB 65; MTCW 1
Prowler, Harley
See Masters, Edgar Lee
Prus, Boleslaw 1845-1912 .... **TCLC 48**
Pryor, Richard (Franklin Lenox Thomas) 1940- **CLC 26**
See also CA 122; 152
Przybyszewski, Stanislaw 1868-1927 TCLC 36
See also CA 160; DLB 66
Pteleon
See Grieve, C(hristopher) M(urray)
See also DAM POET
Puckett, Lute
See Masters, Edgar Lee
Puig, Manuel 1932-1990 CLC 3, 5, 10, 28, 65; **DAM MULT; HLC**
See also CA 45-48; CANR 2, 32, 63; DLB 113; HW; MTCW 1
Pulitzer, Joseph 1847-1911 .... **TCLC 76**
See also CA 114; DLB 23
Purdy, A(lfred) W(ellington) 1918-CLC 3, 6, 14, 50; **DAC; DAM MST, POET**
See also CA 81-84; CAAS 17; CANR 42, 66; DLB 88
Purdy, James (Amos) 1923-CLC 2, 4, 10, 28, 52
See also CA 33-36R; CAAS 1; CANR 19, 51; DLB 2; INT CANR-19; MTCW 1
Pure, Simon
See Swinnerton, Frank Arthur
Pushkin, Alexander (Sergeyevich) 1799-1837 **NCLC 3, 27; DA; DAB; DAC; DAM DRAM, MST, POET; PC 10; SSC 27; WLC**
See also DLB 205; SATA 61
P'u Sung-ling 1640-1715 .... **LC 3; SSC 31**
Putnam, Arthur Lee
See Alger, Horatio, Jr.
Puzo, Mario 1920-CLC 1, 2, 6, 36, 107; **DAM**

NOV, POP
See also CA 65-68; CANR 4, 42, 65; DLB 6; MTCW 1
Pygge, Edward
See Barnes, Julian (Patrick)
Pyle, Ernest Taylor 1900-1945
See Pyle, Ernie
See also CA 115; 160
Pyle, Ernie 1900-1945 .... **TCLC 75**
See also Pyle, Ernest Taylor
See also DLB 29
Pyle, Howard 1853-1911 .... **TCLC 81**
See also CA 109; 137; CLR 22; DLB 42, 188; DLBD 13; MAICYA; SATA 16, 100
Pym, Barbara (Mary Crampton) 1913-1980 **CLC 13, 19, 37, 111**
See also CA 13-14; 97-100; CANR 13, 34; CAP 1; DLB 14, 207; DLBY 87; MTCW 1
Pynchon, Thomas (Ruggles, Jr.) 1937-CLC 2, 3, 6, 9, 11, 18, 33, 62, 72; **DA; DAB; DAC; DAM MST, NOV, POP; SSC 14; WLC**
See also BEST 90:2; CA 17-20R; CANR 22, 46, 73; DLB 2, 173; MTCW 1
Pythagoras c. 570B.C.-c. 500B.C. . **CMLC 22**
See also DLB 176
Q
See Quiller-Couch, SirArthur (Thomas)
Qian Zhongshu
See Ch'ien Chung-shu
Qroll
See Dagerman, Stig (Halvard)
Quarrington, Paul (Lewis) 1953-..... **CLC 65**
See also CA 129; CANR 62
Quasimodo, Salvatore 1901-1968 .... **CLC 10**
See also CA 13-16; 25-28R; CAP 1; DLB 114; MTCW 1
Quay, Stephen 1947- .... **CLC 95**
Quay, Timothy 1947-........................ **CLC 95**
Queen, Ellery .... **CLC 3, 11**
See also Dannay, Frederic; Davidson, Avram; Lee, Manfred B(ennington); Marlowe, Stephen; Sturgeon, Theodore (Hamilton); Vance, John Holbrook
Queen, Ellery, Jr.
See Dannay, Frederic; Lee, Manfred B(ennington)
Queneau, Raymond 1903-1976 CLC 2, 5, 10, 42
See also CA 77-80; 69-72; CANR 32; DLB 72; MTCW 1
Quevedo, Francisco de 1580-1645 ...... **LC 23**
Quiller-Couch, SirArthur (Thomas) 1863-1944 **TCLC 53**
See also CA 118; 166; DLB 135, 153, 190
Quin, Ann (Marie) 1936-1973 .... **CLC 6**
See also CA 9-12R; 45-48; DLB 14
Quinn, Martin
See Smith, Martin Cruz
Quinn, Peter 1947- .... **CLC 91**
Quinn, Simon
See Smith, Martin Cruz
Quiroga, Horacio (Sylvestre) 1878-1937 **TCLC 20; DAM MULT; HLC**
See also CA 117; 131; HW; MTCW 1
Quoirez, Francoise 1935-.................... **CLC 9**
See also Sagan, Francoise
See also CA 49-52; CANR 6, 39, 73; MTCW 1
Raabe, Wilhelm (Karl) 1831-1910 . **TCLC 45**
See also CA 167; DLB 129
Rabe, David (William) 1940-... **CLC 4, 8, 33; DAM DRAM**
See also CA 85-88; CABS 3; CANR 59; DLB 7
Rabelais, Francois 1483-1553 LC 5; **DA; DAB;**

Savan, Glenn 19(?)- .... **CLC 50**

Sayers, Dorothy L(eigh) 1893-1957 **TCLC 2, 15; DAM POP**
    See also CA 104; 119; CANR 60; CDBLB 1914-1945; DLB 10, 36, 77, 100; MTCW 1

Sayers, Valerie 1952- .... **CLC 50**
    See also CA 134; CANR 61

Sayles, John (Thomas) 1950- . **CLC 7, 10, 14**
    See also CA 57-60; CANR 41; DLB 44

Scammell, Michael 1935- .... **CLC 34**
    See also CA 156

Scannell, Vernon 1922- .... **CLC 49**
    See also CA 5-8R; CANR 8, 24, 57; DLB 27; SATA 59

Scarlett, Susan
    See Streatfeild, (Mary) Noel

Scarron
    See Mikszath, Kalman

Schaeffer, Susan Fromberg 1941- **CLC 6, 11, 22**
    See also CA 49-52; CANR 18, 65; DLB 28; MTCW 1; SATA 22

Schary, Jill
    See Robinson, Jill

Schell, Jonathan 1943- .... **CLC 35**
    See also CA 73-76; CANR 12

Schelling, Friedrich Wilhelm Joseph von 1775-1854 .... **NCLC 30**
    See also DLB 90

Schendel, Arthur van 1874-1946 ... **TCLC 56**

Scherer, Jean-Marie Maurice 1920-
    See Rohmer, Eric
    See also CA 110

Schevill, James (Erwin) 1920- .... **CLC 7**
    See also CA 5-8R; CAAS 12

Schiller, Friedrich 1759-1805 . **NCLC 39, 69; DAM DRAM**
    See also DLB 94

Schisgal, Murray (Joseph) 1926- .... **CLC 6**
    See also CA 21-24R; CANR 48

Schlee, Ann 1934- .... **CLC 35**
    See also CA 101; CANR 29; SATA 44; SATA-Brief 36

Schlegel, August Wilhelm von 1767-1845 **NCLC 15**
    See also DLB 94

Schlegel, Friedrich 1772-1829 .... **NCLC 45**
    See also DLB 90

Schlegel, Johann Elias (von) 1719(?)-1749 **LC 5**

Schlesinger, Arthur M(eier), Jr. 1917- **CLC 84**
    See also AITN 1; CA 1-4R; CANR 1, 28, 58; DLB 17; INT CANR-28; MTCW 1; SATA 61

Schmidt, Arno (Otto) 1914-1979 ...... **CLC 56**
    See also CA 128; 109; DLB 69

Schmitz, Aron Hector 1861-1928
    See Svevo, Italo
    See also CA 104; 122; MTCW 1

Schnackenberg, Gjertrud 1953- ...... **CLC 40**
    See also CA 116; DLB 120

Schneider, Leonard Alfred 1925-1966
    See Bruce, Lenny
    See also CA 89-92

Schnitzler, Arthur 1862-1931 **TCLC 4; SSC 15**
    See also CA 104; DLB 81, 118

Schoenberg, Arnold 1874-1951 ...... **TCLC 75**
    See also CA 109

Schonberg, Arnold
    See Schoenberg, Arnold

Schopenhauer, Arthur 1788-1860 .. **NCLC 51**
    See also DLB 90

Schor, Sandra (M.) 1932(?)-1990 ..... **CLC 65**

See also CA 132

Schorer, Mark 1908-1977 .... **CLC 9**
    See also CA 5-8R; 73-76; CANR 7; DLB 103

Schrader, Paul (Joseph) 1946- .... **CLC 26**
    See also CA 37-40R; CANR 41; DLB 44

Schreiner, Olive (Emilie Albertina) 1855-1920 **TCLC 9**
    See also CA 105; 154; DLB 18, 156, 190

Schulberg, Budd (Wilson) 1914- .. **CLC 7, 48**
    See also CA 25-28R; CANR 19; DLB 6, 26, 28; DLBY 81

Schulz, Bruno 1892-1942 **TCLC 5, 51; SSC 13**
    See also CA 115; 123

Schulz, Charles M(onroe) 1922- .... **CLC 12**
    See also CA 9-12R; CANR 6; INT CANR-6; SATA 10

Schumacher, E(rnst) F(riedrich) 1911-1977 **CLC 80**
    See also CA 81-84; 73-76; CANR 34

Schuyler, James Marcus 1923-1991 **CLC 5, 23; DAM POET**
    See also CA 101; 134; DLB 5, 169; INT 101

Schwartz, Delmore (David) 1913-1966 **CLC 2, 4, 10, 45, 87; PC 8**
    See also CA 17-18; 25-28R; CANR 35; CAP 2; DLB 28, 48; MTCW 1

Schwartz, Ernst
    See Ozu, Yasujiro

Schwartz, John Burnham 1965- .... **CLC 59**
    See also CA 132

Schwartz, Lynne Sharon 1939- .... **CLC 31**
    See also CA 103; CANR 44

Schwartz, Muriel A.
    See Eliot, T(homas) S(tearns)

Schwarz-Bart, Andre 1928- .... **CLC 2, 4**

Schwarz-Bart, Simone 1938- .. **CLC 7; BLCS**
    See also BW 2; CA 97-100

Schwob, Marcel (Mayer Andre) 1867-1905 **TCLC 20**
    See also CA 117; 168; DLB 123

Sciascia, Leonardo 1921-1989 . **CLC 8, 9, 41**
    See also CA 85-88; 130; CANR 35; DLB 177; MTCW 1

Scoppettone, Sandra 1936- .... **CLC 26**
    See also AAYA 11; CA 5-8R; CANR 41, 73; SATA 9, 92

Scorsese, Martin 1942- .... **CLC 20, 89**
    See also CA 110; 114; CANR 46

Scotland, Jay
    See Jakes, John (William)

Scott, Duncan Campbell 1862-1947 **TCLC 6; DAC**
    See also CA 104; 153; DLB 92

Scott, Evelyn 1893-1963 .... **CLC 43**
    See also CA 104; 112; CANR 64; DLB 9, 48

Scott, F(rancis) R(eginald) 1899-1985 **CLC 22**
    See also CA 101; 114; DLB 88; INT 101

Scott, Frank
    See Scott, F(rancis) R(eginald)

Scott, Joanna 1960- .... **CLC 50**
    See also CA 126; CANR 53

Scott, Paul (Mark) 1920-1978 ...... **CLC 9, 60**
    See also CA 81-84; 77-80; CANR 33; DLB 14, 207; MTCW 1

Scott, Sarah 1723-1795 .... **LC 44**
    See also DLB 39

Scott, Walter 1771-1832 .. **NCLC 15, 69; DA; DAB; DAC; DAM MST, NOV, POET; PC 13; SSC 32; WLC**
    See also AAYA 22; CDBLB 1789-1832; DLB 93, 107, 116, 144, 159; YABC 2

Scribe, (Augustin) Eugene 1791-1861 **N C L C**

16; **DAM DRAM; DC 5**
    See also DLB 192

Scrum, R.
    See Crumb, R(obert)

Scudery, Madeleine de 1607-1701 .... **LC 2**

Scum
    See Crumb, R(obert)

Scumbag, Little Bobby
    See Crumb, R(obert)

Seabrook, John
    See Hubbard, L(afayette) Ron(ald)

Sealy, I. Allan 1951- .... **CLC 55**

Search, Alexander
    See Pessoa, Fernando (Antonio Nogueira)

Sebastian, Lee
    See Silverberg, Robert

Sebastian Owl
    See Thompson, Hunter S(tockton)

Sebestyen, Ouida 1924- .... **CLC 30**
    See also AAYA 8; CA 107; CANR 40; CLR 17; JRDA; MAICYA; SAAS 10; SATA 39

Secundus, H. Scriblerus
    See Fielding, Henry

Sedges, John
    See Buck, Pearl S(ydenstricker)

Sedgwick, Catharine Maria 1789-1867 **N C L C 19**
    See also DLB 1, 74

Seelye, John (Douglas) 1931- .... **CLC 7**
    See also CA 97-100; CANR 70; INT 97-100

Seferiades, Giorgos Stylianou 1900-1971
    See Seferis, George
    See also CA 5-8R; 33-36R; CANR 5, 36; MTCW 1

Seferis, George .... **CLC 5, 11**
    See also Seferiades, Giorgos Stylianou

Segal, Erich (Wolf) 1937- .. **CLC 3, 10; DAM POP**
    See also BEST 89:1; CA 25-28R; CANR 20, 36, 65; DLBY 86; INT CANR-20; MTCW 1

Seger, Bob 1945- .... **CLC 35**

Seghers, Anna .... **CLC 7**
    See also Radvanyi, Netty
    See also DLB 69

Seidel, Frederick (Lewis) 1936- .... **CLC 18**
    See also CA 13-16R; CANR 8; DLBY 84

Seifert, Jaroslav 1901-1986 .. **CLC 34, 44, 93**
    See also CA 127; MTCW 1

Sei Shonagon c. 966-1017(?) .... **CMLC 6**

Séjour, Victor 1817-1874 .... **DC 10**
    See also DLB 50

Sejour Marcou et Ferrand, Juan Victor
    See Séjour, Victor

Selby, Hubert, Jr. 1928- **CLC 1, 2, 4, 8; SSC 20**
    See also CA 13-16R; CANR 33; DLB 2

Selzer, Richard 1928- .... **CLC 74**
    See also CA 65-68; CANR 14

Sembene, Ousmane
    See Ousmane, Sembene

Senancour, Etienne Pivert de 1770-1846 **NCLC 16**
    See also DLB 119

Sender, Ramon (Jose) 1902-1982 **CLC 8; DAM MULT; HLC**
    See also CA 5-8R; 105; CANR 8; HW; MTCW 1

Seneca, Lucius Annaeus 4B.C.-65 **CMLC 6; DAM DRAM; DC 5**

Senghor, Leopold Sedar 1906- **CLC 54; BLC 3; DAM MULT, POET; PC 25**
    See also BW 2; CA 116; 125; CANR 47, 74; MTCW 1

Serling, (Edward) Rod(man) 1924-1975 **C L C**

See also CA 1-4R

Sigourney, Lydia Howard (Huntley) 1791-1865
   NCLC 21
   See also DLB 1, 42, 73

Siguenza y Gongora, Carlos de 1645-1700**L C
   8**

Sigurjonsson, Johann 1880-1919 ... **TCLC 27**
   See also CA 170

Sikelianos, Angelos 1884-1951 .... **TCLC 39**

Silkin, Jon 1930- .... **CLC 2, 6, 43**
   See also CA 5-8R; CAAS 5; DLB 27

Silko, Leslie (Marmon) 1948-**CLC 23, 74, 114;
   DA; DAC; DAM MST, MULT, POP;
   WLCS**
   See also AAYA 14; CA 115; 122; CANR 45,
   65; DLB 143, 175; NNAL

Sillanpaa, Frans Eemil 1888-1964 ... **CLC 19**
   See also CA 129; 93-96; MTCW 1

Sillitoe, Alan 1928- .... **CLC 1, 3, 6, 10, 19, 57**
   See also AITN 1; CA 9-12R; CAAS 2; CANR
   8, 26, 55; CDBLB 1960 to Present; DLB 14,
   139; MTCW 1; SATA 61

Silone, Ignazio 1900-1978 .... **CLC 4**
   See also CA 25-28; 81-84; CANR 34; CAP 2;
   MTCW 1

Silver, Joan Micklin 1935- .... **CLC 20**
   See also CA 114; 121; INT 121

Silver, Nicholas
   See Faust, Frederick (Schiller)

Silverberg, Robert 1935- **CLC 7; DAM POP**
   See also AAYA 24; CA 1-4R; CAAS 3; CANR
   1, 20, 36; DLB 8; INT CANR-20; MAICYA;
   MTCW 1; SATA 13, 91; SATA-Essay 104

Silverstein, Alvin 1933- .... **CLC 17**
   See also CA 49-52; CANR 2; CLR 25; JRDA;
   MAICYA; SATA 8, 69

Silverstein, Virginia B(arbara Opshelor) 1937-
   CLC 17
   See also CA 49-52; CANR 2; CLR 25; JRDA;
   MAICYA; SATA 8, 69

Sim, Georges
   See Simenon, Georges (Jacques Christian)

Simak, Clifford D(onald) 1904-1988**CLC 1, 55**
   See also CA 1-4R; 125; CANR 1, 35; DLB 8;
   MTCW 1; SATA-Obit 56

Simenon, Georges (Jacques Christian) 1903-
   1989 .. **CLC 1, 2, 3, 8, 18, 47; DAM POP**
   See also CA 85-88; 129; CANR 35; DLB 72;
   DLBY 89; MTCW 1

Simic, Charles 1938- .... **CLC 6, 9, 22, 49, 68;
   DAM POET**
   See also CA 29-32R; CAAS 4; CANR 12, 33,
   52, 61; DLB 105

Simmel, Georg 1858-1918 .... **TCLC 64**
   See also CA 157

Simmons, Charles (Paul) 1924- .... **CLC 57**
   See also CA 89-92; INT 89-92

Simmons, Dan 1948- ...... **CLC 44; DAM POP**
   See also AAYA 16; CA 138; CANR 53

Simmons, James (Stewart Alexander) 1933-
   CLC 43
   See also CA 105; CAAS 21; DLB 40

Simms, William Gilmore 1806-1870 **NCLC 3**
   See also DLB 3, 30, 59, 73

Simon, Carly 1945- .... **CLC 26**
   See also CA 105

Simon, Claude 1913-1984 .. **CLC 4, 9, 15, 39;
   DAM NOV**
   See also CA 89-92; CANR 33; DLB 83; MTCW
   1

Simon, (Marvin) Neil 1927-**CLC 6, 11, 31, 39,
   70; DAM DRAM**
   See also AITN 1; CA 21-24R; CANR 26, 54;

DLB 7; MTCW 1

Simon, Paul (Frederick) 1941(?)- ...... **CLC 17**
   See also CA 116; 153

Simonon, Paul 1956(?)- .... **CLC 30**

Simpson, Harriette
   See Arnow, Harriette (Louisa) Simpson

Simpson, Louis (Aston Marantz) 1923-**CLC 4,
   7, 9, 32; DAM POET**
   See also CA 1-4R; CAAS 4; CANR 1, 61; DLB
   5; MTCW 1

Simpson, Mona (Elizabeth) 1957- .... **CLC 44**
   See also CA 122; 135; CANR 68

Simpson, N(orman) F(rederick) 1919-**CLC 29**
   See also CA 13-16R; DLB 13

Sinclair, Andrew (Annandale) 1935- . **CLC 2,
   14**
   See also CA 9-12R; CAAS 5; CANR 14, 38;
   DLB 14; MTCW 1

Sinclair, Emil
   See Hesse, Hermann

Sinclair, Iain 1943- .... **CLC 76**
   See also CA 132

Sinclair, Iain MacGregor
   See Sinclair, Iain

Sinclair, Irene
   See Griffith, D(avid Lewelyn) W(ark)

Sinclair, Mary Amelia St. Clair 1865(?)-1946
   See Sinclair, May
   See also CA 104

Sinclair, May 1863-1946 .... **TCLC 3, 11**
   See also Sinclair, Mary Amelia St. Clair
   See also CA 166; DLB 36, 135

Sinclair, Roy
   See Griffith, D(avid Lewelyn) W(ark)

Sinclair, Upton (Beall) 1878-1968 **CLC 1, 11,
   15, 63; DA; DAB; DAC; DAM MST, NOV;
   WLC**
   See also CA 5-8R; 25-28R; CANR 7; CDALB
   1929-1941; DLB 9; INT CANR-7; MTCW
   1; SATA 9

Singer, Isaac
   See Singer, Isaac Bashevis

Singer, Isaac Bashevis 1904-1991**CLC 1, 3, 6,
   9, 11, 15, 23, 38, 69, 111; DA; DAB; DAC;
   DAM MST, NOV; SSC 3; WLC**
   See also AITN 1, 2; CA 1-4R; 134; CANR 1,
   39; CDALB 1941-1968; CLR 1; DLB 6, 28,
   52; DLBY 91; JRDA; MAICYA; MTCW 1;
   SATA 3, 27; SATA-Obit 68

Singer, Israel Joshua 1893-1944 .... **TCLC 33**
   See also CA 169

Singh, Khushwant 1915- .... **CLC 11**
   See also CA 9-12R; CAAS 9; CANR 6

Singleton, Ann
   See Benedict, Ruth (Fulton)

Sinjohn, John
   See Galsworthy, John

Sinyavsky, Andrei (Donatevich) 1925-1997
   CLC 8
   See also CA 85-88; 159

Sirin, V.
   See Nabokov, Vladimir (Vladimirovich)

Sissman, L(ouis) E(dward) 1928-1976**CLC 9,
   18**
   See also CA 21-24R; 65-68; CANR 13; DLB 5

Sisson, C(harles) H(ubert) 1914- .... **CLC 8**
   See also CA 1-4R; CAAS 3; CANR 3, 48; DLB
   27

Sitwell, Dame Edith 1887-1964**CLC 2, 9, 67;
   DAM POET; PC 3**
   See also CA 9-12R; CANR 35; CDBLB 1945-
   1960; DLB 20; MTCW 1

Siwaarmill, H. P.

See Sharp, William

Sjoewall, Maj 1935- .... **CLC 7**
   See also CA 65-68; CANR 73

Sjowall, Maj
   See Sjoewall, Maj

Skelton, John 1463-1529 .... **PC 25**

Skelton, Robin 1925-1997 .... **CLC 13**
   See also AITN 2; CA 5-8R; 160; CAAS 5;
   CANR 28; DLB 27, 53

Skolimowski, Jerzy 1938- .... **CLC 20**
   See also CA 128

Skram, Amalie (Bertha) 1847-1905 **TCLC 25**
   See also CA 165

Skvorecky, Josef (Vaclav) 1924- **CLC 15, 39,
   69; DAC; DAM NOV**
   See also CA 61-64; CAAS 1; CANR 10, 34,
   63; MTCW 1

Slade, Bernard .... **CLC 11, 46**
   See also Newbound, Bernard Slade
   See also CAAS 9; DLB 53

Slaughter, Carolyn 1946- .... **CLC 56**
   See also CA 85-88

Slaughter, Frank G(ill) 1908- .... **CLC 29**
   See also AITN 2; CA 5-8R; CANR 5; INT
   CANR-5

Slavitt, David R(ytman) 1935- ..... **CLC 5, 14**
   See also CA 21-24R; CAAS 3; CANR 41; DLB
   5, 6

Slesinger, Tess 1905-1945 .... **TCLC 10**
   See also CA 107; DLB 102

Slessor, Kenneth 1901-1971 .... **CLC 14**
   See also CA 102; 89-92

Slowacki, Juliusz 1809-1849 .... **NCLC 15**

Smart, Christopher 1722-1771 .. **LC 3; DAM
   POET; PC 13**
   See also DLB 109

Smart, Elizabeth 1913-1986 .... **CLC 54**
   See also CA 81-84; 118; DLB 88

Smiley, Jane (Graves) 1949-**CLC 53, 76; DAM
   POP**
   See also CA 104; CANR 30, 50, 74; INT CANR-
   30

Smith, A(rthur) J(ames) M(arshall) 1902-1980
   CLC 15; DAC
   See also CA 1-4R; 102; CANR 4; DLB 88

Smith, Adam 1723-1790 .... **LC 36**
   See also DLB 104

Smith, Alexander 1829-1867 .... **NCLC 59**
   See also DLB 32, 55

Smith, Anna Deavere 1950- .... **CLC 86**
   See also CA 133

Smith, Betty (Wehner) 1896-1972 ..... **CLC 19**
   See also CA 5-8R; 33-36R; DLBY 82; SATA 6

Smith, Charlotte (Turner) 1749-1806 **N C L C
   23**
   See also DLB 39, 109

Smith, Clark Ashton 1893-1961 .... **CLC 43**
   See also CA 143

Smith, Dave .... **CLC 22, 42**
   See also Smith, David (Jeddie)
   See also CAAS 7; DLB 5

Smith, David (Jeddie) 1942-
   See Smith, Dave
   See also CA 49-52; CANR 1, 59; DAM POET

Smith, Florence Margaret 1902-1971
   See Smith, Stevie
   See also CA 17-18; 29-32R; CANR 35; CAP 2;
   DAM POET; MTCW 1

Smith, Iain Crichton 1928-1998 .... **CLC 64**
   See also CA 21-24R; 171; DLB 40, 139

Smith, John 1580(?)-1631 .... **LC 9**
   See also DLB 24, 30

Smith, Johnston

See Crane, Stephen (Townley)

Smith, Joseph, Jr. 1805-1844 .... **NCLC 53**

Smith, Lee 1944-........................ **CLC 25, 73**
See also CA 114; 119; CANR 46; DLB 143; DLBY 83; INT 119

Smith, Martin
See Smith, Martin Cruz

Smith, Martin Cruz 1942- ..... **CLC 25; DAM MULT, POP**
See also BEST 89:4; CA 85-88; CANR 6, 23, 43, 65; INT CANR-23; NNAL

Smith, Mary-Ann Tirone 1944- .... **CLC 39**
See also CA 118; 136

Smith, Patti 1946-............................. **CLC 12**
See also CA 93-96; CANR 63

Smith, Pauline (Urmson) 1882-1959**TCLC 25**

Smith, Rosamond
See Oates, Joyce Carol

Smith, Sheila Kaye
See Kaye-Smith, Sheila

Smith, Stevie .... **CLC 3, 8, 25, 44; PC 12**
See also Smith, Florence Margaret
See also DLB 20

Smith, Wilbur (Addison) 1933-........ **CLC 33**
See also CA 13-16R; CANR 7, 46, 66; MTCW 1

Smith, William Jay 1918- .... **CLC 6**
See also CA 5-8R; CANR 44; DLB 5; MAICYA; SAAS 22; SATA 2, 68

Smith, Woodrow Wilson
See Kuttner, Henry

Smolenskin, Peretz 1842-1885 .... **NCLC 30**

Smollett, Tobias (George) 1721-1771**LC 2, 46**
See also CDBLB 1660-1789; DLB 39, 104

Snodgrass, W(illiam) D(e Witt) 1926-**CLC 2, 6, 10, 18, 68; DAM POET**
See also CA 1-4R; CANR 6, 36, 65; DLB 5; MTCW 1

Snow, C(harles) P(ercy) 1905-1980**CLC 1, 4, 6, 9, 13, 19; DAM NOV**
See also CA 5-8R; 101; CANR 28; CDBLB 1945-1960; DLB 15, 77; DLBD 17; MTCW 1

Snow, Frances Compton
See Adams, Henry (Brooks)

Snyder, Gary (Sherman) 1930-**CLC 1, 2, 5, 9, 32; DAM POET; PC 21**
See also CA 17-20R; CANR 30, 60; DLB 5, 16, 165

Snyder, Zilpha Keatley 1927-........... **CLC 17**
See also AAYA 15; CA 9-12R; CANR 38; CLR 31; JRDA; MAICYA; SAAS 2; SATA 1, 28, 75

Soares, Bernardo
See Pessoa, Fernando (Antonio Nogueira)

Sobh, A.
See Shamlu, Ahmad

Sobol, Joshua .... **CLC 60**

Socrates 469B.C.-399B.C. .... **CMLC 27**

Soderberg, Hjalmar 1869-1941 ..... **TCLC 39**

Sodergran, Edith (Irene)
See Soedergran, Edith (Irene)

Soedergran, Edith (Irene) 1892-1923 . **T C L C 31**

Softly, Edgar
See Lovecraft, H(oward) P(hillips)

Softly, Edward
See Lovecraft, H(oward) P(hillips)

Sokolov, Raymond 1941- .... **CLC 7**
See also CA 85-88

Solo, Jay
See Ellison, Harlan (Jay)

Sologub, Fyodor .... **TCLC 9**

See also Teternikov, Fyodor Kuzmich

Solomons, Ikey Esquir
See Thackeray, William Makepeace

Solomos, Dionysios 1798-1857 .... **NCLC 15**

Solwoska, Mara
See French, Marilyn

Solzhenitsyn, Aleksandr I(sayevich) 1918-**CLC 1, 2, 4, 7, 9, 10, 18, 26, 34, 78; DA; DAB; DAC; DAM MST, NOV; SSC 32; WLC**
See also AITN 1; CA 69-72; CANR 40, 65; MTCW 1

Somers, Jane
See Lessing, Doris (May)

Somerville, Edith 1858-1949 .... **TCLC 51**
See also DLB 135

Somerville & Ross
See Martin, Violet Florence; Somerville, Edith

Sommer, Scott 1951-........................... **CLC 25**
See also CA 106

Sondheim, Stephen (Joshua) 1930-. **CLC 30, 39; DAM DRAM**
See also AAYA 11; CA 103; CANR 47, 68

Song, Cathy 1955- .... **PC 21**
See also CA 154; DLB 169

Sontag, Susan 1933-**CLC 1, 2, 10, 13, 31, 105; DAM POP**
See also CA 17-20R; CANR 25, 51, 74; DLB 2, 67; MTCW 1

Sophocles 496(?)B.C.-406(?)B.C. .. **CMLC 2; DA; DAB; DAC; DAM DRAM, MST; DC 1; WLCS**
See also DLB 176

Sordello 1189-1269 .... **CMLC 15**

Sorel, Julia
See Drexler, Rosalyn

Sorrentino, Gilbert 1929-**CLC 3, 7, 14, 22, 40**
See also CA 77-80; CANR 14, 33; DLB 5, 173; DLBY 80; INT CANR-14

Soto, Gary 1952-. **CLC 32, 80; DAM MULT; HLC**
See also AAYA 10; CA 119; 125; CANR 50, 74; CLR 38; DLB 82; HW; INT 125; JRDA; SATA 80

Soupault, Philippe 1897-1990 .... **CLC 68**
See also CA 116; 147; 131

Souster, (Holmes) Raymond 1921-**CLC 5, 14; DAC; DAM POET**
See also CA 13-16R; CAAS 14; CANR 13, 29, 53; DLB 88; SATA 63

Southern, Terry 1924(?)-1995 .... **CLC 7**
See also CA 1-4R; 150; CANR 1, 55; DLB 2

Southey, Robert 1774-1843 .... **NCLC 8**
See also DLB 93, 107, 142; SATA 54

Southworth, Emma Dorothy Eliza Nevitte 1819-1899 .... **NCLC 26**

Souza, Ernest
See Scott, Evelyn

Soyinka, Wole 1934-**CLC 3, 5, 14, 36, 44; BLC 3; DA; DAB; DAC; DAM DRAM, MST, MULT; DC 2; WLC**
See also BW 2; CA 13-16R; CANR 27, 39; DLB 125; MTCW 1

Spackman, W(illiam) M(ode) 1905-1990**C L C 46**
See also CA 81-84; 132

Spacks, Barry (Bernard) 1931-......... **CLC 14**
See also CA 154; CANR 33; DLB 105

Spanidou, Irini 1946- .... **CLC 44**

Spark, Muriel (Sarah) 1918-**CLC 2, 3, 5, 8, 13, 18, 40, 94; DAB; DAC; DAM MST, NOV; SSC 10**
See also CA 5-8R; CANR 12, 36, 76; CDBLB

1945-1960; DLB 15, 139; INT CANR-12; MTCW 1

Spaulding, Douglas
See Bradbury, Ray (Douglas)

Spaulding, Leonard
See Bradbury, Ray (Douglas)

Spence, J. A. D.
See Eliot, T(homas) S(tearns)

Spencer, Elizabeth 1921- .... **CLC 22**
See also CA 13-16R; CANR 32, 65; DLB 6; MTCW 1; SATA 14

Spencer, Leonard G.
See Silverberg, Robert

Spencer, Scott 1945- .... **CLC 30**
See also CA 113; CANR 51; DLBY 86

Spender, Stephen (Harold) 1909-1995**CLC 1, 2, 5, 10, 41, 91; DAM POET**
See also CA 9-12R; 149; CANR 31, 54; CDBLB 1945-1960; DLB 20; MTCW 1

Spengler, Oswald (Arnold Gottfried) 1880-1936 **TCLC 25**
See also CA 118

Spenser, Edmund 1552(?)-1599**LC 5, 39; DA; DAB; DAC; DAM MST, POET; PC 8; WLC**
See also CDBLB Before 1660; DLB 167

Spicer, Jack 1925-1965 **CLC 8, 18, 72; DAM POET**
See also CA 85-88; DLB 5, 16, 193

Spiegelman, Art 1948- .... **CLC 76**
See also AAYA 10; CA 125; CANR 41, 55, 74

Spielberg, Peter 1929-......................... **CLC 6**
See also CA 5-8R; CANR 4, 48; DLBY 81

Spielberg, Steven 1947-..................... **CLC 20**
See also AAYA 8, 24; CA 77-80; CANR 32; SATA 32

Spillane, Frank Morrison 1918-
See Spillane, Mickey
See also CA 25-28R; CANR 28, 63; MTCW 1; SATA 66

Spillane, Mickey .... **CLC 3, 13**
See also Spillane, Frank Morrison

Spinoza, Benedictus de 1632-1677 .... **LC 9**

Spinrad, Norman (Richard) 1940- .. **CLC 46**
See also CA 37-40R; CAAS 19; CANR 20; DLB 8; INT CANR-20

Spitteler, Carl (Friedrich Georg) 1845-1924 **TCLC 12**
See also CA 109; DLB 129

Spivack, Kathleen (Romola Drucker) 1938-**CLC 6**
See also CA 49-52

Spoto, Donald 1941- .... **CLC 39**
See also CA 65-68; CANR 11, 57

Springsteen, Bruce (F.) 1949- .... **CLC 17**
See also CA 111

Spurling, Hilary 1940-......................... **CLC 34**
See also CA 104; CANR 25, 52

Spyker, John Howland
See Elman, Richard (Martin)

Squires, (James) Radcliffe 1917-1993**CLC 51**
See also CA 1-4R; 140; CANR 6, 21

Srivastava, Dhanpat Rai 1880(?)-1936
See Premchand
See also CA 118

Stacy, Donald
See Pohl, Frederik

Stael, Germaine de 1766-1817
See Stael-Holstein, Anne Louise Germaine Necker Baronn
See also DLB 119

Stael-Holstein, Anne Louise Germaine Necker Baronn 1766-1817 .... **NCLC 3**

See also Stael, Germaine de
See also DLB 192
Stafford, Jean 1915-1979**CLC 4, 7, 19, 68; SSC 26**
See also CA 1-4R; 85-88; CANR 3, 65; DLB 2, 173; MTCW 1; SATA-Obit 22
Stafford, William (Edgar) 1914-1993 **CLC 4, 7, 29; DAM POET**
See also CA 5-8R; 142; CAAS 3; CANR 5, 22; DLB 5, 206; INT CANR-22
Stagnelius, Eric Johan 1793-1823 . **NCLC 61**
Staines, Trevor
See Brunner, John (Kilian Houston)
Stairs, Gordon
See Austin, Mary (Hunter)
Stannard, Martin 1947- .... **CLC 44**
See also CA 142; DLB 155
Stanton, Elizabeth Cady 1815-1902**TCLC 73**
See also CA 171; DLB 79
Stanton, Maura 1946- ....**CLC 9**
See also CA 89-92; CANR 15; DLB 120
Stanton, Schuyler
See Baum, L(yman) Frank
Stapledon, (William) Olaf 1886-1950 . **T C L C 22**
See also CA 111; 162; DLB 15
Starbuck, George (Edwin) 1931-1996**CLC 53; DAM POET**
See also CA 21-24R; 153; CANR 23
Stark, Richard
See Westlake, Donald E(dwin)
Staunton, Schuyler
See Baum, L(yman) Frank
Stead, Christina (Ellen) 1902-1983 **CLC 2, 5, 8, 32, 80**
See also CA 13-16R; 109; CANR 33, 40; MTCW 1
Stead, William Thomas 1849-1912 **TCLC 48**
See also CA 167
Steele, Richard 1672-1729 .... **LC 18**
See also CDBLB 1660-1789; DLB 84, 101
Steele, Timothy (Reid) 1948- .... **CLC 45**
See also CA 93-96; CANR 16, 50; DLB 120
Steffens, (Joseph) Lincoln 1866-1936 . **T C L C 20**
See also CA 117
Stegner, Wallace (Earle) 1909-1993**CLC 9, 49, 81; DAM NOV; SSC 27**
See also AITN 1; BEST 90:3; CA 1-4R; 141; CAAS 9; CANR 1, 21, 46; DLB 9, 206; DLBY 93; MTCW 1
Stein, Gertrude 1874-1946**TCLC 1, 6, 28, 48; DA; DAB; DAC; DAM MST, NOV, POET; PC 18; WLC**
See also CA 104; 132; CDALB 1917-1929; DLB 4, 54, 86; DLBD 15; MTCW 1
Steinbeck, John (Ernst) 1902-1968 **CLC 1, 5, 9, 13, 21, 34, 45, 75; DA; DAB; DAC; DAM DRAM, MST, NOV; SSC 11; WLC**
See also AAYA 12; CA 1-4R; 25-28R; CANR 1, 35; CDALB 1929-1941; DLB 7, 9; DLBD 2; MTCW 1; SATA 9
Steinem, Gloria 1934- .... **CLC 63**
See also CA 53-56; CANR 28, 51; MTCW 1
Steiner, George 1929- ... **CLC 24; DAM NOV**
See also CA 73-76; CANR 31, 67; DLB 67; MTCW 1; SATA 62
Steiner, K. Leslie
See Delany, Samuel R(ay, Jr.)
Steiner, Rudolf 1861-1925 .... **TCLC 13**
See also CA 107
Stendhal 1783-1842**NCLC 23, 46; DA; DAB; DAC; DAM MST, NOV; SSC 27; WLC**

See also DLB 119
Stephen, Adeline Virginia
See Woolf, (Adeline) Virginia
Stephen, SirLeslie 1832-1904 .... **TCLC 23**
See also CA 123; DLB 57, 144, 190
Stephen, Sir Leslie
See Stephen, SirLeslie
Stephen, Virginia
See Woolf, (Adeline) Virginia
Stephens, James 1882(?)-1950 .... **TCLC 4**
See also CA 104; DLB 19, 153, 162
Stephens, Reed
See Donaldson, Stephen R.
Steptoe, Lydia
See Barnes, Djuna
Sterchi, Beat 1949- .... **CLC 65**
Sterling, Brett
See Bradbury, Ray (Douglas); Hamilton, Edmond
Sterling, Bruce 1954- .... **CLC 72**
See also CA 119; CANR 44
Sterling, George 1869-1926 .... **TCLC 20**
See also CA 117; 165; DLB 54
Stern, Gerald 1925- .... **CLC 40, 100**
See also CA 81-84; CANR 28; DLB 105
Stern, Richard (Gustave) 1928- ... **CLC 4, 39**
See also CA 1-4R; CANR 1, 25, 52; DLBY 87; INT CANR-25
Sternberg, Josef von 1894-1969 .... **CLC 20**
See also CA 81-84
Sterne, Laurence 1713-1768 ... **LC 2, 48; DA; DAB; DAC; DAM MST, NOV; WLC**
See also CDBLB 1660-1789; DLB 39
Sternheim, (William Adolf) Carl 1878-1942 **TCLC 8**
See also CA 105; DLB 56, 118
Stevens, Mark 1951- ....**CLC 34**
See also CA 122
Stevens, Wallace 1879-1955 **TCLC 3, 12, 45; DA; DAB; DAC; DAM MST, POET; PC 6; WLC**
See also CA 104; 124; CDALB 1929-1941; DLB 54; MTCW 1
Stevenson, Anne (Katharine) 1933-**CLC 7, 33**
See also CA 17-20R; CAAS 9; CANR 9, 33; DLB 40; MTCW 1
Stevenson, Robert Louis (Balfour) 1850-1894 **NCLC 5, 14, 63; DA; DAB; DAC; DAM MST, NOV; SSC 11; WLC**
See also AAYA 24; CDBLB 1890-1914; CLR 10, 11; DLB 18, 57, 141, 156, 174; DLBD 13; JRDA; MAICYA; SATA 100; YABC 2
Stewart, J(ohn) I(nnes) M(ackintosh) 1906-1994 .... **CLC 7, 14, 32**
See also CA 85-88; 147; CAAS 3; CANR 47; MTCW 1
Stewart, Mary (Florence Elinor) 1916-**CLC 7, 35, 117; DAB**
See also CA 1-4R; CANR 1, 59; SATA 12
Stewart, Mary Rainbow
See Stewart, Mary (Florence Elinor)
Stifle, June
See Campbell, Maria
Stifter, Adalbert 1805-1868**NCLC 41; SSC 28**
See also DLB 133
Still, James 1906- ....**CLC 49**
See also CA 65-68; CAAS 17; CANR 10, 26; DLB 9; SATA 29
Sting 1951-
See Sumner, Gordon Matthew
See also CA 167
Stirling, Arthur
See Sinclair, Upton (Beall)

Stitt, Milan 1941- ....**CLC 29**
See also CA 69-72
Stockton, Francis Richard 1834-1902
See Stockton, Frank R.
See also CA 108; 137; MAICYA; SATA 44
Stockton, Frank R. ....**TCLC 47**
See also Stockton, Francis Richard
See also DLB 42, 74; DLBD 13; SATA-Brief 32
Stoddard, Charles
See Kuttner, Henry
Stoker, Abraham 1847-1912
See Stoker, Bram
See also CA 105; 150; DA; DAC; DAM MST, NOV; SATA 29
Stoker, Bram 1847-1912**TCLC 8; DAB; WLC**
See also Stoker, Abraham
See also AAYA 23; CDBLB 1890-1914; DLB 36, 70, 178
Stolz, Mary (Slattery) 1920- ....**CLC 12**
See also AAYA 8; AITN 1; CA 5-8R; CANR 13, 41; JRDA; MAICYA; SAAS 3; SATA 10, 71
Stone, Irving 1903-1989 .. **CLC 7; DAM POP**
See also AITN 1; CA 1-4R; 129; CAAS 3; CANR 1, 23; INT CANR-23; MTCW 1; SATA 3; SATA-Obit 64
Stone, Oliver (William) 1946- ....**CLC 73**
See also AAYA 15; CA 110; CANR 55
Stone, Robert (Anthony) 1937-**CLC 5, 23, 42**
See also CA 85-88; CANR 23, 66; DLB 152; INT CANR-23; MTCW 1
Stone, Zachary
See Follett, Ken(neth Martin)
Stoppard, Tom 1937-**CLC 1, 3, 4, 5, 8, 15, 29, 34, 63, 91; DA; DAB; DAC; DAM DRAM, MST; DC 6; WLC**
See also CA 81-84; CANR 39, 67; CDBLB 1960 to Present; DLB 13; DLBY 85; MTCW 1
Storey, David (Malcolm) 1933-**CLC 2, 4, 5, 8; DAM DRAM**
See also CA 81-84; CANR 36; DLB 13, 14, 207; MTCW 1
Storm, Hyemeyohsts 1935- ...... **CLC 3; DAM MULT**
See also CA 81-84; CANR 45; NNAL
Storm, Theodor 1817-1888 ....**SSC 27**
Storm, (Hans) Theodor (Woldsen) 1817-1888 **NCLC 1; SSC 27**
See also DLB 129
Storni, Alfonsina 1892-1938 . **TCLC 5; DAM MULT; HLC**
See also CA 104; 131; HW
Stoughton, William 1631-1701 .... **LC 38**
See also DLB 24
Stout, Rex (Todhunter) 1886-1975 ..... **CLC 3**
See also AITN 2; CA 61-64; CANR 71
Stow, (Julian) Randolph 1935- .. **CLC 23, 48**
See also CA 13-16R; CANR 33; MTCW 1
Stowe, Harriet (Elizabeth) Beecher 1811-1896 **NCLC 3, 50; DA; DAB; DAC; DAM MST, NOV; WLC**
See also CDALB 1865-1917; DLB 1, 12, 42, 74, 189; JRDA; MAICYA; YABC 1
Strachey, (Giles) Lytton 1880-1932 **TCLC 12**
See also CA 110; DLB 149; DLBD 10
Strand, Mark 1934- **CLC 6, 18, 41, 71; DAM POET**
See also CA 21-24R; CANR 40, 65; DLB 5; SATA 41
Straub, Peter (Francis) 1943-.. **CLC 28, 107; DAM POP**

Ulibarri, Sabine R(eyes) 1919-CLC 83; DAM MULT
See also CA 131; DLB 82; HW
Unamuno (y Jugo), Miguel de 1864-1936 TCLC 2, 9; DAM MULT, NOV; HLC; SSC 11
See also CA 104; 131; DLB 108; HW; MTCW 1
Undercliffe, Errol
See Campbell, (John) Ramsey
Underwood, Miles
See Glassco, John
Undset, Sigrid 1882-1949TCLC 3; DA; DAB; DAC; DAM MST, NOV; WLC
See also CA 104; 129; MTCW 1
Ungaretti, Giuseppe 1888-1970CLC 7, 11, 15
See also CA 19-20; 25-28R; CAP 2; DLB 114
Unger, Douglas 1952- .... CLC 34
See also CA 130
Unsworth, Barry (Forster) 1930- .... CLC 76
See also CA 25-28R; CANR 30, 54; DLB 194
Updike, John (Hoyer) 1932-CLC 1, 2, 3, 5, 7, 9, 13, 15, 23, 34, 43, 70; DA; DAB; DAC; DAM MST, NOV, POET, POP; SSC 13, 27; WLC
See also CA 1-4R; CABS 1; CANR 4, 33, 51; CDALB 1968-1988; DLB 2, 5, 143; DLBD 3; DLBY 80, 82, 97; MTCW 1
Upshaw, Margaret Mitchell
See Mitchell, Margaret (Munnerlyn)
Upton, Mark
See Sanders, Lawrence
Upward, Allen 1863-1926 .... TCLC 85
See also CA 117; DLB 36
Urdang, Constance (Henriette) 1922-CLC 47
See also CA 21-24R; CANR 9, 24
Uriel, Henry
See Faust, Frederick (Schiller)
Uris, Leon (Marcus) 1924- CLC 7, 32; DAM NOV, POP
See also AITN 1, 2; BEST 89:2; CA 1-4R; CANR 1, 40, 65; MTCW 1; SATA 49
Urmuz
See Codrescu, Andrei
Urquhart, Jane 1949- .... CLC 90; DAC
See also CA 113; CANR 32, 68
Ustinov, Peter (Alexander) 1921- ....CLC 1
See also AITN 1; CA 13-16R; CANR 25, 51; DLB 13
U Tam'si, Gerald Felix Tchicaya
See Tchicaya, Gerald Felix
U Tam'si, Tchicaya
See Tchicaya, Gerald Felix
Vachss, Andrew (Henry) 1942- ...... CLC 106
See also CA 118; CANR 44
Vachss, Andrew H.
See Vachss, Andrew (Henry)
Vaculik, Ludvik 1926- ....CLC 7
See also CA 53-56; CANR 72
Vaihinger, Hans 1852-1933 .... TCLC 71
See also CA 116; 166
Valdez, Luis (Miguel) 1940- .. CLC 84; DAM MULT; DC 10; HLC
See also CA 101; CANR 32; DLB 122; HW
Valenzuela, Luisa 1938- CLC 31, 104; DAM MULT; SSC 14
See also CA 101; CANR 32, 65; DLB 113; HW
Valera y Alcala-Galiano, Juan 1824-1905 TCLC 10
See also CA 106
Valery, (Ambroise) Paul (Toussaint Jules) 1871-1945 .... TCLC 4, 15; DAM POET; PC 9
See also CA 104; 122; MTCW 1

Valle-Inclan, Ramon (Maria) del 1866-1936 TCLC 5; DAM MULT;HLC
See also CA 106; 153; DLB 134
Vallejo, Antonio Buero
See Buero Vallejo, Antonio
Vallejo, Cesar (Abraham) 1892-1938TCLC 3, 56; DAM MULT; HLC
See also CA 105; 153; HW
Valles, Jules 1832-1885 .... NCLC 71
See also DLB 123
Vallette, Marguerite Eymery
See Rachilde
Valle Y Pena, Ramon del
See Valle-Inclan, Ramon (Maria) del
Van Ash, Cay 1918- ....CLC 34
Vanbrugh, Sir John 1664-1726 LC 21; DAM DRAM
See also DLB 80
Van Campen, Karl
See Campbell, John W(ood, Jr.)
Vance, Gerald
See Silverberg, Robert
Vance, Jack ....CLC 35
See also Kuttner, Henry; Vance, John Holbrook
See also DLB 8
Vance, John Holbrook 1916-
See Queen, Ellery; Vance, Jack
See also CA 29-32R; CANR 17, 65; MTCW 1
Van Den Bogarde, Derek Jules Gaspard Ulric Niven 1921-
See Bogarde, Dirk
See also CA 77-80
Vandenburgh, Jane ....CLC 59
See also CA 168
Vanderhaeghe, Guy 1951- ....CLC 41
See also CA 113; CANR 72
van der Post, Laurens (Jan) 1906-1996CLC 5
See also CA 5-8R; 155; CANR 35; DLB 204
van de Wetering, Janwillem 1931- ...CLC 47
See also CA 49-52; CANR 4, 62
Van Dine, S. S. ....TCLC 23
See also Wright, Willard Huntington
Van Doren, Carl (Clinton) 1885-1950 TCLC 18
See also CA 111; 168
Van Doren, Mark 1894-1972 .... CLC 6, 10
See also CA 1-4R; 37-40R; CANR 3; DLB 45; MTCW 1
Van Druten, John (William) 1901-1957TCLC 2
See also CA 104; 161; DLB 10
Van Duyn, Mona (Jane) 1921- CLC 3, 7, 63, 116; DAM POET
See also CA 9-12R; CANR 7, 38, 60; DLB 5
Van Dyne, Edith
See Baum, L(yman) Frank
van Itallie, Jean-Claude 1936- ....CLC 3
See also CA 45-48; CAAS 2; CANR 1, 48; DLB 7
van Ostaijen, Paul 1896-1928 .... TCLC 33
See also CA 163
Van Peebles, Melvin 1932- .CLC 2, 20; DAM MULT
See also BW 2; CA 85-88; CANR 27, 67
Vansittart, Peter 1920- ....CLC 42
See also CA 1-4R; CANR 3, 49
Van Vechten, Carl 1880-1964 ....CLC 33
See also CA 89-92; DLB 4, 9, 51
Van Vogt, A(lfred) E(lton) 1912- ....CLC 1
See also CA 21-24R; CANR 28; DLB 8; SATA 14
Varda, Agnes 1928- ....CLC 16
See also CA 116; 122

Vargas Llosa, (Jorge) Mario (Pedro) 1936- CLC 3, 6, 9, 10, 15, 31, 42, 85; DA; DAB; DAC; DAM MST, MULT, NOV; HLC
See also CA 73-76; CANR 18, 32, 42, 67; DLB 145; HW; MTCW 1
Vasiliu, Gheorghe 1881-1957
See Bacovia, George
See also CA 123
Vassa, Gustavus
See Equiano, Olaudah
Vassilikos, Vassilis 1933- .... CLC 4, 8
See also CA 81-84; CANR 75
Vaughan, Henry 1621-1695 .... LC 27
See also DLB 131
Vaughn, Stephanie ....CLC 62
Vazov, Ivan (Minchov) 1850-1921 . TCLC 25
See also CA 121; 167; DLB 147
Veblen, Thorstein B(unde) 1857-1929 T C L C 31
See also CA 115; 165
Vega, Lope de 1562-1635 .... LC 23
Venison, Alfred
See Pound, Ezra (Weston Loomis)
Verdi, Marie de
See Mencken, H(enry) L(ouis)
Verdu, Matilde
See Cela, Camilo Jose
Verga, Giovanni (Carmelo) 1840-1922T C L C 3; SSC 21
See also CA 104; 123
Vergil 70B.C.-19B.C. ..... CMLC 9; DA; DAB; DAC; DAM MST, POET; PC 12; WLCS
Verhaeren, Emile (Adolphe Gustave) 1855-1916 TCLC 12
See also CA 109
Verlaine, Paul (Marie) 1844-1896NCLC 2, 51; DAM POET; PC 2
Verne, Jules (Gabriel) 1828-1905TCLC 6, 52
See also AAYA 16; CA 110; 131; DLB 123; JRDA; MAICYA; SATA 21
Very, Jones 1813-1880 .... NCLC 9
See also DLB 1
Vesaas, Tarjei 1897-1970 .... CLC 48
See also CA 29-32R
Vialis, Gaston
See Simenon, Georges (Jacques Christian)
Vian, Boris 1920-1959 .... TCLC 9
See also CA 106; 164; DLB 72
Viaud, (Louis Marie) Julien 1850-1923
See Loti, Pierre
See also CA 107
Vicar, Henry
See Felsen, Henry Gregor
Vicker, Angus
See Felsen, Henry Gregor
Vidal, Gore 1925-CLC 2, 4, 6, 8, 10, 22, 33, 72; DAM NOV, POP
See also AITN 1; BEST 90:2; CA 5-8R; CANR 13, 45, 65; DLB 6, 152; INT CANR-13; MTCW 1
Viereck, Peter (Robert Edwin) 1916- . CLC 4
See also CA 1-4R; CANR 1, 47; DLB 5
Vigny, Alfred (Victor) de 1797-1863NCLC 7; DAM POET
See also DLB 119, 192
Vilakazi, Benedict Wallet 1906-1947TCLC 37
See also CA 168
Villa, Jose Garcia 1904-1997 .... PC 22
See also CA 25-28R; CANR 12
Villaurrutia, Xavier 1903-1950 ...... TCLC 80
See also HW
Villiers de l'Isle Adam, Jean Marie Mathias Philippe Auguste, Comte de 1838-1889

NCLC 3; SSC 14
See also DLB 123

Villon, Francois 1431-1463(?) .... **PC 13**
See also DLB 208

Vinci, Leonardo da 1452-1519 .... **LC 12**

Vine, Barbara .... **CLC 50**
See also Rendell, Ruth (Barbara)
See also BEST 90:4

Vinge, Joan (Carol) D(ennison) 1948-**CLC 30; SSC 24**
See also CA 93-96; CANR 72; SATA 36

Violis, G.
See Simenon, Georges (Jacques Christian)

Virgil
See Vergil

Visconti, Luchino 1906-1976 .... **CLC 16**
See also CA 81-84; 65-68; CANR 39

Vittorini, Elio 1908-1966 .... **CLC 6, 9, 14**
See also CA 133; 25-28R

Vivekananda, Swami 1863-1902 .... **TCLC 88**

Vizenor, Gerald Robert 1934-**CLC 103; DAM MULT**
See also CA 13-16R; CAAS 22; CANR 5, 21, 44, 67; DLB 175; NNAL

Vizinczey, Stephen 1933- .... **CLC 40**
See also CA 128; INT 128

Vliet, R(ussell) G(ordon) 1929-1984 **CLC 22**
See also CA 37-40R; 112; CANR 18

Vogau, Boris Andreyevich 1894-1937(?)
See Pilnyak, Boris
See also CA 123

Vogel, Paula A(nne) 1951- .... **CLC 76**
See also CA 108

Voigt, Cynthia 1942- .... **CLC 30**
See also AAYA 3; CA 106; CANR 18, 37, 40; CLR 13, 48; INT CANR-18; JRDA; MAICYA; SATA 48, 79; SATA-Brief 33

Voigt, Ellen Bryant 1943- .... **CLC 54**
See also CA 69-72; CANR 11, 29, 55; DLB 120

Voinovich, Vladimir (Nikolaevich) 1932-**CLC 10, 49**
See also CA 81-84; CAAS 12; CANR 33, 67; MTCW 1

Vollmann, William T. 1959-...**CLC 89; DAM NOV, POP**
See also CA 134; CANR 67

Voloshinov, V. N.
See Bakhtin, Mikhail Mikhailovich

Voltaire 1694-1778 **LC 14; DA; DAB; DAC; DAM DRAM, MST; SSC 12; WLC**

von Aschendrof, BaronIgnatz
See Ford, Ford Madox

von Daeniken, Erich 1935- .... **CLC 30**
See also AITN 1; CA 37-40R; CANR 17, 44

von Daniken, Erich
See von Daeniken, Erich

von Heidenstam, (Carl Gustaf) Verner
See Heidenstam, (Carl Gustaf) Verner von

von Heyse, Paul (Johann Ludwig)
See Heyse, Paul (Johann Ludwig von)

von Hofmannsthal, Hugo
See Hofmannsthal, Hugo von

von Horvath, Odon
See Horvath, Oedoen von

von Horvath, Oedoen
See Horvath, Oedoen von

von Liliencron, (Friedrich Adolf Axel) Detlev
See Liliencron, (Friedrich Adolf Axel) Detlev von

Vonnegut, Kurt, Jr. 1922-**CLC 1, 2, 3, 4, 5, 8, 12, 22, 40, 60, 111; DA; DAB; DAC; DAM MST, NOV, POP; SSC 8; WLC**
See also AAYA 6; AITN 1; BEST 90:4; CA 1-

4R; CANR 1, 25, 49, 75; CDALB 1968-1988; DLB 2, 8, 152; DLBD 3; DLBY 80; MTCW 1

Von Rachen, Kurt
See Hubbard, L(afayette) Ron(ald)

von Rezzori (d'Arezzo), Gregor
See Rezzori (d'Arezzo), Gregor von

von Sternberg, Josef
See Sternberg, Josef von

Vorster, Gordon 1924- .... **CLC 34**
See also CA 133

Vosce, Trudie
See Ozick, Cynthia

Voznesensky, Andrei (Andreievich) 1933-**CLC 1, 15, 57; DAM POET**
See also CA 89-92; CANR 37; MTCW 1

Waddington, Miriam 1917- .... **CLC 28**
See also CA 21-24R; CANR 12, 30; DLB 68

Wagman, Fredrica 1937- .... **CLC 7**
See also CA 97-100; INT 97-100

Wagner, Linda W.
See Wagner-Martin, Linda (C.)

Wagner, Linda Welshimer
See Wagner-Martin, Linda (C.)

Wagner, Richard 1813-1883 .... **NCLC 9**
See also DLB 129

Wagner-Martin, Linda (C.) 1936- ....**CLC 50**
See also CA 159

Wagoner, David (Russell) 1926- **CLC 3, 5, 15**
See also CA 1-4R; CAAS 3; CANR 2, 71; DLB 5; SATA 14

Wah, Fred(erick James) 1939- .... **CLC 44**
See also CA 107; 141; DLB 60

Wahloo, Per 1926-1975 .... **CLC 7**
See also CA 61-64; CANR 73

Wahloo, Peter
See Wahloo, Per

Wain, John (Barrington) 1925-1994 . **CLC 2, 11, 15, 46**
See also CA 5-8R; 145; CAAS 4; CANR 23, 54; CDBLB 1960 to Present; DLB 15, 27, 139, 155; MTCW 1

Wajda, Andrzej 1926- ....**CLC 16**
See also CA 102

Wakefield, Dan 1932- ....**CLC 7**
See also CA 21-24R; CAAS 7

Wakoski, Diane 1937-.**CLC 2, 4, 7, 9, 11, 40; DAM POET; PC 15**
See also CA 13-16R; CAAS 1; CANR 9, 60; DLB 5; INT CANR-9

Wakoski-Sherbell, Diane
See Wakoski, Diane

Walcott, Derek (Alton) 1930-**CLC 2, 4, 9, 14, 25, 42, 67, 76; BLC 3; DAB; DAC; DAM MST, MULT, POET; DC 7**
See also BW 2; CA 89-92; CANR 26, 47, 75; DLB 117; DLBY 81; MTCW 1

Waldman, Anne (Lesley) 1945-...........**CLC 7**
See also CA 37-40R; CAAS 17; CANR 34, 69; DLB 16

Waldo, E. Hunter
See Sturgeon, Theodore (Hamilton)

Waldo, Edward Hamilton
See Sturgeon, Theodore (Hamilton)

Walker, Alice (Malsenior) 1944- **CLC 5, 6, 9, 19, 27, 46, 58, 103; BLC 3; DA; DAB; DAC; DAM MST, MULT, NOV, POET, POP; SSC 5; WLCS**
See also AAYA 3; BEST 89:4; BW 2; CA 37-40R; CANR 9, 27, 49, 66; CDALB 1968-1988; DLB 6, 33, 143; INT CANR-27; MTCW 1; SATA 31

Walker, David Harry 1911-1992 .... **CLC 14**

See also CA 1-4R; 137; CANR 1; SATA 8; SATA-Obit 71

Walker, Edward Joseph 1934-
See Walker, Ted
See also CA 21-24R; CANR 12, 28, 53

Walker, George F. 1947- . **CLC 44, 61; DAB; DAC; DAM MST**
See also CA 103; CANR 21, 43, 59; DLB 60

Walker, Joseph A. 1935- .... **CLC 19; DAM DRAM, MST**
See also BW 1; CA 89-92; CANR 26; DLB 38

Walker, Margaret (Abigail) 1915-1998**CLC 1, 6; BLC; DAM MULT; PC 20**
See also BW 2; CA 73-76; 172; CANR 26, 54, 76; DLB 76, 152; MTCW 1

Walker, Ted .... **CLC 13**
See also Walker, Edward Joseph
See also DLB 40

Wallace, David Foster 1962- .... **CLC 50, 114**
See also CA 132; CANR 59

Wallace, Dexter
See Masters, Edgar Lee

Wallace, (Richard Horatio) Edgar 1875-1932 **TCLC 57**
See also CA 115; DLB 70

Wallace, Irving 1916-1990 . **CLC 7, 13; DAM NOV, POP**
See also AITN 1; CA 1-4R; 132; CAAS 1; CANR 1, 27; INT CANR-27; MTCW 1

Wallant, Edward Lewis 1926-1962**CLC 5, 10**
See also CA 1-4R; CANR 22; DLB 2, 28, 143; MTCW 1

Walley, Byron
See Card, Orson Scott

Walpole, Horace 1717-1797 .... **LC 2**
See also DLB 39, 104

Walpole, Hugh (Seymour) 1884-1941**TCLC 5**
See also CA 104; 165; DLB 34

Walser, Martin 1927- .... **CLC 27**
See also CA 57-60; CANR 8, 46; DLB 75, 124

Walser, Robert 1878-1956 **TCLC 18; SSC 20**
See also CA 118; 165; DLB 66

Walsh, Jill Paton .... **CLC 35**
See also Paton Walsh, Gillian
See also AAYA 11; CLR 2; DLB 161; SAAS 3

Walter, Villiam Christian
See Andersen, Hans Christian

Wambaugh, Joseph (Aloysius, Jr.) 1937-**CLC 3, 18; DAM NOV, POP**
See also AITN 1; BEST 89:3; CA 33-36R; CANR 42, 65; DLB 6; DLBY 83; MTCW 1

Wang Wei 699(?)-761(?) .... **PC 18**

Ward, Arthur Henry Sarsfield 1883-1959
See Rohmer, Sax
See also CA 108

Ward, Douglas Turner 1930- .... **CLC 19**
See also BW 1; CA 81-84; CANR 27; DLB 7, 38

Ward, Mary Augusta
See Ward, Mrs. Humphry

Ward, Mrs. Humphry 1851-1920 .. **TCLC 55**
See also DLB 18

Ward, Peter
See Faust, Frederick (Schiller)

Warhol, Andy 1928(?)-1987 .... **CLC 20**
See also AAYA 12; BEST 89:4; CA 89-92; 121; CANR 34

Warner, Francis (Robert le Plastrier) 1937-**CLC 14**
See also CA 53-56; CANR 11

Warner, Marina 1946- .... **CLC 59**
See also CA 65-68; CANR 21, 55; DLB 194

Warner, Rex (Ernest) 1905-1986 ..... **CLC 45**

See also CA 89-92; 119; DLB 15

Warner, Susan (Bogert) 1819-1885 NCLC 31
See also DLB 3, 42

Warner, Sylvia (Constance) Ashton
See Ashton-Warner, Sylvia (Constance)

Warner, Sylvia Townsend 1893-1978 CLC 7,
19; SSC 23
See also CA 61-64; 77-80; CANR 16, 60; DLB
34, 139; MTCW 1

Warren, Mercy Otis 1728-1814 ...... NCLC 13
See also DLB 31, 200

Warren, Robert Penn 1905-1989CLC 1, 4, 6,
8, 10, 13, 18, 39, 53, 59; DA; DAB; DAC;
DAM MST, NOV, POET; SSC 4; WLC
See also AITN 1; CA 13-16R; 129; CANR 10,
47; CDALB 1968-1988; DLB 2, 48, 152;
DLBY 80, 89; INT CANR-10; MTCW 1;
SATA 46; SATA-Obit 63

Warshofsky, Isaac
See Singer, Isaac Bashevis

Warton, Thomas 1728-1790 ..... LC 15; DAM
POET
See also DLB 104, 109

Waruk, Kona
See Harris, (Theodore) Wilson

Warung, Price 1855-1911 .... TCLC 45

Warwick, Jarvis
See Garner, Hugh

Washington, Alex
See Harris, Mark

Washington, Booker T(aliaferro) 1856-1915
TCLC 10; BLC 3; DAM MULT
See also BW 1; CA 114; 125; SATA 28

Washington, George 1732-1799 .... LC 25
See also DLB 31

Wassermann, (Karl) Jakob 1873-1934 T C L C
6
See also CA 104; 163; DLB 66

Wasserstein, Wendy 1950- ... CLC 32, 59, 90;
DAM DRAM; DC 4
See also CA 121; 129; CABS 3; CANR 53, 75;
INT 129; SATA 94

Waterhouse, Keith (Spencer) 1929-. CLC 47
See also CA 5-8R; CANR 38, 67; DLB 13, 15;
MTCW 1

Waters, Frank (Joseph) 1902-1995 .. CLC 88
See also CA 5-8R; 149; CAAS 13; CANR 3,
18, 63; DLBY 86

Waters, Roger 1944- .... CLC 35

Watkins, Frances Ellen
See Harper, Frances Ellen Watkins

Watkins, Gerrold
See Malzberg, Barry N(athaniel)

Watkins, Gloria 1955(?)-
See hooks, bell
See also BW 2; CA 143

Watkins, Paul 1964- .... CLC 55
See also CA 132; CANR 62

Watkins, Vernon Phillips 1906-1967 CLC 43
See also CA 9-10; 25-28R; CAP 1; DLB 20

Watson, Irving S.
See Mencken, H(enry) L(ouis)

Watson, John H.
See Farmer, Philip Jose

Watson, Richard F.
See Silverberg, Robert

Waugh, Auberon (Alexander) 1939- ..CLC 7
See also CA 45-48; CANR 6, 22; DLB 14, 194

Waugh, Evelyn (Arthur St. John) 1903-1966
CLC 1, 3, 8, 13, 19, 27, 44, 107; DA; DAB;
DAC; DAM MST, NOV, POP; WLC
See also CA 85-88; 25-28R; CANR 22; CDBLB
1914-1945; DLB 15, 162, 195; MTCW 1

Waugh, Harriet 1944- .... CLC 6
See also CA 85-88: CANR 22

Ways, C. R.
See Blount. Roy (Alton). Jr.

Waystaff, Simon
See Swift. Jonathan

Webb, (Martha) Beatrice (Potter) 1858-1943
TCLC 22
See also Potter, (Helen) Beatrix
See also CA 117; DLB 190

Webb, Charles (Richard) 1939- .... CLC 7
See also CA 25-28R

Webb, James H(enry), Jr. 1946- .... CLC 22
See also CA 81-84

Webb, Mary (Gladys Meredith) 1881-1927
TCLC 24
See also CA 123; DLB 34

Webb, Mrs. Sidney
See Webb. (Martha) Beatrice (Potter)

Webb, Phyllis 1927- .... CLC 18
See also CA 104; CANR 23; DLB 53

Webb, Sidney (James) 1859-1947 .. TCLC 22
See also CA 117; 163; DLB 190

Webber, Andrew Lloyd .... CLC 21
See also Lloyd Webber, Andrew

Weber, Lenora Mattingly 1895-1971 CLC 12
See also CA 19-20; 29-32R; CAP 1; SATA 2;
SATA-Obit 26

Weber, Max 1864-1920 .... TCLC 69
See also CA 109

Webster, John 1579(?)-1634(?) ... LC 33; DA;
DAB; DAC; DAM DRAM, MST; DC 2;
WLC
See also CDBLB Before 1660; DLB 58

Webster, Noah 1758-1843 .... NCLC 30
See also DLB 1. 37, 42. 43; 73

Wedekind, (Benjamin) Frank(lin) 1864-1918
TCLC 7; DAM DRAM
See also CA 104; 153; DLB 118

Weidman, Jerome 1913-1998 .... CLC 7
See also AITN 2; CA 1-4R; 171; CANR 1; DLB
28

Weil, Simone (Adolphine) 1909-1943TCLC 23
See also CA 117; 159

Weininger, Otto 1880-1903 .... TCLC 84

Weinstein, Nathan
See West. Nathanael

Weinstein, Nathan von Wallenstein
See West. Nathanael

Weir, Peter (Lindsay) 1944- .... CLC 20
See also CA 113; 123

Weiss, Peter (Ulrich) 1916-1982CLC 3, 15, 51;
DAM DRAM
See also CA 45-48; 106; CANR 3; DLB 69, 124

Weiss, Theodore (Russell) 1916-CLC 3, 8, 14
See also CA 9-12R; CAAS 2; CANR 46; DLB
5

Welch, (Maurice) Denton 1915-1948TCLC 22
See also CA 121; 148

Welch, James 1940- ..... CLC 6, 14, 52; DAM
MULT, POP
See also CA 85-88; CANR 42, 66; DLB 175;
NNAL

Weldon, Fay 1931-..CLC 6, 9, 11, 19, 36, 59;
DAM POP
See also CA 21-24R; CANR 16, 46, 63; CDBLB
1960 to Present; DLB 14, 194; INT CANR-
16; MTCW 1

Wellek, Rene 1903-1995 .... CLC 28
See also CA 5-8R; 150; CAAS 7; CANR 8; DLB
63; INT CANR-8

Weller, Michael 1942- .... CLC 10, 53
See also CA 85-88

Weller, Paul 1958- .... CLC 26

Wellershoff, Dieter 1925-................... CLC 46
See also CA 89-92; CANR 16, 37

Welles, (George) Orson 1915-1985CLC 20, 80
See also CA 93-96; 117

Wellman, John McDowell 1945-
See Wellman, Mac
See also CA 166

Wellman, Mac 1945- .... CLC 65
See also Wellman, John McDowell; Wellman,
John McDowell

Wellman, Manly Wade 1903-1986 .... CLC 49
See also CA 1-4R; 118; CANR 6, 16, 44; SATA
6; SATA-Obit 47

Wells, Carolyn 1869(?)-1942 .... TCLC 35
See also CA 113; DLB 11

Wells, H(erbert) G(eorge) 1866-1946TCLC 6,
12, 19; DA; DAB; DAC; DAM MST, NOV;
SSC 6; WLC
See also AAYA 18; CA 110; 121; CDBLB 1914-
1945; DLB 34, 70, 156, 178; MTCW 1;
SATA 20

Wells, Rosemary 1943- .... CLC 12
See also AAYA 13; CA 85-88; CANR 48; CLR
16; MAICYA; SAAS 1; SATA 18, 69

Welty, Eudora 1909-. CLC 1, 2, 5, 14, 22, 33,
105; DA; DAB; DAC; DAMMST, NOV;
SSC 1, 27; WLC
See also CA 9-12R; CABS 1; CANR 32, 65;
CDALB 1941-1968; DLB 2, 102, 143;
DLBD 12; DLBY 87; MTCW 1

Wen I-to 1899-1946 .... TCLC 28

Wentworth, Robert
See Hamilton, Edmond

Werfel, Franz (Viktor) 1890-1945 ... TCLC 8
See also CA 104; 161; DLB 81, 124

Wergeland, Henrik Arnold 1808-1845N C L C
5

Wersba, Barbara 1932-...................... CLC 30
See also AAYA 2; CA 29-32R; CANR 16, 38;
CLR 3; DLB 52; JRDA; MAICYA; SAAS 2;
SATA 1, 58; SATA-Essay 103

Wertmueller, Lina 1928-................... CLC 16
See also CA 97-100; CANR 39

Wescott, Glenway 1901-1987 .... CLC 13
See also CA 13-16R; 121; CANR 23, 70; DLB
4, 9, 102

Wesker, Arnold 1932-.... CLC 3, 5, 42; DAB;
DAM DRAM
See also CA 1-4R; CAAS 7; CANR 1, 33;
CDBLB 1960 to Present; DLB 13; MTCW 1

Wesley, Richard (Errol) 1945- .... CLC 7
See also BW 1; CA 57-60; CANR 27; DLB 38

Wessel, Johan Herman 1742-1785 .... LC 7

West, Anthony (Panther) 1914-1987 CLC 50
See also CA 45-48; 124; CANR 3, 19; DLB 15

West, C. P.
See Wodehouse, P(elham) G(renville)

West, (Mary) Jessamyn 1902-1984CLC 7, 17
See also CA 9-12R; 112; CANR 27; DLB 6;
DLBY 84; MTCW 1; SATA-Obit 37

West, Morris L(anglo) 1916- .... CLC 6, 33
See also CA 5-8R; CANR 24, 49, 64; MTCW 1

West, Nathanael 1903-1940 TCLC 1, 14, 44;
SSC 16
See also CA 104; 125; CDALB 1929-1941;
DLB 4, 9, 28; MTCW 1

West, Owen
See Koontz, Dean R(ay)

West, Paul 1930- .... CLC 7, 14, 96
See also CA 13-16R; CAAS 7; CANR 22, 53,
76; DLB 14; INT CANR-22

West, Rebecca 1892-1983 ... CLC 7, 9, 31, 50

Williamson, David (Keith) 1942- ..... **CLC 56**
 See also CA 103; CANR 41
Williamson, Ellen Douglas 1905-1984
 See Douglas, Ellen
 See also CA 17-20R; 114; CANR 39
Williamson, Jack .... **CLC 29**
 See also Williamson, John Stewart
 See also CAAS 8; DLB 8
Williamson, John Stewart 1908-
 See Williamson, Jack
 See also CA 17-20R; CANR 23, 70
Willie, Frederick
 See Lovecraft, H(oward) P(hillips)
Willingham, Calder (Baynard, Jr.) 1922-1995
 CLC 5, 51
 See also CA 5-8R; 147; CANR 3; DLB 2, 44;
 MTCW 1
Willis, Charles
 See Clarke, Arthur C(harles)
Willy
 See Colette, (Sidonie-Gabrielle)
Willy, Colette
 See Colette, (Sidonie-Gabrielle)
Wilson, A(ndrew) N(orman) 1950- .. **CLC 33**
 See also CA 112; 122; DLB 14, 155, 194
Wilson, Angus (Frank Johnstone) 1913-1991
 CLC 2, 3, 5, 25, 34; SSC 21
 See also CA 5-8R; 134; CANR 21; DLB 15,
 139, 155; MTCW 1
Wilson, August 1945- ... **CLC 39, 50, 63, 118;**
 BLC 3; DA; DAB; DAC; DAM DRAM,
 MST, MULT; DC 2; WLCS
 See also AAYA 16; BW 2; CA 115; 122; CANR
 42, 54, 76; MTCW 1
Wilson, Brian 1942- .... **CLC 12**
Wilson, Colin 1931- .... **CLC 3, 14**
 See also CA 1-4R; CAAS 5; CANR 1, 22, 33;
 DLB 14, 194; MTCW 1
Wilson, Dirk
 See Pohl, Frederik
Wilson, Edmund 1895-1972 **CLC 1, 2, 3, 8, 24**
 See also CA 1-4R; 37-40R; CANR 1, 46; DLB
 63; MTCW 1
Wilson, Ethel Davis (Bryant) 1888(?)-1980
 CLC 13; DAC; DAM POET
 See also CA 102; DLB 68; MTCW 1
Wilson, John 1785-1854 .... **NCLC 5**
Wilson, John (Anthony) Burgess 1917-1993
 See Burgess, Anthony
 See also CA 1-4R; 143; CANR 2, 46; DAC;
 DAM NOV; MTCW 1
Wilson, Lanford 1937- **CLC 7, 14, 36; DAM**
 DRAM
 See also CA 17-20R; CABS 3; CANR 45; DLB
 7
Wilson, Robert M. 1944- .... **CLC 7, 9**
 See also CA 49-52; CANR 2, 41; MTCW 1
Wilson, Robert McLiam 1964- .... **CLC 59**
 See also CA 132
Wilson, Sloan 1920- .... **CLC 32**
 See also CA 1-4R; CANR 1, 44
Wilson, Snoo 1948- .... **CLC 33**
 See also CA 69-72
Wilson, William S(mith) 1932- .... **CLC 49**
 See also CA 81-84
Wilson, (Thomas) Woodrow 1856-1924 **TCLC**
 79
 See also CA 166; DLB 47
Winchilsea, Anne (Kingsmill) Finch Counte
 1661-1720
 See Finch, Anne
Windham, Basil
 See Wodehouse, P(elham) G(renville)

Wingrove, David (John) 1954- .... **CLC 68**
 See also CA 133
Wintergreen, Jane
 See Duncan, Sara Jeannette
Winters, Janet Lewis .... **CLC 41**
 See also Lewis, Janet
 See also DLBY 87
Winters, (Arthur) Yvor 1900-1968 **CLC 4, 8,**
 32
 See also CA 11-12; 25-28R; CAP 1; DLB 48;
 MTCW 1
Winterson, Jeanette 1959-**CLC 64; DAM POP**
 See also CA 136; CANR 58; DLB 207
Winthrop, John 1588-1649 .... **LC 31**
 See also DLB 24, 30
Wiseman, Frederick 1930- .... **CLC 20**
 See also CA 159
Wister, Owen 1860-1938 .... **TCLC 21**
 See also CA 108; 162; DLB 9, 78, 186; SATA
 62
Witkacy
 See Witkiewicz, Stanislaw Ignacy
Witkiewicz, Stanislaw Ignacy 1885-1939
 TCLC 8
 See also CA 105; 162
Wittgenstein, Ludwig (Josef Johann) 1889-1951
 TCLC 59
 See also CA 113; 164
Wittig, Monique 1935(?)- .... **CLC 22**
 See also CA 116; 135; DLB 83
Wittlin, Jozef 1896-1976 .... **CLC 25**
 See also CA 49-52; 65-68; CANR 3
Wodehouse, P(elham) G(renville) 1881-1975
 CLC 1, 2, 5, 10, 22; DAB; DAC; DAM
 NOV; SSC 2
 See also AITN 2; CA 45-48; 57-60; CANR 3,
 33; CDBLB 1914-1945; DLB 34, 162;
 MTCW 1; SATA 22
Woiwode, L.
 See Woiwode, Larry (Alfred)
Woiwode, Larry (Alfred) 1941- ... **CLC 6, 10**
 See also CA 73-76; CANR 16; DLB 6; INT
 CANR-16
Wojciechowska, Maia (Teresa) 1927-**CLC 26**
 See also AAYA 8; CA 9-12R; CANR 4, 41; CLR
 1; JRDA; MAICYA; SAAS 1; SATA 1, 28,
 83; SATA-Essay 104
Wolf, Christa 1929- .... **CLC 14, 29, 58**
 See also CA 85-88; CANR 45; DLB 75; MTCW
 1
Wolfe, Gene (Rodman) 1931- **CLC 25; DAM**
 POP
 See also CA 57-60; CAAS 9; CANR 6, 32, 60;
 DLB 8
Wolfe, George C. 1954- .... **CLC 49; BLCS**
 See also CA 149
Wolfe, Thomas (Clayton) 1900-1938**TCLC 4,**
 13, 29, 61; DA; DAB; DAC; DAM MST,
 NOV; SSC 33; WLC
 See also CA 104; 132; CDALB 1929-1941;
 DLB 9, 102; DLBD 2, 16; DLBY 85, 97;
 MTCW 1
Wolfe, Thomas Kennerly, Jr. 1930-
 See Wolfe, Tom
 See also CA 13-16R; CANR 9, 33, 70; DAM
 POP; DLB 185; INT CANR-9; MTCW 1
Wolfe, Tom .... **CLC 1, 2, 9, 15, 35, 51**
 See also Wolfe, Thomas Kennerly, Jr.
 See also AAYA 8; AITN 2; BEST 89:1; DLB
 152
Wolff, Geoffrey (Ansell) 1937- .... **CLC 41**
 See also CA 29-32R; CANR 29, 43
Wolff, Sonia

 See Levitin, Sonia (Wolff)
Wolff, Tobias (Jonathan Ansell) 1945- .. **C L C**
 39, 64
 See also AAYA 16; BEST 90:2; CA 114; 117;
 CAAS 22; CANR 54, 76; DLB 130; INT 117
Wolfram von Eschenbach c. 1170-c. 1220
 CMLC 5
 See also DLB 138
Wolitzer, Hilma 1930- .... **CLC 17**
 See also CA 65-68; CANR 18, 40; INT CANR-
 18; SATA 31
Wollstonecraft, Mary 1759-1797 .... **LC 5**
 See also CDBLB 1789-1832; DLB 39, 104, 158
Wonder, Stevie .... **CLC 12**
 See also Morris, Steveland Judkins
Wong, Jade Snow 1922- .... **CLC 17**
 See also CA 109
Woodberry, George Edward 1855-1930
 TCLC 73
 See also CA 165; DLB 71, 103
Woodcott, Keith
 See Brunner, John (Kilian Houston)
Woodruff, Robert W.
 See Mencken, H(enry) L(ouis)
Woolf, (Adeline) Virginia 1882-1941**TCLC 1,**
 5, 20, 43, 56; DA; DAB; DAC; DAM MST,
 NOV; SSC 7; WLC
 See also CA 104; 130; CANR 64; CDBLB
 1914-1945; DLB 36, 100, 162; DLBD 10;
 MTCW 1
Woolf, Virginia Adeline
 See Woolf, (Adeline) Virginia
Woollcott, Alexander (Humphreys) 1887-1943
 TCLC 5
 See also CA 105; 161; DLB 29
Woolrich, Cornell 1903-1968 .... **CLC 77**
 See also Hopley-Woolrich, Cornell George
Wordsworth, Dorothy 1771-1855 .. **NCLC 25**
 See also DLB 107
Wordsworth, William 1770-1850 .. **NCLC 12,**
 38; DA; DAB; DAC; DAM MST, POET;
 PC 4; WLC
 See also CDBLB 1789-1832; DLB 93, 107
Wouk, Herman 1915-**CLC 1, 9, 38; DAM NOV,**
 POP
 See also CA 5-8R; CANR 6, 33, 67; DLBY 82;
 INT CANR-6; MTCW 1
Wright, Charles (Penzel, Jr.) 1935-**CLC 6, 13,**
 28
 See also CA 29-32R; CAAS 7; CANR 23, 36,
 62; DLB 165; DLBY 82; MTCW 1
Wright, Charles Stevenson 1932- ... **CLC 49;**
 BLC 3; DAM MULT, POET
 See also BW 1; CA 9-12R; CANR 26; DLB 33
Wright, Frances 1795-1852 .... **NCLC 74**
 See also DLB 73
Wright, Jack R.
 See Harris, Mark
Wright, James (Arlington) 1927-1980**CLC 3,**
 5, 10, 28; DAM POET
 See also AITN 2; CA 49-52; 97-100; CANR 4,
 34, 64; DLB 5, 169; MTCW 1
Wright, Judith (Arandell) 1915- **CLC 11, 53;**
 PC 14
 See also CA 13-16R; CANR 31, 76; MTCW 1;
 SATA 14
Wright, L(aurali) R. 1939- .... **CLC 44**
 See also CA 138
Wright, Richard (Nathaniel) 1908-1960 **C L C**
 1, 3, 4, 9, 14, 21, 48, 74; BLC 3; DA; DAB;
 DAC; DAM MST, MULT, NOV; SSC 2;
 WLC
 See also AAYA 5; BW 1; CA 108; CANR 64;

Literary Criticism Series
Cumulative Topic Index

This index lists all topic entries in Gale's *Classical and Medieval Literature Criticism, Contemporary Literary Criticism, Literature Criticism from 1400 to 1800, Nineteenth-Century Literature Criticism,* and *Twentieth-Century Literary Criticism.*

Topic Index

Topic Index

Contemporary Literary Criticism
Cumulative Nationality Index

Nationality Index

Nationality Index

        CONTEMPORARY LITERARY CRITICISM

Nationality Index

Nationality Index

Nationality Index

Title Index